Gary Dessler

HUMAN RESOURCE MANAGEMENT

2010 Custom Edition

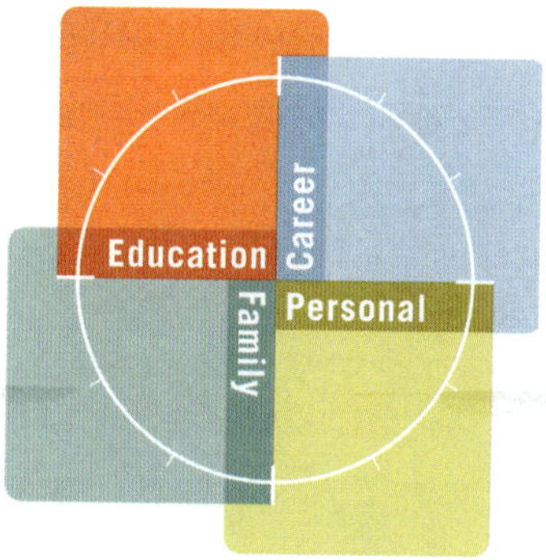

Taken from:
Human Resource Management, Twelfth Edition
by Gary Dessler

1892 STRAYER UNIVERSITY

Learning Solutions

New York Boston San Francisco
London Toronto Sydney Tokyo Singapore Madrid
Mexico City Munich Paris Cape Town Hong Kong Montreal

Cover image: courtesy of Photodisc/Getty Images.

Taken from:

Human Resource Management, Twelfth Edition
by Gary Dessler

Published by Prentice Hall
Upper Saddle River, New Jersey 07458

This special edition published in cooperation with Pearson Learning Solutions.

Pearson Learning Solutions, 501 Boylston Street, Suite 900, Boston, MA 02116
A Pearson Education Company
www.pearsoned.com

Printed in the United States of America

1 2 3 4 5 6 7 8 9 10 V357 15 14 13 12 11 10

000200010270587241

KS

PEARSON

ISBN 10: 0-558-74130-4
ISBN 13: 978-0-558-74130-3

Dedicated to My Parents

Brief Contents

APPENDICES

Contents

APPENDICES

Preface

Human Resource Management provides students in human resource management courses and practicing managers with a complete, comprehensive review of essential personnel management concepts and techniques in a highly readable and understandable form. As this new edition goes to press, I feel even more strongly than I did when I wrote the first that all managers—not just HR managers—need a strong foundation in HR/personnel management concepts and techniques to do their jobs. Because all managers do have personnel-related responsibilities, I again wrote *Human Resource Management,* 12th Edition, for all students of management, not just those who will someday carry the title Human Resource Manager. This edition thus continues to focus on the practical applications that all managers need to manage their HR-related responsibilities. If you used the previous, 11th edition, you should be able to roll over to the 12th more or less seamlessly; the book's chapter outline (as well as the outline for each individual chapter) is more or less the same. However, I've made six changes that both instructors and students should find useful.

NEW TO THE 12TH EDITION

1. **New Evidence-Based Human Resource Management Theme.** The competitive nature of business today means that all managers (including human resource managers) must defend their plans and contributions in measurable terms. Approaching problems scientifically is a learnable skill. I've rewritten Chapter 3, "The Manager's Role in Strategic Human Resource Management," to include material and a new appendix on using tools for evidence-based HR, and I've written new *Evidence-Based HR* features in most chapters to present examples of how managers manage based on facts and evidence.
2. **New Managing HR in Challenging Times Features.** The economic challenges the United States and world faced starting around 2008 prompted most employers to re-think the costs and benefits of how they delivered their human resource services. New *Managing HR in Challenging Times* features in most chapters illustrate the skills managers need to manage human resources in challenging times.
3. **New Chapter: "Managing Human Resources in Entrepreneurial Firms."** Like most people working today, most of the students reading this book either do or will work for small businesses. There are special issues involved with managing human resources in small entrepreneurial firms. I've therefore added a new, final Chapter 18, "Managing Human Resources in Entrepreneurial Firms." It contains special topics that you can use in managing human resources in smaller firms, including using Internet and government tools to support the HR effort.

4. **New Topics.** Although I wrote this book for all managers—not just for future human resource managers—the Society for Human Resource Management recently listed several new suggested competencies for human resource managers. Because it makes sense to do so, I've added discussions of several of these. They include, for example, a discussion of budgets in Chapter 3 (now titled "The Manager's Role in Strategic Human Resource Management") and of coaching and talent management in Chapter 10 (now titled "Coaching, Careers, and Talent Management").
5. **Updates and HR APPs 4 U Features.** You'll find hundreds of *new examples and research references and topics,* including, for example, onboarding and mobile learning. I also updated for this edition many of the book's *figures and tables.* You'll also find in most chapters a new feature, *HR APPS 4 U.* These brief features illustrate how managers use mobile devices to support their HR activities. I also wrote *all new end-of-chapter summaries for every chapter.* These now provide a concise summary and quick learning review of the material in each section of the chapter.
6. **Length and Editing.** Although this 12th edition has one more chapter and a more open design, its total length is actually less than the 11th edition. Two things account for that. One is a somewhat larger trim size. Mostly though, it reflects the heavy editing that I did for this edition. I deleted a great deal of redundant text, rewrote many topics to be more concise, and we worked hard to eliminate typographical errors. I'd appreciate your comments or suggestions; for textbook comments or suggestions it's easiest to reach me at gsdessler@gmail.com.

Everyone involved in creating this book is very proud of what we've achieved. *Human Resource Management* is the number one or one of the top-selling books in this market, and, as you read this, students around the world are using versions of it in many languages, including Thai, French, Spanish, Indonesian, Russian, and both traditional and simplified Chinese. This publication is designed to provide accurate and authoritative information with regard to the subject matter covered, but it is not intended to be a source of legal or other professional advice for any purpose.

KEY 12TH EDITION FEATURES

New Features

First, as noted previously, we've added all new material and/or features on

- evidence-based human resource management,
- managing HR in challenging times,
- entrepreneurship, and
- *HR APPs 4 U.*

Managing the New Workforce Feature

The United States workforce is increasingly diverse. I've revised the 11th edition's *New Workforce* features, and you'll now find *Managing the New Workforce* features in most chapters to illustrate the skills managers need to manage today's diverse employees.

We've also continued several features from the 11th edition, but integrated them into the text, rather than presenting them as boxed features. These include the following three features:

When You're on Your Own: HR for Line Managers and Entrepreneurs Aimed especially at line and small-business managers, *When You're on Your Own* shows managers how to, for instance, recruit and train new employees when their HR department is too busy to help, how to avoid committing management malpractice, how to develop a workable pay plan and testing program, and how to create a simple training program.

Improving Productivity Through HRIS HR managers increasingly rely on information technology to help support their companies' strategic aims. Integrated *Improving Productivity Through HRIS* sections throughout the chapters illustrate how managers use technology to improve the productivity of HR. For example, one Chapter 6 section explains how managers use applicant-tracking systems to compile Web-based resumes to test and prescreen applicants online and to discover candidates' hidden talents.

Know Your Employment Law Today, virtually every HR-related decision managers make has legal implications, a fact underscored by the Human Resource Certification Institute's emphasis, in its exams, on candidates for certification having a solid knowledge of employment law. Many of this edition's chapters therefore contain one or more integrated *Employment Law* sections.

Integrated Strategic HR

This textbook was the first to provide specific, actionable explanations and illustrations showing how to use devices such as the HR Scorecard process (explained fully in Chapter 3) to measure HR's effectiveness in achieving the company's strategic aims. In this edition, a continuing "Hotel Paris" case after the end of each chapter gives readers practice in applying strategic human resource management in action. We cover the core concepts of strategic HR in Chapter 3.

Video and Comprehensive Cases

To provide faculty members with a richer and more flexible textbook, we have video cases—one (or more) at the end of each of the book's five parts and five longer, comprehensive cases in an appendix at the end of the book. The *in-book video cases* provide a basis for in-class discussion of 9 videos available to adopters. I wrote the five *comprehensive cases* to provide students and faculty with an opportunity to discuss and apply the book's concepts and techniques by addressing more comprehensive and realistic case-based issues.

SHRM Guidelines In-Book Study Guide

Several years ago, SHRM, the Society for Human Resource Management, published new HR curriculum guidelines. These contain SHRM's recommended curriculum objectives and guidelines regarding the human resource management curriculum—relevant content, personal competencies, and business knowledge. To enable faculty members who may want to address one or more of these new guidelines to do so, I've included a unique brief in-textbook SHRM study guide. It contains, among other things, discussion and case questions you can use to help cover the new SHRM guidelines' relevant topics and behavioral objectives. It is after Chapter 18, in a separate appendix.

This SHRM study guide is in addition to the SHRM certification exam material we also included in this edition. The profession of HR management is becoming increasingly demanding. Responding to these new demands, many thousands of HR managers have passed the varaious certification exams offered by the Human Resource Certification Institute (HRCI), thus earning the designations Professional in HR (PHR), Senior Professional in HR (SPHR), and Global Professional in HR (GPHR). This edition again contains, in each chapter, an *HRCI-related exercise* students can use to apply their knowledge of that chapter's material within the HRCI exam context, as well as a comprehensive listing of the topics that these exams address, also in this SHRM guidelines appendix.

SUPPLEMENTS

Instructor's Manual This comprehensive supplement provides extensive instructional support. The instructor's manual includes a course planning guide and chapter guides for each chapter in the text. The chapter guides include a chapter outline, lecture notes, answers to discussion questions, definitions to key terms, and references to the figures, tables, cases, and Power Point slides in the text. The instructor's manual also includes a video guide.

Test Item File The test item file contains approximately 110 questions per chapter including multiple-choice, true/false, and short-answer/essay-type questions. Suggested answers, difficulty ratings, AACSB callouts, and page number references are included for all questions.

Videos on DVD The DVD video features video clips that bring HR issues covered in *Human Resource Management,* 12th Edition, to the students' attention and draw them into the text materials. To give you more choices, I've added new videos to the DVD that are not listed or discussed in the textbook itself, so please be sure to check out the DVD.

MyManagementLab MyManagementLab (www.mymanagementlab.com) is an easy-to-use online tool that personalizes course content and provides robust assessment and reporting to measure student and class performance. All the resources you need for course success are in one place—flexible and easily adapted for your course experience. Some of the resources include an e-book version of all chapters, quizzes, video clips, and PowerPoint presentations that engage students while helping them to study independently.

Acknowledgments

Although I am, of course, solely responsible for the content in *Human Resource Management*, I am more pleased with this edition than I have been for many editions, and for that I want to thank several people for their assistance. This includes, first, the faculty who reviewed this and the 11th edition:

Carl P. Borchgrevink, Michigan State University
Jo Ann E. Brown, Radford University
Bruce W. Byars, University of North Dakota
Catherine Giunta, Seton Hill University
Melissa Gruys, Wright State University
Daniel W. Kent, Northern Kentucky University
John N. Kondrasuk, University of Portland
George Thomas Kramer, Craven Community College
Helen LaVan, DePaul University
Amy Rand, Crowder College
Frances Sizemore, Gardner–Webb University
Eric Stark, James Madison University
H. Jeffrey Turner, Mohave Community College
Lei Wang, The University of Texas Pan American
Laura L. Wolfe, Louisiana State University
Tom Zagenczyk, Clemson University

At Pearson/Prentice Hall, I am again grateful for the support and dedicated assistance of a great publishing team. Sally Yagan, Editorial Director; Eric Svendson, Editor in Chief; Jennifer Collins, Acquisitions Editor; Judy Leale, Senior Managing Editor; Kelly Warsak, Production Project Manager; and Susie Abraham, Editorial Project Manager, along with Jen Welsch at BookMasters, worked hard to make this a book that we're all very proud of. Thanks to Nikki Jones, Marketing Manager, and the Pearson sales staff, without whose efforts this book would no doubt languish on the shelf. I want to thank all the people at Pearson International for all their efforts and effectiveness in managing the internationalization of this book.

At home, I want to acknowledge and thank my wife Claudia for her support during the many hours I spent working on this edition. My son Derek, certainly still the best people manager I know and a source of enormous pride, and my daughter-in-law Lisa were always in my thoughts. My parents were always a great source of support and encouragement and would have been very proud to see this book.

Gary Dessler

1 Introduction to Human Resource Management

When it comes to keeping good employees, the restaurant business is a tough sell. The average restaurant's employee turnover is more than 100% per year.[1] That's particularly dangerous in a small service business, where bad service can prompt customers to stay away. Yet the general manager of a Stanford's Restaurant in Lake Oswego, Oregon, estimates his hourly employee turnover is only about 28%. His secret? Mostly simple human resource management practices. For one thing, "I'm selective on who I hire. I'm looking for people who want to stay. . . ."[2] He looks for people who smile easily and are friendly. He tells them during the interview, "If you're not the friendliest employee in the restaurant, you're not going to make it."[3] His success shows that even simple improvements in human resource management can produce big returns.[4]

Source: Courtesy of Claude Dagenais/istockphoto.com.

WHERE ARE WE NOW . . .

The purpose of this chapter is to explain what human resource management is, and why it's important to all managers. We'll see that human resource management activities such as hiring, training, appraising, compensating, and developing employees are part of every manager's job. And we'll see that human resource management is also a separate function, usually with its own human resource or "HR" manager. The main topics we'll cover include the meaning of human resource management; why human resource management is important to all managers; global and competitive trends; human resource management trends; and the plan of this book. The framework below (which introduces each chapter) makes this point: That to formulate and apply HR practices like testing and training you should understand the strategic and legal context in which you're managing.

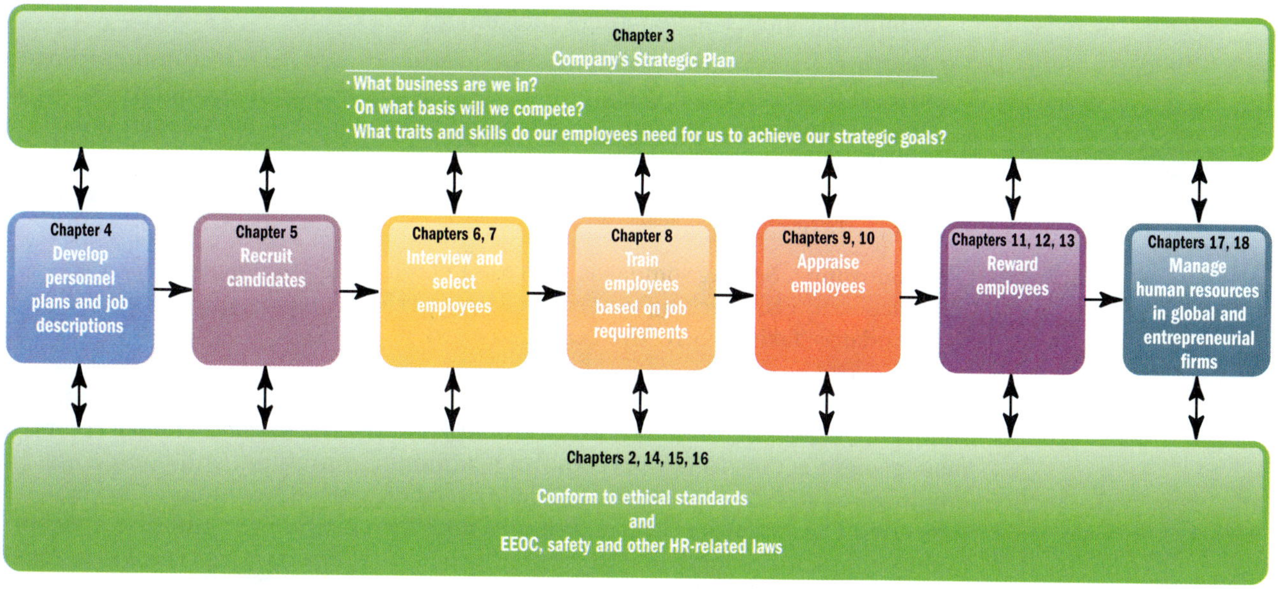

LEARNING OUTCOMES

1. Explain what human resource management is and how it relates to the management process.
2. Show with examples why human resource management is important to all managers.
3. Illustrate the human resources responsibilities of line and staff (HR) managers.
4. Briefly discuss and illustrate each of the important trends influencing human resource management.
5. List and briefly describe important trends in human resource management.
6. Define and give an example of evidence-based human resource management.
7. Outline the plan of this book.

1 Explain what human resource management is and how it relates to the management process.

WHAT IS HUMAN RESOURCE MANAGEMENT AND WHY IS IT IMPORTANT?

What Is Human Resource Management?

Stanford's Restaurant is an *organization.* An **organization** consists of people with formally assigned roles who work together to achieve the organization's goals. A **manager** is the person responsible for accomplishing the organization's goals, and who does so by managing the efforts of the organization's people.

Most experts agree that *managing* involves five functions: planning, organizing, staffing, leading, and controlling. In total, these functions represent the **management process**. Some of the specific activities involved in each function include:

- **Planning.** Establishing goals and standards; developing rules and procedures; developing plans and forecasting.
- **Organizing.** Giving each subordinate a specific task; establishing departments; delegating authority to subordinates; establishing channels of authority and communication; coordinating subordinates' work.
- **Staffing.** Determining what type of people you should hire; recruiting prospective employees; selecting employees; training and developing employees; setting performance standards; evaluating performance; counseling employees; compensating employees.
- **Leading.** Getting others to get the job done; maintaining morale; motivating subordinates.
- **Controlling.** Setting standards such as sales quotas, quality standards, or production levels; checking to see how actual performance compares with these standards; taking corrective action, as needed.

In this book, we are going to focus on one of these functions—the staffing, personnel management, or *human resource management (HRM) function.* **Human resource management** is the process of acquiring, training, appraising, and compensating employees, and of attending to their labor relations, health and safety, and fairness concerns. The topics we'll discuss should therefore provide you with the concepts and techniques you need to perform the "people" or personnel aspects of your management job. These include:

- *Conducting job analyses* (determining the nature of each employee's job)
- *Planning labor needs* and *recruiting* job candidates
- *Selecting* job candidates
- *Orienting and training* new employees
- *Managing wages and salaries* (compensating employees)
- *Providing incentives and benefits*
- *Appraising performance*
- *Communicating* (interviewing, counseling, disciplining)
- *Training and developing* managers
- *Building employee commitment*

And what a manager should know about:

- Equal opportunity and affirmative action
- Employee health and safety
- Handling grievances and labor relations

2 Show with examples why human resource management is important to all managers.

Why Is Human Resource Management Important to All Managers?

Why are these concepts and techniques important to all managers? Perhaps it's easier to answer this by listing some of the personnel mistakes you *don't* want to make while managing. For example, you don't want to:

- Hire the wrong person for the job
- Experience high turnover
- Have your people not doing their best
- Waste time with useless interviews
- Have your company taken to court because of your discriminatory actions
- Have your company cited under federal occupational safety laws for unsafe practices
- Have some employees think their salaries are unfair relative to others in the organization
- Allow a lack of training to undermine your department's effectiveness
- Commit any unfair labor practices

Carefully studying this book will help you avoid mistakes like these. And, more important, it can help ensure that you get results—through people. Remember that you can do everything else right as a manager—lay brilliant plans, draw clear organization charts, set up world-class assembly lines, and use sophisticated accounting controls—but still fail, by hiring the wrong people or by not motivating subordinates. On the other hand, many managers—presidents, generals, governors, supervisors—have been successful even with inadequate plans, organizations, or controls. They were successful because they had the knack of hiring the right people for the right jobs and motivating, appraising, and developing them. Remember as you read this book that *getting results* is the bottom line of managing, and that, as a manager, you will have to get those results through people. As one company president summed up:

> For many years, it has been said that capital is the bottleneck for a developing industry. I don't think this any longer holds true. I think it's the work force and the company's inability to recruit and maintain a good work force that does constitute the bottleneck for production. I don't know of any major project backed by good ideas, vigor, and enthusiasm that has been stopped by a shortage of cash. I do know of industries whose growth has been partly stopped or hampered because they can't maintain an efficient and enthusiastic labor force, and I think this will hold true even more in the future.[5]

We'll see in a moment that because of global competition, technological advances, economic challenges, and the changing nature of work, that president's statement has never been truer than it is today.

HR for Entrepreneurs And here is another reason to study this book. You may well end up as your own human resource manager. More than half the people working in the United States—about 68 million out of 118 million—work for small firms. Small businesses as a group also account for most of the 600,000 or so

organization
People with formally assigned roles who work together to achieve the organization's goals.

manager
The person responsible for accomplishing the organization's goals, and who does so by managing (planning, organizing, staffing, leading, and controlling) the efforts of the organization's people.

management process
The five basic functions of planning, organizing, staffing, leading, and controlling.

human resource management (HRM)
The process of acquiring, training, appraising, and compensating employees, and of attending to their labor relations, health and safety, and fairness concerns.

new businesses created every year. Statistically speaking, therefore, most people graduating from college in the next few years either will work for small businesses or will create new small businesses of their own. Especially if you are managing your own small firm with no human resource manager, you'll have to understand the nuts and bolts of human resource management.[6] We'll focus on *HR for entrepreneurs* in Chapter 18.

Line and Staff Aspects of Human Resource Management

All managers are, in a sense, human resource managers, because they all get involved in activities like recruiting, interviewing, selecting, and training. Yet most firms also have human resource departments with their own top managers. How do the duties of this human resource manager and his or her staff relate to "line" managers' human resource duties? Let's answer this question, starting with a short definition of line versus staff authority.

Authority is the right to make decisions, to direct the work of others, and to give orders. In management, we usually distinguish between line authority and staff authority.

Line authority gives managers the right (or authority) to *issue orders* to other managers or employees. It creates a superior–subordinate relationship. **Staff authority** gives the manager the right (authority) to *advise* other managers or employees. It creates an advisory relationship. **Line managers** have line authority. **Staff managers** have staff authority. The latter generally cannot issue orders down the chain of command (except in their own departments).

In popular usage, managers associate line managers with managing functions (like sales or production) that are crucial for the company's survival. Staff managers generally run departments that are advisory or supportive, like purchasing, human resource management, and quality control. This distinction makes sense as long as the "staff" department is, in fact, purely advisory. However, it's really not the type of department the person is in charge of or its name that determines whether the manager is line or staff. It is the nature of the relationship. The line manager can issue orders. The staff manager can advise.

Human resource managers are usually staff managers. They assist and advise line managers in areas like recruiting, hiring, and compensation. However, line managers still have human resource duties.

3 Illustrate the human resources responsibilities of line and staff (HR) managers.

Line Managers' Human Resource Duties

The direct handling of people has always been an integral part of every line manager's duties, from president down to first-line supervisors. For example, one major company

Line authority gives the manager the right to issue orders.

Source: Courtesy of John A. Rizzo/Getty Images, Inc.–Photodisc/ Royalty Free.

outlines its line supervisors' responsibilities for effective human resource management under these general headings:

1. Placing the right person on the right job
2. Starting new employees in the organization (orientation)
3. Training employees for jobs that are new to them
4. Improving the job performance of each person
5. Gaining cooperation and developing smooth working relationships
6. Interpreting the company's policies and procedures
7. Controlling labor costs
8. Developing the abilities of each person
9. Creating and maintaining department morale
10. Protecting employees' health and physical condition

In small organizations, line managers may carry out all these personnel duties unassisted. But as the organization grows, they need the assistance, specialized knowledge, and advice of a separate human resource staff. The human resource department provides this specialized assistance.

Human Resource Manager's Duties

In providing this specialized assistance, the *human resource manager* carries out three distinct functions:

1. **A line function.** The human resource manager directs the activities of the people in his or her own department, and perhaps in related areas (like the plant cafeteria).
2. **A coordinative function.** The human resource manager also coordinates personnel activities, a duty often referred to as **functional authority** (or functional control). Here he or she ensures that line managers are implementing the firm's human resource policies and practices (for example, adhering to its sexual harassment policies).
3. **Staff (assist and advise) functions.** Assisting and advising line managers is the heart of the human resource manager's job. He or she *advises* the CEO so the CEO can better understand the personnel aspects of the company's strategic options. HR *assists* in hiring, training, evaluating, rewarding, counseling, promoting, and firing employees. It administers the various benefit programs (health and accident insurance, retirement, vacation, and so on). It helps line managers comply with equal employment and occupational safety laws, and plays an important role in handling grievances and labor relations. It carries out an *innovator* role, by providing up-to-date information on current trends and new methods for better utilizing the company's employees (or "human resources"). It plays an *employee advocacy* role, by representing the interests of employees within the framework of its primary obligation to senior management. Although

authority
The right to make decisions, direct others' work, and give orders.

line authority
The authority exerted by an HR manager by directing the activities of the people in his or her own department and in service areas (like the plant cafeteria).

staff authority
Staff authority gives the manager the right (authority) to advise other managers or employees.

line manager
A manager who is authorized to direct the work of subordinates and is responsible for accomplishing the organization's tasks.

staff manager
A manager who assists and advises line managers.

functional authority
The authority exerted by an HR manager as coordinator of personnel activities.

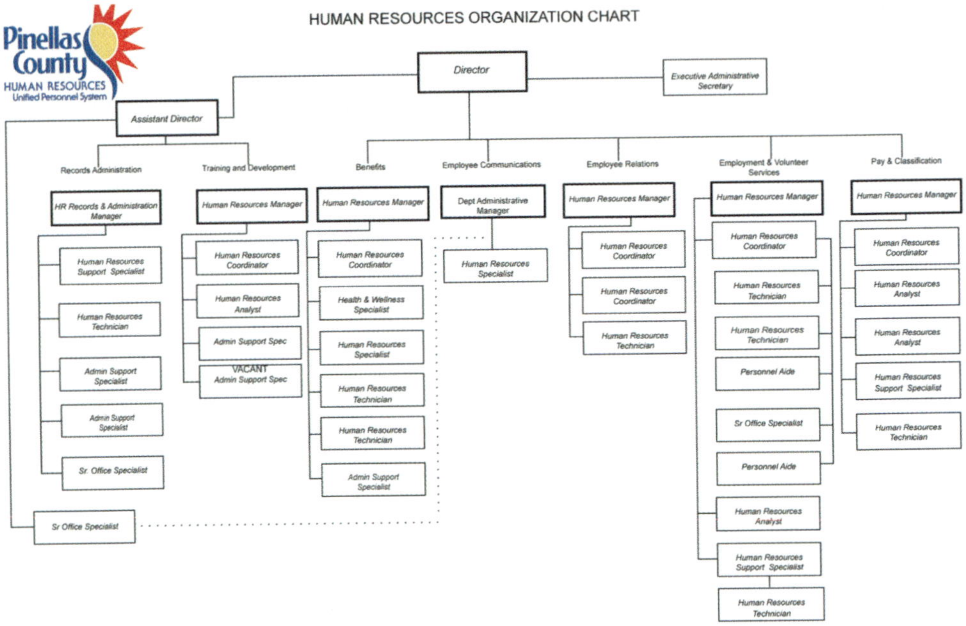

FIGURE 1-1 Human Resources Organization Chart

Source: www.co.pinellas.fl.us/persnl/pdf/orgchart.pdf, accessed April 1, 2009. Used with permission of Pinellas County Govt.

human resource managers generally can't wield line authority (outside their departments), they are likely to exert *implied authority*. This is because line managers know the human resource manager has top management's ear in areas like testing and affirmative action.

The size of the human resource department reflects the size of the employer. For a very large employer, an organization chart like the one in Figure 1-1 would be typical, containing a full complement of specialists for each HR function. At the other extreme, the human resource team for a small manufacturer may contain just five or six (or fewer) staff, and have an organization similar to that in Figure 1-2. There is *generally* about one human resource employee per 100 company employees.

Examples of human resource management specialties include:[7]

- **Recruiters.** Search for qualified job applicants.
- **Equal employment opportunity (EEO) coordinators.** Investigate and resolve EEO grievances; examine organizational practices for potential violations; and compile and submit EEO reports.
- **Job analysts.** Collect and examine information about jobs to prepare job descriptions.
- **Compensation managers.** Develop compensation plans and handle the employee benefits program.
- **Training specialists.** Plan, organize, and direct training activities.
- **Labor relations specialists.** Advise management on all aspects of union–management relations.

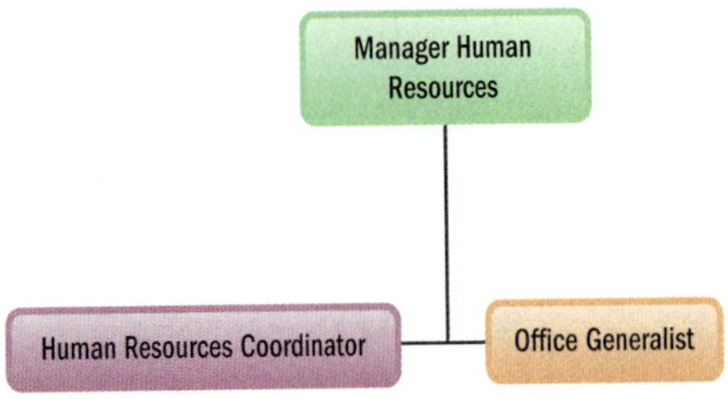

FIGURE 1-2 HR Organization Chart (Small Company)

New Approaches to Organizing HR

Employers are also experimenting with offering human resource services in new ways. For example, some employers organize their HR services around four groups: transactional, corporate, embedded, and centers of expertise.[8]

- The *transactional HR* group focuses on using centralized call centers and outsourcing arrangements with vendors (such as benefits advisors) to provide specialized support in day-to-day transactional HR activities (such as changing benefits plans and providing updated appraisal forms) to the company's employees.
- The *corporate HR* group focuses on assisting top management in "top level" big picture issues such as developing the company's long-term strategic plan.
- The *embedded HR* unit assigns HR generalists (also known as "relationship managers" or "HR business partners") directly to departments like sales and production, to provide the localized human resource management assistance the departments need.
- The *centers of expertise* are like specialized HR consulting firms within the company—for instance, providing specialized assistance in areas such as organizational change.

IBM Example For example, Randy MacDonald, IBM's senior vice president of human resources, says the traditional human resource organization improperly isolates HR functions into "silos" such as recruitment, training, and employee relations. He says this silo approach means there's no one team of human resource specialists focusing on the needs of specific groups of employees.

MacDonald therefore reorganized IBM's human resources function. He segmented IBM's 330,000 employees into three sets of "customers": executive and technical employees, managers, and rank and file. Separate human resource management teams (consisting of recruitment, training, and compensation specialists, for instance) now focus on serving the needs of each employee segment. These specialized teams help ensure that the employees in each segment get precisely the talent, learning, and compensation they require to support IBM's needs.[9]

3 Illustrate the human resources responsibilities of line and staff (HR) managers.

Cooperative Line and Staff HR Management: An Example

Because both line managers and human resource managers have human resource management duties, it is reasonable to ask, "Exactly which HR duties are carried out by line managers and by staff managers?" No one division of responsibilities would apply to all organizations, but we can generalize.

The most important generalization is that the line–staff relationship is generally cooperative.[10] For example, in recruiting and hiring, the line manager describes the qualifications employees need to fill specific positions. Then the human resource team takes over. They develop sources of qualified applicants, and conduct initial screening interviews. They administer the appropriate tests. Then they refer the best applicants to the line manager, who interviews and selects the ones he or she wants. In training, the line manager again describes what he or she expects the employee to be able to do. Then the human resource team devises a training program, which the line manager then (usually) administers.

Some activities are usually HR's alone. For example, 60% of firms assign to human resources the exclusive responsibility for preemployment testing, 75% assign it college recruiting, and 80% assign it insurance benefits administration. But employers split most activities, such as employment interviews, performance appraisal, skills training, job descriptions, and disciplinary procedures, between HR and line managers.[11]

Figure 1-3 illustrates the typical HR–line management partnership. For example, HR alone typically handles interviewing in about 25% of firms. But in about 60% of firms, HR and the other hiring departments both get involved in interviewing.

In summary, human resource management is part of every manager's job. Whether you're a first-line supervisor, middle manager, or president—or whether you're a

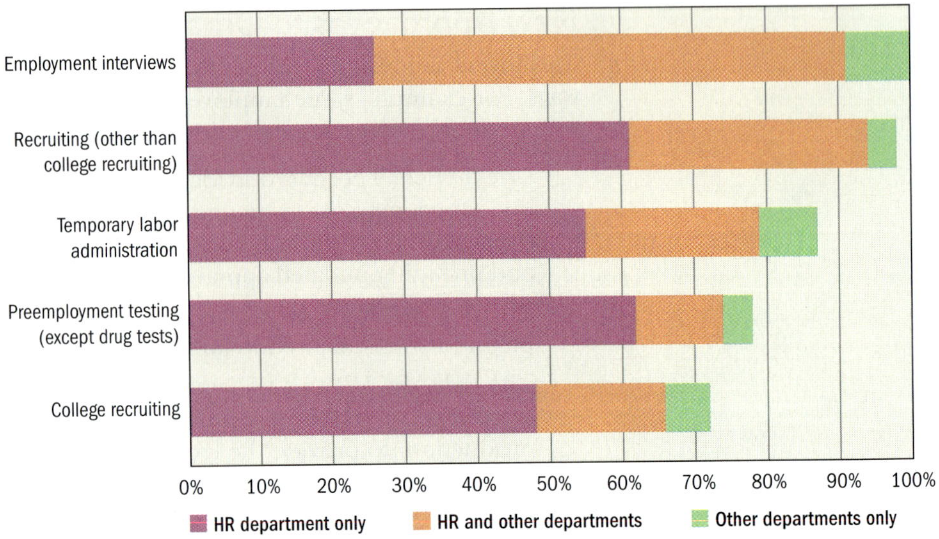

Note: Length of bars represents prevalence of activity among all surveyed employers.

FIGURE 1-3 Employment and Recruiting—Who Handles It? (Percentage of All Employers)

Source: *HR MAGAZINE*, Copyright 2002 by Society for Human Resource Management (SHRM). Reproduced with permission of Society for Human Resource Management (SHRM) in the format Textbook via Copyright Clearance Center.

production manager or county manager (or HR manager)—*getting results through people* is the name of the game. And to do this, you will need a good working knowledge of the human resource management concepts and techniques in this book.

Moving from Line Manager to HR Manager

Which brings us to another reason to be familiar with this book's contents: You may well make a planned (or unplanned) stopover some day as a human resource manager. A survey by a team at the University of Southern California found that about one-fourth of large U.S. businesses appointed managers with no human resource management experience as their top human resource management executives. Reasons given include the fact that these people may give the firms' human resource management efforts a more strategic emphasis, and the possibility that they may sometimes be better equipped to integrate the firm's HR efforts with the rest of the business.[12] In any case, companies often promote their line managers through HR on their way up the corporate ladder. For example, after spending about a year and a half as Walmart's chief human resource officer, the company promoted Lawrence Jackson to run its global procurement division.[13]

However, most top human resource executives do have prior human resource experience. About 80% of those in one survey worked their way up within HR.[14] About 17% of these HR executives had earned the Human Resource Certification Institute's senior professional in human resources (SPHR) designation, and 13% were certified professionals in human resources (PHR).

4 Briefly discuss and illustrate each of the important trends influencing human resource management.

THE TRENDS SHAPING HUMAN RESOURCE MANAGEMENT

Someone always has to staff the organization, so human resource (or "personnel") managers have long played important roles. Working cooperatively with line managers, they've helped administer benefits, screen employees, and recommend appraisal forms, for instance.

However, exactly what they do and how they do it is changing. Some of the reasons for these changes are obvious. For example, employers can now use intranets to let employees change their own benefits plans, something they obviously couldn't do, say, 20 or so years ago. Some other trends shaping human resource management practices are perhaps more subtle. These trends include globalization, technology, deregulation, debt or "leverage," changes in demographics and the nature of work, and economic challenges (summarized in Figure 1-4). We'll discuss these trends next.[15]

FIGURE 1-4 Trends Shaping Human Resource Management

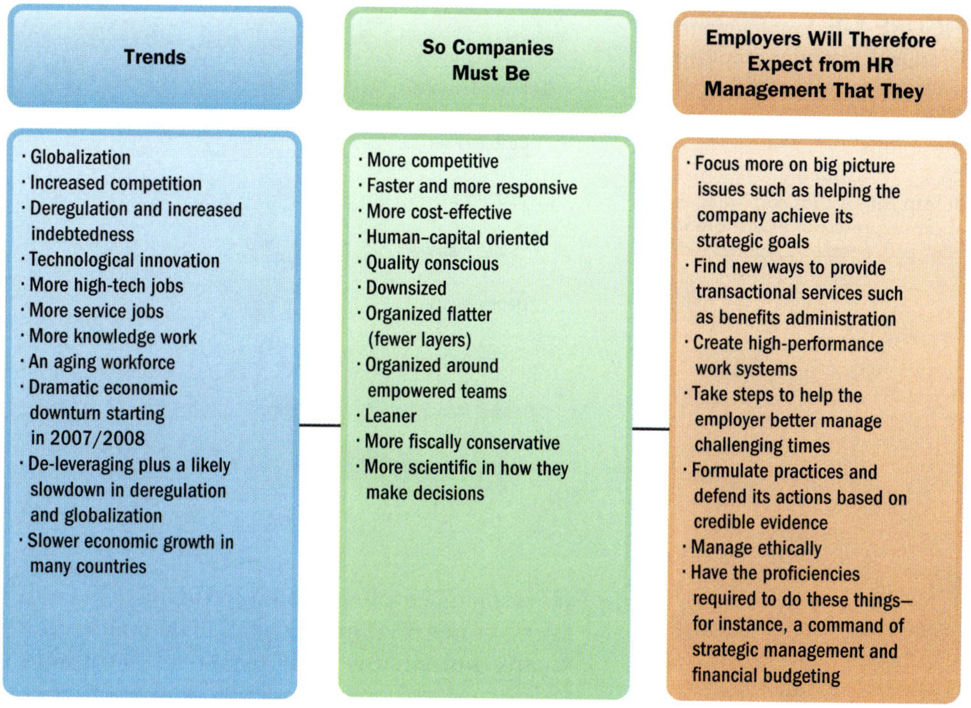

Globalization and Competition Trends

Globalization refers to the tendency of firms to extend their sales, ownership, and/or manufacturing to new markets abroad. Examples surround us. Toyota produces the Camry in Kentucky, while Dell produces PCs in China. Free trade areas—agreements that reduce tariffs and barriers among trading partners—further encourage international trade. NAFTA (the North American Free Trade Agreement) and the EU (European Union) are examples.

Companies expand abroad for several reasons. *Sales expansion* is one. Thus, Google expanded its China presence by initiating its Google China instant messaging service there. Walmart is opening stores in South America. Dell, knowing that China will soon be the world's biggest market for PCs, is aggressively building plants and selling there.

Firms go abroad for other reasons. Some manufacturers seek *new foreign products* and services to sell, and to *cut labor costs.* Thus, some apparel manufacturers design and cut fabrics in Miami, and then have the actual products assembled in Central America, where labor costs are relatively low. Sometimes, it's the prospect of *forming partnerships* that drives firms to do business abroad. Several years ago, IBM sold its PC division to the Chinese firm Lenovo, in part to cement firmer ties with the booming China market.

For businesspeople, globalization's essential characteristic is this: More globalization means more competition, and more competition means more pressure to be "world-class"—to lower costs, to make employees more productive, and to do things better and less expensively. As one expert puts it, "The bottom line is that the growing integration of the world economy into a single, huge marketplace is increasing the intensity of competition in a wide range of manufacturing and service industries."[16] Both workers and companies have to work harder and smarter than they did without globalization.[17]

Because of this, globalization brings both benefits and threats. For *consumers* it means lower prices and higher quality on practically everything from computers to cars, but also the prospect of working harder, and perhaps having less secure jobs. *Job offshoring*—having employees abroad do jobs that, say, Americans formerly did—illustrates this threat. For example, Figure 1-5 illustrates that in the next few

globalization
The tendency of firms to extend their sales, ownership, and/or manufacturing to new markets abroad.

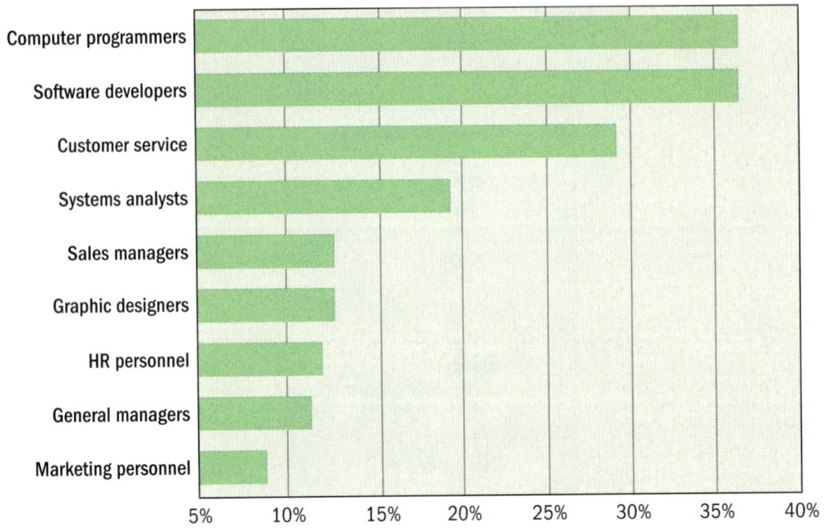

FIGURE 1-5 Employment Exodus: Percent of employers who said they planned as of 2008 to offshore a number of these jobs.

Source: Created from data provided at http://img.icbdr.com/images/aboutus/pressroom/OffshoreStudyFinal.pdf, accessed April 29, 2009.

years, many employers plan to offshore even highly skilled jobs such as sales managers, general managers—and HR managers.[18] For *business owners*, globalization means (potentially) millions of new consumers, but also the considerable threat of facing new and powerful global competitors at home.

For 50 or so years, globalization boomed. For example, the total sum of U.S. imports and exports rose from $47 billion in 1960, to $562 billion in 1980, to about $4.3 *trillion* in 2008.[19] Economic and political philosophies drove this boom. Governments dropped cross-border taxes or tariffs, formed economic "free trade areas" such as NAFTA, and took other steps to encourage the free flow of trade among countries. The fundamental economic rationale was that by doing so, all countries would gain. And indeed, economies around the world, not just in the United States but also in Europe and Asia, did grow rapidly.

Indebtedness ("Leverage") and Deregulation

Other trends contributed to this economic growth. Deregulation was one. In many countries, governments stripped away rules and regulations. In the United States and Europe, for instance, the rules that prevented commercial banks from expanding into new businesses such as stock brokering were relaxed. Giant, multinational "financial supermarkets" such as Citibank quickly emerged. As economies boomed, more businesses and consumers went deeply into debt. Homebuyers bought homes, often with little money down. Banks freely lent money to developers to build more homes. For almost 20 years, U.S. consumers actually spent more than they earned. On a grander scale, the United States itself increasingly became a debtor nation. Its balance of payments (exports minus imports) went from a healthy positive $3.5 billion in 1960, to a not-so-healthy *minus* $19.4 billion in 1980 (imports exceeded exports), to a huge $695 billion deficit in 2008.[20] The only way the country could keep buying more from abroad than it sold was by borrowing money. So, much of the boom was built on debt.

Technological Trends

Everyone knows that technology changed the nature of almost everything we do. We use PDAs to communicate with the office, and plan trips, manage money, and custom-build new computers online.

Similarly, technology changed what businesses do and how they do it. Technology (in the form of Internet-based communications) enabled Dell and thousands of other employers to offshore call center jobs to India. The retailer Zara doesn't need expensive inventories. Zara operates its own Internet-based worldwide distribution network, linked to its checkout registers around the world. When its headquarters in Spain sees a garment "flying" out of a store, Zara's computerized manufacturing system dyes

Source: Courtesy of Paul Thompson; Ecoscene/CORBIS-NY/© Paul Thompson; Ecoscene/CORBIS.

Many blue-collar workers no longer do hard physical labor with dangerous machinery like this. Instead, as explained in the text, Chad Toulouse spends most of his time as a team leader typing commands into computerized machines.

the required fabric, cuts and manufactures the item, and speeds it to that store within days.[21] Companies use virtual online communities to improve efficiency. For example, to win a $300 million navy ship deal, Lockheed-Martin established a virtual design environment with about 200 global suppliers, via a private intranet existing entirely outside the firewalls of the individual companies.

Trends in the Nature of Work

One implication is that technology has also had a huge impact on how people work, and on the skills and training today's workers need.

High-Tech Jobs For example, skilled machinist Chad Toulouse illustrates the modern blue-collar worker. After an 18-week training course, this former college student works as a team leader in a plant where about 40% of the machines are automated. In older plants, machinists would manually control machines that cut chunks of metal into things like engine parts. Today, Chad and his team spend much of their time typing commands into computerized machines that create precision parts for products, including water pumps. Like other modern machinists, he earns about $50,000 per year (including overtime).[22] More and more traditional factory jobs are going high-tech. As the U.S. government's *Occupational Outlook Quarterly* put it, "knowledge-intensive high tech manufacturing in such industries as aerospace, computers, telecommunications, home electronics, pharmaceuticals, and medical instruments" is replacing factory jobs in steel, auto, rubber, and textiles.[23]

Service Jobs Technology is not the only trend driving the change from "brawn to brains." Today over two-thirds of the U.S. workforce is employed in producing and delivering services, not products. Between 2004 and 2014, almost all of the 19 million new jobs added in the United States will be in services, not in goods-producing industries.[24]

Several things account for this.[25] With global competition, more manufacturing jobs are shifting to low-wage countries. For example, Levi Strauss, one of the last major clothing manufacturers in the United States, closed the last of its American plants a few years ago. There has also been a dramatic increase in productivity that lets manufacturers produce more with fewer workers. Just-in-time manufacturing techniques link daily manufacturing schedules more precisely to customer demand, thus squeezing waste out of the system and reducing inventory needs. As manufacturers integrate Internet-based customer ordering with just-in-time manufacturing systems, scheduling becomes even more precise. More manufacturers are collaborating with their suppliers to create integrated supply chains. For example, when a customer orders a Dell computer, the same Internet message that informs Dell's assembly line to produce the order also signals the video screen and keyboard manufacturers to prepare for UPS to pick up their parts at a particular time. The net effect is that manufacturers have been squeezing slack and inefficiencies out of the entire production system, enabling companies to produce more products with fewer employees. So, in America and much of Europe, manufacturing jobs are down, and service jobs up.

Knowledge Work and Human Capital In general, the best jobs that remain require more education and more skills. For example, we saw that automation and just-in-time manufacturing mean that even manufacturing jobs require more reading, mathematics, and communication skills than before.[26]

For managers, this means a growing emphasis on knowledge workers like Chad Toulouse, and therefore on *human capital*.[27] **Human capital** refers to the knowledge,

human capital
The knowledge, education, training, skills, and expertise of a firm's workers.

education, training, skills, and expertise of a firm's workers.[28] Today, as management guru Peter Drucker predicted years ago, "the center of gravity in employment is moving fast from manual and clerical workers to knowledge workers . . . ."[29] Human resource managers recently listed "critical thinking/problem-solving" and "information technology application" as the two applied skills most likely to increase in importance over the next 5 years.[30]

To recap, we're living in a high-tech, competitive world—one that puts a big premium on building and capitalizing on human capital. This makes human resource management skills such as recruiting, screening, training, and paying employees more important to employers.

For example, one bank installed special software that made it easier for its customer service representatives to handle customers' inquiries. However, the bank did not otherwise change the service reps' jobs in any way. Here, the new system did help the service reps handle a few more calls. But otherwise, this bank saw no big performance gains.[31]

A second bank installed the same software. Seeking to capitalize on the new software, this bank upgraded the customer service representatives' jobs. The bank gave them new training, taught them how to sell more of the bank's services, gave them more authority to make decisions, and raised their wages. Here, the new computer system dramatically improved product sales and profitability. The moral is that today's employers need human resource managers who do more than hire and fire employees and monitor benefits. They need ones who have the human resource management skills to create the "human capital" required to compete in a high-tech, competitive world.[32]

Workforce and Demographic Trends

All of this is occurring along with big workforce and demographic trends.

Demographic Trends Most importantly, the U.S. workforce is fast becoming older and more multi-ethnic.[33] Table 1-1, from the U.S. Department of Labor's Bureau of Labor Statistics, provides a bird's-eye view. For example, between 1996 and 2016, the percent of the workforce that it classifies as "white, non-Hispanic" will drop from 75.3% to 64.6%. At the same time, the percent of the workforce that is black will rise from 11.3% to 12.3%; those classified as Asian will rise from 4.3% to 5.3%; and those of Hispanic origin will rise from 9.5% to 16.4%. The percentages of younger workers will fall, while those over 55 years of age will leap from 11.9% of the workforce in 1996 to 22% in 2016. If we go back to 1986, the demographic trends become even more pronounced.

At the same time, demographic trends are making finding, hiring, and supervising employees more challenging.[34] In the United States, experts at the Department of Labor don't expect labor force growth to keep pace with job growth, with an estimated shortfall of about 14 million college-educated workers by 2020.[35] One study of 35 large global companies' senior human resource managers recently said "talent

TABLE 1-1 Demographic Groups as a Percent of the Workforce, 1986–2016

Age, Race, Ethnicity	1986	1996	2006	2016
Age: 16–24	19.8%	15.8%	14.8%	12.7%
25–54	67.5	72.3	68.4	64.6
55+	12.6	11.9	16.8	22.7
White, non-Hispanic	79.8	75.3	69.1	64.6
Black	10.7	11.3	11.4	12.3
Asian	2.9	4.3	4.4	5.3
Hispanic origin	6.9	9.5	13.7	16.4

Source: Adapted from www.bls.gov/emp/emplabor01.pdf, accessed October 20, 2008.

management"—in particular, the acquisition, development and retention of talent to fill the companies' employment needs—ranked as their top concern.[36]

"Generation Y" Furthermore, some experts contend that many younger workers may have different work values than did their parents.[37] Based on one study, older employees are more likely to be work-centric (focusing more on work than on family with respect to career decisions). Younger workers tend to be more family-centric or dual-centric (balancing family and work life).[38] (On the other hand, regardless of the employee's age, "everyone wants to be able to trust their supervisor, no one really likes change, [and] we all like feedback . . . .")[39]

Fortune magazine says that today's "Millennial" or "Generation Y" employees will bring challenges and strengths. It says they may be "the most high maintenance workforce in the history of the world."[40] Referring to them as "the most praised generation," the *Wall Street Journal* explains how Lands' End and Bank of America are teaching their managers to compliment these new employees with quick feedback and recognition.[41] But, as the first generation to grow up using computers and e-mail, their capacity for using information technology will also make them the most high-performing.[42]

Retirees Many human resource professionals call "the aging workforce" the biggest demographic trend affecting employers. The basic problem is that there aren't enough younger workers to replace the projected number of baby boom era older-worker retirees.[43]

Employers are dealing with this challenge in various ways. One survey found that 41% of surveyed employers are bringing retirees back into the workforce, 34% are conducting studies to determine projected retirement rates in the organization, and 31% are offering employment options designed to attract and retain semi-retired workers.[44]

Nontraditional Workers At the same time, there has been a shift to nontraditional workers. Nontraditional workers include those who hold multiple jobs, or who are "contingent" or part-time workers, or who are working in alternative work arrangements (such as a mother–daughter team sharing one clerical job). Today, almost 10% of American workers—13 million people—fit this nontraditional workforce category. Of these, about 8 million are independent contractors who work on specific projects and move on once they complete the projects.

Economic Challenges and Trends

All these trends are occurring in a context of challenge and upheaval. As you can see in Figure 1-6, gross national product (GNP)—a measure of the United States of America's total output—boomed between 2001 and 2007. During this period, home prices (see Figure 1-7) leaped as much as 20% per year. Unemployment remained

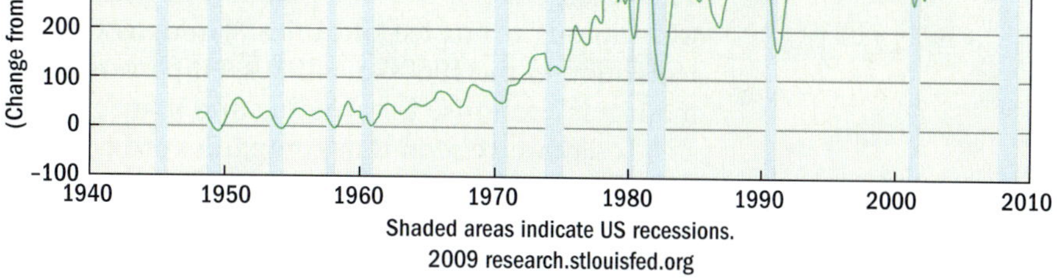

FIGURE 1-6 Gross National Product (GNP)

Source: U.S. Department of Commerce: Bureau of Economic Analysis, http://research.stlouisfed.org/fred2/fredgraph?chart_type=line&s[1][id]=GNP&s[1][transformation]=ch1, accessed April 18, 2009.

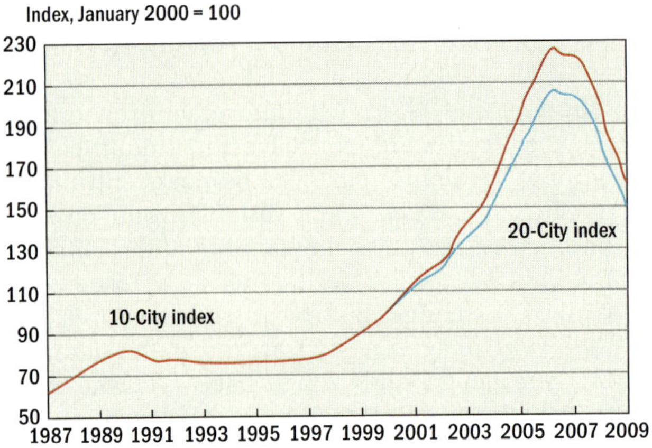

FIGURE 1-7 Case-Shiller Home Price Indexes

Source: S&P, Fiserv, and MacroMarkets, LLC, http://www.clevelandfed.org/research/trends/2009/0309/04ecoact.cfm, accessed April 18, 2009.

docile at about 4.7%.[45] Then, around 2007–2008, all these measures seemingly fell off a cliff. GNP fell. Home prices dropped by 20% or more (depending on city). Unemployment nationwide rose to more than 8%.

Why did all this happen? That is a complicated question, but for one thing, all those years of accumulating excessive debt seems to have run their course. Banks and other financial institutions (such as hedge funds) found themselves with trillions of dollars of worthless loans on their books. Governments stepped in to try to prevent their collapse. Lending dried up. Many businesses and consumers simply stopped buying. The economy tanked.

Economic trends will undoubtedly turn positive again, perhaps even as you read these pages. However, they have certainly grabbed employers' attention. After what the world went through starting in 2007, it's doubtful that the deregulation, leveraging, and globalization that drove economic growth for the previous 50 years will continue unabated. That may mean slower growth for many countries, perhaps for years. This means challenging times ahead for employers. The challenging times mean that for the foreseeable future—and even well after things turn positive—employers will have to be more frugal and creative in managing their human resources than perhaps they've been in the past.

5 List and briefly describe important trends in human resource management.

IMPORTANT TRENDS IN HUMAN RESOURCE MANAGEMENT

Trends like these translate into changes in human resource management practices, and in what employers expect from their human resource managers. We'll look at some specifics.

The New Human Resource Managers

Perhaps the best way to start is with a snapshot of how personnel/human resource management evolved. For much of the twentieth century, personnel/HR managers focused on transactional sorts of issues. In the earliest firms, they first took over hiring and firing from supervisors, ran the payroll department, and administered benefit plans. As technology in areas like testing began to appear, the personnel department began to play an expanded role, for instance in employee selection and training.[46] The emergence of union legislation in the 1930s added "Helping the employer deal with unions" to its list of duties. Then, as Congress passed new equal employment legislation in the 1960s and 1970s, employers began leaning on their human resource managers' expertise for avoiding and managing discrimination claims.[47]

Today, we've seen that companies are competing in a very challenging new environment. Globalization, competition, technology, workforce trends, and economic upheaval confront employers with new challenges. In that context, they expect and demand that their human resource managers exhibit the competencies required to help the company address these new challenges proactively. In practice, this boils down to three things for human resource managers.

They Focus More on Big Picture Issues First, human resource management is more involved in "big picture" issues. Here's a quick example. Several years ago, Wisconsin-based Signicast Corp.'s president, Terry Lutz, and his board decided to build a new, computerized plant. Signicast produces metal parts from a casting process. To compete, the firm needed the new, automated plant. Mr. Lutz and his team understood that "in the real world, new automation technology requires a new kind of employee." They knew the computerized plant was useless without employees who could work in teams, manage their own work, and run the plant's computerized equipment. Lutz and his management team worked closely with and relied on Signicast's human resource management unit to select, train, and organize the tech-friendly people the new plant required.[48] By formulating and executing the hiring and other personnel practices that Signicast needed to make the plant a success, the HR team was supporting Signicast's new strategy.

Therefore, the first change is that today's new human resource managers are involved in more "big picture" issues. They don't just do transactional things like signing onboard new employees. Employers want them to be the firms' *internal consultants,* identifying and institutionalizing changes that help employees better contribute to the company's success, and helping top management formulate and execute its long-term plans or *strategies.*[49]

Two writers summarize this idea by observing that human resource managers are shifting their focus *from* providing transactional services *to* providing top management with decisions that "inform and support."[50] But then, who does the day-to-day transactional things like recruiting and testing employees, and signing them on?

They Find New Ways to Provide Transactional Services The answer is that (second), the new human resource managers also must be adept at offering those traditional "bread and butter" transactional HR services in new ways. We'll see that human resource managers do this in several ways. For example, they *outsource* more of these services (such as benefits administration) to outside vendors.[51] They use *technology* (such as intranet-based Web sites, for instance) to enable employees to self-administer benefits plans. (Table 1-2 lists some important ways employers use technology to support their human resource management activities.[52]) And,

TABLE 1-2 Some Technological Applications to Support HR

Technology	How Used by HR
Application service providers (ASPs) and technology outsourcing	ASPs provide software application, for instance, for processing employment applications. The ASPs host and manage the services for the employer from their own remote computers
Web portals	Employers use these, for instance, to enable employees to sign up for and manage their own benefits packages and to update their personal information
Streaming desktop video	Used, for instance, to facilitate distance learning and training or to provide corporate information to employees quickly and inexpensively
Internet- and network-monitoring software	Used to track employees' Internet and e-mail activities or to monitor their performance
Electronic signatures	Legally valid e-signatures that employers use to more expeditiously obtain signatures for applications and record keeping
Electronic bill presentment and payment	Used, for instance, to eliminate paper checks and to facilitate payments to employees and suppliers
Data warehouses and computerized analytical programs	Help HR managers monitor their HR systems. For example, they make it easier to assess things like cost per hire, and to compare current employees' skills with the firm's projected strategic needs

employers such as Dell set up special *centralized call centers* to answer HR-related inquiries from employees and supervisors.

They Have New Proficiencies[53] Finally, strategizing, internal consulting, and dealing with outside vendors and technology call for new human resource management proficiencies. (The new HR manager "is not your father's HR manager," as one car commercial lamely put it several years ago.) Of course, human resource managers still need skills in areas such as employee selection, training, and compensation. But in addition, they require broader *business knowledge and proficiencies.* For example, to assist top management in formulating strategies, the human resource manager needs to be familiar with strategic planning, marketing, production, and finance.[54] He or she must also be able to "speak the CFO's language," by explaining human resource activities in financially measurable terms, such as return on investment and cost per unit of service.[55]

Studies show that top management and chief financial officers recognize the critical role human resource management can play in achieving a company's strategic goals.[56] Figure 1-8 summarizes some results. It shows they know that human capital—the employees' knowledge, skills, and experiences—can have a big effect on important organizational outcomes such as customer satisfaction and profitability. Partly as a result, human resource executives are increasingly well paid. For example, average total direct compensation for top HR executives was recently more than $1.4 million per year.[57]

Strategic Human Resource Management

The way Signicast Corp.'s Terry Lutz worked with his HR team to design and implement his company's strategy illustrates what managers call "strategic human resource management." We'll see in Chapter 3 (Strategy) that *strategic human resource management* means formulating and executing human resource policies and practices that produce the employee competencies and behaviors the company needs to achieve its strategic aims. Signicast's new strategy required employees with the knowledge, skills, and motivation to run the new automated plant. Signicast's strategic human resource plan therefore included detailed guidelines regarding what skills and knowledge the workers would need, as well as exactly how to recruit, test, select, and train such workers. Signicast's management knew that without the necessary employee knowledge, training, and skills—"human capital"—in place, the new plant could not function. Its strategic human resource plans enabled the company to hire the employees who could exhibit the behaviors the company needed to accomplish its goals (in this case, make the new plant succeed).

FIGURE 1-8 Effects CFOs Believe Human Capital Has on Business Outcomes

Source: Human Capital Management: The CFO's Perspective, CFO Publishing Corp., February 2003. Reprinted with permission.

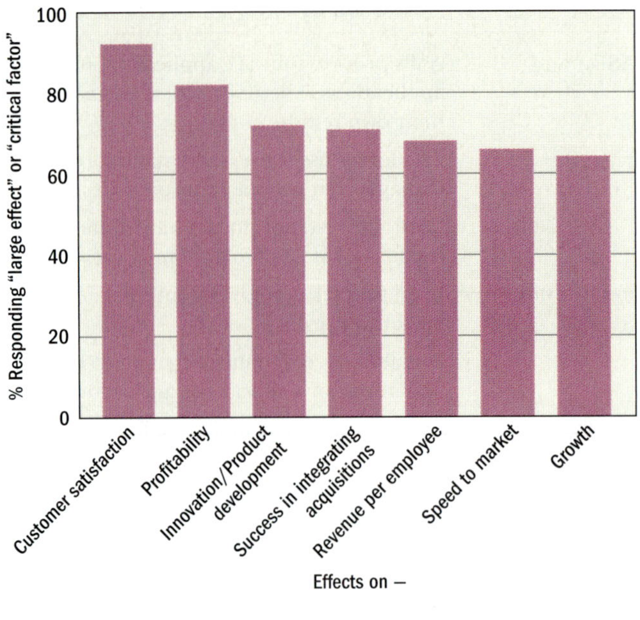

High-Performance Work Systems

The multitude of competitive and economic challenges also means that employers must focus like a laser on *productivity and performance* improvement.

We'll see in this book how human resource practices can improve performance in challenging times. For example, studies of personnel testing's effectiveness conclude that screening applicants with personnel testing can produce employees who perform better.[58] Similarly, well-trained employees perform better than untrained ones, and safe workplaces produce fewer lost-time accidents and accident costs than do unsafe ones. The most productive and highest performing world-class companies, like Toyota, have also long had "high-performance" selection, training, and plant safety programs.

A *high-performance work system* is a set of human resource management policies and practices that together produce superior employee performance. One study focused on 17 manufacturing plants, some of which adopted high-performance work system practices. For example, the high-performance plants paid more (median wages of $16 per hour compared with $13 per hour for all plants), trained more (83% offered more than 20 hours of training per year, compared with 32% for all plants), used more sophisticated recruitment and hiring practices (tests and validated interviews, for instance), and used more self-managing work teams. These plants also had the best overall performance, in terms of higher profits, lower operating costs, and lower turnover.[59] We'll study high-performance work systems more closely in Chapter 3.

6 Define and give an example of evidence-based human resource management.

Evidence-Based Human Resource Management

Saying you have a "high-performance" organization assumes that you can actually measure how you're doing.[60] In today's challenging environment, employers naturally expect that their human resource management teams be able to do this. For example, "How much will that new testing program save us in reduced employee turnover?" "How much more productive will our employees be if we institute that new training program?" And, "How productive is our human resource team, in terms of HR staff per employee, compared to our competitors?"

Providing evidence such as this is the heart of *evidence-based human resource management.* This is the use of data, facts, analytics, scientific rigor, critical evaluation, and critically evaluated research/case studies to support human resource management proposals, decisions, practices, and conclusions.[61] Put simply, evidence-based human resource management is the deliberate use of the best-available evidence in making decisions about the human resource management practices you are focusing on.[62] The evidence may come from *actual measurements* you make (such as, how did the trainees like this program?). It may come from *existing data* (such as, what happened to company profits after we installed this training program?). Or, it may come from published critically evaluated *research studies* (such as, what does the research literature conclude about the best way to ensure that trainees remember what they learn?). The accompanying Evidenced-Based HR feature helps to explain why managers should be evidence-based.

EVIDENCE-BASED HR

Why Should You Be Evidence-Based?

The accompanying text says, "Put simply, evidence-based human resource management is the deliberate use of the best-available evidence in making decisions about the human resource management practices you are focusing on."

Given the fact that (let's face it) so much of management seems to be common sense, you could reasonably ask, "Why should taking an evidence-based approach to making decisions be important to me as a manager?"

One way to answer that is with an example. Let's go back to this chapter's opening vignette, about Stanford's Restaurant in Lake Oswego, Oregon. You'll recall that in the vignette we said that the average restaurant has annual employee turnover of more than 100% per year (which is true) and that the manager of that Stanford

Restaurant estimates his hourly turnover is only about 28% (which we can assume is also true). But after that, we took a small leap of faith. We suggested that his good human resource management practices explained his great results: "For one thing, I'm selective on who I hire. I'm looking for people who want to stay . . . ."[63]

Now, the idea that his restaurant has fewer turnovers because he is careful about whom he hires certainly makes intuitive sense (and, indeed, it's probably true). However, there is really no evidence in the vignette (or in the source from which it came) to support that claim. But then, what else could explain the fact that his turnover is so low? Think about that for a moment. Perhaps Lake Oswego, Oregon, for some reason, has an unusually high unemployment rate, and people there are happy to keep their jobs. Perhaps the manager pays such high salaries that, while he has low turnover, the restaurant itself can never be profitable. Or perhaps the manager only hires people from among his relatives, none of whom are inclined to leave his employ (that's not a serious option). The problem, of course, is that if there *were* some other factors like these that explain this restaurant's low turnover, other restaurant managers who tried this manager's HR practices would discover that his HR practices simply don't work for them. And based on the evidence, we just don't know.

The point is that unless you take a healthy, skeptical, evidence-based approach to what you do as a manager, you may jump to the wrong managerial conclusions. Life is filled with intuitive-sounding insights (such as "opposites attract") that usually turn out to have little or no basis in fact. So as a manager you should always be asking questions like, "What is the evidence for this claim?" and "Did this action really cause this result?" Even experts sometimes are misled. For example, we'll see in Chapter 6 (Testing) that after assuming for years that applicant personality testing improved organizational performance, there is now a vigorous debate in the literature about whether that's even true.

We'll also see (in Chapter 3) that the fundamental requirement for measurability is that the human resource manager needs the numbers. Specifically, he or she needs quantitative performance measures (*metrics*). For example, median HR expenses as a proportion of companies' total operating costs average about 0.8%. There tends to be between 0.9 and 1.0 human resource staff persons per 100 employees (the ratio tends to be lower in retailing and distribution firms and higher in public, state organizations).[64]

Managing Ethics

Every few years (somewhat depressingly), some manager makes the news for his or her unethical practices. There were, for instance, the insider trading scandals of the 1990s, the "Enron scandal" of 2001, the stock options post-dating scandals of the mid-2000s, and the sub-prime and Ponzi scheme scandals just a few years ago. *Ethics* means the standards someone uses to decide what his or her conduct should be. The (seemingly) chronic nature of ethical scandals should give all managers pause. The one sure way to do everything right as a manager and still go down in flames is to let one's ethics lapse.

That certainly applies to human resource management. We'll see in Chapter 14 (Ethics) that six of the ten most serious workplace ethical issues—workplace safety, security of employee records, employee theft, affirmative action, comparable work, and employee privacy rights—were human resource management related.[65] Prosecutors recently filed criminal charges against several Iowa meatpacking plant human resource managers, who allegedly violated employment law by hiring children younger than 16.[66] Every line manager or human resource manager needs to keep in mind the ethical implications of his or her employee-related decisions.

HR Certification

It should not be surprising that as the human resource manager's job becomes more demanding, human resource management is becoming more professionalized. More than 60,000 HR professionals have already passed one or more of the Society for

FIGURE 1-9 Illustrative SHRM® Learning System Module Content

Source: *HR Magazine* Copyright 2004 by Society for Human Resource Management (SHRM). Reproduced with permission of Society for Human Resource Management (SHRM) in the format Textbook via Copyright Clearance Center.

Module 1: Strategic Management
- The Role of Human Resources in Organizations
- The Strategic Planning Process

Organizational Structure and Internal HR Partners
- Measuring Human Resource Effectiveness
- Ethical Issues Affecting Human Resources

Module 2: Workforce Planning and Employment
- Key Legislation Affecting Employee Rights
- Equal Employment Opportunity/Affirmative Action
- Gender Discrimination and Harassment in the Workplace
- Job Analysis and Documentation
- Recruitment
- Selection
- Employment Practices
- Organizational Exit
- Employee Records Management

Module 3: Human Resource Development
- Human Resource Development and the Organization
- Adult Learning and Motivation
- Assessment of HRD Needs
- HRD Program Design and Development
- HRD Program Implementation
- Evaluating HRD Effectiveness
- Career Development
- Organizational Development Initiatives
- Performance Management

Module 4: Compensation and Benefits
- Key Legislation
- Total Compensation and the Strategic Focus of the Organization
- Compensation Systems
- Government-Mandated Benefits
- Compensation and Benefit Programs for Employees
- Evaluating the Total Compensation System and Communicating It to Employees

Module 5: Employee and Labor Relations
- Key Legislation Affecting Employee and Labor Relations
- Positive Employee Relations
- Effective Communication of Laws, Regulations, and Organizational Policies
- Discipline and Formal Complaint Resolution
- Union Organizing
- Unfair Labor Practices
- Collective Bargaining
- Strikes and Secondary Boycotts
- International Employee and Labor Relations

Module 6: Occupational Health, Safety, and Security
- Key Legislation
- Safety
- Health
- Security

Human Resource Management's (SHRM) HR professional certification exams. SHRM's Human Resource Certification Institute offers these exams. Exams test the professional's knowledge of all aspects of human resource management, including ethics, management practices, staffing, development, compensation, labor relations, and health and safety. Those who successfully complete all requirements earn the SPHR (Senior Professional in HR), GPHR (Global Professional in HR), or PHR (Professional in HR) certificate. Figure 1-9 illustrates the body of knowledge in the SHRM certification program. You will find certification-related exercises in the end-of-chapter exercises throughout this book. The test specifications for the HRCI exams, as well as new SHRM-related learning guidelines and exercises for human resource management courses, are in the SHRM appendix at the end of this book. Managers can take an online HRCI assessment exam at www.HRCI.org (or by calling 866-898-HRCI).

7 Outline the plan of this book.

THE PLAN OF THIS BOOK

The Basic Themes and Features

In this book, we'll use several themes and features to emphasize particularly important issues, and to provide continuity from chapter to chapter.

First, human resource management is the *responsibility of every manager*—not just those in human resources. Throughout every page in this book, you'll therefore find an emphasis on practical material that you as a manager will need to perform your day-to-day management responsibilities.

Second, we've seen that the workforce is increasingly diverse. We'll use boxed "Managing the New Workforce" features in most chapters to present snapshots zeroing in on the skills managers need to manage today's diverse employees.

Third, we've seen that the economic challenges the United States and world faced starting around 2008 prompted most employers to re-think the costs and benefits of how they delivered their human resource services. We'll use boxed "Managing HR in Challenging Times" features in most chapters to present snapshots zeroing in on the skills managers need to manage human resources in challenging times.

Fourth, the intensely competitive nature of business today means human resource managers must defend their plans and contributions in measurable terms. Chapter 3 (Strategy) explains how managers do this. We will also use (1) boxed "Evidence-Based HR" features in most chapters to present examples of how managers manage based on facts and evidence, and (2) brief "Research Insights" to illustrate the evidence that supports some of what HR managers do.

CHAPTER CONTENTS OVERVIEW

Following is a brief overview of the chapters and their content.

Part 1: Introduction

Chapter 1: Introduction to Human Resource Management. The manager's human resource management jobs; crucial global and competitive trends; how managers use technology and modern HR measurement systems to create high-performance work systems.

Chapter 2: Equal Opportunity and the Law. What you should know about equal opportunity laws and how they affect activities such as interviewing, selecting employees, and evaluating performance.

Chapter 3: The Manager's Role in Strategic Human Resource Management. What is planning and strategic planning, strategic human resource management, building high-performance HR practices, and tools for evidence-based HR.

Part 2: Recruitment and Placement

Chapter 4: Job Analysis. How to analyze a job; how to determine the human resource requirements of the job, as well as its specific duties and responsibilities.

Chapter 5: Personnel Planning and Recruiting. Human resource planning; determining what sorts of people need to be hired; recruiting them.

Chapter 6: Employee Testing and Selection. Techniques you can use to ensure that you're hiring the right people.

Chapter 7: Interviewing Candidates. How you can interview candidates effectively.

Part 3: Training and Development

Chapter 8: Training and Developing Employees. Providing the training and development to ensure that your employees have the knowledge and skills needed to accomplish their tasks.

Chapter 9: Performance Management and Appraisal. Techniques you can use for appraising employee performance.

Chapter 10: Coaching, Careers, and Talent Management. Coaching employees; managing careers; techniques such as career planning and promotion from within; talent management methods.

Part 4: Compensation

Chapter 11: Establishing Strategic Pay Plans. How to develop equitable pay plans for your employees.

Chapter 12: Pay for Performance and Financial Incentives. Pay-for-performance plans such as financial incentives, merit pay, and incentives that help tie performance to pay.

Chapter 13: Benefits and Services. Providing benefits that make it clear the firm views its employees as long-term investments and is concerned with their welfare.

Part 5: Employee Relations

Chapter 14: Ethics, Justice, and Fair Treatment in HR Management. How you can ensure ethical and fair treatment through grievance and discipline processes.

Chapter 15: Labor Relations and Collective Bargaining. How to deal with unions, including the union organizing campaign, negotiating and agreeing upon a collective bargaining agreement between unions and management, and managing the agreement via the grievance process.

Chapter 16: Employee Safety and Health. How you can make the workplace safe, including the causes of accidents, and laws governing your responsibilities for employee safety and health.

Chapter 17: Managing Global Human Resources. Special topics in managing the HR side of multinational operations.

Chapter 18: Managing Human Resources in Entrepreneurial Firms. Special topics you can use in managing human resources in smaller firms, including using Internet and government tools to support the HR effort, leveraging small size, using professional employer organizations, and managing HR systems, procedures, and paperwork.

The Topics Are Interrelated

In practice, don't think of each of this book's 18 chapters and topics as being unrelated to the others. Each topic interacts with and affects the others, and all should align with the employer's strategic plan. For example, hiring people who don't have the potential to learn the job will doom their performance regardless of how much training they get.

Figure 1-10 summarizes this idea. For example, how you test and interview job candidates (Chapters 6 and 7) and train and appraise job incumbents (Chapters 8

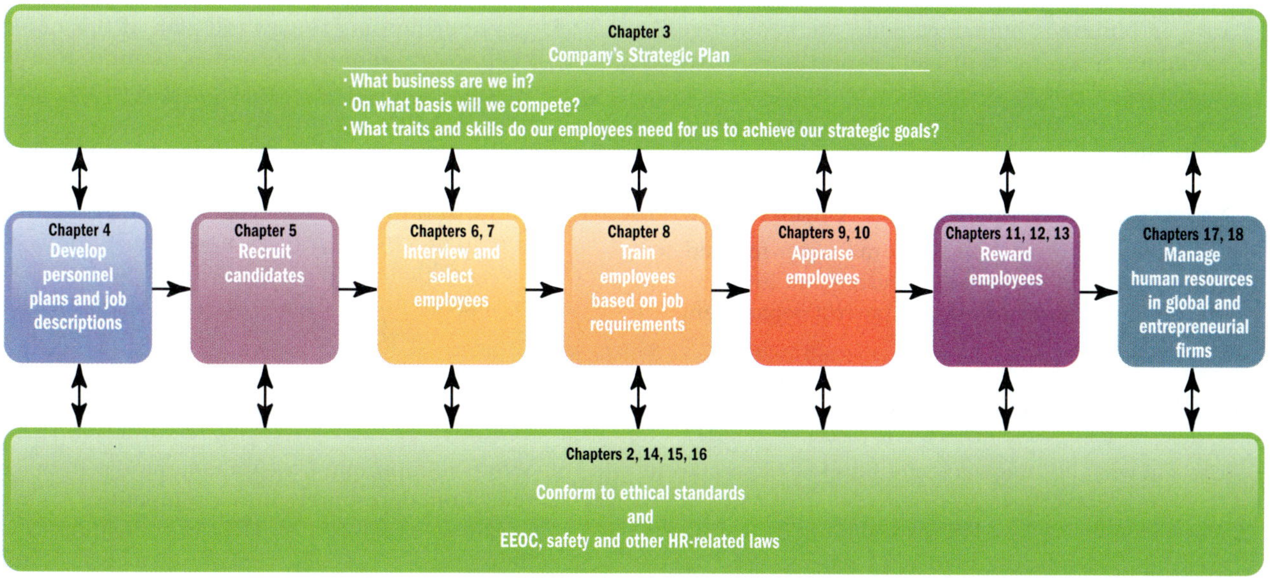

FIGURE 1-10 Strategy and the Basic Human Resource Management Process

and 9) depends on the job's specific duties and responsibilities (Chapter 4). How good a job you do selecting (Chapter 6) and training (Chapter 8) employees will affect how safely they do their jobs (Chapter 16). An employee's performance and thus his or her appraisal (Chapter 9) depends not just on the person's motivation, but also on how well you identified the job's duties (Chapter 4), and screened and trained the employee (Chapters 6 and 7). Furthermore, we saw that how you recruit, select, train, appraise, and compensate employees should make sense in terms of producing the employee behaviors required to support the company's strategic plan.

REVIEW

CHAPTER SECTION SUMMARIES

1. All managers should **understand the importance of human resource management**. Doing so helps managers avoid problems like hiring the wrong person for the job. And more important, it can help ensure that managers get results through people. Line managers' human resource duties include placing the right person on the job, and orienting and training new employees. The human resource manager's duties include supervising his or her own employees, coordinating the company's overall personnel policies, and assisting and advising line managers in the areas of human resource management.
2. **A changing environment today** is influencing what human resource managers do and how they do it. Globalization means more competition, and more competition means more pressure to lower costs and to make employees more productive and quality conscious. Technology is requiring more employees to be technologically well informed and pressuring employers to improve their human resource processes by applying new technological tools. There is more emphasis on "knowledge work" and therefore on building "human capital," the knowledge, education, training, skills, and expertise of a firm's employees. Workforce and demographic changes mean that the workforce is becoming older and more diverse.
3. Changes like these are manifesting themselves in **important trends in human resource management**.
   - Traditionally, personnel/HR managers focused on transactional issues such as hiring and firing employees and running the payroll department.
   - Today, with employers competing in a challenging new environment, employers expect and demand more from their HR managers.
   - For example, they expect their human resource management teams to focus more on big picture issues including instituting human resource policies and practices that support the companies' strategic objectives; to find new, more efficient ways to provide transactional services; and to have new proficiencies, for instance, in terms of strategizing and commanding a broader array of business knowledge.
   - As part of this, employers expect their human resource managers to be able to create high-performance work systems that produce superior employee performance.
   - To do so, HR managers should be able to apply evidence-based human resource management, which means the use of data, facts, analytics, scientific rigor, critical evaluation, and critically evaluated research/case studies to support human resource management proposals, decisions, practices, and conclusions.
4. In understanding the overall **plan of this book**, keep several important themes in mind: that human resource management is the responsibility of every manager, that the workforce is increasingly diverse, that employers and their human resource managers face the need to manage in challenging economic times, and that human resource managers must be able to defend their plans and contributions in measurable terms—to use evidence-based management.

DISCUSSION QUESTIONS

1. Explain what HR management is and how it relates to the management process.
2. Give examples of how HR management concepts and techniques can be of use to all managers.
3. Illustrate the HR management responsibilities of line and staff managers.
4. Why is it important for companies today to make their human resources into a competitive advantage? Explain how HR can contribute to doing this.

INDIVIDUAL AND GROUP ACTIVITIES

1. Working individually or in groups, develop outlines showing how trends like workforce diversity, technological innovation, globalization, and changes in the nature of work have affected the college or university you are attending now. Present in class.
2. Working individually or in groups, contact the HR manager of a local bank. Ask the HR manager how he or she is working as a strategic partner to manage human resources, given the bank's strategic goals and objectives. Back in class, discuss the responses of the different HR managers.
3. Working individually or in groups, interview an HR manager. Based on that interview, write a short presentation regarding HR's role today in building competitive organizations.
4. Working individually or in groups, bring several business publications such as *BusinessWeek* and the *Wall Street Journal* to class. Based on their contents, compile a list titled "What HR Managers and Departments Do Today."
5. Based on your personal experiences, list 10 examples showing how you did use (or could have used) human resource management techniques at work or school.
6. Laurie Siegel, senior vice president of human resources for Tyco International, took over her job just after numerous charges forced the company's previous board of directors and top executives to leave the firm. Hired by new CEO Edward Breen, Siegel had to tackle numerous difficult problems starting the moment she assumed office. For example, she had to help hire a new management team. She had to do something about what the outside world viewed as a culture of questionable ethics at her company. And she had to do something about the company's top management compensation plan, which many felt contributed to the allegations by some that some former company officers had used the company as a sort of private ATM.

   Siegel came to Tyco after a very impressive career. For example, she had been head of executive compensation at Allied Signal, and was a graduate of the Harvard Business School. But, as strong as her background was, she obviously had her work cut out for her when she took the senior vice president of HR position at Tyco.

   Working individually or in groups, conduct an Internet search and library research to answer the following questions: What human resource management–related steps did Siegel take to help get Tyco back on the right track? Do you think she took the appropriate steps? Why or why not? What, if anything, do you suggest she do now?
7. The HRCI "Test Specifications" appendix at the end of this book (pages 699–706) lists the knowledge someone studying for the HRCI certification exam needs to have in each area of human resource management (such as in Strategic Management, Workforce Planning, and Human Resource Development). In groups of four to five students, do four things: (1) Review that appendix now. (2) Identify the material in this chapter that relates to the required knowledge the appendix lists. (3) Write four multiple-choice exam questions on this material that you believe would be suitable for inclusion in the HRCI exam. And (4) if time permits, have someone from your team post your team's questions in front of the class, so the students in other teams can take each others' exam questions.

EXPERIENTIAL EXERCISE

Helping "The Donald"

Purpose: The purpose of this exercise is to provide practice in identifying and applying the basic concepts of human resource management by illustrating how managers use these techniques in their day-to-day jobs.

Required Understanding: Be thoroughly familiar with the material in this chapter, and with at least several episodes of *The Apprentice* or *The Celebrity Apprentice*, the TV shows in which developer Donald Trump starred.

How to Set Up the Exercise/Instructions:

1. Divide the class into teams of three to four students.
2. Read this: As you may know by watching "the Donald" as he organizes his business teams for *The Apprentice* and *The Celebrity Apprentice*, human resource management plays an important role in what Donald Trump and the participants on his separate teams need to do to be successful. For example, Donald Trump needs to be able to appraise each of the participants. And, for their part, the leaders of each of his teams need to be able to staff his or her team with the right participants, and then provide the sorts of training, incentives, and evaluations that help their companies succeed and that therefore make the participants themselves (and especially the team leaders) look like "winners" to Mr. Trump.
3. Watch several of these shows (or reruns of the shows), and then meet with your team and answer the following questions:
   a. What specific HR functions (recruiting, interviewing, and so on) can you identify Donald Trump using on this show? Make sure to give specific examples based on the show.
   b. What specific HR functions (recruiting, selecting, training, etc.) can you identify one or more of the team leaders using to help manage their teams on the show? Again, please give specific answers.
   c. Provide a specific example of how HR functions (such as recruiting, selection, interviewing, compensating, appraising, and so on) contributed to one of the participants coming across as particularly successful to Mr. Trump. Can you provide examples of how one or more of these functions contributed to a participant being told by Mr. Trump, "You're fired"?
   d. Present your team's conclusions to the class.

APPLICATION CASE

Jack Nelson's Problem

As a new member of the board of directors for a local bank, Jack Nelson was being introduced to all the employees in the home office. When he was introduced to Ruth Johnson, he was curious about her work and asked her what the machine she was using did. Johnson replied that she really did not know what the machine was called or what it did. She explained that she had only been working there for 2 months. However, she did know precisely how to operate the machine. According to her supervisor, she was an excellent employee.

At one of the branch offices, the supervisor in charge spoke to Nelson confidentially, telling him that "something was wrong," but she didn't know what. For one thing, she explained, employee turnover was too high, and no sooner had one employee been put on the job than another one resigned. With customers to see and loans to be made, she continued, she had little time to work with the new employees as they came and went.

All branch supervisors hired their own employees without communication with the home office or other branches. When an opening developed, the supervisor tried to find a suitable employee to replace the worker who had quit.

After touring the 22 branches and finding similar problems in many of them, Nelson wondered what the home office should do or what action he should take. The banking firm generally was regarded as being a well-run institution that had grown from 27 to 191 employees during the past 8 years. The more he thought about the matter, the more puzzled Nelson became. He couldn't quite put his finger on the problem, and he didn't know whether to report his findings to the president.

Questions

1. What do you think is causing some of the problems in the bank's home office and branches?
2. Do you think setting up an HR unit in the main office would help?
3. What specific functions should an HR unit carry out? What HR functions would then be carried out by supervisors and other line managers? What role should the Internet play in the new HR organization?

Source: From Claude S. George, *Supervision in Action*, 4th ed., 1985. Adapted by permission of Prentice Hall, Inc., Upper Saddle River, NJ.

CONTINUING CASE

Carter Cleaning Company

Introduction

A main theme of this book is that human resource management activities like recruiting, selecting, training, and rewarding employees is not just the job of a central HR group but rather a job in which every manager must engage. Perhaps nowhere is this more apparent than in the typical small service business. Here the owner/manager usually has no HR staff to rely on. However, the success of his or her enterprise (not to mention his or her family's peace of mind) often depends largely on the effectiveness through which workers are recruited, hired, trained, evaluated, and rewarded. Therefore, to help illustrate and emphasize the front-line manager's HR role, throughout this book we will use a continuing case based on an actual small business in the southeastern United States. Each chapter's segment of the case will illustrate how the case's main player—owner/manager Jennifer Carter—confronts and solves personnel problems each day at work by applying the concepts and techniques of that particular chapter. Here is background information you will need to answer questions that arise in subsequent chapters. (We also present a second, unrelated "application case" case incident in each chapter.)

Carter Cleaning Centers

Jennifer Carter graduated from State University in June 2005, and, after considering several job offers, decided to do what she always planned to do—go into business with her father, Jack Carter.

Jack Carter opened his first laundromat in 1995 and his second in 1998. The main attraction of these coin laundry businesses for him was that they were capital- rather than labor-intensive. Thus, once the investment in machinery was made, the stores could be run with just one unskilled attendant and none of the labor problems one normally expects from being in the retail service business.

The attractiveness of operating with virtually no skilled labor notwithstanding, Jack had decided by 1999 to expand the services in each of his stores to include the dry cleaning and pressing of clothes. He embarked, in other words, on a strategy of "related diversification" by adding new services that were related to and consistent with his existing coin laundry activities. He added these for several reasons. He wanted to better utilize the unused space in the rather large stores he currently had under lease. Furthermore, he was, as he put it, "tired of sending out the dry cleaning and pressing work that came in from our coin laundry clients to a dry cleaner 5 miles away, who then took most of what should have been our profits." To reflect the new, expanded line of services, he renamed each of his two stores Carter Cleaning Centers and was sufficiently satisfied with their performance to open four more of the same type of stores over the next 5 years. Each store had its own on-site manager and, on average, about seven employees and annual revenues of about $500,000. It was this 6-store chain that Jennifer joined after graduating.

Her understanding with her father was that she would serve as a troubleshooter/consultant to the elder Carter with the aim of both learning the business and bringing to it modern management concepts and techniques for solving the business's problems and facilitating its growth.

Questions

1. Make a list of five specific HR problems you think Carter Cleaning will have to grapple with.
2. What would you do first if you were Jennifer?

KEY TERMS

organization, *p. 5*
manager, *p. 5*
management process, *p. 5*
human resource management (HRM), *p. 5*
authority, *p. 7*
line authority, *p. 7*
staff authority, *p. 7*
line manager, *p. 7*
staff manager, *p. 7*
functional authority, *p. 7*
globalization, *p. 11*
human capital, *p. 13*

ENDNOTES

1. Dina Berta, "Paying Attention to Retention," *Nation's Restaurant News* 42, no. 4 (January 28, 2008).
2. Dina Berta, "Motivation Keeps Top Talent Sticking Around," *Nation's Restaurant News* 41, no. 20 (May 14, 2007), pp. 1, 43–44.
3. Ibid.
4. After a larger company bought Stanford's, they apparently introduced new policies. See, for example, www.yelp.com/biz/stanfords-restaurant-and-bar-lake-oswego, accessed March 25, 2009, and www.tripadvisor.com/Restaurant_Review-g51939-d439725-Reviews-Stanford_s_Restaurant_and_Bar-Lake_Oswego_Oregon.html, accessed March 25, 2009.
5. Quoted in Fred K. Foulkes, "The Expanding Role of the Personnel Function," *Harvard Business Review*, March–April, 1975, pp. 71–84. See also Michael Losey, "HR Comes of Age," *HR Magazine* 9 (1998), pp. 40–53.
6. This data comes from "Small Business: A Report of the President" (1998), www.SBA.gov/ADV/stats, accessed March 9, 2006. See also "Statistics of U.S. Businesses and Non-Employer Status," www.SBA.gov/ADV oh/research/data.html, accessed March 9, 2006.
7. Some employers, like Google, are adding "chief sustainability officers" within human resource management who are responsible for fostering the company's environmental sustainability efforts. Nancy Woodward, "New Breed of Human Resource Leader," *HR Magazine*, June 2008, pp. 53–57.
8. See Dave Ulrich, "The New HR Organization," *Workforce Management*, December 10, 2007, pp. 40–44; and Dave Ulrich, "The 21st-Century HR Organization," *Human Resource Management* 47, no. 4 (Winter 2008), pp. 829–850.
9. Robert Grossman, "IBM's HR Takes a Risk," *HR Management*, April 2007, pp. 54–59.
10. In fact, one study found that delegating somewhat more of the HR activities to line managers "had a positive effect on HR managers' perceptions of their units' reputation among line managers." Carol Kulik and Elissa Perry, "When Less Is More: The Effect of Devolution on HR as a Strategic Role and Construed Image," *Human Resource Management* 47, no. 3 (Fall 2008), pp. 541–558.
11. "Human Resource Activities, Budgets, and Staffs, 1999–2000," *BNA Bulletin to Management*, June 20, 2000.
12. Steve Bates, "No Experience Necessary? Many Companies Are Putting Non-HR Executives in Charge of HR with Mixed Results," *HR Magazine* 46, no. 11 (November 2001), pp. 34–41. See also Fay Hansen, "Top of the Class," *Workforce Management*, June 23, 2008, pp. 1, 25–30.
13. Ed Frauenheim, "Wal-Mart HR Chief Makes Early Splash," *Workforce Management*, April 24, 2006, p. 11.
14. "A Profile of Human Resource Executives," *BNA Bulletin to Management*, June 21, 2001, p. S5.
15. For discussions of some other important trends, see, for example, Society for Human Resource Management, "Workplace Trends: An Overview of the Findings of the Latest SHRM Workplace Forecast," *Workplace Visions*, no. 3 (2008), pp. 1–8; and Ed Frauenheim, "Future View," *Workforce Management*, December 15, 2008, pp. 18–23.
16. Ibid., p. 9. See also Society for Human Resource Management, "The Impact of Globalization on HR," *Workplace Visions*, no. 5 (2000), pp. 1–8.
17. See, for example, Society for Human Resource Management, "Promoting Productivity," *Workplace Visions*, no. 1 (2006), pp. 1–8.
18. Roger J. Moncarz, Michael G. Wolf, and Benjamin Wright, "Service-Providing Occupations, Offshoring, and the Labor Market," *Monthly Labor Review*, December 2008 pp. 71–86.
19. www.census.gov/foreign-trade/statistics/historical/gands.pdf, accessed April 23, 2009.
20. Ibid.

21. Kerry Capell, "Zara Thrives by Breaking All the Rules," *BusinessWeek*, October 20, 2008, p. 66.
22. Timothy Appel, "Better Off a Blue-Collar," *The Wall Street Journal*, July 1, 2003, p. B-1.
23. Roger Moncarz and Azure Reaser, "The 2000–10 Job Outlook in Brief," *Occupational Outlook Quarterly*, Spring 2002, pp. 9–44.
24. See "Charting the Projections: 2004–2014," *Occupational Outlook Quarterly*, Winter 2005–2006.
25. Ibid.
26. See, for example, "Engine of Change," *Workforce Management*, July 17, 2006, pp. 20–30.
27. Moncarz and Reaser, "The 2000–10 Job Outlook in Brief."
28. Richard Crawford, *In the Era of Human Capital* (New York: Harper Business, 1991), p. 26.
29. Peter Drucker, "The Coming of the New Organization," *Harvard Business Review*, January–February 1998, p. 45. See also James Guthrie, et al., "Correlates and Consequences of High Involvement Work Practices: The Role of Competitive Strategy," *International Journal of Human Resource Management*, February 2002, pp. 183–197.
30. Society for Human Resource Management, "Workforce Readiness and the New Essential Skills," *Workplace Visions*, no. 2 (2008), p. 5.
31. "Human Resources Wharton," www.knowledge.wharton.upe.edu, accessed January 8, 2006.
32. See, for example, Anthea Zacharatos et al., "High-Performance Work Systems and Occupational Safety," *Journal of Applied Psychology* 90, no. 1 (2005), pp. 77–93.
33. "Charting the Projections: 2004–2014," *Occupational Outlook Quarterly*, Winter 2005–2006, pp. 48–50; and www.bls.gov/emp/emplabor01.pdf, accessed October 20, 2008.
34. As one example, see "Changing Makeup of Workforce Translates into Need for Multilingual Approach by HR," *BNA Bulletin to Management*, January 20, 2008, p. 25.
35. Tony Carnevale, "The Coming Labor and Skills Shortage," *Training & Development*, January 2005, p. 39.
36. "Talent Management Leads in Top HR Concerns," *Compensation & Benefits Review*, May/June 2007, p. 12.
37. For example, see Kathryn Tyler, "Generation Gaps," *HR Magazine*, January 2008, pp. 69–72.
38. Eva Kaplan-Leiserson, "The Changing Workforce," *Training & Development*, February 2005, pp. 10–11. See also S. A. Hewlett, et. al., "How Gen Y & Boomers Will Reshape Your Agenda" [Part of a special section on Managing in the New World], *Harvard Business Review* 87, no. 7/8 (July/August 2009), p. 71–76.
39. Society for Human Resource Management, "Generational Differences: Myths and Realities," *Workplace Visions*, no. 4 (2007), p. 7.
40. By one report, the economic downturn of 2008 made it more difficult for dissatisfied Generation Y employees to change jobs, and is contributing to a buildup of "griping" among some of them. "Generation Y Goes to Work," *The Economist*, January 3, 2009, p. 47.
41. Nadira Hira, "You Raised Them, Now Manage Them," *Fortune*, May 20, 2007, pp. 38–46; Katheryn Tyler, "The Tethered Generation," *HR Magazine*, May 2007, pp. 41–46; Jeffrey Zaslow, "The Most Praised Generation Goes to Work," *The Wall Street Journal*, April 20, 2007, pp. W1, W7; and Rebecca Hastings, "Millennials Expect a Lot from Leaders," *HR Magazine*, January 2008, p. 30.
42. To capitalize on this, more employers are using social networking tools to promote employee interaction and collaboration, particularly among Generation Y employees. "Social Networking Tools Aimed at Engaging Newest Employees," *BNA Bulletin to Management*, September 18, 2007, p. 303.
43. "Talent Management Leads in Top HR Concerns," *Compensation & Benefits Review*, May/June 2007, p. 12.
44. Society for Human Resource Management, Jennifer Schramm, "Exploring the Future of Work," *Workplace Visions*, no. 2 (2005), p. 6; Rainer Strack, Jens Baier, and Anders Fahlander, "Managing Demographic Risk," *Harvard Business Review*, February 2008, pp. 119–128.
45. www.bls.gov/opub/ted/2006/may/wk2/art01.htm, accessed April 18, 2009.
46. "Immigrants in the Workplace," *BNA Bulletin to Management Datagraph*, March 15, 1996, pp. 260–261. See also Tanuja Agarwala, "Human Resource Management: The Emerging Trends," *Indian Journal of Industrial Relations*, January 2002, pp. 315–331.
47. "Human Capital Critical to Success," *Management Review*, November 1998, p. 9. See also "HR 2018: Top Predictions," *Workforce Management* 87, no. 20 (December 15 2008), p. 20–21.
48. Ben Nagler, "Recasting Employees into Teams," *Workforce*, January 1998, pp. 101–106.
49. A recent survey found that HR managers referred to "strategic/critical thinking skills" as the top "most important factor in attaining next HR job." See "Career Development for HR Professionals," *Society for Human Resource Management Research Quarterly*, second quarter 2008, p. 3.
50. John Boudreau and Peter Ramstad, *Beyond HR: The New Science of Human Capital* (Boston: Harvard Business School Publishing Corporation, 2007), p. 9.
51. For example, see Sandra Fisher et al., "Human Resource Issues in Outsourcing: Integrating Research and Practice," *Human Resource Management* 47, no. 3 (Fall 2008), pp. 501–523; and "Sizing Up the HR Outsourcing Market," *HR Magazine*, November 2008, p. 78.
52. Studies suggest that IT usage does support human resource managers' strategic planning. See Victor Haines III and Genevieve LaFleur, "Information Technology Usage and Human Resource Roles and Effectiveness," *Human Resource Management* 47, no. 3 (Fall 2008), pp. 525–540. See also R. Zeidner, "The Tech Effect On Human Resources," *HRMagazine*, (2009 HR Trendbook supp), p. 49–50, 52.
53. Except as noted, most of this section is based on Richard Vosburgh, "The Evolution of HR: Developing HR as an Internal Consulting Organization," *Human Resource Planning* 30, no. 3 (September 2007), pp. 11–24.
54. See, for example, "Employers Seek HR Executives with Global Experience, SOX Knowledge, Business Sense," *BNA Bulletin to Management*, September 19, 2006, pp. 297–298; and Robert Rodriguez, "HR's New Breed," *HR Magazine*, January 2006, pp. 67–71.
55. Susan Wells, "From HR to the Top," *HR Magazine*, June 2003, p. 49.
56. For a contrary view, see for example, P. J. Kiger, "Survey: HR Still Battling for Leaders Respect," *Workforce Management* 87, no. 20 (December 15, 2008), p. 8.
57. Joe Vocino, "High Pay for High-Level HR," *HR Magazine*, June 2006, p. 83; and "The 30 Highest-Paid HR Leaders," *Workforce Management*, September 8, 2008, pp. 38–41.
58. Mitchell Rothstein and Richard Goffin, "The Use of Personality Measures in Personnel Selection: What Does Current Research Support?" *Human Resource Management Review* 16 (2006), pp. 155–180; Helen Shipton et al., "HRM as a Predictor of

Innovation," *Human Resource Management Journal* 16, no. 1 (2006), pp. 3–27; Luc Sels et al., "Unraveling the HRM—Performance Link: Value Creating and Cost-Increasing Effects of Small-Business HRM," *Journal of Management Studies* 43, no. 2 (March 2006), pp. 319–342; and Jaap Paauwe and Paul Boselie, "HRM and Performance: What's Next?" *Human Resource Management Journal* 15, no. 4 (2005), pp. 68–82.

59. "Super Human Resources Practices Result in Better Overall Performance, Report Says," *BNA Bulletin to Management*, August 26, 2004, pp. 273–274. See also Wendy Boswell, "Aligning Employees with the Organization's Strategic Objectives: Out of Line of Sight, Out of Mind," *International Journal of Human Resource Management* 17, no. 9 (September 2006), pp. 1014–1041. A recent study found that some employers, which the researchers called *cost minimizers*, intentionally took a lower cost approach to human resource practices, with mixed results. See Soo Min Toh et al., "Human Resource Configurations: Investigating Fit with the Organizational Context," *Journal of Applied Psychology* 93, no. 4 (2008), pp. 864–882.
60. As one expert puts it, "A great deal of what passes as 'best practice' in HRM most likely is not. In some cases, there is simply no evidence that validates what are thought to be best practices, while in other cases there is evidence to suggest that what are thought to be best practices are inferior practices". Edward Lawler III, "Why HR Practices Are Not Evidence-Based," *Academy of Management Journal* 50, no. 5 (2007), p. 1033.
61. See, for example, www.personneltoday.com/blogs/hcglobal-human-capital-management/2009/02/theres-no-such-thing-as-eviden.html, accessed April 18, 2009.
62. The evidence-based movement began in medicine. In 1996, in an editorial published by the *British Medical Journal*, David Sackett, MD, defined "evidence based medicine" as "use of the best-available evidence in making decisions about patient care" and urged his colleagues to adopt its tenets. "EVIDENCE-BASED TRAINING™: TURNING RESEARCH INTO RESULTS FOR PHARMACEUTICAL SALES TRAINING," An AXIOM White Paper© 2006 AXIOM Professional Health Learning LLC. All rights reserved.
63. Dina Berta, "Motivation Keeps Top Talent Sticking Around," *Nation's Restaurant News* 41, no. 20 (May 14, 2007), pp. 1, 43–44.
64. Chris Brewster et al., "What Determines the Size of the HR Function? A Cross National Analysis," *Human Resource Management* 45, no. 1 (Spring 2006), pp. 3–21. See also Society for Human Resource Management, "SHRM Survey Report, 2006 Strategic HR Management," pp. 18–19.
65. Kevin Wooten, "Ethical Dilemmas in Human Resource Management," *Human Resource Management Review* 11 (2001), p. 161. See also Ann Pomeroy, "The Ethics Squeeze," *HR Magazine* 51, no. 3 (March 2006), pp. 48–55.
66. "Meatpacking Case Highlights HR's Liability," *Workforce Management*, September 20, 2008, p. 6.

2 Equal Opportunity and the Law

As if it didn't face enough challenges with the subprime meltdown a few years ago, Citigroup also faced a possible $1 billion class-action discrimination lawsuit. Several female former employees alleged that the banking giant discriminated against women when cutting jobs in the face of the economic turndown.

Source: Courtesy of Mark Lennihan/AP Wide World Photos.

WHERE ARE WE NOW . . .

Every HR action you take as a manager, from interviewing applicants to training, appraising, and rewarding them, has equal employment implications. Therefore, the purpose of this chapter is to provide you with the knowledge to deal effectively with equal employment questions on the job. It contains fundamental information you will probably have to draw on every day. The main topics we cover are equal opportunity laws enacted from 1964 to 1991, the laws from 1991 to the present, defenses against discrimination allegations, illustrative discriminatory employment practices, and the EEOC enforcement process.

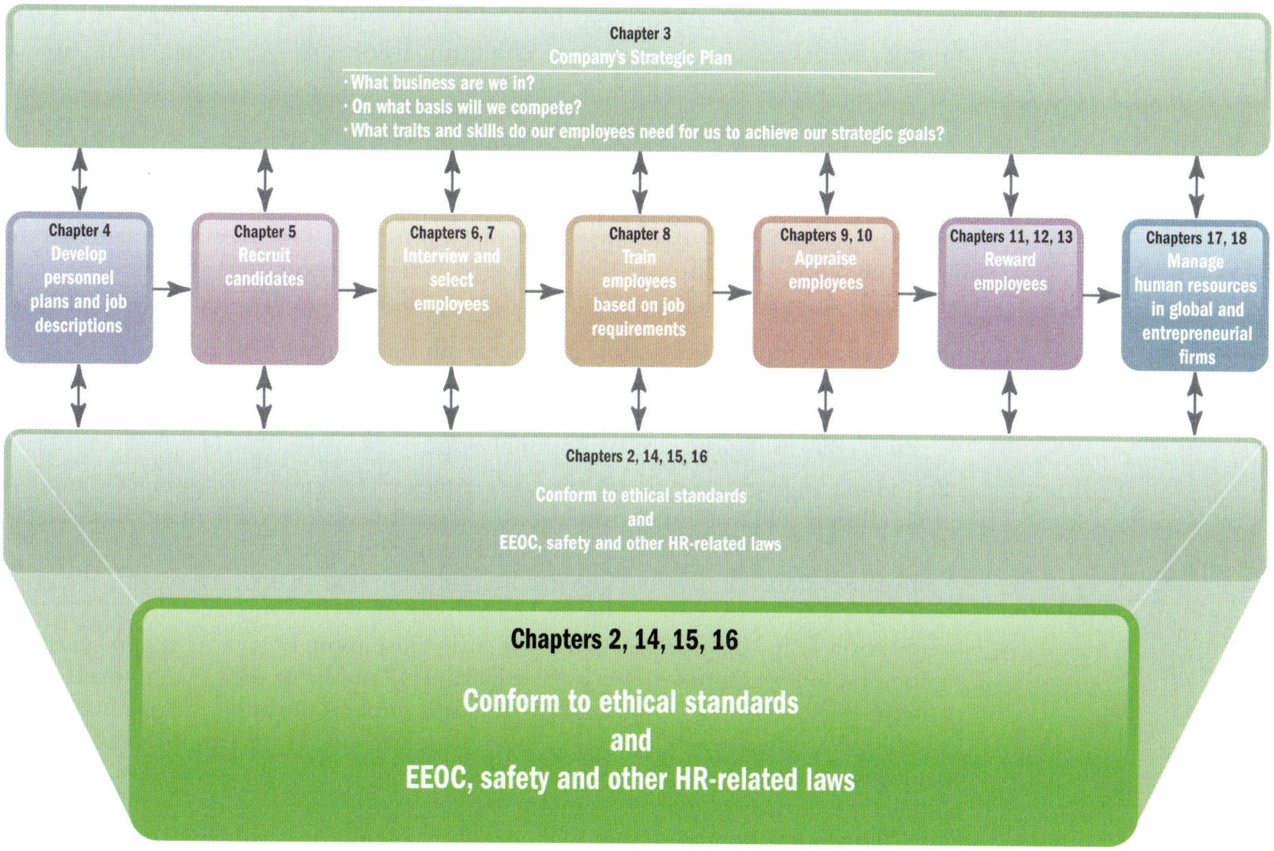

LEARNING OUTCOMES

1. Explain the importance of and list the basic features of Title VII of the 1964 Civil Rights Act and at least five other equal employment laws.
2. Explain how to avoid and deal with accusations of sexual harassment at work.
3. Define *adverse impact* and explain how it is proved.
4. Explain and illustrate two defenses you can use in the event of discriminatory practice allegations.
5. Cite specific discriminatory personnel management practices in recruitment, selection, promotion, transfer, layoffs, and benefits.
6. List the steps in the EEOC enforcement process.
7. Discuss why diversity management is important and how to institutionalize a diversity management program.

1 Explain the importance of and list the basic features of Title VII of the 1964 Civil Rights Act and at least five other equal employment laws.

EQUAL EMPLOYMENT OPPORTUNITY 1964–1991

American race relations were not always as tolerant as Barak Obama's election might suggest. It took centuries of legislative action, court decisions, and evolving public policy to arrive at this point.

Legislation barring discrimination against minorities in the United States is nothing new. The Fifth Amendment to the U.S. Constitution (ratified in 1791) states that "no person shall be deprived of life, liberty, or property, without due process of the law." The Thirteenth Amendment (1865) outlawed slavery, and courts have held that it bars racial discrimination. The Civil Rights Act of 1866 gives all persons the same right to make and enforce contracts and to benefit from U.S. laws.[1] Other laws and various court decisions similarly made discrimination against minorities illegal by the early 1900s, at least in theory.[2]

But as a practical matter, Congress and presidents avoided dramatic action on implementing equal employment until the early 1960s. At that point, civil unrest among minorities and women and changing traditions prompted them to act. Congress passed a multitude of new civil rights laws.

Title VII of the 1964 Civil Rights Act

Title VII of the 1964 Civil Rights Act was one of the first of these 1960s-era laws. As amended by the 1972 Equal Employment Opportunity Act, Title VII states that an employer cannot discriminate based on race, color, religion, sex, or national origin. Specifically, it states that it shall be an unlawful employment practice for an employer:

1. To fail or refuse to hire or to discharge an individual or otherwise to discriminate against any individual with respect to his/her compensation, terms, conditions, or privileges of employment, because of such individual's race, color, religion, sex, or national origin.
2. To limit, segregate, or classify his/her employees or applicants for employment in any way that would deprive or tend to deprive any individual of employment opportunities or otherwise adversely affect his/her status as an employee, because of such individual's race, color, religion, sex, or national origin.

Who Does Title VII Cover?

Title VII covers just about everyone. It bars discrimination on the part of most employers, including all public or private employers of 15 or more persons. It also covers all private and public educational institutions, the federal government, and state and local governments. It bars public and private employment agencies from failing or refusing to refer for employment any individual because of race, color, religion, sex, or national origin. And it bars labor unions with 15 or more members from excluding, expelling, or classifying their membership based on race, color, religion, sex, or national origin.

The EEOC

Title VII established the **Equal Employment Opportunity Commission (EEOC)** to administer and enforce the Civil Rights law at work. The commission itself consists of five members appointed by the president with the advice and consent of the Senate. Each member serves a 5-year term. In popular usage, the EEOC also includes the thousands of staff the EEOC has around the United States. They receive and investigate job discrimination complaints from aggrieved individuals. When the EEOC finds reasonable cause that the charges are justified, it attempts (through conciliation) to reach an agreement. If this fails, it can go to court. The EEOC may file discrimination charges on behalf of aggrieved individuals, or the individuals may file on behalf of themselves.[3] We'll discuss the EEOC procedure later in this chapter.

Executive Orders

Various U.S. presidents signed executive orders expanding equal employment in federal agencies. For example, the Johnson administration (1963–1969) issued Executive Orders 11246 and 11375. These didn't just ban discrimination. They also required that government contractors with contracts of over $50,000 and 50 or more employees take **affirmative action** to ensure employment opportunity for those who may have suffered past discrimination. These orders also established the **Office of Federal Contract Compliance Programs (OFCCP)**.[4] It implements the orders and ensures compliance. For example, it reached a settlement with an aviation contractor to pay more than $240,000 to settle claims that it subjected women and blacks to a "perversely hostile work environment."

Equal Pay Act of 1963

Under the **Equal Pay Act of 1963** (amended in 1972), it is unlawful to discriminate in pay on the basis of sex when jobs involve equal work; require equivalent skills, effort, and responsibility; and are performed under similar working conditions. (Pay differences derived from seniority systems, merit systems, and systems that measure earnings by production quantity or quality or from any factor other than sex do not violate the act.)

Age Discrimination in Employment Act of 1967

The **Age Discrimination in Employment Act of 1967 (ADEA)** made it unlawful to discriminate against employees or applicants who are between 40 and 65 years of age. Subsequent amendments eliminated the age cap, effectively ending most mandatory retirement at age 65. Most states and local agencies, when acting in the role of employer, must also adhere to provisions of the act that protect workers from age discrimination.

You can't get around the ADEA by replacing employees over 40 years of age with those who are also over 40. In *O'Connor v. Consolidated Coin Caterers Corp.*, the U.S. Supreme Court held that an employee who is over 40 years of age might sue for discrimination if a "significantly younger" employee replaces him or her, even if the replacement is also over 40. The Court didn't specify what "significantly younger" meant, but O'Connor had been replaced by someone 16 years younger.[5]

Younger managers may have to especially guard against ageist prejudices. For example, a 54-year-old former manager recently alleged that Google fired him because he wasn't a "cultural fit," according to his own manager. This and other allegedly ageist statements by Google executives prompted the California Court of Appeals to let the manager's case proceed.[6]

The ADEA is a "favored statute" among lawyers. It allows jury trials and double damages to those proving "willful" discrimination.[7]

Vocational Rehabilitation Act of 1973

The **Vocational Rehabilitation Act of 1973** requires employers with federal contracts of more than $2,500 to take affirmative action in employing handicapped persons. It does not require hiring unqualified people. It does require an employer to take steps to accommodate a handicapped worker unless doing so imposes an undue hardship on the employer.

Title VII of the 1964 Civil Rights Act
The section of the act that says an employer cannot discriminate on the basis of race, color, religion, sex, or national origin with respect to employment.

Equal Employment Opportunity Commission (EEOC)
The commission, created by Title VII, is empowered to investigate job discrimination complaints and sue on behalf of complainants.

affirmative action
Steps that are taken for the purpose of eliminating the present effects of past discrimination.

Office of Federal Contract Compliance Programs (OFCCP)
This office is responsible for implementing the executive orders and ensuring compliance of federal contractors.

Equal Pay Act of 1963
The act requiring equal pay for equal work, regardless of sex.

Age Discrimination in Employment Act of 1967 (ADEA)
The act prohibiting arbitrary age discrimination and specifically protecting individuals over 40 years old.

Vocational Rehabilitation Act of 1973
The act requiring certain federal contractors to take affirmative action for disabled persons.

Pregnancy Discrimination Act of 1978

The **Pregnancy Discrimination Act** of 1978 prohibits using pregnancy, childbirth, or related medical conditions to discriminate in hiring, promotion, suspension, or discharge, or in any term or condition of employment. Furthermore, under the act, if an employer offers its employees disability coverage, then it must treat pregnancy and childbirth like any other disability, and include it in the plan as a covered condition.[8]

More women are suing under this act. Pregnancy discrimination claims to the EEOC rose about 39% in the past 10 years, and plaintive victories rose 66%.[9] (Progressive human resources notwithstanding, one firm, an auto dealership, fired an employee after she said she was pregnant. The reason? Allegedly, "in case I ended up throwing up or cramping in one of their vehicles. They said pregnant women do that sometimes, and I could cause an accident, which might mean a lawsuit against them.")[10]

Federal Agency Guidelines

The federal agencies charged with ensuring compliance with these laws and executive orders issue their own implementing guidelines. These spell out recommended procedures for complying with the law.[11]

The EEOC, Civil Service Commission, Department of Labor, and Department of Justice together issued **uniform guidelines**. These set forth "highly recommended" procedures regarding things like employee selection, record keeping, and preemployment inquiries. As an example, they specify that employers must *validate* any employment selection devices (like tests) that screen out disproportionate numbers of women or minorities. And they explain how to validate a selection device. (We explain this procedure in Chapter 6.) The EEOC and other agencies also periodically issue updated guidelines clarifying and revising their positions on matters such as sexual harassment. (The OFCCP has its own guidelines.) The American Psychological Association has its own (non–legally binding) Standards for Educational and Psychological Testing.

Early Court Decisions Regarding Equal Employment Opportunity

Several court decisions between 1964 and 1991 helped clarify courts' interpretations of EEO laws such as Title VII.

Griggs v. Duke Power Company

Griggs was a landmark case, since the Supreme Court used it to define unfair discrimination. Lawyers sued the Duke Power Company on behalf of Willie Griggs, an applicant for a job as a coal handler. The company required its coal handlers to be high school graduates. Griggs claimed this requirement was illegally discriminatory. He said it wasn't related to success on the job, and it resulted in more blacks than whites being rejected for these jobs. Griggs won the case. The Court's decision was unanimous. In his written opinion, Chief Justice Burger laid out three crucial guidelines affecting equal employment legislation.

- First, the Court ruled that the *discrimination does not have to be overt to be illegal.* In other words, the plaintiff does not have to show that the employer intentionally discriminated against the employee or applicant. Instead, the plaintiff just has to show that discrimination took place.
- Second, the Court held that an employment practice (in this case, requiring the high school degree) *must be job related* if it has an unequal impact on members of a **protected class**. (For example, if arithmetic is not required to perform the job, don't test for arithmetic.)
- Third, Chief Justice Burger's opinion placed the *burden of proof on the employer* to show that the hiring practice is job related. Thus, the employer must show that the employment practice (in this case, requiring a high school degree) is

necessary for satisfactory job performance if the practice discriminates against members of a protected class. In the words of Justice Burger,

> The act proscribes not only overt discrimination, but also practices that are fair in form, but discriminatory in operation. The touchstone is business necessity. If an employment practice which operates to exclude Negroes cannot be shown to be related to job performance, the practice is prohibited.[12]

For employers, *Griggs* established these five principles:

1. A test or other selection practice must be job related, and the burden of proof is on the employer.
2. An employer's intent not to discriminate is irrelevant.[13]
3. If a practice is "fair in form but discriminatory in operation," the courts will not uphold it.
4. *Business necessity* is the defense for any existing program that has adverse impact. The court did not define business necessity.
5. Title VII does not forbid testing. However, the test must be job related (valid), in that performance on the test must relate to performance on the job.

Albemarle Paper Company v. Moody In the *Albemarle* case, the Court provided more details on how employers could prove that tests or other screening tools relate to job performance.[14] For example, the Court said that if an employer wants to test candidates for a job, then the employer should first clearly document and understand the job's duties and responsibilities. Furthermore, the job's performance standards should be clear and unambiguous. That way, the employer can identify which employees are performing better than others. The Court's ruling also established the EEOC (now Federal) Guidelines on validation as the procedures for validating employment practices.

EQUAL EMPLOYMENT OPPORTUNITY 1990–91–PRESENT

The Civil Rights Act of 1991

Several subsequent Supreme Court rulings in the 1980s had the effect of limiting the protection of women and minority groups under equal employment laws. For example, they ratcheted up the plaintiff's burden of proving that the employer's acts were in fact discriminatory. This soon prompted Congress to pass a new Civil Rights Act. President George H. W. Bush signed the **Civil Rights Act of 1991 (CRA 1991)** into law in November 1991. The effect of CRA 1991 was to roll back equal employment law to where it stood before the 1980s decisions. In some respects, it even placed more responsibility on employers.

Burden of Proof First, CRA 1991 addressed the issue of *burden of proof*. Burden of proof—what the plaintiff must show to establish possible illegal discrimination, and

Pregnancy Discrimination Act
An amendment to Title VII of the Civil Rights Act that prohibits sex discrimination based on "pregnancy, childbirth, or related medical conditions."

uniform guidelines
Guidelines issued by federal agencies charged with ensuring compliance with equal employment federal legislation explaining recommended employer procedures in detail.

protected class
Persons such as minorities and women protected by equal opportunity laws, including Title VII.

Civil Rights Act of 1991 (CRA 1991)
It places burden of proof back on employers and permits compensatory and punitive damages.

what the employer must show to defend its actions—plays a central role in equal employment cases.[15] Today, in brief, once an aggrieved applicant or employee demonstrates that an employment practice (such as "must lift 100 pounds") has a disparate (or "adverse") impact on a particular group, then the burden of proof shifts to the employer, who must show that the challenged practice is job related.[16] For example, the employer has to show that lifting 100 pounds is actually required for performing the job in question, and that the business could not run efficiently without the requirement—that it is a business necessity.[17]

Money Damages Before CRA 1991, victims of *intentional* discrimination (which lawyers call *disparate treatment*) who had not suffered financial loss and who sued under Title VII could not then sue for compensatory or punitive damages. All they could expect was to have their jobs reinstated (or to get a particular job). They were also eligible for back pay, attorneys' fees, and court costs.

CRA 1991 makes it easier to sue for *money damages* in such cases. It provides that an employee who is claiming intentional discrimination can ask for (1) compensatory damages and (2) punitive damages, if he or she can show the employer engaged in discrimination "with malice or reckless indifference to the federally protected rights of an aggrieved individual."[18]

Mixed Motives Finally, CRA 1991 states:

> An unlawful employment practice is established when the complaining party demonstrates that race, color, religion, sex, or national origin was a motivating factor for any employment practice, even though other factors also motivated the practice.[19]

The last phrase is pivotal. Some employers in so-called **"mixed motive" cases** had taken the position that even though their actions were discriminatory, other factors like the employee's dubious behavior made the job action acceptable. Under CRA 1991, an employer cannot avoid liability by proving it would have taken the same action—such as terminating someone—even without the discriminatory motive.[20] *If there is any such motive, the practice may be unlawful.*[21]

The Americans with Disabilities Act

The **Americans with Disabilities Act (ADA)** of 1990 prohibits employment discrimination against qualified disabled individuals.[22] It prohibits employers with 15 or more workers from discriminating against qualified individuals with disabilities, with regard to applications, hiring, discharge, compensation, advancement, training, or other terms, conditions, or privileges of employment.[23] It also says employers must make "reasonable accommodations" for physical or mental limitations unless doing so imposes an "undue hardship" on the business.

The ADA does not list specific disabilities. Instead, EEOC guidelines say someone is disabled when he or she has a physical or mental impairment that "substantially limits" one or more major life activities. Impairments include any physiological disorder or condition, cosmetic disfigurement, or anatomical loss affecting one or more of several body systems, or any mental or psychological disorder.[24] The act specifies conditions that it does not regard as disabilities, including homosexuality, bisexuality, voyeurism, compulsive gambling, pyromania, and certain disorders resulting from the current illegal use of drugs.[25] The EEOC's position is that the ADA prohibits discriminating against people with HIV/AIDS (and numerous state laws also shield such people).

Mental Impairments and the ADA Mental disabilities account for the greatest number of ADA claims.[26] Under EEOC ADA guidelines, "mental impairment" includes "any mental or psychological disorder, such as . . . emotional or mental illness." Examples include major depression, anxiety disorders, and personality disorders. The ADA also protects employees with intellectual disabilities, including those with IQs below 70–75.[27] The guidelines say employers should be alert to the possibility that traits normally regarded as undesirable (such as chronic lateness, hostility, or poor judgment) may reflect mental impairments. Reasonable accommodation, says the EEOC, might then include providing room dividers, partitions, or other barriers between work spaces.

Qualified Individual Just being disabled doesn't qualify someone for a job, of course. Instead, the act prohibits discrimination against **qualified individuals**—those who, with (or without) a reasonable accommodation, can carry out the *essential functions* of the job. The individual must have the requisite skills, educational background, and experience to do the job. A job function is essential when, for instance, it is the reason the position exists, or it is so highly specialized that the employer hires the person for his or her expertise or ability to perform that particular function.

Reasonable Accommodation If the individual can't perform the job as currently structured, the employer must make a "reasonable accommodation" unless doing so would present an "undue hardship." Reasonable accommodation might include modifying work schedules, or acquiring equipment or other devices (such as voice recognition software) to assist the person.

Attorneys, employers, and the courts continue to work through what "reasonable accommodation" means.[28] An employee with a bad back who worked as a door greeter in a Walmart asked if she could sit on a stool while on duty. The store said no. She sued. The federal district court agreed with Walmart that door greeters must act in an "aggressively hospitable manner," which can't be done sitting on a stool.[29] Standing was an essential job function. You can use technology and common sense to make reasonable accommodation. Figure 2-1 summarizes several examples.

FIGURE 2-1 Examples of How to Provide Reasonable Accommodation

Source: Adapted from *Sexual Harassment Manual for Managers and Supervisors*, published in 1991, by CCH Incorporated, a WoltersKluwer Company, and from www.eeoc.gov/types/sexual_harrasment.html, accessed May 6, 2007.

1. *Follow ADA Accessibility Guidelines, such as regarding*
   - Protruding Objects.
   - Ground and Floor Surfaces
   - Curb Ramps
   - Platform Lifts (Wheelchair Lifts)
   - Doors (width, height of door handles, and so on)
   - Drinking Fountains and Water Coolers
   - Water Closets
2. *Modify Workplace Policies, such as regarding*
   - Eating at the work site
   - Hours of work
   - Leave and attendance
3. *Use Technology, for example,*
   - Employees with *mobility or vision impairments* may benefit from voice recognition software.
   - Word prediction software suggests words based on context with just one or two letters typed.
   - Real-time translation captioning enables employees to participate in meetings.
   - Vibrating text pagers notify employees when messages arrive.
   - Arizona created a disability-friendly Web site, "Arizona@YourService," to help link prospective employees and others to various agencies.

"mixed motive" case
A discrimination allegation case in which the employer argues that the employment action taken was motivated not by discrimination, but by some nondiscriminatory reason such as ineffective performance.

Americans with Disabilities Act (ADA)
The act requiring employers to make reasonable accommodations for disabled employees; it prohibits discrimination against disabled persons.

qualified individuals
Under ADA, those who can carry out the essential functions of the job.

Source: Courtesy of Robin Sachs/PhotoEdit Inc.

Technology enables employers to accommodate disabled employees.

Traditional Employer Defenses Employers traditionally prevailed in almost all—96%—federal circuit court ADA decisions.[30] A main reason is that employees were failing to show that they were disabled and qualified to do the job.[31] Unlike with Title VII of the Civil Rights Act, the employee must establish that he or she has a disability that fits under the ADA. This is more complicated than proving that one is a particular age or race. In one case, a social worker threatened to throw her coworker out a window and to "kick her [butt]." After transfer to another job, a doctor diagnosed her as paranoid. After repeatedly telling her supervisor she was "ready to kill her," she was fired. She sued under ADA. The court dismissed her case because, although she had a debilitating mental illness, ADA does not require retention of employees who make threats.[32] In another case, the court held that the employer did not discriminate against a blind bartender by requiring her to transfer to another job because she was unable to spot underage or intoxicated customers.[33]

A U.S. Supreme Court decision typifies what plaintiffs faced. An assembly worker sued Toyota, arguing that carpal tunnel syndrome prevented her from doing her job.[34] The U.S. Supreme Court ruled that the ADA covers carpal tunnel syndrome only if her impairments affect not just her job performance, but also her daily living activities. The employee admitted that she could perform personal chores such as washing her face and fixing breakfast. The Court said the disability must be central to the employee's daily living (not just job).[35]

The "New" ADA The era in which employers prevail in most ADA claims probably ended January 1, 2009. On that day, the ADA Amendments Act of 2008 (ADAAA) became effective. The EEOC had been interpreting the ADA's "substantially limits" phrase very narrowly. The new ADAAA's basic effect will be to make it much easier for employees to show that their disabilities are limiting. For example, the new act makes it easier for an employee to show that his or her disability is influencing one of the employee's "major life activities." It does this by adding examples like reading, concentrating, thinking, sleeping, and communicating to the list of ADA major life activities. As another example, under the new act, an employee will be considered disabled even if he or she has been able to control his or her impairments through medical or "learned behavioral" modifications. The bottom line is that employers will henceforth have to redouble their efforts to make sure they're complying with the ADA and providing reasonable accommodations.[36]

Many employers simply take a progressive approach. Research shows that common employer concerns about people with disabilities (for instance, that they can't perform physically demanding tasks, are less productive, and have more accidents) are generally baseless.[37] So, for example, Walgreens has a goal of filling at least one-third of the jobs at its two large distribution centers with people with disabilities.[38]

Figure 2-2 summarizes some important ADA guidelines for managers and employers.

FIGURE 2-2 ADA Guidelines For Managers And Employers

Source: Adapted from *Sexual Harassment Manual for Managers and Supervisors,* published in 1991, by CCH Incorporated, a WoltersKluwer Company, and from www.eeoc.gov/types/sexual_harrasment.html, accessed May 6, 2007.

- *Do not* deny a job to a disabled individual if the person is qualified and able to perform the essential job functions.
- *Make* a reasonable accommodation unless doing so would result in undue hardship.
- *You need not* lower existing performance standards or stop using tests for a job. However, those standards or tests must be job related and uniformly applied to all employees and candidates.
- *Know* what you can ask applicants. In general, you may *not* make preemployment inquiries about a person's disability before making an offer. However, you *may* ask questions about the person's ability to perform essential job functions.
- *Review* job application forms, interview procedures, and job descriptions for illegal questions and statements about health, disabilities, medical histories, or previous workers' compensation claims.
- *Itemize* essential job functions on the job descriptions. In virtually any ADA legal action, a central question will be what are the essential functions of the job?
- *Do not* allow misconduct or erratic performance (including absences and tardiness), even if that behavior is linked to the disability.

Genetic Information Nondiscrimination Act of 2008 (GINA)

The Genetic Information Nondiscrimination Act (GINA) prohibits discrimination by health insurers and employers based on people's genetic information. Specifically, it prohibits the use of genetic information in employment, prohibits the intentional acquisition of genetic information about applicants and employees, and imposes strict confidentiality requirements.[39]

State and Local Equal Employment Opportunity Laws

In addition to federal laws, all states and many local governments prohibit employment discrimination.

The effect of the state or local laws is usually to cover employers who federal laws might otherwise miss. Many cover employers (like those with less than 15 employees) not covered by federal legislation.[40] In Arizona, for instance, plaintiffs can bring sexual harassment claims against employers with as few as one employee. Some extend the protection of age discrimination laws to young people, barring discrimination against not only those over 40, but also those under 17. (Here, for instance, it would be illegal to advertise for "mature" applicants, because that might discourage some teenagers from applying.)

State and local equal employment opportunity agencies (often called "Human Resources Commissions" or "Fair Employment Commissions") also play a role in equal employment compliance. When the EEOC receives a discrimination charge, it usually defers it for a limited time to the state and local agencies that have comparable jurisdiction. If that doesn't achieve satisfactory remedies, the charges go back to the EEOC for resolution.

Table 2-1 summarizes selected equal employment opportunity laws, actions, executive orders, and agency guidelines.

2 Explain how to avoid and deal with accusations of sexual harassment at work.

Sexual Harassment

Under Title VII, **sexual harassment** generally refers to harassment on the basis of sex when such conduct has the purpose or effect of substantially interfering with a person's work performance or creating an intimidating, hostile, or offensive work environment. Sexual harassment violates Title VII.

sexual harassment
Harassment on the basis of sex that has the purpose or effect of substantially interfering with a person's work performance or creating an intimidating, hostile, or offensive work environment.

TABLE 2-1 Summary of Important Equal Employment Opportunity Actions

Action	What It Does
Title VII of 1964 Civil Rights Act, as amended	Bars discrimination because of race, color, religion, sex, or national origin; instituted EEOC.
Executive orders	Prohibit employment discrimination by employers with federal contracts of more than $10,000 (and their subcontractors); establish office of federal compliance; require affirmative action programs.
Federal agency guidelines	Indicate guidelines covering discrimination based on sex, national origin, and religion, as well as employee selection procedures; for example, require validation of tests.
Supreme Court decisions: *Griggs v. Duke Power Co., Albemarle v. Moody*	Rule that job requirements must be related to job success; that discrimination need not be overt to be proved; that the burden of proof is on the employer to prove the qualification is valid.
Equal Pay Act of 1963	Requires equal pay for men and women for performing similar work.
Age Discrimination in Employment Act of 1967	Prohibits discriminating against a person age 40 or over in any area of employment because of age.
State and local laws	Often cover organizations too small to be covered by federal laws.
Vocational Rehabilitation Act of 1973	Requires affirmative action to employ and promote qualified handicapped persons and prohibits discrimination against handicapped persons.
Pregnancy Discrimination Act of 1978	Prohibits discrimination in employment against pregnant women, or related conditions.
Vietnam Era Veterans' Readjustment Assistance Act of 1974	Requires affirmative action in employment for veterans of the Vietnam war era.
Ward Cove v. Atonio	Made it more difficult to prove a case of unlawful discrimination against an employer.
Americans with Disabilities Act of 1990	Strengthens the need for most employers to make reasonable accommodations for disabled employees at work; prohibits discrimination.
Civil Rights Act of 1991	Reverses various U.S. Supreme Court decisions; places burden of proof back on employer and permits compensatory and punitive money damages for discrimination.
ADA Amendments Act of 2008	Makes it easier for employee to show that his or her disability "substantially limits" a major life function.
Genetic Information Nondiscrimination Act	Signed into law in May 2008, this prohibits discriminating against employees and applicants based on their genetic information.

Source: The actual laws (and others) can be accessed at www.usa.gov/Topics/Reference_Shelf.shtml#Laws, accessed August 24, 2007.

EEOC guidelines emphasize that employers have an affirmative duty to maintain workplaces free of sexual harassment and intimidation. As we noted earlier, CRA 1991 permits victims of intentional discrimination, including sexual harassment, to have jury trials and to collect compensatory damages for pain and suffering and punitive damages, in cases where the employer acted with "malice or reckless indifference" to the person's rights.[41]

The U.S. Supreme Court held that (in *Oncale v. Sundowner Offshore Services Inc.*) same-sex sexual harassment is also actionable under Title VII.[42] The EEOC's Web site (eeoc.gov) says that in fiscal year 2008, EEOC received 13,867 sexual harassment charges, 15.9% of which males filed.[43]

Minority women are most at risk. One study found "women experienced more sexual harassment than men, minorities experienced more ethnic harassment than whites, and minority women experience more harassment overall than majority men, minority men, and majority women."[44]

The **Federal Violence Against Women Act of 1994** provides another path women can use to seek relief for violent sexual harassment. It provides that a person "who commits a crime of violence motivated by gender and thus deprives another" of her rights shall be liable to the party injured.

What Is Sexual Harassment? EEOC guidelines define sexual harassment as unwelcome sexual advances, requests for sexual favors, and other verbal or physical conduct of a sexual nature that takes place under any of the following conditions:

1. Submission to such conduct is made either explicitly or implicitly a term or condition of an individual's employment.
2. Submission to or rejection of such conduct by an individual is used as the basis for employment decisions affecting such individual.
3. Such conduct has the purpose or effect of unreasonably interfering with an individual's work performance or creating an intimidating, hostile, or offensive work environment.

Proving Sexual Harassment There are three main ways someone can prove sexual harassment.

1. ***Quid Pro Quo.*** The most direct is to prove that rejecting a supervisor's advances adversely affected what the EEOC calls a "tangible employment action" such as hiring, firing, promotion, demotion, and/or work assignment. In one case, the employee showed that continued job success and advancement were dependent on her agreeing to the sexual demands of her supervisors.
2. **Hostile Environment Created by Supervisors.** One need not show that the harassment had tangible consequences such as demotion. For example, in one case the court found that a male supervisor's sexual harassment had substantially affected a female employee's emotional and psychological ability to the point that she felt she had to quit her job. Therefore, even though the supervisor made no direct threats or promises in exchange for sexual advances, his advances interfered with the woman's performance and created an offensive work environment. That was sufficient to prove sexual harassment. Courts generally do not interpret as sexual harassment sexual relationships that arise during the course of employment but that do not have a substantial effect on that employment.[45] The U.S. Supreme Court also held that sexual harassment law doesn't cover ordinary "intersexual flirtation." In his ruling, Justice Antonin Scalia said courts must carefully distinguish between "simple teasing" and truly abusive behavior.[46]
3. **Hostile Environment Created by Coworkers or Nonemployees.** The questionable behavior doesn't have to come from the person's supervisor. For example, one court held that a mandatory sexually provocative uniform led to lewd comments by customers. When the employee said she would no longer wear the uniform, they fired her. The employer couldn't show there was a job-related necessity for requiring the uniform, and only female employees had to wear it. The court thus ruled that the employer, in effect, was responsible for the sexually harassing behavior. Such abhorrent client behavior is more likely when the clients are in positions of power, and when they think no one will penalize them.[47] EEOC guidelines also state that an employer is liable for the sexually harassing acts of its nonsupervisor employees if the employer knew or should have known of the harassing conduct.

When Is the Environment "Hostile"? Hostile environment sexual harassment generally means that the intimidation, insults, and ridicule were sufficiently severe to alter the working conditions. Here courts look at several things. These include whether

Federal Violence Against Women Act of 1994
Provides that a person who commits a crime of violence motivated by gender shall be liable to the party injured.

the discriminatory conduct is *frequent or severe*; whether it is *physically threatening* or humiliating, or a mere offensive utterance; and whether it unreasonably *interferes* with an employee's work performance.[48] Courts also consider whether the employee subjectively *perceives* the work environment as being abusive. For example, did he or she welcome the conduct or immediately show that it was unwelcome?[49]

Supreme Court Decisions The U.S. Supreme Court used a case called *Meritor Savings Bank, FSB v. Vinson* to endorse broadly the EEOC's guidelines on sexual harassment. Two other Supreme Court decisions further clarified sexual harassment law.

In the first, *Burlington Industries v. Ellerth*, the employee accused her supervisor of *quid pro quo* harassment. She said her boss propositioned and threatened her with demotion if she did not respond. He did not carry out the threats, and she was promoted. In the second case, *Faragher v. City of Boca Raton*, the employee accused the employer of condoning a hostile work environment. She said she quit her lifeguard job after repeated taunts from other lifeguards. The Court ruled in favor of the employees in both cases.

Implications The Court's written decisions have two implications for employers and managers. First, in *quid pro quo* cases it is *not* necessary for the employee to suffer a tangible job action (such as a demotion) to win the case.

Second, the Court laid out an important defense against harassment suits. It said the employer must show that it took "reasonable care" to prevent and promptly correct any sexually harassing behavior *and* that the employee unreasonably failed to take advantage of the employer's policy. The implication is that an employer can defend itself against sexual harassment liability by showing two things:

- First, it must show "that the employer exercised reasonable care to prevent and correct promptly any sexually harassing behavior."[50]
- Second, it must demonstrate that the plaintiff "unreasonably failed to take advantage of any preventive or corrective opportunities provided by the employer." The employee's failure to use formal reporting systems would satisfy the second component.

Prudent employers promptly took steps to show they did take reasonable care.[51] Figure 2-3 summarizes steps to take (such as issuing a strong policy statement). Use a form such as in Figure 2-4 to facilitate this process.[52]

FIGURE 2-3 HR in Practice: What Employers Should Do to Minimize Liability in Sexual Harassment Claims

Source: Adapted from *Sexual Harassment Manual for Managers and Supervisors*, published in 1991, by CCH Incorporated, a WoltersKluwer Company, and from www.eeoc.gov/types/sexual_harrassment.html, accessed May 6, 2007.

- *Take all complaints* about harassment seriously.
- *Encourage* the victim to inform the harasser directly that the conduct is unwelcome and must stop, and to use any employer complaint mechanism available.
- *Issue* a strong policy statement condemning such behavior. It should clearly describe the prohibited conduct, assure protection against retaliation, describe a complaint process that provides confidentiality, and provide accessible avenues of complaint and prompt, thorough, impartial investigation and corrective action.
- *Inform* all employees about the policy and of their rights under the policy.
- *Take steps* to prevent sexual harassment from occurring. For example, communicate to employees that the employer will not tolerate sexual harassment, and take immediate action when someone complains.
- *Establish* a management response system that includes an immediate reaction and investigation.
- *Train* supervisors and managers to increase their awareness of the issues.
- *Discipline* managers and employees involved in sexual harassment.
- *Keep thorough records* of complaints, investigations, and actions taken.
- *Conduct* exit interviews that uncover any complaints and that acknowledge by signature the reasons for leaving.
- *Re-publish* the sexual harassment policy periodically.
- *Encourage* upward communication, for instance, through periodic written attitude surveys.
- *Do not* retaliate against someone who files a harassment (or other EEO) complaint.

FIGURE 2-4 Online form to facilitate filing report of harassment.

Source: www.uiowa.edu/~eod/policies/sexual%20%harassment%20form.pdf, accessed April 28, 2009. Used with permission of University of Iowa.

Print Form

The University of Iowa
Office of Equal Opportunity and Diversity
CONFIDENTIAL REPORT OF INFORMAL* SEXUAL HARASSMENT COMPLAINT RESOLUTION
Please complete this form and submit it to the Office of Equal Opportunity and Diversity, 202 Jessup Hall,
As soon as reasonably possible after resolution of the complaint
Due to confidentiality considerations, please do not e-mail these forms.

Date of Incident	Date complaint received

College/Organizational Unit	Department	Today's Date
Name of Individual Completing Report	Title	Campus Telephone #

Consistent with the UI Policy on Sexual Harassment, if the person charged in the complaint has been informed of the existence of the complaint, all parties' names shall be disclosed; if the person charged has not been informed of the existence of the complaint, the parties' names shall not be disclosed.

Name of Complainant(s)

Department | **Gender** ☐ Male ☐ Female ☐ Unknown

Status of Complaint(s): ☐ Academic or Administrative Officer ☐ Faculty ☐ Professional & Scientific ☐ Merit ☐ Student Employee ☐ Undergraduate Student ☐ Graduate Student ☐ Job Applicant ☐ Former Employee ☐ No current University affiliation ☐ Graduate Assistant ☐ Other ________

Ethnicity of Complainant(s): ☐ American Indian or Alaskan Native ☐ White, not of Hispanic Origin ☐ African American and Black, not of Hispanic Origin ☐ Asian or Pacific Islander ☐ Latino or Hispanic

Name of Victim(s) ***(if other than Complainant)***

Department | **Gender** ☐ Male ☐ Female ☐ Unknown

Status of Victim(s): ☐ Academic or Administrative Officer ☐ Faculty ☐ Professional & Scientific ☐ Merit ☐ Student Employee ☐ Undergraduate Student ☐ Graduate Student ☐ Job Applicant ☐ Former Employee ☐ No current University affiliation ☐ Graduate Assistant ☐ Other ________

Ethnicity of Victim(s): ☐ American Indian or Alaskan Native ☐ White, not of Hispanic Origin ☐ African American and Black, not of Hispanic Origin ☐ Asian or Pacific Islander ☐ Latino or Hispanic

Name of Respondent(s)

Department | **Gender** ☐ Male ☐ Female ☐ Unknown

Status of Respondent(s): ☐ Academic or Administrative Officer ☐ Faculty ☐ Professional & Scientific ☐ Merit ☐ Student Employee ☐ Undergraduate Student ☐ Graduate Student ☐ Job Applicant ☐ Former Employee ☐ No current University affiliation ☐ Graduate Assistant ☐ Other ________

Ethnicity of Respondent(s): ☐ American Indian or Alaskan Native ☐ White, not of Hispanic Origin ☐ African American and Black, not of Hispanic Origin ☐ Asian or Pacific Islander ☐ Latino or Hispanic

DEFINITION: The University's Policy on Sexual Harassment defines sexual harassment as persistent, repetitive or egregious conduct directed at a specific individual or group of individuals that a reasonable person would interpret, in the full context in which the conduct occurs, as harassment of a sexual nature, when:

1. submission to such conduct is made or threatened to be made explicitly or implicitly a term or condition of an individual's employment, education, on campus living environment, or participation in a University activity;
2. submission to or rejection of such conduct is used or threatened to be used as a basis for a decision affecting an individual employment, education, on-campus living environment, or participation in a University activity; or
3. such conduct has the purpose or effect of unreasonably interfering with work or educational performance, or of creating an intimidating or offensive environment for employment, education, on-campus living, or participation in a University activity.

M:\KLast\Forms\sexual harassment form.doc, Page 1

(continued)

When the Law Isn't Enough Unfortunately, two practical considerations often trump the legal requirements. First, harassers sometimes don't realize that their abominable behavior is offending others. For example, men don't view harassment the same as do women.[53] Specifically, "women perceive a broader range of socio-sexual behaviors as harassing," particularly when those behaviors involve "hostile work environment harassment, derogatory attitudes toward women, dating pressure, or physical sexual contact."[54] Sexual harassment training and policies can reduce this problem.[55]

A second reason the usual precautions may not suffice is that employees are reluctant to use them. One study surveyed about 6,000 U.S. military employees. It turned out that reporting harassment often triggered retaliation, and could harm the victim "in terms of lower job satisfaction and greater psychological distress." Under such conditions, the most "reasonable" thing to do was to avoid reporting. "The few women who do formally complain do so only after encountering frequent, severe sexual harassment; at that point, considerable damage may have already

FIGURE 2.4 *(continued)*

For the purposes of this form, "informational complaints" are those handled by department or units outside the Office of Equal Opportunity and Diversity. Pursuant to the UI Policy on Sexual Harassment, any academic or administrative officer who becomes aware of allegations of sexual harassment by any means ***must*** consult with the Office of Equal Opportunity and Diversity regarding appropriate steps.

Forms of Sexual Harassment: (check all forms of unwelcome behavior that apply)

☐ **Verbal Harassment**	☐ **Physical Harassment**	☐ **Visual Harassment**
☐ comments of a sexual nature ☐ unwelcome advances ☐ derogatory sex based comments ☐ verbal threats ☐ other (explain)	☐ unwelcome contact ☐ physical gestures ☐ exhibitionism ☐ stalking ☐ assault ☐ other (explain)	☐ written ☐ pictures/photos ☐ posters ☐ electronic/computer ☐ other (explain)
☐ **Conditioning employment or educational benefits on submitting to sexual requests**	☐ **retaliation for complaining about sexual harassment**	☐ **Other (explain)**

Please provide summary of the nature of the allegations below (attach additional pages if necessary):

Outcome (check only one):

☐ Founded	☐ unfounded	☐ resolved/negotiated settlement
☐ complaint pending	☐ complaint withdrawn	☐ referred to another office
☐ Other		

Discipline (check all that apply):

☐ apology	☐ educational program	☐ counseling
☐ verbal reprimand	☐ written reprimand	☐ reassignment
☐ suspension	☐ no contact order	☐ termination
☐ other (explain)		
☐ **sanctions applied under the Code of Student Life** (explain)**		

*To your knowledge, has this complaint been referred to another office? ☐ Yes ☐ No If yes, please indicate where:
☐ Office of Equal Opportunity and Diversity ☐ Office of Student Services ☐ other (specify)

** For Office of Student Services use only: Date report Completed

Please return this form to the Office of Equal Opportunity and Diversity, 202 Jessup Hall.
Due to confidentiality considerations, please do not e-mail these forms.
Thank you for your assistance in resolving the complaint.

M:\KLast\Forms\sexual harassment form.doc, Page 2

occurred."[56] The bottom line is that most sexual harassment victims don't sue or complain. Instead, they quit or try to avoid their harassers. The solution is to execute zealously the policies in Figure 2-3.

What the Employee Can Do First, remember that courts generally look to whether *the harassed employee used the employer's reporting procedures to file a complaint promptly.* In that context, the steps an employee can take include the following:

1. File a verbal contemporaneous complaint or protest with the harasser and the harasser's boss, stating that the unwanted overtures should cease because the conduct is unwelcome.
2. Write a letter to the accused. This may be a polite, low-key letter that does three things: provides a detailed statement of the facts as the writer sees them; describes his or her feelings and what damage the writer thinks has been done;

Employees who believe they are victims of harassment should have a mechanism for filing a complaint.

and states that he or she would like to request that the future relationship be on a purely professional basis. Deliver this letter in person, with a witness, if necessary.

3. If the unwelcome conduct does not cease, file verbal and written reports regarding the unwelcome conduct and unsuccessful efforts to get it to stop with the harasser's manager and/or the human resource director.
4. If the letters and appeals to the employer do not suffice, the accuser should turn to the local office of the EEOC to file the necessary claim.
5. If the harassment is of a serious nature, the employee can also consult an attorney about suing the harasser for assault and battery, intentional infliction of emotional distress, injunctive relief, and to recover compensatory and punitive damages.

Globalization complicates the task of applying equal employment laws, as the accompanying "Managing the New Workforce" feature shows.

Managing the New Workforce

Enforcing Equal Employment Laws with International Employees

Most employers' workforces are increasingly international, and this complicates applying equal employment laws. For example, do U.S. EEO laws cover your foreign employees legally working in the United States?

In practice, the answer depends on the interplay of U.S. laws, international treaties, and the laws of the countries in which the U.S. firms are doing business. For example, Title VII, the ADEA, and ADA cover all U.S. citizens employed outside the United States by a U.S. firm or by a U.S.-controlled company.[57] But the laws of the country in which the U.S. citizen is working may take precedence. For instance, some foreign countries have statutes prohibiting the employment of women in management positions. There is also the practical difficulty of enforcing U.S. laws abroad. For example, it's not easy for the EEOC to review the organizational structure of an overseas employer.[58]

Here are some guidelines for applying EEO laws in an international context.[59]

- U.S. EEO laws *do* apply inside the United States when the employer is a U.S. entity and the employee is *not* a U.S. citizen but *is* legally authorized to work in the United States. In some cases, U.S. laws may apply to workers who are *not* authorized to work in the United States.[60]
- U.S. EEO laws *do* apply to jobs located inside the United States when the employer is a foreign entity *not* exempted by a treaty and the employee is authorized to work in the United States.
- U.S. EEO laws *do not* apply to jobs located outside the United States when the employer is a foreign entity, even if the employee is a U.S. citizen.
- U.S. EEO laws *do not* apply to foreign citizens in jobs located outside the United States, even if the employer is a U.S. entity.
- U.S. EEO laws *do* apply to jobs located outside the United States when the employer is a U.S. entity and the employee is a U.S. citizen, if compliance with U.S. laws would *not* violate foreign laws.

3 Define *adverse impact* and explain how it is proved.

DEFENSES AGAINST DISCRIMINATION ALLEGATIONS

To understand how employers defend themselves against employment discrimination claims, we should first briefly review some basic legal terminology.

Discrimination law distinguishes between disparate *treatment* and disparate *impact*. *Disparate treatment* means intentional discrimination. It "requires no more than a finding that women (or protected minority group members) were intentionally treated differently because of their gender" (or minority status). Disparate treatment "exists where an employer treats an individual differently because that individual is a member of a particular race, religion, gender, or ethnic group."[61] Having a rule that says "we do not hire bus drivers over 60 years of age" exemplifies this.

Disparate impact means that "an employer engages in an employment practice or policy that has a greater adverse impact (effect) on the members of a protected group under Title VII than on other employees, regardless of intent."[62] A rule that says "employees must have college degrees to do this particular job" exemplifies this (because more white males than some minorities earn college degrees).

Disparate impact claims do not require proof of discriminatory intent. Instead, the plaintiff must show that the apparently neutral employment practice (such as requiring a college degree) creates an **adverse impact**—a significant disparity—between the proportion of (say) minorities in the available labor pool and the proportion you hire. So, the key here is to show that the employment practice caused an adverse impact. If it has, then the employer will probably have to defend itself (for instance, by arguing that there is a business necessity for the practice).

The Central Role of Adverse Impact

Showing adverse impact therefore plays a central role in discriminatory practice allegations. Employers may not institute an employment practice that causes a disparate impact on a particular class of people unless they can show that the practice is job related and necessary.[63] Under Title VII and CRA 1991, a person who believes that (1) he or she was a victim of unintentional discrimination because of an employer's practices need only (2) establish a *prima facie* case of discrimination. This means showing, for instance, that the employer's selection procedures (like requiring a college degree for the job) did have an adverse impact on the protected minority group. Adverse impact "refers to the total employment process that results in a significantly higher percentage of a protected group in the candidate population being rejected for employment, placement, or promotion."[64] Then the burden of proof shifts to the employer.

So, for example, if a minority applicant feels he or she was a victim of discrimination, the person need only show that the employer's selection process resulted in an adverse impact on his or her group. (For example, if 80% of the white applicants passed the test, but only 20% of the black applicants passed, a black applicant has a *prima facie* case proving adverse impact.) Then the burden of proof shifts to the employer. It becomes the employer's task to prove that its test (or application blank or the like) is a valid predictor of performance on the job (and that it applied its selection process fairly and equitably to both minorities and nonminorities).

How Can Someone Show Adverse Impact?

An applicant or employee can use one of four methods to show that one of an employer's procedures (such as a selection test) has an adverse impact on a protected group.

1. **Disparate Rejection Rates. Disparate rejection rates** can be shown by comparing the rejection rates for a minority group and another group (usually the remaining nonminority applicants).

   Federal agencies use a **"4/5ths rule"** to assess disparate rejection rates: "A selection rate for any racial, ethnic, or sex group which is less than four-fifths or 80% of the rate for the group with the highest rate will generally be regarded as evidence of adverse impact, while a greater than four-fifths rate will generally not be regarded as evidence of adverse impact." For example, suppose the employer hires 60% of male applicants, but only 30% of female applicants. Four-fifths of 60% would be 48%. Since 30% is less than 48%, adverse impact exists as far as these federal agencies are concerned.[65]

2. **Restricted Policy.** The **restricted policy** approach means demonstrating that the employer's policy intentionally or unintentionally excluded members of a protected group. Here the problem is usually obvious—such as policies against hiring bartenders less than six feet tall. Evidence of restricted policies such as these is enough to prove adverse impact and to expose an employer to litigation.
3. **Population Comparisons.** This approach compares (1) the percentage of Hispanic (or black or other minority/protected group) and white workers in the organization with (2) the percentage of the corresponding group in the labor market. The EEOC usually defines labor market as the U.S. Census data for that Standard Metropolitan Statistical Area.

   Yet "labor market," of course, varies with the job. For some jobs, such as laborer or secretary, it makes sense to compare the percentage of minority employees with the percentage of minorities in the surrounding community, since they will come from that community. But for jobs such as engineer, recruiting may be nationwide. Determining whether an employer has enough black engineers might thus involve determining the number available nationwide, not in the surrounding community.
4. **McDonnell-Douglas Test.** Lawyers in disparate impact cases use approaches 1 through 3 to test whether an employer's policies or actions have the effect of unintentionally screening out disproportionate numbers of women or minorities. Lawyers use the McDonnell-Douglas test for showing (intentional) disparate treatment, rather than (unintentional) disparate impact.

   This test grew out of a case at the former McDonnell-Douglas Corporation. The applicant was qualified but the employer rejected the person and continued seeking applicants. Did this show that the hiring company intentionally discriminated against the female or minority candidate? The U.S. Supreme Court set four rules for applying the McDonnell-Douglas test:

   a. that the person belongs to a protected class;
   b. that he or she applied and was qualified for a job for which the employer was seeking applicants;
   c. that, despite this qualification, he or she was rejected; and
   d. that, after his or her rejection, the position remained open and the employer continued seeking applications from persons with the complainant's qualifications.

   If the plaintiff meets all these conditions, then a *prima facie* case of disparate treatment is established. At that point, the employer must articulate a legitimate nondiscriminatory reason for its action, and produce evidence but not prove that it acted based on such a reason. If it meets this relatively easy standard, the plaintiff then has the burden of proving that the employer's articulated reason is merely a pretext for engaging in unlawful discrimination.

adverse impact
The overall impact of employer practices that result in significantly higher percentages of members of minorities and other protected groups being rejected for employment, placement, or promotion.

disparate rejection rates
A test for adverse impact in which it can be demonstrated that there is a discrepancy between rates of rejection of members of a protected group and of others.

4/5ths rule
Federal agency rule that minority selection rate less than 80% (4/5ths) that of group with highest rate evidences adverse impact.

restricted policy
Another test for adverse impact, involving demonstration that an employer's hiring practices exclude a protected group, whether intentionally or not.

Adverse Impact Example Assume you turn down a member of a protected group for a job with your firm. You do this based on a test score (although it could have been interview questions or something else). Further, assume that this person feels he or she was discriminated against due to being in a protected class, and decides to sue your company.

Basically, all he or she must do is show that your human resources procedure (such as the selection test) had an adverse impact on members of his or her minority group. The plaintiff can apply three approaches here. These are disparate rejection rates, restricted policy, or population comparisons. Once the person proves adverse impact (to the court's satisfaction), the burden of proof shifts to the employer. The employer must defend against the discrimination charges.

Note that there is nothing in the law that says that because one of your procedures has an adverse impact on a protected group, you can't use the procedure. In fact, it may well happen that some tests screen out disproportionately higher numbers of, say, blacks than they do whites. What the law does say is that once your applicant has made his or her case (showing adverse impact), the burden of proof shifts to you. Now you (or your company) must defend use of the procedure.

There are then two basic defenses employers use to justify an employment practice that has an adverse impact on members of a minority group: the bona fide occupational qualification (BFOQ) defense and the business necessity defense.

4 Explain and illustrate two defenses you can use in the event of discriminatory practice allegations.

Bona Fide Occupational Qualification

An employer can claim that the employment practice is a **bona fide occupational qualification (BFOQ)** for performing the job. Title VII specifically permits this defense. Title VII provides that "it should not be an unlawful employment practice for an employer to hire an employee . . . on the basis of religion, sex, or national origin *in those certain instances where religion, sex, or national origin is a bona fide occupational qualification* reasonably necessary to the normal operation of that particular business or enterprise."

However, courts usually interpret the BFOQ exception narrowly. It is usually a defense to a disparate treatment case based upon direct evidence of *intentional* discrimination, rather than to disparate impact (unintentional) cases. As a practical matter, employers use it mostly as a defense against charges of intentional discrimination based on age.

Age as a BFOQ The Age Discrimination in Employment Act (ADEA) permits disparate treatment in those instances when age is a BFOQ.[66] For example, age is a BFOQ when the Federal Aviation Agency sets a compulsory retirement age of 65 for commercial pilots.[67] Actors required for youthful or elderly roles suggest other instances when age may be a BFOQ. However, courts set the bar high: The reason for the age limit must go to the essence of the business. A court said a bus line's maximum-age hiring policy for bus drivers was a BFOQ. The court said the essence of the business was safe transportation of passengers, and given that, the employer could strive to employ the most qualified persons available.[68]

Employers who use the BFOQ defense here admit they base their personnel decisions on age. However, they seek to justify them by showing that the decisions were reasonably necessary to normal business operations (for instance, the bus line arguing its age requirement is necessary for safety).[69]

Religion as a BFOQ Religion may be a BFOQ in religious organizations or societies that require employees to share their particular religion. For example, religion may be a BFOQ when hiring persons to teach in a religious school. However, remember courts construe the BFOQ defense very narrowly.

Gender as a BFOQ Gender may be a BFOQ for positions like actor, model, and restroom attendant requiring physical characteristics possessed by one sex. However, for most jobs today, it's difficult to claim that gender is a BFOQ. For example, gender is not a BFOQ for parole and probation officers.[70] It is not a BFOQ for positions just because the positions require lifting heavy objects.

National Origin as a BFOQ A person's country of national origin may be a BFOQ. For example, an employer who is running the Chinese pavilion at a fair might claim that Chinese heritage is a BFOQ for persons to deal with the public.

Business Necessity

"Business necessity" is a defense created by the courts. It requires showing that there is an overriding business purpose for the discriminatory practice and that the practice is therefore acceptable.

It's not easy to prove business necessity.[71] The Supreme Court made it clear that business necessity does not encompass such matters as avoiding an employer inconvenience, annoyance, or expense. For example, an employer can't generally discharge employees whose wages have been garnished merely because garnishment (requiring the employer to divert part of the person's wages to pay his or her debts) creates an inconvenience. The Second Circuit Court of Appeals held that business necessity means an "irresistible demand." It said the practice "must not only directly foster safety and efficiency" but also be essential to these goals.[72] Furthermore, "the business purpose must be sufficiently compelling to override any racial impact. . . ."[73]

However, many employers have used the business necessity defense successfully. In an early case, *Spurlock v. United Airlines*, a minority candidate sued United Airlines. He said that its requirements that pilot candidates have 500 flight hours and college degrees were unfairly discriminatory. The court agreed that the requirements did have an adverse impact on members of the person's minority group. But it held that in light of the cost of the training program and the huge human and economic risks in hiring unqualified candidates, the selection standards were a business necessity and were job related.[74]

In general, when a job requires a small amount of skill and training, the courts closely scrutinize any preemployment standards or criteria that discriminate against minorities. Employers in such cases have a heavy burden to demonstrate that the practices are job related. There is a correspondingly lighter burden when the job requires a high degree of skill, and when the economic and human risks of hiring an unqualified applicant are great.[75]

Attempts by employers to show that their selection tests or other employment practices are *valid* are examples of the business necessity defense. Here the employer must show that the test or other practice is job related—in other words, that it is a valid predictor of performance on the job. Where the employer can establish such validity, the courts have generally supported using the test or other employment practice as a business necessity. In this context, *validity* means the degree to which the test or other employment practice is related to or predicts performance on the job; Chapter 6 explains validation.

bona fide occupational qualification (BFOQ)
Requirement that an employee be of a certain religion, sex, or national origin where that is reasonably necessary to the organization's normal operation. Specified by the 1964 Civil Rights Act.

Other Considerations in Discriminatory Practice Defenses

There are three other points to remember about discrimination charges:

1. First, *good intentions are no excuse.* As the Supreme Court held in the *Griggs* case,

   > Good intent or absence of discriminatory intent does not redeem procedures or testing mechanisms that operate as built-in headwinds for minority groups and are unrelated to measuring job capability.

2. Second, one *cannot hide behind collective bargaining agreements* (for instance, by claiming that a union agreement necessitates some discriminatory practice). Courts hold that equal employment opportunity laws take precedence over the rights embodied in a labor contract.[76]
3. Third, a strong defense *is not your only recourse.* When confronted with the fact that one or more personnel practices is discriminatory, the employer can also respond by agreeing to eliminate the illegal practice and (when required) by compensating the people discriminated against.

5 Cite specific discriminatory personnel management practices in recruitment, selection, promotion, transfer, layoffs, and benefits.

ILLUSTRATIVE DISCRIMINATORY EMPLOYMENT PRACTICES

A Note on What You Can and Cannot Do

Before proceeding, we should review what federal fair employment laws allow (and do not allow) you to say and do.

Federal laws like Title VII usually don't expressly ban preemployment questions about an applicant's race, color, religion, sex, or national origin. In other words, "with the exception of personnel policies calling for outright discrimination against the members of some protected group," it's not the questions but their impact.[77] For example, it isn't illegal to ask a job candidate about her marital status (although such a question might seem discriminatory). You can ask. However, you should be prepared to show either that you do not discriminate or that you can defend the practice as a BFOQ or business necessity.

But, in practice, there are two reasons to avoid such questions. First, although federal law may not bar such questions, many state and local laws do.

Second, the EEOC has said that it will disapprove of such practices, so just asking the questions may draw its attention. Put another way, these are potentially "problem questions." They may identify and/or adversely affect an applicant as a member of a protected group. They become illegal if a complainant can show you use them to screen out a greater proportion of his or her protected group's applicants, and you can't prove the practice is required as a business necessity or BFOQ.

Let's look now at some of the potentially discriminatory practices to avoid.[78]

Recruitment

Word of Mouth You cannot rely upon word-of-mouth dissemination of information about job opportunities when your workforce is all (or mostly all) white or all members of some other class such as all female, all Hispanic, and so on. Doing so reduces the likelihood that others will become aware of the jobs and thus apply for them.

Misleading Information It is unlawful to give false or misleading information to members of any group, or to fail or refuse to advise them of work opportunities and the procedures for obtaining them.

Help Wanted Ads "Help wanted—male" and "help wanted—female" ads are violations unless gender is a bona fide occupational qualification for the job. The same applies to ads that suggest age discrimination. For example, you cannot advertise for a "young" man or woman.

Selection Standards

Educational Requirements

Courts have found educational qualifications to be illegal when (1) minority groups are less likely to possess the educational qualifications (such as a high school degree) and (2) such qualifications are also not job related. However, there may be jobs of course for which educational requirements (such as college degrees for pilot candidates) are a necessity.

Tests

Courts deem tests unlawful if they disproportionately screen out minorities or women *and* they are not job related. According to former Chief Justice Burger,

> Nothing in the [Title VII] act precludes the use of testing or measuring procedures; obviously they are useful. What Congress has forbidden is giving these devices and mechanisms controlling force unless they are demonstrating a reasonable measure of job performance.

Preference to Relatives

Do not give preference to relatives of current employees with respect to employment opportunities if your current employees are substantially nonminority.

Height, Weight, and Physical Characteristics

Physical requirements such as minimum height are unlawful unless the employer can show they're job related. For example, a U.S. Appeals Court recently upheld a $3.4 million jury verdict against Dial Corp. Dial rejected 52 women for entry-level jobs at a meat processing plant because they failed strength tests, although strength was not a job requirement.[79] *Maximum* weight rules generally don't trigger adverse legal rulings. To qualify for reasonable accommodation, obese applicants must be at least 100 pounds above their ideal weight or there must be a physiological cause for their disability. However, legalities aside, managers should be vigilant.[80] Studies leave little doubt that obese individuals are less likely to be hired, less likely to receive promotions, more likely to get less desirable sales assignments, and more likely to receive poor customer service as customers.[81]

Arrest Records

Unless the job requires security clearance, you should not ask an applicant whether he or she has been arrested or spent time in jail, or use an arrest record to disqualify a person automatically. There are several reasons. Various racial minorities are more likely than whites to have arrest records.[82] There is always a presumption of innocence until proven guilty. And arrest records in general are not valid for predicting job performance. Thus, disqualifying applicants based on arrest records adversely impacts minorities. You can ask about conviction records. Then determine on a case-by-case basis whether the facts justify refusal to employ an applicant in a particular position.

Application Forms

Employment applications generally shouldn't contain questions about applicants' disabilities, workers' compensation history, age, arrest record, or U.S. citizenship. In general it's best to collect personal information required for legitimate tax or benefit reasons (such as who to contact in case of emergency) after you hire the person.[83] (Note that equal employment laws discourage employers from asking for such information, but no such laws prohibit applicants from offering it. One study examined 107 résumés from Australian managerial applicants. Many provided information regarding marital status, ethnicity, age, and gender.)[84]

Discharge Due to Garnishment

A disproportionate number of minorities suffer garnishment procedures (in which creditors make a claim to some of the person's wages). Therefore, firing a minority member whose salary is garnished is illegal, unless you can show some overriding business necessity.

Sample Discriminatory Promotion, Transfer, and Layoff Practices

Fair employment laws protect not just job applicants but also current employees. For example, the Equal Pay Act requires that equal wages be paid for substantially similar work performed by men and women. Therefore, courts may hold that any employment practices regarding pay, promotion, termination, discipline, or benefits that

1. are applied differently to different classes of persons;
2. adversely impact members of a protected group; and
3. cannot be shown to be required as a BFOQ or business necessity are illegally discriminatory.

Personal Appearance Regulations and Title VII

Employees sometimes file suits against employers' dress and appearance codes under Title VII. They usually claim sex discrimination, but sometimes claim racial discrimination. A sampling of court rulings follows:[85]

- **Dress.** In general, employers do not violate the Title VII ban on sex bias by requiring all employees to dress conservatively. For example, a supervisor's suggestion that a female attorney tone down her attire was permissible when the firm consistently sought to maintain a conservative dress style and counseled men to dress conservatively.
- **Hair.** Again, courts usually favor employers. For example, employer rules against facial hair do not constitute sex discrimination because they discriminate only between clean-shaven and bearded men, discrimination not qualified as sex bias under Title VII. Courts have also rejected arguments that prohibiting cornrow hair styles infringed on black employees' expression of cultural identification.
- **Uniforms.** When it comes to discriminatory uniforms and/or suggestive attire, however, courts frequently side with employees. For example, requiring female employees (such as waitresses) to wear sexually suggestive attire as a condition of employment has been ruled as violating Title VII in many cases.[86]

What the Supervisor Should Keep in Mind

The human resource manager certainly plays a big role in helping the company avoid practices like these, but at the end of the day, the first-line supervisor usually triggers the problem. You make an ill-informed or foolish comment, and the employee is quick to sue. Even something apparently "nondiscriminatory"—like telling a female candidate you'd be concerned about her safety on the job after dark—might trigger a claim.

This is, therefore, a good point at which to emphasize two things. First, carefully learning this chapter's contents is important. For example, *understand the questions* you can and cannot ask when interviewing applicants, and know what *constitutes* sexual harassment, and *how* equal *employment opportunity law affects all your human resources decisions*, including those relating to appraisal, compensation, promotions, disciplinary procedures, and employee dismissals. There is no substitute for that knowledge. Good intentions (as we saw) are no excuse.

Second, if that's not sufficient warning, consider this: The courts may hold you (not just your employer) personally liable for your injudicious actions. *Management malpractice* is conduct (really, aberrant conduct) on the part of the manager that has serious consequences for the employee's personal or physical well-being, or which, as one court put it, "exceeds all bounds usually tolerated by society."[87] In one outrageous example, the employer demoted a manager to janitor and took other steps to humiliate the person. The jury subsequently awarded the former manager $3.4 million. Supervisors who commit management malpractice may be personally liable for paying a portion of the judgment.

6 List the steps in the EEOC enforcement process.

THE EEOC ENFORCEMENT PROCESS

Even prudent employers eventually face employment discrimination claims and have to deal with EEOC officials. We'll see that all managers (not just human resource managers) play important roles in this process. All managers should therefore have a working knowledge of the following EEOC claim and enforcement process. Figure 2-5 provides an overview of the process.[88]

The process consists of these steps:

- **File Charge.** The process begins when someone files a claim with the EEOC. Under CRA 1991, the discrimination claim must be filed within 300 days (when there is a similar state law) or 180 days (where there is no similar state law) after the alleged incident took place (2 years for the Equal Pay Act).[89] Either the aggrieved person or a member of the EEOC who has reasonable cause to believe that a violation occurred must file the claim in writing and under oath.[90] The number of private-sector discrimination charges filed with the EEOC climbed to 95,402 in fiscal year 2008, up more than 15% from the previous year.[91]
- **Charge Acceptance.** The EEOC's common practice is to accept a charge and orally refer it to the state or local agency on behalf of the charging party. If the agency waives jurisdiction or cannot obtain a satisfactory solution, the EEOC processes it upon the expiration of the deferral period. It does not require filing a new charge.[92]
- **Serve Notice.** After a charge is filed (or the state or local deferral period has ended), the EEOC has 10 days to serve notice on the employer. Figure 2-6 (page 55) summarizes important questions an employer should ask after receiving a bias complaint from the EEOC. They include, for example, "To what protected group does the worker belong?"
- **Investigation/Fact-Finding Conference.** The EEOC then investigates the charge to determine whether there is reasonable cause to believe it is true; it has 120 days to make this determination. Early in the investigation, the EEOC holds an initial *fact-finding conference.* The EEOC calls these "informal meetings" for defining issues and determining whether there's a basis for negotiation. However, the EEOC's real focus here is often on settlement. Its investigators use the conferences to find weak spots in each party's position. They use these as leverage to push for a settlement.
- **Cause/No Cause.** If it finds no reasonable cause, the EEOC must dismiss the charge, and must issue the charging party a Notice of Right to Sue. The person then has 90 days to file a suit on his or her own behalf.
- **Conciliation.** If the EEOC does find cause, it has 30 days to work out a conciliation agreement. The EEOC conciliator meets with the employee to determine what remedy would be satisfactory. It then tries to negotiate a settlement with the employer. If both parties accept the remedy, they sign and submit a conciliation agreement to the EEOC for approval. If the EEOC cannot obtain an acceptable conciliation agreement, it may sue the employer in a federal district court. The EEOC is also using outside mediators to settle claims in selected cities (more on this in a moment).
- **Notice to Sue.** If this conciliation is not satisfactory, the EEOC may bring a civil suit in a federal district court, or issue a Notice of Right to Sue to the person who filed the charge.

The Equal Employment Opportunity Commission voted unanimously in 2006 to focus more on big, "systemic" cases, those that reflect a pattern or practice of alleged discrimination.[93] Its systemic cases task force recently issued specific recommendations the EEOC can use to uncover and remedy systemic discrimination.[94] In a suit apparently prompted by its subsequent "Eradicating Racism from Employment" campaign, the EEOC recently claimed that Walgreens used race to determine who to assign to low-performing stores in African American communities.[95]

FIGURE 2-5 The EEOC Charge-Filing Process

Note: Parties may settle at any time.

Source: Based on information at www.eeoc.gov.

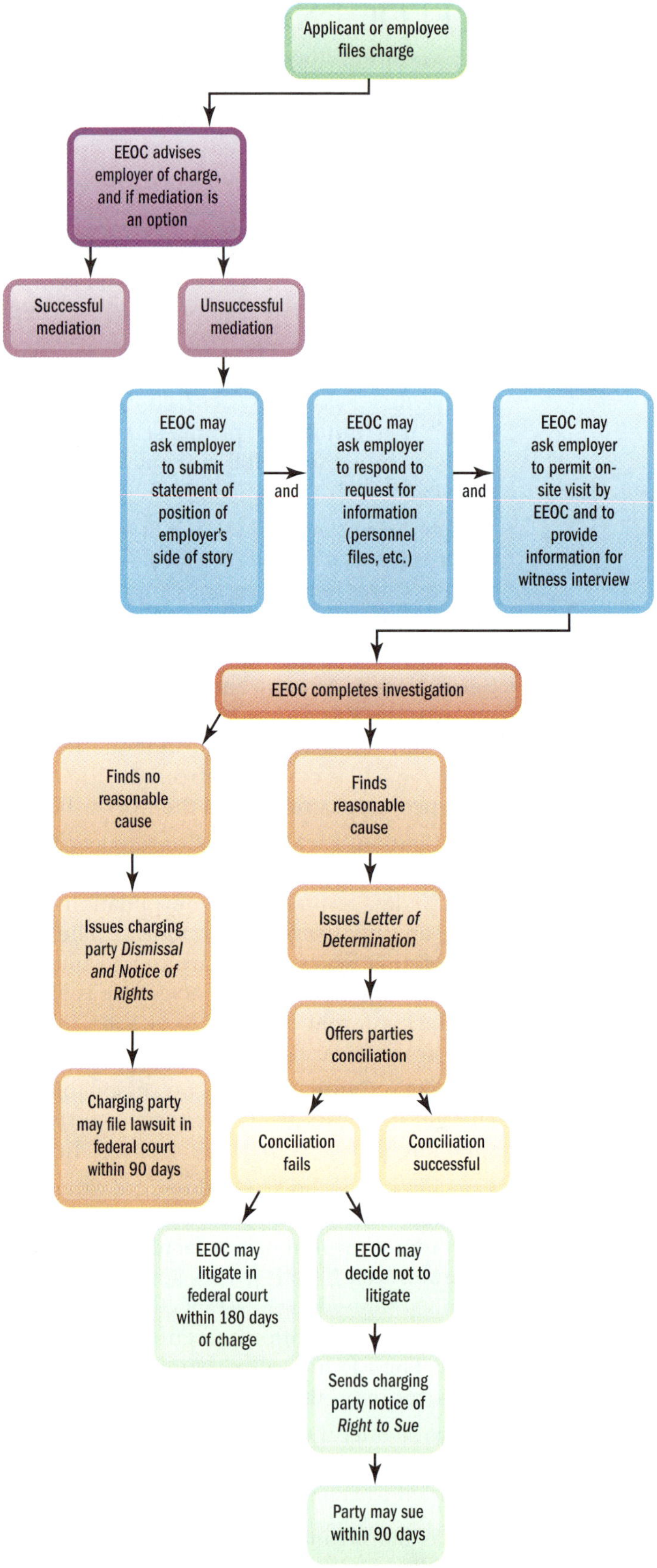

Voluntary Mediation

The EEOC refers about 10% of its charges to a voluntary mediation mechanism. This is "an informal process in which a neutral third party assists the opposing parties to reach a voluntary, negotiated resolution of a charge of discrimination."[96]

FIGURE 2-6 Questions to Ask When an Employer Receives Notice That EEOC Has Filed a Bias Claim

Source: Fair Employment Practices Summary of Latest Developments, January 7, 1983, p. 3, Bureau of National Affairs, Inc. (800-372-1033); Kenneth Sovereign, *Personnel Law* (Upper Saddle River, NJ: Prentice Hall, 1999), pp. 36–37; "EEOC Investigations—What an Employer Should Know," Equal Employment Opportunity Commission (www.eoc.gov/employers/investigations.html), accessed May 6, 2007.

1. Exactly what is the charge and is your company covered by the relevant statutes? (For example, Title VII and the Americans with Disabilities Act generally apply only to employees with 15 or more employees; the Age Discrimination in Employment Act applies to employers with 20 or more employees; but the Equal Pay Act applies to virtually all employers with one or more employees.) Did the employee file his or her charge on time, and was it processed in a timely manner by the EEOC?
2. What protected group does the employee belong to? Is the EEOC claiming disparate impact or disparate treatment?
3. Are there any obvious bases upon which you can challenge and/or rebut the claim? For example, would the employer have taken the action if the person did not belong to a protected group? Does the person's personnel file support the action taken by the employer? Conversely, does it suggest the possibility of unjustified discriminatory treatment?
4. If it is a sexual harassment claim, are there offensive comments, calendars, posters, screensavers, and so on, on display in the company?
5. In terms of the practicality of defending your company against this claim, who are the supervisors who actually took the allegedly discriminatory actions and how effective will they be as potential witnesses? Have you received an opinion from legal counsel regarding the chances of prevailing? Even if you do prevail, what do you estimate will be the out-of-pocket costs of taking the charge through the judicial process? Would you be better off settling the case, and what are the prospects of doing so in a way that will satisfy all parties?

If the plaintiff and employer both agree to mediation, the mediation session usually lasts up to 4 hours. If the parties don't reach agreement (or one of the parties rejects participation), the EEOC processes the charge through its usual mechanisms.[97]

In the 4 years after the EEOC launched its mediation program, its offices had already conducted more than 44,000 mediations and settled more than 30,000 charges through the program. By then, the EEOC had also signed numerous *National Universal Agreement to Mediate* (NUAM) agreements with firms including Ford Motor Company,[98] as well as local agreements with participating employers. Under NUAM, the EEOC refers all eligible discrimination charges filed against these employers directly to the commission's mediation unit.[99]

Faced with an offer to mediate, the employer has three options: Agree to mediate the charge; make a settlement offer without mediation; or prepare a "position statement" for the EEOC. If the employer does not mediate or make an offer, the position statement is required. It should include a robust defense, including information relating to the company's business and the charging party's position; a description of any rules or policies and procedures that are applicable; and the chronology of the offense that led to the adverse action.[100]

Mandatory Arbitration of Discrimination Claims

Many employers, to avoid EEO litigation, require applicants and employees to agree to arbitrate such claims. The U.S. Supreme Court's decisions (in *Gilmer v. Interstate/Johnson Lane Corp.* and similar cases) make it clear that "employment discrimination plaintiffs [employees] may be compelled to arbitrate their claims under some circumstances."[101] Given this, the following suggestions are in order:[102]

- Employers "may wish to consider inserting a mandatory arbitration clause in their employment applications or employee handbooks."[103]
- To protect such a process against appeal, the employer should institute steps to protect against arbitrator bias; allow the arbitrator to offer a claimant broad relief (including reinstatement); and allow for a reasonable amount of prehearing discovery (fact finding).

FIGURE 2-7 Management Guidelines for Addressing EEOC Claims

Sources: "Tips for Employers On Dealing with EEOC Investigations", *BNA Fair Employment Practices*, October 31, 1996, p. 130; "Conducting Effective Investigations of Employee Bias Complaints," *BNA Fair Employment Practices*, July 13, 1995, p. 81; Commerce Clearing House, *Ideas and Trends*, January 23, 1987, pp. 14–15; http://eeoc.gov/employers/investigations.html, accessed October 4, 2009.

During the EEOC Investigation:

Conduct your own investigation to get the facts.
Ensure that there is information in the EEOC's file *demonstrating lack of merit* of the charge.
Limit the information supplied to only those issues raised in the charge itself.
Get as much information as possible about the *charging party's claim.*
Meet with the employee who made the complaint to clarify all the relevant issues. For example, what happened? Who was involved?
Remember that *the EEOC can only ask employers* to submit documents and ask for the testimony of witnesses under oath. It cannot compel employers.
It may be useful to give the EEOC a *position statement.* It should contain words to the effect that "the company has a policy against discrimination and would not discriminate in the manner charged in the complaint." Support the statement with documentation.

During the Fact-Finding Conference:

Because the only official record is the notes the EEOC investigator takes, *keep your own records.*
Bring an *attorney.*
Make sure you are *fully informed* of the charges and facts of the case.
Before appearing, *witnesses (especially supervisors) need to be aware* of the legal significance of the facts they will present.

During the EEOC Determination and Attempted Conciliation:

If there is a finding of cause, *review it carefully,* and point out inaccuracies in writing to the EEOC.
Use this letter to try again to convince the parties that the charge is *without merit.*
Conciliate prudently. If you have properly investigated and evaluated the case, there may be no real advantage in settling at this stage.
Remember: It is likely (based on the statistics) that *no suit will be filed* by the EEOC.

- Employers should review all employment discrimination suits filed against them to determine whether they involve an employee who is subject to an agreement to arbitrate; they should then decide whether to move to compel arbitration of the claim.[104]

After an expensive EEO lawsuit, Rockwell International implemented a grievance procedure that provides for binding arbitration as the last step. Called (as is traditional) an **alternative dispute resolution or ADR program**, Rockwell gradually extended the program to all nonunion employees at some locations. New hires at Rockwell must sign the agreement as a condition of employment. Current employees must sign it prior to promotion or transfer.[105] ADR plans are popular, although the EEOC generally opposes such plans for handling bias claims.[106] Figure 2-7 sums up guidelines employers should follow in addressing EEOC claims.

7 Discuss why diversity management is important and how to institutionalize a diversity management program.

DIVERSITY MANAGEMENT AND AFFIRMATIVE ACTION PROGRAMS

To a real extent, demographic changes and globalization are rendering moot the motives that drove equal employment legislation. In other words, employers now have little choice but to willingly push for more diversity. In this context, **diversity** refers to the variety or multiplicity of demographic features that characterize a company's workforce, particularly in terms of race, sex, culture, national origin, handicap, age, and religion.[107] White males no longer dominate the labor force, and women and minorities represent the lion's share of labor force growth over the near future. Furthermore, globalization requires employers to hire minority members with the cultural and language skills to deal with customers abroad. As the *Wall Street Journal* put it: "As companies do more and more business around the world, diversity isn't simply a matter of doing what is fair or good public relations. It's a business imperative."[108]

Unfortunately, everyone knows that having workforce diversity doesn't necessarily mean having a smoothly functioning cadre of employees. Intuitively at least, most would assume that diversity provides at least the potential for arguments and conflict. However, the evidence doesn't necessarily support that, as the accompanying Evidenced-Based HR feature explains.

EVIDENCE-BASED HR

Will Workforce Diversity Cause Problems for Our Company?

As intuitively obvious as it sounds, the research evidence does not support the idea that diversity necessarily triggers problems for employers. Much of the earlier research did conclude that diversity is a "double-edged sword"—specifically, that diversity in work groups leads to more high-quality solutions, but also to reduced group cohesion.[109] However, recent reviews of the research provide little or no evidence to support the idea that diversity has "much of an influence on group cohesion or performance."[110] Similarly, another study found "few positive or negative direct effects of diversity on performance."[111]

No one is quite sure what accounts for this. Perhaps the effect of diversity on work-group cohesion and performance has been overstated. Perhaps "over time the negative outcomes associated with diversity decrease because people get to know each other."[112] Perhaps the measures of diversity are inconsistent. A reasonable conclusion is that if you do most everything else right—hire the right people, train them, appraise and reward everyone fairly—diversity's potential negative effects will fade away.

Managing Diversity

Managing diversity means maximizing diversity's potential benefits (greater cultural awareness, and broader language skills, for instance) while minimizing the potential barriers (such as prejudices and bias) that can undermine the company's performance.[113]

Legislatures and courts determine the nature and scope of many "diversity management" programs. For example, we've devoted most of this chapter to the legally compulsory actions employers must take to minimize employment discrimination.

The problem is that while compulsory actions can reduce some blatant diversity barriers, taking a diverse workforce and blending it into a close-knit and productive one requires more. Briefly, a *diversity management program* to achieve this kind of blending usually starts at the top and includes the following elements:

- **Provide strong leadership.** Companies with exemplary reputations in managing diversity typically have CEOs who champion diversity's benefits. For example, they take strong stands on advocating the need for and advantages of a diverse workforce. And, they act as role models for exemplifying pro-diversity behaviors, such as by promoting employees evenhandedly.
- **Assess the situation.** The diversity management program itself typically starts with the company assessing the current state of affairs with respect to diversity. In particular, how diverse are we, and are there any diversity-related issues we need to address? Common tools here include equal employment hiring and retention metrics, employee attitude surveys, management and employee evaluations, and focus groups.[114]

alternative dispute resolution or ADR program
Grievance procedure that provides for binding arbitration as the last step.

diversity
Diversity generally refers to the variety or multiplicity of demographic features that characterize a company's workforce, particularly in terms of race, sex, culture, national origin, handicap, age, and religion.

managing diversity
Maximizing diversity's potential benefits while minimizing its potential barriers.

- **Provide diversity training and education.** If the assessment reveals issues to address, some change program is in order. This normally involves employee training and education—for instance, having employees discuss with expert trainers the values of diversity and the types of behaviors and prejudices that may undermine it.[115] Diversity training often aims at sensitizing all employees to the need to value differences and build self-esteem, and at generally creating a more smoothly functioning and hospitable environment for the firm's diverse workforce. In creating diversity management programs, don't ignore the obvious. For example, training immigrants in their native languages can facilitate learning and ensure compliance with matters such as safety rules and harassment policies, and thus ease their entry into your workforce.[116]
- **Change culture and management systems.** To reinforce the training, management should reinforce the words of the training with deeds. For example, change the bonus plan to incentivize managers to improve their departments' employee attitude survey scores. Supervisor resistance is a potential issue. One study, in a large British retailer, found that usual diversity instructions like "recognize and respond to individual differences" conflicted with the supervisor's inclinations to treat everyone evenhandedly.[117]
- **Evaluate the diversity management program.** For example, do employee attitude surveys now indicate any improvement in employees' attitudes toward diversity?

A big part of managing diversity involves overcoming barriers to inclusion—to bringing all employees "under the same tent," in a matter of speaking. Figure 2-8 illustrates strategies for overcoming barriers to inclusion, such as learning about other cultures and helping all employees to better understand the causes of prejudice.

How can one tell if the diversity initiatives are effective? There are some commonsense questions to ask:

- Are there women and minorities reporting directly to senior managers?
- Do women and minorities have a fair share of the job assignments that are the traditional stepping-stones to successful careers in the company?
- Do women and minorities have equal access to international assignments?
- Is the employer taking steps (including providing developmental opportunities) that ensure that female and minority candidates will be in the company's career development pipeline?
- Are turnover rates for female and minority managers the same or lower than those for white male managers?[118]

Source: Courtesy of Alamy Images Royalty Free/JUPITERIMAGES/Brand X/Alamy.

Diversity management can blend a diverse workforce into a close-knit and productive community.

Workforce Diversity in Practice

In practice, employers combine several elements in developing their programs. Baxter Healthcare Corporation started by adopting a strong company policy: "Baxter International believes that a multi-cultural employee population is essential to the company's leadership in healthcare around the world." Baxter publicized this philosophy throughout the company. It then took steps to foster diversity and to manage it. These steps included evaluating diversity program efforts, recruiting minority members to the board of directors, formally interacting with representative minority groups and networks, and offering diversity training programs.

Other employers facilitate the organizing of minority employees' "networks." The networks' aims are to help minority employees connect better to each other and to provide mutually beneficial information, social support, and mentoring.[119]

FIGURE 2-8 Strategies That Overcome Barriers to Inclusion

Source: Reprinted by permission from Managing Diversity by Norma Carr-Ruffino. Copyright © 2005 by Norma Carr-Rufino. By permission of Pearson Custom Publishing, a Pearson Education Company.

Inclusive Strategies	Barriers to Inclusion
At the Personal Level	
Become aware of prejudice and other barriers to valuing diversity	Stereotypes, prejudices
Learn about other cultures and groups	Past experiences and influences
Serve as an example, walk the talk	Stereotyped expectations and perceptions
Participate in managing diversity	Feelings that tend to separate, divide
At the Interpersonal Level	
Facilitate communication and interactions in ways that value diversity	Cultural differences
Encourage participation	Group differences
Share your perspective	Myths
Facilitate unique contributions	Relationship patterns based on exclusion
Resolve conflicts in ways that value diversity	
Accept responsibility for developing common ground	
At the Organizational Level	
All employees have access to networks and focus groups	Individuals who get away with discriminating and excluding
All employees take a proactive role in managing diversity and creating a more diverse workplace culture	A culture that values or allows exclusion
All employees are included in the inner circle that contributes to the bottom-line success of the company	Work structures, policies, and practices that discriminate and exclude
All employees give feedback to management	
All employees are encouraged to contribute to change	

IBM created several minority task forces for groups such as women and Native Americans. In the ensuing 10 or so years, the task forces expanded IBM's multicultural markets. For example, one team decided to focus on expanding IBM's market among multicultural and women-owned businesses. They did this in part by providing ". . . much-needed sales and service support to small midsize business, a niche well populated with minority and female buyers." As a result, this market grew from $10 million to more than $300 million in revenue in just 3 years.[120] As another example, Longo Toyota in El Monte, California, built its competitive strategy on its employees' diversity.[121] With a 60-person sales force that speaks more than 20 languages, Longo's staff provides a powerful competitive advantage for serving an increasingly diverse customer base.

Some employers encourage diversity through *affirmative action programs.* Affirmative action means making an extra effort to hire and promote those in protected groups, particularly when those groups are underrepresented. We turn to this next.

Equal Employment Opportunity Versus Affirmative Action

Equal employment opportunity aims to ensure that anyone, regardless of race, color, disability, sex, religion, national origin, or age, has an equal opportunity based on his or her qualifications. *Affirmative action* goes beyond this by having the employer take actions (in recruitment, hiring, promotions, and compensation) to eliminate the current effects of past discrimination.

Affirmative action is still a significant workplace issue today. The incidences of major court-mandated affirmative action programs are down, but courts still use them. Furthermore, many employers must still engage in voluntary programs. For example, Executive Order 11246 (issued in 1965) requires federal contractors to take affirmative action to improve employment opportunities for groups such as women and racial minorities. EO 11246 covers about 26 million workers—about 22% of the U.S. workforce.[122]

Steps in an Affirmative Action Program

Under guidelines such as EO 11246, the key aims of affirmative action programs are (1) to use numerical analysis to determine which (if any) target groups the firm is underutilizing relative to the relevant labor market, and (2) to eliminate the barriers to equal employment. Many employers pursue these aims with a **good faith effort strategy**; this emphasizes identifying and eliminating the obstacles to hiring and promoting women and minorities, and increasing the minority or female applicant flow. Reasonable steps to take would include those in Figure 2-9.

Recruiting Minorities Online

One step is to direct recruiting ads to one or more of the online minority-oriented job markets. For example, Recruiting-Online lists dozens of online diversity candidate resources (www.recruiting-online.com/course55.html). Diversity candidate Web sites with job banks include the National Urban League, Hispanic Online, Latino Web, Society of Hispanic Engineers, Gay.com, Association for Women in Science, and Minorities Job Bank.

The National Urban League's Web site is a good example (www.nul.org). Clicking on its Career Center tab brings you to a page with five options: Job Search; Post a Job; Resume Center; Job Agents; and Career Resources. The Job Agents section lets job seekers create their own job profiles. It then searches for employers' listings that may match, and sends a message to the job seeker when it finds a match.

Avoiding employee resistance to affirmative action programs is important. Studies suggest that current employees need to believe the program is fair. *Transparent*

FIGURE 2-9 Steps in an Affirmative Action Program

1. Issue a written equal employment policy indicating that firm is an equal employment opportunity employer and the employer's commitment to affirmative action.
2. Demonstrate top-management support for the equal employment policy—for instance, appoint a high-ranking EEO administrator.
3. Publicize internally and externally the equal employment policy and affirmative action commitment.
4. Survey current minority and female employment by department and job classification to determine where affirmative action programs are especially desirable.
5. Carefully analyze employer human resources practices to identify and eliminate hidden barriers.
6. Review, develop, and implement specific HR programs to improve female and minority utilization.
7. Use focused recruitment to find qualified applicants from the target group(s).
8. Establish an internal audit and reporting system to monitor and evaluate progress.
9. Develop support for the affirmative action program, inside the company and in the community.

selection procedures (making it clear what selection tools and standards the company uses) help in this regard. *Communication* is also crucial. Make clear that the program doesn't involve preferential selection standards. Provide details on the qualifications of all new hires (both minority and nonminority). *Justifications* for the program should emphasize redressing past discrimination and the practical value of diversity, not underrepresentation.[123]

Improving Productivity Through HRIS: Measuring Diversity

There are many ways to measure the performance of an employer's equal employment and diversity efforts. These might include, for example, the number of EEOC claims per year; the cost of HR-related litigation; and various measures for analyzing the survival and loss rate among new diverse employee groups.

Even for a company with a few hundred employees, keeping track of such metrics is expensive. HR software is one solution. One package called "Measuring Diversity Results" provides HR managers with several diversity-related software options. These aim to boost the accuracy of the information at the manager's disposal and reduce the costs of collecting and compiling it. Among other things, diversity management packages like this let the manager more easily calculate things like the cost per diversity hire; a workforce profile index; the numeric impact of voluntary turnover among diverse employee groups; and such things as direct and indirect replacement cost per hire.

Reverse Discrimination

Particularly with the U.S. workforce becoming increasingly diverse, courts have been grappling with the use of quotas (or defacto quotas) in hiring, and particularly with claims of **reverse discrimination** (discriminating against *non*minority applicants and employees). Many cases addressed these issues, but until recently, few consistent answers emerged.

In one of the first and most notable such cases, *Bakke v. Regents of the University of California* (1978), the University of California at Davis Medical School denied admission to white student Allen Bakke, allegedly because of the school's affirmative action quota system, which required that a specific number of openings go to minority applicants. In a 5-to-4 vote, the U.S. Supreme Court struck down the policy that made race the only factor in considering applications for a certain number of class openings and thus allowed Bakke's admission.

Bakke was followed by many other cases. For example, in June 2001, the U.S. Supreme Court refused to hear Texas's challenge to a ruling that one of its law school affirmative action programs, which gives special consideration to black and Mexican American student applicants, discriminated against whites. In 2003, the U.S. Supreme Court decided against the University of Michigan's quota-based admissions programs. In June 2007, the Court ruled against race-based school assignment (busing) plans.[124]

In June 2009, the U.S. Supreme Court ruled in an important reverse discrimination suit brought by Connecticut firefighters. In *Ricci v. DeStefano,* 19 white firefighters and one Hispanic firefighter say the city of New Haven should have promoted them based on their successful test scores. The city argued that certifying the tests would have left them vulnerable to lawsuits from minorities for violating Title VII.[125] The Court ruled in favor of the (predominantly white) plaintiffs. In New Haven's desire to avoid making promotions that might appear to have an adverse impact on minorities, Justice Kennedy wrote that "The city rejected the test results solely because the higher scoring candidates were white." The consensus of observers was that the decision would make it much harder for employers to ignore the results obtained by valid tests, even if the results dispropotionately impact minorities.[126]

good faith effort strategy
An affirmative action strategy that emphasizes identifying and eliminating the obstacles to hiring and promoting women and minorities, and increasing the minority or female applicant flow.

reverse discrimination
Claim that due to affirmative action quota systems, white males are discriminated against.

Cultures," *Journal of Applied Psychology* 90, no. 1 (2005), pp. 182–192.

57. "We're a Multinational Corporation with U.S. Citizens Working in Several Countries. Do Laws Such as the Fair Labor Standards Act or the Family and Medical Leave Act Apply to Them?" *HR Magazine*, February 2008, p. 333.
58. Based on Gregory Baxter, "Over There: Enforcing the 1991 Civil Rights Act Abroad," *Employee Relations Law Journal* 1, no. 2 (Autumn 1993), pp. 257–266.
59. "Expansion of Employment Laws Abroad Impacts U.S. Employers, " *BNA Bulletin to Management*, April 11, 2006, p. 119; Richard Posthuma, Mark Roehling, and Michael Campion, "Applying U.S. Employment Discrimination Laws to International Employers: Advice for Scientists and Practitioners," *Personnel Psychology*, 2006, 59, pp. 705–739.
60. Guidelines based on Richard Posthuma et al., "Applying U.S. Employment Discrimination Laws to International Employees: Advice for Scientists and Practitioners," *Personnel Psychology* 59 (2006), p. 710. Reprinted by permission of Wiley Blackwell.
61. John Moran, *Employment Law* (Upper Saddle River, NJ: Prentice Hall, 1997), p. 166.
62. "The Eleventh Circuit Explains Disparate Impact, Disparate Treatment," p. 102.
63. Moran, *Employment Law*, p. 168.
64. John Klinefelter and James Thompkins, "Adverse Impact in Employment Selection," *Public Personnel Management*, May/June 1976, pp. 199–204.
65. One study found that using the 4/5ths rule often resulted in false-positive ratings of adverse impact, and that incorporating tests of statistical significance could improve the accuracy of applying the 4/5ths rule. See Philip Roth, Philip Bobko, and Fred Switzer, "Modeling the Behavior of the 4/5ths Rule for Determining Adverse Impact: Reasons for Caution," *Journal of Applied Psychology* 91, no. 3 (2006), pp. 507–522.
66. The ADEA does not just protect against intentional discrimination (disparate treatment). Under a recent Supreme Court decision (*Smith v. Jackson*, Miss., 2005), it also covers employer practices that seem neutral but that actually bear more heavily on older workers (disparate impact). "Employees Need Not Show Intentional Bias to Bring Claims Under ADEA, High Court Says," *BNA Bulletin to Management* 56, no. 14 (April 5, 2005), p. 105.
67. The Fair Treatment for Experienced Pilots Act raised commercial pilots' mandatory retirement age from 60 to 65 in 2008. Allen Smith, "Congress Gives Older Pilots a Reprieve," *HR Magazine*, February 2008, p. 24.
68. *Usery v. Tamiami Trail Tours*, 12FEP cases 1233.
69. Alternatively, an employer faced with an age discrimination claim may raise the FOA (factors other than age) defense. Here, it argues that its actions were "reasonable" based on some factor other than age, such as the terminated person's poor performance.
70. Ledvinka, *Federal Regulation*.
71. Howard Anderson and Michael Levin-Epstein, *Primer of Equal Employment Opportunity* (Washington, DC: The Bureau of National Affairs, 1982), pp. 13–14.
72. *U.S. v. Bethlehem Steel Company*, 3FEP cases 589.
73. *Robinson v. Lorillard Corporation*, 3FEP cases 653.
74. *Spurlock v. United Airlines*, 5FEP cases 17.
75. Anderson and Levin-Epstein, *Primer of Equal Employment Opportunity*, p. 14.
76. This isn't ironclad, however. For example, the U.S. Supreme Court, in *Stotts*, held that a court cannot require retention of black employees hired under a court's consent decree in preference to higher-seniority white employees who were protected by a bona fide seniority system. It's unclear whether this decision also extends to personnel decisions not governed by seniority systems. *Firefighters Local 1784 v. Stotts* (*BNA*, April 14, 1985).
77. Ledvinka and Gatewood, "EEO Issues with Preemployment Inquiries," pp. 22–26.
78. Ibid.
79. "Eighth Circuit OKs $3.4 Million EEOC Verdict Relating to Pre-Hire Strength Testing Rules," *BNA Bulletin to Management*, November 28, 2006, p. 377.
80. Svetlana Shkolnikova, "Weight Discrimination Could Be as Common as Racial Bias," www.usatoday.com/news/health/weightloss/2008-05-20-overweight-bias_N.htm, accessed January 21, 2009.
81. Jenessa Shapiro et al., "Expectations of Obese Trainees: How Stigmatized Trainee Characteristics Influence Training Effectiveness," *Journal of Applied Psychology* 92, no. 1 (2007), pp. 239–249. See also Lisa Finkelstein et al., "Bias Against Overweight Job Applicants: Further Explanations of When and Why," *Human Resource Management* 46, no. 2 (Summer 2007), pp. 203–222.
82. "EEOC Weighs Guidance on Use of Criminal Records in Hiring," *BNA Bulletin to Management*, November 20, 2008, p. 383.
83. See for example, http://www.eeoc.gov/policy/docs/guidance-inquiries.html, accessed June 28, 2009.
84. Lynn Bennington and Ruth Wein, "Aiding and Abetting Employer Discrimination: The Job Applicant's Role," *Employer Responsibilities and Rights* 14, no. 1 (March 2002), pp. 3–16.
85. This is based on *BNA Fair Employment Practices*, April 13, 1989, pp. 45–47.
86. Eric Matusewitch, "Tailor Your Dress Codes," *Personnel Journal* 68, no. 2 (February 1989), pp. 86–91; Matthew Miklave, "Sorting Out a Claim of Bias," *Workforce* 80, no. 6 (June 2001), pp. 102–103.
87. Kenneth Sovereign, *Personnel Law*, 4th edition (Upper Saddle River, NJ: Prentice Hall, 1999), p. 220.
88. Prudent employers often purchase employment practices liability insurance to insure against some or all of the expenses involved with defending against discrimination, sexual harassment, and wrongful termination–type claims. Antone Melton-Meaux, "Maximizing Employment Practices Liability Insurance Coverage," *Compensation & Benefits Review*, May/June 2008, pp. 55–59.
89. In 2007, the U.S. Supreme Court, in *Ledbetter v. Goodyear Tire & Rubber Company,* held that employees claiming Title VII pay discrimination must file their claims within 180 days of when they first receive the allegedly discriminatory pay. As of 2009, Congress was working to formulate new legislation enabling employees to file claims anytime, as long as the person was still receiving an "infected" paycheck.
90. Litigants must watch the clock. In an equal pay decision, the U.S. Supreme Court held (in *Ledbetter v. Goodyear Tire & Rubber Company*) that the employee must file a complaint within 180 (or 300) days of the employer's decision to pay the allegedly unfair wage. The clock starts with that first pay decision, not with the subsequent paychecks that the employee

receives. "Justices Rule 5–4 Claim-Filing Period Applies to Pay Decision, Not Subsequent Paycheck," *BNA Bulletin to Management* 58, no. 23 (June 5, 2007), pp. 177–184.

91. "EEOC Charges Pace Climbed to Record High During Fiscal 2008," *BNA Bulletin to Management*, December 2, 2008, p. 389.
92. If the charge was filed initially with a state or local agency within 180 days after the alleged unlawful practice occurred, the charge may then be filed with the EEOC within 30 days after the practice occurred or within 30 days after the person received notice that the state or local agency has ended its proceedings.
93. "EEOC Turning Attention to Broader Cases," *Workforce Management*, April 24, 2006, p. 6; "EEOC's Focus on Systemic Cases Increases Need for Preventing Bias," *BNA Human Resources Report*, May 22, 2006, p. 533.
94. Jonathan Segal, "Land Executives, Not Lawsuits," *HR Magazine* 51, no. 10 (October 2006), pp. 123–130.
95. Mark Schoeff, Jr., "Walgreens Suit Reflects EEOC's Latest Strategies," *Workforce Management*, March 20, 2007, p. 8.
96. www.eeoc.gov/mediate/facts.html, accessed June 29, 2009.
97. "EEOC's New Nationwide Mediation Plan Offers Option of Informal Settlements," *BNA Fair Employment Practices*, February 18, 1999, p. 21.
98. Kathryn Tyler, "Mediating a Better Outcome," *HR Magazine*, November 2007, pp. 63–66.
99. "EEOC Has 18 Nationwide, 300 Local Accords with Employers to Mediate Job Bias Claims Charges," *BNA Human Resources Report*, October 13, 2003, p. H-081.
100. Timothy Bland, "Sealed Without a Kiss," *HR Magazine*, October 2000, pp. 85–92.
101. Stuart Bompey and Michael Pappas, "Is There a Better Way? Compulsory Arbitration of Employment Discrimination Claims After Gilmer," *Employee Relations Law Journal* 19, no. 3 (Winter 1993–1994), pp. 197–216.
102. These are based on ibid., pp. 210–211.
103. Ibid.
104. Ibid., p. 210.
105. David Nye, "When the Fired Fight Back," *Across-the-Board*, June 1995, pp. 31–34.
106. "EEOC Opposes Mandatory Arbitration," *BNA Fair Employment Practices*, July 24, 1997, p. 85.
107. Michael Carrell and Everett Mann, "Defining Work-Force Diversity in Public Sector Organizations," *Public Personnel Management* 24, no. 1 (Spring 1995), pp. 99–111. See also Richard Koonce, "Redefining Diversity," *Training and Development Journal*, December 2001, pp. 22–33.
108. Carol Heimowitz, "The New Diversity," *The Wall Street Journal*, November 14, 2005, p. R1.
109. Lisa Hope Pelled, Kathleen Eisenhardt, and Katherine Xin, "Exploring the Black Box: An Analysis of Work Group Diversity, Conflict, and Performance," *Administrative Science Quarterly* 44, no. 1 (March 1999) p. na. in http://findarticles.com/p/articles/mi_m4035/is_1_44/ai_54482491/?tag=content;col1, accessed June 29, 2009; Sheila Simsarian Webber and Lisa M. Donahue, "Impact of Highly and Less Job-Related Diversity on Work Group Cohesion and Performance: A Meta-Analysis," *Journal of Management* 27 (2001), pp. 141–162.
110. Definitions of diversity vary. These researchers actually focused on two types of diversity: highly job-related and less job-related diversity. Sheila Simsarian Webber and Lisa M. Donahue, "Impact of Highly and Less Job-Related Diversity on Work Group Cohesion and Performance: A Meta-Analysis," *Journal of Management* 27 (2001), pp. 141–162.
111. Thomas Kochan et al., "The Effects of Diversity on Business Performance: Report of the Diversity Research Network," *Human Resource Management* 42, no. 1 (Spring 2003), pp. 3–21.
112. Sheila Simsarian Webber and Lisa M. Donahue, "Impact of Highly and Less Job-Related Diversity on Work Group Cohesion and Performance: A Meta-Analysis," *Journal of Management* 27 (2001), pp. 141–162.
113. Brian O'Leary and Bart Weathington, "Beyond the Business Case for Diversity in Organizations," *Employee Responsibilities and Rights* 18, no. 4 (December 2006), pp. 283–292.
114. Patricia Digh, "Creating a New Balance Sheet: The Need for Better Diversity Metrics," *Mosaics* (Society for Human Resource Management, October 1999), p. 1. See also Richard Bucher, *Diversity Consciousness* (Upper Saddle River, NJ: Prentice Hall, 2004), pp. 109–137.
115. Robert Grossman, "Is Diversity Working?" *HR Magazine*, March 2000, pp. 47–50.
116. Carol Hastings, "Tapping into Your Foreign-Born, Spanish-Speaking Workforce," *Mosaics* (Society for Human Resource Management, July/August 2002), no. 3, p. 1.
117. Carley Foster and Lynette Harris, "Easy to Say, Difficult to Do: Diversity Management in Retail," *Human Resource Management Journal* 15, no. 3 (2005), pp. 4–17.
118. Bill Leonard, "Ways to Tell if a Diversity Program Is Measuring Up," *HR Magazine*, July 2002, p. 21.
119. Raymond Friedman and Brooks Holtom, "The Effects of Network Groups on Minority Employee Turnover Intentions," *Human Resource Management* 41, no. 4 (Winter 2002), pp. 405–421.
120. David Thomas, "Diversity as Strategy," *Harvard Business Review*, September 2004, pp. 98–104. See also J. T. Childs Jr., "Managing Global Diversity at IBM: A Global HR Topic That Has Arrived," *Human Resource Management* 44, no. 1 (Spring 2005), pp. 73–77.
121. Orlando Richard, "Racial Diversity, Business Strategy, and Firm Performance: A Resource Based View," *Public Personnel Management* 24, no. 1 (Spring 1995), pp. 99–111.
122. David Harrison et al., "Understanding Attitudes Toward Affirmative Action Programs in Employment: Summary and Meta-Analysis of 35 Years of Research," *Journal of Applied Psychology* 91, no. 5 (2006), pp. 10, 1013–1036; and Margaret Fiester et al., "Affirmative Action, Stock Options, I-9 Documents," *HR Magazine*, November 2007, p. 31.
123. David Harrison et al., "Understanding Attitudes Toward Affirmative Action Programs in Employment: Summary and Meta-Analysis of 35 Years of Research," *Journal of Applied Psychology* 91, no. 5 (2006), pp. 10, 113, 1013–1036.
124. "Lawyers, Scholars Differ on Likely Impact of Affirmative Action Rulings on Workplace," *BNA Fair Employment Practices*, July 3, 2003, pp. 79–80.
125. http://newsfeedresearcher.com/data/articles_n17/tests-city-court.html, accessed April 24, 2009.
126. Adam Liptak, "Supreme Court Finds Bias Against White Firefighters," *The New York Times*, June 30, 2009, pp. A1, A13.
127. J. Coil and C. Rice, "Managing work-force diversity in the nineties: The impact of the Civil Rights Act of 1991. *Employee Relations Law Journal*, 18(4) p. 548.
128. Ibid., p. 560.
129. Ibid., pp. 562–563.

3 The Manager's Role in Strategic Human Resource Management

John Rauls, sales manager for High Point Auto Dealers, came out unnerved from his meeting with the CEO. With sales down 30% and the economy worsening, the CEO told his managers that High Point had a new strategic plan. After 8 years of opening new showrooms throughout South Florida, survival now was key. High Point had to consolidate and shrink its operations. The company would reduce its workforce by 20%, cut expenses by half, close three showrooms, and take steps to build sales at its remaining dealerships. In 3 days, Rauls and the other managers had to submit detailed lists of personnel actions they'd take to implement the CEO's new plan. Rauls wondered, "Where should I start? What am I supposed to do?"

Source: Courtesy of Juice Images Limited/Alamy Images.

WHERE ARE WE NOW . . .

Managers must adapt their departments' personnel activities to the requirements of their companies' strategic plans. For example, who you hire and how you train and pay them should make sense in terms of your company's strategic aims. The main purpose of this chapter is to explain the fundamentals of strategic human resource planning. We'll explain the "hierarchy of goals," the overall planning process, and the manager's roles in strategic planning, strategic human resource management, and creating high-performance organizations. We'll also see that managers should make decisions based on evidence; the appendix to this chapter presents an overview of how to measure human resource management activities.

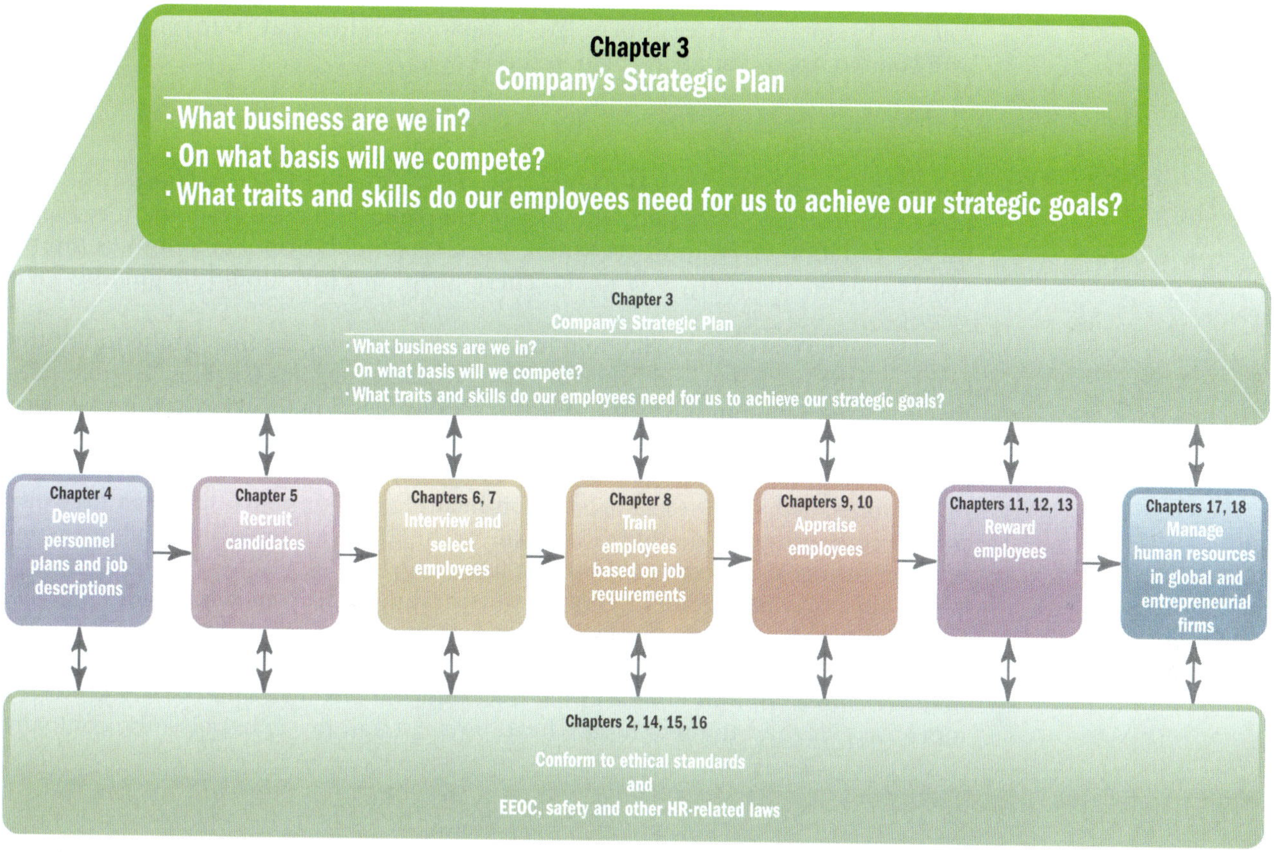

LEARNING OUTCOMES

1. Explain why strategic planning is important to all managers.
2. Outline the basic steps in the management planning process.
3. List the main contents of a typical business plan.
4. Answer the question, "What should a manager do to set 'smart' motivational goals?"
5. Explain with examples each of the seven steps in the strategic planning process.
6. List with examples the main generic types of corporate strategies and competitive strategies.
7. Define strategic human resource management and give an example of strategic human resource management in practice.
8. Briefly describe three important strategic human resource management tools.
9. Explain with examples why metrics are essential for identifying and creating high-performance human resource policies and practices.

1 Explain why strategic planning is important to all managers.

WHY STRATEGIC PLANNING IS IMPORTANT TO ALL MANAGERS

You may not realize it when you're managing, but your company's strategic plan is guiding much of what you do. Management expert Peter Drucker once said that management ". . . is the responsibility for execution." What he means is that as a manager you'll be judged on at least one thing—on the extent to which you accomplished your unit's goals. Organizations exist to achieve some purpose, and if they fail to achieve their ends, to that extent they have failed. As Drucker also said, "There has to be something to point to and say, [we] have not worked in vain." Those aims or goals—and the hard work you put into accomplishing them—all depend on your company's plan. All your personnel and other decisions—what sorts of people you hire and how you hire them, what you train them to do, and how you appraise and reward them, for instance—depend on the goals that trickled down to you from your firm's overall plan. We'll look more closely at your role in working with your company's strategic plan in this chapter.

The Hierarchy of Goals

Lets start with a bird's eye view of why strategic planning is important to you. It is important because, as we said, in well-run companies the goals from the very top of the organization down to where you're working should form a more-or-less unbroken chain (or "hierarchy") of goals. These goals, in turn, should be guiding what you do.

The hierarchy of goals diagram in Figure 3-1 summarizes this. At the top of the company, the president and his or her staff set strategic goals (such as "Double sales revenue to $16 million in fiscal year 2011"). Lower-level managers (in this case, vice presidents) then set goals (such as "Add one production line at plant A"). These goals should flow from and make sense in terms of the goals at the next level up. (In other words, "What must I as production head do to help make sure that the company accomplishes its 'double sales' goal?") Then the vice presidents' subordinates set their own goals, and so on down the line.

In this way, management creates a hierarchy or chain of departmental goals, from the top down to the lowest-ranked managers, and even employees. Then, if everyone does his or her job—if each salesperson sells his or her quota, and the sales manager hires enough good salespeople, and the HR manager creates the right incentive plan, and the purchasing head buys enough raw materials—the company

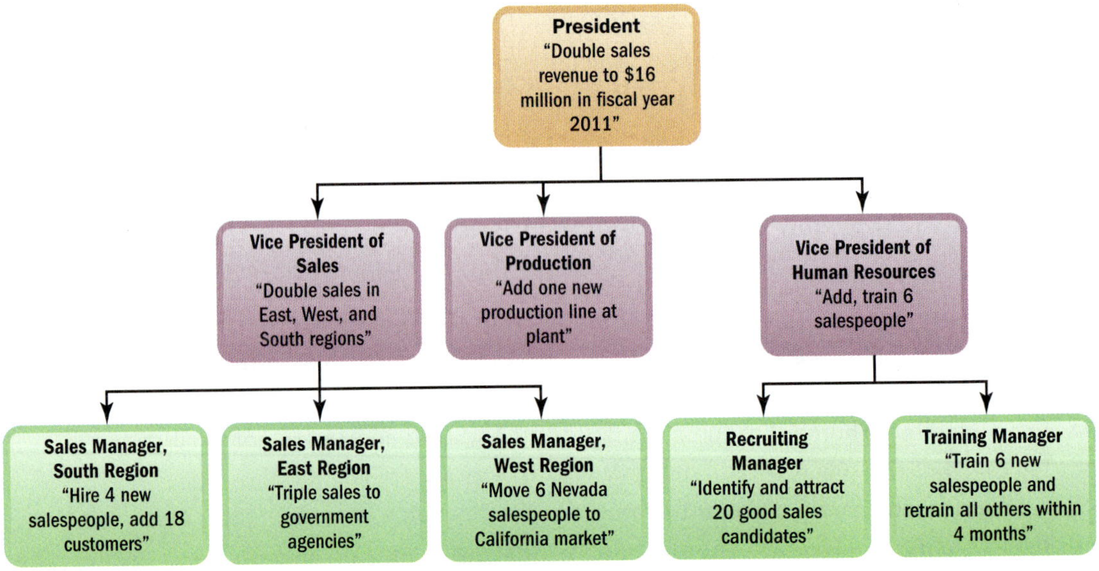

FIGURE 3-1 Sample Hierarchy of Goals Diagram for a Company

and the CEO should also accomplish the overall, company-wide strategic goals. You could therefore say with great certainty that without a clear plan at the top, no one in the company (including you and the other managers) would have the foggiest notion of what to do. At best, you'd all be working at cross-purposes. Let's look next at the basic planning process.

FUNDAMENTALS OF MANAGEMENT PLANNING

People make plans every day, often without giving it a thought. We plan our routes to school, what courses to take, and what to do on Saturday night. Underlying all those plans, however, is an often unstated planning process.

2 Outline the basic steps in the management planning process.

The Planning Process

Consider how you might create a plan for your career. You might:

1. Tentatively *set an objective,* such as "to work as a management consultant."
2. *Make forecasts,* for instance, of industry trends and to check your basic assumptions about things like your strengths and weaknesses to determine your consulting prospects.
3. *Determine what your alternatives are for getting from where you are now to where you want to be.* Your aim here is to help you identify what courses of action (including college major and summer experiences) will get you to your goal best.
4. *Evaluate your alternatives.*
5. Finally, implement and evaluate *your plan.*

That is all there is to the planning process. It hardly matters whether you're planning your career, a trip abroad, or how to sell your company's new product. The basic planning process always involves setting objectives, forecasting and assessing your basic planning "premises" or assumptions, determining alternative courses of action, evaluating which options are best, and then choosing and implementing your plan.

The process is the same when managers plan for their firms, with one small complication. There is usually a *hierarchical aspect* to managerial planning. Top management approves a long-term or strategic plan. Then each department, working with top management, creates its own budgets and other plans to fit and to contribute to the company's long-term plan.

3 List the main contents of a typical business plan.

Putting Together the Business Plan

All this planning produces a business plan. The **business plan** provides a comprehensive view of the firm's situation today and of its company-wide and departmental goals and plans for the next 3 to 5 years. Managers most often use the term "business plan" in relation to smaller businesses. It is the plan that investors or lenders want to see before offering money to the firm. However, even Dell or Microsoft has versions of such comprehensive plans. They often label it their "long-term" or perhaps "strategic" plan.

Figure 3-2 displays the contents of a typical business plan. There are no rigid rules regarding what such plans contain. However, they usually include, at a minimum, a (1) *description of the business* (including ownership and products or services), (2) *the marketing plan,* (3) *the financial plan,* and (4) *the management* and/or *personnel plan.* Notice that the business plan invariably guides every functional department in the firm, from sales and marketing to manufacturing and finance.

business plan
Provides a comprehensive view of the firm's situation today and of its company-wide and departmental goals and plans for the next 3 to 5 years.

FIGURE 3-2 Business Plan Table of Contents

Sources: Adapted from Marc Dollinger, *Entrepreneurship* (Upper Saddle River, NJ, 2003), pp. 430–431; Thomas Zimmerer and Norman Scarborough, *Entrepreneurship and Small Business Management* (Upper Saddle River, NJ, 2008), pp. 154–156; Peggy Lambing and Charles Kuehl, *Entrepreneurship* (Upper Saddle River, NJ, 2000), pp. 131–132; Business Plan Pro, Palo Alto Software, Palo Alto, CA.

1.0 Executive Summary
- 1.1 Company Name and Address
- 1.2 Brief History and Description of Business
- 1.3 Brief Overview of Markets and Trends
- 1.4 Brief Strategy and Keys to Success
- 1.5 Critical Risks and Assumptions

2.0 Vision and Mission Statement
- 2.1 Management's Vision for the Company
- 2.2 "What Business Are We In?"

3.0 Company Products and Services
- 3.1 Product and Service Description
- 3.2 Customer Benefits
- 3.3 Technology

4.0 Market and Competitive Analysis
- 4.1 Overall Market and Target Market
  - 4.1.1 Market Needs
  - 4.1.2 Market Size and Trends
  - 4.1.3 Historical and Projected Market Growth
- 4.2 Industry Analysis
  - 4.2.1 SWOT Analysis
  - 4.2.2 Major Industry Participants
  - 4.2.3 Economic, Competitive, Other Trends
  - 4.2.4 Main Competitors

5.0 Business Strategy and Marketing Plan
- 5.1 Value Proposition: Why Buy From Us?
- 5.2 Competitive Advantages
- 5.3 Marketing Targets and Strategy
  - 5.3.1 Pricing Strategy
  - 5.3.2 Advertising and Promotion Strategy
  - 5.3.3 Distribution Strategy
  - 5.3.4 Marketing Programs
  - 5.3.5 Sales Strategy

6.0 Production Plan
- 6.1 Production Processes
- 6.2 Quality Assurance

7.0 Organization and Management Summary
- 7.1 Organizational Charts and Structure
- 7.2 Personnel Plan

8.0 Financial Plan
- 8.1 Important Assumptions
- 8.2 Income Statement
- 8.3 Balance Sheet
- 8.4 Breakeven Analysis
- 8.5 Projected Profit and Loss
- 8.6 Projected Cash Flow
- 8.7 Business Ratios
- 8.8 Insurance Requirements

The Marketing Plan To have a successful business, you need customers. And to have customers, you need a plan for marketing products or services to them. The marketing plan specifies the nature of the *product* or service (for instance its variety, quality, design, and features). It also shows the approaches the company plans to take with respect to *pricing* and *promoting* the product or service, and getting it sold and *delivered* to the customers. (Marketing managers call these "the four Ps"—product, price, promotion, and place.)

The Personnel/Human Resource Plan Anything the company does, or plans to do, will require managers and other personnel, and therefore a personnel plan. For example, a consulting company's projected number of clients will help determine how many consultants and support staff it needs at each stage of the plan.

The Production/Operations Plan Implementing the marketing plan will necessitate having productive assets. For example, it takes factories and machines to assemble Dell's PCs. Dell must therefore plan for how it will meet its projected demand for factories and facilities to take orders for, build, and distribute its PCs.

The Financial Plan "What's the bottom line?" is the first question most managers and bankers ask. The question underscores a truism about business and management. At the end of the day, most of managers' plans, goals, and accomplishments end up expressed in financial terms.

The financial plan (see Figure 3-3) is the vehicle for doing so. For example, a projected (or "pro forma" or planned) profit and loss (P&L) statement shows the revenue, cost, and profit (or loss) implications of a company's marketing, production, and personnel plans. The P&L says this: If your plans work out as you anticipate, these are the revenues, costs, and profits or losses you should produce each month (or quarter, or year). It shows you the bottom line.

4 Answer the question, "What should a manager do to set 'smart' motivational goals?"

How Managers Set Objectives

Financial goals are the bottom line of planning. The whole point of planning is to decide what the company is to do, and then to express what you want all its employees to do, in terms of goals.

Setting SMART Goals Setting effective goals is therefore an essential management skill. Experienced managers have a simple and effective way to check whether their goals are good or not—they use the acronym "SMART." They say good goals

FIGURE 3-3 Acme Consulting Profit and Loss

Source: Business Plan Pro, Palo Alto Software, Palo Alto, CA.

Pro Forma Profit and Loss (Income Statement)	2010	2011	2012
Sales	$592,000	$875,000	$1,100,000
Direct Cost of Sales	$159,000	$219,000	$ 289,000
Other	$ 0	$ 0	$ 0
Total Cost of Sales	$159,000	$219,000	$ 289,000
Gross Margin	$433,000	$656,000	$ 811,000
Gross Margin %	73.14%	74.97%	73.73%
Operating Expenses:			
Advertising/Promotion	$ 36,000	$ 40,000	$ 44,000
Public Relations	$ 30,000	$ 30,000	$ 33,000
Travel	$ 90,000	$ 60,000	$ 110,000
Miscellaneous	$ 6,000	$ 7,000	$ 8,000
Payroll Expense	$194,750	$377,000	$ 432,000
Payroll Burden	$ 27,265	$ 52,780	$ 60,480
Depreciation	$ 3,600	$ 0	$ 0
Leased Equipment	$ 18,000	$ 7,000	$ 7,000
Utilities	$ 0	$ 12,000	$ 12,000
Insurance	$ 0	$ 2,000	$ 2,000
Rent	$ 0	$ 0	$ 0
Other	$ 0	$ 0	$ 0
Contract/Consultants	$ 0	$ 0	$ 0
Total Operating Expenses	$423,615	$587,780	$ 708,480
Profit Before Interest and Taxes	$ 9,385	$ 68,220	$ 102,520
Interest Expense Short-Term	$ 1,800	$ 6,400	$ 10,400
Interest Expense Long-Term	$ 5,000	$ 5,000	$ 5,000
Taxes Incurred	$ 646	$ 14,205	$ 21,780
Net Profit	$ 1,939	$ 42,615	$ 65,340
Net Profit/Sales	0.33%	4.87%	5.94%

are *specific* (make clear what to achieve), ***measurable, attainable; relevant*** (in terms of what you're setting the goal for), and ***timely*** (they have deadlines and milestones).

For example, suppose you have an automobile salesperson who has been selling about half the cars he should be selling, and also selling too many easier-to-sell fuel-efficient cars, leaving the gas guzzlers in the back of the showroom. Here, an *in*effective "un-smart" goal might be, "Rick, you've got to double the number of vehicles you sell next month." That goal ("double the number") is fairly specific (it would be better if he also knew what kinds of cars you wanted him to sell) and is measurable. Whether it's attainable is debatable (given his performance to date). It's not relevant in terms of what you're setting the goal for (namely, also getting Rick to sell some gas guzzlers). It is timely, in that you said he must sell them in the next month.

What would be a better way to formulate Rick's goal? Perhaps this: "Rick, by the end of this June, 2 months from today, you've got to sell double the total number of vehicles you sold in the last 2 months, and three-quarters of those new vehicles must come from the gas guzzlers we have in inventory." This goal is specific, measurable, probably more attainable (given his shaky performance), relevant, and timely.

How to Set Motivational Goals Goals are only useful if employees are motivated to achieve them. Research known as the *goal-setting studies* provides useful insights into setting motivational goals. They suggest the following:[1]

- **Assign Specific Goals.** Employees who have *specific goals* usually perform better than those who do not. Setting specific goals with subordinates (rather than setting no goals or telling them to "do their best") is probably the simplest effective way to motivate subordinates.
- **Assign Measurable Goals.** Always try to express the goal in terms of numbers, and include target dates or deadlines.
- **Assign Challenging but Doable Goals.** Goals should be challenging, but not so difficult that they appear impossible or unrealistic.
- **Encourage Participation.** Throughout your management career, you'll face this decision: Should I just *tell* my employees what their goals are, or should I let them *participate* in setting their goals? Participatively set goals do not consistently result in higher performance than assigned goals, nor do assigned goals consistently result in higher performance than participatively set ones. *But when (as is usually the case) the participatively set goals are more difficult than the assigned ones, participatively set goals usually produce higher performance.* And of course, participation usually reduces employee resistance. So participation is usually best.

Using Management by Objectives With **management by objectives (MBO)**, the supervisor and subordinate jointly set goals for the latter and periodically assess progress toward those goals. You can engage in a modest MBO program by setting goals with your subordinates and periodically providing feedback. However, "MBO" usually refers to a formal organizationwide program in which managers at each organizational level meet with subordinates to hammer out goals that make sense in terms of each department's assigned goal(s). The process typically includes using special forms and assessing employees' progress frequently.

Peter Drucker, the creator of MBO, emphasizes thinking of it as a philosophy, not as a rigid sequence of steps. The point, he says, is that "the goals of each manager's job must be defined by the contribution he or she has to make to the success of the larger unit of which they are part." In other words, what each manager does must make sense in terms of the company's overall plan. In any case, the MBO process typically consists of five steps:

1. **Set organization goals.** Top management sets strategic goals for the company.
2. **Set department goals.** Department heads and their superiors jointly set supporting goals for their departments.
3. **Discuss department goals.** Department heads present department goals and ask all subordinates to develop their own individual goals.

FIGURE 3-4 Management Objectives Grid

Company-Wide or Departmental Objective: *Double sales revenue to $16 million in fiscal year 2011.*				
Managers' or Subordinates' Objectives in Support of Above Objective	**Manager or Subordinate Responsible**	**Start Date**	**End Date**	**Progress as of:**
Double sales in East, West, and South regions	Vice President of Sales	8/1/09	7/31/10	President checked 11/09, sales up 60%.
Add one new production line at plant	Vice President of Production	8/1/09	10/31/09	President checked 9/09, work 80% done.
Add and train six new salespeople	Vice President of Human Resources	8/1/09	9/3/09	President checked 9/30/09, all hired, new people trained.

4. **Set individual goals.** Goals are set for each subordinate, and a timetable is assigned for accomplishing those goals.
5. **Give feedback.** Supervisor and subordinate meet periodically to review the subordinate's performance and to monitor and analyze progress toward his or her goals.

MBO has benefits. It provides a simple process for working through how the goals at each level will relate to those above and to those below. It also capitalizes on the advantages of employee participation. The downside is that MBO is time-consuming. These programs often involve numerous meetings among employees and supervisors, and then extensively documenting each person's goals in various electronic or hard-copy formats. All that takes time.

Using the Management Objectives Grid With or without MBO, every manager needs a system for organizing how his or her subordinates' goals dovetail with those of the company. The *management objectives grid* provides an easy way to do this. Figure 3-4 provides an example. This spells out each department manager's assigned goals in support of achieving the firm's overall goals. In this case, one long-term top management goal is to "Double sales revenue to $16 million in fiscal year 2011." The grid in Figure 3-4 summarizes the goals each department needs to achieve if the firm is to meet its overall $16 million sales goal.

Managers use the management objectives grid for four things. As the top manager, use it to show each of your department manager's goals and *to list their supporting goals*. As a department manager, use it *to clarify what your own goals should be*, given the company's goals, and to summarize for your subordinates *what their goals are*, in light of your department's goal(s). And finally, any manager may use the grid's start and end dates as a quick way *to track subordinates' progress*.

THE STRATEGIC MANAGEMENT PROCESS

In practice, determining what the company's long-term, overall plan should be requires some special tools. For example, you need to be able to systematically review the competitive landscape and analyze what your best strategic, long-term courses of action might be. *Strategic planning*, which we turn to now, provides these special tools. We'll start with some definitions.

management by objectives (MBO)
A technique in which supervisor and subordinate jointly set goals for the latter and periodically assess progress toward those goals.

Introduction

A **strategic plan** is the company's plan for how it will match its internal strengths and weaknesses with external opportunities and threats in order to maintain a competitive advantage. The essence of strategic planning is to ask, "Where are we now as a business, where do we want to be, and how should we get there?" The manager then formulates specific (human resources and other) strategies to take the company from where it is now to where he or she wants it to be. When Yahoo! tries to figure out whether to sell its search business to Microsoft, or Citibank ponders whether to get out of the brokerage business, they're engaged in strategic planning. A **strategy** is a course of action. If Yahoo! decides it must raise money and focus more on applications like Yahoo! Finance, one strategy might be to sell Yahoo! Search. **Strategic management** is the process of identifying and executing the organization's strategic plan, by matching the company's capabilities with the demands of its environment.

5 Explain with examples each of the seven steps in the strategic planning process.

Figure 3-5 sums up the strategic management process. This includes (1) defining the business and developing a mission, (2) evaluating the firm's internal and external strengths, weaknesses, opportunities, and threats, (3) formulating a new business direction, (4) translating the mission into strategic goals, and (5) formulating strategies or courses of action. Step (6) and step (7) then entail implementing and then evaluating the strategic plan. Let's look at each step.

Step 1: Define the Current Business A logical place to start is by defining one's current business. Specifically, what products do we sell, where do we sell them, and how do our products or services differ from our competitor's For example, Rolex and Casio both sell watches. But there the similarity ends. Rolex sells a limited line of expensive watches. Casio sells a variety of relatively inexpensive but innovative specialty watches with features like compasses and altimeters.

Step 2: Perform External and Internal Audits The next step is to ask, "Are we heading in the right direction?" No one is immune to competitive pressures. Yahoo!'s search tool was on top of the world until Google came along. Amazon's Kindle Reader launch forced even more bookstores to close. Prudent managers periodically assess what's happening in their environments. You need to audit the firm's environment, and strengths and weaknesses.

You can use two tools to help here. The *environmental scanning worksheet* in Figure 3-6 is a simple guide for compiling relevant information about the company's environment. This includes things like economic, competitive, and political trends that may affect the company. The *SWOT chart* in Figure 3-7 is the 800-pound gorilla of strategic planning; everyone uses it. Managers use it to compile and organize the company strengths, weaknesses, opportunities, and threats. The idea, of course, is to create a strategy that makes sense in terms of the company's strengths, weaknesses, opportunities, and threats.

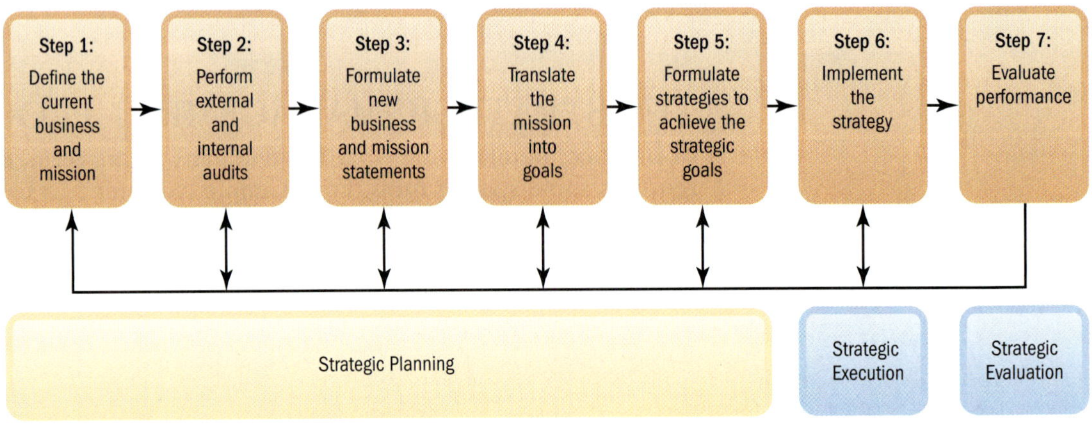

FIGURE 3-5 The Strategic Management Process

FIGURE 3-6 Worksheet for Environmental Scanning

Economic Trends
(such as recession, inflation, employment, monetary policies)

____
____
____
____

Competitive and Market Trends
(such as market/customer trends, entry/exit of competitors, new products from competitors)

____
____
____
____

Political Trends
(such as legislation and regulation/deregulation)

____
____
____
____

Technological Trends
(such as introduction of new production/distribution technologies, rate of product obsolescence, trends in availability of supplies and raw materials)

____
____
____
____

Social Trends
(such as demographic trends, mobility, education, evolving values)

____
____
____
____

Geographic Trends
(such as opening/closing of new markets, factors affecting current plant/office facilities location decisions)

____
____
____
____

Leveraging Strategy experts counsel against blindly avoiding strategies that may seem to be beyond the company's capabilities. They argue there are times when, to pursue great opportunities, you should underplay the firm's weaknesses, and instead capitalize on ("leverage")—some unique company strength.

For example, strategy experts Hamel and Prahalad say that if modest resources were an insurmountable deterrent, GM would not have been put on the defensive by smaller firms such as Honda. And, Apple—competing against giants like Microsoft and IBM—capitalized on its competitive strengths (including very creative employees) in innovating products like the iPhone.

strategic plan
The company's plan for how it will match its internal strengths and weaknesses with external opportunities and threats in order to maintain a competitive advantage.

strategy
A course of action the company can pursue to achieve its strategic aims.

strategic management
The process of identifying and executing the organization's strategic plan, by matching the company's capabilities with the demands of its environment.

FIGURE 3-7 SWOT Matrix, with Generic Examples

Potential Strengths	Potential Weaknesses
• Market leadership	• Large inventories
• Strong research and development	• Excess capacity for market
• High-quality products	• Management turnover
• Cost advantages	• Weak market image
• Patents	• Lack of management depth
Potential Opportunities	**Potential Threats**
• New overseas markets	• Market saturation
• Failing trade barriers	• Threat of takeover
• Competitors failing	• Low-cost foreign competition
• Diversification	• Slower market growth
• Economy rebounding	• Growing government regulation

Step 3: Formulate a New Direction The question now is, based on the environmental scan and SWOT analysis, what should our new business be, in terms of three things—what products we will sell, where we will sell them, and how our products or services will differ from competitors' products?

Managers sometimes formulate a *vision statement* to summarize how they see the essence of their business down the road. The **vision statement** is a general statement of the firm's intended direction and shows, in broad terms, "what we want to become."[2] Rupert Murdoch, chairman of News Corporation (which owns MySpace.com, the Fox network, and many newspapers and satellite TV businesses), has a vision of an integrated, global satellite-based news-gathering, entertainment, and multimedia firm. PepsiCo's latest vision is "Performance with Purpose." PepsiCo's CEO Indra Nooyi says the company's executives choose businesses to be in and make decisions based on Performance with Purposes' three pillars, namely, human sustainability, environmental sustainability, and talent sustainability.[3]

Whereas vision statements usually describe in broad terms what the business should be, the company's **mission statement** summarizes your answer to the question, "What business are we in?" Managers often use the mission statement to pinpoint whether and how the company will *vertically integrate* (thus Apple opened its own retail stores), as well as the firm's *product scope (diversity), geographic coverage,* and *competitive advantage.* Several years ago, Ford adapted what was for several years a powerful competitive advantage for them—"Where Quality Is Job One."

Step 4: Translate the Mission into Strategic Goals Next, translate the mission—such as *vertical integration, product scope (diversity), geographic coverage,* and *competitive advantage*—into strategic goals or objectives. For example, saying your advantage is "to make quality job one" is one thing; operationalizing that mission for your managers is another. The company and its managers need strategic goals. At Ford, for example, what exactly did "Quality Is Job One" mean for each department in terms of how they would boost quality? The answer is that its managers had to meet strict goals such as "no more than 1 initial defect per 10,000 cars."

Step 5: Formulate Strategies to Achieve the Strategic Goals Next, the manager chooses strategies—courses of action—that will enable the company to achieve its strategic goals. For example, what strategies could Ford pursue to hit its goal of no more than 1 initial defect per 10,000 cars? Perhaps open two new high-tech plants, reduce the number of car lines to better focus on just a few, and pursue a partnership with a firm known for quality cars, like Honda.

Step 6: Implement the Strategies Strategy implementation or execution means translating the strategies into action. The company's managers do this by actually hiring (or firing) people, building (or closing) plants, and adding (or eliminating) products and product lines.

Step 7: Evaluate Performance Things don't always turn out as planned. For example, some years ago Ford bought Jaguar and Land Rover as a way to reduce reliance on lower-profit cars. With auto competition brutal, Ford announced in 2009 it was selling Jaguar and Land Rover (to Tata, a company in India). It wants to focus its scarce resources on modernizing and turning around its struggling North American operations. Like all companies, Ford continually needs to assess its strategic decisions.

Improving Productivity Through HRIS: Using Computerized Business Planning Software

Business planning software packages are available to assist the manager in writing strategic and business plans. CheckMATE (www.chechmateplan.com) uses strategic planning tools such as SWOT analysis to enable even users with no prior planning experience to develop sophisticated strategic plans.[4] *Business Plan Pro* from Palo Alto Software contains all the information and planning aids you need to create a business plan. It contains 30 sample plans, step-by-step instructions (with examples) for creating each part of a plan (executive summary, market analysis, and so on), financial planning spreadsheets, easy-to-use tables (for instance, for making sales forecasts), and automatic programs for creating color 3-D charts for showing things like monthly sales and yearly profits.

6 List with examples the main generic types of corporate strategies and competitive strategies.

Types of Strategies

In practice, managers use three types of strategies, one for each level of the company. There is *corporate-wide* strategic planning, business unit (or *competitive*) strategic planning, and *functional* (or departmental) strategic planning (see Figure 3-8). We'll look at each.

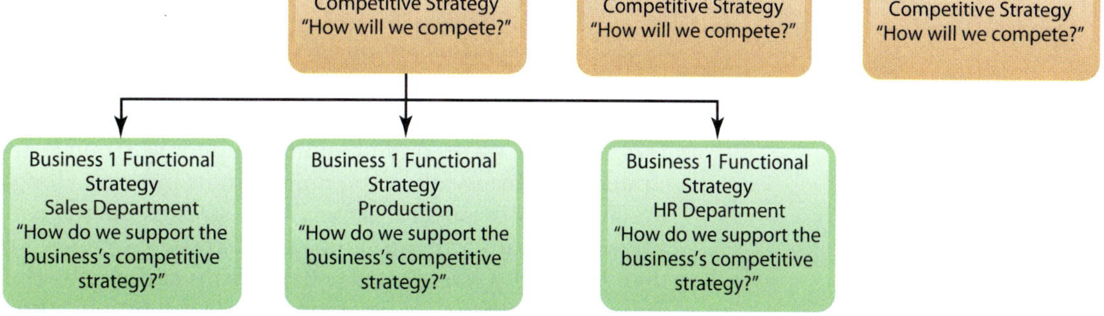

FIGURE 3-8 Type of Strategy at Each Company Level

vision statement
A general statement of the firm's intended direction and shows, in broad terms, "what we want to become."

mission statement
Summarizes your answer to the question, "What business are we in?"

Corporate Strategy The question here is, "How many and what kind of businesses should we be in?" For example, PepsiCo doesn't just make Pepsi-Cola. Instead, PepsiCo is comprised of four main businesses: Frito-Lay North America, PepsiCo Beverages North America, PepsiCo International, and Quaker Oats North America.[5]

PepsiCo therefore needs a *corporate-level strategy*. A company's **corporate-level strategy** identifies the portfolio of businesses that, in total, comprise the company and the ways in which these businesses relate to each other. There are several standard corporate strategy possibilities:

- With a *concentration* (single business) strategy, the company offers one product or product line, usually in one market. WD-40 Company (which makes a spray hardware lubricant) is one example. Concentrating in a single business doesn't mean the firm can't grow. Some grow through *market penetration*. This means boosting sales of current products by more aggressively selling and marketing into the firm's current markets. Firms can also achieve growth through *product development*, which means developing improved products for current markets. A third option is *horizontal integration*, which means acquiring control of competitors in the same or similar markets with the same or similar products.
- A *diversification* corporate strategy implies that the firm will expand by adding new product lines. PepsiCo is diversified. Over the years, PepsiCo added chips and Quaker Oats. Such *related diversification* means diversifying so that a firm's lines of business still possess some kind of fit. *Conglomerate diversification* means diversifying into products or markets not related to the firm's current businesses or to one another.
- A *vertical integration* strategy means the firm expands by, perhaps, producing its own raw materials, or selling its products direct. Thus, Apple opened its open Apple stores.
- *Consolidation*—reducing the company's size.
- *Geographic expansion*—for instance, taking the business abroad, as PepsiCo also did.

Competitive Strategy On what basis will each of our businesses compete? Each of these businesses (such as Frito-Lay) needs its own *business-level/competitive strategy*. A **competitive strategy** identifies how to build and strengthen the business's long-term competitive position in the marketplace.[6] It identifies, for instance, how Pizza Hut will compete with Papa John's or how Walmart competes with Target.

Managers endeavor to achieve competitive advantages for each of their businesses. We can define **competitive advantage** as any factors that allow a company to differentiate its product or service from those of its competitors to increase market share. Managers use several standard competitive strategies to achieve competitive advantage:

- *Cost leadership* means becoming the low-cost leader in an industry. Walmart is a classic example. It maintains its competitive advantage through its satellite-based distribution system, careful (usually suburban) site location, and expert control of purchasing and sales costs.
- *Differentiation* is a second possible competitive strategy. In a differentiation strategy, the firm seeks to be unique in its industry along dimensions that are widely valued by buyers.[7] Thus, Volvo stresses the safety of its cars, Papa John's stresses fresh ingredients, and Target stresses somewhat more upscale brands than Walmart. Like Mercedes-Benz, firms can usually charge a premium if they successfully stake a claim to being substantially different from competitors in some coveted way.
- *Focusers* carve out a market niche (like Ferrari). They compete by providing a product or service that specify customers can get in no other way.

HUMAN RESOURCES AS A COMPETITIVE ADVANTAGE When you think of some of the companies with the clearest competitive strategies, those competitive strategies usually depend on highly trained and committed employees. That's why many managers rightfully believe that their employees' capabilities and motivation represent an indispensable source of competitive advantage. For example, Apple's renown for innovative products would be impossible to maintain without the competitive advantage it has in the form of its creative and brilliant engineers. Similarly, Toyota's low-cost, high-quality cars aren't just the result of sophisticated machines. Instead, they're a result of intensely committed and highly trained employees, all working hard and with self-discipline to produce the best cars that they can at the lowest possible cost.

Functional Strategy Finally, what do our strategic choices (such as maintaining the lowest costs) mean for each of the departments that actually must do the work? Each individual business (like PepsiCo's Frito-Lay and Quaker Oats) is made up of departments such as manufacturing, sales, and human resource management. Each department must have marching orders under the plan. **Functional strategies** identify the broad activities that each department will pursue in order to help the business accomplish its competitive goals.

Each department's functional strategy should make sense in terms of the business/competitive strategy. For example, what would Ford's emphasis on "Quality Is Job One" mean for its human resources department? Probably, that HR would have to create a more quality-capable workforce by raising hiring standards, instituting new testing and training practices, and formulating a merit pay plan tying raises partly to performance.

Strategic Fit Strategic planning expert Michael Porter calls the idea that each department's strategy needs to fit the parent business's competitive aims "strategic fit." For example, Southwest Airlines is a low-cost leader. It therefore molds its functional departments' activities to deliver low-cost, convenient service on its routes. Southwest's ground crew department gets fast 15-minute turnarounds at the gate. That way, Southwest can keep its planes flying longer hours and have more departures with less aircraft. Its purchasing and marketing departments shun frills like meals and premium classes of service.

Figure 3-9 graphically illustrates how Southwest Airline's activities fit the firm's low-cost strategy. The larger (pink) circles represent the pivotal aims that support Southwest's low-cost system. These pivotal aims include limited passenger services and frequent reliable departures. Southwest's departments each must support these aims. For example, "limited passenger service" means no seat assignments. "Highly productive ground crews" means high compensation, flexible union contracts, and employee stock ownership, or in summary:

High Pay > Highly Productive Ground Crews > Frequent Departures > Low Costs

The Top Manager's Role in Strategic Planning

Ultimately, devising a strategic plan is top management's responsibility. Because the consequences of a poor choice can be dire, few top managers would delegate the job of deciding how the company should match its internal strengths and weaknesses with its external opportunities and threats to maintain a competitive advantage. *Top management* must decide what businesses the company will be in and where, and on

corporate-level strategy
Type of strategy that identifies the portfolio of businesses that, in total, comprise the company and the ways in which these businesses relate to each other.

competitive strategy
A strategy that identifies how to build and strengthen the business's long-term competitive position in the marketplace.

competitive advantage
Any factors that allow an organization to differentiate its product or service from those of its competitors to increase market share.

functional strategy
Strategy that identifies the broad activities that each department will pursue in order to help the business accomplish its competitive goals.

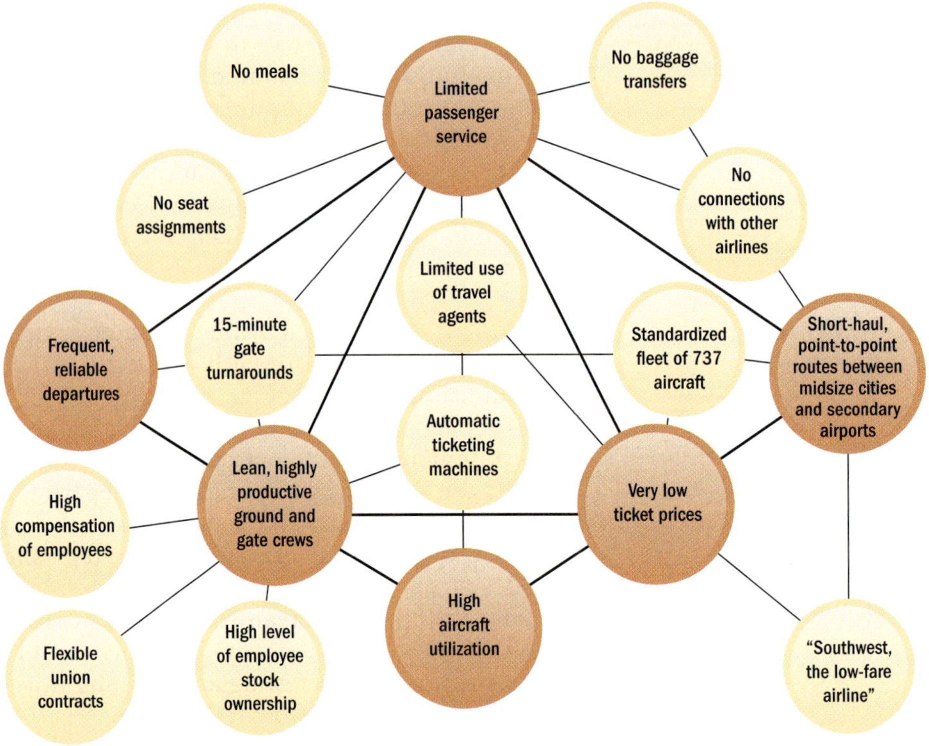

FIGURE 3-9 Southwest Airlines' Activity System

Note: Companies like Southwest tailor all their activities so that they fit and contribute to making their strategies a reality.

Source: Reprinted by permission of *Harvard Business Review*. From "What Is Strategy?" by Michael E. Porter, November–December 1996. Copyright © 1996 by the President and Fellows of Harvard College. All Rights Reserved.

what basis it will compete. Southwest Airlines' top managers could never let lower-level managers make strategic decisions (such as unilaterally deciding that instead of emphasizing low cost, they were going to retrofit the planes with first-class cabins and fancy frills).

Departmental Managers' Strategic Planning Roles

But what of all the company's other, departmental, managers, like those for sales, manufacturing, and human resource management? They also play big roles in strategic planning and management. Specifically, they *help the top managers devise* the strategic plan, formulate *functional, departmental plans* that support the overall strategic plan, and then *execute* the plans. We'll look at each.

They Help Devise the Strategic Plan

It would be reckless for any top executive to formulate a strategic plan without the input of his or her lower-level managers. Few people know as much about the firm's competitive pressures, vendor capabilities, product and industry trends, and employee capabilities and concerns than do the company's department managers. So in practice, devising the strategic plan almost invariably involves frequent meetings and discussions among and between levels of managers. The top managers then lean heavily on the information from these interactions to hammer out their strategic plan.

Understanding the strategic management process should better prepare you to know how to prepare for these meetings. Remember the heart of strategic planning is gathering information on the company's strengths, weaknesses, opportunities, and threats. A complete listing of possible issues is beyond the scope of this book. However, the sales manager, for instance, should bring to the table a thorough understanding of what customers are buying which products, who the company's keenest competitors are, what makes them dangerous (in a competitive sense), and which markets seem to be growing fastest or slowing. The manufacturing manager needs to know what the company can do to improve its production costs and quality, whether outsourcing production or perhaps purchasing finished products might be superior to producing them internally, and what competitors are doing in terms of producing their products.

Similarly, the human resource manager is in a good position to supply competitive intelligence. Details regarding competitors' incentive plans, employee opinion surveys that elicit information about customer complaints, and information about pending legislation such as labor laws are examples. And of course, human resource managers should be the masters of information about current employees' strengths and weaknesses. Input like this should all help win human resource managers a "seat at the (top management strategic planning) table." As other examples,

> From public information and legitimate recruiting and interview activities, you ought to be able to construct organization charts, staffing levels, and group missions for the various organizational components of each of your major competitors. Your knowledge of . . . who reports to whom can give important clues as to a competitor's strategic priorities. You may even know the track record and characteristic behavior of the executives.[8]

The accompanying "Managing the New Workforce" feature further illustrates how human resource managers help devise (and execute) strategic plans.

Managing the New Workforce

Dealing with Offshoring

In the film *Slumdog Millionaire*, the hero works in an Indian call center. Here, hundreds of his colleagues spend their days juggling calls from client companies' users around the world. The client companies *offshored* this call-handling task to the call center's relatively low-paid employees.

Offshoring increasingly plays a role in employers' competitive strategies. **Offshoring** is the exporting of jobs from developed countries to countries where labor and other costs are lower.[9] When a pharmaceuticals company decides to have its drugs produced in China, or you find yourself on the phone with a call center employee in Bangalore, India, offshoring is taking place.

Historically, offshoring involved mostly lower skilled manufacturing jobs as, say, clothing manufacturers chose to assemble their garments abroad. Increasingly, however, employers—seeking to reduce costs and stay competitive—are offshoring thousands of higher skilled jobs, for instance, in financial, legal, and security analysis.

The human resource manager plays a role at each stage of the offshoring decision. For example, the CEO should have the human resource team involved in the earliest stages of gathering information about things like the educational and pay levels of the countries to which the firm is thinking of offshoring jobs. However, HR's main involvement is usually once the company decides to offshore. For example, the human resource management team needs to establish policies governing things like compliance with ethical safety and work standards, and pay levels. Human resource management's involvement back home may be even more crucial. Current, home-country employees and their unions may well resist the transfer of work. Maintaining employee commitment and open communications with employees is therefore important.[10]

They Formulate Supporting, Functional/Departmental Strategies In addition to helping top management devise the overall plan, department managers (as we explained earlier in this chapter) also must translate the firm's strategic choices (such as becoming a low-cost leader) into functional strategies. For example, Walmart's cost leadership strategy means its purchasing department must pursue

offshoring
The exporting of jobs from developed countries to countries where labor and other costs are lower.

forcefully buying the lowest-costs goods it can find. To ensure that it does, the purchasing department institutes purchasing guidelines, or *policies*, in terms of what buyers should pay, and how vendors bid for Walmart's business.

Deciding how to translate the company's strategy into departmental strategies and policies is always critical. Functional managers, therefore, need both a good grasp of strategic planning and of what options are best for translating the company's strategic plan into department initiatives.

They Execute the Plans Whereas it would be reckless for top management to devise a plan without lower-level managers' advice, it would simply be impossible for them to execute the plan without the active assistance of all the company's other managers and employees. Except in the tiniest of companies, no top manager could ever expect to do everything alone. With careful oversight, they therefore rely on their subordinate managers to do the planning, organizing, staffing, leading, and controlling that are required to execute the company's and each department's plans and goals.

STRATEGIC HUMAN RESOURCE MANAGEMENT

7 Define strategic human resource management and give an example of strategic human resource management in practice.

We've seen that once a company decides how it's going to compete, it turns to formulating departmental strategies to support its competitive aims. One of those departments is human resource management.

Every company needs its human resource management policies and activities to make sense in terms of its broad strategic aims. **Strategic human resource management** means formulating and executing human resource policies and practices that produce the employee competencies and behaviors the company needs to achieve its strategic aims. Figure 3-10 demonstrates the relationship between human resource strategy and the company's strategic plans.

The basic idea behind strategic human resource management is simple: In formulating human resource management policies and activities, the manager's aim must be to produce the employee skills and behaviors that the company needs to achieve its strategic aims. Figure 3-11 graphically outlines this idea. Management formulates a *strategic plan.* That strategic plan implies certain *workforce requirements.* (For example, do we need more computer-literate employees for our new machines?) Given these workforce requirements, human resource management formulates *HR strategies (policies and practices)* to produce the desired workforce skills, competencies, and behaviors. Finally, the human resource manager identifies the measures he or she can use to gauge the extent to which its new policies and practices are actually producing the required employee skills and behaviors. These

FIGURE 3-10 Linking Company-Wide and HR Strategies
Source: © Gary Dessler, Ph.D., 2007.

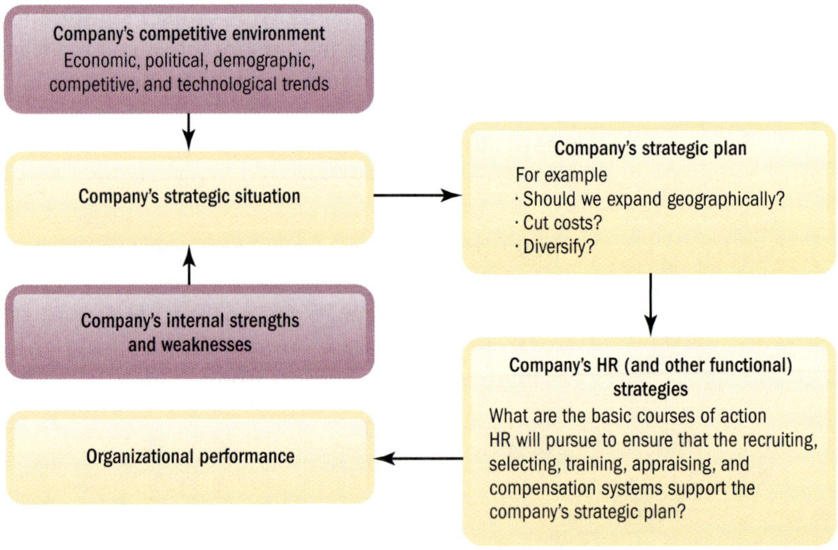

FIGURE 3-11 Basic Model of How to Align HR Strategy and Actions with Business Strategy

Source: Adapted from Garrett Walker and J. Randal MacDonald, "Designing and Implementing an HR Scorecard," *Human Resources Management* 40, no. 4 (2001), p. 370.

measures might include, for instance, "hours of computer training per employee," "productivity per employee," and (via customer surveys) "customer satisfaction."

Shanghai Portman Hotel Example

Several years ago, the Ritz-Carlton Company took over managing the Portman Hotel in Shanghai. The new management decided to improve significantly the hotel's level of service. In doing so, Shanghai Portman's new top executive, Mark DeCocinis, followed a similar strategic HR process to the one we just outlined. For example:

- *Strategically*, he and Ritz-Carlton management set out to make the Shanghai Portman an outstanding property by offering superior customer service.
- To achieve this, Shanghai Portman employees would have to exhibit new *skills and behaviors.* They would genuinely have to care for customers, for instance, and the Portman would have to train and motivate them to be proactive about providing superior customer service.
- To produce these employee skills and behaviors, Mark DeCocinis introduced the Ritz-Carlton Company's *human resource system* to the Portman. He knew its policies and practices produced the high-quality service behaviors his hotel required. For example, DeCocinis and his managers personally interviewed each candidate. They delved into each candidate's values, selecting only employees who cared for and respected others: "Our selection focuses on talent and personal values because these are things that can't be taught . . . it's about caring for and respect and others."[11]

Their efforts paid off. Over the past few years, various publications have named the Shanghai Portman Ritz-Carlton "best employer in Asia," "overall best business hotel in Asia," and "best business hotel in China." Profits have soared. Effective strategic human resource management helped turn Shanghai's Portman into a premier hotel.

Human Resource Strategies and Policies

Managers call the specific human resource management policies and practices they use to support their strategic aims *human resource strategies.*[12] The Shanghai Portman's

strategic human resource management
Formulating and executing human resource policies and practices that produce the employee competencies and behaviors the company needs to achieve its strategic aims.

human resource strategy was to produce the service-oriented employee behaviors the hotel needed to improve significantly the hotel's level of service. Its HR policies therefore included installing the Ritz-Carlton Company's human resource system, having top management personally interview each candidate, and selecting only employees who cared for and respected others.

Albertsons Example Several years ago, Albertsons Markets had to improve performance, and fast. With 2,500 stores and 230,000 workers, it faced competition not only from grocery chains, but also from Walmart and online sites. Albertsons' overall strategy included reducing costs, maximizing financial returns, becoming more customer-focused, enhancing technology, and energizing employees. Albertsons turned to its human resource managers to help achieve these strategic aims. Albertsons' human resource team took steps to help the company cut costs, and hire and motivate customer-focused applicants. Its human resource strategy meant instituting new screening, training, pay, and other human resources policies and practices, and using more technology to support and reduce the costs of HR activities.[13]

Employers also adjust their strategies and policies to the realities of the economic challenges that they face. The accompanying "Managing HR in Challenging Times" feature shows how employers were adjusting their HR policies as the U.S. slipped into recession.

MANAGING HR IN CHALLENGING TIMES

Adjusting HR Policies to Challenging Times

Given the events in 2008 in the economy and financial markets, what changes have you made or do you expect to make in HR policies?

	Already made change (December)	Already made change (October)	Expect to make change in next 12 months (December)	Expect to make change in next 12 months (October)	No change expected (December)	No change expected (October)
Add/increase restrictions to company travel policy	48%	34%	16%	21%	36%	45%
Hiring freeze	47%	30%	18%	25%	35%	45%
Layoffs/reduction in force	39%	19%	23%	26%	38%	55%
Downgrade or cancel company holiday party	35%	19%	8%	18%	57%	64%
Increase communication to employees about their benefits	32%	35%	35%	35%	33%	31%
Eliminate or reduce the hiring of seasonal workers	28%	17%	16%	18%	56%	65%
Organization-wide restructuring	23%	14%	21%	23%	57%	64%
Eliminate or reduce training	23%	10%	18%	18%	59%	72%
Raise employee contribution to health care premiums	20%	21%	17%	25%	63%	54%
Increase communication to employees about their pay	16%	18%	43%	37%	41%	45%
HR function restructuring	14%	15%	21%	19%	66%	66%
Salary freeze	13%	4%	19%	12%	67%	84%
Mandatory holiday shutdown	13%	6%	5%	2%	83%	92%
Reduce or eliminate other employee programs	12%	8%	12%	11%	75%	81%
Salary reductions	5%	2%	6%	4%	89%	94%
Early retirement window	3%	4%	6%	5%	92%	91%
Reduce employer 401(k)/403(b) match	3%	2%	7%	4%	90%	94%
Reduced workweek	2%	4%	6%	4%	93%	92%

As you can see in this table, as the United States slipped into recession, employers began adjusting their HR policies to adapt them to the new strategic and economic realities.

Source: Watson Wyatt, *Effect of Economic Crisis on HR Programs, Update*, December 2008, p. 5.

Strategic HR in Action: Improving Mergers and Acquisitions

As the credit crisis worsened a few years ago, Merrill Lynch looked to Bank of America (BOA) to throw it a lifeline, and BOA obliged by buying Merrill. Within 2 months, that purchase wasn't looking so attractive. Dozens of top Merrill managers had quit, and costs were skyrocketing. BOA's experience isn't unique. Until recently, it appears that only about half of all mergers and acquisitions achieved their anticipated goals.[14]

When mergers and acquisitions do fail, it's often not due to financial or technical issues but to personnel-related ones. These may include, for example, employee resistance, mass exits by high-quality employees, and declining morale and productivity.[15] As one study concluded some years ago, mergers and acquisitions often fail due to "a lack of adequate preparation of the personnel involved and a failure to provide training which fosters self-awareness, cultural sensitivity, and a spirit of cooperation."[16]

Using HRM It's ironic that, until recently, top executives rarely involved their human resource managers in planning the merger or acquisition. Surveys by consultants Towers Perrin found that prior to 2000, human resource executives played limited roles in merger and acquisition (M&A) planning and due diligence. They tended to get involved only when management began integrating the two companies into one. Today, by contrast "close to two thirds of the [survey] participants are involved in M&A due diligence now."[17]

So, it's probably not surprising that there's been a rise in M&A success as employers have called in their human resource experts earlier. For example, a more recent survey concluded that almost 80% of recent mergers and acquisitions had satisfactory results.[18] Another survey found that mergers in which top management asked human resource management to apply its expertise consistently outperformed those in which HR was less involved.[19] Figure 3-12 summarizes the findings.

How can good human resource practices work such apparent magic? Let's look at some examples.

Due Diligence Stage Before finalizing a deal, it is usual for the acquirer (or merger partners) to perform "due diligence" reviews to assure they know what they're getting into. For the human resource teams, due diligence includes reviewing things like organizational culture and structure, employee compensation and benefits, labor relations, pending employee litigation, human resource policies and procedures, and key employees.[20] Employee benefits are one obvious example. For example, do the target firm's health insurance contracts have termination clauses that could eliminate coverage for all employees if you lay too many off after the merger?[21]

Integration Stage There are critical human resource issues during the first few months of a merger or acquisition. These include choosing the top management team, ensuring top management leadership, communicating changes effectively to employees, retaining key talent, and aligning cultures.[22]

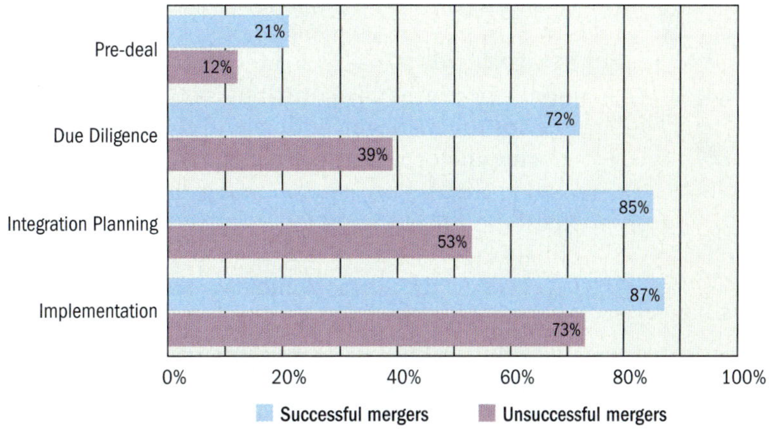

FIGURE 3-12 Percent of Successful Mergers in Which HR Manager Was Involved

Source: HR Magazine by Schmidt. Copyright 2001 by Society for Human Resource Management (SHRM). Reproduced with permission of Society for Human Resource Management (SHRM) in the format Textbook via Copyright Clearance Center.

Using HR Consultants Several global human resource consulting companies, such as Towers Perrin, provide merger-related human resource management services. The services they provide help to illustrate human resource experts' potential role in facilitating mergers and acquisitions.

- **Manage the deal costs.** For example, Towers Perrin consultants identify and quantify people-related costs, risks, and potential synergies. These range from pension issues to items such as redundancy costs and stock options.
- **Manage the messages.** "We support our clients in rapidly developing and deploying an employee communication strategy."
- **Secure the top team and key talent.** They help clients to identify key talent, and then develop suitable retention strategies.
- **Define and implement an effective HR service delivery strategy.** Towers Perrin helps their clients plan out how they're going to implement the delivery of HR services, such as in combining payroll systems.
- **Develop a workable change management plan.** "Especially in cross-border transactions, we assist companies in understanding and managing the cultural differences they face as part of the deal."
- **Design and implement the right staffing model.** Help companies design the organization structure and determine which employee is best for which role.
- **Aligning total rewards.** "When integration [of pay plans] is desirable, we help companies' benchmarking and integration of compensation and benefit programs."[23]

Shaws Example Shaws Supermarkets acquired Star Markets several years ago. At the time, Shaws had 126 stores and Star had 54.[24] The two firms' human resource management teams played an important role in this successful acquisition. For example, they worked to:

- develop preliminary organizational designs,
- identify the members of the top three levels of management,
- assess critical managers and employees,
- create retention policies for key people,
- plan for and execute the separation of redundant staff,
- develop a total rewards strategy for the combined company, and
- integrate payroll benefits and human resource information systems.[25]

8 Briefly describe three important strategic human resource management tools.

Strategic Human Resource Management Tools

Managers use several tools to help them translate the company's broad strategic goals into specific human resource management policies and activities. Three important tools include the strategy map, the HR Scorecard, and the digital dashboard.

Strategy Map The **strategy map** shows the "big picture" of how each department's performance contributes to achieving the company's overall strategic goals. It helps the manager understand the role his or her department plays in helping to execute the company's strategic plan.

Figure 3-13 presents a strategy map example, in this case for Southwest Airlines. Recall Southwest has a low-cost leader strategy. The strategy map for Southwest succinctly lays out the hierarchy of main activities required for Southwest Airlines to succeed. At the top is achieving company-wide, strategic financial goals. Then the strategy map shows the chain of activities that help Southwest Airlines achieve these goals. For example, as we saw earlier in this chapter, to boost revenues and profitability Southwest needs to fly fewer planes (to keep costs down), maintain low prices, and maintain on-time flights.

FIGURE 3-13 Strategy Map for Southwest Airlines
Source: Adapted from "Creating a Strategy Map," Ravi Tangri;Team@TeamCHRYSALIS.com.

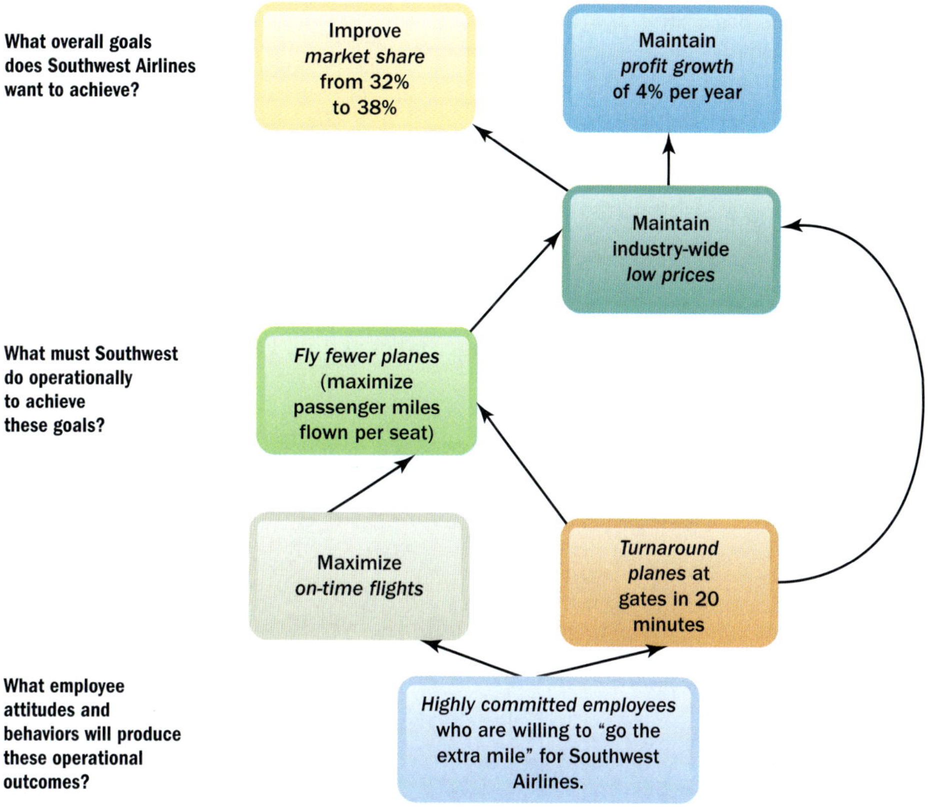

In turn (further down the strategy map), on-time flights and low prices require fast turnaround. And, fast turnaround requires motivated ground and flight crews. The strategy map helps each department (including HR) visualize what it needs to do to support Southwest's low-cost strategy.

The HR Scorecard Many employers quantify and computerize the map's activities. The HR Scorecard helps them to do so. The **HR Scorecard** is not a scorecard. It refers to a process for *assigning financial and nonfinancial goals or metrics* to the human resource management–related chain of activities required for achieving the company's strategic aims and for *monitoring results*.[26] (Metrics for Southwest might include airplane turnaround time, percent on-time flights, and ground crew productivity.) Simply put, the idea is to take the strategy map and to quantify it.

Managers use special scorecard software to facilitate this. The computerized scorecard process helps you to quantify the relationships between (1) the HR activities (amount of testing, training, and so forth), (2) the resulting employee behaviors (customer service, for instance), and (3) the resulting firm-wide strategic outcomes and performance (such as customer satisfaction and profitability).[27] Figure 3-14 summarizes this process.

HR APPs 4 U

Mobile Access to Strategy Maps

Managers can access their companies' strategy maps while on-the-go. They can use the ActiveStrategy Company's *ActiveStrategy Enterprise* to create and automate their strategy maps, and to access them through iPhone or similar devices.[28]

Digital Dashboards The saying "a picture is worth a thousand words" explains the purpose of the digital dashboard. A **digital dashboard** presents the manager with desktop graphs and charts, and so a computerized

strategy map
A strategic planning tool that shows the "big picture" of how each department's performance contributes to achieving the company's overall strategic goals.

HR scorecard
A process for *assigning financial and nonfinancial goals or metrics* to the human resource management–related chain of activities required for achieving the company's strategic aims and for *monitoring results*.

digital dashboard
Presents the manager with desktop graphs and charts, and so a computerized picture of where the company stands on all those metrics from the HR Scorecard process.

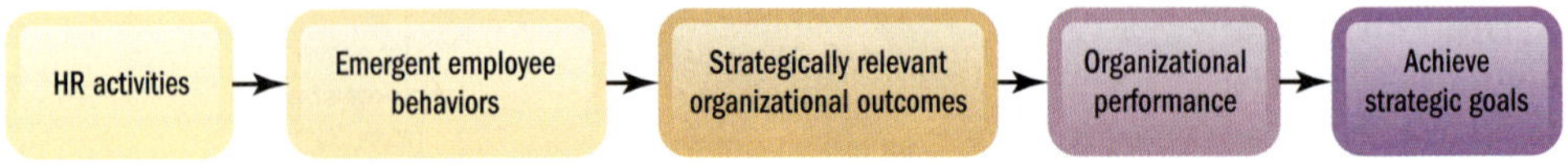

FIGURE 3-14 The Basic HR Scorecard Relationships

picture of where the company stands on all those metrics from the HR Scorecard process. As in the illustration just below, a top manager's dashboard for Southwest Airlines might display on the PC screen real-time trends for strategy map activities such as fast turnaround, attracting and keeping customers, and on-time flights. This gives the manager time to take corrective action. For example, if ground crews are turning planes around slower today, financial results tomorrow may decline unless the manager takes action. Figure 3-15 summarizes the three tools.

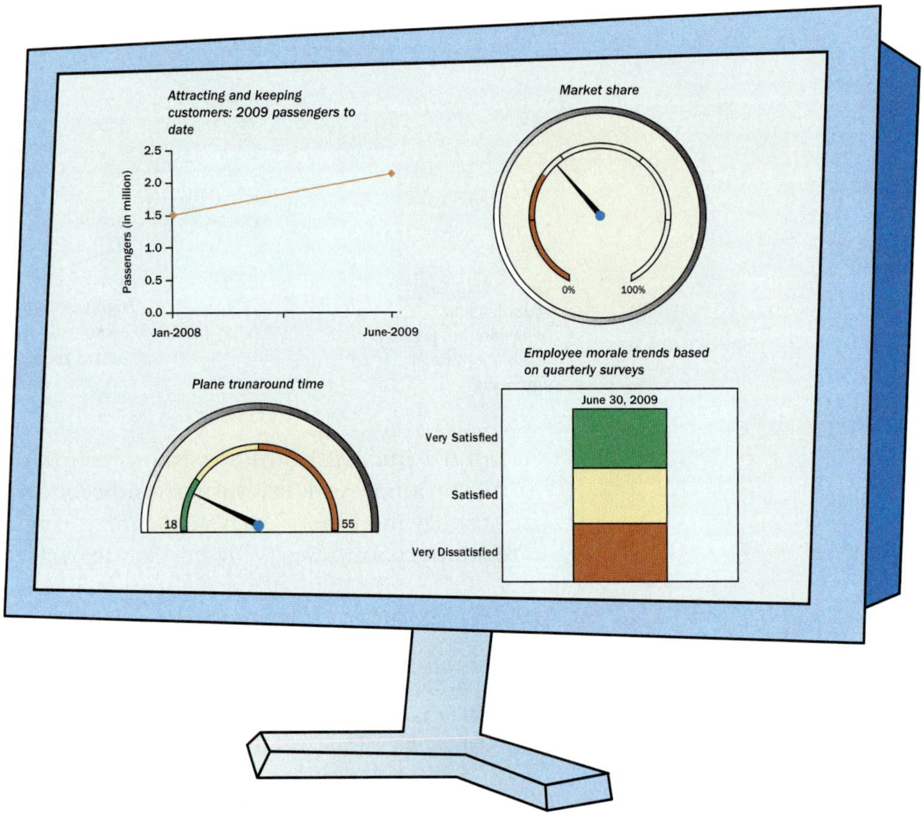

Translating Strategy into Human Resource Policies and Practices: Einstein Medical Example

Albert Einstein Healthcare Network (Einstein Medical) illustrates how managers translate strategic plans into human resource policies and practices.[29] Einstein's new CEO saw that intense competition, medical technology changes, and the growth of managed care meant that his company needed a new strategic plan. At the time, Einstein Medical was a single acute care hospital, treating just the seriously ill.

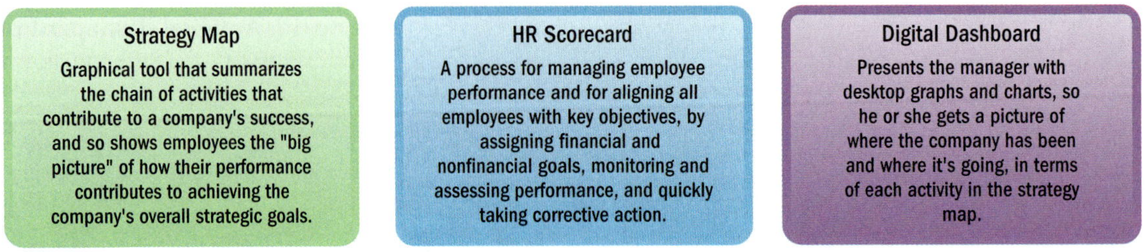

FIGURE 3-15 Three Important Strategic HR Tools

New Strategy The essence of the CEO's new strategy was to change Einstein into a network of health care facilities providing a full range of high-quality services in local markets. Based on that, he decided that to achieve Einstein Medical's strategic aims, its new HR and other strategies would have to produce three important organizational outcomes: produce new services (*initiate*), capitalize on opportunities (*adapt*), and offer consistently high-quality services (*deliver*).

New Employee Competencies and Behaviors The CEO then asked, "What sorts of employee values, competencies, skills, and behaviors would Einstein Medical need in order to produce these three outcomes?" They would have to be *dedicated* to Einstein's focus on initiate, adapt, and deliver. They would have to take personal *accountability* for their results. They would have to be able and willing *to apply new knowledge* and skills in a constant search for innovative solutions. And they would have to be *resilient*, for instance, in terms of moving from job to job, as Einstein's needs changed.

New Human Resource Policies and Practices Given these desired employee values and competencies, Einstein Medical's human resource managers could ask, "What specific HR policies and practices would help Einstein create a dedicated, accountable, innovative, and resilient workforce?" The answer was to implement several new human resource programs:

- New *training programs* aimed at assuring that employees clearly understood the company's new vision and what it would require of all employees.
- *Enriching work* involved providing employees with more challenge and responsibility through flexible assignments.
- Providing *appropriate returns* involved tying employees' rewards to organization-wide results (such as initiating new services).
- *Improved selection, orientation, and dismissal procedures* also helped Einstein build a more dedicated, resilient, accountable, and generative workforce.

In sum, Einstein's managers knew they could not execute their new strategy without new employee competencies and behaviors. In turn, promoting these competencies and behaviors required implementing new human resource policies and practices. They could then choose measures (such as "hours of training per employee per year") to monitor the new HR strategies' actual progress, and track these on digital dashboards, if they so chose. (The Hotel Paris Case at the end of this chapter explains the HR Scorecard process in more detail.)

BUILDING YOUR OWN HIGH-PERFORMANCE WORK SYSTEM

No two companies have the exact same human resource practices and polices. For example, a low-cost leader will have different testing, training, and pay policies than will one that makes luxury goods.

What are High-Performance Work Systems?

However, many experts agree that certain human resource management policies and practices do distinguish many high-performing companies. Managers call these sets of practices *high-performance work systems* (HPWS). A **high-performance work system** is a set of human resource management policies and practices that promote organizational effectiveness.

high-performance work system
A set of human resource management policies and practices that promote organizational effectiveness.

High-performance work systems became popular in the 1990s. Faced with global competition from the Toyotas of the world, U.S. companies needed ways to improve quality, productivity, and responsiveness. The U.S. Department of Labor listed several characteristics of high-performance work organizations. These include multi-skilled work teams, empowered front-line workers, extensive training, labor–management cooperation, commitment to quality, and customer satisfaction.[30]

9 Explain with examples why metrics are essential for identifying and creating high-performance human resource policies and practices.

High-Performance Human Resource Policies and Practices

Studies show that in terms of policies and practices, high-performance work systems do differ from less productive ones. Table 3-1 illustrates this. For example, high-performing companies start with more job candidates, use more selection tests, and spend many more hours training employees. This table demonstrates four things about high-performing firms' human resource management systems.

First, it helps demonstrate why *metrics* are important. A **human resource metric** is the quantitative measure of some human resource management yardstick such as employee turnover, hours of training per employee, or qualified applicants per position. (In Table 3-1, the high-performing company metric for the yardstick "Number of qualified applicants per position" is 36.55.) You can use such metrics to assess your own company's HR performance, and to compare one company's with another's. Using concrete, quantifiable evidence like this is the heart of evidence-based management. Recall that *evidence-based management* is the use of data, facts, analytics, scientific rigor, critical evaluation, and critically evaluated research/case studies to support human resource management proposals, decisions, practices,

TABLE 3-1 Comparison of Selected Human Resource Practices in High-Performance and Low-Performance Companies

	Low-Performance Company HR System Bottom 10% (42 firms)	High-Performance Company HR System Top 10% (43 firms)
Sample HR Practices		
Number of qualified applicants per position (*recruiting*)	8.24	36.55
Percentage hired based on a validated *selection* test	4.26	29.67
Percentage of jobs filled from within	34.90	61.46
Percentage in a *formal HR plan* including recruitment, *development*, and succession	4.79	46.72
Number of hours of *training* for new employees (less than 1 year)	35.02	116.87
Number of hours of *training* for experienced employees	13.40	72.00
Percentage of employees receiving a regular *performance appraisal*	41.31	95.17
Percentage of workforce whose *merit increase* or *incentive pay* is tied to performance	23.36	87.27
Percentage of the workforce eligible for *incentive pay*	27.83	83.56
Percentage of difference in incentive pay between a low-performing and high-performing employee	3.62	6.21
Percentage of the workforce routinely working in a self-managed, *cross-functional*, or *project team*	10.64	42.28
Firm Performance		
Employee turnover	34.09	20.87
Sales per employee	$158,101	$617,576
Market value to book value	3.64	11.06

Source: Adapted from Brian Becker, Mark Huselid, and Dave Ulrich, *The HR Scorecard: Linking People, Strategy, and Performance* (Boston: Harvard Business School Press, 2001), pp. 16–17.

and conclusions.[31] (This chapter's appendix, "Tools for Evidence-Based Human Resource Management," provides you with some tools you can use here.)

Second, Table 3-1 illustrates *the things human resource systems must do* to be high-performance systems. For example, they hire based on validated selection tests, fill more jobs from within, organize work around self-managing teams, and extensively train employees.

Third, the table illustrates that high-performance practices generally *aspire to help workers to manage themselves.* The point of the recruiting, screening, training, and other human resources practices is to foster a trained, empowered, self-motivated, and flexible workforce.[32]

Fourth, Table 3-1 highlights *the notable differences* between high-performance and low-performance companies' human resource management systems. (For example, high-performing companies have more than four times the number of qualified applicants per job than do low performers.) The idea that "better" companies' human resource practices are measurably different from low performers' underlies the human resource management benchmarking movement. *Benchmarking* means comparing and analyzing the practices of high-performing companies to your own in order to understand what they do that makes them better.[33]

The Evidence The research evidence does seem to demonstrate that companies using high-performance policies and practices like those in Table 3-1 do perform significantly better. For example, based on studies of more than 2,800 companies, one researcher concludes, "high-performance HR practices, [particularly] combined with new technology, produce better productivity, quality, sales, and financial performance."[34] Another team of researchers, studying the productivity of 308 companies over 22 years, concluded that empowerment, teamwork, and extensive training—outcomes that high-performance work practices usually aspire to achieve—produced significant performance benefits.[35]

The Line Manager's Role in Building a High-Performance Work System

That a human resource manager can influence things like "number of qualified applicants per position" and "percentage of jobs filled from within" is apparent. After all, those are exactly the sorts of activities that human resource managers oversee.

Not so apparent is that *every* department manager and supervisor can play an important role in activities like these and thus build, within his or her own departmental domain, a higher performing organization.

Table 3-1 again provides a sort of road map for doing so. This shows, for instance, that more applicants, more testing, more formal appraisals, better training, and more incentive plans usually correlate with higher performance. You don't have to be a human resource manager to influence activities like these. Every sales manager, production manager, and accounting manager can influence the number of job applicants they get, the testing they do, the quality training they provide, and the sorts of incentives they offer to their employees. The whole point of this book is to show you how to do this. For instance, we will see how to boost the chances that you'll have more applicants, improve your batting average in interviewing candidates, and select the best. We'll explain how to spot applicant dishonestly, list the mistakes to avoid in appraising performance, and list dozens of incentives all supervisors can use (quite aside from the company's formal pay plan). All managers are "human resource managers" because no manager can excel without applying the sorts of tools and techniques you'll find in the following chapters.

human resource metric
The quantitative measure of some human resource management yardstick such as employee turnover, hours of training per employee, or qualified applicants per position.

REVIEW

CHAPTER SECTION SUMMARIES

1. **Strategic planning is important to all managers.** All managers' personnel and other decisions should be consistent with the goals that cascade down from the firm's overall strategic plan. Those goals form a hierarchy, starting with the president's overall strategic goals (such as double sales revenue to $16 million) and filtering down to what each individual manager needs to do in order to support that overall company goal.
2. Because each manager needs to make his or her decisions within the context of the company's plans, it's important for all managers to understand the **fundamentals of management planning.** The management planning process includes setting an objective, making forecasts, determining what your alternatives are, evaluating your alternatives, and implementing and evaluating your plan. The business plan itself typically includes a description of the business, the marketing plan, the production plan, the financial plan, and the personnel plan. Setting effective objectives is an integral part of effective managerial planning. "Smart" goals are specific, measurable, attainable, relevant, and timely. Motivational goals tend to be specific, measurable, challenging but doable, and (usually) a product of employee participation.
3. Again, because all managers operate within the framework of their company's overall plans, it's important for all managers to be familiar with the **strategic management process.**
   - A strategic plan is the company's plan for how it will match its internal strengths and weaknesses with external opportunities and threats in order to maintain a competitive advantage. A strategy is a course of action.
   - Strategic management is the process of identifying and executing the organization's strategic plan. Basic steps in the strategic management process include defining the current business, performing an external and internal audit, formulating a new direction, translating the mission into strategic goals, formulating strategies to achieve the strategic goals, implementing strategies, and evaluating performance.
   - We distinguished among corporate-level, competitive-level, and functional strategies. Corporate strategies include, among others, diversification strategies, vertical integration, horizontal integration, geographic expansion, and consolidation. The main competitive strategies include cost leadership, differentiation, and focuser. Functional strategies reflect the specific departmental policies that are necessary for executing the businesses's competitive strategies.
   - Department managers play an important role in strategic planning in terms of devising the strategic plan, formulating supporting functional/departmental strategies, and of course in executing the company's plans.
4. Each function or department in the business needs its own functional strategy, and **strategic human resource management** means formulating and executing human resource policies and practices that produce the employee competencies and behaviors the company needs to achieve its strategic aims. Human resource strategies are the specific human resource management policies and practices managers use to support their strategic aims. The Shanghai Portman Hotel and Albertsons Markets are two examples of strategic human resource planning. Another is the use of HR consultants in improving mergers and acquisitions, for instance with respect to managing the deal's costs, and aligning the total rewards necessary for the new entity. Important and popular strategic human resource management tools include the strategy map, the HR Scorecard, and digital dashboards.
5. In today's competitive environment, it's important for all managers to understand they have a role in building, even within their own departments, **high-performance work systems**. In brief, a high-performance work system is a set of human resource management policies and practices that promote organizational effectiveness. Human resource metrics (quantitative measures of some human resource management yardstick such as employee turnover) are critical in creating high-performance human resource policies and practices. This is because they enable managers to benchmark their own practices against those of successful organizations.

DISCUSSION QUESTIONS

1. Give an example of hierarchical planning in an organization.
2. What are the main components of a business plan? Describe each briefly.
3. How would you set motivational goals?
4. What is the difference between a strategy, a vision, and a mission? Give one example of each.

5. Define and give at least two examples of the cost leadership competitive strategy and the differentiation competitive strategy.
6. Explain how human resources management can be instrumental in helping a company create a competitive advantage.
7. What is a high-performance work system? Provide several specific examples of the typical components in a high-performance work system.
8. Define what an HR Scorecard is, and briefly explain each of the seven steps in the strategic management process.

INDIVIDUAL AND GROUP ACTIVITIES

1. With three or four other students, form a strategic management group for your college or university. Your assignment is to develop the outline of a strategic plan for the college or university. This should include such things as mission and vision statements; strategic goals; and corporate, competitive, and functional strategies. In preparing your plan, make sure to show the main strengths, weaknesses, opportunities, and threats the college faces, and which prompted you to develop your particular strategic plans.
2. Using the Internet or library resources, analyze the annual reports of five companies. Bring to class examples of how those companies say they are using their HR processes to help the company achieve its strategic goals.
3. Interview an HR manager and write a short report on "The Strategic Roles of the HR Manager at XYZ Company."
4. Using the Internet or library resources, bring to class and discuss at least two examples of how companies are using an HR Scorecard to help create HR systems that support the company's strategic aims. Do all managers seem to mean the same thing when they refer to "HR Scorecards"? How do they differ?
5. It is probably safe to say that your career plan is one of the most important plans you'll ever create. Unfortunately, most people never lay out such a plan, or they don't realize they need one until it is too late. Using the concepts and techniques in this chapter, develop an outline of a career plan for yourself, one that has sufficient detail to provide direction for your career decisions over the next 5 years. Make sure to include an executive assignment action plan and measurable goals and/or milestones.
6. The HRCI "Test Specifications" appendix at the end of this book (pages 699–706) lists the things someone studying for the HRCI certification exam needs to know in each area of human resource management (such as in Strategic Management, Workforce Planning, and Human Resource Development). In groups of four to five students, do four things: (1) review that appendix now; (2) identify the material in this chapter that relates to the required knowledge the appendix lists; (3) write four multiple choice exam questions on this material that you believe would be suitable for inclusion in the HRCI exam; and (4) if time permits, have someone from your team post your team's questions in front of the class, so the students in other teams can take each others' exam questions.

EXPERIENTIAL EXERCISE

Developing an HR Strategy for Starbucks

By 2009, Starbucks was facing serious challenges. Sales per store were stagnant or declining, and its growth rate and profitability were down. Many believed that its introduction of breakfast foods had diverted its "baristas" from their traditional jobs as coffee-preparation experts. McDonald's and Dunkin Donuts were introducing lower priced but still high-grade coffees. Starbucks' former CEO stepped back into the company's top job. You need to help him formulate a new direction for his company.

Purpose: The purpose of this exercise is to give you experience in developing an HR strategy, in this case, by developing one for Starbucks.

Required Understanding: You should be thoroughly familiar with the material in this chapter.

How to Set Up the Exercise/Instructions: Set up groups of three or four students for this exercise. You are probably already quite familiar with what it's like to have a cup of coffee or tea in a Starbucks coffee shop, but if not, spend some time in one prior to this exercise. Meet in groups and develop an outline for an HR strategy for Starbucks Corp. Your outline should include four basic elements: a basic business/competitive strategy for Starbucks, workforce requirements (in terms of employee competencies and behaviors) this strategy requires, specific HR policies and the activities necessary to produce these workforce requirements, and suggestions for metrics to measure the success of the HR strategy.

APPLICATION CASE

Siemens Builds a Strategy-Oriented HR System

Siemens is a 150-year-old German company, but it's not the company it was even a few years ago. Until recently, Siemens focused on producing electrical products. Today the firm has diversified into software, engineering, and services. It is also global, with more than 400,000 employees working in 190 countries. In other words, Siemens became a world leader by pursuing a corporate strategy that emphasized diversifying into high-tech products and services, and doing so on a global basis.

With a corporate strategy like that, human resource management plays a big role at Siemens. Sophisticated engineering and services require more focus on employee selection, training, and compensation than in the average firm, and globalization requires delivering these services globally. Siemens sums up the basic themes of its HR strategy in several points. These include:

1. **A living Company is a learning Company.** The high-tech nature of Siemens' business means that employees must be able to learn on a continuing basis. Siemens uses its system of combined classroom and hands-on apprenticeship training around the world to help facilitate this. It also offers employees extensive continuing education and management development.
2. **Global teamwork is the key to developing and using all the potential of the firm's human resources.** Because it is so important for employees throughout Siemens to feel free to work together and interact, employees have to understand the whole process, not just bits and pieces. To support this, Siemens provides extensive training and development. It also ensures that all employees feel they're part of a strong, unifying corporate identity. For example, HR uses cross-border, cross-cultural experiences as prerequisites for career advances.
3. **A climate of mutual respect is the basis of all relationships—within the Company and with society.** Siemens contends that the wealth of nationalities, cultures, languages, and outlooks represented by its employees is one of its most valuable assets. It therefore engages in numerous HR activities aimed at building openness, transparency, and fairness, and supporting diversity.

Questions

1. Based on the information in this case, provide examples, for Siemens, of at least four strategically required organizational outcomes, and four required workforce competencies and behaviors.
2. Identify at least four strategically relevant HR system policies and activities that Siemens has instituted in order to help human resource management contribute to achieving Siemens' strategic goals.
3. Provide a brief illustrative outline of a strategy map for Siemens.

CONTINUING CASE

The Carter Cleaning Company

The High-Performance Work System

As a recent graduate and as a person who keeps up with the business press, Jennifer is familiar with the benefits of programs such as total quality management and high-performance work systems.

Jack has actually installed a total quality program of sorts at Carter, and it has been in place for about 5 years. This program takes the form of employee meetings. Jack holds employee meetings periodically, but particularly when there is a serious problem in a store—such as poor-quality work or machine breakdowns. When problems like these arise, instead of trying to diagnose them himself or with Jennifer, he contacts all the employees in that store and meets with them as soon as the store closes. Hourly employees get extra pay for these meetings. The meetings have been useful in helping Jack to identify and rectify several problems. For example, in one store all the fine white blouses were coming out looking dingy. It turned out that the cleaner-spotter had been ignoring the company rule that required cleaning ("boiling down") the perchloroethylene cleaning fluid before washing items like these. As a result, these fine white blouses were being washed in cleaning fluid that had residue from other, earlier washes.

Jennifer now wonders whether these employee meetings should be expanded to give the employees an even bigger role in managing the Carter stores' quality. "We can't be everywhere watching everything all the time," she said to her father. "Yes, but these people only earn about $8 to $15 per hour. Will they really want to act like mini-managers?" he replied.

Questions

1. Would you recommend that the Carters expand their quality program? If so, specifically what form should it take?
2. Assume the Carters want to institute a high-performance work system as a test program in one of their stores. Write a one-page outline summarizing what such a program would consist of.

KEY TERMS

TRANSLATTING STRATEGY INTO HR POLICIES & PRACTICES CASE

The Hotel Paris Case

Introduction: The 8-Step HR Scorecard Process

We saw that Einstein Medical's managers used a simple, logical, and subjective process to translate strategy into required human resource policies and activities. This is perfectly acceptable. Increasingly, however, many companies are turning to a more rigorous methodology called the HR Scorecard process. We'll illustrate that newer approach next.

There are eight steps in the HR Scorecard process.[36] They are as follows:

Step 1: Define the Business Strategy. Translating strategy into human resource policies and activities starts by defining the company's strategic plans. For Einstein Medical, they included becoming a comprehensive health care network.

Step 2: Outline the Company's Value Chain. As in Figure 3-16, we can think of any business as consisting of a chain of necessary activities. The company's **value chain** identifies the primary activities that create value for customers and the related support activities.[37] These activities might include bringing supplies and materials into the company's warehouse; bringing these materials to the shop floor and designing the product to customers' specifications; and the various marketing, sales, and distribution activities that attract customers and get the company's product to them.

Outlining the company's value chain (in this case for a hotel, Figure 3-16) shows the business's chain of essential activities. This can help managers better understand the activities that drive performance in their company. In other words, it is a tool for identifying, isolating, visualizing, and analyzing the firm's most important activities and strategic costs.

Step 3: Outline a Strategy Map. You can use this information to help construct your strategy map. As we saw, this diagram summarizes the chain of major interrelated activities that contribute to a company's success. Figure 3-13 (page 91) presented a strategy map for Southwest Airlines.

Step 4: Identify the Strategically Required Organizational Outcomes. Every company must produce strategically relevant outcomes if it is to achieve its strategic goals. At Einstein Medical, "new services delivered" was one such required organizational outcome. At Dell, receiving *quick, competent, and courteous technical advice by phone* is one such outcome. The strategy map and value chain from the preceding steps helps the manager identify these core outcomes.

Step 5: Identify the Required Workforce Competencies and Behaviors. Here, ask, "What competencies and behaviors must our employees exhibit if our company is to produce the strategically relevant organizational outcomes, and thereby achieve its strategic goals?" At Einstein Medical, employees had to take *personal accountability* for their results, and be willing to work proactively to *find innovative solutions.*

Step 6: Identify the Required HR System Policies and Activities. Once the human resource manager knows the required employee competencies and behaviors, he or she can turn to identifying the HR activities and policies that will help to produce them. For example, at Einstein Medical, these included new training and pay plans.

value chain
Identifies the primary activities that create value for customers and the related support activities.

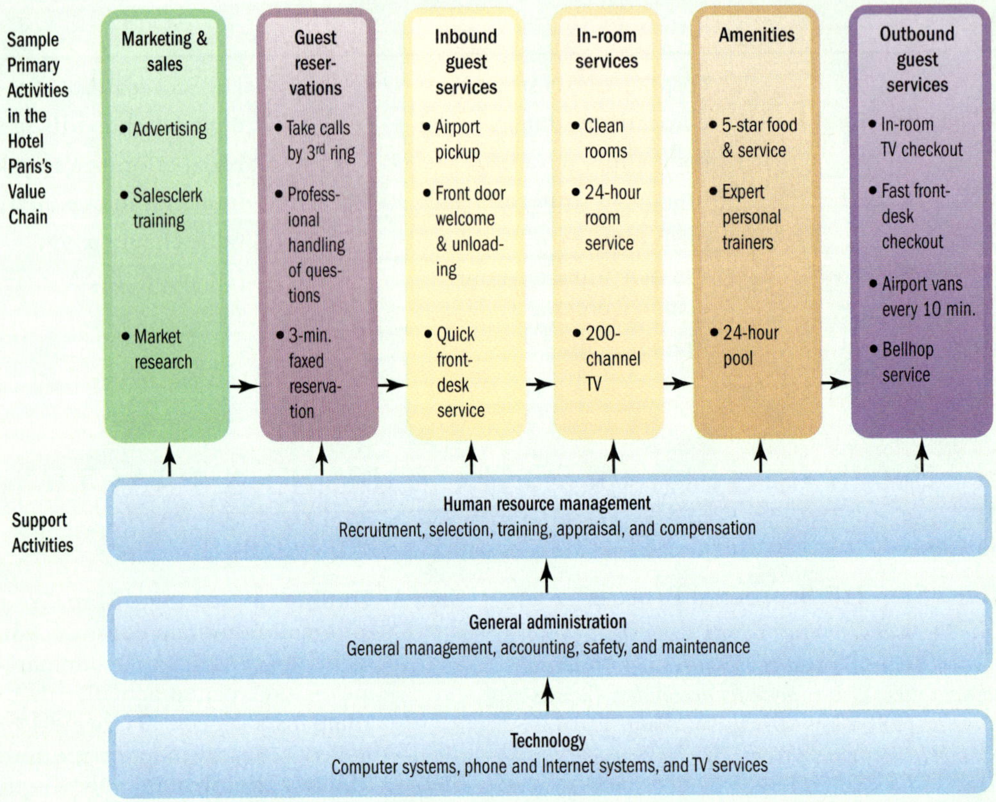

FIGURE 3-16 Simple Value Chain for "The Hotel Paris"
Source: © Gary Dessler, Ph.D.

In this step, one should be specific. It is not enough to say, "We need new training programs or disciplinary processes." Instead, the manager must now ask, "Exactly what sorts of new training programs do we need to produce the sorts of employee competencies and behaviors that we seek?"

Step 7: Choose HR Scorecard Measures. We saw that many managers quantify and computerize this chain of strategic goals, employee competencies, and required HR practices. The HR Scorecard process helps them to do so. Recall that the HR Scorecard is a process for assigning financial and nonfinancial goals or *metrics* to the HR-related chain of activities required for achieving the company's strategic aims and for monitoring results.

The task here is to choose the appropriate metrics. For example, if we decide to "improve the disciplinary system," how precisely will we measure improvement? Perhaps we would use the metric, "number of grievances." Table 3-1 (page 94) presents some performance measures.

Step 8: Summarize the Scorecard Measures in a Digital Dashboard. We saw that a digital dashboard presents the manager, via a PC desktop screen containing graphs and charts, with a bird's eye view of how the human resource management function is doing.

The Hotel Paris International

Let us demonstrate how this HR Scorecard process works by considering a fictitious company, the Hotel Paris International (Hotel Paris). Starting as a single hotel in a Paris suburb in 1990, the Hotel Paris now comprises a chain of nine hotels, with two in France, one each in London and Rome, and others in New York, Miami, Washington, Chicago, and Los Angeles. As a corporate strategy, the Hotel Paris's management and owners want to continue to expand geographically. They believe doing so will let them capitalize on their reputation for good service by providing multi-city alternatives for their satisfied guests. The problem is their reputation for good service, has been deteriorating. If they cannot improve service it would be unwise for them to expand, since their guests might actually prefer other hotels after trying the Hotel Paris.

The Strategy Top management, with input from the human resources and other managers, and with the board of directors' approval, chooses a new competitive strategy and formulates new strategic goals. They decide: "The Hotel Paris International will use superior guest services to differentiate the Hotel Paris properties, and to thereby increase the length of stays and the return rate of guests, and thus boost revenues and profitability." All Hotel Paris managers—including the director of HR services—must now formulate strategies that support this competitive strategy.

The Value Chain Based on discussions with other managers, the HR director, Lisa Cruz, outlines the company's value chain (see Figure 3-16). This should help her identify the HR activities that are crucial to helping the hotel achieve its strategic goals. In a service business, the "product" is satisfied guests. Producing satisfied guests requires attending to all those activities along the hotel's value chain where there is an opportunity to affect the guests' experiences. For the Hotel Paris, there are *inbound logistics activities* such as getting the guest from the airport and checked in. There are *operations activities* such as cleaning the guest's room. There are *outbound logistics activities* such as picking up baggage and getting the person checked out and to his or her plane. There are *marketing and sales activities* aimed at attracting guests to the hotel. There are *service activities* that provide post-stay services, such as travel awards to guests for multiple stays. And there are various *support activities*, such as purchasing, information systems, and human resources.

The Strategically Required Organizational Outcomes The Hotel Paris's basic strategy is to use superior guest services to expand geographically. Each step in the hotel's value chain provides opportunities for improving guest service. For Lisa Cruz, reviewing the hotel's value chain makes it clear that achieving the hotel's strategic aims necessitates achieving a number of required organizational outcomes. For example, Lisa and her management colleagues must take steps that produce *fewer customer complaints* and more written compliments, more frequent *guest returns* and longer stays, and higher *guest expenditures* per visit.

The Strategically Relevant Workforce Competencies and Behaviors Therefore, the question facing Lisa is this: What are the competencies and behaviors that our hotel's employees will have to exhibit if we are to produce required organizational outcomes such as fewer customer complaints, more compliments, and more frequent guest returns? Thinking through the sorts of activities that occur at each step in the hotel's value chain helps Lisa answer that question. For example, the hotel's required employee competencies and behaviors would include "high-quality front-desk customer service," "taking calls for reservations in a friendly manner," "greeting guests at the front door," and "processing guests' room service meals efficiently." All require motivated, high-morale employees.

The Strategically Relevant HR System Policies and Activities The HR manager's task now is to identify the human resource policies and activities that will enable the hotel to produce these crucial workforce competencies and behaviors. As one example, "high-quality front-desk customer service" is one such required behavior. From this, Lisa identifies human resource activities to produce such front-desk customer service efforts. For example, she decides to *institute practices to improve the disciplinary fairness and justice in the company*, with the aim of *improving employee morale*. Her assumption is that enhanced fairness will produce higher morale and that higher morale will produce improved front-desk service.

The HR Scorecard Finally, Lisa may (or may not) decide to computerize all these cause-and-effect links among the HR activities, the workforce behaviors, and the organizational outcomes, using scorecard software to present results on digital dashboards. With a computerized scorecard software package, Lisa need not limit herself to assessing the effects of the handful of employee behaviors (such as percentage of calls answered on time). Instead, she could include metrics covering dozens of activities, from recruitment and selection through training, appraisal, compensation, and labor relations. Her HR Scorecard model could also include the effects of all these activities on a variety of workforce competencies and behaviors, and thus on organizational outcomes and on the company's performance. In this way, her HR Scorecard would become a comprehensive model representing the value-adding effects of the full range of Hotel Paris human resource activities.

How We Will Use the Hotel Paris Case in This Book

We will use a "Translating Strategy into HR Policies and Practices: The Hotel Paris Case" in the end-of-chapter material of each chapter (starting with this chapter). These cases demonstrate how the Hotel Paris's HR director uses the concepts and techniques from that chapter to create a human resource management system that helps the Hotel Paris achieve its strategic goals. Table 3-2 presents some of the metrics that Lisa could use to measure human resource activities (by chapter). For example, she could endeavor to improve workforce competencies and behaviors by instituting (as per Chapter 5, "Personnel Planning and Recruiting") improved recruitment processes, and measure the latter in terms of "number of qualified applicants per position." Similarly, she may recommend to management that they change the firm's pay policies (see Chapter 11, "Establishing Strategic Pay Plans") so that the "target percentile for total compensation is in the top 25%." She could then show that doing so will have favorable effects on employee morale, and on employee service behavior, customer satisfaction, and the hotel chain's performance. In practice, all the HR functions we discuss in this book influence employee competencies and behaviors, and, thereby, organizational outcomes and performance.

Questions

1. Draw a simple strategy map for the Hotel Paris. Specifically, summarize in your own words an example of the hierarchy of links among the hotel's *HR practices*, necessary *workforce competencies* and behaviors, and required *organizational outcomes*.
2. Using Table 3-1 (page 94), list at least five specific metrics the Hotel Paris could use to measure its HR practices.

TABLE 3-2 Examples of HR System Activities the Hotel Paris Can Measure as Related to Each Chapter in This Book

Chapter	Strategic Activities Metrics
2. EEOC	Number EEOC claims/year; cost of HR-related litigation; % minority/women promotions
3. Strategy	% employees who can quote company strategy/vision
4. Job Analysis	% employees with updated job descriptions
5. Recruiting	Number applicants per recruiting source; number qualified applicants/position
6. Testing	% employees hired based on validated employment test
7. Interview	% applicants receiving structured interview
8. Training	Number hours training/employee/year; number hours training new employee
9. Appraisal	Number employees getting feedback; % appraisals completed on time
10. Career Management	% employees with formal career/development plan
11. Compensation	Target percentile for total compensation (pay in top 25%)
12. Incentives	% workforce eligible for merit pay
13. Benefits	% employees 80% satisfied with benefits
14. Ethics	Number grievances/year; % employees able to quote ethics code
15. Labor Relations	% workforce in unions
16. Health and Safety	Number safety training programs/year; $ accident costs/year; hours lost time due to accidents
17. Global	% expatriates receiving predeparture screening, counseling
18. Entrepreneurship	Employee turnover
Overall HR Metrics	HR cost/employee; HR expense/total expenses; turnover costs

Appendix for Chapter 3

Tools for Evidence-Based Human Resource Management

Most CEOs won't accept subjective, off-the-cuff explanations for the worth of projects you ask them to implement, or for sizing up your team's success. That is why quantitative, data-based analysis and decision making is a hallmark of successful human resource management. Managers should make decisions based on the evidence. We saw that *evidence-based human resource management* is the use of data, facts, analytics, scientific rigor, critical evaluation, and critically evaluated research/case studies to support human resource management proposals, decisions, practices, and conclusions.[38] We'll focus here on two critical tools managers use for taking an evidence-based approach: *human resource audits* and *benchmarking*. But let's first look at how managers can be more scientific.

EVIDENCE-BASED HR AND THE SCIENTIFIC WAY OF DOING THINGS

What Is Science?

When we say that you should take an evidence-based approach to human resource management, you probably sense that doing so is similar to taking a scientific approach. If so, you would be right, and so we should look briefly at what "science" means.

When most people hear the word "science," probably the first thing that springs to mind is subject matter such as physics, biology, geology, and psychology. (That's probably why, when most people think of "science," it also conjures up visions of people in labs, hunched over chemicals.) But while all of these are indeed "sciences," science is something more. Stripped to its essentials, science is a way of going about doing something—in other words, a methodology. However, it is a very special methodology. As that scientist in the lab knows, the methodology of science has some very strict ground rules, and it's these ground rules that make the scientific method so special.

The Ground Rules of Science

In brief, the ground rules of science include *objectivity, experimentation, quantification, explanation, prediction,* and *replication*. In gathering his or her evidence, the scientist needs to be *objective*, or there's no way to trust his or her conclusions. (For example, a medical school recently disciplined several of its professors. These doctors had failed to reveal that they were on the payroll of the drug company who supplied the drugs—the results of which the doctors were studying.)

Scientists also ply their trade through *experimentation*. Basically, an experiment is a test the scientist sets up in such a way as to ensure (to the extent possible) that he or she understands the reasons for the results that he or she obtains. (For example, our scientist would want to make sure that mixing, say, two chemicals caused his or her results, rather than some third chemical that unknowingly slipped into the test tube.) In conducting his or her experiment, the scientist will typically follow four steps.

1. Setting up a *hypothesis* (a tentative explanation of what to expect, usually based on prior theories and observations).
2. Developing a *method* for testing the hypothesis (most importantly, a method that helps ensure that extraneous explanations such as contaminants can't confuse the experiment's results).
3. Gathering the *data* (which means actually making the observations and measuring what you find). And finally,
4. Drawing *conclusions* based on the findings.

You can see then that scientists also usually ply their trade through *quantification.* Quantification means that they measure, or assign numerical values to, the phenomenon that they're studying. They need evidence.

The dual aims of science are *explanation* and *prediction.* In particular, the point of being scientific is to help you to make predictions—in other words, anticipate a particular outcome. (For example, you own a small business and a vendor suggests that you pay her $10,000 per year to use a personnel test to identify high-potential sales candidates. You conduct a study [we'll explain how in Chapter 5]. You conclude that by using that test, you can predict with high accuracy which candidates will succeed. How many extra sales will that produce? You decide based on the evidence that the $10,000 would be well spent.) Hopefully, your study will also help you *explain* your results, in other words to answer, "Why." For example, "This test identifies people who are highly self-confident, and that's a trait you need to be a great salesperson in my business."

Finally, scientific endeavors are subject to *replication,* which means the ability to repeat or duplicate your findings. If you are the only person who can get those results with your study, there's reason for all to be skeptical about your conclusions. So, to sum up, science is a methodology or way of doing things characterized by *objectivity, experimentation, quantification, explanation, prediction,* and *replication.*

Why Should a Manager Be Scientific?

For managers, the key point of being "scientific" is to make sure you maintain a sense of skepticism, by always questioning and measuring what you hear, read, and do at work. You want to be sure, "What is the cause, and what is the effect?" The problem is that *things aren't always as they appear,* and what's "*intuitively obvious*" can be misleading. You even have to question your *experts.* (Recall the opening vignette from Chapter 1, which implied that good staffing practices reduced the Stanford Restaurant's turnover, but with little in the way of evidence.) Opportunities to err are always there. "Will buying that new machine really save $20,000? What's the evidence?" "Is this incentive plan really boosting sales?" "We've spent $40,000 in the past 5 years on our tuition-refund plan; what (if anything) did we get out of it?" "Joe says Mike caused the machine to fail; was it really him?" And (focusing specifically on HR), just how effective *are* our human resource management activities? How does what we spend on human resource management compare to our competitors? How can we change our human resource practices to boost company-wide productivity? We'll turn to this next.

CONDUCTING THE HUMAN RESOURCE MANAGEMENT AUDIT

What Are HR Audits?

Within the human resource management area, numbers-based analyses often start with HR managers conducting *human resource audits* of all or part of their operations. One practitioner describes an **HR audit** as an analysis by which an organization measures where it currently stands and determines what it has to accomplish to improve its HR function.[39]

Types of HR Audits

Most such audits involve reviewing all or most aspects of the company's human resource function, usually by using a checklist.[40] However, the situation may require one or more specialized audits, too.[41] These may include the following:

1. **Compliance audits**—in particular, how well are we complying with relevant laws and regulations?
2. **Best practices audits**—in particular, how do our recruitment practices, hiring practices, and so on compare to those of "best practices" companies?
3. **Strategic audits**—in particular, are our human resource management practices helping us to achieve our strategic goals, by fostering the required employee behaviors?

4. **Function specific audits**—audits here concentrate on one or more specific human resource management areas, such as compensation, or training and development.

Many employers conduct these audits routinely, say every 2 to 3 years. On the other hand, problems or issues may prompt the manager to conduct an unscheduled audit. Illustrative problems or questions here might include the following: Are we administering our human resource management function as productively as we might be? Are best practice companies employing best HR practices we might benefit from? Did our key human resource projects or initiatives last year produce the results we intended? What improvements can we institute within HR to reduce costs while improving the value HR adds to our company? Are there any persistent safety and health issues we may need to address? Are their issues such as low morale or poor performance that might respond to improved HR practices?[42]

Legal compliance requires auditing. With respect to employment law compliance, most problem areas (also known as lawsuits) involve a handful of sources.[43] These include:

- Hiring (including job descriptions and application forms)
- Performance evaluations
- Employee discipline (evidence, rules, procedures)
- Terminations (proper warnings, and so on)
- Miscalculation of exempt and nonexempt jobs
- Inadequate personnel files, including performance documentation
- Inadequate time records (for instance, plant personnel improperly checking in early)
- Insufficient documentation (for instance, missing I-9 forms)

The HR Audit Process

In conducting an HR audit, the basic approach is to use a checklist-type questionnaire. The team may also interview selected HR employees, and managers in other (non-HR) areas, to better assess the human resource function's effectiveness.

We can summarize the basic audit process as follows:[44]

1. **Decide on the scope of the audit.** For example, will we focus on all HR functions, or just on one or two, or perhaps just on legal compliance issues?
2. **Draft an audit team.** Identify the members of the HR audit team, who the leaders are, and who the team reports to.
3. **Compile the checklists and other tools that are available.** For example, what do we now have in terms of internal checklists or other materials, and checklists from corporate counsel? What packaged software HR audit checklist programs are available?
4. **Know your budget.** Familiarize yourself with the audit's likely costs, and ascertain the budget before moving too far ahead.
5. **Consider the legalities.** Understand that what you unearth during the HR audit may be discoverable by opposing counsel in the event of a lawsuit. At a minimum, discuss the proposed audit with attorneys.
6. **Get top management support.** Top management needs to be committed to the audit and to remedying any problems.

HR audit
An analysis by which an organization measures where it currently stands and determines what it has to accomplish to improve its HR function.

7. **Develop the audit checklist.** From various sources, including internal company checklists, packaged software programs, and reviews of other firms' best practices, have the audit team create an audit questionnaire. This is usually a series of checklists. The team will use these to guide them in reviewing the areas they're about to audit. (For example, one checklist may cover what items should and should not be in the personnel file.)[45]
8. **Use the questionnaire to collect the data** about the company and its HR practices.
9. **Benchmark the findings** by comparing them with human resource benchmark standards.
10. **Provide feedback** about the results to senior management.
11. **Create action plans** aimed at improving areas the audit singles out.

Illustrative HR Audit Checklist Items In practice, many employers use off-the-shelf checklists from an HR audit software package to conduct the audit, at least for the legal compliance questions. The accompanying image illustrates one example.[46]

Source: www.blr.com/product.cfm/product/30519900, accessed May 2, 2008.

Three illustrative sets of HR audit checklist areas and checklist items would include the following:

Personnel Files Do our files contain information including resumes and applications, offer letters, job descriptions, performance evaluations, benefit enrollment forms, payroll change notices and/or documentation related to personnel actions, documents regarding performance issues, employee handbook acknowledgements, Form I-9, medical information (related to a medical leave of absence or FMLA leave), and workers' compensation information?[47]

Wage and Hour Compliance Is our time record-keeping process in compliance with state and federal law (for instance check-in/checkout no more then 3 minutes before starting/stopping work)? Do we conduct a random audit of timecards to ensure that practices are as they should be?[48]

Headcount How many employees are currently on staff? How many employees of these are

Regular
Probationary
Temporary
Full Time
Part Time
Exempt
Nonexempt[49]

HR METRICS AND BENCHMARKING

Whether you are conducting an HR audit or simply gathering evidence to ascertain, say, if your training efforts are paying off, you will probably want to *benchmark*—compare your results to those of comparable companies. Many private human resource management consulting firms (such as Hewitt Associates) compile and offer such comparables data, as does the Society of Human Resource Management. We'll discuss in this section various types of HR metrics, benchmarks, and HR measurement systems.[50]

Types of Metrics Metrics are the fundamental financial and nonfinancial measures you will use to assess your unit's status and progress. Employment-related metrics range from broad, overall organizational measures down to ones that focus narrowly on specific human resource management functions and activities.

Figures 3A-1 and 3A-2 contain examples of broader measures. Figure 3A-1 gives an overall sense for how efficient an employer's human resource unit is. For example, a company with about 300 employees should have (at the median) just under 1 (0.94) HR employee per company employee.

Figure 3A-2 gives a quick impression of how productive the company is—in this case, in terms of sales per full-time equivalent employee (two part-timers might equal one full-time equivalent employee, for instance). Thus, *sales per employee* provides a rough but useful first approximation for how the company is doing. If, say, the typical Office Depot was generating $90,000 per employee, while Staples was generating significantly less, it would prompt questions at Staples like, "Are we overstaffed at headquarters?" "Do we have too many employee per store?" and "Can we do anything (like more training, or incentives) to boost sales per Staples employee?"

Figures 3A-3 and 3A-4 illustrate more narrowly focused human resource management metrics. Figure 3A-3 shows target executive bonus percentages for different-size companies. For example, for a firm with about 200 employees, the median executive bonus is about 14% of the executive's compensation. Figure 3A-4 summarizes several typical HR metrics. These include absence rate, cost per hire, and health care costs per employee.[51]

Benchmarking in Action As you can see, metrics are rarely useful by themselves. Whether it is HR metrics, financial ratios, or some other, managers generally want to "know how we're doing" in relation to something. That "something" may be historical company figures or benchmark-able (i.e., comparable) figures from other companies.[52]

SHRM provides a customized benchmarking service; this enables employers to compare their HR-related metric results with other companies (see Figure 3A-5). It provides benchmark figures for various industries including construction and mining, educational services, finance, manufacturing, and numerous others. The employer can request the comparable figures not just by industry, but broken down by employee size, company revenue, industry sectors, and geographic region (see http://shrm.org/research/benchmarks).

FIGURE 3A-1 HR-to-Employee Ratios (by Organizational Size)

Source: SHRM Human Capital Benchmarking Study: 2007 Executive Summary.

Organizational Size	n	25th Percentile	Median	75th Percentile
Total	751	0.73	1.12	1.88
Fewer than 100	209	1.52	2.41	3.45
100 to 249	230	0.74	1.00	1.65
250 to 499	100	0.67	0.94	1.32
500 to 999	55	0.60	0.83	1.27
1,000 to 2,499	76	0.50	0.79	1.04
2,500 to 7,499	57	0.40	0.72	1.19
7,500 or more	24	0.36	0.72	1.06

FIGURE 3A-2 Revenue per FTE (by Industry)

Note: Industries with fewer than 10 organizations were omitted from the table. They were agriculture, forestry, fishing and hunting; insurance; real estate; and utilities.

Source: SHRM Human Capital Benchmarking Study: 2007 Executive Summary.

	n	25th Percentile	Median	75th Percentile
All industries	828	$ 88,497	$200,000	$539,087
Accommodations, food and drinking places	34	$ 43,478	$ 72,140	$400,000
Biotechnology	10	$ 90,909	$267,857	$448,430
Construction, mining, oil and gas	31	$125,000	$274,725	$555,556
Educational services	17	$ 73,171	$150,000	$261,216
Finance	30	$ 38,462	$155,956	$904,762
Government	34	$125,000	$241,270	$564,972
Health care services	71	$ 71,429	$140,167	$448,430
High-tech	55	$ 97,959	$208,421	$787,402
Manufacturing (durable goods)	95	$146,990	$264,368	$625,000
Manufacturing (nondurable goods)	44	$153,406	$287,088	$603,198
Publishing and broadcasting	22	$ 94,076	$166,667	$518,129
Pharmaceutical	12	$ 70,378	$312,927	$792,398
Retail trade	58	$111,111	$311,741	$614,704
Services (nonprofit)	70	$ 67,692	$128,606	$425,532
Services (profit)	161	$100,000	$200,000	$535,714
Telecommunications	16	$ 92,151	$112,401	$431,115
Transportation and warehousing	29	$ 90,909	$358,852	$600,000
Government agency (all industries)	40	$ 80,179	$239,048	$508,444
Nonprofit organization (all industries)	136	$ 68,934	$123,833	$394,560
Privately owned for-profit organization (all industries)	444	$107,787	$236,255	$655,914
Publicly owned for-profit organization (all industries)	206	$ 66,667	$195,890	$460,829

Figures 3A-6 and 3A-7 illustrate two of the many sets of comparable benchmark measures the SHRM survey benchmark service would provide to a specific employer who uses its service. Figure 3A-6 shows HR expense data—in this case, HR expenses, HR expenses to operating expenses, and HR expenses per full-time employee for firms comparable to this client. Figure 3A-7 shows important recruitment performance benchmarks, such as time (required) to fill open positions, and cost per hire.

FIGURE 3A-3 2007 Target Bonus Percentage for Executives (Percent of Total Compensation, by Organizational Size)

Source: SHRM Human Capital Benchmarking Study: 2007 Executive Summary.

	n	25th Percentile	Median	75th Percentile
All sizes	319	10%	18%	30%
Fewer than 100	78	8%	15%	25%
100 to 249	99	7%	14%	20%
250 to 499	38	15%	23%	30%
500 to 999	24	13%	20%	30%
1,000 to 2,499	33	11%	23%	30%
2,500 to 7,499	31	20%	25%	40%
7,500 or more	16	18%	28%	40%

HR Metrics

Absence Rate	[(# days absent in month) ÷ (Ave. # of employees during mo.) × (# of workdays)] × 100	Measures absenteeism. Determine whether your company has an absenteeism problem. Analyze why and how to address issue. Analyze further for effectiveness of attendance policy and effectiveness of management in applying policy. See white paper titled *Absenteeism: Analyzing Work Absences.*
Cost per Hire	(Advertising + Agency fees + Employee referrals + Travel cost of applicants and staff + Relocation costs + Recruiter pay and benefits) ÷ Number of hires	Costs involved with a new hire. Use *EMA/Cost per Hire Staffing Metrics Survey* as a benchmark for your organization. Can be used as a measurement to show any substantial improvements to savings in recruitment/retention costs. Determine what your recruiting function can do to increase savings/reduce costs, etc.
Health Care Costs per Employee	Total cost of health care ÷ Total employees	Per capita cost of employee benefits. Indicates cost of health care per employee. See BLS's publications titled *Employer Costs for Employee Compensation* and *Measuring Trends in the Structure and Levels of Employer Costs for Employee Compensation* for additional information on this topic.
HR Expense Factor	HR expense ÷ Total operating expense	HR expenses in relation to the total operating expenses of organization. In addition, determine if expenditures exceeded, met, or fell below budget. Analyze HR practices that contributed to savings, if any.
Human Capital ROI	Revenue − (Operating expense − [Compensation cost + Benefit cost]) ÷ (Compensation cost + Benefit cost)	Return on investment ratio for employees. Did organization get a return on their investment? Analyze causes of positive/negative ROI metric. Use analysis as opportunity to optimize investment with HR practices such as recruitment, motivation, training, and development. Evaluate whether HR practices are having a causal relationship in positive changes to improving metric.

FIGURE 3A-4 Sample Metrics from SHRM Measurements Library
Source: SHRM, http://shrm.org.

FIGURE 3A-5 Highlights of SHRM® Customized Benchmarking Service
Source: SHRM, www.shrm.org/research/benchmarks.

CUSTOMIZED BY INDUSTRY/EMPLOYEE SIZE/REVENUE SIZE/GEORGRAPHIC REGION/GOVERNMENT/FOR-PROFIT/NONPROFIT/PUBLIC/PRIVATE . . . PLUS MORE

Fill the gap between expensive benchmarking services and going it alone with SHRM's affordable, high-quality customized benchmarking reports.

- Justify additional HR staff
- Defend recruiting and HR budgets
- Make the case for better 401(k) matching
- Devise competitive health care plans
- Brief board members about return on investment
- Conduct due diligence for mergers, reorganizations, and acquisitions

Whether your company size is 50 employees, 10,000, or more, we will help you choose a customized report that compares your organization's key benchmarks with similar organizations. In just days, you will receive your benchmarking report, along with guidelines on how to understand and use the data, definitions, and metric calculations.

- Database of more than 3,000 organizations
- Customize based on two cuts of the data (industry, employee size or other cuts)
- *More than 100 benchmarks!*

    Health Care
    Retirement
    Employment
    HR Expenses
    Disability & Life Insurance

(*continued*)

FIGURE 3A-5 *(continued)*

Turnover
and coming soon:
HR Staff Salaries

- SHRM member price:
  From $245
- Receive up to 21 SPHR/PHR recertification credits

CHECK OUR WEB SITE FOR A LISTING OF ALL THE CUSTOMIZABLE BENCHMARKS YOU CAN RECEIVE.

FIGURE 3A-6 SHRM Customized Human Capital Benchmarking Report for [Your Organization's Name Here]

Source: SHRM Human Capital Benchmarking Study: 2007.

HR Expense Data			
	2006 HR Expenses	2006 HR Expense to Operating Expenses	2006 HR Expense per FTE
n	12	11	12
25th percentile	$320,000	5.15%	$1,358
Median	$548,215	12.86%	$2,044
75th percentile	$700,000	16.67%	$3,550
Average	$533,421	12.66%	$2,341

FIGURE 3A-7 SHRM Customized Human Capital Benchmarking Report for [Your Organization's Name Here]

Source: SHRM Human Capital Benchmarking Study: 2007.

Employment Data						
	2006 Number of Positions Filled	2006 Time-to-Fill	2006 Cost-per- Hire	2006 Annual Turnover Overall Rate	2006 Annual Voluntary Turnover Rate	2006 Annual Involuntary Turnover Rate
n	16	16	14	16	14	16
25th Percentile	35	27 days	$1,000	5%	5%	1%
Median	48	55 days	$3,050	18%	18%	4%
75th Percentile	97	60 days	$7,000	20%	20%	9%
Average	65	47 days	$3,918	16%	16%	5%

Part I Video Cases Appendix

Video 1: Introduction to Human Resource Management and Strategic Human Resource Management

VIDEO TITLE: SHOWTIME

Showtime Networks operates cable networks and pay-per-view cable channels across the United States and in several countries abroad. As this video illustrates, its HR function supports corporate strategy by helping to determine what kind of employees are needed to keep the company in peak performance, and then by providing the company and its employees with the HR activities that these employees need to do their jobs. For example, you'll see that Showtime offers many development and training programs, as well as personal development–type activities including mentoring programs and career-oriented development activities. The firm's performance management process (which the employees helped develop) focuses specifically on the work activities and results that help achieve departmental and corporate goals. In this video, Matthew, the firm's CEO, emphasizes that it's essential to use human resources as a strategic partner, and the video then goes on to provide something of a summary of the basic human resource management functions.

Discussion Questions

1. What concrete evidence do you see in this video that HR at Showtime helps the company achieve its strategic goals?
2. What specific HR functions does the video mention, at least in passing?
3. Why do you think management at Showtime places such a heavy emphasis on personal development and quality of work issues such as open-door policies, mentoring programs, and allowing employees to swap jobs?

Video 2: Managing Equal Opportunity and Diversity

VIDEO TITLE: IQ SOLUTIONS

IQ Solutions is in the business of providing health care system services. It says one of its aims is lessening the inequality that they say exists in America's health care system, and the company uses its very diverse employee base to better serve and attract a broad client base. Employees at IQ Solutions work together in teams to achieve the company's goals. As we see in this video, the company itself is indeed very diverse: for example, employees speak about 18 languages. The company capitalizes on this diversity in many ways. For example, they let their employees share their ethnically unique holidays, and provide special training and other benefits that support diversity.

Discussion Questions

1. To what extent does diversity management at IQ Solutions contribute to the company achieving its strategic goals?
2. Based upon what you read in this part of the book, which diversity management programs can you identify in use at IQ Solutions?

ENDNOTES

1. See, for example, Gary Latham and Gary Yukl, "A Review of Research on the Application of Goal Setting in Organizations," *Academy of Management Journal* 18, no. 4 (1964), p. 824. See also Gary Latham and Terrence A. Mitchell, "Importance of Participative Goal Setting and Anticipated Rewards on Goal Difficulty and Job Performance," *Journal of Applied Psychology* 63 (1978), pp. 163–171; Sandra Hart, William Moncrief, and A. Parasuraman, "An Empirical Investigation of Sales People's Performance, Effort, and Selling Method During a Sales Contest," *Journal of the Academy of Marketing Science*, Winter 1989, pp. 29–39.
2. See, for example, Fred David, *Strategic Management* (Upper Saddle River, NJ: Prentice Hall, 2007), p. 11.
3. Tony Bingham and Pat Galagan, "Doing Good While Doing Well," *Training & Development*, June 2008, p. 33.
4. www.checkmateplan.com, accessed April 24, 2009.
5. www.pepsico.com/PEP_Company/Overview, accessed December 7, 2007.
6. Paul Nutt, "Making Strategic Choices," *Journal of Management Studies*, January 2002, pp. 67–96.
7. Michael Porter, *Competitive Strategy* (New York: The Free Press, 1980), p. 14.
8. Samuel Greengard, "You're Next! There's No Escaping Merger Mania!" *Workforce*, April 1997, pp. 52–62. The extent to which top executives rely on HR managers to support their strategic planning efforts is a matter of debate. Many employers still view HR managers mostly as strategy executors. On the other hand, a recent study found that 71% of the management teams do see HR as a "strategic player." See Patrick Kiger, "Survey: HR Still Battling for Leaders' Respect," *Workforce Management*, December 15, 2008, p. 8. See also E. E., Lawler, et. al., "What Makes HR a Strategic Partner?," *People & Strategy* 32, no. 1 (2009), p. 14.
9. SHRM Research, "Offshoring," *Workplace Visions*, no. 2 (2004), p. 1.
10. Ibid, p. 7.
11. Arthur Yeung, "Setting Up for Success: How the Portman Ritz-Carlton Hotel Gets the Best from Its People," *Human Resource Management* 45, no. 2 (Summer 2006), pp. 67–75.
12. See, for example, Evan Offstein, Devi Gnyawali, and Anthony Cobb, "A Strategic Human Resource Perspective of Firm Competitive Behavior," *Human Resource Management Review* 15 (2005), pp. 305–318.
13. "Automation Improves Retailer's Hiring Efficiency and Quality," *HR Focus* 82, no. 2 (February 2005), p. 3.
14. Bou-Wen Lin et al., "Mergers and Acquisitions as a Human Resource Strategy," *International Journal of Manpower* 27, no. 2 (2006), p. 127.
15. Andy Cook, "Make Sure You Get a Prenup," *European Venture Capital Journal*, December/January 2007, p. 76. See http://www.accessmylibrary.com/coms2/summary_0286-29140938_ITM, accessed June 29, 2009.

16. Quoted in Bou-Wen Lin et al., "Mergers and Acquisitions as a Human Resource Strategy," *International Journal of Manpower* 27, no. 2 (2006), pp. 129–130.
17. www.towersPerrin.com, accessed December 4, 2007.
18. Ibid.
19. Jeffrey Schmidt, "The Correct Spelling of M&A Begins with HR," *HR Magazine*, June 2001, pp. 102–108. See also Wendy Boswell, "Aligning Employees with the Organization's Strategic Objectives: Out of Line of Sight, Out of Mind," *International Journal of Human Resource Management* 17, no. 9 (September 2006), pp. 1014–1041.
20. "Mergers & Acquisitions: Managing the HR issues," *The M&A Spotlight*, January 1, 2007.
21. Leah Carlson, "Smooth Transition: HR Input Can Prevent Benefits Blunders During M&As," *Employee Benefit News*, June 1, 2005.
22. www.towersPerrin.com, accessed December 4, 2007. See also Ingmar Bjorkman, "The HR Function in Large-Scale Mergers and Acquisitions: The Case of Nordea," *Personnel Review* 35, no. 6 (2006), pp. 654–671; and Elina Antila and Anne Kakkonen, "Factors Affecting the Role of HR Managers in International Mergers and Acquisitions: A Multiple Case Study," *Personnel Review* 37, no. 3 (2008), pp. 280–299.
23. This is paraphrased or quoted from "HR Services, Service Offerings: Mergers, Acquisitions and Restructuring," www.towersPerrin.com, accessed December 4, 2007.
24. "Mergers & Acquisitions: Managing the HR Issues," *The M&A Spotlight*, January 1, 2007.
25. Ibid. See also Ruth Bramson, "HR's Role in Mergers and Acquisitions," www.findarticles.com, accessed November 5, 2009.
26. When focusing on HR activities, managers call this an "HR Scorecard." When applying the same process broadly to all the company's activities, including, for example, sales, production, and finance, managers call it the "balanced scorecard process."
27. The idea for the HR Scorecard derives from a broader measurement tool managers call the "balanced scorecard." This does for the company as a whole what the HR Scorecard does for HR, summarizing instead the impact of various functions including HRM, sales, production, and distribution. The "balanced" in balanced scorecard refers to a balance of goals—financial and nonfinancial.
28. www.activestrategy.com/solutions/strategy_mapping.aspx, accessed March 24, 2009.
29. Richard Shafer et al., "Crafting a Human Resource Strategy to Foster Organizational Agility: A Case Study," *Human Resource Management* 40, no. 3 (Fall 2001), pp. 197–211.
30. "With High-Performance Work Organizations, Adversaries No More," *Work & Family Newsbrief*, August 2003, p. 5. See also Karen Kroll, "Repurposing Metrics for HR," *HR Magazine* 51, no. 7 (July 2006), www.SHRM.org/HR magazine/articles, accessed February 4, 2008.
31. See, for example, www.personneltoday.com/blogs/hcglobal-human-capital-management/2009/02/theres-no-such-thing-as-eviden.html, accessed April 18, 2009.
32. Robert McNabb and Keith Whitfield, "Job Evaluation and High-Performance Work Practices: Compatible or Conflictual?" *Journal of Management Studies* 38, no. 2 (March 2001), p. 294.
33. See, for example, John Sullivan, "The Last Word," *Workforce Management*, November 19, 2007, p. 42.
34. Alexander Colvin et al., "How High-Performance Human Resource Practices and Workforce Unionization Affect Managerial Pay," *Personnel Psychology* 54 (2001), pp. 903–934.
35. Kamal Birdi, Chris Clegg, Malcolm Patterson, Andrew Robinson, Chris Stride, Toby Wall, and Steven Wood, "The Impact of Human Resource and Operational Management Practices on Company Productivity: A Longitudinal Study," *Personnel Psychology* 61 (2008), pp. 467–501. In fact, these researchers concluded that worker empowerment, teamwork, and training had much greater effects on employee and company performance than did the sorts of manufacturing initiatives such as quality management, just-in-time, supply chain partnering, and advanced manufacturing technology that companies often institute in efforts to improve productivity and performance.
36. This section is adapted in part from Brian Becker, Mark Huselid, and Dave Ulrich, *The HR Scorecard: Linking People, Strategy, and Performance* (Boston: Harvard Business School Press, 2001).
37. Arthur Thompson Jr. and A. J. Strickland III, *Strategic Management: Concepts and Cases* (New York: McGraw-Hill, 2001), pp. 129–131.
38. See, for example, www.personneltoday.com/blogs/hcglobal-human-capital-management/2009/02/theres-no-such-thing-as-eviden.html, accessed April 18, 2009.
39. Lin Grensing-Pophal, "HR Audits: Know the Market, Land Assignments," SHRM Consultants Forum (December 2004), http://moss07.shrm.org/hrdisciplines/consultants/Articles/Pages/CMS_010705.aspx, accessed February 2, 2008.
40. Bill Coy, "Introduction to the Human Resources Audit," La Piana Associates, Inc., www.lapiana.org/consulting, accessed May 1, 2008.
41. The following is based on Teresa Daniel, "HR Compliance Audits: 'Just Nice' or Really Necessary?" SHRM White Paper (November 2004), http://moss07.shrm.org/Research/Articles/Articles/Pages/CMS_010198.aspx, accessed February 2, 2008.
42. See, for example, Dana R. Scott, "Take the Time to Audit Your Human Resources Practices," *New Hampshire Business Review*, August 17, 2007.
43. Teresa Daniel, "HR Compliance Audits: 'Just Nice' or Really Necessary?" SHRM White Paper (November 2004), http://moss07.shrm.org/Research/Articles/Articles/Pages/CMS_010198.aspx, accessed February 2, 2008. See also Dana Scott, "Conducting a Human Resources Audit," *New Hampshire Business Review*, August 2007.
44. See Teresa Daniel, op. cit.; Dana Scott, op. cit.; "Start Your HR Audit with This Checklist," *HR Focus* 84, no. 6 (June 2007), pp. 1, 11, 13–15; and Bill Coy, "Introduction to the Human Resources Audit," La Piana Associates, Inc., www.lapiana.org/consulting, accessed May 1, 2008.
45. For additional detailed information on conducting HR audits, see, for example, http://SHRM.org/HR tools/toolkits_published, accessed February 2, 2008.
46. http://www.blr.com/product.cfm/product/30519900, accessed May 2, 2008.
47. Dana Scott, "Conducting a Human Resources Audit," *New Hampshire Business Review*, August 2007.
48. Ibid.
49. Bill Coy, "Introduction to the Human Resources Audit," La Piana Associates, Inc., www.lapiana.org/consulting, accessed May 1, 2008.

50. See, for example, "Using HR Performance Metrics to Optimize Operations and Profits," *PR Newswire,* February 27, 2008; and "How to 'Make Over' Your HR Metrics," *HR Focus* 84, no. 9 (September 2007), p. 3.

51. For additional information on HR metrics, see, for example, Karen M. Kroll, "Repurposing Metrics for HR: HR Professionals Are Looking Through a People-Focused Lens at the CFO's Metrics on Revenue and Income per FTE," *HR Magazine* 51, no. 7 (July 2006), p. 64(6); and http://shrm.org/metrics/library_published over/measurement systems_TOC.asp, accessed February 2, 2008.

52. See, for example, "Benchmarking for Functional HR Metrics," *HR Focus* 83, no. 11 (November 2006), p. 1.

4 Job Analysis

When Daimler opened its Mercedes Benz assembly plant in Alabama, its managers faced a dilemma. They could not hire, train, or pay the plant employees unless the managers knew what each employee was expected to do—they needed, for each person, a list of job duties, a "job description." But in this plant, self-managing teams of employees would assemble the vehicles, and their jobs and duties might change every day. How do you list job duties when the duties are a moving target?[1]

Source: Courtesy of Jim West/Alamy Images.

WHERE ARE WE NOW . . .

The human resource management process really begins with deciding what the job entails. Therefore, we now embark on the details of human resource management. The main purpose of this chapter is to show you how to analyze a job and write job descriptions. We'll see that analyzing jobs involves determining in detail what the job entails and what kind of people the firm should hire for the job. We discuss several techniques for analyzing jobs, and explain how to draft job descriptions and job specifications. Then, in Chapter 5 (Personnel Planning and Recruiting), we'll turn to the methods managers use to actually find the employees they need.

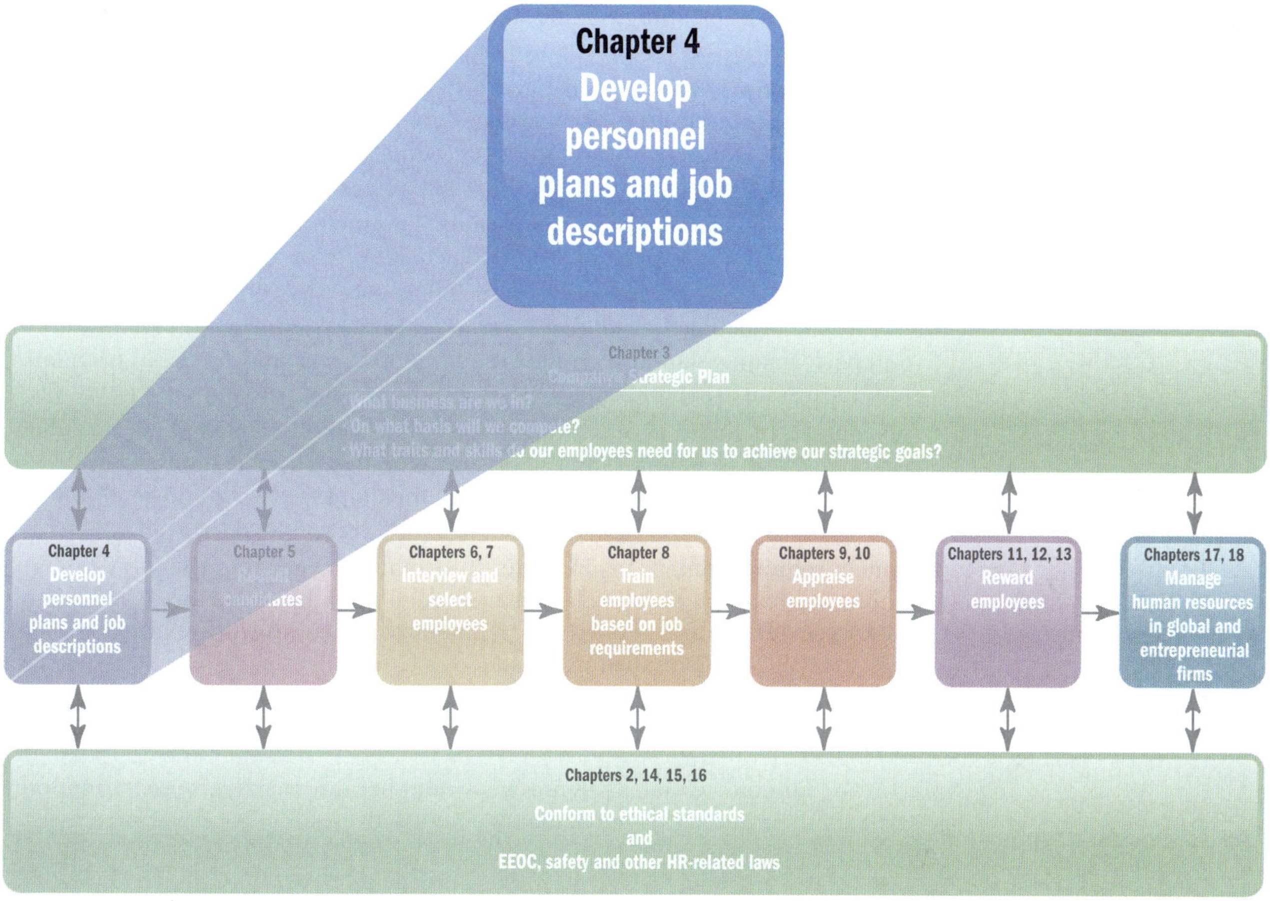

LEARNING OUTCOMES

1. Discuss the nature of job analysis, including what it is and how it's used.
2. Use at least three methods of collecting job analysis information, including interviews, questionnaires, and observation.
3. Write job descriptions, including summaries and job functions, using the Internet and traditional methods.
4. Write a job specification.
5. Explain job analysis in a "worker-empowered" world, including what it means and how it's done in practice.

1 Discuss the nature of job analysis, including what it is and how it's used.

THE BASICS OF JOB ANALYSIS

Organizations consist of jobs that have to be staffed. **Job analysis** is the procedure through which you determine the duties of these positions and the characteristics of the people to hire for them.[2] Job analysis produces information for writing **job descriptions** (a list of what the job entails) and **job specifications** (what kind of people to hire for the job). We'll see in a moment that every manager should understand the mechanics of analyzing jobs. Virtually every personnel-related action you take—interviewing applicants, and training and appraising employees, for instance—depends on knowing what the job entails and what human traits one needs to do the job well.[3]

The supervisor or human resources specialist normally collects one or more of the following types of information via the job analysis:

- **Work activities.** First, he or she collects information about the job's actual work activities, such as cleaning, selling, teaching, or painting. This list may also include how, why, and when the worker performs each activity.
- **Human behaviors.** The specialist may also collect information about human behaviors the job requires, like sensing, communicating, deciding, and writing. Included here would be information regarding job demands such as lifting weights or walking long distances.
- **Machines, tools, equipment, and work aids.** This includes information regarding tools used, materials processed, knowledge dealt with or applied (such as finance or law), and services rendered (such as counseling or repairing).
- **Performance standards.** The employer may also want information about the job's performance standards (in terms of quantity or quality levels for each job duty, for instance). Management will use these standards to appraise employees.
- **Job context.** Included here is information about such matters as physical working conditions, work schedule, and the organizational and social context—for instance, the number of people with whom the employee would normally interact. Information regarding incentives might also be included here.
- **Human requirements.** This includes information regarding the job's human requirements, such as job-related knowledge or skills (education, training, work experience) and required personal attributes (aptitudes, physical characteristics, personality, interests).

Uses of Job Analysis Information

As Figure 4-1 summarizes, job analysis is important because managers use it to support just about all their human resource management activities.

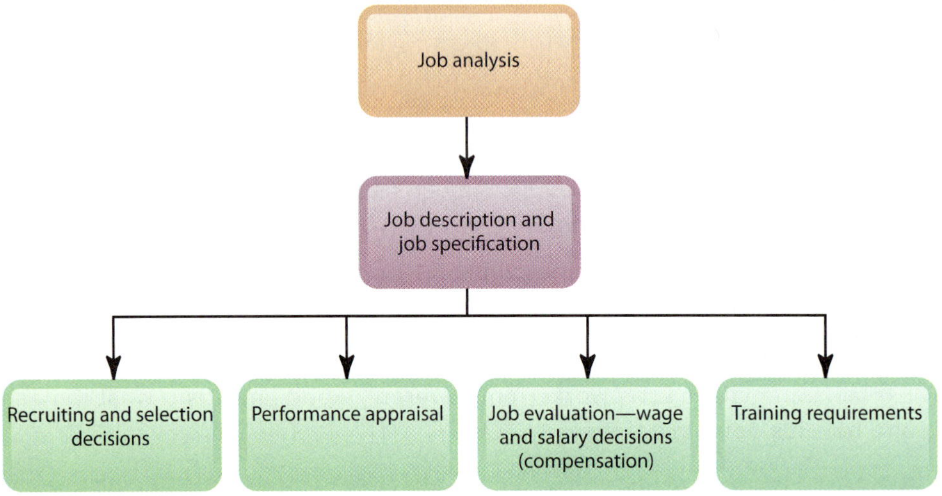

FIGURE 4-1 Uses of Job Analysis Information

Recruitment and Selection Job analysis provides information about what duties the job entails and what human characteristics are required to perform these activities. This information, in the form of job descriptions and specifications, helps managers decide what sort of people to recruit and hire.

Compensation Compensation (such as salary and bonus) usually depends on the job's required skill and education level, safety hazards, degree of responsibility, and so on—all factors you assess through job analysis. Furthermore, many employers group jobs into classes (say, secretary III and IV) for pay purposes. Job analysis provides the information to determine the relative worth of each job—and thus its appropriate class.

Training The job description lists the job's specific duties and requisite skills—and therefore the training—that the job requires.

Performance Appraisal A performance appraisal compares each employee's actual performance with his or her performance standards. Doing so requires knowledge of the job's duties and standards. Managers use job analysis to learn what these duties and standards are.

Discovering Unassigned Duties Job analysis can also help reveal unassigned duties. For example, your company's production manager says she's responsible for a dozen or so duties, such as production scheduling and raw material purchasing. Missing, however, is managing raw material inventories. On further study, you learn that none of the other manufacturing people are responsible for inventory management, either. You've uncovered an essential unassigned duty, thanks to job analysis.

EEO Compliance Job analysis plays a big role in EEO compliance. U.S. Federal Agencies' Uniform Guidelines on Employee Selection stipulate that job analysis is a crucial step in validating all major human resources activities.[4] For example, to comply with the Americans with Disabilities Act, employers should know each job's essential job functions—which in turn requires a job analysis.

Steps in Job Analysis

There are six steps in doing a job analysis. Let's look at each of them.

Step 1: Decide how you'll use the information, since this will determine the data you collect and how you collect them. Some data collection techniques—like interviewing the employee and asking what the job entails—are good for writing job descriptions and selecting employees for the job. Other techniques, like the position analysis questionnaire we describe later, do not provide qualitative information for job descriptions. Instead, they provide numerical ratings for each job; these can be used to compare jobs for compensation purposes.

Step 2: Review relevant background information such as organization charts, process charts, and job descriptions.[5] **Organization charts** show the organization-wide division of work, how the job in question relates to other jobs, and where the job fits in the overall organization. The chart should show the title of each position and, by means of interconnecting lines, who reports to whom and with whom the job incumbent communicates.

job analysis
The procedure for determining the duties and skill requirements of a job and the kind of person who should be hired for it.

job description
A list of a job's duties, responsibilities, reporting relationships, working conditions, and supervisory responsibilities—one product of a job analysis.

job specifications
A list of a job's "human requirements," that is, the requisite education, skills, personality, and so on—another product of a job analysis.

organization chart
A chart that shows the organization-wide distribution of work, with titles of each position and interconnecting lines that show who reports to and communicates with whom.

A **process chart** provides a more detailed picture of the work flow. In its simplest form a process chart (like that in Figure 4-2) shows the flow of inputs to and outputs from the job you're analyzing. (In Figure 4-2, the quality control clerk is expected to review components from suppliers, check components going to the plant managers, and give information regarding component's quality to these managers.) Finally, the existing job description, if there is one, usually provides a starting point for building the revised job description.

Step 3: Select representative positions. There may be too many similar jobs to analyze them all. For example, it is usually unnecessary to analyze the jobs of 200 assembly workers when a sample of 10 jobs will do.

Step 4: Actually analyze the job—by collecting data on job activities, required employee behaviors, working conditions, and human traits and abilities needed to perform the job. For this step, use one or more of the job analysis methods we'll explain in the next section of this chapter.

Step 5: Verify the job analysis information with the worker performing the job and with his or her immediate supervisor. This will help confirm that the information is factually correct and complete. This review can also help gain the employee's acceptance of the job analysis data and conclusions, by giving that person a chance to review and modify your description of the job activities.

Step 6: Develop a job description and job specification. These are two tangible products of the job analysis. The *job description* (to repeat) is a written statement that describes the activities and responsibilities of the job, as well as its important features, such as working conditions and safety - hazards. The *job specification* summarizes the personal qualities, traits, skills, and background required for getting the job done. It may be in a separate document or in the same document as the job description.

A Quicker Approach for Supervisors

Job analysis can be a time-consuming process. It might take a few days to interview five or six employees and their managers, and to explain to them the process and the reason for the analysis. The department manager wouldn't have the time for that. An abbreviated but still useful process would take just several hours. The steps might include:

1. Greet participants.
2. Briefly explain the job analysis process and the participants' roles in this process.
3. Spend about 15 minutes interviewing the employees to get agreement on a basic summary of the job.
4. Identify the job's broad areas of responsibility, such as "accounting" and "supervisory."

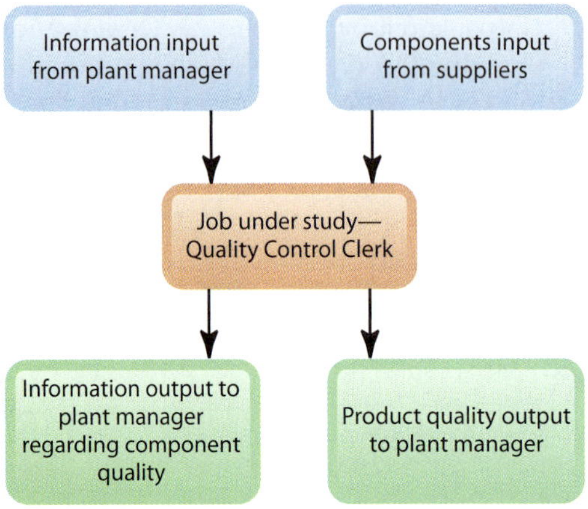

FIGURE 4-2 Process Chart for Analyzing a Job's Workflow

Source: Compensation Management: Rewarding Performance by Richard J. Henderson. Reprinted by permission of Pearson Education, Upper Saddle River, NJ.

5. Identify tasks within each area, using a flip chart interactively with the employees, or collaboration software.
6. Print the task list and get the group to sign off on it.[6]

Job Analysis Guidelines

Before actually analyzing the job, using one or more of the tools we turn to in the following section, keep four practical guidelines in mind.

- Make the job analysis a *joint effort by a human resources specialist, the worker, and the worker's supervisor.* The human resource manager might observe the worker doing the job, and have both the supervisor and worker fill out job questionnaires. Based on all that, the specialist lists the job's duties and required human traits. The supervisor and worker then review and verify the HR manager's list of the job's activities and duties.
- If there are several employees doing the same job in different departments, *collect job analysis information from employees in different departments,* not just one. The way someone with a particular job title spends his or her time is not necessarily the same from department to department.
- *Make sure the questions and process are clear* to the employees. (For example, some might not know what you mean when you ask about the job's "mental demands.") Catch problems early.
- *Use several different tools for the job analysis.* Generally try not to rely just on a questionnaire, for instance, but perhaps supplement your survey results with a short follow-up interview. (The problem is that each tool has potential drawbacks.) For example, in a group interview, some workers may feel pressure to go along with the group's consensus. It's therefore ideal to use several sources and/or tools. We'll turn to these tools next.

2 Use at least three methods of collecting job analysis information, including interviews, questionnaires, and observation.

METHODS FOR COLLECTING JOB ANALYSIS INFORMATION

There are various ways (interviews, or questionnaires, for instance) to collect information on a job's duties, responsibilities, and activities. We discuss the most important ones in this section.

In practice, you could use any one of them, or combine several. The basic rule is to use those that best fit your purpose. Thus, an interview might be best for creating a list of job duties and job description. The more quantitative position analysis questionnaire may be best for quantifying each job's relative worth for pay purposes.

Interviews, questionnaires, observations, and diary/logs are the most popular methods for gathering job analysis data. They all provide realistic information about what job incumbents actually do. Managers use these methods for developing job descriptions and job specifications.

The Interview

Job analysis interviews range from completely unstructured interviews ("Tell me about your job") to highly structured ones containing hundreds of specific items to check off.

Managers may conduct individual interviews with each employee, group interviews with groups of employees who have the same job, and/or supervisor

process chart
A work-flow chart that shows the flow of inputs to and outputs from a particular job.

Source: Courtesy of David Mager/Pearson Learning Photo Studio.

It is helpful to spend several minutes prior to collecting job analysis information explaining the process that you will be following.

interviews with one or more supervisors who know the job. They use group interviews when a large number of employees are performing similar or identical work, since it can be a quick and inexpensive way to gather information. As a rule, the workers' immediate supervisor attends the group session; if not, you can interview the supervisor separately to get that person's perspective on the job's duties and responsibilities.

Whichever kind of interview you use, you need to be sure the interviewee fully understands the reason for the interview. There's a tendency for workers to view such interviews, rightly or wrongly, as "efficiency evaluations." If so, interviewees may hesitate to describe their jobs accurately.

Typical Questions Some typical interview questions include the following:

What is the job being performed?

What are the major duties of your position? What exactly do you do?

What physical locations do you work in?

What are the education, experience, skill, and [where applicable] certification and licensing requirements?

In what activities do you participate?

What are the job's responsibilities and duties?

What are the basic accountabilities or performance standards that typify your work?

What are your responsibilities? What are the environmental and working conditions involved?

What are the job's physical demands? The emotional and mental demands?

What are the health and safety conditions?

Are you exposed to any hazards or unusual working conditions?

Structured Interviews You can also use a structured or checklist format to guide the interview. Figure 4-3 presents one example, in this case, a job analysis information sheet. It includes a series of questions regarding matters like the general purpose of the job; supervisory responsibilities; job duties; and education, experience, and skills required. Of course, structured lists are not just for interviews: Job analysts who collect information by personally observing the work or by using questionnaires—two methods explained later—can also use structured lists like these.[7] Figure 4-4 is a questionnaire intended for completing online.

Pros and Cons The interview's wide use reflects its advantages. It's a simple and quick way to collect information, including information that might not appear on a written form. For instance, a skilled interviewer can unearth important activities that occur only occasionally, or informal contacts that wouldn't be obvious from the organization chart. The interview also provides an opportunity to explain the need for and functions of the job analysis. The employee can also vent frustrations that might otherwise go unnoticed by management.

Distortion of information is the main problem—whether due to outright falsification or honest misunderstanding.[8] Job analysis is often a prelude to changing a job's pay rate. Employees therefore may legitimately view the interview as a sort of "efficiency evaluation" that may affect their pay. They may then tend to exaggerate certain responsibilities while minimizing others. In one study, researchers listed possible job duties either as simple task statements ("record phone messages and other routine information") or as ability statements ("ability to record phone

FIGURE 4-3 Job Analysis Questionnaire for Developing Job Descriptions

Source: www.hr.blr.com. Reprinted with permission of the publisher Business and Legal Resources, Inc., Old Saybrook, CT. BLR® (Business & Legal Resources, Inc.).

Job Analysis Information Sheet

Job Title____________________ **Date** __________

Job Code________________ **Dept.** ______________

Superior's Title ________________________

Hours Worked _____ **AM to** _____ **PM**

Job Analyst's Name ______________________

1. **What is the job's overall purpose?**

2. **If the incumbent supervises others,** list them by job title; if there is more than one employee with the same title, put the number in parentheses following.

3. **Check those activities** that are part of the incumbent's supervisory duties.
   - ❐ Training
   - ❐ Performance appraisal
   - ❐ Inspecting work
   - ❐ Budgeting
   - ❐ Coaching and/or counseling
   - ❐ Others (please specify) ________________

4. **Describe the type and extent of supervision** received by the incumbent.

5. **JOB DUTIES:** Describe briefly WHAT the incumbent does and, if possible, HOW he/she does it. Include duties in the following categories:
   a. daily duties (those performed on a regular basis every day or almost every day)

   b. periodic duties (those performed weekly, monthly, quarterly, or at other regular intervals)

   c. duties performed at irregular intervals

6. Is the incumbent performing duties he/she considers unnecessary? If so, describe.

7. Is the incumbent performing duties not presently included in the job description? If so, describe.

8. **EDUCATION:** Check the box that indicates the educational requirements for the job (not the educational background of the incumbent).
   - ❐ No formal education required
   - ❐ Eighth grade education
   - ❐ High school diploma (or equivalent)
   - ❐ 2-year college degree (or equivalent)
   - ❐ 4-year college degree (or equivalent)
   - ❐ Graduate work or advanced degree Specify: __________
   - ❐ Professional license Specify: __________

messages and other routine information"). Respondents were more likely to include and report the ability-based versions of the statements. There may be a tendency for people to inflate their job's importance when abilities are involved, to impress the perceptions of others.[9] Employees will even puff up their job titles to make their jobs seem more important.[10] Obtaining valid information can thus be a slow process, and prudent analysts get multiple inputs.

FIGURE 4-3 *(continued)*

9. **EXPERIENCE:** Check the amount of experience needed to perform the job.

❒ None	❒ Less than one month
❒ One to six months	❒ Six months to one year
❒ One to three years	❒ Three to five years
❒ Five to ten years	❒ More than ten years

10. **LOCATION:** Check location of job and, if necessary or appropriate, describe briefly.

❒ Outdoor	❒ Indoor
❒ Underground	❒ Excavation
❒ Scaffold	❒ Other (specify)

11. **ENVIRONMENTAL CONDITIONS:** Check any objectionable conditions found on the job and note afterward how frequently each is encountered (rarely, occasionally, constantly, etc.).

❒ Dirt	❒ Dust
❒ Heat	❒ Cold
❒ Noise	❒ Fumes
❒ Odors	❒ Wetness/humidity
❒ Vibration	❒ Sudden temperature changes
❒ Darkness or poor lighting	❒ Other (specify)

12. **HEALTH AND SAFETY:** Check any undesirable health and safety conditions under which the incumbent must perform and note how often they are encountered.

❒ Elevated workplace	❒ Mechanical hazards
❒ Explosives	❒ Electrical hazards
❒ Fire hazards	❒ Radiation
❒ Other (specify)	

13. **MACHINES, TOOLS, EQUIPMENT, AND WORK AIDS:** Describe briefly what machines, tools, equipment, or work aids the incumbent works with on a regular basis:

____

14. Have concrete work standards been established (errors allowed, time taken for a particular task, etc.)? If so, what are they?

____

15. Are there any personal attributes (special aptitudes, physical characteristics, personality traits, etc.) required by the job?

____

16. Are there any exceptional problems the incumbent might be expected to encounter in performing the job under normal conditions? If so, describe.

____

17. Describe the successful completion and/or end results of the job.

____

18. What is the seriousness of error on this job? Who or what is affected by errors the incumbent makes?

____

19. To what job would a successful incumbent expect to be promoted?

____

[**Note:** this form is obviously slanted toward a manufacturing environment, but it can be adapted quite easily to fit a number of different types of jobs.]

Interviewing Guidelines To get the best information possible, keep several things in mind when conducting a job analysis interview.

- Quickly establish rapport with the interviewee. Know the person's name, speak in easily understood language, briefly review the interview's purpose, and explain how the person was chosen for the interview.

- Preferably follow a structured guide or checklist, one that lists questions and provides space for answers. This ensures you'll identify crucial questions ahead of time and that all interviewers (if more than one) cover all the required questions. (However, also make sure to provide some open-ended questions like, "Was there anything we didn't cover with our questions?")
- When duties are not performed in a regular manner—for instance, when the worker doesn't perform the same duties repeatedly many times a day—ask the worker to list his or her duties in order of importance and frequency of occurrence. This will ensure that you don't overlook crucial but infrequently performed activities—like a nurse's occasional emergency room duties.
- After completing the interview, review and verify the data. Specifically, review the information with the worker's immediate supervisor and with the interviewee.

Questionnaires

Having employees fill out questionnaires to describe their job-related duties and responsibilities is another popular way to obtain job analysis information.

You have to decide how structured the questionnaire should be and what questions to include. Some questionnaires are very structured checklists. Here each employee gets an inventory of perhaps hundreds of specific duties or tasks (such as "change and splice wire"). He or she is asked to indicate whether or not he or she performs each task and, if so, how much time is normally spent on each. At the other extreme, the questionnaire can be open-ended and simply ask the employee to "describe the major duties of your job."

In practice, the best questionnaire often falls between these two extremes. As illustrated in Figure 4-3, a typical job analysis questionnaire might include several open-ended questions (such as "state your jobs' overall purpose") as well as structured questions (concerning, for instance, previous education required). Figure 4-4 is another example.

Whether structured or unstructured, questionnaires have pros and cons. A questionnaire is a quick and efficient way to obtain information from a large number of employees; it's less costly than interviewing hundreds of workers, for instance. However, developing the questionnaire and testing it (perhaps by making sure the workers understand the questions) can be time-consuming. And as with interviews, employees may distort their answers, consciously or unconsciously.

Observation

Direct observation is especially useful when jobs consist mainly of observable physical activities—assembly-line worker and accounting clerk are examples. On the other hand, observation is usually not appropriate when the job entails a lot of mental activity (lawyer, design engineer). Nor is it useful if the employee only occasionally engages in important activities, such as a nurse who handles emergencies. And *reactivity*—the worker's changing what he or she normally does because you are watching—can also be a problem.

Managers often use direct observation and interviewing together. One approach is to observe the worker on the job during a complete work cycle. (The *cycle* is the time it takes to complete the job; it could be a minute for an assembly-line worker or an hour, a day, or longer for complex jobs.) Here you take notes of all the job activities. Then, after accumulating as much information as practical, you interview the worker. Ask the person to clarify points not understood and to explain what other activities he or she performs that you didn't observe. You can also observe and interview simultaneously, asking questions while the worker performs his or her job.

NEW COLLEGE OF FLORIDA
POSITION DESCRIPTION USPS & OPS

CURRENT DESCRIPTIVE DATA		FOR COMPLETION BY HR UPON FINAL ACTION							Position Number:		
		Approved Class Title:							Approved Class Code:		
1. Position Number:	2. Requested Classification Action: (__) Establish Position (__) Update (__) Change	Transaction:							Effective Date:		
3. Class Code:	4. Class Title:										
5. Department:	6. Department Head:	Org ID#:			Fund Code	FTE	Pay Plan		Pay Grade	EEO-6 Code	CBU Code
7. Grant Funded:	8. Contract:										
9. City: Sarasota	10. County: Sarasota	Signature of HR Director:							Date:		

ATTACH AN ADDITIONAL SHEET IF NEEDED TO PROPERLY DESCRIBE THE POSITION

In accordance with the Americans with Disabilities Act (ADA), identify essential functions of the job required to be performed with or without reasonable accommodations. Requests for reasonable accommodations to facilitate the performance of essential functions will be given careful consideration. **For purposes of the ADA, these functions are marginal only to individuals who are unable to perform the functions with or without reasonable accommodations because of a covered disability.

11. Describe functions in terms of outcomes/results rather than method used or how a job is normally accomplished.

11a. Essential Functions of the Job:* (List % of time for each function. Total % of time should add up to 100%.)

11b. Marginal Functions of the Job:

12. List the class titles and position numbers of positions under the direct supervision of this position.

13. List machines and equipment used regularly and percentage of time in the operations of each.

14. Describe the type and extent of instructions normally given to the incumbent of this position by the immediate supervisor.

14a. Working Hours (including any variations, split shifts, on call status, and/or rotations):

14b. Total hours per week:

FIGURE 4-4 Example of Position/Job Description Intended for Use Online

Source: www.ncf.edu/humanresources/documents/A&P%20Final.doc, accessed May 10, 2007.

15. **Education/Training/Experience** - In order of importance, state any specific education, training and experience and knowledge, skills and abilities required for this position. Note that these requirements must be related to the essential functions and at least equal to the minimum qualifications stated on the official class specification.

Specialized Minimum Qualifications:

Preferred Qualifications:

Knowledge, Skills, & Abilities:

Language Skills:

Mathematical Skills:

Reasoning Ability:

Computer Skills:

16. **Required Licenses/Certifications and Other Specific Requirements of Law** - Review the statements below and check all that apply.

17. **Other Characteristics of the Position** - Describe physical, mental and environmental factors critical to the satisfactory performance of the functions of the position or other characteristics which have not otherwise been described above.

Physical Demands: The physical demands described here are representative of those that must be met by an employee to successfully perform the essential functions of this job. Reasonable accommodations may be made to enable individuals with disabilities to perform the essential functions.

Work Environment:

_____ This position requires a post-offer employment physical	_____ This position requires a police background check	_____ This position requires fingerprinting	_____ This position required licensure, certification or other special requirements, as specified below
_____ This position requires a child care provider security check as required under Sections 402.305 and 402.3055, Florida Statutes	_____ This position is responsible for meeting the requirements of Section 215.422, Florida Statutes, as amended, regarding the approval and/or processing of vendors' invoices and/or distribution of warrants to vendors	_____ This position requires a classified driver's license appropriate to the type of vehicle operated in accordance with Section 332.60, Florida Statutes	_____ Other, as specified below

FIGURE 4-4 *(continued)*

Participant Diary/Logs

Another method is to ask workers to keep a **diary/log** of what they do during the day. For every activity engaged in, the employee records the activity (along with the time) in a log. This can produce a very complete picture of the job, especially when supplemented with subsequent interviews with the worker and the supervisor. The employee, of course, might try to exaggerate some activities and underplay others. However, the detailed, chronological nature of the log tends to mediate against this.

Diary/logs have gone high-tech. Some firms give employees pocket dictating machines and pagers. Then at random times during the day, they page the workers, who dictate what they are doing at that time. This approach can avoid one pitfall of the traditional diary/log method: relying on workers to remember what they did hours earlier when they complete their logs at the end of the day.

Quantitative Job Analysis Techniques

Qualitative methods like interviews and questionnaires are not always suitable. For example, if your aim is to compare jobs for pay purposes, a mere listing of duties may not suffice. You may need to say that, in effect, "Job A is twice as challenging as Job B, and so is worth twice the pay." To do this, it helps to have quantitative ratings for each job. The position analysis questionnaire and the Department of Labor approach are quantitative methods for doing this.

Position Analysis Questionnaire

The **position analysis questionnaire (PAQ)** is probably the most popular quantitative job analysis tool, and consists of a detailed questionnaire containing 194 items (see Figure 4-5 for a sample).[11] The 194 items (such as "written materials") each represent a basic element that may or may not play a role in the job. The 194 items each belong to one of five PAQ basic activities: (1) having decision-making/communication/social responsibilities, (2) performing skilled activities, (3) being physically active, (4) operating vehicles/equipment, and (5) processing information (Figure 4-5 illustrates this last activity). The final PAQ "score" shows the job's rating on each of these five activities. The job analyst decides if each of the 194 items plays a role and, if so, to what extent. In Figure 4-5, for example, "written materials" received a rating of 4. Since the scale ranges from 1 to 5, a 4 suggests that written materials (such as books and reports) do play a significant role in this job. The analyst can use an online version of the PAQ (see www.paq.com) for each job he or she is analyzing.

The PAQ's strength is in classifying jobs. With scores for each job's decision-making, skilled activity, physical activity, vehicle/equipment operation, and information-processing characteristics, you can quantitatively compare jobs relative to one another,[12] and then assign pay for each job.[13]

Department of Labor (DOL) Procedure

Experts at the U.S. Department of Labor did much of the early work developing job analysis.[14] They used their results to compile what was for many years the bible of job descriptions, the *Dictionary of Occupational Titles.* This mammoth book contained detailed information on virtually every job in America. We'll see in a moment that Internet-based tools have largely replaced the *Dictionary.* However, the U.S. Department of Labor job analysis procedure still offers a good example of how to quantitatively rate, classify, and compare different jobs, based on the DOL's "data, people, and things" ratings.

It works as follows. As Table 4-1 shows, the DOL method uses a set of standard basic activities called *worker functions* to describe what a worker must do with respect to data, people, and things. With respect to data, for instance, the functions include synthesizing, coordinating, and copying. With respect to people, they include

FIGURE 4-5 Portion of a Completed Page from the Position Analysis Questionnaire The 194 PAQ elements are grouped into six dimensions. This exhibits of the "information input" questions or elements. Other PAQ pages contain questions regarding mental processes, work output, relationships with others, job context, and other job characteristics.

Information Input

1 Information Input

1.1 Sources of Job Information

Rate each of the following items in terms of the extent to which it is used by the worker as a source of information in performing his job.

	Extent of Use (U)
NA	Does not apply
1	Nominal/very infrequent
2	Occasional
3	Moderate
4	Considerable
5	Very substantial

1.1.1 Visual Sources of Job Information

1	4	Written materials (books, reports, office notes, articles, job instructions, signs, etc.)
2	2	Quantitative materials (materials which deal with quantities or amounts, such as graphs, accounts, specifications, tables of numbers, etc.)
3	1	Pictorial materials (pictures or picture-like materials used as sources of information, for example, drawings, blueprints, diagrams, maps, tracing, photographic films, x-ray films, TV pictures, etc.)
4	1	Patterns/related devices (templates, stencils, patterns, etc., used as sources of information when observed during use; do not include here materials described in item 3 above)
5	2	Visual displays (dials, gauges, signal lights, radarscopes, speedo-meters, clocks, etc.)
6	5	Measuring devices (rulers, calipers, tire pressure gauges, scales, thickness gauges, pipettes, thermometers, protractors, etc., used to obtain visual information about physical measurements; do not include here devices describe in item 5 above)
7	4	Mechanical devices (tools, equipment, machinery, and other mechanical devices which are sources of information when observed during use of operation)
8	3	Materials in process (parts, material, objects, etc., which are sources of information when being modified, worked on, or otherwise processed, such as bread dough being mixed, workpiece being turned in a lathe, fabric being cut, shoe being resoled, etc.)
9	4	Materials not in process (parts, materials, objects, etc., not in the process of being changed or modified, which are sources of information when being inspected, handled, packaged, distributed, or selected, etc., such as items or materials in inventory, storage, or distribution channels, items being inspected, etc.)
10	3	Features of nature (landscapes, fields, geological samples, vegetation, cloud formations, and other features of nature which are observed or inspected to provide information)
11	2	Man-made features of environment (structures, buildings, dams, highways, bridges, docks, railroads, and other "man-made" or altered aspects of the indoor environment which are observed or inspected to provide job information; do not consider equipment, machines, etc., that an individual uses in his work, as covered by item 7)

mentoring, negotiating, and supervising. With respect to things, the basic functions include manipulating, tending, and handling.

Each worker function has an importance rating. Thus, "coordinating" is 1, whereas "copying" is 5. If you were analyzing the job of a receptionist/clerk, for

diary/log
Daily listings made by workers of every activity in which they engage along with the time each activity takes.

position analysis questionnaire (PAQ)
A questionnaire used to collect quantifiable data concerning the duties and responsibilities of various jobs.

TABLE 4-1 Basic Department of Labor Worker Functions

Basic Activities	Data	People	Things
	0 Synthesizing	0 Mentoring	0 Setting up
	1 Coordinating	1 Negotiating	1 Precision working
	2 Analyzing	2 Instructing	2 Operating/controlling
	3 Compiling	3 Supervising	3 Driving/operating
	4 Computing	4 Diverting	4 Manipulating
	5 Copying	5 Persuading	5 Tending
	6 Comparing	6 Speaking/signaling	6 Feeding/offbearing
		7 Serving	7 Handling
		8 Taking instructions/helping	

Note: Determine employee's job "score" on data, people, and things by observing his or her job and determining, for each of the three categories, which of the basic functions illustrates the person's job. "0" is high; "6," "8," and "7" are lows in each column.

example, you might label the job 5, 6, 7, to represent copying data, speaking/signaling people, and handling things. On the other hand, you might code a psychiatric aide in a hospital 1, 7, 5 in relation to data, people, and things. In practice, you would score each task that the worker performed as part of his or her job in terms of data, people, and things. Then you would use the highest combination (say 4, 6, 5) to rate the overall job, since this is the highest level that you would expect a successful job incumbent to attain. If you were selecting a worker for that 4, 6, 5 job, you'd expect him or her to be able to at least compute (4), speak/signal (6), and tend (5). If you were comparing jobs for pay purposes, then a 4, 6, 5 job should rank higher (see Table 4-1) than a 6, 8, 6 job. You can then present a summary of the job along with its 3-digit rating on a form such as in Figure 4-6.

Another technique, *functional job analysis,* is similar to the DOL method. However, it rates the job not just on data, people, and things, but also on the extent to which performing the task also requires four other things—specific instructions, reasoning and judgment, mathematical ability, and verbal and language facilities.

Internet-Based Job Analysis

Methods such as questionnaires and interviews present some drawbacks. For example, face-to-face interviews and observations can be time-consuming. And collecting the information from geographically dispersed employees can be challenging.[15]

Conducting the job analysis via the Internet is an obvious solution. Therefore, "[t]he use of online methodologies for surveys, including job analysis surveys, has increased dramatically in recent years, and most companies choose to use the Internet or intranet to collect this type of data."[16] Most simply, the human resource department can distribute standardized job analysis questionnaires to geographically disbursed employees via their company intranets, with instructions to complete the forms and return them by a particular date.

Of course, the instructions should be clear, and it's best to test the process first. Most importantly, without a job analyst actually sitting there with the employee or supervisor, there's always a chance that the employees won't cover important points or that misunderstandings will cloud the results.

U.S. Navy Example The U.S. Navy used the Web to do a job analysis. Being long-distance, collecting the data presented a special challenge. The challenge was

FIGURE 4-6 Sample Report Based on Department of Labor Job Analysis Technique

Job Analysis Schedule

1. Established Job Title DOUGH MIXER
2. Ind. Assign (bake prod.)
3. SIC Code(s) and Title(s) 2051 Bread and other bakery products

4. JOB SUMMARY:

Operates mixing machine to mix ingredients for straight and sponge (yeast) doughs according to established formulas, directs other workers in fermentation of dough, and curls dough into pieces with hand cutter.

5. WORK PERFORMED RATINGS:

	D	P	(T)
Worker Functions	Data	People	Things
	5	6	2

Work Field Cooking, Food Preparing

6. WORKER TRAITS RATING (to be filled in by analyst):

Training time required
Aptitudes
Temperaments
Interests
Physical demands
Environment conditions

"to develop a system that would allow the collection of job-related information with minimal intervention and guidance, so that the system could be used in a distributed manner."[17] Therefore, the Navy's consultants did not ask the job incumbents or their supervisors about the jobs as a whole, but rather duty by duty. To keep ambiguities to a minimum, they had the employees complete structured job analysis forms step-by-step, as follows:

- First the online form *shows workers a set of general work activities* from the Department of Labor online O*NET work activities list. (Figure 4-7 lists some of these activities, such as "Information Input Category" and "Interacting with Others Category." You can access the others at http://online.onetcenter.org.)
- Then the form directs them to *select those general work activities* that are important to their job.
- Then the form asks them to *list specific duties* of their jobs that fit each of those selected work activities. For example, suppose an employee chose "getting information" as a work activity that was important to his or her job. In this final step, he or she would list next to "getting information" one or more specific job duties from the job, perhaps such as "watch for new orders from our vendors and bring them to the boss's attention."

Again, the main issue with online job analysis is to make sure you've stripped the process of as many ambiguities as possible. The Navy's method proved to be an effective way to collect job-related related information online.[18]

FIGURE 4-7 Selected O*NET General Work Activities Categories

Information input category

Where and how are the information and data gained that are needed to perform the job?

- Getting information: observing, receiving, and otherwise obtaining information from all relevant sources
- Identifying objects, actions, and events: identifying information by categorizing, estimating, recognizing differences or similarities, and detecting changes in circumstances or events

Interacting with others category

What interactions with other persons or supervisory activities occur while performing this job?

- Assisting and caring for others: providing personal assistance, medical attention, emotional support, or other personal care to others such as coworkers, customers, or patients
- Coaching and developing others: identifying the developmental needs of others and coaching, mentoring, or otherwise helping others to improve their knowledge or skills

Mental processes category

What processing, planning, problem-solving, decision-making, and innovating activities are performed with job-relevant information?

- Analyzing data or information: identifying the underlying principles, reasons, or facts of information by breaking down information or data into separate parts
- Making decisions and solving problems: analyzing information and evaluating results to choose the best solution and solve problems

Work output category

What physical activities are performed, what equipment and vehicles are operated, and what complex/technical activities are accomplished as job outputs?

- Controlling machines and processes: using either control mechanisms or direct physical activity to operate machines or processes (not including computers or vehicles)
- Interacting with computers: using computers and computer systems (including hardware and software) to write software, set up functions, or enter data

3 Write job descriptions, including summaries and job functions, using the Internet and traditional methods.

WRITING JOB DESCRIPTIONS

The employer almost always uses the job analysis to (at least) produce a job description. A job description is a written statement of what the worker actually does, how he or she does it, and what the job's working conditions are. You use this information to write a job specification; this lists the knowledge, abilities, and skills required to perform the job satisfactorily.

There is no standard format for writing a job description. However, most descriptions contain sections that cover:

1. Job identification
2. Job summary
3. Responsibilities and duties
4. Authority of incumbent
5. Standards of performance
6. Working conditions
7. Job specifications

Figures 4-8 and 4-9 present two sample forms of job descriptions.

Job Identification

As in Figure 4-8, the job identification section (on top) contains several types of information.[19] The *job title* specifies the name of the job, such as supervisor of data processing operations, or inventory control clerk. The FLSA status section identifies the job as exempt or nonexempt. (Under the Fair Labor Standards Act, certain positions,

JOB TITLE: Telesales Respresentative	**JOB CODE:** 100001
RECOMMENDED SALARY GRADE:	**EXEMPT/NONEXEMPT STATUS:** Nonexempt
JOB FAMILY: Sales	**EEOC:** Sales Workers
DIVISION: Higher Education	**REPORTS TO:** District Sales Manager
DEPARTMENT: In-House Sales	**LOCATION:** Boston
	DATE: April 2009

SUMMARY (Write a brief summary of job.)

The person in this position is responsible for selling college textbooks, software, and multimedia products to professors, via incoming and outgoing telephone calls, and to carry out selling strategies to meet sales goals in assigned territories of smaller colleges and universities. In addition, the individual in this position will be responsible for generating a designated amount of editorial leads and communicating to the publishing groups product feedback and market trends observed in the assigned territory.

SCOPE AND IMPACT OF JOB

Dollar responsibilities (budget and/or revenue)

The person in this position is responsible for generating approximately $2 million in revenue, for meeting operating expense budget of approximately $4000, and a sampling budget of approximately 10,000 units.

Supervisory responsibilities (direct and indirect)

None

Other

REQUIRED KNOWLEDGE AND EXPERIENCE (Knowledge and experience necessary to do job)

Related work experience

Prior sales or publishing experience preferred. One year of company experience in a customer service or marketing function with broad knowledge of company products and services is desirable.

Formal education or equivalent

Bachelor's degree with strong academic performance or work equivalent experience.

Skills

Must have strong organizational and persuasive skills. Must have excellent verbal and written communications skills and must be PC proficient.

Other

Limited travel required (approx 5%)

(continued)

FIGURE 4-8 Sample Job Description, Pearson Education
Source: Courtesy of HR Department, Pearson Education.

primarily administrative and professional, are exempt from the act's overtime and minimum wage provisions.) *Date* is the date the job description was actually approved.

There may also be a space to indicate who approved the description and perhaps a space that shows the location of the job in terms of its facility/division and department/section. This section might also include the immediate supervisor's title and information regarding salary and/or pay scale. There might also be space for the grade/level of the job, if there is such a category. For example, a firm may classify programmers as programmer II, programmer III, and so on.

PRIMARY RESPONSIBILITIES (List in order of importance and list amount of time spent on task.)

Driving Sales (60%)

- Achieve quantitative sales goal for assigned territory of smaller colleges and universities.
- Determine sales priorities and strategies for territory and develop a plan for implementing those strategies.
- Conduct 15–20 professor interviews per day during the academic sales year that accomplishes those priorities.
- Conduct product presentations (including texts, software, and Web site); effectively articulate author's central vision of key titles; conduct sales interviews using the PSS model; conduct walk-through of books and technology.
- Employ telephone selling techniques and strategies.
- Sample products to appropriate faculty, making strategic use of assigned sampling budgets.
- Close class test adoptions for first edition products.
- Negotiate custom publishing and special packaging agreements within company guidelines.
- Initiate and conduct in-person faculty presentations and selling trips as appropriate to maximize sales with the strategic use of travel budget. Also use internal resources to support the territory sales goals.
- Plan and execute in-territory special selling events and book-fairs.
- Develop and implement in-territory promotional campaigns and targeted email campaigns.

Publishing (editorial/marketing) 25%

- Report, track, and sign editorial projects.
- Gather and communicate significant market feedback and information to publishing groups.

Territory Management 15%

- Track and report all pending and closed business in assigned database.
- Maintain records of customer sales interviews and adoption situations in assigned database.
- Manage operating budget strategically.
- Submit territory itineraries, sales plans, and sales forecasts as assigned.
- Provide superior customer service and maintain professional bookstore relations in assigned territory.

Decision-Making Responsibilities for This Position:

Determine the strategic use of assigned sampling budget to most effectively generate sales revenue to exceed sales goals.
Determine the priority of customer and account contacts to achieve maximum sales potential.
Determine where in-person presentations and special selling events would be most effective to generate most sales.

Submitted By: Jim Smith, District Sales Manager	Date: April 10, 2007
Approval:	Date:
Human Resources:	Date:
Corporate Compensation:	Date:

FIGURE 4-8 *(continued)*

Job Summary

The job summary should of course summarize the essence of the job, and include only its major functions or activities. Thus (in Figure 4-8), the telesales rep ". . . is responsible for selling college textbooks . . . ." For the job of materials manager, the summary might state that the "materials manager purchases economically, regulates deliveries of, stores, and distributes all material necessary on the production line." For the job of mailroom supervisor, "the mailroom supervisor receives, sorts, and delivers all incoming mail properly, and he or she handles all outgoing mail including the accurate and timely posting of such mail."[20]

FIGURE 4-9 Marketing Manager Description from Standard Occupational Classification

Source: www.bls.gov/soc/soc_a2c1.htm, accessed May 10, 2007.

U.S. Department of Labor
Bureau of Labor Statistics
Standard Occupational Classification

www.bls.gov | Advanced Search | A-Z Index

BLS Home | Programs & Surveys | Get Detailed Statistics | Glossary | What's New | Find It! In DOL

11-2021 Marketing Managers

Determine the demand for products and services offered by a firm and its competitors and identify potential customers. Develop pricing strategies with the goal of maximizing the firm's profits or share of the market while ensuring the firm's customers are satisfied. Oversee product development or monitor trends that indicate the need for new products and services.

While it's common to do so, include general statements like "performs other assignments as required" with care. Such statements do give supervisors more flexibility in assigning duties. Some experts, however, state unequivocally that "one item frequently found that should never be included in a job description is a 'cop-out clause' like 'other duties, as assigned,'"[21] since this leaves open the nature of the job—and the people needed to staff it. To avoid any ambiguities, it's advisable to make it clear in the job summary that the employer expects the job incumbent to carry out his or her duties efficiently, attentively, and conscientiously.

Relationships

There may be a "relationships" statement (not in the example) that shows the jobholder's relationships with others inside and outside the organization. For a human resource manager, such a statement might look like this:[22]

Reports to: Vice president of employee relations.

Supervises: Human resource clerk, test administrator, labor relations director, and one secretary.

Works with: All department managers and executive management.

Outside the company: Employment agencies, executive recruiting firms, union representatives, state and federal employment offices, and various vendors.[23]

Responsibilities and Duties

This is the heart of the job description. It should present a list of the job's significant responsibilities and duties. As in Figure 4-8, list each of the job's major duties separately, and describe it in a few sentences. In the figure, for instance, the job's duties include "achieve quantitative sales goal . . ." and "determine sales priorities . . . ." Typical duties for other jobs might include maintaining balanced and controlled inventories, making accurate postings to accounts payable, maintaining favorable purchase price variances, and repairing production-line tools and equipment.

This section may also define the limits of the jobholder's authority, including his or her decision-making authority, direct supervision of other personnel, and budgetary authority. For example, the jobholder might have authority to approve purchase requests up to $5,000, grant time off or leaves of absence, discipline department personnel, recommend salary increases, and interview and hire new employees.

Usually, the manager's basic question here is, "How do I determine what the job's duties are and should be?" The first answer is, from the *job analysis* itself; this should reveal what the employees on each job are doing now. Second, the manager will turn to various sources of standardized job description information. As mentioned, for many

TABLE 4-2 SOC Major Groups of Jobs

11-0000	Management Occupations
13-0000	Business and Financial Operations Occupations
15-0000	Computer and Mathematical Occupations
17-0000	Architecture and Engineering Occupations
19-0000	Life, Physical, and Social Science Occupations
21-0000	Community and Social Services Occupations
23-0000	Legal Occupations
25-0000	Education, Training, and Library Occupations
27-0000	Arts, Design, Entertainment, Sports, and Media Occupations
29-0000	Health Care Practitioners and Technical Occupations
31-0000	Health Care Support Occupations
33-0000	Protective Service Occupations
35-0000	Food Preparation and Serving-Related Occupations
37-0000	Building and Grounds Cleaning and Maintenance Occupations
39-0000	Personal Care and Service Occupations
41-0000	Sales and Related Occupations
43-0000	Office and Administrative Support Occupations
45-0000	Farming, Fishing, and Forestry Occupations
47-0000	Construction and Extraction Occupations
49-0000	Installation, Maintenance, and Repair Occupations
51-0000	Production Occupations
53-0000	Transportation and Material Moving Occupations
55-0000	Military Specific Occupations

Note: Within these major groups are 96 minor groups, 449 broad occupations, and 821 detailed occupations.

years the U.S. Labor Department's *Dictionary of Occupational Titles* was the basic source managers both within and outside the government turned to for standard job descriptions. However, the government replaced the *Dictionary* with several tools. The **Standard Occupational Classification (SOC)** (www.bls.gov/soc/socguide.htm) classifies all workers into one of 23 major groups of jobs (see Table 4-2). These in turn contain 96 minor groups of jobs, and these in turn include 821 detailed occupations, such as the marketing manager description in Figure 4-9. The employer can use standard descriptions like these to identify a job's specific duties and responsibilities, such as "Determine the demand for products." The employer may also use other popular sources of job description information, such as www.jobdescription.com. O*NET online, as noted, is another option for finding job duties. We'll turn to this in a moment.

The list of job duties looms large in employers' efforts to comply with ADA regulations: See the accompanying "Managing the New Workforce" feature.

Standards of Performance and Working Conditions

Some managers want the job description to contain a "standards of performance" section. This lists the standards the company expects the employee to achieve under each of the job description's main duties and responsibilities. It guides both the employee and manager in assessing how the former is performing.

Setting standards is never easy. However, most managers soon learn that just telling subordinates to "do their best" doesn't provide enough guidance. One straightforward way of setting standards is to finish the statement, "I will be completely satisfied with your work when . . . ." This sentence, if completed for each duty listed in the job description, should result in a usable set of performance standards.[24] Here are some examples:

Duty: Accurately Posting Accounts Payable

1. Post all invoices received within the same working day.
2. Route all invoices to proper department managers for approval no later than the day following receipt.
3. An average of no more than three posting errors per month.

Managing the New Workforce

Writing Job Descriptions That Comply with the ADA

Congress enacted the Americans with Disabilities Act (ADA) to reduce or eliminate serious problems of discrimination against disabled individuals. Under the ADA, the individual must have the requisite skills, educational background, and experience to perform the job's essential functions. A job function is essential when it is the reason the position exists or when the function is so specialized that the firm hired the person doing the job for his or her expertise or ability to perform that particular function. If the disabled individual can't perform the job as currently structured, the employer is required to make a "reasonable accommodation," unless doing so would present an "undue hardship."

As we said earlier, the ADA does not require job descriptions, but it's probably advisable to have them. Virtually all ADA legal actions will revolve around the question, "What are the essential functions of the job?" Without a job description that lists such functions, it will be hard to convince a court that the functions are essential to the job. The corollary is that you should clearly identify the essential functions: Don't just list them among the job description's other duties.

Essential job functions are the job duties that employees must be able to perform, with or without reasonable accommodation.[25] Is a function essential? Questions to ask include:

1. What three or four main activities actually constitute the job? Is each really necessary? (For example, a secretary types, files, answers the phone, takes dictation.)
2. What is the relationship between each task? Is there a special sequence that the tasks must follow?
3. Do the tasks necessitate sitting, standing, crawling, walking, climbing, running, stooping, kneeling, lifting, carrying, digging, writing, operating, pushing, pulling, fingering, talking, listening, interpreting, analyzing, seeing, coordinating, etc.?
4. Can the performance of that job function be distributed among any other employees?
5. How much time is spent on the job performing each particular function?
6. Would removing a function fundamentally alter the job?
7. What happens if a task is not completed on time?
8. Does the position actually exist to perform that function?
9. Are employees in the position actually required to perform the function?[26]
10. What is the degree of expertise or skill required to perform the function?
11. What is the actual work experience of present or past employees in the job?
12. What is the amount of time an individual actually spends performing the function?
13. What are the consequences of not requiring the performance of the function?

Standard Occupational Classification (SOC) Classifies all workers into one of 23 major groups of jobs that are subdivided into minor groups of jobs and detailed occupations.

Duty: Meeting Daily Production Schedule

1. Produces no less than 426 units per working day.
2. Next workstation rejects no more than an average of 2% of units.
3. Weekly overtime does not exceed an average of 5%.

The job description may also list the working conditions involved on the job. These might include things like noise level, hazardous conditions, or heat.

Using the Internet for Writing Job Descriptions

Most employers probably still write their own job descriptions, but more are turning to the Internet. One site, www.jobdescription.com, illustrates why. The process is simple. Search by alphabetical title, keyword, category, or industry to find the desired job title. This leads you to a generic job description for that title—say, "Computers & EDP systems sales representative." You can then use the wizard to customize the generic description for this position. For example, you can add specific information about your organization, such as job title, job codes, department, and preparation date. And you can indicate whether the job has supervisory abilities, and choose from a number of possible desirable competencies and experience levels.

O*Net

The U.S. Department of Labor's occupational information network, called O*NET, is an increasingly popular Web tool (you'll find it at http://online.onetcenter.org). It allows users (not just managers, but workers and job seekers) to see the most important characteristics of various occupations, as well as the experience, education, and knowledge required to do each job well. Both the Standard Occupational Classification and O*NET include the specific tasks associated with many occupations. O*NET also lists skills, including *basic skills* such as reading and writing, *process skills* such as critical thinking, and *transferable skills* such as persuasion and negotiation.[27] You'll also see that an O*NET job listing includes information on worker requirements (required knowledge, for instance), occupation requirements (such as compiling, coding, and categorizing data, for instance), and experience requirements (including education and job training). You can also use O*NET to check the job's labor market characteristics, such as employment projections and earnings data.[28]

How to Use O*Net

Many managers and small business owners face two hurdles when doing job analyses and job descriptions. First, they need a streamlined approach for developing a job description. Second, they fear that they will overlook duties that subordinates should be assigned.

You have three good options. The *Standard Occupational Classification*, mentioned earlier, provides detailed descriptions of thousands of jobs and their human requirements. Web sites like www.jobdescription.com provide customizable descriptions by title and industry. And the Department of Labor's O*NET is a third option. We'll focus here on how you can write a job description using O*NET (http://online.onetcenter.org).[29]

Step 1: Decide on a Plan. Ideally, the jobs you need should flow from your departmental or company plans. Therefore, you may want to review your plan. What do you expect your sales to be next year, and in the next few years? What areas or departments do you think will have to be expanded or reduced? What kinds of new positions do you think you'll need?

Step 2: Develop an Organization Chart. You may want to write an organization chart. Start with the organization as it is now. Then (depending upon how far you're planning), produce a chart showing how you'd like your chart to look in the future (say, in a year or two). Microsoft's MS Word includes an organization charting function. Software packages such as *OrgPublisher* from TimeVision of Irving, Texas, are another option.[30]

Step 3: Use a Simplified Job Analysis Questionnaire. Next, gather preliminary information about the job's duties. (You can use one of the more comprehensive job analysis questionnaires, as in Figure 4-3, but that in Figure 4-10 is simpler

FIGURE 4-10 Preliminary Job Description Questionnaire

Source: Reprinted from www.hr.blr.com with the permission of the publisher. Business and Legal Resources, Inc., Old Saybrook, CT. BLR® (Business & Legal Resources, Inc.).

Instructions: Distribute copies of this questionnaire to supervisors, managers, personnel staff members, job analysts, and others who may be involved in writing job descriptions. Ask them to record their answers to these questions in writing.

1. What is the job title? ______________________
2. Summarize the job's more important, regularly performed/duties in a Job Summary.
3. In what department is the job located? ______________
4. What is the title of the supervisor or manager to whom the job holder must report?
5. Does the job holder supervise other employees? If so, give their job titles and a brief description of their responsibilities.

Position Supervised	Responsibilities

6. What essential function duties does the job holder perform regularly? List them in order of importance.

Duty	Percentage of Time Devoted to This Duty
1.	
2.	
3.	
4.	
5.	
6.	

7. Does the job holder perform other duties periodically? Infrequently? If so, please list, indicating frequency.
8. What are the working conditions? List such items as noise, heat, outside work, and exposure to bad weather.
9. How much authority does the job holder have in such matters as training or guiding other people?
10. How much education, experience, and skill are required for satisfactory job performance?
11. At what stage is the job holder's work reviewed by the supervisor?
12. What machines or equipment is the job holder responsible for operating?
13. If the job holder makes a serious mistake or error in performing required duties, what would be the cost to management?

and satisfactory for our purposes here.) Fill in the required information. This includes the job's duties divided into daily duties, periodic duties, and duties performed at irregular intervals.

Step 4: Obtain Job Duties from O*NET. The list of job duties you uncovered in the previous step may or may not be complete. We'll therefore use O*NET to compile a more complete list. (Refer to A, B, and C examples below as you read along.)

Start by going to http://online.onetcenter.org (A). Here, click on *Find Occupations.* Assume you want to create job descriptions for a retail salesperson. Type in *Retail Sales* for the occupational titles drop-down box.

This brings you to the *Find Occupations Search Result* (B).

Clicking on *Retail Salespersons*-summary produces the job summary and specific occupational duties for retail salespersons (C). For a small store, you might want to combine the duties of the "retail salesperson" with those of "first-line supervisors/ managers of retail sales workers."

Step 5: List the Job's Human Requirements from O*NET. Next, return to the *Snapshot* (summary) *for Retail Salesperson* (C). Here, instead of choosing occupation-specific information, click, for example, *Worker Experiences, Occupational Requirements,* and *Worker Characteristics.* Use this information to help develop a job specification for your job. Use this information for recruiting, selecting, and training your employees.

Step 6: Finalize the Job Description. Finally, perhaps using Figure 4-10 as a guide, write an appropriate job summary for the job. Then use the information obtained in steps 4 and 5 above to create a complete listing of the tasks, duties, and human requirements of each of the jobs you will need to fill.

Shown in the following three screen captures, below, O*Net easily allows the user to develop job descriptions.

A

B

o•net® OnLine

Occupational Information Network

O*NET OnLine

Related Links | OnLine Help |

Find Occupations | Skills Search | Crosswalk

Job Family Search Results for:

Sales and Related (30 matches)

Sales and Related [Go]

O*NET-SOC Code	O*NET-SOC Title	Reports (help)		
41-1011.00	First-Line Supervisors/Managers of Retail Sales Workers	Summary	Details	Custom
41-1012.00	First-Line Supervisors/Managers of Non-Retail Sales Workers	Summary	Details	Custom
41-2011.00	Cashiers	Summary	Details	Custom
41-2012.00	Gaming Change Persons and Booth Cashiers	Summary	Details	Custom
41-2021.00	Counter and Rental Clerks	Summary	Details	Custom
41-2022.00	Parts Salespersons	Summary	Details	Custom
41-2031.00	Retail Salespersons	Summary	Details	Custom
41-3011.00	Advertising Sales Agents	Summary	Details	Custom
41-3021.00	Insurance Sales Agents	Summary	Details	Custom
41-3031.00	Securities, Commodities, and Financial Services Sales Agents	Summary	Details	Custom
41-3031.01	Sales Agents, Securities and Commodities	Summary	Details	Custom
41-3031.02	Sales Agents, Financial Services	Summary	Details	Custom
41-3041.00	Travel Agents	Summary	Details	Custom
41-3099.99	Sales Representatives, Services, All Other	Summary	Details	Custom
41-4011.00	Sales Representatives, Wholesale and Manufacturing, Technical and Scientific Products	Summary	Details	Custom
41-4011.01	Sales Representatives, Agricultural	Summary	Details	Custom
41-4011.02	Sales Representatives, Chemical and Pharmaceutical	Summary	Details	Custom
41-4011.03	Sales Representatives, Electrical/Electronic	Summary	Details	Custom

C

Updated 2003

Summary Report for:

41-2031.00 - Retail Salespersons

Sell merchandise, such as furniture, motor vehicles, appliances, or apparel in a retail establishment.

Tasks | Knowledge | Skills | Abilities | Work Activities | Work Context | Job Zone | Interests | Work Styles | Work Values | Related Occupations | Wages & Employment

Tasks

- Greet customers and ascertain what each customer wants or needs.
- Open and close cash registers, performing tasks such as counting money, separating charge slips, coupons, and vouchers, balancing cash drawers, and making deposits.
- Maintain knowledge of current sales and promotions, policies regarding payment and exchanges, and security practices.
- Compute sales prices, total purchases and receive and process cash or credit payment.
- Maintain records related to sales.
- Watch for and recognize security risks and thefts, and know how to prevent or handle these situations.
- Recommend, select, and help locate or obtain merchandise based on customer needs and desires.
- Answer questions regarding the store and its merchandise.
- Describe merchandise and explain use, operation, and care of merchandise to customers.
- Ticket, arrange and display merchandise to promote sales.

back to top

Knowledge

Customer and Personal Service — Knowledge of principles and processes for providing customer and personal services. This includes customer needs assessment, meeting quality standards for services, and evaluation of customer satisfaction.

Sales and Marketing — Knowledge of principles and methods for showing, promoting, and selling products or services. This includes marketing strategy and tactics, product demonstration, sales techniques, and sales control systems.

Administration and Management — Knowledge of business and management principles involved in strategic planning, resource allocation, human resources modeling, leadership technique, production methods, and coordination of people and resources.

Education and Training — Knowledge of principles and methods for curriculum and training design, teaching and instruction for individuals and groups, and the measurement of training effects.

Mathematics — Knowledge of arithmetic, algebra, geometry, calculus, statistics, and their applications.

English Language — Knowledge of the structure and content of the English language including the meaning and spelling of words, rules of composition, and grammar.

4 Write a job specification.

WRITING JOB SPECIFICATIONS

The job specification takes the job description and answers the question, "What human traits and experience are required to do this job effectively?" It shows what kind of person to recruit and for what qualities you should test that person. The job specification may be a section of the job description, or a separate document. Often—as in Figure 4-8 on pages 131–132—the employer presents it as part of the job description.[31]

Filling jobs with untrained employees requires identifying the personal traits that predict performance.

Source: Courtesy of Mark Richards/Photo Edit Inc.

Specifications for Trained Versus Untrained Personnel

Writing job specifications for trained employees is relatively straightforward. For example, suppose you want to fill a position for a bookkeeper (or counselor or programmer). In cases like these, your job specifications might focus mostly on traits like length of previous service, quality of relevant training, and previous job performance. Thus, it's usually not too difficult to determine the human requirements for placing already trained people on a job.

The problems are more complex when you're filling jobs with untrained people (with the intention of training them on the job). Here you must specify qualities such as physical traits, personality, interests, or sensory skills that imply some potential for performing or for being trained to do the job.

For example, suppose the job requires detailed manipulation in a circuit board assembly line. Here you might want to ensure that the person scores high on a test of finger dexterity. Your goal, in other words, is to identify those personal traits—those human requirements—that validly predict which candidates would do well on the job and which would not. Employers identify these human requirements either through a subjective, judgmental approach or through statistical analysis (or both). Let's examine both approaches.

Specifications Based on Judgment

Most job specifications come from the educated guesses of people like supervisors and human resource managers. The basic procedure here is to ask, "What does it take in terms of education, intelligence, training, and the like to do this job well?"

There are several ways to get these "educated guesses." You could simply review the job's duties, and deduce from those what human traits and skills the job requires. You can also choose them from the competencies listed in Web-based job descriptions like those at www.jobdescription.com. (For example, a typical job description there lists competencies like "Generates creative solutions" and "Manages difficult or emotional customer situations.") O*NET online is another option. Job listings there include complete lists of required educational and other experience and skills.

Use Common Sense

In any case, use common sense when compiling your list. Don't ignore the behaviors that may apply to almost any job but that might not normally surface through a job analysis.

Industriousness is an example. Who wants an employee who doesn't work hard? One researcher collected supervisor ratings and other information from 18,000 employees in 42 different hourly entry-level jobs in predominantly retail settings.[32] Regardless of the job, here are the work behaviors (with examples) that he found to be important to all jobs:

Job-Related Behavior	Some Examples
Industriousness	Keeps working even when other employees are standing around talking; takes the initiative to find another task when finished with regular work.
Thoroughness	Cleans equipment thoroughly, creating a more attractive display; notices merchandise out of place and returns it to the proper area.
Schedule flexibility	Accepts schedule changes when necessary; offers to stay late when the store is extremely busy.
Attendance	Arrives at work on time; maintains good attendance.
Off-task behavior (reverse)	Uses store phones to make personal unauthorized calls; conducts personal business during work time; lets joking friends be a distraction and interruption to work.
Unruliness (reverse)	Threatens to bully another employee; refuses to take routine orders from supervisors; does not cooperate with other employees.
Theft (reverse)	(As a cashier) Underrings the price of merchandise for a friend; cheats on reporting time worked; allows nonemployees in unauthorized areas.
Drug misuse (reverse)	Drinks alcohol or takes drugs on company property; comes to work under the influence of alcohol or drugs.

Here's another example, which focused on 50 testing engineers at a Volvo plant in Sweden. When asked what determined job competence for a testing engineer, most of the engineers listed obvious criteria such as "to make the engine perform according to specifications." But the most effective testing engineers defined the job's main task differently: "to make sure the engine provides a customer with a good driving experience." As a result, these engineers worked hard to develop their knowledge of customers' driving needs, even when it meant reaching out to people outside their own group, such as designers or marketers. So, the job specifications for engineers turned out to be quite different from what the initial job analysis survey revealed.[33]

Job Specifications Based on Statistical Analysis

Basing job specifications on statistical analysis is the more defensible approach, but it's also more difficult. The aim here is to determine statistically the relationship between (1) some *predictor* (human trait, such as height, intelligence, or finger dexterity), and (2) some indicator or *criterion* of job effectiveness, such as performance as rated by the supervisor.

The procedure has five steps: (1) analyze the job and decide how to measure job performance; (2) select personal traits like finger dexterity that you believe should predict successful performance; (3) test candidates for these traits; (4) measure these candidates' subsequent job performance; and (5) statistically analyze the relationship between the human trait (finger dexterity) and job performance. Your objective is to determine whether the former predicts the latter.

This method is more defensible than the judgmental approach because equal rights legislation forbids using traits that you can't prove distinguish between high and low job performers. For example, hiring standards that discriminate based on sex, race, religion, national origin, or age may have to be shown to predict job performance. Ideally, you do this with a statistical validation study, as in the 5-step approach outlined earlier. In practice, most employers probably rely more on judgmental approaches.

5 Explain job analysis in a "worker-empowered" world, including what it means and how it's done in practice.

JOB ANALYSIS IN A WORKER-EMPOWERED WORLD

We usually think of a "job" as a more or less unchanging specific set of duties that one carries out for pay. However, over the past few years, that concept has been changing quite dramatically. Indeed, for employees at many firms like Google, what they do on their jobs changes almost every day. This has prompted managers to re-think how they conduct job analyses. After all, how can you conduct a job analysis if the duties the job entails today may be different tomorrow?

From Specialized to Enriched Jobs

The evolution of "job" from a narrow list of duties to what it is today took place over many years. Early economists such as Adam Smith wrote enthusiastically of how specialized jobs (doing the same small thing repeatedly) were more efficient (as in, "practice makes perfect").

By the mid-1900s, other writers were reacting to what they viewed as the "dehumanizing" aspects of pigeonholing workers into highly repetitive jobs. Many proposed solutions like job enlargement. **Job enlargement** means assigning workers additional same-level activities. Thus, the worker who previously only bolted the seat to the legs might attach the back as well. **Job rotation** means systematically moving workers from one job to another.

Psychologist Frederick Herzberg argued that the best way to motivate workers is through job enrichment. **Job enrichment** means redesigning jobs in a way that increases the opportunities for the worker to experience feelings of responsibility, achievement, growth, and recognition. It does this by *empowering* the worker—for instance, by giving the worker the skills and authority to inspect the work, instead of having supervisors do that. Herzberg said empowered employees would do their jobs well because they wanted to, and quality and productivity would rise. That philosophy, in one form or another, is the theoretical basis for the team-based self-managing jobs in many factories around the world, like Daimler's new plant in Alabama.

Daimler Alabama Example

When Daimler opened its new Mercedes-Benz factory in Alabama, it designed a modern factory.[34] The system Daimler chose is similar to the "lean production systems" that Japanese manufacturers like Toyota use. It emphasizes *just-in-time* inventory methods, so that inventories stay negligible due to the arrival "just in time" of parts. It also organizes employees into *work teams*, and emphasizes that all employees must dedicate themselves to *continuous improvement*.

Job analysis plays a reduced role in this factory. There are a relatively few job descriptions covering all jobs, and each is fairly broad. Without detailed descriptions showing what "my job" is, it's easier for employees to move from job to job within their teams. Not being pigeonholed also encourages employees to look beyond their own jobs to find ways to improve things. For instance, one team found a $.23 plastic prong that worked better than the one for $2.50 the plant was using to keep car doors open during painting.

Other Changes at Work

Just as teamwork and worker empowerment improved Daimler's bottom line, employers have instituted other changes in how they organize work. For example, instead of seven or more management layers, *flat organizations* (with just three or four levels) are more prevalent. This puts top managers in closer touch with customers. However, the remaining managers also each tend to supervise more subordinates. Their subordinates, now with less oversight, end up with more responsibilities.

Reengineering (technically, "business process reengineering") is another change. In many companies, work processes look like relay races. For example, for a bank to approve a loan application, the application might go from applications, to credit analysis, to loan approval, to the loan closing group. This is time-consuming. *Reengineering* means redesigning a business process so that small multidisciplinary self-managing teams get the task done together, all at once. Since team members often share duties, they tend to be more multi-skilled than if they only had to do, say, loan analysis.

The bottom line is that whether due to teamwork, fewer supervisors, or reengineering, many jobs today are more likely to change daily and to be broader (in terms of duties) than in the past. As a result, many employers and job analysts say that how we do job analyses must change.[35] They say that compiling a list of job duties for jobs that may change daily is counterproductive. The alternative is to create job descriptions that are based on competencies—on what employees in these jobs must be able to do—rather than on lists of specific duties. The result is competency-based job analysis.

Competency-Based Job Analysis

Competencies are demonstrable characteristics of the person that make performance possible. That is a mouthful, so let us be more specific. Job competencies are always observable and measurable behaviors. To determine what a job's required competencies are, you should ask, "In order to perform this job competently, what should the employee be able to do?" We can say that **competency-based job analysis** means describing the job in terms of measurable, observable, behavioral competencies (knowledge, skills, and/or behaviors) that an employee doing that job must exhibit to do the job well. This contrasts with describing jobs in terms of job duties and responsibilities.[36] Traditional job analysis is more job-focused (what are this job's duties?). Competency-based analysis is more worker-focused: Here you ask, "What must these employees be competent to do in order to perform this multi-skilled job?"

Examples of Competencies

In practice, you might list a job's required competencies in two or three clusters. For example, you might list the job's required competencies in terms of *general competencies* (such as reading, writing, and mathematical reasoning), *leadership competencies* (such as leadership, strategic thinking, and teaching others), and *technical competencies* (programming in xtml, or writing advertising copy, for instance).

So, *technical competencies* for the job of systems engineer might include the following:

- Design complex software applications, establish protocols, and create prototypes.
- Establish the necessary platform requirements to efficiently and completely coordinate data transfer.
- Prepare comprehensive and complete documentation including specifications, flow diagrams, process patrols, and budgets.[37]

Similarly, for a corporate treasurer, technical competencies might include:

- Formulate trade recommendations by studying several computer models for currency trends.
- Recommend specific trades and when to make them.
- Present recommendations and persuade others to follow the recommended course of action.[38]

In practice, competency-based analysis usually comes down to identifying the basic skills an employee needs to do the job. Where can you find lists of skills for various jobs? For one source, O*NET lists various skills within six skill groups (accessible at http://online.onetcenter.org/skills). A sampling includes:

"Mathematics—using mathematics to solve problems"

"Speaking—talking to others to convey information effectively"

"Complex problem-solving—identifying complex problems and reviewing related information to develop and evaluate options and implement solutions"

"Negotiation—bringing others together and trying to reconcile differences"

job enlargement
Assigning workers additional same-level activities.

job rotation
Systematically moving workers from one job to another.

job enrichment
Redesigning jobs in a way that increases the opportunities for the worker to experience feelings of responsibility, achievement, growth, and recognition.

competency-based job analysis
Describes the job in terms of measurable, observable, behavioral competencies (knowledge, skills, and/or behaviors) that an employee doing that job must exhibit to do the job well.

How to Write Job Competencies-Based Job Descriptions

Defining the job's competencies and writing them up involves a process that is similar in most respects to traditional job analysis. In other words, you might interview job incumbents and their supervisors, ask open-ended questions regarding job responsibilities and activities, and perhaps identify critical incidents that pinpoint success on the job. But there the similarity ends. Instead of compiling lists of job duties, you will ask, *"In order to perform this job competently, the employee should be able to . . . ?"* You can use your knowledge of the job to answer this, or use a list like that mentioned at O*NET. There are also off-the-shelf competencies databanks. One is that of the Department of Labor's Office of Personnel Management (see www.opm.gov).

BP Example As we said, competency-based analysis usually comes down to identifying the basic skills an employee needs to do the job. For example, British Petroleum's (BP's) exploration division managers wanted a more efficient, faster acting, flatter organization and empowered employees. To accomplish this, senior managers wanted to shift employees' attention from a job description–type "that's-not-my-job" mentality to one that would motivate them to acquire the new skills they needed to carry out their broader responsibilities.

The solution was a skills matrix, similar to the one shown in Figure 4-11. BP created skills matrices for various jobs for two groups of employees: those on a management track and those whose aims lay elsewhere (such as to stay in engineering). HR prepared a matrix for each job or job family (such as drilling managers). As in Figure 4-11, each matrix listed (1) the basic skills needed for that job (such as technical expertise) and (2) the minimum level of each skill required for that job or job family. The emphasis is no longer on specific job duties. Instead, the focus is on developing the new skills needed for the employees' broader and empowered responsibilities.

The skills matrix method prompted other HR-related changes in this division. For example, the firm instituted a new *skills-based pay plan* that awards raises based on skills improvement. *Performance appraisals* now focus more on skills employees acquired. And *training* emphasizes developing broad skills like leadership and planning—skills applicable across a wide range of responsibilities and jobs.

In Summary: Why Competency Analysis?

To sum up, there are two reasons to consider describing jobs in terms of competencies rather than (or in addition to) duties.

First, traditional job descriptions may actually backfire if a *high-performance work system* is your goal. Here the whole thrust is to encourage employees to work in a self-motivated way. Employers do this by empowering employees, organizing the work around teams, encouraging team members to rotate freely among jobs, and pushing more responsibility for things like day-to-day supervision down to the workers. Employees must be enthusiastic about learning and moving among jobs. Giving someone a job description with a list of specific duties may simply breed a

FIGURE 4-11 The Skills Matrix for One Job at BP

Note: The light purple boxes indicate the minimum level of skill required for the job.

H	H	H	H	H	H	H
G	G	G	G	G	G	G
F	F	F	F	F	F	F
E	E	E	**E**	E	E	E
D	D	D	D	**D**	**D**	D
C	**C**	C	C	C	C	**C**
B	B	**B**	B	B	B	B
A	A	A	A	A	A	A
Technical expertise	Business awareness	Communication and interpersonal	Decision-making and initiative	Leadership and guidance	Planning and organizational ability	Problem-solving

"that's-not-my-job" attitude. The important thing is to ensure that each worker has the skills he or she needs to move among the jobs.

Second, describing jobs in terms of skills can help the company support its strategic aims. As an example, Canon's competitive strategy emphasizes miniaturization and precision manufacturing. Encouraging employees to develop their skills in these two areas helps ensure Canon has the skills it needs to execute its strategy.

REVIEW

CHAPTER SECTION SUMMARIES

1. All managers need to be familiar with **the basics of job analysis**
   - Job analysis is the procedure through which you determine the duties of the department's positions and the characteristics of the people to hire for them.
   - Job descriptions are a list of what the job entails, while job specifications identify what kind of people to hire for the job.
   - The job analysis itself involves collecting information on matters such as work activities, required human behaviors, and machines, tools, and equipment used.
   - Managers use job analysis information in recruitment and selection, compensation, training, and performance appraisal.
   - The basic steps in job analysis include deciding the use of the job analysis information, reviewing relevant background information including organization charts, analyzing the job, verifying the information, and developing job descriptions and job specifications.
2. There are various **methods for collecting job analysis information**. These include interviews, questionnaires, observation, participant diary/logs, and quantitative techniques such as position analysis questionnaires. Employers increasingly collect information from employees via the Internet.
3. Managers should be familiar with the process for **writing job descriptions**. While there is no standard format, most descriptions contain sections that cover job identification, a job summary, a listing of responsibilities and duties, the job incumbent's authority, and performance standards. The job description may also contain information regarding the job's working conditions, and the job specifications. Many employers use Internet sources such as jobdescription.com to facilitate writing job descriptions.
4. In **writing job specifications**, it's important to distinguish between specifications for trained versus untrained personnel. For trained employees, the process is relatively straightforward, because you're looking primarily for traits like experience. For untrained personnel, it's necessary to identify traits that might predict success of the job. Most job specifications come from the educated guesses of people like supervisors, and are based mostly on judgment. Some employers use statistical analyses to identify predictors or human traits that are related to success on the job.
5. As workers increasingly work in teams and with less supervision, understanding how to deal with **job analysis in a worker-empowered world** has become more important. In particular, more employers are moving toward competency-based job analysis, which means describing the job in terms of measurable, observable, behavioral competencies (such as specific skills) that an employee doing the job must exhibit to do the job well. With the job of, say, a team member possibly changing daily, it's more important to identify the skills the employee may need to move among jobs on the team than to box the employee in with a traditional job analysis listing of duties.

DISCUSSION QUESTIONS

1. What items are typically included in the job description?
2. What is job analysis? How can you make use of the information it provides?
3. We discussed several methods for collecting job analysis data—questionnaires, the position analysis questionnaire, and so on. Compare and contrast these methods, explaining what each is useful for and listing the pros and cons of each.
4. Describe the types of information typically found in a job specification.
5. Explain how you would conduct a job analysis.
6. Do you think companies can really do without detailed job descriptions? Why or why not?
7. In a company with only 25 employees, is there less need for job descriptions? Why or why not?

INDIVIDUAL AND GROUP ACTIVITIES

1. Working individually or in groups, obtain copies of job descriptions for clerical positions at the college or university where you study, or the firm where you work. What types of information do they contain? Do they give you enough information to explain what the job involves and how to do it? How would you improve on the description?
2. Working individually or in groups, use O*NET to develop a job description for your professor in this class. Based on that, use your judgment to develop a job specification. Compare your conclusions with those of other students or groups. Were there any significant differences? What do you think accounted for the differences?
3. The HRCI "Test Specifications" appendix at the end of this book (pages 699–706) lists the knowledge someone studying for the HRCI certification exam needs to have in each area of human resource management (such as in Strategic Management, Workforce Planning, and Human Resource Development). In groups of four to five students, do four things: (1) review that appendix now; (2) identify the material in this chapter that relates to the required knowledge in the appendix lists; (3) write four multiple-choice exam questions on this material that you believe would be suitable for inclusion in the HRCI exam; and (4) if time permits, have someone from your team post your team's questions in front of the class, so the students in other teams can take each others' exam questions.

EXPERIENTIAL EXERCISE

The Instructor's Job Description

Purpose: The purpose of this exercise is to give you experience in developing a job description, by developing one for your instructor.

Required Understanding: You should understand the mechanics of job analysis and be thoroughly familiar with the job analysis questionnaires. (See Figures 4-3 and 4-10.)

How to Set Up the Exercise/Instructions: Set up groups of four to six students for this exercise. As in all exercises in this book, the groups should be separated and should not converse with each other. Half of the groups in the class will develop the job description using the job analysis questionnaire (Figure 4-3), and the other half of the groups will develop it using the job description questionnaire (Figure 4-10). Each student should review his or her questionnaire (as appropriate) before joining his or her group.

1. Each group should do a job analysis of the instructor's job: Half of the groups will use the Figure 4-3 job analysis questionnaire for this purpose, and half will use the Figure 4-10 job description questionnaire.
2. Based on this information, each group will develop its own job description and job specification for the instructor.
3. Next, each group should choose a partner group, one that developed the job description and job specification using the alternate method. (A group that used the job analysis questionnaire should be paired with a group that used the job description questionnaire.)
4. Finally, within each of these new combined groups, compare and critique each of the two sets of job descriptions and job specifications. Did each job analysis method provide different types of information? Which seems superior? Does one seem more advantageous for some types of jobs than others?

APPLICATION CASE

Tropical Storm Wilma

In August 2005, tropical storm Wilma hit North Carolina and the Optima Air Filter Company. Many employees' homes were devastated, and the firm found that it had to hire almost three completely new crews, one for each of its shifts. The problem was that the "old-timers" had known their jobs so well that no one had ever bothered to draw up job descriptions for them. When about 30 new employees began taking their places, there was general confusion about what they should do and how they should do it.

The storm quickly became old news to the firm's out-of-state customers, who wanted filters, not excuses. Phil Mann, the firm's president, was at his wits' end. He had about 30 new employees, 10 old-timers, and his original factory supervisor, Maybelline. He decided to meet with Linda Lowe, a consultant from the local university's business school. She immediately had the old-timers fill out a job questionnaire that listed all their duties. Arguments ensued almost at once: Both Phil and Maybelline thought the old-timers were exaggerating to make themselves look more important, and the old-timers insisted that the lists faithfully reflected their duties. Meanwhile, the customers clamored for their filters.

Questions

1. Should Phil and Linda ignore the old-timers' protests and write up the job descriptions as they see fit? Why? Why not? How would you go about resolving the differences?
2. How would you have conducted the job analysis? What should Phil do now?

CONTINUING CASE

Carter Cleaning Company

The Job Description

Based on her review of the stores, Jennifer concluded that one of the first matters she had to attend to involved developing job descriptions for her store managers.

As Jennifer tells it, her lessons regarding job descriptions in her basic management and HR management courses were insufficient to fully convince her of the pivotal role job descriptions actually played in the smooth functioning of an enterprise. Many times during her first few weeks on the job, Jennifer found herself asking one of her store managers why he was violating what she knew to be recommended company policies and procedures. Repeatedly, the answers were either "Because I didn't know it was my job" or "Because I didn't know that was the way we were supposed to do it." Jennifer knew that a job description, along with a set of standards and procedures that specified what was to be done and how to do it, would go a long way toward alleviating this problem.

In general, the store manager is responsible for directing all store activities in such a way that quality work is produced, customer relations and sales are maximized, and profitability is maintained through effective control of labor, supply, and energy costs. In accomplishing that general aim, a specific store manager's duties and responsibilities include quality control, store appearance and cleanliness, customer relations, bookkeeping and cash management, cost control and productivity, damage control, pricing, inventory control, spotting and cleaning, machine maintenance, purchasing, employee safety, hazardous waste removal, human resource administration, and pest control.

The questions that Jennifer had to address follow.

Questions

1. What should be the format and final form of the store manager's job description?
2. Is it practical to specify standards and procedures in the body of the job description, or should these be kept separate?
3. How should Jennifer go about collecting the information required for the standards, procedures, and job description?
4. What, in your opinion, should the store manager's job description look like and contain?

TRANSLATING STRATEGY INTO HR POLICIES & PRACTICES CASE

The Hotel Paris Case

Job Descriptions

The Hotel Paris's competitive strategy is "To use superior guest service to differentiate the Hotel Paris properties, and to thereby increase the length of stay and return rate of guests, and thus boost revenues and profitability." HR manager Lisa Cruz must now formulate functional policies and activities that support this competitive strategy, by eliciting the required employee behaviors and competencies.

As an experienced human resource director, the Hotel Paris's Lisa Cruz knew that recruitment and selection processes invariably influenced employee competencies and behavior and, through them, the company's bottom line. Everything about the workforce—its collective skills, morale, experience, and motivation—depended on attracting and then selecting the right employees.

In reviewing the Hotel Paris's employment systems, she was therefore concerned that virtually all the company's job descriptions were out of date, and that many jobs had no descriptions at all. She knew that without accurate job descriptions, all her improvement efforts would be in vain. After all, if you don't know a job's duties, responsibilities, and human requirements, how can you decide who to hire or how to train them? To create human resource policies and practices that would produce employee competencies and behaviors needed to achieve the hotel's strategic aims, Lisa's team first had to produce a set of usable job descriptions.

A brief analysis, conducted with her company's CFO, reinforced that observation. They chose departments across the hotel chain that did and did not have updated job descriptions. Although they understood that many other factors might be influencing the results, they believed that the relationships they observed did suggest that having job descriptions had a positive influence on various employee behaviors and competencies. Perhaps having the descriptions facilitated the employee selection process, or perhaps the departments with the descriptions just had better managers.

She knew the Hotel Paris's job descriptions would have to include traditional duties and responsibilities. However, most should also include several competencies unique to each job. For example, job descriptions for the front-desk clerks might include "able to check a guest in or out in 5 minutes or less." Most service employees' descriptions included the competency, "able to exhibit patience and guest supportiveness even when busy with other activities."

Questions

In teams or individually:

1. Based on the hotel's stated strategy, list at least four important employee behaviors for the Hotel Paris's staff.
2. If time permits, spend some time prior to class observing the front-desk clerk at a local hotel. In any case, create a job description for a Hotel Paris front desk clerk.

KEY TERMS

job analysis, *p. 117*
job description, *p. 117*
job specifications, *p. 117*
organization chart, *p. 117*
process chart, *p. 119*
diary/log, *p. 127*
position analysis questionnaire (PAQ), *p. 127*
Standard Occupational Classification (SOC), *p. 135*
job enlargement, *p. 143*
job rotation, *p. 143*
job enrichment, *p. 143*
competency-based job analysis, *p. 143*

ENDNOTES

1. Daimler is now expanding this plant; see www.autoblog.com/2009/03/23/rumormill-mercedes-benz-expected-to-expand-alabama-plant, accessed March 25, 2009.
2. For a good discussion of job analysis, see James Clifford, "Job Analysis: Why Do It, and How Should It Be Done?" *Public Personnel Management* 23, no. 2 (Summer 1994), pp. 321–340; and "Job Analysis," www.paq.com/index.cfm?FuseAction=bulletins.job-analysis, accessed February 3, 2009.
3. One writer recently called job analysis, "The hub of virtually all human resource management activities necessary for the successful functioning organizations". See Parbudyal Singh, "Job Analysis for a Changing Workplace," *Human Resource Management Review* 18 (2008), p. 87.
4. James Clifford, "Manage Work Better to Better Manage Human Resources: A Comparative Study of Two Approaches to Job Analysis," *Public Personnel Management*, Spring 1996, pp. 89–102.
5. Richard Henderson, *Compensation Management: Rewarding Performance* (Upper Saddle River, NJ: Prentice Hall, 1994), pp. 139–150. See also T. A. Stetz, et. al, "New Tricks for an Old Dog: Visualizing Job Analysis Results," *Public Personnel Management* 38, no. 1 (Spring 2009), pp. 91–100.
6. Darin Hartley, "Job Analysis at the Speed of Reality," *Training & Development*, September 2004, pp. 20–22.
7. See Henderson, *Compensation Management*, pp. 148–152.
8. Wayne Cascio, *Applied Psychology in Human Resource Management* (Upper Saddle River, NJ: Prentice Hall, 1998), p. 142. See also M. K. Lindell, C. S. Clause, C. J. Brandt, and R. S. Landis, "Relationships Between Organizational Content and Job Analysis Task Ratings," *Journal of Applied Psychology* 83, no. 5 (1998), pp. 769–776.
9. Frederick Morgeson et al., "Self Presentation Processes in Job Analysis: A Field Experiment Investigating Inflation in Abilities, Tasks, and Competencies," *Journal of Applied Psychology* 89, no. 4 (November 4, 2004): 674–686; and Frederick Morgeson and Stephen Humphrey, "The Work Design Questionnaire (WDQ): Developing and Validating a Comprehensive Measure for Assessing Job Design and the Nature of Work," *Journal of Applied Psychology* 91, no. 6 (2006), pp. 1321–1339.
10. Arthur Martinez et al., "Job Title Inflation," *Human Resource Management Review* 18 (2008), pp. 19–27.
11. Note that the PAQ (and other quantitative techniques) can also be used for job evaluation, which is explained in Chapter 11.
12. Again, we will see that job evaluation is the process through which jobs are compared to one another and their values determined. Although usually viewed as a job analysis technique, the PAQ is, in practice, actually as much or more of a job evaluation technique and could therefore be discussed in either this chapter or in Chapter 11. For a discussion of how to use PAQ for classifying jobs for pay purposes, see Edwin Cornelius III, Theodore Carron, and Marianne Collins, "Job Analysis Models and Job Classification," *Personnel Psychology* 32 (Winter 1979), pp. 693–708. See also Edwin Cornelius III, Frank Schmidt, and Theodore Carron, "Job Classification Approaches and the Implementation of Validity Generalization Results," *Personnel Psychology* 37, no. 2 (Summer 1984), pp. 247–260.
13. Jack Smith and Milton Hakel, "Convergence Among Data Sources, Response Bias, and Reliability and Validity of a Structured Job Analysis Questionnaire," *Personnel Psychology* 32 (Winter 1979), pp. 677–692. See also Edwin Cornelius III, Angelo DeNisi, and Allyn Blencoe, "Expert and Naïve Raters Using the PAQ: Does It Matter?" *Personnel Psychology* 37, no. 3 (Autumn 1984), pp. 453–464; Robert J. Harvey et al., "Dimensionality of the Job Element Inventory: A Simplified Worker-Oriented Job Analysis Questionnaire," *Journal of Applied Psychology*, November 1988, pp. 639–646; Frederick Morgeson and Stephen Humphrey, "The Work Design Questionnaire (WDQ): Developing and Validating a Comprehensive Measure for Assessing Job Design and the Nature of Work," *Journal of Applied Psychology* 91, no. 6 (2006), pp. 1321–1339; www.paq.com/index.cfm?FuseAction=bulletins.job-analysis, accessed February 3, 2009.
14. www.paq.com/index.cfm?FuseAction=bulletins.job-analysis, accessed February 3, 2009.
15. Roni Reiter-Palmon et al., "Development of an O*NET Web-Based Job Analysis and Its Implementation in the U.S. Navy: Lessons Learned," *Human Resource Management Review* 16 (2006), pp. 294–309.
16. Ibid., p. 294.
17. Ibid., p. 295.
18. Digitizing the information also enables the employer to quantify, tag, and electronically store and access it more readily. Lauren McEntire et al., "Innovations in Job Analysis: Development and Application of Metrics to Analyze Job Data," *Human Resource Management Review* 16 (2006), pp. 310–323.
19. Regarding this discussion, see Henderson, *Compensation Management*, pp. 175–184. See also Louisa Wah, "The Alphabet Soup of Job Titles," *Management Review* 87, no. 6, 01-JUN-98, pp. 40–43.
20. James Evered, "How to Write a Good Job Description," *Supervisory Management*, April 1981, pp. 14–19; Roger J. Plachy, "Writing Job Descriptions That Get Results," *Personnel*, October 1987, pp. 56–58. See also Matthew Mariani, "Replace with a database: O*NET replaces the Dictionary of Occupational Titles," *Occupational Outlook Quarterly* 43, no. 1 (March 1999), pp. 2–9.

21. Ibid., p. 16.
22. Ibid.
23. Ibid.
24. Deborah Kearney, *Reasonable Accommodations: Job Descriptions in the Age of ADA, OSHA, and Workers Comp* (New York: Van Nostrand Reinhold, 1994), p. 9. See also Paul Starkman, "The ADA's Essential Job Function Requirements: Just How Essential Does an Essential Job Function Have to Be?" *Employee Relations Law Journal* 26, no. 4 (Spring 2001), pp. 43–102.
25. Michael Esposito, "There's More to Writing Job Descriptions Than Complying with the ADA," *Employment Relations Today*, Autumn 1992, p. 279. See also Richard Morfopoulos and William Roth, "Job Analysis and the Americans with Disabilities Act," *Business Horizons* 39, no. 6 (November 1996), pp. 68–72; and Krystin Mitchell, George Alliger, and Richard Morfopoulos, "Toward an ADA-Appropriate Job Analysis," *Human Resource Management Review* 7, no. 1 (Spring 1997), pp. 5–16.
26. James Evered, "How to Write a Good Job Description," p. 18.
27. See, for example, Christelle Lapolice et al., "Linking O*NET Descriptors to Occupational Literacy Requirements Using Job Component Validation," *Personnel Psychology* 61 (2008), pp. 405–441.
28. Matthew Mariani, "Replace with a database: O*NET replaces the Dictionary of Occupational Titles," *Occupational Outlook Quarterly* 43, no. 1 (March 1999), pp. 2–9.
29. O*Net™ is a trademark of the U.S. Department of Labor, Employment, and Training Administration.
30. Jorgen Sandberg, "Understanding Competence at Work," *Harvard Business Review*, March 2001, p. 28. Other organization chart software vendors include Nakisa, Aquire, and HumanConcepts. See "Advanced Org Charting," *Workforce Management*, May 19, 2008, p. 34.
31. Based on Ernest J. McCormick and Joseph Tiffin, *Industrial Psychology* (Upper Saddle River, NJ: Prentice Hall, 1974), pp. 56–61.
32. Steven Hunt, "Generic Work Behavior: An Investigation into the Dimensions of Entry-Level, Hourly Job Performance," *Personnel Psychology* 49 (1996), pp. 51–83.
33. David Shair, "Wizardry Makes Charts Relevant," *HR Magazine*, April 2000, p. 127.
34. Lindsay Chappell, "Mercedes Factories Embrace a New Order," *Automotive News*, May 28, 2001.
35. Jeffrey Shippmann et al., "The Practice of Competency Modeling," *Personnel Psychology* 53, no. 3 (2000), p. 703.
36. Ibid.
37. Adapted from Richard Mirabile, "Everything You Wanted to Know About Competency Modeling," *Training & Development* 51, no. 8 (August 1997), pp. 73–78.
38. Dennis Kravetz, "Building a Job Competency Database: What the Leaders Do," Kravetz Associates (Bartlett, Illinois, 1997).

5 Personnel Planning and Recruiting

With more than 110 restaurants and adding 20 more per year, The Cheesecake Factory must attract and hire 24,000 people per year. For Ed Eynon, Cheesecake's senior vice president for human resources, that means casting a wide net when it comes to recruiting—"You don't find all the people you need from one source," he says. So, having the right recruiting sources is crucial to The Cheesecake Factory's success.[1]

Source: Courtesy of Chris Howarth/USA/Alamy Images.

WHERE ARE WE NOW . . .

In Chapter 4, we discussed job analysis and the methods managers use to create job descriptions and job specifications. The purpose of this chapter is to improve your effectiveness in recruiting candidates. The topics we discuss include personnel planning and forecasting, recruiting job candidates, and developing and using application forms. Then, in Chapter 6, we'll turn to the methods managers use to select the best employees from this applicant pool.

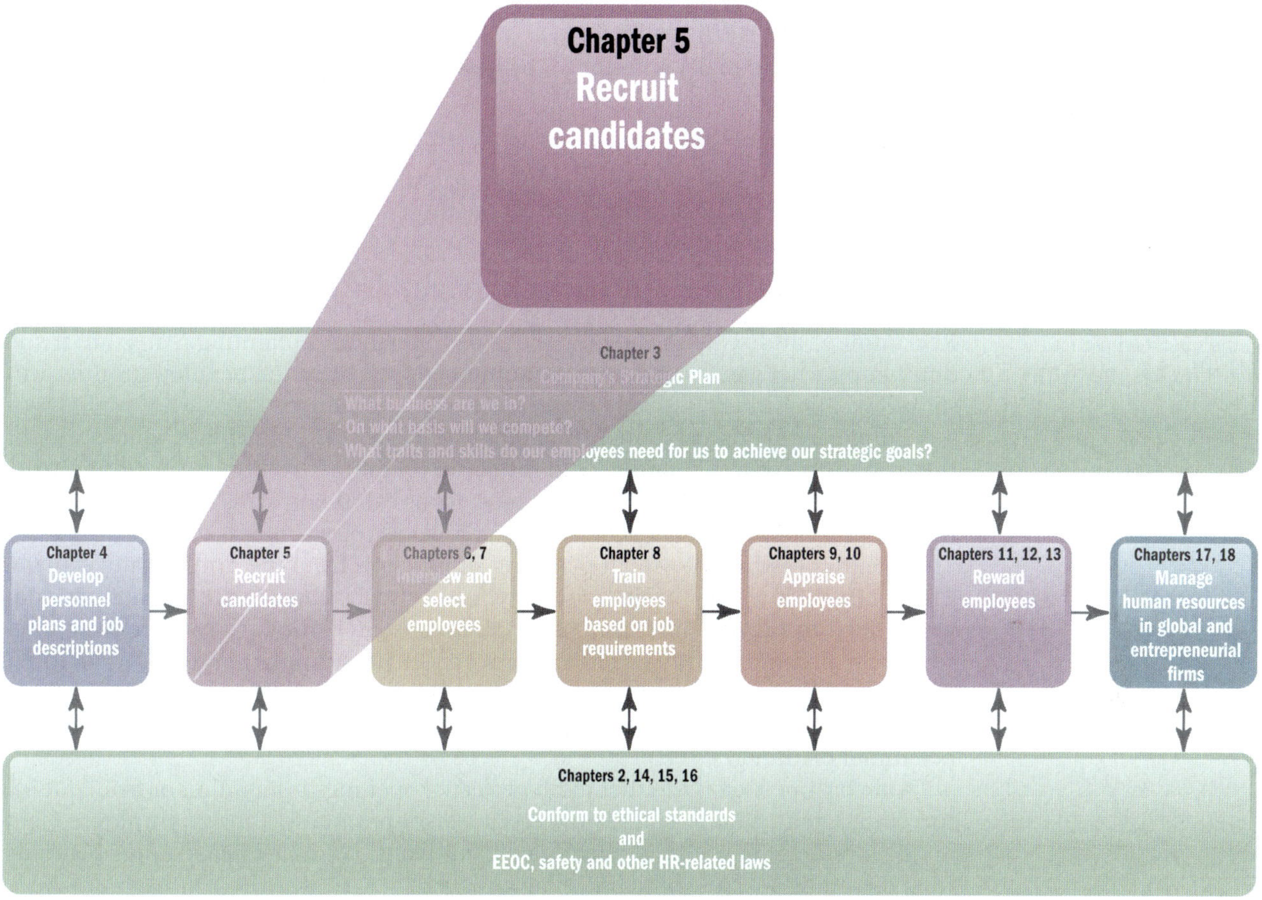

LEARNING OUTCOMES

1. List the steps in the recruitment and selection process.
2. Explain the main techniques used in employment planning and forecasting.
3. Explain and give examples for the need for effective recruiting.
4. Name and describe the main internal sources of candidates.
5. List and discuss the main outside sources of candidates.
6. Develop a help wanted ad.
7. Explain how to recruit a more diverse workforce.

1 List the steps in the recruitment and selection process.

THE RECRUITMENT AND SELECTION PROCESS

Job analysis identifies the duties and human requirements for each of the company's jobs. The next step is to decide how many of these jobs you need to fill, and to recruit and select employees for them. The best way to envision *recruitment and selection* is as a series of hurdles (Figure 5-1):

1. Decide what positions to fill, through *personnel planning and forecasting.*
2. Build a pool of candidates for these jobs, by *recruiting* internal or external candidates.
3. Have candidates complete *application forms* and perhaps undergo initial screening interviews.
4. Use *selection tools* like tests, background investigations, and physical exams to identify viable candidates.
5. Decide who to make an offer to, by having the supervisor and perhaps others *interview* the candidates.

This chapter focuses on personnel planning and on recruiting employees. Chapter 6 addresses selection techniques, including tests, background checks, and physical exams. Chapter 7 focuses on interviewing—by far the most widely used selection technique.

2 Explain the main techniques used in employment planning and forecasting.

PLANNING AND FORECASTING

Recruitment and selection ideally starts with personnel planning. After all, if you don't know what your team's employment needs will be in the next few months, why should you be hiring?

Employment (or personnel) planning is the process of deciding what positions the firm will have to fill, and how to fill them. It embraces all future positions, from maintenance clerk to CEO. However, most firms call the process of deciding how to fill executive jobs *succession planning.*

In either case, employment planning should flow from the firm's strategic plans. Thus plans to enter new businesses or reduce costs all influence the types of positions you'll need to fill (or eliminate). At IBM, for instance, human resource executives review with finance and other executives the personnel ramifications of their company's strategic plans.[2] In other words, "What sorts of skills and competencies will we need to execute our plans?" Figure 5-2 summarizes the link between strategic and personnel planning.

One big question is whether to fill projected openings from within or from outside the firm. Each option requires different personnel plans. *Current* employees may require training, development, and coaching plans. Going *outside* requires planning what recruiting sources you'll use.

Like all good plans, personnel plans require some forecasts or estimates, in this case, of three things: *personnel needs,* the *supply of inside* candidates, and the likely *supply of outside* candidates. We'll start with personnel needs.

FIGURE 5-1 Steps in Recruitment and Selection Process. The recruitment and selection process is a series of hurdles aimed at selecting the best candidate for the job.

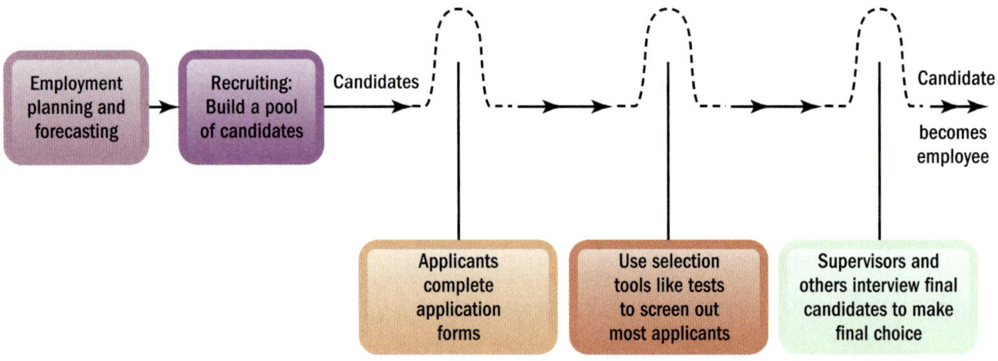

The recruitment and selection process is a series of hurdles aimed at selecting the best candidate for the job.

FIGURE 5-2 Linking Employer's Strategy to Plans

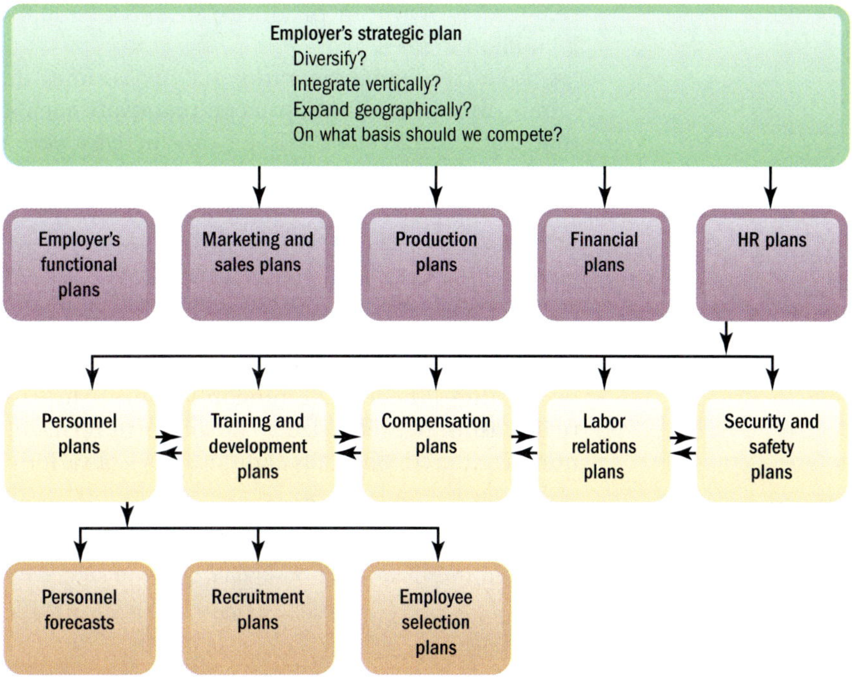

Forecasting Personnel Needs

How many people do you need? Managers consider several factors.[3] For example, when Dan Hilbert took over staffing at Valero Energy, he reviewed Valero's demographics, growth plans, and turnover history. He discovered that projected employment shortfalls were four times more than Valero could fill with its current recruitment procedures. He turned to formulating new personnel plans for boosting employee retention and recruiting and screening more candidates.[4]

As we explained in Chapter 3 on business planning, the basic process of deciding personnel needs is to forecast revenues first. Then estimate the size of the staff required to support this sales volume. However, managers obviously need to consider other factors too. These include projected turnover, decisions to upgrade (or downgrade) products or services, productivity changes, and financial resources. There are several simple tools for projecting personnel needs, as follows.

Trend Analysis

Trend analysis means studying variations in your firm's employment levels over the last few years. For example, you might compute the number of employees at the end of each of the last 5 years, or perhaps the number in each subgroup (like sales, production, secretarial, and administrative). The aim is to identify trends that might continue into the future.

Trend analysis can provide an initial estimate of future staffing needs, but employment levels rarely depend just on the passage of time. Other factors (like changes in sales volume and productivity) also affect staffing needs.

Ratio Analysis

Another simple approach, **ratio analysis**, means making forecasts based on the historical ratio between (1) some causal factor (like sales volume) and (2) the number of employees required (such as number of salespeople). For example, suppose a salesperson traditionally generates $500,000 in sales. If the sales revenue to salespeople ratio remains the same, you would require six new salespeople next

employment (or personnel) planning
The process of deciding what positions the firm will have to fill, and how to fill them.

trend analysis
Study of a firm's past employment needs over a period of years to predict future needs.

ratio analysis
A forecasting technique for determining future staff needs by using ratios between, for example, sales volume and number of employees needed.

year (each of whom produces an extra $500,000) to produce a hoped-for extra $3 million in sales.

Like trend analysis, ratio analysis assumes that productivity remains about the same—for instance, that you can't motivate each salesperson to produce much more than $500,000 in sales. If sales productivity were to rise or fall, the ratio of sales to salespeople would change.

The Scatter Plot A **scatter plot** shows graphically how two variables—such as sales and your firm's staffing levels—are related. If they are, then if you can forecast the business activity (like sales), you should also be able to estimate your personnel needs.

For example, suppose a 500-bed hospital expects to expand to 1,200 beds over the next 5 years. The human resource director wants to forecast how many registered nurses they'll need. The human resource director realizes she must determine the relationship between size of hospital (in terms of number of beds) and number of nurses required. She calls eight hospitals of various sizes and gets the following figures:

Size of Hospital (Number of Beds)	Number of Registered Nurses
200	240
300	260
400	470
500	500
600	620
700	660
800	820
900	860

Figure 5-3 shows hospital size on the horizontal axis. It shows number of nurses on the vertical axis. If these two factors are related, then the points will tend to fall along a straight line, as they do here. If you carefully draw in a line to minimize the distances between the line and each one of the plotted points, you will be able to estimate the number of nurses needed for each hospital size. Thus, for a 1,200-bed hospital, the human resource director would assume she needs about 1,210 nurses.

While simple, tools like scatter plots have drawbacks.[5]

1. They generally focus on historical sales/personnel relationships and assume that the firm's existing activities will continue as is.
2. They tend to support compensation plans that reward managers for managing ever-larger staffs, irrespective of the company's strategic needs.
3. They tend to institutionalize existing ways of doing things, even in the face of change.

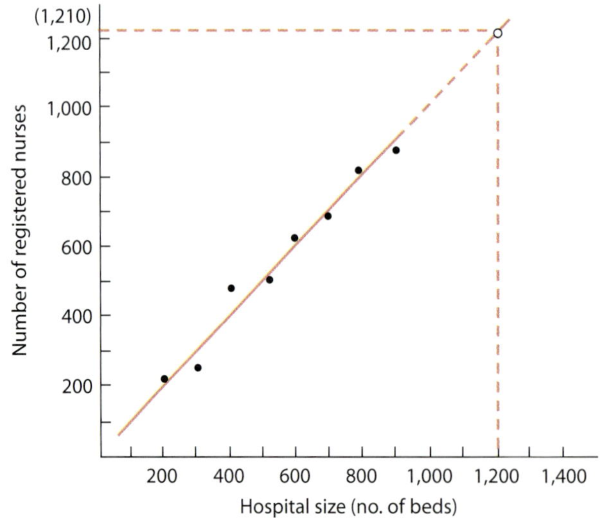

FIGURE 5-3 Determining the Relationship Between Hospital Size and Number of Nurses

Note: After fitting the line, you can project how many employees you'll need, given your projected volume.

Using Computers to Support Forecasting Personnel Needs

Computerized forecasts enable the manager to build more variables into his or her personnel projections.[6] Newer systems particularly rely on mathematically setting clear goals, such as reducing amount of inventory on hand.[7] Other variables might include direct labor hours required to produce one unit of product (a measure of productivity), and minimum, maximum, and probable sales projections. Based on such input, a typical program generates average staff levels required to meet product demands, as well as separate forecasts for direct labor (such as assembly workers), indirect staff (such as secretaries), and exempt staff (such as executives).

With programs like these, employers can more accurately translate desired and/or projected productivity and sales levels into forecasted personnel needs. And, they can estimate the effects of various productivity and sales level assumptions on personnel requirements.[8] Many firms use computerized employee forecasting systems particularly for estimating short-term needs. In retailing, for instance, labor scheduling systems help retailers estimate required staffing needs based on sales forecasts and estimated store traffic.

Whichever forecasting tool you use, *managerial judgment* should play a big role. It's rare that any historical trend, ratio, or relationship will simply continue. You will therefore have to modify the forecast based on subjective factors—such as the feeling that more employees will be quitting—you believe will be important.

Forecasting the Supply of Inside Candidates

Knowing your staffing needs satisfies only half the staffing equation. Next, you have to estimate the likely supply of both inside and outside candidates. Most firms start with the inside candidates.

The main task here is determining which current employees might be qualified for the projected openings. For this you need to know current employees' skills sets—their current qualifications. Sometimes it's obvious how you have to proceed. For example, when Bill Gates needed someone to lead Microsoft's new user interface project, his first question was, "Where's Kai-Fu?" His firm's voice recognition expert, Kai-Fu Lee, was in China at the time, establishing a new research lab for the firm.[9] (Kai-Fu later became head of Google Greater China.)

Sometimes who to choose is not so obvious. Here, managers turn to **qualifications (or skills) inventories**. These contain data on employees' performance records, educational background, and promotability. Whether manual or computerized, these help managers determine which employees are available for promotion or transfer.

Manual Systems and Replacement Charts

Department managers or owners of smaller firms often use manual devices to track employee qualifications. Thus a *personnel inventory and development record form* compiles qualifications information on each employee. The information includes education, company-sponsored courses taken, career and development interests, languages, desired assignments, and skills. **Personnel replacement charts** (Figure 5-4) are another option, particularly for the firm's top positions. They show the present performance and promotability for each position's potential replacement. As an alternative, you can develop a **position replacement card**. Here, create a card for each position, showing possible replacements as well as their present performance, promotion potential, and training.

scatter plot
A graphical method used to help identify the relationship between two variables.

qualifications (or skills) inventories
Manual or computerized records listing employees' education, career and development interests, languages, special skills, and so on, to be used in selecting inside candidates for promotion.

personnel replacement charts
Company records showing present performance and promotability of inside candidates for the most important positions.

position replacement card
A card prepared for each position in a company to show possible replacement candidates and their qualifications.

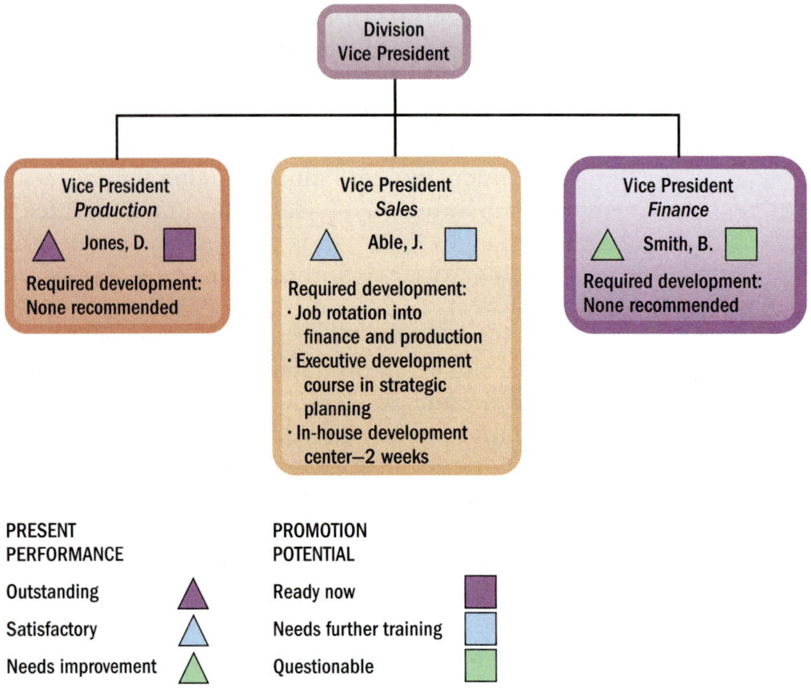

FIGURE 5-4 Management Replacement Chart Showing Development Needs of Potential Future Divisional Vice Presidents

Computerized Skills Inventories Larger firms obviously can't track the qualifications of hundreds or thousands of employees manually. Larger employers therefore computerize this information, using various packaged software systems. Increasingly, they also link skills inventories with their other human resources systems. So, for instance, an employee's skills inventory might automatically update each time he is trained or appraised.

The usual process is for the employee, the supervisor, and human resource manager to enter information about the employee's background, experience, and skills via the company intranet. Then, when a manager needs a person for a position, he or she uses key words to describe the position's specifications (for instance, in terms of education and skills). The computerized skills inventory then produces a list of qualified candidates. Computerized skills inventory data typically include items like *work experience codes, product knowledge*, the employee's *level of familiarity* with the employer's product lines or services, the person's *industry experience*, and *formal education*.

Keeping the Information Private The employer should secure all its employee data.[10] Much of the data is personal (such as Social Security numbers and illnesses). Legislation gives employees legal rights regarding who has access to information about them. The legislation includes the Federal Privacy Act of 1974 (applies to federal workers), the New York Personal Privacy Act of 1985, HIPAA (regulates use of medical records), and the Americans with Disabilities Act. Employers should keep their manual records under lock and key.

Internet access makes it relatively easy for more people to access the firm's computerized files.[11] One solution is to incorporate an access matrix in the database management system. These define the rights of users to various kinds of access (such as "read only" or "write only") to each database element. (So, those in accounting might *read only* information such as an employee's address.) Figure 5-5 summarizes some guidelines for keeping employee data safe. A growing problem is that peer-to-peer file-sharing applications jump firewalls and give outsiders quick access. Pfizer Inc. lost personal data on about 17,000 current and former employees this way.[12]

Forecasting the Supply of Outside Candidates

If there won't be enough inside candidates to fill the anticipated openings (or you want to go outside for another reason), you will turn to outside candidates.

FIGURE 5-5 Keeping Data Safe

Source: *HR Magazine* by Caternicchia. Copyright 2005 by Society for Human Resource Management (SHRM). Reproduced with permission of Society for Human Resource Management (SHRM) in the format Textbook via Copyright Clearance Center.

Since intruders can strike from outside an organization or from within, HR departments can help screen out potential identity thieves by following four basic rules:

- Perform background checks on anyone who is going to have access to personal information.
- If someone with access to personal information is out sick or on leave, don't hire a temporary employee to replace him or her. Instead, bring in a trusted worker from another department.
- Perform random background checks such as random drug tests. Just because someone passed 5 years ago doesn't mean their current situation is the same.
- Limit access to information such as SSNs, health information, and other sensitive data to HR managers who require it to do their jobs.

If you are drawing up a personnel plan (say, for the coming fiscal year), you may want to estimate how difficult it will be to find good outside candidates. For example, unemployment rates of more than 9% in the United States in late 2009 signaled to HR managers that finding good candidates would be easier.[13]

Information like this is easy to find, both online and in print format. For example, look for economic projections online, for instance, from the U.S. Congressional Budget Office (www.cbo.gov/showdoc.cfm?index=1824&sequence=0) and the Bureau of Labor Statistics (www.bls.gov/news.release/ecopro.toc.htm). For hard-copy formats, *BusinessWeek* presents a weekly snapshot of the economy on its Outlook page, as well as a yearly forecast in December.

Your planning may also require that you forecast specific occupations such as nurse, computer programmer, or teacher. Recently, for instance, there has been an undersupply of nurses. O*NET (discussed in Chapter 4) includes projections for most occupations. The U.S. Bureau of Labor Statistics publishes annual occupational projections both online and in the *Monthly Labor Review* and in *Occupational Outlook Quarterly*.

3 Explain and give examples for the need for effective recruiting.

THE NEED FOR EFFECTIVE RECRUITING

Assuming the company authorizes you to fill a position, the next step is to build up, through recruiting, an applicant pool. **Employee recruiting** means finding and/or attracting applicants for the employer's open positions.

Why Recruiting Is Important

It's hard to overemphasize the importance of effective recruiting. If only two candidates apply for two openings, you may have little choice but to hire them. But if 10 or 20 applicants appear, you can use techniques like interviews and tests to screen out all but the best.

Even high unemployment doesn't necessarily mean that it is easy to find good candidates. For example, a survey during an earlier slowdown (2003–2004) found that about half of respondents said they had "difficulty" finding qualified applicants. About 40% said it was "hard to find" good candidates.[14]

What Makes Effective Recruiting a Challenge?

It's easy to assume that recruiting is easy—that all you need do is place a few ads on the Web. Nothing could be farther from the truth. Several things make it more complex.

employee recruiting
Finding and/or attracting applicants for the employer's open positions.

- First, we'll see that some recruiting methods are superior to others, depending on the type of job for which you are recruiting.
- Second, the success you have recruiting depends greatly on nonrecruitment issues and policies. For example, paying 10% more than most firms in your locale should, other things being equal, help you build a bigger applicant pool faster.[15]
- Third, you know by now that employment law prescribes what you can and cannot do when recruiting. For example, managers can't rely on word-of-mouth dissemination of information about job opportunities when the workforce is substantially all white or all members of some other class, such as Hispanic.[16] Similarly, gender-specific ads that call for "busboy" or "firemen" obviously raise red flags.

Organizing How You Recruit

Should you centralize your firm's recruitment efforts, or let each plant or office do their own recruiting? More firms are centralizing it, for four good reasons. *First,* doing so makes it easier to apply the company's *strategic priorities* company-wide. For example, several years ago, GM centralized recruitment because it wanted to strengthen its employment image. They felt too many potential applicants viewed (rightly or wrongly) GM as old-fashioned. GM's central "talent acquisition department" now handles all of GM's North American plant recruiting.[17] *Second,* recruiting centrally *reduces duplication* (having several recruitment offices instead of one). *Third,* centralized recruiting makes it easier to ensure that recruitment experts who know EEO law are doing the recruiting.

But when it comes down to it, the widening *use of the Internet* probably trumps these other reasons. It's simply much easier for employers to recruit centrally now that so much recruiting is on the Net.[18] The accountants Deloitte & Touche Tohmatsu recently created a global recruitment site, thus eliminating the need to maintain 35 separate local recruiting Web sites.[19] Retailer 7-Eleven's site presents its worldwide job openings and lets prospective employees apply online.

The Supervisor's Role

The human resource manager charged with recruiting for an open job is seldom very familiar with the job itself. Someone has to tell this person what the position really entails, and what key things too look or watch out for. Only the position's supervisor can do this.

The supervisor therefore needs to know what sorts of questions to anticipate (and here your knowledge of job analysis should serve you well). For example, in addition to what the job entails now and its job specifications, the recruiter might want to know about the supervisor's leadership style and about the work group—is it a tough group to get along with, for instance?

The Recruiting Yield Pyramid

Some employers use a **recruiting yield pyramid** to calculate the number of applicants they must generate to hire the required number of new employees. In Figure 5-6, the company knows it needs 50 new entry-level accountants next year. From experience, the firm also knows the following:

- The ratio of offers made to actual new hires is 2 to 1.
- The ratio of candidates interviewed to offers made is 3 to 2.
- The ratio of candidates invited for interviews to candidates interviewed is about 4 to 3.
- Finally, the firm knows that of six leads that come in from all its recruiting sources, only one applicant typically gets invited for an interview—a 6-to-1 ratio.

Given these ratios, the firm knows it must generate 1,200 leads to be able to invite 200 viable candidates to its offices for interviews. The firm will then get to interview about 150 of those invited, and from these it will make 100 offers, and so on.

FIGURE 5-6 Recruiting Yield Pyramid

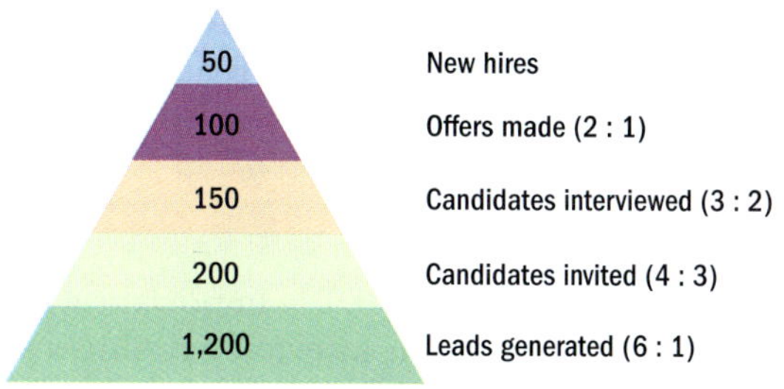

4 Name and describe the main internal sources of candidates.

INTERNAL SOURCES OF CANDIDATES

Recruiting typically brings to mind Monster.com, employment agencies, and classified ads, but internal sources—in other words, current employees or "hiring from within"—is often the best source of candidates.

Using Internal Sources: Pros and Cons

Filling open positions with inside candidates has several advantages. First, there is really no substitute for knowing a candidate's *strengths and weaknesses*, as you should after working with them for some time. Current employees may also be more *committed* to the company. *Morale* may rise if employees see promotions as rewards for loyalty and competence. And inside candidates should require *less orientation* and (perhaps) training than outsiders.

However, hiring from within can also backfire. Employees who apply for jobs and don't get them may become *discontented;* telling them why you rejected them and what remedial actions they might take is crucial. And too often internal recruiting is something of a *waste of time.* Many employers require managers to post job openings and interview all inside candidates. Yet the manager often knows ahead of time who he or she wants to hire. Requiring the person to interview a stream of unsuspecting inside candidates can be a waste of time for all concerned. *Inbreeding* is another potential drawback. When all managers come up through the ranks, they may have a tendency to maintain the status quo, when a new direction is required.

Finding Internal Candidates

Hiring from within ideally relies on job posting and the firm's skills inventories. **Job posting** means publicizing the open job to employees (usually by literally posting it on company intranets or bulletin boards). These postings list the job's attributes, like qualifications, supervisor, work schedule, and pay rate.

Qualifications skills banks also play a role. For example, the database may reveal persons who have potential for further training or who have the right background for the open job.

Rehiring

Should you rehire someone who left your employ? It depends. On the plus side, former employees are known quantities (more or less) and are already familiar with how you do things. On the other hand, employees who you let go may return with less-than-positive attitudes. And hiring former employees who resigned back into better positions may signal current employees that the best way to get ahead is to leave.

In any event, you can reduce the chance of adverse reactions.[20] After employees have been back on the job for a certain period, credit them with the years of service

recruiting yield pyramid
The historical arithmetic relationships between recruitment leads and invitees, invitees and interviews, interviews and offers made, and offers made and offers accepted.

job posting
Publicizing an open job to employees (often by literally posting it on bulletin boards) and listing its attributes, like qualifications, supervisor, working schedule, and pay rate.

they had accumulated before they left. In addition, inquire (before rehiring them) about what they did during the layoff and how they feel about returning: "You don't want someone coming back who feels they've been mistreated," said one manager.[21]

Succession Planning

Hiring from within is particularly important when it involves filling the employer's top positions. Filling them internally requires **succession planning**—the ongoing process of systematically identifying, assessing, and developing organizational leadership to enhance performance.[22] About 36% of employers have formal succession planning programs.[23] Succession planning entails three steps: identifying key needs, creating and assessing candidates, and selecting those who will fill the key positions.

Identify Key Needs

First, based on the company's plans, top management and the HR director identify what the company's future key position needs will be, and formulate job descriptions and specifications for them. (Thus, plans to expand abroad may suggest bulking up the international division.[24])

Develop Inside Candidates

After identifying future key positions, management turns to creating candidates for these jobs. "Creating" means identifying potential internal (and perhaps external) candidates for the future key positions, and then providing them with the developmental experiences they require to be viable candidates. Employers develop high-potential employees through internal training and cross-functional experiences, job rotation, external training, and global/regional assignments.[25]

Assess and Choose

Finally, succession planning requires assessing these candidates and selecting those who will actually fill the key positions.[26]

Improving Productivity Through HRIS: Succession Planning Systems

More large employers rely on software to facilitate the succession planning process. For example, when Larry Kern became president of Dole Food Co., Inc., Dole was highly decentralized. Kern's strategy involved improving financial performance by reducing redundancies and centralizing certain activities, including succession planning.[27]

Web technology helped Dole do this. It contracted with application system providers (ASPs) to handle things like payroll management. For succession management, Dole chose software from Pilat NAI, which keeps all the data on its own servers for a monthly fee.

The Pilat succession planning system is easy for Dole's managers to use. They access the program via the Web using a password. They fill out online résumés for themselves, including career interests, and note special considerations such as geographic restrictions. The managers also assess themselves on four competencies. When the manager completes his or her input, the program automatically notifies that manager's boss. The latter then assesses his or her subordinate and indicates whether the person should be promoted. This assessment and the online résumés then go automatically to the division head and the divisional HR director. Dole's senior vice president for human resources for North America then uses the information to create a career development plan for each manager, including seminars and other programs.[28]

5 List and discuss the main outside sources of candidates.

OUTSIDE SOURCES OF CANDIDATES

Firms can't always get all the employees they need from their current staff, and sometimes they just don't want to. We'll look at the sources firms use to find outside candidates next.

Recruiting via the Internet

Most people today go online to look for jobs. For most employers and for most jobs, Internet-based recruiting is by far the recruiting source of choice.[29] For example, The Cheesecake Factory gets about a third of its management applicants via the Web. Most employers recruit through their own Web sites, or use job boards. Figure 5-7 highlights some top online recruiting job boards.

Other Online Options There are online alternatives to placing ads on job boards. Newer sites capitalize on social networking. Users register by supplying their name,

FIGURE 5-7 Some Top Online Recruiting Job Boards

Source: www.quintcareers.com/top_10_sites.html, accessed April 28, 2009. Used with permission of QuintCareers.com.

succession planning
The ongoing process of systematically identifying, assessing, and developing organizational leadership to enhance performance.

location, and the kind of work they do on sites like Monster Networking and LinkedIn.com. These sites facilitate developing personal relationships for networking and employee referrals.[30] Accountants Deloitte & Touche asked employees to make short videos describing their experiences with Deloitte. It then took the 14 best (of 400 submitted) and posted them on YouTube.[31] Monster has a video product that helps employers integrate streaming video into their job postings.[32] MySpace and Facebook both make it easy to start a company networking site, which some employers may use for recruiting purposes.[33] McDonald's posted employee testimonials on networking sites like Second Life as a way to attract applicants.[34] Other managers simply do keyword searches on online databases. For example, one HR manager found that a keyword search of the HotJobs database produced 52 résumés. "I find more qualified candidates by searching for résumés than posting ads," he says.[35]

HR APPs 4 U

Posting and Accessing Job Openings

CareerBuilder.com iPhone App—"Jobs"[37]

The CareerBuilder.com iPhone application offers a unique way to search nearly 2 million jobs on CareerBuilder.com, the largest U.S. job site. Users may search for jobs by keyword, read job descriptions and salaries, save jobs to a list of favorites, and e-mail job links to anyone on their contact list.

The application also takes advantage of the iPhone's geo-location capabilities. Users may direct it to search only for jobs in the region where they are located.

Finally, the application integrates Google Maps by displaying a map of the city each job is located in. For more about CareerBuilder.com, please visit the Web site. And the app—it's free.

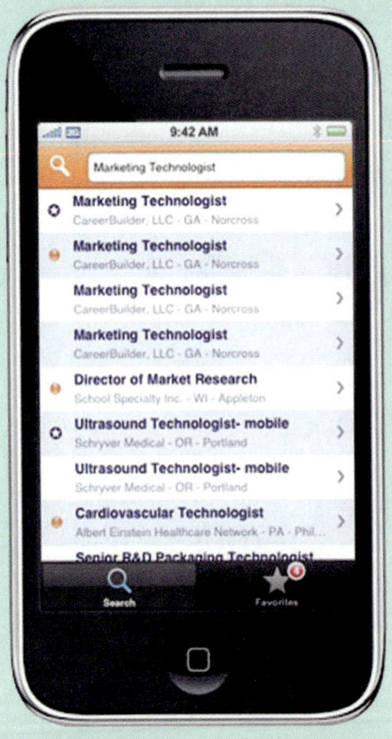

Source: http://www.careerbuilder.com/MarketingWeb/iPhone/CBJobsApplication.aspx?cbRecursionCnt=1&cbsid=7fd458dafd4a444fb192d9a24ceed771-291142537-wx-6&ns_siteid=ns_us_g_careerbuilder_iphone, accessed March 23, 2009.

The Dot-Jobs Domain The new *dot-jobs* domain gives job seekers a one-click conduit for finding jobs at the employers who register at www.goto.jobs. For example, applicants seeking a job at Disneyland can go to www.Disneyland.jobs. This takes them to Disney's Disneyland recruiting Web site.

Virtual Job Fairs Virtual (fully online) job fairs are another option. For example, the magazine *PR Week* organized such a fair for about a dozen public relations employers. At a virtual job fair, online visitors see a very similar setup to a regular job fair. They can listen to presentations, visit booths, leave résumés and business cards, participate in live chats, and get contact information from recruiters, HR managers, and even hiring managers.[36]

Pros Internet recruiting is a cost-effective way to publicize openings; it generates more responses quicker and for a longer time at less cost than just about any other method. For example, Marsha Wheatley, human resource director for the Washington, DC–based American Crop Protection Association, no longer runs $400 ads in the *Washington Post* for professionals. Instead, ads on WashingtonPost.com cost only $200. "Instead of a tiny ad that says, 'ACPA needs an accountant,' I get a whole page to describe the job, give information about the association, and include a link to our Web site."[38] She estimates that she averages nine times as many applicants via the online ad.

Cons Internet recruiting has two big potential problems—discrimination and overload.

First, fewer older people use the Internet, so online application gathering may inadvertently exclude disproportionate numbers of older applicants (and certain minorities). To prove they've complied with EEO laws, employers should keep track of each applicant's race, sex, and ethnic group. The EEO says that, to be an "applicant," he or she must meet three conditions: he or she must express interest in employment; the employer must have taken steps to fill a specific job; and the individual must have followed the employer's standard application procedure.[39]

The second challenge is Internet overload: Employers end up deluged with résumés. There are several ways to handle this. Realism helps. The Cheesecake Factory posts detailed job duties listings, so those not interested need not apply. Another approach is to have job seekers complete a short online prescreening questionnaire. Then use these to identify those that may proceed in the hiring process.[40] Most employers also use applicant tracking systems, to which we now turn.

Using Applicant Tracking

Web-based ads tend to generate so many applicants that most firms are installing applicant tracking systems to support their on- and offline recruiting efforts. **Applicant tracking systems** (from firms such as Taleo Corporation [formerly Recruitsoft, Inc.] and iTrack Solutions) are online systems that help employers attract, gather, screen, compile, and manage applicants.[41] They also provide other services, including requisitions management (for monitoring the firm's open jobs), applicant data collection (for scanning applicants' data into the system), and reporting (to create various recruiting-related reports such as cost per hire and hire by source).[42] Most are from *application service providers* (ASPs). The latter are companies that provide employers with online services by enabling the employer's applicants or employees to use the ASP's servers as if they're using the employer's own. Thus, applicants who log on to take a test at the employer are actually taking the test at the ASP's site.[43]

SUTTER HEALTH EXAMPLE For example, with 10,000 job openings per year, Sutter Health Corporation turned to online recruiting. But this actually complicated things.[44] Sutter Health had so many résumés coming in by e-mail and through its Web site (more than 300,000 per year) that the applications ended up in a pile, waiting for Sutter affiliates' HR departments to get to them.

Sutter Health's solution was to sign on with Taleo Corporation of San Francisco. Taleo is a recruiting applications service provider (ASP). It now does all the work of hosting Sutter Health's job site. Taleo doesn't just post Sutter Health job openings and collect its résumés; it also gives Sutter Health an automated way to evaluate, rank, and match IT and other job candidates with specific openings. For example, Taleo's system automatically screens incoming résumés, compares them with Sutter's job requirements, and flags high-priority applicants. This helped Sutter cut its recruiting process from weeks to days.

Improving Online Recruiting Effectiveness

Planning your online recruiting effort is crucial. For one thing, some estimate that employers have only a few minutes "before online applicants will turn their attention elsewhere."[45] Employers therefore need to make it easy for applicants to use their Web sites to hunt for jobs; most of Standard & Poor's 500 companies place employment information one click away from their home pages.[46] Applicants can submit their résumés online at almost all *Fortune* 500 Web sites. Fewer give job seekers the option of completing online applications, although that's what most applicants prefer.[47]

One survey of 256 alumni from graduate business schools showed why many firms' Web-based recruiting turned them off. The objections included the following:

- Job openings lacked relevant information (such as job descriptions).
- It was often difficult to format résumés and post them in the form required.
- Many respondents expressed concerns about the privacy of the information.
- Poor graphics often made it difficult to use the Web site.
- Slow feedback from the employers (in terms of follow-up responses and receiving online applications) was annoying.[48]

applicant tracking systems
Online systems that help employers attract, gather, screen, compile, and manage applicants.

FIGURE 5-8 Ineffective and Effective Web Ads

Ineffective Ad, Recycled from Magazine to the Web	Effective Web Ad (Space Not an Issue)
Process Engineer Pay: $65k–$85k/year	Do you want to help us make this a better world?
Immediate Need in Florida for a Wastewater Treatment Process Engineer. Must have a min. 4–7 years Industrial Wastewater exp. Reply KimGD@WatersCleanX.com	We are one of the top wastewater treatment companies in the world, with installations from Miami to London to Beijing. We are growing fast and looking for an experienced process engineer to join our team. If you have at least 4–7 years' experience designing processes for wastewater treatment facilities and a dedication to make this a better world, we would like to hear from you. Pay range depending on experience is $65,000–$85,000. Please reply in confidence to KimGD@WatersCleanX.com

Furthermore, the best Web ads don't just transpose newspaper ads to the Web. As one specialist put it, "getting recruiters out of the 'shrunken want ad mentality' is a big problem." Figure 5-8 is an example of recycling a print ad to the Web. The ineffective Web ad has needless abbreviations, and doesn't say much about why the job seeker should want that job.[49]

Now look at the effective Web ad in Figure 5-8. It uses compelling keywords such as "make this a better world." It provides good reasons to work for this company. It starts with an attention-grabbing heading and uses the extra space to provide more specific job information. Similarly, the Cheesecake Factory doesn't just post short print-type help wanted ads on the Web. For most jobs, it includes the entire job description.[50] Ideally, an ad also should provide a way (such as a checklist of the job's human requirements) for potential applicants to gauge the extent to which the job is a good fit.[51]

Finally, online recruiting requires caution on the part of applicants. Many job boards don't check the legitimacy of the "recruiters" who place ads. Many applicants submit personal details such as Social Security numbers, not realizing that the sites they're using are actually run by ASPs, rather than the firm to which they're applying.[52] U.S. laws generally do not prohibit job boards from sharing your data with other sources. One job board reportedly had personal information on more than 1 million subscribers stolen.[53]

Challenging times are shifting the sort of online and other recruiting employers do. The accompanying "Managing HR in Challenging Times" feature addresses this.

MANAGING HR IN CHALLENGING TIMES

Reducing Recruitment Costs

Challenging economic times are prompting employers to rethink how they go about recruiting, with an emphasis on cost cutting. For those using traditional job boards, one expert says employers should be proactive about asking for deals with recruitment sites. For example, negotiate a 1-year discount on a shorter contract. Beyond that, employers are turning to free (or almost free) recruitment options. For example, free or low-cost recruitment resources include Craigslist and Jobbing.com. In these challenging times, more employers are also focusing on their states' one-stop career centers, not for just nonexempt employees, but for professional and administrative employees as well.[54]

6 Develop a help wanted ad.

Advertising

While Web-based recruiting is rapidly replacing help wanted ads, a glance at almost any paper or business or professional magazine will confirm that print ads are still popular. To use help wanted ads successfully, employers have to address two issues: the advertising medium and the ad's construction.

The Media

The best medium—the local paper, the *Wall Street Journal*, the Web (or some other)—depends on the positions for which you're recruiting. For example, the local newspaper is often the best source for local blue-collar help, clerical employees, and lower-level administrative employees. On the other hand, if recruiting for workers with special skills—such as furniture finishers—you'd probably want to advertise in the Carolinas or Georgia, even if your plant is in Tennessee. The point is to target your ads where they'll reach your prospective employees.

For specialized employees, you can advertise in trade and professional journals like *American Psychologist, Sales Management, Chemical Engineering,* and *Women's Wear Daily*. Help wanted ads in papers like the *Wall Street Journal* and the *International Herald Tribune* can be good sources of middle- or senior-management personnel. Most of these print outlets now include online ads with the purchase of print help wanted ads.

Technology lets companies be more creative about the media they use.[55] For example, Electronic Arts (EA), a video-game publisher, uses its products to help solicit job applicants. EA includes information about its internship program on the back of its video game manuals. Thanks to nontraditional techniques like these, EA has a database of more than 200,000 potential job candidates. It also uses tracking software to identify potential applicants with specific skills, and to facilitate ongoing e-mail communications with everyone in its database.

Constructing (Writing) the Ad

Experienced advertisers use the guide AIDA (attention, interest, desire, action) to construct ads. Of course, you must attract attention to the ad, or readers may just miss or ignore it. Figure 5-9 shows an ad from one classified section. Why does this ad attract attention? The phrase "next key player" certainly helps. Employers usually advertise key positions in display ads like this.

FIGURE 5-9 Help Wanted Ad that Draws Attention

Source: Giombetti Associates, Hampden, MA. Reprinted with permission.

Are You Our Next Key Player?

PLANT CONTROLLER — **Northern New Jersey**

Are you looking to make an impact? Can you be a strategic business partner and team player, versus a classic, "bean counter"? Our client, a growing **Northern New Jersey** manufacturer with two locations, needs a high-energy, self-initiating, technically competent Plant Controller. Your organizational skills and strong understanding of general, cost, and manufacturing accounting are a must. We are not looking for a delegator, this is a hands-on position. If you have a positive can-do attitude and have what it takes to drive our accounting function, read on!

Responsibilities and Qualifications:

- Monthly closings, management reporting, product costing, and annual budget.
- Accurate inventory valuations, year-end physical inventory, and internal controls.
- 4-year Accounting degree, with 5–8 years experience in a manufacturing environment.
- Must be proficient in Microsoft Excel and have general computer skills and aptitude.
- Must be analytical and technically competent, with the leadership ability to influence people, situations, and circumstances.

If you have what it takes to be our next key player, tell us in your cover letter, *"Beyond the beans, what is the role of a Plant Controller?"* Only cover letters addressing that question will be considered. Please indicate your general salary requirements in your cover letter and email or fax your resume and cover letter to:

Ross Giombetti
Giombetti Associates
2 Allen Street, P.O. Box 720
Hampden, MA 01036
Email: Rossgiombetti@giombettiassoc.com
Fax: (413) 566-2009

Next, develop interest in the job. You can create interest with lines such as "are you looking to make an impact?" or use other aspects of the job, such as its location.

Create desire by spotlighting words such as *travel* or *challenge.* As an example, having a graduate school nearby may appeal to engineers and professional people.

Finally, the ad should prompt action with a statement like "call today." (Of course, the ad should also comply with equal employment laws, avoiding features like "man wanted.")

In general, more information is better than less. Job applicants view ads with more specific job information as more attractive and more credible.[56] If the job has big drawbacks, then (depending on your risk preferences) consider a realistic ad. When the New York City Administration for Children's Services was having problems with employee retention, it began using these ads: "Wanted: men and women willing to walk into strange buildings in dangerous neighborhoods, [and] be screamed at by unhinged individuals . . . ." Realism reduces applicants, but improves employee retention.[57]

Employment Ads and Image Employers should try to create the right impressions of their companies through their job postings, Web sites, and other means. If possible, all applicants should also receive a response and, preferably, a personalized one rather than a generic, automated one.[58] For example, Barnes & Noble wants employees who are passionate about books and who generally have scholarly backgrounds. Employees here tend to wear collared shirts and have a clean-cut look. Barnes & Noble's ads tend to project this image.[59]

Employment Agencies

There are three main types of employment agencies: (1) public agencies operated by federal, state, or local governments; (2) agencies associated with nonprofit organizations; and (3) privately owned agencies.

Public and Nonprofit Agencies Every state has a public, state-run employment service agency. The U.S. Department of Labor supports these agencies, in part through grants, and in part through other assistance such as a nationwide computerized job bank. The National Job Bank enables agency counselors to advise applicants about available jobs not just in their local area, but in other states as well.

Some employers have had mixed experiences with public agencies. For one thing, applicants for unemployment insurance are required to register and to make themselves available for job interviews. Some of these people are not interested in getting back to work, so employers can end up with applicants who have little desire for immediate employment. And fairly or not, employers probably view some of these local agencies as lethargic in their efforts to fill area employers' jobs.

Yet these agencies are actually quite useful. Beyond just filling jobs, for instance, counselors will visit an employer's work site, review the employer's job requirements, and even assist the employer in writing job descriptions. Most states have turned their local state employment service agencies into "one-stop" shops—neighborhood training/employment/educational services centers.[60] One user said of the Queens New York Career Center in Jamaica: "I love it: I've made this place like a second home."[61] Services available to employers include recruitment services, tax credit information, training programs, and access to local and national labor market information.[62] More employers should be taking advantage of these centers (formerly the "unemployment offices" in many cities).

Most (nonprofit) professional and technical societies, such as the Institute for Electrical and Electronic Engineers (IEEE), have units that help members find jobs. Many special public agencies place people who are in special categories, such as those who are disabled.

Private Agencies Private employment agencies are important sources of clerical, white-collar, and managerial personnel. They charge fees (set by state law and posted in their offices) for each applicant they place. Most are "fee-paid" jobs, in which the employer pays the fee.

Why use an agency? Reasons include:

1. Your firm doesn't have its own human resources department and feels it can't do a good job recruiting and screening.
2. You must fill a particular opening quickly.
3. There is a perceived need to attract a greater number of minority or female applicants.
4. You want to reach currently employed individuals, who might feel more comfortable dealing with agencies than with competing companies.
5. You want to cut down on the time you're devoting to recruiting.[63]

Yet using employment agencies requires avoiding potential pitfalls. For example, the employment agency's screening may let poor applicants go directly to the supervisors responsible for hiring, who may in turn naively hire them. Conversely, improper screening at the agency could block potentially successful applicants.

To help avoid problems:

1. Give the agency an accurate and complete job description.
2. Make sure tests, application blanks, and interviews are part of the agency's selection process.
3. Periodically review EEOC data on candidates accepted or rejected by your firm, and by the agency.
4. Screen the agency. Check with other managers to find out which agencies have been the most effective at filling the sorts of positions you need filled. Review the Internet and classified ads to discover the agencies that handle the positions you seek to fill.
5. Make sure to supplement the agency's reference checking by conscientiously checking at least the final candidate's references yourself.

Temp Agencies and Alternative Staffing

Employers increasingly supplement their permanent workforces by hiring contingent or temporary workers, often through temporary help employment agencies. Also known as *part-time* or *just-in-time workers*, the contingent workforce is big and growing.

The contingent workforce isn't limited to clerical or maintenance staff. It includes thousands of engineering, science, or management support occupations, such as temporary chief financial officers, human resource managers, and CEOs.

Employers can hire temp workers either through direct hires or through temporary staff agencies. Direct hiring involves simply hiring workers and placing them on the job. The employer usually pays these people directly, as it does all its employees, but classifies them separately, as casual, seasonal, or temporary employees, and often pays few if any benefits.[64] The other approach is to have a temp agency supply the employees. Here the agency handles all the recruiting, screening, and payroll administration for the temps. Thus, Nike hired Kelly Services to manage Nike's temp needs.

Pros and Cons

Employers have long used "temps" to fill in for permanent employees who were out sick or on vacation. But today's desire for ever-higher productivity also contributes to temp workers' growing popularity. Productivity is measured in terms of output per hour paid for, and temps are generally paid only when they're working—not for days off, in other words. Many firms also use temporary hiring to give prospective employees a trial run before hiring them as regular employees.[65]

The benefits don't come without a price. Temps may be more productive, but generally cost employers 20% to 50% more than comparable permanent workers (per hour or per week), since the agency gets a fee. Furthermore, "people have a psychological reference point to their place of employment. Once you put them in the contingent category, you're saying they're expendable."[66]

When working with temporary agencies, ensure that basic policies and procedures are in place, including:

- **Invoicing.** Get a sample copy of the agency's invoice. Make sure it fits your company's needs.
- **Time sheets.** With temps, the time sheet is not just a verification of hours worked. Once the worker's supervisor signs it, it's usually an agreement to pay the agency's fees.
- **Temp-to-perm policy.** What is the policy if the client wants to hire one of the agency's temps as a permanent employee?
- **Recruitment of and benefits for temp employees.** Find out how the agency plans to recruit employees and what sorts of benefits it pays.
- **Dress code.** Specify the appropriate attire at each of your offices or plants.
- **Equal employment opportunity statement.** Get a document from the agency stating that it is not discriminating when filling temp orders.
- **Job description information.** Ensure the agency understands the job to be filled and the sort of person, in terms of skills and so forth, you want to fill it.[67]

What Supervisors Should Know About Temporary Employees' Concerns

To make temporary relationships as successful as possible, managers supervising temps should understand these employees' main concerns. In one survey, six key concerns emerged. They said they were:

1. Treated by employers in a dehumanizing, impersonal, and ultimately discouraging way.
2. Insecure about their employment and pessimistic about the future.
3. Worried about their lack of insurance and pension benefits.
4. Misled about their job assignments and in particular about whether temporary assignments were likely to become full-time.
5. "Underemployed" (particularly those trying to return to the full-time labor market).
6. In general angry toward the corporate world; participants repeatedly expressed feelings of alienation and disenchantment.[68]

Legal Guidelines

Several years ago, federal agents rounded up about 250 illegal "contract" cleaning workers in 60 Walmart stores. The raid underscores that you

The numbers of temporary and freelance workers are increasing all over the world. Alemi Takada is a noted Japanese freelance animator who manages her workload and does projects for companies all over the world through an Internet agency that represents about 15,000 freelancers in media and publishing.

Source: Courtesy of Stuart Isett/ZUMA Press-Gamma.

have to understand the status of the contract employees who work on your premises handling activities like security, food service, or after-hours store cleaning.[69] The fact that they actually work for another, temp-type company is no excuse. For purposes of most employment laws, with certain limited exceptions, employees of temporary staffing firms working in an employer's workplace will be considered to be employees both of the agency and of the employer.[70]

Largely, it comes down to how much control you really exert over the so-called temporary workers. The more control the manager exercises over the "temps," the more likely it is that the court will view the temporary employees as regular employees. (Among other things, that may make them eligible for benefits. Microsoft had to pay a $97 million settlement several years ago to employees it had mischaracterized as "temporary.")

Therefore, if your company uses contract workers who are actually paid and employed by a staffing firm, *the basic rule is to treat the temporary employee as if the temp agency is in fact his or her employer.* The temporary employee's direct supervisor should be particularly aware of what to avoid. For example, don't train or negotiate pay directly with the workers; let the temp firm do that. Figure 5-10 summarizes some other legal guidelines for dealing with temporary workers.

Alternative Staffing Temporary employees are examples of **alternative staffing**—basically, the use of nontraditional recruitment sources. Other alternative staffing arrangements include "in-house temporary employees" (people employed directly by the company, but on an explicit short-term basis) and "contract technical employees" (highly skilled workers like engineers, who are supplied for long-term projects under contract from an outside technical services firm).

Offshoring and Outsourcing Jobs

Outsourcing and offshoring are perhaps the most extreme examples of alternative staffing. Rather than bringing people in to do the company's jobs, outsourcing and offshoring send the jobs out. *Outsourcing* means having outside vendors supply services (such as benefits management, market research, or manufacturing) that the company's own employees previously did in-house. *Offshoring* is a narrower term. It means having outside vendors *abroad* supply services that the company's own employees previously did in-house.

FIGURE 5-10 10 Things Managers Should Avoid When Supervising Temporary Employees

Source: Adapted from Bohner and Selasco, "Beware the Legal Risks of Hiring Temps," *Workforce*, October 2000, p. 53.

DO NOT:

1. **Train your contingent workers.** Ask their staffing agency to handle training.
2. **Negotiate the pay rate of your contingent workers.** The agency should set pay.
3. **Coach a contingent worker on his/her job performance.** Instead, call the person's agency and request that it do so.
4. **Negotiate a contingent worker's vacations or personal time off.** Direct the worker to his or her agency.
5. **Routinely include contingent workers in your company's employee functions.**
6. **Issue company business cards, nameplates, or employee badges to contingent workers without HR and legal approval.**
7. **Discuss harassment or discrimination issues with contingent workers.**
8. **Discuss job opportunities and the contingent worker's suitability for them directly.** Instead, refer the worker to publicly available job postings.
9. **Terminate a contingent worker directly.** Contact the agency to do so.
10. **Assume you can dismiss these employees arbitrarily**, or ignore federal wage and hour laws. Temporary workers, like all workers, have significant legal rights.

alternative staffing
The use of nontraditional recruitment sources.

Outsourcing and offshoring are both contentious. Particularly in challenging economic times, employees, unions, legislators, and even many business owners feel that "shipping jobs out" (particularly overseas) is ill-advised. That notwithstanding, employers are sending more jobs out, and not just blue-collar jobs. As explained in Chapter 1, current projections show that about 3 million white-collar jobs ranging from call center employee to radiologist moved abroad in the past few years. For example, GE's transportation division announced that it was shifting 17 mid-level drafting jobs from Pennsylvania to India.[71]

Sending out jobs, particularly overseas, presents employers with some special challenges. One is the potential for political tension in countries such as India. Others include the likelihood of cultural misunderstandings (such as between your home-based customers and the employees abroad); security and information privacy concerns; the need to deal with foreign contract, liability, and legal systems issues; and the fact that the offshore employees need special training (for instance, in using pseudonyms like "Jim" without discomfort). Rising overseas wages (call center hourly wages in India rose from $2 an hour in 1998 to $6 in 2008, for instance), higher oil prices, and quality issues are prompting more U.S. employers to bring their jobs back home.[72] The bottom line is that neither outsourcing nor offshoring always brings all the savings one would have hoped for, and both require careful consideration of human resource issues.

Executive Recruiters

Executive recruiters (also known as *headhunters*) are special employment agencies retained by employers to seek out top-management talent for their clients. The percentage of your firm's positions filled by these services might be small. However, these jobs include key executive and technical positions. For executive positions, headhunters may be your only source of candidates. The employer always pays the fees.

There are two types of executive recruiters—contingent and retained. Members of the Association of Executive Search Consultants usually focus on executive positions paying $150,000 or more, and on "*retained* executive search." They are paid regardless of whether the employer hires the executive through the search firm's efforts. *Contingency-based recruiters* tend to handle junior- to middle-level management job searches in the $50,000 to $150,000 range. Whether retained or contingent, fees are beginning to drop from the usual 30% or more of the executive's first-year pay.[73] Top recruiters (all retained) include Heidrick and Struggles, Egon Zehander International, Russell Reynolds, and Spencer Stuart.[74]

Executive recruiters are using more technology and becoming more specialized. The challenging part of recruiting has always been finding potential candidates—to find, say, "a sales manager with experience in chemical engineered products." Not surprisingly, Internet-based databases now dramatically speed up such searches. Executive recruiters are also becoming more specialized. The large ones are creating new businesses aimed at specialized functions (such as sales) or industries (such as oil products). So, it's advisable to look first for one that specializes in your field.

Pros and Cons Recruiters bring a lot to the table. They have many contacts and are especially adept at finding qualified employed candidates who aren't actively looking to change jobs. They can keep your firm's name confidential until late into the search process. The recruiter can save top management's time by finding and screening an applicant pool. The recruiter's fee might actually turn out to be small when you compare it to the executive time saved.

The big issue is ensuring that the recruiter really understands your needs and then delivers properly vetted candidates who fill the bill. As an employer, it is essential to explain completely what sort of candidate is required—and why. Recruiters also claim that what their clients say they want is often not really what the clients want. Therefore, be prepared for some in-depth dissecting of your request. Some recruiters also may be more interested in persuading you to hire a candidate than in finding one who will really do the job. Understand that one or two of the "final candidates" may actually just be fillers to make the recruiter's one "real" candidate look better.

Guidelines In choosing a recruiter, guidelines include:[75]

1. Make sure the firm is capable of conducting a thorough search. Under their ethics code, a recruiter can't approach the executive talent of a former client for a period of 2 years after completing a search for that client. Since former clients are off limits for 2 years, the recruiter must search from a constantly diminishing pool.[76]
2. Meet the individual who will actually handle your assignment.
3. Make sure to ask how much the search firm charges. Get the agreement in writing.[77]
4. Make sure the recruiter and you see eye to eye on what sort of person you need for the position.
5. *Never* rely solely on the executive recruiter (or other search professional, such as employment agency) to do all the reference checking. Certainly, let them check the candidates' references, but get notes of these references in writing from the recruiter (if possible). And, in any event, make sure to check at least the final candidate's references yourself.

Should You Do Your Own Executive Recruiting? Although most large firms don't think twice about hiring executive search firms, small-firm owners will understandably hesitate before committing to a $70,000 or so search fee for a marketing manager. Yet not doing so can be shortsighted.

Executive search is not like recruiting supervisors or data entry clerks. For one thing, the person you seek is probably not reading the want ads. What you'll end up with is a drawer of résumés of people who are, for one reason or another, unsuited for your job.

If you do decide to do the job yourself (or even if you use a recruiter), retain an industrial psychologist. He or she should spend 4 or 5 hours assessing the problem-solving ability, personality, interests, and energy level of the two or three candidates in which you are most interested.

Exercise special care when recruiting applicants from competing companies. Always check to ascertain if noncompete or nondisclosure agreements bar them from talking with you. Even without a written contract, courts generally hold that employees have a duty of loyalty to their current employers during their employment. If you participate in any breach of that loyalty, you may share in the liability.[78]

If you're a department manager with an open position to fill in a *Fortune* 500 company, even you may have a dilemma. Your human resource office may do little more than place some ads on recruiting Web sites. What to do? Use word of mouth to "advertise" your open position. Make sure everyone in your company who may know of a candidate knows that the position is open. Contact your friends and colleagues in other firms to watch out for possible candidates. And perhaps push for retaining an executive recruiter.

On-Demand Recruiting Services

On-demand recruiting services (ODRS) provide short-term specialized recruiting assistance to support specific projects without the expense of retaining traditional search firms. They are recruiters who are paid by the hour or project, instead of a

on-demand recruiting services (ODRS)
A service that provides short-term specialized recruiting to support specific projects without the expense of retaining traditional search firms.

percentage fee. For example, when the human resource manager for a biotech firm had to hire several dozen people with scientific degrees and experience in pharmaceuticals, she decided an ODRS firm was her best option. A traditional recruiting firm might charge 20% to 30% of each hire's salary, a prohibitive amount for a small company. The ODRS firm charged by time, rather than per hire. It handled recruiting and prescreening, and left the client with a short list of qualified candidates.[79]

College Recruiting

College recruiting—sending an employer's representatives to college campuses to prescreen applicants and create an applicant pool from the graduating class—is an important source of management trainees and professional and technical employees. One study several years ago concluded, for instance, that new college graduates filled about 38% of all externally filled jobs requiring a college degree.[80]

The problem is that on-campus recruiting is expensive and time-consuming. Schedules must be set well in advance, company brochures printed, interview records kept, and much time spent on campus. And recruiters themselves are sometimes ineffective, or worse. Some recruiters are unprepared, show little interest in the candidate, and act superior. Many don't screen candidates effectively. Employers need to train recruiters in how to interview candidates, how to explain what the company has to offer, and how to put candidates at ease. And even more than usual, the recruiter needs to be personable and preferably have a history of attracting good candidates.[81]

On-Campus Recruiting Goals

The campus recruiter has two main goals. One is to determine if a candidate is worthy of further consideration. Usual traits to assess include communication skills, education, experience, and interpersonal skills. The other aim is to attract good candidates. A sincere and informal attitude, respect for the applicant, and prompt follow-up letters can help sell the employer to the interviewee.

Employers should choose their recruiters and schools carefully. Factors in selecting schools include the school's reputation and the performance of previous hires from that source.

Building close ties with a college's career center can help employers achieve these goals. Doing so provides recruiters with useful feedback regarding things like labor market conditions and the effectiveness of one's on- and offline recruiting ads.[82] Shell Oil reduced the list of schools its recruiters visit, using factors such as quality of academic program, number of students enrolled, and diversity of the student body.[83]

The On-Site Visit

Employers generally invite good candidates to the office or plant for an on-site visit.

There are several ways to make this visit fruitful. The invitation letter should be warm and friendly but businesslike, and should give the person a choice of dates to visit. Have someone meet the applicant, preferably at the airport or at his or her hotel, and act as host. A package containing the applicant's schedule as well as other information regarding the company—such as annual reports and employee benefits—should be waiting for the applicant at the hotel.

Plan the interviews and adhere to the schedule. Avoid interruptions; give the candidate the undivided attention of each person with whom he or she interviews. Have another recently hired graduate host the candidate's lunch. Make any offer as soon as possible, preferably at the time of the visit. If this is not possible, tell the candidate when to expect a decision. Frequent follow-ups to "find out how the decision process is going" may help to tilt the applicant in your favor.

A study of 96 graduating students from a major Northeastern university reveals some other things for which to watch out. For example, 53% said "on-site visit opportunities to meet with people in positions similar to those applied for, or with higher-ranking persons" had a positive effect. Fifty-one percent mentioned "impressive hotel/dinner arrangements and having well-organized site arrangements." On the other hand, make sure the visit is professional. "Disorganized, unprepared interviewer behavior, or uninformed, useless answers" turned off 41%. Forty percent mentioned "unimpressive cheap hotels, disorganized arrangements, or inappropriate behavior of hosts" as negatives.[84]

Internships Many college students get their jobs through college internships. Internships can be win–win situations. For students, it may mean being able to hone business skills, learn more about potential employers, and discover their career likes (and dislikes). And employers can use the interns to make useful contributions while evaluating them as possible full-time employees. One survey reports that employers offer jobs to more than 70% of their interns.[85]

Referrals and Walk-Ins

Employee referral campaigns are an important recruiting option. Here the firm posts announcements of openings and requests for referrals on its Web site, bulletin, and/or wallboards. The firm offers prizes or cash awards for referrals that lead to hiring. AmeriCredit uses its "You've got friends, we want to meet them" employee referral program. Employees making a successful referral receive $1,000 awards, with the payments spread over a year. As the head of recruiting says, "Quality people know quality people."[86] The Container Store uses a successful variant of the employee referral campaign. They train their employees to recruit new employees from among the firm's customers.

Pros and Cons The biggest advantage here is that referrals tend to generate "more applicants, more hires, and a higher yield ratio (hires/applicants)."[87] Current employees will usually provide accurate information about the job applicants they are referring, since they're putting their own reputations on the line. The new employees may also come with a more realistic picture of what the firm is like. Referrals can also facilitate diversifying your workforce. One survey found 70% of minority/ethnic candidates search for jobs on corporate Web sites. However, only 6% listed "corporate Web site" as one of the top five ways they actually found jobs; 25% listed referrals.[88] A survey by the Society for Human Resource Management (SHRM) found that of 586 employer respondents, 69% said employee referral programs are more cost-effective than other recruiting practices and 80% specifically said they are more cost-effective than employment agencies. On average, referral programs cost around $400–$900 per hire in incentives and rewards.[89]

There are a few things to avoid. If morale is low, you probably should address that prior to asking for referrals. And if you don't hire someone, explain to your employee/referrer why you did not hire his or her candidate. And we saw that relying on referrals might be discriminatory.

Walk-ins Particularly for hourly workers, walk-ins—direct applications made at your office—are a big source of applicants. From a practical point of view, simply posting a "Help Wanted" sign outside the door may be the most cost-effective way of attracting good local applicants. Treat walk-ins courteously and diplomatically, for the sake of both the employer's community reputation and the applicant's self-esteem. Many employers give every walk-in a brief interview, even if it is only to get information on the applicant "in case a position should be open in the future." Particularly in challenging times, you'll also receive many unsolicited application letters

college recruiting
Sending an employer's representatives to college campuses to prescreen applicants and create an applicant pool from the graduating class.

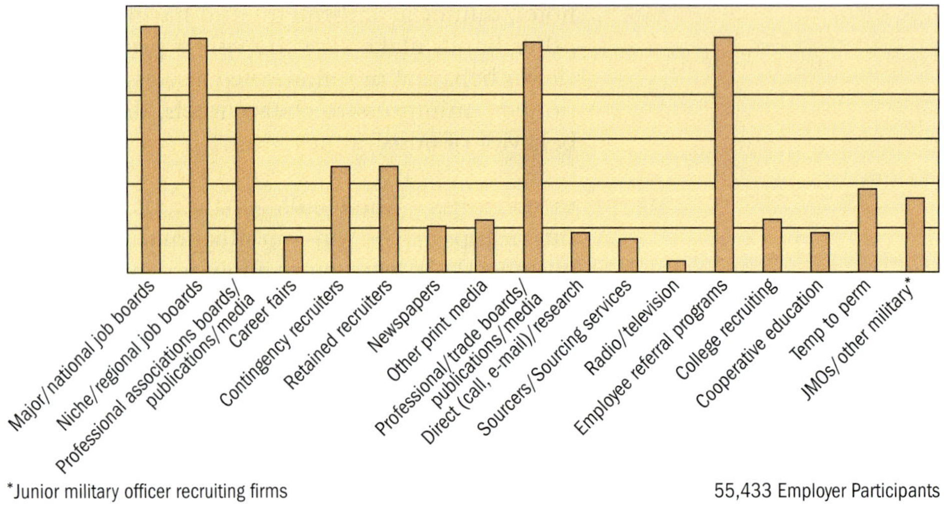

FIGURE 5-11 Relative Recruiting Source Effectiveness Based on New Hires

Note: Internet job boards continue to be the most effective sources followed by employee referral programs and professional and trade media and associations.

Source: © Staffing.org, Inc., 2007. All Rights Reserved. The 2007 Recruiting Metrics and Performance Benchmark Report, 2nd Ed., is sponsored by NAS Recruitment Communications. Used with permission of Staffing.org, Inc.

from professional and white-collar applicants. These can be good sources of leads. Good business practice requires answering all letters of inquiry from applicants promptly and courteously.

Telecommuters

Telecommuters are another option. For example, JetBlue Airways uses at-home agents to handle its reservation needs. These JetBlue employee "crewmembers" live in the Salt Lake City area and work out of their homes. They use JetBlue-supplied computers and technology, and receive JetBlue training.[90]

Military Personnel

Returning and discharged U.S. military personnel provide an excellent source of trained recruits. Several military branches have programs to facilitate soldiers finding jobs. For example, the U.S. Army's Partnership for Youth Success enables someone entering the Army to select a post-army corporate partner for an employment interview as a way to help soldiers find a job after leaving the Army.[91]

Recruiting Source Use and Effectiveness

Figure 5-11 summarizes a survey of best recruiting sources. Internet job boards garnered the most votes, followed by professional/trade job boards and employee referral programs.[92]

Research also reveals several guidelines employers can use to improve their recruiting efforts' effectiveness (see Table 5-1). For example, referrals from current employees yield applicants who are less likely to leave and more likely to perform better.[93] The accompanying "Evidence-Based HR" feature explains how to assess your firm's recruiting effectiveness.

Evidence-Based HR

Measuring Recruiting Effectiveness

Even small employers may spend tens of thousands of dollars per year recruiting applicants, yet few firms assess their recruitment efforts' effectiveness. Is it more cost-effective for us to advertise for applicants on the Web or in Sunday's paper? Should we use this employment agency or that one? One survey found that only about 44% of the 279 firms surveyed made formal attempts to evaluate their recruitment efforts.[94] Such inattention flies in the face of common sense.[95]

In terms of what to measure, one question is "How many applicants did we generate through each of our recruitment sources?"[96] The problem is that more is not always better. The employer needs qualified, hirable applicants, not just applicants. An Internet ad may generate thousands of applicants, many from so far away that there's no chance they're viable. Even with computerized prescreening and tracking software, there are still more applicants to correspond with and screen.[97] The applicant tracking system should help compare recruiting sources, but about 30% of them lack the necessary tools to effectively pinpoint source of hire.[98] And realistically, the manager looking to hire five engineers probably won't be twice as selective with 20,000 applicants as with 10,000. So, it is not just quantity but quality. It's therefore wise to compare your recruiting sources with measures of how employees from these sources did after about a year on the job.

GE Medical Example

GE Medical hires about 500 technical workers a year to make sophisticated medical devices such as CT scanners. GE Medical must compete for talent with the likes of Microsoft. However, it has cut its hiring costs by 17%, reduced time to fill the positions by 20% to 30%, and cut in half the percentage of new hires who don't work out.[99]

GE Medical accomplished this in part by applying some of its purchasing techniques to its dealings with recruiters. For example, it called a meeting and told 20 recruiters that it would work with only the 10 best. To measure "best," the company created measurements inspired by manufacturing techniques, such as "percentage of résumés that result in interviews" and "percentage of interviews that lead to offers." Similarly, GE Medical discovered that current employees are very effective as references. For instance, GE Medical interviews just 1% of applicants whose résumés it receives, while 10% of employee referrals result in actual hires. So GE Medical took steps to double the number of employee referrals. It simplified the referral forms, eliminated bureaucratic submission procedures, and added a small reward like a Sears gift certificate for referring a qualified candidate. GE also upped the incentive—$2,000 if someone referred is hired, and $3,000 if he or she is a software engineer.

TABLE 5-1 Recruitment Research Findings: Practical Applications for Managers

Recruitment Research Finding[a]	Practical Applications for Managers
The recruitment source affects the characteristics of applicants you attract.	Use sources such as referrals from current employees that yield applicants more likely to be better performers.
Recruitment materials have a more positive impact if they contain more specific information.	Provide applicants with information on aspects of the job that are important to them, such as salary, location, and diversity.
Organizational image influences applicants' initial reactions.	Ensure all communications regarding an organization provide a positive message regarding the attractiveness of the organization as a place to work.
Applicants with a greater number of job opportunities are more attentive to early recruitment activities.	Ensure initial recruitment activities (e.g., Web site, brochure, on-campus recruiting) are attractive to candidates.
Realistic job previews that highlight both the advantages and the disadvantages of the job reduce subsequent turnover.	Provide applicants with a realistic picture of the job and organization, not just the positives.
Applicants will infer (perhaps erroneous) information about the job and company if the information is not clearly provided by the company.	Provide clear, specific, and complete information in recruitment materials so that applicants do not make erroneous inferences about the job or the employer.
Recruiter warmth has a large and positive effect on applicants' decisions to accept a job.	Choose individuals who have contact with applicants for their interpersonal skills.

[a] Selected research principles from Taylor & Collins (2000).

Source: Adapted from Ann Marie Ryan and Nancy Tippins, "Attracting and Selecting: What Psychological Research Tells Us," *Human Resource Management* 43, no. 4 (Winter 2004), p. 311.

Improving Productivity Through HRIS: An Integrated Approach to Recruiting

Ideally, an employer's computerized recruitment system should include several elements:

- A *requisition management system*, which facilitates requisition, routing, approval, and posting of job openings
- A *recruiting solution*, including job advertisement, recruitment marketing, applicant tracking, and online recruitment vendor management, to increase and improve applicant pool quality
- *Screening services*, such as skills and behavioral assessment services
- *Hiring management* software to capture and manage candidate information[100]

Some employers have separate tools or systems for each element. However, several ATS providers integrate these elements into one comprehensive employee recruitment system.

7 Explain how to recruit a more diverse workforce.

RECRUITING A MORE DIVERSE WORKFORCE

As we explained in Chapter 2, recruiting a diverse workforce isn't just socially responsible. Given globalization and the rapid increase in minority, older worker, and women candidates, it is a necessity. The recruiting tools we have described to this point are certainly useful for minority and other applicants, too. However, in general, recruiting a more diverse workforce requires several special steps, to which we now turn.[101]

Single Parents

About two-thirds of all single parents are in the workforce today. Being a single parent isn't easy, and recruiting and keeping them requires understanding the problems they face in balancing work and family life.[102] In one survey,

> Many described falling into bed exhausted at midnight without even minimal time for themselves . . . They often needed personal sick time or excused days off to care for sick children. As one mother noted, "I don't have enough sick days to get sick."[103]

Source: Courtesy of Getty Images, Inc.-Taxi.

Not just single parents, but also their children may occasionally need some extra support.

Given such concerns, the first step in attracting (and keeping) single parents is to make the workplace as user friendly for single parents as practical.[104] Many firms have family friendly programs but these may not be extensive enough for single parents. For example, *flextime* programs provide employees some flexibility (such as 1-hour windows at the beginning or end of the day) around which to build their workdays. The problem is that for many single parents this limited flexibility may not be enough in the face of the "patchwork child care" and conflicting work–home pressures that many face.[105]

Flexible work schedules and child-care benefits are thus just two big single-parent magnets. In addition, employers should train their supervisors; surveys suggest that a supportive attitude on the supervisor's part can go far toward making the single parent's work–home balancing act more bearable.

Older Workers

When it comes to hiring older workers, employers don't have much choice.[106] Over the next few years, the fastest-growing labor force segment will be those from 45 to 64 years old. Those age 25 to 34 will decline by almost 3 million, reflecting fewer births in the late 1960s and early 1970s. On the positive side, a survey by AARP and SHRM concluded that older workers tend to have lower absenteeism rates, more reliability, and better work habits than younger workers.[107] Firms like Home Depot capitalize on this by hiring older employees, who "serve as a powerful draw to baby boomer shoppers by mirroring their knowledge and perspective . . . ."[108]

It therefore makes sense for employers to encourage older workers to stay (or to come to work at the company). Doing so involves several things. The big one is probably to provide opportunities for flexible (and often abbreviated) work schedules. One survey found that flexibility was the main concern for 71% of baby boomers, with those who continue working preferring to do so part time.[109] At Wrigley Company, workers over 65 can progressively shorten their work schedules; another company uses "mini shifts" to accommodate those interested in working less than full time. Other suggestions include the following:

- Train managers to address age bias in the workplace.
- Phased retirement that allows workers to ease out of the workforce.
- Portable jobs for "snowbirds" who wish to live in warmer climates in the winter.
- Part-time projects for retirees.
- Full benefits for part-timers.[110]

As always in recruiting, projecting the right image is essential. For example, one study examined the impact of various practices on the likelihood of attracting retirees interested in bridge employment (work after formal retirement). The researchers found that writing the ad so that it sent the message "we're older-worker friendly" was important. The most effective ads emphasized schedule flexibility, and accentuated the firm's equal opportunity employment statement. This was much more effective than adding statements alluding to giving retirees opportunities to transfer their knowledge to the new work setting.[111] The accompanying "Managing the New Workforce" feature explains another important issue.

Managing the New Workforce

Supervising Older Workers

Recruiting and hiring older employees is one thing; supervising them—especially when they're 20 or 30 years older than their supervisors—can be a challenge.

Gregg Levin's experiences provide an example. Levin, 31, is chief executive of Perfect Curve, a company in Sudbury, Massachusetts, that makes racks for baseball caps and related products. His father—one of his employees—doesn't use a computer, but instead "takes out his legal pad and spends an hour on something that takes me 4½ minutes on a computer," says Gregg. Maintaining authority is one of the challenges in a situation like this. Gregg Levin does this in part by dressing up: "I'm always in a suit and tie," he says. "If I'm going to represent my company, I've got to do it in a mature manner."

Mary Rodas was in a similar situation when, at 24, she helped start kardz.com (which then morphed into YourFreePresentation) and then became its vice president. Kardz.com delivered inexpensive gifts matched with greeting cards. Her five subordinates at that time were much older than she was. "When people meet me, their first reaction is: 'Who's this little kid?' Or else they say, 'Can I speak to your boss?' And I point to myself and say, 'That's her.'" She says she earns respect through hard work and getting to know her workers. "I know my business, and with time people realize that I'm talking to them as an individual and an equal. I've been in this industry for 11 years [she created a balloon ball at age 11 that brought in $70 million in sales for a toy company in New York]; I know what I'm doing."[112]

Recruiting Minorities

The same prescriptions that apply to recruiting older workers apply to recruiting minorities. If there is a basic guideline, it is this: Take the goal of recruiting more minorities seriously, and pursue that goal energetically. In practice, this requires a three-part effort: Understand the recruitment barriers, formulate the required recruitment plans, and institute the specific day-to-day programs.[113]

Understand

Understanding the barriers that prevent minorities from applying comes first. For example, many minority applicants don't meet the educational or experience standards for the job, so many companies offer remedial training in basic arithmetic and writing. For many, lack of role models is a problem. For example, among life insurers and other financial services firms, a lack of women role models makes many hesitate to accept jobs as sales agents. In one retail chain, it was a lack of role models (plus what the one manager called a "rather macho culture") that stopped women from applying. Sometimes (as we saw) it's a lack of schedule flexibility, given the responsibility for caring and schooling of the children.

Plan

After recognizing what the potential impediments are, you can turn to formulating plans for attracting and retaining minorities and women. This may include, for instance, developing flexible work options, redesigning jobs, and offering flexible benefits plans.

Implement

Finally, translate these personnel plans into recruitment programs. For example, decide what your ads will say, and what recruiting sources you will use. Many Hispanic (and other) job seekers check with friends or relatives as a strategy for looking for jobs, so encouraging your Hispanic employees to assist in your recruitment efforts makes sense. Other firms collaborate with professional organizations such as the black MBA Association, the National Society of Hispanic MBAs, and the Organization of Chinese Americans. Specialized job search Web sites are another option.[114]

Welfare-to-Work

Some companies report difficulty in hiring and assimilating people previously on welfare. Applicants sometimes lack basic work skills (such as reporting for work on time, working in teams, and "taking orders without losing their temper").[115] The key to a welfare-to-work program's success seems to be the employer's pretraining program. Here, participants get counseling and basic skills training over several weeks.[116] For example, Marriott International hired 600 welfare recipients under its Pathways to Independence program. The heart of the program is six weeks of preemployment training. This focuses on work and life skills and aims to rebuild self-esteem and instill positive attitudes about work.[117]

The Disabled

The EEOC estimates that nearly 70% of the disabled are jobless, but it certainly doesn't have to be that way.[118] The research is quite persuasive regarding the fact that in terms of virtually all work criteria, employees with disabilities are capable workers. Thousands of employers in the United States and elsewhere have found that disabled employees provide an excellent and largely untapped source of competent, efficient labor for jobs ranging from information technology to creative advertising to receptionist.

Employers can do several things to tap this huge potential workforce. The U.S. Department of Labor's Office of Disability Employment Policy offers several programs, including one that helps link disabled college undergraduates who are looking for summer internships with potential employers.[119] All states have local agencies (such as "Corporate Connections" in Tennessee) that provide placement services and other recruitment and training tools and information for employers seeking to hire the disabled. Employers also must use common sense. For example, employers who only post job openings online may miss potential employees who are visually impaired.[120]

DEVELOPING AND USING APPLICATION FORMS

Purpose of Application Forms

With a pool of applicants, the prescreening process can begin. The **application form** is usually the first step in this process (some firms first require a brief, prescreening interview or online test).

A filled-in application provides four types of information. First, you can make judgments on *substantive matters*, such as whether the applicant has the education and experience to do the job. Second, you can draw conclusions about the applicant's *previous progress* and growth, especially important for management candidates. Third, you can draw tentative conclusions about the applicant's *stability* based on previous work record (although years of downsizing suggest the need for caution here). Fourth, you may be able to use the data in the application to *predict* which candidates will succeed on the job and which will not.

In practice, most organizations need several application forms. For technical and managerial personnel, the form may require detailed answers to questions about education and training. The form for hourly factory workers might focus on tools and equipment. Figure 5-12 presents one employer's approach to collecting application form information—the employment application for the FBI. In practice, most employers encourage online applications.

Application Guidelines

Managers should keep several practical guidelines in mind. In the "Employment History" section, request detailed information on each prior employer, including the name of the supervisor and his or her telephone number; this is essential for reference checking. Also, in signing the application, the applicant should certify his or her understanding that falsified statements may be cause for dismissal, that investigation of credit and employment and driving record is authorized, that a medical examination may be required, that drug screening tests may be required, and that employment is for no definite period.

Reviewing the Completed Form

Always make sure applicants complete the form and sign a statement on it indicating that the information is true. The court will almost always support a discharge for falsifying information when applying for work.[121] Furthermore, doing a less-than-complete job of filling in the form may reflect poor work habits. Some applicants simply scribble "see résumé attached" on the application. This is not acceptable. You need the signed, completed form.

Application Forms and EEO Law

Carefully review application forms to ensure that they comply with equal employment laws. Questions to beware of include:

Education. A question on the dates of attendance and graduation from various schools is one potential violation, insofar as it may reflect the applicant's age.

Arrest record. The courts have usually held that employers violate Title VII by disqualifying applicants from employment because of an arrest. This item has an adverse impact on minorities, and employers usually can't show it's required as a business necessity.

application form
The form that provides information on education, prior work record, and skills.

FIGURE 5-12 FBI Employment Application

Source: www.fbijobs.gov/employment/ fd646c.pdf, accessed April 28, 2009.

FEDERAL BUREAU OF INVESTIGATION

Preliminary Application for
Honors Internship Program
(Please Type or Print in Ink)

Date: ______________

FIELD OFFICE USE ONLY

HP

Div: **Program:**

I. PERSONAL HISTORY

Name in Full (Last, First, Middle, Maiden)	List College(s) attended, Major, Degree (if applicable), Grade Point Average
Birth Date (Month, Day, Year) Birth Place:	Social Security Number: (Optional)

Current Address

Street ______ Apt. No. ______ Home Phone ______ Area Code ______ Number ______

City ______ State ______ Zip Code ______ Work Phone ______ Area Code ______ Number ______

Are you: Licensed Driver ☐ Yes ☐ No U. S. Citizen ☐ Yes ☐ No

Have you served on active duty in the Armed Forces of the United States? ☐ Yes ☐ No	Branch of military service and dates of active duty:	Type of Discharge

How did you learn or become interested in the FBI Honors Internship Program?

Do you have a foreign language background? ☐ Yes ☐ No List proficiency for each language on reverse side.

Have you ever been arrested or charged with any violation including traffic, but excluding parking tickets? ☐ Yes ☐ No If so, list all such matters even if found not guilty, not formally charged, no court appearance, or matter settled by payment of fine or forfeiture of collateral. Include date, place, charge, disposition, details, and police agency on reverse side.

II. EMPLOYMENT HISTORY

Identify your most recent three years FULL-TIME work experience, after high school (excluding summer, part-time and temporary employment).

From	To	Description of Work	Name/Location of Employer

III. PERSONAL DECLARATIONS

Persons with a disability who require an accommodation to complete the application process are required to notify the FBI of their need for the accommodation.

Have you used marijuana during the last three years or more than 15 times? ☐ Yes ☐ No

Have you used any illegal drug(s) or combination of illegal drugs, other than marijuana, more than 5 times or during the last 10 years? ☐ Yes ☐ No

All Information provided by applicants concerning their drug history will be subject to verification by a preemployment polygraph examination.

Do you understand all prospective FBI employees will be required to submit to an urinalysis for drug abuse prior to employment? ☐ Yes ☐ No

I am aware that willfully withholding information or making false statements on this application constitutes a violation of Section 1001, Title 18, U.S. Code and if appointed, will be the basis for dismissal from the Federal Bureau of Investigation. I agree to these conditions and I hereby certify that all statements made by me on this application are true and complete, to the best of my knowledge.

____

Signature of Applicant as usually written. **(Do Not Use Nickname)**

The Federal Bureau of Investigation is an equal opportunity employer.

Notify in case of emergency. It is generally legal to require the name, address, and phone number of a person to notify in case of emergency. However, asking the relationship of this person could indicate the applicant's marital status or lineage.

Membership in organizations. Some forms ask the applicant to list memberships in clubs, organizations, or societies. Employers should include instructions not to include organizations that would reveal race, religion, physical handicaps, marital status, or ancestry.

Physical handicaps. It is usually illegal to require the listing of an applicant's physical handicaps or past illnesses unless the application blank specifically asks only for those that "may interfere with your job performance." Similarly, it is generally illegal to ask whether the applicant has ever received workers' compensation.

Marital status. In general, the application should not ask whether an applicant is single, married, divorced, separated, or living with anyone, or the names, occupations, and ages of the applicants' spouse or children.

FIGURE 5-13 Sample Acceptable Questions Once Conditional Offer Is Made

Source: Kenneth Sovereign, *Personnel Law*, 4th edition, © 1999. Reprinted by permission of Pearson Education, Inc., Upper Saddle River, NJ.

1. Do you have any responsibilities that conflict with the job vacancy?
2. How long have you lived at your present address?
3. Do you have any relatives working for this company?
4. Do you have any physical defects that would prevent you from performing certain jobs where, to your knowledge, vacancies exist?
5. Do you have adequate means of transportation to get to work?
6. Have you had any major illness (treated or untreated) in the past 10 years?
7. Have you ever been convicted of a felony or do you have a history of being a violent person? (This is a very important question to avoid a negligent hiring or retention charge.)
8. What is your educational background? (The information required here would depend on the job-related requirements of the position.)

Housing. Asking whether an applicant *owns, rents,* or *leases* a house may also be discriminatory. It can adversely affect minority groups and is difficult to justify on business necessity.

Two-Stage Process In choosing what to ask on the application, some experts suggest using a two-stage process. Use the first stage to determine if the applicant is qualified. Here, limit application form questions to identification and work history, and to questions that help you to determine if he or she has the skills for the job. This stage includes interviews and testing.

If the answer is "Yes, I believe this person is qualified," then make a conditional job offer, but make it clear that failing to meet any of the following "second stage" conditions may result in rejection. Then, you may ask acceptable conditional job offer questions like those in Figure 5-13, such as "Do you have adequate means of transportation to get to work?"

Video Résumés More candidates are submitting video résumés, a practice replete with benefits and threats. About half of responding employers in one survey thought video résumés might give employers a better feel for the candidate. The danger is that a video résumé makes it more likely that rejected candidates may claim discrimination.[122]

Using Application Forms to Predict Job Performance

It is possible to use application form information to predict which candidates will be successful and which won't, in much the same way that one might use tests for screening. The basic process involves conducting statistical studies to analyze the relationship between (1) biodata responses on the application form (distance from work, for instance) and (2) measures of success on the job.

Here, it is important to choose the biodata items (such as "does not own automobile" or "not living at home") with two things in mind. First, of course, equal employment law limits the items you'll want to use (don't use age, race, or gender, for instance). And, noninvasive questions are best. In one study, subjects perceived items such as "dollar sales achieved" and "grade point average in math" as legitimate, and not invasive. Other items such as "birth order" and "frequent dates in high school" were more invasive, and unacceptable.[123]

Mandatory Arbitration

Many employers, cognizant of the high costs of employment litigation, require applicants to agree in writing to mandatory arbitration should a dispute arise. The practice is a matter of debate.

Different federal courts have taken different positions on the enforceability of these "mandatory alternative dispute resolution" clauses. The basic situation now is that they are generally enforceable, with two big caveats.

First, it had better be a fair process.[124] For example, the agreement should be a signed and dated separate agreement. Use simple wording. Provide for reconsideration and judicial appeal if there is an error of law.[125] The employer must absorb most of the cost of the arbitration process. The arbitration process should be reasonably swift. The employee, if he or she prevails, should be eligible to receive the full remedies that he or she would have had if he or she had had access to the courts.

Second, mandatory arbitration clauses turn some candidates off. In one study, 389 MBA students read simulated employment brochures. Mandatory employment arbitration had a significantly negative impact on the attractiveness of the company as a place to work.[126]

REVIEW

CHAPTER SECTION SUMMARIES

1. The **recruitment and selection process** entails five main steps: decide what positions to fill; build a pool of candidates for these jobs; have candidates complete application forms; use selection tools; and decide to whom to make an offer, in part by having the supervisor and others interview the candidates.
2. Recruitment and selection starts with **personnel planning and forecasting**. Personnel planning is the process of deciding what positions the firm will have to fill, and how to fill them. This often starts by forecasting personnel needs, perhaps using trend analysis, ratio analysis, scatter plots, or computerized software packages. The other side of the equation is forecasting the supply of inside candidates. Here employers use manual systems and replacement charts, and computerized skills inventories. Forecasting the supply of outside candidates is important, particularly when entering periods of economic expansion where unemployment is low and good candidates are more difficult to come by.
3. All managers need to understand why **effective recruiting is important**. Without enough candidates, employers cannot effectively screen the candidates or hire the best. Some employers use a recruiting yield pyramid to estimate how many applicants they need to generate in order to fill predicted job openings.
4. Filling open positions with **internal sources of candidates** has several advantages. For example, you're probably already more familiar with their strengths and weaknesses, and they require less orientation. Finding internal candidates often utilizes job posting. For filling the company's projected top-level positions, succession planning—the ongoing process of systematically identifying, assessing, and developing organizational leadership to enhance performance—is the process of choice.
5. Employers use a variety of **outside sources of candidates** when recruiting applicants.
   - Of these, recruiting via the Internet using job boards such as Monster.com represents the leading source. It is quick and cost-effective. One downside is too many applicants from too far away, but employers use applicant tracking software to screen online applicants.
   - Other sources include advertising and employment agencies (including public and nonprofit agencies, and private agencies).
   - Employers increasingly turn to temporary agencies and other alternative staffing methods to hire "alternative" types of employees, such as contract employees for special projects.
   - Executive recruiters, a special type of employment agency, are invaluable for finding and helping the employer hire top-level professionals and executives. However, the employer needs to ensure that the recruiter is conducting a thorough search and carefully checking references.
   - Other outside sources include college recruiting, referrals and walk-ins, and military personnel.
6. Understanding how to **recruit a more diverse workforce** is important. Whether the target is the single parent, older workers, or minorities, the basic rule is to understand their special needs and to create a set of policies and practices that create a more hospitable environment in which they can work.
7. The recruitment process inevitably includes **developing and using application forms** to collect essential background information about the applicant. The application should enable you to make judgments on substantial matters such as the person's education and to identify the person's job references and supervisors. Of course, it's important to make sure the application complies with equal employment laws, for instance with respect to questions regarding physical handicaps.

DISCUSSION QUESTIONS

1. What are the pros and cons of five sources of job candidates?
2. What are the four main types of information that application forms provide?
3. How, specifically, do equal employment laws apply to personnel recruiting activities?
4. What are five things employers should keep in mind when using Internet sites to find job candidates?
5. What are the five main things you would do to recruit and retain a more diverse workforce?

INDIVIDUAL AND GROUP ACTIVITIES

1. Bring to class several classified and display ads from the Sunday help wanted ads. Analyze the effectiveness of these ads using the guidelines discussed in this chapter.
2. Working individually or in groups, develop a 5-year forecast of occupational market conditions for five occupations such as accountant, nurse, and engineer.
3. Working individually or in groups, visit the local office of your state employment agency. Come back to class prepared to discuss the following questions: What types of jobs seem to be available through this agency, predominantly? To what extent do you think this particular agency would be a good source of professional, technical, and/or managerial applicants? What sorts of paperwork are applicants to the state agency required to complete before their applications are processed by the agency? What other services does the office provide? What other opinions did you form about the state agency?
4. Working individually or in groups, find at least five employment ads, either on the Internet or in a local newspaper, that suggest that the company is family friendly and should appeal to women, minorities, older workers, and single parents. Discuss what they're doing to be family friendly.
5. Working individually or in groups, interview a manager between the ages of 25 and 35 at a local business who manages employees age 40 or older. Ask the manager to describe three or four of his or her most challenging experiences managing older employees.
6. The HRCI "Test Specifications" appendix at the end of this book (pages 699–706) lists the knowledge someone studying for the HRCI certification exam needs to have in each area of human resource management (such as in Strategic Management, Workforce Planning, and Human Resource Development). In groups of four to five students, do four things: (1) Review that appendix now. (2) Identify the material in this chapter that relates to the required knowledge the appendix lists. (3) Write four multiple-choice exam questions on this material that you believe would be suitable for inclusion in the HRCI exam. And (4) if time permits, have someone from your team post your team's questions in front of the class, so the students in other teams can take each others' exam questions.

EXPERIENTIAL EXERCISE

The Nursing Shortage

As of October 2009, U.S. unemployment was still disappointingly high, and employers were still obviously holding back on their hiring. However, while many people were unemployed, that was not the case with nurse professionals. Virtually every hospital was aggressively recruiting nurses. Many were turning to foreign-trained nurses, for example, by recruiting nurses in the Philippines. Experts expected nurses to be in very short supply for years to come.

Purpose: The purpose of this exercise is to give you experience in creating a recruitment program.

Required Understanding: You should be thoroughly familiar with the contents of this chapter, and with the nurse recruitment program of a hospital such as Lenox Hill Hospital in New York (see http://lenoxhillhospital.org/careers_default.aspx).

How to Set Up the Exercise/Instructions: Set up groups of four to five students for this exercise. The groups should work separately and should not converse with each other. Each group should address the following tasks:

1. Based on information available on the hospital's Web site, create a hard-copy ad for the hospital to place in the Sunday edition of the *New York Times*. Which (geographic) editions of the *Times* would you use, and why?
2. Analyze the hospital's current online nurses' ad. How would you improve on it?
3. Prepare in outline form a complete nurses' recruiting program for this hospital, including all recruiting sources your group would use.

APPLICATION CASE

Finding People Who Are Passionate About What They Do

Trilogy Enterprises Inc. of Austin, Texas, is a fast-growing software company, and provides software solutions to giant global firms for improving sales and performance. It prides itself on its unique and unorthodox culture. Many of its approaches to business practice are unusual, but in Trilogy's fast-changing and highly competitive environment, they seem to work.

There is no dress code and employees make their own hours, often very long. They tend to socialize together (the average age is 26), both in the office's well-stocked kitchen and on company-sponsored events and trips to places like local dance clubs and retreats in Las Vegas and Hawaii. An in-house jargon has developed, and the shared history of the firm has taken on the status of legend. Responsibility is heavy and comes early, with a "just do it now" attitude that dispenses with long apprenticeships. New recruits are given a few weeks of intensive training, known as "Trilogy University" and described by participants as "more like boot camp than business school." Information is delivered as if with "a fire hose," and new employees are expected to commit their expertise and vitality to everything they do. Jeff Daniel, director of college recruiting, admits the intense and unconventional firm is not the employer for everybody. "But it's definitely an environment where people who are passionate about what they do can thrive."

The firm employs about 700 such passionate people. Trilogy's managers know the rapid growth they seek depends on having a staff of the best people they can find, quickly trained and given broad responsibility and freedom as soon as possible. CEO Joe Liemandt says, "At a software company, people are everything. You can't build the next great software company, which is what we're trying to do here, unless you're totally committed to that. Of course, the leaders at every company say, 'People are everything.' But they don't act on it."

Trilogy makes finding the right people (it calls them "great people") a company-wide mission. Recruiters actively pursue the freshest, if least experienced, people in the job market, scouring college career fairs and computer science departments for talented overachievers with ambition and entrepreneurial instincts. Top managers conduct the first rounds of interviews, letting prospects know they will be pushed to achieve but will be well rewarded. Employees take top recruits and their significant others out on the town when they fly into Austin for the standard, 3-day preliminary visit. A typical day might begin with grueling interviews but end with mountain biking, rollerblading, or laser tag. Executives have been known to fly out to meet and woo hot prospects who couldn't make the trip.

One year, Trilogy reviewed 15,000 résumés, conducted 4,000 on-campus interviews, flew 850 prospects in for interviews, and hired 262 college graduates, who account for over a third of its current employees. The cost per hire was $13,000; Jeff Daniel believes it was worth every penny.

Questions

1. Identify some of the established recruiting techniques that apparently underlie Trilogy's unconventional approach to attracting talent.
2. What particular elements of Trilogy's culture most likely appeal to the kind of employees it seeks? How does it convey those elements to job prospects?
3. Would Trilogy be an appealing employer for you? Why or why not? If not, what would it take for you to accept a job offer from Trilogy?
4. What suggestions would you make to Trilogy for improving its recruiting processes?

Source: Chuck Salter, "Insanity, Inc.," *Fast Company*, January 1999, pp. 101–108; and www. trilogy.com/sections/careers/work, accessed August 24, 2007.

CONTINUING CASE

Carter Cleaning Company

Getting Better Applicants

If you were to ask Jennifer and her father what the main problem was in running their firm, their answer would be quick and short: hiring good people. Originally begun as a string of coin-operated laundromats requiring virtually no skilled help, the chain grew to six stores, each heavily dependent on skilled managers, cleaner–spotters, and pressers. Employees generally have no more than a high school education (often less), and the market for them is very competitive. Over a typical weekend, literally dozens of want ads for experienced pressers or cleaner–spotters can be found in area newspapers. All these people usually are paid around $15.00 per hour, and they change jobs frequently. Jennifer and her father thus face the continuing task of recruiting and hiring qualified workers out of a pool of individuals they feel are almost nomadic in their propensity to move from area to area and job to job. Turnover in their stores (as in the stores of many of their competitors) often approaches 400%. "Don't talk to me about human resources planning and trend analysis," says Jennifer. "We're fighting an economic war and I'm happy just to be able to round up enough live applicants to be able to keep my trenches fully manned."

In light of this problem, Jennifer's father asked her to answer the following questions:

Questions

1. First, how would you recommend we go about reducing the turnover in our stores?
2. Provide a detailed list of recommendations concerning how we should go about increasing our pool of acceptable job applicants so we no longer face the need to hire almost anyone who walks in the door. (Your recommendations regarding the latter should include completely worded online and hard-copy advertisements and recommendations regarding any other recruiting strategies you would suggest we use.)

TRANSLATING STRATEGY INTO HR POLICIES & PRACTICES CASE

The Hotel Paris Case

The New Recruitment Process

The Hotel Paris's competitive strategy is "To use superior guest service to differentiate the Hotel Paris properties, and to thereby increase the length of stay and return rate of guests, and thus boost revenues and profitability." HR manager Lisa Cruz must now formulate functional policies and activities that support this competitive strategy, by eliciting the required employee behaviors and competencies.

As a longtime HR professional, Lisa Cruz was well aware of the importance of effective employee recruitment. If the Hotel Paris didn't get enough applicants, it could not be selective about who to hire. And, if it could not be selective about who to hire, it wasn't likely that the hotels would enjoy the customer-oriented employee behaviors that the company's strategy relied on. She was therefore disappointed to discover that the Hotel Paris was paying virtually no attention to the job of recruiting prospective employees. Individual hotel managers slapped together help wanted ads when they had positions to fill, and no one in the chain had any measurable idea of how many recruits these ads were producing, or which recruiting approaches worked the best (or worked at all). Lisa knew that it was time to step back and get control of the Hotel Paris's recruitment function.

As they reviewed the details of the Hotel Paris's current recruitment practices, Lisa Cruz and the firm's CFO became increasingly concerned. What they found, basically, was that the recruitment function was unmanaged, totally. The previous HR director had simply allowed the responsibility for recruiting to remain with each separate hotel, and the hotel managers, not being human resources professionals, usually took the path of least resistance when a job became available, such as by placing help wanted ads in their local papers. There was no sense of direction from the Hotel Paris's headquarters regarding what sorts of applicants the company preferred, what media and alternative sources of recruits its managers should use, no online recruiting, and no measurement at all of recruitment process effectiveness. The company ignored recruitment-source metrics that other firms used effectively, such as number of qualified applicants per position, percentage of jobs filled from within, the offer-to-acceptance ratio, acceptance by recruiting source, turnover by recruiting source, and selection test results by recruiting source.

It was safe to say that achieving the Hotel Paris's strategic aims depended on the quality of the people that it attracted to and then selected for employment at the firm. "What we want are employees who will put our guests first, who will use initiative to see that our guests are satisfied, and who will work tirelessly to provide our guests with services that exceed their expectations" said the CFO. Lisa and the CFO both knew this process had to start with better recruiting. The CFO gave her the green light to design a new recruitment process.

Questions

1. Given the hotel's stated employee preferences, what recruiting sources would you suggest they use, and why?
2. What would a Hotel Paris help wanted ad look like?
3. How would you suggest they measure the effectiveness of their recruiting efforts?

KEY TERMS

employment (or personnel) planning, *p. 153*
trend analysis, *p. 153*
ratio analysis, *p. 153*
scatter plot, *p. 155*
qualifications (or skills) inventories, *p. 155*
personnel replacement charts, *p. 155*
position replacement card, *p. 155*
employee recruiting, *p. 157*
recruiting yield pyramid, *p. 159*
job posting, *p. 159*
succession planning, *p. 161*
applicant tracking systems, *p. 163*
alternative staffing, *p. 169*
on-demand recruiting services (ODRS), *p. 171*
college recruiting, *p. 173*
application form, *p. 179*

ENDNOTES

1. "Help Wanted—and Found," *Fortune*, October 2, 2006, p. 40; www.cakecareers.com, accessed March 25, 2009.
2. "More Companies Turn to Workforce Planning to Boost Productivity and Efficiency," The Conference Board, press release/news, August 7, 2006; Carolyn Hirschman, "Putting Forecasting in Focus," *HR Magazine*, March 2007, pp. 44–49.
3. Jones Shannon, "Does HR Planning Improve Business Performance?" *Industrial Management*, January/ February 2003, p. 20. See also Michelle Harrison et al., "Effective Succession Planning" *Training & Development*, October 2006, pp. 22–23.
4. Carolyn Hirschman, "Putting Forecasting in Focus," *HR Magazine*, March 2007, pp. 44–49.
5. Shannon, "Does HR Planning Improve Business Performance?" p. 16.
6. See, for example, Fay Hansen, "The Long View," *Workforce Management*, April 20, 2008, pp. 1, 14.
7. Chaman Jain and Mark Covas, "Thinking About Tomorrow: Seven Tips for Making Forecasting More Effective," *The Wall Street Journal*, July 7, 2008, p. 10.
8. For an example of a computerized, supply chain–based personnel planning system, see Dan Kara, "Automating the Service Chain," *Software Magazine* 20 (June 2000), pp. 3, 42.
9. John Markoff, "Bill Gates's Brain Cells, Dressed Down for Action," *The New York Times*, March 25, 2001, pp. B1, B12.
10. For a recent discussion see, for example, "Pitfalls Abound for Employers Lacking Electronic Information Retention Policies," *BNA Bulletin to Management*, January 1, 2008, pp. 1–2.
11. Ibid. See also Bill Roberts, "Risky Business," *HR Magazine*, October 2006, pp. 69–72.
12. "Traditional Security Insufficient to Halt File-Sharing Threat," *BNA Bulletin to Management*, January 20, 2008, p. 39.
13. See, for example, Society for Human Resource Management, "HR's Insight into the Economy," *Workplace Visions* 4 (2008), p. 5.
14. "Employers Still in Recruiting Bind Should Seek Government Help, Chamber Suggests," *BNA Bulletin to Management*, May 29, 2003, pp. 169–170. See also D. Mattioli, "Only the Employed Need Apply," *Wall Street Journal* (Eastern Edition) (June 30, 2009), p. D1.
15. Tom Porter, "Effective Techniques to Attract, Hire, and Retain 'Top Notch' Employees for Your Company," *San Diego Business Journal* 21, no. 13 (March 27, 2000), p. b36.
16. Jonathan Segal, "Land Executives, Not Lawsuits," *HR Magazine*, October 2006, pp. 123–130.
17. Michelle Martinez, "Recruiting Here and There," *HR Magazine*, September 2002, p. 95.
18. Ibid.
19. Jessica Marquez, "A Global Recruiting Site Helps Far-Flung Managers at the Professional Services Company Acquire the Talent They Need—and Saves One Half-Million Dollars a Year," *Workforce Management*, March 13, 2006, p. 22.
20. "Hiring Works the Second Time Around," *BNA Bulletin to Management*, January 30, 1997, p. 40.
21. Ibid.
22. Where *succession planning* aims to identify and develop employees to fill specific slots, talent management is a broader activity. *Talent management* involves identifying, recruiting, hiring, and developing high-potential employees. Soonhee Kim, "Linking Employee Assessments to Succession Planning," *Public Personnel Management* 32, no. 4 (Winter 2003), pp. 533–547. See also Michael Laff, "Talent Management: From Hire to Retire,"*Training & Development*, November 2006, pp. 42–48.
23. "Succession Management: Identifying and Developing Leaders," *BNA Bulletin to Management* 21, no. 12 (December 2003). BNA Inc., 1231 25th St. NW Washington, DC 20037.
24. Quoted in Susan Wells, "Who's Next," *HR Magazine*, November 2003, p. 43. See also Christee Atwood, "Implementing Your Succession Plan," *Training & Development*, November 2007, pp. 54–57.
25. See "Succession Management: Identifying and Developing Leaders," *BNA Bulletin to Management* 21, no. 12 (December 2003), p. 15.
26. Soonhee Kim, "Linking Employee Assessments to Succession Planning," *Public Personnel Management*, Winter 2003.
27. Bill Roberts, "Matching Talent with Tasks," *HR Magazine*, November 2002, pp. 91–96.
28. Ibid., p. 34.
29. See, for example, J. De Avila, "Beyond Job Boards: Targeting the Source," *Wall Street Journal* (Eastern Edition) (July 2, 2009), pp. D1, D5, and C. Fernandez-Araoz, et. al., "The Definitive Guide to Recruiting in Good Times and Bad" [Financial crisis spotlight], *Harvard Business Review* 87, no. 5 (May 2009), pp. 74–84.
30. Jennifer Berkshire, "Social Network Recruiting," *HR Magazine*, April 2005, pp. 95–98. See also S. DeKay, "Are Business-Oriented Social Networking Web Sites Useful Resources for Locating Passive Jobseekers? Results of a Recent Study," *Business Communication Quarterly* 72, no. 1 (March 2009), pp. 101–105.
31. Josee Rose, "Recruiters Take Hip Path to Fill Accounting Jobs," *The Wall Street Journal*, September 18, 2007, p. 38.
32. Gina Ruiz, "Firms Tapping Web Videos to Lure Jobseekers," *Workforce Management*, October 8, 2007, p. 12.
33. Ed Frauenheim, "Social Revolution," *Workforce*, October 20, 2007, p. 30.
34. "Innovative HR Programs Cultivate Successful Employees," *Nation's Restaurant News* 41, no. 50 (December 17, 2007), p. 74.
35. Sarah Gale, "Internet Recruiting: Better, Cheaper, Faster," *Workforce*, December 2001, p. 76. See also J. De Avila, "Beyond Job Boards: Targeting the Source," *Wall Street Journal* (Eastern Edition) (July 2, 2009), pp. D1, D5.
36. Elizabeth Agnvall, "Job Fairs Go Virtual," *HR Magazine*, July 2007, p. 85.
37. Reprinted from www.careerbuilder.com/MarketingWeb/iPhone/CBJobsApplication.aspx?cbRecursionCnt=1&cbsid=7fd458dafd4a444fb192d9a24ceed771-291142537-wx-6&ns_siteid=ns_us_g_careerbuilder_iphone, accessed March 23, 2009.
38. Ibid., p. 75.
39. "EEOC Issues Much Delayed Definition of 'Applicant,'" *HR Magazine*, April 2004, p. 29; Valerie Hoffman and Greg Davis, "OFCCP's Internet Applicant Definition Requires Overhaul of Recruitment and Hiring Policies," *Society for Human Resources Management Legal Report*, January/February 2006, p. 2.

40. This carries legal risks, particularly if the device disproportionately screens out minority or female applicants. Lisa Harpe, "Designing an Effective Employment Prescreening Program," *Employment Relations Today* 32, no. 3 (Fall 2005), pp. 43–51.
41. William Dickmeyer, "Applicant Tracking Reports Make Data Meaningful," *Workforce*, February 2001, pp. 65–67.
42. Paul Gilster, "Channel the Resume Flood with Applicant Tracking Systems," *Workforce*, January 2001, pp. 32–34; William Dickmeyer, "Applicant Tracking Reports Make Data Meaningful," *Workforce*, February 2001, pp. 65–67.
43. Note that the U.S. Department of Labor's office of federal contract compliance programs recently announced it would review federal contractors' online application tracking systems to ensure they're providing equal opportunity to qualify prospective applicants with disabilities. "Feds Want a Look at Online Job Sites," *HR Magazine*, November 2008, p. 12.
44. Maria Seminerio, "E-Recruiting Takes Next Step," *eWeek*, April 23, 2001, pp. 49–51.
45. Dawn Onley, "Improving Your Online Application Process," *HR Magazine* 50, no. 10 (October 2005), p. 109.
46. "Does Your Company's Website Click with Job Seekers?" *Workforce*, August 2000, p. 260.
47. "Study Says Career Web Sites Could Snare More Job Seekers," *BNA Bulletin to Management*, February 1, 2001, p. 36.
48. Daniel Feldman and Brian Klaas, "Internet Job Hunting: A Field Study of Applicant Experiences with Online Recruiting," *Human Resource Management* 41, no. 2 (Summer 2002), pp. 175–192.
49. Sarah Gale, "Internet Recruiting: Better, Cheaper, Faster," p. 75.
50. "Help Wanted—and Found," *Fortune*, October 2, 2006, p. 40.
51. James Breaugh, "Employee Recruitment: Current Knowledge and Important Areas for Future Research," *Human Resource Management Review* 18 (2008), p. 114.
52. "Job Seekers' Privacy Has Been Eroded with Online Job Searchers, Report Says," *BNA Bulletin to Management*, November 20, 2003, p. 369.
53. James Breaugh, op. cit.
54. See, for example, Rita Zeidner, "Strategies for Saving in a Down Economy," *HR Magazine*, February 2009, p. 31.
55. Eric Krell, "Recruiting Outlook: Creative HR for 2003," *Workforce*, December 2002, pp. 40–44.
56. James Breaugh, op. cit., p. 111.
57. James Breaugh, op. cit., p. 113.
58. Bill Roberts, "Manage Candidates Right from the Start," *HR Magazine*, October 2008, pp. 73–76.
59. Sarah Gale, "The Bookstore Battle," *Workforce Manage-ment*, January 2004, pp. 51–56. See also David Allen et al., "Recruitment Communication Media: Impact on Prehire Outcomes," *Personnel Psychology* 57 (2004), pp. 143–171.
60. Find your nearest one-stop center at www.servicelocator. org.
61. Susan Saulney, "New Jobless Centers Offer More Than a Benefit Check," *The New York Times*, September 5, 2001, p. A1.
62. Lynn Doherty and E. Norman Sims, "Quick, Easy Recruitment Help: From a State?" *Workforce*, May 1998, p. 36.
63. Ibid.
64. Robert Bohner Jr. and Elizabeth Salasko, "Beware the Legal Risks of Hiring Temps," *Workforce*, October 2002, pp. 50–57. See also Fay Hansen, "A Permanent Strategy for Temporary Hires," *Workforce Management*, February 26, 2007, p. 27.
65. John Zappe, "Temp-to-Hire Is Becoming a Full-Time Practice at Firms," *Workforce Management*, June 2005, pp. 82–86.
66. Shari Cauldron, "Contingent Workforce Spurs HR Planning," *Personnel Journal*, July 1994, p. 60.
67. This is based on or quoted from Nancy Howe, "Match Temp Services to Your Needs," *Personnel Journal*, March 1989, pp. 45–51. See also Richard Vosburgh, "The Evolution of HR: Developing HR as an Internal Consulting Organization," *Human Resource Planning* 30, no. 3 (September 2007), pp. 11–12; and Stephen Miller, "Collaboration Is Key to Effective Outsourcing," *HR Magazine* 58 (2008), pp. 60–61.
68. Daniel Feldman, Helen Doerpinghaus, and William Turnley, "Managing Temporary Workers: A Permanent HRM Challenge," *Organizational Dynamics* 23, no. 2 (Fall 1994), p. 49. See also Kathryn Tyler, "Treat Contingent Workers with Care," *HR Magazine*, March 2008, p. 75.
69. Carolyn Hirschman, "Are Your Contractors Legal?" *HR Magazine*, March 2004, pp. 59–63.
70. Ibid.
71. This section is based on Robyn Meredith, "Giant Sucking Sound," *Forbes* 172, no. 6 (September 29, 2003), p. 158; Jim McKay, "Inevitable Outsourcing, Offshoring Stirred Passions at Pittsburgh Summit," *Knight Ridder/Tribune Business News*, March 11, 2004; Peter Panepento, "General Electric Transportation to Outsource Drafting Jobs to India," *Knight Ridder/Tribune Business News*, May 5, 2004; Julie Harbin, "Recent Survey Charts Execs' Willingness to Outsource Jobs," *San Diego Business Journal* 25, no. 14 (April 5, 2004), pp. 8–10; and Pamela Babcock, "America's Newest Export: White-Collar Jobs," *HR Magazine* 49, no. 4 (April 2004), pp. 50–57.
72. "Economics of Offshoring Shifting, as Some Reconsider Ventures," *BNA Bulletin to Management*, September 23, 2008, p. 311.
73. Susan Wells, "Slow Times for Executive Recruiting," *HR Magazine*, April 2003, pp. 61–67.
74. "Leading Executive Search Firms," *Workforce Management*, June 25, 2007, p. 24.
75. Michelle Martinez, "Working with an Outside Recruiter? Get It in Writing," *HR Magazine*, January 2001, pp. 98–105.
76. See, for example, Stephenie Overman, "Searching for the Top," *HR Magazine*, January 2008, p. 49.
77. Bill Leonard, "Recruiting from the Competition," *HR Magazine*, February 2001, pp. 78–86. See also G. Anders, "Secrets of the Talent Scouts," *New York Times* (Late New York Edition) (March 15, 2009), pp. 1, 7 (Sec 3).
78. Jonathan Segal, "Strings Attached," *HR Magazine*, February 2005, pp. 119–123.
79. Martha Frase-Blunt, "A Recruiting Spigot," *HR Magazine*, April 2003, pp. 71–79.
80. Sara Rynes, Marc Orlitzky, and Robert Bretz Jr., "Experienced Hiring Versus College Recruiting: Practices and Emerging Trends," *Personnel Psychology* 50 (1997), pp. 309–339. See also Lisa Munniksma, "Career Matchmakers: Partnering with Collegiate Career Centers Offers Recruiters Access to Rich Source of Applicants," *HR Magazine* 50, no. 2 (February 2005), p. 93.

81. See, for example, James Breaugh, "Employee Recruitment: Current Knowledge and Important Areas for Future Research," *Human Resource Management Review* 18 (2008), p. 111.
82. Lisa Munniksma, "Career Matchmakers," *HR Magazine*, February 2005, pp. 93–96.
83. Joe Mullich, "Finding the Schools That Yield the Best Job Applicant ROI," *Workforce Management*, March 2004, pp. 67–68.
84. Wendy Boswell et al., "Individual Job Choice Decisions and the Impact of Job Attributes and Recruitment Practices: A Longitudinal Field Study," *Human Resource Management* 42, no. 1 (Spring 2003), pp. 23–37. See also James Breaugh, "Employee Recruitment: Current Knowledge and Important Areas for Future Research," *Human Resource Management Review* 18 (2008), p. 115.
85. Roseanne Geisel, "Interns on the Payroll," *HR Magazine* 49, no. 12 (December 2004), p. 89; "Internships Growing in Popularity Among Companies Seeking Fresh Talent and Ideas," *BNA Bulletin to Management*, March 20, 2007, pp. 89–90.
86. Michelle Martinez, "The Headhunter Within," *HR Magazine*, August 2001, pp. 48–56. See also Jennifer Taylor Arnold, "Customers as Employees," *HR Magazine*, April 2007, pp. 77–82.
87. James Breaugh, "Employee Recruitment: Current Knowledge and Important Areas for Future Research," *Human Resource Management Review* 18 (2008), p. 109.
88. Ruth Thaler-Carter, "Your Recruitment Advertising," *HR Magazine*, June 2001, pp. 93–100.
89. "Tell a Friend: Employee Referral Programs Earn High Marks for Low Recruiting Costs," *BNA Bulletin to Management*, June 28, 2001, p. 201.
90. Martha Frase-Blunt, "Call Centers Come Home," *HR Magazine*, January 2007, pp. 85–90.
91. Theresa Minton-Eversole, "Mission: Recruitment," *HR Magazine*, January 2009, pp. 43–45.
92. "The 2007 Recruiting Metrics and Performance Benchmark Report, 2nd ed.," Staffing.org, Inc., 2007.
93. Ann Marie Ryan and Nancy Tippins, "Attracting and Selecting: What Psychological Research Tells Us," *Human Resource Management* 43, no. 4 (Winter 2004), p. 311.
94. Kevin Carlson et al., "Recruitment Evaluation: The Case for Assessing the Quality of Applicants Attracted," *Personnel Psychology* 55 (2002), pp. 461–490. For a recent survey of recruiting source effectiveness, see "The 2007 Recruiting Metrics and Performance Benchmark Report, 2nd ed.," Staffing.org, Inc., 2007.
95. Ibid., p. 461.
96. Ibid., p. 466.
97. Ibid., p. 466.
98. Gino Ruiz, "Special Report: Talent Acquisition," *Workforce Management*, July 23, 2007, p. 39.
99. Thomas Stewart, "In Search of Elusive Tech Workers," *Fortune*, February 16, 1998, pp. 171–172.
100. Quoted or paraphrased from Robert Neveu, "Making the Leap to Strategic Recruiting," special advertising supplement to *Workforce Management*, 2005, p. 3.
101. "Internship Programs Help These Recruiters Toward Qualified Students with Disabilities," *BNA Bulletin to Management*, July 17, 2003, p. 225.
102. Unless otherwise noted, this section is based on Judith Casey and Marcie Pitt-Catsouphes, "Employed Single Mothers: Balancing Job and Home Life," *Employee Assistance Quarterly* 9, no. 324 (1994), pp. 37–53.
103. Ibid., p. 42.
104. "Barclaycard Helps Single Parents to Find Employment," *Personnel Today*, November 7, 2006.
105. Susan Glairon, "Single Parents Need More Flexibility at Work, Advocate in Denver Says," *Daily Camera*, February 8, 2002.
106. Sandra Block and Stephanie Armour, "Many Americans Retire Years Before They Want To," *USA Today*, July 26, 2006, http://usatoday.com, accessed December 23, 2007.
107. Phaedra Brotherton, "Tapping into an Older Workforce," *Mosaics* (Society for Human Resource Management, March/April 2000). See also Thomas Ng and Daniel Feldman, "The Relationship of Age to Ten Dimensions of Job Performance," *Journal of Applied Psychology* 90, no. 2 (2008), pp. 392–423.
108. Sue Shellenbarger, "Gray Is Good: Employers Make Efforts to Retain Older, Experienced Workers," *The Wall Street Journal*, December 1, 2005.
109. Alison Wellner, "Tapping a Silver Mine," *HR Magazine*, March 2002, p. 29.
110. Sue Shellenbarger, op. cit. See also Robert Grossman, "Keep Pace with Older Workers," *HR Magazine*, May 2008, pp. 39–46.
111. Gary Adams and Barbara Rau, "Attracting Retirees to Apply: Desired Organizational Characteristics of Bridge Employment," *Journal of Organizational Behavior* 26, no. 6 (September 2005), pp. 649–660.
112. Susan Sweetser, "Women in Financial Services—An Ideal Match," *National Underwriter Life & Health—Financial Services Edition* 1, no. 2 (January 12, 2004), pp. 14–16; Charles Lauer, "Keeping the Women on Board: Hospitals Must Work Overtime to Retain the Majority of Their Employees," *Modern Health Care* 33, no. 40 (October 6, 2003), p. 21.
113. Abby Ellin, "Supervising the Graybeards," *The New York Times*, January 16, 2000, p. B16; Derek Avery and Patrick McKay, "Target Practice: An Organizational Impression Management Approach to Attracting Minority and Female Job Applicants," *Personnel Psychology* 59 (2006), pp. 157–189.
114. "Recruitment: B&Q in Search of Female Managers," *Personnel Today*, September 2, 2003, p. 4; Dina Berta, "Brinker International's Gomez Keeps Recruitment of Women, Minorities on Company's Front Burner," *Nation's Restaurant News* 37, no. 46 (November 17, 2003), p. 16.
115. "Welfare-to-Work: No Easy Chore," *BNA Bulletin to Management*, February 13, 1997, p. 56.
116. Herbert Greenberg, "A Hidden Source of Talent," *HR Magazine*, March 1997, pp. 88–91.
117. "Welfare to Work: No Easy Chore," p. 56.
118. Linda Moore, "Firms Need to Improve Recruitment, Hiring of Disabled Workers, EEO Chief Says," *Knight Ridder/Tribune Business News*, November 5, 2003. See also "Recruiting Disabled More Than Good Deed, Experts Say," *BNA Bulletin to Management*, February 27, 2007, p. 71.
119. "Students with Disabilities Available," *HR Briefing*, June 15, 2002, p. 5.
120. Moore, "Firms Need to Improve Recruitment."
121. Kenneth Sovereign, *Personnel Law* (Upper Saddle River, NJ, Pearson, 1999), p. 51.
122. Kathy Gurchiek, "Video Resumes Spark Curiosity, Questions," *HR Magazine*, May 2007, pp. 28–30; "Video Resumes Can

Illuminate Applicants' Abilities, but Pose Discrimination Concerns," *BNA Bulletin to Management,* May 20, 2007, pp. 169–170.

123. Fred Mael, Mary Connerley, and Ray Morath, "None of Your Business: Parameters of Biodata Invasiveness," *Personnel Psychology* 49 (1996), pp. 613–650.

124. "Supreme Court Denies Circuit City's Bid for Review of Mandatory Arbitration," *BNA Bulletin to Management,* June 6, 2002, p. 177.

125. "Supreme Court Gives the Employers Green Light to Hold Most Employees to Arbitration Pacts," *BNA Bulletin to Management,* March 29, 2001, pp. 97–98.

126. Douglas Mahony et al., "The Effects of Mandatory Employment Arbitration Systems on Applicants Attraction to Organizations," *Human Resource Management* 44, no. 4 (Winter 2005), pp. 449–470.

6 Employee Testing and Selection

After growing quickly for several years, Google changed its employee screening process. At first, candidates went through a dozen or more grueling in-person interviews. Then, the firm's selection team would routinely reject candidates with years of work experience if they had just average college grades. But, as Google's new HR head said, "Everything works if you're trying to hire 500 people a year, or 1,000." Once it was hiring thousands of people per year, it couldn't let such a slow hiring process bog it down. Google therefore reduced the interview load (to about five on average) and no longer put as much weight on college grade point averages.[1]

Source: Courtesy of Paul Sakuma/AP Wide World Photos.

WHERE ARE WE NOW . . .

Chapter 5 focused on the methods managers use to build an applicant pool. The purpose of Chapter 6 is to explain how to use various tools to select the best candidates for the job. The main topics we'll cover include the selection process, basic testing techniques, background and reference checks, ethical and legal questions in testing, types of tests, and work samples and simulations. In Chapter 7, we will turn to the techniques you can use to improve your skills with what is probably the most widely used screening tool, the selection interview.

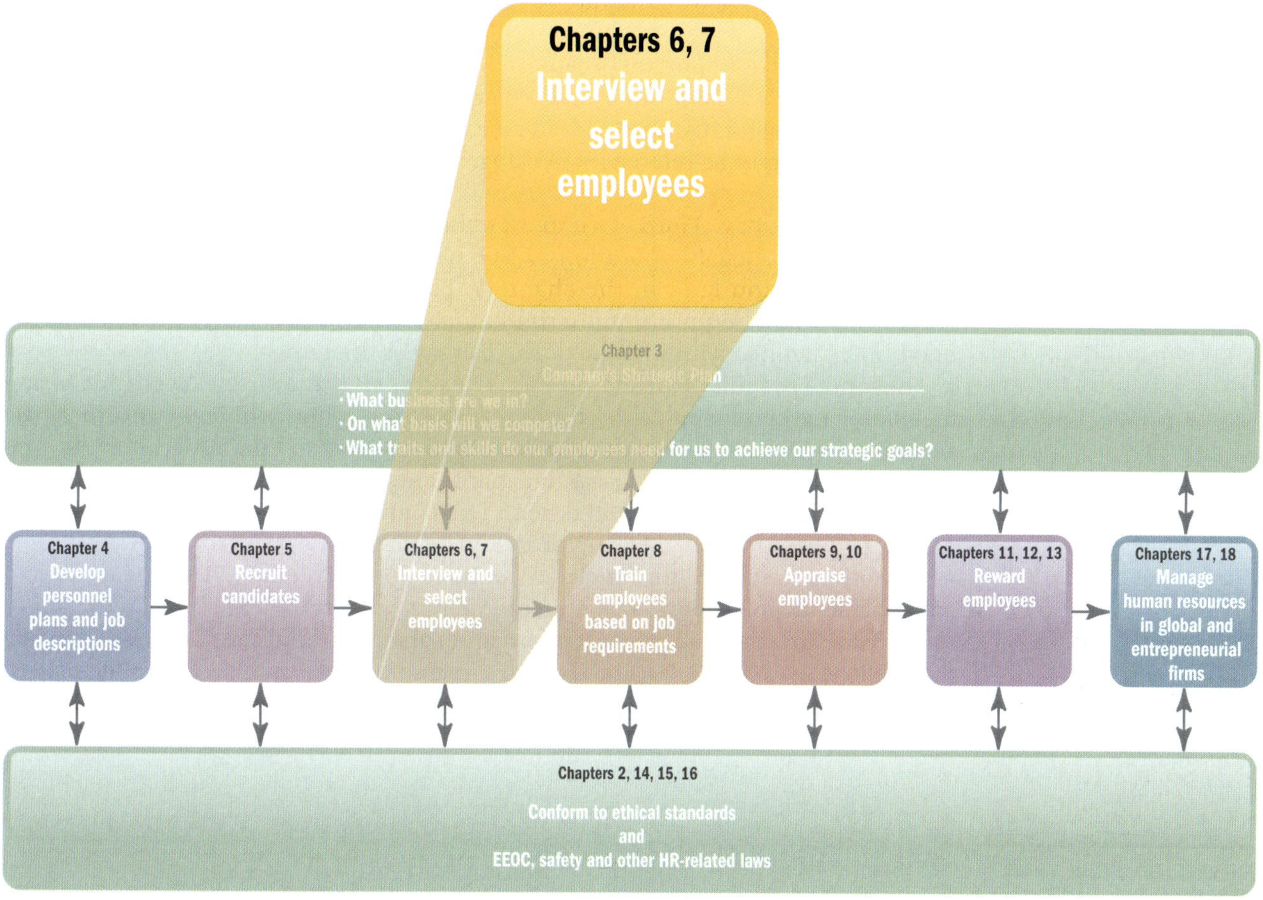

LEARNING OUTCOMES

1. Explain what is meant by reliability and validity.
2. Explain how you would go about validating a test.
3. Cite and illustrate our testing guidelines.
4. Give examples of some of the ethical and legal considerations in testing.
5. List eight tests you could use for employee selection, and how you would use them.
6. Give two examples of work sample/simulation tests.
7. Explain the key points to remember in conducting background investigations.

WHY CAREFUL SELECTION IS IMPORTANT

Once you review your applicants' résumés, the next step is selecting the best candidates for the job. This usually means whittling down the applicant pool by using the screening tools we cover in this chapter: tests, assessment centers, and background and reference checks. Then the supervisor can interview likely candidates and decide who to hire. Nothing you do at work is more important than hiring the right employees. It is important for three main reasons: performance, costs, and legal obligations.

Performance First, your own performance always depends on your subordinates. Employees with the right skills will do a better job for you and the company. Employees without these skills or who are abrasive or obstructionist won't perform effectively, and your own performance and the firm's will suffer. The time to screen out undesirables is before they are in the door, not after.

Cost Second, it is important because it's costly to recruit and hire employees. Hiring and training even a clerk can cost $5,000 or more in fees and supervisory time. The total cost of hiring a manager could easily be 10 times as high once you add search fees, interviewing time, reference checking, and travel and moving expenses.

Legal Obligations Third, it's important because mismanaging the hiring process has three serious legal implications: EEO, negligent hiring, and defamation (we'll discuss defamation later in the chapter). First, (as we saw in Chapter 2), equal employment laws require nondiscriminatory selection procedures. The manager needs to be familiar with what he or she can say or do here.[2]

Second, someone can sue an employer for *negligent hiring*. **Negligent hiring** means hiring employees with criminal records or other problems who then use access to customers' homes (or similar opportunities) to commit crimes.[3] In one case, *Ponticas v. K.M.S. Investments*, an apartment manager with a passkey entered a woman's apartment and assaulted her.[4] The court found the apartment complex's owner negligent for not checking properly the manager's background.[5]

Avoiding negligent hiring claims requires good screening. This means taking "reasonable" action to investigate the candidate's background. Specifically, ". . . make a systematic effort to gain relevant information about the applicant, verify documentation, follow up on missing records or gaps in employment, and keep a detailed log of all attempts to obtain information, including the names and dates for phone calls or other requests."[6]

1 Explain what is meant by reliability and validity.

BASIC TESTING CONCEPTS

A test is, basically, a sample of a person's behavior. Using a test (or any selection tool) assumes the tool is both reliable and valid. Few things illustrate evidence-based HR—the deliberate use of the best-available evidence in making decisions about the human resource management practices you are focusing on—as do checking for reliability and validity.

Reliability

Reliability is a test's first requirement and refers to its consistency: A reliable test is one that yields consistent scores when a person takes two alternate forms of the test or when he or she takes the same test on two or more different occasions.[7]

Reliability is very important. If a person scores 90 on an intelligence test on a Monday and 130 when retested on Tuesday, you probably wouldn't have much faith in the test.

There are several ways to estimate consistency or reliability. You could administer the same test to the same people at two different points in time, comparing their test scores at time two with their scores at time one; this would be a *retest estimate.*

Or you could administer a test and then administer what experts believe to be an equivalent test later; this would be an *equivalent form estimate.* The Scholastic Assessment Test (SAT) is an example of the latter.

A test's internal consistency is another reliability measure. For example, a psychologist includes 10 items on a test of vocational interests, believing that they all measure, in various ways, the test taker's interest in working outdoors. You administer the test and then statistically analyze the degree to which responses to these 10 items vary together. This would provide a measure of the internal reliability of the test. Psychologists refer to this as an *internal comparison estimate.* Internal consistency is one reason that you find apparently repetitive questions on some test questionnaires.

Many things could cause a test to be unreliable. For example, the questions may do a poor job of sampling the material; test one focuses more on Chapters 1, 3, 5, and 7, while test two focuses more on Chapters 2, 4, 5, and 8. Or there might be errors due to changes in the testing conditions; for instance, the room one test is given in may be noisy.

Validity

Reliability, while indispensable, only tells you that the test is measuring something consistently. It does not prove that you are measuring what you intend to measure. A mismanufactured 33-inch yardstick will consistently tell you that 33-inch boards are 33 inches long. Unfortunately, if what you're looking for is a board that is 1 yard long, then your 33-inch yardstick, though reliable, is misleading you by 3 inches.

What you need is a valid yardstick. *Validity* tells you whether the test (or yardstick) is measuring what you think it's supposed to be measuring.[8]

A test, as we said, is a sample of a person's behavior, but some tests are more clearly representative of the behavior being sampled than others. A typing test, for example, clearly corresponds to an on-the-job behavior. At the other extreme, there may be no apparent relationship between the items on the test and the behavior. This is the case with projective personality tests. Thus, in the Rorschach Test sample in Figure 6-1, the psychologist asks the person to explain how he or she interprets an ambiguous picture. The psychologist uses that interpretation to

FIGURE 6-1 A Slide from the Rorschach Test

Source: http://en.wikipedia.org/wiki/File:Rorschach1.jpg, accessed July 27, 2009.

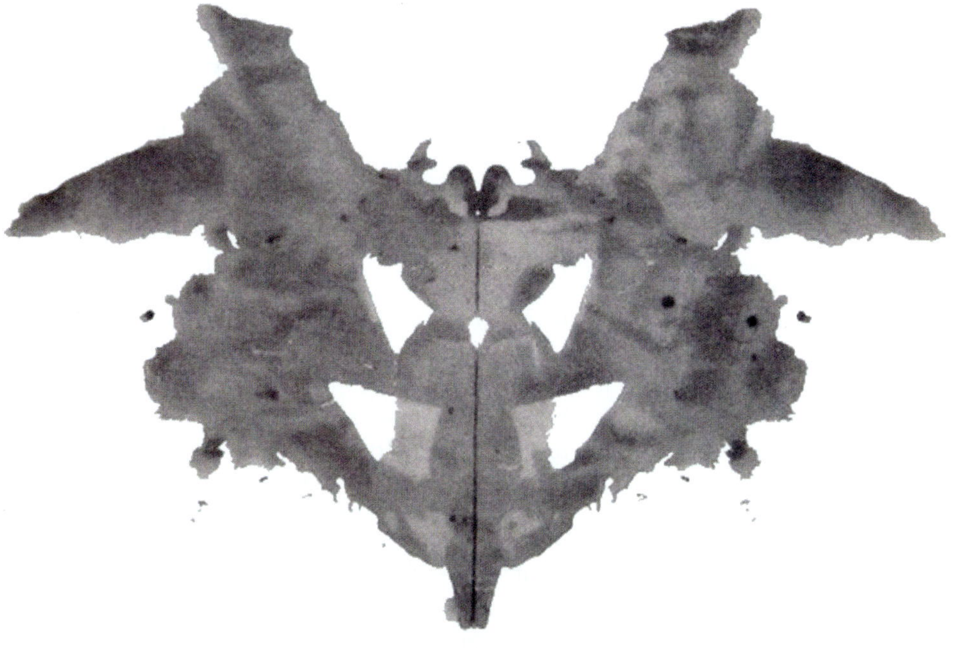

negligent hiring
Hiring workers with questionable backgrounds without proper safeguards.

reliability
The consistency of scores obtained by the same person when retested with the identical tests or with alternate forms of the same test.

draw conclusions about the person's personality and behavior. In such tests, it is more difficult to prove that the tests are measuring what they are said to measure, in this case, some trait of the person's personality—that they're valid.

Test Validity

Test validity answers the question "Does this test measure what it's supposed to measure?" Put another way, *validity* refers to the correctness of the inferences that we can make based on the test. For example, if Jane gets a higher score on mechanical comprehension tests than Jim does, can we be sure that Jane possesses more mechanical comprehension than Jim does?[9] With employee selection tests, *validity* often refers to evidence that the test is job related—in other words, that performance on the test is a valid predictor of subsequent performance on the job. A selection test must be valid since, without proof of validity, there is no logical or legally permissible reason to continue using it to screen job applicants. You would not be too comfortable taking the GRE if you didn't think that your score on the GRE predicted, in some valid way, your likely performance in graduate school. Equal employment law (as we explained in Chapter 2) requires valid tests. In employment testing, there are two main ways to demonstrate a test's validity: **criterion validity** and **content validity**.[10]

Criterion Validity

Demonstrating *criterion validity* means demonstrating that those who do well on the test also do well on the job, and that those who do poorly on the test do poorly on the job. Thus, the test has validity to the extent that the people with higher test scores perform better on the job. In psychological measurement, a *predictor* is the measurement (in this case, the test score) that you are trying to relate to a *criterion*, such as performance on the job. The term *criterion validity* reflects that terminology.

Content Validity

Employers demonstrate the *content validity* of a test by showing that the test constitutes a fair sample of the job's content. The basic procedure here is to identify job tasks that are critical to performance, and then randomly select a sample of those tasks to test. In selecting students for dental school, many schools give applicants chunks of chalk, and ask them to carve something that looks like a tooth. If the content you choose for the test is a representative sample of what the person needs to know for the job, then the test is probably content valid. Clumsy dental students need not apply.

Demonstrating content validity sounds easier than it is in practice. Demonstrating that (1) the tasks the person performs on the test are really a comprehensive and random sample of the tasks performed on the job and (2) the conditions under which the person takes the test resemble the work situation is not always easy. For many jobs, employers opt to demonstrate other evidence of a test's validity—most often, criterion validity.

2 Explain how you would go about validating a test.

Evidence-Based HR: How to Validate a Test

In order for a selection test to be useful, you want to know (you need evidence) that scores on the test relate in a predictable way to performance on the job. Thus, other things being equal, students who score high on the graduate admissions tests also do better in graduate school. Applicants who score high on mechanical comprehension tests perform better as engineers. In other words, you should validate the test before using it by ensuring that scores on the test are a good predictor of some *criterion* like job performance—thus demonstrating the test's *criterion validity*.[11] At best, invalid tests are a waste of time. At worst, they may be discriminatory. Tests you buy "off the shelf" should include information on their validity. The Society for Industrial and Organizational Psychology says that "Experienced and knowledgeable test publishers have (and are happy to provide) information on the validity of their testing products."[12] But ideally, you should revalidate the tests for the job(s) at hand.

An industrial psychologist usually conducts the validation study. The human resource department coordinates the effort. Strictly speaking, the supervisor's role is just to make sure that the job's human requirements and performance standards are clear to the psychologist. But in practice, anyone using tests (or test results) should know something about validation. Then you can better understand how to use tests and interpret their results. The validation process consists of five steps:

Step 1: Analyze the Job. The first step is to analyze the job and write job descriptions and job specifications. The point is to specify the human traits and skills you believe are required for adequate job performance. For example, must an applicant be verbal, a good talker? Must the person assemble small, detailed components? These requirements become the *predictors*. These are the human traits and skills you believe predict success on the job.

In this first step, you also must define what you mean by "success on the job," since it's this success for which you want predictors. The standards of success are *criteria*. Here you could use production-related criteria (quantity, quality, and so on), personnel data (absenteeism, length of service, and so on), or judgments of worker performance (by persons like supervisors). For an assembler's job, your predictors might include manual dexterity and patience. Specific criteria then might include number of rejects produced per hour.

Choosing the right criteria (measures of performance) is important. One study involved 212 gas utility company employees. The researchers found a significant relationship between the test and two performance criteria—supervisor ratings of performance and objective productivity indices. However, there was virtually no relationship between the same test and two other performance criteria, namely, an objective quality index or employee performance self-ratings.[13]

Step 2: Choose the Tests. Once you know the predictors (such as mechanical comprehension) you want to use, the next step is to decide how to test for them. Employers usually base this choice on experience, previous research, and "best guesses." They usually don't start with just one test. Instead, they choose several tests and combine them into a test battery. The test battery aims to measure an array of possible predictors, such as aggressiveness, extroversion, and numerical ability.

What tests are available and where do you get them? Given the EEO and ethical issues involved, the best advice is probably to use a professional, such as a licensed industrial psychologist. However, many firms publish tests. Psychological Assessment Resources, Inc., in Odessa, Florida, is typical. It publishes and distributes many tests. Some of these are available to virtually any purchaser. Others are available only to qualified buyers (such as those with degrees in psychology or counseling). Figure 6-2 presents several Web sites that provide information about tests or testing programs.

Some companies publish employment tests that are generally available to almost anyone. For example, Wonderlic, Inc., publishes a well-known intellectual capacity test and other tests, including aptitude test batteries and interest inventories. G. Neil Company of Sunrise, Florida, offers employment testing materials including, for example, a clerical skills test, telemarketing ability test, service ability test, management ability test, team skills test, and sales abilities test. Again, though, don't let the widespread availability of tests blind you to this fact: You should use tests in a manner consistent with equal employment laws, and in a manner that is ethical and protects the test taker's privacy. We'll return to this point in a moment.

Step 3: Administer the Test. Next, administer the selected test(s). You have two choices here. One option is to administer the tests to employees currently

test validity
The accuracy with which a test, interview, and so on measures what it purports to measure or fulfills the function it was designed to fill.

criterion validity
A type of validity based on showing that scores on the test (predictors) are related to job performance (criterion).

content validity
A test that is content valid is one that contains a fair sample of the tasks and skills actually needed for the job in question.

FIGURE 6-2 Examples of Web Sites Offering Information on Tests or Testing Programs

- www.hr-guide.com/data/G371.htm
  Provides general information and sources for all types of employment tests.
- http://ericae.net
  Provides technical information on all types of employment and nonemployment tests.
- www.ets.org/testcoll
  Provides information on more than 20,000 tests.
- www.kaplan.com
  Information from Kaplan test preparation on how various admissions tests work.
- www.assessments.biz
  One of many firms offering employment tests.

on the job. You then compare their test scores with their current performance; this is *concurrent (at the same time) validation.* Its main advantage is that data on performance are readily available. The disadvantage is that current employees may not be representative of new applicants (who, of course, are really the ones for whom you are interested in developing a screening test). Current employees have already had on-the-job training and screening by your existing selection techniques.

Predictive validation is the second and more dependable way to validate a test. Here you administer the test to applicants before you hire them. Then hire these applicants using only existing selection techniques, not the results of the new tests. After they have been on the job for some time, measure their performance and compare it to their earlier test scores. You can then determine whether you could have used their performance on the new test to predict their subsequent job performance.

Step 4: Relate Your Test Scores and Criteria. The next step is to ascertain if there is a significant relationship between scores (the predictor) and performance (the criterion). The usual way to do this is to determine the statistical relationship between (1) scores on the test and (2) job performance using correlation analysis, which shows the degree of statistical relationship.

If there is a correlation between test and job performance, you can develop an **expectancy chart.** This presents the relationship between test scores and job performance graphically. To do this, split the employees into, say, five groups according to test scores, with those scoring the highest fifth on the test, the second highest fifth, and so on. Then compute the percentage of high job performers in each of these five test score groups and present the data in an expectancy chart like that in Figure 6-3. In this case, someone scoring in the top fifth of the test has a 97% chance of being

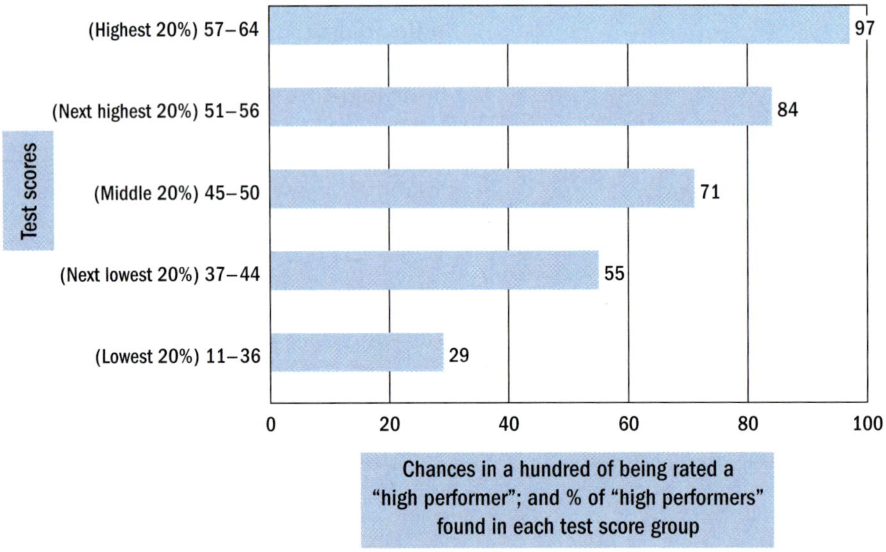

FIGURE 6-3 Expectancy Chart

Note: This expectancy chart shows the relation between scores made on the Minnesota Paper Form Board and rated success of junior draftspersons.

Example: Those who score between 37 and 44 have a 55% chance of being rated above average and those scoring between 57 and 64 have a 97% chance.

TABLE 6-1 Testing Program Guidelines

1. *Use tests as supplements.* Don't make tests your only selection tool; use them to supplement other tools like interviews and background checks.
2. *Validate the tests.* It's best to validate them in your own organization. However, the fact that the same tests have proven valid in similar organizations—called *validity generalization*—is usually adequate.
3. *Monitor your testing/selection program.* Ask questions such as, "What proportions of minority and nonminority applicants are rejected at each stage of the hiring process?" and "Why am I using this test—what does it mean in terms of actual behavior on the job?"
4. *Keep accurate records.* Record why you rejected each applicant. A general note such as "not sufficiently well qualified" is not enough. Your reasons for rejecting the person may be subject to validation at a later date.
5. *Use a certified psychologist.* Developing, validating, and using selection standards (including tests) generally require a qualified psychologist. Most states require persons who offer psychological services to the public to be certified or licensed. A Ph.D. degree (the bachelor's degree is never sufficient) is usually one qualification. Potential consultants should provide evidence of similar work and experience in test validation, and demonstrate familiarity with federal and state equal rights laws and regulations.
6. *Manage test conditions.* Administer tests in areas that are reasonably private, quiet, well lighted, and ventilated, and make sure all applicants take the tests under the same test conditions. Once completed, keep test results confidential. Give them only to individuals with a legitimate need for the information and the ability to understand and interpret the scores (including the applicant). Train your supervisors regarding test results confidentiality.
7. *Revalidate periodically.* Employers' needs and applicants' aptitudes change over time. You should have your testing program revalidated periodically.

a high performer, while one scoring in the lowest fifth has only a 29% chance of being a high performer.[14]

Step 5: Cross-Validate and Revalidate. Before using the test, you may want to check it by "cross-validating"—in other words, by again performing steps 3 and 4 on a new sample of employees. At a minimum, have someone revalidate the test periodically.

Table 6-1 summarizes important testing guidelines. such as "use tests as supplements."

3 Cite and illustrate our testing guidelines.

Who Scores the Test?

Tests come from test publishers, who provide various services, including automated scoring and test interpretation. Some tests (such as the 16PF® Personality Profile, for measuring creativity, independence, leadership, and self-control) are professionally scored and interpreted. Wonderlic, Inc., lets an employer administer the 16PF. The employer then faxes (or scans) the answer sheet to Wonderlic, which scores the candidate's profile and faxes (or scans) back the interpretive report in one day. Psychologists also easily score many psychological tests, including the MMPI personality test, online or using interpretive Windows-based software. However, managers can easily score many tests, like the Wonderlic Personnel Test, themselves.

Research Insight: What Tests Do Applicants Like?

In a nutshell, applicants like tests that they think are fair.[15] Following good test practices—a quiet test-taking environment, privacy, and so on—is important.[16] Another factor is the obviousness

expectancy chart
A graph showing the relationship between test scores and job performance for a group of people.

of the link between the test and performing the job (in other words, the test's "face validity"). For example, in one study, students' reactions were highly favorable toward interviews and work sample tests, both of which had obvious links to the job.[17] They were moderately favorable toward biographical information and written ability tests. They were neutral toward personality and honesty tests, and negative toward graphology. Fairness in selection is important because "applicants who hold positive perceptions about selection are more likely to view the organization favorably and report stronger intentions to accept job offers and recommend the employer to others."[18]

4 Give examples of some of the ethical and legal considerations in testing.

Test Takers' Individual Rights and Test Security

Test takers have rights to privacy and feedback under the American Psychological Association's (APA) standard for educational and psychological tests; these guide psychologists but are *not* legally enforceable. Test takers have the following rights:

- The right to the confidentiality of test results.
- The right to informed consent regarding use of these results.
- The right to expect that only people qualified to interpret the scores will have access to them, or that sufficient information will accompany the scores to ensure their appropriate interpretation.
- The right to expect the test is fair to all. For example, no one taking it should have prior access to the questions or answers.

A complete discussion of the APA's "Ethical Principles of Psychologists and Code of Conduct" is beyond the scope of this book. But some of the points it addresses include competence, integrity, respect for people's dignity, maintaining expertise, nondiscrimination, sexual harassment, personal problems and conflicts, avoiding harm, misuse of psychologists' influence, exploitation of relationships, competent and appropriate use of assessments and interventions, obsolete tests, minimizing intrusions on privacy, and reporting ethical violations.[19] Anyone using tests, including supervisors, should keep issues like those in mind. The accompanying "Managing the New Workforce" feature illustrates why.

Managing the New Workforce

Bias Against Working Mothers

Would you hire someone's mother? As silly as that question seems, managers should be aware of a sad fact: Employers tend to view working mothers negatively.[20]

Here's an example. Researchers gave 100 MBA students (34% female, and all of whom worked full time) copies of a job description summary. The job was assistant vice president of financial affairs. The MBA students also got a "promotion applicant information form" to evaluate for each fictitious "applicant." These included researcher-created information such as marital status and supervisor comments. Some "applicants" were mothers.

The student-evaluators were biased against the mothers. They viewed them as less competent and were less likely to recommend them for the job. As the researchers say, "These data are consistent with mounting evidence that women suffer disadvantages in the workplace when they are mothers, a problem that has been termed 'the maternal wall.'"[21]

Privacy Issues Common sense suggests that managers should keep their knowledge of employees' test results private. However, there are also privacy protections embedded in U.S. and common law. Certain U.S. Supreme Court decisions do protect individuals from intrusive governmental action in a variety of contexts.[22] Furthermore, the Federal Privacy Act gives federal employees the right to inspect their personnel files, and limits the disclosure of personnel information without the employee's consent, among other things.[23]

We'll also see that common law provides some protection against disclosing information about employees to people outside the company. The main application here involves defamation (either libel or slander), but there are privacy issues, too.[24] The bottom line is this:

1. Make sure you understand the need to keep employees' information confidential.
2. Adopt a "need to know" policy. For example, if an employee has been rehabilitated after a period of drug use and that information is not relevant to his or her functioning in the workplace, then a new supervisor may not "need to know."

How Do Employers Use Tests at Work?

About 41% of companies that the American Management Association surveyed tested applicants for basic skills (defined as the ability to read instructions, write reports, and do arithmetic adequate to perform common workplace tasks).[25] About 67% of the respondents required employees to take job skills tests, and 29% required some form of psychological measurement.[26] To see what such tests are like, try the short test in Figure 6-4 to find out how prone you might be to on-the-job accidents.

Tests are not just for lower-level workers. For example, Barclays Capital gives graduate and undergraduate job candidates aptitude tests instead of first-round interviews.[27] In general, as work demands increase (in terms of skill requirements, training, and pay), employers tend to rely more on testing in the selection process.[28] Employers don't use tests just to find good employees, but also to screen out bad ones. By one account, about 30% of all employees say they've stolen from their employers; about 41% are managers.[29] In retail, employers apprehended about one out of every 28 workers for stealing.[30] No wonder prudent employers test their applicants. We'll look at three examples.

Outback Steakhouse Example

Outback Steakhouse began using preemployment tests in 1991, just 2 years after the company started. The testing is apparently

FIGURE 6-4 Sample Test
Source: Courtesy of NYT Permissions.

CHECK YES OR NO	YES	NO
1. You like a lot of excitement in your life.		
2. An employee who takes it easy at work is cheating on the employer.		
3. You are a cautious person.		
4. In the past three years you have found yourself in a shouting match at school or work.		
5. You like to drive fast just for fun.		

Analysis: According to John Kamp, an industrial psychologist, applicants who answered no, yes, yes, no, no to questions 1, 2, 3, 4, and 5 are statistically likely to be absent less often, to have fewer on-the-job injuries, and, if the job involves driving, to have fewer on-the-job driving accidents. Actual scores on the test are based on answers to 130 questions.

quite successful. While annual turnover rates for hourly employees may reach 200% in the restaurant industry, Outback's turnover ranges from 40% to 60%. Outback is looking for employees who are highly social, meticulous, sympathetic, and adaptable, and uses a test to screen out applicants who don't fit the Outback culture. This personality assessment test is part of a three-step preemployment process. Applicants take the test, and managers then compare the candidates' results to the profile for Outback Steakhouse employees. Those who score low on certain traits (like compassion) don't move to the next step. Those who score high move on to be interviewed by two managers. The latter focus on behavioral questions such as "What would you do if a customer asked for a side dish we don't have on the menu?"[31]

City Garage Example City Garage, a 200-employee chain of 25 auto service and repair shops in Dallas–Fort Worth, implemented a computerized testing program to improve its operations. The original hiring process consisted of a paper-and-pencil application and one interview, immediately followed by a hire/don't hire decision. The result was high turnover, and too few managers to staff new stores. This inhibited the firm's growth strategy.

City Garage's top managers' solution was to purchase the Personality Profile Analysis online test from Dallas-based Thomas International USA. After a quick application and background check, likely candidates take the 10-minute, 24-question PPA. City Garage staff then enter the answers into the PPA Software system, and test results are available in less than 2 minutes. These show whether the applicant is high or low in four personality characteristics; it also produces follow-up questions about areas that might cause problems. For example, applicants might be asked how they've handled possible weaknesses such as lack of patience in the past. If candidates answer those questions satisfactorily, they're asked back for extensive, all-day interviews, after which hiring decisions are made.

Capital One Example Several years ago, Capital One Financial was using three paper-and-pencil tests: a cognitive skills test, a math test, and a biodata job history (which the firm used to predict job stability).[32] The process was inefficient: "In Tampa, we were having to process several thousand people a month just to hire 100." The company's new online system eliminates the paper-and-pencil process. Call center applicants working online complete the application and the upgraded math and biodata tests (which might include number of years on last job, and distance from the nearest Capital One office, for instance). They also take an online role-playing call simulation. They put on a headset, and the program plays seven different customer situations. Applicants (playing the role of operators) answer multiple-choice questions online as to how they would respond.

Source: Courtesy of William Thomas Cain/Bloomberg News.

Person taking a Web-based employment test.

Computerized and Online Testing

As you can see from the previous examples, computerized and/or online testing is increasingly replacing conventional paper-and-pencil and manual tests. Many firms such as FedEx have applicants take online or offline computerized tests—sometimes by phone, using the touch-tone keypad, sometimes online—to prescreen applicants quickly prior to more in-depth interviews and background checks.[33] Service firms like Unicru process and score online preemployment tests from employers' applicants. The applicant tracking systems we discussed in Chapter 5 (Recruiting) often include an online prescreening test.[34]

Most of the tests we describe on the following pages are available in computerized form. For example, candidates for architectural certification solve online architectural problems, such as designing building layouts to fit specified space constraints.[35]

5 List eight tests you could use for employee selection, and how you would use them.

TYPES OF TESTS

We can conveniently classify tests according to whether they measure cognitive (mental) abilities, motor and physical abilities, personality and interests, or achievement.[36] We'll look at each.

HR APPs 4 U

Testing via the iPhone

Vendors are making tests available for applicants to take via their iPhones. For example, the top of the screen grab below illustrates one app, in this case for an online typing test you can take on an iPhone.[37]

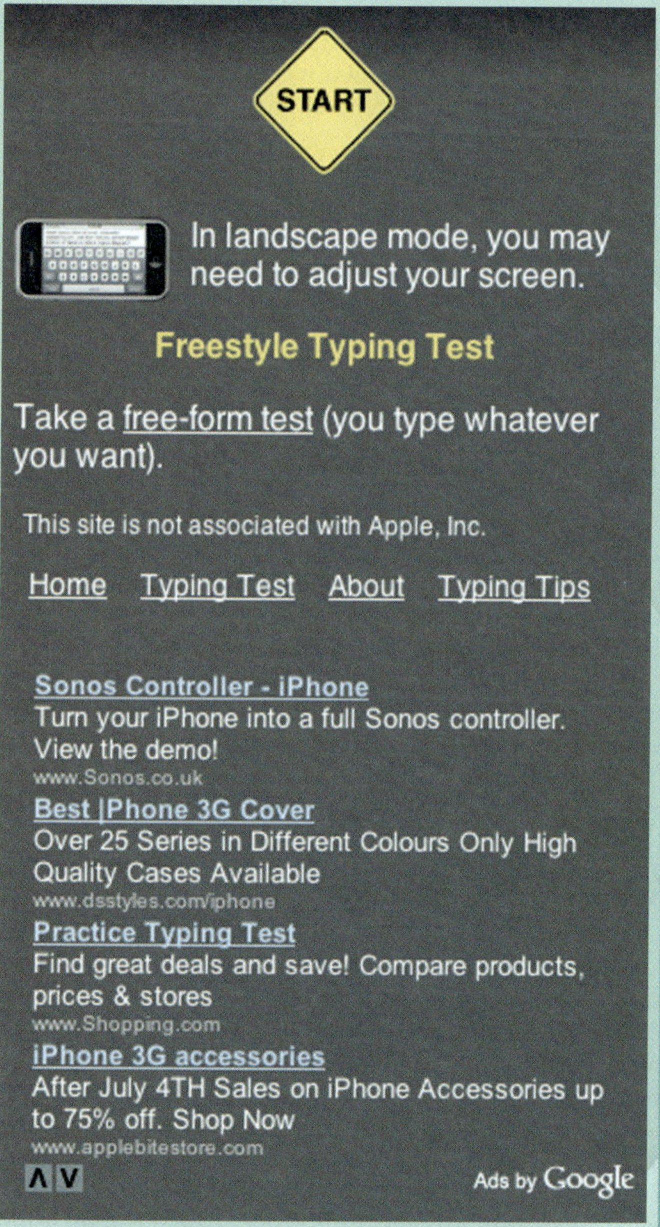

Source: http://www.iphonetypingtest.com, accessed March 23, 2009.

Tests of Cognitive Abilities

Cognitive tests include tests of general reasoning ability (intelligence) and tests of specific mental abilities like memory and inductive reasoning.

Intelligence Tests Intelligence (IQ) tests are tests of general intellectual abilities. They measure not a single trait but rather a range of abilities, including memory, vocabulary, verbal fluency, and numerical ability.

Originally, IQ (intelligence quotient) was literally a quotient. The procedure was to divide a child's mental age (as measured by the intelligence test) by his or her chronological age, and then multiply the results by 100. If an 8-year-old child answered questions as a 10-year-old might, his or her IQ would be 10 divided by 8, times 100, or 125.

For adults, of course, the notion of mental age divided by chronological age wouldn't make sense. Therefore, an adult's IQ score is actually a "derived" score. It reflects the extent to which the person is above or below the "average" adult's intelligence score.

Intelligence is often measured with individually administered tests like the Stanford-Binet Test or the Wechsler Test. Employers can administer other IQ tests such as the Wonderlic to groups of people. Other intelligence tests include the Kaufman Adolescent and Adult Intelligence Test, the Slosson Intelligence Test, the Wide Range Intelligence Test, and the Comprehensive Test of Nonverbal Intelligence.

Specific Cognitive Abilities There are also measures of specific mental abilities, such as inductive and deductive reasoning, verbal comprehension, memory, and numerical ability.

Psychologists often call such tests *aptitude tests*, since they purport to measure aptitude for the job in question. Consider the Test of Mechanical Comprehension in Figure 6-5, which tests applicants' understanding of basic mechanical principles. This may reflect a person's aptitude for jobs—like that of machinist or engineer—that require mechanical comprehension. Other tests of mechanical aptitude include the Mechanical Reasoning Test and the SRA Test of Mechanical Aptitude. The revised Minnesota Paper Form Board Test consists of 64 two-dimensional diagrams cut into separate pieces. It provides insights into an applicant's mechanical spatial ability; you'd use it for screening applicants for jobs such as designers, draftspeople, or engineers.

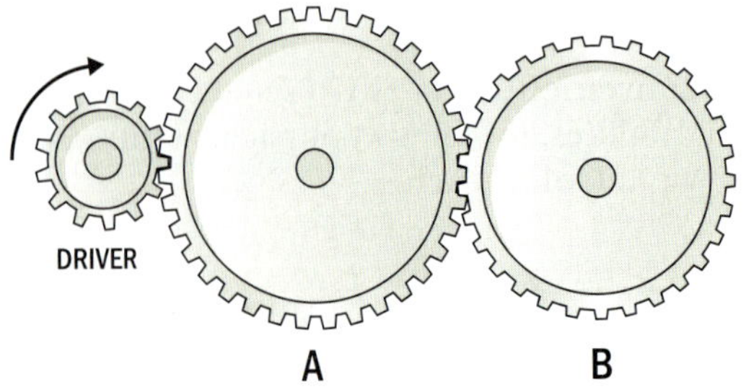

FIGURE 6-5 Type of Question Applicant Might Expect on a Test of Mechanical Comprehension

Tests of Motor and Physical Abilities

You might also want to measure motor abilities, such as finger dexterity, manual dexterity, and (if hiring pilots) reaction time. The Crawford Small Parts Dexterity Test is an example. It measures the speed and accuracy of simple judgment as well as the speed of finger, hand, and arm movements. Other tests include the Stromberg Dexterity Test, the Minnesota Rate of Manipulation Test, and the Purdue Peg Board. The Roeder Manipulative Aptitude Test screens individuals for jobs where dexterity is a main requirement.

Tests of physical abilities may also be required. These include static strength (such as lifting weights), dynamic strength (like pull-ups), body coordination (as in jumping rope), and stamina.[38] Lifeguards, for example, must show they can swim a course before they're hired.

Measuring Personality and Interests

A person's cognitive and physical abilities alone seldom explain his or her job performance. Other factors, like motivation and interpersonal skills, are very important. As one consultant put it, most people are hired based on qualifications, but most are fired for nonperformance. And nonperformance "is usually the result of personal characteristics, such as attitude, motivation, and especially, temperament."[39] Even some online dating services, like eHarmony.com, have prospective members take online personality tests and reject those who its software judges as unmatchable.[40]

Employers use personality tests to measure and predict such intangibles. For example, as part of its selection process for CEO, Hewlett-Packard put its finalists through a 2-hour, 900-question personality test. Candidates had to indicate whether statements like "When I bump into a piece of furniture, I usually get angry" were true or false.[41] Other firms such as Acxiom Corp. use tests like the Myers-Briggs or Birkman Method personality assessment to help new employees better understand the tasks at which they're best.[42]

What Do Personality Tests Measure?

Personality tests measure basic aspects of an applicant's personality, such as introversion, stability, and motivation.

Some of these tests are *projective*. The psychologist presents an ambiguous stimulus (like an inkblot or clouded picture) to the person. The person then reacts to it. Since the pictures are ambiguous, the person supposedly projects into the picture his or her attitudes. A security-oriented person might describe the ink blot in Figure 6-1 (page 193) as "A giant insect coming to get me." Other projective techniques include Make a Picture Story (MAPS), House-Tree-Person (H-T-P), and the Forer Structured Sentence Completion Test.

Other personality tests are *self-reported*: Applicants fill them out themselves. The Guilford-Zimmerman Survey measures personality traits like emotional stability versus moodiness, and friendliness versus criticalness. The Minnesota Multiphasic Personality Inventory (MMPI) taps traits like hypochondria and paranoia. The Interpersonal Style Inventory is a self-report inventory composed of 300 true/false items covering scales such as sociable, sensitive, deliberate, stable, conscientious, trusting, and directive. The Wonderlic Personal Characteristics Inventory measures five personality dimensions. The Sales Achievement Predictor rates the applicant as highly recommended, recommended, or not recommended for sales. You'll find sample personality tests online at www.psychtests.com. Figure 6-6 presents sample personality test items.

FIGURE 6-6 Sample Online Personality Test Questions

Source: Elaine Pulakos, "Selection Assessment Methods," SHRM Foundation, 2005, p. 9.

HumanMetrics

Jung Typology Test™

After completing the questionnaire, you will obtain:

- Your type formula according to Carl Jung and Isabel Myers-Briggs typology along with the strengths of the preferences
- The description of your personality type
- The list of occupations and educational institutions where you can get relevant degree or training, most suitable for your personality type - Jung Career Indicator™

For Organizations and Professionals

Organizations and specialists interested in Jung personality assessments for team building, candidate assessment, leadership, career development, psychographics - visit **HRPersonality™** for practical and validated instruments and professional services.

1. You are almost never late for your appointments
   ○YES ○NO
2. You like to be engaged in an active and fast-paced job
   ○YES ○NO
3. You enjoy having a wide circle of acquaintances
   ○YES ○NO
4. You feel involved when watching TV soaps
   ○YES ○NO
5. You are usually the first to react to a sudden event: the telephone ringing or unexpected question
   ○YES ○NO
6. You are more interested in a general idea than in the details of its realization
   ○YES ○NO
7. You tend to be unbiased even if this might endanger your good relations with people
   ○YES ○NO
8. Strict observance of the established rules is likely to prevent a good outcome
   ○YES ○NO
9. It's difficult to get you excited
   ○YES ○NO
10. It is in your nature to assume responsibility
    ○YES ○NO
11. You often think about humankind and its destiny
    ○YES ○NO
12. You believe the best decision is one that can be easily changed
    ○YES ○NO
13. Objective criticism is always useful in any activity
    ○YES ○NO
14. You prefer to act immediately rather than speculate about various options
    ○YES ○NO
15. You trust reason rather than feelings
    ○YES ○NO
16. You are inclined to rely more on improvisation than on careful planning
    ○YES ○NO
17. You spend your leisure time actively socializing with a group of people, attending parties, shopping, etc.
    ○YES ○NO
18. You usually plan your actions in advance
    ○YES ○NO
19. Your actions are frequently influenced by emotions
    ○YES ○NO
20. You are a person somewhat reserved and distant in communication
    ○YES ○NO
21. You know how to put every minute of your time to good purpose
    ○YES ○NO
22. You readily help people while asking nothing in return
    ○YES ○NO
23. You often contemplate about the complexity of life
    ○YES ○NO
24. After prolonged socializing you feel you need to get away and be alone
    ○YES ○NO
25. You often do jobs in a hurry
    ○YES ○NO
26. You easily see the general principle behind specific occurrences
    ○YES ○NO
27. You frequently and easily express your feelings and emotions
    ○YES ○NO
28. You find it difficult to speak loudly
    ○YES ○NO

(continued)

The "Big Five" What traits to measure? Industrial psychologists often focus on the "big five" personality dimensions: extraversion, emotional stability/neuroticism, agreeableness, conscientiousness, and openness to experience.[43]

> Neuroticism represents a tendency to exhibit poor emotional adjustment and experience negative effects, such as anxiety, insecurity, and hostility. Extraversion represents a tendency to be sociable, assertive, active, and to experience positive effects, such as energy and zeal. Openness to experience is the disposition to be imaginative, nonconforming, unconventional, and autonomous. Agreeableness is the tendency to be trusting, compliant, caring, and gentle. Conscientiousness is comprised of two related facets: achievement and dependability.[44]

Do Personality Tests Predict Performance? It seems to make sense that personality tests would predict performance. After all, wouldn't an extroverted person do better in sales?

FIGURE 6-6 *(continued)*

29. You get bored if you have to read theoretical books
○YES ○NO
30. You tend to sympathize with other people
○YES ○NO
31. You value justice higher than mercy
○YES ○NO
32. You rapidly get involved in social life at a new workplace
○YES ○NO
33. The more people with whom you speak, the better you feel
○YES ○NO
34. You tend to rely on your experience rather than on theoretical alternatives
○YES ○NO
35. You like to keep a check on how things are progressing
○YES ○NO
36. You easily empathize with the concerns of other people
○YES ○NO
37. Often you prefer to read a book than go to a party
○YES ○NO
38. You enjoy being at the center of events in which other people are directly involved
○YES ○NO
39. You are more inclined to experiment than to follow familiar approaches
○YES ○NO
40. You avoid being bound by obligations
○YES ○NO
41. You are strongly touched by the stories about people's troubles
○YES ○NO
42. Deadlines seem to you to be of relative, rather than absolute, importance
○YES ○NO
43. You prefer to isolate yourself from outside noises
○YES ○NO
44. It's essential for you to try things with your own hands
○YES ○NO
45. You think that almost everything can be analyzed
○YES ○NO
46. You do your best to complete a task on time
○YES ○NO
47. You take pleasure in putting things in order
○YES ○NO
48. You feel at ease in a crowd
○YES ○NO
49. You have good control over your desires and temptations
○YES ○NO
50. You easily understand new theoretical principles
○YES ○NO
51. The process of searching for solution is more important to you than the solution itself
○YES ○NO
52. You usually place yourself nearer to the side than in the center of the room
○YES ○NO
53. When solving a problem you would rather follow a familiar approach than seek a new one
○YES ○NO
54. You try to stand firmly by your principles
○YES ○NO
55. A thirst for adventure is close to your heart
○YES ○NO
56. You prefer meeting in small groups to interaction with lots of people
○YES ○NO
57. When considering a situation you pay more attention to the current situation and less to a possible sequence of events
○YES ○NO
58. You consider the scientific approach to be the best
○YES ○NO
59. You find it difficult to talk about your feelings
○YES ○NO
60. You often spend time thinking of how things could be improved
○YES ○NO
61. Your decisions are based more on the feelings of a moment than on the careful planning
○YES ○NO
62. You prefer to spend your leisure time alone or relaxing in a tranquil family atmosphere
○YES ○NO
63. You feel more comfortable sticking to conventional ways
○YES ○NO
64. You are easily affected by strong emotions
○YES ○NO
65. You are always looking for opportunities
○YES ○NO
66. Your desk, workbench etc. is usually neat and orderly
○YES ○NO
67. As a rule, current preoccupations worry you more than your future plans
○YES ○NO
68. You get pleasure from solitary walks
○YES ○NO
69. It is easy for you to communicate in social situations
○YES ○NO
70. You are consistent in your habits
○YES ○NO
71. You willingly involve yourself in matters which engage your sympathies
○YES ○NO
72. You easily perceive various ways in which events could develop
○YES ○NO

Score It!

disclaimer contact us

In fact, personality traits do often correlate with job performance. In one study, extraversion, conscientiousness, and openness to experience were strong predictors of leadership.[45] In another study, neuroticism was negatively related to motivation, while conscientiousness was positively related to it.[46] And, "in personality research, conscientiousness has been the most consistent and universal predictor of job performance."[47] So to paraphrase Woody Allen, it does seem that "90% of success is just showing up."

Other traits correlate with occupations. For example, extraversion correlates with success in sales and management jobs.[48] The responsibility, socialization, and self-control scales of the California Psychological Inventory predicted dysfunctional job behaviors among law enforcement officers.[49] Emotional stability, extroversion, and agreeableness predicted whether expatriates would leave their overseas assignments early.[50]

Caveats But there are three big things to watch out for when using personality tests at work. *First,* remember projective tests are difficult to interpret. An expert must analyze the test taker's interpretations and reactions and infer from them his or her personality. The usefulness of such tests then assumes that you can find a relationship between a measurable personality trait (like introversion) and success on the job. Measuring aberrant behavior is a particular challenge.

Second, personality tests are more likely to trigger legal challenges. For example, one U.S. court of appeals said the MMPI is a medical test because it can screen out applicants perceived to have a psychological impairment; therefore, use before an employment offer might violate the ADA.[51]

Third, there is a big debate about whether self-report personality tests generally predict performance at all. The journal *Personnel Psychology* recently convened a panel of distinguished industrial psychologists who said using self-report personality tests in selection "should be reconsidered."[52] They went on to say that if you carefully conduct predictive validation studies with actual job candidates, it turns out validity is very low.[53] In response, other experts call such concerns "unfounded."[54] At a minimum, the bottom line seems to be to make sure that any personality tests you use actually do predict performance.

Interest Inventories **Interest inventories** compare your interests with those of people in various occupations. Thus, a person who takes the Strong-Campbell Interests Inventory would receive a report comparing his or her interests to those of people already in occupations like accounting, engineering, or management. Someone taking the self-administered Self-Directed Search (SDS) (www.self-directed-search.com) receives an interests code to use in identifying likely high-potential occupations.

Interest inventories have many uses. They're irreplaceable in career planning, since a person will likely do better in jobs that involve activities in which he or she is interested. They're also useful as selection tools. If you can select people whose interests are roughly the same as those of successful incumbents in the jobs for which you're recruiting, it's more likely that those applicants will be successful.

Achievement Tests

Achievement tests measure what someone has learned. Most of the tests you take in school are achievement tests. They measure your "job knowledge" in areas like economics, marketing, or human resources. Achievement tests are also popular at work. For example, the Purdue Test for Machinists and Machine Operators tests the job knowledge of experienced machinists with questions like, "What is meant by 'tolerance'?" Other tests are available for other occupations. In addition to job knowledge, achievement tests measure the applicant's abilities; a typing test is one example.

interest inventory
A personal development and selection device that compares the person's current interests with those of others now in various occupations so as to determine the preferred occupation for the individual.

WORK SAMPLES AND SIMULATIONS

With **work samples,** you present examinees with situations representative of the job for which they're applying, and evaluate their responses.[55] Experts consider these (and *simulations,* like the assessment centers we also discuss in this section) to be tests. However, they differ from most tests, because they measure job performance directly. For example, work samples for a cashier may include operating a cash register and counting money; for a clerical position, work samples would include a typing test and proofreading.[56]

6 Give two examples of work sample/simulation tests.

Using Work Sampling for Employee Selection

The **work sampling technique** tries to predict job performance by requiring job candidates to perform one or more samples of the job's basic tasks.

Work sampling has several advantages. It measures actual job tasks, so it's harder to fake answers. The work sample's content—the actual tasks the person must perform—is not as likely to be unfair to minorities (as might a personnel test that possibly emphasizes middle-class concepts and values).[57] Work sampling doesn't delve into the applicant's personality, so there's almost no chance of applicants viewing it as an invasion of privacy. Designed properly, work samples also exhibit better validity than do other tests designed to predict performance.

Basic Procedure The basic procedure is to select a sample of several tasks crucial to performing the job, and then to test applicants on them.[58] An observer monitors performance on each task, and indicates on a checklist how well the applicant performs. Here is an example. In creating a work sampling test for maintenance mechanics, experts first listed all possible job tasks (like "install pulleys and belts" and "install and align a motor"). Four crucial tasks were installing pulleys and belts, disassembling and installing a gearbox, installing and aligning a motor, and pressing a bushing into a sprocket.

They then broke down these four tasks into the steps required to complete each step. Mechanics could perform each step in a slightly different way, of course. Since some approaches were better than others, the experts gave a different weight to different approaches.

Figure 6-7 shows one of the steps required for installing pulleys and belts—"checks key before installing." As the figure shows, possible approaches here include checking the key against (1) the shaft, (2) the pulley, or (3) neither. The right of the figure lists the weights (scores) reflecting the worth of each method. The applicant performs the task, and the observer checks off the approach used.

Management Assessment Centers

A **management assessment center** is a 2- to 3-day simulation in which 10 to 12 candidates perform realistic management tasks (like making presentations) under the observation of experts who appraise each candidate's leadership potential. The center itself may be a simple conference room, but more likely a special room with a one-way mirror to facilitate observation. Typical simulated tasks include:

- **The in-basket.** This exercise confronts the candidate with an accumulation of reports, memos, notes of incoming phone calls, letters, and other materials collected in the actual or computerized in-basket of the simulated job he or she is about to start. The candidate must take appropriate action on each item. Trained evaluators then review the candidate's efforts.
- **Leaderless group discussion.** Trainers give a leaderless group a discussion question and tell members to arrive at a group decision. They then evaluate each

FIGURE 6-7 Example of a Work Sampling Question

Checks key before installing against:

__shaft	score 3
__pulley	score 2
__neither	score 1

Note: This is one step in installing pulleys and belts.

group member's interpersonal skills, acceptance by the group, leadership ability, and individual influence.

- **Management games.** Participants solve realistic problems as members of simulated companies competing in a marketplace. They may have to decide, for instance, how to advertise, and how much inventory to stock.
- **Individual presentations.** Here trainers evaluate each participant's communication skills and persuasiveness by having each make an assigned oral presentation.
- **Objective tests.** An assessment center typically includes tests of personality, mental ability, interests, and achievements.
- **The interview.** Most also require an interview between at least one trainer and each participant, to assess the latter's interests, past performance, and motivation.

Supervisor recommendations usually play a big role in choosing center participants. Line managers usually act as assessors and typically arrive at their ratings through a consensus process.[59]

Effectiveness Many firms use assessment centers. For example, The Cheesecake Factory created its Professional Assessment and Development Center to help select promotable managers. Candidates spend 2 days of exercises, simulations, and classroom learning to see if they have the skills for key management positions.[60]

Most experts view assessment centers as effective for selecting management candidates, but are they worth their cost? They are expensive to develop, take much longer than conventional tests, require managers acting as assessors, and often require psychologists. However, studies suggest they are worth it.[61] One study of 40 police candidates found that such centers are worth the extra cost: "Assessment center performance shows a unique and substantial contribution to the prediction of future police work success, justifying the usage of such method." In this study, peers' evaluations of candidates during the center proved especially useful.[62]

Situational Testing and Video-Based Situational Testing

Situational tests require examinees to respond to situations representative of the job. Work sampling (discussed earlier) and some assessment center tasks (such as in-baskets) fall in this category. So do video-based tests and miniature job training (described next), and the situational interviews we address in Chapter 7.[63]

The **video-based simulation** presents the candidate with several online or PC-based video situations, each followed by one or more multiple-choice questions. For example, the scenario might depict an employee handling a situation on the job. At a critical moment, the scenario ends and the video asks the candidate to choose from several courses of action. For example:

(*A manager is upset about the condition of the department and takes it out on one of the department's employees.*)

Manager: Well, I'm glad you're here.

Associate: Oh? Why is that?

Manager: Look at this place, that's why! I take a day off and come back to find the department in a mess. You should know better.

Associate: But I didn't work late last night.

Manager: Maybe not. But there have been plenty of times before when you've left this department in a mess.

work samples
Actual job tasks used in testing applicants' performance.

work sampling technique
A testing method based on measuring performance on actual basic job tasks.

management assessment center
A simulation in which management candidates are asked to perform realistic tasks in hypothetical situations and are scored on their performance. It usually also involves testing and the use of management games.

situational test
A test that requires examinees to respond to situations representative of the job.

video-based simulation
A situational test in which examinees respond to video simulations of realistic job situations.

(*The scenario stops here.*)

If you were this associate, what would you do?

a. Let the other associates responsible for the mess know that you had to take the heat.

b. Straighten up the department, and try to reason with the manager later.

c. Suggest to the manager that he talk to the other associates who made the mess.

d. Take it up with the manager's boss.[64]

The Miniature Job Training and Evaluation Approach

Miniature job training and evaluation means training candidates to perform several of the job's tasks, and then evaluating the candidates' performance prior to hire. The approach assumes that a person who demonstrates that he or she can learn and perform the sample of tasks will be able to learn and perform the job itself. This approach tests applicants with actual samples of the job, so it's inherently content relevant and valid. The big problem is the expense involved in the individual instruction and training.

Honda Example

Honda successfully used miniature job training. When Honda built a new plant in Alabama, it had to hire thousands of new employees. Few people there had worked in manufacturing. Honda's recruiting ad sought applicants for a free training program Honda was offering as a precondition for applying for jobs at the new plant. Applicants needed at least a high school diploma or GED, employment for the past 2 years with no unexplainable gaps, and Alabama residency. Eighteen thousand people applied.

First Honda and the Alabama state employment agency screened the applicants by eliminating those who lacked the education or experience. They then gave preference to applicants near the plant. About 340 applicants per 6-week session received special training at a new facility, two evenings a week. This included classroom instruction, videos of Honda employees in action, and actually practicing particular jobs. (Thus, "miniature job training and evaluation.") Some candidates who watched the videos dropped out when they saw the work's pace.

During training, special assessors from the Alabama state agency scrutinized and rated the trainees. They then invited those who graduated to apply for jobs at the plant. Honda employees (from HR and departmental representatives) then interviewed the candidates, reviewed their training records, and decided who to hire. New employees get a one-time drug test, but there are no other paper-and-pencil tests or credentials required. New hires get a 3-day orientation. Then, assistant managers in each department coordinate their day-to-day training.[65]

Source: Courtesy of Billy Brown Photography, Inc.

Employers such as Honda train and then have applicants perform several of the job tasks, and then evaluate the candidates before hiring them.

Realistic Job Previews

Sometimes, a dose of realism makes the best screening tool. For example, Walmart found that many new associates quit within the first 90 days. Walmart began explicitly explaining and asking about work schedules and work preferences; turnover improved.[66] In general, applicants who receive realistic job previews are more likely to turn down job offers, but firms are more likely to have lower turnover.[67]

HR in Practice: Testing Techniques for Managers

You may find that even in the largest company, when it comes to screening employees, you're more or less on your own. The human resource department may work with you to design and administer screening tests. But more often HR may do little more than place the ads, do some prescreening (for instance, typing tests for clerical applicants), and run background checks and drug and physical exams.

That leaves you with a problem. Suppose you are, say, the marketing manager, and you want to screen your job applicants more formally. It is possible to buy or devise your own test battery, but caution is required. Purchasing and then using, for instance, packaged intelligence tests or psychological tests could be a problem. Doing so may violate company policy, raise validity questions, and even expose your employer to EEO liability.

A preferred approach is to devise and use screening tools, the face validity of which is obvious. For example, create a work sampling test. Thus, it is reasonable for the marketing manager to ask an advertising applicant to spend an hour designing an ad, or to ask a marketing research applicant to spend a half hour outlining a marketing research program for a hypothetical product.

Summary

Table 6-2 summarizes the validity, cost, and potential adverse impact of several popular assessment methods.

TABLE 6-2 Evaluation of Assessment Methods on Four Key Criteria

Assessment Method	Validity	Adverse Impact	Costs (Develop/ Administer)	Applicant Reactions
Cognitive ability tests	High	High (against minorities)	Low/low	Somewhat favorable
Job knowledge test	High	High (against minorities)	Low/low	More favorable
Personality tests	Low to moderate	Low	Low/low	Less favorable
Biographical data inventories	Moderate	Low to high for different types	High/low	Less favorable
Integrity tests	Moderate to high	Low	Low/low	Less favorable
Structured interviews	High	Low	High/high	More favorable
Physical fitness tests	Moderate to high	High (against females and older workers)	High/high	More favorable
Situational judgment tests	Moderate	Moderate (against minorities)	High/low	More favorable
Work samples	High	Low	High/high	More favorable
Assessment centers	Moderate to high	Low to moderate, depending on exercise	High/high	More favorable
Physical ability tests	Moderate to high	High (against females and older workers)	High/high	More favorable

Note: There was limited research evidence available on applicant reactions to situational judgment tests and physical ability tests. However, because these tests tend to appear very relevant to the job, it is likely that applicant reactions to them would be favorable.

Source: Elaine Pulakos, *Selection Assessment Methods*, SHRM Foundation, 2005, p. 17. Reprinted by permission of Society for Human Resource Management via Copyright Clearance Center.

miniature job training and evaluation
Training candidates to perform several of the job's tasks, and then evaluating the candidates' performance prior to hire.

7 Explain the key points to remember in conducting background investigations.

BACKGROUND INVESTIGATIONS AND OTHER SELECTION METHODS

Testing is only part of an employer's selection process. Other tools may include background investigations and reference checks, preemployment information services, honesty testing, graphology, and substance abuse screening.

Why Perform Background Investigations and Reference Checks?

One of the easiest ways to avoid hiring mistakes is to check the candidate's background thoroughly. Doing so is cheap and (if done right) useful. There's usually no reason why even supervisors in large companies can't check the references of someone they're about to hire, as long as they know the rules.

Most employers therefore check and verify the job applicant's background information and references. In one survey of about 700 human resource managers, 87% said they conduct reference checks, 69% conduct background employment checks, 61% check employee criminal records, 56% check employees' driving records, and 35% sometimes or always check credit.[68] Commonly verified data include legal eligibility for employment (in compliance with immigration laws), dates of prior employment, military service (including discharge status), education, identification (including date of birth and address to confirm identity), county criminal records (current residence, last residence), motor vehicle record, credit, licensing verification, Social Security number, and reference checks.[69] With diploma mills proliferating, it's necessary to check academic backgrounds.[70] Some employers are checking executive candidates' civil litigation records, with the candidate's prior approval.[71]

Why Check?

There are two main reasons to check backgrounds—to verify the applicant's information (name and so forth) and to uncover damaging information.[72] Lying on one's application isn't unusual. A survey found that 23% of 7,000 executive résumés contained exaggerated or false information.[73]

Even relatively sophisticated companies fall prey to criminal employees, in part because they haven't conducted proper background checks. In Chicago, a pharmaceutical firm discovered it had hired gang members in mail delivery and computer repair. The crooks were stealing close to a million dollars a year in computer parts, and then using the mail department to ship them to a nearby computer store they owned.[74]

How deeply you search depends on the position you seek to fill. For example, a credit and education check is more important for hiring an accountant than a groundskeeper. In any case, also periodically check the credit ratings of employees (like cashiers) who have easy access to company assets, and the driving records of employees who routinely use company cars.

Effectiveness

Most managers don't view references as very useful. In one older study, only about half the managers said that reference letters were at least "somewhat valuable." Asked whether they preferred written or telephone references, 72% favored the telephone reference, because it allows a more candid assessment and provides a more personal exchange. In fact, reference letters ranked lowest—seventh out of seven—as selection tools. Ranked from top to bottom, the tools were interview, application form, academic record, oral referral, aptitude and achievement tests, psychological tests, and reference letters.[75] Another survey found that only 11% of respondents said the information they get about a candidate's violent or "bizarre" behavior is adequate. Of the types of information sought in background checks, only three were ranked by more than half of respondents as ones for which they received adequate information: dates of employment (96%), eligibility for rehire (65%), and job qualifications (56%).[76]

It's obvious why background checks have bad reputations. For one thing, many supervisors don't want to damage a former employee's chances for a job; others might prefer giving an incompetent employee good reviews if it will get rid of him or her. Even when checking references via phone, therefore, you have to be careful to ask the right questions.

The other reason is legal. Employers providing references generally cannot be successfully sued for defamation unless the employee can show "malice"—that is, ill will, culpable recklessness, or disregard of the employee's rights.[77] But the managers and companies providing the references understandably still don't want the grief. Let's look at why.

The Legal Dangers and How to Avoid Them

In practice (as most people instinctively know), giving someone a bad reference can drag you into a legal mess. For example, if the courts believe you gave the bad reference to retaliate for the employee previously filing an EEOC claim, they might let him or her sue you.[78]

Defamation

That is just the tip of the iceberg. Being sued for defamation is the real danger. First-line supervisors and managers, not just employers, are potentially at risk. Various federal laws[79] give individuals and students the right to know the nature and substance of information in their credit files and files with government agencies, and to review records pertaining to them from any private business that contracts with a federal agency. So, it's quite possible the person you're describing will see your comments and decide you defamed him or her. Common law (in particular, the tort of defamation) applies to any information you supply. A communication is *defamatory* if it is false and tends to harm the reputation of another by lowering the person in the estimation of the community or by deterring other persons from associating or dealing with him or her.

The person alleging defamation has various legal remedies, including suing the source of the reference for defamation.[80] In one case, a court awarded a man $56,000 after a company turned him down for a job because, among other things, the former employer called him a "character." As if that's not enough, there are companies that, for a small fee, will call former employers on behalf of employees who believe they're getting bad references. One supervisor thought his previous employer might bad-mouth him. He hired BadReferences.com to investigate. BadReferences.com (which uses trained court reporters for its investigations) found that a supervisor at the company suggested that the employee was "a little too obsessive . . . and not comfortable with taking risks, or making big decisions." The former employee sued his previous employer, demanding an end to defamation and $45,000 in compensation.[81]

Privacy

Furthermore, truth is not always a defense. Some states recognize common law as it applies to invasion of privacy. Employees can sue employers for disclosing to a large number of people true but embarrassing private facts about the employee. Here truth is no defense.

One case involved a supervisor in a shouting match with an employee. The supervisor yelled out that the employee's wife had been having sexual relations with certain people. The employee and his wife sued the employer for invasion of privacy. The jury found the employer liable for invasion of the couple's privacy. It awarded damages to both of them, as well as damages for the couple's additional claim that the supervisor's conduct amounted to an intentional infliction of emotional distress.[82]

The net result is that most employers and managers are very restrictive about who can give references, and what they can say. As a rule, employers should ensure that only authorized managers provide information. Other suggested guidelines for defensible references include "Don't volunteer information," "Avoid vague statements," and "Do not answer trap questions such as, 'Would you rehire this person?'" In practice, many firms have a policy of not providing any information about former employees except for their dates of employment, last salary, and position titles.[83]

However, *not* disclosing relevant information can be dangerous, too. In one Florida case, a company fired an employee for allegedly bringing a handgun to work. After his next employer fired him (for absenteeism), he returned to that company and shot several employees before taking his own life. The injured parties and the relatives of the murdered employees sued the previous employer, who had provided the employee with a clean letter of recommendation allegedly because that first employer didn't want to anger the employee over his firing.

How to Check a Candidate's Background

Which brings us back to this point: In practice, the references you receive may not be very useful. There are several things that managers and employers can do to get better information.

Most employers at least try to verify an applicant's current (or former) position and salary with his or her current (or former) employer by phone (assuming you cleared doing so with the candidate). Others call the applicant's current and previous supervisors to try to discover more about the person's motivation, technical competence, and ability to work with others (although again, many employers have policies against providing such information). Some employers get background reports from commercial credit rating companies for information about credit standing, indebtedness, reputation, character, and lifestyle. Figure 6-8 shows one form you can use for phone references.

More employers are Googling applicants or checking social networking sites. After online searches, recruiters found that 31% of applicants had lied about their qualifications and 19% had posted information about their drinking or drug use.[84] On Facebook.com, one employer found that a candidate had described his interests as smoking pot and shooting people. The student may have been kidding, but didn't get the job.[85] An article called "References You Can't Control" notes that you can use social networking sites to identify an applicant's former colleagues, and thus contact them.[86]

Googling is probably safe enough, but checking social networking sites raises legal issues. For example, while the Fair Credit Reporting Act refers more to getting official reports, it's probably best to get the candidate's prior approval for social networking searches.[87] And, of course, do not use a pretext or fabricate an identity.[88]

HR in Practice: Making the Background Check More Valuable

Is there any way to obtain better information? Yes.

- First, include on the application form a statement for applicants to sign explicitly authorizing a background check, such as:

  > I hereby certify that the facts set forth in the above employment application are true and complete to the best of my knowledge. I understand that falsified statements or misrepresentation of information on this application or omission of any information sought may be cause for dismissal, if employed, or may lead to refusal to make an offer and/or to withdrawal of an offer. I also authorize investigation of credit, employment record, driving record, and, once a job offer is made or during employment, workers' compensation background if required.

- Second (since telephone references apparently produce assessments that are more candid), it's probably best to rely on telephone references. Use a form, such as the one in Figure 6-8. Remember that you can probably get relatively accurate information regarding dates of employment, eligibility for rehire, and job qualifications. It's more difficult to get other background information (such as reasons for leaving a previous job).[89]
- Third, persistence and attentiveness to potential red flags improves results. For example, if the former employer hesitates or seems to qualify his or her answer when you ask, "Would you rehire?" don't just go on to the next question. Try to

FIGURE 6-8 Reference Checking Form

Source: Society for Human Resource Management, © 2004. Reproduced with permission of Society for Human Resource Management in the Format Textbook via Copyright Clearance Center.

(Verify that the applicant has provided permission before conducting reference checks.)

Candidate Name ______________________________

Reference Name ______________________________

Company Name ______________________________

Dates of Employment
From: ______________ To: ______________

Position(s) Held ______________________________

Salary History ______________________________

Reason for Leaving ______________________________

Explain the reason for your call and verify the above information with the supervisor (including the reason for leaving)

____

1. Please describe the type of work for which the candidate was responsible.

____

2. How would you describe the applicant's relationships with coworkers, subordinates (if applicable), and with superiors?

____

3. Did the candidate have a positive or negative work attitude? Please elaborate.

____

4. How would you describe the quantity and quality of output generated by the former employee?

____

5. What were his/her strengths on the job?

____

6. What were his/her weaknesses on the job?

____

7. What is your overall assessment of the candidate?

____

8. Would you recommend him/her for this position? Why or why not?

____

9. Would this individual be eligible for rehire? Why or why not?

____

Other comments?

____

unearth what the applicant did to make the former employer pause. If he says, "Joe requires some special care," say, "Special care?"

- Fourth, compare the application to the résumé; people tend to be more imaginative on their résumés than on their application forms, where they must certify the information.
- Fifth, try to ask open-ended questions (such as, "How much structure does the applicant need in his/her work?") in order to get the references to talk more about the candidate.[90] But in asking for information:

  Only ask for and obtain information that you're going to use.

  Remember that using arrest information is highly suspect.

  Use information that is specific and job related.

  Keep information confidential.
- Sixth, use the references offered by the applicant as a source for other references. You might ask each of the applicant's references, "Could you give me the name of another person who might be familiar with the applicant's performance?" In that way, you begin getting information from references that may be more objective, because they did not come directly from the applicant.

Using Preemployment Information Services

It is easy to have employment screening services check out applicants. Numerous firms do this. Top providers include Kroll Background Screenings Group (www.Krollworldwide.com), Hirecheck (www.hirecheck.com), ChoicePoint (www.choicepoint.com), and First Advantage (www.FADV.com).[91] They use databases to access information about matters such as workers' compensation and credit histories, and conviction and driving records. For example, a South Florida firm advertises that for less than $50 it will do a criminal history report, motor vehicle/driver's record report, and (after the person is hired) a workers' compensation claims report history, plus confirm identity, name, and Social Security number. There are thousands of databases and sources for finding background information, including sex offender registries, workers' compensation histories, and sources for criminal, employment, and educational histories.[92]

Use Caution

There are two reasons to use caution when delving into an applicant's criminal, credit, and workers' compensation histories.[93] First (as discussed in Chapter 2), it can be tricky complying with EEO laws. For example, the ADA prohibits employers from making preemployment inquiries into the existence, nature, or severity of a disability. Therefore, asking about a candidate's previous workers' compensation claims before offering the person a job is usually unlawful. Similarly, asking about arrest records may be discriminatory. Never authorize an unreasonable investigation.

Second, various federal and state laws govern how employers acquire and use applicants' and employees' background information. At the federal level, the Fair Credit Reporting Act is the main directive. In addition, at least 21 states impose their own requirements. Compliance with these laws essentially involves four steps, as follows:

Step 1: Disclosure and authorization. Before requesting reports, the employer must disclose to the applicant or employee that a report will be requested and that the employee/applicant may receive a copy. (Do this on the application.)

Step 2: Certification. The employer must certify to the reporting agency that the employer will comply with the federal and state legal requirements—for example, that the employer obtained written consent from the employee or applicant.

Step 3: Providing copies of reports. Under federal law, the employer must provide copies of the report to the applicant or employee if adverse action (such as withdrawing an offer of employment) is contemplated.[94]

Step 4: Notice after adverse action. After the employer provides the employee or applicant with copies of the consumer and investigative reports and a "reasonable period" has elapsed, the employer may take an adverse action (such as withdrawing an offer). If the employer anticipates taking an adverse action, the employee or applicant must receive an adverse action notice. This notice contains information such as the name of the consumer reporting agency. The employee/applicant then has various remedies under the applicable laws.[95]

The Polygraph and Honesty Testing

Some firms still use the polygraph (or lie detector) for honesty testing, although the law severely restricts its use. The polygraph is a device that measures physiological changes like increased perspiration. The assumption is that such changes reflect changes in emotional state that accompany lying.

Complaints about offensiveness plus grave doubts about the polygraph's accuracy culminated in the Employee Polygraph Protection Act of 1988.[96] With a few exceptions, the law prohibits employers from conducting polygraph examinations of all job applicants and most employees. (Also prohibited are other mechanical or electrical devices that attempt to measure honesty or dishonesty, including psychological stress evaluators and voice stress analyzers. Federal laws don't prohibit paper-and-pencil tests and chemical testing [as for drugs].)

Who Can Use the Polygraph?

Local, state, and federal government employers (including the FBI) can use polygraphs, but state laws restrict many local and state governments. Private employers can use polygraph testing, but only under strictly limited circumstances. The latter include those with

- National defense or security contracts
- Nuclear power–related contracts with the Department of Energy
- Access to highly classified information
- Counterintelligence-related contracts with the FBI or Department of Justice
- Private businesses (1) hiring private security personnel, (2) hiring persons with access to drugs, or (3) doing ongoing investigations involving economic loss or injury to an employer's business, such as a theft

However, even if used for ongoing investigations of theft, the law restricts employers' rights. To administer a polygraph test for an ongoing investigation, an employer must meet four standards:

1. First, the employer must show that it suffered an economic loss or injury.
2. Second, it must show that the employee in question had access to the property.
3. Third, it must have a reasonable suspicion before asking the employee to take the polygraph.
4. Fourth, the employee must receive the details of the investigation before the test, as well as the questions to be asked on the polygraph test.

Paper-and-Pencil Honesty Tests

The Polygraph Protection Act triggered a burgeoning market for paper-and-pencil (or online) honesty tests. These are psychological tests designed to predict job applicants' proneness to dishonesty and other forms of counterproductivity.[97] Most measure attitudes regarding things like tolerance of others who steal, acceptance of rationalizations for theft, and admission of theft-related activities. Tests include the Phase II profile. London House, Inc., and Stanton Corporation publish similar tests.[98] (See www.queendom.com/tests/career/honesty_access.html for an example.)

Psychologists initially raised concerns about paper-and-pencil honesty tests, but studies support these tests' validity. One early study illustrates their potential usefulness.

The study involved 111 employees hired by a convenience store chain to work at store or gas station counters.[99] The firm estimated that "shrinkage" equaled 3% of sales, and believed that internal theft accounted for much of this. Scores on an honesty test successfully predicted theft here, as measured by termination for theft. One large review of such tests concluded that the "pattern of findings" regarding the usefulness of such tests "continues to be consistently positive."[100]

Checking for Honesty: What You Can Do With or without testing, there's a lot a manager or employer can do to screen out dishonest applicants or employees. Specifically:

- **Ask blunt questions.**[101] Says one expert, there is nothing wrong with asking the applicant direct questions, such as, "Have you ever stolen anything from an employer?" "Have you recently held jobs other than those listed on your application?" "Have you ever been fired or asked to leave a job?" "What reasons would past supervisors give if they were asked why they let you go?" "Have past employers ever disciplined you or warned you about absences or lateness?" And, "Is any information on your application misrepresented or falsified?"
- **Listen, rather than talk.** Allow the applicant to do the talking so you can learn as much about the person as possible.
- **Do a credit check.** Include a clause in your application giving you the right to conduct background checks, including credit checks and motor vehicle reports.
- **Check all employment and personal references.**
- **Use paper-and-pencil honesty tests and psychological tests.**
- **Test for drugs.** Devise a drug-testing program and give each applicant a copy of the policy.
- **Establish a search-and-seizure policy and conduct searches.** Give each applicant a copy of the policy and require each to return a signed copy. The policy should state, "All lockers, desks, and similar property remain the property of the company and may be inspected routinely."

Honesty testing still requires some caution. Having just taken and "failed" what is fairly obviously an "honesty test," the candidate may leave the premises feeling his or her treatment was less than proper. Some "honesty" questions also pose invasion-of-privacy issues. And there are state laws to consider. For instance, Massachusetts and Rhode Island limit paper-and-pencil honesty testing.

Graphology

Graphology refers to the use of handwriting analysis to determine the writer's basic personality traits. Graphology thus has some resemblance to projective personality tests, although graphology's validity is highly suspect.

In graphology, the handwriting analyst studies an applicant's handwriting and signature to discover the person's needs, desires, and psychological makeup. According to the graphologist, the writing in Figure 6-9 exemplifies traits such as "independence" and "isolation."

Graphology's place in screening sometimes seems schizophrenic. Studies suggest it is generally not valid, or that when graphologists do accurately size up candidates, it's because they are also privy to other background information. Yet some firms continue to use graphology—indeed, to swear by it. It tends to be bigger in Europe, where "countries like France or Germany have one central graphology institute, which serves as the certifying body."[102] Fike Corporation in Blue Springs, Missouri, a 325-employee maker of valves and other industrial products, uses profiles based on handwriting samples to design follow-up interviews. Exchange Bank in Santa Rosa, California, uses it as one element for screening officer candidates.[103]

FIGURE 6-9 "The Uptight Personality"

Source: http://www.graphicinsight.co.za/writing samples.htm#The%20Uptight%20 Personality%2, accessed March 28, 2009. Used with permission of www.graphicinsight.co.za.

The Uptight Personality

From The Graphology Review No 17

"The following sample shows several uptight tendencies. We see independence, a critical, rather severe attitude and an economy of feeling. Notice too, how the words are separated by large spaces indicating that the writer has a feeling of personal isolation."

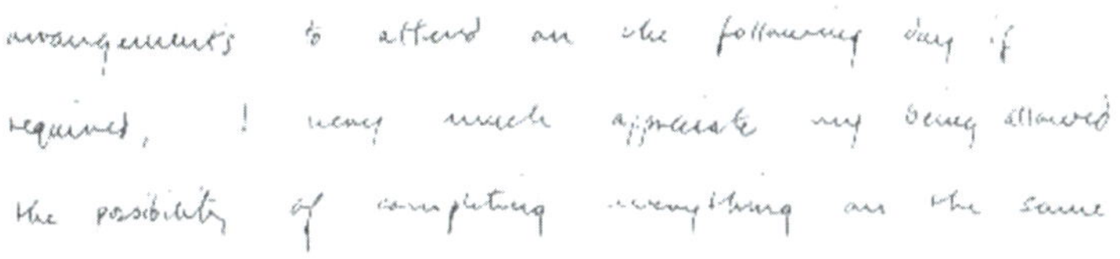

"Here are some of the handwriting indicators for the uptight personality as discussed in The Graphology Review No 17;"

- Small to middle size handwriting
- Upright slant
- Narrow letters
- Angular connections
- Economical use of space on the page
- Although the words here are not extremely cramped they are certainly not expansive. The spacing between the letters is very economical."

Physical Exams

Once the employer extends the person a job offer, a medical exam is often the next step in the selection (although it may also occur after the new employee starts work).

There are several reasons for preemployment medical exams: to verify that the applicant meets the position's physical requirements, to discover any medical limitations you should consider in placing him or her, and to establish a baseline for future insurance or compensation claims. By identifying health problems, the examination can also reduce absenteeism and accidents and, of course, detect communicable diseases.

The issue here is the ADA. Under the Americans with Disabilities Act, an employer cannot reject someone with a disability if he or she is otherwise qualified and can perform the essential job functions with reasonable accommodation. Recall that the ADA permits a medical exam during the period between the job offer and commencement of work if such exams are standard practice for all applicants for that job category.[104]

Substance Abuse Screening

Many employers conduct drug screenings. The most common practice is to test candidates just before they're formally hired. Many also test current employees when there is reason to believe the person has been using drugs—after a work accident, or in the presence of obvious behavioral symptoms such as chronic lateness. Some firms routinely administer drug tests on a random or periodic basis, while others require drug tests when they transfer or promote employees to new positions.[105]

Some Practical Considerations Drug testing, while ubiquitous, is neither as simple nor effective as it might appear at first. You need to consider several things. First, no drug test is foolproof. Some urine sample tests can't distinguish between legal and illegal substances; for example, Advil and Nuprin can produce positive results for marijuana. One medical review officer also notes that "anyone" can go online and purchase drug-free samples to try to beat the tests.[106] In fact, "there is a swarm of products that promise to help employees (both male and female) beat drug tests."[107] The alternative, hair follicle testing, requires a small sample of hair, which the lab analyzes.[108] Hair follicle testing is (in a way) less intrusive than urinalysis, but actually produces more personal information: A 3-inch segment will record 6 months of drug use. And here, too, classified ads advertise chemicals to rub on the scalp to fool the test.

There's also the question of what is the bottom line.[109] Unlike roadside breathalyzers police give to DUI drivers, tests for drugs indicate only whether drug residues are present, not impairment (or, for that matter, habituation or addiction).[110] Some therefore argue that testing is not justifiable on the grounds of boosting workplace safety.[111] Many feel the testing procedures themselves are degrading and intrusive. Many employers reasonably counter that they don't want drug-prone employees on their premises.

Drug testing raises legal issues, too.[112] Several federal (and many state) laws affect workplace drug testing. As an example, under the ADA, a court would probably consider a former drug user (who no longer uses illegal drugs and has successfully completed or is participating in a rehabilitation program) a qualified applicant with a disability.[113] Under the Drug Free Workplace Act of 1988, federal contractors must maintain a workplace free from illegal drugs. Under the U.S. Department of Transportation workplace regulations, firms with more than 50 eligible employees in transportation industries (mass transit workers, school bus drivers, and so on) must conduct alcohol testing on workers with sensitive or safety-related jobs.[114]

What to Do if an Employee Tests Positive What should one do when a job candidate tests positive? Most companies will not hire such candidates, and a few will immediately fire current employees who test positive. Current employees have more legal recourse. Employers must tell them the reason for dismissal if the reason is a positive drug test.[115]

However, where sensitive jobs are concerned, courts tend to side with employers. In one case, the U.S. Court of Appeals for the First Circuit ruled that Exxon acted properly in firing a truck driver who failed a drug test. Exxon's drug-free workplace program included random testing of employees in safety-sensitive jobs. The employee drove a tractor-trailer carrying 12,000 gallons of flammable motor fuel and tested positive for cocaine. The union representing the employee challenged the firing, and an arbitrator reduced the penalty to a 2-month suspension. The appeals court reversed the arbitrator's decision. It ruled that the employer acted properly in firing the truck driver, given the circumstances.[116]

Complying with Immigration Law

Employees hired in the United States must prove they are eligible to work in the United States. A person does not have to be a U.S. citizen to be employable. However, employers should ask a person they're about to hire whether he or she is a U.S. citizen or an alien lawfully authorized to work in the United States. To comply with this law, employers should follow procedures outlined in the so-called I-9 Employment Eligibility Verification form (see Figure 6-10).[117] More employers are using the federal government's voluntary electronic employment verification program, E-Verify.[118] Federal contractors must use it.[119]

Proof of Eligibility Applicants can prove their eligibility for employment in two ways. One is to show a document (such as a U.S. passport or alien registration card with photograph) that proves both the person's identity and employment eligibility. The other is to show a document that proves the person's identity, along with a second document showing the person's employment eligibility, such as a work permit.[120] In any case, it's always advisable to get two forms of proof of identity from everyone.

Some documents may be fakes. For example, a few years ago Immigration and Naturalization Service (INS) agents seized more than 2 million counterfeit

FIGURE 6-10 Procedure in Complying with Immigration Law

1. Hire only citizens and aliens lawfully authorized to work in the United States.
2. Advise all new job applicants of your policy.
3. Require all new employees to complete and sign the verification form (the "I-9 form") designated by the Immigration and Naturalization Service (INS) to certify that they are eligible for employment.
4. Examine documentation presented by new employees, record information about the documents on the verification form, and sign the form.
5. Retain the form for 3 years or for 1 year past the employment of the individual, whichever is longer.
6. If requested, present the form for inspection by INS or Department of Labor officers. No reporting is required.

documents ranging from green cards and Social Security cards to driver's licenses, from nine different states. The federal government is tightening restrictions on hiring undocumented workers. Realizing that many documents (such as Social Security cards) are faked, the government is putting the onus on the employers to make sure whom they're hiring. The Department of Homeland Security presses criminal charges against suspected employer-violators.[121]

Employers can protect themselves in several ways. First, they can use E-Verify. Then, systematic background checks are important. Preemployment screening should include employment verification, criminal record checks, drug screens, and reference checks. You can verify Social Security numbers by calling the Social Security Administration. Employers can avoid accusations of discrimination by verifying the documents of all applicants, not just those they may think suspicious.[122]

Avoiding Discrimination In any case, employers should not use the I-9 form to discriminate based on race or country of national origin. The requirement to verify eligibility does not provide any basis to reject an applicant just because he or she is a foreigner, or not a U.S. citizen, or an alien residing in the United States, as long as that person can prove his or her identity and employment eligibility. The latest I-9 forms contain a prominent "antidiscrimination notice."[123] Since 2001, there has been a significant rise in allegations of religious and national origin discrimination, among both employees and applicants.

Improving Productivity Through HRIS: Using Automated Applicant Tracking and Screening Systems

The applicant tracking systems we introduced in Chapter 5 (Recruiting) do more than compile incoming Web-based résumés and track applicants during the hiring process. They should also help with the testing and screening. Here are three examples.

First, most employers also use their applicant tracking systems (ATS) to "knock out" applicants who don't meet minimum, nonnegotiable job requirements, like submitting to drug tests or holding driver's licenses.

Second, employers use ATS to test and screen applicants online. This includes Web-based skills testing (in accounting, for instance), cognitive skills testing (such as for mechanical comprehension), and even psychological testing. For example, Recreation Equipment, Inc., wanted to identify applicants who were team-oriented. Its applicant tracking system helps it do that.[124] Many online testing systems don't require an up-front cost or long-term commitment. Employers pay perhaps $25 per lower-level employee screened.[125]

Third, the newer systems don't just screen out candidates, but discover "hidden talents." Thanks to the Internet, applicants often send their résumés out hoping a shotgun approach will help them hit a match. For most employers, this is a screening nuisance. But a good ATS can identify required talents in the applicant that even the applicant didn't know existed when he or she applied. Figure 6-11 lists what the effective ATS should do.[126]

FIGURE 6-11 Checklist: What to Look For in an Applicant Tracking System (ATS)

The employer thinking of adopting an ATS should seek one that meets several minimum functionality requirements. Among other things, the ATS should be:

- Easy to use.
- Capable of being integrated into the company's existing HRIS platform, so that, for instance, data on a newly hired candidate can flow seamlessly into the HRIS payroll system.
- Able to capture, track, and report applicant EEO data.
- Able to provide employee selection performance metrics reports, including "time to fill," "cost to hire," and "applicant source statistics."
- Able to facilitate scheduling and tracking of candidate interviews, e-mail communications, and completed forms, including job offers.
- Able to provide automated screening and ranking of candidates based upon job skill profiles.
- Able to provide an internal job posting service that supports applications from current employees and employee referral programs.
- Able to cross-post jobs to commercial job boards such as www.monster.com.
- Able to integrate the ATS job board with your company's own Web site, for instance, by linking it to your site's "careers" section.
- Able to provide for requisition creation and sign-off approvals.

REVIEW

CHAPTER SECTION SUMMARIES

1. Careful **employee selection is important** for several reasons. Your own performance always depends on your subordinates; it is costly to recruit and hire employees; and mismanaging the hiring process has various legal implications including equal employment, negligent hiring, and defamation.
2. Whether you are administering tests or making decisions based on test results, managers need to understand several **basic testing concepts**. Reliability refers to a test's consistency, while validity tells you whether the test is measuring what you think it's supposed to be measuring. Criterion validity means demonstrating that those who do well on the test also do well on the job while content validity means showing that the test constitutes a fair sample of the job's content. Validating a test involves analyzing the job, choosing the tests, administering the test, relating your test scores and criteria, and cross-validating and revalidating. Test takers have rights to privacy and feedback as well as to confidentiality.
3. Whether administered via paper and pencil, by computer, or online, we discussed several main **types of tests**. Tests of cognitive abilities measure things like reasoning ability and include intelligence tests and tests of specific cognitive abilities such as mechanical comprehension. There are also tests of motor and physical abilities, and measures of personality and interests. With respect to personality, psychologists often focus on the "big five" personality dimensions: extroversion, emotional stability/neuroticism, agreeableness, conscientiousness, and openness to experience. Achievement tests measure what someone has learned.
4. With **work samples and simulations,** you present examinees with situations representative of the jobs for which they are applying. One example is the management assessment center, a 2- to 3-day simulation in which 10 to 12 candidates perform realistic management tasks under the observation of experts who appraise each candidate's leadership potential. Video-based situational testing and the miniature job training and evaluation approach are two other examples.
5. Testing is only part of an employer's selection process; you also want to conduct **background investigations and other selection procedures**.
   - The main point of doing a background check is to verify the applicant's information and to uncover potentially damaging information. However, care must be taken, particularly when giving a reference, that the employee not be defamed and that his or her privacy rights are maintained.
   - Given former employers' reluctance to provide a comprehensive report, those checking references need to do several things. Make sure the applicant explicitly authorizes a background check, use a checklist or form for obtaining telephone references, and be persistent and attentive to potential red flags.
   - Given the growing popularity of computerized employment background databases, many or most employers use preemployment information services to obtain background information.
   - For many types of jobs, honestly testing is essential and paper-and-pencil tests have proven useful.

- Most employers also require that new hires, before actually coming on board, take physical exams and substance abuse screening. It's essential to comply with immigration law, in particular by having the candidate complete an I-9 Employment Eligibility Verification Form and submit proof of eligibility.

DISCUSSION QUESTIONS

1. What is the difference between reliability and validity? In what respects are they similar?
2. Explain how you would go about validating a test. How can this information be useful to a manager?
3. Explain why you think a certified psychologist who is specifically trained in test construction should (or should not) be used by a small business that needs a test battery.
4. Give some examples of how to use interest inventories to improve employee selection. In doing so, suggest several examples of occupational interests that you believe might predict success in various occupations, including college professor, accountant, and computer programmer.
5. Why is it important to conduct preemployment background investigations? Outline how you would go about doing so.
6. Explain how you would get around the problem of former employers being unwilling to give bad references on their former employees.
7. How can employers protect themselves against negligent hiring claims?

INDIVIDUAL AND GROUP ACTIVITIES

1. Write a short essay discussing some of the ethical and legal considerations in testing.
2. Working individually or in groups, develop a list of specific selection techniques that you would suggest your dean use to hire the next HR professor at your school. Explain why you chose each selection technique.
3. Working individually or in groups, contact the publisher of a standardized test such as the Scholastic Assessment Test and obtain from it written information regarding the test's validity and reliability. Present a short report in class discussing what the test is supposed to measure and the degree to which you think the test does what it is supposed to do, based on the reported validity and reliability scores.
4. The HRCI "Test Specifications" appendix at the end of this book (pages 699–706) lists the knowledge someone studying for the HRCI certification exam needs to have in each area of human resource management (such as in Strategic Management, Workforce Planning, and Human Resource Development). In groups of four to five students, do four things: (1) Review that appendix now. (2) Identify the material in this chapter that relates to the required knowledge the appendix lists. (3) Write four multiple-choice exam questions on this material that you believe would be suitable for inclusion in the HRCI exam. And (4) if time permits, have someone from your team post your team's questions in front of the class, so the students in other teams can take each others' exam questions.

EXPERIENTIAL EXERCISE

A Test for a Reservation Clerk

Purpose: The purpose of this exercise is to give you practice in developing a test to measure *one specific ability* for the job of airline reservation clerk for a major airline. If time permits, you'll be able to combine your tests into a test battery.

Required Understanding: Your airline has decided to outsource its reservation jobs to Asia. You should be fully acquainted with the procedure for developing a personnel test and should read the following description of an airline reservation clerk's duties:

Customers contact our airline reservation clerks to obtain flight schedules, prices, and itineraries. The reservation clerks look up the requested information on our airline's online flight schedule systems, which are updated continuously. The reservation clerk must speak clearly, deal courteously and expeditiously with the customer, and be able to find quickly alternative flight arrangements in order to provide the customer with the itinerary that fits his or her needs. Alternative flights and prices must be found quickly, so that the customer is not kept waiting, and so that our reservations operations group maintains its efficiency standards. It is often necessary to look under various routings, since there may be a dozen or more alternative routes between the customer's starting point and destination.

You may assume that we will hire about one-third of the applicants as airline reservation clerks. Therefore, your objective is to create a test that is useful in selecting a third of those available.

How to Set Up the Exercise/Instructions: Divide the class into teams of five or six students. The ideal candidate will obviously need to have a number of skills and abilities to perform this job well. Your job is to select a single ability and to develop a test to measure that ability. Use only the materials available in the room, please. The test should permit quantitative scoring and may be an individual or a group test.

Please go to your assigned groups. As per our discussion of test development in this chapter, each group should make a list of the abilities relevant to success in the airline reservation clerk's job. Each group should then rate the importance of these abilities on a 5-point scale. Then, develop a test to measure what you believe to be the top-ranked ability. If time permits, the groups should combine the various tests from each group into a test battery. If possible, leave time for a group of students to take the test battery.

APPLICATION CASE

Where's My Czar?

A few years ago, President George W. Bush's White House team made what would seem to be a questionable hiring decision. It's not clear how much screening they did, or who did it, but almost as soon as the White House recommended the business executive to be the administration's assistant commerce secretary for manufacturing ("manufacturing czar"), he had to withdraw his name from consideration.

The candidate withdrew his name after blistering criticism from Democratic nominee John Kerry. Among other things, the President's manufacturing czar was supposed to develop strategies for beefing up U.S. manufacturing capacity and creating more manufacturing jobs in the United States (a crucial task, given the almost 3 million jobs the United States had lost in the previous 3 years). But, it turned out that this executive ran a manufacturing business that had set up plants in China, and outsourced a portion of his company's jobs there. Senator Kerry said this man therefore hardly seemed like the ideal person to champion keeping jobs in the United States.

The Bush administration said the candidate's withdrawal was related to political issues and not the fuss raised by Kerry. In an interview on CNBC, Commerce Secretary Don Evans said that the administration would continue to look for candidates. For a White House team known for working hard to be very corporate in the way it does things, the situation must have been somewhat embarrassing. Now, Mr. Bush has asked for your advice.

Questions

1. What should this position's job description look like?
2. What are the ideal job specifications for the person in this position?
3. How should we have gone about recruiting and screening for this position? What selection tools, specifically, would you use?
4. Where do you think we went wrong?

CONTINUING CASE

Honesty Testing at Carter Cleaning Company

Jennifer Carter, of the Carter Cleaning Centers, and her father have what the latter describes as an easy but hard job when it comes to screening job applicants. It is easy because for two important jobs—the people who actually do the pressing and those who do the cleaning-spotting—the applicants are easily screened with about 20 minutes of on-the-job testing. As with typists, as Jennifer points out, "Applicants either know how to press clothes fast enough or how to use cleaning chemicals and machines, or they don't, and we find out very quickly by just trying them out on the job." On the other hand, applicant screening for the stores can also be frustratingly hard because of the nature of some of the other qualities that Jennifer would like to screen for. Two of the most critical problems facing her company are employee turnover and employee honesty. Jennifer and her father sorely need to implement practices that will reduce the rate of employee turnover. If there is a way to do this through employee testing and screening techniques, Jennifer would like to know about it because of the management time and money that are now being wasted by the never-ending need to recruit and hire new employees. Of even greater concern to Jennifer and her father is the need to institute new practices to screen out those employees who may be predisposed to steal from the company.

Employee theft is an enormous problem for the Carter Cleaning Centers, and one that is not just limited to employees who handle the cash. For example, the cleaner–spotter and/or the presser often open the store themselves, without a manager present, to get the day's work started, and it is not unusual to have one or more of these people steal supplies or "run a route." Running a route means that an employee canvasses his or her neighborhood to pick up people's clothes for cleaning and then secretly cleans and presses them in the Carter store, using the company's supplies, gas, and power. It would also not be unusual for an unsupervised person (or his or her supervisor, for that matter) to accept a 1-hour rush order for cleaning or laundering, quickly clean and press the item, and return it to the customer for payment without making out a proper ticket for the item posting the sale. The money, of course, goes into the worker's pocket instead of into the cash register.

The more serious problem concerns the store manager and the counter workers who actually have to handle the cash. According to Jack Carter, "You would not believe the creativity employees use to get around the management controls we set up to cut down on employee theft." As one extreme example of this felonious creativity, Jack tells the following story: "To cut down on the amount of money my employees were stealing, I had a small sign painted and placed in front of all our cash registers. The sign said: YOUR ENTIRE ORDER FREE IF WE DON'T GIVE YOU A CASH REGISTER RECEIPT WHEN YOU PAY. CALL 552–0235. It was my intention with this sign to force all our cash-handling employees to give receipts so the cash register would record them for my accountants. After all, if all the cash that comes in is recorded in the cash register, then we should have a much better handle on stealing in our stores. Well, one of our managers found a diabolical way around this. I came into the store one night and noticed that the cash register this particular manager was using just didn't look right, although the sign was placed in front of it. It turned out that every afternoon at about 5:00 P.M. when the other employees left, this character would pull his own cash register out of a box that he hid underneath our supplies. Customers coming in would notice the sign and, of course, the fact that he was meticulous in ringing up every sale. But unknown to them and us, for about 5 months the sales that came in for about an hour every day went into his cash register, not mine. It took us that long to figure out where our cash for that store was going."

Here is what Jennifer would like you to answer:

Questions

1. What would be the advantages and disadvantages to Jennifer's company of routinely administering honesty tests to all its employees?
2. Specifically, what other screening techniques could the company use to screen out theft-prone and turnover-prone employees, and how exactly could these be used?
3. How should her company terminate employees caught stealing, and what kind of procedure should be set up for handling reference calls about these employees when they go to other companies looking for jobs?

TRANSLATING STRATEGY INTO HR POLICIES & PRACTICES CASE

The Hotel Paris Case

Testing

The Hotel Paris's competitive strategy is "To use superior guest service to differentiate the Hotel Paris properties, and to thereby increase the length of stay and return rate of guests, and thus boost revenues and profitability." HR manager Lisa Cruz must now formulate functional policies and activities that support this competitive strategy, by eliciting the required employee behaviors and competencies. The HR Scorecard (inside back cover) outlines the relationships involved.

As she considered what she had to do next, Lisa Cruz, the Hotel Paris's HR director, knew that employee selection had to play a central role in her plans. The Hotel Paris currently had an informal screening process in which local hotel managers obtained application forms, interviewed applicants, and checked their references. However, a pilot project using an employment test for service people at the Chicago hotel had produced startling results. Lisa found consistent, significant relationships between test performance and a range of employee competencies and behaviors such as speed of check-in/out, employee turnover, and percentage of calls answered with the required greeting. Clearly, she was onto something. She knew that employee capabilities and behaviors like these translated into just the sorts of improved guest services the Hotel Paris needed to execute its strategy. She therefore had to decide what selection procedures would be best.

Lisa's team, working with an industrial psychologist, wants to design a test battery that they believe will produce the sorts of high-morale, patient, people-oriented employees they are looking for. It should include, at a minimum, a work sample test for front-desk clerk candidates and a personality test aimed at weeding out applicants who lack emotional stability.

Questions

1. Provide a detailed example of the front-desk work sample test.
2. Provide a detailed example of two possible personality test questions.
3. What other tests would you suggest to Lisa, and why would you suggest them?

KEY TERMS

negligent hiring, *p. 193*
reliability, *p. 193*
test validity, *p. 195*
criterion validity, *p. 195*
content validity, *p. 195*
expectancy chart, *p. 197*
interest inventory, *p. 205*
work samples, *p. 207*
work sampling technique, *p. 207*
management assessment center, *p. 207*
situational test, *p. 207*
video-based simulation, *p. 207*
miniature job training and evaluation, *p. 209*

ENDNOTES

1. Kevin Delaney, "Google Adjusts Hiring Process as Needs Grow," *The Wall Street Journal*, October 23, 2006, pp. B1, B8; http://googleblog.blogspot.com/2009/01/changes-to-recruiting.html, accessed March 25, 2009.
2. Even if they use a third party to prepare an employment test, contractors are "ultimately responsible" for ensuring the tests' job relatedness and EEO compliance. "DOL Officials Discuss Contractors' Duties on Validating Tests," *BNA Bulletin to Management*, September 4, 2007, p. 287. Furthermore, enforcement units are increasing their scrutiny of employers who rely on tests and screening. See "Litigation Increasing with Employer Reliance on Tests, Screening," *BNA Bulletin to Management*, April 8, 2008, p. 119. However, see also C. Tuna et. al., "Job-Test Ruling Cheers Employers," *Wall Street Journal* (July 1, 2009), p. B1–2.
3. See, for example, Ann Marie Ryan and Marja Lasek, "Negligent Hiring and Defamation: Areas of Liability Related to Pre-Employment Inquiries," *Personnel Psychology* 44, no. 2 (Summer 1991), pp. 293–319. See also Jay Stuller, "Fatal Attraction," *Across the Board* 42, no. 6 (November, December 2005), pp. 18–23.
4. Also see, for example, Ryan Zimmerman, "Wal-Mart to Toughen Job Screening," *The Wall Street Journal*, July 12, 2004, pp. B1–B8.
5. Negligent hiring highlights the need to think through what the job's human requirements really are. For example, "non-rapist" isn't likely to appear as a required knowledge, skill, or ability in a job analysis of an apartment manager, but in situations like this screening for such tendencies is obviously required.
6. Fay Hansen, "Taking 'Reasonable' Action to Avoid Negligent Hiring Claims," *Workforce Management*, September 11, 2006, p. 31.
7. Kevin Murphy and Charles Davidshofer, *Psychological Testing: Principles and Applications* (Upper Saddle River, NJ: Prentice Hall, 2001), p. 73.
8. W. Bruce Walsh and Nancy Betz, *Tests and Assessment* (Upper Saddle River, NJ: Prentice Hall, 2001).
9. Murphy and Davidshofer, *Psychological Testing*, p. 74.
10. A third, less-used way to demonstrate a test's validity is *construct validity*. A construct is an abstract trait such as happiness or intelligence. Construct validity generally addresses the question of "validity of measurement," in other words, of whether the test is really measuring, say, intelligence. To prove construct validity, an employer has to prove that the test measures the construct. Federal agency guidelines make it difficult to prove construct validity, however, and as a result few employers use this approach as part of their process for satisfying the federal guidelines. See James Ledvinka, *Federal Regulation of Personnel and Human Resource Management* (Boston: Kent, 1982), p. 113; and Murphy and Davidshofer, *Psychological Testing*, pp. 154–165.
11. The procedure you would use to demonstrate content validity differs from that used to demonstrate criterion validity (as described in steps 1 through 5). Content validity tends to emphasize judgment. Here, you first do a careful job analysis to identify the work behaviors required. Then combine several samples of those behaviors into a test. A typing and computer skills test for a clerk would be an example. The fact that the test is a comprehensive sample of actual, observable, on-the-job behaviors is what lends the test its content validity.
12. www.siop.org/workplace/employment%20testing/information_to_consider_when_cre.aspx, accessed March 22, 2009.
13. Murphy and Davidshofer, *Psychological Testing*, p. 73. See also Chad Van Iddekinge and Robert Ployhart, "Developments in the Criterion-Related Validation of Selection Procedures: A Critical Review and Recommendations for Practice," *Personnel Psychology* 60, no. 1 (2008), pp. 871–925.
14. Experts sometimes have to develop separate expectancy charts and cutting points for minorities and nonminorities if the validation studies indicate that high performers from either group (minority or nonminority) score lower (or higher) on the test.
15. Mark Schmit and Ann Marie Ryan, "Applicant Withdrawal: The Role of Test-Taking Attitudes and Racial Differences," *Personnel Psychology* 50 (1997), pp. 855–876. See also Anthony Celani, "In Justice We Trust: A Model of the Role of Trust in the Organization in Applicant Reactions to the Selection Process," *Human Resource Management Review* 18 (2008), pp. 63–76.
16. Robert Ployhart and Ann Marie Ryan, "Applicants' Reactions to the Fairness of Selection Procedures: The Effects of Positive Rule Violations and Time of Measurement," *Journal of Applied Psychology* 83, no. 1 (1998), pp. 3–16.
17. Walsh and Betz, *Tests and Assessment*, p. 425.
18. John Hausknecht et al., "Applicant Reactions to Selection Procedures: An Updated Model and Meta-Analysis," *Personnel Psychology* 57 (2004), pp. 639–683; See also A. M. Forsberg et. al., "Perceived Fairness of a Background Information Form and a Job Knowledge Test," *Public Personnel Management* 38, no. 1 (Spring 2009), p. 33–46.
19. From "Ethical Principles of Psychologists and Code of Conduct," *American Psychologist* 47 (1992), pp. 1597–1611.
20. Madeline Heilman and Tyler Okimoto, "Motherhood: A Potential Source of Bias in Employment Decisions," *Journal of Applied Psychology* 93, no. 1 (2008), pp. 189–198.
21. Ibid., p. 196.
22. Susan Mendelsohn and Kathryn Morrison, "The Right to Privacy at the Work Place, Part I: Employee Searches," *Personnel*, July 1988, p. 20. See also Talya Bauer et al., "Applicant Reactions to Selection: Development of the Selection Procedural Justice Scale," *Personnel Psychology* 54 (2001), pp. 387–419.
23. Mendelsohn and Morrison, "The Right to Privacy in the Work Place," p. 22.
24. Kenneth Sovereign, *Personnel Law* (Upper Saddle River, NJ: Prentice Hall, 1999), pp. 204–206.
25. "One-Third of Job Applicants Flunked Basic Literacy and Math Tests Last Year, American Management Association Survey Finds," American Management Association, www.amanet.org/press/amanews/bjp2001.htm, accessed January 11, 2008.
26. Ibid. See also Alison Wolf and Andrew Jenkins, "Explaining Greater Test Use for Selection: The Role of HR Professionals in a World of Expanding Regulation," *Human Resource Management Journal* 16, no. 2 (2006), pp. 193–213.
27. Rachel Emma Silverman, "Sharpen Your Pencil," *The Wall Street Journal*, December 5, 2000.
28. Steffanie Wilk and Peter Capelli, "Understanding the Determinants of Employer Use of Selection Methods," *Personnel Psychology* 56 (2003), p. 117.

29. Kevin Hart, "Not Wanted: Thieves," *HR Magazine*, April 2008, p. 119.
30. Sarah Needleman, "Businesses Say Theft by Their Workers Is Up," *The Wall Street Journal*, December 11, 2008, p. B8.
31. Sarah Gale, "Three Companies Cut Turnover with Tests," *Workforce*, Spring 2002, pp. 66–69.
32. Gilbert Nicholson, "Automated Assessments for Better Hires," *Workforce*, December 2000, pp. 102–107.
33. Scott Hayes, "Kinko's Dials into Automated Applicants Screening," *Workforce*, November 1999, pp. 71–73; Gilbert Nicholson, "Automated Assessments for Better Hires," *Workforce*, December 2000, pp. 102–107. Proctored Web-based and paper-and-pencil tests of applicants produce similar results, for instance, on personality and judgment tests. However, a timed test may take longer for applicants on the Web, due to downloading problems and the fact that there are fewer items presented on the viewable page. Similarly, test takers generally find it more difficult to go back and review their results on the Web-based tests. Proctoring is another problem. There is "currently no way to completely prevent [online] test takers from cheating or copying items during testing" or to ensure there's not someone looking over the test taker's shoulder. See Robert Ployhart et al., "Web-Based and Paper-and-Pencil Testing of Applicants in a Proctored Setting: Are Personality, Biodata and Situational Judgment Tests Comparable?" *Personnel Psychology* 56 (2003), pp. 733–752; Denise Potosky and Philip Bobko, "Selection Testing Via the Internet: Practical Considerations and Exploratory Empirical Findings," *Personnel Psychology* 57 (2004), p. 1025.
34. Requiring job seekers to complete prescreening questionnaires and screening selected applicants out on this basis carries legal and business consequences. See, for example, Lisa Harpe, "Designing an Effective Employment Prescreening Program," *Employment Relations Today* 32, no. 3 (Fall 2005), pp. 41–43.
35. Brian O'Leary et al., "Selecting the Best and Brightest," *Human Resource Management* 41, no. 3 (Fall 2002), pp. 25–34.
36. Except as noted, this is based largely on Laurence Siegel and Irving Lane, *Personnel and Organizational Psychology* (Burr Ridge, IL: McGraw-Hill, 1982), pp. 170–185. See also Cabot Jaffee, "Measurement of Human Potential," *Employment Relations Today* 17, no. 2 (Summer 2000), pp. 15–27; Maureen Patterson, "Overcoming the Hiring Crunch; Tests Deliver Informed Choices," *Employment Relations Today* 27, no. 3 (Fall 2000), pp. 77–88; Kathryn Tyler, "Put Applicants' Skills to the Test," *HR Magazine*, January 2000, p. 74; Murphy and Davidshofer, *Psychological Testing*, pp. 215–403; Elizabeth Schoenfelt and Leslie Pedigo, "A Review of Court Decisions on Cognitive Ability Testing, 1992–2004," *Review of Public Personnel Administration* 25, no. 3 (2005), pp. 271–287.
37. www.iphonetypingtest.com, accessed March 23, 2009.
38. As an example, results of meta-analyses in one study indicated that isometric strength tests were valid predictors of both supervisory ratings of physical performance and performance on work simulations. See Barry R. Blakley, Miguel Quinones, Marnie Swerdlin Crawford, and I. Ann Jago, "The Validity of Isometric Strength Tests," *Personnel Psychology* 47 (1994), pp. 247–274.
39. William Wagner, "All Skill, No Finesse," *Workforce*, June 2000, pp. 108–116. See also, for example, James Diefendorff and Kajal Mehta, "The Relations of Motivational Traits with Workplace Deviance," *Journal of Applied Psychology* 92, no. 4 (2007), pp. 967–977.
40. James Spencer, "Sorry, You're Nobody's Type," *The Wall Street Journal*, July 30, 2003, p. D1.
41. Cora Daniels, "Does This Man Need a Shrink?" *Fortune*, February 5, 2001, pp. 205–206.
42. Toddi Gutner, "Applicants' Personalities Put to the Test," *The Wall Street Journal*, August 20, 2008, p. D4.
43. See, for example, Joyce Hogan et al., "Personality Measurement, Faking, and Employee Selection," *Journal of Applied Psychology* 92, no. 5 (2007), pp. 1270–1285; and Colin Gill and Gerard Hodgkinson, "Development and Validation of the Five Factor Model Questionnaire (FFMQ): An Adjectival-Based Personality Inventory for Use in Occupational Settings," *Personnel Psychology* 60 (2007), pp. 731–766.
44. Timothy Judge et al., "Personality and Leadership: A Qualitative and Quantitative Review," *Journal of Applied Psychology* 87, no. 4 (2002), p. 765.
45. Ibid.
46. Timothy Judge and Remus Ilies, "Relationship of Personality to Performance Motivation: A Meta Analytic Review," *Journal of Applied Psychology* 87, no. 4 (2002), pp. 797–807.
47. L. A. Witt et al., "The Interactive Effects of Conscientiousness and Agreeableness on Job Performance," *Journal of Applied Psychology* 87, no. 1 (2002), pp. 164–169.
48. Murray Barrick et al., "Personality and Job Performance: Test of the Immediate Effects of Motivation Among Sales Representatives," *Journal of Applied Psychology* 87, no. 1 (2002), p. 43.
49. Charles Sarchione et al., "Prediction of Dysfunctional Job Behaviors Among Law-Enforcement Officers," *Journal of Applied Psychology* 83, no. 6 (1998), pp. 904–912. See also W. A., Scroggins et. al., "Psychological Testing in Personnel Selection, Part III: The Resurgence of Personality Testing," *Public Personnel Management* 38, no. 1 (Spring 2009), p. 67–77.
50. Paula Caligiuri, "The Big Five Personality Characteristics as Predictors of Expatriate Desire to Terminate the Assignment and Supervisor Rated Performance," *Personnel Psychology* 53 (2000), pp. 67–68. For some other examples, see Ryan Zimmerman, "Understanding the Impact of Personality Traits on Individuals' Turnover Decisions: A Meta-Analytic Path Model," *Personnel Psychology* 60, no. 1 (2008), pp. 309–348.
51. Diane Cadrain, "Reassess Personality Tests After Court Case," *HR Magazine* 50, no. 9 (September 2005), p. 30.
52. Frederick Morgeson et al., "Reconsidering the Use of Personality Tests in Personnel Selection Contexts," *Personnel Psychology* 60 (2007), p. 683.
53. Frederick Morgeson et al., "Are We Getting Fooled Again? Coming to Terms with Limitations in the Use of Personality Tests for Personnel Selection," *Personnel Psychology* 60 (2007), p. 1046.
54. Robert Tett and Neil Christiansen, "Personality Tests at the Crossroads: A Response to Morgeson, Campion, Dipboye, Hollenbeck, Murphy, and Schmitt," *Personnel Psychology* 60 (2007), p. 967. See also Deniz Ones et al., "In Support of Personality Assessment in Organizational Settings," *Personnel Psychology* 60 (2007), pp. 995–1027.
55. Jeff Weekley and Casey Jones, "Video-Based Situational Testing," *Personnel Psychology* 50 (1997), p. 25.
56. Elaine Pulakos, *Selection Assessment Methods*, SHRM Foundation, 2005, p. 14.

57. However, studies suggest that blacks may be somewhat less likely to do well on work sample tests than are whites. See, for example, Philip Roth, Philip Bobko, and Lynn McFarland, "A Meta-Analysis of Work Sample Test Validity: Updating and Integrating Some Classic Literature," *Personnel Psychology* 58, no. 4 (Winter 2005), pp. 1009–1037; and Philip Roth et al., "Work Sample Tests in Personnel Selection: A Meta-Analysis of Black–White Differences in Overall and Exercise Scores," *Personnel Psychology* 60, no. 1 (2008), pp. 637–662.
58. Siegel and Lane, *Personnel and Organizational Psychology*, pp. 182–183.
59. Annette Spychalski, Miguel Quinones, Barbara Gaugler, and Katja Pohley, "A Survey of Assessment Center Practices in Organizations in the United States," *Personnel Psychology* 50, no. 1 (Spring 1997), pp. 71–90. See also Winfred Arthur Jr. et al., "A Meta Analysis of the Criterion Related Validity of Assessment Center Data Dimensions," *Personnel Psychology* 56 (2003), pp. 124–154.
60. "Help Wanted—and Found," *Fortune*, October 2, 2006, p. 40.
61. See, for example, John Meriac et al., "Further Evidence for the Validity of Assessment Center Dimensions: A Meta-Analysis of the Incremental Criterion-Related Validity of Dimension Ratings," *Journal of Applied Psychology* 93, no. 5 (2008), pp. 1042–1052.
62. Kobi Dayan et al., "Entry-Level Police Candidate Assessment Center: An Efficient Tool or a Hammer to Kill a Fly?" *Personnel Psychology* 55 (2002), pp. 827–848.
63. Weekley and Jones, "Video-Based Situational Testing," p. 26.
64. Ibid., p. 30.
65. Robert Grossman, "Made from Scratch," *HR Magazine*, April 2002, pp. 44–53.
66. Coleman Peterson, "Employee Retention, The Secrets Behind Wal-Mart's Successful Hiring Policies," *Human Resource Management* 44, no. 1 (Spring 2005), pp. 85–88. See also Murray Barrick and Ryan Zimmerman, "Reducing Voluntary, Avoidable Turnover Through Selection," *Journal of Applied Psychology* 90, no. 1 (2005), pp. 159–166.
67. James Breaugh, "Employee Recruitment: Current Knowledge and Important Areas for Future Research," *Human Resource Management Review* 18 (2008), pp. 106–107.
68. "Internet, E-Mail Monitoring Common at Most Workplaces," *BNA Bulletin to Management*, February 1, 2001, p. 34. See also "Are Your Background Checks Balanced? Experts Identify Concerns over Verifications," *BNA Bulletin to Management*, May 13, 2004, p. 153.
69. Merry Mayer, "Background Checks in Focus," *HR Magazine*, January 2002, pp. 59–62; and Carroll Lachnit, "Protecting People and Profits with Background Checks," *Workforce*, February 2002, p. 52.
70. Bill Leonard, "Fraud Factories," *HR Magazine*, September 2008, pp. 54–58.
71. Matthew Heller, "Special Report: Background Checking," *Workforce Management*, March 3, 2008, pp. 35–54.
72. Seymour Adler, "Verifying a Job Candidate's Background: The State of Practice in a Vital Human Resources Activity," *Review of Business* 15, no. 2 (Winter 1993), p. 6.
73. Heller, "Special Report: Background Checking," p. 35.
74. This is based on Samuel Greengard, "Have Gangs Invaded Your Workplace?" *Personnel Journal*, February 1996, pp. 47–48.
75. Thomas von der Embse and Rodney Wyse, "Those Reference Letters: How Useful Are They?" *Personnel* 62, no. 1 (January 1985), pp. 42–46.
76. "Reference Checks Hit Wall of Silence," *BNA Bulletin to Management*, July 6, 1995, p. 216.
77. Ibid., p. 55.
78. For example, one U.S. Court of Appeals found that bad references might be grounds for a suit when they are retaliations for the employee having previously filed an EEOC claim. "Negative Reference Leads to Charge of Retaliation," *BNA Bulletin to Management*, October 21, 2004, p. 344.
79. Laws that affect references include the Privacy Act of 1974 (which applies only to federal workers), the Fair Credit Reporting Act of 1970, the Family Education Rights and Privacy Act of 1974 (and Buckley Amendment of 1974), and the Freedom of Information Act of 1966.
80. For additional information, see Lawrence E. Dube Jr., "Employment References and the Law," *Personnel Journal* 65, no. 2 (February 1986), pp. 87–91. See also Mickey Veich, "Uncover the Resume Ruse," *Security Management*, October 1994, pp. 75–76.
81. Eileen Zimmerman, "A Subtle Reference Trap for Unwary Employers," *Workforce*, April 2003, p. 22.
82. *Kehr v. Consolidated Freightways of Delaware*, Docket No. 86–2126, July 15, 1987, U.S. Seventh Circuit Court of Appeals. Discussed in *Commerce Clearing House, Ideas and Trends*, October 16, 1987, p. 165.
83. James Bell, James Castagnera, and Jane Patterson Young, "Employment References: Do You Know the Law?" *Personnel Journal* 63, no. 2 (February 1984), pp. 32–36. In order to demonstrate defamation, several elements must be present: (a) the defamatory statement must have been communicated to another party; (b) the statement must be a false statement of fact; (c) injury to reputation must have occurred; and (d) the employer must not be protected under qualified or absolute privilege. For a discussion, see Ryan and Lasek, "Negligent Hiring and Defamation," p. 307. See also James Burns Jr., "Employment References: Is There a Better Way?" *Employee Relations Law Journal* 23, no. 2 (Fall 1997), pp. 157–168.
84. "Vetting via Internet Is Free, Generally Legal, but Not Necessarily Smart Hiring Strategy," *BNA Bulletin to Management*, February 20, 2007, pp. 57–58.
85. Alan Finder, "When a Risqué Online Persona Undermines a Chance for a Job," *The New York Times*, June 11, 2006, p. 1.
86. Anjali Athavaley, "Job References You Can't Control," *The Wall Street Journal*, September 27, 2007, p. B1.
87. Rita Zeidner, "How Deep Can You Probe?" *HR Magazine*, October 1, 2007, pp. 57–62.
88. "Web Searches on Applicants Are Potentially Perilous for Employers," *BNA Bulletin to Management*, October 14, 2008, p. 335.
89. See Paul Taylor et al., "Dimensionality and the Validity of a Structured Telephone Reference Check Procedure," *Personnel Psychology* 57 (2004), pp. 745–772, for a discussion of checking other work habits and traits.
90. "Getting Applicant Information Difficult but Still Necessary," *BNA Bulletin to Management*, February 5, 1999, p. 63. See also Robert Howie and Laurence Shapiro, "Pre-Employment Criminal Background Checks: Why Employers Should Look Before They Leap," *Employee Relations Law Journal*, Summer 2002, pp. 63–77.
91. "Top Employee Background Checking and Screening Providers," *Workforce Management*, November 7, 2005, p. 14.
92. Lachnit, "Protecting People and Profits with Background Checks," p. 50.

93. Jeffrey M. Hahn, "Pre-Employment Information Services: Employers Beware?" *Employee Relations Law Journal* 17, no. 1 (Summer 1991), pp. 45–69. See also "Pre-Employment Background Screenings Have Evolved, But So Have Liability Risks," *BNA Bulletin to Management*, November 1, 2005, p. 345.
94. Under California law, applicants or employees must have the option of requesting a copy of the report regardless of action.
95. Teresa Butler Stivarius, "Background Checks: Steps to Basic Compliance in a Multistate Environment," *Society for Human Resource Management Legal Report*, March–April 2003, pp. 1–8.
96. Polygraphs are still widely used in law enforcement and reportedly are quite useful. See, for example, Laurie Cohen, "The Polygraph Paradox," *The Wall Street Journal*, March 22, 2008, p. A1.
97. John Jones and William Terris, "Post-Polygraph Selection Techniques," *Recruitment Today*, May–June 1989, pp. 25–31.
98. Norma Fritz, "In Focus: Honest Answers—Post Polygraph," *Personnel*, April 1989, p. 8. See also Richard White Jr., "Ask Me No Questions, Tell Me No Lies: Examining the Uses and Misuses of the Polygraph," *Public Personnel Management* 30, no. 4 (Winter 2001), pp. 483–493.
99. John Bernardin and Donna Cooke, "Validity of an Honesty Test in Predicting Theft Among Convenience Store Employees," *Academy of Management Journal* 36, no. 5 (1993), pp. 1097–1108.
100. Judith Collins and Frank Schmidt, "Personality, Integrity, and White Collar Crime: A Construct Validity Study," *Personnel Psychology* 46 (1993), pp. 295–311; Paul Sackett and James Wanek, "New Developments in the Use of Measures of Honesty, Integrity, Conscientiousness, Dependability, Trustworthiness, and Reliability for Personnel Selection," *Personnel Psychology* 49 (1996), p. 821. Some suggest that by possibly signaling mental illness, integrity tests may conflict with the Americans with Disabilities Act, but one review concludes these tests pose little such legal risk to employers. Christopher Berry et al., "A Review of Recent Developments in Integrity Test Research," *Personnel Psychology* 60, no. 2 (Summer 2007), pp. 271–301.
101. These are based on "Divining Integrity Through Interviews," *BNA Bulletin to Management*, June 4, 1987, p. 184; and *Commerce Clearing House, Ideas and Trends*, December 29, 1998, pp. 222–223. See also Bridget A. Styers and Kenneth S. Shultz, "Perceived Reasonableness of Employment Testing Accommodations for Persons with Disabilities," *Public Personnel Management* 38, no. 3 (Fall 2009), p. 71–91.
102. Bill Leonard, "Reading Employees," *HR Magazine*, April 1999, pp. 67–73.
103. Ibid.
104. Mick Haus, "Pre-Employment Physicals and the ADA," *Safety and Health*, February 1992, pp. 64–65. See also Bridget A. Styers and Kenneth S. Shultz, "Perceived Reasonableness of Employment Testing Accommodations for Persons with Disabilities," *Public Personnel Management* 38, no. 3 (Fall 2009), p. 71–91.
105. Scott MacDonald, Samantha Wells, and Richard Fry, "The Limitations of Drug Screening in the Workplace," *International Labor Review* 132, no. 1 (1993), p. 98. Not all agree that drug testing is worthwhile. See, for example, Mark Karper, Clifford Donn, and Marie Lyndaker, "Drug Testing in the Transportation Industry: The Maritime Case," *Employee Responsibilities and Rights* 71, no. 3 (September 1994), pp. 219–233.
106. "Drug Testing: The Things People Will Do," *American Salesman* 46, no. 3 (March 2001), p. 20.
107. Diane Cadrain, "Are Your Employees' Drug Tests Accurate?" *HR Magazine*, January 2003, pp. 40–45.
108. Chris Berka and Courtney Poignand, "Hair Follicle Testing—An Alternative to Urinalysis for Drug Abuse Screening," *Employee Relations Today*, Winter 1991–1992, pp. 405–409.
109. MacDonald et al., "The Limitations of Drug Screening," pp. 102–104.
110. R. J. McCunney, "Drug Testing: Technical Complications of a Complex Social Issue," *American Journal of Industrial Medicine* 15, no. 5 (1989), pp. 589–600; discussed in MacDonald et al., "The Limitations of Drug Screening," p. 102.
111. MacDonald et al., "The Limitations of Drug Screening," p. 103.
112. This is based on Ann M. O'Neill, "Legal Issues Presented by Hair Follicle Testing," *Employee Relations Today*, Winter 1991–1992, pp. 411–415.
113. Ibid., p. 413.
114. Richard Lisko, "A Manager's Guide to Drug Testing," *Security Management* 38, no. 8 (August 1994), p. 92. See also Randall Kesselring and Jeffrey Pittman, "Drug Testing Laws and Employment Injuries," *Journal of Labor Research*, Spring 2002, pp. 293–301.
115. Michael A. McDaniel, "Does Pre-Employment Drug Use Predict On-the-Job Suitability?" *Personnel Psychology* 41, no. 4 (Winter 1988), pp. 717–729.
116. *Exxon Corp. v. Esso Workers Union, Inc.*, CA1#96–2241, 7/8/97; discussed in *BNA Bulletin to Management*, August 7, 1997, p. 249.
117. These are quoted from *Commerce Clearing House, Ideas and Trends*, May 1, 1987, pp. 70–71.
118. "Conflicting State E-Verify Laws Troubling for Employers," *BNA Bulletin to Management*, November 4, 2008, p. 359.
119. "President Bush Signs Executive Order: Federal Contractors Must Use E-Verify," *BNA Bulletin to Management*, June 17, 2008, p. 193.
120. Note that the acceptable documents on page 3 of the current (as of 2009) I-9 form do not reflect the current list of acceptable documents. For this, refer to the Web site of the U.S. Department of Homeland Security. Margaret Fiester et al., "Affirmative Action, Stock Options, I-9 Documents," *HR Magazine*, November 2007, p. 32.
121. Susan Ladika, "Trouble on the Hiring Front," *HR Magazine*, October 2006, pp. 56–62.
122. Russell Gerbman, "License to Work," *HR Magazine*, June 2000, pp. 151–160.
123. "As E-Verify, No Match Rules, I-9 Evolve, Employers Need to Stay on Top of Issues," *BNA Bulletin Management*, April 15, 2008, p. 121.
124. Note that unproctored Internet tests raise serious questions in employment settings. Nancy Tippins et al., "Unproctored Internet Testing in Employment Settings," *Personnel Psychology* 59 (2006), pp. 189–225.
125. Jennifer Taylor Arnold, "Getting Facts Fast," *HR Magazine*, February 2008, p. 58.
126. From Bob Neveu, "Applicant Tracking's Top 10: Do You Know What to Look for in Applicant Tracking Systems?" *Workforce*, October 2002, p. 10.

7 Interviewing Candidates

Careerbuilder.com conducted a survey of more than 400 hiring managers, asking them to share "the most memorable blunders" that caused them to reject a particular candidate. Job interviews scored high on the list. For example, several job candidates displayed stunningly arrogant attitudes during their interviews. Some samples: "He asked me to speed up the interview because he had a lunch date." "He told me the only reason he was here was because his mother wanted him to get a job." "The candidate used profanity when describing something negative about a previous boss." "One candidate did not wear shoes to the interview."[1]

Source: Courtesy of Ilene MacDonald/Alamy Images.

WHERE ARE WE NOW . . .

Chapter 6 focused on important tools managers use to select employees. Now we'll turn to one of these tools—interviewing candidates. The main topics we'll cover include types of interviews, things that undermine interviewing's usefulness, and designing and conducting effective selection interviews. In Chapter 8, we'll turn to making sure your new employees have the skills they need to perform their jobs.

Before proceeding, we should answer an obvious question. If the interview is only one of several selection tools, why devote a whole chapter to this one tool? One answer is that interviews *are the most widely used selection procedure.* Not all managers use tests or even reference checks. However, it would be highly unusual for you not to interview someone before hiring him or her. The other answer is that most people *think they're better interviewers than they really are.* In one study, less than 34% of interviewers had formal interview training, for instance, in how to structure an interview. However, "interviewers were confident [erroneously] that they could identify the best candidates regardless of the amount of interview structure employed."[2]

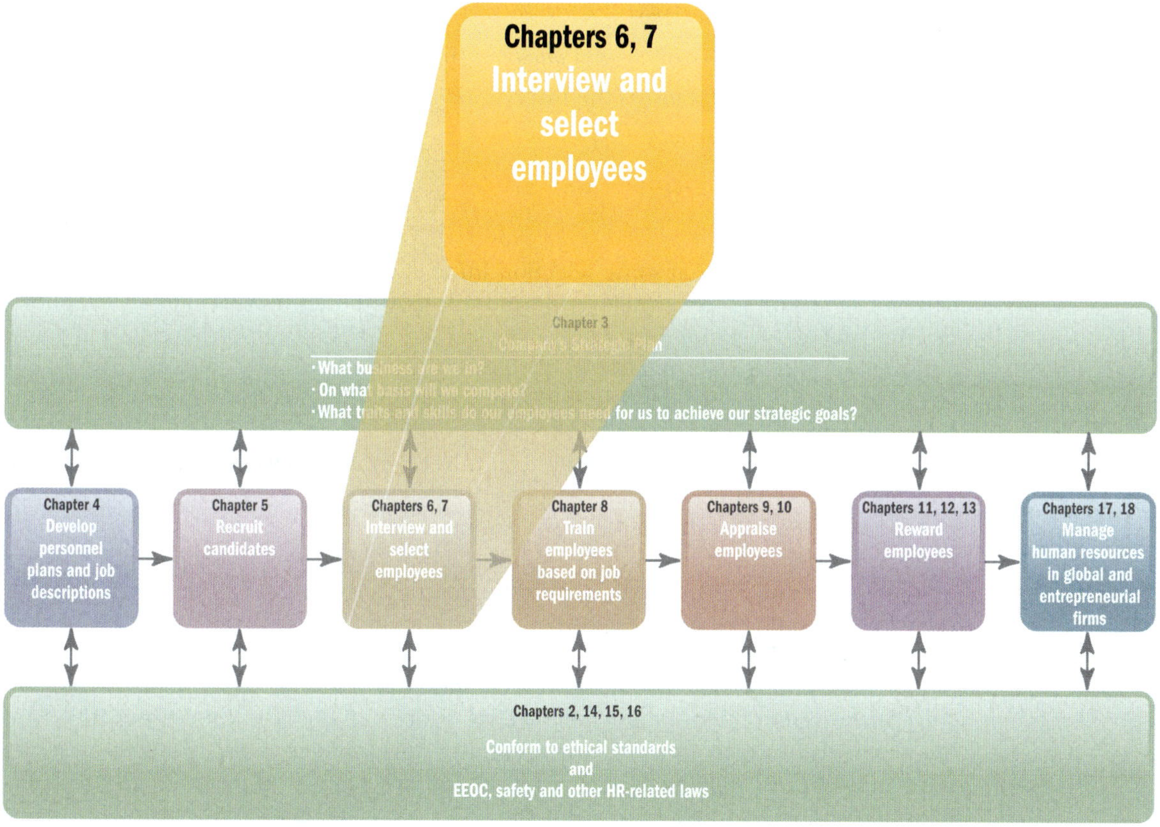

LEARNING OUTCOMES

1. List the main types of selection interviews.
2. List and explain main errors that can undermine an interview's usefulness.
3. Define a structured situational interview.
4. Explain and illustrate each guideline for being a more effective interviewer.
5. Give several examples of situational questions, behavioral questions, and background questions that provide structure.
6. List the steps in a streamlined interview process.
7. List guidelines for interviewees.

1 List the main types of selection interviews.

BASIC TYPES OF INTERVIEWS

An interview is more than a discussion. An *interview* is a procedure designed to obtain information from a person through oral responses to oral inquiries. A *selection interview* (which we'll focus on in this chapter) is a selection procedure designed to predict future job performance on the basis of applicants' oral responses to oral inquiries.[3] Let's look first at the basic types of employment interviews.

Types of Employment Interviews

Managers use several interviews at work. For example, an *appraisal interview* is a discussion, following a performance appraisal, in which supervisor and employee discuss the employee's ratings and possible remedial actions. When an employee leaves a firm, one often conducts an *exit interview.* This aims at eliciting information that might provide some insight into what's right or wrong about the firm. Many techniques in this chapter apply to appraisal and exit interviews. However, we'll postpone a fuller discussion of these two interviews until Chapters 9 and 10, and focus here on selection interviews.

We can classify selection interviews according to

1. How *structured* they are
2. Their "content"—the *types of questions* they contain
3. How the firm *administers* the interviews

Let's look at each.

Structured Versus Unstructured Interviews

You've probably seen that some selection interviews are more structured or methodical than others are. In **unstructured (or nondirective) interviews,** the manager follows no set format. A few questions might be specified in advance, but they're usually not, and there is seldom a formal guide for scoring "right" or "wrong" answers. This type of interview could even be described as little more than a general conversation.[4] Most selection interviews probably fall in this category.

At the other extreme, in **structured (or directive) interviews,** the employer lists the questions ahead of time, and may even list and score possible answers for appropriateness.[5] McMurray's Patterned Interview was one early example. The interviewer followed a printed form to ask a series of questions, such as "How was the person's present job obtained?" Comments printed beneath the questions (such as "Has he/she shown self-reliance in getting his/her jobs?") then guide the interviewer in evaluating the answers. Some experts still restrict the term "structured interview" to interviews like these, which are based on carefully selected job-oriented questions with predetermined answers.

But in practice, interview structure is a matter of degree. Sometimes the manager may just want to ensure he or she has a standard set of questions to ask so as to avoid skipping any questions. Here, the interviewer might just choose questions from a list like that in Figure 7-3 (page 244). The structured applicant interview guide in Figure 7-A1 (pages 254–256) illustrates a more structured approach. As a third example, the Department of Homeland Security uses the structured guide in Figure 7-1 to help screen Coast Guard officer candidates. It contains a formal candidate rating procedure; it also enables geographically disbursed interviewers to complete the form over the Web.[6]

Which to Use?

There's no doubt that structured interviews are superior. In structured interviews, all interviewers generally ask all applicants the same questions. Partly because of this, these interviews tend to be more reliable and valid. Structured interviews can also help less talented interviewers conduct better interviews. Standardizing the interview also increases consistency across candidates, enhances job relatedness, reduces overall subjectivity and thus the potential for bias, and may "enhance the ability to withstand legal challenge."[7]

U.S. Department of Homeland Security CG-5527 (06-04)	Officer Programs Applicant Interview Form	1. Date:

2. Name of Applicant (Last, First, MI)

3. **Overall Impression:** Compare this applicant to others you have interviewed or known. (Note: Scores of 4 through 7 constitute a recommendation for selection.)

NOT RECOMMENDED			RECOMMENDED			
Unsatisfactory 1☐	Limited Potential 2☐	Fair Performer 3☐	Good Performer 4☐	Excellent Performer 5☐	Exceptional Performer 6☐	Distinguished Performer 7☐

Comments:

4. **Performance of Duties:** Measures an applicant's ability to manage and to get things done.

Unsatisfactory 1☐ Limited Potential 2☐ Fair Performer 3☐ Good Performer 4☐ Excellent Performer 5☐ Exceptional Performer 6☐ Distinguished Performer 7☐

Comments:

5. **Communication Skills:** Measures an applicant's ability to communicate in a positive, clear, and convincing manner.

Unsatisfactory 1☐ Limited Potential 2☐ Fair Performer 3☐ Good Performer 4☐ Excellent Performer 5☐ Exceptional Performer 6☐ Distinguished Performer 7☐

Comments:

6. Names of Board Members	7. Rank	8. Command/Unit	9. Signature	10. Career Total of Interviews Conducted

PREVIOUS EDITIONS ARE OBSOLETE

CONTINUED ON REVERSE

Reset

(*continued*)

FIGURE 7-1 Officer Programs Applicant Interview Form
Source: http://www.uscg.mil/forms/ cg/CG5527.pdf, accessed May 9, 2007.

EEOC Aspects of Interviews That last point is important. No one wants to have someone sue for discrimination, let alone lose the suit. A study of federal district court cases involving alleged employment interview discrimination therefore is relevant. It's clear the courts will look at whether the interview process is structured and consistently applied. For example, did you (1) have objective/job-related questions,

unstructured (or nondirective) interview
An unstructured conversational-style interview in which the interviewer pursues points of interest as they come up in response to questions.

structured or directive interview
An interview following a set sequence of questions.

FIGURE 7-1 *(continued)*

Page 2 - CG-5527 (06-04)

11. Leadership Skills: Measures an applicant's ability to support, develop, direct, and influence others in performing work.

Unsatisfactory	Limited Potential	Fair Performer	Good Performer	Excellent Performer	Exceptional Performer	Distinguished Performer
1☐	2☐	3☐	4☐	5☐	6☐	7☐

Comments:

12. Personal and Professional Qualities: Measures qualities which illustrate the applicant's character.

Unsatisfactory	Limited Potential	Fair Performer	Good Performer	Excellent Performer	Exceptional Performer	Distinguished Performer
1☐	2☐	3☐	4☐	5☐	6☐	7☐

Comments:

Reset

INSTRUCTIONS

The Officer Programs Applicant Interview Form is designed to help Officer Programs selection panels select applicants to be Coast Guard officers. The form is heavily based on the Officer Evaluation Report (OER) and the scale for each category is based on OER performance standards. While it should be remembered that applicants are not yet Coast Guard officers, they should have had opportunities to exhibit qualities that show they possess the character and potential necessary to be successful officers. Provide written comments in support of numeric markings for each category. Base these comments on what you observe during the interview or see in the supporting documentation in the applicant's package. Much like an OER, both the numerical evaluation and written comments are used by selection panels. Officer interview boards should review Article 4.B.2 of the Recruiting Manual, COMDTINST M1100.2 (series) and Articles 1.B.8 and 1.B.9 of the Personnel Manual, COMDTINST M1000.6 (series), which provide guidance on officer interviews.

1. Date of interview.
2. Self-explanatory.
3. Marks in the **Overall Impression** block should summarize the interview board's recommendation of the applicant's suitability for service as a Coast Guard Officer, and therefore should be completed last. Scores of 4 through 7 constitute a recommendation for selection.

4-5. Self-explanatory.

6. Last name, first name, and middle initial.

7-9. Self-explanatory.

10. Interviewer's career total of officer applicant interview boards.

11-12. Self-explanatory.

PREVIOUS EDITIONS ARE OBSOLETE

(2) standardize interview administration, and (3) preferably use multiple interviewers?[8] Also, ". . . endeavor to make it clear to applicants that the interview process is fair, that the interviewer treats the interviewee with courtesy and respect, and that the interviewer is willing to explain the interview process and the nature and rationale for the questions."[9]

However, blindly following a structured format isn't advisable either. Doing so may not provide enough opportunity to pursue points of interest as they develop. Therefore, the interviewer should always leave an opportunity to ask follow-up questions and pursue points of interest as they develop.

Interview Content (What Types of Questions to Ask)

We can also classify interviews based on the "content" or the types of questions you ask. Many (probably most) interviewers tend to ask relatively unfocused questions. These might include "What are your main strengths and weaknesses?" and "What do you want to be doing 5 years from now?" Generally, questions like these don't provide much useful insight into how the person will do on the job. At work, *situational, behavioral,* and *job-related* questions are most important.

Situational Questions In a **situational interview,** you ask the candidate what his or her behavior *would be* in a given situation.[10] For example, you might ask a supervisory candidate how he or she would act in response to a subordinate coming to work late 3 days in a row.

Behavioral Questions Whereas situational interviews ask applicants to describe how they would react to a hypothetical situation today or tomorrow, **behavioral interview** questions ask applicants to describe *how they reacted* to actual situations in the past.[11] For example, when Citizen's Banking Corporation in Flint, Michigan, found that 31 of the 50 people in its call center quit in one year, Cynthia Wilson, the center's head, switched to behavioral interviews. Many of those who left did so because they didn't enjoy fielding questions from occasionally irate clients. So Wilson no longer tries to predict how candidates will act based on asking them if they want to work with angry clients. Instead, she asks behavioral questions like, "Tell me about a time you were speaking with an irate person, and how you turned the situation around." Wilson says this makes it much harder to fool the interviewer, and, indeed, only four people left her center in the following year.[12] In summary, *situational* questions start with phrases such as, "Suppose you were faced with the following situation . . . What would you do?" *Behavioral* questions start with phrases like, "Can you think of a time when . . . What did you do?"[13] More employers today are using (or planning to use) behavioral interviews.[14]

Behavioral or situational interviews can be hard on applicants. "It's pretty intense," said one applicant for a consultant's job with Accenture, the consulting firm. "You can pretty much fake one or two answers, but the third time they come back to it, you pretty much can't. You're pulling from real life, and you're nervous. [The interviewer] asked how I would prepare for something important. He came back to that again and again to make sure what I said was true. The whole time they are writing constantly."[15]

Other Types of Questions In a **job-related interview,** the interviewer asks applicants questions about relevant past experiences. The questions here don't revolve around hypothetical or actual situations or scenarios. Instead, the interviewer asks job-related questions such as, "Which courses did you like best in business school?" The aim is to draw conclusions about, say, the candidate's ability to handle the financial aspects of the job the employer seeks to fill.

There are other, lesser-used types of questions. In a **stress interview,** the interviewer seeks to make the applicant uncomfortable with occasionally rude questions. The aim is supposedly to spot sensitive applicants and those with low (or high) stress tolerance. The interviewer might first probe for weaknesses in the applicant's background, such as a job that the applicant left under questionable circumstances. You then zero in on these weaknesses, hoping to get the candidate to lose his or her composure. Thus, a candidate for a customer relations manager position who obligingly mentions having had four jobs in the past 2 years might be told that frequent job changes reflect irresponsible and immature behavior. If the applicant then responds with a reasonable explanation of why the job changes were necessary, the interviewer might pursue another topic. On the other hand, if the formerly tranquil applicant reacts explosively with anger and disbelief, the interviewer might deduce that the person has a low tolerance for stress.

situational interview
A series of job-related questions that focus on how the candidate would behave in a given situation.

behavioral interview
A series of job-related questions that focus on how the candidate reacted to actual situations in the past.

job-related interview
A series of job-related questions that focus on relevant past job-related behaviors.

stress interview
An interview in which the applicant is made uncomfortable by a series of often rude questions. This technique helps identify hypersensitive applicants and those with low or high stress tolerance.

Stress interviews may help unearth hypersensitive applicants who might overreact to mild criticism with anger and abuse. However, the stress interview's invasive and ethically questionable nature demands that the interviewer be both skilled in its use and sure the job really calls for a thick skin and an ability to handle stress. This is definitely not an approach for amateur interrogators or for those without the skills to keep the interview under control.

Puzzle questions are popular. Recruiters like to use them to see how candidates think under pressure. For example, an interviewer at Microsoft asked a tech service applicant this: "Mike and Todd have $21 between them. Mike has $20 more than Todd does. How much money has Mike, and how much money has Todd?"[16] (You'll find the answer two paragraphs below.)

How Should We Administer the Interview?

Employers also administer interviews in various ways: *one-on-one or by a panel of interviewers; sequentially or all at once*; and *computerized or personally.*

Most selection interviews are *one-on-one* and *sequential.* In a one-on-one interview, two people meet alone, and one interviews the other by seeking oral responses to oral inquiries. Employers tend to schedule these interviews *sequentially.* In a *sequential (or serial) interview,* several persons interview the applicant, in sequence, one-on-one, and then make their hiring decision. In an **unstructured sequential interview**, each interviewer generally just asks questions as they come to mind. In a **structured sequential interview**, each interviewer rates the candidates on a standard evaluation form, using standardized questions. The hiring manager then reviews and compares the evaluations before deciding whom to hire.[17] (Answer: Mike had $20.50, Todd $.50.)

Panel Interviews

A **panel interview**, also known as a board interview, is an interview conducted by a team of interviewers (usually two to three), who together interview each candidate and then combine their ratings into a final panel score. This contrasts with the *one-on-one interview* (in which one interviewer meets one candidate) and a *serial interview* (where several interviewers assess a single candidate one-on-one, sequentially).[18]

The panel format enables interviewers to ask follow-up questions, much as reporters do in press conferences. This may elicit more meaningful responses than are normally produced by a series of one-on-one interviews. On the other hand, some candidates find panel interviews more stressful, so they may actually inhibit responses. (An even more stressful variant is the **mass interview**. Here a panel interviews several candidates simultaneously. The panel poses a problem, and then watches to see which candidate takes the lead in formulating an answer.)

It's not clear whether as a rule panel interviews are more or less reliable and valid than sequential interviews, because how the employer actually does the panel interview determines this. For example, *structured* panel interviews are more reliable and valid than unstructured ones. Specifically, panel interviews in which members use scoring sheets with descriptive scoring examples for sample answers are more reliable and valid than those that don't. And, training the panel interviewers may boost the interview's reliability.[19]

Phone Interviews

Employers do some interviews entirely by *telephone.* These can actually be more accurate than face-to-face interviews for judging an applicant's conscientiousness, intelligence, and interpersonal skills. Here, neither party need worry about things like appearance or handshakes, so each can focus on substantive answers. Or perhaps candidates—somewhat surprised by an unexpected call from the recruiter—just give answers that are more spontaneous.[20] In a typical study, interviewers tended to evaluate applicants more favorably in telephone versus face-to-face interviews, particularly where the interviewees were less physically attractive. However, the interviewers came to about the same conclusions regarding the interviewees whether the interview was face-to-face or by *videoconference.* The applicants themselves preferred the face-to-face interviews.[21]

HR APPs 4 U

iPhone Job Interviews

More employers and job interviewees are using iPhone and similar devices to conduct job interviews—sometimes, video job interviews—via cell phone. As one blogger recently noted, "I've even had several phone interviews in the car with one company while driving up for an on-site interview with a second company. Now that's multi-tasking."[22] To help this process along, designers are making more job interviewing apps available through Apple's iPhone App Store. One is from *Martin's iPhone Apps.* For people seeking technical jobs, this app includes hundreds of potential interview questions, taken from a range of categories, such as Brain Teasers, Algorithms, C/C++, and Personal.[23]

Video/Web-Assisted Interviews Firms have long used the Web to do selection interviews (particularly the initial, prescreening interviews), and with the widespread use of Skype™-type products, their use is growing. For instance, Cisco Systems, Inc. (which in 2006 expanded its core business to include videoconferencing equipment) equips Cisco recruiters with PC video cameras, so they can conduct preliminary interviews online. Applicants use their own camera-supported PC (or go to a local FedEx Office or similar business). Then, at the appointed time, he or she links to Cisco via Web video. Cisco doesn't eliminate face-to-face interviews. However, the video interviews do reduce travel and recruiting expenses, and make things easier for candidates. And that's especially important today, which the accompanying "Managing HR in Challenging Times" feature explains.

Managing HR in Challenging Times

Acing the Skype Interview

With employers cutting their recruitment budgets, more are conducting at least the initial screening interviews over the Internet. Web cam prices are now well below $100 and new recruitment sites (such as Inovahire.com) post free Web cam conferencing. And increasingly, with free applications like Skype so widely used, there's no reason for not doing the first few interviews via Skype.

Having a Skype job interview probably doesn't require too many special preparations for the employer, but according to Career FAQs (www.careerfaqs.com) there are important things that interviewees should keep in mind. (Most apply to the interviewers, too.) Many of these may seem obvious. However, it's often the obvious things we tend to overlook. Here's what Career FAQs suggests.[24]

- **Make sure you look presentable.** You might feel silly sitting at home wearing a suit, but it could make all the difference.
- **Clean up the room.** Whether the interview is from your own home or a busy office environment, the interviewer does not want to see you sitting in front of a pile of junk.
- **Test first.** As Career FAQs says, "Five minutes before the video interview is not a good time to realize that your Internet is down, Skype isn't working, or your pet rabbit has chewed through the microphone cord."
- **Do a dry run.** Try recording yourself before the interview to try answering some imaginary questions.
- **Relax.** The golden rule with a Skype interview is to treat it like any other face-to-face meeting. There is a real person on the other end of the call, so treat them like one. Smile, look confident and enthusiastic, try to make eye contact, and don't shout, but do speak clearly.

unstructured sequential interview
An interview in which each interviewer forms an independent opinion after asking different questions.

structured sequential interview
An interview in which the applicant is interviewed sequentially by several persons; each rates the applicant on a standard form.

panel interview
An interview in which a group of interviewers questions the applicant.

mass interview
A panel interviews several candidates simultaneously.

Computerized Interviews Some firms computerize part of the interview process. A *computerized selection interview* is one in which a job candidate's oral and/or computerized replies are obtained in response to computerized oral, visual, or written questions and/or situations. Most computerized interviews present the applicant with a series of questions regarding his or her background, experience, education, skills, knowledge, and work attitudes that relate to the job for which the person has applied.[25] Some (video-based) computerized interviews also confront candidates with realistic scenarios (such as irate customers) to which they must respond.

Typical computerized interviews present questions in a multiple-choice format, one at a time. The applicant has to respond to the questions on the screen by pressing a key. A sample interview question for a person applying for a job as a retail store clerk might be:

How would your supervisor rate your customer service skills?

a. Outstanding

b. Above average

c. Average

d. Below average

e. Poor[26]

Questions on computerized interviews come in rapid sequence and require the applicant to concentrate.[27] The typical computerized interview program measures the response time to each question. A delay in answering certain questions such as "Can you be trusted?" flags a potential problem.

Great Western Bank Example Here's how such a system works at Great Western Bank. When Bonnie Dunn, 20 years old, tried out for a teller's job at Great Western Bank, she faced a lineup of tough customers.[28] One young woman sputtered contradictory instructions about depositing a check and then blew her top when Bonnie didn't handle the transaction fast enough. Another customer had an even shorter fuse: "You people are unbelievably slow," he said.

Both tough customers appeared on a computer screen, as part of a 20-minute computerized job interview. Ms. Dunn sat in front of a personal computer, responding via a touch screen and a microphone. She was tested on making change and on sales skills, as well as keeping cool in tense situations.

When applicants sit down facing the computer at Great Western's bank branches, they hear it say, "Welcome to the interactive assessment aid." The computer doesn't understand what applicants say at that point, although it records their comments for evaluation later. To begin the interview, applicants touch a label on the screen, eliciting an ominous foreword: "We'll be keeping track of how long it takes you and how many mistakes you make. Accuracy is more important than speed."

First, the computer tests the applicant on money skills, asking him or her to cash a check for $192.18, including at least three $5 bills and two dollars in quarters. Then, when an angry customer appears on the screen, the system expects candidates to grab the microphone and mollify him. Later, a bank official who listens to the recorded interviews gives applicants 5 points for maintaining a friendly tone of voice, plus up to 15 points for apologizing, promising to solve the customer's problem, and, taking a cue from the screen, suggesting that in the future he use the bank's deposit-only line.

The touchy young woman on the screen is tougher. Speaking fast, she says she wants to cash a $150 check, get $40 in cash, and put $65 in savings and the rest in checking. As an applicant struggles to sort that out, she quickly adds, "No, it has to be $50 in checking because I just wrote a check this morning." If the applicant then touches a label on the screen that says "?" the woman fumes, "How many times do I have to tell you?"

Great Western reports success with its system. It dramatically reduced useless personal interviewing of unacceptable candidates. And, partly because the candidates see what the job is really like, those hired are reportedly 26% less likely to quit or be dismissed within 90 days of hiring.

Pic 'n Pay Stores Example Employers often use computer-aided interviews to pre-screen candidates. Pic 'n Pay stores, a chain of 915 self-service shoe stores headquartered in North Carolina, gives job applicants an 800 number to dial for a computerized interview. The interview contains 100 questions and lasts about 10 minutes. Applicants press 1 for *yes* and 0 for *no*. Every applicant then gets a follow-up live telephone interview, from one of the firm's six dedicated interviewers.

Three Ways to Make the Interview Useful

Interviews hold an ironic place in the hiring process: Everyone uses them, but they're generally not too useful. The knack is in doing them properly. If you do, then the interview is generally a much better predictor of performance than previously thought and is comparable with many other selection techniques.[29] There are three things to keep in mind.

Structure the Interview First, you should *structure the interview*.[30] Structured interviews (particularly structured interviews using situational questions) are more valid than unstructured interviews for predicting job performance. They are more valid partly because they are more reliable—for example, the same interviewer administers the interview more consistently from candidate to candidate.[31] Situational interviews yield a higher mean validity than do job-related (or behavioral) interviews, which in turn yield a higher mean validity than do "psychological" interviews (which focus more on motives and interests).[32]

Be Careful What Sorts of Traits You Try to Assess Interviews are better for revealing some traits than others. A typical study illustrates this. Interviewers were able to size up the interviewee's extraversion and agreeableness. What they could *not* assess accurately were the traits that often matter most on jobs—like conscientiousness and emotional stability.[33] The implication seems to be, don't focus (as many do) on hard-to-assess traits like conscientiousness or intelligence.[34] Limit yourself mostly to situational and job knowledge questions that help you assess how the candidate will actually respond to typical situations on that job. We'll explain how to do this later in the chapter.

Beware of Committing Interviewing Errors Third, understand and avoid the *various errors that can undermine* any interview's usefulness. We turn to these next.

2 List and explain main errors that can undermine an interview's usefulness.

WHAT ERRORS CAN UNDERMINE AN INTERVIEW'S USEFULNESS?

One reason selection interviews tend to be less than useful is that managers make predictable, avoidable errors. We'll look at these next.

First Impressions (Snap Judgments)

Perhaps the most consistent research finding is that interviewers tend to jump to conclusions—make snap judgments—about candidates during the first few minutes of the interview (or even before the interview starts, based on test scores or résumé data). One researcher estimates that in 85% of the cases, interviewers had made up their minds before the interview even began, based on first impressions the interviewers gleaned from candidates' applications and personal appearance.[35] In a typical study, giving interviewers the candidates' test scores biased the ultimate assessment of the candidates.[36]

First impressions are especially damaging when the prior information about the candidate is negative. In one study, interviewers who previously received unfavorable reference letters about applicants gave those applicants less credit for past successes and held them more personally responsible for past failures after the interview. And the interviewers' final decisions (to accept or reject those applicants) always reflected what they expected of the applicants based on the references, quite aside from the applicants' actual interview performance.[37]

Add to this two more interviewing facts. First, interviewers are more influenced by unfavorable than favorable information about the candidate. Second, their impressions are much more likely to change from favorable to unfavorable than from unfavorable to favorable. Indeed, many interviewers really search more for negative information, often without realizing it.

The bottom line is that most interviews are probably loaded against the applicant. An applicant who starts well could easily end up with a low rating because unfavorable information tends to carry more weight in the interview. And pity the poor interviewee who starts out poorly. It's almost impossible to overcome that first bad impression.[38] Here's how one London-based psychologist who interviewed the chief executives of 80 top companies put it:

> "Really, to make a good impression, you don't even get time to open your mouth. . . . An interviewer's response to you will generally be preverbal—how you walk through the door, what your posture is like, whether you smile, whether you have a captivating aura, whether you have a firm, confident handshake. You've got about half a minute to make an impact and after that all you are doing is building on a good or bad first impression. . . . It's a very emotional response."[39]

Not Clarifying What the Job Requires

Interviewers who don't have an accurate picture of what the job entails and what sort of candidate is best suited for it usually make their decisions based on incorrect impressions or stereotypes of what a good applicant is. They then erroneously match interviewees with their incorrect stereotypes. You should clarify what sorts of traits you're looking for, and why, before starting the interview.

One classic study involved 30 professional interviewers.[40] Half got just a brief description of the jobs for which they were recruiting: It said, the "eight applicants here represented by their application blanks are applying for the position of secretary." The other 15 interviewers got much more explicit job information, in terms of typing speed and bilingual ability, for instance.

More job knowledge translated into better interviews. The 15 interviewers who had more job information generally all agreed among themselves about each candidate's potential; those without complete job information did not. The latter also didn't discriminate as well among applicants—they tended to give them all high ratings.

Candidate-Order (Contrast) Error and Pressure to Hire

Candidate-order (or contrast) error means that the order in which you see applicants affects how you rate them. In one study, managers had to evaluate a candidate who was "just average" after first evaluating several "unfavorable" candidates. They scored the average candidate more favorably than they might otherwise have done because, in contrast to the unfavorable candidates, the average one looked better than he actually was. This contrast effect can be huge: In some early studies, evaluators based only a small part of the applicant's rating on his or her actual potential.[41]

Pressure to hire accentuates this problem. Researchers told one group of managers to assume they were behind in their recruiting quota. They told a second group they were ahead of their quota. Those "behind" evaluated the same recruits much more highly than did those "ahead."[42]

Nonverbal Behavior and Impression Management

The applicant's nonverbal behavior (smiling, avoiding your gaze, and so on) can also have a surprisingly large impact on his or her rating. In one study, 52 human resource specialists watched videotaped job interviews in which *the applicants' verbal content was identical*, but their nonverbal behavior differed markedly. Researchers told applicants in one group to exhibit minimal eye contact, a low energy level, and low voice modulation. Those in a second group demonstrated the opposite behavior. Twenty-three of the 26 personnel specialists who saw the high-eye-contact, high-energy-level candidate would have invited him or her for a second interview. None who saw the low-eye-contact, low-energy-level candidate would have recommended a second interview.[43] It certainly seems to pay interviewees to "look alive."

In another study, interviewers listened to audio interviews and watched video interviews. Vocal cues (such as the interviewee's pitch, speech rates, and pauses) and visual cues (such as smiling and body orientation) correlated with the evaluator's judgments of whether the interviewees could be liked and trusted.[44]

Nonverbal behaviors are probably so important because interviewers infer your personality from the way you act in the interview. In one study, 99 graduating college seniors completed questionnaires both before and after their job interviews; the questionnaires included measures of personality, among other things.[45] The students then reported their success in generating follow-up interviews and job offers. The interviewee's personality, particularly his or her level of extraversion, had a pronounced influence on whether or not he or she received follow-up interviews and job offers.[46] Extraverted applicants seem particularly prone to self-promotion, and self-promotion is strongly related to the interviewer's perceptions of candidate–job fit.[47]

Impression Management Clever candidates capitalize on that fact. One study found that some used ingratiation to persuade interviewers to like them. For instance, the interviewers praised them or appeared to agree with their opinions. Ingratiation also involves, for example, agreeing with the recruiter's opinions and thus signaling that they share similar beliefs. Sensing that a perceived similarity in attitudes may influence how the interviewer rates them, some interviewees try to emphasize (or fabricate) such similarities.[48] Others make self-promoting comments about their own accomplishments.[49] Self-promotion means promoting one's own skills and abilities to create the impression of competence.[50] Psychologists call using techniques like ingratiation and self-promotion "impression management."

Effect of Personal Characteristics: Attractiveness, Gender, Race

Unfortunately, physical attributes such as applicants' attractiveness, gender, disability, or race may also distort their assessments.[51] For example, people usually ascribe more favorable traits and more successful life outcomes to attractive people.[52] In one study, subjects had to evaluate candidates for promotion based on photographs. They perceived men as being more suitable for hire and more likely to advance to a next executive level than they did equally qualified women; they preferred more attractive candidates (especially men) to less attractive ones.[53] "Even when female managers exhibited the same career-advancing behaviors as

candidate-order (or contrast) error
An error of judgment on the part of the interviewer due to interviewing one or more very good or very bad candidates just before the interview in question.

male managers, they still earned less money and were offered fewer career-progressing transfer opportunities."[54] Similarly, race can play a role, depending on how you conduct the interview. In one study, for example, the white members of a racially balanced interview panel rated white candidates higher, while the black interviewers rated black candidates higher. (In all cases, by the way, *structured* interviews produced less of a difference between minority and white interviewees than did unstructured interviews.)[55]

In general, candidates evidencing various attributes and disabilities (such as child-care demands, HIV-positive status, and being wheelchair-bound) had less chance of obtaining a positive decision, even when the person performed very well in the structured interview.[56] (Because the applicant's "race, gender, hair style, teeth and even facial tics" can influence the interview process in a discriminatory way, the European Community even considered requiring that employers conduct recruitment interviews with screens between the applicant and the interviewers, or over a room-to-room speakerphone.)[57] The "Managing the New Workforce" feature expands on this topic.

Managing the New Workforce

Applicant Disability and the Employment Interview

A study by the Research and Evaluation Center at the National Center for Disability Services provides some insight into what disabled people who use "assistive technology" at work expect and prefer from interviewers.[58] Researchers surveyed 40 disabled people from various occupations to arrive at their conclusions. The basic finding was that the disabled people felt that interviewers tend to avoid directly addressing the disability, and therefore make their decisions without all the facts.

What the disabled people prefer is an open discussion, one that would allow the employer to clarify his or her concerns and reach a knowledgeable conclusion. Among the questions disabled persons said they would like interviewers to ask were these:

- Is there any kind of setting or special equipment that will facilitate the interview process for you?
- Is there any specific technology that you currently use or have used in previous jobs that assists the way you work?
- Other than technology, what other kind of support did you have in previous jobs? If none, is there anything that would benefit you?
- Is there any technology that you don't currently have that would be helpful in performing the duties of this position?
- In the past, did you experience any problems between your technology and the company's information systems?
- Do you foresee your technology needs changing in the near future? Why and how?
- Discuss a barrier or obstacle, if any, that you have encountered in any of your previous jobs. How was that addressed?
- Do you anticipate any transportation or scheduling issues with the work schedule expected of this position?

Also, keep in mind that under the Americans with Disabilities Act, the interviewer must limit his or her questions to whether the applicant has any physical or mental impairment that may interfere with his or her ability to perform the job's essential tasks.[59]

Employment discrimination is abhorrent, but the use of employment discrimination "testers" makes nondiscriminatory interviewing even more important. As defined by the EEOC, testers are "individuals who apply for employment which they do not intend to accept, for the sole purpose of uncovering unlawful discriminatory hiring practices."[60] Although they're not really seeking employment, testers have legal standing with the courts and with the EEOC.[61]

For example, a private, nonprofit civil rights group sent four university students—two white, two black—to an employment agency, supposedly in pursuit of a job. The civil rights group gave the four "testers" backgrounds and training to make them appear almost indistinguishable from each other in terms of qualifications. The white tester/applicants got interviews and job offers, while the black tester/applicants got neither interviews nor offers.[62]

Interviewer Behavior

Finally, the *interviewer's* behavior also affects the interviewee's performance and rating.

Consider some examples. Some interviewers inadvertently telegraph the expected answers,[63] as in: "This job calls for handling a lot of stress. You can do that, can't you?" Even subtle cues (like a smile or nod) can telegraph the desired answer.[64] Some interviewers talk so much that applicants have no time to answer questions. At the other extreme, some interviewers let the applicant dominate the interview, and so don't ask all their questions.[65] When interviewers have favorable pre-interview impressions of the applicant, they tend to act more positively toward that person (smiling more, for instance), possibly because they want to increase the chance that the applicant will accept the job.[66] Other interviewers play district attorney. It's smart to be alert for inconsistencies, but uncivil to play "gotcha" by gleefully pouncing on them. Some interviewers play amateur psychologist, unprofessionally probing for hidden meanings in everything the applicant says.[67] And, some interviewers are simply inept, unable to formulate decent questions, while others are good at drawing out the best in interviewees.

In summary, potential interviewing errors to avoid include:

- First impressions (snap judgments)
- Not clarifying what the job involves and requires
- Candidate-order error and pressure to hire
- Nonverbal behavior and impression management
- The effects of interviewees' personal characteristics
- The interviewer's inadvertent behaviors

3 Define a structured situational interview.

HOW TO DESIGN AND CONDUCT AN EFFECTIVE INTERVIEW

There are two basic ways to avoid interview errors. One is obvious: Keep them in mind and avoid them (don't make snap judgments, for instance). The second is not so obvious: Use structured interviews. The single biggest rule for conducting effective selection interviews is to structure the interview around job-relevant situational and behavioral questions. We'll look next at how to do this.

The Structured Situational Interview

There is little doubt that the **structured situational interview**—a series of job-relevant questions with predetermined answers that interviewers ask of all applicants for the job—produces superior results.[68] Ideally, the basic idea is to write situational (what

structured situational interview
A series of job-relevant questions with predetermined answers that interviewers ask of all applicants for the job.

would you do), or behavioral (what did you do), or job knowledge questions, *and* have job experts (like those supervising the job) also write answers for these questions, rated from good to poor. The people who interview and rate the applicants then use rating sheets anchored with examples of good or bad answers to rate the interviewees' answers.[69]

In creating structured situational interviews, people familiar with the job develop questions based on the job's actual duties. They then reach consensus on what are and are not acceptable answers. The procedure is as follows.[70]

Step 1: Analyze the job. Write a job description with a list of job duties, required knowledge, skills, abilities, and other worker qualifications.

Step 2: Rate the job's main duties. Identify the job's main duties. To do so, rate each job duty based on its importance to job success and on the time required to perform it compared to other tasks.

Step 3: Create interview questions. Create interview questions based on actual job duties, with more questions for the important duties. Recall that *situational questions* pose a hypothetical job situation, such as "What would you do if the machine suddenly began heating up?" *Job knowledge questions* assess knowledge essential to job performance (such as "What is HTML?"). *Willingness questions* gauge the applicant's willingness and motivation to meet the job's requirements—to do repetitive physical work or to travel, for instance. *Behavioral questions,* of course, ask candidates how they've handled similar situations.

The people who create the questions usually write them in terms of critical incidents. For example, for a supervisory candidate, the interviewer might ask this situational question:

> Your spouse and two teenage children are sick in bed with colds. There are no relatives or friends available to look in on them. Your shift starts in 3 hours. What would you do in this situation?

Step 4: Create benchmark answers. Next, *for each question,* develop ideal (benchmark) answers for good (a 5 rating), marginal (a 3 rating), and poor (a 1 rating). For example, consider the preceding situational question, where the spouse and children are sick. Three benchmark answers (from low to high) for the example question might be, "I'd stay home—my spouse and family come first" (1); "I'd phone my supervisor and explain my situation" (3); and "Since they only have colds, I'd come to work" (5).

Step 5: Appoint the interview panel and conduct interviews. Employers generally conduct structured situational interviews using a panel, rather than one-on-one. The panel usually consists of three to six members, preferably the same ones who wrote the questions and answers. It may also include the job's supervisor and/or incumbent, and a human resources representative. The same panel interviews all candidates for the job.[71]

The panel members generally review the job description, questions, and benchmark answers before the interview. One panel member introduces the applicant, and asks all questions of all applicants in this and succeeding candidates' interviews (to ensure consistency). However, all panel members record and rate the applicant's answers on the rating scale sheet. They do this by indicating where the candidate's answer to each question falls relative to the ideal poor, marginal, or good answers. At the end of the interview, someone answers any questions the applicant has.[72]

Web-based programs help interviewers design and organize behaviorally based selection interviews. For example, SelectPro (www.selectpro.net) enables interviewers to create behavior-based selection interviews, custom interview guides, and automated online interviews.

4 Explain and illustrate each guideline for being a more effective interviewer.

How to Conduct an Effective Interview

You may not have the time or inclination to create a full-blown, structured situational interview. However, there is still a lot you can do to make your interviews more systematic and effective.

Step 1: First, make sure you know the job. Do not start the interview unless you understand the job and what human skills you're looking for. Study the job description and understand what traits and skills the ideal employee in that job should have.

5 Give several examples of situational questions, behavioral questions, and background questions that provide structure.

Step 2: Structure the interview. *Any* structuring is usually better than none. If pressed for time, you can do several things to ask more consistent and job-relevant questions, without developing a full-blown structured interview.[73] Any of these will help. They include:[74]

- Base questions on *actual job duties.* This will minimize irrelevant questions.
- Use *job knowledge, situational, or behavioral questions,* and know enough about the job to be able to evaluate the interviewee's answers. Questions that simply ask for opinions and attitudes, goals and aspirations, and self-descriptions and self-evaluations allow candidates to present themselves in an overly favorable manner or avoid revealing weaknesses.[75] Figure 7-2 illustrates structured interview questions.
- *Use the same questions* with all candidates. When it comes to asking questions, the prescription is "the more standardized, the better." Using the same questions with all candidates improves reliability. It also reduces bias because of the obvious fairness of giving all the candidates the exact same opportunity.
- Use *descriptive rating scales* (excellent, fair, poor) to rate answers. For each question, if possible, have several ideal answers and a score for each. Then you can rate each candidate's answers against this scale.
- If possible, use a *standardized interview form.* Interviews based on structured guides like the one in Figure 7A-1 (pages 254–256 usually result in better interviews.[76] At the very least, list your questions before the interview.

Step 3: Get organized. The interview should take place in a private room where telephone calls are not accepted and you can minimize interruptions. Prior to the interview, review the candidate's application and résumé, and note any areas that are vague or that may indicate strengths or weaknesses.

FIGURE 7-2 Examples of Questions That Provide Interview Structure

Source: Michael Campion, David Palmer, and James Campion, "A Review of Structure in the Selection Interview," *Personnel Psychology,* 1997, p. 668. Reprinted by permission of Wiley–Blackwell.

Situational Questions

1. Suppose a coworker was not following standard work procedures. The coworker was more experienced than you and claimed the new procedure was better. Would you use the new procedure?
2. Suppose you were giving a sales presentation and a difficult technical question arose that you could not answer. What would you do?

Behavioral (Past Behavior) Questions

3. Based on your past work experience, what is the most significant action you have ever taken to help a coworker?
4. Can you provide an example of a specific instance where you developed a sales presentation that was highly effective?

Background Questions

5. What work experiences, training, or other qualifications do you have for working in a teamwork environment?
6. What experience have you had with direct point-of-purchase sales?

Job Knowledge Questions

7. What steps would you follow to conduct a brainstorming session with a group of employees on safety?
8. What factors should you consider when developing a television advertising campaign?

Note: These questions provide structure, insofar as they are job-related and the employer can be consistent in asking them of all candidates.

In one study, about 39% of the 191 respondents said interviewers were unprepared or unfocused.[77]

Step 4: Establish rapport. The main reason for the interview is to find out about the applicant. To do this, start by putting the person at ease. Greet the candidate and start the interview by asking a noncontroversial question, perhaps about the weather or the traffic conditions that day. As a rule, all applicants—even unsolicited drop-ins—should receive friendly, courteous treatment, not only on humanitarian grounds but also because your reputation is on the line.

Step 5: Ask questions. Try to follow the situational, behavioral, and job knowledge questions you wrote out ahead of time. You'll find a sampling of other technical questions (such as "What did you most enjoy about your last job?") in Figure 7-3. In actually asking the questions, sensible guidelines include the following.

Don't ask questions that the candidate can just answer with a yes or no.
Don't put words in the applicant's mouth or telegraph the desired answer.
Don't interrogate the applicant as if the person is on trial, and don't be patronizing, sarcastic, or inattentive.
Don't monopolize the interview by rambling, nor let the applicant dominate the interview.
Do ask open-ended questions.
Do listen to the candidate to encourage him or her to express thoughts fully.
Do draw out the applicant's opinions and feelings by repeating the person's last comment as a question (e.g., "You didn't like your last job?").
Do ask for examples.[78] For instance, if the candidate lists a specific strength, follow up with, "What are specific examples of that?"
Do ask, "If I were to arrange for an interview with your boss, what's your best guess as to what he or she would say as your strengths, weaker points, and overall performance?"[79]

FIGURE 7-3 Suggested Supplementary Questions for Interviewing Applicants

Source: Reprinted from http://hr.blr.com with permission of the publisher Business and Legal Resources, Inc. 141 Mill Rock Road East, Old Saybrook, CT © 2004. BLR© (Business and Legal Resources, Inc.).

1. How did you choose this line of work?
2. What did you enjoy most about your last job?
3. What did you like least about your last job?
4. What has been your greatest frustration or disappointment on your present job? Why?
5. What are some of the pluses and minuses of your last job?
6. What were the circumstances surrounding your leaving your last job?
7. Did you give notice?
8. Why should we be hiring you?
9. What do you expect from this employer?
10. What are three things you will not do in your next job?
11. What would your last supervisor say your three weaknesses are?
12. What are your major strengths?
13. How can your supervisor best help you obtain your goals?
14. How did your supervisor rate your job performance?
15. In what ways would you change your last supervisor?
16. What are your career goals during the next 1–3 years? 5–10 years?
17. How will working for this company help you reach those goals?
18. What did you do the last time you received instructions with which you disagreed?
19. What are some of the things about which you and your supervisor disagreed? What did you do?
20. Which do you prefer, working alone or working with groups?
21. What motivated you to do better at your last job?
22. Do you consider your progress on that job representative of your ability? Why?
23. Do you have any questions about the duties of the job for which you have applied?
24. Can you perform the essential functions of the job for which you have applied?

Source: Courtesy of Dorling Kindersley Media Library/© Dorling Kindersley.

Go into the interview with an accurate picture of the traits of an ideal candidate, know what you're going to ask, and be prepared to keep an open mind about the candidate.

Step 6: Take brief, unobtrusive notes during the interview. Doing so may help avoid making a snap decision based on inadequate information early in the interview, and may also help jog your memory once the interview is complete. Take notes, but not copious ones, instead noting just the key points of what the interviewee says.[80]

Step 7: Close the interview. Leave time to answer any questions the candidate may have and, if appropriate, to advocate your firm to the candidate.

Try to end the interview on a positive note. Tell the applicant whether there is any interest and, if so, what the next step will be. Make rejections diplomatically—for instance, "Although your background is impressive, there are other candidates whose experience is closer to our requirements." If the applicant is still under consideration but you can't reach a decision now, say so. If your policy is to inform candidates of their status in writing, do so within a few days of the interview. Remember, as one recruiter says, "An interview experience should leave a lasting, positive impression of the company, whether the candidate receives and accepts an offer or not."[81]

In rejecting a candidate, one perennial question is, should you provide an explanation or not? In one study, rejected candidates who received an explanation detailing why the employer rejected them felt that the rejection process was fairer. These people were also more likely to give the employer a better recommendation, and to apply again for jobs with the firm. Unfortunately, providing detailed explanations may not be practical. As the researchers put it,

> "We were unsuccessful in a number of attempts to secure a site for our applied study. Of three organizations that expressed interest in our research, all eventually declined to participate in the study because they were afraid that any additional information in the rejection letters might increase legal problems. They were reluctant to give rejected applicants information that can be used to dispute the decision."[82]

Step 8: Review the interview. After the candidate leaves, review your interview notes, score the interview guide answers (if you used one), and review the interview while it's fresh.

6 List the steps in a streamlined interview process.

Using a Streamlined Interview Process[83]

Managers are busy people, and you may not always have the time or inclination to follow all the preceding steps. If so, here, from one employment expert, is a streamlined approach that may come in handy.

1. **Prepare for the Interview** Prepare for the interview by thinking through the skills and traits the job requires. Focus on four basic required factors—knowledge and experience, motivation, intellectual capacity, and personality. To do this, ask yourself the following questions:
   - **Knowledge and experience:** What must the candidate know to perform the job? What experience absolutely is necessary to perform the job?
   - **Motivation:** What should the person like doing to enjoy this job? Is there anything the person should not dislike? Are there any essential goals or aspirations the person should have? Are there any unusual energy demands on the job?
   - **Intellectual capacity:** Are there any specific intellectual aptitudes required (mathematical, mechanical, and so on)? How complex are the problems the person must solve? What must a person be able to demonstrate he or she can do intellectually? How should the person solve problems (cautiously, deductively, and so on)?
   - **Personality factor:** What are the critical personality qualities needed for success on the job (ability to withstand boredom, decisiveness, stability, and so

on)? How must the job incumbent handle stress, pressure, and criticism? What kind of interpersonal behavior is required in the job up the line, at peer level, down the line, and outside the firm with customers?

2. **Formulate Questions to Ask in the Interview** Next, formulate a combination of situational and behavioral questions, plus open-ended questions like those in Figure 7-3, to probe the candidate's suitability for the job. For example:
   - **Intellectual factor:** Here, assess such things as complexity of tasks the person has performed, grades in school, test results (including scholastic aptitude tests, and so on), and how the person organizes his or her thoughts and communicates.
   - **Motivation factor:** Probe such areas as the person's likes and dislikes (for each thing done, what he or she liked or disliked about it); aspirations (including the validity of each goal in terms of the person's reasoning about why he or she chose it); and energy level, perhaps by asking what he or she does on, say, a "typical Tuesday."
   - **Personality factor:** Here, probe by looking for self-defeating behaviors (aggressiveness, compulsive fidgeting, and so on) and by exploring the person's past interpersonal relationships. Ask questions about the person's past interactions (working in a group at school, working with fraternity brothers or sorority sisters, leading the work team on the last job, and so on). Also, try to judge the person's behavior in the interview itself—is the candidate personable? Shy? Outgoing?
   - **Knowledge and experience factor:** Here, probe with situational questions such as "How would you organize such a sales effort?" "How would you design that kind of Web site?"
3. **Conduct the Interview**
   - **Have a plan.** Devise and use a chronological plan to guide the interview. According to interviewing expert John Drake, significant areas to cover include the candidate's:
     - College experiences
     - Work experiences—summer, part-time
     - Work experience—full-time (one by one)
     - Goals and ambitions
     - Reactions to the job you are interviewing for
     - Self-assessments (by the candidate of his or her strengths and weaknesses)
     - Military experiences
     - Present outside activities[84]
   - **Follow your plan.** Perhaps start with an open-ended question for each topic, such as, "Could you tell me about what you did when you were in high school?" Keep in mind that you are trying to elicit information about four main traits—intelligence, motivation, personality, and knowledge and experience. You can then accumulate the information in each of these four areas as the person answers. Follow up on particular areas that you want to pursue by asking questions like, "Could you elaborate on that, please?"
4. **Match the Candidate to the Job** Finally, draw conclusions about the person's relevant intellectual capacity, knowledge and experience, motivation, and personality. How appropriate is this person for the job? Compare your conclusions to both the job description and the list of behavioral requirements you developed when preparing for the interview. This should provide a rational basis for matching the candidate to the job.

You might use an interview evaluation form to compile your impressions (for instance, see Figure 7-4).

FIGURE 7-4 Interview Evaluation Form

Source: Reprinted from http://hr.blr.com with permission of the publisher Business and Legal Resources Inc. 141 Mill Rock Road East, Old Saybrook, CT © 2004. BLR© (Business and Legal Resources, Inc.).

Name of candidate:
Date interviewed:
Position:

Completed by:
Date:

Instructions: Circle one number for each criterion, then add them together for a total.

KNOWLEDGE OF SPECIFIC JOB AND JOB-RELATED TOPICS

0. No knowledge evident.
1. Less than we would prefer.
2. Meets requirements for hiring.
3. Exceeds our expectations of average candidates.
4. Thoroughly versed in job and very strong in associated areas.

EXPERIENCE

0. None for this job; no related experience either.
1. Would prefer more for this job. Adequate for job applied for.
2. More than sufficient for job.
3. Totally experienced in job.
4. Strong experience in all related areas.

COMMUNICATION

0. Could not communicate. Will be severely impaired in most jobs.
1. Some difficulties. Will detract from job performance.
2. Sufficient for adequate job performance.
3. More than sufficient for job.
4. Outstanding ability to communicate.

INTEREST IN POSITION AND ORGANIZATION

0. Showed no interest.
1. Some lack of interest.
2. Appeared genuinely interested.
3. Very interested. Seems to prefer type of work applied for.
4. Totally absorbed with job content. Conveys feeling only this job will do.

OVERALL MOTIVATION TO SUCCEED

0. None exhibited.
1. Showed little interest in advancement.
2. Average interest in advancement.
3. Highly motivated. Strong desire to advance.
4. Extremely motivated. Very strong desire to succeed and advance.

POISE AND CONFIDENCE

0. Extremely distracted and confused. Displayed uneven temper.
1. Sufficient display of confusion or loss of temper to interfere with job performance.
2. Sufficient poise and confidence to perform job.
3. No loss of poise during interview. Confidence in ability to handle pressure.
4. Displayed impressive poise under stress. Appears unusually confident and secure.

COMPREHENSION

0. Did not understand many points and concepts.
1. Missed some ideas or concepts.
2. Understood most new ideas and skills discussed.
3. Grasped all new points and concepts quickly.
4. Extremely sharp. Understood subtle points and underlying motives.

_____ **TOTAL POINTS**

ADDITIONAL REMARKS:

7 List guidelines for interviewees.

Guidelines for Interviewees

Before you get into a position where you have to interview others, you will probably have to navigate some interviews yourself. It's therefore useful to apply some of what we said in this chapter to navigating your own interviews.

Interviewers may well assess your skills and technical expertise through tests and a study of your educational and work history. They will tend to use the interview to try to determine what you are like as a person. In other words, information regarding how you get along with other people and your desire to work is often most important in the interview. They will look first at how you behave. Specifically, they will note whether you respond concisely, cooperate fully in answering questions, state personal opinions when relevant, and keep to the subject at hand; these are very important elements in influencing the interviewer's decision.

There are seven things to do to get an extra edge in the interview.

1. **Preparation is essential.** Before the interview, learn all you can about the employer, the job, and the people doing the recruiting. On the Web or at the library, look through business periodicals to find out what is happening in the employer's field. Who is the competition? How are they doing? Try to unearth the employer's problems. Be ready to explain why you think you would be able to solve such problems, citing some of your *specific accomplishments* to make your case.
2. **Uncover the interviewer's real needs.** Spend as little time as possible answering your interviewer's first questions and as much time as possible getting him or her to describe his or her needs. Determine what the person is expecting to accomplish, and the type of person he or she feels is needed. Use open-ended questions here such as, "Could you tell me more about that?"
3. **Relate yourself to the interviewer's needs.** Once you know the type of person your interviewer is looking for and the sorts of problems he or she wants solved, you are in a good position to describe your own accomplishments *in terms of the interviewer's needs.* Start by saying something like, "One of the problem areas you've said is important to you is similar to a problem I once faced." Then state the problem, describe your solution, and reveal the results.
4. **Think before answering.** Answering a question should be a three-step process: Pause—Think—Speak. *Pause* to make sure you understand what the interviewer is driving at, *think* about how to structure your answer, and then *speak.* In your answer, try to emphasize how hiring you will help the interviewer solve his or her problem.
5. **Remember that appearance and enthusiasm are important.** Appropriate clothing, good grooming, a firm handshake, and energy are important. Remember that your *nonverbal behavior* may broadcast more about you than the verbal content of what you say. Maintaining eye contact is very important. In addition, speak with enthusiasm, nod agreement, and remember to take a moment to frame your answer (pause, think, speak) so that you sound articulate and fluent.
6. **Make a good first impression.** Remember, studies show that in most cases interviewers make up their minds about the applicant during the early minutes of the interview. A good first impression may turn to bad during the interview, but it is unlikely. Bad first impressions are almost impossible to overcome. Experts suggest paying attention to the following key interviewing considerations:
    - Appropriate clothing
    - Good grooming
    - A firm handshake
    - The appearance of controlled energy
    - Pertinent humor and readiness to smile
    - A genuine interest in the employer's operation and alert attention when the interviewer speaks
    - Pride in past performance
    - An understanding of the employer's needs and a desire to serve them
    - The display of sound ideas
7. **Ask questions.** Sample questions you can ask are presented in Figure 7-5.

FIGURE 7-5 Interview Questions to Ask

Source: Job Search: The Complete Manual for Job Seekers by Rust, H. Lee. Copyright 1990 by AMACOM Books. Reproduced with the permission of AMACOM Books in the format print/electronic usage via Copyright Clearance Center.

1. What is the first problem that needs the attention of the person you hire?
2. What other problems need attention now?
3. What has been done about any of these to date?
4. How has this job been performed in the past?
5. Why is it now vacant?
6. Do you have a written job description for this position?
7. What are its major responsibilities?
8. What authority would I have? How would you define its scope?
9. What are the company's 5-year sales and profit projections?
10. What needs to be done to reach these projections?
11. What are the company's major strengths and weaknesses?
12. What are its strengths and weaknesses in production?
13. What are its strengths and weaknesses in its products or its competitive position?
14. Whom do you identify as your major competitors?
15. What are their strengths and weaknesses?
16. How do you view the future for your industry?
17. Do you have any plans for new products or acquisitions?
18. Might this company be sold or acquired?
19. What is the company's current financial strength?
20. What can you tell me about the individual to whom I would report?
21. What can you tell me about other persons in key positions?
22. What can you tell me about the subordinates I would have?
23. How would you define your management philosophy?
24. Are employees afforded an opportunity for continuing education?
25. What are you looking for in the person who will fill this job?

REVIEW

CHAPTER SECTION SUMMARIES

1. A selection interview is a selection procedure designed to predict future job performance based on applicants' oral responses to oral inquiries, and we discussed several **basic types of interviews**. There are structured versus unstructured interviews. We also distinguished between interviews based on the types of questions (such as situational versus behavioral) and on how you administer the interview, such as one-on-one, sequentially, or even via computer, video, or telephone. However you decide to conduct the interview, or structure the interview, be careful what sorts of traits you try to assess, and beware of committing the sorts of interviewing errors we touch on next.
2. One reason selection interviews are often less useful than they should be is that managers make predictable **errors that undermine an interview's usefulness**. They jump to conclusions or make snap judgments based on preliminary information, they don't clarify what the job really requires, they succumb to candidate-order error and pressure to hire, and they let a variety of nonverbal behaviors and personal characteristics undermine the validity of the interview.
3. There are two basic ways to **avoid interview errors**. One is to keep them in mind, and the second is to use structured interviews.
   - The structured situational interview is a series of job-related questions with predetermined answers that interviewers ask of all applicants for the job. Steps in creating a structured situational interview include analyzing the job, rating the job's main duties, creating interview questions, creating benchmark enters, and appointing the interview panel and conducting interviews.
4. Steps in **conducting an effective interview** include making sure you know the job, structuring the interview, getting organized, asking questions, taking brief unobtrusive notes during the interview, and reviewing the interview.
   - We presented a streamlined interview process. This involves preparing for the interview by formulating knowledge, motivation, intellectual capacity, and personality factor questions and identifying specific factors to probe in the interview (such as the complexity of the jobs the person performed); conducting the interview using a plan (from college to current job); and then matching the candidate to the job.
   - From the point of view of an interviewee, remember that preparation is essential. You should uncover the interviewer's real needs, relate yourself to those needs, think before answering, remember that appearance and enthusiasm are important, and make a good first impression.

DISCUSSION QUESTIONS

1. Explain and illustrate the basic ways in which you can classify selection interviews.
2. Briefly describe each of the following types of interviews: unstructured panel interviews, structured sequential interviews, job-related structured interviews.
3. For what sorts of jobs do you think computerized interviews are most appropriate? Why?
4. Why do you think situational interviews yield a higher mean validity than do job-related or behavioral interviews, which in turn yield a higher mean validity than do psychological interviews?
5. Similarly, how would you explain the fact that structured interviews, regardless of content, are more valid than unstructured interviews for predicting job performance?
6. Briefly discuss and give examples of at least five common interviewing mistakes. What recommendations would you give for avoiding these interviewing mistakes?
7. Briefly discuss what an interviewer can do to improve his or her performance.

INDIVIDUAL AND GROUP ACTIVITIES

1. Prepare and give a short presentation titled "How to Be Effective as an Employment Interviewer."
2. Use the Internet to find employers who now do preliminary selection interviews via the Web. Print out and bring examples to class. Do you think these interviews are useful? Why or why not? How would you improve them?
3. In groups, discuss and compile examples of "the worst interview I ever had." What was it about these interviews that made them so bad? If time permits, discuss as a class.
4. In groups, prepare an interview (including a sequence of at least 20 questions) you'll use to interview candidates for the job of teaching a course in human resources management. Each group should present their interview questions in class.
5. Some firms swear by unorthodox interview methods. For example, Tech Planet, of Menlo Park, California, uses weekly lunches and "wacky follow-up sessions" as substitutes for first-round job interviews. During the informal meals, candidates are expected to mingle, and the Tech Planet employees they meet at the luncheons then review them. One Tech Planet employee asks candidates to ride a unicycle in her office to see if "they'll bond with the corporate culture or not." Toward the end of the screening process, the surviving group of interviewees has to solve brainteasers, and then openly evaluate their fellow candidates' strengths and weaknesses. What do you think of a screening process like this? Specifically, what do you think are its pros and cons? Would you recommend a procedure like this? If so, what changes, if any, would you recommend?[85]
6. Several years ago, Lockheed Martin Corp. sued the Boeing Corp. in Orlando, Florida, accusing it of using Lockheed's trade secrets to help win a multibillion-dollar government contract. Among other things, Lockheed Martin claimed that Boeing had obtained those trade secrets from a former Lockheed Martin employee who switched to Boeing.[86] But in describing methods companies use to commit corporate espionage, one writer says that hiring away the competitor's employees or hiring people to through go its dumpster are just the most obvious methods companies use to commit corporate espionage. As he says, "one of the more unusual scams—sometimes referred to as 'help wanted'—uses a person posing as a corporate headhunter who approaches an employee of the target company with a potentially lucrative job offer. During the interview, the employee is quizzed about his responsibilities, accomplishments and current projects. The goal is to extract important details without the employee realizing there is no job."[87]

   Assume that you are the owner of a small high-tech company that is worried about the possibility that one or more of your employees may be approached by one of these sinister "headhunters." What would you do (in terms of employee training, or a letter from you, for instance) to try to minimize the chance that one of your employees will fall into that kind of a trap? Also, compile a list of 10 questions that you think such a corporate spy might ask one of your employees.
7. The HRCI "Test Specifications" appendix at the end of this book (pages 699–706) lists the knowledge someone studying for the HRCI certification exam needs to have in each area of human resource management (such as in Strategic Management, Workforce Planning, and Human Resource Development). In groups of four to five students, do four things: (1) Review that appendix now. (2) Identify the material in this chapter that relates to the required knowledge the appendix lists. (3) Write four multiple-choice exam questions on this material that you believe would be suitable for inclusion in the HRCI exam. And (4) if time permits, have someone from your team post your team's questions in front of the class, so the students in other teams can take each others' exam questions.

EXPERIENTIAL EXERCISE

The Most Important Person You'll Ever Hire

Purpose: The purpose of this exercise is to give you practice using some of the interview techniques you learned from this chapter.

Required Understanding: You should be familiar with the information presented in this chapter, and read this: For parents, children are precious. It's therefore interesting that parents who hire "nannies" to take care of their children usually do little more than ask several interview questions and conduct what is often, at best, a perfunctory reference check. Given the often questionable validity of interviews, and the (often) relative inexperience of the father or mother doing the interviewing, it's not surprising that many of these arrangements end in disappointment. You know from this chapter that it is difficult to conduct a valid interview unless you know exactly what you're looking for and, preferably, structure the interview. Most parents simply aren't trained to do this.

How to Set Up the Exercise/Instructions:

1. Set up groups of five or six students. Two students will be the interviewees, while the other students in the group will serve as panel interviewers. The interviewees will develop an interviewer assessment form, and the panel interviewers will develop a structured situational interview for a "nanny."
2. Instructions for the interviewees: The interviewees should leave the room for about 20 minutes. While out of the room, the interviewees should develop an "interviewer assessment form" based on the information presented in this chapter regarding factors that can undermine the usefulness of an interview. During the panel interview, the interviewees should assess the interviewers using the interviewer assessment form. After the panel interviewers have conducted the interview, the interviewees should leave the room to discuss their notes. Did the interviewers exhibit any of the factors that can undermine the usefulness of an interview? If so, which ones? What suggestions would you (the interviewees) make to the interviewers on how to improve the usefulness of the interview?
3. Instructions for the interviewers: While the interviewees are out of the room, the panel interviewers will have 20 minutes to develop a short structured situational interview form for a "nanny." The panel interview team will interview two candidates for the position. During the panel interview, each interview should be taking notes on a copy of the structured situational interview form. After the panel interview, the panel interviewers should discuss their notes. What were your first impressions of each interviewee? Were your impressions similar? Which candidate would you all select for the position and why?

APPLICATION CASE

The Out-of-Control Interview

Maria Fernandez is a bright, popular, and well-informed mechanical engineer who graduated with an engineering degree from State University in June 2009. During the spring preceding her graduation, she went out on many job interviews, most of which she thought were conducted courteously and were reasonably useful in giving both her and the prospective employer a good impression of where each of them stood on matters of importance to both of them. It was, therefore, with great anticipation that she looked forward to an interview with the one firm in which she most wanted to work: Apex Environmental. She had always had a strong interest in cleaning up the environment and firmly believed that the best use of her training and skills lay in working for a firm like Apex, where she thought she could have a successful career while making the world a better place.

The interview, however, was a disaster. Maria walked into a room where five men—the president of the company, two vice presidents, the marketing director, and another engineer—began throwing questions at her that she felt were aimed primarily at tripping her up rather than finding out what she could offer through her engineering skills. The questions ranged from being unnecessarily discourteous ("Why would you take a job as a waitress in college if you're such an intelligent person?") to being irrelevant and sexist ("Are you planning on settling down and starting a family anytime soon?"). Then, after the interview, she met with two of the gentlemen individually (including the president), and the discussions focused almost exclusively on her technical expertise. She thought that these later discussions went fairly well. However, given the apparent aimlessness and even mean-spiritedness of the panel interview, she was astonished when several days later she got a job offer from the firm.

The offer forced her to consider several matters. From her point of view, the job itself was perfect. She liked what she would be doing, the industry, and the firm's location. And in fact, the president had been quite courteous in subsequent discussions, as had been the other members of the management team. She was left wondering whether the panel interview had been intentionally tense to see how she'd stand up under pressure, and, if so, why they would do such a thing.

Questions

1. How would you explain the nature of the panel interview Maria had to endure? Specifically, do you think it reflected a well-thought-out interviewing strategy on the part of the firm or carelessness on the part of the firm's management? If it were carelessness, what would you do to improve the interview process at Apex Environmental?

2. Would you take the job offer if you were Maria? If you're not sure, what additional information would help you make your decision?
3. The job of applications engineer for which Maria was applying requires (a) excellent technical skills with respect to mechanical engineering, (b) a commitment to working in the area of pollution control, (c) the ability to deal well and confidently with customers who have engineering problems, (d) a willingness to travel worldwide, and (e) a very intelligent and well-balanced personality. List 10 questions you would ask when interviewing applicants for the job.

CONTINUING CASE

Carter Cleaning Company

The Better Interview

Like virtually all the other HR-related activities at Carter Cleaning Centers, the company currently has no organized approach to interviewing job candidates. Store managers, who do almost all the hiring, have a few of their own favorite questions that they ask. But in the absence of any guidance from top management, they all admit their interview performance leaves something to be desired. Similarly, Jack Carter himself is admittedly most comfortable dealing with what he calls the "nuts and bolts" machinery aspect of his business and has never felt particularly comfortable having to interview management or other job applicants. Jennifer is sure that this lack of formal interviewing practices, procedures, and training account for some of the employee turnover and theft problems. Therefore, she wants to do something to improve her company's batting average in this important area. Here are her questions:

Questions

1. In general, what can Jennifer do to improve her employee interviewing practices? Should she develop interview forms that list questions for management and nonmanagement jobs? If so, how should these look and what questions should be included? Should she initiate a computer-based interview approach? If so, why and how?
2. Should she implement an interview training program for her managers, and if so, specifically what should be the content of such a training program? In other words, if she did decide to start training her management people to be better interviewers, what should she tell them and how should she tell it to them?

TRANSLATING STRATEGY INTO HR POLICIES & PRACTICES CASE

The Hotel Paris Case

The New Interviewing Program

The Hotel Paris's competitive strategy is "To use superior guest service to differentiate the Hotel Paris properties, and to thereby increase the length of stay and return rate of guests, and thus boost revenues and profitability." HR manager Lisa Cruz must now formulate functional policies and activities that support this competitive strategy, by eliciting the required employee behaviors and competencies.

One thing that concerned Lisa Cruz was the fact that the Hotel Paris's hotel managers varied widely in their interviewing and hiring skills. Some were quite effective; most were not. Furthermore, the company did not have a formal employment interview training program, nor, for that matter, did it have standardized interview packages that hotel managers around the world could use.

As an experienced HR professional, Lisa knew that the company's new testing program would go only so far. She knew that, at best, employment tests explained perhaps 30% of employee performance. It was essential that she and her team design a package of interviews that her hotel managers could use to assess—on an interactive and personal basis—candidates for various positions. It was only in that way that the hotel could hire the sorts of employees whose competencies and behaviors would translate into the kinds of outcomes—such as improved guest services—that the hotel required to achieve its strategic goals.

Lisa receives budgetary approval to design a new employee interview system. She and her team start by reviewing the job descriptions and job specifications for the positions of front-desk clerk, assistant manager, security guard, valet/door person, and housekeeper. Focusing on developing structured interviews for each position, the team sets about devising interview questions. For example, for the front-desk clerk and assistant manager, they formulate several *behavioral questions*, including, "Tell me about a time when you had to deal with an irate person, and what you did." And, "Tell me about a time when you had to deal with several conflicting demands at once, such as having to study for several final exams at the same time, while working. How did you handle the situation?" They also developed a number of *situational questions*, including, "Suppose you have a very pushy incoming guest who insists on being checked in at once, while at the same time you're trying to process the checkout for another guest who must be at the airport in 10 minutes. How would you handle the situation?"

Questions

1. For the job of security guard or valet, develop five situational, five behavioral, and five job knowledge questions, with descriptive good/average/poor answers.
2. Combine your questions into a complete interview that you would give to someone who must interview candidates for these jobs.

KEY TERMS

unstructured (or nondirective) interview, *p. 231*

structured (or directive) interview, *p. 231*

situational interview, *p. 233*

behavioral interview, *p. 233*

job-related interview, *p. 233*

stress interview, *p. 233*

unstructured sequential interview, *p. 235*

structured sequential interview, *p. 235*

panel interview, *p. 235*

mass interview, *p. 235*

candidate-order (or contrast) error, *p. 239*

structured situational interview, *p. 241*

Appendix for Chapter 7

Interview Guide

FIGURE 7A-1 Structured Interview Guide

Source: Copyright 1992. The Dartnell Corporation, Chicago, IL. Adapted with permission.

APPLICANT INTERVIEW GUIDE

To the interviewer: This Applicant Interview Guide is intended to assist in employee selection and placement. If it is used for all applicants for a position, it will help you to compare them, and it will provide more objective information than you will obtain from unstructured interviews.

Because this is a general guide, all of the items may not apply in every instance. Skip those that are not applicable and add questions appropriate to the specific position. Space for additional questions will be found at the end of the form.

Federal law prohibits discrimination in employment on the basis of sex, race, color, national origin, religion, disability, and in most instances, age. The laws of most states also ban some or all of the above types of discrimination in employment as well as discrimination based on marital status or ancestry. Interviewers should take care to avoid any questions that suggest that an employment decision will be made on the basis of any such factors.

Job Interest

Name ______________________ Position applied for ______________

What do you think the job (position) involves? ______________________

Why do you want the job (position)? ______________________

Why are you qualified for it? ______________________

What would your salary requirements be? ______________________

What do you know about our company? ______________________

Why do you want to work for us? ______________________

Current Work Status

Are you now employed? _____ Yes _____ No. If not, how long have you been unemployed? __________

Why are you unemployed? ______________________

If you are working, why are you applying for this position? ______________________

When would you be available to start work with us? ______________________

Work Experience

(Start with the applicant's current or last position and work back. All periods of time should be accounted for. Go back at least 12 years, depending upon the applicant's age. Military service should be treated as a job.)

Current or last employer ______________________ Address ______________________

Dates of employment: from ______________ to ______________

Current or last job title ______________________

What are (were) your duties? ______________________

Have you held the same job throughout your employment with that company? _____ Yes _____ No. If not, describe the various jobs you have had with that employer, how long you held each of them, and the main duties of each. ______________________

What was your starting salary? ________ What are you earning now? ________ Comments ________

____

Name of your last or current supervisor ______________________

What did you like most about that job? ______________________

What did you like least about it? ______________________

Why are you thinking of leaving? ______________________

Why are you leaving right now? ______________________

Interviewer's comments or observations ______________________

____

(continued)

FIGURE 7A-1 *(continued)*

What did you do before you took your last job? ____________________

Where were you employed? ____________________

Location ____________________ Job title ____________________

Duties ____________________

Did you hold the same job throughout your employment with that company? ______ Yes ______ No. If not, describe the jobs you held, when you held them, and the duties of each. ____________________

____

What was your starting salary? ______________ What was your final salary? ______________

Name of your last supervisor ____________________

May we contact that company? ______ Yes ______ No

What did you like most about that job? ____________________

What did you like least about that job? ____________________

Why did you leave that job? ____________________

Would you consider working there again? ____________________

Interviewer: If there is any gap between the various periods of employment, the applicant should be asked about them. ____________________

Interviewer's comments or observations ____________________

____

What did you do prior to the job with that company? ____________________

What other jobs or experience have you had? Describe them briefly and explain the general duties of each.

____

Have you been unemployed at any time in the last five years? ____ Yes ____ No. What efforts did you make to find work? ____________________

What other experience or training do you have that would help qualify you for the job applied for? Explain how and where you obtained this experience or training. ____________________

____

Educational Background

What education or training do you have that would help you in the job for which you have applied? ______

____

Describe any formal education you have had. (Interviewer may substitute technical training, if relevant.) ____

____

Off-Job Activities

What do you do in your off-hours? ___ Part-time job ___ Athletics ___ Spectator sports ___ Clubs ___ Other

Please explain. ____________________

Interviewer's Specific Questions

Interviewer: Add any questions to the particular job for which you are interviewing, leaving space for brief answers.

(Be careful to avoid questions that may be viewed as discriminatory.)

____

____

____

Personal

Would you be willing to relocate? _____ Yes _____ No

Are you willing to travel? _____ Yes _____ No

(continued)

FIGURE 7A-1 *(continued)*

What is the maximum amount of time you would consider traveling? ______________________

____

Are you able to work overtime? ______________________

What about working on weekends? ______________________

Self-Assessment

What do you feel are your strong points? ______________________

____

What do you feel are your weak points? ______________________

____

Interviewer: Compare the applicant's responses with the information furnished on the application for employment.

Clear up any discrepancies. ______________________

____

Before the applicant leaves, the interviewer should provide basic information about the organization and the job opening, if this has not already been done. The applicant should be given information on the work location, work hours, the wage or salary, type of remuneration (salary or salary plus bonus, etc.), and other factors that may affect the applicant's interest in the job.

Interviewer's Impressions

Rate each characteristic from 1 to 4, with 1 being the highest rating and 4 being the lowest.

Personal Characteristics	1	2	3	4	Comments
Personal appearance					
Poise, manner					
Speech					
Cooperation with interviewer					
Job-Related Characteristics					
Experience for this job					
Knowledge of job					
Interpersonal relationships					
Effectiveness					

Overall Rating for Job

1	2	3	4	5
___ Superior	___ Above Average	___ Average	___ Marginal	___ Unsatisfactory
	(well qualified)	(qualified)	(barely qualified)	

Comments or remarks ______________________

____

____

Interviewer ____________ Date ____________

Part II Video Cases Appendix

Video 3: The HR Manager's Job, Job Analysis, Personnel Planning, and Recruitment

VIDEO TITLE: RECRUITMENT AND PLACEMENT

In this video, Paul, the vice president of human resources at BMG, faces the possibility that the wrong person was hired for a job. The senior director of music placement accuses Paul of sending her candidates that do not meet the criteria set by her department. A discussion takes place between the two, detailing information about the role of HR in the hiring process and the recruitment process, in general. The video also delves into some of the technological aspects of recruiting.

As Paul explains, "When we get a recruitment request, we ask for job specifications, we interview several candidates, and we provide the hiring department with a short list of candidates." So, as Paul says, if the candidate turns out to be inadequate, it's not HR's problem: It's "your fault, since your supervisors picked him." She makes the point that "you only recruited in *Rolling Stone* magazine." Paul agrees, but points out that they did get 60 candidates. Furthermore, recruiting more extensively would involve considerably more cost. Again, though, one of the main issues revolves around whether the job specifications (criteria) are correct and whether there was an agreement on those job specs between HR and the hiring managers.

Discussion Questions

1. Do you agree or disagree with BMG's HR vice president when she tells the hiring manager that "your department picked him, so if the candidate did not work out, it's your fault, not ours." What, if anything, does an approach like that say about the extent to which HR in this company views itself is a strategic partner?
2. If you had been in HR's shoes in this company, what, if anything, would you have done differently to make sure you understood the job specifications? And, whose responsibility was it to come up with those job specifications—HR, the hiring department, or both in partnership?
3. Do you think one good solution would be raising the salary of the position in order to get better candidates? If so, do you think it's really practical to do so?
4. Based on what you read in this textbook, how much legitimacy is there to the accusation that BMG did not throw out a wide enough net in recruiting (given the fact that they did get 60 candidates)?

ENDNOTES

1. "Hiring Managers Reveal Top Five Biggest Mistakes Candidates Make During Job Interviews in Careerbuilder.com Survey," *Internet Wire*, January 21, 2004, www.careerbuilder.com/Article/CB-502-Getting-Hired-Weirdest-Interview-Behavior/?ArticleID=502&cbRecursionCnt=1&cbsid=43dae5840a2348648a1e0a3e58100610-291329855-wh-6&ns_siteid=ns_us_g_careerbuilder_intervi, accessed March 25, 2009.
2. Derek Chapman and David Zweig, "Developing a Nomological Network for Interview Structure: Antecedents and Consequences of the Structured Selection Interview," *Personnel Psychology* 58 (2005), pp. 673–702.
3. Michael McDaniel et al., "The Validity of Employment Interviews: A Comprehensive Review and Meta-Analysis," *Journal of Applied Psychology* 79, no. 4 (1994), p. 599. See also Laura Graves and Ronald Karren, "The Employee Selection Interview: A Fresh Look at an Old Problem," *Human Resource Management* 35, no. 2 (Summer 1996), pp. 163–180. For an argument against holding selection interviews, see D. Heath et. al., "Hold the Interview," *Fast Company*, no. 136 (June 2009), pp. 51–52.
4. Duane Schultz and Sydney Schultz, *Psychology and Work Today* (Upper Saddle River, NJ: Prentice Hall, 1998), p. 830. A study found that interview structure "was best described by four dimensions: questioning consistency, evaluation standardization, question sophistication, and rapport building." Chapman and Zweig, op. cit.
5. McDaniel et al., "The Validity of Employment Interviews," p. 602.
6. We'll see later in this chapter that there are other ways to "structure" selection interviews. Many of them have nothing to do with using structured guides like these.
7. Laura Gollub Williamson et al., "Employment Interview on Trial: Linking Interview Structure with Litigation Outcomes," *Journal of Applied Psychology* 82, no. 6 (1996), p. 908.
8. Richard Posthuma, Frederick Morgeson, and Michael Campion, "Beyond Employment Interview Validity: A Comprehensive Narrative Review of Trends over Time," *Personnel Psychology*, 55 (2002), p. 47. See also Frederick P. Morgeson, Matthew H. Reider, and Michael A. Campion, "Review of Research on Age Discrimination in the Employment Interview," *Journal of Business & Psychology* 22, no. 3 (March 2008) pp. 223–232.
9. Postuma, Morgeson, and Campion, op. cit.
10. Williamson et al., op. cit.
11. McDaniel et al., "The Validity of Employment Interviews," pp. 602.
12. Bill Stoneman, "Matching Personalities with Jobs Made Easier with Behavioral Interviews," *American Banker*, November 30, 2000, p. 8a.
13. Paul Taylor and Bruce Small, "Asking Applicants What They Would Do Versus What They Did: A Meta-Analytic Comparison of Situational and Past Behavior Employment Interview Questions," *Journal of Occupational and Organizational Psychology* 75, no. 3 (September 2002), pp. 277–295.
14. Aparna Nancherla, "Anticipated Growth in Behavioral Interviewing," *Training & Development*, April 2008, p. 20.
15. "Job Hunt as Head Trip? More Companies Use Behavioral Interviews to Screen Candidates," *Los Angeles Times*, May 20, 2001, p. W.1.
16. Martha Frase-Blunt, "Games Interviewers Play," *HR Magazine*, January 2001, pp. 104–114.
17. Kevin Murphy and Charles Davidshofer, *Psychological Testing* (Upper Saddle River, NJ: Prentice Hall, 2001), pp. 430–431.
18. Marlene Dixon et al., "The Panel Interview: A Review of Empirical Research and Guidelines for Practice," *Public Personnel Management* 31, no. 3 (Fall 2002), pp. 397–429.
19. Ibid. See also M. Ronald Buckley, Katherine A. Jackson, and Mark C. Bolino, "The Influence of Relational Demography on Panel Interview Ratings: A Field Experiment," *Personnel Psychology* 60, no. 3 (Autumn 2007), pp. 627–646.
20. "Phone Interviews Might Be the Most Telling, Study Finds," *BNA Bulletin to Management*, September 1998, p. 273.
21. Susan Strauss et al., "The Effects of Videoconference, Telephone, and Face-to-Face Media on Interviewer and Applicant Judgments in Employment Interviews," *Journal of Management* 27, no. 3 (2001), pp. 363–381. If the employer records a video interview with the intention of sharing it with hiring managers who don't participate in the interview, it's advisable to first obtain the candidate's written permission. Matt Bolch, "Lights, Camera . . . Interview!" *HR Magazine*, March 2007, pp. 99–102.
22. www.kpao.org/blog/2008/11/iphone-the-perfect-job-interview-tool.html, accessed March 23, 2009.
23. http://pcworld.about.com/gi/dynamic/offsite.htm?site=http://www.martinreddy.net/iphone/interview, accessed July 5, 2009.
24. These are quoted or adapted from www.careerfaqs.com.au/getthatjob_video_interview.asp, accessed March 2, 2009.
25. Douglas Rodgers, "Computer-Aided Interviewing Overcomes First Impressions," *Personnel Journal*, April 1987, pp. 148–152; see also Linda Thornburg, "Computer-Assisted Interviewing Shortens Hiring Cycle," *HR Magazine*, February 1998, p. 73ff.
26. Rogers, op. cit.
27. Gary Robins, "Dial-an-Interview," *Stores*, June 1994, pp. 34–35.
28. This is quoted from or paraphrased from William Bulkeley, "Replaced by Technology: Job Interviews," *The Wall Street Journal*, August 22, 1994, pp. B1, B7.
29. For example, structured employment interviews using either situational questions or behavioral questions tend to yield high criterion-related validities (.63 versus .47). This is particularly so where the raters can use descriptively anchored rating scale answer sheets; these use short descriptors to illustrate good, average, or poor

performance. Paul Taylor and Bruce Small, "Asking Applicants What They Would Do Versus What They Did Do: A Meta-Analytic Comparison of Situational and Past Behaviour Employment Interview Questions," *Journal of Occu pational and Organizational Psychology* 75, no. 3, (2002), pp. 277–294.

30. Williamson, "Employment Interview on Trial," p. 900.
31. Frank Schmidt and Ryan Zimmerman, "A Counterintuitive Hypothesis About Employment Interview Validity and Some Supporting Evidence," *Journal of Applied Psychology* 89, no. 3 (2004), pp. 553–561.
32. This validity discussion and these findings are based on McDaniel et al., "The Validity of Employment Interviews," pp. 607–610; the validities for situational, job-related, and psychological interviews were (.50), (.39), and (.29), respectively.
33. Murray Barrick et al., "Accuracy of Interviewer Judgments of Job Applicant Personality Traits," *Personnel Psychology* 53 (2000), pp. 925–951.
34. For example, with respect to the usefulness of selection interviews for assessing candidate intelligence or cognitive ability, see Christopher Berry et al., "Revisiting Interview–Cognitive Ability Relationships: Attending to Specific Range Restriction Mechanisms in Meta-Analysis," *Personnel Psychology* 60 (2007), pp. 837–874.
35. McDaniel et al., "The Validity of Employment Interviews," p. 608.
36. Anthony Dalessio and Todd Silverhart, "Combining Biodata Test and Interview Information: Predicting Decisions and Performance Criteria," *Personnel Psychology* 47 (1994), p. 313.
37. S. W. Constantin, "An Investigation of Information Favorability in the Employment Interview," *Journal of Applied Psychology* 61 (1976), pp. 743–749. It should be noted that a number of the studies discussed in this chapter involve having interviewers evaluate interviews based on written transcripts (rather than face to face) and that a study suggests that this procedure may not be equivalent to having interviewers interview applicants directly. See Charles Gorman, William Glover, and Michael Doherty, "Can We Learn Anything About Interviewing Real People from 'Interviews' of Paper People? A Study of the External Validity Paradigm," *Organizational Behavior and Human Performance* 22, no. 2 (October 1978), pp. 165–192. See also John Binning et al., "Effects of Pre-Interview Impressions on Questioning Strategies in Same and Opposite Sex Employment Interviews," *Journal of Applied Psychology* 73, no. 1 (February 1988), pp. 30–37; and Sebastian Fisicaro, "A Reexamination of the Relation Between Halo Error and Accuracy," *Journal of Applied Psychology* 73, no. 2 (May 1988), pp. 239–246.
38. David Tucker and Patricia Rowe, "Relationship Between Expectancy, Causal Attribution, and Final Hiring Decisions in the Employment Interview," *Journal of Applied Psychology* 64, no. 1 (February 1979), pp. 27–34. See also Robert Dipboye, Gail Fontenelle, and Kathleen Garner, "Effect of Previewing the Application on Interview Process and Outcomes," *Journal of Applied Psychology* 69, no. 1 (February 1984), pp. 118–128.
39. Anita Chaudhuri, "Beat the Clock: Applying for Job? A New Study Shows That Interviewers Will Make Up Their Minds About You Within a Minute," *The Guardian*, June 14, 2000, pp. 2–6.
40. John Langdale and Joseph Weitz, "Estimating the Influence of Job Information on Interviewer Agreement," *Journal of Applied Psychology* 57 (1973), pp. 23–27.
41. R. E. Carlson, "Effects of Applicant Sample on Ratings of Valid Information in an Employment Setting," *Journal of Applied Psychology* 20 (1967), pp. 259–280.
42. R. E. Carlson, "Selection Interview Decisions: The Effects of Interviewer Experience, Relative Quota Situation, and Applicant Sample on Interview Decisions," *Personnel Psychology* 20 (1967), pp. 259–280.
43. See, for example, Scott T. Fleischmann, "The Messages of Body Language in Job Interviews," *Employee Relations* 18, no. 2 (Summer 1991), pp. 161–166; James Westphal and Ithai Stern, "Flattery Will Get You Everywhere (Especially if You're a Male Caucasian): How Ingratiation, Board Room Behavior, and a Demographic Minority Status Affect Additional Board Appointments at U.S. Companies," *Academy of Management Journal* 50, no. 2 (2007), pp. 267–288.
44. Tim DeGroot and Stephan Motowidlo, "Why Visual and Vocal Interview Cues Can Affect Interviewers' Judgments and Predicted Job Performance," *Journal of Applied Psychology*, December 1999, pp. 968–984.
45. David Caldwell and Jerry Burger, "Personality Characteristics of Job Applicants and Success in Screening Interviews," *Personnel Psychology* 51 (1998), pp. 119–136.
46. Ibid., p. 130.
47. Amy Kristof-Brown et al., "Applicant Impression Management: Dispositional Influences and Consequences for Recruiter Perceptions of Fit and Similarity," *Journal of Management* 28, no. 1 (2002), pp. 27–46. See also Lynn McFarland et al., "Impression Management Use and Effectiveness Across Assessment Methods," *Journal of Management* 29, no. 5 (2003), pp. 641–661.
48. Posthuma, Morgeson, and Campion, "Beyond Employment Interview Validity," 1–87.
49. C. K. Stevens and A. L. Kristof, "Making the Right Impression: A Field Study of Applicant Impression Management During Interviews," *Journal of Applied Psychology* 80, pp. 587–606; Schultz and Schultz, *Psychology and Work Today*, p. 82. See also Jay Stuller, "Fatal Attraction," *Across the Board* 42, no. 6 (November/December 2005), pp. 18–23.
50. Chad Higgins and Timothy Judge, "The Effect of Applicant Influence Tactics on Recruiter Perceptions of Fit and Hiring Recommendations: A Field Study," *Journal of Applied Psychology* 89, no. 4 (2004), pp. 622–632. Some researchers in this area question results like these. The problem is that much of the other interviewing research uses students as raters and hypothetical jobs, so it's not clear that we can apply the findings to the real world. For example, "In operational settings, where actual jobs are at stake, faking or socially desirable responding may be more likely to distort personality measurement and obscure relationships." Richard Posthuma, Frederick Morgeson, and Michael Campion, "Beyond Employment Interview Validity: A Comprehensive Narrative

Review of Recent Trends over Time," *Personnel Psychology* 55 (2002), p. 30. But, realistically, anyone who has been through an interview probably recognizes that such impression management goes on (and probably works, at least up to a point).

51. See, for example, Madeline Heilmann and Lois Saruwatari, "When Beauty Is Beastly: The Effects of Appearance and Sex on Evaluations of Job Applicants for Managerial and Nonmanagerial Jobs," *Organizational Behavior and Human Performance* 23 (June 1979), pp. 360–372; and Cynthia Marlowe, Sandra Schneider, and Carnot Nelson, "Gender and Attractiveness Biases in Hiring Decisions: Are More Experienced Managers Less Biased?" *Journal of Applied Psychology* 81, no. 1 (1996), pp. 11–21.
52. Marlowe et al., "Gender and Attractiveness Biases," p. 11.
53. Ibid., p. 18.
54. Ibid., p. 11.
55. Allen Huffcutt and Philip Roth, "Racial Group Differences in Employment Interview Evaluations," *Journal of Applied Psychology* 83, no. 2 (1998), pp. 179–189.
56. N. S. Miceli et al., "Potential Discrimination in Structured Employment Interviews," *Employee Responsibilities and Rights* 13, no. 1 (March 2001), pp. 15–38.
57. "Screens Can Be a Key to Unbiased Interview Process," *Personnel Today*, April 1, 2003, p. 3.
58. Andrea Rodriguez and Fran Prezant, "Better Interviews for People with Disabilities," *Workforce*, workforce.com, accessed November 14, 2003.
59. Pat Tammaro, "Laws to Prevent Discrimination Affect Job Interview Process," *The Houston Business Journal*, June 16, 2000, p. 48.
60. This is based on John F. Wymer III and Deborah A. Sudbury, "Employment Discrimination: 'Testers'—Will Your Hiring Practices 'Pass'?" *Employee Relations Law Journal* 17, no. 4 (Spring 1992), pp. 623–633.
61. Bureau of National Affairs, *Daily Labor Report*, December 5, 1990, p. D1.
62. Wymer and Sudbury, "Employment Discrimination," p. 629.
63. Arthur Pell, "Nine Interviewing Pitfalls," *Managers Magazine*, January 1994, p. 20.
64. Thomas Dougherty, Daniel Turban, and John Callender, "Confirming First Impressions in the Employment Interview: A Field Study of Interviewer Behavior," *Journal of Applied Psychology* 79, no. 5 (1994), p. 663.
65. See Pell, "Nine Interviewing Pitfalls," p. 29; Parth Sarathi, "Making Selection Interviews Effective," *Management and Labor Studies* 18, no. 1 (1993), pp. 5–7.
66. Posthuma, Morgeson, and Campion, "Beyond Employment Interview Validity," pp. 1–87.
67. Pell, "Nine Interviewing Pitfalls," p. 30.
68. This section is based on Elliot Pursell et al., "Structured Interviewing," *Personnel Journal* 59 (November 1980), pp. 907–912; and G. Latham et al., "The Situational Interview," *Journal of Applied Psychology* 65 (1980), pp. 422–427. See also Campion, Pursell, and Brown, "Structured Interviewing," pp. 25–42.
69. Taylor and Small, "Asking Applicants What They Would Do Versus What They Did," pp. 277–295. Structured employment interviews using either situational questions or behavioral questions tend to yield high validities. However, structured interviews with situational question formats yield the higher ratings. This may be because interviewers get more consistent (reliable) responses with situational questions (which force all applicants to apply the same scenario) than they do with behavioral questions (which require each applicant to find applicable experiences). However, there is some evidence that for higher-level positions, situational question–based interviews are inferior to behavioral question–based ones, possibly because the situations are "just too simple to allow any real differentiation among candidates for higher level positions." Allen Huffcutt et al., "Comparison of Situational and Behavioral Description Interview Questions for Higher Level Positions," *Personnel Psychology* 54, no. 3 (2001), p. 619.
70. See also Phillip Lowry, "The Structured Interview: An Alternative to the Assessment Center?" *Public Personnel Management* 23, no. 2 (Summer 1994), pp. 201–215. See also Steven Maurer, "The Potential of the Situational Interview: Existing Research and Unresolved Issues," *Human Resource Management Review* 7, no. 2 (Summer 1997), pp. 185–201; and Todd Maurer and Jerry Solamon, "The Science and Practice of a Structured Employment Interview Coaching Program," *Personnel Psychology* 59, no. 2 (Summer 2006), pp. 433–456.
71. Pursell et al., "Structured Interviewing," p. 910.
72. From a speech by industrial psychologist Paul Green and contained in *BNA Bulletin to Management*, June 20, 1985, pp. 2–3.
73. Williamson et al., "Employment Interview on Trial," p. 901; Michael Campion, David Palmer, and James Campion, "A Review of Structure in the Selection Interview," *Personnel Psychology* 50 (1997), pp. 655–702. See also Todd Maurer and Jerry Solamon, "The Science and Practice of a Structured Employment Interview Coaching Program," *Personnel Psychology* 59 (2006), pp. 433–456.
74. Unless otherwise specified, the following are based on Williamson et al., "Employment Interview on Trial," pp. 901–902.
75. Campion, Palmer, and Campion, "A Review of Structure," p. 668.
76. Carlson, "Selection Interview Decisions," pp. 259–280.
77. "The Tables Have Turned," *American Management Association International*, September 1998, p. 6.
78. Pamela Kaul, "Interviewing Is Your Business," *Association Management*, November 1992, p. 29. See also Nancy Woodward, "Asking for Salary Histories," *HR Magazine*, February 2000, pp. 109–12. Gathering information about specific interview dimensions such as social ability, responsibility, and independence (as is often done with structured interviews) can improve interview accuracy, at least for more complicated jobs. See also Andrea Poe, "Graduate Work: Behavioral Interviewing Can Tell You If an Applicant Just Out of College Has Traits Needed for the Job," *HR Magazine* 48, no. 10 (October 2003): 95–96.
79. Edwin Walley, "Successful Interviewing Techniques," *The CPA Journal* 63 (September 1993), p. 70.
80. Catherine Middendorf and Therese Macan, "Note Taking in the Employment Interview: Effects on Recall and Judgment," *Journal of Applied Psychology* 87, no. 2 (2002), pp. 293–303.

81. Kristen Weirick, "The Perfect Interview," *HR Magazine*, April 2008, p. 85.
82. Stephen Gilliland et al., "Improving Applicants' Reactions to Rejection Letters: An Application of Fairness Theory," *Personnel Psychology* 54 (2001), pp. 669–703.
83. This is based on John Drake, *Interviewing for Managers: A Complete Guide to Employment Interviewing* (New York: AMACOM, 1982).
84. Ibid.
85. Kris Maher, "New High-Tech Recruiting Tools: Unicycles, Yahtzee and Silly Putty," *The Wall Street Journal*, June 6, 2000, p. B14; see also Paul McNamara, "Extreme Interview," *Network World*, June 25, 2001, p. 65.
86. Tim Barker, "Corporate Espionage Takes Center Stage with Boeing Revelation," *Knight Ridder/Tribune Business News*, June 15, 2003.
87. Ibid.

8 Training and Developing Employees

In a Stanford University Hospital virtual training room, residents and medical students rush to save a virtual patient. They use virtual reality headsets to control their on-screen avatars. The avatars are computerized simulations dressed in medical scrubs. Each avatar has a different role, such as nurse or emergency room technician. The residents and medical students use their keypads to control their avatars in a virtual reality trauma center. One avatar props up the patient; another rushes to clear his airway. On the screen, the patient's vital signs react fittingly to the medical students' decisions. Then instructors replay the scenario, showing trainees what they did right and wrong.[1] Training, as we'll see in this chapter, is increasingly high-tech.

Source: Courtesy of Getty Images–Stockbyte, Royalty Free.

WHERE ARE WE NOW . . .

Chapters 6 and 7 focused on the methods managers use to interview and select employees. Once employees are on board, the employer must train them. The purpose of this chapter is to increase your effectiveness in training employees. The main topics we'll cover include orienting employees, the training process, analyzing training needs, implementing training and development programs, and evaluating the training effort. Then, in Chapter 9, we'll turn to appraising employees.

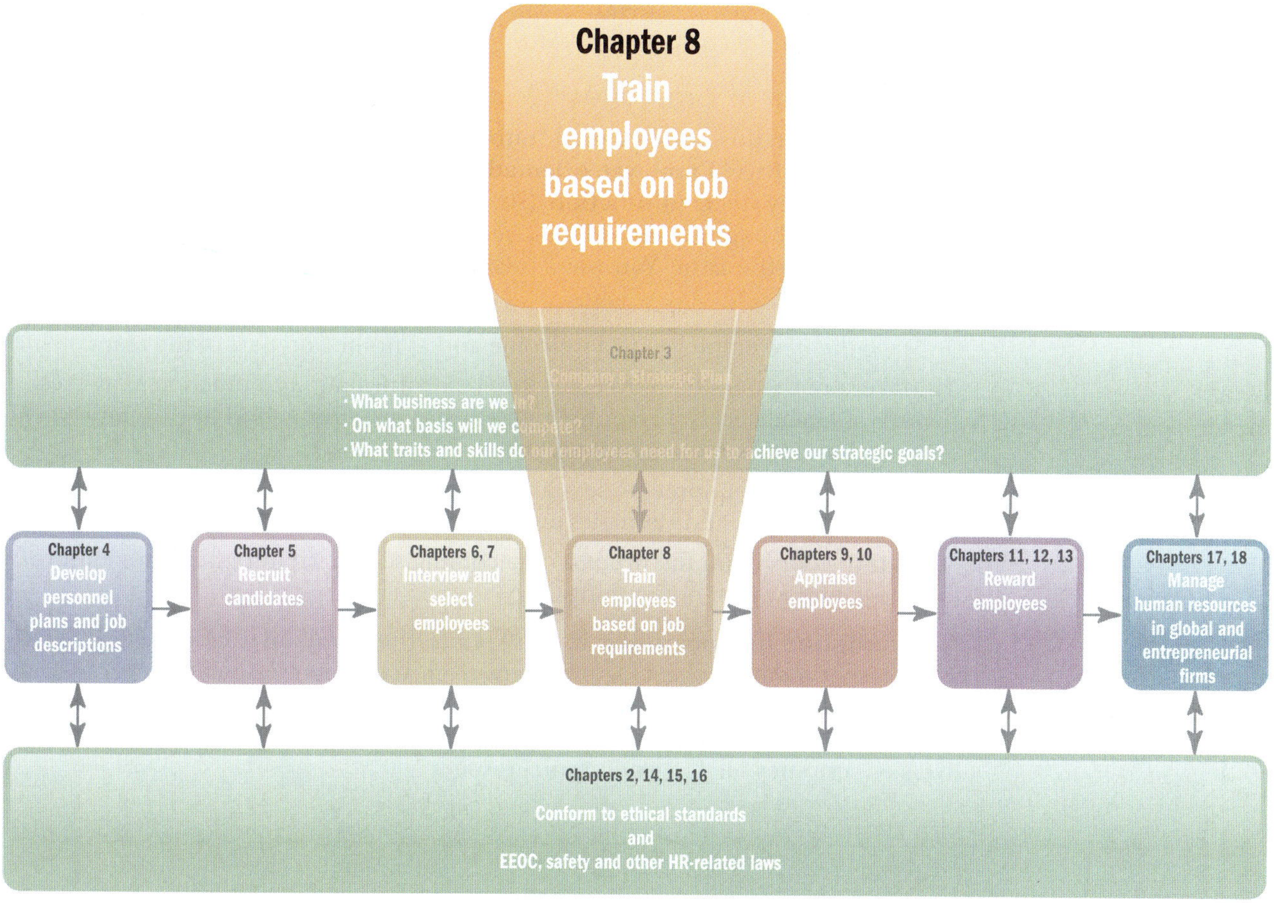

LEARNING OUTCOMES

1. Summarize the purpose and process of employee orientation.
2. List and briefly explain each of the four steps in the training process.
3. Discuss how you would motivate trainees.
4. Describe and illustrate how you would identify training requirements.
5. Explain how to distinguish between problems you can fix with training and those you can't.
6. Explain how to use five training techniques.
7. List and briefly discuss four management development programs.
8. List and briefly discuss the importance of the eight steps in leading organizational change.
9. Answer the question, "What is organizational development and how does it differ from traditional approaches to organizational change?"

INTRODUCTION TO ORIENTING AND TRAINING EMPLOYEES

Carefully selecting employees doesn't guarantee they'll perform effectively. Even high-potential employees can't do their jobs if they don't know what to do or how to do it. Making sure your employees do know what to do and how to do it is the purpose of orientation and training. The human resources department usually designs the company's orientation and training programs, but the rubber hits the road with the department supervisor. He or she does most of the day-to-day orienting and training. Every manager therefore needs to know how to orient and train employees. We will start with orientation.

1 Summarize the purpose and process of employee orientation.

The Purposes of Employee Orientation/Onboarding

Employee orientation (often called "onboarding" today) involves more than what most people realize.[2] **Employee orientation** still provides new employees with the information they need to function (such as computer passwords and company rules); ideally, though, it should also help new employees start getting emotionally attached to the firm. You want to accomplish four things by orienting new employees:

1. Make the new employee feel welcome and at home and part of the team.
2. Make sure the new employee has the basic information to function effectively, such as e-mail access, personnel policies and benefits, and what the employer expects in terms of work behavior.
3. Help the new employee understand the organization in a broad sense (its past, present, culture, and strategies and vision of the future).
4. Start the person on the process of becoming socialized into the firm's culture, values, and ways of doing things.[3]

Getting the new employee to appreciate the company's culture and values distinguishes today's *onboarding* programs from traditional orientation.[4] For example, the Mayo Clinic's new "heritage and culture" program now emphasizes core Mayo Clinic values such as teamwork, personal responsibility, innovation, integrity, diversity, customer service, and mutual respect.[5]

The Orientation Process

The length of the orientation program depends on what you cover. Traditional orientation programs take several hours. The human resource specialist (or, in smaller firms, the office manager) usually performs the first part of the orientation by explaining basic matters like working hours, benefits, and vacations. That person then introduces the new employee to his or her new supervisor. The supervisor continues the orientation by explaining (see Figure 8-1) the organization of the department and by introducing the person to his or her new colleagues, familiarizing the new employee with the workplace, and helping to reduce first-day jitters. Supervisors need to be vigilant. Follow up on and encourage new employees to engage in activities (such as taking breaks with current employees) that will enable each to "learn the ropes" and become productive. In firms like Toyota Motor USA, onboarding-type orientations take up to a week. These may include videos, lectures by company officers, and exercises covering matters like company history, vision, and values.

At a minimum, as in Figure 8-1, an orientation typically includes information on employee benefits, personnel policies, the daily routine, company organization and operations, safety measures and regulations, and a facilities tour.[6] New employees should receive (and sign for) print or Internet-based employee handbooks covering matters like these.

UNIVERSITY *of* CALIFORNIA, SAN DIEGO
MEDICAL CENTER

NEW EMPLOYEE DEPARTMENTAL ORIENTATION CHECKLIST
(Return to Human Resources within 10 days of Hire)

NAME:	HIRE DATE:	SSN:	JOB TITLE:
DEPARTMENT:	NEO DATE:	DEPARTMENTAL ORIENTATION COMPLETED BY:	

TOPIC	DATE REVIEWED	N/A
1. HUMAN RESOURCES INFORMATION		
a. Departmental Attendance Procedures and UCSD Medical Center Work Time & Attendance Policy	a. ________	☐
b. Job Description Review	b. ________	☐
c. Annual Performance Evaluation and Peer Feedback Process	c. ________	☐
d. Probationary Period Information	d. ________	☐
e. Appearance/Dress Code Requirements	e. ________	☐
f. Annual TB Screening	f. ________	☐
g. License and/or Certification Renewals	g. ________	☐
2. DEPARTMENT INFORMATION		
a. Organizational Structure-Department Core Values Orientation	a. ________	☐
b. Department/Unit Area Specific Policies & Procedures	b. ________	☐
c. Customer Service Practices	c. ________	☐
d. CQI Effort and Projects	d. ________	☐
e. Tour and Floor Plan	e. ________	☐
f. Equipment/Supplies	f. ________	☐
• Keys issued	________	☐
• Radio Pager issued	________	☐
• Other ________	________	☐
g. Mail and Recharge Codes	g. ________	☐
3. SAFETY INFORMATION		
a. Departmental Safety Plan	a. ________	☐
b. Employee Safety/Injury Reporting Procedures	b. ________	☐
c. Hazard Communication	c. ________	☐
d. Infection Control/Sharps Disposal	d. ________	☐
e. Attendance at annual Safety Fair (mandatory)	e. ________	☐
4. FACILITES INFORMATION		
a. Emergency Power	a. ________	☐
b. Mechanical Systems	b. ________	☐
c. Water	c. ________	☐
d. Medical Gases	d. ________	☐
e. Patient Room	e. ________	☐
• Bed	________	☐
• Headwall	________	☐
• Bathroom	________	☐
• Nurse Call System	________	☐
5. SECURITY INFORMATION		
a. Code Triage Assignment	a. ________	☐
b. Code Blue Assignment	b. ________	☐
c. Code Red – Evacuation Procedure	c. ________	☐
d. Code 10 – Bomb Threat Procedure	d. ________	☐
e. Departmental Security Measures	e. ________	☐
f. UCSD Emergency Number 6111 or 911	f. ________	☐

This generic checklist may not constitute a complete departmental orientation or assessment. Please attach any additional unit specific orientation material for placement in the employee's HR file

I have been oriented on the items listed above________________________________

D1999(R7-01) **WHITE** – HR Records (8912) **Yellow** – Department Retains

FIGURE 8-1 New Employee Departmental Orientation Checklist
Source: Used with permission of UC San Diego Medical Center.

employee orientation
A procedure for providing new employees with basic background information about the firm.

The Employee Handbook Note that under certain conditions, courts may find that the employee handbook's contents represent legally binding employment commitments. Therefore, employers often include disclaimers. These make it clear that statements of company policies, benefits, and regulations do not constitute the terms and conditions of an employment contract, either expressed or implied. Also, companies generally do not insert statements such as "No employee will be fired without just cause" or statements that imply or state that employees have tenure. Indeed, it's best to emphasize that the employment relationship is strictly "at-will."

Orientation Technology Employers use technology to support orientation. For example, some provide incoming managers with preloaded personal digital assistants. These contain information such as on key contacts, and even digital images of key employees.[7] Other employers put all or some of their orientation media on the Web. At the University of Cincinnati, new employees spend about 45 minutes online learning about their new employer's mission, organization, and policies and procedures. IBM uses virtual environments like Second Life to support orientation, particularly for employees abroad. The new employees choose virtual avatars, which then interact with other company avatars, for instance to learn how to enroll for benefits.[8]

HR APPs 4 U

Mobile Company Directory

With Workday's iPhone app, employers can provide their employees easy mobile access to their employee directories. Users can search their company's worker directory for names, images, and contact information; call or e-mail coworkers directly; and view physical addresses on Google Maps.[9]

The Training Process

Directly after orientation, training should begin. **Training** means giving new or current employees the skills they need to perform their jobs. This might mean showing a new Web designer the intricacies of your site, a new salesperson how to sell your firm's product, or a new supervisor how to complete the firm's weekly payroll sheets. It might involve simply having the current jobholder explain the job to the new hire, or a multi-week training process including classroom or Internet classes.

In any case, training is a hallmark of good management, and a task that managers ignore at their peril. Having high-potential employees doesn't guarantee they'll succeed. Instead, they must know what you want them to do and how you want them to do it. If they don't, they will improvise or do nothing useful at all.

Inadequate training can also expose employers to **negligent training** liability. As one expert puts it, "It's clear from the case law that where an employer fails to train adequately and an employee subsequently does harm to third parties, the court will find the employer liable."[10] Employers should confirm the applicant/employee's claims of skill and experience, provide adequate training (particularly where employees use dangerous equipment), and evaluate the training to ensure that it's actually reducing risks.

Aligning Strategy and Training Employers today want to make sure their training programs are supporting their firms' strategic goals.[11] As one trainer said, "We sit down with management and help them identify strategic goals and objectives and the skills and knowledge needed to achieve them."[12]

For example, Caterpillar Inc. created Caterpillar University to oversee all its training and development programs. The university has a board of directors comprised of company executives. They set the university's policies and oversee "the alignment of the corporation's learning needs with the enterprises' business strategy."[13] As another example, when Wisconsin-based Signicast Corp. decided to build a new, high-tech plant, the firm's president worked closely with his HR team to create the hiring and training policies and programs to hire train these new employees.

One survey found that "establishing a linkage between learning and organizational performance" was the number-one pressing issue facing training professionals.[14] Training experts today increasingly use the phrase "workplace learning and performance" in lieu of training to underscore training's dual aims of employee learning and organizational performance.[15] Training has an impressive record of influencing performance, scoring higher than appraisal and feedback and just below goal setting in its effect on productivity.[16]

For whatever reason, training is booming. Companies spend on average $1,103 per employee for training per year and offer each about 28 hours of training.[17]

2 List and briefly explain each of the four steps in the training process.

The Four-Step Training Process

Training programs consist of four steps.

1. In the first, *needs analysis* step, you identify the specific knowledge and skills the job requires, and compare these with the prospective trainees' knowledge and skills.
2. In the second, *instructional design* step, you formulate specific, measurable knowledge and performance training objectives, review possible training program content (including workbooks, exercises, and activities), and estimate a budget for the training program.
3. The third step is to *implement* the program, by actually training the targeted employee group using methods such as on-the-job or online training.
4. Finally, in an *evaluation* step, you assess the program's success (or failures).

Unfortunately, only about 10% to 35% of trainees are transferring what they learned in training to their jobs a year after training. Improving on that sad statistic requires taking special steps at each stage of training. *Prior to training*, get trainee and supervisor input in designing the program, institute a training attendance policy, and encourage employees to participate. *During training*, provide trainees with training experiences and conditions (surroundings, equipment) that resemble the actual work environment. *After training*, reinforce what trainees learned, for instance, by appraising and rewarding employees for using new skills, and by making sure that they have the tools and materials they need to use their new skills.[18]

3 Discuss how you would motivate trainees.

Training, Learning, and Motivation

Municipalities running driver education programs for traffic violators know there's often no better way to get a learner's attention than by presenting a terrifying filmed accident. In other words, they start the training, not with a lecture but by making the material meaningful. They know that driver training is futile if the driver either cannot or will not benefit from the program.

The same is true in schools and at work. Students need the ability to benefit from the training, and must want to benefit from it; learning requires both ability and motivation. In terms of *ability*, the learner–trainee needs (among other things) the required reading, writing, and mathematics skills, and the educational level, intelligence, and knowledge base. At work, employee selection should serve this function. (At school, admissions tests like the SAT supposedly serve a similar screening function.)

But as every student (and driver's ed program) knows, the learner must also be motivated to learn the material. No manager should want to waste his or her time showing a disinterested employee how to do something. Making the material meaningful—graphically making the point, "why should I learn this?"—is one way to do this. We can summarize motivational points as follows.

Make the Learning Meaningful

Learners are always more motivated to learn something that has meaning for them. Therefore:

1. At the start of training, provide a bird's-eye view of the material that you are going to present. For example, show why it's important, and provide an overview.[19]
2. Use a variety of familiar examples.

training
The process of teaching new or current employees the basic skills they need to perform their jobs.

negligent training
A situation where an employer fails to train adequately, and the employee subsequently harms a third party.

3. Organize the information so you can present it logically, and in meaningful units.
4. Use terms and concepts that are already familiar to trainees.
5. Use as many visual aids as possible.
6. Again, create a perceived training need in trainees' minds.[20] In one study, pilots who experienced pretraining, accident-related events subsequently learned more from an accident-reduction training program than did those experiencing fewer such events.[21] Similarly, "before the training, managers need to sit down and talk with the trainee about why they are enrolled in the class, what they are expected to learn, and how they can use it on the job."[22]

Make Skills Transfer Easy Make it easy to *transfer* new skills and behaviors from the training site to the job site:

1. Maximize the similarity between the training situation and the work situation.
2. Provide adequate practice.
3. Label or identify each feature of the machine and/or step in the process.
4. Direct the trainees' attention to important aspects of the job. For example, if you're training a customer service rep to handle calls, explain the different types of calls he or she will encounter.[23]
5. Provide "heads-up" information. For example, supervisors often face stressful conditions. You can reduce the negative impact of such events by letting supervisory trainees know they might occur.[24]
6. Trainees learn best at their own pace. If possible, let them pace themselves.

Reinforce the Learning Make sure the learner gets plenty of feedback. In particular:

1. Trainees learn best when the trainers immediately reinforce correct responses, perhaps with a quick "well done."
2. The schedule is important. The learning curve goes down late in the day, so that "full day training is not as effective as half the day or three-fourths of the day."[25]

Because so much research is available on how people learn, training design is an area ripe for evidence-based HR. The accompanying "Evidence-Based HR" feature illustrates this.

EVIDENCED-BASED HR

Sounds and Shortcuts: How to Design the Training Format to Improve Training Results[26]

When designing training programs, evidence-based HR means, among other things, designing the program based on the best available research evidence. For example, there is considerable evidence regarding how to improve the odds that trainees remember what you're presenting to them. The following are important examples of these principles.

Audio narration is better than just text. Specifically, combining audio narration in e-learning programs with on-screen text improves learning by at least 41%.

"Bells and whistles" (such as sound effects or interesting visuals that are not directly related to content) actually reduce learning outcomes by about 20%.

Spread *practice exercises* throughout a lesson, and throughout a curriculum, rather than grouping them together at the end.

A *conversational writing* style is better than a formal style.

Use mnemonic devices such as *acronyms* (for example, *"ROY G BIV"* helps us to remember the colors of a rainbow); doing so dramatically improves knowledge retention.

4 Describe and illustrate how you would identify training requirements.

ANALYZING TRAINING NEEDS AND DESIGNING THE PROGRAM

Most managers have an intuitive feel for what they want their subordinates to learn when they're training them. For instance, they may want the new clerk to learn the company's filing system or the new engineer to learn the correct procedure for responding to a customer's request for a proposal. However, taking a purely informal, intuitive approach to what you want your employees to learn risks missing important tasks. For this reason, most experienced trainers first go through a formal needs analysis process.

How you analyze training needs depends on whether you're training new or current employees. The main task in analyzing *new* employees' training needs is to determine what the job entails and to break it down into subtasks, each of which you then teach to the new employee.

Analyzing *current* employees' training needs is more complex, since here you have the added task of deciding whether training is the solution. For example, performance may be down because the standards aren't clear or because the person isn't motivated.

Task Analysis: Assessing New Employees' Training Needs

Particularly with lower-level workers, it's common to hire inexperienced personnel and train them. Your aim here is to give these new employees the skills and knowledge they need to do the job. You use task analysis to determine the new employees' training needs.

Task analysis is a detailed study of the job to determine what specific skills—like Java (in the case of a Web developer) or interviewing (in the case of a supervisor)—the job requires. Job descriptions and job specifications are important here. These list the job's specific duties and skills, which are the basic reference points in determining the training required. You can also uncover training needs by reviewing performance standards, performing the job, and questioning current job holders and their supervisors.[27]

Some managers supplement the job description and specification with a *task analysis record form.* This consolidates information regarding required tasks and skills in a form that's especially helpful for determining training requirements. As Table 8-1 illustrates, the task analysis record form contains six types of information, such as "Skills required."

Competency Models

Many employers develop competency models for jobs.[28] The **competency model** consolidates, usually in one diagram, a precise overview of the competencies (for example, in terms of knowledge, skills, and behaviors) someone would need to do a job well. As an example, Figure 8-2 shows an illustrative competency model for a human resource manager.[29] In this case, the model shows three things. At the top of the pyramid, it shows four *roles* we would expect the human resource manager to fill—line, staff, coordinative, and strategic. Beneath that, it shows the *areas of expertise* in which he or she must be expert to fill these roles, such as an expertise in HR practices and strategic planning. Next step down are basic *competencies* one would need to exhibit the required expertise and to fill the HR manager's roles. For our human resource manager, these competencies include interpersonal competencies (such as communicating), business management competencies (such as financial analysis), and personal competencies (such as exercising good judgment based on evidence).

task analysis
A detailed study of a job to identify the specific skills required.

competency model
A graphic model that consolidates, usually in one diagram, a precise overview of the competencies (the knowledge, skills, and behaviors) someone would need to do a job well.

TABLE 8-1 Sample Task Analysis Record Form

Task List		When and How Often Performed	Quantity and Quality of Performance	Conditions Under Which Performed	Skills or Knowledge Required	Where Best Learned
1.	Operate paper cutter	4 times per day		Noisy pressroom: distractions		
1.1	Start motor					
1.2	Set cutting distance		± tolerance of 0.007 in.		Read gauge	On the job
1.3	Place paper on cutting table		Must be completely even to prevent uneven cut		Lift paper correctly	On the job
1.4	Push paper up to cutter				Must be even	On the job
1.5	Grasp safety release with left hand		100% of time, for safety		Essential for safety	On the job but practice first with no distractions
1.6	Grasp cutter release with right hand				Must keep both hands on releases	On the job but practice first with no distractions
1.7	Simultaneously pull safety release with left hand and cutter release with right hand					
1.8	Wait for cutter to retract		100% of time, for safety		Must keep both hands on releases	On the job but practice first with no distractions
1.9	Retract paper				Wait until cutter retracts	On the job but practice first with no distractions
1.10	Shut off		100% of time, for safety			On the job but practice first with no distractions
2.	Operate printing press					
2.1	Start motor					

Note: Task analysis record form showing some of the tasks and subtasks performed by a printing press operator.

Again, the point of the competency model is to compile in one place a picture of the competencies one needs to do a job well. For our HR manager, this would include, for instance, knowledge and skills in areas such as HR practices, strategic planning, financial analysis, and ethics. A competency model need not follow any specific format. The important thing is that it presents a bird's-eye view of the job's required competencies.

At Sharp Electronics, creating competency models starts with trainers meeting with senior executives to crystallize the firm's strategy and objectives. This helps the trainers understand the skills Sharp's employees need to achieve the company's strategic goals. Then they conduct behavioral interviews with each job's top performers, and focus groups. Their aim is to identify the competencies (such as "demonstrates creativity" and "focuses on the customer") that together will comprise the job's competency model.[30]

5 Explain how to distinguish between problems you can fix with training and those you can't.

Performance Analysis: Assessing Current Employees' Training Needs

For under-performing current employees, you can't assume that training is the problem: Is it lack of training, or something else? **Performance analysis** is the process of verifying that there is a performance deficiency and determining whether the employer should correct such deficiencies through training or some other means (like transferring the employee).

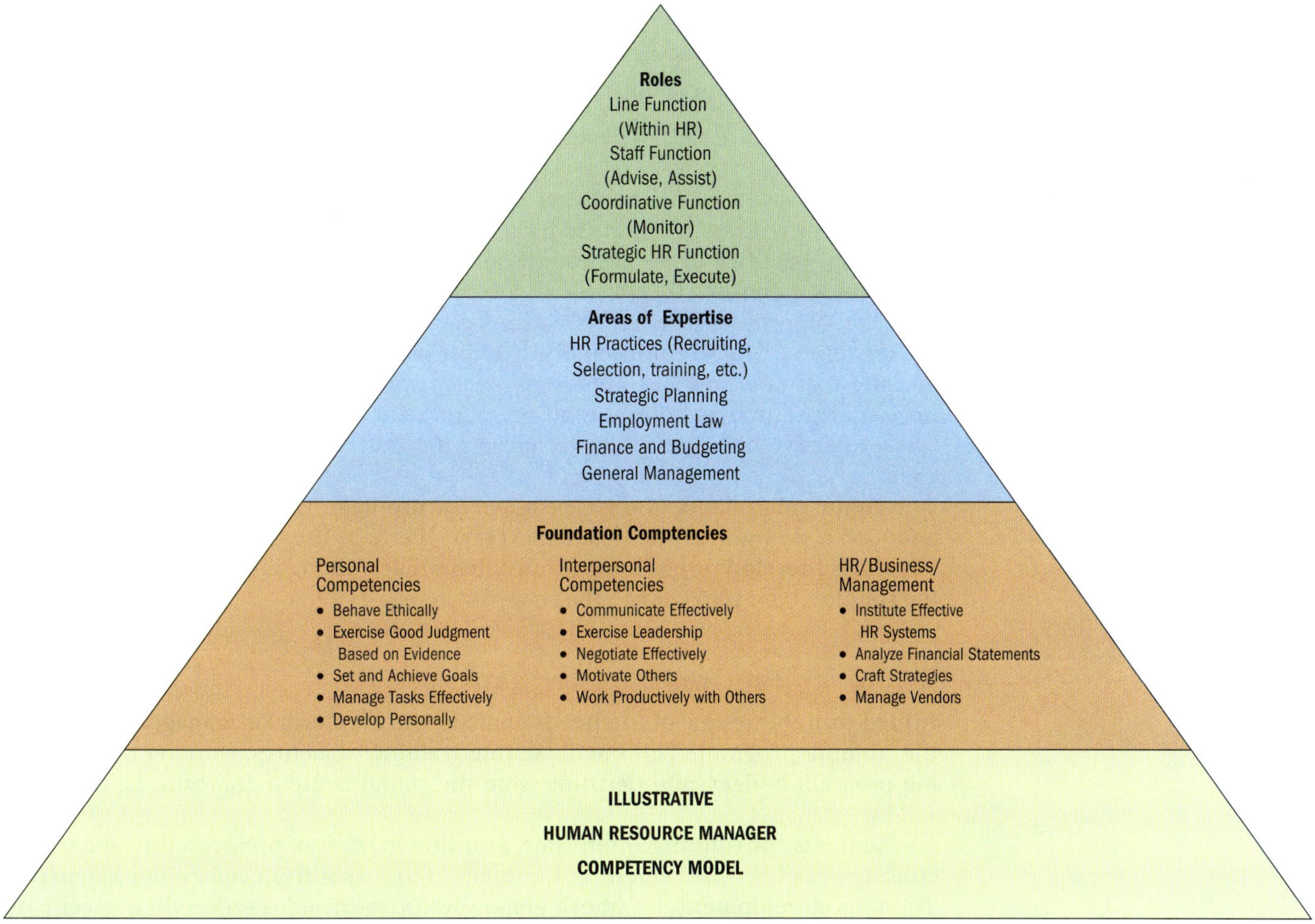

FIGURE 8-2 Example of Competency Model for Human Resource Manager

The first step in performance analysis is usually to compare the person's actual performance to what it should be. Doing so helps to confirm that there is a performance deficiency, and may also help the manager to identify its cause. Examples of performance deficiency might be:

I expect each salesperson to make 10 new contracts per week, but John averages only six.

Other plants our size average no more than two serious accidents per month; we're averaging five.

There are several ways to identify how a current employee is doing. These include reviewing:

- Performance appraisals
- Job-related performance data (including productivity, absenteeism and tardiness, grievances, waste, late deliveries, product quality, downtime, repairs, equipment utilization, and customer complaints)
- Observations by supervisors or other specialists
- Interviews with the employee or his or her supervisor
- Tests of things like job knowledge, skills, and attendance

performance analysis
Verifying that there is a performance deficiency and determining whether that deficiency should be corrected through training or through some other means (such as transferring the employee).

- Attitude surveys
- Individual employee daily diaries
- Assessment center results
- Special "performance gap" analytical software, such as from Saba Software, Inc.

Can't Do/Won't Do The heart of performance analysis is determining why performance is down. It is futile to train an employee whose work actually is deficient because of insufficient motivation. Distinguishing between can't-do and won't-do problems is therefore crucial.

First, determine whether it is a *can't-do* problem and, if so, its specific causes. For example: The employees don't know what to do or what your standards are; there are obstacles in the system such as lack of tools or supplies; there are no job aids (such as color-coded wires that show assemblers which wire goes where); you've hired people who haven't the skills to do the job; or inadequate training.

On the other hand, it might be a *won't-do* problem. Here employees could do a good job if they wanted to. One expert says, "Perhaps the biggest trap that trainers fall into is [developing] training for problems that training just won't fix."[31] Perhaps the solution here is to change the reward system.

Designing the Training Program

Armed with the results of the needs analysis, the employer or manager can design the training program. This entails setting training objectives, working out a training program budget, and deciding what the actual content and training methods will be.

Requests for training often start with line managers presenting problems or concerns, such as "we're getting too many complaints from call center callers."[32] Training, development, or (more generally) *instructional objectives* then specify in measurable terms what the trainee should be able to accomplish after successfully completing the training program.[33] For example:

> The technical service representative will be able to adjust the color guidelines on this HP Officejet All-in-One printer copier within 10 minutes according to the device's specifications.

For all but the most trivial training programs, the employer will also want to see and approve a *training budget* for the program. Typical costs include the development costs (of having, say, a human resource specialist working on the program for a week or two), the direct and indirect (overhead) costs of the trainers' time, participant compensation (for the time they're actually being trained), and the cost of evaluating the program.

In turn, the budget will help determine the actual *design* of the program. In this case, "design" means deciding on the actual content (the courses and step-by-step instructions, for instance) as well as on how to deliver the training—on-the-job or via the Web, for instance.

Some employers create their own training content, but there is also a vast selection of online and offline content from which to choose. You'll find turnkey, off-the-shelf programs on virtually any topic—from occupational safety to sexual harassment to Web design—from tens of thousands of online and offline providers. (See, for example, the American Society for Training and Development's Infoline at www.astd.org, www.trainerswarehouse.com, and www.gneil.com, among thousands of such suppliers.) As other examples, the professional development site saba.com offers Web-based courses for employees. Many firms, including HRDQ of King of Prussia, Pennsylvania, and American Media, Inc., of West Des Moines, Iowa, provide turnkey training packages.[34] These include trainer's guide, self-study book, and video.

Challenging times prompt employers to turn to sources of free or low-cost training, as the accompanying "Managing HR in Challenging Times" feature explains.

Most employers can build training programs like this one based on existing online and offline content offered by training content providers.

Source: Courtesy of Kim Kulish/CORBIS-NY

MANAGING HR IN CHALLENGING TIMES

Free Training Alternatives

When the economy sours, training and development are often the first human resource management activities to face the axe. Recently, for instance, "morale and team building," "professional development," and "all staff training" (on issues like anti-harassment and diversity) were the three most likely cuts HR managers were going to make (followed by recruitment, office refreshments, and human resource technology).[35]

There are, however, numerous no-cost training alternatives employers can turn to. For example, some states, including Pennsylvania, have free training programs for in-state employers. In Pennsylvania, the Workforce and Economic Development Network of Pennsylvania (WEDnetPA) provides in-state employers with grants of up to $450 per employee for basic skills training (www.wednetpa.com). Web sites such as free-training.com (www.free-training.com) are another option. The federal government's Small Business Administration (www.SBA.gov/training) provides a virtual campus that offers online courses, workshops, publications, and learning tools aimed at supporting entrepreneurs.

6 Explain how to use five training techniques.

IMPLEMENTING TRAINING PROGRAMS

With the program designed and budgeted and objectives set, you can turn to implementing the training program. This means actually doing the training, using one or more of the training methods we turn to now. We'll start with simpler, low-tech methods and proceed to computer-based ones.

On-the-Job Training

On-the-job training (OJT) means having a person learn a job by actually doing it. Every employee, from mailroom clerk to CEO, gets on-the-job training when he or she joins a firm. In many firms, OJT is the only training available.[36] (Or worse: All too often the supervisor simply says, "Here's your desk; get started.")

on-the-job training
Training a person to learn a job while working on it.

Types of On-the-Job Training The most familiar on-the-job training is the *coaching or understudy method.* Here, an experienced worker or the trainee's supervisor trains the employee. This may involve simply acquiring skills by observing the supervisor, or (preferably) having the supervisor or job expert show the new employee the ropes, step-by-step. The Men's Wearhouse, with more than 455 stores nationwide, makes extensive use of on-the-job training. Every manager is formally accountable for the development of his or her direct subordinates.[37] *Job rotation,* in which an employee (usually a management trainee) moves from job to job at planned intervals, is another OJT technique. *Special assignments* similarly give lower-level executives firsthand experience in working on actual problems.

Perhaps most importantly, don't take the success of an on-the-job training effort for granted. Train the trainers themselves (often the employees' supervisors), and provide the training materials. Trainers should know, for instance, the principles of motivating learners. Because low expectations on the trainer's part may translate into poor trainee performance, supervisor/trainers should emphasize the high expectations they have for their trainees' success.

The OJT Process Here are some steps to help ensure OJT success.

Step 1: Prepare the Learner

1. Put the learner at ease.
2. Explain why he or she is being taught.
3. Create interest and find out what the learner already knows about the job.
4. Explain the whole job and relate it to some job the worker already knows.
5. Place the learner as close to the normal working position as possible.
6. Familiarize the worker with equipment, materials, tools, and trade terms.

Step 2: Present the Operation

1. Explain quantity and quality requirements.
2. Go through the job at the normal work pace.
3. Go through the job at a slow pace several times, explaining each step. Between operations, explain the difficult parts, or those in which errors are likely to be made.
4. Again, go through the job at a slow pace several times; explain the key points.
5. Have the learner explain the steps as you go through the job at a slow pace.

Step 3: Do a Tryout

1. Have the learner go through the job several times, slowly, explaining each step to you. Correct mistakes and, if necessary, do some of the complicated steps the first few times.
2. Run the job at the normal pace.
3. Have the learner do the job, gradually building up skill and speed.
4. As soon as the learner demonstrates ability to do the job, let the work begin, but don't abandon him or her.

Step 4: Follow-Up

1. Designate to whom the learner should go for help.
2. Gradually decrease supervision, checking work from time to time.
3. Correct faulty work patterns before they become a habit. Show why the method you suggest is superior.
4. Compliment good work.[38]

Apprenticeship Training

Apprenticeship training is a process by which people become skilled workers, usually through a combination of formal learning and long-term on-the-job training. It traditionally involves having the learner/apprentice study under the tutelage of a master craftsperson. When steelmaker Dofasco discovered that many of their employees would be retiring during the next 5 to 10 years, the company decided to revive its apprenticeship training. Applicants are prescreened. New recruits then spend about 32 months in an internal apprenticeship training program, learning various jobs under the tutelage of experienced employees.[39]

The U.S. Department of Labor's National Apprenticeship System promotes apprenticeship programs. More than 460,000 apprentices participate in 28,000 programs, and registered programs can receive federal and state contracts and other assistance.[40] Figure 8-3 lists popular recent apprenticeships.

Informal Learning

Surveys from the American Society for Training and Development estimate that as much as 80% of what employees learn on the job they learn not through formal training but through informal means, including performing their jobs on a daily basis in collaboration with their colleagues.[41]

Although managers don't manage informal learning, there's still much they can do to ensure that it occurs. Most of the steps are simple. For example, Siemens Power Transmission and Distribution in Raleigh, North Carolina, places tools in cafeteria areas to take advantage of the work-related discussions taking place. Even installing whiteboards with markers can facilitate informal learning.

Job Instruction Training

Many jobs (or parts of jobs) consist of a logical sequence of steps that one best learns step-by-step. This step-by-step training is called **job instruction training (JIT)**. First, list all necessary steps in the job (in this case for a mechanical paper cutter) each in

FIGURE 8-3 Some Popular Apprenticeships

Source: www.doleta.gov/oa, accessed July 3, 2009.

The U.S. Department of Labor's Registered Apprenticeship program offers access to 1,000 career areas, including the following top occupations:

- Able seaman
- Carpenter
- Chef
- Child care development specialist
- Construction craft laborer
- Dental assistant
- Electrician
- Elevator constructor
- Fire medic
- Law enforcement agent
- Over-the-road truck driver
- Pipefitter

apprenticeship training
A structured process by which people become skilled workers through a combination of classroom instruction and on-the-job training.

job instruction training (JIT)
Listing each job's basic tasks, along with key points, in order to provide step-by-step training for employees.

its proper sequence. Then list a corresponding "key point" (if any) beside each step. The steps in such a *job instruction training sheet* show trainees what to do, and the key points show how it's to be done—and why.

Steps	Key Points
1. Start motor	None
2. Set cutting distance	Carefully read scale—to prevent wrong-sized cut
3. Place paper on cutting table	Make sure paper is even—to prevent uneven cut
4. Push paper up to cutter	Make sure paper is tight—to prevent uneven cut
5. Grasp safety release with left hand	Do not release left hand—to prevent hand from being caught in cutter
6. Grasp cutter release with right hand	Do not release right hand—to prevent hand from being caught in cutter
7. Simultaneously pull cutter and safety releases	Keep both hands on corresponding releases—avoid hands being on cutting table
8. Wait for cutter to retract	Keep both hands on releases—to avoid having hands on cutting table
9. Retract paper	Make sure cutter is retracted; keep both hands away from releases
10. Shut off motor	None

Figure 8-4 shows the step-by-step graphical instructions UPS uses to train new drivers in how to park their trucks and disembark.

Lectures

Although some correctly view lectures as being boring, studies and practical experience show that they can be effective.[42] Lecturing is a quick and simple way to present knowledge to large groups of trainees, as when the sales force needs to learn a new product's features. Here are some guidelines for presenting a lecture:[43]

- Don't start out on the wrong foot. For instance, don't open with an irrelevant joke or by saying something like, "I really don't know why I was asked to speak here today."

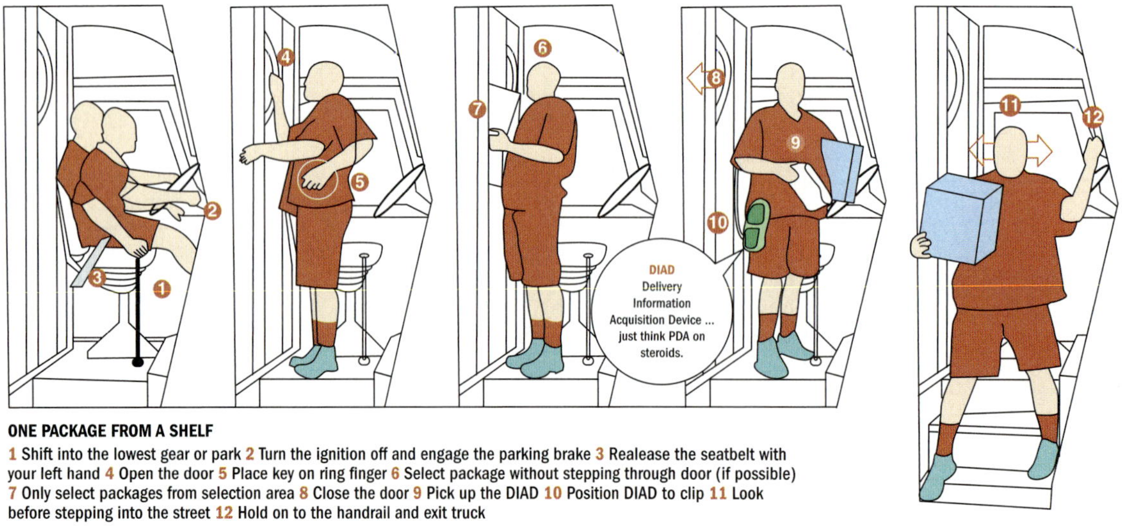

FIGURE 8-4 Job Instruction Training at UPS

Source: Nadira Hira, "The Making of a UPS Driver," *Fortune*, November 12, 2007, page 120.

- Give your listeners signals. For instance, if you have a list of items, start by saying something like, "There are four reasons why the sales reports are necessary . . . . The first . . ."
- Be alert to your audience. Watch body language for negative signals like fidgeting and crossed arms.
- Maintain eye contact with the audience during your presentation.
- Make sure everyone in the room can hear. Repeat questions that you get from trainees before you answer.
- Control your hands. Get in the habit of leaving them hanging naturally at your sides.
- Talk from notes rather than from a script. Write out clear, legible notes on large index cards or on PowerPoint slides. Use these as an outline.
- Break a long talk into a series of 5-minute talks. Speakers often give a short overview introduction and then spend the rest of a 1-hour presentation going point by point through their material. Experts suggest breaking the long talk into a series of 5-minute talks, each with its own introduction. Write brief PowerPoint slides, and spend about a minute on each. Each introduction highlights what you'll discuss, why it's important to the audience, and your credibility—why they should listen to you.[44]
- Practice. If possible, rehearse under conditions similar to those under which you will actually give your presentation.

Programmed Learning

Whether the medium is a textbook, PC, or the Internet, **programmed learning** (or *programmed instruction*) is a step-by-step, self-learning method that consists of three parts:

1. Presenting questions, facts, or problems to the learner
2. Allowing the person to respond
3. Providing feedback on the accuracy of answers

Generally, programmed learning presents facts and follow-up questions frame by frame. When the learner responds, subsequent frames provide feedback on the answer's accuracy. What the next question is often depends on how the learner answers the previous question.

Programmed learning's main advantage is that it reduces training time.[45] It also facilitates learning by letting trainees learn at their own pace, get immediate feedback, and reduce their risk of error. The problem is that trainees do not learn much more from programmed learning than they would from a textbook. You must therefore weigh the cost of developing the programmed instruction against the faster but not improved learning.

Intelligent tutoring systems take programmed learning one step further. They are computerized, supercharged, programmed instruction programs. In addition to the usual programmed learning, intelligent tutoring systems learn what questions and approaches worked and did not work for the learner, and therefore adjust the suggested instructional sequence to the trainee's unique needs.

programmed learning
A systematic method for teaching job skills, involving presenting questions or facts, allowing the person to respond, and giving the learner immediate feedback on the accuracy of his or her answers.

Audiovisual-Based Training

Audiovisual-based training techniques like DVDs, films, PowerPoint, and audiotapes are widely used.[46] The Ford Motor Company uses videos in its dealer training sessions to simulate problems and reactions to various customer complaints, for example.

Audiovisuals are more expensive than lectures but offer advantages. Of course, they usually tend to be more interesting. In addition, consider using them in the following situations:

1. When there is a need to illustrate how to follow a certain sequence over time, such as when teaching machine repair. The stop-action, instant replay, and fast- or slow-motion capabilities of audiovisuals can be useful here.
2. When there is a need to expose trainees to events not easily demonstrable in live lectures, such as a visual tour of a factory or open-heart surgery.
3. When you need organizationwide training and it is too costly to move the trainers from place to place.

Vestibule Training

Vestibule training is a method in which trainees learn on the actual or simulated equipment they will use on the job, but are trained off the job (perhaps in a separate room or *vestibule*). Vestibule training is necessary when it's too costly or dangerous to train employees on the job. Putting new assembly-line workers right to work could slow production, for instance, and when safety is a concern—as with pilots—simulated training may be the only practical alternative. As an example, UPS uses a life-size learning lab to provide a 40-hour, 5-day realistic training program for driver candidates.[47]

Teletraining and Videoconferencing

With *teletraining*, a trainer in a central location teaches groups of employees at remote locations via televised hookups. Honda America began by using satellite television to train engineers. Now its Ohio-based subsidiary purchases seminars from the National Technological University. This is a provider of satellite education that uses courses from various universities and specialized teaching organizations.

Videoconferencing allows people in one location to communicate live with people in another city or country, or with groups in several cities. This may simply involve using PC-based video cameras and several remote trainees, or a dozen or more learners taking a class in a videoconference lecture room. Here, keypads allow audience interactivity.

Electronic Performance Support Systems (EPSS)

People don't remember everything they learn. Dell, for example, introduces about 80 new products per year, so it's unrealistic to expect Dell's technical support people to know everything about every product. Dell's training therefore focuses on providing its employees with the general knowledge they need every day, such as Dell's rules, culture and values, and systems and work processes. Performance support systems then deliver the rest of what they need to know, when they need it.[48]

Electronic performance support systems (EPSS) are computerized tools and displays that automate training, documentation, and phone support.[49] When you call a Dell service rep about a problem with your new computer, he or she is probably asking questions prompted by an EPSS; it takes you both, step-by-step, through an analytical sequence. Without the EPSS, Dell would have to train its service reps to memorize an unrealistically large number of solutions. Aetna Insurance cut its 13-week instructor-led training course for new call center employees by about 2 weeks by providing the employees with performance support tools.[50]

Performance support systems are modern job aids. A **job aid** is a set of instructions, diagrams, or similar methods available at the job site to guide the worker.[51] Job aids work particularly well on complex jobs that require multiple steps, or where it's dangerous to forget a step. Airline pilots use job aids (such as a checklist of things to do prior to takeoff). GM's former Electromotive Division gave workers job aids in the form of diagrams. These show, for example, where the locomotive wiring runs and which color wires go where.

Computer-Based Training

With computer-based training, trainers use interactive computer-based and/or DVD systems to increase knowledge or skills.[52]

We'll see that computer-based training (CBT) is increasingly interactive and realistic. For example, *interactive multimedia training* integrates the use of text, video, graphics, photos, animation, and sound to produce a complex training environment with which the trainee interacts.[53] In training a physician, for instance, an interactive multimedia training system lets a medical student take a hypothetical patient's medical history, conduct an examination, and analyze lab tests. Then, by clicking the "examine chest" button, the student can choose a type of chest examination and even hear the sounds of the person's heart. The medical student can then interpret the sounds and draw conclusions upon which to base a diagnosis. *Virtual reality training* takes this realism a step further. Table 8-2 summarizes the main terminology of computer-based training.

Simulated Learning

"Simulated learning" means different things to different people. A recent survey asked training professionals what experiences qualified as simulated learning experiences. The percentages of trainers choosing each experience were:

- Virtual reality-type games, 19%
- Step-by-step animated guide, 8%
- Scenarios with questions and decision trees overlaying animation, 19%
- Online role-play with photos and videos, 14%
- Software training including screenshots with interactive requests, 35%
- Other, 6%[54]

Virtual reality puts the trainee in an artificial three-dimensional environment that simulates events and situations that might be experienced on the job.[55] Sensory devices transmit how the trainee is responding to the computer, and the trainee "sees, feels and hears" what is going on, assisted by special goggles and auditory and sensory devices.[56]

The U.S. Armed Forces use simulation-based training programs for soldiers and officers. For example, the army developed video-game-type training programs called Full-Spectrum Command and Full-Spectrum Warrior for training troops in urban warfare. According to one description, the two games offer extremely realistic features, within a context that emphasizes real-time leadership and decision-making skills.[57]

electronic performance support systems (EPSS)
Sets of computerized tools and displays that automate training, documentation, and phone support, integrate this automation into applications, and provide support that's faster, cheaper, and more effective than traditional methods.

job aid
A set of instructions, diagrams, or similar methods available at the job site to guide the worker.

TABLE 8-2 Names and Descriptions of Various Computer-Based Training Techniques

PI	Computer-based programmed instruction (PI) programs consist of text, graphics, and perhaps multimedia enhancements that are stored in memory and connected to one another electronically. Material to be learned is grouped into chunks of closely related information. Typically, the computer-based PI program presents the trainees with the information in the chunk, and then tests them on their retention of the information. If they have not retained the material, they are cycled back to the original information, or to remedial information. If they have retained the information, they move on to the next information to be learned.
CBT	Training provided in part or in whole through the use of a computer. *Computer-based training* is the term most often used in private industry or the government for training employees using computer-assisted instruction.
CMI	Computer-managed instruction (CMI) uses a computer to manage the administrative functions of training, such as registration, record keeping, scoring, and grading.
ICAI	When the computer-based training system is able to provide some of the primary characteristics of a human tutor, it is often referred to as an intelligent computer-assisted instruction (ICAI) system. It is a more advanced form of PI. Expert systems are used to run the tutoring aspect of the training, monitor trainee knowledge within a programmed knowledge model, and provide adaptive tutoring based on trainee responses.
ITS	Intelligent tutoring systems (ITS) make use of artificial intelligence to provide tutoring that is more advanced than ICAI type tutoring. ITS "learns" through trainee responses the best methods of facilitating the trainee's learning.
Simulations	Computer simulations provide a representation of a situation and the tasks to be performed in the situation. The representation can range from identical (e.g., word processing training) to fairly abstract (e.g., conflict resolution). Trainees perform the tasks presented to them by the computer program and the computer program monitors their performance.
Virtual Reality	Virtual reality is an advanced form of computer simulation, placing the trainee in a simulated environment that is "virtually" the same as the physical environment. This simulation is accomplished by the trainee wearing special equipment such as headgear, gloves, and so on, that controls what the trainee is able to see, feel, and otherwise sense. The trainee learns by interacting with objects in the electronic environment to achieve some goal.

Source: P. Nick Blanchard and James Thacker, *Effective Training: Systems, Strategies, and Practices* (Upper Saddle River, NJ: Pearson, 2003), p. 144. Reprinted by permission.

As at Stamford University, employers use computerized simulations to inject more realism into their training. For example, Orlando-based Environmental Tectonics Corporation created an Advanced Disaster Management simulation for emergency medical response trainees. One of the simulated scenarios involves a passenger plane crashing into a runway. So realistic that it's "unsettling," trainees including firefighters and airport officials respond to the simulated crash's sights and sounds via pointing devices and radios.[58] IBM created *IBM at Play*. This uses video-game technology and three-dimensional virtual environments to facilitate training.[59] When Cisco Systems decided it needed a better way to train the tens of thousands of Cisco trainees for Cisco certification exams it turned to gaming. Cisco embedded the learning within a video-game-like atmosphere that included music, graphics, and sound effects.[60] Training simulations are expensive, but for larger companies the cost per employee is usually reasonable.[61]

One way to reduce the cost is to capitalize on virtual environments such as Second Life. For example, British Petroleum uses Second Life to train new gas station employees. The aim here is to show new gas station employees how to use the safety features of gasoline storage tanks. BP built three-dimensional renderings of the tank systems in Second Life. Trainees could use these to "see" underground and observe the effects of using the safety devices.[62]

In general, interactive technologies like these reduce learning time by an average of 50%.[63] Other advantages include instructional consistency (computers, unlike human trainers, don't have good days and bad days), mastery of learning (if the trainee doesn't learn it, he or she generally can't move on to the next step), increased retention, and increased trainee motivation (resulting from responsive feedback).

Specialist multimedia software houses like Graphic Media of Portland, Oregon, produce much of the content for these programs. They produce both custom titles and generic programs like a $999 package for teaching workplace safety.

Internet-Based Training

Internet or Web-based learning is rapidly replacing other types of training. Thus, Delta Air Lines customer service personnel receive much of their annual required FAA training via the Internet. Prior to online training, employees had to travel to one of five training centers, keeping them away from their jobs for at least the day.[64]

There are basically two ways to make online courses available to employees. First, the employer can encourage and/or facilitate having its employees take relevant online courses from its own online (intranet) offerings, or from the hundreds of online training vendors on the Web. For example, the employer might arrange with www.puresafety.com to let its employees take one or more occupational safety courses from those puresafety.com offers.

Learning Portals The second main approach is to arrange with an online training vendor to make its courses available via the employer's intranet-based learning portal. A *learning portal* is a section of an employer's Web site that offers employees online access to many or all of the training courses they need to succeed at their jobs. Most often, the employer contracts with applications service providers (ASP) like those we list in Figure 8-5. When employees go to their firm's learning portal, they actually access the menu of training courses that the ASP company contracted with the employer to offer.

Improving Productivity Through HRIS: Learning Management Systems

Learning management systems (LMS) play an important role in Internet training. They are special software packages that support Internet training by helping employers identify training needs, and in scheduling, delivering, assessing, and managing the online training itself. For example, General Motors uses a new LMS to help its dealers in Africa and the Middle East deliver training. The Internet-based LMS includes a course catalog, supervisor approved self-enrollment, and pre-and post-course tests. Dealers, supervisors, and employees review the list of courses on the LMS. They then choose courses based upon their needs, for instance, in specific areas such as automobile transmissions and sales management. The system then automatically schedules the individual's training.[65] Blackboard and WebCT are two familiar college-oriented learning management systems.

The movement today is toward integrating the e-learning system with the company's overall, enterprisewide information systems. In that way, for instance, employers can automatically update skills inventory and succession plans as employees complete their training.[66]

The Virtual Classroom

Conventional Web-based learning tends to be limited to the sorts of online learning with which many college students are already familiar—reading PowerPoint presentations, participating in instant message type chat rooms, and taking online exams, for instance.

The virtual classroom takes online learning to a new level. A **virtual classroom** uses special collaboration software to enable multiple remote learners, using

virtual classroom
Teaching method thatuses special collaboration software to enable multiple remote learners, using their PCs or laptops, to participate in live audio and visual discussions, communicate via written text, and learn via content such as PowerPoint slides.

FIGURE 8-5 Partial List of E-Learning Vendors

Source: Google. http://www.google.com/permissions/index.html, accessed January 19, 2008.

E-learning Companies

Reference > Education > Distance Learning > Online Teaching and Learning > E-learning Companies — Go to Directory Home

Categories

Course Authoring (71)
E-learning Portals (60)
E-learning Research (23)
Learning Management Systems (73)
Online Classrooms (18)

Related Categories:
Computers > Education > Commercial Services > Training Companies > Self-Study (49)
Reference > Education > Distance Learning > Online Courses (281)
Reference > Education > Distance Learning > Services (34)
Reference > Knowledge Management > Business and Companies (124)

Web Pages — **Viewing in Google PageRank order** — View in alphabetical order

Skillsoft - http://www.skillsoft.com
Providers of enterprise e-learning, a fully integrated student environment and courseware to support e-Learning initiatives in enterprises.

Plateau Systems - http://www.plateau.com
Corporate learning solutions deployed at enterprises across the world enabling global organizations to increase productivity and save millions of training dollars.

Academee - http://www.academee.com
Integrated learning programmes, blending consultancy, online e-learning and face-to-face classroom courses for management and professional development.

Enspire Learning - http://www.enspire.com
Enspire Learning develops custom e-learning courses that include interactive multimedia, simulations, and engaging scenarios.

Ninth House Network - http://www.ninthhouse.com/
A leading e-learning broadband environment for organizational development, delivering to the desktop experiential, interactive programs that leverage the world's foremost business thinkers.

Futurate Ltd - http://www.futurate.com/
Developers of eLearning content and systems that are engaging and accessible to all. They offer a 'full service' from consultancy to implementation and maintenance.

PrimeLearning - http://www.primelearning.com
E-learning company that specialises in business and professional skills courses provided off the self or can be custom made.

Intellinex - http://www.intellinex.com
Provider of e-Learning solutions for workers in Global 2000 companies, government, and educational institutions. Courseware covers PC and business skills applications.

Allen Communication - http://www.allencomm.com
Provides e-Learning solutions including learning portals, strategic planning for training, courseware development and authoring / design tools.

The Learning House, Inc. - http://www.learninghouse.com
Learning House, Inc. is an eLearning services company that creates off the shelf and custom online degree and professional development courses.

DefinITion - http://www.definition.be
DefinITion design and development e-learning courses for companies. The company is based in Belgium and their services include consultancy and support.

Intrac Design Inc - http://www.intrac.biz
The development and delivery of customizable training programs for live classroom and e-learning delivery.

Seward, Inc. - http://www.sewardinc.com
Seward, Inc. provide engaging, instructionally sound, cost-effective training solutions ranging from soft skills involved in sales to the most technically exacting fields of medicine, engineering, and finance.

Silverchair Learning Systems - http://www.silverchairlearning.com
Online employee education exclusively for the Senior Care industry.

Tata Interactive Systems - http://www.tatainteractivesystems.com
Developer of custom e-learning solutions for corporate, educational and governmental organizations.

Little Planet Learning - http://www.littleplanet.com
Provides design and development of learning experiences delivered live and through elearning, computer and web based training (CBT and WBT), and multimedia programs.

Employment Law Learning Technologies - http://www.elt-inc.com
Online compliance training for managers and employees on critical US employment law / HR topics, including harassment, discrimination, privacy and diversity.

their PCs or laptops, to participate in live audio and visual discussions, communicate via written text, and learn via content such as PowerPoint slides.

The virtual classroom combines the best of Web-based learning offered by systems like Blackboard and WebCT with live video and audio. For example, Elluminate Live! enables learners to communicate with clear, two-way audio; build communities with user profiles and live video; collaborate with chat and shared whiteboards; and learn with shared applications such as PowerPoint slides.[67]

Using Internet-Based Learning

Whether to use e-learning often comes down to efficiency. Web learning doesn't necessarily teach faster or better. In one review of the evidence, Web-based instruction was a bit more effective than classroom instruction for teaching memory of facts and principles, and Web-based instruction and classroom instruction were equally effective for teaching information about how to perform a task or action.[68] But of course, the need to teach large numbers of students remotely, or to enable students to study at their leisure, often makes e-learning so much more efficient that the small differences in Web-based versus classroom learning become somewhat meaningless.[69]

HR APPs 4 U

Mobile Learning

Mobile learning (or "on-demand learning") means delivering learning content on demand via mobile devices like cell phones, laptops, and iPhones, wherever and whenever the learner has the time and desire to access it.[72] For example, using dominKnow's (www.dominknow.com) iPod touch and iPhone-optimized Touch Learning Center Portal, trainees can log in and take full online courses.[73]

Employers use mobile learning to deliver "corporate training and downloads on everything from how to close an important sales deal to optimizing organizational change to learning business Spanish . . . you can be . . . riding your bike" while listening to the training program.[74] Financial services firm Capital One purchased 3,000 iPods for trainees who had enrolled in one of 20 instructor-led courses at its Capital One University. The training department then had an Internet audio book provider create an audio learning site within Capital One's firewall. Employees used it to download the instructor-requested books and other materials to their iPods.[75] IBM uses mobile learning to deliver just-in-time information (for instance about new product features) to its sales force. To increase such learning's accessibility, IBM's training department often breaks up, say, an hour program into 10-minute pieces. That way, employees needn't put away a full hour to listen.[76] JP Morgan encourages employees to use instant messaging as a quick learning device, for instance, to quickly update colleagues about new products.

In practice, many employers opt for "blended learning." Here, the trainees make use of several delivery methods (such as manuals, in-class lectures, self-guided e-learning programs, and Web-based seminars or "webinars") to learn the material.[70] Intuit (which makes software such as TurboTax) uses instructor-led classroom training for bringing in new distributors and getting them up to speed. Then, they use their virtual classroom systems to provide additional training, for monthly meetings with distributors, and for short classes on special software features.[71]

Lifelong and Literacy Training Techniques

Lifelong learning means providing employees with continuing learning experiences over their tenure with the firm, with the aims of ensuring they have the opportunity to learn the skills they need to do their jobs and to expand their horizons. For example, one senior waiter at the Rhapsody restaurant in Chicago received his undergraduate degree and began work toward a master of social work using the lifelong learning account (LiLA) program his employer offers. Somewhat similar to 401(k) plans, employers and employees contribute to LiLA plans (without the tax advantages of 401(k) plans), and the employee can use these funds to better himself or herself.[77] Lifelong learning may thus range from basic remedial skills (for instance, English as a second language) to college.

Literacy Training

By one estimate, about 39 million people in the United States have learning disabilities. This makes it challenging to read, write, or do arithmetic.[78] Yet today's emphasis on teamwork and quality requires that employees read, write, and understand numbers. A recent study called the American workforce ill-prepared.[79]

Employers often turn to private firms like Education Management Corporation to provide the requisite education.[80] Another simple literacy training approach is to have supervisors teach basic skills by giving employees writing and speaking exercises.[81] One way to do this is to convert materials used in the employee's job into instructional tools. For example, if an employee needs to use a manual to find out how to change a part, teach that person how to use the index to locate the relevant section. Another approach is to bring in outside professionals (such as teachers from a local high school) to teach, say, remedial reading or writing. Having employees attend adult education or high school evening classes is another option.

Literacy training is sometimes one aspect of diversity training programs, as the "Managing the New Workforce" feature illustrates.

lifelong learning
Provides employees with continuing learning experiences over their tenure with the firm, with the aims of ensuring they have the opportunity to learn the skills they need to do their jobs and to expand their occupational horizons.

Managing the New Workforce

Diversity Training

With an increasingly diverse workforce, we saw in Chapter 2 that more firms are implementing diversity training programs. *Diversity training* aims to create better cross-cultural sensitivity, with the goal of fostering more harmonious working relationships among a firm's employees. Such training typically includes improving interpersonal skills, understanding and valuing cultural differences, improving technical skills, socializing employees into the corporate culture, indoctrinating new workers into the U.S. work ethic, improving English proficiency and basic math skills, and improving bilingual skills for English-speaking employees.[82] But with minorities the fastest-growing part of the U.S. workforce, language training no longer means just teaching English. In many industries or locales, customers speak a variety of languages, and for a company to thrive, its workforce may have to be bilingual or multilingual.[83]

Adams Mark Hotel & Resorts conducted a diversity training seminar for about 11,000 employees. It combined lectures, video, and employee role playing to emphasize sensitivity to race and religion.[84] However, most employers can probably opt for an off-the-shelf diversity training program such as *F.A.I.R.: A practical approach to diversity and the workplace*, from VisionPoint productions. The package includes a facilitator and discussion guide, participant materials and workbook, a DVD with print materials, PowerPoint slides, and two videos (the purchase price for the entire program is about $1,000). The first video provides an overview of diversity, explains what it means to be "culturally competent," and addresses the various categories of diversity such as race, religion, ethnicity, gender, and age. The second presents four vignettes illustrating such things as the importance of communicating, the potential pitfalls of stereotyping people, and bias in action (such as a worker whose colleagues treat his religion's holidays with less seriousness then their own).[85]

HR in Practice: Creating Your Own Training Program

Although it would certainly be ideal if supervisors could tap into their companies' packaged training programs to train the new people that they hire, the fact is that many times they cannot. Often, you hire and are responsible for the performance of a new employee, only to find that your company provides little or no specialized training, beyond the new person's introductory orientation. If so, you have several options.

First, there are (as we noted earlier) hundreds of suppliers of prepackaged training solutions. These range from self-study programs from the American Management Association (www.amanet.org) and SHRM (www.shrm.org) to specialized programs (for example, trade journals like *EHS Today* (for environmental, health, and safety managers, http://ehstoday.com/) that contain information on specialized packaged training program suppliers. Firms like elearningdepot.com offer online courses.

Second, managers can create their own training programs, using the following process.

Step 1: Set Training Objectives First, write out the training objectives. Be specific and specify the conditions under which the employee should achieve the objective.

Step 2: Use a Detailed Job Description A detailed job description is the heart of any training program. It should list the daily and periodic tasks of each job, along with a summary of the steps in each task.

Step 3: Develop an Abbreviated Task Analysis Record Form You can use an abbreviated version of the Task Analysis Record Form (Table 8-1, page 270) containing just four columns. In the first column, list *tasks* (including what the employee is to perform in terms of each of the main tasks, step-by-step). In column 2, list *performance standards* (in terms of quantity, quality, accuracy, and so on). In column 3, list *trainable skills* required, things the employee must know or do to perform the task. (Here list the specific knowledge and skills, such as "Keep both hands on the wheel," that you want to stress.) In the fourth column, list *aptitudes required*. These are the human aptitudes (such as mechanical comprehension) that employees need to be trained for the job.

Step 4: Develop a Job Instruction Sheet Next, write a job instruction sheet. As explained on pages 275–276, this sheet shows the steps in each task as well as key points for each.

Step 5: Compile Training Program for the Job At a minimum, your training package should include the job description, abbreviated Task Analysis Record Form, and job instruction sheet, all compiled in a training manual. The latter should also contain a summary of the training program's objectives, and a list of the trainable skills required for the trainee. The manual might also contain an introduction to the job and an explanation of how the job fits with other jobs in the plant or office.

A simple but effective on-the-job training program using employees as trainers requires only the materials we just listed. However, the nature of the job (or the number of trainees) may require purchasing special media, or a PowerPoint slide presentation, for instance.

7 List and briefly discuss four management development programs.

IMPLEMENTING MANAGEMENT DEVELOPMENT PROGRAMS

It's not always easy to tell where "training" leaves off and "management development" begins. The latter, however, tends to emphasize both long-term development and a focus on developing current or future managers. **Management development** is any attempt to improve managerial performance by imparting knowledge, changing attitudes, or increasing skills. The management development process consists of (1) assessing the company's strategic needs (for instance, to fill future executive openings or to boost competitiveness), (2) appraising managers' current performance, and then (3) developing the managers (and future managers).[86] As we explained in Chapter 5, (Planning and Recruiting), development is usually part of the employer's *succession planning*. Succession planning refers to the process through which a company plans for and fills senior-level openings.[87]

Succession planning and management development both stem from the employer's strategy, vision, and personnel plans. For example, strategies to enter new businesses or expand overseas imply that the employer will need managers who have the skills to manage these new businesses.

Some management development programs are company-wide and involve all or most new (or potential) managers. Thus, new MBAs may join GE's management development program and rotate through various assignments and educational experiences. The dual aims are identifying their management potential and giving them breadth of experience (in, say, production and finance). The firm may then slot superior candidates onto a "fast track," a development program that prepares them more quickly for senior-level commands.

management development
Any attempt to improve current or future management performance by imparting knowledge, changing attitudes, or increasing skills.

Other development programs aim to fill specific top positions, such as CEO. For example, GE spent years developing, testing, and watching potential replacements for CEO before finally choosing Jeffrey Immelt.

In any case, assessment is usually part of development programs. At frozen foods manufacturer Schawn, a committee of senior executives first whittles 40 or more development candidates down to about 10. Then the program begins with a 1-day assessment by outside consultants of each manager's leadership strengths and weaknesses. The assessment involves managers addressing problems such as employee conflict. The consultants assess 15 leadership competencies. This assessment becomes the basis for each manager's individual development plan. Action-learning (practical) projects then supplement individual and group training activities.[88]

A recent survey listed the most popular management development activities. The most popular include classroom-based learning, executive coaching, action learning, 360° feedback, experiential learning, off-site retreats (where managers meet with colleagues for learning), mentoring, and job rotation.[89] We'll look at some of these.

Managerial On-the-Job Training

Managerial on-the-job training methods include job rotation, the coaching/understudy approach, and action learning.

Job Rotation

Job rotation means moving managers from department to department to broaden their understanding of the business and to test their abilities. The trainee may be a recent college graduate, and spend several months in each department, learning the department's business by actually doing it. Or he or she may be a senior manager being groomed for CEO by being exposed to a range of domestic and foreign challenges.

Coaching/Understudy Approach

Here the trainee works directly with a senior manager or with the person he or she is to replace; the latter is responsible for the trainee's coaching. Normally, the understudy relieves the executive of certain responsibilities, giving the trainee a chance to learn the job.

Action Learning

Action learning programs give managers and others released time to work analyzing and solving problems in departments other than their own. The basics include carefully selected teams of 5 to 25 members, assigning the teams real-world business problems that extend beyond their usual areas of expertise, and structured learning through coaching and feedback. The employer's senior managers usually choose the projects and decide whether to accept the teams' recommendations.[90] Many major firms around the world, from GE to Samsung, use action learning.[91] For example, Pacific Gas & Electric Company's (PG&E) Action-Forum Process has three phases:

1. A "framework" phase of 6 to 8 weeks—basically, an intense planning period during which the team defines and collects data on an issue;
2. The action forum—2 to 3 days at PG&E's learning center discussing the issue and developing action-plan recommendations; and
3. Accountability sessions, when the teams meet with the leadership group at 30, 60, and 90 days to review their action plans.

Off-the-Job Management Training and Development Techniques

There are also many off-the-job techniques for training and developing managers.

The Case Study Method

As most everyone knows, the **case study method** presents a trainee with a written description of an organizational problem. The person then analyzes the case, diagnoses the problem, and presents his or her findings and solutions in a discussion with other trainees.

Integrated case scenarios expand the case analysis concept by creating long-term, comprehensive case situations. For example, the FBI Academy created an integrated case scenario. It starts with "a concerned citizen's telephone call and ends 14 weeks later with a simulated trial. In between is the stuff of a genuine investigation, including a healthy sampling of what can go wrong in an actual criminal inquiry." To create such scenarios, scriptwriters (often employees in the firm's training group) write the scripts. The scripts include themes, background stories, detailed personnel histories, and role-playing instructions. The scenarios aim to develop specific training skills, such as interviewing witnesses.[92]

Management Games With computerized **management games**, trainees divide into five- or six-person groups, each of which competes with the others in a simulated marketplace. Each group typically must decide, for example, (1) how much to spend on advertising, (2) how much to produce, (3) how much inventory to maintain, and (4) how many of which product to produce. Usually, the game compresses a 2- or 3-year period into days, weeks, or months. As in the real world, each company team usually can't see what decisions (such as to boost advertising) the other firms have made, although these decisions do affect their own sales.

Management games are effective. People learn best by being involved, and games gain such involvement. They also help trainees develop their problem-solving skills, and to focus attention on planning rather than just putting out fires. The groups also usually elect their own officers and organize themselves. This can develop leadership skills and foster cooperation and teamwork.

Outside Seminars Many companies and universities offer Web-based and traditional classroom management development seminars and conferences. For example, the American Management Association provides thousands of courses in areas ranging from accounting and controls to assertiveness training, basic financial skills, information systems, and total quality management.[93] Specialized associations, such as SHRM, provide specialized seminars for their profession's members.

University-Related Programs Many universities provide executive education and continuing education programs in leadership, supervision, and the like. These can range from 1- to 4-day programs to executive development programs lasting 1 to 4 months.

The Advanced Management Program of Harvard's Graduate School of Business Administration is a well-known example.[94] Students are experienced managers from around the world. It uses cases and lectures to provide them with the latest management skills. When Hasbro wanted to improve its executives' creativity skills, it turned to Dartmouth University's Amos Tuck Business School. Tuck provided a "custom approach to designing a program that would be built from the ground up to suit Hasbro's specific needs."[95]

job rotation
A management training technique that involves moving a trainee from department to department to broaden his or her experience and identify strong and weak points.

action learning
A training technique by which management trainees are allowed to work full-time analyzing and solving problems in other departments.

case study method
A development method in which the manager is presented with a written description of an organizational problem to diagnose and solve.

management game
A development technique in which teams of managers compete by making computerized decisions regarding realistic but simulated situations.

Video-linked university programs are another option. For example, a video link between California State University, Sacramento, and a Hewlett-Packard facility in Roseville, California, allows HP employees to take courses at their facility.

Role Playing

The aim of **role playing** is to create a realistic situation and then have the trainees assume the parts (or roles) of specific persons in that situation.

Figure 8-6 presents a role from a classic role-playing exercise called the New Truck Dilemma. When combined with the general instructions and other roles, role playing can trigger spirited discussions among the role player/trainees. The aim is to develop trainees' skills in areas like leadership and delegating. For example, a supervisor could experiment with both a considerate and an autocratic leadership style, whereas in the real world the person might not have the luxury of experimenting. It may also train someone to be more aware of and sensitive to others' feelings.[96]

Behavior Modeling

Behavior modeling involves (1) showing trainees the right (or "model") way of doing something, (2) letting trainees practice that way, and then (3) giving feedback on the trainees' performance. Behavior modeling training is one of the most widely used, well researched, and highly regarded psychologically based training interventions.[97] The basic procedure is as follows:

1. **Modeling.** First, trainees watch live or video examples showing models behaving effectively in a problem situation. Thus, the video might show a supervisor effectively disciplining a subordinate, if teaching "how to discipline" is the aim of the training program.
2. **Role playing.** Next, the trainees are given roles to play in a simulated situation; here, they practice and rehearse the effective behaviors demonstrated by the models.
3. **Social reinforcement.** The trainer provides reinforcement in the form of praise and constructive feedback based on how the trainee performs in the role-playing situation.
4. **Transfer of training.** Finally, trainees are encouraged to apply their new skills when they are back on their jobs.

Corporate Universities

Many firms, particularly larger ones, establish **in-house development centers** (often called *corporate universities*). GE, Caterpillar, and IBM are some examples. In-house development centers typically offer a catalogue of courses and programs aimed at supporting the employers' management development needs. They typically do not produce all (or most) of their own training and development programs, although some do. Employers are increasingly collaborating with academic institutions, and with training and

FIGURE 8-6 Typical Role in a Role-Playing Exercise

Source: From Maier, Norman. *Psychology of Industrial Organizations,* 5e. © 1982 Wadsworth, a part of Cengage Learning, Inc. Reproduced by permission.www.cengage.com/permissions.

Walt Marshall—Supervisor of Repair Crew

You are the head of a crew of telephone maintenance workers, each of whom drives a small service truck to and from the various jobs. Every so often you get a new truck to exchange for an old one, and you have the problem of deciding which of your crew members you should give the new truck. Often there are hard feelings, since each seems to feel entitled to the new truck, so you have a tough time being fair. As a matter of fact, it usually turns out that whatever you decide is considered wrong by most of the crew. You now have to face the issue again because a new truck, a Chevrolet, has just been allocated to you for assignment.

In order to handle this problem you have decided to put the decision up to the crew. You will tell them about the new truck and will put the problem in terms of what would be the fairest way to assign the truck. Do not take a position yourself, because you want to do what they think is most fair.

development program providers and Web-based educational portals, to create packages of programs and materials.[98]

For many firms, learning portals are becoming their virtual corporate universities. While firms such as GE have long had their own bricks-and-mortar corporate universities, learning portals let even smaller firms have corporate universities. Bain & Company, a management consulting firm, has such a Web-based virtual university for its employees. It provides a means not only for coordinating all the company's training efforts, but also for delivering Web-based modules that cover topics from strategic management to mentoring.[99]

Executive Coaches Many firms retain executive coaches to develop their top managers' effectiveness. An **executive coach** is an outside consultant who questions the executive's boss, peers, subordinates, and (sometimes) family in order to identify the executive's strengths and weaknesses, and to counsel the executive so he or she can capitalize on those strengths and overcome the weaknesses.[100] Executive coaching can cost as much as $50,000 per executive. Experts therefore recommend using formal assessments prior to coaching, to uncover strengths and weaknesses and to provide more focused coaching.[101]

Executive coaching can be effective. Participants in one study included about 1,400 senior managers who had received "360 degree" performance feedback from bosses, peers, and subordinates. About 400 worked with an executive coach to review the feedback. Then, about a year later, these 400 managers and about 400 who didn't receive coaching again received multisource feedback. The managers who received executive coaching were more likely to set more effective, specific goals for their subordinates, and to have received improved ratings from subordinates and supervisors.[102]

The coaching field is unregulated, so managers should do their due diligence. The International Coach Federation is one trade group.

The SHRM Learning System SHRM, the Society for Human Resource Management, encourages HR professionals to qualify for certification by taking examinations. The society offers several preparatory training programs. The self-study option includes text and DVD. The college/university option provides classroom interaction with instructors and other students.

8 List and briefly discuss the importance of the eight steps in leading organizational change.

MANAGING ORGANIZATIONAL CHANGE PROGRAMS

Several years ago, Intel Corp. carried out a major reorganization that one writer says "may have badly damaged employee development, morale and the company's culture of innovation."[103] Managing change is important in today's challenging environment. Professor Edward Lawler concluded that as more employers face the need to adapt to rapid competitive change, "focusing on strategy, organizational development, and organizational change is a high payoff activity for the HR organization."[104] But (although human resource management plays a role in executing change programs), it is always the line manager who must formulate the change program and execute the changes day-to-day.

role playing
A training technique in which trainees act out parts in a realistic management situation.

behavior modeling
A training technique in which trainees are first shown good management techniques in a film, are asked to play roles in a simulated situation, and are then given feedback and praise by their supervisor.

in-house development center
A company-based method for exposing prospective managers to realistic exercises to develop improved management skills.

executive coach
An outside consultant who questions the executive's associates in order to identify the executive's strengths and weaknesses, and then counsels the executive so he or she can capitalize on those strengths and overcome the weaknesses.

What to Change

The first question is, "What should we change?" For example, when she became CEO of a troubled Avon Products Company some years ago, Andrea Jung knew she had a problem. Sales reps were leaving, customers were demanding more effective products, and the firm's whole "back end" operation—the purchasing, order-taking, distribution system—lacked automation.

Faced with situations like these, managers like Andrea Jung can change one or more of five aspects of their companies—their *strategy, culture, structure, technologies,* or the *attitudes and skills* of the employees.

Organizational turnarounds often start with a change in the firm's strategy, mission, and vision—with *strategic change.* For example, faced with competition from firms like Estée Lauder, Avon under Ms. Jung more than doubled its expenditures on new-product development, with the aim of introducing new products that created younger-looking skin. Avon also expanded its strategy to selling through select department stores, rather than just door-to-door. Yet strategic change isn't always the most pressing issue. When he took over as IBM's CEO in the 1990s, Louis Gerstner famously said, "The last thing IBM needs now is a vision." What IBM did need first was *cultural* change. Gerstner believed IBM's employees had become too complacent. He instituted new incentive and other plans to focus them more on the competition.

Back at Avon, its expansion to department stores demanded *structural change*—in other words, reorganizing the company's departmental structure, coordination, span of control, reporting relationships, tasks, and decision-making procedures. Ms. Jung's turnaround strategy also demanded *technological change,* as Ms. Jung guided Avon to automate its purchasing/distribution chain.

Of course, strategic, cultural, structural, and technological changes like these, no matter how logical, will fail without the employees' active support. As one example of many, a nationwide beverage distributor encountered significant opposition from its sales force several years ago when it moved from its paper-based sales management system to wireless laptops.[105] Organizational change therefore invariably involves bringing about *changes in the employees* themselves and in their attitudes, skills, and behaviors.[106]

Unfortunately, getting that active support (or at least silent compliance) from your employees is easier said than done. The manager invariably runs into employee resistance. Knowing how to deal with that resistance is the heart of implementing an organizational change program.

Source: Courtesy of Mario Tama/Getty Images.

CEO Andrea Jung initiated a renewal program at Avon Products that demanded strategic change (doubling expenditures on new-product development) and cultural change (selling through retail outlets, not just door-to-door), as well as structural and technological changes to fulfill the new goals.

Lewin's Change Process

Often, the trickiest part of implementing an organizational change is overcoming employees' resistance to it. The change may require the cooperation of dozens or even hundreds of managers and supervisors, many of whom might well view the change as detrimental to their peace of mind. Resistance may therefore be formidable.

Psychologist Kurt Lewin formulated a model of change to summarize what he believed was the basic process for implementing a change with minimal resistance. To Lewin, all behavior in organizations was a product of two kinds of forces: those striving to maintain the status quo and those pushing for change. Implementing change thus meant either reducing the forces for the status quo or building up the forces for change. Lewin's process consisted of three steps:

1. *Unfreezing* means reducing the forces that are striving to maintain the status quo, usually by presenting a provocative problem or event to get people to recognize the need for change and to search for new solutions.

2. *Moving* means developing new behaviors, values, and attitudes. The manager may accomplish this through organizational structure changes, and sometimes through the other organizational development techniques (such as the team building) we'll discuss later.
3. *Refreezing* means building in the reinforcement to make sure the organization doesn't slide back into its former ways of doing things.

Leading Organizational Change[107]

Of course, the challenge is in the details. An 8-step process for leading organizational change follows.[108]

Unfreezing Stage

1. *Establish a sense of urgency.* Most managers start by creating a sense of urgency. This often takes creativity. For example, the CEO might present executives with a (fictitious) analyst's report describing the firm's imminent demise.
2. *Mobilize commitment* through joint diagnosis of problems. Having established a sense of urgency, the leader may then create one or more task forces to diagnose the problems facing the company. Such teams can produce a shared understanding of what they can and must improve, and thereby mobilize commitment.

Moving Stage

3. *Create a guiding coalition.* No one can really implement major organizational change alone. Most CEOs create a guiding coalition of influential people. They work together as a team to act as missionaries and implementers.
4. *Develop and communicate a shared vision.* Your organizational renewal may require a new vision. For example, when Barry Gibbons became CEO of Spec's Music Stores some years ago, his vision of Spec's offering a diversified blend of concerts and retail music helped provide this direction. Guidelines here are *keep it simple* (for example, "We are going to become faster than anyone else in our industry at satisfying customer needs."), *use multiple forums* (meetings, e-mails, formal and informal interaction), and *lead by example* ("walk your talk"—make sure your behaviors and decisions are consistent with the vision).[109]
5. *Help employees make the change.* Are there impediments to change? Does a lack of skills stand in the way? Do policies, procedures, or the firm's organization make it difficult to act? Do intransigent managers discourage employees from acting? If so, address the impediments. When he was CEO at the former Allied Signal, Lawrence Bossidy put every one of his 80,000 people through quality improvement training.
6. *Consolidate gains* and produce more change. Aim for attainable short-term accomplishments. Use the credibility from these to change all the systems, structures, and policies that don't fit well with the company's new vision. Continue to produce more change, for instance by hiring and promoting new people.[110]

Refreezing Stage

7. *Reinforce the new ways of doing things* with changes to the company's systems and procedures. Use new appraisal systems and incentives to reinforce the desired behaviors. Reinforce the new culture by ensuring that the firm's managers take steps to role-model and communicate the company's new values.

8. Finally, the leader must *monitor and assess progress.* In brief, this involves comparing where the company is today with where it should be, based on measurable milestones. Avon Product's Ms. Jung knew Avon had to increase its new products. She instituted many changes, and then asked, "How many new products has the company introduced?" "How many new door-to-door sales reps has the firm added?"

9 Answer the question, "What is organizational development and how does it differ from traditional approaches to organizational change?"

Using Organizational Development

There are many ways to reduce the resistance often associated with organizational change. Among the many suggestions are that managers impose rewards or sanctions that guide employee behaviors, explain why the change is needed, negotiate with employees, give inspirational speeches, or ask employees to help design the change.[111] Organizational development (OD) taps into the latter. **Organizational development** is a change process through which employees formulate the change that's required and implement it, often with the assistance of trained consultants. As an approach to changing organizations, OD has several distinguishing characteristics:

1. It usually involves *action research,* which means collecting data about a group, department, or organization, and feeding the information back to the employees so they can analyze it and develop hypotheses about what the problems in the unit might be.
2. It applies behavioral science knowledge to improve the organization's effectiveness.
3. It changes the organization in a particular direction—toward empowerment, improved problem solving, responsiveness, quality of work, and effectiveness.

There are four basic categories of OD applications: human process, technostructural, human resource management, and strategic applications (see Table 8-3). Action research—getting the employees themselves to review the required data and to design and implement the solutions—is the basis of all four.

Human Process Applications

Human process OD techniques aim at improving human relations skills. The goal is to give employees the insight and skills required to analyze their own and others' behavior more effectively, so they can then solve interpersonal and intergroup problems. These problems might include, for instance, conflict among employees. Applications here include sensitivity training, team building, and survey research.

Sensitivity, laboratory, or *t-group* (the *t* is for "training") training's basic aim is to increase the participant's insight into his or her own behavior by encouraging an open expression of feelings in the trainer-guided t-group. Typically, 10 to 15 people meet, usually away from the job, with no specific agenda. Instead, the focus is on the feelings and emotions of the members in the group at the meeting. The facilitator encourages participants to portray themselves as they feel the group rather than in terms of past behaviors. The t-group's success depends on the feedback each person gets from the others, and on the participants' willingness to be candid. The process requires that participants feel safe enough to expose their feelings.[112]

T-group training is controversial. Its personal nature suggests that participation should be voluntary. Some view it as unethical because you can't consider participation "suggested" by one's superior as voluntary.[113] Others argue that it can actually be a dangerous exercise if led by an inadequately prepared trainer.

TABLE 8-3 Examples of OD Interventions

Interventions
Human Process
T-groups
Process consultation
Third-party intervention
Team building
Organizational confrontation meeting
Survey research
Technostructural
Formal structural change
Differentiation and integration
Cooperative union–management projects
Quality circles
Total quality management
Work design
Human Resource Management
Goal setting
Performance appraisal
Reward systems
Career planning and development
Managing workforce diversity
Employee wellness
Strategic
Integrated strategic management
Culture change
Strategic change
Self-designing organizations

Team building is another option. According to experts French and Bell, the typical team-building meeting begins with the consultant interviewing each of the group members and the leader before the meeting.[114] They are asked what their problems are, how they think the group functions, and what obstacles are keeping the group from performing better. The consultant then categorizes the interview data into themes (such as "inadequate communications") and presents the themes to the group at the start of the meeting. The group ranks the themes in terms of importance, and the most important ones become the agenda for the meeting. The group then explores and discusses the issues, examines the underlying causes of the problems, and begins devising solutions.

Survey research, another human process OD technique, requires that employees throughout the organization complete attitude surveys. The facilitator then uses those data as a basis for problem analysis and action planning. Surveys are a convenient way to unfreeze a company's management and employees. They provide a comparative, graphic illustration of the fact that the organization does have problems to solve.[115]

Technostructural Interventions OD practitioners also get involved in changing firms' structures, methods, and job designs, using an assortment of technostructural

organizational development
A special approach to organizational change in which employees themselves formulate and implement the change that's required.

interventions. For example, in a *formal structural change* program, the employees collect data on the company's existing organizational structure; they then jointly redesign and implement a new one.

Human Resource Management Applications OD practitioners use action research to enable employees to analyze and change their firm's human resources practices. Targets of change here might include the performance appraisal and reward systems, as well as installing diversity programs.

Strategic OD Applications *Strategic interventions* aim to use action research to improve a company's strategic management. *Integrated strategic management* is one example. It consists of four steps: managers and employees (1) analyze current strategy and organizational structure, (2) choose a desired strategy and organizational structure, and (3) design a strategic change plan—"an action plan for moving the organization from its current strategy and organizational design to the desired future strategy and design."[116] Finally, (4) the team oversees implementing the strategic change and reviewing the results.[117]

EVALUATING THE TRAINING EFFORT

With today's emphasis on evidence-based management and measuring results, it is crucial that the manager evaluate the training program. There are several things you can measure: participants' *reactions* to the program, what (if anything) the trainees *learned* from the program, and to what extent their on-the-job *behavior* or *results* changed as a result of the program. In one survey of about 500 U.S. organizations, 77% evaluated their training programs by eliciting reactions, 36% evaluated learning, and about 10% to 15% assessed the program's behavior and/or results.[118] Computerization facilitates evaluation. For example, Bovis Lend Lease uses learning management system software to monitor which employees are taking which courses, and the extent to which they're improving their skills.[119]

There are two basic issues to address when evaluating training programs. The first is the design of the evaluation study and, in particular, whether to use controlled experimentation. The second issue is, "What should we measure?"

Designing the Study

In evaluating the training program, the first question should be how to design the evaluation study. Your basic concern here is this: How can we be sure that the training caused the results? The *time series design* is one option. Here, as in Figure 8-7, you take a series of measures before and after the training program. This can provide at least an initial reading on the program's effectiveness.[120] However, you can't be sure from this that the training (rather than, say, a new pay plan) caused any change.

Controlled experimentation is therefore the evaluation process of choice. A controlled experiment uses both a training group and a control group that receives no training. Data (for instance, on quantity of sales or quality of service) are obtained both before and after the group is exposed to training and before and after a corresponding work period in the control group. This makes it possible to determine the extent to which any change in the training group's performance resulted from the training, rather than from some organizationwide change like a raise in pay. (The pay raise should have affected employees in both groups equally.)[121]

This controlled approach is feasible, but, in terms of current practice, few firms use it. Most simply measure trainees' reactions to the program; some also measure the trainees' job performance before and after training.[122]

FIGURE 8-7 Using a Time Series Graph to Assess a Training Program's Effects

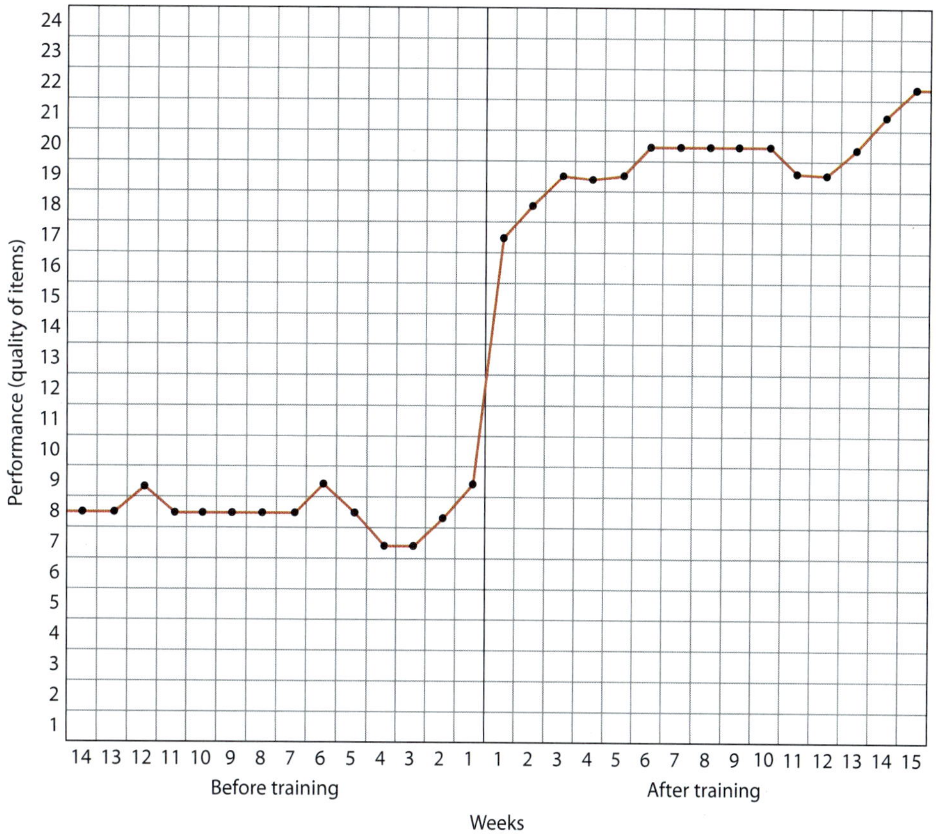

Training Effects to Measure

You can actually measure four basic categories of training outcomes:

1. **Reaction.** Evaluate trainees' reactions to the program. Did they like the program? Did they think it worthwhile?
2. **Learning.** Test the trainees to determine whether they learned the principles, skills, and facts they were supposed to learn.
3. **Behavior.** Ask whether the trainees' on-the-job behavior changed because of the training program. For example, are employees in the store's complaint department more courteous toward disgruntled customers?
4. **Results.** Probably most important, ask, "What results did we achieve, in terms of the training objectives previously set?" For example, did the number of customer complaints diminish? Reactions, learning, and behavior are important. But if the training program doesn't produce measurable results, then it probably hasn't achieved its goals.[123]

Evaluating any of these four is straightforward. For example, Figure 8-8 presents one page from a sample evaluation questionnaire for assessing trainees' reactions. Similarly, you might assess trainees' learning by testing their new knowledge. The employer can assess the trainees' behavioral change directly or indirectly. Indirectly, you might assess the effectiveness of, say, a supervisory performance appraisal

controlled experimentation
Formal methods for testing the effectiveness of a training program, preferably with before-and-after tests and a control group.

OPM **INSTRUCTOR HANDOUTS** ***United States Office of Personnel Management***

TRAINING EVALUATION FORM

TITLE OF COURSE: **"Work and Family Issues — A Module for Supervisors and Managers"**
NAME OF INSTRUCTOR:

DATE OF TRAINING
Started:__________
Ended:__________

NAME: (Optional)	**POSITION TITLE/GRADE:**	
AGENCY:	**OFFICE PHONE:** (Optional)	**OFFICE ADDRESS:** (Optional)

Rate Your Knowledge and Skill Level
(Circle your rating)

Before this course Low ------------------------------------High
1 2 3 4 5

After this course Low ------------------------------------High
1 2 3 4 5

Overall, how would you rate this course?

__ Excellent __Very Good __ Good

__ Fair __ Poor

EVALUATION OF COURSE
(Check appropriate box)

ITEMS OF EVALUATION How did the course sharpen your knowledge or skills in:	Excellent	Very Good	Good	Fair	Poor	Not Applicable
1. What work and family programs are	°	°	°	°	°	°
2. Who uses work and family programs	°	°	°	°	°	°
3. How to recognize/solve work/family issues	°	°	°	°	°	°
4. Helping you take practical steps on the job	°	°	°	°	°	°

RATING OF INSTRUCTOR

1. Presentation, organization, delivery	°	°	°	°	°	°
2. Knowledge and command of the subject	°	°	°	°	°	°
3. Use of audio-visuals or other training aids	°	°	°	°	°	°
4. Stimulation of an open exchange of ideas, participation, & group interaction	°	°	°	°	°	°

STRONG POINTS OF THE COURSE
°
°
°

WEAK POINTS OF THE COURSE
°
°
°

ADDITIONAL DATA YOU WOULD LIKE TO HAVE COVERED IN COURSE
°
°
°

ADDITIONAL COMMENTS/OR RECOMMENDATIONS

FIGURE 8-8 A Sample Training Evaluation Form
Source: www.opm.gov/ Employment_and_Benefits/WorkLife.

training program by asking that person's subordinates questions like, "Did your supervisor take the time to provide you with examples of good and bad performance when he or she appraised your performance most recently?" Or, you can directly assess a training program's results, for instance, by measuring, say, the percentage of phone calls answered correctly.

REVIEW

CHAPTER SECTION SUMMARIES

1. Getting your new employee on board and up to speed begins with **orienting and training** him or her. Employee orientation means providing new employees with the information they need to function, and helping them start being emotionally attached to the firm. This may simply involve providing them with brief written orientation materials and an employee handbook, but sometimes involves a formal process aimed at instilling in the employee the company's cherished values. The four-step training process includes needs analysis, instructional design, implementation, and evaluation. Trainees need to be motivated to learn. Ensuring that they are motivated involves making the learning meaningful, making skills transfers easy, and reinforcing the learning.
2. Before training employees, it's necessary to **analyze their training needs and design the training program**. In training new employees, employers use task analysis—basically, a detailed study of the job—to determine what skills the job requires. For current employees, performance analysis is required, specifically to verify that there is performance efficiency and to determine if training is the solution. Distinguishing between can't do and won't do problems is the main issue here. Once you understand the issues, you can design a training program, which means identifying specific training objectives, clarifying a training budget, and then actually designing the program in terms of the actual content.
3. With this in place, you can turn to **implementing the training program**. Specific training methods include on-the-job training, apprenticeship training, informal learning, job instruction training, lectures, programmed learning, audiovisual-based training, vestibule training, videoconferencing, electronic performance support systems, and computer-based training. Computerized training is increasingly popular, with many packaged programs available. Frequently, programs today are Internet-based, with employees accessing packaged online programs, backed up by learning management systems, through their company's learning portals. Employers also increasingly use mobile learning, for instance, delivering short courses and explanations to employees' iPods. With increasing demands for technologically literate employees, lifelong learning can help ensure employees have the basic educational backgrounds they need to succeed on their jobs. Diversity training aims to create better cross-cultural sensitivity with the goal of fostering more harmonious working relationships.
4. Most training methods are useful for all employees, but some are particularly appropriate for **management development programs**. Like all employees, new managers often get on-the-job training, for instance, via job rotation and coaching. In addition, it's usual to supply various off-the-job training and development opportunities—for instance, using the case study method, management games, outside seminars, university-related programs, corporate universities, executive coaches, and (for human resource managers) the SHRM learning system.
5. When facing economic, competitive, or other challenges, managers have to execute **organizational change programs**. These may aim at changing the company's strategy, culture, structure, technologies, or the attitudes and skills of the employees. Often, the trickiest part of organizational change is overcoming employees' resistance to it. With that in mind, steps in an effective organizational change program include establishing a sense of urgency, mobilizing commitment, creating a guiding coalition, developing and communicating a shared vision, helping employees make the change, consolidating gains, reinforcing a new ways of doing things, and monitoring and assessing progress. Organizational development is a special approach to organizational change, one that involves action research, which means collecting data about a group and feeding the information back to the employees so they can analyze it and develop hypotheses about what the problems might be.
6. Whatever the training program, it's important to **evaluate the training effort**. You can measure reaction, learning, behavior, or results, ideally using a control group that is not exposed to training, in parallel with the group that you're training.

DISCUSSION QUESTIONS

1. "A well-thought-out orientation program is essential for all new employees, whether they have experience or not." Explain why you agree or disagree with this statement.
2. Explain how you would apply our "motivation points" (pages 267–268) in developing a lecture, say, on orientation and training.
3. John Santos is an undergraduate business student majoring in accounting. He just failed the first accounting course, Accounting 101. He is understandably upset. How would you use performance analysis to identify what, if any, are John's training needs,
4. What are some typical on-the-job training techniques? What do you think are some of the main drawbacks of relying on informal on-the-job training for breaking new employees into their jobs?
5. One reason for implementing global training programs is the need to avoid business losses "due to cultural insensitivity." What sort of cultural insensitivity do you think is referred to, and how might that translate into lost business? What sort of training program would you recommend to avoid such cultural insensitivity?
6. Describe the pros and cons of five management development methods.
7. Do you think job rotation is a good method to use for developing management trainees? Why or why not?

INDIVIDUAL AND GROUP ACTIVITIES

1. You're the supervisor of a group of employees whose task is to assemble disk drives that go into computers. You find that quality is not what it should be and that many of your group's devices have to be brought back and reworked; your boss says, "You'd better start doing a better job of training your workers."
   a. What are some of the staffing factors that could be contributing to this problem?
   b. Explain how you would go about assessing whether it is in fact a training problem.
2. Pick out some task with which you are familiar—mowing the lawn, making a salad, or studying for a test—and develop a job instruction sheet for it.
3. Working individually or in groups, develop a short, programmed learning program on the subject "Guidelines for Giving a More Effective Lecture."
4. Find a provider of management development seminars. Obtain copies of its recent listings of seminar offerings. At what levels of managers are the offerings aimed? What seem to be the most popular types of development programs? Why do you think that's the case?
5. Working individually or in groups, develop several specific examples to illustrate how a professor teaching human resource management could use at least four of the techniques described in this chapter in teaching his or her HR course.
6. Working individually or in groups, develop an orientation program for high school graduates entering your university as freshmen.
7. The HRCI "Test Specifications" appendix at the end of this book (pages 699–706) lists the knowledge someone studying for the HRCI certification exam needs to have in each area of human resource management (such as in Strategic Management, Workforce Planning, and Human Resource Development). In groups of four to five students, do four things: (1) Review that appendix now. (2) Identify the material in this chapter that relates to the required knowledge the appendix lists. (3) Write four multiple-choice exam questions on this material that you believe would be suitable for inclusion in the HRCI exam. And (4) if time permits, have someone from your team post your team's questions in front of the class, so the students in other teams can take each others' exam questions
8. The U.S.-led coalition in Iraq sent hundreds of trainers to that country to train new cadres of Iraqi workers, from teachers to police officers. Perhaps no training task was more pressing than that involved in creating the country's new police force. These were the people who were to help the coalition bring security to Iraq. However, many new officers had no experience in police work. There were language barriers between trainers and trainees. And some trainees found themselves quickly under fire from insurgents when they went as trainees out into the field. Based on what you learned about training from this chapter, list the five most important things you would tell the officer in charge of training (a former U.S. big-city police chief) to keep in mind as he designs the training program.

EXPERIENTIAL EXERCISE

Flying the Friendlier Skies

Purpose: The purpose of this exercise is to give you practice in developing a training program for the job of airline reservation clerk for a major airline.

Required Understanding: You should be fully acquainted with the material in this chapter and should read the following description of an airline reservation clerk's duties:

Customers contact our airline reservation clerks to obtain flight schedules, prices, and itineraries. The reservation clerks look up the requested information on our airline's online flight schedule systems, which are updated continuously. The reservation clerk must deal courteously and expeditiously with the customer, and be able to find quickly alternative flight arrangements in order to provide the customer with the itinerary that fits his or her needs. Alternative flights and prices must be found quickly, so that the customer is not kept waiting, and so that our reservations operations group maintains its efficiency standards. It is often necessary to look under various routings, since there may be a dozen or more alternative routes between the customer's starting point and destination.

You may assume that we just hired 30 new clerks, and that you must create a 3-day training program.

How to Set Up the Exercise/Instructions: Divide the class into teams of five or six students.

Airline reservation clerks obviously need numerous skills to perform their jobs. JetBlue Airlines has asked you to develop quickly the outline of a training program for its new reservation clerks. You may want to start by listing the job's main duties and by reviewing any work you may have done for the exercise at the end of Chapter 6. In any case, please produce the requested outline, making sure to be very specific about what you want to teach the new clerks, and what methods and aids you suggest using to train them.

APPLICATION CASE

Reinventing the Wheel at Apex Door Company

Jim Delaney, president of Apex Door, has a problem. No matter how often he tells his employees how to do their jobs, they invariably "decide to do it their way," as he puts it, and arguments ensue between Jim, the employee, and the employee's supervisor. One example is the door-design department, where the designers are expected to work with the architects to design doors that meet the specifications. While it's not "rocket science," as Jim puts it, the designers invariably make mistakes—such as designing in too much steel, a problem that can cost Apex tens of thousands of wasted dollars, once you consider the number of doors in, say, a 30-story office tower.

The order processing department is another example. Jim has a very specific and detailed way he wants the order written up, but most of the order clerks don't understand how to use the multipage order form. They simply improvise when it comes to a detailed question such as whether to classify the customer as "industrial" or "commercial."

The current training process is as follows. None of the jobs has a training manual per se, although several have somewhat out-of-date job descriptions. The training for new people is all on the job. Usually, the person leaving the company trains the new person during the 1- or 2-week overlap period, but if there's no overlap, the new person is trained as well as possible by other employees who have filled in occasionally on the job in the past. The training is the same throughout the company—for machinists, secretaries, assemblers, engineers, and accounting clerks, for example.

Questions

1. What do you think of Apex's training process? Could it help to explain why employees "do things their way"? If so, how?
2. What role should job descriptions play in training at Apex?
3. Explain in detail what you would do to improve the training process at Apex. Make sure to provide specific suggestions, please.

CONTINUING CASE

Carter Cleaning Company

The New Training Program

The Carter Cleaning Centers currently have no formal orientation or training policies or procedures, and Jennifer believes this is one reason why the standards to which she and her father would like employees to adhere are generally not followed.

The Carters would prefer that certain practices and procedures be used in dealing with the customers at the front counters. For example, all customers should be greeted with what Jack refers to as a "big hello." Garments they drop off should immediately be inspected for any damage or unusual stains so these can be brought to the customer's attention, lest the customer later return to pick up the garment and erroneously blame the store. The garments are then supposed to be immediately placed together in a nylon sack to separate them from other customers' garments. The ticket also has to be carefully written up, with the customer's name and telephone number and the date precisely and clearly noted on all copies. The counterperson is also supposed to take the opportunity to try to sell the customer additional services such as waterproofing, or simply notify the customer that "Now that people are doing their spring cleaning, we're having a special on drapery cleaning all this month." Finally, as the customer leaves, the counterperson is supposed to make a courteous comment like "Have a nice day" or "Drive safely." Each of the other jobs in the stores—pressing, cleaning and spotting, periodically maintaining the coin laundry equipment, and so forth—similarly contain certain steps, procedures, and most importantly, standards the Carters would prefer to see upheld.

The company has had problems, Jennifer feels, because of a lack of adequate employee training and orientation. For example, two new employees became very upset last month when they discovered that they were not paid at the end of the week, on Friday, but instead were paid (as are all Carter employees) on the following Tuesday. The Carters use the extra two days in part to give them time to obtain everyone's hours and compute their pay. The other reason they do it, according to Jack, is that "frankly, when we stay a few days behind in paying employees it helps to ensure that they at least give us a few days' notice before quitting on us. While we are certainly obligated to pay them anything they earn, we find that psychologically they seem to be less likely to just walk out on us Friday evening and not show up Monday morning if they still haven't gotten their pay from the previous week. This way they at least give us a few days' notice so we can find a replacement."

There are other matters that could be covered during orientation and training, says Jennifer. These include company policy regarding paid holidays, lateness and absences, health benefits (there are none, other than workers' compensation), substance abuse, and eating or smoking on the job (both forbidden), and general matters like the maintenance of a clean and safe work area, personal appearance and cleanliness, time sheets, personal telephone calls, and personal e-mail.

Jennifer believes that implementing orientation and training programs would help to ensure that employees know how to do their jobs the right way. And she and her father further believe that it is only when employees understand the right way to do their jobs that there is any hope their jobs will be accomplished the way the Carters want them to be accomplished.

Questions

1. Specifically, what should the Carters cover in their new employee orientation program and how should they convey this information?
2. In the HR management course Jennifer took, the book suggested using a job instruction sheet to identify tasks performed by an employee. Should the Carter Cleaning Centers use a form like this for the counterperson's job? If so, what should the form look like, say, for a counter person?
3. Which specific training techniques should Jennifer use to train her pressers, her cleaner–spotters, her managers, and her counterpeople? Why should these training techniques be used?

TRANSLATING STRATEGY INTO HR POLICIES & PRACTICES CASE

The Hotel Paris Case

The New Training Program

The Hotel Paris's competitive strategy is "To use superior guest service to differentiate the Hotel Paris properties, and to thereby increase the length of stay and return rate of guests, and thus boost revenues and profitability." HR manager Lisa Cruz must now formulate functional policies and activities that support this competitive strategy, by eliciting the required employee behaviors and competencies.

As she reviewed her company's training processes, Lisa had reasons to be concerned. For one thing, the Hotel Paris relied almost exclusively on informal on-the-job training. New security guards attended a 1-week program offered by a law enforcement agency, but all other new hires, from assistant manager to housekeeping crew, learned the rudiments of their jobs from their colleagues and their supervisors, on the job. Lisa noted that the drawbacks of this informality were evident when she compared the Hotel Paris's performance on various training metrics with those of other hotels and service firms. For example, in terms of number of hours training per employee per year, number of hours training for new employees, cost per trainee hour, and percent of payroll spent on training, the Hotel Paris was far from the norm when benchmarked against similar firms.

Indeed, as Lisa and the CFO reviewed the measures of the Hotel Paris's current training efforts, it was clear that (when compared to similar companies) some changes were in order. Most other service companies provided at least 40 hours of training per employee per year, while the Hotel Paris offered, on average, no more than 5 or 6 hours. Similar firms offered at least 40 hours of training per new employee, while the Hotel Paris offered, at most, 10. Even the apparently "good" metrics comparisons simply masked poor results. For example, whereas most service firms spend about 8% of their payrolls on training, the Hotel Paris spent less than 1%. The problem, of course, was that the Hotel Paris's training was nonexistent. Given this and the commonsense links between (1) employee training and (2) employee performance, the CFO gave his go-ahead for Lisa and her team to design a comprehensive package of training programs for all Hotel Paris employees.

Questions

1. Based on what you read in this chapter, what do you suggest Lisa and her team do first with respect to training? Why?
2. Have Lisa and the CFO sufficiently investigated whether training is really called for? Why? What would you suggest?
3. Based on what you read in this chapter and what you may access via the Web, develop a detailed training program for one of these hotel positions: security guard, housekeeper, or valet/door person.

KEY TERMS

employee orientation, *p. 265*
training, *p. 267*
negligent training, *p. 267*
task analysis, *p. 269*
competency model, *p. 269*
performance analysis, *p. 271*
on-the-job training (OJT), *p. 273*
apprenticeship training, *p. 275*
job instruction training (JIT), *p. 275*
programmed learning, *p. 277*
electronic performance support systems (EPSS), *p. 279*
job aid, *p. 279*
virtual classroom, *p. 281*
lifelong learning, *p. 283*
management development, *p. 285*
job rotation, *p. 287*
action learning, *p. 287*
case study method, *p. 287*
management game, *p. 287*
role playing, *p. 289*
behavior modeling, *p. 289*
in-house development center, *p. 289*
executive coach, *p. 289*
organizational development, *p. 293*
controlled experimentation, *p. 295*

ENDNOTES

1. David Raths, "Virtual Reality in the OR," *Training & Development*, August 2006. For a slide show of a similar training process see, http://www.slideshare.net/magistra12/a-second-life-virtual-clinic-for-medical-student-training-presentation, accessed October 27, 2009.
2. Marjorie Derven, "Management Onboarding," *Training & Development*, April 2008, pp. 49–52.
3. Sabrina Hicks, "Successful Orientation Programs," *Training & Development*, April 2000, p. 59. See also Howard Klein and Natasha Weaver, "The Effectiveness of an Organizational Level Orientation Program in the Socialization of New Hires," *Personnel Psychology* 53 (2000), pp. 47–66; and Laurie Friedman, "Are You Losing Potential New Hires at Hello?" *Training & Development*, November 2006, pp. 25–27.
4. Charlotte Garvey, "The Whirlwind of a New Job," *HR Magazine*, June 2001, p. 111. See also Talya Bauer et al., "Newcomer Adjustment During Organizational Socialization: A Meta-Analytic Review of Antecedents, Outcomes, and Methods," *Journal of Applied Psychology* 92, no. 3 (2007), pp. 707–721.
5. Sheila Hicks et al., "Orientation Redesign," *Training & Development*, July 2006, pp. 43–46.

6. See, for example, John Kammeyer-Mueller and Connie Wanberg, "Unwrapping the Organizational Entry Process: Disentangling Multiple Antecedents and Their Pathways to Adjustments," *Journal of Applied Psychology* 88, no. 5 (2003), pp. 779–794.
7. See Darin Hartley, "Technology Kicks Up Leadership Development," *Training & Development*, March 2004, pp. 22–24.
8. Ed Frauenheim, " IBM Learning Programs Get a 'Second Life,'" *Workforce Management*, December 11, 2006, p. 6. See also J. T. Arnold, "Gaming Technology Used To Orient New Hires," *HRMagazine* (2009 HR Trendbook supp), pp. 36, 38.
9. www.workday.com/company/news/workdaymobility.php, accessed March 24, 2009.
10. Mindy Chapman, "The Return on Investment for Training," *Compensation & Benefits Review*, January/February 2003, pp. 32–33.
11. Rita Smith, "Aligning Learning with Business Strategy," *Training & Development*, November 2008, pp. 41–43.
12. Christine Ellis and Sarah Gale, "A Seat at the Table," *Training*, March 2001, pp. 90–96.
13. Christopher Glynn, "Building a Learning Infrastructure," *Training & Development*, January 2008, pp. 38–43.
14. Nancy DeViney and Brenda Sugrue, "Learning Outsourcing: A Reality Check," *Training & Development*, December 2004, p. 41. See also "How Are Organizations Training Today?," *HR Focus* 86, no. 7 (July 2009), pp. S2–53.
15. Brenda Sugrue et al., "What in the World Is WLP?" *Training & Development*, January 2005, pp. 51–54.
16. "Companies Invested More in Training Despite Economic Setbacks, Survey Says," *BNA Bulletin to Management*, March 7, 2002, p. 73; "Employee Training Expenditures on the Rise," *American Salesman* 49, no. 1 (January 2004), pp. 26–28.
17. "Companies Invested More in Training Despite Economic Setbacks, Survey Says," op. cit.; Andrew Paradise, "The 2008 ASTD State of the Industry Report Shows Sustained Support for Corporate Learning," *Training & Development*, November 2008, pp. 45–51.
18. Alan Saks and Monica Belcourt, "An Investigation of Training Activities and Transfer of Training in Organizations," *Human Resource Management* 45, no. 4 (Winter 2006), pp. 629–648. The percentage of managers transferring behaviors from training to the job may be as low as 10% to 20%. See George Vellios, "On the Level," *Training & Development*, December 2008, pp. 26–29. See also K. Lee, "Implement Training Successfully," *Training* (Minneapolis, Minn.) 46, no. 5 (June 2009), p. 16.
19. Ibid., p. 90.
20. Kenneth Wexley and Gary Latham, *Developing and Training Human Resources in Organizations* (Upper Saddle River, NJ: Prentice Hall, 2002), p. 305.
21. Ibid.
22. Kathryn Tyler, "Focus on Training," *HR Magazine*, May 2000, pp. 94–102.
23. Janice A. Cannon-Bowers et al., "Framework for Understanding Pre-Practice Conditions and Their Impact on Learning," *Personnel Psychology* 51 (1998), pp. 291–320.
24. Ibid., p. 305.
25. Ibid.
26. This is adapted from "Evidence-Based Training™: Turning Research into Results for Pharmaceutical Sales Training," An AXIOM White Paper © 2006 AXIOM Professional Health Learning LLC. All rights reserved.
27. P. Nick Blanchard and James Thacker, *Effective Training: Systems, Strategies and Practices* (Upper Saddle River, NJ: Prentice Hall, 1999), pp. 138–139. See also Matthew Casey and Dennis Doverspike, "Training Needs Analysis and Evaluation for New Technologies Through the Use of Problem Based Inquiry," *Performance Improvement Quarterly* 18, no. 1 (2005), pp. 110–124.
28. Marjorie Derven, "Lessons Learned: Using Competency Models to Target Training Needs," *Training & Development*, December 2008, p. 70.
29. See, for example, Jennifer Salopek, "Keeping It Real," *Training & Development*, August 2008, p. 44.
30. Richard Montier et al., "Competency Models Develop Top Performance," *Training & Development*, July 2006, pp. 47–50.
31. Tom Barron, "When Things Go Haywire," *Training & Development*, February 1999, pp. 25–27.
32. Jay Bahlis "Blueprint for Planning Learning," *Training & Development*, March 2008, pp. 64–67.
33. P. Nick Blanchard and James Thacker, *Effective Training: Systems, Strategies, and Practices* (Upper Saddle River, NJ: Prentice Hall, 2007), p. 8.
34. See, for example, the HRDQ Winter 2008 catalog, www.HRDQ.com.
35. Rita Zeidner, "Strategies for Saving in a Down Economy," *HR Magazine*, February 2009, p. 33. See also K. Giacalone, "Making New Employees Successful in Any Economy," *T+D* 63, no. 6 (June 2009), pp. 36–39.
36. Kenneth Wexley and Gary Latham, op cit., pp. 78–79.
37. Donna Goldwasser, "Me a Trainer?" *Training*, April 2001, pp. 60–66.
38. Four steps in on-the-job training based on William Berliner and William McLarney, *Management Practice and Training* (Burr Ridge, IL: McGraw-Hill, 1974), pp. 442–443. See also Robert Sullivan and Donald Miklas, "On-the-Job Training That Works," *Training & Development Journal* 39, no. 5 (May 1985), pp. 118–120; Stephen B. Wehrenberg, "Supervisors as Trainees: The Long-Term Gains of OJT," *Personnel Journal* 66, no. 4 (April 1987), pp. 48–51.
39. Cindy Waxer, "Steelmaker Revives Apprentice Program to Address Graying Workforce, Forge Next Leaders," *Workforce Management*, January 30, 2006, p. 40.
40. Kermit Kaleba, "New Changes to Apprenticeship Program Could Be Forthcoming," *Training & Development*, February 2008, p. 14.
41. Robert Weintraub and Jennifer Martineau, "The Just in Time Imperative," *Training & Development*, June 2002, p. 52; and Andrew Paradise, "Informal Learning: Overlooked or Overhyped?" *Training & Development*, July 2008, pp. 52–53.
42. Arthur Winfred Jr. et al., "Effectiveness of Training in Organizations: A Meta Analysis of Design and Evaluation Features," *Journal of Applied Psychology* 88, no. 2 (2003), pp. 234–245.
43. Donald Michalak and Edwin G. Yager, *Making the Training Process Work* (New York: Harper & Row, 1979), pp. 108–111. See also Richard Wiegand, "Can All Your Trainees Hear You?" *Training & Development Journal* 41, no. 8 (August 1987), pp. 38–43.
44. Jacqueline Schmidt and Joseph Miller, "The Five-Minute Rule for Presentations," *Training & Development*, March 2000, pp. 16–17.
45. G. N. Nash, J. P. Muczyk, and F. L. Vettori, "The Role and Practical Effectiveness of Programmed Instruction," *Personnel Psychology* 24 (1971), pp. 397–418; Duane

Schultz and Sydney Ellen Schultz, *Psychology and Work Today* (Upper Saddle River, NJ: Prentice Hall, 1998), pp. 181–183.

46. Wexley and Latham, *Developing and Training*, pp. 131–133. See also Teri O. Grady and Mike Matthews, "Video . . . Through the Eyes of the Trainee," *Training* 24, no. 7 (July 1987), pp. 57–62; "New ARTBA PPE Video and Laborers' Night Work Suggestions Highlight Construction Safety Advances," *EHS Today* 2, no. 7 (July 2009), p. 51.
47. Paula Ketter, "What Can Training Do for Brown?" *Training & Development*, May 2008, pp. 30–36.
48. Tyler, "Focus on Training," p. 96. See also Allison Rossett and Erica Mohr, "Performance Support Tools: Where Learning, Work, and Results Converge," *Training & Development*, February 2004, pp. 35–37.
49. Craig Marion, "What Is the EPSS Movement and What Does It Mean to Information Designers?" August 20, 1999, www.chesco.com/~cmarion/pcd/epssimplications.html.
50. Josh Bersin and Karen O'Leonard, "Performance Support Systems," *Training & Development*, April 2005, p. 68.
51. Blanchard and Thacker, *Effective Training*, p. 163.
52. Dina Berta, "Computer-Based Training Clicks with Both Franchisees and Their Employees," *Nation's Restaurant News*, July 9, 2001, pp. 1, 18; see also Daniel Cable and Charles Parsons, "Socialization Tactics and Person–Organization Fit," *Personnel Psychology*, 54 (2001), pp. 1–23.
53. P. Nick Blanchard and James Thacker, *Effective Training: Systems, Strategies, and Practices* (Upper Saddle River, NJ: Pearson, 2003), p. 247; see also Michael Laff, "Simulations: Slowly Proving Their Worth," *Training & Development*, June 2007, pp. 30–34.
54. Laff, op. cit.
55. Blanchard and Thacker, op cit., p. 248.
56. Ibid., p. 249. See also Kim Kleps, "Virtual Sales Training Scores a Hit," *Training & Development*, December 2006, pp. 63–64.
57. Paul Harris, "Simulation: The Game Is On," *Training & Development*, October 2003, p. 49. See also Jenni Jarventaus, "Virtual Threat, Real Sweat," *Training & Development*, May 2007, pp. 72–78.
58. Jarventaus, op. cit.
59. Ed Frauenheim, "IBM Learning Programs Get a 'Second Life,'" *Workforce Management*, December 11, 2006, p. 6.
60. Clark Aldrich, "Engaging Mini-Games Find Niche in Training," *Training & Development*, July 2007, pp. 22–24; and "Cisco's Global Training Machine," *Workforce Management*, November 17, 2008, p. 30.
61. "What Do Simulations Cost?" *Training & Development*, June 2007, p. 88; see also Paul Harris, "Immersive Learning Seeks a Foothold," *Training & Development*, January 2009, pp. 40–45; and R. S Polimeni et al., "Using Computer Simulations to Recruit and Train Generation Y Accountants," *The CPA Journal* 79, no. 5 (May 2009), pp. 64–68.
62. Pat Galagan, "Second That," *Training & Development*, February 2008, pp. 34–37.
63. See for example, Rockley Miller, "New Training Looms," *Hotel and Motel Management*, April 4, 1994, pp. 26, 30; Albert Ingram, "Teaching with Technology," *Association Management* 48 (June 1996), pp. 31–34; Sandra Vera-Munoz, et al., "Enhancing Knowledge Sharing in Public Accounting Firms," *Accounting Horizons* 20, no. 2 (June 2006), pp. 133–155.
64. Ellen Zimmerman, "Better Training Is Just a Click Away," *Workforce*, January 2001, pp. 36–42.
65. John Zonneveld, "GM Dealer Training Goes Global," *Training & Development*, December 2006, pp. 47–51.
66. "The Next Generation of Corporate Learning," *Training & Development*, June 2003, p. 47.
67. Traci Sitzmann et al., "The Comparative Effectiveness of Web-Based and Classroom Instruction: A Meta-Analysis," *Personnel Psychology* 59 (2006), pp. 623–664.
68. Ibid.
69. For a list of guidelines for using e-learning, see, for example, Mark Simon, "E-Learning No How," *Training & Development*, January 2009, pp. 34–39.
70. "The Next Generation of Corporate Learning," *Training & Development*, June 2004, p. 47; and Jennifer Hofmann and Nanatte Miner, "Real Blended Learning Stands Up," *Training & Development*, September 2008, pp. 28–31.
71. Ruth Clark, "Harnessing the Virtual Classroom," *Training & Development*, November 2005, pp. 40–46.
72. Jennifer Taylor Arnold, "Learning On-the-Fly," *HR Magazine*, September 2007, p. 137.
73. www.dominknow.com, accessed March 23, 2009.
74. Elizabeth Agnvall, "Just-in-Time Training," *HR Magazine*, May 2006, pp. 67–78.
75. Ibid.
76. For a similar program, at Accenture, see Don Vanthournout and Dana Koch, "Training at Your Fingertips," *Training & Development*, September 2008, pp. 52–57.
77. Susan Ladika, "When Learning Lasts a Lifetime," *HR Magazine*, May 2008, p. 57.
78. Paula Ketter, "The Hidden Disability," *Training & Development*, June 2006, pp. 34–40.
79. Jeremy Smerd, "New Workers Sorely Lacking Literacy Skills," *Workforce Management*, December 10, 2008, p. 6.
80. Jennifer Salopek, "The Growth of Succession Management," *Training & Development*, June 2007, pp. 22–24; and Kermit Kaleba, "Businesses Continue to Push for Lifelong Learning," *Training & Development*, June 2007, p. 14.
81. Rita Zeidner, "One Workforce—Many Languages," *HR Magazine*, January 2009, pp. 33–37.
82. Matthew Reis, "Do-It-Yourself Diversity," *Training & Development*, March 2004, pp. 80–81.
83. "Adams Mark Hotel & Resorts Launches Diversity Training Program," *Hotel and Motel Management* 216, no. 6 (April 2001), p. 15.
84. Valerie Frazee, "Workers Learn to Walk So They Can Run," *Personnel Journal*, May 1996, pp. 115–120. See also Kathryn Tyler, "I Say Potato, You Say Patata: As Workforce and Customer Diversity Grow, Employers Offer Foreign Language Training to Staff," *HR Magazine* 49, no. 1 (January 2004), pp. 85–87.
85. Jennifer Salopek, "Trends: Lost in Translation," *Training & Development*, December 2003, p. 15.
86. For a discussion of leadership development tools, see John Beeson, "Building Bench Strength: A Tool Kit for Executive Development," *Business Horizons* 47, no. 6 (November 2004), pp. 3–9. See also Rita Smith and Beth Bledsoe, "Grooming Leaders for Growth," *Training & Development*, August 2006, pp. 47–50.
87. Paula Caligiuri, "Developing Global Leaders," *Human Resource Management Review* 16 (2006), pp. 219–228.
88. Ann Pomeroy, "Head of the Class," *HR Magazine*, January 2005, p. 57.
89. Mike Czarnowsky, "Executive Development," *Training & Development*, September 2008, pp. 44–45.
90. "Thrown into Deep End, Workers Surface as Leaders," *BNA Bulletin to Management*, July 11, 2002, p. 223. See also Ann Locke and Arlene Tarantino, "Strategic Leadership

Development," *Training & Development*, December 2006, pp. 53–55.

91. Michael Marquardt, "Harnessing the Power of Action Learning," *Training & Development*, June 2004, pp. 26–32.
92. Chris Whitcomb, "Scenario-Based Training at the FBI," *Training & Development*, June 1999, pp. 42–46. See also Michael Laff, "Serious Gaming: The Trainer's New Best Friend," *Training & Development*, January 2007, pp. 52–57.
93. American Management Association, *Catalog of Seminars*, April–December 2003.
94. For a list of Harvard programs, see, for example, their intensive 2-day conferences in the 2008 brochure from their Center for Management Research, "Programs on Leadership for Senior Executives," 2008, www.execseminars.com.
95. Ann Pomeroy, "Head of the Class," *HR Magazine*, January 2005, p. 57. See also Michael Laff, "Centralized Training Leads to Nontraditional Universities," *Training & Development*, January 2007, pp. 27–29; and Chris Musselwhite, "University Executive Education Gets Real," *Training & Development*, May 2006, p. 57.
96. Norman Maier, Allen Solem, and Ayesha Maier, *The Role Play Technique* (San Diego, CA: University Associates, 1975), pp. 2–3. See also Alan Test, "Why I Do Not Like to Role Play," *American Salesman*, August 1994, pp. 7–20.
97. Paul Taylor et al., "A Meta-Analytic Review of Behavior Modeling Training," *Journal of Applied Psychology* 90, no. 4 (2005), pp. 692–719.
98. Martha Peak, "Go Corporate U!" *Management Review* 86, no. 2 (February 1997), pp. 33–37. See also Jeanne Meister, "Universities Put to the Test," *Workforce Management*, December 11, 2006, pp. 27–30.
99. Russell Gerbman, "Corporate Universities 101," *HR Magazine*, February 2000, pp. 101–106.
100. "Executive Coaching: Corporate Therapy," *The Economist*, November 15, 2003, p. 61. See also Steve Gladis, "Executive Coaching Builds Steam in Organizations," *Training & Development*, December 2007, pp. 59–61.
101. "As Corporate Coaching Goes Mainstream, Key Prerequisite Overlooked: Assessment," *BNA Bulletin to Management*, May 16, 2006, p. 153.
102. James Smither et al., "Can Working with an Executive Coach Improve Multisource Feedback Ratings over Time?" *Personnel Psychology* 56, no. 1 (Spring 2003), pp. 23–44.
103. Ed Fraeuenheim, "Lost in the Shuffle," *Workforce Management*, January 14, 2008, p. 13.
104. Paul Harris, "A New Market Emerges," *Training & Development*, September 2003, pp. 30–38. For an example of a successful organizational change, see Jordan Mora et al., "Recipe for Change," *Training & Development*, March 2008, pp. 42–46.
105. Gina Gotsill and Meryl Natchez, "From Resistance to Acceptance: How to Implement Change Management," *Training & Development*, November 2007, pp. 24–26.
106. Edward Lawler III and Susan Mohrman, "Beyond the Vision: What Makes HR Effective?" *Human Resource Planning* 23, no. 4 (December 2000), p. 10.
107. The steps are based on Michael Beer, Russell Eisenstat, and Bert Spector, "Why Change Programs Don't Produce Change," *Harvard Business Review*, November–December 1990, pp. 158–166; Thomas Cummings and Christopher Worley, *Organization Development and Change* (Minneapolis, MN: West Publishing Company, 1993); John P. Kotter, "Leading Change: Why Transformation Efforts Fail," *Harvard Business Review*, March–April 1995, pp. 59–66; and John P. Kotter, *Leading Change* (Boston: Harvard Business School Press, 1996). Change doesn't necessarily have to be painful. See, for example, Eric Abrahamson, "Change Without Pain," *Harvard Business Review*, July–August 2000, pp. 75–79. See also David Herold et al., "Beyond Change Management: A Multilevel Investigation of Contextual and Personal Influences on Employees' Commitment to Change," *Journal of Applied Psychology* 92, no. 4 (2007), p. 949.
108. Ibid. Note that some people are more open to change than are others. As just one example, self-esteem and optimism were related to higher levels of change acceptance in one recent study: Connie Wanberg, "Predictors and Outcomes of Openness to Changes in a Reorganizing Workplace," *Journal of Applied Psychology* 85, no. 1 (2000), pp. 132–142.
109. Kotter, "Leading Change," p. 85.
110. Beer, Eisenstat, and Spector, "Why Change Programs Don't Produce Change," p. 164.
111. Stacie Furst and Daniel Cable, "Employee Resistance to Organizational Change: Managerial Influence Tactics and Leader Member Exchange," *Journal of Applied Psychology* 3, no. 2 (2008), p. 453.
112. Beer, Eisenstat, and Spector, "Why Change Programs Don't Produce Change," p. 164.
113. Robert J. House, *Management Development* (Ann Arbor, MI: Bureau of Industrial Relations, University of Michigan, 1967), p. 71; Louis White and Kevin Wooten, "Ethical Dilemmas in Various Stages of Organizational Development," *Academy of Management Review* 8, no. 4 (1983), pp. 690–697.
114. Wendell French and Cecil Bell Jr., *Organization Development* (Upper Saddle River, NJ: Prentice Hall, 1995), pp. 171–193.
115. Benjamin Schneider, Steven Ashworth, A. Catherine Higgs, and Linda Carr, "Design Validity, and Use of Strategically Focused Employee Attitude Surveys," *Personnel Psychology* 49 (1996), pp. 695–705.
116. Cummings and Worley, *Organization Development and Change*, p. 501.
117. For a description of how to make OD a part of organizational strategy, see Aubrey Mendelow and S. Jay Liebowitz, "Difficulties in Making OD a Part of Organizational Strategy," *Human Resource Planning* 12, no. 4 (1995), pp. 317–329.
118. Wexley and Latham, *Developing and Training Human Resources in Organizations*, p. 128.
119. Todd Raphel, "What Learning Management Reports Do for You," *Workforce*, June 2001, pp. 56–58.
120. Wexley and Latham, 2002, op cit., p. 153.
121. See, for example, Charlie Morrow, M. Quintin Jarrett, and Melvin Rupinski, "An Investigation of the Effect and Economic Utility of Corporate-Wide Training," *Personnel Psychology* 50 (1997), pp. 91–119.
122. See, for example, Antonio Aragon-Sanchez et al., "Effects of Training on Business Results," *International Journal of Human Resource Management* 14, no. 6 (September 2003), pp. 956–980.
123. A recent review concluded that the relationship of training to human resource outcomes and organizational performance is positive, but that training "is only very weakly related to financial outcomes." Given this, managers may want to assess training results not just in terms of employee behavior and performance, but company financial performance as well. See Phyllis Tharenou et al., "A Review and Critique of Research on Training and Organizational Level Outcomes," *Human Resource Management Review* 17 (2007), pp. 251–273.

9 Performance Management and Appraisal

As the United States invested billions of dollars supporting General Motors and Chrysler awhile ago, Congress and the White House began grappling with the details of how actually to oversee those huge investments. Some reasonably asked, "How should we assess these executives' performance?" "Do we just look at GM's and Chrysler's overall financial performance?" "Are there other bases on which we can appraise their efforts?" Unfortunately, most members of Congress soon decided that employee appraisal was not one of their areas of expertise.

Source: Courtesy of Gerald Herbert/AP Wide World Photos.

WHERE ARE WE NOW . . .

Chapters 6–8 explained selecting, training, and developing employees. After employees have been on the job for some time, you should appraise their performance. The purpose of this chapter is to show you how to do that. The main topics we cover include the performance appraisal process, appraisal methods, appraisal performance problems and solutions, performance management, and the appraisal interview. Career planning is a logical consequence of appraisal: We'll turn to career and talent planning in Chapter 10.

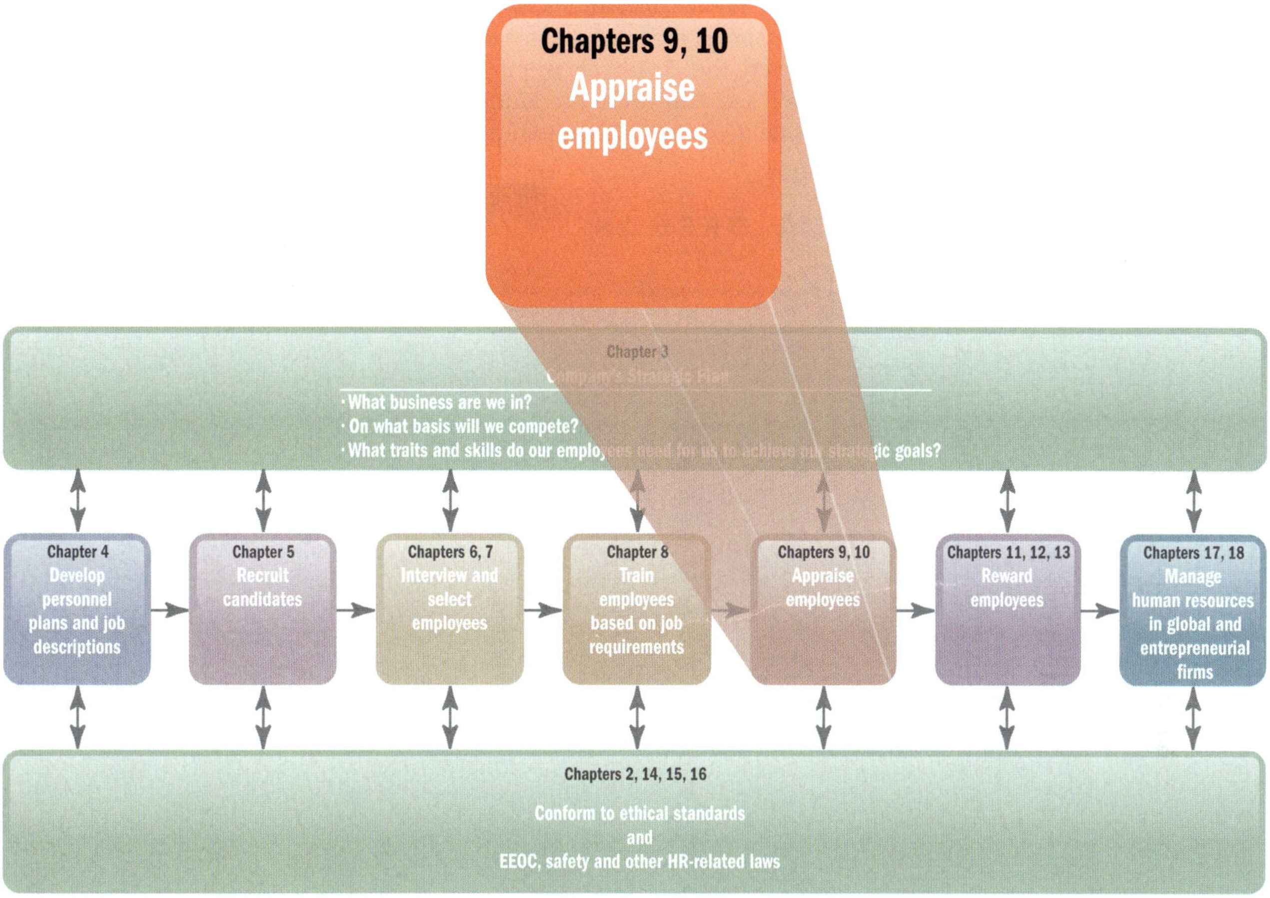

LEARNING OUTCOMES

1. Define performance management and discuss how it differs from performance appraisal.
2. Set effective performance appraisal standards.
3. Describe the appraisal process.
4. Develop, evaluate, and administer at least four performance appraisal tools.
5. Explain and illustrate the problems to avoid in appraising performance.
6. Discuss the pros and cons of using different raters to appraise a person's performance.
7. Perform an effective appraisal interview.

1 Define performance management and discuss how it differs from performance appraisal.

BASIC CONCEPTS IN PERFORMANCE MANAGEMENT AND APPRAISAL

Every manager needs some way to appraise employees' performance. If employees' performance is good, you'll want to reinforce it, and if it's bad, you'll want to take corrective action. **Performance appraisal** means evaluating an employee's current and/or past performance relative to his or her performance standards. Stripped to its essentials, performance appraisal always involves (1) setting work standards, (2) assessing the employee's actual performance relative to those standards, and (3) providing feedback to the employee with the aim of motivating him or her to eliminate performance deficiencies or to continue to perform above par.

For most people, "performance appraisal" brings to mind appraisal tools like the appraisal form in Figure 9-1, but appraisal is more than forms. For one thing, "appraisal" also assumes that the employees knew what their performance standards were, and received the feedback required to remove performance deficiencies. For another, we'll see that there are automated means of continuously monitoring performance that bypass forms altogether. (As explained later in this chapter,

FIGURE 9-1 Online Faculty Evaluation Form

Source: Used with permission of Central Oregon Community College.

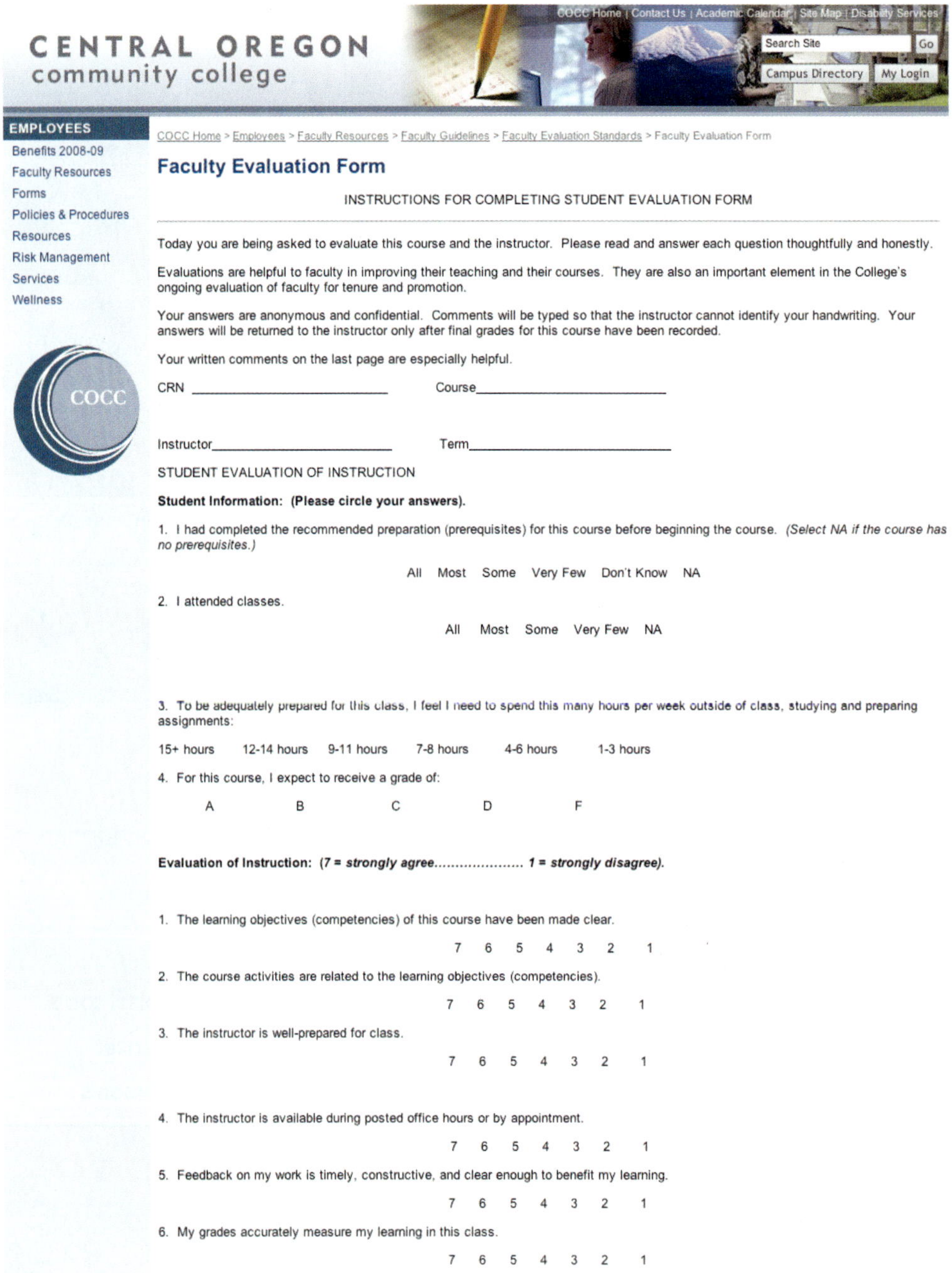

CENTRAL OREGON community college

COCC Home | Contact Us | Academic Calendar | Site Map | Disability Services

Search Site Go

Campus Directory My Login

EMPLOYEES
Benefits 2008-09
Faculty Resources
Forms
Policies & Procedures
Resources
Risk Management
Services
Wellness

COCC

COCC Home > Employees > Faculty Resources > Faculty Guidelines > Faculty Evaluation Standards > Faculty Evaluation Form

Faculty Evaluation Form

INSTRUCTIONS FOR COMPLETING STUDENT EVALUATION FORM

Today you are being asked to evaluate this course and the instructor. Please read and answer each question thoughtfully and honestly.

Evaluations are helpful to faculty in improving their teaching and their courses. They are also an important element in the College's ongoing evaluation of faculty for tenure and promotion.

Your answers are anonymous and confidential. Comments will be typed so that the instructor cannot identify your handwriting. Your answers will be returned to the instructor only after final grades for this course have been recorded.

Your written comments on the last page are especially helpful.

CRN ______________________ Course______________________

Instructor______________________ Term______________________

STUDENT EVALUATION OF INSTRUCTION

Student Information: (Please circle your answers).

1. I had completed the recommended preparation (prerequisites) for this course before beginning the course. *(Select NA if the course has no prerequisites.)*

   All Most Some Very Few Don't Know NA

2. I attended classes.

   All Most Some Very Few NA

3. To be adequately prepared for this class, I feel I need to spend this many hours per week outside of class, studying and preparing assignments:

   15+ hours 12-14 hours 9-11 hours 7-8 hours 4-6 hours 1-3 hours

4. For this course, I expect to receive a grade of:

   A B C D F

Evaluation of Instruction: ***(7 = strongly agree.................... 1 = strongly disagree).***

1. The learning objectives (competencies) of this course have been made clear.

   7 6 5 4 3 2 1

2. The course activities are related to the learning objectives (competencies).

   7 6 5 4 3 2 1

3. The instructor is well-prepared for class.

   7 6 5 4 3 2 1

4. The instructor is available during posted office hours or by appointment.

   7 6 5 4 3 2 1

5. Feedback on my work is timely, constructive, and clear enough to benefit my learning.

   7 6 5 4 3 2 1

6. My grades accurately measure my learning in this class.

   7 6 5 4 3 2 1

FIGURE 9-1 *(continued)*

7. The instructor creates a learning environment in which diverse points of view are respected and can be freely expressed.

7 6 5 4 3 2 1

8. Based on what I have learned, I would recommend this course to other students.

7 6 5 4 3 2 1

COMMENTS

Your written comments are especially helpful. Comments will be typed so that the instructor cannot identify your handwriting. Your answers will be returned to the instructor only after final grades for this course have been recorded.

1. What are the most valuable aspects of this course and/or the way the course was taught?

2. Even excellent courses can be improved. Can you give some constructive suggestions for making the course better?

3. Do you wish to comment on any of your ratings in the "Evaluation of Instruction" section on the Previous page? If so, please state the item number to which your comment refers.

performance management is one of these automated means). But first, let's focus on traditional performance appraisal, starting with how to set appraisable goals for employees.

Defining the Employee's Goals and Work Standards

2 Set effective performance appraisal standards.

Employees should know ahead of time the basis upon which you're going to appraise them. In practice, this means one of two things. Many managers simply use appraisal forms with preprinted generic criteria like "quality of work" or "gets along with others." The generic criteria become the de facto standards by which you appraise your employees.

The second basic approach is to appraise them relative to specific standards that you expect them to achieve, such as "add 10 new customers next year." This sounds simple, but in practice, clarifying what you expect from employees is tricky. Job descriptions are rarely the answer. Employers usually write job descriptions not for specific jobs, but for groups of jobs, and the descriptions rarely include specific goals. Your sales manager's job description may list duties like "motivate sales force." But, you may expect your sales manager to personally sell at least $600,000 worth of products per year by handling the division's two largest accounts and to keep the sales force happy.

As we saw in Chapter 3 (Strategic Planning), setting motivational goals is an art. The most straightforward way to do this (for a sales manager job, for instance) is to set measurable goals or standards for each duty. For example, you might measure "motivate sales force" in terms of turnover (on the assumption that less than 10% of the sales force will quit in any given year if morale is high).[1] We've already explained how to set effective goals in Chapter 3. In brief, we said there that the guidelines for doing so include:

- **Set SMART goals.** These are **s***pecific,* **m***easurable,* **a***ttainable,* **r***elevant,* and **t***imely.*
- **Assign specific goals.** Employees who have *specific goals* usually perform better than those who do not.
- **Assign measurable goals.** Always try to express the goal in terms of numbers, and include target dates or deadlines.
- **Assign challenging but doable goals.** Make them challenging, but not so difficult that they appear impossible or unrealistic.
- **Encourage participation.** Participatively set goals usually produce higher performance.

performance appraisal
Evaluating an employee's current and/or past performance relative to his or her performance standards.

TECHNIQUES FOR APPRAISING PERFORMANCE

Although many progressive employers, such as Toyota, have essentially eliminated formal appraisals, doing so may not be practical for most employers. At firms like Toyota, eliminating appraisals is a by-product of a broader effort. New employees endure a week or more of screening, and then several weeks of training. Enormous efforts go into fostering employee commitment and teamwork. Incentives support company-oriented thinking. "Appraisals" then mainly involve having teammates continuously assessing each other, day-to-day. Not all employers can or necessarily would benefit from such systems. Conventional appraisals are therefore still the norm. They are also, as most people know, more often than not occasions for tension and grief.[2]

Why Appraise Performance?

There are four reasons to appraise subordinates' performance.

- First, from a practical point of view, most employers still base pay and promotional decisions on the employee's appraisal.[3]
- Second, the appraisal lets the boss and subordinate develop a plan for correcting any deficiencies, and to reinforce the things the subordinate does right.
- Third, appraisals should serve a useful career planning purpose. They provide an opportunity to review the employee's career plans in light of his or her exhibited strengths and weaknesses.
- Fourth, we'll see later in this chapter that appraisals play an integral role in the employer's performance management process. Performance management is the *continuous* process of identifying, measuring, and developing the performance of individuals and teams and *aligning* their performance with the organization's *goals.*

Source: Courtesy of Getty Images–Stockbyte, Royalty Free.

Supervisors must be familiar with appraisal techniques, understand and avoid problems that can cripple appraisals, and know how to conduct appraisals fairly.

Realistic Appraisals

In reviewing the appraisal tools we discuss here, don't miss the forest for the trees. It doesn't matter which tool you use if you're less than candid when your subordinate is underperforming. Not all managers are devotees of such candor, but some firms, like GE, are famous for hard-hearted appraisals. GE's former CEO Jack Welch once said, for instance, that there's nothing crueler than telling someone who's doing a mediocre job that he or she is doing well.[4] Someone who might have had the chance to correct bad behavior or find a more appropriate vocation may instead spend years in a dead-end situation, only to have to leave when a more demanding boss comes along.

There are many practical motivations for giving soft appraisals: the fear of having to hire and train someone new; the appraisee's unpleasant reactions; or a company appraisal process that's not conducive to candor, for instance. Ultimately, it is the person doing the appraising who must decide if the potential negatives of less-than-candid appraisals outweigh the assumed benefits. They rarely do.

The Supervisor's Role

Appraising performance is both a difficult and an essential supervisory skill. The supervisor—not HR—usually does the actual appraising, and a supervisor who rates his or her employees too high or too low (or all average) is doing a disservice to them and to the company. Supervisors must therefore be familiar with appraisal techniques, understand and avoid problems that can cripple appraisals, and know how to conduct appraisals fairly.

The human resources department serves a policy-making and advisory role. Generally, human resource managers provide the advice and assistance regarding the appraisal tool to use, but leave final decisions on procedures to operating division heads. (In some firms, human resources prepares detailed forms and procedures for all departments.) The human resource team should also be responsible for training supervisors to improve their appraisal skills, for monitoring the appraisal system's effectiveness, and for ensuring that it complies with EEO laws.

3 Describe the appraisal process.

Steps in Appraising Performance

Effective appraisals begin long before the actual appraisal.

First, make sure you define the employee's job and performance criteria. *Defining the job* means making sure that you and your subordinate agree on his or her duties and job standards and on the appraisal method you will use.

Then, some time later, *appraising performance* means comparing your subordinate's actual performance to the standards; this usually involves some rating form.

Finally, an effective appraisal requires a *feedback session*. Here, you and the subordinate discuss his or her performance and progress, and make plans for any development required.

The manager generally conducts the actual appraisal using a predetermined and formal tool like one or more of those described next. The two basic questions in designing the actual appraisal tool are *what to measure* and *how to measure* it. For example, in terms of *what to measure*, we may measure, as noted, the employee's performance in terms of generic dimensions such as quality and timeliness of work, or with respect to achieving specific goals. In terms of *how to measure* it, there are various methodologies, including graphic rating scales, the alternation ranking method, and "MBO." We'll start with graphic rating scales.

4 Develop, evaluate, and administer at least four performance appraisal tools.

Graphic Rating Scale Method

The **graphic rating scale** is the simplest and most popular method for appraising performance. Figure 9-2 shows one graphic rating scale. A graphic rating scale lists traits (such as "communication" or "teamwork") and a range of performance values (from "unsatisfactory" to "outstanding," or "below expectations" to "role model") for each trait. The supervisor rates each subordinate by circling or checking the score that best describes the subordinate's performance for each trait. The assigned values for the traits are then totaled.

What to Measure?

Graphic rating-type forms typically measure one or more of four job-relevant dimensions.

- As in Figure 9-2, the manager may opt to assess *generic job dimensions* such as communications, teamwork, know-how, and quantity.
- Another option is to appraise the *job's actual duties*. For example, Figure 9-3 shows part of an appraisal form for a pizza chef. This form assesses the job's main sets of job-specific duties, one of which is "Maintain adequate inventory of pizza dough." Here you would assess how well the employee did in exercising each of these duties.

graphic rating scale
A scale that lists a number of traits and a range of performance for each. The employee is then rated by identifying the score that best describes his or her level of performance for each trait.

Sample Performance Rating Form

Employee's Name ______________________ Level: Entry-level employee

Manager's Name ______________________

Key Work Responsibilities	Results/Goals to be Achieved
1. ______________	1. ______________
2. ______________	2. ______________
3. ______________	3. ______________
4. ______________	4. ______________

Communication

1	2	3	4	5
Below Expectations Even with guidance, fails to prepare straight-forward communications, including forms, paperwork, and records, in a timely and accurate manner; products require minimal corrections. Even with guidance, fails to adapt style and materials to communicate straightforward information.		**Meets Expectations** With guidance, prepares straightforward communications, including forms, paperwork, and records, in a timely and accurate manner; products require minimal corrections. With guidance, adapts style and materials to communicate straightforward information.		**Role Model** Independently prepares communications, such as forms, paperwork, and records, in a timely, clear, and accurate manner; products require few, if any, corrections. Independently adapts style and materials to communicate information.

Organizational Know-How

1	2	3	4	5
Below Expectations <performance standards appear here>		**Meets Expectations** <performance standards appear here>		**Role Model** <performance standards appear here>

Personal Effectiveness

1	2	3	4	5
Below Expectations <performance standards appear here>		**Meets Expectations** <performance standards appear here>		**Role Model** <performance standards appear here>

Teamwork

1	2	3	4	5
Below Expectations <performance standards appear here>		**Meets Expectations** <performance standards appear here>		**Role Model** <performance standards appear here>

Achieving Business Results

1	2	3	4	5
Below Expectations <performance standards appear here>		**Meets Expectations** <performance standards appear here>		**Role Model** <performance standards appear here>

FIGURE 9-2 Sample Graphic Rating Performance Rating Form

Source: Elaine Pulakos, "Performance Management," SHRM Foundation, 2004, pp. 16–17.

- *Competency-based appraisal forms* are another option. Here, you focus on the extent to which the employee exhibits the *competencies* essential for the job. For example, what is one competency a nurse supervisor should bring to the job? One might be, "builds a culture that is open and receptive to improved clinical care." Why focus on competencies? Suppose this hospital's strategy includes improving quality of care. Then focusing the nurse supervisor on improving his or her clinical care competency may be more

FIGURE 9-3 One Item from an Appraisal Form Assessing Employee Performance on Specific Job-Related Duties

Position: Pizza Chef			
Duty 1: Maintain adequate inventory of pizza dough		**Rating**	
Each round pizza dough must be between 12 and 14 ounces each, kneaded at least 2 minutes before being placed in the temperature and humidity-controlled cooler, and kept there for at least 5 hours prior to use. There should be enough, but no more for each day's demand.	Needs improvement	Satisfactory	Excellent

supportive of the hospital's strategy than is assessing duties like "supervise one dozen nurses."[5]

- Or, you might rate how well the employee did with respect to achieving specific objectives, such as "sell $600,000 worth of products per year."

Some graphic rating forms assess several things. For example, Figure 9-4 (Sections I and II) assesses the employee's performance relating to both competencies and objectives. With respect to *competencies*, the employee is expected to develop and exhibit competencies (Section II) such as "identifies and analyzes problems" (Problem Solving), and "maintains harmonious and effective work relationships with co-workers and constituents" (Teamwork). The employee and supervisor

SECTION I **Responsibilities/Objectives and Performance Standards in Support of Departmental Goals "Maximizing one's professional qualifications to make a difference"**

Primary Performance Expectations: Responsibilities/Objectives and Standards	Mid-Year Progress Notes	End of Period Rating of Success and Effectiveness Comment and Place X on Scale to Rate (Not Strong — Very Strong)
Objective 1:		├──┼──┼──┼──┤
Objective 2:		├──┼──┼──┼──┤
Objective 3:		├──┼──┼──┼──┤
Objective 4:		├──┼──┼──┼──┤
Objective 5:		├──┼──┼──┼──┤

Objectives for new rating period reviewed and agreed to:				Mid-Year Review:			
Evaluator	Date	Employee	Date	Evaluator	Date	Employee	Date

FIGURE 9-4 Appraisal Form for Assessing Both Competencies and Specific Objectives

Source: www;case.edu/finadmin/humres/policies/perfexempt.pdf, accessed May 17, 2007. Used with permission of Case Western Reserve University.

SECTION II **Performance Competencies**
"Making a Difference by Working and Learning Together."

	Mid-Year Progress Notes	End of Period Rating of Success and Effectiveness Comment and Place X on Scale to Rate Not Strong — Very Strong
Job Knowledge/Competency: Demonstrates the knowledge and skills necessary to perform the job effectively. Understands the expectations of the job and remains current regarding new developments in areas of responsibility. Performs responsibilities in accordance with job procedures and policies. Acts as a resource person upon whom others rely for assistance.		
Quality/Quantity of Work: Completes assignments in a thorough, accurate, and timely manner that achieves expected outcomes. Exhibits concern for the goals and needs of the department and others that depend on services or work products. Handles multiple responsibilities in an effective manner. Uses work time productively.		
Planning/Organization: Establishes clear objectives and organizes duties for self based on the goals of the department, division, or management center. Identifies resources required to meet goals and objectives. Seeks guidance when goals or priorities are unclear.		
Initiative/Commitment: Demonstrates personal responsibility when performing duties. Offers assistance to support the goals and objectives of the department and division. Performs with minimal supervision. Meets work schedule/attendance expectations for the position.		
Problem Solving/Creativity: Identifies and analyzes problems. Formulates alternative solutions. Takes or recommends appropriate actions. Follows up to ensure problems are resolved.		
Teamwork and Cooperation: Maintains harmonious and effective work relationships with co-workers and constituents. Adapts to changing priorities and demands. Shares information and resources with others to promote positive and collaborative work relationships.		
Interpersonal Skills: Deals positively and effectively with coworkers and constituents. Demonstrates respect for all individuals.		
Communication (Oral and Written): Effectively conveys information and ideas both orally and in writing. Listens carefully and seeks clarification to ensure understanding.		

Competencies Reviewed and Discussed: Mid-Year Review	
Evaluator Date	Employee Date

FIGURE 9-4 *(continued)*

would fill in the *objectives* section (Section I) at the start of the year, and then assess results and set new ones as part of the next appraisal.

Alternation Ranking Method

Ranking employees from best to worst on a trait or traits is another option. Since it is usually easier to distinguish between the worst and best employees, an **alternation ranking method** is most popular. First, list all subordinates to be rated, and then cross out the names of any not known well enough to rank. Then, on a form like that in Figure 9-5, indicate the employee who is the highest on the characteristic being measured and the one who is the lowest. Then choose the next highest and the next lowest, alternating between highest and lowest until all employees have been ranked.

Paired Comparison Method

The **paired comparison method** helps make the ranking method more precise. For every trait (quantity of work, quality of work, and so on), you pair and compare every subordinate with every other subordinate.

FIGURE 9-5 Scale for Alternate Ranking of Appraisee

ALTERNATION RANKING SCALE

Trait: ______________________

For the trait you are measuring, list all the employees you want to rank. Put the highest-ranking employee's name on line 1. Put the lowest-ranking employee's name on line 20. Then list the next highest ranking on line 2, the next lowest ranking on line 19, and so on. Continue until all names are on the scale.

Highest-ranking employee

1. ______________	11. ______________
2. ______________	12. ______________
3. ______________	13. ______________
4. ______________	14. ______________
5. ______________	15. ______________
6. ______________	16. ______________
7. ______________	17. ______________
8. ______________	18. ______________
9. ______________	19. ______________
10. ______________	20. ______________

Lowest-ranking employee

Suppose you have five employees to rate. In the paired comparison method, you make a chart, as in Figure 9-6, of all possible pairs of employees for each trait. Then, for each trait, indicate (with a + or –) who is the better employee of the pair. Next, add up the number of +'s for each employee. In Figure 9-6, Maria ranked highest (has the most + marks) for quality of work, whereas Art was ranked highest for creativity.

FIGURE 9-6 Ranking Employees by the Period Comparison Method

Note: + means "better than." – means "worse than." For each chart, add up the number of +'s in each column to get the highest ranked employee.

FOR THE TRAIT "QUALITY OF WORK"

As Compared to:	Employee rated: A Art	B Maria	C Chuck	D Diane	E José
A Art		+	+	–	–
B Maria	–		–	–	–
C Chuck	–	+		+	–
D Diane	+	+	–		+
E José	+	+	+	–	

Maria ranks highest here

FOR THE TRAIT "CREATIVITY"

As Compared to:	Employee rated: A Art	B Maria	C Chuck	D Diane	E José
A Art		–	–	–	–
B Maria	+		–	+	+
C Chuck	+	+		–	+
D Diane	+	–	+		–
E José	+	–	–	+	

Art ranks highest here

alternation ranking method
Ranking employees from best to worst on a particular trait, choosing highest, then lowest, until all are ranked

paired comparison method
Ranking employees by making a chart of all possible pairs of the employees for each trait and indicating which is the better employee of the pair.

Forced Distribution Method

The **forced distribution method** is similar to grading on a curve. With this method, you place predetermined percentages of ratees into several performance categories. The proportions in each category need not be symmetrical; GE used top 20%, middle 70%, and bottom 10% for managers.

Many companies use forced ranking. Sun Microsystems force-ranks its 43,000 employees. Managers appraise employees in groups of about 30, and those in the bottom 10% of each group get 90 days to improve. If they're still in the bottom 10% in 90 days, they can resign and take severance pay. Some decide to stay, but "if it doesn't work out," the firm fires them without severance.[6] This dismissal policy seems somewhat standard. It reflects the fact that top employees often outperform average or poor ones by as much as 100%.[7] About a fourth of *Fortune* 500 companies including Microsoft, Conoco, and Intel use versions of forced distribution.[8]

As most students know, forced grading systems are unforgiving. With forced distribution, you're either in the top 5% or 10% (and thus get that "A"), or you're not. And, if you're in the bottom 5% or 10%, you get an "F," no questions asked. Your professor hasn't the wiggle room to give everyone As, Bs, and Cs. Some students must fail. One survey found that 77% of responding employers using this approach were at least "somewhat satisfied" with forced ranking, while the remaining 23% were dissatisfied. The biggest complaints: 44% said it damages morale. Forty-seven percent said it creates interdepartmental inequities: "High performing teams must cut 10% of their workers while low performing teams are still allowed to retain 90% of theirs."[9] Some writers refer unkindly to forced rankings as "Rank and Yank."[10]

Given this, employers need to be doubly careful to protect such appraisals from managerial abuse. To protect against unfairness and bias claims, managers should take several steps.[11] Appoint a review committee to review any employee's low ranking. Train raters to be objective, and consider using multiple raters in conjunction with the forced distribution approach.

Attempting to install forced ranking in a previously more laid-back environment can be risky; Jacques Nasser, a former Ford CEO, famously left in part due to resistance to his advocacy of such a plan. GE, which first popularized forced ranking, has been injecting more flexibility. For instance, it now tells managers to use more common sense in assigning rankings, and no longer strictly adheres to its famous 20/70/10 split.[12] And remember that distinguishing between top and bottom performers is usually not even the problem: "The challenge is to differentiate meaningfully between the other 80%."[13]

Critical Incident Method

With the **critical incident method**, the supervisor keeps a log of positive and negative examples (critical incidents) of a subordinate's work-related behavior. Every 6 months or so, supervisor and subordinate meet to discuss the latter's performance, using the incidents as examples.

Compiling incidents is useful. It provides examples of good and poor performance the supervisor can use to explain the person's rating. It makes the supervisor think about the subordinate's appraisal all during the year (so the rating does not just reflect the employee's most recent performance). And the list provides examples of what specifically the subordinate can do to eliminate deficiencies. The downside is that without some numerical rating, this method is not too useful for comparing employees or for salary decisions.

In any case, it is common to accumulate incidents, so as to illustrate the reasons behind the employee's ratings. In Table 9-1, one of the assistant plant manager's continuing duties was to supervise procurement and to minimize inventory costs. The critical incident log shows that the assistant plant manager let inventory storage costs rise 15%; this provides an example of what performance she must improve in the future.

TABLE 9-1 Examples of Critical Incidents for Assistant Plant Manager

Continuing Duties	Targets	Critical Incidents
Schedule production for plant	90% utilization of personnel and machinery in plant; orders delivered on time	Instituted new production scheduling system; decreased late orders by 10% last month; increased machine utilization in plant by 20% last month
Supervise procurement of raw materials and inventory control	Minimize inventory costs while keeping adequate supplies on hand	Let inventory storage costs rise 15% last month; overordered parts "A" and "B" by 20%; underordered part "C" by 30%
Supervise machinery maintenance	No shutdowns due to faulty machinery	Instituted new preventative maintenance system for plant; prevented a machine breakdown by discovering faulty part

Narrative Forms

All or part of the written appraisal may be in narrative form. Figure 9-7 presents one example. Here, the person's supervisor is responsible for assessing the employee's past performance and required areas of improvement. The supervisor's narrative assessment aids the employee in understanding where his or her performance was good or bad, and how to improve that performance.

Behaviorally Anchored Rating Scales

A **behaviorally anchored rating scale (BARS)** is an appraisal tool that anchors a numerical rating scale with specific examples of good or poor performance. Its proponents say it provides better, more equitable appraisals than do the other tools we discussed.[14]

Developing a BARS typically requires five steps:

1. **Write critical incidents.** Ask persons who know the job (jobholders and/or supervisors) to describe specific illustrations (critical incidents) of effective and ineffective job performance.
2. **Develop performance dimensions.** Have these people group the incidents into 5 or 10 dimensions; then define each dimension, such as "salesmanship skills."
3. **Reallocate incidents.** To verify these groupings, have another team of people who also know the job reallocate the original critical incidents. They get the cluster definitions (from step 2) and the critical incidents, and must reassign each incident to the cluster they think it fits best. Retain a critical incident if, say, 50% to 80% of this second team assigns it to the same cluster as did the first group.

forced distribution method
Similar to grading on a curve; predetermined percentages of ratees are placed in various performance categories.

critical incident method
Keeping a record of uncommonly good or undesirable examples of an employee's work-related behavior and reviewing it with the employee at predetermined times.

behaviorally anchored rating scale (BARS)
An appraisal method that aims at combining the benefits of narrative critical incidents and quantified ratings by anchoring a quantified scale with specific narrative examples of good and poor performance.

FIGURE 9-7 Appraisal-Coaching Worksheet

Source: Reprinted from www.HR.BLR.com with permission of the publisher *Business and Legal Resources, Inc.* 141 Mill Rock Road East, Old Saybrool, CT © 2004. BLR® (Business & Legal Resources, Inc.).

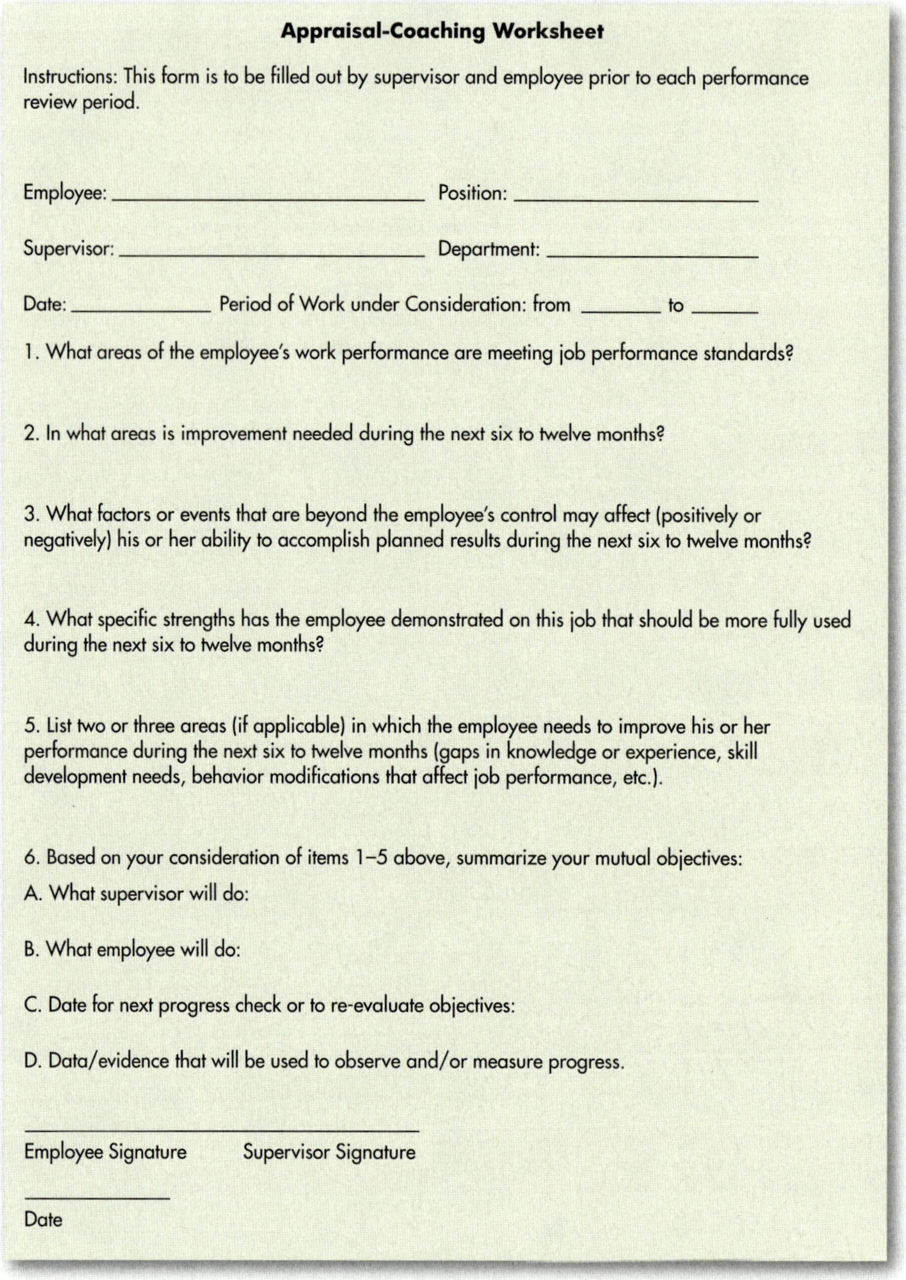

Appraisal-Coaching Worksheet

Instructions: This form is to be filled out by supervisor and employee prior to each performance review period.

Employee: ______________________ Position: ____________________

Supervisor: ______________________ Department: ____________________

Date: __________ Period of Work under Consideration: from ______ to ______

1. What areas of the employee's work performance are meeting job performance standards?

2. In what areas is improvement needed during the next six to twelve months?

3. What factors or events that are beyond the employee's control may affect (positively or negatively) his or her ability to accomplish planned results during the next six to twelve months?

4. What specific strengths has the employee demonstrated on this job that should be more fully used during the next six to twelve months?

5. List two or three areas (if applicable) in which the employee needs to improve his or her performance during the next six to twelve months (gaps in knowledge or experience, skill development needs, behavior modifications that affect job performance, etc.).

6. Based on your consideration of items 1–5 above, summarize your mutual objectives:

A. What supervisor will do:

B. What employee will do:

C. Date for next progress check or to re-evaluate objectives:

D. Data/evidence that will be used to observe and/or measure progress.

____

Employee Signature Supervisor Signature

____

Date

4. **Scale the incidents.** This second group then rates the behavior described by the incident as to how effectively or ineffectively it represents performance on the dimension (7- to 9-point scales are typical).
5. **Develop a final instrument.** Choose about six or seven of the incidents as the dimension's behavioral anchors.[15] Figure 9-8 presents an example.

Research Insight Three researchers developed a BARS for grocery checkout clerks.[16] They collected many critical incidents, and then grouped or clustered these into eight performance dimensions:

Knowledge and Judgment

Conscientiousness

Skill in Human Relations

Skill in Operation of Register

Skill in Bagging

Organizational Ability of Checkstand Work

Skill in Monetary Transactions

Observational Ability

They then developed behaviorally anchored rating scales (similar to the one in Figure 9-8) for each of these dimensions. Each contained a scale (ranging from 1 to 9) for rating performance from "extremely poor" to "extremely good." Then a specific critical incident (such as "by knowing the price of items, this checker would be expected to look for mis-marked and unmarked items") helped anchor or specify what was meant by "extremely good" (9) performance. Similarly, they used several other critical incident anchors along the performance scale from (8) down to (1).

Advantages It takes more time to develop a BARS, but the tool has advantages.

1. **A more accurate gauge.** People who know and do the job and its requirements better than anyone develop the BARS. This should produce a good gauge of job performance.
2. **Clearer standards.** The critical incidents along the scale illustrate what to look for in terms of superior performance, average performance, and so forth.
3. **Feedback.** The critical incidents make it easier to explain the ratings to appraisees.
4. **Independent dimensions.** Systematically clustering the critical incidents into five or six performance dimensions (such as "salesmanship skills") should help

FIGURE 9-8 Example of a Behaviorally Anchored Rating Scale for the Dimension *Salesmanship Skills*

SALESMANSHIP SKILLS

Grocery Store Checkout Clerk: *Conscientiousness* Being careful and precise in checking out the customer's groceries. Being meticulous in ensuring prices are accurately charged and that coupons are rung up correctly.

Extremely Good 9

Carefully but expeditiously checked the date of each coupon to ensure it was still valid.

8

Looked for unmarked items and had a bagger go back to check the price when received an item with an unmarked price.

7

Checked sales flyer when customer pointed out an item was on sale.

6

Weighed produce but failed to check price listed per pound, instead depending on memory

5

Asked clerk at next register for price of unmarked item.

4

Noticed unmarked item and asked customer what the price should be.

3

Instead of checking item, rang up produce item as "plain" rather than as "deluxe", undercharging by 40%.

2

Seen talking on cell phone and texting while checking customer's groceries, failing to charge for six items as a result.

Extremely Poor 1

EXPERIENTIAL EXERCISE

Grading the Professor

Purpose: The purpose of this exercise is to give you practice in developing and using a performance appraisal form.

Required Understanding: You are going to develop a performance appraisal form for an instructor and should therefore be thoroughly familiar with the discussion of performance appraisals in this chapter.

How to Set Up the Exercise/Instructions: Divide the class into groups of four or five students.

1. First, based on what you now know about performance appraisal, do you think Figure 9-1 is an effective scale for appraising instructors? Why? Why not?
2. Next, your group should develop its own tool for appraising the performance of an instructor. Decide which of the appraisal tools (graphic rating scales, alternation ranking, and so on) you are going to use, and then design the instrument itself.
3. Next, have a spokesperson from each group post his or her group's appraisal tool on the board. How similar are the tools? Do they all measure the same factors? Which factor appears most often? Which do you think is the most effective tool on the board?
4. The class should select the top 10 factors from all of the appraisal tools presented to create what the class perceives to be the most effective tool for appraising the performance of the instructor.

APPLICATION CASE

Appraising the Secretaries at Sweetwater U

Rob Winchester, newly appointed vice president for administrative affairs at Sweetwater State University, faced a tough problem shortly after his university career began. Three weeks after he came on board in September, Sweetwater's president, Rob's boss, told Rob that one of his first tasks was to improve the appraisal system used to evaluate secretarial and clerical performance at Sweetwater U. The main difficulty was that the performance appraisal was traditionally tied directly to salary increases given at the end of the year. Therefore, most administrators were less than accurate when they used the graphic rating forms that were the basis of the clerical staff evaluation. In fact, what usually happened was that each administrator simply rated his or her clerk or secretary as "excellent." This cleared the way for all support staff to receive a maximum pay increase every year.

But the current university budget simply did not include enough money to fund another "maximum" annual increase for every staffer. Furthermore, Sweetwater's president felt that the custom of providing invalid feedback to each secretary on his or her year's performance was not productive, so he had asked the new vice president to revise the system. In October, Rob sent a memo to all administrators, telling them that in the future no more than half the secretaries reporting to any particular administrator could be appraised as "excellent." This move, in effect, forced each supervisor to begin ranking his or her secretaries for quality of performance. The vice president's memo met widespread resistance immediately—from administrators, who were afraid that many of their secretaries would begin leaving for more lucrative jobs, and from secretaries, who felt that the new system was unfair and reduced each secretary's chance of receiving a maximum salary increase. A handful of secretaries had begun quietly picketing outside the president's home on the university campus. The picketing, caustic remarks by disgruntled administrators, and rumors of an impending slowdown by the secretaries (there were about 250 on campus) made Rob Winchester wonder whether he had made the right decision by setting up forced ranking. He knew, however, that there were a few performance appraisal experts in the School of Business, so he decided to set up an appointment with them to discuss the matter.

He met with them the next morning. He explained the situation as he had found it: The current appraisal system had been set up when the university first opened 10 years earlier. A committee of secretaries had developed it. Under that system, Sweetwater's administrators filled out forms similar to the one shown in Table 9-2. This once-a-year appraisal (in March) had run into problems almost immediately, since it was apparent from the start that administrators varied widely in their interpretations of job standards, as well as in how conscientiously they filled out the forms and supervised their secretaries. Moreover, at the end of the first year it became obvious to everyone that each secretary's salary increase was tied directly to the March appraisal. For example, those rated "excellent" received the maximum increases, those rated "good" received smaller increases, and those given neither rating received only the standard across-the-board cost-of-living increase. Since universities in general—and Sweetwater, in particular—have paid secretaries somewhat lower salaries than those prevailing in private industry, some secretaries left in a huff that first year. From that time on, most administrators simply rated all secretaries excellent in order to reduce staff turnover, thus ensuring each a maximum increase. In the process, they also avoided the hard feelings aroused by the significant performance differences otherwise highlighted by administrators.

Two Sweetwater experts agreed to consider the problem, and in 2 weeks they came back to the vice president with the following recommendations. First, the form used to rate the secretaries was grossly insufficient. It was unclear what "excellent" or "quality of work" meant, for example. They recommended instead a form like that in Figure 9-2. In addition, they recommended that the vice president rescind his earlier memo and no longer attempt to force university administrators to arbitrarily rate at least half their secretaries as something less than excellent. The two consultants pointed out that this was, in fact, an unfair procedure since it was quite possible that any particular administrator might have staffers who were all or virtually all excellent—or conceivably, although less likely, all below standard. The experts said that the way to get all the administrators to take the appraisal process more seriously was to stop tying it to salary increases. In other words, they recommended that every administrator fill out a form like that in Figure 9-2 for each secretary at least once a year and then use this form as the basis of a counseling session. Salary increases would have to be made on some basis other than the performance appraisal, so that administrators would no longer hesitate to fill out the rating forms honestly.

Rob thanked the two experts and went back to his office to ponder their recommendations. Some of the recommendations (such as substituting the new rating form for the old) seemed to make sense. Nevertheless, he still had serious doubts as to the efficacy of any graphic rating form, particularly compared with his original, preferred forced ranking approach. The experts' second recommendation—to stop tying the appraisals to automatic salary increases—made sense but raised at least one very practical problem: If salary increases were not to be based on performance appraisals, on what were they to be based? He began wondering whether the experts' recommendations weren't simply based on ivory tower theorizing.

Questions

1. Do you think that the experts' recommendations will be sufficient to get most of the administrators to fill out the rating forms properly? Why? Why not? What additional actions (if any) do you think will be necessary?
2. Do you think that Vice President Winchester would be better off dropping graphic rating forms, substituting instead one of the other techniques we discussed in this chapter, such as a ranking method? Why?
3. What performance appraisal system would you develop for the secretaries if you were Rob Winchester? Defend your answer.

CONTINUING CASE

Carter Cleaning Company

The Performance Appraisal

After spending several weeks on the job, Jennifer was surprised to discover that her father had not formally evaluated any employee's performance for all the years that he had owned the business. Jack's position was that he had "a hundred higher-priority things to attend to," such as boosting sales and lowering costs, and, in any case, many employees didn't stick around long enough to be appraisable anyway. Furthermore, contended Jack, manual workers such as those doing the pressing and the cleaning did periodically get positive feedback in terms of praise from Jack for a job well done, or criticism, also from Jack, if things did not look right during one of his swings through the stores. Similarly, Jack was never shy about telling his managers about store problems so that they, too, got some feedback on where they stood.

This informal feedback notwithstanding, Jennifer believes that a more formal appraisal approach is required. She believes that there are criteria such as quality, quantity, attendance, and punctuality that should be evaluated periodically even if a worker is paid on piece rate. Furthermore, she feels quite strongly that the managers need to have a list of quality standards for matters such as store cleanliness, efficiency, safety, and adherence to budget on which they know they are to be formally evaluated.

Questions

1. Is Jennifer right about the need to evaluate the workers formally? The managers? Why or why not?
2. Develop a performance appraisal method for the workers and managers in each store.

TRANSLATING STRATEGY INTO HR POLICIES & PRACTICES CASE

The Hotel Paris Case

The New Performance Management System

The Hotel Paris's competitive strategy is "To use superior guest service to differentiate the Hotel Paris properties, and to thereby increase the length of stay and return rate of guests, and thus boost revenues and profitability." HR manager Lisa Cruz must now formulate functional policies and activities that support this competitive strategy, by eliciting the required employee behaviors and competencies.

Lisa knew that the Hotel Paris's performance appraisal system was archaic. When the founders opened their first hotel, they went to an office-supply store and purchased a pad of performance appraisal forms. The hotel chain uses these to this day. Each form is a two-sided page. Supervisors indicate whether the employee's performance in terms of various standard traits including quantity of work, quality of work, and dependability was excellent, good, fair, or poor. Lisa knew that, among other flaws, this appraisal tool did not force either the employee or the supervisor to focus the appraisal on the extent to which the employee was helping the Hotel Paris to achieve its strategic goals. She wanted a system that focused the employee's attention on taking those actions that would contribute to helping the company achieve its goals, for instance, in terms of improved customer service.

Lisa and her team also wanted a performance management system that focused on both competencies and objectives. In designing the new system, their starting point was the job descriptions they had created for the hotel's employees. These descriptions each included required competencies. Consequently, using a form similar to Figure 9-4 (page 311), the front-desk clerks' appraisals now focus on competencies such as "able to check a guest in or out in 5 minutes or less." Most service employees' appraisals include the competency, "able to exhibit patience and guest support even when busy with other activities." There were other required competencies. For example, the Hotel Paris wanted all service employees to show initiative in helping guests, to be customer-oriented, and to be team players (in terms of sharing information and best practices). Each of these competencies derives from the hotel's aim of becoming more service-oriented.

Questions

1. Pick out one job, such as front-desk clerk. Based on any information you have (including job descriptions you may have created in other chapters) write a list of duties, competencies, and performance standards for that chosen job.
2. Based on that, create a performance appraisal form for appraising that job.

KEY TERMS

performance appraisal, *p. 307*
graphic rating scale, *p. 309*
alternation ranking method, *p. 313*
paired comparison method, *p. 313*
forced distribution method, *p. 315*
critical incident method, *p. 315*
behaviorally anchored rating scale (BARS), *p. 315*
electronic performance monitoring (EPM), *p. 319*
unclear standards, *p. 321*
halo effect, *p. 321*
central tendency, *p. 323*
strictness/leniency, *p. 323*
bias, *p. 323*
appraisal interview, *p. 329*
performance management, *p. 331*

ENDNOTES

1. See, for example, Doug Cederblom and Dan Pemerl, "From Performance Appraisal to Performance Management: One Agency's Experience," *Personnel Management* 31, no. 2 (Summer 2002), pp. 131–140.
2. For a recent discussion of this, see, for example, Samuel Culbert, "Get Rid of the Performance Review!" *The Wall Street Journal*, October 20, 2008, p. 4; and J. Pfeffer, "Low Grades for Performance Reviews," *Business Week*, no. 4141 (August 3, 2009), p. 68.
3. Experts debate the pros and cons of tying appraisals to pay decisions. One side argues that doing so distorts the appraisals. A recent study concludes the opposite. Based on an analysis of surveys from more than 24,000 employees in more than 6,000 workplaces in Canada, the researchers concluded (1) linking the employees' pay to their performance appraisals contributed to improved pay satisfaction; (2) even when appraisals are *not* directly tied to pay, appraisals contributed to pay satisfaction, "probably through mechanisms related to perceived organizational justice"; and (3) whether or not the employees received performance pay, "individuals who do not receive performance appraisals are significantly less satisfied with their pay." Mary Jo Ducharme et al., "Exploring the Links Between Performance Appraisals and Pay Satisfaction," *Compensation & Benefits Review*, September/October 2005, pp. 46–52. See also Robert Morgan, "Making the Most of Performance Management Systems," *Compensation & Benefits Review*, September/October 2006, pp. 22–27.
4. John (Jack) Welch, broadcast interview at Fairfield University, C-Span, May 5, 2001.
5. Howard Risher, "Getting Serious About Performance Management," *Compensation & Benefits Review*, November/December 2005, pp. 18–26.
6. Del Jones, "More Firms Cut Workers Ranked at Bottom to Make Way for Talent," *USA Today*, May 30, 2001, p. B01.
7. Steve Bates, "Forced Ranking," *HR Magazine*, June 2003, pp. 63–68.
8. Steven Cullen et al., "Forced Distribution Rating Systems and the Improvement of Workforce Potential: A Baseline Simulation," *Personnel Psychology* 58 (2005), p. 1.
9. "Survey Says Problems with Forced Ranking Include Lower Morale and Costly Turnover," *BNA Bulletin to Management*, September 16, 2004, p. 297.
10. Steve Bates, "Forced Ranking: Why Grading Employees on a Scale Relative to Each Other Forces a Hard Look at Finding

Keepers, Losers May Become Weepers," *HR Magazine* 48, no. 6 (June 2003), p. 62. See also D. J. Schleicher et. al., "Rater Reactions to Forced Distribution Rating Systems," *Journal of Management* 35, no. 4 (August 2009), pp. 899–927.

11. "Straight Talk About Grading Employees on a Curve," *BNA Bulletin to Management*, November 1, 2001, p. 351.
12. Jena McGregor, "The Struggle to Measure Performance," *BusinessWeek*, January 9, 2006, p. 26.
13. Clinton Wingrove, "Developing an Effective Blend of Process and Technology in the New Era of Performance Management," *Compensation & Benefits Review*, January/February 2003, p. 26.
14. See, for example, Timothy Keaveny and Anthony McGann, "A Comparison of Behavioral Expectation Scales and Graphic Rating Scales," *Journal of Applied Psychology* 60 (1975), pp. 695–703. See also John Ivancevich, "A Longitudinal Study of Behavioral Expectation Scales: Attitudes and Performance," *Journal of Applied Psychology* 30, no. 3 (Autumn 1986), pp. 619–628.
15. Based on Donald Schwab, Herbert Heneman III, and Thomas DeCotiis, "Behaviorally Anchored Scales: A Review of the Literature," *Personnel Psychology*, 28 (1975), pp. 549–562. For a discussion, see also Uco Wiersma and Gary Latham, "The Practicality of Behavioral Observation Scales, Behavioral Expectation Scales, and Trait Scales," *Personnel Psychology* 30, no. 3 (Autumn 1986), pp. 619–689.
16. Lawrence Fogli, Charles Hulin, and Milton Blood, "Development of First Level Behavioral Job Criteria," *Journal of Applied Psychology* 55 (1971), pp. 3–8. See also Joseph Maiorca, "How to Construct Behaviorally Anchored Rating Scales (BARS) for Employee Evaluations," *Supervision*, August 1997, pp. 15–19.
17. Kevin R. Murphy and Joseph Constans, "Behavioral Anchors as a Source of Bias in Rating," *Journal of Applied Psychology* 72, no. 4 (November 1987), pp. 573–577; Aharon Tziner, "A Comparison of Three Methods of Performance Appraisal with Regard to Goal Properties, Goal Perception, and Ratee Satisfaction," *Group & Organization Management* 25, no. 2 (June 2000), pp. 175–191.
18. www.employeeappraiser.com/index.php, accessed January 10, 2008.
19. www.halogensoftware.com/products/halogen-eappraisal, accessed January 10, 2008.
20. Drew Robb, "Appraising Appraisal Software," HR *Magazine*, October 2008, p. 68.
21. Drew Robb, "Building a Better Workforce," *HR Magazine*, October 2004, pp. 87–94.
22. See, for example, Stoney Alder and Maureen Ambrose, "Towards Understanding Fairness Judgments Associated with Computer Performance Monitoring: An Integration of the Feedback, Justice, and Monitoring Research," *Human Resource Management Review* 15, no. 1 (March 2005), pp. 43–67.
23. See, for example, John Aiello and Y. Shao, "Computerized Performance Monitoring," Paper presented at the Seventh Conference of the Society for Industrial and Organizational Psychology, Montreal, Quebec, Canada, May 1992.
24. Rasha Madkour, "NASA Shooting Suspect Received Poor Job Review and Feared Being Fired, Police Say," Associated Press, April 21, 2007.
25. See, for example, Adrienne Fox, "Curing What Ails Performance Reviews," *HR Magazine*, January 2009, pp. 52–55.
26. Andrew Solomonson and Charles Lance, "Examination of the Relationship Between True Halo and Halo Effect in Performance Ratings," *Journal of Applied Psychology* 82, no. 5 (1997), pp. 665–674.
27. Manuel London, Edward Mone, and John C. Scott, "Performance Management and Assessment: Methods for Improved Rater Accuracy and Employee Goal Setting," *Human Resource Management* 43, no. 4 (Winter 2004), pp. 319–336.
28. Ted Turnasella, "Dagwood Bumstead, Will You Ever Get That Raise?" *Compensation & Benefits Review*, September–October 1995, pp. 25–27. See also Solomonson and Lance, "Examination of the Relationship Between True Halo and Halo Effect," pp. 665–674.
29. I. M. Jawahar and Charles Williams, "Where All the Children Are Above Average: The Performance Appraisal Purpose Effect," *Personnel Psychology* 50 (1997), p. 921.
30. Annette Simmons, "When Performance Reviews Fail," *Training & Development* 57, no. 9 (September 2003), pp. 47–53.
31. "Flawed Ranking System Revives Workers' Bias Claim," *BNA Bulletin to Management*, June 28, 2005, p. 206.
32. Karen Lyness and Madeline Heilman, "When Fit Is Fundamental: Performance Evaluations and Promotions of Upper-Level Female and Male Managers," *Journal of Applied Psychology* 91, no. 4 (2006), pp. 767–775.
33. Madeleine Heilman et al., "Penalties for Success: Reactions to Women Who Succeed at Male Gender Type Tasks," *Journal of Applied Psychology* 89, no. 3 (2004), pp. 416–427. Managers may not rate successful female managers negatively (for instance, in terms of likability and boss desirability) when they see the woman as supportive, caring, and sensitive to their needs. Madeleine Heilmann and Tyler Okimoto, "Why Are Women Penalized for Success at Male Tasks? The Implied Communality Deficit," *Journal of Applied Psychology* 92, no. 1 (2007), pp. 81–92.
34. Gary Greguras et al., "A Field Study of the Effects of Rating Purpose on the Quality of Multisource Ratings," *Personnel Psychology* 56 (2003), pp. 1–21.
35. Jane Halpert, Midge Wilson, and Julia Hickman, "Pregnancy as a Source of Bias in Performance Appraisals," *Journal of Organizational Behavior* 14 (1993), pp. 649–663.
36. Ibid., p. 655.
37. Clinton Wingrove, "Developing an Effective Blend of Process and Technology," pp. 25–30.
38. Joanne Sammer, "Calibrating Consistency," *HR Magazine*, January 2008, pp. 73–74.
39. Angelo DeNisi and Lawrence Peters, "Organization of Information in Memory and the Performance Appraisal Process: Evidence from the Field," *Journal of Applied Psychology* 81, no. 6 (1996), pp. 717–737. See also A. Fox, "Curing What Ails Performance Reviews," *HR Magazine* 54, no. 1 (January 2009), pp. 52–56.
40. Juan Sanchez and Phillip De La Torre, "A Second Look at the Relationship Between Rating and Behavioral Accuracy in Performance Appraisal," *Journal of Applied Psychology* 81, no. 1 (1996), p. 7. See also "How To . . . Improve Appraisals," *People Management* 15, no. 3 (January 29, 2009), p. 57.

41. David Martin et al., "The Legal Ramifications of Performance Appraisal: The Growing Significance," *Public Personnel Management* 29, no. 3 (Fall 2000), pp. 381–383.
42. Jon Werner and Mark Bolino, "Explaining U.S. Courts of Appeals' Decisions Involving Performance Appraisal: Accuracy, Fairness, and Validation," *Personnel Psychology* 50 (1997), pp. 1–24.
43. Wayne Cascio and H. John Bernardin, "Implications of Performance Appraisal Litigation for Personnel Decisions," *Personnel Psychology*, Summer 1981, pp. 211–212; Gerald Barrett and Mary Kernan, "Performance Appraisal and Terminations: A Review of Court Decisions Since *Brito v. Zia* with Implications for Personnel Practices," *Personnel Psychology* 40, no. 3 (Autumn 1987), pp. 489–504; Elaine Pulakos, *Performance Management*, SHRM Foundation, 2004.
44. Vanessa Druskat and Steven Wolf, "Effects and Timing of Developmental Peer Appraisals in Self-Managing Workgroups," *Journal of Applied Psychology* 84, no. 1 (1999), pp. 58–74.
45. R. G. Downey, F. F. Medland, and L. G. Yates, "Evaluation of a Peer Rating System for Predicting Subsequent Promotion of Senior Military Officers," *Journal of Applied Psychology* 61 (April 1976); see also Julie Barclay and Lynn Harland, "Peer Performance Appraisals: The Impact of Rater Competence, Rater Location, and Rating Correctability on Fairness Perceptions," *Group & Organization Management* 20, no. 1 (March 1995), pp. 39–60.
46. Chockalingam Viswesvaran, Deniz Ones, and Frank Schmidt, "Comparative Analysis of the Reliability of Job Performance Ratings," *Journal of Applied Psychology* 81, no. 5 (1996), pp. 557–574. See also Kevin Murphy et al., "Raters Who Pursue Different Goals Give Different Ratings," *Journal of Applied Psychology* 89, no. 1 (2004), pp. 158–164.
47. George Thornton III, "Psychometric Properties of Self-Appraisal of Job Performance," *Personnel Psychology* 33 (Summer 1980), p. 265. See also Cathy Anderson, Jack Warner, and Cassie Spencer, "Inflation Bias in Self-Assessment Evaluations: Implications for Valid Employee Selection," *Journal of Applied Psychology* 69, no. 4 (November 1984), pp. 574–580; and Shaul Fox and Yossi Dinur, "Validity of Self-Assessment: A Field Evaluation," *Personnel Psychology* 41, no. 3 (Autumn 1988), pp. 581–592. Yet, such findings may be culturally related. One study compared self and supervisor ratings in "other-oriented" cultures (as in Asia, where values tend to emphasize teams). It found here that self and supervisor ratings were related. M. Audrey Korsgaard et al., "The Effect of Other Orientation on Self–Supervisor Rating Agreement," *Journal of Organizational Behavior* 25, no. 7 (November 2004), pp. 873–891.
48. Forest Jourden and Chip Heath, "The Evaluation Gap in Performance Perceptions: Illusory Perceptions of Groups and Individuals," *Journal of Applied Psychology* 81, no. 4 (August 1996), pp. 369–379. See also Sheri Ostroff, "Understanding Self-Other Agreement: A Look at Rater and Ratee Characteristics, Context, and Outcomes," *Personnel Psychology* 57, no. 2 (Summer 2004), pp. 333–375.
49. Richard Reilly, James Smither, and Nicholas Vasilopoulos, "A Longitudinal Study of Upward Feedback," *Personnel Psychology* 49 (1996), pp. 599–612.
50. Ibid., p. 599.
51. The evidence from another study suggests also that "... upward and peer 360-degree ratings may be biased by rater affect [whether the rater likes the ratee]; therefore, at this point, these ratings should be used for the sole purpose of providing ratees with developmental feedback." David Antonioni and Heejoon Park, "The Relationship Between Rater Affect and Three Sources of 360-Degree Feedback Ratings," *Journal of Management* 27 no. 4 (2001) pp. 479–495.
52. "360-Degree Feedback on the Rise, Survey Finds," *BNA Bulletin to Management*, January 23, 1997, p. 31. See also Christopher Mabey, "Closing the Circle: Participant Views of a 360-Degree Feedback Program," *Human Resource Management Journal* 11, no. 1 (2001), pp. 41–53.
53. Carol Hymowitz, "Managers See Feedback from Their Staffers as the Most Valuable," *The Wall Street Journal* (Eastern Edition), November 11, 2003, p. B1.
54. Terry Beehr et al., "Evaluation of 360-Degree Feedback Ratings: Relationships with Each Other and with Performance and Selection Predictors," *Journal of Organizational Behavior* 22, no. 7 (November 2001), pp. 775–778.
55. Christine Hagan et al., "Predicting Assessment Center Performance with 360-Degree, Top-Down, and Customer-Based Competency Assessments," *Human Resource Management* 45, no. 3 (Fall 2006), pp. 357–390.
56. James Smither et al., "Does Performance Improve Following Multi-Source Feedback? A Theoretical Model, Meta Analysis, and Review of Empirical Findings," *Personnel Psychology* 58 (2005), pp. 33–36.
57. Bruce Pfau and Ira Kay, "Does a 360-Degree Feedback Negatively Affect the Company Performance?" *HR Magazine*, June 2002, pp. 55–59.
58. Maury Peiperl, "Getting 360-Degree Job Feedback Right," *Harvard Business Review*, January 2001, p. 147. See also Leanne Atwater et al., "Multisource Feedback: Lessons Learned and Implications for Practice," *Human Resource Management* 46, no. 2 (Summer 2007), p. 285.
59. Brian Smith et al., "Current Trends in Performance Appraisal: An Examination of Managerial Practice," *SAM Advanced Management Journal* 61, no. 3 (Summer 1996), p. 16; "Companies Appraise to Improve Development," *Personnel Today*, February 25, 2003, p. 51.
60. Herman Aguinis, *Performance Management* (Upper Saddle River, NJ: Prentice Hall, 2007), p. 2.
61. Howard Risher, "Getting Serious About Performance Management," *Compensation & Benefits Review*, November/December 2005, p. 19.
62. Clinton Wingrove, "Developing an Effective Blend of Process and Technology in the New Era of Performance Management," *Compensation & Benefits Review*, January/February 2003, p. 27.
63. These are quoted or paraphrased from Howard Risher, "Getting Serious About Performance Management," *Compensation & Benefits Review*, November/December 2005, p. 19.
64. Mushin Lee and Byoungho Son, "The Effects of Appraisal Review Content on Employees' Reactions and Performance," *International Journal of Human Resource Management* 1 (February 1998), p. 283; David Antonioni, "Improve the Management Process Before Discontinuing Performance Appraisals," *Compensation & Benefits Review*, May–June 1994, p. 29; Jonathan Siegel, "86 Your Appraisal Process?" *HR Magazine*, October 2000, pp. 199–206; Steve

Bates, "Performance Appraisals: Some Improvement Needed," *HR Magazine,* April 2003, p. 12.

65. Robert Kaplan and David Norton, "The Office of Strategy Management," *Harvard Business Review,* October 2005, pp. 72–80.
66. Michael Mankins and Richard Steele, "Turning Great Strategy into Great Performance," *Harvard Business Review,* July/August 2005, pp. 65–72.
67. www.activestrategy.com/eventsandnews/pressreleases/050108.aspx, accessed March 23, 2009.
68. D. Bradford Neary, "Creating a Company-Wide, Online, Performance Management System: A Case at TRW, Inc.," *Human Resource Management* 41, no. 4 (Winter 2002), pp. 491–498.

10 Coaching, Careers, and Talent Management

Reviewing demographic trends, pharmacy chain CVS knew it had a problem. As a retail chain, CVS relied on an army of young people to staff its stores—to restock shelves, be cashiers, and serve as clerks in each store's various departments. The problem was that the number of young people entering the workforce was shrinking, while the number of older ones was rising. CVS executives knew they needed some way to tap into this growing pool of older workers.[1]

Source: Courtesy of Masterfile Royalty Free Division.

WHERE ARE WE NOW . . .

Chapter 9 focused on appraising employees' performance. After appraising performance, the manager typically needs to deal with several issues. The employee may require coaching, as well as career advice and mentoring. And, the manager and employer may want to review the employee's performance in the context of the company's overall talent management needs. The main purpose of this chapter is to help you be more effective at coaching and mentoring employees, and at supporting their career planning needs. The main topics we'll address include coaching employees, the basics and methods of career planning and mentoring, and talent management. The appendix to this chapter provides specific career management and job search tools and techniques. This chapter completes Part 3, which addressed training, appraisal, and development. Once you've trained, appraised, and coached employees, you turn to the question of how to pay them, the topic we cover in the following three chapters.

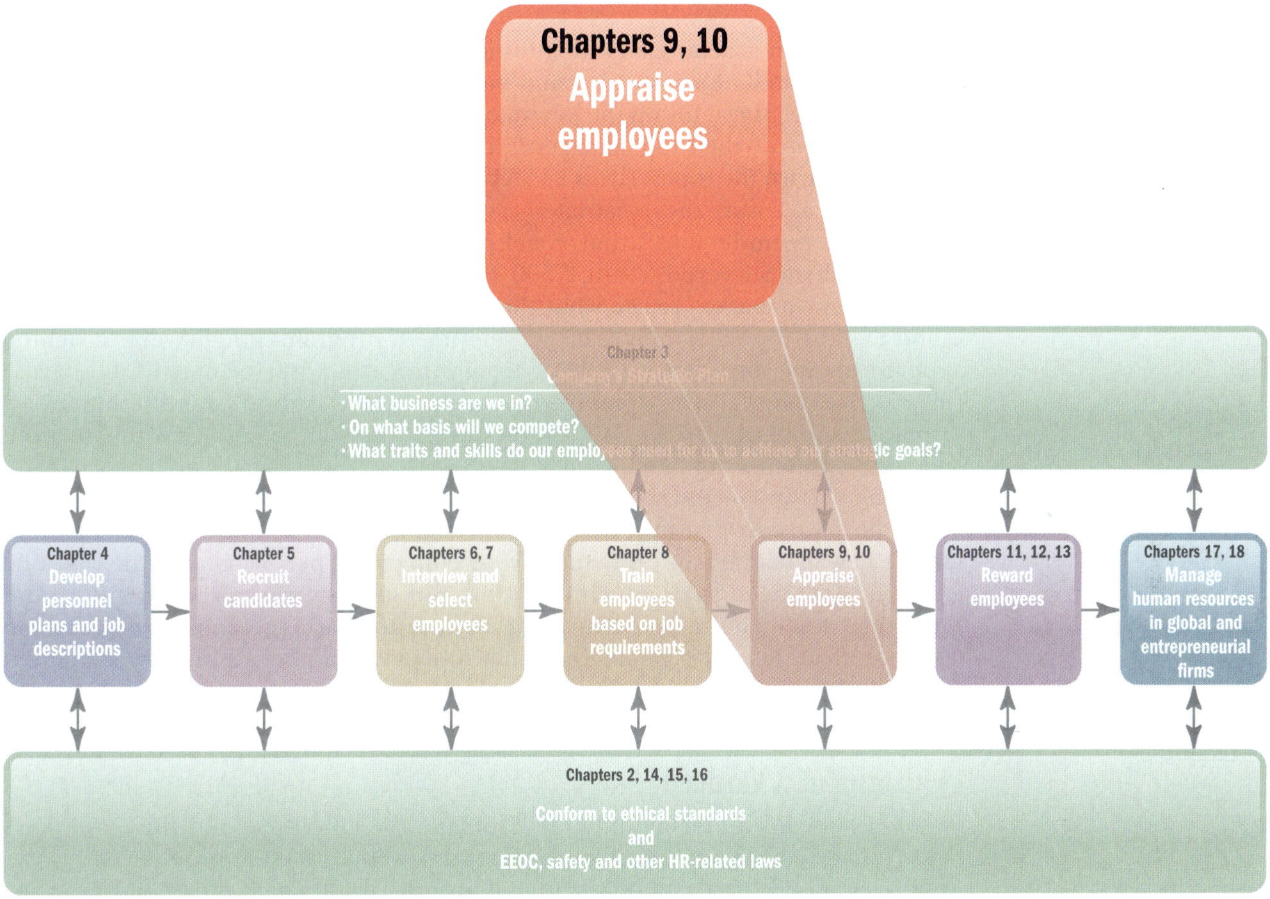

LEARNING OUTCOMES

1. Compare and contrast coaching and mentoring and describe the importance of each.
2. Compare employers' traditional and career planning–oriented HR focuses.
3. Explain the employee's, manager's, and employer's career development roles.
4. Describe the issues to consider when making promotion decisions.
5. List and briefly explain at least four methods for better managing retirements.
6. Define talent management and give an example of an actual talent management system.

1 Compare and contrast coaching and mentoring and describe the importance of each.

IMPROVING YOUR COACHING SKILLS

Great supervisors tend to be great coaches, because they bring out the best in their employees. Coaching and the closely related *mentoring* are thus key supervisory skills. **Coaching** means educating, instructing, and training subordinates.

Mentoring means advising, counseling, and guiding. Coaching focuses on teaching shorter-term job-related skills; mentoring, on helping employees navigate longer-term career hazards. Supervisors have coached and mentored employees from the dawn of management (in Greek mythology, *Mentor* advised Odysseus's son Telemachus). But with more managers leading highly trained employees and self-managing teams, supporting, coaching, and mentoring are fast replacing formal authority and giving orders for getting things done.

Coaching and mentoring require both analytical and interpersonal skills. They require *analysis* because it's futile to teach or advise someone if you don't know what the problem is. They require *interpersonal* skills because it's equally futile to know the problem if you can't get the person to listen or change.

Coaching's Importance

Managers rely on coaching and mentoring for some of their most important duties. For example, you'll need coaching and mentoring skills when appraising employees, and coaching is crucial for on-the-job training.[2] We saw that many firms use executive coaches to improve their top managers' performance. You may have to mentor a new employee to learn the ropes. Firms like AT&T assign mentors to those employees they send abroad, to ensure the expatriates' careers stay on track while they're gone.

Employers understand that coaching and mentoring are important. One consulting firm surveyed about 2,500 senior human resource and training and development managers to see what their training programs offered.[3] The survey found that the top skills their firms' development programs taught were "coaching a performance problem" (72%), "communicating performance standards" (69%), "coaching a development opportunity" (69%), and "conducting a performance appraisal" (67%). We'll look more closely at coaching in this section, and address mentoring later in the chapter.

Some performance situations don't require coaching. For example, if your new employee learns the first time through how to do the job, if your current employees use the new machine flawlessly, and if your employee's performance review is faultless, you won't need to do much coaching. But things rarely go so smoothly. And when they don't, you're probably going to have to coach the employee. Coaching does not mean just telling someone what to do. We can best think of coaching in terms of a four-step process: *preparation, planning, active coaching,* and *follow-up.*[4]

Preparing to Coach

Preparation means understanding the problem, the employee, and the employee's skills. Your aim here is to formulate a hypothesis about what the problem is.

Preparation is partly an observational process. You'll watch the employee to see what he or she is doing, and observe the workflow and how coworkers interact with the employee. In addition to observation, you may review (as we explained in Chapter 8, Training) objective data on things like productivity, absenteeism and tardiness, accidents, grievances, waste, product quality, downtime, repairs, customer complaints, and the employee's previous performance reviews and training.

In formulating your hypothesis, it can help to apply the *ABC (antecedents, behavior, consequences) approach.* The basic idea of ABC is that poor skills and motivation don't always explain poor performance. Faced with a performance problem, first review the *antecedents*—those things that come before the person does the job. Does the employee know what the performance standards are? Does he or she now that they're not being met?

Next review the employee's *behavior.* Here, particularly ask, "Could this person do the job if he or she wanted to?" For example, was training adequate? Does the person have the necessary aptitudes? Does he or she have the tools and raw materials to do the job?

Finally, think through, from the employee's vantage point, the *consequences* of doing the job right. Do you reward the person for doing well? Might there be negative consequences (like complaints from peers) for performing to standard?

Planning

Perhaps the most powerful way to get someone to change is to obtain his or her enthusiastic agreement on what change is required. This requires reaching agreement on the problem and on what to change. In practice, you'll then lay out a change plan in the form of *Steps to Take, Measures of Success,* and *Date to Complete.*

Getting agreement on these items requires all the interpersonal communications skills you can muster. Figure 10-1 presents, in the form of guidelines (such as "make yourself clear"), a short course in interpersonal communications.

Active Coaching

With agreement on a plan, you can start the actual "educating, instructing, and training"—namely, coaching. Here you are, in essence, in the role of teacher. Your toolkit will include what you learned about on-the-job training in Chapter 8 ("review the job description," "use a job instruction sheet," and so on). However, interpersonal communications skills are the heart of effective coaching. As one writer says, "[a]n effective coach offers ideas and advice in such a way that the subordinate can hear them, respond to them, and appreciate their value."[5]

FIGURE 10-1 A Short Course in Improving Interpersonal Communications

Make Yourself Clear. For example, if you mean immediately, say "immediately," don't leave the timing open-ended or say something like, "as soon as you can."

Be Consistent. Much of what the other person "hears" reflects not just your words but your (nonverbal) tone, expression, and eye contact. Therefore, make sure your tone, expression, and words send a consistent meaning.

Consider the Distractions. In delivering your message, consider the potential distractions (such as background noise), for instance, by speaking louder.

Confirm, "Message received." Pilots and flight controllers know to confirm and reconfirm the message. You should do the same.

Do Not Attack the Person's Defenses. Remember not to attack the other person's defenses (as in "you just can't stand being blamed for anything").

Use "Active Listening." Use these "active listening" tools:

- ***Listen for total meaning.*** If your employee says, "We can't sell that much," strive to understand the underlying feelings (such as the pressure): "I know how you feel, so let's see what we can work out."
- ***Reflect feelings.*** For example, "They're pushing you pretty hard, aren't they?"
- ***Show that you are listening with an open mind.*** Do not rush to interrupt the person, or to finish his or her sentences.
- ***Encourage the speaker to talk.*** Ask open-ended questions, and confirm your understanding by summarizing what the employee said.

coaching
Educating, instructing, and training subordinates.

mentoring
Advising, counseling, and guiding.

Follow-Up

Bad habits sometimes reemerge. It's therefore necessary to re-observe the person's progress periodically.

Figure 10-2 presents a self-evaluation checklist for assessing your coaching skills.

FIGURE 10-2 Coach's Self-Evaluation Checklist

Source: Based on Richard Luecke, *Coaching and Mentoring* (Boston: Harvard Business School Press, 2004), pp. 8–9.

Coach's Self-Evaluation Checklist

The questions below relate to the skills and qualities needed to be an effective coach. Use this tool to evaluate your own effectiveness as a coach.

Question	Yes	No
1. Do you show interest in career development, not just short-term performance?		
2. Do you provide both support and autonomy?		
3. Do you set high yet attainable goals?		
4. Do you serve as a role model?		
5. Do you communicate business strategies and expected behaviors as a basis for establishing objectives?		
6. Do you work with the individual you are coaching to generate alternative approaches or solutions which you can consider together?		
7. Before giving feedback, do you observe carefully, and without bias, the individual you are coaching?		
8. Do you separate observations from judgments or assumptions?		
9. Do you test your theories about a person's behavior before acting on them?		
10. Are you careful to avoid using your own performance as a yardstick to measure others?		
11. Do you focus your attention and avoid distractions when someone is talking to you?		
12. Do you paraphrase or use some other method to clarify what is being said in a discussion?		
13. Do you use relaxed body language and verbal cues to encourage a speaker during conversations?		
14. Do you use open-ended questions to promote sharing of ideas and information?		
15. Do you give specific feedback?		
16. Do you give timely feedback?		
17. Do you give feedback that focuses on behavior and its consequences (rather than on vague judgments)?		
18. Do you give positive as well as negative feedback?		
19. Do you try to reach agreement on desired goals and outcomes rather than simply dictate them?		
20. Do you try to prepare for coaching discussions in advance?		
21. Do you always follow up on a coaching discussion to make sure progress is proceeding as planned?		
TOTALS		

When you have these characteristics and use these strategies, people trust you and turn to you for both professional and personal support.
If you answered ***"yes"*** *to most of these questions, you are probably an effective coach.*
If you answered ***"no"*** *to same or many of these questions, you may want to consider how you can further develop your coaching skills.*

Source: Harvard ManageMentor® *Coaching.*

CAREER MANAGEMENT BASICS

Employers and employees tend to view performance reviews from different points of view. Employers of course are often preoccupied with getting the employee's performance aligned with the company's standards and needs. Employees will want to know what the review means in terms of their careers. Those conducting appraisals therefore need to know something about careers and career planning.

Career Terminology

We may define **career** as the "occupational positions a person has had over many years." Many people look back on their careers, knowing that what they might have achieved they did achieve, and that their career goals were satisfied. Others are less fortunate and feel that, at least in their careers, their lives and their potential went unfulfilled.

Knowing this, many employers work hard to support their employees' career needs. Some institute formal *career management* processes, while others do little. We can define **career management** as a process for enabling employees to better understand and develop their career skills and interests and to use these skills and interests most effectively within the company and after they leave the firm. Specific career management activities might include providing realistic career-oriented appraisals, posting open jobs, and offering formal career development activities. **Career development** is the lifelong series of activities (such as workshops) that contribute to a person's career exploration, establishment, success, and fulfillment. **Career planning** is the formal process through which someone becomes aware of his or her personal skills, interests, knowledge, motivations, and other characteristics; acquires information about opportunities and choices; identifies career-related goals; and establishes action plans to attain specific goals.

Careers Today

Careers today are not what they were several years ago. Not too long ago, people viewed careers as a sort of upward staircase from job to job, more often than not with one or at most a few firms. Today, recessions, mergers, outsourcing, consolidations, and more or less endless downsizings have changed the ground rules. Many people do still move up from job to job. But more often employees find themselves having to reinvent themselves. For example, the sales rep, laid off by a publishing firm that's just merged, may reinvent her career as an account executive at a media-oriented accounting firm.[6]

Careers today differ in other ways from a few years ago. With more women pursuing professional and managerial careers, families must balance the challenges associated with dual career pressures. At the same time, what people want from their careers seems to be changing. Baby boomers—those retiring in the next few years—tended to be job- and employer-focused. Those entering the job market now often value work arrangements that provide more opportunities for balanced lives.

career
The occupational positions a person has had over many years.

career management
The process for enabling employees to better understand and develop their career skills and interests, and to use these skills and interests more effectively.

career development
The lifelong series of activities that contribute to a person's career exploration, establishment, success, and fulfillment.

career planning
The deliberate process through which someone becomes aware of personal skills, interests, knowledge, motivations, and other characteristics and establishes action plans to attain specific goals.

These changes have big implications for employers. A few years ago, the assumption (the "psychological contract") between employer and employee was, often, "Be loyal to us, and we'll take care of you." Today, employees know they must take care of themselves. The psychological contract is more like, "I'll do my best for you, but I expect you to provide the development and learning that will prepare me for the day I must move on, and for having the work–life balance that I desire."[7] John Madigan, human resources vice president for the Hartford Insurance Company's 3,500-member IT group, discovered how important such development activities can be. Of the employees who left Hartford IT, "Ninety percent . . . talked about [the lack of] career and professional development and the level of support their managers gave them in this area," he says.[8]

2 Compare employers' traditional and career planning–oriented HR focuses.

Employer Career Efforts Today

Recognizing these changes, many employers have added a career aspect to their human resource activities. They use human resource activities not just to support the employer's needs, but also to facilitate career self-analysis and development.[9] Table 10-1 summarizes this. For example, instead of just using appraisals to align the employees' performance with the job's standards, there is more emphasis on using them to help the employee better plan and adjust his or her career planns.

We'll see in a moment that such career development–oriented programs needn't be complicated. Even just receiving performance feedback, having individual development plans, and having access to nontechnical skills training is enough for most employees. Yet, only about a fourth of the respondents in one survey even had individual development plans.[10] Figure 10-3 illustrates a simple career planning form.[11]

John Madigan's experience at Hartford Insurance illustrates why employers also benefit from offering career development. The employees, armed with better insights about their occupational strengths, should be *better equipped* to serve the company.[12] Supporting your employees' career development may also *boost employee commitment* and support your *recruitment* and *retention* efforts. As one expert said, "The most attractive proposition an employer can make today is that in 5 years the employee will have more knowledge and be more employable than now. That should be the acid test for any career development program."[13]

Ideally, the employer, employee, and manager all play roles in planning, guiding, and developing the employee's career (see Table 10-2). We'll look at each.

TABLE 10-1 Traditional Versus Career Development Focus

HR Activity	Traditional Focus	Career Development Focus
Human resource planning	Analyzes jobs, skills, tasks—present and future. Projects needs. Uses statistical data.	Adds information about individual interests, preferences, and the like to replacement plans.
Recruiting and placement	Matching organization's needs with qualified individuals.	Matches individual and jobs based on variables including employees' career interests and aptitudes.
Training and development	Provides opportunities for learning skills, information, and attitudes related to job.	Provides career path information. Adds individual development plans.
Performance appraisal	Rating and/or rewards.	Adds development plans and individual goal setting.
Compensation and benefits	Rewards for time, productivity, talent, and so on.	Adds tuition reimbursement plans, compensation for non–job-related activities such as United Way.

Source: Adapted from Fred L. Otte and Peggy G. Hutcheson, *Helping Employees Manage Careers* (Upper Saddle River, NJ: Prentice Hall, 1992), p. 10, and www.ge.com.cn/careers/career_management.html, accessed May 18, 2007.

FIGURE 10-3 Employee Career Development Plan

Source: Reprinted from www.HR.BLR.com with permission of the publisher *Business and Legal Resources, Inc.*, 141 Mill Rock Road East, Old Saybrook, CT © 2004. BLR© (Business and Legal Resources, Inc.).

Employee Career Development Plan

Employee: ____________ **Position:** ____________

Manager: ____________ **Department:** ____________

Date of Appraisal: ____________

1. What is the next logical step up for this employee, and when do you think he or she will be ready for it?

Probable Next Job:	When Ready:			
	Now	6 Months	1 Year	2 Years
1.	☐	☐	☐	☐
2.	☐	☐	☐	☐
3.	☐	☐	☐	☐

2. What is the highest probable promotion within five years?

3. What does this employee need to prepare for promotion?

- Knowledge: ____________

  Action Plan: ____________

- Still Training: ____________

  Action Plan: ____________

- Management Training: ____________

  Action Plan: ____________

3 Explain the employee's, manager's, and employer's career development roles.

The Employee's Role

Although the employer and manager have roles in guiding employees' careers, no employee should ever abandon this task to others. For the employee, *career planning* means matching individual strengths and weaknesses with occupational opportunities and threats. In other words, the person wants to pursue occupations, jobs, and a career that capitalize on his or her interests, aptitudes, values, and skills. He or she also wants to choose occupations, jobs, and a career that make sense in terms of projected future demand for various types of occupations. The consequences of a bad choice (or of no choice) are too severe to leave to others.

Of course, career planning is no guarantee. A few years ago, a career as a systems analyst or computer engineer was a ticket to success; then many firms began outsourcing these jobs to Asia. But uncertainties like these only highlight the need to be best positioned to move when a career change is required. Luck, as someone once said, comes to those who are best prepared. The appendix to this chapter, "Managing Your Career and Finding a Job" (see page 367), explains the career planning process from the employee's point of view.

TABLE 10-2 Roles in Career Development

Individual

- Accept responsibility for your own career.
- Assess your interests, skills, and values.
- Seek out career information and resources.
- Establish goals and career plans.
- Utilize development opportunities.
- Talk with your manager about your career.
- Follow through on realistic career plans.

Manager

- Provide timely and accurate performance feedback.
- Provide developmental assignments and support.
- Participate in career development discussions with subordinates.
- Support employee development plans.

Employer

- Communicate mission, policies, and procedures.
- Provide training and development opportunities, including workshops.
- Provide career information and career programs.
- Offer a variety of career paths.
- Provide career-oriented performance feedback.
- Provide mentoring opportunities to support growth and self-direction.
- Provide employees with individual development plans.
- Provide academic learning assistance programs.

Source: Adapted from Fred L. Otte and Peggy G. Hutcheson, *Helping Employees Manage Careers* (Upper Saddle River, NJ: Prentice Hall, 1992), p. 56; www.ge.com.cn/careers/career_management.html; and www_03.ibm.com/employment/us.cd_career_dev.shtml, accessed May 18, 2007.

CAREER MANAGEMENT METHODS

At work, as we've said both the employer and the employee's supervisor play important roles in the employee's career development. We'll look at what exactly employers and managers can do next.

The Employer's Role

As you can see in Table 10-3, employers' career development efforts range from simple to comprehensive. For example, job postings and tuition reimbursement plans are simple ways to support employees' career development needs. At the other extreme, many firms, like Sun Microsystems, have comprehensive formal programs. Sun (now part of Oracle) maintains a career development center staffed by counselors. It helps employees fill development gaps and choose appropriate Sun career opportunities. Sun believes its program helps explain why its average employee tenure of 4 years is more than twice that estimated at other Silicon Valley firms.[14]

Other employer career efforts include career centers and career workshops. *Career centers* may include a Web-based or offline library of career development materials, career workshops, workshops on related topics (such as time management), and individual career coaches for career guidance. (The employer may organize an online career center using tools like those in the chapter appendix.) First USA Bank has what it calls the "Opportunity Knocks" program. Its aim is to help employees crystallize their career goals and achieve them within the company. In addition to career development training and follow-up support, the program includes special career development facilities at work sites that employees

TABLE 10-3 Possible Employer Career Planning and Development Practices

Job postings
Formal education/tuition reimbursement
Performance appraisal for career planning
Counseling by manager
Lateral moves/job rotations
Counseling by HR
Preretirement programs
Succession planning
Formal mentoring
Common career paths
Dual ladder career paths
Career booklets/pamphlets
Written individual career plans
Career workshops
Assessment center
Upward appraisal
Appraisal committees
Training programs for managers
Orientation/induction programs
Special needs (highfliers)
Special needs (dual-career couples)
Diversity management
Expatriation/repatriation

Source: Yehuda Baruch, "Career Development in Organizations and Beyond: Balancing Traditional and Contemporary Viewpoints," *Human Resource Management Review,* 16 (2006), p. 131.

can use on company time. The latter contain materials such as career assessment and planning tools.[15]

Career Planning Workshops A career planning workshop is "a planned learning event in which participants are expected to be actively involved, completing career planning exercises and inventories and participating in career skills practice sessions."[16] A typical workshop includes a self-assessment, an environmental assessment, and goal-setting and action-planning segments. See Figure 10-4 for a typical agenda.

A survey illustrates the popularity of various employer career practices. The researchers studied 524 organizations in the United Kingdom to determine how they used 17 career management practices. "Posting job openings" was the most widespread practice. The other top career practices, in descending order, were formal education; career-oriented performance appraisals; counseling by managers; lateral, developmental moves; counseling by HR; retirement preparation; and succession planning.[17]

Some Innovative Employer Career Initiatives

Employers also use innovative career development initiatives of one sort or another. We'll look at several next.

Lifelong Learning Budgets As we explained in Chapter 8 (Training), several employers including IBM now provide 401(k)–type lifelong learning accounts for their employees. Both employers and employees contribute, and the employees can tap into these to get the career-related education and development they desire.[18]

FIGURE 10-4 Sample Agenda—Two-Day Career Planning Workshop

Source: Fred L. Otte and Peggy Hutcheson, *Helping Employees Manage Careers* (Upper Saddle River, NJ: Prentice Hall), 1992, pp. 22–23.

Before the program—Two weeks prior to the workshop participants receive a letter confirming their participation in the program and package of work to be completed before coming to the workshop. The exercises in this package include skills inventory, values identification, life accomplishments inventory, and a reading describing career direction options.

Day 1

8:30–10:00 Introduction and Overview of Career Planning

Welcome and Introduction to Program
- Welcome by general manager
- Overview of agenda and outcomes
- Participant introductions (statements of expectations for the program)

Overview of Career Development
- Company's philosophy
- Why career planning is needed
- What career planning is and is not
- Career planning model

10:00–Noon Self-Assessment: Part 1

Individual Self-Assessment: Values
- Values card sort exercise
- Reconciling with values pre-work
- Introduce career planning summary work sheet

Individual Self-Assessment: Skills
- Motivated skills exercise
- Examining life accomplishments (synthesize with pre-work)
- Identifying accomplishment themes
- Preferred work skills (from pre-work inventory)
- Fill in career planning summary work sheet

1:00–3:00 Self-Assessment: Part 2

Individual Self-Assessment: Career Anchors
- Career anchoring pattern exercise
- Small group discussions
- Fill in career planning summary work sheet

Individual Self-Assessment: Preferences
- What success means to me
- Skills, knowledge, personal qualities
- Fill in career planning summary work sheet

Individual Self-Assessment: Career Path Pattern
- Synthesize with direction options from pre-work
- Fill in career planning summary work sheet

3:30–4:30 Environmental Assessment

Information About the Company
Goals, growth areas, expectations, turnover, competition for jobs, skills for the future
Fill in career planning summary work sheet
Personal career profile
Reality test, how you see self at this point by sharing

Day 2

8:30–10:00 Goal Setting

Warm-Up Exercise
Review of where we've been and where we're going
Setting goals—where do I want to be?
Creating an ideal future
Future skills and accomplishments
Desired lifestyle
Life and career goals

10:15–1:30 Environmental Assessment: Part 2

Career resources in the company
Introduce support services and hand out information
Marketing yourself—what it takes to achieve your goals here
Describe resource people who will be with the group for lunch and brainstorm questions/issues to be discussed
Lunch with resource people
Review lunch discussions

1:30–4:30 Developing Career Action Plans

Making career decisions
Identifying long-range alternatives
Identifying short-range alternatives
Improving career decisions
Decision styles and ways to enhance them
Creating your career plan
Reconciling your goals with options
Next career steps
Development action plan
Contingency planning
Making it happen — Making commitments to next steps
Summary and adjourn

Role Reversal Have employees temporarily work in different jobs in order to develop a better appreciation of their occupational strengths and weaknesses.

Organize Career Success Teams Here, small groups of employees meet periodically to support one another in achieving their career goals.

Provide Career Coaches For example, Allmerica Financial Corp. hired 20 career development coaches to assist its 850-person information technology staff. The coaches helped individual employees identify their development needs and obtain the training, professional development, and networking opportunities that they need to satisfy those needs.[19]

Career coaches generally help employees create 1- to 5-year plans showing where their careers with the firm may lead. Then, the employer and employee base the latter's development plans on what he or she will need to move up.[20]

Offer Online Programs

For example, WorkforceVision from Criterion, Inc., supplies online systems that help the employer analyze an employee's training needs. Clicking on the employee's name launches his or her work history, competencies, career path, and other information. For each competency (such as leadership and customer focus), a bar chart graphically shows a "gap analysis" highlighting the person's strengths and weaknesses. The firm can then organize developmental activities around the person's needs.[21]

Commitment-Oriented Career Development Efforts

The globalization of the world economy was a boon in many ways. For products and services ranging from cars to computers to air travel, it powered lower prices, better quality, and higher productivity and (in many countries) higher living standards. However the same cost-efficiencies, belt-tightening, and productivity improvements that globalization produced also triggered numerous workforce dislocations. The desire for efficiencies drove firms to "do more with less." And with every bankruptcy, buyout, and merger, more employees found themselves out of work.

This understandably undermines employee commitment. As noted earlier in this chapter, the "psychological contract" changed. Now, many employees ask, "Why should I be loyal to you if you're just going to dump me when you decide to cut costs again?" To paraphrase the author of the book *Pack Your Own Parachute*, employees today thus tend to think of themselves as free agents, there to do a good job but also to prepare for the next likely move, to another firm. In this environment, many employees expect their employers to provide an opportunity for them to broaden their career options. That is why (as we said earlier in this chapter), "The most attractive proposition an employer can make today is that in 5 years the employee will have more knowledge and be more employable than now. . . ."[22]

We've seen there are many things that the employer can do to improve the employee's development and career prospects, from job postings and tuition reimbursement to career planning workshops. The main thing is that the employer's career development efforts, taken as a whole, should send the signal that the employer cares about the employee's career success, and thus deserves the employee's commitment. Of all the opportunities an employer and supervisor have for supporting employees' career development needs, probably none is as important as a career-oriented appraisal.

Career-Oriented Appraisals

In brief, if you use the performance review only to tell the employee how he or she is doing, you'll miss an opportunity to support the employee's career development. Performance appraisals are not just about telling someone how he or she has done. They also provide an opportunity to discuss and link the employee's performance, career interests, and developmental needs into a coherent career plan.

Many employers have formal programs to do this. For example, JCPenney's managerial performance appraisal form contains a listing of all the Penney's jobs by title, function, and level that employees could conceivably want to consider. The company trains its supervisors to link the employee's performance, career interests, and corporate needs, and develop a career plan including development activities for the employee.

On the other hand, even a simple form like the one in Figure 10-5 can suffice. The main thing is to help the manager and employee translate the latter's performance-based experiences for the year into tangible development plans and goals.

While all employees have much in common, a diverse workforce often brings to the workplace some special career development needs. The accompanying "Managing the New Workforce" feature addresses this.

HR Management Checklists

A. Employee's Major Strengths
1. ____
2. ____
3. ____

B. Areas for Improvement/Development
1. ____
2. ____
3. ____

C. Development Plans: Areas for Development
1. ____
2. ____
3. ____
4. ____

Development Strategy: ____

D. Employee's Comments on This Review: ____

E. Reviewer's Comments: ____

Growth potential in present position and future growth potential for increased responsibilities: ____

Employer's Signature: ____ Date: ____
Reviewer's Signature: ____ Date: ____
Reviewer's Manager's Signature: ____ Date: ____

FIGURE 10-5 Sample Performance Review Development Plan

Source: Reprinted from www.HR.BLR.com with permission of the publisher *Business and Legal Resources, Inc.*, 141 Mill Rock Road East, Old Saybrook, CT © 2004. BLR© (Business and Legal Resources, Inc.).

Managing the New Workforce

Different Career Development Needs

Women and men face different challenges as they advance through their careers. Women report greater barriers (such as being excluded from informal networks) than do men, and greater difficulty getting developmental assignments and geographic mobility opportunities. Women have to be more proactive to get such assignments.[23]

In these matters, minority women seem particularly at risk. Over the past few years, the percent of African American, Asian American, and Hispanic women in the U.S. workforce grew by 35%, 78%, and 25%, respectively. Yet women of color hold only a small percentage of professional and managerial private-sector positions.

One survey asked minority women what they saw as the barriers to a successful career. The minority women reported that the main barriers to advancement included not having an influential mentor (47%), lack of informal networking with influential colleagues (40%), lack of company role models for members of the same racial or ethnic group (29%), and a lack of high-visibility assignments (28%).[24]

Unfortunately, many career development programs are not consistent with the needs of minority and nonminority women. For example, many such programs underestimate the role played by family responsibilities in many women's (and men's) lives. Similarly, some programs assume that career paths are continuous; however, the need to stop working for a time to attend to family needs often punctuates the career paths of many people of color and women (and perhaps men).[25] And, in any case, several types of career development programs—fast-track programs, individual career counseling, and career planning workshops—are less available to women than to men.[26] Many refer to this totality of subtle and not-so-subtle barriers to women's' career progress as the *glass ceiling*.

Given all this, the most important thing the employer and manager can do is to take the career needs of women and minority employees seriously. Some specific steps include the following.

Eliminate Institutional Barriers Many practices (such as required late-night meetings) may seem gender neutral but in fact disproportionately affect women and minorities.

Improve Networking and Mentoring To improve female employees' networking opportunities, Marriott International instituted a series of leadership conferences for women. Speakers offered practical tips for career advancement, and shared their experiences. More important, the conferences provided informal opportunities—over lunch, for instance—for the Marriott women to meet and forge business relationships.

Abolish the Glass Ceiling Eliminating glass ceiling barriers requires more than an order from the CEO, because the problem is usually systemic. As one expert puts it, "the roots of gender discrimination are built into a platform of work practices, cultural norms, and images that appear unbiased . . . People don't even notice them, let alone question them." These range from the late-night meetings mentioned earlier to golf course memberships.

Adopt Flexible Career Tracks Inflexible promotional ladders (such as "you must work 8 years of 70-hour weeks to apply for partner) can put women—who often have more responsibility for child-raising chores—at a disadvantage. In many large accounting firms, for instance, "more men successfully logged the dozen or so years normally needed to apply for a position as partner. But fewer women stuck around, so fewer applied for or earned these prized positions."[27] One solution is to institute career tracks (including reduced hours and more flexible year-round work schedules) that enable women to periodically reduce their time at work, but remain on a partner track.

The Manager's Role

It's hard to overestimate the impact that a supervisor can have on his or her employee's career development. With little or no additional effort than realistic performance reviews and candid career advice, a competent supervisor can help the employee get on and stay on the right career track. At the other extreme, an uncaring or unsupportive supervisor may look back on years of having inhibited his or her employees' career development.

Whether or not the employer has a career development program, the individual manager can do several things to support his or her subordinates' career development needs. For example, when the subordinate first begins his or her job, make sure (through orientation and training) that he or she gets off to a good start.

Schedule regular performance appraisals and, at these reviews, focus on the extent to which the employee's current skills and performance are consistent with the person's career goals. Provide the employee with an informal career development plan like that in Figure 10-5. Keep subordinates informed about how they can utilize the firm's current career-related benefits, and encourage them to do so.[28] And, perhaps most importantly, know how to provide mentoring assistance. Let's look at this next.

Building Your Mentoring Skills

Mentoring traditionally means having experienced senior people advising, counseling, and guiding employees' longer-term career development. An employee who agonizes over which career to pursue or how to navigate office politics might need mentoring.

Mentoring may be formal or informal. Informally, mid- and senior-level managers may voluntarily help less-experienced employees—for instance, by giving them career advice and helping them to navigate office politics. Many employers also have formal mentoring programs. For instance, the employer may pair protégés with potential mentors, and provide training to help mentor and protégé better understand their respective responsibilities. Either formal or informal, studies show that having a mentor give career-related guidance and act as a sounding board can significantly enhance one's career satisfaction and success.[29]

Mentoring Caveats

For the supervisor, mentoring is both valuable and dangerous. It can be valuable insofar as it allows you to impact, in a positive way, the careers and lives of your less experienced subordinates and colleagues. The danger lies on the other side of that same coin. *Coaching* focuses on daily tasks that you can easily re-learn, so coaching's downside is usually limited. *Mentoring* focuses on relatively hard-to-reverse longer-term issues, and often touches on the person's psychology (motives, needs, aptitudes, and how one gets along with others, for instance). Because the supervisor is usually not a psychologist or trained career advisor, he or she must be extra cautious in the mentoring advice he or she gives.

The Effective Mentor

Research on what supervisors can do to be better mentors reveals few surprises. Effective mentors *set high standards,* are willing to *invest the time* and effort the mentoring relationship requires, and actively *steer protégés* into important projects, teams, and jobs.[30] Effective mentoring requires *trust,* and the level of trust reflects the mentor's *professional competence, consistency, ability to communicate,* and readiness to *share control.*[31]

On the other hand, the findings on what *employers* can do to make mentoring programs more effective are somewhat counterintuitive.[32] We can summarize the findings as follows:

- **Require mentoring?** It made little difference in the extent or quality of mentoring whether the protégés volunteered to take part, or were assigned formally to mentors.
- **Provide mentoring training?** Keep it to a minimum. The more hours spent on mentor training, the more mentors reported poorer mentoring relationships. "This might be related to resentment about time spent on training or unduly raised expectations."[33]
- **Does distance matter?** No. The long-distance mentoring participants may even have worked harder at their relationship to compensate for the distance.
- **Same or different departments?** Mentoring was more useful when mentors and protégés were in the same department.
- **Big or small difference in rank?** Protégés prefer mentors closer to their own level. This should make first-line supervisors particularly valuable as mentors.

The Protégé's Responsibilities

Effective mentoring is a two-way street. It's important to have effective mentors. But as the one with the most to gain, the protégé is still largely responsible for making the relationship work. Suggestions for protégés include:

- **Choose an appropriate potential mentor.** The mentor should be objective enough to offer good career advice. Many people seek out someone who is one or two levels above their current boss.
- **Don't be surprised if you're turned down.** Not everyone is willing to undertake this time-consuming commitment.
- **Make it easier for a potential mentor to agree to your request.** Do so by making it clear ahead of time what you expect in terms of time and advice.
- **Respect the mentor's time.** Be selective about the work-related issues that you bring to the table. The mentoring relationship generally should not involve personal problems or issues.[34]

Improving Productivity Through HRIS: Career Planning and Development

Realistically, it doesn't make much sense to isolate activities like career planning, succession planning, performance appraisal, and training from each other. For example, the employee's career planning and development needs should reflect the strengths and weaknesses that the performance appraisal brings to light. Similarly, eliminating the weaknesses should involve helping the employee tap into the firm's training and development offerings. At the same time, top management and HR need an integrated, bird's-eye view of their employees' career interests, progress, and appraisal results to expedite the succession planning process.

The bottom line is that more employers are integrating their career planning and development systems with their firms' performance appraisal, succession planning, and training and development information systems. For example, Alyeska, the company that manages the trans-Alaska pipeline, has a user-friendly portal that lets employees "see their full training history, development plans and upcoming deadlines, register for courses, or do career planning—usually without having to ask for help."[35] At the same time, "managers can get a quick picture of the training needs for a particular group, or see all the employees who have a specific qualification."[36]

Various software systems enable employers to integrate appraisal, career development, training, and succession planning. One is Kenexa CareerTracker. CareerTracker "helps organizations optimize workforce productivity by providing an easily accessible platform for ongoing employee performance management, succession planning, and career development."[37]

4 Describe the issues to consider when making promotion decisions.

EMPLOYER LIFE-CYCLE CAREER MANAGEMENT

An employee's tenure with a firm tends to follow a familiar life cycle, from employment interview to first job, promotion, transfer, and perhaps retirement. The employer's career development responsibilities change as the employee moves through this cycle. For example, before hiring, realistic job previews can help candidates gauge whether the job is for them, and particularly whether its demands are a good fit with a candidate's skills and interests. Once on board, one's first job can be crucial for building confidence and a more realistic picture of what the employee can and cannot do. Therefore, providing challenging first jobs and providing an experienced mentor who can help the person learn the ropes are important. Tactics like these can help prevent **reality shock**, a phenomenon that occurs

reality shock
Results of a period that may occur at the initial career entry when the new employee's high job expectations confront the reality of a boring or otherwise unattractive work situation.

when a new employee's expectations and enthusiasm confront the reality of a boring or otherwise unattractive work situation. Next, career-oriented appraisals are important, as are activities such as job rotation, job postings, promotion-from-within policies, development, and career management. We've discussed many of these.

Promotions and transfers are particularly important aspects of most people's careers. **Promotions** traditionally refer to advancements to positions of increased responsibility; **transfers** are reassignments to similar positions in other parts of the firm. We'll look at each.

Making Promotion Decisions

Most people hope for promotions, which usually mean more pay, responsibility, and (often) job satisfaction. For employers, promotions can provide opportunities to reward exceptional performance, and to fill open positions with tested and loyal employees. Yet the promotion process isn't always a positive experience. Unfairness, arbitrariness, or secrecy can diminish the effectiveness of the process. Several decisions, therefore, loom large in any firm's promotion process.

Decision 1: Is Seniority or Competence the Rule?

Probably the most important decision is whether to base promotion on seniority or competence, or some combination of the two.

Today's focus on competitiveness favors competence. However, a company's ability to use competence as the criterion depends on several things. Union agreements sometimes contain clauses that emphasize seniority, such as, "In the advancement of employees, employees with the highest seniority will be given preference, where skills and performance are approximately equal." And civil service regulations that stress seniority rather than competence often govern promotions in many public-sector organizations.

Decision 2: How Should We Measure Competence?

If the firm opts for competence, how should it define and measure competence? The question highlights an important managerial adage called the "Peter Principle," after its founder. In brief, the Peter Principle says that companies often promote competent employees up to their "level of incompetence," where they then sit, sometimes underperforming for years. The point is that defining and measuring *past* performance is relatively straightforward: Define the job, set standards, and use one or more appraisal tools to record performance. But promotions should require something more. You also need a valid procedure for predicting the candidate's future performance.

For better or worse, most employers use prior performance as a guide, and assume that (based on exemplary prior performance) the person will do well on the new job. This is the simplest procedure. Many others use tests or assessment centers to evaluate promotable employees and to identify those with executive potential.

Given the public safety issues involved, police departments and the military tend to take a relatively systematic approach when evaluating candidates for promotion to command positions. For the police, traditional promotional reviews include a written knowledge test, an assessment center, credit for seniority, and a score based on recent performance appraisal ratings. Others include a personnel records review. This includes evaluation of job-related influences such as supervisory-related education and experience, ratings from multiple sources, and systematic evaluation of behavioral evidence.[38]

Decision 3: Is the Process Formal or Informal?

Many firms have informal promotion processes. They may or may not post open positions, and key managers may use their own "unpublished" criteria to make decisions. Here employees may (reasonably) conclude that factors like "who you know" are more important than performance, and that working hard to get ahead—at least in this firm—is futile.

Other employers set formal, published promotion policies and procedures. Employees receive a *formal promotion policy* describing the criteria by which the firm awards promotions. A *job posting policy* states the firm will post open positions and their requirements, and circulate these to all employees. As explained in Chapter 5, many employers also maintain *employee qualification databanks* and use replacement charts and computerized employee information systems.

Decision 4: Vertical, Horizontal, or Other? Promotions aren't necessarily straightforward. For example, how do you motivate employees with the prospect of promotion when your firm is downsizing? And how do you provide promotional opportunities for those, like engineers, who may have little or no interest in managerial roles?

Several options are available. Some firms, such as the exploration division of British Petroleum (BP), create two parallel career paths, one for managers and another for "individual contributors" such as high-performing engineers. At BP, individual contributors can move up to nonsupervisory but senior positions, such as "senior engineer." These jobs have most of the financial rewards attached to management-track positions at that level.

Another option is to move the person horizontally. For instance, move a production employee to human resources, to develop his or her skills and to test and challenge his or her aptitudes. And, in a sense, "promotions" are possible even when leaving the person in the same job. For example, you can usually enrich the job and provide training to enhance the opportunity for assuming more responsibility.

Sources of Bias in Promotion Decisions

Women and people of color still experience relatively less career progress in organizations, and bias and more subtle barriers are often the cause. Yet (as we noted earlier in this chapter) this is not necessarily the result of decision makers' racist sentiments. Instead, secondary factors—such as having few people of color employed in the hiring department—may be the cause. In any case, the bottom line seems to be that whether it's bias or some other reason, questionable barriers like these still exist. Employers and supervisors need to identify and abolish them.

Similarly, women still don't make it to the top of the career ladder in numbers proportionate to their numbers in U.S. industry. Women constitute more than 40% of the workforce, but hold less than 2% of top management positions. Blatant or subtle discrimination accounts for much of this. Some hiring managers erroneously believe that "women belong at home and are not committed to careers." The "old-boy network" of informal (mostly male) friendships forged over lunch, at social events, or at club meetings is still a problem. A lack of female mentors makes it harder for women to find the role models and supporters they need to help guide their careers. More women than men must also make the "career versus family" decision, since the responsibilities of raising children still fall disproportionately on women. As mentioned earlier, special networking and mentoring opportunities can reduce some of these problems, as can more flexible employment policies. For example, when the accounting firm Deloitte & Touche noticed it was losing good female auditors, it instituted a new flexible/reduced work schedule. This enabled many working mothers who might otherwise have left to stay with the firm.[39]

promotions
Advancements to positions of increased responsibility.

transfers
Reassignments to similar positions in other parts of the firm.

Source: Courtesy of David Young-Wolff/ PhotoEdit Inc.

Employers are transferring employees less often, partly because of family resistance.

Promotions and the Law

In general, the employer's promotion processes must comply with all the same antidiscrimination laws as do procedures for recruiting and selecting employees or any other HR actions. But beyond that general caveat, there are several specific things to keep in mind regarding promotion decisions.

One concerns *retaliation*. Most federal and state employment laws contain anti-retaliation provisions. For example, one U.S. Circuit Court of Appeals allowed a claim of retaliation to proceed when a female employee provided evidence that her employer turned her down for promotion because a supervisor she had previously accused of sexual harassment made comments that persuaded her current supervisor not to promote her.[40] The evidence confirmed that, in a meeting at which supervisors reviewed the person's performance, the former supervisor (and object of the sexual harassment accusation) made comments regarding the employee's "ability to work effectively with others."

A second concerns using inconsistent, unsystematic processes to decide who to promote. For example, one employer turned down the 61-year-old applicant for a promotion because of his interview performance; the person who interviewed him said he did not "get a real feeling of confidence" from the candidate.[41] In this case, "the court made it clear that while subjective reasons can justify adverse employment decisions, an employer must articulate any clear and reasonably specific factual bases upon which it based its decision." In other words, you should be able to provide objective evidence supporting your subjective assessment for promotion.

Managing Transfers

A *transfer* is a move from one job to another, usually with no change in salary or grade. Employers may transfer a worker to vacate a position where he or she is no longer needed, to fill one where he or she is needed, or more generally to find a better fit for the employee within the firm. Many firms today boost productivity by consolidating positions. Transfers are a way to give displaced employees a chance for another assignment or, perhaps, some personal growth. Employees seek transfers for many reasons, including personal enrichment, more interesting jobs, greater convenience—better hours, location of work, and so on—or to jobs offering greater advancement possibilities.

Many firms have had policies of routinely transferring employees from locale to locale, either to expose them to a wider range of jobs or to fill open positions with trained employees. Such easy-transfer policies have fallen into some disfavor. This is partly because of the high cost of relocating employees (moving expenses and buying the employee's current home, for instance), and partly because firms assume that frequent transfers adversely affect transferees' family lives.

5 List and briefly explain at least four methods for better managing retirements.

Managing Retirements

For many employees, years of appraisals and career planning end with retirement.

Retirement planning is a significant long-term issue for employers. In the United States, the number of 25- to 34-year-olds is growing relatively slowly, and the number of 35- to 44-year olds is declining. So, with many employees in their 50s and 60s moving toward traditional retirement age, employers face a longer-term labor shortage: ". . . companies have been so focused on downsizing to contain costs that they largely neglected a looming threat to their competitiveness . . . a severe shortage of talented workers."[42]

Many have wisely chosen to fill their staffing gaps in part with current or soon-to-be retirees. Fortuitously, 78% of employees in one survey said they expect to continue working in some capacity after normal retirement age (64% said they want to do so part-time). Only about a third said they plan to continue work for financial reasons; about 43% said they just wanted to remain active.[43]

The bottom line is that "retirement planning" is no longer just for helping current employees slip into retirement.[44] It can also enable the employer to retain, in some capacity, the skills and brain power of those who would normally retire and leave the firm. A reasonable first step is to conduct numerical analyses of pending retirements. This should include a demographic analysis (including a census of the company's employees), a determination of the average retirement age for the company's employees, and a review of how retirement is going to affect the employer's health care and pension benefits. The employer can then determine the extent of the "retirement problem," and take fact-based steps to address it.[45]

Methods Employers seeking to recruit and/or retain retirees need to take several steps. The general idea is to institute human resource policies that encourage and support older workers. Not surprisingly, studies show that employees who are more committed and loyal to the employer are more likely to stay beyond their normal retirement age.[46] Beyond that, specific suggestions include:

- **Create a culture that honors experience.** For example, the CVS pharmacy chain knows that traditional recruiting media such as help-wanted signs might not attract older workers; CVS thus works through The National Council on Aging, city agencies, and community organizations to find new employees. They also made it clear to retirees that they welcome older workers: "I'm too young to retire. [CVS] is willing to hire older people. They don't look at your age but your experience," said one dedicated older worker.[47]
- **Modify selection procedures.** For example, one British bank stopped using psychometric tests, replacing them with role-playing exercises to gauge how candidates deal with customers.
- **Offer flexible or part-time work.** Companies "need to design jobs such that staying on is more attractive than leaving." One of the simplest ways to do this is through flexible work, specifically, making both where one works (as with telecommuting) and when the work is performed flexible.[48]
- **Phased retirement.** Many employers are implementing phased retirement programs. These combine reduced work hours, job changes, reduced responsibilities, and sometimes transitioning to independent contractor status.

Preretirement Counseling Aside from special programs (such as phased retirement), most companies offer some preretirement counseling. The aim is to help prospective retirees better prepare for their retirements. Counseling typically covers matters such as benefits advice, second careers, and so on, such as:

Explanation of Social Security benefits (reported by 97% of those with preretirement education programs)

Leisure time counseling (86%)

Financial and investment counseling (84%)

Health counseling (82%)

Psychological counseling (35%)

Counseling for second careers outside the company (31%)

Counseling for second careers inside the company (4%)

Financial and investment counseling deserves special mention. The accompanying "Managing HR in Challenging Times" feature addresses this.

Managing HR in Challenging Times

More retirees today rely on their own savings and investments, rather than their employer's pension. Because employees invest much of these funds in market-sensitive equities, employees—even those several years away from retirement—should be monitoring and managing their retirement accounts. This is particularly so in economically challenging times, when the traditional "buy and hold" strategy seems at least temporarily to have worked to many peoples' disadvantage. Employers can play an important role in two ways. They can make available to their employees investment education and advice from third-party advisors. And they can make it easier for employees to monitor and manage their invested funds. For example, American Express introduced an online asset allocation tool for use by its employer–clients' retirement plan participants. The Web-based tool "Retirement Guidance Planner" lets an employer's retirement plan participants calculate and keep track of progress toward retirement income goals and more easily allocate assets among different investments online.[49] Many firms, including Vanguard and Fidelity, offer similar online programs.

6 Define talent management and give an example of an actual talent management system.

TALENT MANAGEMENT

In an ideal world, an employer would be able to integrate the entire process of hiring, training, appraising, and developing and rewarding employees to maximize each employee's contribution while minimizing the total costs of that process. New integrated computerized systems enable employers to move closer to accomplishing that.

What Is Talent Management?

Talent management is the automated end-to-end process of planning, recruiting, developing, managing, and compensating employees throughout the organization.[50]

Because talent management involves recruiting, hiring, and developing high potential employees, it requires coordinating several human resource activities, in particular workforce acquisition, assessment, development, and retention.[51] In simplest terms, talent management simply "refers to the process of attracting, selecting, training, developing, and promoting employees through an organization."[52] But again, the main thing driving the talent management movement is the availability of new talent management information systems; these integrate talent management–related system components like succession planning, recruitment, learning, and employee pay, enabling seamless updating of data among them. Figure 10-6 summarizes this idea.

FIGURE 10-6 The Talent Management Process

Talent management is, in a sense, career management from the employer's point of view. The employee wants to align his or her skills, training, performance feedback, and development in such a way as to have a successful career. The employer, for its part, wants to integrate the same functions to ensure that it is using its corporate talent in the best possible way. One survey of CEOs of large companies said they typically spent between 20% and 40% of their time on talent management.[53] Another survey of human resource executives found that for about 62% of respondents, "talent management" issues were the most pressing ones they faced.[54]

Talent Management Systems

While employers have long "managed their talent" without computerized systems, talent management today is usually information technology–based. Several software providers offer specialized talent management suites. The suites include and integrate underlying talent management components such as e-recruiting, e-training, performance reviews, and rewards. Some examples follow.

- Talent Management Solutions' (www.talentmanagement101.com) talent management suite includes e-recruiting software, employee performance management, a learning management system, and compensation management. Among other things, Talent Management Solutions' suite of programs "relieves the stress of writing employee performance reviews by automating the task" and ensures "that all levels of the organization are aligned—all working for the same goals."[55]
- SilkRoad Technology's talent management solution includes applicant tracking, onboarding, performance management, compensation, and employee Internet.[56]
- Info HCM Talent Management "includes several upgrades including tracking and monitoring performance metrics, interactive online training via WebEx, support for e-commerce integration to enable training . . . and full localization for additional countries including Spanish, French, and Chinese."[57]
- Workstream's new talent management suite includes "industry leading compensation, performance, development, competencies, knowledge management and rewards applications."[58]

REVIEW

CHAPTER SECTION SUMMARIES

1. Getting employees to do better requires **improving your coaching skills**. Ideally, the coaching process involves preparation (in terms of analyzing the issues), developing an improvement plan, active coaching, and follow-up.
2. Employees ultimately need to take responsibility for their own careers, but employers and managers also need to understand what **career management methods** are available. These include establishing company-based career centers, offering career planning workshops, providing employee development budgets, and offering online career development workshops and programs. Perhaps the simplest and most direct is to make the appraisal itself career-oriented, in so far as the appraisal feedback is a link to the employee's aspirations and plans. Supervisors can play a major role in their employee's career development. For example, make sure the employee gets the training he or she requires, and make sure appraisals are discussed in the context of the employee's career aspirations. Effective mentors set high standards, invest the time, steer protégés into important projects, and exhibit professional competence and consistency.

talent management
The automated end-to-end process of planning, recruiting, developing, managing, and compensating employees throughout the organization.

3. An employee's tenure with the firm tends to follow a familiar **career management life cycle,** from first job to promotion, transfer, and perhaps retirement. Questions on promotion decisions include the following: Is seniority or competence the rule, how should we measure competence, is the process formal or informal, and will the "promotion" be vertical, horizontal, or some other? Because women and people of color still experience relatively less career progress, employers and supervisors need to identify and abolish sources of bias. Managing retirements is an increasingly important issue with so many baby boom–era employees now preparing to retire. Because there may not be enough younger employees to replace those retiring, many employers are encouraging retirees to remain with the firm in some capacity. Attracting and keeping retirees means taking steps like creating a culture that honors experience, modifying selection procedures, and offering flexible part-time work.
4. **Talent management** is the automated process of planning, recruiting, developing, managing, and compensating employees throughout the organization. The main thing driving the talent management movement is the availability of new talent management information systems. These integrate succession planning, recruitment, learning, and employee pay, enabling the employer to maintain a more integrated system and set of decisions. For example, SilkRoad Technologies' talent management system includes applicant tracking, onboarding, performance management, compensation, and employee Internet.

DISCUSSION QUESTIONS

1. What is the employee's role in the career development process? The manager's role? The employer's role?
2. Describe the specific corporate career development initiatives that an employer can take.
3. What are four specific steps employees can take to support diverse employees' career progress?
4. Give several examples of career development activities that employers can use to foster employee commitment.

INDIVIDUAL AND GROUP ACTIVITIES

1. Write a 1-page essay titled, "Where I Would Like to Be Career-Wise 10 Years from Today."
2. Explain the career-related factors to keep in mind when making the employee's first assignments.
3. In groups of four or five students, meet with several administrators and faculty members in your college or university and, based on this, write a 2-page paper on the topic "the faculty promotion process at our college." What do you think of the process? Could you make any suggestions for improving it?
4. In groups of four or five students, at your place of work or at your college, interview the HR manager with the aim of writing a 2-page paper addressing the topic "steps we are taking in this organization to enhance diversity through career management."
5. Develop a résumé for yourself, using the guidelines presented in this chapter's appendix.
6. Working individually or in groups, choose three occupations (such as management consultant, HR manager, or salesperson) and use some of the sources described in the appendix to this chapter to make an assessment of the future demand for this occupation in the next 10 years or so. Does this seem like a good occupation to pursue? Why or why not?
7. The HRCI "Test Specifications" appendix at the end of this book (pages 699–706) lists the knowledge someone studying for the HRCI certification exam needs to have in each area of human resource management (such as in Strategic Management, Workforce Planning, and Human Resource Development). In groups of four to five students, do four things: (1) Review that appendix now. (2) Identify the material in this chapter that relates to the required knowledge the appendix lists. (3) Write four multiple-choice exam questions on this material that you believe would be suitable for inclusion in the HRCI exam. And (4) if time permits, have someone from your team post your team's questions in front of the class, so the students in other teams can take each others' exam questions
8. A survey of recent college graduates in the United Kingdom found that although many hadn't found their first jobs, most were already planning "career breaks" and to keep up their hobbies and interests outside work. As one report of the findings put it, "the next generation of workers is determined not to wind up on the hamster wheel of long hours with no play."[59] Part of the problem seems to be that many already see their friends "putting in more than 48 hours a week" at work. Career experts reviewing the results concluded that many of these recent college grads "are not looking for high-pay, high-profile jobs anymore."[60] Instead, they seem to be looking to "compartmentalize" their lives; to keep the number of hours they spend at work down, so they can maintain their hobbies and outside interests. So, do you think these findings are as popular in the United States as they appear to be in the United Kingdom? If so, if you were mentoring one of these people at work, what three specific bits of career advice would you give him or her?

EXPERIENTIAL EXERCISE

Where Am I Going . . . and Why?

Purpose: The purpose of this exercise is to provide you with experience in analyzing your career preferences.

Required Understanding: Students should be thoroughly familiar with the "Managing Your Career and Finding a Job" appendix to this chapter.

How to Set Up the Exercise/Instructions: Using at least three of the methods described in this chapter's appendix (identify your occupational orientation, identify your career directions, and so forth), analyze your career-related inclinations (you can take the self-directed search for about $10 www.self-directed-search.com). Based on this analysis, answer the following questions (you may, if you wish, do this analysis in teams of three or four students).

1. What does your research suggest to you about what would be your preferable occupational options?
2. Based on research sources like those we listed in the appendix to this chapter, what are the prospects for these occupations?
3. Given these prospects and your own occupational inclinations, outline a brief, 1-page career plan for yourself, including current occupational inclinations, career goals, and an action plan listing four or five development steps you will need to take in order to get from where you are now career-wise to where you want to be, based on your career goals.

APPLICATION CASE

The Mentor Relationship Turns Upside Down

"I wish I could talk this problem over with Walter," Carol Lee thought. Walter Lemaire had been her mentor for several years at Larchmont Consulting, yet now he was her problem.

Carol thought back to the beginning of her association with Larchmont and with Walter. She had joined the firm as a writer and editor; her job during those early years had been to revise and polish the consultants' business reports. The work brought her into frequent contact with Walter, who was a senior vice president at the time. Carol enjoyed discussing the consultants' work with him, and when she decided to try to join the consulting team, she asked for his help. Walter became her mentor as well as her boss and guided her through her successful transition to consultant and eventually partner.

At each promotion to various supervisory jobs along the way to partner, Carol cemented her relationship with her new subordinates by meeting with each person individually to forge a new working relationship. Her career prospered, and when Walter moved on to run a start-up software publishing venture for Larchmont, Carol was promoted to take his place. However, his new venture faltered, and the partners decided someone else would have to step in. Despite the fact that Carol was much younger than Walter and once had worked for him, she was given the assignment of rescuing the start-up operation.

Carol's discomfort over the assignment only grew as she began to review the history of the new venture. Her rescue mission was going to entail undoing much of what Walter had done, reversing his decisions about everything from product design to marketing and pricing. Carol was so reluctant to second-guess her old mentor and boss that she found herself unable to discuss any of her proposed solutions with him directly. She doubted that any of her experience had prepared her to assume the role of Walter's boss, and in these difficult circumstances her need to turn the operation around would be, she felt, like "pouring salt on his wounds."

Questions

1. What is Carol's role in Walter's career development now? Should Larchmont have any such role? Why or why not?
2. What advice would you offer Carol for approaching Walter?
3. If Carol has to dismiss Walter, how specifically would you suggest she proceed?
4. Assume Carol has heard a rumor that Walter has considered resigning. What should she do about it?

Note: The incident in this case is based on an event at an unidentified firm described in Jennifer Frey, "Pride and Your Promotion," *Working Woman*, October 1996.

CONTINUING CASE

Carter Cleaning Company

The Career Planning Program

Career planning has always been a pretty low-priority item for Carter Cleaning, since "just getting workers to come to work and then keeping them honest is enough of a problem," as Jack likes to say. Yet Jennifer thought it might not be a bad idea to give some thought to what a career planning program might involve for Carter. Many of their employees had been with them for years in dead-end jobs, and she frankly felt a little badly for them: "Perhaps we could help them gain a better perspective on what they want to do," she thought. And she definitely believed that the store management group needed better career direction if Carter Cleaning was to develop and grow.

Questions

1. What would be the advantages to Carter Cleaning of setting up a career planning program?
2. Who should participate in the program? All employees? Selected employees?
3. Outline and describe the career development program you would propose for the cleaners, pressers, counterpeople, and managers at the Carter Cleaning Centers.

TRANSLATING STRATEGY INTO HR POLICIES & PRACTICES CASE

The Hotel Paris CASE

The New Career Management System

The Hotel Paris's competitive strategy is "To use superior guest service to differentiate the Hotel Paris properties, and to thereby increase the length of stay and return rate of guests, and thus boost revenues and profitability." HR manager Lisa Cruz must now formulate functional policies and activities that support this competitive strategy, by eliciting the required employee behaviors and competencies.

Lisa Cruz knew that as a hospitality business, the Hotel Paris was uniquely dependent upon having committed, high-morale employees. In a factory or small retail shop, the employer might be able to rely on direct supervision to make sure that the employees were doing their jobs. But in a hotel, just about every employee is "on the front line." There is usually no one there to supervise the limousine driver when he or she picks up a guest at the airport, or when the valet takes the guest's car, or the front-desk clerk signs the guest in, or the housekeeping clerk needs to handle a guest's special request. If the hotel wanted satisfied guests, they had to have committed employees who did their jobs as if they owned the company, even when the supervisor was nowhere in sight. But for the employees to be committed, Lisa knew the Hotel Paris had to make it clear that the company was also committed to its employees.

From her experience, she knew that one way to do this was to help her employees have successful and satisfying careers, and she was therefore concerned to find that the Hotel Paris had no career management process at all. Supervisors weren't trained to discuss employees' developmental needs or promotional options during the performance appraisal interviews. Promotional processes were informal. And the firm did not attempt to provide any career development services that might help its employees to develop a better understanding of what their career options were, or should be. Lisa was sure that committed employees were the key to improving the experiences of its guests, and that she couldn't boost employee commitment without doing a better job of attending to her employees' career needs.

For Lisa and the CFO, their preliminary research left little doubt about the advisability of instituting a new career management system at the Hotel Paris. The CFO therefore gave the go-ahead to design and institute a new Hotel Paris career management program. Lisa and her team knew that they already had some of the building blocks in place, thanks to the new performance management system they had instituted just a few weeks earlier (as noted in the previous chapter). For example, the new performance management system required that the supervisor appraise the employee based on goals and competencies that were driven by the company's strategic needs; and the appraisal itself produced new goals for the coming year and specific development plans for the employee.

Questions

1. "Many hotel jobs are inherently 'dead end'; maids, laundry workers, and valets, for instance, either have no great aspirations to move up, or are just using these jobs temporarily, for instance to help out with household expenses." First, do you agree with this statement—why, or why not? Second, list three specific career activities you would recommend Lisa implement for these employees.
2. Build on the company's current performance management system by recommending two other specific career development activities the hotel should implement.
3. What specific career development activities would you recommend in light of the fact that the Paris's hotels and employees are disbursed around the world?

KEY TERMS

Appendix for Chapter 10

Managing Your Career and Finding a Job

With the dislocations occurring throughout our economy, managing your career has never been as important as it is today.[61] The individual must be responsible for creating and managing his or her own career. And, in today's job marketplace, knowing how to find or get a job is crucial.

Identify Your Career Stage

Each person's career goes through stages, and the stage you are in will influence your knowledge of and preference for various occupations. The main stages of this **career cycle** follow.[62]

Growth Stage

The **growth stage** lasts roughly from birth to age 14 and is a period during which the person develops a self-concept by identifying with and interacting with other people such as family, friends, and teachers. Toward the beginning of this period, role playing is important, and children experiment with different ways of acting; this helps them to form impressions of how other people react to different behaviors and contributes to their developing a unique self-concept or identity. Toward the end of this stage, the adolescent (who by this time has developed preliminary ideas about what his or her interests and abilities are) begins to think realistically about alternative occupations.

Exploration Stage

The **exploration stage** is the period (roughly from ages 15 to 24) during which a person seriously explores various occupational alternatives. The person attempts to match these alternatives with what he or she has learned about them and about his or her own interests and abilities from school, leisure activities, and work. Tentative broad occupational choices are made during the beginning of this period. Then toward the end of this period, a seemingly appropriate choice is made and the person tries out for a beginning job.

Probably the most important task the person has in this and the preceding stage is that of developing a realistic understanding of his or her abilities and talents. Similarly, the person must make sound educational decisions based on reliable sources of information about occupational alternatives.

Establishment Stage

The **establishment stage** spans roughly ages 24 to 44 and is the heart of most people's work lives. During this period, a suitable occupation is found (hopefully) and the person engages in those activities that help him or her earn a permanent place in it. Often, and particularly in the professions, the person locks onto a chosen occupation early. But in most cases, this is a period of testing. The person is continually testing his or her capabilities and ambitions against those of the initial occupational choice.

The establishment stage is itself comprised of three substages. The **trial substage** lasts from about ages 25 to 30. During this period, the person determines whether or not the chosen field is suitable; if it is not, several changes might be attempted. (Jane Smith might have her heart set on a career in retailing, for example, but after several months of constant travel as a newly hired assistant buyer for a department

career cycle
The various stages a person's career goes through.

growth stage
The period from birth to age 14 during which a person develops a self-concept by identifying with and interacting with other people.

exploration stage
The period (roughly from ages 15 to 24) during which a person seriously explores various occupational alternatives.

establishment stage
Spans roughly ages 24 to 44 and is the heart of most people's work lives.

trial substage
Period that lasts from about ages 25 to 30 during which the person determines whether or not the chosen field is suitable; if not, changes may be attempted.

store, she might decide that a less travel-oriented career such as one in market research is more in tune with her needs.) Roughly, between the ages of 30 and 40, the person goes through a **stabilization substage**. Here firm occupational goals are set and the person does more explicit career planning to determine the sequence of promotions, job changes, and/or any educational activities that seem necessary for accomplishing these goals.

Finally, somewhere between the mid-30s and mid-40s, the person may enter the **midcareer crisis substage**. During this period, people often make a major reassessment of their progress relative to original ambitions and goals. They may find that they are not going to realize their dreams (such as being company president) or that having been accomplished, their dreams are not all they were purported to be. Also during this period, people have to decide how important work and career are to be in their lives. It is often during this midcareer substage that some people face, for the first time, the difficult choices between what they really want, what really can be accomplished, and how much must be sacrificed to achieve it.

Maintenance Stage

Between the ages of 45 and 65, many people simply slide from the stabilization substage into the **maintenance stage**. During this latter period, the person has typically created a place in the world of work and most efforts are directed now at maintaining that place.

Decline Stage

As retirement age approaches, there is often a deceleration period in the **decline stage**. Here many people face the prospect of having to accept reduced levels of power and responsibility and learn to accept and develop new roles as mentor and confidante for those who are younger. There is then probably retirement, after which the person hopefully finds alternative uses for the time and effort formerly expended on his or her occupation.

Evidence-Based HR: Making Career Choices

It is unfortunate but true that many people don't put much thought into their careers. Some choose majors based on class scheduling preferences, favorite professors, or unstated psychological motives. Others stumble into jobs because "that's all that was available." If there was ever anything that cried out for evidence-based decisions, it is choosing your career. The first and essential step here is to learn as much as possible about your interests, aptitudes, and skills.

Identify Your Occupational Orientation

Career-counseling expert John Holland says that personality (including values, motives, and needs) is one career choice determinant. For example, a person with a strong social orientation might be attracted to careers that entail interpersonal rather than intellectual or physical activities and to occupations such as social work. Based on research with his Vocational Preference Test (VPT), Holland found six basic personality types or orientations (see www.self-directed-search.com.)[63]

1. **Realistic orientation.** These people are attracted to occupations that involve physical activities requiring skill, strength, and coordination. Examples include forestry, farming, and agriculture.

2. **Investigative orientation.** Investigative people are attracted to careers that involve cognitive activities (thinking, organizing, understanding) rather than affective activities (feeling, acting, or interpersonal and emotional tasks). Examples include biologist, chemist, and college professor.

3. **Social orientation.** These people are attracted to careers that involve interpersonal rather than intellectual or physical activities. Examples include clinical psychology, foreign service, and social work.

4. **Conventional orientation.** A conventional orientation favors careers that involve structured, rule-regulated activities, as well as careers in which it is expected that the employee subordinate his or her personal needs to those of the organization. Examples include accountants and bankers.

FIGURE 10A-1 Choosing an Occupational Orientation

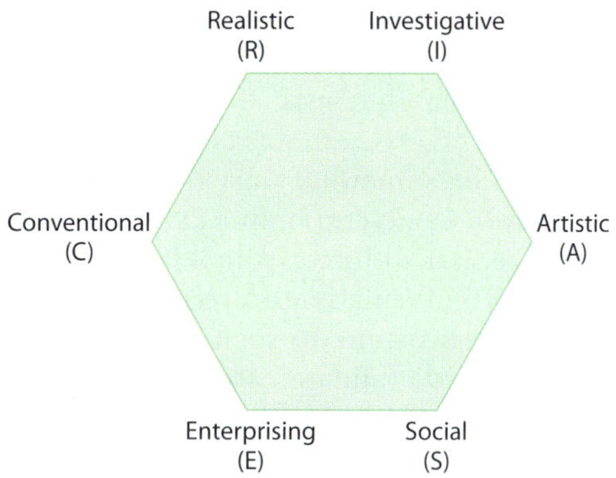

5. **Enterprising orientation.** Verbal activities aimed at influencing others characterize enterprising personalities. Examples include managers, lawyers, and public relations executives.

6. **Artistic orientation.** People here are attracted to careers that involve self-expression, artistic creation, expression of emotions, and individualistic activities. Examples include artists, advertising executives, and musicians.

Most people have more than one occupational orientation (they might be social, realistic, and investigative, for example), and Holland believes that the more similar or compatible these orientations are, the less internal conflict or indecision a person will face in making a career choice. To help illustrate this, Holland suggests placing each orientation in one corner of a hexagon, as in Figure 10A-1. As you can see, the model has six corners, each of which represents one personal orientation (for example, enterprising). According to Holland's research, the closer two orientations are in this figure, the more compatible they are. If your number-one and number-two orientations fall side by side, you will have an easier time choosing a career. However, if your strong orientations turn out to be opposite (such as realistic and social), you may experience more indecision in making a career choice because your interests are driving you toward different types of careers. In Table 10A-1, we

TABLE 10A-1 Example of Some Occupations That May Typify Each Occupational Theme

Realistic	Investigative	Artistic	Social	Enterprising	Conventional
				A wide range of managerial occupations, including:	
Engineers	Physicians	Advertising executives	Auto Sales dealers	Military officers	Accountants
Carpenters	Psychologists	Public relations executives	School administrators	Chamber of commerce executives	Bankers
	Research and development managers			Investment managers	Credit managers
				Lawyers	

stabilization substage
Firm occupational goals are set and the person does more explicit career planning.

midcareer crisis substage
Period during which people often make major reassessments of their progress relative to original ambitions and goals.

maintenance stage
Period between ages 45 and 65 when many people slide from the stabilization substage into an established position and focus on maintaining that place.

decline stage
Period where many people face having to accept reduced levels of power and responsibility, and must learn to develop new roles as mentors or confidantes for younger people.

have summarized some of the occupations found to be the best match for each of these six orientations. You can, for about $10.00, take Holland's SDS online (see www.self-directed-search.com).

The SDS (Self-Directed Search) has an excellent reputation, but the career seeker needs to be somewhat wary of some of the other online career assessment sites. One study of 24 no-cost online career assessment Web sites concluded that they were easy to use, but suffered from a lack of validation, limited confidentiality controls, and limited information on test interpretation. However, a number of online career assessment instruments such as the Career Key (www.careerkey.org/English) do reportedly provide validated and useful information.[64]

Identify Your Career Directions MBA students at the Harvard Business School sometimes take a quiz to help them identify career directions and make career choices in which they'll be happy.[65] To take a short-form version of this quiz, you'll need three types of information. First (see Figure 10A-2), this approach assumes that all executive work is based on one or more of eight core activities such as "quantitative analysis" and "managing people." Begin by reading each of those activities.

Next (see Figure 10A-3), quickly go through each of the second figure's pairs of statements and indicate which one is more interesting to you. Then add the letters for your total score on each core function and record that score in the second figure.

Then, use Figure 10A-4 to see what kind of successful businesspeople share your career direction's interests. For example, if you scored high in Figure 10A-3 on "Enterprise Control" and "Managing People," then CEOs, presidents, division managers, and general managers are the sorts of people whose career interests are most similar to yours.

Identify Your Skills Successful performance also depends on ability. You may have a conventional orientation, but whether you have *the skills* to be an accountant, banker, or credit manager will largely determine which occupation you ultimately choose. Therefore, you have to identify your skills.

Business Career Interest Inventory (BC II)

Part 1: *All executive work is based on one or more of the following eight core activities. Read them.*

Application of Technology: Taking an engineering-like approach to business problems and using technology to solve them (operations process analysis, process redesign, production planning).

Quantitative Anaysis: Problem-solving that relies on mathmatical and financial analysis (determining the most advantageous debt/equity structure, analyzing market research).

Theory Development and Conceptual Thinking: Taking a broadly conceptual, quasi-academic approach to business problems (developing a new general economic theory or model of market behavior).

Creative Production: Highly creative activities (the generation of new business ideas such as line extensions or additional markets, the development of new marketing concepts).

Counseling and Mentoring: Developing a variety of personal relationships in the workplace and helping others in their careers (human-resources coaching, training, and mentoring).

Managing People: Accomplishing business goals through working directly with people (particularly as a front-line manager, team leader, director, or direct supervisor).

Enterprise Control: Having ultimate stategy and decision-making authority as well as resource control for an operation (as a division manager, president, CEO, partner in a professional firm, or entrepreneur).

Influence Through Language and Ideas: Exercising influence through the skillful use of persuasion (negotiating, deal-making, sales functions, and relationship development).

FIGURE 10A-2 Finding the Job You *Should* Want (Part 1)

Source: James Waldroop and Timothy Butler, "Finding the Job You *Should* Want," *Fortune*, March 2, 1998, p. 211.

Part 2: *Reread the brief description of the eight sets of activities on the previous page, then quickly go through each of the following pairs and indicate which one is more interesting to you by placing the bold letter for that choice in the box to the left. Don't leave any out and don't record any ties. Mark your first intuitive response.*

☐ 1. Creative **P**roduction or **I**nfluence Through Language and Ideas

☐ 2. **M**anaging People or Creative **P**roductions

☐ 3. **E**nterprise Control or **A**pplication of Technology

☐ 4. **T**heory Development or Creative **P**roduction

☐ 5. **M**anaging People or **C**ounseling and Mentoring

☐ 6. **Q**uantitative Analysis or **T**heory Development

☐ 7. **I**nfluence Through Language and Ideas or **E**nterprise Control

☐ 8. **Q**uantitative Analysis or **E**nterprise Control

☐ 9. **A**pplication of Technology or **I**nfluence Through Language and Ideas

☐ 10. **I**nfluence Through Language and Ideas or **Q**uantitative Analysis

☐ 11. **T**heory Development or **C**ounseling and Mentoring

☐ 12. **A**pplication of Technology or Creative **P**roduction

☐ 13. **A**pplication of Technology or **M**anaging People

☐ 14. **T**heory Development or **I**nfluence Through Language and Ideas

☐ 15. Creative **P**roduction or **C**ounseling and Mentoring

☐ 16. **C**ounseling and Mentoring or **Q**uantitative Analysis

☐ 17. **T**heory Development or **E**nterprise Control

☐ 18. **E**nterprise Control or Creative **P**roduction

☐ 19. **M**anaging People or **T**heory Development

☐ 20. **A**pplication of Technology or **T**heory Development

☐ 21. **E**nterprise Control or **C**ounseling and Mentoring

☐ 22. Creative **P**roduction or **Q**uantitative Analysis

☐ 23. **C**ounseling and Mentoring or **I**nfluence Through Language and Ideas

☐ 24. **Q**uantitative Analysis or **M**anaging People

☐ 25. **E**nterprise Control or **M**anaging People

☐ 26. **A**pplication of Technology or **C**ounseling and Mentoring

☐ 27. **M**anaging People or **I**nfluence Through Language and Ideas

☐ 28. **A**pplication of Technology or **Q**uantitative Analysis

Add the bold letters for your total score on each core function and record that score below:

☐ **Application of Technology**	☐ **Theory Development and Conceptual Thinking**
☐ **Counseling and Mentoring**	☐ **Enterprise Control**
☐ **Quantitative Analysis**	☐ **Creative Production**
☐ **Managing People**	☐ **Influence Through Language and Ideas**

Based on the scores above, identify your most significant interests. Most people will find one to three clear leaders. What does it all mean? Turn the page to find out.

FIGURE 10A-3 Finding the Job You *Should* Want (Part 2)

Source: James Waldroop and Timothy Butler, "Finding the Job You *Should* Want," *Fortune*, March 2, 1998, p. 212.

An Exercise One useful exercise for identifying occupational skills is to take a blank piece of paper and head it "The School or Occupational Tasks I Was Best At." Then write a short essay that describes the tasks. Make sure to go into as much detail as you can about your duties and responsibilities and what you found enjoyable about each task that. (In writing your essay, by the way, notice that it's not necessarily the most enjoyable *job* you've had, but the most enjoyable *task* you've had to perform; you may have had jobs that you really didn't like except for one of the specific duties or tasks in the job, which you really enjoyed.) Next, on other sheets of paper, do the same thing for two other tasks you have had. Now go through your three essays and underline the skills that you mentioned the most often. For example, did you enjoy putting

FIGURE 10A-4 Finding the Job You *Should* Want (Part 3)

Source: James Waldroop and Timothy Butler, "Finding the Job You *Should* Want," *Fortune*, March 2, 1998, p. 214. Copyright © 1998 Time Inc. Reprinted by permission.

Part 3: *Now that you know which combinations you prefer, see what kind of successful business people share your interests.*

ENTERPRISE CONTROL and MANAGING PEOPLE: CEOs, presidents, division managers, and general managers who enjoy both strategy and the operations aspects of the position—the CEO who enjoys playing the COO role as well.

ENTERPRISE CONTROL and QUANTITATIVE ANALYSIS: Investment bankers, other financial professionals who enjoy deal making, partners in Big Six firms, top-level executives in commercial and investment banks, investment managers.

APPLICATION OF TECHNOLOGY and QUANTITATIVE ANALYSIS: Individual contributors who have a strong interest in engineering analysis (systems analysis, tech consultants, process consultants); production and operations managers.

CREATIVE PRODUCTION and INFLUENCE THROUGH LANGUAGE AND IDEAS: Advertising executives, brand managers, corporate trainers, salespeople, public relations specialists; people in the fashion, entertainment, and media industries.

COUNSELING AND MENTORING and MANAGING PEOPLE: Human resources managers, managers who enjoy coaching and developing the people reporting to them, managers in nonprofit organizations with an altruistic mission.

ENTERPRISE CONTROL and INFLUENCE THROUGH LANGUAGE AND IDEAS: Executives (CEOs, presidents, general managers) whose leadership style relies on persuasion and consensus building, marketing managers, salespeople.

APPLICATION OF TECHNOLOGY and ENTERPRISE CONTROL: Managers and senior executives in high technology, telecommunications, biotech, information systems (internally or consulting), and other engineering-related fields.

THEORY DEVELOPMENT and QUANTITATIVE ANALYSIS: Economic-model builders quantitative analysis, "knowledge base" consultants, market forecasters, business professors.

CREATIVE PRODUCTION and ENTERPRISE CONTROL: Solo entrepreneurs, senior executives in industries where the product or service is of a creative nature (fashion, entertainment, advertising, media).

CREATIVE PRODUCTION: Entrepreneurs who partner with a professional manager, short-term project managers, new-product developers, advertising "creatives," individual contributors in fashion, entertainment, and media.

together and coordinating the school play when you worked in the principal's office one year? Did you especially enjoy the hours you spent in the library doing research for your boss when you worked one summer as an office clerk?[66]

Aptitudes and Special Talents For career planning purposes, a person's aptitudes are usually measured with a test battery such as the general aptitude test battery (GATB), which most states' One-Stop Career Centers make available. This instrument measures various aptitudes including intelligence and mathematical ability. You can also use specialized tests, such as for mechanical comprehension. However, even Holland's Self-Directed Search will provide some insights into your aptitudes.[67]

Identify Your Career Anchors Edgar Schein says that career planning is a continuing process of discovery—one in which a person slowly develops a clearer occupational self-concept in terms of what his or her talents, abilities, motives, needs, attitudes, and values are. Schein also says that as you learn more about yourself, it becomes apparent that you have a dominant **career anchor**, a concern or value that you will not give up if a [career] choice has to be made.

Career anchors, as their name implies, are the pivots around which a person's career swings; a person becomes conscious of them because of learning, through experience, about his or her talents and abilities, motives and needs, and attitudes and values. Based on his research at the Massachusetts Institute of Technology, Schein believes that career anchors are difficult to predict because they are evolutionary and a product of a process of discovery. Some people may never find out what their career anchors are until they have to make a major choice—such as whether to take the promotion to the headquarters staff or strike out on their own by starting a business. It is at this point that all the person's past work experiences, interests, aptitudes, and orientations converge into a meaningful pattern that helps show what (career anchor) is the most important factor in driving the person's career choices.

Based on his study of MIT graduates, Schein identified five career anchors.[68]

TECHNICAL/FUNCTIONAL COMPETENCE People who had a strong technical/functional career anchor tended to avoid decisions that would drive them toward general management. Instead, they made decisions that would enable them to remain and grow in their chosen technical or functional fields.

MANAGERIAL COMPETENCE Other people show a strong motivation to become managers and their career experience enabled them to believe they had the skills and values required. A management position of high responsibility is their ultimate goal. When pressed to explain why they believed they had the skills necessary to gain such positions, many in Schein's research sample answered that they were qualified because of what they saw as their competencies in a combination of three areas. These were (1) *analytical competence* (ability to identify, analyze, and solve problems under conditions of incomplete information and uncertainty); (2) *interpersonal competence* (ability to influence, supervise, lead, manipulate, and control people at all levels); and (3) *emotional competence* (the capacity to be stimulated by emotional and interpersonal crises rather than exhausted or debilitated by them, and the capacity to bear high levels of responsibility without becoming paralyzed).

CREATIVITY Some of the graduates had gone on to become successful entrepreneurs. To Schein, these people seemed to have a need "to build or create something that was entirely their own product—a product or process that bears their name, a company of their own, or a personal fortune that reflects their accomplishments." For example, one graduate had become a successful purchaser, restorer, and renter of townhouses in a large city; another had built a successful consulting firm.

AUTONOMY AND INDEPENDENCE Some seemed driven by the need to be on their own, free of the dependence that can arise when a person elects to work in a large organization where promotions, transfers, and salary decisions make them subordinate to others. Many of these graduates also had a strong technical/functional orientation. Instead of pursuing this orientation in an organization, they had decided to become consultants, working either alone or as part of a relatively small firm. Others had become professors of business, freelance writers, and proprietors of a small retail business.

SECURITY A few of the graduates were mostly concerned with long-run career stability and job security. They seemed willing to do what was required to maintain job security, a decent income, and a stable future in the form of a good retirement program and benefits. For those interested in *geographic security*, maintaining a stable, secure career in familiar surroundings was generally more important than pursuing superior career choices, if choosing the latter meant injecting instability or insecurity into their lives by forcing them to pull up roots and move to another city. For others, security meant *organizational security*. They might today opt for government jobs, where tenure still tends to be a way of life. They were much more willing to let their employers decide what their careers should be.

career anchors
Pivots around which a person's career swings; require self-awareness of talents and abilities, motives and needs, and attitudes and values.

ASSESSING CAREER ANCHORS To help you identify career anchors, take a few sheets of blank paper and write out your answers to the following questions:[69]

1. What was your major area of concentration (if any) in high school? Why did you choose that area? How did you feel about it?
2. What is (or was) your major area of concentration in college? Why did you choose that area? How did you feel about it?
3. What was your first job after school? (Include military, if relevant.) What were you looking for in your first job?
4. What were your ambitions or long-range goals when you started your career? Have they changed? When? Why?
5. What was your first major change of job or company? What were you looking for in your next job?
6. What was your next major change of job, company, or career? Why did you initiate or accept it? What were you looking for? (Do this for each of your major changes of job, company, or career.)
7. As you look back over your career, identify some times you have especially enjoyed. What was it about those times that you enjoyed?
8. As you look back, identify some times you have not especially enjoyed. What was it about those times you did not enjoy?
9. Have you ever refused a job move or promotion? Why?
10. Now review all your answers carefully, as well as the descriptions for the five career anchors (managerial competence, technical/functional, security, creativity, autonomy). Based on your answers to the questions, rate, for yourself, each of the anchors from 1 to 5 (1 equals low importance; 5 equals high importance).

    Managerial competence ______________

    Technical/functional competence ______________

    Security ______________

    Creativity ______________

    Autonomy ______________

What Do You Want to Do?

We have explained occupational orientations, skills, aptitudes, and career anchors and the role these play in choosing a career. Now, another exercise can prove enlightening. On a sheet of paper, answer the question: "If I could have any kind of job, what would it be?" Invent your own job if need be, and don't worry about what you can do—just what you want to do.[70]

Identify High-Potential Occupations

Learning about your skills and interests is only half the job of choosing an occupation. You also have to identify those occupations that are right (given your occupational orientations, skills, career anchors, and occupational preferences) as well as those that will be in high demand in the years to come.

Not surprisingly, the most efficient way to learn about, compare, and contrast occupations is through the Internet. The U.S. Department of Labor's online *Occupational Outlook Handbook* (www.bls.gov/oco), is updated each year, and provides detailed descriptions and information on hundreds of occupations (see Figure 10A-5). The New York State Department of Labor http://nycareerzone.org) similarly provides excellent information on careers categorized in clusters, such as Arts and Humanities, Business and Information Systems, and Engineering and Technology. Both these sites include information regarding demand for and employment prospects for the occupations they cover. Figure 10A-6 lists some other sites to turn to both for occupational information and for information on where to turn to when searching for a job—the subject to which we ourselves now turn.

The U.S. government's One-Stop Career Centers are another excellent source. In them, job seekers can now apply for unemployment benefits, register with the state job service, talk to career counselors, use computers to write résumés and access the Internet, take tests, and use career libraries, which offer books and videos

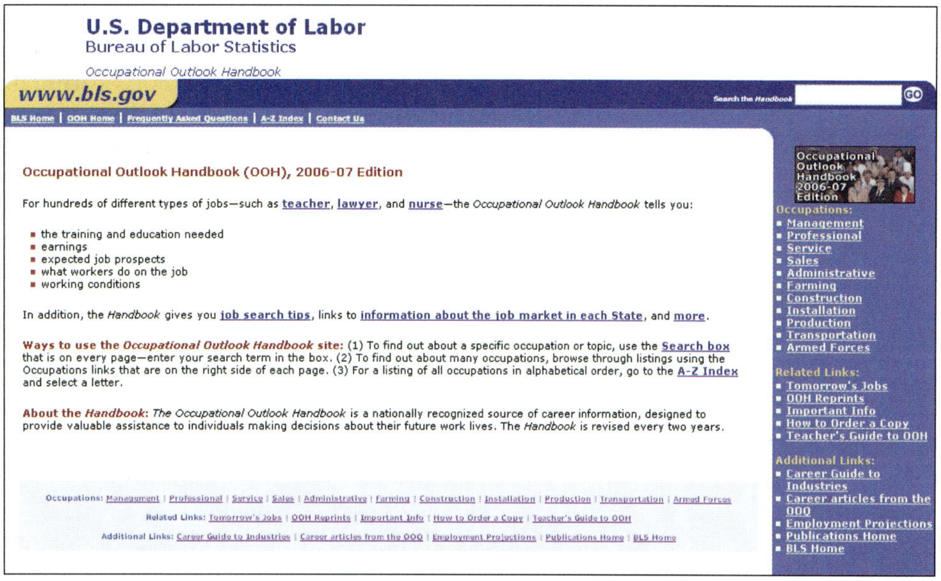

FIGURE 10A-5 Occupational Outlook Handbook Online

Source: www.bls.gov//oco, accessed May 18, 2007.

on various employment topics. In some centers, job hunters can even make use of free telephones, fax machines, and photocopiers to facilitate job searches.

Finding the Right Job You have identified your occupational orientation, skills, and career anchors and have picked out the occupation you want and made plans for a career. If necessary, you have embarked on the required education and training. Your next step is to find a job that you want in the company and locale in which you want to work.

Before leaving a current job, however, make sure leaving is what you want. Many people make the mistake of changing jobs or occupations when a smaller change would suffice. Dissatisfied at work, they assume it must be the job or the occupation. But, why decide to switch from being a lawyer to a teacher, when it's not the profession but that law firm's 80-hour weeks that's the problem?

The employee needs to use a process of elimination. For example, you may like your occupation and employer, but not how your specific job is structured. Others may find their employers' ways of doing things are the problem. Or, it may in fact be the occupation.

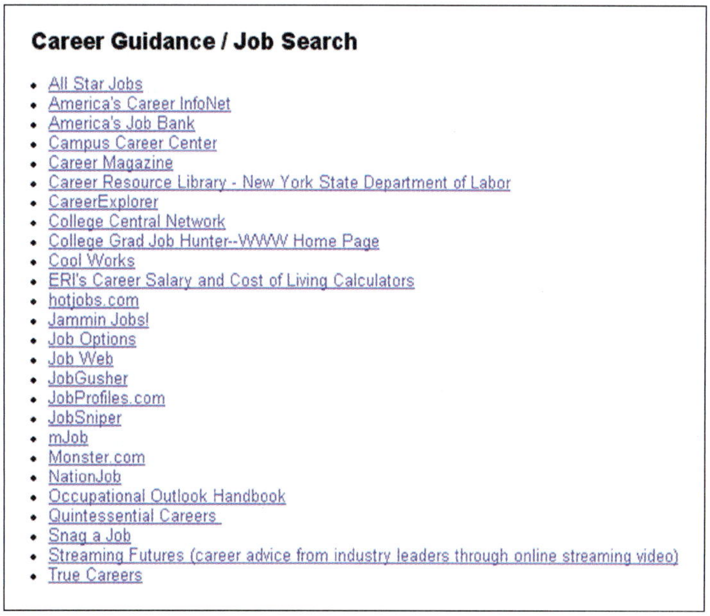

FIGURE 10A-6 Some Online Sources of Occupational Information

Source: Printed with permission from Mapping Your Future, a public service Web site providing career, college, financial aid, and financial literacy information and services to students, families, and schools (http://mapping-your-future.org/features/resources.cfm#CareerGuidance/JobSearch), accessed August 25, 2007.

In any case, the solution needs to fit the cause. For example, if, after thinking it through, you are satisfied with your occupation and where you work, but not with your job as it's organized now, try reconfiguring it. For example, consider alternative work arrangements such as flexible hours or telecommuting; delegate or eliminate the job functions you least prefer; and seek out a "stretch assignment" that will let you work on something you find more challenging.[71]

Job Search Techniques

DO YOUR OWN LOCAL RESEARCH Finding a job in a new geographic location is a challenge. One way to proceed is to find out all you can about the companies in that area that appeal to you, and the people you have to contact in those companies to get the job you want. Sometimes this research is decidedly low-tech. For example, the reference librarian in one Fairfax County, Virginia, library suggested the following sources for patrons seeking information about local businesses:

Industrial Directory of Virginia
Industrial Directory of Fairfax County
Principal Employers of the Washington Metro Area
The Business Review of Washington

Other general reference materials you can use include *Who's Who in Commerce and Industry, Who's Who in America, Who's Who in the East,* and *Poor's Register.* Using these guides, you can find the person in each organization ultimately responsible for hiring people in the position you seek.

ONLINE JOB BOARDS But the Internet is generally a better bet, especially if you're in one city and your ideal job would be in another. Most of the large online job search sites such as Monster.com (and those in Figure 10A-6) have local-area search capabilities, for instance. Use the *Wall Street Journal*'s career Web site (www.careerjournal.com) to search for jobs by occupation and location. And, most newspapers have their own (or links to) online local job listings. Remember to use social networking sites such as linked-in.

In addition to job boards (like Monster) and specialized ones (like www.theladder.com), most large companies, industries, and crafts have their own specialized sites.[72] For example, the Air Conditioning Contractors in America (www.acca.org/careers) and Financial Executives International (www.fei.org) make it easy for industry employers and prospective employees to match their needs. Remember (as we explained in the *HR APPs 4 U* in Chapter 5 (Recruiting) to use mobile services, for instance accessing jobs via the Careerbuilder iPhone portal.

When job hunting, you can post your résumé on the Web. But although many people do so, Web-based résumés can cause problems. "Once I put my résumé on the Internet, I couldn't do anything to control it," said one technical consultant after his boss had stumbled across the fact that, several months before, he had been job hunting. If you do post your résumé on the Web, experts suggest taking precautions. At a minimum, date your résumé (in case it lands on your boss's desk 2 years from now). Also insert a disclaimer forbidding unauthorized transmission by headhunters; check ahead of time to see who has access to the database on which you're posting your résumé; and try to cloak your identity by listing your capabilities but not your name or employer—just an anonymous e-mail account to receive inquiries.[73]

PERSONAL CONTACTS Generally, the most popular way to seek job interviews is to rely on personal contacts such as friends and relatives.[74] So, let as many responsible people as possible know that you are looking for a job and also what kind of job you want. (Beware, though, if you are currently employed and don't want your job search getting back to your current boss. If that is the case, better just pick out two or three very close friends and tell them it is essential that they be discreet in seeking a job for you.)

No matter how close your friends or relatives are to you, by the way, you don't want to impose too much on them. It is usually best to ask them for the name of someone they think you should talk to in the kind of firm in which you'd like to work, and then do the digging yourself.

ANSWERING ADVERTISEMENTS Most experts agree that answering ads is a low-probability way to get a job, and it becomes increasingly less likely that you will get a job this way as the level of jobs increases. Answering ads, in other words, is fine for jobs that pay under $30,000 per year, but it's highly unlikely that as you move up in management you are going to get your job by simply answering classified ads. Nevertheless, good sources of classified ads for professionals and managers include the *New York Times*, the *Wall Street Journal*, and specialized journals in your field that list job openings. All these sources also post the positions online, of course.

In responding to ads, be sure to create the right impression with the materials you submit; check the typing, style, grammar, neatness, and so forth, and check your résumé to make sure it is geared to the job for which you are applying. In your cover letter, be sure to have a paragraph or so in which you specifically address why your background and accomplishments are appropriate to the advertised position you must respond clearly to the company's identified needs.[75]

Be very careful in replying to blind ads, however (those with just a post office box). Some executive search firms and companies will run ads even when no position exists just to gauge the market, and there is always the chance that you will blunder into responding to your own firm.

EMPLOYMENT AGENCIES Agencies are especially good at placing people in jobs paying up to about $60,000, but they can be useful for higher-paying jobs as well. The employer usually pays the fees for professional and management jobs. Assuming you know the job you want, review a few back issues of your paper's Sunday classified ads to identify the agencies that consistently handle the positions you want. Approach three or four initially, preferably in response to specific ads, and avoid signing any contract that gives an agency the exclusive right to place you.

EXECUTIVE RECRUITERS We've seen that employers retain executive recruiters to seek out top talent for their clients; employers always pay any fees. They do not do career counseling, but if you know the job you want, it pays to contact a few. Send your résumé and a cover letter summarizing your objective in precise terms, including job title and the size of company desired, work-related accomplishments, current salary, and salary requirements. Firms are listed under "Executive Search Consultants." However, beware, because some firms today call themselves executive search or career consultants but do no searches: They just charge a (often hefty) fee to help you manage your search. Remember that with a search firm you never pay a fee.

What sorts of things will the headhunter look for? Ten important items include:[76]

- You have demonstrated the ability to get results.
- You come well recommended by your peers and competitors.
- You understand who the search consultant works for and what he is trying to do.
- You are likeable and presentable, and your ego is in check.
- You can think strategically and understand how to institute change in an organized direction.
- You have achieved the results you have because of the way you treat others, not in spite of it.
- You can sell yourself concisely.
- You have at least some of the key specific experiences that the job entails.
- You are honest, and even take the time when a recruiter calls to give them other sources that you believe are high potential.
- You know who you are and what you want.[77]

CAREER COUNSELORS Career counselors will not help you find a job per se; rather, they specialize in aptitude testing and career counseling. They are listed under "Career Counseling" or "Vocational Guidance." Their services usually cost

$300 or so and include psychological testing and interviews with an experienced career counselor. Check the firm's services, prices, and history as well as the credentials of the person you will be dealing with.

EXECUTIVE MARKETING CONSULTANTS Executive marketing consultants manage your job-hunting campaign. They generally are not recruiters and do not have jobs to fill. Depending on the services you choose, your cost will range from $400 to $5,000 or more. The process may involve months of weekly meetings. Services include résumé and letter writing, interview skill building, and developing a full job-hunting campaign. Before approaching a consultant, though, you should definitely do in-depth self-appraisal (as explained in this chapter) and read books like Richard Bolles's *The Quick Job Hunting Map* and *What Color Is Your Parachute?*

Then check out three or four of these firms (they may also be listed under "Executive Search Consultants") by visiting each and asking: What exactly is your program? How much does each service cost? Are there any extra costs, such as charges for printing and mailing résumés? What does the contract say? After what point will you get no rebate if you're unhappy with the services? Then review your notes, check the Better Business Bureau, and decide which of these firms (if any) is for you.

EMPLOYERS' WEB SITES With more and more companies listing job openings on their Web sites, any serious job hunter should be using this valuable source. Doing so requires some special résumé preparations, as we'll see next.

Writing Your Résumé

Your résumé is probably your most important selling document, one that can determine whether you get offered a job interview. Here are some résumé pointers, as offered by employment counselor Richard Payne and other experts.[78] Figure 10A-7 presents one example of an effective résumé.

FIGURE 10A-7 Partial Example of a Good Résumé

Source: Adapted from Richard Payne, *How to Get a Better Job Quicker* (New York: Signet), 1988, pp. 80–81.

CONRAD D. STAPLETON
77 Pleasantapple Way
Coltsville, NY 10176
747-1012 conrad@Pearson.com

CONFIDENTIAL

JOB OBJECTIVE	*Senior Production Manager* in a situation requiring extensive advertising and promotion experience.
PRESENT POSITION	VALUE-PLUS DIVISION, INTERCONTINENTAL CORPORATION
2000–Present	*Product Manager,* NEW PRODUCTS, LAUDRYON SOAP and CARBOLENE CLEANER, reporting to Group Product Manager.
	Recommended and obtained test market authorization, then managed all phases of development of THREE test brands, scheduled for introduction during Fall/Winter 2003. Combined first year national volume projects to $20 million, with advertising budget of $6 million. Concurrently developing several new products for 2004 test marketing.
	Also responsible for two established brands: LAUNDRYON SOAP, a $7 million brand, and CARBOLENE CLEANER, a $4 million regional brand. Currently work with three advertising agencies on test and established brands.
1997–2000	*Product Manager,* WEEKENDER PAINTS, a $6 million brand.
	Developed and implemented a repositioning of this brand (including new copy and new package graphics) to counter a 10-year sales downtrend averaging 10% a year. Repositioning increased test market volume 16%, and national volume 8% the following year.
	Later initiated development of new, more competitive copy than advertising used during repositioning. Test area sales increased 35%. National airing is scheduled for Fall 1999.
	Developed plastic packaging that increased test market volume 10%.
	Also developed and implemented profit improvement projects which increased net profit 33%.
1996	*Product Manager,* SHINEZY CAR WASH, a $4 million brand.
	Initiated and test marketed an improved aerosol formula and a liquid refill. Both were subsequently expanded nationally and increased brand volume 26%.
	RICHARDS-DONALDS COMPANY

INTRODUCTORY INFORMATION Start your résumé with your name, home and e-mail addresses, and telephone number. Using your office phone number can indicate either that (1) your employer knows you are leaving or (2) you don't care whether he or she finds out. You're usually better off using your home or cell phone number.

JOB OBJECTIVE Next, state your job objective. This should summarize in one sentence the specific position you want, where you want to do it (type and size of company), and a special reason an employer might have for wanting you to fill the job. For example, "Production manager in a medium-size manufacturing company in a situation in which strong production scheduling and control experience would be valuable." Always try to put down the most senior title you know you can expect to secure, keeping in mind the specific job for which you are applying.

JOB SCOPE Indicate the scope of your responsibility in each of your previous jobs, starting with your most recent position. For each of your previous jobs, write a paragraph that shows job title, whom you reported to directly and indirectly, who reported to you, how many people reported to you, the operational and human resource budgets you controlled, and what your job entailed (in one sentence).

YOUR ACCOMPLISHMENTS Next (and this is very important), indicate your "worth" in each of the positions you held. This is the heart of your résumé. It shows for each of your previous jobs: (1) the concrete action you took and why you took it and (2) the specific result of your action—the "payoff." For example, "As production supervisor, I introduced a new process to replace costly hand soldering of component parts. The new process reduced assembly time per unit from 30 to 10 minutes and reduced labor costs by more than 60%." Use several of these worth statements for each job.

LENGTH Keep your résumé to two pages or less, and list education, military service (if any), and personal background (hobbies, interests, associations) on the last page.

PERSONAL DATA Do not put personal data regarding age, marital status, or dependents on top of page one. If you must include it, do so at the end of the résumé, where it will be read after the employer has already formed an opinion of you.

Finally, two last points. First, do not produce a slipshod résumé: Avoid overcrowded pages, difficult-to-read copies, typographical errors, and other problems of this sort. Second, do not use a make-do résumé—one from 10 years ago. Produce a new résumé for each job you are applying for, gearing your job objective and worth statements to the job you want.

MAKE YOUR RÉSUMÉ SCANNABLE For many job applications, it's important to write a scannable résumé, in other words, one that is electronically readable by a computer system. Many medium- and larger-sized firms that do extensive recruiting and hiring—especially online and with the aid of applicant tracking systems—now use software to quickly and automatically review large numbers of résumés, screening out those that don't seem to match (often based on the absence of certain key words that the employer is looking for).

There are several guidelines to keep in mind for writing scannable résumés.[79] We can summarize these as follows:

Use type no smaller than 10 points and no larger than 14 points.

Do not use italicized type, and do not underline words.

Use type styles that work well for résumés and can be scanned as well as read, such as Helvetica, Futura, Optima, Times Roman, New Century Schoolbook, Courier, Univers, and Bookman.

When submitting hard copies, make sure they are high-resolution documents. Documents produced on a laser printer work best. Many photocopies and faxes are not clean enough for scanning.

Make sure to present your qualifications using powerful key words appropriate to the job or jobs for which you are applying. For example, trainers might use key words and phrases such as computer-based training, interactive video, and group facilitator.

ONLINE BIOS Today, employers often encourage or require their professionals and managers to post brief biographies on corporate intranets or Web sites. These bios let other employees know about their colleagues' expertise. Tips for writing such bios include:[80]

Fill it with details. "The more information you enter, the more likely a person seeking someone with your background will find you. . . ."

Avoid touchy subjects. For example, avoid discussing religion and politics.

Look the part. Your profile may require posting photos. If so, dress in professional attire.

Make it search friendly. Make sure your profile contains the key words you think someone searching for someone with your background and expertise would be looking for, such as "manager," "supervisor," or "engineer."

Use abbreviations. Abbreviations are important. For example, someone searching the site might more readily punch in "MBA" than "Masters in Business Administration."

Say it with numbers. Describe specifically how your work has contributed to your current employer's and past employer's bottom lines.

Proofread. Carefully proofread your online profile, as you would your résumé.

Handling the Interview

You have done all your homework and now the big day is almost here; you have an interview next week with the person who is responsible for hiring for the job you want. What must you do to excel in the interview? Here are some suggestions.

Prepare, Prepare, Prepare. First, remember that preparation is essential. Before the interview, learn all you can about the employer, the job, and the people doing the recruiting. Search the Internet (or your library) to find out what is happening in the employer's field. Who is the competition? How are they doing?

Uncover the Interviewer's Needs. Spend as little time as possible answering your interviewer's first questions and as much time as possible getting the person to describe his or her needs—what the person is looking to get accomplished and the type of person needed. Use open-ended questions, such as "Could you tell me more about that?"

Relate Yourself to the Person's Needs. Once you understand the type of person your interviewer is looking for and the sorts of problems he or she wants solved, you are in a good position to describe your own accomplishments in terms of the interviewer's needs. Start by saying something like, "One of the problem areas you've indicated is important to you is similar to a problem I once faced." Then state the problem, describe your solution, and reveal the results.

Think Before Answering. Answering a question should be a three-step process: pause, think, speak. Pause to make sure you understand what the interviewer is driving at, think about how to structure your answer, and then speak. In your answer, try to emphasize how hiring you will help the interviewer solve his or her problem.

Make a Good Appearance and Show Enthusiasm. Appropriate clothing, good grooming, a firm handshake, and the appearance of controlled energy are important. Remember that studies of interviews show that in almost 80% of the cases, interviewers make up their minds about the applicant during the first few moments of the interview. A good first impression may turn bad during the interview, but it is unlikely. Bad first impressions are almost impossible to overcome.

Part III Video Cases Appendix

Video 4: The HR Manager's Job, Job Analysis, Training and Developing Employees

VIDEO TITLE: TRAINING AND DEVELOPMENT

In this video, the director of training and development turns a somewhat confrontational meeting with the firm's marketing director into something more positive. The marketing director is making the case that there are several performance problems among employees of the company, and that she believes that inadequate training and development is the reason why. For her part, the training and development manager, Jenny Herman, says that she understands that the company, Loews Hotels, is getting complaints from customers, but that the firm's training program has been following the employee performance standards now in place. The problem is "there are standards, but employees are still falling down." After discussing the matter between the two of them, they agree that the training and development program was not revised for the company's new needs, and that among other things Jenny would "like to revise the new hire certification process." She emphasizes that "we need to hear more from the field what the training and development needs are, and then try these out, and then roll out the final program."

Discussion Questions

1. Could the inadequate performance be a result, not of inadequate training, but of something else—such as inadequate motivation or inadequate employee selection?
2. How would you go about finding out, based upon what you read in this part of the book?
3. The concluding discussion of the video about how human resource managers actually choose training techniques raises some useful questions. For example, do you agree that classroom training is particularly appropriate for hotel employees "because they like classroom training?"

Video 5: Performance Management and Appraisal, Career Management

VIDEO TITLE: ERNST & YOUNG

Ernst & Young, a large U.S. accounting firm, increased its employee retention rate by 5% through a human resource initiative "to put people first." By creating a performance feedback–rich culture, building great résumés for its 160,000 people in New York City and around the world, and giving them time and freedom to pursue personal goals, Ernst & Young executed its "people first" idea and thereby created a more motivated workforce. In this video, you'll see the company uses mandatory goal setting, provides employees with learning opportunities in their areas of interest, and measures HR processes using an employee survey to evaluate the workplace environment. While the first segment of this video is necessarily relevant for our needs, the segment on Ernst & Young, in which Kevin, the senior auditor, describes his experience at Ernst & Young, illustrates both what performance management means in practice, and the effect that it can have on employees.

Discussion Questions

1. In what ways do the HR practices of Ernst & Young (such as goal setting and providing people with learning opportunities in their areas of interest) illustrate what performance management means in practice?
2. How important do you think it is that Ernst & Young measure HR practices using an employee survey? Why? How would you do so?
3. What role should such a survey play in the firm's performance management program, and in its strategic human resource efforts?

ENDNOTES

1. www.cvscaremark.com/careers/seniors, accessed March 25, 2009.
2. Donna Goldwasser, "Me, a Trainer?" *Training*, April 2001, pp. 60–66.
3. Ann Pace, "Coaching Gains Ground," *Training & Development* 62, no. 7 (July 21, 2008). Accessed from http://findarticles.com/p/articles/mi_m4467/is_200807/ai_n27996020/, July 28, 2009.
4. This is based on Richard Luecke, *Coaching and Mentoring* (Boston: Harvard Business School Press, 2004), pp. 8–9.
5. Ibid., p. 9.
6. For example, see Phyllis Moen and Patricia Roehling, *The Career Mystique* (Boulder, CO: Rowman & Littlefield Publishers, 2005).
7. See, for example, Andreas Liefooghe et al., "Managing the Career Deal: The Psychological Contract as a Framework for Understanding Career Management, Organizational Commitment and Work Behavior," *Journal of Organizational Behavior* 26, no. 7 (November 2005), pp. 821–838.
8. Carla Joinson, "Career Management and Commitment," *HR Magazine*, May 2001, pp. 60–64.
9. Jan Selmer, "Usage of Corporate Career Development Activities by Expatriate Managers and the Extent of Their International Adjustment," *International Journal of Commerce and Management* 10, no. 1 (Spring 2000), p. 1.
10. Carla Joinson, "Employee, Sculpt Thyself with a Little Help," *HR Magazine*, May 2001, pp. 61–64.
11. Jim Bright, "Career Development: Empowering Your Staff to Excellence," *Journal of Banking and Financial Services* 17, no. 3 (July 2003), p. 12.
12. Barbara Greene and Liana Knudsen, "Competitive Employers Make Career Development Programs a Priority," *San Antonio Business Journal* 15, no. 26 (July 20, 2001), p. 27.
13. Bright, "Career Development: Empowering Your Staff to Excellence," p. 12.
14. "Career Guidance Steers Workers Away from Early Exits," *BNA Bulletin to Management*, September 7, 2000, p. 287.
15. Patrick Kiger, "First USA Bank, Promotions and Job Satisfaction," *Workforce*, March 2001, pp. 54–56.
16. Fred Otte and Peggy Hutcheson, *Helping Employees Manage Careers* (Upper Saddle River, NJ: Prentice Hall, 1992), p. 143.
17. Yehuda Baruch and Maury Peiperl, "Career Management Practices: An Empirical Survey and Implications," *Human Resource Management* 39, no. 4 (Winter 2000), pp. 347–366.
18. Greene and Knudsen, "Competitive Employers Make Career Development Programs a Priority," p. 27.
19. Julekha Dash, "Coaching to Aid IT Careers, Retention," *Computerworld*, March 20, 2000, p. 52.
20. David Foote, "Wanna Keep Your Staff Happy? Think Career," *Computerworld*, October 9, 2000, p. 38.
21. Jim Meade, "Boost Careers and Succession Planning," *HR Magazine*, October 2000, pp. 175–178.
22. Bright, "Career Development: Empowering Your Staff to Excellence," p. 12.
23. Karen Lyness and Donna Thompson, "Climbing the Corporate Ladder: Do Female and Male Executives Follow the Same Route?" *Journal of Applied Psychology* 85, no. 1 (2000), pp. 86–101.
24. "Minority Women Surveyed on Career Growth Factors," *Community Banker* 9, no. 3 (March 2000), p. 44.
25. In Ellen Cook et al., "Career Development of Women of Color and White Women: Assumptions, Conceptualization, and Interventions from an Ecological Perspective," *Career Development Quarterly* 50, no. 4 (June 2002), pp. 291–306.
26. Jan Selmer and Alicia Leung, "Are Corporate Career Development Activities Less Available to Female Than to Male Expatriates?" *Journal of Business Ethics*, March 2003, pp. 125–137.
27. Kathleen Melymuka, "Glass Ceilings & Clear Solutions," *Computerworld*, May 29, 2000, p. 56.
28. Bill Hayes, "Helping Workers with Career Goals Boosts Retention Efforts," *Boston Business Journal* 21, no. 11 (April 20, 2001), p. 38.
29. Michael Doody, "A Mentor Is a Key to Career Success," *Health-Care Financial Management* 57, no. 2 (February 2003), pp. 92–94.
30. Luecke, op. cit., pp. 100–101.
31. Ferda Erdem and Janset Özen Aytemur, "Mentoring—A Relationship Based on Trust: Qualitative Research," *Public Personnel Management* 37 no. 1 (Spring 2008), pp. 55–65.
32. Charles Woodruffe and Victoria McFarland, "What Makes a Successful Mentoring Scheme? The Answer May Surprise You . . . ," *People Management* 12, no. 25 (December 2006), p. 48.
33. Ibid.
34. "Preparing Future Leaders in Health-Care," *Leaders*, c/o Witt/Kieffer, 2015 Spring Road, Suite 510, Oak Brook, IL 60523.
35. Tim Harvey, "Enterprise Training System Is Trans Alaska Pipeline's Latest Safety Innovation," *Pipeline and Gas Journal* 229, no. 12 (December 2002), pp. 28–32.
36. Ibid.
37. "Kenexa Announces a Latest Version of Kenexa Career Tracker," *Internet Wire*, March 22, 2004.
38. George Thornton III and David Morris, "The Application of Assessment Center Technology to the Evaluation of Personnel Records," *Public Personnel Management* 30, no. 1 (Spring 2001), p. 55.
39. Robin Shay, "Don't Get Caught in the Legal Wringer When Dealing with Difficult to Manage Employees," http://www.shrm.org ttp://moss07.shrm.org/Publications/hrmagazine/EditorialContent/Pages/0702toc.aspx, accessed July 28, 2009.

WHERE

Once you'
course, few
sense in te
purpose of
evaluation-
online and
developing
on pay-for-

Chapter 4
Develop personnel plans and job descriptions

LEARNIN

1. List the
2. Define
3. Explain
4. Explain
5. Explain
6. Explain oversig

40. Maria Danaher, "Unclear Promotion Procedures Smack of Discrimination," www.shrm.org, downloaded March 2, 2004.
41. In Susan Wells, "Smoothing the Way," *HR Magazine*, June 2001, pp. 52–58.
42. Ken Dychtwald et al., "It's Time to Retire Retirement," *Harvard Business Review*, March 2004, p. 49.
43. "Employees Plan to Work Past Retirement, but Not Necessarily for Financial Reasons," *BNA Bulletin to Management*, February 19, 2004, pp. 57–58. See also Mo Wang, "Profiling Retirees in the Retirement Transition and Adjustment Process: Examining the Longitudinal Change Patterns of Retirees' Psychological Well-Being," *Journal of Applied Psychology* 92, no. 2 (2007), pp. 455–474.
44. See, for example, Matt Bolch, "Bidding Adieu," *HR Magazine*, June 2006, pp. 123–127; and Claudia Deutsch, "A Longer Goodbye," *The New York Times*, April 20, 2008, pp. H1, H10.
45. Luis Fleites and Lou Valentino, "The Case for Phased Retirement," *Compensation & Benefits Review*, March/April 2007, pp. 42–46.
46. Andrew Luchak et al., "When Do Committed Employees Retire? The Effects of Organizational Commitment on Retirement Plans Under a Defined Benefit Pension Plan," *Human Resource Management* 47, no. 3 (Fall 2008), pp. 581–599.
47. Dychtwald et al., op. cit., 52.
48. Ibid.
49. "American Express Adds Tools to Retirement Section," *Financial Net News* 6, no. 17 (April 30, 2001), p. 3. See also Catherine Dalton, "The Art of the Graceful Exit," *Business Horizons* 48, no. 2 (March 2005), pp. 91–93.
50. www.talentmanagement101.com, accessed December 10, 2007.
51. "Talent Management Is on HR's Agenda for 2007 and Beyond," *HR Focus* 84, no. 4 (April 2007), p. 8. See also Andrew Paradise, "Talent Management Defined," *Training & Development* 63, no. 5 (May 2009), pp. 68–69.
52. www.successfactors.com/info/en/talent-management/?source=Google_ppc&kw=Talent%20Management&gclid=CNzA-YmRgpkCFQS7sgodnkdLnw, accessed March 1, 2009.
53. Michael Laff, "Talent Management: From Hire to Retire," *Training & Development*, November 2006, pp. 42–48.
54. "Survey: Talent Management a Top Concern," http://www.channelinsider.com/c/a/News/Survey-Talent-Management-a-Top-Concern/, accessed July 28, 2009.
55. www.talentmanagement101.com, downloaded December 10, 2007.
56. www.silkroadtech.com, accessed December 10, 2007.
57. "Software Facilitates Talent Management," http://news.thomasnet.com/fullstory/517396, accessed July 28, 2009.
58. "Work Stream to Announce 'Project X'—Their Next-Generation Talent Management Solutions—at HR Technology Conference & Exposition, October 10, 2007, in Chicago, Illinois," http://www.workstreaminc.com/company/pr2007/prsept26_07.asp, accessed July 28, 2009.
59. "New Trend in Career Hunt," *Europe Intelligence Wire*, February 10, 2004.
60. Ibid.
61. Rebecca Sohn, "Career Management in a Jobless Economy," *Westchester County Business Journal* 43, no. 14 (April 5, 2004), p. 4. See also P. Bronson, "What Should I Do With My Life Now?," *Fast Company*, no. 134 (April 2009), pp. 35–37.
62. The classic discussion of career stages is in Donald Super et al., *Vocational Development: A Framework for Research* (New York: Teachers College Press, 1975); and Edgar Schein, *Career Dynamics: Matching Individual and Organizational Needs* (Reading, MA: Addison-Wesley, 1978).
63. John Holland, *Making Vocational Choices: A Theory of Careers* (Upper Saddle River, NJ: Prentice Hall, 1973).
64. Edward Levinson et al., "A Critical Evaluation of the Web-Based Version of the Career Key," *Career Development Quarterly* 50, no. 1 (September 1, 2002), pp. 26–36.
65. This is based on James Waldroop and Timothy Butler, "Finding the Job You *Should* Want," *Fortune*, March 2, 1998, pp. 211–214.
66. Richard Bolles, *What Color Is Your Parachute?* (Berkeley, CA: Ten Speed Press, 2003), pp. 5–6.
67. Ibid., p. 5. Researchers and career specialists worked with the U.S. government's O*NET to devise a methodology that will enable individuals to make better use of O*NET in identifying and choosing career paths. See, for example, Patrick Converse et al., "Matching Individuals to Occupations Using Abilities and the O*NET: Issues and an Application in Career Guidance," *Personnel Psychology* 57 (2004), pp. 451–47.
68. Edgar Schein, *Career Dynamics* (Reading, MA; Addison-Wesley, 1978), pp. 128–129; and Edgar Schein, "Career Anchors Revisited: Implications for Career Development in the 21st Century," *Academy of Management Executive* 10, no. 4 (1996), pp. 80–88.
69. Ibid., pp. 257–262. For a test of Schein's career anchor concept, see Yvon Martineau et al., "Multiple Career Anchors of Québec Engineers: Impact on Career Path and Success," *Relations Industrielles/Industrial Relations* 60, no. 3 (Summer 2005), pp. 45, 455–482.
70. This example is based on Richard Bolles, *The Three Boxes of Life* (Berkeley, CA: Ten Speed Press, 1976). See also Richard Bolles, *What Color Is Your Parachute?*
71. Deb Koen, "Revitalize Your Career," *Training & Development*, January 2003, pp. 59–60. See also R. Zeidner, "When It Doesn't Pay to Stay," *HR Magazine* 54, no. 1 (January 2009), p. 26.
72. "Resume Banks Launched," *Financial Executives* 17, no. 6 (September 2001), p. 72; James Siegel, "The ACCA Launches Online Career Center," *A/C, Heating & Refrigeration News*, June 16, 2003, p. 5.
73. "Read This Before You Put a Resume Online," *Fortune*, May 24, 1999, pp. 290–291. See also N. Amare et. al., "Writing for the Robot: How Employer Search Tools Have Influenced Resume Rhetoric and Ethics," *Business Communication Quarterly* 72, no. 1 (March 2009), pp. 35–60.
74. See John Wareham, "How to Make a Headhunter Call You," *Across-the-Board* 32, no. 1 (January 1995), pp. 49–50; and Deborah Wright Brown and Alison Konrad, "Job Seeking in a Turbulent Environment: Social Networks and the Importance of Cross-Industry Ties to an Industry Change," *Human Relations* 54, no. 8 (August 2001), p. 1018. See also "Best Headhunters for 2009 [Tables]," *Asiamoney* 20, no. 1 (February 2009), pp. 37, 40–42.
75. See, for example, "Job Search Tips: The America's Intelligence Wire," May 17, 2004; and "What to Do When Your Job Search Stalls," *BusinessWeek Online*, March 16, 2004.
76. John Rau, "And the Winner Is . . . ," *Across-the-Board* 54, no. 10 (November/December 1997), pp. 38–42.
77. Based on ibid., pp. 32–42.
78. Richard Payne, "How to Get a Better Job Quicker" (New York, Mentor, 1987), pp. 54–87. See also Larry Salters, "Resume Writing for the 1990s," *Business and Economics Review* 40, no. 3 (April 1994), pp. 11–18.
79. Erica Gordon Sorohan, "Electrifying a Job Search," *Training & Development*, October 1994, pp. 7–9; "Electronic Resumes Help Searchers Get in Job Hunt," Knight Ridder/Tribune Business News, April 6, 2004, ITEM 04097013.
80. Sarah Needleman, "Posting a Job Profile Online? Keep It Polished," *The Wall Street Journal*, August 29, 2006, p. B7.

1 List the basic factors determining pay rates

BASIC FACTORS IN DETERMINING PAY RATES

Employee compensation refers to all forms of pay going to employees and arising from their employment. It has two main components, **direct financial payments** (wages, salaries, incentives, commissions, and bonuses) and **indirect financial payments** (financial benefits like employer-paid insurance and vacations).

In turn, there are two basic ways to make direct financial payments to employees: base them on increments of time or on performance. Time-based pay is still the foundation of most employers' pay plans. Blue-collar and clerical workers get hourly or daily wages, for instance, and others, like managers or Web designers, tend to be salaried and paid by the week, month, or year. The second direct payment option is to pay for performance. Piecework is an example. It ties compensation to the amount of production (or number of "pieces") the worker turns out. For instance, you divide a worker's target hourly wage by the standard number of units he or she is to produce in one hour. Then, for each unit he or she produces, the person earns the calculated rate per piece. Sales commissions are another example of performance-based (in this case, sales-based) compensation. Of course, employers also devise pay plans in which employees receive some combination of time-based pay plus incentives.

In this chapter, we explain how to formulate plans for paying employees a time-based wage or salary; subsequent chapters cover performance-based financial incentives and bonuses (Chapter 12) and employee benefits (Chapter 13).

Several factors determine the design of any pay plan: legal, union, company strategy and policy, and equity. We'll start with legal factors.

Legal Considerations in Compensation

Various laws specify things like minimum wages, overtime rates, and benefits.[2] For example, the 1931 **Davis-Bacon Act** allows the secretary of labor to set wage rates for laborers and mechanics employed by contractors working for the federal government. Amendments provide for paid employee benefits. The 1936 **Walsh-Healey Public Contract Act** sets basic labor standards for employees working on any government contract that amounts to more than $10,000. It contains minimum wage, maximum hour, and safety and health provisions, and requires time-and-a-half pay for work over 40 hours a week. **Title VII of the 1964 Civil Rights Act** makes it unlawful for employers to discriminate against any individual with respect to hiring, compensation, terms, conditions, or privileges of employment because of race, color, religion, sex, or national origin.[3] We'll look next at other important compensation-related laws.

The 1938 Fair Labor Standards Act

The **Fair Labor Standards Act**, originally passed in 1938 and since amended many times, contains minimum wage, maximum hours, overtime pay, equal pay, record-keeping, and child labor provisions that are familiar to most working people.[4] It covers the majority of U.S. workers—virtually all those engaged in the production and/or sale of goods for interstate and foreign commerce. In addition, agricultural workers and those employed by certain larger retail and service companies are included. State fair labor standards laws cover most employers not covered by the Fair Labor Standards Act (FLSA).[5]

One familiar provision governs *overtime pay*. It says employers must pay overtime at a rate of at least one-and-a-half times normal pay for any hours worked over 40 in a workweek. Thus, if a worker covered by the act works 44 hours in one week, he or she must be paid for 4 of those hours at a rate equal to one-and-a-half times the hourly or weekly base rate the person would have earned for 40 hours. For example, if the person earns $8 an hour (or $320 for a 40-hour week), he or she would be paid at the rate of $12 per hour (8 times 1.5) for each of the 4 overtime hours worked, or a total of $48 for the extra 4 hours. If the employee instead receives time off for the overtime hours, the employer must also compute the

HR APPs 4 U

Mobile PDA Handheld Timesheet Solutions

Keeping track of employees' hours when they're working out of the office isn't easy. That's why vendors such as Pacific Timesheet (www.pacifictimesheet.com) provide mobile payroll time sheets. Employees who work outside can access and fill these in via their iPhones or similar devices. This improves attendance and payroll accuracy, reduces the need to adjust payrolls, and helps eliminate overpaying overtime.[7]

number of hours granted off at the one-and-a-half-times rate. So the person would get 6 hours off for the 4 hours of overtime, in lieu of overtime pay. Employers need to monitor when employees clock in and out, lest they become obligated for unexpected additional demands for overtime pay.[6]

Violating the FLSA's provisions is inadvisable, but even giant firms make errors. Walmart recently agreed to pay up to $640 million to settle 63 wage and hour suits alleging infractions, such as failing to pay overtime and not providing required meal breaks.[8] A great many employers today pay people as "independent contractors" rather than as employees. Strictly speaking, these people are like consultants, not covered by the FLSA. The accompanying "Managing the New Workforce" feature explains about paying this new kind of worker.

Managing the New Workforce

The Independent Contractor

Whether the person is an employee or an *independent contractor* is a continuing issue for employers. For example, FedEx Ground is battling many lawsuits as it defends its right to maintain the status of its roughly 15,000 delivery truck owner-operators as independent contractors (it recently won one such case).[9]

The problem is that many so-called independent contractor relationships aren't independent contractor relationships. There is no single rule or test for determining whether an individual is an independent contractor or a bona fide employee. Instead, the courts will look at the total activity or situation. The major consideration is this: The more the employer controls what the worker does and how he or she does it, the more likely it is that the courts will find the worker is actually an employee. Figure 11-1 lists some factors the courts will consider here.

For employers, there are advantages to claiming that someone is an independent contractor. For one thing, the FLSA's overtime and most other requirements do not apply. For another, the employer does not have to pay unemployment compensation payroll taxes, Social Security taxes, or city, state, and federal income taxes or compulsory workers' compensation for that worker. If the person is truly an independent contractor, the relationship can also be advantageous to him or her. For example, it gives the worker more flexibility regarding things like when and where he or she works, and often gives the person more options, for instance, in terms of deducting business expenses.

employee compensation
All forms of pay or rewards going to employees and arising from their employment.

direct financial payments
Pay in the form of wages, salaries, incentives, commissions, and bonuses.

indirect financial payments
Pay in the form of financial benefits such as insurance.

Davis-Bacon Act (1931)
A law that sets wage rates for laborers employed by contractors working for the federal government.

Walsh-Healey Public Contract Act (1936)
A law that requires minimum wage and working conditions for employees working on any government contract amounting to more than $10,000.

Title VII of the 1964 Civil Rights Act
This act makes it unlawful for employers to discriminate against any individual with respect to hiring, compensation, terms, conditions, or privileges of employment because of race, color, religion, sex, or national origin.

Fair Labor Standards Act (1938)
This act provides for minimum wages, maximum hours, overtime pay, and child labor protection. The law, amended many times, covers most employees.

Independent Contractor

Managers are to use the following checklist to classify individuals as independent contractors. If more than three questions are answered "yes," the manager will confer with human resources regarding the classification. (EE = Employees, IC = Independent Contractors)

Factors which show control:

	Yes/EE	No/IC	N/A
1. Worker must comply with instructions.	☐	☐	☐
2. Worker is trained by person hired.	☐	☐	☐
3. Worker's services are integrated in business.	☐	☐	☐
4. Worker must personally render services.	☐	☐	☐
5. Worker cannot hire or fire assistants.	☐	☐	☐
6. Work relationship is continuous or indefinite.	☐	☐	☐
7. Work hours are present.	☐	☐	☐
8. Worker must devote full time to this business.	☐	☐	☐
9. Work is done on the employer's premises.	☐	☐	☐
10. Worker cannot control order or sequence.	☐	☐	☐
11. Worker submits oral or written reports.	☐	☐	☐
12. Worker is paid at specific intervals.	☐	☐	☐
13. Worker's business expenses are reimbursed.	☐	☐	☐
14. Worker is provided with tools or materials.	☐	☐	☐
15. Worker has no significant investment.	☐	☐	☐
16. Worker has no opportunity for profit/loss.	☐	☐	☐
17. Worker is not engaged by many different firms.	☐	☐	☐
18. Worker does not offer services to public.	☐	☐	☐
19. Worker may be discharged by employer.	☐	☐	☐
20. Worker can terminate without liability.	☐	☐	☐

FIGURE 11-1 Independent Contractor

Source: Reprinted from www.HR.BLR.com with permission of the publisher *Business and Legal Resources Inc.*, 141 Mill Rock Road East, Old Saybrook, CT © 2004. BLR© (Business and Legal Resources, Inc.).

Penalties for the employer who misclassifies an employee as an independent contractor can be severe. For example, the employer can be liable retroactively for the IRS taxes that it did not withhold (plus penalties), as well as for overtime pay, unemployment compensation taxes, and back Social Security taxes plus interest. Microsoft paid almost $97 million to settle one such suit, for instance.[10]

The FLSA also sets a *minimum wage*, which sets a floor for employees covered by the act (and usually bumps up wages for practically all workers when Congress raises the minimum). The minimum wage for the majority of those covered by the act was $7.25 in 2009.[11] Many states have their own minimum wage laws. About 80 localities, including Boston and Chicago, require businesses that have contracts with the city to pay employees wages ranging from $8 to $12 an hour.[12] *Child labor provisions* prohibit employing minors between 16 and 18 years old in hazardous occupations, and carefully restrict employment of those under 16.

Exempt/Nonexempt Specific categories of employees are *exempt* from the FLSA or certain provisions of the act, and particularly from the act's overtime provisions—they are "exempt employees." A person's exemption depends on his or her responsibilities, duties, and salary. Bona fide executive, administrative (like office managers), and professional employees (like architects) are generally exempt from the minimum wage and overtime requirements of the act.[13] A white-collar worker earning more than $100,000 and performing any one exempt administrative, executive, or professional duty is automatically ineligible for overtime pay. Other employees can generally earn up to $23,660 per year and still automatically get overtime pay (so most employees earning less than $455 per week are nonexempt and earn overtime).[14] Figure 11-2 lists some examples of typically exempt and nonexempt jobs.

If an employee is exempt from the FLSA's minimum wage provisions, then he or she is also exempt from its overtime pay provisions. However, certain employees are *always* exempt from overtime pay provisions. They include, among others, agricultural employees, live-in household employees, taxicab drivers, and motion picture theater employees.[15]

Identifying exemptions is tricky. As noted, some jobs—for example, top managers and lawyers—are clearly exempt, while others—such as office workers earning less than $23,660 per year—are clearly nonexempt. Unfortunately, beyond the obvious categorizations, it's advisable to review the job before classifying it as exempt or nonexempt. Figure 11-3 presents a procedure for making this decision. In all but the clearest situations, carefully review the job description. Make sure, for instance, that the job currently does, in fact, require that the person perform, say, an exempt-type supervisory duty.[16]

FLSA exemption lawsuits are on the rise. For example, sales reps for a drug firm argue in one suit that the FLSA "outside salesperson" exemption doesn't cover them because they market and advise—not sell—drugs to doctors.[17] More "administrative secretaries" are arguing that the administrative exemption does not apply because they don't make decisions that influence their firms' finances. "Supervisors" are

FIGURE 11-2 Some Typical Exempt, Nonexempt Job Titles

Source: Exempt, Nonexempt Examples by Jeffrey Friedman, "The Fair Labor Standards Act Today: A Primer," *Compensation* (January/February 2002), p. 53, Reprinted by Permission of Sage Publications, Inc. Copyright © 2002, Sage Publications.

EXEMPT	NONEXEMPT
Attorneys	Paralegals
Physicians	Accounting clerks
Pharmacists	Newspaper writers
Engineers	Working supervisor
Teachers	Management trainees
Scientists	Secretaries
Computer systems analysts	Clerical employees
General managers	
Personnel directors	
Accountants	
Purchasing agents	

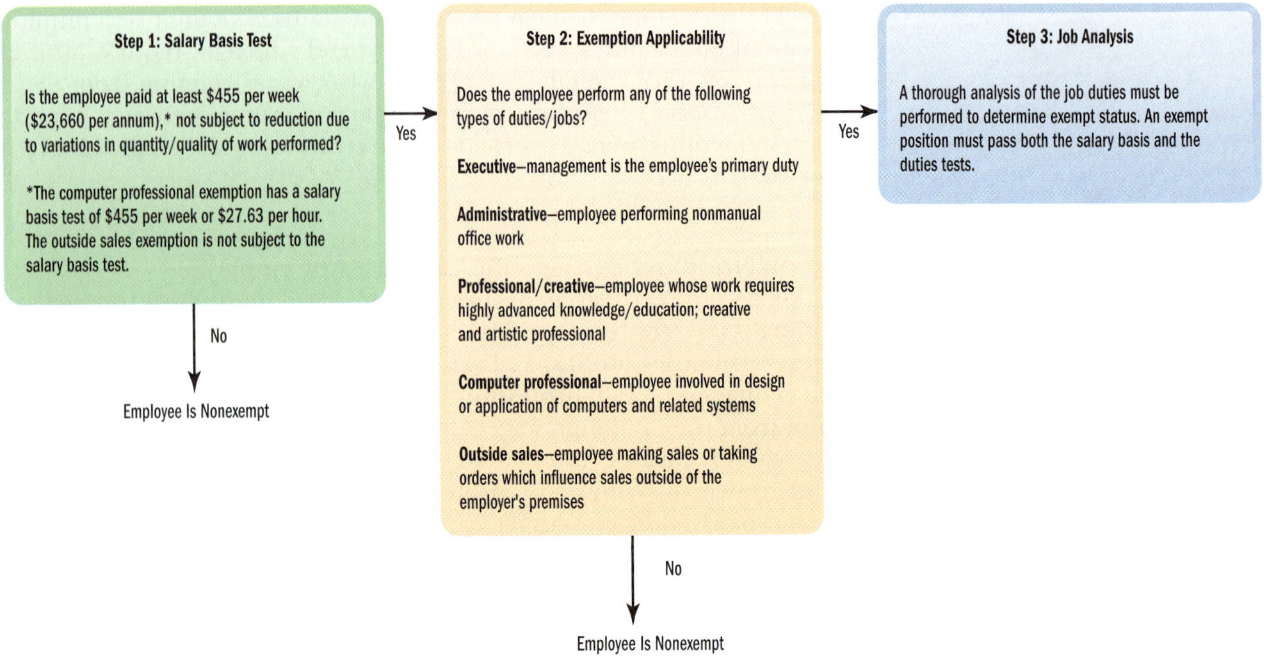

FIGURE 11-3 Who Is Exempt? Who Is Not Exempt?

saying they don't really themselves supervise two or more employees.[18] So, again, it's not the title; it is what the employees actually do.[19]

1963 Equal Pay Act The **Equal Pay Act**, an amendment to the Fair Labor Standards Act, states that employees of one sex may not be paid wages at a rate lower than that paid to employees of the opposite sex for doing roughly equivalent work. Specifically, if the work requires equal skills, effort, and responsibility and involves similar working conditions, employees of both sexes must receive equal pay, unless the differences in pay stem from a seniority system, a merit system, the quantity or quality of production, or "any factor other than sex."

Source: Courtesy of Michael Newman/PhotoEdit Inc.

Two executives discuss a print layout; one happens to be in a wheelchair. Federal law mandates that the wheelchair-bound employee not suffer discrimination in compensation.

1974 Employee Retirement Income Security Act The **Employee Retirement Income Security Act (ERISA)** provided for the creation of government-run, employer-financed corporations to protect employees against the failure of their employers' pension plans. In addition, it sets regulations regarding vesting rights (*vesting* refers to the equity or ownership the employees build up in their pension plans should their employment terminate before retirement). ERISA also regulates *portability rights* (the transfer of an employee's vested rights from one organization to another). It also contains fiduciary standards to prevent dishonesty in pension plan funding.

Other Legislation Affecting Compensation Various other laws influence compensation decisions. For example, the *Age Discrimination in Employment Act* prohibits age discrimination against employees who are 40 years of age and older in all aspects of employment, including compensation.[20] The *Americans with Disabilities Act* prohibits discrimination against qualified persons with disabilities in all aspects of employment, including compensation. The *Family and Medical Leave Act* aims to entitle eligible employees, both men and women, to take up to 12 weeks of unpaid, job-protected leave for the birth of a child or for the care of a child, spouse, or parent. And various executive orders require employers that are federal government contractors or subcontractors to not discriminate, and to take affirmative action in certain employment areas, including compensation.

Each state has its own *workers' compensation laws.* Among other things, these aim to provide prompt, sure, and reasonable income to victims of work-related accidents. The *Social Security Act of 1935* (as amended) provides for unemployment compensation for workers unemployed through no fault of their own for up to 26 weeks, and for retirement benefits. (We'll discuss Social Security benefits in Chapter 13.) The federal wage garnishment law limits the amount of an employee's earnings that employers can withhold (garnish) per week, and protects the worker from discharge due to garnishment.

Union Influences on Compensation Decisions

Unions and labor relations laws also influence pay plan design. The National Labor Relations Act of 1935 (Wagner Act) and related legislation and court decisions legitimized the labor movement. It gave unions legal protection, and granted employees the right to unionize, to bargain collectively, and to engage in concerted activities for the purpose of collective bargaining or other mutual aid or protection. Historically, the wage rate has been the main issue in collective bargaining. However, unions also negotiate other pay-related issues, including time off with pay, income security (for those in industries with periodic layoffs), cost-of-living adjustments, and health care benefits.

The Wagner Act created the National Labor Relations Board (NLRB) to oversee employer practices and ensure that employees receive their rights. Its rulings underscore the need to involve union officials in developing the compensation package. For example, employers must give the union a written explanation of the employer's "wage curves"—the graph that relates job to pay rate. The union is also entitled to know its members' salaries.[21]

Competitive Strategy, Corporate Policies, and Compensation

The compensation plan should advance the firm's strategic aims—management should produce an *aligned reward strategy.* This means creating a bundle of rewards—a total reward package including wages, incentives, and benefits—that aims to produce the employee behaviors the firm needs to support and achieve its competitive strategy.[22] Table 11-1 lists the sorts of questions to ask here.

The employer's compensation strategy will manifest itself in *pay policies.* For example, a top hospital like Johns Hopkins might have a policy of starting nurses at a wage 20% above the prevailing market wage.

TABLE 11-1 Developing an Aligned Reward Strategy

Questions to Ask:

1. What must our company do (for instance in terms of improving customer service), to be successful in fulfilling its mission or achieving its desired competitive position?
2. What are the employee behaviors or actions necessary to successfully implement this competitive strategy?
3. What compensation programs should we use to reinforce those behaviors? What should be the purpose of each program in reinforcing each desired behavior?
4. What measurable requirements should each compensation program meet to be deemed successful in fulfilling its purpose?
5. How well do our current compensation programs match these requirements?

Source: Adapted from Jack Dolmat-Connell, "Developing a Reward Strategy That Delivers Shareholder and Employee Value," *Compensation & Benefits Review*, March–April 1999, p. 51.

Equal Pay Act (1963)
An amendment to the Fair Labor Standards Act designed to require equal pay for women doing the same work as men.

Employee Retirement Income Security Act (ERISA)
The law that provides government protection of pensions for all employees with company pension plans. It also regulates vesting rights (employees who leave before retirement may claim compensation from the pension plan).

IBM Example IBM provides a classic example of how managers use compensation policy to support their strategic aims.[23] When he became CEO in the1990s, Louis Gerstner believed IBM's employees had become too complacent. He instituted four new incentive and other pay policies to focus his employees more on the competition. These policies were:

1. **Pay to market.** The company switched from its previous single pay plan (for non-sales employees) to different pay plans and merit budgets for different job families (accountants, engineers, and so on). This enabled IBM to pay different job families in a more market-oriented way.
2. **Fewer, "broadband" jobs.** IBM's old system slotted IBM's jobs into 24 narrow wage grades. This tended to focus employees' attention on doing just their relatively narrow jobs. The new plan slotted all jobs into one of just 10 grades based on three factors (skills, leadership requirements, and scope/impact). In the United States, the number of separate job titles dropped from more than 5,000 to fewer than 1,200. Each employee ended up with a broader set of job duties.
3. **Let managers manage.** The previous compensation plan based raises on a complex formula that linked performance appraisal scores to salary increases measured in tenths of a percent. The new system was streamlined. Managers get a budget and some coaching, the essence of which is: "Either differentiate the pay you give to stars versus acceptable performers or the stars won't be around long."
4. **Incentivize employees.** As IBM was floundering in the early 1990s, every nonexecutive employee's cash compensation (outside the sales division) consisted of base salary (plus overtime, shift premiums, and some other adjustments). Soon after he arrived, Gerstner had all employees paid in part based on incentives.

Types of Pay Policies As at IBM, managers need to formulate pay policies covering a range of issues. One is whether to emphasize *seniority* or *performance*. For example, it takes 18 years for a U.S. federal employee to progress from step 1 to step 9 of the government's pay scale. Seniority-based pay may be advantageous to the extent that seniority is an objective standard. One disadvantage is that top performers may get the same raises as poor ones. Seniority-based pay might seem to be a relic reserved for some government agencies and unionized firms. However, one recent survey found that 60% of employees responding thought high-seniority employees got the most pay. Only about 35% said their companies paid high performers more.[24]

How to distinguish between *high and low performers* is a related policy issue. For example, for many years Payless ShoeSource was paternal in how it distributed raises—it paid everyone about the same. However, after seeing its market share drop over several years, management decided on a turnaround plan. The plan necessitated revising its compensation policies to differentiate more aggressively between top performers and others.[25] Other pay policies usually cover *how to award salary increases and promotions, overtime pay, probationary pay, leaves for military service, jury duty,* and *holidays.* Of course, the level of economic activity will also influence how much employers should pay, as the accompanying "Managing HR in Challenging Times" feature explains.

Managing HR in Challenging Times

Salary and Incentives in Tough Times

Not surprisingly, one way that employers deal with economically challenging times is by cutting back on salary increases and merit pay. Surveys by human resource management consulting companies such as Hewitt Associates and Mercer showed that as the recent recession deepened, at least half the employers in America (and more abroad) were planning to cut salary increases. On average, the survey suggested that salaried exempt employees' raises would drop from about 3.8% in

2008 to about 2.5% in 2009, while about 10% of U.S. employers surveyed were instituting pay freezes.

Interestingly though, the challenging times were also prompting employers to pay closer attention to their highest performing employees. For example, many were establishing special funds to reward high-performing employees with such items as long-term equity grants and retention bonuses.[26]

Pay Raises Employers compute pay raises in one of two ways. Many have *merit pay* policies. We'll discuss these in Chapter 12 (Incentives), but the basic idea is to tie each employee's annual raise to the employee's performance. Some employers award raises *across-the-board* (such as a 3% raise to all employees). The latter avoids the aggravation that often accompanies awarding differential raises, helps keep all employees even with inflation, and may even be required by a union or civil-service agreement. The problem is that higher-performing employees usually should earn more.

Salary Compression How to handle salary compression is a key policy issue. **Salary compression** means longer-term employees' salaries are lower than those of workers entering the firm today, and is a creature of inflation. Prices (and starting salaries) go up faster than the company's salaries, and firms need a policy to handle it. On the one hand, you don't want to treat current employees unfairly or to have them leave with their expertise. However, mediocre performance, not salary compression, may explain some low salaries. One policy is to install a more aggressive merit pay program. Other policies allow supervisors to recommend "equity" adjustments for selected employees who are highly valued victims of pay compression.

Geography How to account for geographic differences in cost of living is another big pay policy issue. For example, the average base pay for an executive secretary ranges from $37,300 in Albuquerque, New Mexico, to $41,900 (Tampa, Florida), $59,800 (New York, New York), and $60,100 (San Francisco, California).[27]

Employers handle cost-of-living differentials in several ways. One is to give the transferred person a nonrecurring payment, usually in a lump sum or perhaps spread over 1 to 3 years. Others pay a differential for ongoing costs in addition to a one-time allocation. For example, one employer pays a differential of $6,000 per year to people earning $35,000 to $45,000 whom it transfers from Atlanta to Minneapolis. Others simply raise the employee's base salary.

The problem is more complicated when you're sending employees overseas. Most multinational enterprises set expatriates' salaries according to their home-country base pay. (Thus, a French manager assigned to Kiev by a U.S. multinational will generally have a base salary that reflects the salary structure in the manager's home country, in this case, France.) In addition, the person typically gets allowances including cost-of-living, relocation, housing, education, and hardship allowances (the latter for countries with a relatively hard quality of life, such as Zambia).[28] The employer also usually pays any extra tax burdens resulting from taxes the manager is liable for over and above those he or she would have to pay in the home country.

Equity and Its Impact on Pay Rates

In studies at Emory University, researchers investigated how capuchin monkeys reacted to inequitable pay. They trained monkeys to trade pebbles for food. Some monkeys got grapes in return for pebbles; others got cucumber slices. Those receiving

salary compression
A salary inequity problem, generally caused by inflation, resulting in longer-term employees in a position earning less than workers entering the firm today.

the sweeter grapes willingly traded in their pebbles. But if a monkey receiving a cucumber slice saw one of its neighbors get grapes, it slammed down the pebble or refused to eat the cucumber.[29] The moral seems to be that even lower primates are genetically programmed to demand fair treatment when it comes to pay.

Equity Theory of Motivation Higher up the primate line, *the equity theory of motivation* postulates that people are strongly motivated to maintain a balance between what they perceive as their inputs or contributions, and their rewards. Equity theory states that if a person perceives an inequity, a tension or drive will develop in the person's mind, and the person will be motivated to reduce or eliminate the tension and perceived inequity. Research tends to support equity theory, particularly as it applies to people who are underpaid.[30] One recent study found that turnover of retail buyers is significantly lower when the buyers perceive fair treatment in the amount or rewards and in the methods by which employers allocate rewards.[31]

With respect to compensation, managers should address four forms of equity: *external, internal, individual,* and *procedural.*[32]

- *External equity* refers to how a job's pay rate in one company compares to the job's pay rate in other companies.
- *Internal equity* refers to how fair the job's pay rate is when compared to other jobs within the same company (for instance, is the sales manager's pay fair, when compared to what the production manager is earning?).
- *Individual equity* refers to the fairness of an individual's pay as compared with what his or her coworkers are earning for the same or very similar jobs within the company, based on each individual's performance.
- *Procedural equity* refers to the "perceived fairness of the processes and procedures used to make decisions regarding the allocation of pay."[33]

Addressing Equity Issues Managers use various methods to address each of these equity issues. For example, they use salary surveys (surveys of what other employers are paying) to monitor and maintain external equity. They use job analysis and job evaluation comparisons of each job to maintain internal equity. They use performance appraisal and incentive pay to maintain individual equity. And they use communications, grievance mechanisms, and employees' participation in developing the company's pay plan to help ensure that employees view the pay process as transparent and procedurally fair.

Some firms administer surveys to monitor employees' pay satisfaction. Questions typically include, "How satisfied are you with your pay?" and "What factors do you believe are used when your pay is determined?" In addressing pay dissatisfaction, employers need to solve the right problem. Potential sources of dissatisfaction include amount of pay and benefits, and how both raises and the overall pay plan are administered. Addressing the wrong issue may mean the employees remain dissatisfied.[34]

When inequities do arise, conflicts ensue. To head off discussions that might prompt feelings of internal inequity, some firms maintain strict secrecy over pay rates, with mixed results. But for external equity, online pay sites like Salary.com make it easy for employees to discover that they could earn more elsewhere. And one study recently found that it's not just paying too little that can reduce morale. Overpaying people relative to what they think they're worth can backfire too, perhaps "due to feelings of guilt or discomfort."[35]

ESTABLISHING PAY RATES

The process of establishing pay rates while ensuring external, internal, and (to some extent) procedural equity consists of five steps:

1. Conduct a salary survey of what other employers are paying for comparable jobs (to help ensure external equity).

2. Determine the worth of each job in your organization through job evaluation (to ensure internal equity).
3. Group similar jobs into pay grades.
4. Price each pay grade by using wave curves.
5. Fine-tune pay rates.

We start with the salary survey.

Step 1. The Salary Survey

It's difficult to set pay rates if you don't know what others are paying, so **salary surveys**—surveys of what others are paying—play a big role in pricing jobs. Virtually every employer conducts at least an informal telephone, newspaper, or Internet salary survey.[36]

Employers use salary surveys in three ways. First, they use survey data to price **benchmark jobs**. Benchmark jobs are the anchor jobs around which they slot their other jobs, based on each job's relative worth to the firm. (*Job evaluation,* explained next, helps determine the relative worth of each job.) Second, employers typically price 20% or more of their positions directly in the marketplace (rather than relative to the firm's benchmark jobs), based on a formal or informal survey of what comparable firms are paying for comparable jobs. (Google might do this for jobs like Web programmer, whose salaries fluctuate widely and often.) Third, surveys also collect data on benefits like insurance, sick leave, and vacations to provide a basis for decisions regarding employee benefits.

Salary surveys can be formal or informal. *Informal* phone or Internet surveys are good for checking specific issues, such as when a bank wants to confirm the salary at which to advertise a newly open teller's job, or whether some banks are really paying tellers an incentive. Some large employers can afford to send out their own *formal* surveys to collect compensation information from other employers. Most of these ask about things like number of employees, overtime policies, starting salaries, and paid vacations.

Commercial, Professional, and Government Salary Surveys

Many employers use surveys published by consulting firms, professional associations, or government agencies. For example, the U.S. Department of Labor's Bureau of Labor Statistics' (BLS) *National Compensation Survey (NCS)* provides comprehensive reports of occupational earnings, compensation cost trends, and benefits (http://www.bls.gov/bls/wages.htm).

Detailed occupational earnings are available from this survey for over 800 occupations in the United States, regions, states, and many metropolitan areas (http://stats.bls.gov/oes/current/oes_nat.htm). The Current Employment Statistics survey is a monthly survey of the payroll records of business establishments that provides data on earnings of production and nonsupervisory workers at the national level. This provides information about earnings as well as production bonuses, commissions, and cost-of-living increases. The National Compensation Survey–Benefits provides information on the share of workers who participate in specified benefits, such as health care, retirement plans, and paid vacations. These data also show the details of those benefits, such as amounts of paid leave. Internationally, the BLS reports comparative hourly compensation costs in local currencies and U.S. dollars for production workers and all employees in manufacturing in its International Labor Comparisons Tables.

salary survey
A survey aimed at determining prevailing wage rates. A good salary survey provides specific wage rates for specific jobs. Formal written questionnaire surveys are the most comprehensive, but telephone surveys and newspaper ads are also sources of information.

benchmark job
A job that is used to anchor the employer's pay scale and around which other jobs are arranged in order of relative worth.

Private consulting and/or executive recruiting companies like Hay Associates, Heidrick and Struggles, and Hewitt Associates publish data covering compensation for top and middle management and members of boards of directors. Professional organizations like the Society for Human Resource Management and the Financial Executives Institute publish surveys of compensation practices among members of their associations.

Watson Wyatt Data Services of Rochelle Park, New Jersey, publishes several compensation surveys.[37] Its top management compensation surveys cover dozens of top positions, including chief executive officer, top real estate executive, top financial executive, top sales executive, and top claims executive, all categorized by function and industry. Watson Wyatt also offers middle management compensation surveys, supervisory management compensation surveys, sales and marketing personnel surveys, professional and scientific personnel surveys, and surveys of technician trades, skilled trades, and office personnel, among others. The surveys generally cost about $700 each, but can help employers avoid the dual hazards of (1) paying too much or (2) suffering turnover due to uncompetitive pay.

Using the Internet to Do Compensation Surveys A rapidly expanding array of Internet-based options makes it easy for anyone to access published compensation survey information. Table 11-2 shows some popular salary survey Web sites.

Many of these sites, such as Salary.com, provide national salary levels for jobs that the site then arithmetically adjusts to each locale based on cost-of-living formulas. To get a real-time picture of what employers in your area are actually paying for, say, accounting clerks, it's useful to access the online Internet sites of one or two of your local newspapers. For example, the *South Florida Sun-Sentinel* (and many papers) uses a site called careerbuilder.com. It lists career opportunities—in other words, just about all the jobs listed in the newspaper by category and, in many instances, their wage rates (www.sun-sentinel.com/classified/jobs). From this listing, you'll find jobs listed for "Accounts receivable clerks—$10.00 per hour," "Accounting clerk—$25k," "Accounting clerk—credit clerk, to $22k," and "Accounts payable clerk, $22–26k," among many others. Switching to the *Miami Herald*'s Web site (http://www.miamiherald.com/jobs/) similarly takes you to the local careerbuilder site, and a list of several dozen related-job listings. For example, there is a "Payroll clerk, Doral area, $25k," an "Accounting clerk—City of Hialeah starting at $594 biweekly," and "Accounting assistant—Miami Lakes area, to $29k."

TABLE 11-2 Some Pay Data Web Sites

Sponsor	Internet Address	What It Provides	Downside
Salary.com	Salary.com	Salary by job and zip code, plus job and description, for hundreds of jobs	Adapts national averages by applying local cost-of-living differences
Wageweb	www.wageweb.com	Average salaries for more than 150 clerical, professional, and managerial jobs	Charges for breakdowns by industry, location, etc.
U.S. Office of Personnel Management	www.opm.gov/oca/09Tables/index.asp	Salaries and wages for U.S. government jobs, by location	Limited to U.S. government jobs
Job Smart	http://jobstar.org/tools/salary/sal-prof.php	Profession-specific salary surveys	Necessary to review numerous salary surveys for each profession
cnnmoney.com	cnnmoney.com	Input your current salary and city, and this gives you comparable salary in destination city	Based on national averages adapted to cost-of-living differences

The Internet also provides numerous fee-based sources of international salary data. For example, William M. Mercer, Inc. (www.mercer.com) publishes an annual global compensation planning report summarizing compensation trends for more than 40 countries plus representative pay data for four common benchmark jobs.[38]

As we said, employers usually use salary survey data to price benchmark jobs, around which other jobs are then slotted based on the job's relative worth. Determining the relative worth of a job is the purpose of job evaluation, which we address next.

2 Define and give an example of how to conduct a job evaluation.

Step 2. Job Evaluation

Job evaluation aims to determine a job's relative worth. The job evaluation is a formal and systematic comparison of jobs to determine the worth of one job relative to another. Job evaluation eventually results in a wage or salary structure or hierarchy (this shows the pay rate for various jobs or groups of jobs). The basic principle of job evaluation is this: Jobs that require greater qualifications, more responsibilities, and more complex job duties should receive more pay than jobs with lesser requirements.[39] The basic procedure is to compare the jobs in relation to one another—for example, in terms of required effort, responsibility, and skills. Suppose you know (based on your salary survey) how to price key benchmark jobs, and then use job evaluation to determine the relative worth of all the other jobs in your firm relative to these key jobs. You are then well on your way to being able to price all the jobs in your organization equitably.

Compensable Factors

You can use two basic approaches to compare several jobs. First, you can take an intuitive approach. You might decide that one job is more important than another and not dig any deeper into why. As an alternative, you could compare the jobs by focusing on certain basic factors the jobs have in common. Compensation management specialists call these **compensable factors**. They are the factors that establish how the jobs compare to one another, and that determine the pay for each job.

Some employers develop their own compensable factors. However, most use factors popularized by packaged job evaluation systems or by federal legislation. For example, the Equal Pay Act emphasizes four compensable factors—skills, effort, responsibility, and working conditions. The method popularized by the Hay consulting firm emphasizes three factors: know-how, problem solving, and accountability. Walmart bases its wage structure on knowledge, problem-solving skills, and accountability requirements.

Identifying compensable factors plays a central role in job evaluation. You usually compare each job with all comparable jobs using the same compensable factors. However, the compensable factors you use depend on the job and the job evaluation method. For example, you might choose to include "decision making" for a manager's job, though it might be inappropriate for a cleaner's job.[40]

Preparing for the Job Evaluation

Job evaluation is a judgmental process and demands close cooperation among supervisors, HR specialists, and employees and union representatives. The main steps include identifying the need for the program, getting cooperation, and then choosing an evaluation committee. The committee then performs the actual evaluation.

Identifying the need for job evaluation should not be difficult. For example, dissatisfaction reflected in high turnover, work stoppages, or arguments may result from paying employees different rates for similar jobs. Managers may express uneasiness

job evaluation
A systematic comparison done in order to determine the worth of one job relative to another.

compensable factor
A fundamental, compensable element of a job, such as skills, effort, responsibility, and working conditions.

with an informal way of assigning pay rates, accurately sensing that a more systematic assignment would be more equitable.

Next (since employees may fear that a systematic evaluation of their jobs may reduce their pay rates), *getting employees to cooperate* in the evaluation is important. You can tell employees that because of the impending job evaluation program, pay rate decisions will no longer be made just by management whim; that job evaluation will provide a mechanism for considering the complaints they have been expressing; and that no current employee's rate will be adversely affected because of the job evaluation.

Third, *choose a job evaluation committee.* There are two reasons for doing so. First, those evaluating jobs should include several people who are familiar with the jobs in question, each of whom may have a different perspective regarding the nature of the jobs. Second, if the committee is composed at least partly of employees, the committee approach can foster greater employee acceptance of the job evaluation results.

So the composition of the committee is important. The group usually consists of about five members, most of whom are employees. Management has the right to serve on such committees, but employees may view this with suspicion. However, a human resource specialist can usually be justified as perhaps being more impartial than line managers, and can provide expert assistance. Perhaps have this person serve in a non-voting capacity. Union representation is possible. In most cases, though, the union's position is that it is accepting the results of the job evaluation only as an initial decision and is reserving the right to appeal actual job pricing decisions through grievance or bargaining channels.[41] Once appointed, each committee member should receive a manual explaining the job evaluation process and instructions that explain how to conduct the job evaluation.

The evaluation committee performs three main functions. First, it usually identifies 10 or 15 key *benchmark jobs.* These will be the first jobs they'll evaluate and will serve as the anchors or benchmarks against which the relative importance or value of all other jobs can be compared. Next, the committee may select *compensable factors* (although the human resources department will usually choose these as part of the process of determining the specific job evaluation technique the firm will use). Finally, the committee performs its most important function—actually *evaluating the worth of each job.* For this, the committee will probably use one of the following methods: ranking, job classification, point method, or factor comparison.

Job Evaluation Methods: Ranking The simplest job evaluation method ranks each job relative to all other jobs, usually based on some overall factor like "job difficulty." There are several steps in the job **ranking method**.

The job evaluation committee typically includes at least several employees, and has the important task of evaluating the worth of each job using compensable factors.

Source: Courtesy of Rob Lewine Photography.

1. **Obtain job information.** Job analysis is the first step: Job descriptions for each job are prepared, and the information they contain about the job's duties is usually the basis for ranking jobs. (Sometimes job specifications are also prepared. However, the ranking method usually ranks jobs based on the whole job, rather than on several compensable factors. Therefore, job specifications, which tend to list job demands in terms of compensable factors such as problem solving, decision making, and skills, are not as important with this method as they are for other job evaluation methods.)
2. **Select and group jobs.** It is usually not practical to make a single ranking for all jobs in an organization. The usual procedure is to rank jobs by department or in clusters (such as factory workers or clerical workers). This eliminates the need for direct comparison of, say, factory jobs and clerical jobs.
3. **Select compensable factors.** In the ranking method, it is common to use just one factor (such as job difficulty) and to rank jobs based on the whole job. Regardless of the number of factors you choose, it's advisable to explain the definition of the factor(s) to the evaluators carefully so that they all evaluate the jobs consistently.
4. **Rank jobs.** For example, give each rater a set of index cards, each of which contains a brief description of a job. Then they rank these cards from lowest to highest. Some managers use an "alternation ranking method" for making the procedure more accurate. Here you take the cards, first choosing the highest and the lowest, then the next highest and next lowest, and so forth, until you've ranked all the cards. Table 11-3 illustrates a job ranking. Jobs in this small health facility rank from orderly up to office manager. The corresponding pay scales are on the right. After ranking, it is possible to slot additional jobs between those already ranked and to assign an appropriate wage rate.
5. **Combine ratings.** Usually, several raters rank the jobs independently. Then the rating committee (or the employer) can simply average the raters' rankings.

This is the simplest job evaluation method, as well as the easiest to explain. And it usually takes less time than other methods.

Some of its drawbacks derive more from how it's used than from the method itself. For example, there's a tendency to rely too heavily on "guesstimates" (of things like overall difficulty), since ranking usually does not use compensable factors. Similarly, ranking provides no yardstick for quantifying the value of one job relative to another. For example, job number 4 may in fact be five times "more valuable" than job number 5, but with the ranking method all you know is that one job ranks higher than the other. Ranking is usually more appropriate for small employers that can't afford the time or expense of developing a more elaborate system.

TABLE 11-3 Job Ranking by Olympia Health Care

Ranking Order	Annual Pay Scale
1. Office manager	$43,000
2. Chief nurse	42,500
3. Bookkeeper	34,000
4. Nurse	32,500
5. Cook	31,000
6. Nurse's aide	28,500
7. Orderly	25,500

ranking method
The simplest method of job evaluation that involves ranking each job relative to all other jobs, usually based on overall difficulty.

Job Evaluation Methods: Job Classification **Job classification** (or **job grading**) is a simple, widely used method in which raters categorize jobs into groups; all the jobs in each group are of roughly the same value for pay purposes. The groups are called **classes** if they contain similar jobs or **grades** if they contain jobs that are similar in difficulty but otherwise different. Thus, in the federal government's pay grade system, a "press secretary" and a "fire chief" might both be graded "GS-10" (GS stands for "General Schedule"). On the other hand, in its job class system, the state of Florida might classify all "secretary IIs" in one class, all "maintenance engineers" in another, and so forth.

In practice, there are several ways to categorize jobs. One is to write class or grade descriptions (similar to job descriptions) and place jobs into classes or grades based on how well they fit these descriptions. A second is to write a set of compensable factor-based rules for each class (for instance, how much independent judgment, skill, physical effort, and so on, does the class of jobs require?). Then categorize the jobs according to these rules.

The most popular procedure is to choose compensable factors and then develop class or grade descriptions for each class or grade in terms of the amount or level of the compensable factor(s) in those jobs. For example, the U.S. government's classification system uses the following compensable factors: (1) difficulty and variety of work, (2) supervision received and exercised, (3) judgment exercised, (4) originality required, (5) nature and purpose of interpersonal work relationships, (6) responsibility, (7) experience, and (8) knowledge required. Based on these compensable factors, raters write a **grade definition** like that in Figure 11-4. This one shows one grade description (GS-7) for the federal government's pay grade system. Then the evaluation committee reviews all job descriptions and slots each job into its appropriate grade, by comparing each job description to the rules in each grade description. For instance, the federal government system classifies the positions automotive mechanic, welder, electrician, and machinist in grade GS-10.

The classification method has several advantages. The main one is that most employers usually end up grouping jobs into classes anyway, regardless of the evaluation method they use. They do this to avoid having to work with and price separately dozens or hundreds of jobs. Of course, the job classification automatically groups the employer's jobs into classes. The disadvantages are that it is difficult to write the class or grade descriptions, and considerable judgment is required to apply them. Yet many employers use this method with success.

Job Evaluation Methods: Point Method The **point method** is a quantitative technique. It involves identifying (1) several compensable factors, each having several degrees, as well as (2) the degree to which each of these factors is present in the job. Assume there are five degrees of "responsibility" a job could contain. Further, assume you assign a different number of points to each degree of each factor. Once the evaluation committee determines the degree to which each compensable factor (like "responsibility" and "effort") is present in the job, it can calculate a total point value for the job by adding up the corresponding points for each factor. The result is a quantitative point rating for each job. The point

FIGURE 11-4 Example of a Grade Level Definition

Source: www.opm.gov/fedclass/gscler.pdf. Accessed May 18, 2007.

Grade	Nature of Assignment	Level of Responsibility
GS-7	Performs specialized duties in a defined functional or program area involving a wide variety of problems or situations; develops information, identifies interrelationships, and takes actions consistent with objectives of the function or program served.	Work is assigned in terms of objectives, priorities, and deadlines; the employee works independently in resolving most conflicts; completed work is evaluated for conformance to policy; guidelines, such as regulations, precedent cases, and policy statements require considerable interpretation and adaptation.

method is probably the most widely used job evaluation method; the appendix to this chapter explains it in detail.

Job Evaluation Methods: Factor Comparison The **factor comparison method** is a refinement of the ranking method. With the ranking method, you generally look at each job as an entity and rank the jobs on some overall factor like job difficulty. With the factor comparison method, you rank each job several times—once for each of several compensable factors. For example, you might first rank jobs in terms of the compensable factor "skill." Then rank them according to their "mental requirements," and so forth. Then combine the rankings for each job into an overall numerical rating for the job. This too is a widely used method, also found in more detail in the appendix to this chapter.

Computerized Job Evaluations Using more quantitative job evaluation methods such as point or factor comparison can be time-consuming. Accumulating the information about "how much" of each compensable factor the job contains involves a tedious process in which evaluation committees debate the level of each compensable factor in a job. They then write down their consensus judgments and manually compute each job's point values or rankings.

Computer-aided job evaluation can streamline this process. Most of these computerized systems have two main components. There is, first, a structured questionnaire. This contains items such as "enter total number of employees who report to this position." Second, all such systems use statistical models. These allow the computer program to price jobs more or less automatically, by assigning points or factor comparison rankings to things like number of employees reporting to the positions, pay rates of benchmark jobs, and current pay.

3 Explain in detail how to establish pay rates.

Step 3. Group Similar Jobs into Pay Grades

Once the committee has used job evaluation to determine the relative worth of each job, it can turn to the task of assigning pay rates to each job; however, it will usually want to first group jobs into **pay grades**.[42] Of course, it could just assign pay rates to each individual job. But for a large employer, such a plan would be difficult to administer, since there might be different pay rates for hundreds or even thousands of jobs. And even in smaller organizations, there's a tendency to try to simplify wage and salary structures as much as possible. Therefore, the committee will probably group similar jobs (in terms of their ranking or number of points, for instance) into grades for pay purposes. So, instead of having to deal with hundreds of pay rates, it might only have to focus on, say, 10 or 12.

A pay grade is comprised of jobs of approximately equal difficulty or importance as established by job evaluation. If the committee used the point method, then the pay grade consists of jobs falling within a range of points. With the ranking method, the grade consists of all jobs that fall within two or three ranks. The classification method automatically categorizes jobs into classes or grades. (With the factor

job classification (or grading) method
A method for categorizing jobs into groups.

classes
Grouping jobs based on a set of rules for each group or class, such as amount of independent judgment, skill, physical effort, and so forth, required. Classes usually contain similar jobs.

grades
A job classification system like the class system, although grades often contain dissimilar jobs, such as secretaries, mechanics, and firefighters. Grade descriptions are written based on compensable factors listed in classification systems.

grade definition
Written descriptions of the level of, say, responsibility and knowledge required by jobs in each grade. Similar jobs can then be combined into grades or classes.

point method
The job evaluation method in which a number of compensable factors are identified and then the degree to which each of these factors is present on the job is determined.

factor comparison method
A widely used method of ranking jobs according to a variety of skill and difficulty factors, then adding up these rankings to arrive at an overall numerical rating for each given job.

pay grade
A pay grade is comprised of jobs of approximately equal difficulty.

comparison method, the grade consists of a specified range of pay rates, as the appendix to this chapter explains.) Ten to 16 grades per "job cluster" (a *cluster* is a logical grouping, such as factory jobs, clerical jobs, and so on) are now common. However, as we'll explain shortly, there's a trend toward including more jobs—and a broader range of jobs—within each cluster.

Step 4. Price Each Pay Grade—Wage Curves

The next step is to assign pay rates to your pay grades. (Of course, if you chose not to slot jobs into pay grades, you would have to assign individual pay rates to each individual job.) You'll typically use a *wage curve* to help assign pay rates to each pay grade (or to each job).

The **wage curve** shows the pay rates currently paid for jobs in each pay grade, relative to the points or rankings assigned to each job or grade by the job evaluation. Figure 11-5 presents an example. Note that it shows pay rates on the vertical axis, and pay grades (in terms of points) along the horizontal axis. The purpose of the wage curve is to show the relationships between (1) the value of the job as determined by one of the job evaluation methods and (2) the current average pay rates for your grades.

The pay rates on the wage curve are traditionally those now paid by the employer. However, if there is reason to believe the current pay rates are out of step with the market rates for these jobs, choose benchmark jobs within each pay grade, and price them via a compensation survey. These new market-based pay rates then replace the current rates on the wage curve. Then slot in your other jobs (and their pay rates) around the benchmark jobs.[43]

Here is how to price jobs with a wage curve. First, find the average pay for each pay grade, since each of the pay grades consists of several jobs. Next, plot the average pay rates for each pay grade as was done in Figure 11-5. Then fit a line, called a *wage curve*, through the points just plotted. You can do this freehand or by using a statistical method. Finally, price the jobs. For this, wages along the wage line are the target wages or salary rates for the jobs in each pay grade. If the current rates being paid for any of your jobs or grades fall well above or below the wage line, raises or a pay freeze for that job may be in order. Your next step, then, is to fine-tune your pay rates.

Step 5. Fine-Tune Pay Rates

Fine-tuning involves (1) developing *pay ranges* and (2) correcting *out-of-line rates.*

Developing Pay Ranges

Most employers do not pay just one rate for all jobs in a particular pay grade. For example, GE Medical won't want to pay all its accounting

FIGURE 11-5 Plotting a Wage Curve

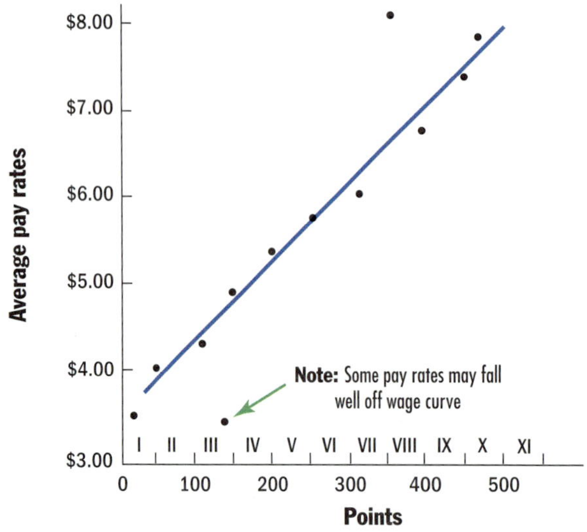

clerks, from beginners to long tenure, at the same rate. Instead, employers develop vertical pay (or "rate") ranges for each of the horizontal pay grades (or pay classes). These **pay ranges** often appear as vertical boxes within each grade, showing minimum, maximum, and midpoint pay rates for that grade, as in Figure 11-6. (Specialists call this graph a *wage structure.* It graphically depicts the range of pay rates—in this case, per hour—paid for each pay grade.) Alternatively, you may depict the pay range for each class or grade as steps or levels. Here you will have specific corresponding pay rates for each step within each grade in tabular form. Table 11-4 shows the pay rates and steps for some federal government grades. As of the time of this pay schedule, for instance, employees in positions classified in grade GS-10 could be paid annual salaries between $45,095 and $58,622, depending on the level or step at which they were hired into the grade, the amount of time they were in the grade, and their merit increases (if any).

The wage line or curve usually anchors the pay rate for each pay range. The firm might then arbitrarily decide on a maximum and minimum rate for each grade, such as 15% above and below the wage line. As an alternative, some employers allow the pay range for each grade to become wider (covering more pay rates) for the higher pay ranges, reflecting the greater demands and performance variability inherent in more complex jobs. As in Figure 11-6, most employers structure their pay ranges to overlap a bit, so an employee in one grade who has more experience or seniority may earn more than an entry-level position in the next higher pay grade.

FIGURE 11-6 Wage Structure

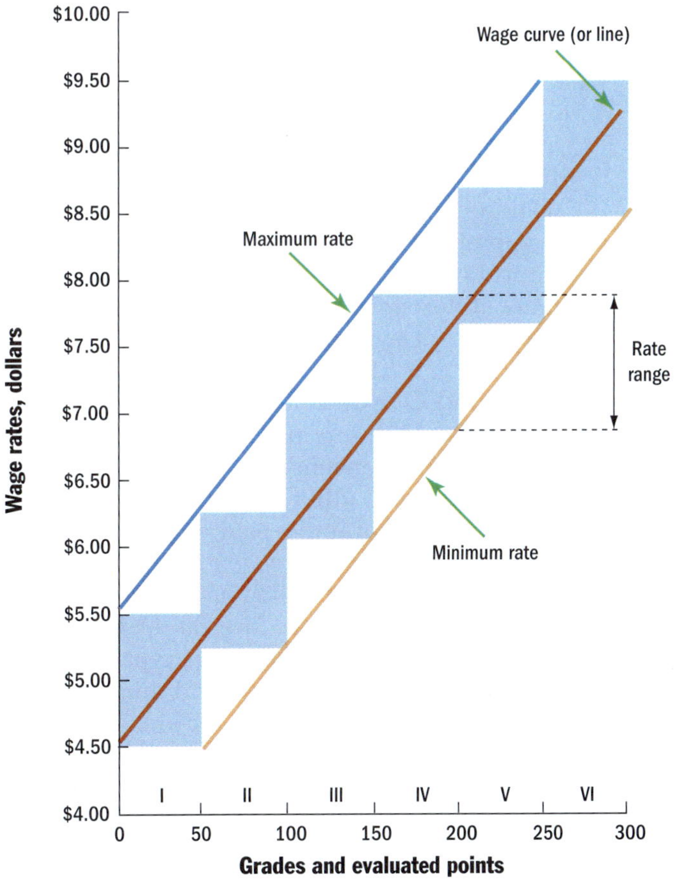

wage curve
Shows the relationship between the value of the job and the average wage paid for this job.

pay ranges
A series of steps or levels within a pay grade, usually based upon years of service.

TABLE 11-4 Federal Government Pay Scales

SALARY TABLE 2009-GS

INCORPORATING THE 2.90% GENERAL SCHEDULE INCREASE EFFECTIVE JANUARY 2009

Annual Rates by Grade and Step

Grade	Step 1	Step 2	Step 3	Step 4	Step 5	Step 6	Step 7	Step 8	Step 9	Step 10
1	17540	18126	18709	19290	19873	20216	20792	21373	21396	21944
2	19721	20190	20842	21396	21635	22271	22907	23543	24179	24815
3	21517	22234	22951	23668	24385	25102	25819	26536	27253	27970
4	24156	24961	25766	26571	27376	28181	28986	29791	30596	31401
5	27026	27927	28828	29729	30630	31531	32432	33333	34234	35135
6	30125	31129	32133	33137	34141	35145	36149	37153	38157	39161
7	33477	34593	35709	36825	37941	39057	40173	41289	42405	43521
8	37075	38311	39547	40783	42019	43255	44491	45727	46963	48199
9	40949	42314	43679	45044	46409	47774	49139	50504	51869	53234
10	45095	46598	48101	49604	51107	52610	54113	55616	57119	58622
11	49544	51195	52846	54497	56148	57799	59450	61101	62752	64403
12	59383	61362	63341	65320	67299	69278	71257	73236	75215	77194
13	70615	72969	75323	77677	80031	82385	84739	87093	89447	91801
14	83445	86227	89009	91791	94573	97355	100137	102919	105701	108483
15	98156	101428	104700	107972	111244	114516	117788	121060	124332	127604

There are several reasons to use pay ranges for each pay grade. First, it lets the employer take a more flexible stance in the labor market. For example, it makes it easier to attract experienced, higher-paid employees into a pay grade at the top of the range, since the starting salary for the pay grade's lowest step may be too low to attract them. Pay ranges also let companies provide for performance differences between employees within the same grade or between those with different seniorities.

Correcting Out-of-Line Rates The wage rate for a particular job may now fall well off the wage line or well outside the rate range for its grade, as shown in Figure 11-5. This means that the average pay for that job is currently too high or too low, relative to other jobs in the firm. For underpaid jobs, the solution is clear: Raise the wages of underpaid employees to the minimum of the rate range for their pay grade.

Current pay rates falling above the rate range are a different story. These are "red circle," "flagged," or "overrates," and there are several ways to cope with this problem. One is to freeze the rate paid to these employees until general salary increases bring the other jobs into line. A second option is to transfer or promote the employees involved to jobs for which you can legitimately pay them their current pay rates. The third option is to freeze the rate for 6 months, during which time you try to transfer or promote the overpaid employees. If you cannot, then cut the rate you pay these employees to the maximum in the pay range for their pay grade.

HR in Practice: Developing a Workable Pay Plan

Developing a pay plan is as important in a small firm as a large one. Paying overly high wages may be unnecessarily expensive, and paying less may guarantee inferior help and high turnover. Furthermore, internally inequitable wage rates will reduce morale and cause endless badgering by employees demanding raises "the same as Joe down the hall." The owner who wants to concentrate on major issues like sales would thus do well to install a rational pay plan. Here's a simplified approach.

Wage Surveys First, conduct a wage survey. Four sources can be especially useful. We saw that the Internet and Web sites like Salary.com can yield a wealth of information on area pay rates The Sunday classified newspaper ads should yield useful information on wages offered for jobs similar to those you are trying to price. Local Job Service "One Stop" offices can provide valuable information, as they compile extensive information on pay ranges and averages for many of the jobs listed on in BLS online wage surveys. Finally, local employment agencies, always eager to establish ties that could grow into business relationships, should be able to provide good data.

Smaller firms are using the Internet for wage surveys in other ways. For example, StockHouse Media Corp. has 210 employees from the United States to Canada, Japan, and Singapore. The firm's global HR director makes extensive use of the Web for determining salaries for all the firm's personnel. For example, she reviews the sites of professional groups like the Society for Human Resource Management, and surfs the Internet to monitor rates and trends by periodically checking job boards, company Web sites, and industry associations. "We source information that is both industry related as well as functionally related and of varying geographies, such as state, provincial, countrywide versus marketing, sales, HR, tech, etc.," she says.[44]

Job Evaluation If you employ more than 20 employees or so, conduct at least a rudimentary job evaluation. You will need job descriptions, since these will be the source of data regarding the nature and worth of each job. Checking a Web site like JobDescription.com can be useful here.

You may find it easier to split employees into three clusters—managerial/professional, office/clerical, and plant personnel. For each of the three groups, choose compensable factors and then rank or assign points to each job based on the job evaluation. For each job or class of jobs (such as assemblers), you will want to create a pay range. In general, you should choose as the midpoint of that range the average salary you're now paying for that job or job class. Then produce a range of about 30% around this average, broken into five steps. (Thus, the assemblers in one pay grade might earn from $8.00 to $11.60 per hour, in five steps.)

Pay Policies As noted earlier, compensation policies are important. For example, you need a policy on when to award raises. Many small business owners make the mistake of appraising employees on their anniversary date, a year after they are hired. The problem here is that the raise for one employee then becomes the standard for the next, as employees have time to compare notes. This produces a never-ending cycle of appraisals and posturing for ever-higher raises.

The better alternative is to have a policy of once-a-year raises following a standard 1-week appraisal period, preferably about 4 weeks before you produce the budget for next year. In this way, you deal with the administrative headache of conducting appraisals and awarding raises during a 1-week (or 2-week) period, and the raises are known before the budget is compiled. Other required compensation policies include amount of holiday and vacation pay (as explained in Chapter 13), overtime pay policy, method of pay (weekly, biweekly, monthly), garnishments, and time card or sign-in sheet procedures. Use the checklist in Figure 11-7 to judge the new plan's completeness.

FIGURE 11-7 Compensation Administration Checklist
A good compensation administration program is comprehensive and flexible and ensures optimum performance from employees at all levels. This checklist may be used to evaluate a company's program. The more questions answered "yes," the more thorough has been the planning for compensation administration.

Source: Reprinted from www.HR.BLR.com with permission of the publisher *Business and Legal Resources Inc.*, 141 Mill Rock Road East, Old Saybrook, CT © 2004. BLR© (Business and Legal Resources, Inc.).

	Yes	No
• Is your plan for salary administration in writing?	☐	☐
• Do you have stated goals for your plan, such as:		
–Compliance with applicable law?	☐	☐
–Consistently rewarding performance?	☐	☐
–Attracting quality employees?	☐	☐
–Reducing turnover?	☐	☐
• Does your plan include the following topics:	☐	☐
–Annual wage and hour surveys?	☐	☐
–Explanations for salary schedules?	☐	☐
–Evaluations of job classifications?	☐	☐
–Premium, bonus, vacation pay?	☐	☐
–Paid medical leave, long-term disability?	☐	☐
–Temporary positions, part-time positions?	☐	☐
• Is there a written analysis for each job in your company?	☐	☐
• Does each analysis include a listing of the following job requirements:	☐	☐
–Knowledge/skills/experience/personal characteristics?	☐	☐
• Do you periodically review and update each job description?	☐	☐
• Have you set salary ranges for each job category?	☐	☐
• Do you provide regular, written performance evaluations for employees?	☐	☐
• Are the evaluations used to decide promotions and pay increases?	☐	☐
• Do you communicate your job evaluation plan to your employees through:	☐	☐
–Orientation/supervisors?	☐	☐
–Bulletin boards/handbooks?	☐	☐
• Have you developed a written system of merit increases?	☐	☐
• Do you have stated goals for the system, such as:	☐	☐
–Increase productivity/quality?	☐	☐
–Reduce errors/cost?	☐	☐
• Do you respond to suggestions from employees about your compensation plan?	☐	☐

4 Explain how to price managerial and professional jobs.

PRICING MANAGERIAL AND PROFESSIONAL JOBS

Developing compensation plans for managers or professionals is similar in many respects to developing plans for any employee. The basic aim is the same: to attract and keep good employees. And job evaluation—classifying jobs, ranking them, or assigning points to them, for instance—is about as applicable to managerial and professional jobs (below the top executive levels) as to production and clerical ones.

There are some big differences, though. Managerial jobs tend to stress harder-to-quantify factors like judgment and problem solving more than do production and clerical jobs. There is also more emphasis on paying managers and professionals based on results—based on their performance or on what they can do—rather than on the basis of static job demands like working conditions. And there is the challenge of having to compete in the marketplace for executives who by some standards still have the pay of rock stars. So, job evaluation, although still important, usually plays a secondary role to non-salary issues like bonuses, incentives, market rates, and benefits.

Compensating Executives and Managers

Compensation for a company's top executives usually consists of four main elements: base pay, short-term incentives, long-term incentives, and executive benefits/perquisites or "perks."[45] *Base pay* includes the person's fixed salary as well as, often, guaranteed bonuses such as "10% of pay at the end of the fourth fiscal quarter, regardless of whether or not the company makes a profit." *Short-term incentives* are usually cash or stock bonuses for achieving short-term goals, such as year-to-year increases in sales revenue. *Long-term incentives* aim to encourage the executive to take actions that drive up the value of the company's stock and include things like stock options; these generally give the executive the right to purchase stock at a specific price for a specific period. Finally, *executive benefits and perks* might include supplemental executive retirement pension plans, supplemental life insurance, and health insurance without a deductible or coinsurance. With so many complicated elements, employers must also be alert to the tax and securities law implications of their executive compensation decisions.[46]

What Determines Executive Pay?

For top executive jobs (especially the CEO), job evaluation typically has little relevance. One recent study concluded that three main factors, *job complexity* (span of control, the number of functional divisions over which the executive has direct responsibility, and management level), the employer's *ability to pay* (total profit and rate of return), and the executive's *human capital* (educational level, field of study, work experience) accounted for about two-thirds of executive compensation variance.[47] The traditional wisdom is that company size and performance significantly affect top managers' salaries. Yet studies from the early 2000s showed that size and performance explained only about 30% of CEO pay: "In reality, CEO pay is set by the board taking into account a variety of factors such as the business strategy, corporate trends, and most importantly where they want to be in a short and long term."[48] In practice, CEOs may have considerable influence over the boards of directors who theoretically set their pay. So, their pay sometimes doesn't reflect strictly arms-length negotiations.[49]

Shareholder activism and government oversight have tightened the restrictions on what companies pay top executives. For example, shareholders in pharmaceuticals firm GlaxoSmithKline voted to reject the board's recommendation to pay its chief executive $35 million if he lost his job.[50] There is no doubt that as a general trend most employers, particularly large ones, are linking executive pay more to financial performance.[51]

Elements of Executive Pay

Salary is traditionally the cornerstone of executive compensation. On it, employers layer benefits, incentives, and perquisites—all normally conferred in proportion to base pay. Executive compensation emphasizes performance incentives more than do other employees' pay plans, since organizational results are likely to reflect executives' contributions more directly than lower-echelon employees' are.[52] Indeed, boards are boosting the emphasis on performance-based pay (in part due to shareholder activism). The big issue here is identifying the appropriate performance standards and then determining how to link these to pay. Typical short-term measures of shareholder value include revenue growth and operating profit margin. Long-term shareholder value measures include rate of return above some predetermined base, and what compensation experts call *economic value added.* We'll discuss such short and long-term incentives in Chapter 12.

Performance-based pay can focus a manager's attention. When heavy truck production tumbled, CEO Joseph Magliochetti saw sales of auto-parts maker Dana Corp. drop by 6%, and profits by 44%. At the end of the year, he still got his $850,000 salary. But his board eliminated his bonus and stock grant, which the year before had earned him $1.8 million. The board said he had failed to beat the profit goals it had set for him.[53]

Managerial Job Evaluation Many employers use job evaluation for pricing managerial jobs (at least, below the top jobs) in most large firms. The basic approach is to classify all executive and management positions into a series of grades, each with a salary range.

As with nonmanagerial jobs, one alternative is to rank the executive and management positions in relation to each other, grouping those of equal value. However, firms also use the job classification and point evaluation methods, with compensable factors like position scope, complexity, and difficulty. Job analysis, salary surveys, and the fine-tuning of salary levels around wage curves also play roles.

Compensating Professional Employees

Compensating professional employees like engineers and scientists presents unique problems.[54] Analytical jobs like these emphasize creativity and problem solving, compensable factors not easily compared or measured. Furthermore, how do you measure performance? For example, the success of an engineer's invention depends on many factors, like how well the firm markets it.

Employers can use job evaluation for professional jobs. Compensable factors here tend to focus on problem solving, creativity, job scope, and technical knowledge and expertise. Firms use the point method and factor comparison methods, although job classification seems most popular. (Here, recall that you slot jobs into grades based on grade descriptions.) Yet in practice, firms rarely rely on just job evaluation for pricing professional jobs, since it is difficult to quantify the factors, such as creativity, that make a difference in professional work.

Most employers use a market-pricing approach. They price professional jobs in the marketplace as best they can, to establish the values for benchmark jobs. Then they slot these benchmark jobs and their other professional jobs into a salary structure. Each professional discipline (like engineering or R&D) usually ends up having four to six grade levels, each with a broad salary range. This helps employers remain competitive when bidding for professionals whose skills and attainments vary widely, and who literally have global employment possibilities.[55]

5 Explain the difference between competency-based and traditional pay plans.

COMPETENCY-BASED PAY

Introduction

We've seen that employers traditionally base a job's pay rate on the relative worth of the job. The job evaluation committee compares jobs using compensable factors such as effort and responsibility. This allows them (1) to compare jobs to one another (as in, "based on its duties, this job seems to require about twice the effort of that one"), and (2) to assign internally equitable pay rates for each job. Therefore, the pay rate for the job principally depends on the job itself, not on who is doing it.

For reasons we'll explain shortly, an increasing number of compensation experts and employers are moving away from assigning pay rates to jobs based on the jobs' numerically rated, intrinsic duties. Instead, they advocate basing the job's pay rate on the level of "competencies" the job demands of those who fill it.[56] "Title and tenure have been replaced with performance and competencies" is how one expert puts it.[57] Compensation specialists call this second approach *competency-based pay.*

What Is Competency-Based Pay?

In brief, **competency-based pay** means the company pays for the employee's range, depth, and types of skills and knowledge, rather than for the job title he or she holds.[58] Experts variously call this competence-, knowledge-, or skill-based pay. With competency-based pay, an employee in a class I job who could (but may not have to at the moment) do class II work gets paid as a class II worker, not a class I.

Different organizations define "competencies" in somewhat different ways. Most, like the U.S. Office of Personnel Management, use "competencies" synonymously with the knowledge, or skills, or abilities required to do the job. Another approach is to express competencies in terms of measurable behaviors, such as "design a Web site."[59] Here, you would identify the job's required competencies by completing the phrase, "In order to perform this job competently, the employee should be able to. . . ."[60] We can simply define **competencies** as demonstrable knowledge, skills, or behaviors that enable performance.[61]

In practice, competency-based pay usually comes down to using one or both of two basic types of pay programs: *pay for knowledge* or *skill-based pay*.[62] Pay-for-knowledge pay plans reward employees for learning organizationally relevant knowledge—for instance, Microsoft pays new programmers more as they learn the intricacies of Windows. Skill-based pay tends to be used more for workers with manual jobs—thus, carpenters earn more as they become more proficient at finishing cabinets.

In sum, probably the biggest difference between traditional and competency-based pay is this:

- Traditional job evaluation–based pay plans tie the worker's pay to the worth of the job based on the job description—pay here is more *job oriented.*
- Competence-based pay ties the worker's pay to his or her competencies—pay is more *person oriented.* Employees here are paid based on what they know or can do—even if, at the moment, they don't have to do it.

Why Use Competency-Based Pay?

Why pay employees based on the skill, knowledge, or competency level they achieve, rather than based on the duties of the jobs to which they're assigned? For example, why pay an Accounting Clerk III who has achieved a certain mastery of accounting techniques the same (or more than) someone who is an Accounting Clerk IV?

The main reason is that traditional pay plans may actually backfire if a *high-performance work system* is your goal. The whole thrust of these systems is to encourage employees to work in a self-motivated way. Employers do this by organizing the work around teams, by encouraging team members to rotate freely among jobs (each with its own skill set), by pushing more responsibility for things like day-to-day supervision down to the workers, and by organizing work around projects or processes where jobs may blend or overlap. In such systems, you obviously want employees to be enthusiastic about learning and moving among other jobs. Pigeonholing workers by classifying them too narrowly into jobs based on the job's points may actually discourage such enthusiasm and flexibility.

Studies do suggest that quantitative types of job evaluation (such as the point or factor comparison methods) may conflict with the high-performance work approach.[63] In one study, the researchers found that

> "Workplaces in which the high-performance approach has been most fully implemented are less likely to have the more formal, analytical type of job evaluation. Furthermore, those [workplaces] with both analytical job evaluation and the high-performance work system are less likely to have high above average financial performance than those with either of these on a single basis."[64]

Qualitative job evaluation methods such as classifying, grading, or ranking jobs were less of a problem. Point plans may breed more of an "it's not my job" attitude.

competency-based pay
Where the company pays for the employee's range, depth, and types of skills and knowledge, rather than for the job title he or she holds.

competencies
Demonstrable knowledge, skills, or behaviors, that enable performance.

Experts give two more reasons for paying based on competencies rather than job duties. First, paying for competencies *enables companies to encourage employees* to develop the competencies the companies require to achieve their strategic aims. For example, Canon Corp. needs competencies in miniaturization and precision manufacturing to design and produce its cameras and copiers. It thus makes sense for Canon to reward some employees based on the skills and knowledge they develop in these two strategically crucial areas.

Second, paying for measurable and influence-able competencies provides a focus for the employer's *performance management* process. For example, at Canon, this might mean focusing hiring, training, and appraising (and rewards) on employees achieving higher levels of miniaturization and precision manufacturing competencies.

Competency-Based Pay in Practice

In practice, any skill/competency/knowledge-based pay program generally contains five main elements, which are listed as follows:

1. A system for defining specific required skills
2. A process for tying the person's pay to his or her skill level
3. A training system that lets employees acquire the skills
4. A formal skills competency testing system
5. A work design that lets employees move among jobs to permit work assignment flexibility[65]

General Mills Example

For example, a General Mills manufacturing plant pays workers based on attained skill levels.[66] Management created four clusters of jobs, corresponding to the plant's four production areas: mixing, filling, packaging, and materials. Within each cluster, workers could attain three levels of skill. Level 1 indicates limited ability, such as knowledge of basic facts and ability to perform simple tasks without direction.[67] Level 2 means the employee attained partial proficiency and could (for instance) apply technical principles on the job. Attaining Level 3 means the employee is fully competent in the area and could, for example, analyze and solve production problems. Each of the four production clusters had a different average wage rate. There were, therefore, 12 pay levels in the plant (four clusters with three pay levels each).

General Mills set the wages for each cluster's three levels in part by making the pay for the lowest of the three pay levels in each cluster equal to the average entry-level pay rate for similar jobs in the community. A new employee could start in any cluster, but always at Level 1. If after several weeks he or she was certified at the next higher skill level, General Mills raised his or her salary. Employees freely rotated from cluster to cluster, as long as they could achieve Level 2 performance within their current cluster.

The Bottom Line on Competency-Based Pay

Competency-based pay has detractors. Some note that competency-based pay "ignores the cost implications of paying [employees] for knowledge, skills and behaviors even if they are not used."[68] There may also be simpler ways to encourage the necessary learning. For example, one aerospace firm has a quasi–skill-based pay program. All exempt employees negotiate "learning contracts" with their supervisors. The employees then get raises for meeting skills-improvement objectives.[69] Whether skill-based pay improves productivity is an open question. When used in conjunction with team-building and worker involvement programs, it appears to lead to higher quality and lower absenteeism.[70] However, even with the advent of approaches like competency-based pay, there is actually today "a renewed interest in the job of evaluation and market pricing."[71] In

Many employers, such as General Mills, pay certain workers based on attained skill levels.

Source: Courtesy of Mark Richards/PhotoEdit Inc.

economically challenging times, it may be that the purported efficiencies of job evaluation–based pay plans outweigh the flexibility of other approaches to determining pay.

6 Explain the importance today of broadbanding, comparable worth, and board oversight of executive pay.

SPECIAL TOPICS IN COMPENSATION

How employers pay employees has been evolving. We can sum up the main changes as follows:

- We've seen that there is somewhat less emphasis on the job's duties, and more on the person's skills and competencies and how these fit with the firm's strategic needs.
- We've seen that there is less emphasis on seniority, and more on the employee's performance.
- There is less emphasis on narrowly defined pay ranges and jobs, and more on broader jobs and pay ranges.
- There is increased interest in ensuring that men and women are paid comparably for essentially the same work.
- There is more emphasis on board oversight and regulation of executive pay.

We'll look at the last three of these topics—broadbanding, comparable worth, and board oversight of executive pay—next.[72] We'll address performance-based pay in Chapter 12.

Broadbanding

Most firms end up with pay plans that slot jobs into classes or grades, each with its own vertical pay rate range. For example, the U.S. government's pay plan consists of 18 main grades (GS-1 to GS-18), each with its own pay range. For an employee whose job falls in one of these grades, the pay range for that grade dictates his or her minimum and maximum salary.

The question is, "How wide should the salary grades be, in terms of the number of job evaluation points they include?" (For example, might the U.S. government want to collapse its 18 salary grades into six or seven broader bands?) There is a downside to having (say, 18) narrow grades. For instance, if you want someone whose job is in grade 2 to fill in for a time in a job that happens to be in grade 1, it's difficult to reassign that person without lowering his or her salary. Similarly, if you want the person to learn about a job that happens to be in grade 3, the employee might object to the reassignment without a corresponding raise to grade 3 pay. Traditional grade pay plans thus breed inflexibility.

That is why some firms are broadbanding their pay plans. **Broadbanding** means collapsing salary grades into just a few wide levels or bands, each of which contains a relatively wide range of jobs and pay levels. Figure 11-8 illustrates this. In this case, the company's previous six pay grades are consolidated into two broad grades or "broadbands."

A company may create broadbands for all its jobs, or for specific groups such as managers or professionals. The pay rate range of each broadband is relatively large, since it ranges from the minimum pay of the lowest grade the firm merged into the broadband up to the maximum pay of the highest merged grade. Thus, for example, instead of having 10 salary grades, each of which contains a salary range of $15,000, the firm might collapse the 10 grades into three broadbands, each with a set of jobs such that the difference between the lowest- and highest-paid jobs might be $40,000 or more. For the jobs that fall in this broadband, there is therefore a much wider range of pay rates. You can move an employee from job to job within the broadband more easily, without worrying about the employee's moving outside the relatively narrow rate range associated with a traditional narrow pay grade. Broadbanding therefore breeds flexibility.

Pros and Cons

Companies create broadbands for several reasons. The basic advantage is that it injects greater flexibility into employee assignments.[73] It is especially sensible where firms organize into self-managing teams. The new, broad salary bands can include both supervisors and subordinates and also facilitate moving employees slightly up or down along the pay scale, without bumping the person into a new salary range. For example, "the employee who needs to spend time in a lower-level job to develop a certain skill set can receive higher-than-usual pay for the work, a circumstance considered impossible under traditional pay systems."[74] Similarly, one expert argues that traditional quantitative evaluation plans actually reward inadaptability.[75] He says that jobs narrowly defined by compensable factors such as "know-how" are unlikely to encourage job incumbents to be

FIGURE 11-8 Broadbanded Structure and How It Relates to Traditional Pay Grades and Ranges

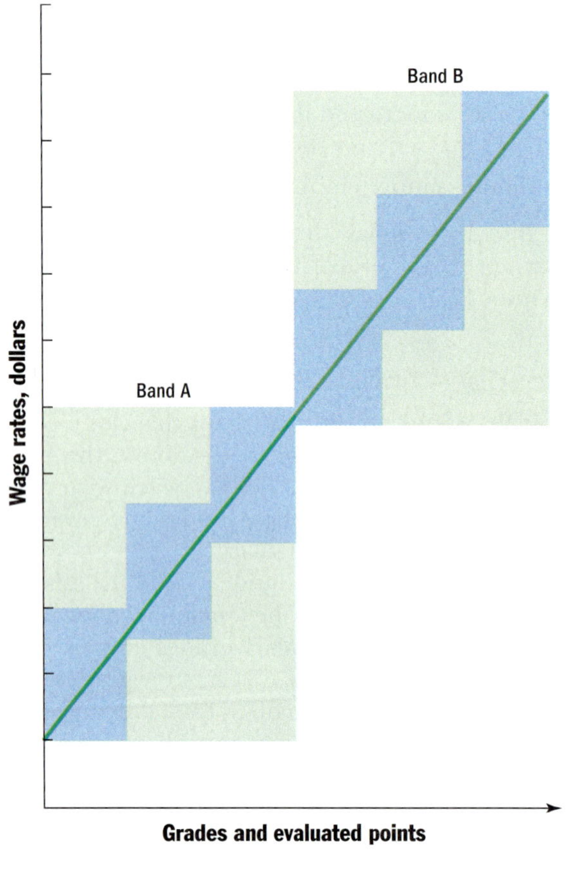

flexible. Instead, the tendency may be for workers to take a "that's not my job" attitude and to concentrate on their specific tasks.

However, broadbanding can be unsettling, particularly for new employees. For example, The Home Depot has used broadbanding for more than 10 years, and "when employees want to learn something new, they play to the level [on that project] that they're capable of," says the firm's head of information systems. Moving among jobs is motivating once you get used to it. However, it can make a new employee feel adrift: "There's a sense of permanence in the set of job responsibilities often attached to job titles," he says. That sense of permanence isn't nearly as clear when employees move frequently from project to project and job to job.[76]

Use A survey of 783 employers found that about 15% were using broadbanding.[77] One British company does so to support its strategy of cutting costs and flattening and downsizing the organization. The flattening meant fewer job titles, each of which had broader responsibilities, and broadbanding made it easier to get employees to assume their new, broader roles. Dow Jones & Company implemented broadbanding for its 1,000 IT professionals several years ago.

Note that even with competence/skill-based pay and broadbanding, 60% to 70% of U.S. firms use quantitative point and factor comparison plans to create pay structures. Job evaluation's relative ease of use and familiarity are probably the main reasons. And neither skill-based pay nor broadbanding eliminates the need for evaluating the worth of one job relative to others.[78]

Comparable Worth

Comparable worth refers to the requirement to pay men and women equal wages for jobs that are of *comparable* (rather than strictly *equal*) value to the employer. Thus, comparable worth may mean comparing quite dissimilar jobs, such as nurses to truck mechanics or secretaries to technicians. The question "comparable worth" seeks to address is this: Should you pay women who are performing jobs *equal* to men's or just *comparable* to men's the same as men? If it's only for equal jobs, then the tendency may be to limit women's pay to that of the other, lower-paid jobs in which women tend to predominate.

County of Washington v. Gunther (1981) was a pivotal case for comparable worth. It involved Washington County, Oregon, prison matrons who claimed sex discrimination. The county had evaluated comparable but non-equal men's jobs as having 5% more "job content" (based on a point evaluation system) than the women's jobs, but paid the men 35% more.[79] Should the women matrons not be paid more than they were, even though the comparable (in terms of points) men's jobs were "unequal" to (not the same as) theirs? After seesawing through the courts to the U.S. Supreme Court, Washington County finally agreed to pay 35,000 employees in female-dominated jobs almost $500 million in pay raises over 7 years to settle the suit.

Comparable worth has implications for job evaluation. Virtually every comparable worth case that reached a court involved the use of the point method of job evaluation. By assigning points to dissimilar jobs, point plans facilitate comparability ratings among different jobs. Should employers still use point-type plans? Perhaps the wisest approach is for employers to price their jobs as they see fit (with or without point plans), but to ensure that women have equal access to all jobs. In other words, eliminate the wage discrimination issue by eliminating sex-segregated jobs.

broadbanding
Consolidating salary grades and ranges into just a few wide levels or "bands," each of which contains a relatively wide range of jobs and salary levels.

comparable worth
The concept by which women who are usually paid less than men can claim that men in comparable rather than in strictly equal jobs are paid more.

The Pay Gap All this notwithstanding, those formulating pay raises for women need to keep in mind that women in the United States earn only about 77% as much as men, although the gap is narrowing a bit.[80]

What accounts for the difference? One pay specialist cites four factors:

1. Women's starting salaries are traditionally lower because employers traditionally view them as having less leverage.
2. Salary increases for women in professional jobs do not reflect their above-average performance (men with equal performance receive bigger raises).
3. In white-collar jobs, men tend to change jobs more frequently, which enables them to be promoted to higher-level jobs over women with more seniority.
4. In blue-collar jobs, women tend to be placed in departments with lower-paying jobs.[81]

Education may reduce the wage gap. Studies suggest that schooling's impact on earnings is greater for females than for males, other things equal. This may be because education reduces the male–female earnings gap attributable to female discrimination.[82] But, education aside, the managers making the pay decisions are primarily responsible for identifying and rectifying problem pay rates.

Board Oversight of Executive Pay

For 15 years, the board of directors of UnitedHealth Group Inc. supported its CEO, with almost $2 billion in compensation. Then, the board ousted him, allegedly because, as the *Wall Street Journal* put it, "his explanation for a pattern of unusually well-timed stock option grants didn't add up."[83]

There are various reasons why boards are clamping down on executive pay. The economic downturn that began around 2008 exposed the enormous disconnect between what many executives were earning and their performance. The U.S. government's "pay czar" was soon overseeing certain pay awards in firms which had U.S. treasury loans. As of 2007, the Securities and Exchange Commission (SEC) required filing more compensation-related information, including a detailed listing of all individual "perks" or benefits if they total more than $100,000.[84] As of 2005, the Financial Accounting Standards Board required that most public companies recognize as an expense the fair value of the stock options they grant.[85] The Sarbanes-Oxley Act makes executives personally liable, under certain conditions, for corporate financial oversight lapses. Writing in the *Harvard Business Review*, the chief justice of Delaware's Supreme Court said that governance issues, shareholder activism, and other changes have "created a new set of expectations for directors."[86] Yet none of these SEC or legislative actions seem (in retrospect) to have prevented some employers from dramatically overpaying their executives. The net result is that lawyers specializing in executive pay suggest that boards of directors (board compensation committees usually make executive pay decisions in large firms)[87] ask themselves these questions:

- Has our compensation committee thoroughly identified its duties and processes?
- Is our compensation committee using the appropriate compensation advisors? (Government regulators and commentators strongly encourage this.)
- Are there particular executive compensation issues that our committee should address?[88]
- Do our procedures demonstrate diligence and independence? (This demands careful deliberations and records.)
- Is our committee appropriately communicating its decisions? How will shareholders react?[89]

Tomorrow's Pay Programs

It's always risky to forecast the future, but several pay-related trends seem certain.[90] Companies around the world will continue to face severe economic and competitive challenges. There will be what consultants McKinsey & Co. calls a "war for talent" as companies vie to hire and retain top employees. With reduced Social Security and company pensions, employees will increasingly have to accumulate their own wealth for retirement. And younger "Generation Y" applicants will enter the workforce with greater expectations for recognition and feedback than did their predecessors.

Tomorrow's pay programs will therefore probably exhibit several features. Every company has jobs that are strategically crucial to their futures, and others, which while important, are supportive. Employers will have to identify the strategically crucial jobs and pay them at premium levels. To engage the new millennial employees, it's essential that they know what's expected of them, and that they get continuing constructive feedback about their performance. Pay for performance will continue to be the key, and as one expert puts it, "incentives should be a component of every compensation package."[91] Employers will have to be creative about providing rewards like stock ownership options to provide young talent with the opportunity to create wealth through their employment. And nonfinancial rewards including personal recognition will grow in importance as supplements to financial rewards.

Improving Productivity Through HRIS: Automating Compensation Administration

Usually, the employer identifies set times during the year (called "focal reviews") when all the firm's managers review employees' performance and match these with budgetary constraints and formulate pay raise recommendations for the coming year.[92] As employers moved toward linking their compensation plans more closely to strategic considerations, the job of developing salary raise recommendations has become more complex. It's no longer just a case of allocating raises across the board, or based on performance appraisals. Instead, numerous issues (including strategic concerns, geographic considerations, paying employees based on competencies, and the need to factor in various elements including bonus payments and stock option grants) make allocating raises while staying within budget a challenge.

Making raise decisions has always been cumbersome. Traditionally, employers used spreadsheets to administer these compensation decisions. The human resource department would create individual spreadsheets for each manager. The manager would then use these spreadsheets to record their salary increase recommendations for their subordinates. Human resources would then compile the spreadsheets by unit, department, division, and, finally, companywide to add up who was spending what. This was a labor-intensive and costly process.

Today, companies more often use server-based intranet compensation planning programs to keep track of who can spend what, and who is spending what. This Web-based method has many advantages. The employer can quickly update its compensation programs (such as how much is available, and how much can each manager allocate for various criteria) without having to modify the software on individual managers' computers. And automating the system reduces costs by eliminating manual processes. For example, one company estimated that it cost them about $35 to complete a single manual compensation transaction (such as combining the raise budgets for two departments), but about $16 if it automated this process. Using a centralized application saves money in other ways. For example, employers often assign pay raise budgets to all their managers, only to find that (once the various department budgets all come together) the accumulated excess raises the amount to millions of dollars. This generally doesn't happen with an automated system. And, a compensation administration system that is compatible with the employer's HRIS can also automatically administer other pay actions, such as updating employees' pay checks.

REVIEW

CHAPTER SECTION SUMMARIES

1. In establishing strategic pay plans, managers first need to understand some **basic factors in determining pay rates.** Employee compensation includes both direct financial payments and indirect financial statements. The factors determining the design of any pay plan include legal, union, company strategy/policy, and equity. Legal considerations include, most importantly, the Fair Labor Standards Act, which governs matters such as minimum wages and overtime pay. Specific categories of employees are exempt from the act or certain provisions of the act, particularly its overtime provisions. The Equal Pay Act of 1963 and the Employee Retirement Income Security Act are other important laws.
2. The process of **establishing pay rates** while ensuring external, internal, and procedural equity consists of five steps: conducting a salary survey, determining the worth of each job, doing a job evaluation, grouping jobs comprised of approximately equal difficulty and pricing each pay grade with wage curves, and fine-tuning pay rates.
   - Salary surveys may be informal phone or Internet surveys, or formal surveys conducted by the employer or utilizing commercial, professional, and/or government salary surveys.
   - Job evaluation is a systematic comparison done in order to determine the worth of one job relative to another based on compensable factors.
   - Compensable factors refer to compensable elements of a job such as skills and efforts.
   - Popular job evaluation methods include ranking, job classification, the point method, and factor comparison. With ranking, for instance, you conduct a job analysis, group jobs by department, and have raters rank jobs.
   - Once the committee uses job evaluation to determine the relative worth of each job, it can turn to the task of assigning pay rates to each job; it would usually first want to group jobs into pay grades to streamline the process.
   - The team can then use wage curves to price each grade and then fine-tune pay rates.
3. **Pricing managerial and professional jobs** involves some special issues. Managerial pay typically consists of base pay, short-term incentives, long-term incentives, and executive benefits and, particularly at the top levels, doesn't lend itself to job evaluation but rather to understanding the job's complexity, the employer's ability to pay, and the need to be competitive in attracting top talent.
4. More employers are moving from paying jobs based on their intrinsic duties toward **paying jobs based on the competencies** the job requires. The main reason for doing so is to encourage employees to develop the competencies they need to move seamlessly from job to job. At General Mills, for instance, certain plant personnel are paid based on the skill levels they attain.
5. We addressed several important **special topics in compensation**. Broadbanding means consolidating several rates and ranges into a few wide levels or "bands," each of which contains a relatively wide range of jobs in salary levels. Broadbanding encourages employees to move freely from job to job and facilitates implementing team-based high-performance management systems. Comparable worth refers to the requirement to pay men and women equal pay for jobs that are of comparable rather than strictly equal value to the employee. With many stockholders concerned with excessive executive remuneration, board oversight of executive pay has become an important issue, and boards of directors need to make sure they use qualified advisers and exercise diligence and independence in formulating executive pay plans.

DISCUSSION QUESTIONS

1. What is the difference between exempt and non-exempt jobs?
2. Should the job evaluation depend on an appraisal of the jobholder's performance? Why? Why not?
3. What is the relationship between compensable factors and job specifications?
4. Compare and contrast the following methods of job evaluation: ranking, classification, factor comparison, and point method.
5. What are the pros and cons of broadbanding, and would you recommend your current employer (or some other firm you're familiar with) use it? Why or why not?
6. It was recently reported in the news that the average pay for most university presidents was around $250,000 per year, but that a few earned much more. For example, the new president of Vanderbilt received $852,000 in one year. Discuss why you would (or would not) pay university presidents as much or more than many corporate CEOs.
7. Do small companies need to develop a pay plan? Why or why not?

INDIVIDUAL AND GROUP ACTIVITIES

1. Working individually or in groups, conduct salary surveys for the following positions: entry-level accountant and entry-level chemical engineer. What sources did you use, and what conclusions did you reach? If you were the HR manager for a local engineering firm, what would you recommend that you pay for each job?
2. Working individually or in groups, develop compensation policies for the teller position at a local bank. Assume that there are four tellers: two were hired in May and the other two were hired in December. The compensation policies should address the following: appraisals, raises, holidays, vacation pay, overtime pay, method of pay, garnishments, and time cards.
3. Working individually or in groups, access relevant Web sites to determine what equitable pay ranges are for these jobs: chemical engineer, marketing manager, and HR manager, all with a bachelor's degree and 5 years' experience. Do so for the following cities: New York, New York; San Francisco, California; Houston, Texas; Denver, Colorado; Miami, Florida; Atlanta, Georgia; Chicago, Illinois; Birmingham, Alabama; Detroit, Michigan; and Washington, D.C. For each position in each city, what are the pay ranges and the average pay? Does geographical location impact the salaries of the different positions? If so, how?
4. The "HRCI Test Specifications Appendix" (pages 699–706) lists the knowledge someone studying for the HRCI certification exam needs to have in each area of human resource management (such as in Strategic Management, Workforce Planning, and Human Resource Development). In groups of four to five students, do four things: (1) Review that appendix now. (2) Identify the material in this chapter that relates to the required knowledge the appendix lists. (3) Write four multiple-choice exam questions on this material that you believe would be suitable for inclusion in the HRCI exam. And (4) if time permits, have someone from your team post your team's questions in front of the class, so the students in other teams can take each others' exam questions.
5. Some of America's executives have come under fire recently because their pay seemed to some to be excessive, given their firms' performances. To choose just two of very many: one Citigroup division head was due a $97 million bonus in 2009, and Merrill Lynch paid tens of millions in bonuses soon after Bank of America rescued it. However, big institutional investors are no longer sitting back and not complaining. For example, TV's *Nightly Business Line* says that pension manager TIAA-CREF is talking to 50 companies about executive pay. And the U.S. government's "pay czar" is looking to roll back some such payouts. Do you think they are right to make a fuss? Why?

EXPERIENTIAL EXERCISE

Ranking the College's Administrators

Purpose: The purpose of this exercise is to give you experience in performing a job evaluation using the ranking method.

Required Understanding: You should be thoroughly familiar with the ranking method of job evaluation and obtain job descriptions for your college's dean, department chairperson, director of admissions, library director, registrar, and your professor.

How to Set Up the Exercise/Instructions: Divide the class into groups of four or five students. The groups will perform a job evaluation of the positions of dean, department chairperson, and professor using the ranking method.

1. Perform a job evaluation by ranking the jobs. You may use one or more compensable factors.
2. If time permits, a spokesperson from each group can put his or her group's rankings on the board. Did the groups end up with about the same results? How did they differ? Why do you think they differed?

APPLICATION CASE

Salary Inequities at Acme Manufacturing

Joe Black was trying to figure out what to do about a problem salary situation he had in his plant. Black recently took over as president of Acme Manufacturing. The founder and former president, Bill George, had been president for 35 years. The company was family owned and located in a small eastern Arkansas town. It had approximately 250 employees and was the largest employer in the community. Black was a member of the family that owned Acme, but he had never worked for the company prior to becoming president. He had an MBA and a law degree, plus 5 years of management experience with a large manufacturing organization, where he was senior vice president for human resources before making his move to Acme.

A short time after joining Acme, Black started to notice that there was considerable inequity in the pay structure for salaried employees. A discussion with the human resources director led him to believe that salaried employees' pay was very much a matter of individual bargaining with the past president. Hourly paid factory employees were not part of the problem because they were unionized and their wages were set by collective bargaining. An examination of the salaried payroll showed that there were 25 employees, ranging in pay from that of the president to that of the receptionist. A closer examination showed that 14 of the salaried employees were female. Three of these were front-line factory supervisors and one was the human resources director. The other 10 were nonmanagement.

This examination also showed that the human resources director appeared underpaid, and that the three female supervisors earned somewhat less than any male supervisor did. However, there were no similar supervisory jobs with both male and female job incumbents. When asked, the HR director said she thought the female supervisors may have been paid at a lower rate mainly because they were women, and perhaps George, the former president, did not think that women needed as much money because they had working husbands. However, she added she personally thought that they were paid less because they supervised less-skilled employees than did the male supervisors. Black was not sure that this was true.

The company from which Black had moved had a good job evaluation system. Although he was thoroughly familiar with and capable in this compensation tool, Black did not have time to make a job evaluation study at Acme. Therefore, he decided to hire a compensation consultant from a nearby university to help him. Together, they decided that all 25 salaried jobs should be in the same job evaluation cluster; that a modified ranking method of job evaluation should be used; and that the job descriptions recently completed by the HR director were current, accurate, and usable in the study.

The job evaluation showed that the HR director and the three female supervisors were being underpaid relative to comparable male salaried employees.

Black was not sure what to do. He knew that if the underpaid female supervisors took the case to the local EEOC office, the company could be found guilty of sex discrimination and then have to pay considerable back wages. He was afraid that if he gave these women an immediate salary increase large enough to bring them up to where they should be, the male supervisors would be upset and the female supervisors might comprehend the total situation and want back pay. The HR director told Black that the female supervisors had never complained about pay differences.

The HR director agreed to take a sizable salary increase with no back pay, so this part of the problem was solved. Black believed he had four choices relative to the female supervisors:

1. To do nothing
2. To gradually increase the female supervisors' salaries
3. To increase their salaries immediately
4. To call the three supervisors into his office, discuss the situation with them, and jointly decide what to do

Questions

1. What would you do if you were Black?
2. How do you think the company got into a situation like this in the first place?
3. Why would you suggest Black pursue the alternative you suggested?

Source: This case was prepared by Professor James C. Hodgetts of the Fogelman College of Business and Economics of the University of Memphis. All names are disguised. Used by permission.

CONTINUING CASE

Carter Cleaning Company

The New Pay Plan

Carter Cleaning Centers does not have a formal wage structure nor does it have rate ranges or use compensable factors. Wage rates are based mostly on those prevailing in the surrounding community and are tempered with an attempt on the part of Jack Carter to maintain some semblance of equity between what workers with different responsibilities in the stores are paid.

Carter does not make any formal surveys when determining what his company should pay. He peruses the want ads almost every day and conducts informal surveys among his friends in the local chapter of the laundry and cleaners trade association. While Jack has taken a "seat-of-the-pants" approach to paying employees, his salary schedule has been guided by several basic pay policies. Although many of his colleagues adhere to a policy of paying minimum rates, Jack has always followed a policy of paying his employees about 10% above what he feels are the prevailing rates, a policy that he believes reduces turnover while fostering employee loyalty. Of somewhat more concern to Jennifer is her father's informal policy of paying men about 20% more than women for the same job. Her father's explanation is, "They're stronger and can work harder for longer hours, and besides they all have families to support."

Questions

1. Is the company at the point where it should be setting up a formal salary structure based on a complete job evaluation? Why?
2. Is Jack Carter's policy of paying 10% more than the prevailing rates a sound one, and how could that be determined?
3. Similarly, is Carter's male–female differential wise? If not, why not?
4. Specifically, what would you suggest Jennifer do now with respect to her company's pay plan?

TRANSLATING STRATEGY INTO HR POLICIES & PRACTICES CASE

The Hotel Paris Case

The New Compensation Plan

The Hotel Paris's competitive strategy is "To use superior guest service to differentiate the Hotel Paris properties, and to thereby increase the length of stay and return rate of guests, and thus boost revenues and profitability." HR manager Lisa Cruz must now formulate functional policies and activities that support this competitive strategy, by eliciting the required employee behaviors and competencies.

Like several other HR systems at the Hotel Paris, the compensation program was unplanned and unsophisticated. The company has a narrow target range for what it will pay employees in each job category (front-desk clerk, security guard, and so forth). Each hotel manager decides where to start a new employee within that narrow pay range. The company has given little thought to tying general pay levels or individual employees' pay to the company's strategic goals. For example, the firm's policy is simply to pay its employees a "competitive salary," by which it means about average for what other hotels in the city are paying for similar jobs. Lisa knows that pay policies like these may actually run counter to what the company wants to achieve strategically, in terms of creating an extraordinarily service-oriented workforce. How can you hire and retain a top workforce, and channel their behaviors toward high-quality guest services, if you don't somehow link performance and pay? She and her team therefore turn to the task of assessing and redesigning the company's compensation plan.

Even a casual review by Lisa Cruz and the CFO made it clear that the company's compensation plan wasn't designed to support the firm's new strategic goals. For one thing, they knew that they should pay somewhat more, on average, than did their competitors if they expected employees to consistently exceed expectations when it came to serving guests. Yet their review of a variety of metrics (including the Hotel Paris's salary/competitive salary ratios, the total compensation expense per employee, and the target percentile for total compensation) suggested that in virtually all job categories the Hotel Paris paid no more than average, and, occasionally, paid somewhat less.

The current compensation policies had also bred what one hotel manager called an "I don't care" attitude on the part of most employees. What she meant was that most Hotel Paris employees quickly learned that regardless of what their performance was, they always ended up being paid about the same as employees who performed better and worse than they did. So, the firm's compensation plan actually was dysfunctional: It was not channeling employees' behaviors toward those required to achieve the company's goals. In some ways, it was doing the opposite.

Lisa and the CFO knew they had to institute a new, strategic compensation plan. They wanted a plan that improved employee morale, contributed to employee commitment, reduced employee turnover, and rewarded (and thus encouraged) the sorts of service-oriented behaviors that boosted guest satisfaction. After meeting with the company's CEO and the board, the CFO gave Lisa the go-ahead to redesign the company's compensation plan, with the overall aim of creating a new plan that would support the company's strategic aims.

Questions

1. Draw a diagram showing with arrows how compensation at Hotel Paris should influence employee performance, which should in turn influence Hotel Paris performance. Include at each level examples of relevant compensation policies, employee behavior, and Hotel Paris outcomes.
2. Would you suggest that Hotel Paris implement a competency-based pay plan for its nonmanagerial staff? Why or why not?
3. Devise a ranking job evaluation system for the Hotel Paris's nonmanagerial employees (housekeepers, valets, front-desk clerks, phone operators, waitstaff, groundskeepers, and security guards) and use it to show the worth of these jobs relative to one another.

KEY TERMS

employee compensation, *p. 387*
direct financial payments, *p. 387*
indirect financial payments, *p. 387*
Davis-Bacon Act (1931), *p. 387*
Walsh-Healey Public Contract Act (1936), *p. 387*
Title VII of the 1964 Civil Rights Act, *p. 387*
Fair Labor Standards Act (1938), *p. 387*
Equal Pay Act (1963), *p. 391*
Employee Retirement Income Security Act (ERISA), *p. 391*
salary compression, *p. 393*
salary survey, *p. 395*
benchmark job, *p. 395*
job evaluation, *p. 397*
compensable factor, *p. 397*
ranking method, *p. 399*
job classification (or grading) method, *p. 401*
classes, *p. 401*
grades, *p. 401*
grade definition, *p. 401*
point method, *p. 401*
factor comparison method, *p. 401*
pay grade, *p. 401*
wage curve, *p. 403*
pay ranges, *p. 403*
competency-based pay, *p. 409*
competencies, *p. 409*
broadbanding, *p. 413*
comparable worth, *p. 413*

Appendix for Chapter 11

Quantitative Job Evaluation Methods

Using the Factor Comparison Job Evaluation Method The factor comparison technique is a quantitative job evaluation method. It has many variations and appears to be the most accurate, the most complex, and one of the most widely used job evaluation methods.

It is actually a refinement of the ranking method and entails deciding which jobs have more of certain compensable factors. With the ranking method, you generally look at each job as an entity and rank the jobs. With the factor comparison method, you rank each job *several times—once for each compensable factor you choose.* For example, jobs might be ranked first in terms of the factor "skill." Then they are ranked according to their "mental requirements." Next they are ranked according to their "responsibility," and so forth. Then these rankings are combined for each job into an overall numerical rating for the job. Here are the required steps.

Step 1. Obtain Job Information This method requires a careful, complete job analysis. First, job descriptions are written. Then job specifications are developed, preferably in terms of the compensable factors the job evaluation committee has decided to use. For the factor comparison method, these compensable factors are usually (1) mental requirements, (2) physical requirements, (3) skill requirements, (4) responsibility, and (5) working conditions. Typical definitions of each of these five factors are presented in Figure 11A-1.

FIGURE 11A-1 Sample Definitions of Five Factors Typically Used in Factor Comparison Method

Source: Jay L. Otis and Richard H. Leukart, *Job Evaluation: A Basis for Sound Wage Administration*, p. 181. © 1954, revised 1983. Reprinted by permission of Prentice Hall, Upper Saddle River, NJ.

1. Mental Requirements

Either the possession of and/or the active application of the following:

A. (inherent) Mental traits, such as intelligence, memory, reasoning, facility in verbal expression, ability to get along with people, and imagination.

B. (acquired) General education, such as grammar and arithmetic; or general information as to sports, world events, etc.

C. (acquired) Specialized knowledge such as chemistry, engineering, accounting, advertising, etc.

2. Skill

A. (acquired) Facility in muscular coordination, as in operating machines, repetitive movements, careful coordinations, dexterity, assembling, sorting, etc.

B. (acquired) Specific job knowledge necessary to the muscular coordination only; acquired by performance of the work and not to be confused with general education or specialized knowledge. It is very largely training in the interpretation of sensory impressions.

Examples

1. In operating an adding machine, the knowledge of *which* key to depress for a subtotal would be skill.
2. In automobile repair, the ability to determine the significance of a certain knock in the motor would be skill.
3. In hand-firing a boiler, the ability to determine from the appearance of the firebed how coal should be shoveled over the surface would be skill.

3. Physical Requirements

A. Physical effort, such as sitting, standing, walking, climbing, pulling, lifting, etc.; both the amount exercised and the degree of the continuity should be taken into account.

B. Physical status, such as age, height, weight, sex, strength, and eyesight.

FIGURE 11A-1 *(continued)*

4. Responsibilities

A. For raw materials, processed materials, tools, equipment, and property.
B. For money or negotiable securities.
C. For profits or loss, savings or method improvement.
D. For public contact.
E. For records.
F. For supervision.

1. Primarily the complexity of supervision *given* to subordinates; the number of subordinates is a secondary feature. Planning, direction, coordination, instruction, control, and approval characterize this kind of supervision.
2. Also, the degree of supervision *received*. If Jobs A and B gave no supervision to subordinates, but A received much closer immediate supervision than B, then B would be entitled to a higher rating than A in the supervision factor.

To summarize the four degrees of supervision:
Highest degree—gives much—gets little
High degree—gives much—gets much
Low degree—gives none—gets little
Lowest degree—gives none—gets much

5. Working Conditions

A. Environmental influences such as atmosphere, ventilation, illumination, noise, congestion, fellow workers, etc.
B. Hazards—from the work or its surroundings.
C. Hours.

Step 2. Select Key Benchmark Jobs Next, the job evaluation committee selects 15 to 25 key jobs. These jobs will have to be representative benchmark jobs, acceptable reference points that represent the full range of jobs to be evaluated.

Step 3. Rank Key Jobs by Factor Here evaluators are asked to rank the key jobs on each of the five factors (mental requirements, physical requirements, skill requirements, responsibility, and working conditions). This ranking procedure is based on job descriptions and job specifications. Each committee member usually makes this ranking individually, and then a meeting is held to develop a consensus on each job. The result of this process is a table, as in Table 11A-1. This shows how each key job ranks on each of the five compensable factors.

Step 4. Distribute Wage Rates by Factors This is where the factor comparison method gets a bit more complicated. In this step, the committee members have to divide up the present wage now being paid for each key job, distributing it among the five compensable factors. They do this in accordance with their judgments about the importance to the job of each factor. For example, if the

TABLE 11A-1 Ranking Key Jobs by Factors[1]

	Mental Requirements	Physical Requirements	Skill Requirements	Responsibility	Working Conditions
Welder	1	4	1	1	2
Crane operator	3	1	3	4	4
Punch press operator	2	3	2	2	3
Security guard	4	2	4	3	1

[1] 1 is high, 4 is low.

TABLE 11A-2 Ranking Key Jobs by Wage Rates[1]

	Hourly Wage	Mental Requirements	Physical Requirements	Skill Requirements	Responsibility	Working Conditions
Welder	$9.80	4.00(1)	0.40(4)	3.00(1)	2.00(1)	0.40(2)
Crane operator	5.60	1.40(3)	2.00(1)	1.80(3)	0.20(4)	0.20(4)
Punch press operator	6.00	1.60(2)	1.30(3)	2.00(2)	0.80(2)	0.30(3)
Security guard	4.00	1.20(4)	1.40(2)	0.40(4)	0.40(3)	0.60(1)

[1]1 is high, 4 is low.

present wage for the job of laborer in Mexico is $4.26, our evaluators might distribute this wage as follows:

Mental requirements	$0.36
Physical requirements	$2.20
Skill requirements	$0.42
Responsibility	$0.28
Working conditions	$1.00
Total	$4.26

You make such a distribution for all key jobs.

Step 5. Rank Key Jobs According to Wages Assigned to Each Factor Here you again rank each job, factor by factor, but the ranking is based on the wages assigned to each factor. As shown in Table 11A-2, for example, for the "mental requirements" factor, the welder job ranks first, whereas the security guard job ranks last.

Each member of the committee first makes this distribution working independently. Then the committee meets and arrives at a consensus concerning the money to be assigned to each factor for each key job.

Step 6. Compare the Two Sets of Rankings to Screen Out Unusable Key Jobs You now have two sets of rankings for each key job. One was your original ranking (from step 3). This shows how each job ranks on each of the five compensable factors. The second ranking reflects for each job the wages assigned to each factor. You can now draw up a table like the one in Table 11A-3.

For each factor, this shows both rankings for each key job. On the left is the ranking from step 3. On the right is the ranking based on wages paid. For each factor, the ranking based on the amount of the factor (from step 3) should be about the same as the ranking based on the wages assigned to the job (step 5). (In this case

TABLE 11A-3 Comparison of Factor and Wage Rankings

	Mental Requirements		Physical Requirements		Skill Requirements		Responsibility		Working Conditions	
	A[1]	$[2]	A[1]	$[2]	A[1]	$[2]	A[1]	$[2]	A[1]	$[2]
Welder	1	1	4	4	1	1	1	1	2	2
Crane operator	3	3	1	1	3	3	4	4	4	4
Punch press operator	2	2	3	3	2	2	2	2	3	3
Security guard	4	4	2	2	4	4	3	3	1	1

[1]Amount of each factor based on step 3.
[2]Ratings based on distribution of wages to each factor from step 5.

they are.) If there's much of a discrepancy, it suggests that the key job might be unusable, and from this point on, it is no longer used as a key job. (Many managers don't bother to screen out unusable key jobs. To simplify things, they skip over our steps 5 and 6, going instead from step 4 to step 7; this is an acceptable alternative.)

Step 7. Construct the Job-Comparison Scale Once you've identified the usable, true key jobs, the next step is to set up the job-comparison scale (Table 11A-4). (Note that there's a separate column for each of the five comparable factors.) To develop it, you'll need the assigned wage tables from steps 4 and 5.

For each of the factors for all key jobs, you write the job next to the appropriate wage rate. Thus, in the assigned wage rate table (Table 11A-2), the welder job has $4.00 assigned to the factor "mental requirements." Therefore, on the job-comparison

TABLE 11A-4 Job (Factor)-Comparison Scale

	Mental Requirements	Physical Requirements	Skill Requirements	Responsibility	Working Conditions
.20				Crane Operator	Crane Operator
.30					Punch Press Operator
.40		Welder	Security Guard	Security Guard	Welder
.50					
.60					Security Guard
.70					
.80				Punch Press Operator	
.90					
1.00				(Plater)	
1.10					
1.20	Security Guard				
1.30		Punch Press Operator			
1.40	Crane Operator	Security Guard	(Inspector)	(Plater)	
1.50		(Inspector)			(Inspector)
1.60	Punch Press Operator				
1.70	(Plater)				
1.80			Crane Operator	(Inspector)	
1.90					
2.00		Crane Operator	Punch Press Operator	Welder	
2.20		(Plater)			
2.40	(Inspector)				(Plater)
2.60					
2.80					
3.00			Welder		
3.20					
3.40					
3.60					
3.80					
4.00	Welder				
4.20					
4.40					
4.60					
4.80					

scale (Table 11A-4), write "welder" in the "mental requirements" factor column, next to the "$4.00" row. Do the same for all factors for all key jobs.

Step 8. Use the Job-Comparison Scale Now all the other jobs to be evaluated can be slotted, factor by factor, into the job-comparison scale. For example, suppose you have a job of plater that you want to slot in. You decide where the "mental requirements" of the plater job would fit as compared with the "mental requirements" of all the other jobs listed. It might, for example, fit between punch press operator and inspector. Similarly, you would ask where the "physical requirements" of the plater's job fit as compared with the other jobs listed. Here you might find that it fits just below crane operator. You would do the same for each of the remaining three factors.

An Example Let us work through an example to clarify the factor comparison method. We'll just use four key jobs to simplify the presentation—you'd usually start with 15 to 25 key jobs.

Step 1: First, we do a job analysis.

Step 2: Here we select our four key jobs: welder, crane operator, punch press operator, and security guard.

Step 3: Based on the job descriptions and specifications, here we rank key jobs by factor, as in Table 11A-1.

Step 4: Here we distribute wage rates by factor, as in Table 11A-2.

Step 5: Then we rank our key jobs according to wage rates assigned to each key factor. These rankings are shown in parentheses in Table 11A-2.

Step 6: Next compare your two sets of rankings (see Table 11A-3). In each left-hand column (marked A) is the job's ranking from step 3 based on the amount of the compensable factor. In each right-hand column (marked $) is the job's ranking from step 5 based on the wage assigned to that factor. In this case, there are no differences between any of the pairs of A (amount) and $ (wage) rankings, so all our key jobs are usable. If there had been any differences (for example, between the A and $ rankings for the welder job's "mental requirements" factor), we would have dropped that job as a key job.

Step 7: Now we construct our job-comparison scale as in Table 11A-4. For this, we use the wage distributions from step 4. For example, let us say that in steps 4 and 5 we assigned $4.00 to the "mental requirements" factor of the welder's job. Therefore, we now write "welder" on the $4.00 row under the "mental requirements" column as in Table 11A-4.

Step 8: Now all our other jobs can be slotted, factor by factor, into our job-comparison scale. We do not distribute wages to each of the factors for our other jobs to do this. We just decide where, factor by factor, each of our other jobs should be slotted. We've done this for two other jobs in the factor comparison scale: They're shown in parentheses. Now we also know what the wages for these two jobs should be, and we can do the same for all our jobs.

A Variation There are several variations to this basic factor comparison method. One converts the dollar values on the factor comparison chart (Table 11A-4) to points. (You can do this by multiplying each of the dollar values by 100, for example.) The main advantage in making this change is that your system would no longer be "locked in" to your present wage rates. Instead, each of your jobs would be compared with one another, factor by factor, in terms of a more constant point system.

Pros and Cons We've presented the factor comparison method at some length because it is (in one form or another) a very widely used job evaluation method. Its wide use derives from several advantages: First, it is an accurate, systematic, quantifiable method for which detailed, step-by-step instructions are available. Second, jobs are compared to other jobs to determine a relative value. Thus, in the job-comparison scale you not only see that a welder requires more mental ability than a plater, but you also can determine about *how much* more mental ability is required—apparently about twice as much ($4.00 versus $1.70). (This type of calibration is not possible with the ranking or classification methods.) Third, this is also a fairly easy job evaluation system to explain to employees.

Complexity is probably the most serious disadvantage of the factor comparison method. Although it is fairly easy to explain the factor comparison scale and its rationale to employees, it is difficult to show them how to build one. In addition, the use of the five factors is an outgrowth of the technique developed by its originators. However, using the same five factors for all organizations and for all jobs in an organization may not always be appropriate.

The Point Method of Job Evaluation The point method is widely used. It requires identifying several compensable factors (like skills and responsibility), each with several degrees, and also the degree to which each of these factors is present in the job. A different number of points are usually assigned for each degree of each factor. So once you determine the degree to which each factor is present in the job, you need only add up the corresponding number of points for each factor and arrive at an overall point value for the job.[93] Here are the steps:

STEP 1. DETERMINE CLUSTERS OF JOBS TO BE EVALUATED Because jobs vary widely by department, you usually will not use one point-rating plan for all jobs in the organization. Therefore, the first step is usually to cluster jobs, for example, into shop jobs, clerical jobs, sales jobs, and so forth. Then the committee will generally develop a point plan for one group or cluster at a time.

STEP 2. COLLECT JOB INFORMATION This means performing a job analysis and writing job descriptions and job specifications.

STEP 3. SELECT COMPENSABLE FACTORS Here select compensable factors, like problem solving, physical requirements, or skills. Each cluster of jobs may require its own compensable factors.

STEP 4. DEFINE COMPENSABLE FACTORS Next, carefully define each compensable factor. This is done to ensure that the evaluation committee members will each apply the factors with consistency. Figure 11A-2 (top) shows one such definition. The definitions are often drawn up or obtained by the human resource specialist.

STEP 5. DEFINE FACTOR DEGREES Next define each of several degrees for each factor so that raters may judge the amount or degree of a factor existing in a job. Thus, for the factor "complexity" you might choose to have six degrees, ranging from "seldom confronts new problems" through "uses independent judgment." (Definitions for each degree are shown in Figure 11A-2.) The number of degrees usually does not exceed five or six, and the actual number depends mostly on judgment. Thus, if all employees work either in a quiet, air-conditioned office or in a noisy, hot factory, then two degrees would probably suffice for the factor "working conditions." You need not have the same number of degrees for each factor, and you should limit degrees to the number necessary to distinguish among jobs.

STEP 6. DETERMINE RELATIVE VALUES OF FACTORS The next step is to decide how much weight (or how many total points) to assign to each factor. This is important because for each cluster of jobs some factors are bound to be more important than others. Thus, for executives the "mental requirements" factor would carry far more weight than would "physical requirements." The opposite might be true of factory jobs.

FIGURE 11A-2 Example of One Factor (Complexity/Problem Solving) in a Point Factor System

Source: Richard W. Beatty and James R. Beatty, "Job Evaluation," in Ronald A. Berk (ed.), *Performance Assessment: Methods and Applications* (Baltimore, MD: Johns Hopkins University Press, 1986), p. 322. Reprinted by permission.

The mental capacity required to perform the given job as expressed in resourcefulness in dealing with unfamiliar problems, interpretation of data, initiation of new ideas, complex data analysis, creative or developmental work.

Level	Point Value	Description of Characteristics and Measures
0	0	Seldom confronts problems not covered by job routine or organizational policy; analysis of data is negligible. *Benchmark*: Telephone operator/receptionist.
1	40	Follows clearly prescribed standard practice and demonstrates straightforward application of readily understood rules and procedures. Analyzes noncomplicated data by established routine. *Benchmark*: Statistical clerk, billing clerk.
2	80	Frequently confronts problems not covered by job routine. Independent judgment exercised in making minor decisions where alternatives are limited and standard policies established. Analysis of standardized data for information of or use by others. *Benchmark*: Social worker, executive secretary.
3	120	Exercises independent judgment in making decisions involving nonroutine problems with general guidance only from higher supervision. Analyzes and evaluates data pertaining to nonroutine problems for solution in conjunction with others. *Benchmark*: Nurse, accountant, team leader.
4	160	Uses independent judgment in making decisions that are subject to review in the final stages only. Analyzes and solves nonroutine problems involving evaluation of a wide variety of data as a regular part of job duties. Makes decisions involving procedures. *Benchmark*: Associate director, business manager, park services director.
5	200	Uses independent judgment in making decisions that are not subject to review. Regularly exercises developmental or creative abilities in policy development. *Benchmark*: Executive director.

The evaluation committee generally does the work of determining the relative values or weights that should be assigned to each of the factors. The committee members carefully study factor and degree definitions and then determine the relative value of the factors for the cluster of jobs under consideration. Here is one method for doing this:

First, assign a value of 100% to the highest-ranking factor. Then assign a value to the next highest factor as a percentage of its importance to the first factor, and so forth. For example,

Decision making	100%
Problem solving	85%
Knowledge	60%

Next, sum up the total percentage (in this case 100% + 85% + 60% = 245%). Then convert this 245% to a 100% system as follows:

Decision making:	100 ÷ 245 = 40.82 = 40.8%
Problem solving:	85 ÷ 245 = 34.69 = 34.7%
Knowledge:	60 ÷ 245 = 24.49 = 24.5%
Totals	100.0%

STEP 7. ASSIGN POINT VALUES TO FACTORS AND DEGREES In step 6, total weights were developed for each factor in percentage terms. Now assign points to each factor as in Table 11A-5. For example, suppose it is decided to use a total number of 500 points in the point plan. Because the factor "decision making" had a weight of 40.8%, it would be assigned a total of 40.8% × 500 = 204 points.

Thus, it was decided to assign 204 points to the decision-making factor. This automatically means that the highest degree for the decision-making factor would also carry 204 points. Then assign points to the other degrees for this factor, usually in equal amounts from the lowest to the highest degree. For example, divide 204 by the number of degrees (say, 5); this equals 40.8. Then the lowest degree here would carry about 41 points. The second degree would carry 41 plus 41, or 82 points. The third degree would carry 123 points. The fourth degree would carry 164 points. Finally, the fifth and highest degree would carry 204 points. Do this for each factor (as in Table 11A-5).

STEP 8. WRITE THE JOB EVALUATION MANUAL Developing a point plan like this usually culminates in a *point manual* or *job evaluation manual.* This simply consolidates the factor and degree definitions and point values into one convenient manual.

STEP 9. RATE THE JOBS Once the manual is complete, the actual evaluations can begin. Raters (usually the committee) use the manual to evaluate jobs. Each job based on its job description and job specification is evaluated factor by factor to determine the number of points that should be assigned to it. First, committee members determine the degree (first degree, second degree, and so on) to which each factor is present in the job. Then they note the corresponding points (see Table 11A-5) that were previously assigned to each of these degrees (in step 7). Finally, they add up the points for all factors, arriving at a total point value for the job. Raters generally start with rating key jobs and obtain consensus on these. Then they rate the rest of the jobs in the cluster.

"PACKAGED" POINT PLANS Developing a point plan of one's own can obviously be a time-consuming process. For this reason a number of groups (such as the National Electrical Manufacturer's Association and the National Trade Association) have developed standardized point plans. These have been used or adapted by thousands of organizations. They contain ready-made factor and degree definitions and point assessments for a wide range of jobs and can often be used with little or no modification.

PROS AND CONS Point systems have their advantages, as their wide use suggests. This is a quantitative technique that is easily explained to and used by employees. On the other hand, it can be difficult to develop a point plan, and this is one reason many organizations have opted for ready-made plans. In fact, the availability of a number of ready-made plans probably accounts in part for the wide use of point plans in job evaluation.

TABLE 11A-5 Evaluation Points Assigned to Factors and Degrees

	First-Degree Points	Second-Degree Points	Third-Degree Points	Fourth-Degree Points	Fifth-Degree Points
Decision making	41	82	123	164	204
Problem solving	35	70	105	140	174
Knowledge	24	48	72	96	123

ENDNOTES

1. Elayne Robertson Demby, "Two Stores Refused to Join the Race to the Bottom for Benefits and Wages," *Workforce Management*, February 2004, pp. 57–59; www.wegmans.com/webapp/wcs/stores/servlet/CategoryDisplay?langId=-1&storeId=10052&catalogId=10002&categoryId=256548, accessed March 25, 2009.
2. Richard Henderson, *Compensation Management* (Reston, VA: Reston Publishing, 1980); see also Barry Gerhart and Sara Rynes, *Compensation: Theory, Evidence, and Strategic Implications* (Thousand Oaks, CA: Sage Publications, 2003); and Joseph Martocchio, *Strategic Compensation* (Upper Saddle River, NJ: Prentice Hall, 2006), pp. 67–94.
3. In a recent case, *Ledbetter v. Goodyear Tire & Rubber Co.*, the U.S. Supreme Court notably restricted the amount of time (to 180 or 300 days) after each allegedly discriminatory pay decision under Title VII to file or forever lose the claim. Congress subsequently passed and President Obama assigned a new law significantly expanding the amount of time to file such claims. See, for example, "Following *Ledbetter* Ruling, Issue of Workers Sharing Pay Information Takes Center Stage," *BNA Bulletin to Management*, July 17, 2007, p. 225.
4. The recently approved Genetic Information Nondiscrimination Act amended the Fair Labor Standards Act to increase penalties for the death or serious injury of employees under age 18. Allen Smith, "Penalties for Child Labor Violations Increase," *HR Magazine*, July 2008, p. 19.
5. Also note that 18 states have their own rules governing overtime. The states are Alaska, Arkansas, California, Colorado, Connecticut, Hawaii, Illinois, Kentucky, Maryland, Minnesota, Montana, New Jersey, North Dakota, Oregon, Pennsylvania, Washington, West Virginia, and Wisconsin. "DOL's Final Rule Is Not the Final Word on Overtime for Employers in 18 States," *BNA Bulletin to Management*, June 3, 2004, pp. 55, 177.
6. Employers should be vigilant about employees who arrive early or leave late, lest the extra time spent on the employer's property obligate the employer to compensate the employee for that time. For example, a diligent employee may get dropped off at work early and spend, say, 20 minutes before his or her day actually starts doing work-related chores such as compiling a list of clients to call that day. Although there is no hard and fast rule, some courts follow the rule that employees who arrive 15 or more minutes early are presumed to be working unless the employer can prove otherwise. If using time clocks, employers should always instruct employees not to clock in more than 5–10 minutes early (or out 5–10 minutes late). Kenneth Sovereign, *Personnel Law* (Upper Saddle River, NJ: Prentice Hall, 1999), p. 215.
7. www.pacifictimesheet.com/timesheet_products/pacific_timesheet_handheld_pda_field_data_entry_software.htm, accessed March 23, 2009.
8. "Wal-Mart to Settle 63 Wage and Hour Suits, Paying up to $640 Million to Resolve Claims," *BNA Bulletin to Management*, January 13, 2009, p. 11.
9. "FedEx Ground in Reverse on Driver Status," *Workforce Management*, April 21, 2008, p. 4. In April 2009, one jury in Seattle ruled in favor of FedEx, deeming the drivers to be independent contractors. In another case, a jury in California ruled instead for the drivers. Alex Roth, "Verdict Backs FedEx in Labor Case," *The New York Times*, April 2, 2009, p. B4.
10. "Microsoft Agrees to Pay $96.9 Million to Settle Contingent Workers' Lawsuits," *BNA Bulletin to Management*, December 14, 2000, p. 395.
11. "Senate Passes Minimum Wage Increase That Includes Small-Business Tax Provisions," *BNA Bulletin to Management*, February 6, 2007, p. 41; www.dol.gov/esa/whd/flsa, accessed August 12, 2007.
12. Society for Human Resource Management, "The Evolution of Compensation," *Workplace Visions*, 2002, p. 2; www.dol.gov/esa/minwage/america.htm, accessed June 3, 2004.
13. For a description of exemption requirements, see Jeffrey Friedman, "The Fair Labor Standards Act Today: A Primer," *Compensation*, January/February 2002, pp. 51–54. See also www.shrm.org/issues/FLSA, accessed August 12, 2007; and www.dol.gov/esa/whd/flsa, accessed August 12, 2007.
14. "Employer Ordered to Pay $2 Million in Overtime," *BNA Bulletin to Management*, September 26, 1996, pp. 308–309. See also "Restaurant Managers Awarded $2.9 Million in Overtime Wages for Nonmanagement Work," *BNA Bulletin to Management*, August 30, 2001, p. 275.
15. Because the overtime and minimum wage rules only changed in 2004, exactly how to apply these rules is still in a state of flux. If there's doubt about exemption eligibility, it's probably best to check with the local Department of Labor Wage and Hour office. See, for example, "Attorneys Say FLSA Draws a Fine Line Between Exempt/Nonexempt Employees," *BNA Bulletin to Management*, July 5, 2005, p. 219; "DOL Releases Letters on Administrative Exemption, Overtime," *BNA Bulletin to Management*, October 18, 2005, p. 335.
16. See, for example, Jeffrey Friedman, "The Fair Labor Standards Act Today: A Primer," *Compensation*, January/February 2002, p. 53; Andre Honoree, "The New Fair Labor Standards Act Regulations and the Sales Force: Who Is Entitled to Overtime Pay?" *Compensation & Benefits Review*, January/February 2006, p. 31; www.shrm.org/issues/FLSA, accessed August 12, 2007; www.dol.gov/esa/whd/flsa, accessed August 12, 2007.
17. "Drug Sales Reps Raise Questions About Outside Sales Exemption," *BNA Bulletin to Management*, April 1, 2008, p. 111.
18. Diane Cadrain, "Guard Against FLSA Claims," *HR Magazine*, April 2008, pp. 97–100.
19. For another example, this one involving technical writers working for Sun Microsystems, see "Court Certifies Class of Technical Writers Working for Sun Microsystems", *BNA Bulletin to Management*, May 20, 2008, p. 161.
20. Robert Nobile, "How Discrimination Laws Affect Compensation," *Compensation & Benefits Review*, July/August 1996, pp. 38–42.
21. Henderson, *Compensation Management*, pp. 101–127; see also Barry Hirsch and Edward Schumacher, "Unions, Wages, and Skills," *Journal of Human Resources* 33, no. 1 (Winter 1998), p. 115.
22. See, for example, Robert Heneman, "Implementing Total Rewards of Strategies," Society for Human Resource Management, www.shrm.org/foundation, accessed March 2, 2009.

23. See for example, Andrew Richter, "Paying the People in Black at Big Blue," *Compensation & Benefits Review*, May/June 1998, p. 51; and Bobby Watson, Jr. and Gangaram Singh, "Global Pay Systems: Compensation in Support of Multinational Strategy," *Compensation & Benefits Review*, Jan/Feb 2005, pp. 33–36.
24. Peg Buchenroth, "Driving Performance: Making Pay Work for the Organization," *Compensation & Benefits Review*, May/June 2006, pp. 30–35.
25. Jessica Marquez, "Raising the Performance Bar," *Workforce Management*, April 24, 2006, pp. 31–32.
26. http://markets.on.nytimes.com/research/stocks/news/press_release.asp?docKey=600-200902040900BIZWIRE_USPR_____BW5153-7ENARVBIKO0QHDGGFHUTBKEMIS&provider=Businesswire&docDate=February%204%2C%202009&press_symbol=US%3BHEW, accessed March 21, 2009; www.shrm.org/hrdisciplines/benefits/Articles/Pages/AmericanstoSeeLowestPayRaisesinThreeDecades.aspx, accessed March 21, 2009.
27. "Salaries for Similar Jobs Very Significantly Across the United States," *Compensation & Benefits Review*, January/February 2006, p. 9.
28. Bobby Watson Jr. and Gangaram Singh, "Global Pay Systems: Compensation in Support of Multinational Strategy," *Compensation & Benefits Review*, January/February 2005, pp. 33–36.
29. Nicholas Wade, "Play Fair: Your Life May Depend on It," *The New York Times*, September 12, 2003, p. 12.
30. Robert Bretz and Stephen Thomas, "Perceived Inequity, Motivation, and Final Offer Arbitration in Major League Baseball," *Journal of Applied Psychology*, June 1992, pp. 280–289.
31. James DeConinck and Duane Bachmann, "An Analysis of Turnover Among Retail Buyers," *Journal of Business Research* 58, no. 7 (July 2005), pp. 874–882.
32. David Terpstra and Andre Honoree, "The Relative Importance of External, Internal, Individual, and Procedural Equity to Pay Satisfaction," *Compensation & Benefits Review*, November/December 2003, pp. 67–74.
33. Ibid., p. 68.
34. Millicent Nelson et al., "Pay Me More: What Companies Need to Know About Employee Pay Satisfaction," *Compensation & Benefits Review*, March/April 2008, pp. 35–42.
35. Michael Harris et al., "Keeping up with the Joneses: A field study of the relationships among upward, lateral, and downward comparisons and pay level satisfaction," *Journal of Applied Psychology* 93, no. 3 (2008), pp. 665–673.
36. Henderson, *Compensation Management*, pp. 260–269. See also "Web Access Transforms Compensation Surveys," *Workforce Management*, April 24, 2006, p. 34.
37. For more information on these surveys, see the company's brochure, "Domestic Survey References," Watson Wyatt Data Services, 218 Route 17 North, Rochelle Park, NJ 07662. See http://www.watsonwyatt.com/search/publications.asp?ArticleID=21432, accessed October 29, 2009.
38. "International Sources of Salary Data," *Compensation & Benefits Review*, May/June 1998, p. 23. For current international salary data see, ibid.
39. Martocchio, *Strategic Compensation*, p. 138. See also Nona Tobin, "Can Technology Ease the Pain of Salary Surveys?" *Public Personnel Management* 31, no. 1 (Spring 2002), pp. 65–78.
40. You may have noticed that job analysis as discussed in Chapter 4 can be a useful source of information on compensable factors, as well as on job descriptions and job specifications. For example, a quantitative job analysis technique like the position analysis questionnaire generates quantitative information on the degree to which the following five basic factors are present in each job: having decision-making/communication/social responsibilities, performing skilled activities, being physically active, operating vehicles or equipment, and processing information. As a result, a job analysis technique like the PAQ is actually as (or some say, more) appropriate as a job evaluation technique (than for job analysis) in that jobs can be quantitatively compared to one another on those five dimensions and their relative worth thus ascertained. Another point worth noting is that you may find that a single set of compensable factors is not adequate for describing all your jobs. This is another reason why many managers therefore divide their jobs into job clusters. For example, you might have a separate job cluster for factory workers, for clerical workers, and for managerial personnel. You would then probably have a somewhat different set of compensable factors for each job cluster.
41. Michael Carrell and Christina Heavrin, *Labor Relations and Collective Bargaining* (Upper Saddle River, NJ: Prentice Hall, 2004) pp. 300–303.
42. If you used the job classification method, then of course the jobs are already classified.
43. In other words, on the graph, plot the benchmark jobs' points (as determined by job evaluation) and their corresponding market pay rates (as determined by the salary survey). Then slot in the other jobs based on their evaluations, to determine what their target pay rates should be.
44. Susan Marks, "Can the Internet Help You Hit the Salary Mark?" *Workforce*, January 2001, pp. 86–93.
45. Mark Meltzer and Howard Goldsmith, "Executive Compensation for Growth Companies," *Compensation & Benefits Review*, November/December 1997, pp. 41–50; Joseph Martocchio, *Strategic Compensation* (Upper Saddle River, NJ: Prentice Hall, 2006) pp. 421–428. See also Martin J. Conyon, "Executive Compensation and Incentives," *The Academy of Management Perspectives* 20, no. 1 (February 2006), p. 25(20); and "Realities of Executive Compensation—2006/2007 Report on Executive Pay and Stock Options," www. watsonwyatt.com/research/resrender.asp?id=2006-US-0085&page=1, accessed May 20, 2007.
46. Douglas Tormey, "Executive Compensation: Creating a 'Legal' Checklist," *Compensation & Benefits Review*, July/August 1996, pp. 12–36. See also Bruce Ellig, "Executive Pay: A Primer," *Compensation & Benefits Review*, January/February 2003, pp. 44–50.
47. Syed Tahir Hijazi, "Determinants of Executive Compensation and Its Impact on Organizational Performance," *Compensation & Benefits Review* 39, no. 2 (March–April 2007), p. 58(9).
48. James Reda, "Executive Pay Today and Tomorrow," *Corporate Board* 22, no. 126 (January 2001), p. 18.
49. For example, one book argues that executives of large companies use their power to have themselves compensated in ways that are not sufficiently related to performance. Lucian Bebchuk and Jesse Fried, *Pay Without Performance: The Unfulfilled Promise of Executive Compensation* (Boston: Harvard University Press, 2004).

50. "Revolting Shareholders," *The Economist*, May 24, 2003, p. 13.
51. "Executive Pay Remains Linked to Performance," *Compensation & Benefits Review*, March/April 2008, p. 10. See also "Appraising and Rewarding Managerial Performance in Challenging Economic Times: Part 2," *Journal of Compensation & Benefits* 25, no. 4 (July/August 2009), p. 5–12.
52. See, for example, Fay Hansen, "Current Trends in Compensation and Benefits," *Compensation & Benefits Review* 36, no. 2 (March/April 2004), pp. 7–8.
53. Louis Lavelle, "While the CEO Gravy Train May Be Slowing Down, It Hasn't Jumped the Rails," *BusinessWeek*, April 16, 2001, pp. 76–80. See also K. Dillon, "The Coming Battle over Executive Pay," *Harvard Business Review* 87, no. 9 (September 2009), pp. 96–103.
54. See, for example, Martocchio, *Strategic Compensation*; and Patricia Zingheim and Jay Schuster, "Designing Pay and Rewards in Professional Services Companies," *Compensation & Benefits Review*, January/February 2007, pp. 55–62.
55. Dimitris Manolopoulos, "What Motivates Research and Development Professionals? Evidence from Decentralized Laboratories in Greece," *International Journal of Human Resource Management* 17, no. 4 (April 2006), pp. 616–647.
56. See, for example, Robert Heneman and Peter LeBlanc, "Development of and Approach for Valuing Knowledge Work," *Compensation & Benefits Review*, July/August 2002, p. 47.
57. Kevin Foote, "Competencies in the Real World: Performance Management for the Rationally Healthy Organization," *Compensation & Benefits Review*, July/August 2001, p. 25.
58. Gerald Ledford Jr., "Paying for the Skills, Knowledge, and Competencies of Knowledge Workers," *Compensation & Benefits Review*, July/August 1995, p. 56; see also Richard Sperling and Larry Hicks, "Trends in Compensation and Benefits Strategies," *Employment Relations Today* 25, no. 2 (Summer 1998), pp. 85–99.
59. Foote, "Competencies in the Real World," p. 29. See also B. Lokshin et. al., "Crafting Firm Competencies to Improve Innovative Performance," *European Management Journal* 27, no. 3 (June 2009), pp. 187–196.
60. Duncan Brown, "Using Competencies and Rewards to Enhance Business Performance and Customer Service at The Standard Life Assurance Company," *Compensation & Benefits Review*, July/August 2001, pp. 17, 19.
61. Ledford, "Three Case Studies on Skill-Based Pay," *Compensation & Benefits Review*, March/April 1991, p. 12. See also Kathryn Cofsky, "Critical Keys to Competency-Based Pay," *Compensation & Benefits Review*, November/December 1993, pp. 46–52; Brian Murray and Barry Gerhart, "Skill-Based Pay and Skills Seeking," *Human Resource Management Review* 10, no. 3 (2000), pp. 271–287.
62. Joseph Martocchio, *Strategic Compensation*, p. 168.
63. Robert McNabb and Keith Whitfield, "Job Evaluation and High-Performance Work Practices: Compatible or Conflictual?" *Journal of Management Studies* 38, no. 2 (March 2001), pp. 294–311.
64. Ibid., p. 293.
65. Ledford, "Three Case Studies on Skill-Based Pay," p. 12. See also Cofsky, "Critical Keys to Competency-Based Pay," pp. 46–52; Murray and Gerhart, "Skill-Based Pay and Skills Seeking," pp. 271–287.
66. Gerald Ledford Jr. and Gary Bergel, "Skill-Based Pay Case Number 1: General Mills," *Compensation & Benefits Review*, March/April 1991, pp. 24–38; see also Gerald Barrett, "Comparison of Skill-Based Pay with Traditional Job Evaluation Techniques," *Human Resource Management Review* 1, no. 2 (Summer 1991), pp. 97–105; Barbara Dewey, "Changing to Skill-Based Pay: Disarming the Transition Land Mines," *Compensation & Benefits Review*, January/February 1994, pp. 38–43.
67. This is based on Ledford and Bergal, "Skill-Based Pay Case Number 1," pp. 28–29.
68. Robert Heneman and Peter LeBlanc, "Work Evaluation Addresses the Shortcomings of Both Job Evaluation and Market Pricing," *Compensation & Benefits Review*, January/February 2003, p. 8.
69. Ledford, "Paying for the Skills, Knowledge, and Competencies of Knowledge Workers," p. 55.
70. Kevin Parent and Caroline Weber, "Case Study: Does Paying for Knowledge Pay Off?" *Compensation & Benefits Review*, September/October 1994, pp. 44–50; and Edward Lawler III, Gerald Ledford, Jr. and Lei Chang, "Who Uses Skill-Based Pay, and Why?" *Compensation & Benefits Review*, November/December 1996, pp. 20–26.
71. John Kilgour, "Job Evaluation Revisited: The Point Factor Method," *Compensation & Benefits Review*, July/August 2008, p. 37.
72. Patricia Zingheim and Jay Schuster, "The Next Decade for Pay and Rewards," *Compensation & Benefits Review*, January/February 2005, p. 29; and Patricia Zingheim and Jay Schuster, "What Are Key Pay Issues Right Now," *Compensation & Benefits Review*, May/June 2007, pp. 51–55. See also "A Framework for Understanding New Concepts in Compensation Management," *Benefits & Compensation Digest* 46, no. 9 (September 2009), pp. Front Cover, 13–16.
73. David Hofrichter, "Broadbanding: A 'Second Generation' Approach," *Compensation & Benefits Review*, September/October 1993, pp. 53–58. See also "The Future of Salary Management," *Compensation & Benefits Review*, July/August 2001, pp. 7–12.
74. Ibid., p. 55.
75. For example, see Sandra Emerson, "Job Evaluation: A Barrier to Excellence?" *Compensation & Benefits Review*, January/February 1991, pp. 39–52; Nan Weiner, "Job Evaluation Systems: A Critique," *Human Resource Management Review* 1, no. 2 (Summer 1991), pp. 119–132; and Brian Klaas, "Compensation in the Jobless Organization," *Human Resource Management Review* 12, no. 1 (Spring 2002), pp. 43–62.
76. Dawne Shand, "Broadbanding the IT Worker," *Computerworld* 34, no. 41 (October 9, 2000).
77. "Broadbanding Pay Structures Does Not Receive Flat-Out Support from Employers, Survey Finds," *BNA Bulletin to Management*, January 13, 2000, p. 11.
78. Emerson, "Job Evaluation," p. 39.
79. *County of Washington v. Gunther*, U.S. Supreme Court, no. 80–426, June 8, 1981.
80. "Generation X Women Earn More Than Predecessors," *BNA Bulletin to Management*, June 6, 2002, p. 181.
81. "Women Still Earned Less Than Men, BLS Data Show," *BNA Bulletin to Management*, June 8, 2000, p. 72. However, there is some indication that there is less gender-based pay gap among full-time workers ages 21 to 35 living alone. Kent

Hoover, "Study Finds No Pay Gap for Young, Single Workers," *Tampa Bay Business Journal* 20, no. 19 (May 12, 2000), p. 10.
82. Christopher Dougherty, "Why Are the Returns to Schooling Higher for Women Than for Men?" *Journal of Human Resources* 40, no. 4 (Fall 2005), pp. 969–988.
83. James Bandler and Charles Forelle, "How a Giant Insurer Decided to Oust Hugely Successful CEO," *The Wall Street Journal*, December 7, 2006, p. A1.
84. Jennifer Dudley, "The New Executive Compensation Rule: The Tough Disclosures," *Compensation & Benefits Review*, July/August 2007, pp. 28–34.
85. Mark Poerio and Eric Keller, "Executive Compensation 2005: Many Forces, One Direction," *Compensation & Benefits Review*, May/June 2005, pp. 34–40.
86. Ibid., p. 38.
87. Society for Human Resource Management, "Changing Leadership Strategies," *Workplace Visions*, no. 1 (2008), p. 3.
88. For a discussion of some of the issues that go into hammering out an executive employment agreement, see, for example, Jonathan Cohen and Laura Clark, "Is the Executive Employment Agreement Dead?" *Compensation & Benefits Review*, July/August 2007, pp. 50–55.
89. Ibid. See also Brent Longnecker and James Krueger, "The Next Wave of Compensation Disclosure," *Compensation & Benefits Review*, January/February 2007, pp. 50–54.
90. This is based on Howard Risher, "Planning and Managing Tomorrow's Pay Programs," *Compensation & Benefits Review*, July/August 2008, pp. 30–35.
91. Ibid., p. 35.
92. Al Wright, "Tools for Automating Complex Compensation Programs," *Compensation & Benefits Review*, November/December 2003, pp. 53–61.
93. For a discussion, see, for example, Roger Plachy, "The Point Factor Job Evaluation System: A Step-by-Step Guide, Part I," *Compensation & Benefits Review*, July/August 1987, pp. 12–27; Roger Plachy, "The Case for Effective Point-Factor Job Evaluation, Viewpoint I," *Compensation & Benefits Review*, March/April 1987, pp. 45–48; Roger Plachy, "The Point-Factor Job Evaluation System: A Step-by-Step Guide, Part II," *Compensation & Benefits Review*, September/October 1987, pp. 9–24; and Alfred Candrilli and Ronald Armagast, "The Case for Effective Point-Factor Job Evaluation, Viewpoint II," *Compensation & Benefits Review*, March/April 1987, pp. 49–54. See also Robert J. Sahl, "How to Install a Point-Factor Job Evaluation System," *Personnel* 66, no. 3 (March 1989), pp. 38–42.

12 Pay for Performance and Financial Incentives

Grilled some time ago by a Congress outraged by the huge bonuses AIG was paying to certain employees, Treasury Secretary Timothy Geithner seemed to agree that under the circumstances, the bonuses were an injustice. In his comments, he pointed out that AIG's old bonus plan actually seemed to be dysfunctional, insofar as it apparently encouraged the huge risk taking that had just about brought AIG down.

Source: Courtesy of Andy Kropa/Redux Pictures.

WHERE ARE WE NOW . . .

Chapter 11 focused on developing the overall pay plan and on salaries and wages. Incentives play an important role in any pay plan. The main purpose of this chapter is to explain how managers use performance-based incentives to motivate employees. After a brief overview of motivation theories, we'll discuss incentives for individual employees, and then for managers and executives, salespeople, and professionals, as well as organizationwide incentive plans. In Chapter 13 (Benefits and Services), we'll turn to the financial and nonfinancial benefits and services, which are the final part of the employee's compensation package.

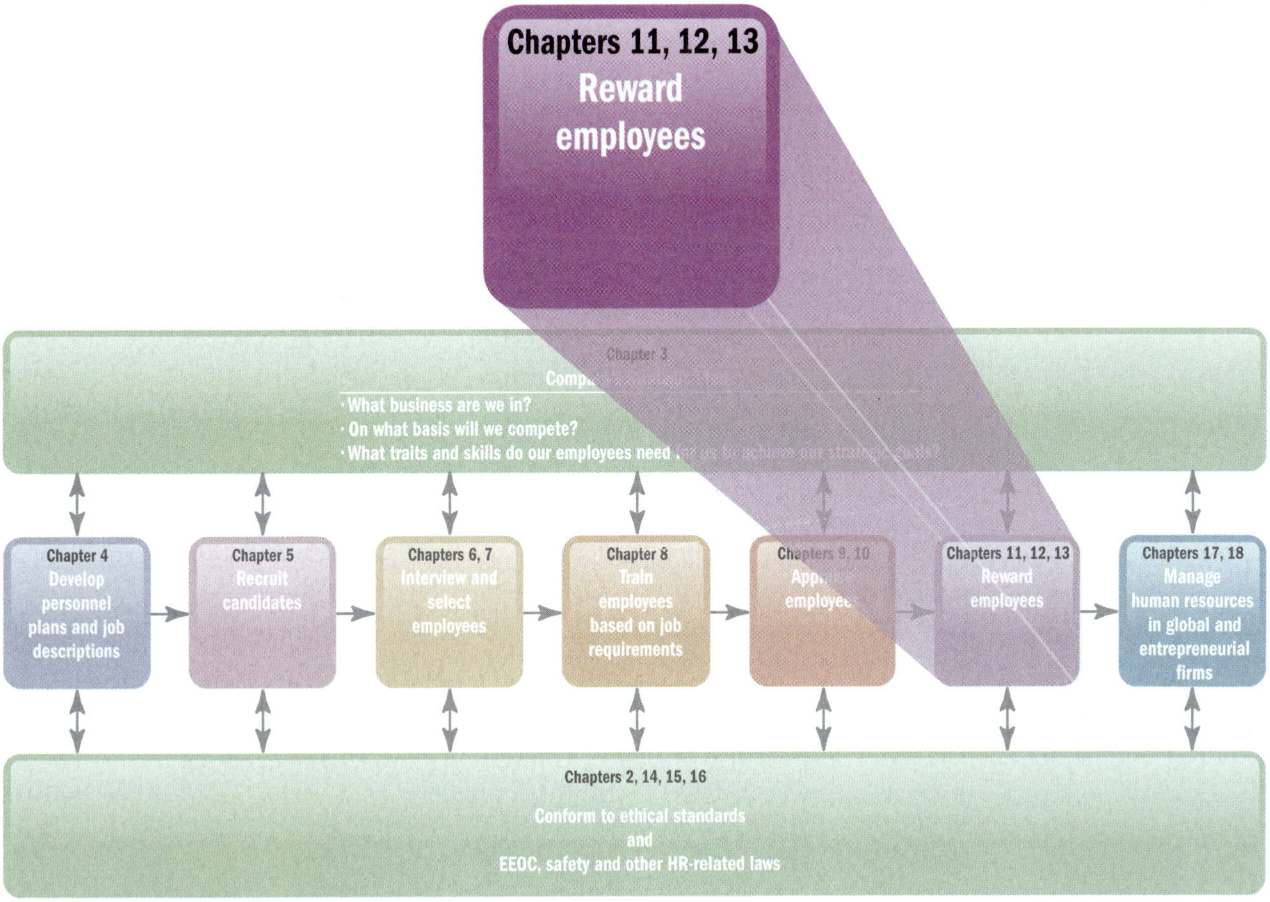

LEARNING OUTCOMES

1. Explain how you would apply five motivation theories in formulating an incentive plan.
2. Discuss the main incentives for individual employees.
3. Discuss the pros and cons of commissions versus straight pay incentives for salespeople.
4. Describe the main incentives for managers and executives.
5. Name and define the most popular organizationwide variable pay plans
6. Outline the steps in designing effective incentive plans.

MONEY AND MOTIVATION

Frederick Taylor popularized using **financial incentives**—financial rewards paid to workers whose production exceeds some predetermined standard—in the late 1800s. As a supervisory employee of the Midvale Steel Company, Taylor was concerned with what he called "systematic soldiering"—the tendency of employees to work at the slowest pace possible and to produce at the minimum acceptable level. What especially intrigued him was the fact that some of these workers had the energy to run home and work on their houses, even after a 12-hour day. Taylor knew that if he could harness this energy during the workday, Midvale Steel could achieve huge productivity gains.

In pursuing that aim, Taylor turned to financial incentives. At the time, primitive incentive plans were already in use, but were generally ineffective (because employers arbitrarily changed incentive rates). Taylor made three contributions. He saw the need for formulating what he called a **fair day's work**, namely standards of output for a job, which he devised for each job based on careful, scientific analysis. He spearheaded the **scientific management movement**, a management approach that emphasized improving work methods through observation and analysis. And, he popularized the use of incentive pay as a way to reward employees who produced over standard.

Linking Performance and Pay

Today, as we explained in Chapter 11, incentive pay—tying workers' pay to their performance—is widely popular.[1] The problem is that doing so is easier said than done. Many such programs are ineffective, and some are disastrous (one plan, at Levi Strauss, is widely assumed to have been the last nail in the coffin of Levi's U.S.-based production). As logical as it seems to link pay to performance, many (or most) of these programs simply don't work. Mercer Consulting found that just 28% of the 2,600 U.S. workers it surveyed said they were personally motivated by their companies' incentive plans. "Employees don't see a strong connection between pay and performance, and their performance is not particularly influenced by the company's incentive plan," said one Mercer expert.[2] About 83% of companies with such programs say their programs are only somewhat successful or not successful at all.[3]

We'll see that there are many reasons for such dismal results. Many employers, perhaps ignorant of Taylor and history, institute and change their plans' standards arbitrarily. Others ignore the fact that incentive pay is, at its heart, psychologically based. Therefore, not everyone reacts to a reward in the same way, and not all rewards are suited to all situations.[4] Compensation experts therefore argue that managers should understand the motivational bases of incentive plans.[5] We'll review some of this basic motivation information next.

Motivation and Incentives

1 Explain how you would apply five motivation theories in formulating an incentive plan.

Several motivation theories have particular relevance to designing incentive plans. These include theories associated with the psychologists Abraham Maslow, Frederick Herzberg, Edward Deci, Victor Vroom, and B. F. Skinner.

The Hierarchy of Needs and Abraham Maslow

Abraham Maslow made what may be the most popular observation on what motivates people. He said that people have a hierarchy of five types of needs: *physiological* (food, water, warmth), *security* (a secure income, knowing one has a job), *social* (friendships and camaraderie), *self-esteem* (respect), and *self-actualization* (becoming the person you believe you can become). According to Maslow's *prepotency process principle*, people are motivated first to satisfy each lower-order need and then, in sequence, each of the higher-level needs. For example, if someone is out of work and insecure, getting a job may drive everything he or she does. (So, during periods of high unemployment, one may see even former executives taking low-level jobs to make ends meet.) A secure employee may then turn to being concerned with building friendships, getting respect, and going to school to get the degree required to be a top executive. We usually envision Maslow's hierarchy of needs as a stepladder or pyramid.

Maslow's theory has many practical implications. For example, insecure employees won't be as concerned with doing jobs that might be "beneath them"; and, don't try to motivate someone with more challenging work if he or she doesn't earn enough to pay the bills.

Motivators and Frederick Herzberg Frederick Herzberg said the best way to motivate someone is to organize the job so that doing it provides the feedback and challenge that helps satisfy the person's "higher-level" needs for things like accomplishment and recognition. These needs are relatively insatiable, says Herzberg, so recognition and challenging work provide a sort of built-in motivation generator. Satisfying "lower level" needs for things like better pay and working conditions just keeps the person from becoming dissatisfied.

Herzberg says the factors ("hygienes") that satisfy lower-level needs are different from those ("motivators") that satisfy or partially satisfy higher-level needs. If *hygiene* factors (factors outside the job itself, such as working conditions, salary, and incentive pay) are inadequate, employees become dissatisfied. However, adding more of these hygienes (like incentives) to the job (supplying what Herzberg calls "extrinsic motivation") is an inferior way to try to motivate someone, because lower-level needs are quickly satisfied. Soon the person simply says, in effect, "What have you done for me lately? I want another raise."

Instead of relying on hygienes, says Herzberg, managers interested in creating a self-motivated workforce should emphasize "job content" or *motivator* factors. Managers do this by enriching workers' jobs so that the jobs are more challenging, and by providing feedback and recognition—they make doing the job intrinsically motivating, in other words. Here, just doing the job provides the motivation. Among other things, Herzberg's theory makes the point that relying exclusively on financial incentives is risky. The employer should also provide the recognition and challenging work that most people desire.

Demotivators and Edward Deci Psychologist Edward Deci's work highlights another potential downside to relying too heavily on extrinsic rewards: They may backfire. Deci found that extrinsic rewards could at times actually detract from the person's intrinsic motivation.[6] For example, a Samaritan who risks danger by rushing to an accident victim's aid might be insulted if the victim said, "Thanks, here's some money for your trouble." The point may be stated thusly: Be cautious in devising incentive pay for highly motivated employees, lest you inadvertently demean and detract from the desire they have to do the job out of a sense of responsibility.

Expectancy Theory and Victor Vroom Another important motivational fact is that, in general, people won't pursue rewards they find unattractive, or where the odds of success are very low. Psychologist Victor Vroom's expectancy motivation theory echoes these commonsense observations. He says a person's motivation to exert some level of effort depends on three things: the person's **expectancy** (in terms of probability) that his or her effort will lead to performance;[7] **instrumentality**, or the perceived connection (if any) between successful performance and actually obtaining the rewards;

financial incentives
Financial rewards paid to workers whose production exceeds some predetermined standard.

fair day's work
Output standards devised based on careful, scientific analysis.

scientific management
Management approach based on improving work methods through observation and analysis.

expectancy
A person's expectation that his or her effort will lead to performance.

instrumentality
The perceived relationship between successful performance and obtaining the reward.

and **valence**, which represents the perceived value the person attaches to the reward.[8] In Vroom's theory, motivation is thus a product of three things: Motivation = $(E \times I \times V)$, where, of course, E represents expectancy, I instrumentality, and V valence. If E or I or V is zero or inconsequential, there will be no motivation.

Vroom's theory has three implications for how managers design incentive plans.

- First, if employees don't *expect* that effort will produce performance, no motivation will occur. So, managers must ensure that their employees have the skills to do the job, and believe they can do the job. Thus training, job descriptions, and confidence building and support are important in using incentives.
- Second, Vroom's theory suggests that employees must see the *instrumentality* of their efforts—they must believe that successful performance will in fact lead to getting the reward. Managers can accomplish this, for instance, by creating easy to understand incentive plans.
- Third, the reward itself must be of *value* to the employee. So ideally, the manager should take into account individual employee preferences.

Behavior Modification/Reinforcement and B. F. Skinner

Using incentives also assumes you know something about how consequences affect behavior.[9] Psychologist B. F. Skinner's findings provide the foundation for much of what we know about this. Managers apply Skinner's principles by using *behavior modification.* **Behavior modification** means changing behavior through rewards or punishments that are contingent on performance. For managers, behavior modification boils down to following two main principles: (1) That behavior that appears to lead to a positive consequence (reward) tends to be repeated, while behavior that appears to lead to a negative consequence (punishment) tends not to be repeated; and (2) that, therefore, managers can get someone to change his or her behavior by providing the properly scheduled rewards (or punishment).

Incentive Pay Terminology

Managers often use two terms synonymously with incentive plans.[10] Traditionally, all incentive plans are *pay-for-performance* plans. They all tie employees' pay to the employees' performance. **Variable pay** is more specific: It is usually an incentive plan that ties a group or team's pay to some measure of the firm's (or the facility's) overall profitability;[11] *profit-sharing plans* (discussed later) are one example.[12] However, confusing as it may be, some experts do use the term "variable pay" to include incentive plans for individual employees.[13]

To arrange our discussion, we will organize the following sections around individual employee incentive and recognition programs, sales compensation programs, management and executive incentive compensation programs, and team and organizationwide incentive programs.

Employee Incentives and the Law

Walmart recently paid a large settlement because allegedly it had not properly computed overtime pay. Their problem points up a critical aspect of incentive pay. Under the Fair Labor Standards Act, if the performance-based pay is in the form of a prize or cash award, the employer generally must *include the value of that award* when calculating the worker's overtime pay for that pay period.[14] Employers pay overtime rates to nonexempt employees based on the employees' previous week's earnings. Unless you structure the incentive bonuses properly, the bonus itself becomes part of the week's wages. Suppose someone earning \$10 per hour for a 40-hour week also earns performance incentive pay of \$80 for the week, or \$480 total. Further, assume she also works 2 hours overtime that week. The overtime rate for the 2 hours she works overtime that week equals 1.5 times \$12, or \$18; you must include the average \$2 per hour (\$80 divided by 40 hours) she earned in incentive pay.

Certain bonuses are excludable from overtime pay calculations. For example, Christmas and gift bonuses that are not based on hours worked, or are so substantial that employees don't consider them a part of their wages, do not have to be included in overtime pay calculations. Similarly, purely discretionary bonuses in which the employer retains discretion over how much if anything to pay are excludable.

Other types of incentive pay *must* be included. Under the Fair Labor Standards Act (FLSA), bonuses to include in overtime pay computations include those promised to newly hired employees; those provided for in union contracts or other agreements; and those announced to induce employees to work more productively, steadily, rapidly, or efficiently or to induce them to remain with the company. Such bonuses would include many of those we turn to next, such as individual and group production bonuses, bonuses for quality and accuracy of work, efficiency bonuses, attendance bonuses, and sales commissions.

2 Discuss the main incentives for individual employees.

INDIVIDUAL EMPLOYEE INCENTIVE AND RECOGNITION PROGRAMS

Several incentive plans are particularly suited for use with individual employees.

Piecework Plans

Piecework is the oldest and still most popular individual incentive plan. Here you pay the worker a sum (called a *piece rate*) for each unit he or she produces. Thus, if Tom the Web surfer gets $0.40 for each e-mail sales lead he finds for the firm, he would make $40 for bringing in 100 a day and $80 for 200.

In a perfect world, developing a workable piece rate plan requires industrial engineering (that's how Frederick Taylor got his start). The crucial issue is the production standard, and industrial engineers often set this—for instance, in terms of a standard number of e-mail leads per hour or a standard number of minutes per e-mail lead. In Tom's case, a job evaluation indicated that his Web surfing job was worth $8 an hour. The industrial engineer determined that 20 good leads per hour was the standard production rate. Therefore, the piece rate (for each lead) was $8 divided by 20, or $0.40 per sales lead. (Of course, we need to ensure that Tom makes at least the minimum wage, so we'd probably pay him $7.25 per hour—the minimum wage in July 2009—whether or not he brought in 18 leads, and then pay him $0.40 per lead for each over 18.) But in practice, most employers set the piece rates more informally.

Straight Piecework

Piecework generally implies **straight piecework**, which entails a strict proportionality between results and rewards regardless of output. However, some piecework plans allow for sharing productivity gains between employer and worker; here, the worker receives extra income for some above-normal production.[15] So, if Tom starts bringing in 30 leads per hour instead of the "standard" 20, his piece rate for leads above 25 might bump to $.45 each.

Standard Hour Plans

The **standard hour plan** is like the piece rate plan, with one difference. Instead of getting a rate per piece, the worker gets a premium equal to the percent by which his or her performance exceeds the standard. So if Tom's standard is 160 leads per day (and thus $64 per day), and he brings in 200 leads, he'd get

valence
The perceived value a person attaches to the reward.

behavior modification
Using contingent rewards or punishment to change behavior.

variable pay
Any plan that ties pay to productivity or profitability, usually as one-time lump payments.

piecework
A system of pay based on the number of items processed by each individual worker in a unit of time, such as items per hour or items per day.

straight piecework
An incentive plan in which a person is paid a sum for each item he or she makes or sells, with a strict proportionality between results and rewards.

standard hour plan
A plan by which a worker is paid a basic hourly rate but is paid an extra percentage of his or her rate for production exceeding the standard per hour or per day. Similar to piecework payment but based on a percent premium.

an extra 25% (40/160), or $80 total for the day. Some firms find that expressing the incentive in percentages reduces the workers' tendency to link their production standard to pay (thus making the standard easier to change). It also eliminates the need to recalculate piece rates whenever hourly wage rates are changed.

Pros and Cons Piecework plans are understandable, appear equitable in principle, and can be powerful incentives, since rewards are proportionate to performance.

But from the time of Taylor, managers have seen piecework's disadvantages. Workers on piecework may resist attempts to revise production standards, even if the change is justified. Since piecework plans usually tie incentive pay to quantity produced, employees may well downplay quality, or resist switching from job to job (since doing so could reduce productivity).[16] Attempts to introduce new technology or processes may trigger resistance, for much the same reason.

In some industries, the term *piecework* has a dreadful reputation. For example, some garment manufacturers had operators assemble items (like shirts) in their homes, and paid them for each piece they completed. Unfortunately, the hourly pay for this work didn't always fulfill the Wage and Hour Act's minimum wage requirements. In one case, an electronics firm had a woman who assembled cables for the firm during the day take home parts to assemble at night. Working at home, she allegedly averaged only $2 to $2.50 an hour for the piecework.[17]

For these and other reasons, more employers are moving to other plans.[18] We'll look at these on the following pages.

Merit Pay as an Incentive

Merit pay or a **merit raise** is any salary increase the firm awards to an individual employee based on his or her individual performance. It is different from a bonus in that it usually becomes part of the employee's base salary, whereas a bonus is a one-time payment. Although the term *merit pay* can apply to the incentive raises given to any employee—exempt or nonexempt, office or factory, management or nonmanagement—the term is more often used for white-collar employees and particularly professional, office, and clerical employees.

Merit pay is the subject of much debate. Advocates argue that awarding pay raises across the board (without regard to individual merit) may actually detract from performance, by showing employees they'll be rewarded regardless of how they perform.

Detractors present good reasons why merit pay can backfire. One, certainly, is the dubious nature of many appraisal processes. Since many appraisals are unfair, so too will be the merit pay you base them on.[19] Similarly, supervisors often give most employees about the same rating and raise, either because of a reluctance to alienate some employees or to give everyone a raise that will help them stay even with the cost of living. (Alienating employees is a real problem. Almost every employee thinks he or she is above average, so getting a below-average merit increase can be demoralizing.) One study focused on performance ratings and merit pay raises for 218 workers in a nuclear waste facility. The researchers found a "very modest relationship between merit pay increase and performance rating."[20] Research into the effects of tying merit pay increases to teachers' or faculty members' research and/or teaching performance suggest that merit pay is more clearly linked with research productivity than with teaching effectiveness.[21]

The solution is not to throw out merit raises, but to design them to be more effective. Among other things, this means establishing effective appraisal procedures and ensuring that managers in fact tie merit pay awards to performance.

Merit Pay Options Two adaptations of merit pay plans are popular. One awards merit raises in a lump sum once a year and does *not* make the raise part of the employee's salary (making them, in effect, short-term bonuses for lower-level workers). Traditional merit increases are cumulative, but these *lump-sum merit raises* are not. This produces two potential benefits. First, the merit raise is not baked into the employee's salary, so you need not pay it year after year. Lump-sum merit increases can also be more dramatic motivators than a traditional merit raise. For example, a 5% lump-sum merit payment to a $30,000 employee is $1,500 cash, as opposed to a traditional weekly merit payout of $29 for 52 weeks.

The other adaptation ties merit awards to both individual and organizational performance. Table 12-1 presents a sample matrix for doing so. In this example, you might measure the company's performance by, say, rate of return, or sales divided by payroll costs. Company performance and the employee's performance (using his or her performance appraisal) receive equal weight in computing the merit pay. Here an outstanding performer would receive 70% of his or her maximum lump-sum award even if the organization's performance were marginal. However, employees with marginal or unacceptable performance would get no lump-sum awards even in years in which the firm's performance was outstanding. The bonus plan at Discovery Communications is an example. Executive assistants can receive bonuses of up to a maximum of 10% of their salaries. The boss's evaluation of the assistant's individual performance accounts for 80% of the potential bonus; 10% is based on how the division does, and 10% on how the company as a whole does.[22]

Incentives for Professional Employees

Professional employees are those whose work involves the application of learned knowledge to the solution of the employer's problems. They include lawyers, doctors, economists, and engineers.

Making incentive pay decisions for professional employees can be challenging. For one thing, firms usually pay professionals well anyway. For another, they're already driven by the desire to produce high-caliber work and receive recognition from colleagues. In some cases (as psychologists such as Deci would argue), offering financial rewards to people like these may actually diminish their intrinsic motivation—not add to it.

However, it would be unrealistic to assume that people like the systems analysts and programmers at Microsoft and Google work only for professional gratification. A survey of 300 IT departments found that 77% were paying bonuses and incentives, including stock options and profit sharing, to IT professionals.[23] Texas Instruments

TABLE 12-1 Merit Award Determination Matrix (an Example)

The Employee's Performance Rating (Weight = 0.50)	*The Company's Performance (Weight = 0.50)*				
	Outstanding	Excellent	Good	Marginal	Unacceptable
Outstanding	1.00	0.90	0.80	0.70	0.00
Excellent	0.90	0.80	0.70	0.60	0.00
Good	0.80	0.70	0.60	0.50	0.00
Marginal	—	—	—	—	—
Unacceptable	—	—	—	—	—

To determine the dollar value of each employee's award: (1) multiply the employee's annual, straight-time wage or salary as of June 30 times his or her maximum incentive award (as determined by management or the board—such as, "10% of each employee's pay") and (2) multiply the resultant product by the appropriate percentage figure from this table. For example, if an employee had an annual salary of $20,000 on June 30 and a maximum incentive award of 7% and if her performance and the organization's performance were both "excellent," the employee's award would be $1,120: ($20,000 × 0.07 × 0.80 = $1,120).

merit pay (merit raise)
Any salary increase awarded to an employee based on his or her individual performance.

began offering stock option grants to about a third of its engineers when it discovered it was losing about 15% of them to the competition.[24] Several firms, including IBM and Motorola, award bonuses to employees whose work wins patents for the firms.[25]

Nonfinancial and Recognition-Based Awards

Recognition programs are one of several types of nonfinancial incentives. The term *recognition program* usually refers to formal programs, such as employee-of-the-month programs. *Social recognition program* generally refers to informal manager–employee exchanges such as praise, approval, or expressions of appreciation for a job well done. *Performance feedback* means providing quantitative or qualitative information on task performance for the purpose of changing or maintaining performance; showing workers a graph of how their performance is trending is an example.[26]

Studies show that recognition has a positive impact on performance, either alone or in conjunction with financial rewards.[27] In one survey, 89% of surveyed companies reported having recognition programs in place, for things ranging from exceptional performance to attendance, safety, sales, and major life events.[28] At American Skandia, which provides insurance and financial planning products and services, customer service reps who exceed standards receive a plaque, a $500 check, their photo and story on the firm's internal Web site, and a dinner for themselves and their teams.[29] Most employers combine financial and nonfinancial awards. One survey of 235 managers found that the most-used rewards to motivate employees (top–down, from most used to least) were:[30]

- Employee recognition
- Gift certificates
- Special events
- Cash rewards
- Merchandise incentives
- E-mail/print communications
- Training programs
- Work/life benefits
- Variable pay
- Group travel
- Individual travel
- Sweepstakes

HR in Practice: Incentives Managers Can Use

As you can see, the individual line manager should not rely just on the employer's incentive plans for motivating subordinates. Those plans may not be very complete, and there are simply too many opportunities to motivate employees every day to let those opportunities pass. There are three guides to follow.

First, the best option for motivating employees is also the simplest—*make sure the employee has a doable goal* and that he or she agrees with that. It makes little sense to try to motivate employees with financial incentives if they don't know their goals or don't agree with them. Psychologist Edwin Locke and his colleagues have consistently found that specific, challenging goals lead to higher task performance than specific, unchallenging goals, or vague goals or no goals.

Second, *recognizing an employee's contribution* is a powerful motivation tool. Studies (and theories like those of Maslow and Herzberg) show that recognition has a positive impact on performance, either alone or in combination with financial rewards. For example, in one study, combining financial rewards with recognition produced a 30% performance improvement in service firms, almost twice the effect of using each reward alone.

Third, remember you can use *social recognition* (such as compliments) as positive reinforcement on a day-to-day basis. Figure 12-1 presents a short list.[31]

FIGURE 12-1 Social Recognition and Related Positive Reinforcement Managers Can Use

Source: Bob Nelson, *1001 Ways to Reward Employees* (New York: Workman Pub, 1994), p. 19; Sunny C. L. Fong and Margaret A. Shaffer, "The Dimensionality and Determinants of Pay Satisfaction: A Cross-Cultural Investigation of a Group Incentive Plan," *International Journal of Human Resource Management* 14, no. 4 (June 2003), p. 559.

- Challenging work assignments
- Freedom to choose own work activity
- Having fun built into work
- More of preferred task
- Role as boss's stand-in when he or she is away
- Role in presentations to top management
- Job rotation
- Encouragement of learning and continuous improvement
- Being provided with ample encouragement
- Being allowed to set own goals
- Compliments
- Expression of appreciation in front of others
- Note of thanks
- Employee-of-the-month award
- Special commendation
- Bigger desk
- Bigger office or cubicle

Online and IT-Supported Awards

If there's a downside to incentive programs, it's that they can be expensive and complicated to administer.[32] For example, with more than 1,000 sales representatives, First Tennessee Bank was having problems managing its sales incentive programs.[33] Tracking the performance of dozens or hundreds of measures and then computing individual employees' incentives is time-consuming. Bank employees had to enter by hand sales information for each of the 1,000 sales reps onto Excel spreadsheets. The process, said one officer, "had begun to spiral out of control." As one solution, vendors provide *enterprise incentive management* (EIM) systems. These automate the planning, analysis, and management of incentive compensation plans.[34]

Administering recognition programs is similarly challenging. If a company has an Employee Anniversary Recognition Program, for instance, someone (probably in human resources) needs to compile a prizes catalog, distribute it, and keep track of who gets what. Many firms—including Levi Strauss & Co., Barnes & Noble, Citibank, and Walmart—now join with online awards firms to expedite the whole process. Management consultant Hewitt Associates uses www.bravanta.com/recognition/ to help its managers more easily recognize exceptional employee service with special awards. Additional Internet incentive/recognition sites include www.terryberry.com/OnlineRecognition.htm, www.premierechoiceaward.com/secure/home.asp, www.giveanything.com, www.incentivecity.com, www.netcentives.com, and www.kudoz.com.

3 Discuss the pros and cons of commissions versus straight pay incentives for salespeople.

INCENTIVES FOR SALESPEOPLE

Sales compensation plans typically rely heavily on incentives in the form of sales commissions. However, some salespeople get straight salaries, and most receive a combination of salary and commissions.

Salary Plan

Some firms pay salespeople fixed salaries (perhaps with occasional incentives in the form of bonuses, sales contest prizes, and the like).[35] Straight salaries particularly make sense when the main task involves prospecting (finding new clients) or account servicing (such as participating in trade shows).

The straight salary approach makes it easier to switch territories or to reassign salespeople, and it can foster sales staff loyalty. The main disadvantage, of course, is that straight salary can demotivate potentially high-performing salespeople.[36]

Commission Plan

Straight commission plans pay salespeople for results, and only for results. Under these plans, salespeople have the greatest incentive. Commission plans tend to attract high-performing salespeople who see that effort clearly produces rewards. Sales costs are proportionate to sales rather than fixed, and the company's fixed sales costs are thus lower. It's a plan that's easy to understand and compute.

However, problems abound. Salespeople tend to focus on making the sale and on high-volume items, and may neglect nonselling duties like servicing small accounts, cultivating dedicated customers, and pushing hard-to-sell items. Wide variations in pay may occur; this can make some feel the plan is inequitable. Misjudging sales potential can lead to excessively high commissions and to the need to cut commission rates. In addition, salespersons' pay may be excessive in boom times and low in recessions. Furthermore, sales performance—like any performance—reflects not just motivation, but ability, too. If the person hasn't the sales skills, commissions won't produce sales.[37] Similarly, many find working without a financial safety net can be unsettling. As one sales representative in a study put it,

> If I go on vacation, I lose money. If I'm sick, I lose money. If I'm not willing to drop everything on a moment's notice to close with a customer, I lose money. I can't see how anyone could stay in this job for long. It's like a trapeze act and I'm working without a net.[38]

Combination Plan

Most companies pay salespeople a combination of salary and commissions, usually with a sizable salary component. An incentive mix of about 70% base salary/30% incentive seems typical; this cushions the salesperson's downside risk (of earning nothing), while limiting the risk that the commissions could get out of hand from the firm's point of view.[39]

Combination plans have pros and cons. They give salespeople a floor to their earnings, let the company specify what services the salary component is for (such as servicing current accounts), and still provide an incentive for superior performance. However, the salary component isn't tied to performance, so the employer is obviously trading away some incentive value. Combination plans also tend to become complicated, and misunderstandings can result.

The latter might not be a problem with a simple salary-plus-commission plan, but most plans are not so simple. For example, in a "commission-plus-drawing-account" plan, the salesperson is paid based on commissions. However, he or she can draw on future earnings to get through low sales periods. Similarly, in the "commission-plus-bonus" plan, the firm pays its salespeople mostly based on commissions. However, they also get a small bonus for directed activities like selling slow-moving items.

An example can help illustrate the complexities of the typical combination plan. In one company, the following three-step formula is applied:

Step 1: For sales volume up to $18,000 a month, pay base salary plus 7% of gross profits plus 0.5% of gross sales.

Step 2: For sales volume from $18,000 to $25,000 a month, pay base salary plus 9% of gross profits plus 0.5% of gross sales.

Step 3: More than $25,000 a month, pay base salary plus 10% of gross profits plus 0.5% of gross sales.

In all cases, base salary is paid every 2 weeks, while the earned percentage of gross profits and gross sales is paid monthly.[40]

Maximizing Sales Force Results

In setting sales quotas and commission rates, the employer wants to motivate sales activity but avoid having commissions become excessive. Unfortunately, there is a tendency to set commission rates informally, without considering how much each sale must contribute to covering expenses. Employers often discover that they barely break even on a sale once all commissions are paid.[41] Setting effective quotas is an art. Questions to ask include, Are quotas communicated to the sales force within 1 month of the start of the period? Does the sales force know how their quotas are set? Do you combine bottom–up information (like account forecasts) with top–down requirements (like the company business plan)? Are returns and de-bookings reasonably low? And, has your firm generally avoided compensation-related lawsuits?[42] One expert suggests the following rule as to whether the sales incentive plan is effective: 75% or more of the sales force achieving quota or better, 10% of the sales force achieving higher performance level (than previously), and 5% to 10% of the sales force achieving below-quota performance and receiving performance development coaching.[43]

A recent survey of sales effectiveness by consultants Watson Wyatt reveals that, among other things, salespeople at high-performing companies:

- Receive 38% of their total cash compensation in the form of *sales-related variable pay* (compared with 27% for salespeople at low-performing companies)
- Are twice as likely to receive stock, *stock options*, or other equity pay as are their counterparts at low-performing companies (36% versus 18%)
- Spend 264 more hours per year on *high-value sales activities* (e.g., prospecting, making sales presentations, and closing) than salespeople at low-performing companies
- Spend 40% more time each year with their *best potential customers*—qualified leads and prospects they know—than salespeople at low-performing companies
- Compared with salespeople at low-performing companies, spend nearly 25% *less time on administration*, allowing them to allocate more time to core sales activities, such as prospecting leads and closing sales[44]

The accompanying "Evidence-Based HR" feature explains how the sales manager can gather evidence on and analyze these issues, such as, "How much time is my sales force spending with their best potential customers?"

EVIDENCE-BASED HR

How Effective Are Your Incentives?

Somewhat astonishingly, given the amount of money employers pay out in commissions, most still track sales performance and sales commissions much as they did decades ago, using spreadsheets (although now computerized ones). But to maximize performance, the sales manager typically needs evidence, such as: Do the sales team members understand the compensation plans? Do they know how we measure and reward performance? Are quotas set fairly? Is there a positive correlation between performance and commission earnings? Are commissions more than covering total salespersons expenses? And, does our commission plan maximize sales of our most profitable products?[45] It is difficult or impossible to gather this evidence or answer these questions because the spreadsheets don't easily support these types of analyses.

Gathering this evidence and conducting these analyses require software programs that we mentioned earlier in this chapter, namely enterprise incentive management applications.[46] Several vendors supply these systems. One is VUE Software™, which supplies VUE Compensation Management®.[47] With the aid of charts such as that in the accompanying illustration, VUE Compensation Management® enables the sales manager to conduct the necessary analyses. For example, he or she can trend and analyze compensation and performance data, conduct "what-if" analyses and reports, do trend analysis for performance data, and model changes to existing compensation plans.[48]

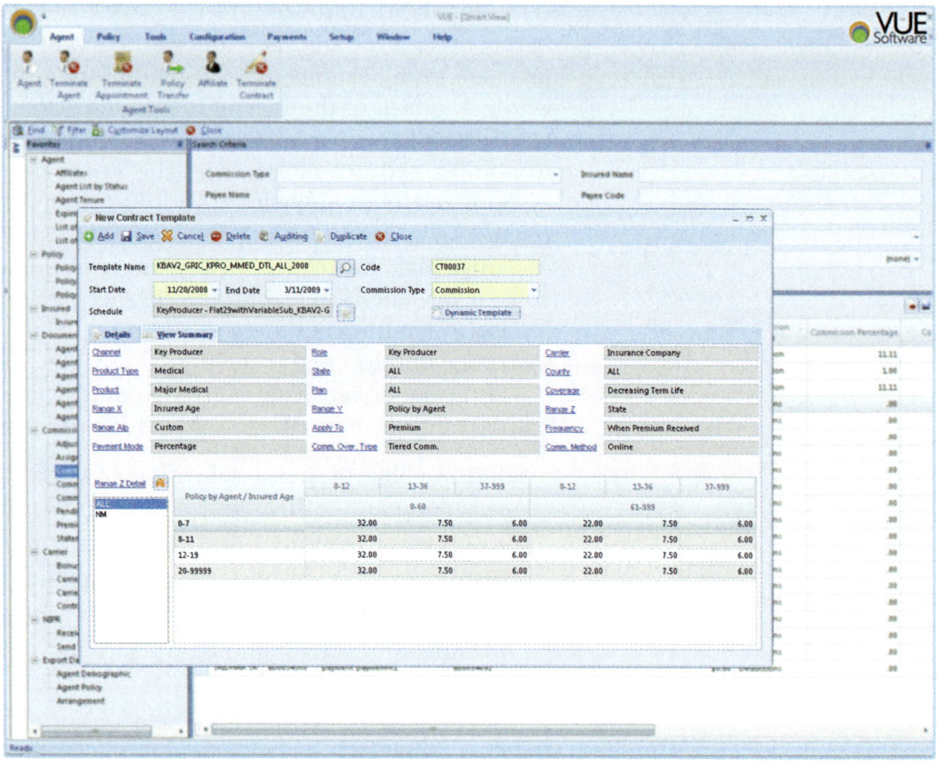

Source: Used with permission of Computer Solutions & Software International, Inc.

How to Sell Cars Commission rates vary by industry. However, a look at how auto dealers set salespersons' commission rates provides some insights into how to set rates to achieve specific aims. Compensation for car salespeople ranges from 100% commission to a small base salary with commission accounting for most of total compensation. Traditionally, dealers base commissions on the car's net profit when delivered to the buyer. This promotes precisely the sorts of behaviors the car dealer wants to encourage. For example, it encourages the salesperson to hold firm on the retail price, and to push "after-sale products" like floor mats, side moldings, undercoating, and car alarms. Car dealers also use short-term incentives. For helping sell slow-moving vehicles, the salesperson may be offered a "spiff"—a car dealer term for an extra incentive bonus over commission.

Commission plans still predominate in auto dealerships, but they're not as popular as they were. Many dealerships are substituting salary plus bonus plans for commissions. The transition to salary plus bonus reflects the growing emphasis on "one price no hassle" pricing, and the desire on the part of more dealers to make the purchase process less tense.[49]

4 Describe the main incentives for managers and executives

INCENTIVES FOR MANAGERS AND EXECUTIVES

Managers play a crucial role in divisional and company-wide profitability, and most firms therefore put considerable thought into how to reward them. Most managers get short-term and long-term incentives in addition to salary.[50] For firms offering short-term incentive plans, virtually all—96%—provide those incentives in cash. For those offering long-term incentives, about 48% offer them as stock options. The latter are to motivate and reward management for long-term corporate growth, prosperity, and shareholder value. A recent Mercer Consultants survey found that the average CEO pay mix was 16% salary, 22% bonus, and 62% long-term incentives.[51] Employers generally pay out bonus and short-term incentive awards in cash. Long-term incentives more often take the form of company stock, sometimes stock options. About 69% of companies in one survey had short-term incentives, although nearly a third of those said they didn't consider them effective in boosting employee performance.[52]

Sarbanes-Oxley

The Sarbanes-Oxley Act of 2002 affects how employers formulate their executive incentive programs. Congress passed Sarbanes-Oxley to inject a higher level of responsibility into executives' and board members' decisions. It makes them personally liable for violating their fiduciary responsibilities to their shareholders. The act also requires CEOs and CFOs of a public company to repay any bonuses, incentives, or equity-based compensation received from the company during the 12-month period following the issuance of a financial statement that the company must restate due to material noncompliance with a financial reporting requirement stemming from misconduct.[53]

We'll look at short- and long-term incentives.

Short-Term Incentives: The Annual Bonus

As noted, most firms have **annual bonus** plans aimed at motivating managers' short-term performance. Short-term bonuses can easily result in plus or minus adjustments of 25% or more to total pay. Three factors influence one's bonus: eligibility, fund size, and individual performance.

Eligibility

Most firms base bonus eligibility on a combination of factors, including job level/title, base salary, and other considerations (such as key jobs having a special impact on profits). Some simply base eligibility on job level or job title, or salary.[54]

The percentage size of the bonus is usually greater for top-level executives. Thus, an executive earning $250,000 in salary may be able to earn another 80% of his or her salary as a bonus, while a manager in the same firm earning $100,000 can earn only another 30%. Similarly, a supervisor might be able to earn up to 15% of his or her base salary in bonuses. A typical breakdown might be executives, 45% of base salary; managers, 25%; and supervisory personnel, 12%.

Source: Courtesy of Bill Aron/PhotoEdit Inc.

Even in a retail store, it would not be unusual to compensate the store manager partly based on the store's short-term sales and profit performance.

Fund Size

The employer must also decide the total amount of bonus money to make available—fund size. There are no hard-and-fast rules about the proportion of profits to pay out. One alternative is to reserve a minimal amount of the profits, say, 10%, for safeguarding stockholders' investments, and then to establish a fund for bonuses equal to, say, 20% of the corporate operating profit before taxes in excess of this safeguard amount. So here, if the operating profits were $200,000 (after putting away 10% to safeguard stockholders), then the management bonus fund might be 20% of $200,000 or $40,000. Other illustrative formulas might include:

- Twelve percent of net earnings after deducting 6% of net capital
- Ten percent of the amount by which net income exceeds 5% of stockholders' equity

annual bonus
Plans that are designed to motivate short-term performance of managers and are tied to company profitability.

Some firms don't use a formula at all, but make that decision on a discretionary basis.[55]

Individual Performance The third task is deciding the actual individual awards. Typically, the employer sets a target bonus (as well as maximum bonus, perhaps double the target bonus) for each eligible position. The actual award then reflects the manager's performance. For example, having previously decided which of one or more financial performance measures (return on assets, revenue growth, and so on) to use to measure each manager's performance, the firm computes preliminary total bonus estimates, and compares the total amount of money required with the bonus fund available.[56] If necessary, it then adjusts the individual bonus estimates. In any case, the basic rule should be that outstanding managers should receive at least their target bonuses, and marginal ones should receive at best below-average awards. Give the money you save from the poor performers to the outstanding ones.

One complication is whether managers will receive bonuses based on individual performance, corporate performance, or both. Firms usually tie top-level executive bonuses mostly to overall corporate results (or divisional results if the executive heads a major division). This makes sense because the company's results are largely their own. But as one moves farther down the chain of command, corporate profits become a less accurate gauge of a manager's contribution. For, say, supervisors or the heads of functional departments, it often makes more sense to tie the bonus more closely to individual performance.

Many firms therefore end up tying short-term bonuses to both organizational and individual performance. Perhaps the simplest method is the *split-award plan.* This makes the manager eligible for two bonuses, one based on his or her individual effort and one based on the organization's overall performance. Thus, a manager might be eligible for an individual performance bonus of up to $10,000, but receive only $2,000 at the end of the year, based on his or her individual performance evaluation. But the person might also receive a second bonus of $3,000, based on the firm's profits for the year.

One drawback to this approach is that it may give marginal performers too much—for instance, someone could get a company-based bonus, even if his or her own performance is mediocre. One way to avoid this is to use the *multiplier method.* In other words, make the bonus a product of both individual and corporate performance. As Table 12-2 illustrates, multiply the target bonus by 1.00, .80, or zero (if the firm's performance is excellent, and the person's performance is excellent, good, fair, or poor). Here a manager whose own performance is poor does not even receive the company-based bonus. As the accompanying "Managing HR in Challenging Times" feature illustrates, differentials like these become more pronounced when economies turn down.

TABLE 12-2 Multiplier Approach to Determining Annual Bonus

Individual Performance (Based on Appraisal, Weight = 0.50)	*Company Performance (Based on Sales Targets, Weight = 0.50)*			
	Excellent	Good	Fair	Poor
Excellent	1.00	0.90	0.80	0.70
Good	0.80	0.70	0.60	0.50
Fair	0.00	0.00	0.00	0.00
Poor	0.00	0.00	0.00	0.00

Note: To determine the dollar amount of a manager's award, multiply the maximum possible (target) bonus by the appropriate factor in the matrix.

Managing HR in Challenging Times

Incentives for Top Performers

In challenging times, employers tend to reduce the pool of dollars available for raises, but that's not necessarily true for all employees. As one expert from the consulting firm Mercer puts it, "In this less than robust economic environment . . . top-performing employees are an organization's best competitive weapon and they are rewarding them accordingly."[57]

So as the United States slipped into recession, employers were broadening the performance differentials they awarded to top performers. For example, in 2009, expected base pay increases for the highest ranked employees were 5.6%, compared with only 0.6% for the lowest rated employees. Middle rated employees could expect about 3.3%. The same is true for incentive payouts. For example, the highest-paid office clerical employees could expect short-term incentive payouts of 13%, while lowest rated employees could expect 3%, and mid-rated employees 8%.[58] So the bottom line seems to be that in challenging times it's even more important to focus on keeping and incentivizing your top employees.[59]

Long-Term Incentives

Employers use long-term incentives to inject a long-term perspective into their executives' decisions. With only short-term criteria to shoot for, a manager could conceivably boost profitability by reducing plant maintenance, for instance; this tactic might catch up with the company 2 or 3 years later. Long-term incentives are also "golden handcuffs"—they motivate executives to stay with the company by letting them accumulate capital (usually options to buy company stock) that they can only cash in after a certain number of years. Popular long-term incentives include cash, stock, stock options, stock appreciation rights, and phantom stock. We'll look at each.

Stock Options A **stock option** is the right to purchase a specific number of shares of company stock at a specific price during a specific period. The executive thus hopes to profit by exercising his or her option to buy the shares in the future but at today's price. The assumption is that the price of the stock will go up. Unfortunately, this depends partly on considerations outside the manager's control, such as general economic and market conditions. When the market plummets, employers must scramble to sweeten their managers' stock option plans. When employers don't, the evidence suggests that the executives do leave.[60] When stock markets dropped in 2008–2009, many employers including Intel modified option plans to increase the chances for a payout.[61]

Stock Option Problems The chronic problem with stock options is that they often reward even managers who have lackluster performance, but there are also other issues. Many blame stock options for contributing to corporate scandals, in which executives allegedly manipulated the dates they received their options to maximize their returns. Options may (and probably do, based on the evidence) also encourage executives to take perilous risks in pursuit of higher (at least short-term) profits.[62] Their stock options provide an incentive to go for spectacular results, but since they have not actually bought the stock yet, they don't risk their own money. (One solution is to draft the option plan so that it forces recipients to convert their options to stock more quickly.[63])

stock option
The right to purchase a stated number of shares of a company stock at today's price at some time in the future.

Other Stock Plans In any case, there is a trend toward using new types of compensation, tied more explicitly to performance goals. Instead of stock options, more firms are granting various types of *performance shares* such as performance-contingent restricted stock; the executive receives his or her shares only if he or she meets the preset performance targets.[64] As other examples, with *indexed options*, the option's exercise price fluctuates with the performance of, say, a market index. Then, if the company's stock does no better than the index, the manager's options are worthless. With *premium priced options*, the exercise price is higher than the stock's closing price on the date of the grant, so the executive can't profit from the options until the stock makes significant gains.[65]

Stock appreciation rights permit the recipient to exercise the stock option (by buying the stock) or to take any appreciation in the stock price in cash, stock, or some combination of these. A *performance achievement plan* awards shares of stock for the achievement of predetermined financial targets, such as profit or growth in earnings per share. With *restricted stock plans*, the firm usually awards shares without cost to the executive: The employee can sell the stock (for which he or she paid nothing), but is restricted from doing so for, say, 5 years. Under *phantom stock plans*, executives receive not shares but "units" that are similar to shares of company stock. Then at some future time, they receive value (usually in cash) equal to the appreciation of the "phantom" stock they own.

Other Executive Incentives

Companies also provide various incentives to persuade executives not to leave the firm. This is especially important when there is reason to believe another company is stalking the firm and wants to buy it. **Golden parachutes** (as opposed to golden handcuffs) are extraordinary payments companies make to executives in connection with a change in ownership or control of a company. For example, a company's golden parachute clause might state that, with a change in ownership of the firm, the executive would receive a one-time payment of $2 million.[66]

Other firms, perhaps more dubiously, guarantee large loans as incentives to directors and officers, for instance, to buy company stock. Thus, directors and officers of Conseco owed the company more than $500 million for such loans when shares of the company stock dropped precipitously.[67]

Strategy and the Executive's Total Rewards Package

Few human resource practices have as profound an impact on strategic success as the company's long-term incentives. Whether expanding through joint ventures abroad, consolidating operations, or pursuing growth, few firms can fully implement strategies in just 1 or 2 years. Therefore, the long-term signals you send managers and executives regarding what you will (or won't) reward can have a big effect on whether the firm's strategy succeeds.

Employers designing long-term incentives thus disregard their firm's strategy at their peril. The executives' *total reward package*—base salary, short- and long-term incentives, and perks—must align with each other and with the goal of achieving the company's strategic aims. Compensation experts suggest first defining the strategic context for the executive compensation plan. In other words, "What is our strategy and what are our strategic goals?" Then create the compensation package, through a strategy-mapping–type process. First decide what long-term behaviors (boosting sales, cutting costs, and so on) the executives must exhibit to achieve the firm's strategic goals. Then shape each component of the executive total compensation package (base salary, short- and long-term incentives, and perks) and group them into a balanced plan that makes sense in terms of motivating the executive to achieve these aims. The rule is this: Each pay component should help focus the manager's attention on the behaviors required to achieve the company's strategic goals.[68]

5 Name and define the most popular organizationwide variable pay plans.

TEAM AND ORGANIZATIONWIDE INCENTIVE PLANS

We've focused to this point on individual employee incentives such as piecework, commissions, and executive bonuses. Let's look now at incentives for teams, and for all employees company-wide.

How to Design Team Incentives

Firms increasingly rely on teams to manage their work. They therefore need incentive plans that encourage teamwork and focus team members' attention on performance. **Team (or group) incentive plans** pay incentives to the team based on the team's performance.

The main question here is how to reward the team's performance, and the wrong choice can prove lethal. Levi Strauss installed a team incentive plan that rewarded the team as a whole for its output, neglecting the fact that some employees worked harder than others did. The faster ones soon slowed down, production declined, and Levi's (as noted earlier) ended up closing its U.S. factories.

So, the main thing is to make sure you have all your team pulling together. Yet the usual approach is still to tie rewards to some overall standard of group performance, such as "total labor hours per car." Doing so avoids the need for a precisely engineered piecework standard (in terms of wheels installed per hour, for instance).[69] One company established such an overall standard for its teams. If the firm reached 100% of its goal, the employees would share in about 5% of the improvement (in labor costs saved). The firm divided the 5% pool by the number of employees to compute the value of a "share." If the firm achieved less than 100% of its goal, the bonus pool was less. The results of this plan—in terms of changing employee attitudes and focusing teams on strategic goals—were reportedly "extraordinary."[70]

Engineered Standards

Given the costs and the risks, it's sensible to analyze the situation. Some employers set an engineered production standard based on the output of the group (again, such as in terms of wheels installed per hour). The employer typically uses either the piece rate or standard hour plan, but the latter is more prevalent. All team members then typically receive the same share of the team's incentive pay. Occasionally, the employer may want to pay all team members according to some other formula. For instance, instead of paying everyone on the team based on how well the team as a whole does, pay everyone based on how well the *best* team member does. This counterintuitive sounding option may make sense when an employer has reason to believe the new team incentive plan might demotivate high-performing team members. That's what happened at Levi's, for instance.

Pros and Cons of Team Incentives

Team incentives often make sense. They reinforce team planning and problem solving, and can help ensure collaboration. In Asia in general (and Japan in particular), the tendency is to reward the group—to reduce jealousy, to make group members indebted to one another, and to encourage a sense of cooperation. Team incentives also facilitate training, since each member has an interest in getting new members trained as fast as possible.

The main disadvantage is what you might call the Levi's problem: that a good worker's pay may not be proportionate to his or her personal efforts. Workers who share in the team-based pay but who don't put their hearts into it ("free riders") represent the other side of the coin. The accompanying "Evidence-Based HR" feature illustrates this.

golden parachutes
Payments companies make in connection with a change in ownership or control of a company.

team (or group) incentive plan
A plan in which a production standard is set for a specific work group, and its members are paid incentives if the group exceeds the production standard.

Team incentives can foster a sense of cooperation and unanimity.

Source: Courtesy of Jose Luis Pelaez, Inc./CORBIS–NY.

Evidence-Based HR

Inequities That Undercut Team Incentives

Although about 85% of large employers reportedly use some type of group- or team-based incentives, studies suggest that team incentives are often counterproductive. What are the main things for which to beware? A researcher studied business students enrolled in a graduate online MBA program.[71] She devised a method for systematically categorizing their qualitative observations about the team incentives they'd experienced.

The fundamental problem was inequity. In many cases, each team member's financial compensation was the same, although one or two people "did the lion's share of the work." In other cases, the employer chose one or two team members for promotion, leaving others to feel they'd worked hard to support someone else's career. The bottom line seems to be that unless you actively minimize inequities, it's probably best to pay employees based on their individual contributions to the team, rather than on collective team performance.

Aside from avoiding inequities, the other thing to keep in mind is that successful teamwork reflects more than team incentives. Companies such as Toyota screen, hire, train, and cultivate workers to be team members, so the incentives are just one component.

Many employers take the team incentive idea to the next logical level and institute incentive plans in which all or most employees participate. **Organizationwide incentive plans** are plans in which all or most employees can participate, and which generally tie the reward to some measure of company-wide performance. Also called *variable pay plans*, they include profit sharing, Scanlon/gainsharing plans, and employee stock ownership (ESOP) plans. We'll look at them next.

Profit-Sharing Plans

Profit-sharing plans are plans in which all or most employees receive a share of the firm's annual profits. Research on such plans' effectiveness is sketchy. One study concludes that there is ample evidence that profit-sharing plans boost productivity and morale, but that their effect on profits is insignificant, once you factor in the costs of the plans' payouts.[72]

There are several types of profit-sharing plans. With *current profit-sharing* or cash plans, employees share in a portion of the employer's profits quarterly or annually.

In cash plans, the firm simply distributes a percentage of profits (usually 15% to 20%) as profit shares to employees at regular intervals. The Home Depot instituted such a cash program for all its store workers. Starting in 2003, it started paying store associates a bonus if their stores meet certain financial goals. In one recent year, The Home Depot distributed a total of $90 million under that company-wide incentive plan.[73]

With *deferred profit-sharing* plans, the employer puts cash awards into trust accounts for the employees' retirement.[74] Here the employer generally distributes the awards based on a percentage of the employee's salary, or some measure of the employee's contribution to company profits.[75] There is a tax advantage, since employees' income taxes on the distributions are deferred, often until the employee retires.

Thermacore Example Thermacore, Inc., provides an example. All employees are eligible and all receive the same amount of bonus regardless of total compensation, seniority, or position. The bonus pool is based on pretax income minus a minimum, threshold guarantee to the stockholders (typically 15% of the firm's equity at the beginning of the year). The amount of income to place in the bonus pool is determined by multiplying (1) company income (less the 15%-of-equity guarantee) by (2) an "employee bonus pool percentage rate" established by the board of directors and senior management. Regular employees then receive a full share, and part-time employees receive a share based on the percentage of time worked.

Scanlon Plans

Few would argue with the idea that the most powerful way of ensuring employee commitment is to synchronize the company's goals with those of its employees—in other words, to ensure that by pursuing his or her goals, the worker pursues the employer's goals as well. Experts have proposed many techniques for attaining this ideal state. However, few plans are used as widely or successfully as the **Scanlon plan**, an incentive plan developed in 1937 by Joseph Scanlon, a United Steel Workers Union official.[76] It is still popular today.

The Scanlon plan is remarkably progressive, considering that it is now more than 70 years old. Scanlon plans have five basic features.[77] The first is Scanlon's *philosophy of cooperation*. This philosophy assumes that managers and workers must rid themselves of the "us" and "them" attitudes that normally inhibit employees from developing a sense of ownership in the company.

A second feature is what its practitioners call *identity*. This means that in order to focus employee involvement, the company must articulate its mission or purpose, and employees must understand how the business operates in terms of customers, prices, and costs. *Competence* is a third basic feature. The program, say three experts, "explicitly recognizes that a Scanlon plan demands a high level of competence from employees at all levels."[78] This suggests careful selection and training.

The fourth feature of the plan is the *involvement system*. Employees present improvement suggestions to the appropriate departmental-level committees, which transmit the valuable ones to the executive-level committee. The latter then decides whether to implement the suggestion.

The fifth element of the plan is the *sharing of benefits formula*. If a suggestion is implemented and successful, all employees usually share in 75% of the savings. For example, assume that the normal monthly ratio of payroll costs to sales is 50%. (Thus, if sales are $600,000, payroll costs should be $300,000.) Assume the firm

organizationwide incentive plans
Incentive plans in which all or most employees can participate.

profit-sharing plan
A plan whereby employees share in the company's profits.

Scanlon plan
An incentive plan developed in 1937 by Joseph Scanlon and designed to encourage cooperation, involvement, and sharing of benefits.

implements suggestions that result in payroll costs of $250,000 in a month when sales were $550,000 and payroll costs therefore should have been $275,000 (50% of sales). The savings attributable to these suggestions is $25,000 ($275,000 minus $250,000). Workers would typically split 75% of this ($18,750), while $6,250 would go to the firm. In practice, the firm sets aside a portion, usually one-quarter of the $18,750, for the months in which payroll costs exceed the standard.

Other Gainsharing Plans

The Scanlon plan is one early version of what we call today a **gainsharing plan**. Gainsharing is an incentive plan that engages many or all employees in a common effort to achieve a company's productivity objectives, with any resulting cost-savings gains shared among employees and the company.[79] In addition to the Scanlon plan, other popular gainsharing plans include the Lincoln, Rucker, and Improshare plans.

The basic difference among these plans is the formula employers use to determine employee bonuses. The Scanlon formula divides payroll expenses by total sales (or, sometimes, by total sales plus increases in inventory). The Rucker plan uses a value-added formula. Here the employer divides the value added for the period (basically net sales minus the cost of materials, supplies, and services such as utilities) by total payroll expenses. With the Improshare plan, the bonus depends on the difference between how many labor hours the company should have used for the period, compared with how many it actually used. In one version of the *Lincoln incentive system*, first instituted at the Lincoln Electric Company of Ohio, employees work on a guaranteed piecework basis. The company distributes total annual profits (less taxes, 6% dividends to stockholders, and a reserve) each year among employees based on their merit rating. Most firms using them implement customized versions of these plans. Recent results—from various efforts in hospitals, as well as manufacturing plants—suggest quite clearly that gainsharing plans can improve productivity and patient care, and reduce grievances, but often also entail considerable implementation costs.[80]

There are eight basic steps in implementing a gainsharing plan:[81]

1. Establish general plan objectives, such as boosting productivity or lowering labor costs.
2. Choose specific performance measures. For example, use productivity measures such as labor hours per unit produced.
3. Decide the portion of gains employees will receive. In the Scanlon example mentioned earlier, employees receive about 75% of the gains.
4. Decide on a method for dividing and distributing the employees' share of the gains. Popular methods include equal percentage of pay or equal shares.
5. Choose the form of payment. This is usually cash, but occasionally is common stock.
6. Decide how often to pay bonuses. Firms tend to pay based on financial performance measures annually and on labor productivity measures quarterly or monthly.
7. Develop the involvement system. The most commonly used elements include steering committees, update meetings, suggestion systems, and problem-solving teams.
8. Implement the plan.

At-Risk Pay Plans

At-risk variable pay plans (sometimes called *risk-sharing plans*) are plans that put some portion of the employee's weekly, monthly, or yearly pay at risk. If employees meet or exceed their goals, they earn back not only the portion of their pay that was at risk, but also an incentive. If they fail to meet their goals, they forego some of the pay they would normally have earned. One DuPont division set employee's at-risk pay at 6%. Employees could then match or exceed their usual full pay if their department reached certain predetermined financial goals.

Employee Stock Ownership Plans

Employee stock ownership plans (ESOPs) are company-wide plans in which the employer contributes shares of its own stock (or cash to be used to purchase such stock) to a trust established to purchase shares of the firm's stock for employees. The firm generally makes these contributions annually in proportion to total employee compensation, with a limit of 15% of compensation. The trust holds the stock in individual employee accounts and distributes it to employees upon retirement (or other separation from service), assuming the person has worked long enough to earn ownership of the stock. (*Stock options*, as discussed earlier in this chapter, go directly to the employees individually to use as they see fit, rather than into a retirement trust.)

ESOPs are quite popular. The company gets a tax deduction equal to the fair market value of the shares it transfers to the trustee, and can claim an income tax deduction for dividends paid on ESOP-owned stock. Employees, as noted, aren't taxed until they receive a distribution from the trust, usually at retirement. The Employee Retirement Income Security Act (ERISA) allows a firm to borrow against employee stock held in trust and then repay the loan in pretax rather than after-tax dollars, another tax incentive for using such plans.[82]

ESOPs can also help the shareholders of closely held corporations (in which, for instance, a family owns virtually all the shares) to diversify their assets. They do this by placing some of their own shares of the company's stock into the ESOP trust and purchasing other marketable securities for themselves in their place.[83]

Research suggests that ESOPs do encourage employees to develop a sense of ownership in and commitment to the firm. However, those responsible for the funds—usually, the firm's top executives—must be fastidious in executing their fiduciary responsibilities for the fund.[84]

Broad-Based Stock Options

Many companies have offered "broad-based stock option plans" in which all or most employees can participate. The basic thinking is that sharing ownership in the company with employees makes motivational and practical sense.[85]

Employers seem to be cutting back on these. For example, Time Warner, Microsoft, Aetna, and Charles Schwab announced they were discontinuing distributing stock options to most employees. Some of them, including Microsoft, are instead awarding stock. With current tax laws, companies must show the options as an expense when awarded, reducing their attractiveness as a "costless" reward. Microsoft and others apparently feel awarding stock instead of stock options is a more direct and immediate way to link pay to performance.[86]

6 Outline the steps in designing effective incentive plans.

DESIGNING EFFECTIVE INCENTIVE PROGRAMS

As we saw at the start of this chapter, roughly 70% of employees feel that their firms' incentive plans are ineffective. We turn here to why such plans fail, and to how to improve their effectiveness.[87] We'll start with an example.

gainsharing plan
An incentive plan that engages employees in a common effort to achieve productivity objectives and share the gains.

at-risk variable pay plans
Plans that put some portion of the employee's weekly pay at risk, subject to the firm's meeting its financial goals.

employee stock ownership plan (ESOP)
A corporation contributes shares of its own stock to a trust in which additional contributions are made annually. The trust distributes the stock to employees on retirement or separation from service.

Research Insight: The Impact of Financial and Nonfinancial Incentives

Two researchers studied the impact of financial and nonfinancial incentives on business performance in 21 stores of a fast-food franchise in the Midwest.[88] The researchers carefully compared performance over time in stores that did and did not use financial and nonfinancial incentives. Each store had about 25 workers and two managers. The researchers trained the managers to identify observable, measurable employee behaviors that were currently deficient but that could influence store performance. Example behaviors included "keeping both hands moving at the drive-through window," "working during idle time," and "repeating the customer's order back to him or her."[89] Then they instituted the incentive plans. The researchers measured store performance in terms of gross profitability (revenue minus expenses), drive-through time, and employee turnover.

Financial Incentives

Some employees in some of the stores received financial incentives for exhibiting the desired behaviors. The financial incentives consisted of lump-sum bonuses in the workers' paychecks. For example, if the manager observed a work team exhibiting up to 50 behaviors during the observation period, he or she added $25 to the paychecks of all store employees that period; 50 to 100 behaviors added $50 per paycheck, and more than 100 behaviors added $75 per paycheck. Payouts rose over time as the employees learned more about the behaviors they were to exhibit.

Nonfinancial Incentives

The researchers also trained the managers in some stores to deliver nonfinancial incentives in the form of feedback and recognition. For example, for *performance feedback* managers maintained charts showing the drive-through times at the end of each day. They placed the charts by the time clocks, so all the store employees could keep track of their store's performance on things like drive-through times. The researchers also trained managers to administer *recognition* to employees, such as, "I noticed that today the drive-through times were really good. That is great since that is what we're really focusing on these days."[90]

Results

Both the financial and nonfinancial incentives improved employee and store performance.[91] For example, store profits rose 30% for those units where managers used financial rewards. Store profits rose 36% for those units where managers used nonfinancial rewards. During the same 9-month period, drive-through times decreased 19% for the financial incentives group, and 25% for the nonfinancial incentives groups. Turnover improved 13% for the financial incentives group, and 10% for the nonfinancial incentives group.

The Five Building Blocks of Effective Incentive Plans

The incentive plans in this study exhibited the characteristics of great incentive plans. We can summarize these as follows:

1. **Ask: Does it make sense to use incentives here?** [92] It makes more sense to use an incentive plan when:
   - Motivation (and not ability) is the problem.
   - There is a clear relationship between employee effort and quantity or quality of output.
   - The job is standardized.
   - The work flow is regular.
   - The employees can control the work you plan to incentivize.
   - Delays are few or consistent.
2. **Link the incentive with your strategy.** Link the incentive to behavior that is critical for achieving strategic goals.[93] For example, one incentive program at

Sun Microsystems (now part of Oracle) supported Sun's customer satisfaction goals. Employees received incentives based on improvements in activities like on-time delivery and customer returns.[94]

3. **Make sure the program is motivational.** Victor Vroom would say there should be a clear link between *effort and performance*, and between *performance and reward*, and that the reward must be *attractive* to the employee.
4. **Set complete standards.** For example, don't just pay for quantity if quality is an issue, too.
5. **Be scientific.** Don't waste money on incentives that seem logical but that may not be contributing to performance. *Gather evidence* and analyze the effects of the incentive plan over time, to ascertain whether it is indeed influencing the measures (such as employee turnover, and so on) that you intended to improve through your plan.[95]

Incentive Plans in Practice: Nucor

Nucor Corp. is the largest steel producer in the United States. It also has the highest productivity and lowest labor cost per ton in the American steel industry.[96] Employees can earn bonuses of 100% or more of base salary, and all Nucor employees participate in one of four performance-based incentive plans. With the *production incentive plan*, operating and maintenance employees and supervisors get weekly bonuses based on their work groups' productivity. The *department manager incentive plan* pays department managers annual incentive bonuses based mostly on the ratio of net income to dollars of assets employed for their division. With the *professional and clerical bonus plan*, employees who are not in one of the two previous plans get bonuses based on their divisions' net income return on assets.[97] Finally, under the *senior officer incentive plan*, Nucor senior managers (whose base salaries are lower than those in comparable firms) get bonuses based on Nucor's annual overall percentage of net income to stockholders equity.[98] Nucor also divides 10% of its operating profits yearly among all employees (except senior officers). Depending on company performance, this may be from 1% to over 20% of an employee's pay.

REVIEW

CHAPTER SECTION SUMMARIES

1. In designing an effective financial incentive plan, it's important to understand the relationship between **money and motivation**.
   - Abraham Maslow said that people have a hierarchy of five types of needs and that people are first motivated to satisfy each lower order need.
   - Frederick Hertzberg said the best way to motivate someone is to organize the job so that it provides the feedback and challenge that helps satisfy the person's higher-level needs.
   - Edward Deci found that extrinsic rewards may actually detract from a person's intrinsic motivation.
   - Victor Vroom's expectancy motivation theory says a person's motivation depends on expectancy, instrumentality, and valence.
   - Psychologist B. F. Skinner's behavior modification–based approach means changing behavior through rewards or punishments that are contingent on performance.
2. Several incentive plans are particularly suited for **individual employee incentives and recognition programs**. Piecework is an incentive plan in which a person is paid a sum for each item he or she makes. Merit pay refers to any salary increase awarded to an employee based on his or her individual performance. Nonfinancial and recognition-based awards are increasingly important and include awards in the form of employee recognition, gift certificates, and individual travel. Many employers use enterprise incentive management systems to automate the planning, analysis, and management of their incentive plans.
3. **Incentives for salespeople** are typically sales commissions. Although the percentage of pay in the form of sales commission may vary from zero to 100%, a survey found that salespeople at high-performing companies receive about 38% of their total cash compensation in the form of sales-related variable pay.

4. Managers take many things into consideration when formulating **incentives for managers and executives**. Most firms have annual bonus plans aimed at motivating managers' short-term performance. Here the actual award often depends on some combination of individual performance and organizational performance, so that, for instance, high-performing managers get a bonus even if the company itself underperforms. Long-term incentives include stock options, "golden parachutes," and stock appreciation rights.
5. With more employers organizing their efforts around teams, **team and organizationwide incentive plans are more important**. With team incentive plans, the main question is whether to reward members based on individual or team performance; both have pros and cons. Organizationwide incentive plans are plans in which all or most employees can participate. These include profit-sharing plans in which employees share in the company's profits; gainsharing plans, including the Scanlon plan, engage employees in a common effort to achieve productivity objectives and thereby share the gains. Employee stock ownership plans are company-wide plans in which the employer contributes shares of its own stock to a trust established to purchase shares of the firm's stock for employees.
6. Because so many incentive plans fail, **designing effective incentive programs** is crucial. Five important building blocks include determining whether using incentives makes sense, linking the incentive with your strategy, making sure the program is motivational, setting complete standards, and being scientific in terms of analyzing the effects of the incentive plan.

DISCUSSION QUESTIONS

1. Compare and contrast six types of incentive plans.
2. Explain five reasons why incentive plans fail.
3. Describe the nature of some important management incentives.
4. When and why would you pay a salesperson a combined salary and commission?
5. What is merit pay? Do you think it's a good idea to award employees merit raises? Why or why not?
6. In this chapter, we listed a number of guidelines for not instituting a pay-for-performance plan. Do you think these points make sense in terms of motivation theory? Why or why not?
7. What is a Scanlon plan? Based on what you've read in this chapter, what features of an effective incentive program does the Scanlon plan include?
8. Give four examples of when you would suggest using team or group incentive programs rather than individual incentive programs.

INDIVIDUAL AND GROUP ACTIVITIES

1. Working individually or in groups, create an incentive plan for the following positions: chemical engineer, plant manager, used-car salesperson. What factors did you have to consider in reaching your conclusions?
2. A state university system in the Southeast instituted a "Teacher Incentive Program" (TIP) for its faculty. Faculty committees within each university's colleges were told to award $5,000 raises (not bonuses) to about 40% of their faculty members based on how good a job they did teaching undergraduates, and how many courses they taught per year. What are the potential advantages and pitfalls of such an incentive program? How well do you think it was accepted by the faculty? Do you think it had the desired effect?
3. The "HRCI Test Specifications Appendix" (pages 699–706) lists the knowledge someone studying for the HRCI certification exam needs to have in each area of human resource management (such as in Strategic Management, Workforce Planning, and Human Resource Development). In groups of four to five students, do four things: (1) Review that appendix now. (2) Identify the material in this chapter that relates to the required knowledge the appendix lists. (3) Write four multiple-choice exam questions on this material that you believe would be suitable for inclusion in the HRCI exam. And (4) if time permits, have someone from your team post your team's questions in front of the class, so the students in other teams can take each others' exam questions.
4. Several years ago, the pension plan of the Utility Workers Union of America proposed that shareholders change the corporate bylaws of Dominion Resources, Inc., so that in the future, management had to get shareholder approval of executive pay exceeding $1 million, as well as detailed information about the firm's executive incentive plans. Many unions—most of which have pension funds with huge investments in U.S. companies—are taking similar steps. They point out that, usually, under Internal Revenue Service regulations, corporations can't deduct more than $1 million in pay for any of a company's top five paid executives. Under the new rules the unions are pushing, boards of directors will no longer be able to approve executive pay above $1 million; instead, shareholders would have to vote on it. In terms of effectively running a company, what do you think are the pros and cons of the unions' recommendations? Would you vote for or against the unions' recommendation? Why or why not?

TABLE 12-3 Express Auto Compensation System

Express Auto Team	Responsibility of Team	Current Compensation Method
1. Sales force	Persuade buyer to purchase a car.	Very small salary (minimum wage) with commissions. Commission rate increases with every 20 cars sold per month.
2. Finance office	Help close the sale; persuade customer to use company finance plan.	Salary, plus bonus for each $10,000 financed with the company.
3. Detailing	Inspect cars delivered from factory, clean, and make minor adjustments.	Piecework paid on the number of cars detailed per day.
4. Mechanics	Provide factory warranty service, maintenance, and repair.	Small hourly wage, plus bonus based on (1) number of cars completed per day and (2) finishing each car faster than the standard estimated time to repair.
5. Receptionists/phone service personnel	Primary liaison between customer and sales force, finance, and mechanics.	Minimum wage.

EXPERIENTIAL EXERCISE

Motivating the Sales Force at Express Auto

Purpose: The purpose of this exercise is to give you practice developing an incentive plan.

Required Understanding: Be thoroughly familiar with this chapter, and read the following:

Express Auto, an automobile mega-dealership with more than 600 employees that represents 22 brands, has just received a very discouraging set of survey results. Customer satisfaction scores have fallen for the ninth straight quarter. Customer complaints include:

- It was hard to get prompt feedback from mechanics by phone.
- Salespeople often did not return phone calls.
- The finance people seemed "pushy."
- New cars were often not properly cleaned or had minor items that needed immediate repair or adjustment.
- Cars often had to be returned to have repair work redone.

Table 12-3 describes Express Auto's current compensation system.

How to Set Up the Exercise/Instructions: Divide the class into groups of four to five students. One or more groups should analyze each of the five teams in column one. Each student group should analyze the compensation package for its Express Auto team. Each group should address these questions:

1. In what ways might your team's compensation plan contribute to the customer service problems?
2. What recommendations would you make to improve the compensation system in a way that would likely improve customer satisfaction?

APPLICATION CASE

Inserting the Team Concept into Compensation—or Not

In his new position at Hathaway Manufacturing, one of the first things Sandy Caldwell wanted to do was improve productivity through teamwork at every level of the firm. As the new human resource manager for the suburban plant, Sandy set out to change the culture to accommodate the team-based approach he had become so enthusiastic about in his most recent position.

Sandy started by installing the concept of team management at the highest level, to oversee the operations of the entire plant. The new management team consisted of manufacturing, distribution, planning, technical, and human resource plant managers. Together they developed a new vision for the 500-employee facility, which they expressed in the simple phrase "Excellence Together." They drafted a new mission statement for the firm that focused on becoming customer driven and team based, and that called upon employees to raise their level of commitment and begin acting as "owners" of the firm.

The next step was to convey the team message to employees throughout the company. The communication process went surprisingly well, and Sandy was happy to see his idea of a "workforce of owners" begin to take shape.

Teams trained together, developed production plans together, and embraced the technique of 360-degree feedback, in which an employee's performance evaluation is obtained from supervisors, subordinates, peers, and internal or external customers. Performance and morale improved, and productivity began to tick upward. The company even sponsored occasional celebrations to reward team achievements, and the team structure seemed firmly in place.

Sandy decided to change one more thing. Hathaway's long-standing policy had been to give all employees the same annual pay increase. But Sandy felt that in the new team environment, outstanding performance should be the criterion for pay raises. After consulting with CEO Regina Cioffi, Sandy sent a memo to all employees announcing the change to team-based pay for performance.

The reaction was immediate and 100% negative. None of the employees was happy with the change, and among their complaints, two stood out. First, because the 360-degree feedback system made everyone responsible in part for someone else's performance evaluation, no one was comfortable with the idea that pay raises might also be linked to peer input. Second, there was a widespread perception that the way the change was decided upon, and the way it was announced, put the firm's commitment to team effort in doubt. Simply put, employees felt left out of the decision process.

Sandy and Regina arranged a meeting for early the next morning. Sitting in her office, they began a painful debate. Should the new policy be rescinded as quickly as it was adopted, or should it be allowed to stand?

Questions

1. Does the pay-for-performance plan seem like a good idea? Why or why not?
2. What advice would you give Regina and Sandy as they consider their decision?
3. What mistakes did they make in adopting and communicating the new salary plan? How might Sandy have approached this major compensation change a little differently?
4. Assuming the new pay plan is eventually accepted, how would you address the fact that in the new performance evaluation system, employees' input affects their peers' pay levels?

Note: The incident in this case is based on an actual event at Frito-Lay's Kirkwood, New York, plant, as reported in C. James Novak, "Proceed with Caution When Paying Teams," *HR Magazine*, April 1997, p. 73.

CONTINUING CASE

Carter Cleaning Company

The Incentive Plan

The question of whether to pay Carter Cleaning Center employees an hourly wage or an incentive of some kind has always intrigued Jack Carter.

His basic policy has been to pay employees an hourly wage, except that his managers do receive an end-of-year bonus depending, as Jack puts it, "on whether their stores do well or not that year."

However, he is considering using an incentive plan in one store. Jack knows that a presser should press about 25 "tops" (jackets, dresses, blouses) per hour. Most of his pressers do not attain this ideal standard, though. In one instance, a presser named Walt was paid $8 per hour, and Jack noticed that regardless of the amount of work he had to do, Walt always ended up going home at about 3:00 P.M., so he earned about $300 at the end of the week. If it was a holiday week, for instance, and there were a lot of clothes to press, he might average 22 to 23 tops per hour (someone else did pants) and so he'd earn perhaps $300 and still finish up each day in time to leave by 3:00 P.M. so he could pick up his children at school. But when things were very slow in the store, his productivity would drop to perhaps 12 to 15 pieces an hour, so that at the end of the week he'd end up earning perhaps $280, and in fact not go home much earlier than he did when it was busy.

Jack spoke with Walt several times, and while Walt always promised to try to do better, it gradually became apparent to Jack that Walt was simply going to earn his $300 per week no matter what. Though Walt never told him so directly, it dawned on Jack that Walt had a family to support and was not about to earn less than his "target" wage, regardless of how busy or slow the store was. The problem was that the longer Walt kept pressing each day, the longer the steam boilers and compressors had to be kept on to power his machines, and the fuel charges alone ran close to $6 per hour. Jack clearly needed some way short of firing Walt to solve the problem, since the fuel bills were eating up his profits.

His solution was to tell Walt that, instead of an hourly $8 wage, he would henceforth pay him $0.33 per item pressed. That way, said Jack to himself, if Walt presses 25 items per hour at $0.33 he will in effect get a small raise. He'll get more items pressed per hour and will therefore be able to shut the machines down earlier.

On the whole, the experiment worked well. Walt generally presses 25 to 35 pieces per hour now. He gets to leave earlier, and with the small increase in pay, he generally earns his target wage. Two problems have arisen, though. The quality of Walt's work has dipped a bit, plus his manager has to spend a minute or two each hour counting the number of pieces Walt pressed that hour. Otherwise, Jack is fairly pleased with the results of his incentive plan, and he's wondering whether to extend it to other employees and other stores.

Questions

1. Should this plan be extended to pressers in the other stores?
2. Should other employees (cleaner–spotters, counterpeople) be put on a similar plan? Why? Why not? If so, how, exactly?

3. Is there another incentive plan you think would work better for the pressers? Describe it.
4. A store manager's job is to keep total wages to no more than 30% of sales and to maintain the fuel bill and the supply bill at about 9% of sales each. Managers can also directly affect sales by ensuring courteous customer service and by ensuring that the work is done properly. What suggestions would you make to Jennifer and her father for an incentive plan for store managers or front desk clerks?

TRANSLATING STRATEGY INTO HR POLICIES & PRACTICES CASE

The Hotel Paris Case

The New Incentive Plan

The Hotel Paris's competitive strategy is "To use superior guest service to differentiate the Hotel Paris properties, and to thereby increase the length of stay and return rate of guests, and thus boost revenues and profitability." HR manager Lisa Cruz must now formulate functional policies and activities that support this competitive strategy, by eliciting the required employee behaviors and competencies.

One of Lisa Cruz's biggest pay-related concerns is that the Hotel Paris compensation plan does not link pay to performance in any effective way. Because salaries were historically barely competitive, supervisors tended to award merit raises across the board. So, employees who performed well got only about the same raise as did those who performed poorly. Similarly, there was no bonus or incentive plan of any kind aimed at linking employee performance to strategically relevant employee capabilities and behaviors such as greeting guests in a friendly manner or providing expeditious check-ins and checkouts.

Based on their analysis, Lisa Cruz and the CFO concluded that by any metric, their company's incentive plan was inadequate. The percentage of the workforce whose merit increase or incentive pay is tied to performance is effectively zero, because managers awarded merit pay across the board. No more than 5% of the workforce (just the managers) was eligible for incentive pay. And, the percentage of difference in incentive pay between a low-performing and a high-performing employee was less than 2%. Lisa knew from industry studies that in top firms, more than 80% of the workforce had merit pay or incentive pay tied to performance. She also knew that in high-performing firms, there was at least a 5% or 6% difference in incentive pay between a low-performing and a high-performing employee. The CFO authorized Lisa to design a new strategy-oriented incentive plan for the Hotel Paris's employees. Their overall aim was to incentivize the pay plans of just about all the company's employees.

Lisa and the company's CFO laid out three measurable criteria that the new incentive plan had to meet. First, at least 90% (and preferably all) of the Hotel Paris's employees must be eligible for a merit increase or incentive pay that is tied to performance. Second, there must be at least a 10% difference in incentive pay between a low-performing and high-performing employee. Third, the new incentive plan had to include specific bonuses and evaluative mechanisms that linked employee behaviors in each job category with strategically relevant employee capabilities and behaviors. For example, front-desk clerks were to be rewarded in part based on the friendliness and speed of their check-ins and checkouts, and the housecleaning crew was to be evaluated and rewarded in part based on the percentage of room-cleaning infractions.

Questions

1. Discuss what you think of the measurable criteria that Lisa and the CFO set for their new incentive plan.
2. Given what you know about the Hotel Paris's strategic goals, list three or four specific behaviors you would incentivize for each of the following groups of employees: front-desk clerks, hotel managers, valets, housekeepers.
3. Lay out a complete incentive plan (including all long- and short-term incentives) for the Hotel Paris's hotel managers.

KEY TERMS

financial incentives, *p. 435*
fair day's work, *p. 435*
scientific management movement, *p. 435*
expectancy, *p. 435*
instrumentality, *p. 435*
valence, *p. 437*
behavior modification, *p. 437*
variable pay, *p. 437*
piecework, *p. 437*
straight piecework, *p. 437*
standard hour plan, *p. 437*
merit pay (merit raise), *p. 439*
annual bonus, *p. 445*
stock option, *p. 447*
golden parachutes, *p. 449*
team (or group) incentive plan, *p. 449*
organizationwide incentive plans, *p. 451*
profit-sharing plan, *p. 451*
Scanlon plan, *p. 451*
gainsharing plan, *p. 453*
at-risk variable pay plans, *p. 453*
employee stock ownership plan (ESOP), *p. 453*

ENDNOTES

1. Even the traditional holiday bonus is being replaced by performance-based pay. A survey by consultants Hewitt Associates found that only about 5% of employers surveyed would distribute holiday cash bonuses. About 78% said they were offering performance-based awards, up from 51% about 15 years previously. "Cash Bonuses Are Ghosts of Holidays Past, Survey Says," *BNA Bulletin to Management,* December 13, 2005, p. 396. See also "Aligning Rewards with the Changing Employment Deal: 2006/2007 Strategic Rewards®Report," www.watsonwyatt.com/research/resrender.asp?id=2006-US-0038&page=1, accessed May 20, 2007.
2. "Few Employees See the Pay for Performance Connection," *Compensation & Benefits Review* 17, no. 2 (June 2003); "Most Workers Not Motivated by Cash," *Incentive Today,* July–August 2004, p. 19; and "Pay-for-Performance Plans' Impact Uncertain: Study," *Modern Healthcare,* May 24, 2004, p. 34.
3. Kathy Chu, "Employers See Lackluster Results Linking Salary to Performance," *The Wall Street Journal,* June 15, 2004, p. D2.
4. Ted Turnasella, "Pay and Personality," *Compensation & Benefits Review,* March/April 2002, pp. 45–59.
5. Jason Shaw et al., "Reactions to Merit Pay Increases: A Longitudinal Test of a Signal Sensitivity Perspective," *Journal of Applied Psychology* 88, no. 3 (2003), pp. 538–544.
6. See, for example, Edward Deci, *Intrinsic Motivation* (New York: Plenum, 1975).
7. Ruth Kanfer, "Motivation Theory," in Harry C. Triandis, Marvin D. Dunnette, and Leaetta M. Hough, *Handbook of Industrial and Organizational Psychology,* (Palo Alto, CA: Consulting Psychologists Press, c1990–c1994), p. 113.
8. For a discussion, see John P. Campbell and Robert Prichard, "Motivation Theory in Industrial and Organizational Psychology," in Marvin Dunnette (ed.), *Industrial and Organizational Psychology* (Chicago: Rand McNally, 1976), pp. 74–75; and Kanfer, op cit. pp. 115–116.
9. See, for example, Aubrey Daniels et al., "The Leader's Role in Pay Systems and Organizational Performance," *Compensation & Benefits Review,* May/June 2006, pp. 58–60; and Suzanne Peterson and Fred Luthans, "The Impact of Financial and Non-Financial Incentives on Business Unit Outcomes Over Time," *Journal of Applied Psychology* 91, no. 1 (2006), pp. 156–165.
10. See, for example, Mary Ducharme and Mark Podolsky, "Variable Pay: Its Impact on Motivation and Organisation Performance," *International Journal of Human Resources Development and Management* 6 (May 9, 2006), p. 68.
11. Ibid.
12. "Employers Use Pay to Lever Performance," *BNA Bulletin to Management,* August 21, 1997, p. 272.
13. See, for example, Kenan Abosch, "Variable Pay: Do We Have the Basics in Place?" *Compensation & Benefits Review,* July/August 1998, pp. 2–22.
14. See, for example, Diane Cadrain, "Cash Versus Non-Cash Rewards," *HR Magazine,* April 2003, pp. 81–87.
15. Richard Henderson, *Compensation Management* (Upper Saddle River, NJ: Prentice Hall, 2000), p. 463.
16. For a discussion of these, see Thomas Wilson, "Is It Time to Eliminate the Piece Rate Incentive System?" *Compensation & Benefits Review,* March/April 1992, pp. 43–49.
17. K. Oanh Ha, "California Workers Named in Articles Not Asked to Help in Piecework Probe," *Knight Ridder/Tribune News,* March 23, 2000, item 0008408e.
18. William Atkinson, "Incentive Pay Programs That Work in Textile," *Textile World* 151, no. 2 (February 2001), pp. 55–57.
19. See, for example, "Bias Creeps into Bonus Process, MIT Study Finds," *Workforce Management,* September 20, 2008, pp. 8–9.
20. The average uncorrected cross-sectional correlation was 17. Michael Harris et al., "A Longitudinal Examination of a Merit Pay System: Relationships Among Performance Ratings, Merit Increases, and Total Pay Increases," *Journal of Applied Psychology* 83, no. 5 (1998), pp. 825–831.
21. Eric R. Schulz and Denise Marie Tanguay, "Merit Pay in a Public Higher Education Institution: Questions of Impact and Attitudes," *Public Personnel Management* 35, no. 1 (Spring 2006), p. 71(18); Thomas S. Dee and Benjamin J. Keys, "Does Merit Pay Reward Good Teachers? Evidence from a Randomized Experiment," *Journal of Policy Analysis & Management* 23, no. 3 (Summer 2004), pp. 471–488. See also David N. Figlio and Lawrence W. Kenny, "Individual Teacher Incentives and Student Performance," *Journal of Public Economics* 91, no. 5–6 (June 2007), p. 901(14).
22. Jonathan Glater, "Varying the Recipe Helps TV Operations Solve Morale Problem," *The New York Times,* March 7, 2001, p. C1.
23. Esther Shein, "Team Spirit: IT Is Getting Creative with Compensation to Foster Collaboration," *PC Week,* May 11, 1998, pp. 69–72. See also Fay Hansen, "Short-Term Incentive Programs Are Most Effective in Driving IT Performance," *Compensation & Benefits Review,* November/December 2003, pp. 11–12.
24. Ann Harrington, "Saying 'We Love You' with Stock Options," *Fortune,* October 11, 1999, p. 316.
25. Betty Sosnin, "A Pat(ent) on the Back," *HR Magazine,* March 2000, pp. 107–8, 110, 112.
26. Suzanne Peterson and Fred Luthans, "The Impact of Financial and Nonfinancial Incentives on Business Unit Outcomes Over Time," *Journal of Applied Psychology* 91, no. 1 (2006), p. 158.
27. See, for example, ibid., pp. 156–165.
28. "Employee Recognition," *WorldatWork,* April 2008, at http://www.worldatwork.org/waw/adimLink?id=25653, accessed November 3, 2009.
29. See, for example, Leslie Yerkes, *Fun Works: Creating Places Where People Love to Work,* (San Francisco, CA: Berrett-Koehler Publishers, 2007).
30. Charlotte Huff, "Recognition That Resonates," *Workforce Management,* September 11, 2006, pp. 25–29. See also Scott Jeffrey and Victoria Schaffer, "The Motivational Properties of Tangible Incentives," *Compensation & Benefits Review,* May/June 2007, pp. 44–50.
31. Bob Nelson, *1001 Ways to Reward Employees* (New York : Workman Pub., 1994), p. 19. See also Sunny C. L. Fong and Margaret A. Shaffer, "The Dimensionality and Determinants of Pay Satisfaction: A Cross-Cultural Investigation of a Group Incentive Plan," *International Journal of Human Resource Management* 14, no. 4 (June 2003), p. 559(22).
32. William Bulkeley, "Incentives Systems Fine-Tune Pay/Bonus Plans," *The Wall Street Journal,* August 16, 2001, p. B4.
33. Jeremy Wuittner, "Plenty of Incentives to Use E.I.M. Software Systems," *American Banker* 168, no. 129 (July 8, 2003), p. 680.

34. Nina McIntyre, "Using EIM Technology to Successfully Motivate Employees," *Compensation & Benefits Review*, July/August 2001, pp. 57–60.
35. Straight salary by itself is not, of course, an incentive compensation plan as we use the term in this chapter.
36. Sonjun Luo, "Does Your Sales Incentive Plan Pay for Performance?" *Compensation & Benefits Review*, January/February 2003, pp. 18–24.
37. Ibid., pp. 331–345. See also James M. Pappas and Karen E. Flaherty, "The Moderating Role of Individual-Difference Variables in Compensation Research," *Journal of Managerial Psychology* 21, no. 1 (January 2006), pp. 19–35; and T. B. Lopez, C. D. Hopkins, and M. A. Raymond, "Reward Preferences of Salespeople: How Do Commissions Rate?" *Journal of Personal Selling & Sales Management* 26, no. 4 (Fall 2006), p. 381(10).
38. David Harrison, Meghan Virick, and Sonja William, "Working Without a Net: Time, Performance, and Turnover Under Maximally Contingent Rewards," *Journal of Applied Psychology* 81, no. 4 (1996), p. 332.
39. Bill O'Connell, "Dead Solid Perfect: Achieving Sales Compensation Alignment," *Compensation & Benefits Review*, March/April 1996, pp. 46–47. See also C. Albrech, "Moving to a Global Sales Incentive Compensation Plan," *Compensation & Benefits Review* 41, no. 4 (July/August 2009), p. 52.
40. In the salary bonus plan, salespeople are paid a base salary and are then paid a bonus for carrying out specific activities.
41. Leslie Stretch, "From Strategy to Profitability: How Sales Compensation Management Drives Business Performance," *Compensation & Benefits Review*, May/June 2008, pp. 32–37.
42. S. Scott Sands, "Ineffective Quotas: The Hidden Threat to Sales Compensation Plans," *Compensation & Benefits Review* (March/April 2000): 35–42. See also "Driving Profitable Sales Growth: 2006/2007 Report on Sales Effectiveness," http://www.watsonwyatt.com/research/resrender.asp?id=2006-US-0060&page=1, accessed May 20, 2007.
43. Peter Gundy, "Sales Compensation Programs: Built to Last," *Compensation & Benefits Review* (September/October 2002): 21–28. See also T. B. Lopez, C. D. Hopkins, M. A. Raymond, "Reward Preferences of Salespeople: How Do Commissions Rate?", *Journal of Personal Selling & Sales Management* 26, no. 4 (Fall 2006), p. 381(10).
44. "Driving Profitable Sales Growth: 2006/2007 Report on Sales Effectiveness," www.watsonwyatt.com/research/resrender.asp?id=2006-US-0060&page=1, accessed May 20, 2007.
45. Bob Conlin, "Best Practices for Designing New Sales Compensation Plans," *Compensation & Benefits Review*, March/April 2008, p. 51.
46. Ibid, p. 53.
47. www.vuesoftware.com/Product/Compensation_Management.aspx, accessed March 4, 2009.
48. Ibid.
49. Peter Glendinning, "Kicking the Tires of Automotive Sales Compensation," *Compensation & Benefits Review*, September/October 2000, pp. 47–53; and Michele Marchetti, "Why Sales Contests Don't Work," *Sales and Marketing Management* 156 (January 2004), p. 19. See also "Salary and Bonus Gain Favor in Sales Pay (for Motor Vehicle Salespeople)," *Automotive News* 75, no. 5915 (February 5, 2001), p. 50.
50. Mark Meltzer and Howard Goldsmith, "Executive Compensation for Growth Companies," *Compensation & Benefits Review*, November/December 1997, pp. 41–50; and Barbara Kiviat, "Everyone into the Bonus Pool," *Time* 162, no. 24 (December 15, 2003), p. A5.
51. www.mercer.com/pressrelease/details.jhtml/dynamic/idContent/1263210, accessed January 2, 2007.
52. "Short-Term Incentives Considered Ineffective, Survey Reveals," *Society for Human Resource Management*, January 2000, p. 5. See also Steven Balsam and Setiyono Miharjo, "The Effect of Equity Compensation on Voluntary Executive Turnover," *Journal of Accounting and Economics* 43, no. 1 (March 2007), p. 95(25).
53. See "The Impact of Sarbanes-Oxley on Executive Compensation," www.thelenreid.com, downloaded December 11, 2003. See also Brent Longnecker and James Krueger, "The Next Wave of Compensation Disclosure," *Compensation & Benefits Review*, January/February 2007, pp. 50–54.
54. Meltzer and Goldsmith, "Executive Compensation for Growth Companies," pp. 44–45. See also Robert E. Wood et al., "Bonuses, Goals, and Instrumentality Effects," *Journal of Applied Psychology* 84, no. 5 (1999), pp. 703–720.
55. Ibid., pp. 188. Meltzer and Goldsmith, "Executive Compensation for Growth Companies," p. 44. Fay Hansen, "Salary and Wage Trends," *Compensation & Benefits Review*, March/April 2004, pp. 9–10.
56. Bruce Ellig, "Executive Pay Financial Measurements," *Compensation & Benefits Review*, September/October 2008, pp. 42–49.
57. "Base Pay Will Rise More Slowly in 2009," *Compensation & Benefits Review*, November/December 2008, p. 5.
58. Ibid.
59. Employers need to beware of piling so many new stock incentives on top performers during challenging times that when buoyant economic times return, the employees receive a windfall. See, for example, Jack Dolmat-Connell et al., "Potential Implications of the Economic Downturn for Executive Compensation," *Compensation & Benefits Review* 41, no. 1 (January/February 2009), pp. 33–38.
60. Benjamin Dunford et al., "Underwater Stock Options and Voluntary Executive Turnover: A Multidisciplinary Perspective Integrating Behavioral and Economic Theories," *Personnel Psychology* 61 (2008), pp. 687–726.
61. Phred Dvorak, "Slump Yields Employee Rewards," *The Wall Street Journal*, October 10, 2008, p. B2; Don Clark and Jerry DiColo, "Intel to Let Workers Exchange Options," *The Wall Street Journal*, March 24, 2009, p. B3.
62. Wm. Gerard Sanders and Donald Hambrick, "Swinging for the Fences: The Effects of CEO Stock Options on Company Risk-Taking and Performance," *Academy of Management Journal* 50, no. 5 (2007), pp. 1055–1078.
63. "Study Finds That Directly Owning Stock Shares Leads to Better Results," *Compensation & Benefits Review*, March/April 2001, p. 7. See also Ira Kay, "Whither the Stock Option? While Stock Options Lose More Luster as Executive Motivators, Compensation Committees Face Challenges, Including Selecting Other Forms of Stock Incentives," *Financial Executive* 20, no. 2 (March–April 2004), p. 46(3); and Lucian A. Bebchuk and Jesse M. Fried, "Pay Without Performance: Overview of the Issues," *Academy of Management Perspectives*, Feb. 2006, v20 i1 p. 5(20).
64. www.mercer.com/pressrelease/details.jhtml/dynamic/idContent/1263210, accessed January 2, 2007.
65. Louis Lavelle, "How to Halt the Options Express," *BusinessWeek*, September 9, 2002.

66. Under IRS regulations, companies cannot deduct all golden parachute payments made to executives, and the executive must pay a 20% excise tax on the golden parachute payments. "Final Regs Issued for Golden Parachute Payments," *Executive Tax and Management Report* 66, no. 17 (September 2003), p. 1.
67. "Conseco Not Alone on Executive Perks," *Knight-Ridder/Tribune Business News*, August 28, 2003, item 03240015. See also "Realities of Executive Compensation—2006/2007 Report on Executive Pay and Stock Options," www.watsonwyatt.com/research/resrender.asp?id=2006-US-0085&page=1), accessed May 20, 2007.
68. Meltzer and Goldsmith, "Executive Compensation for Growth Companies," pp. 41–50. See also Patricia Zingheim and Jay Schuster, "Designing Pay and Rewards in Professional Companies," *Compensation & Benefits Review*, January/February 2007, pp. 55–62; and Ronald Bottano and Russell Miller, "Making Executive Compensation Count: Tapping into the New Long-Term Incentive Portfolio," *Compensation & Benefits Review*, July/August 2007, pp. 43–47.
69. Other suggestions are as follows: equal payments to all members on the team; differential payments to team members based on their contributions to the team's performance; and differential payments determined by a ratio of each group member's base pay to the total base pay of the group. See Kathryn Bartol and Laura Hagmann, "Team Based Pay Plans: A Key to Effective Team Work," *Compensation & Benefits Review*, November–December 1992, pp. 24–29. See also Charlotte Garvey, "Steer Teams with the Right Pay," *HR Magazine*, May 2002, pp. 70–71, and K. Merriman, "On the Folly of Rewarding Team Performance, While Hoping for Teamwork," *Compensation & Benefits Review* 41, no. 1 (January/February 2009), pp. 61–66.
70. Richard Seaman, "The Case Study: Rejuvenating an Organization with Team Pay," *Compensation & Benefits Review*, September/October 1997, pp. 25–30. See also Peter Wright, Mark Kroll, Jeffrey A. Krug, and Michael Pettus, "Influences of Top Management Team Incentives on Firm Risk Taking," *Strategic Management Journal* 28, no. 1 (January 2007), pp. 81–89.
71. K. Merriman, "On the Folly of Rewarding Team Performance, While Hoping for Teamwork," *Compensation & Benefits Review*, January/February 2009, pp. 61–66.
72. Seongsu Kim, "Does Profit Sharing Increase Firms' Profits?" *Journal of Labor Research*, Spring 1998, pp. 351–371. See also Jacqueline Coyle-Shapiro et al., "Using Profit-Sharing to Enhance Employee Attitudes: A Longitudinal Examination of the Effects on Trust and Commitment," *Human Resource Management* 41, no. 4 (Winter 2002), pp. 423–449.
73. Kaja Whitehouse, "More Companies Offer Packages Linking Pay Plans to Performance," *The Wall Street Journal*, December 13, 2005, p. B4.
74. Under the U.S. tax code, "any arrangement that provides for the deferral of compensation in a year later than the year in which the compensation was earned may be considered a deferred compensation arrangement." Steven Friedman, "2008 Compliance Strategies for Employers in Light of Final 409A Regulations," *Compensation & Benefits Review*, March/April 2008, p. 27.
75. Joseph Martocchio, *Strategic Compensation* (Upper Saddle River, NJ: Prentice Hall, 2006), pp. 163–165.
76. Brian Graham-Moore and Timothy Ross, *The Scanlon Way to Improved Productivity: A Practical Guide* (New York: Wiley, 1978), p. 2.
77. These are based in part on Steven Markham, K. Dow Scott, and Walter Cox Jr., "The Evolutionary Development of a Scanlon Plan," *Compensation & Benefits Review*, March/April 1992, pp. 50–56. See also Woodruff Imberman, "Are You Ready to Boost Productivity with a Gainsharing Plan? To Survive and Prosper in Our Hyper-competitive Environment, Board Converters Must Motivate Employees at All Levels," *Official Board Markets* 82, no. 47 (November 25, 2006), p. 5(2); and James Reynolds and Daniel Roble, "Combining Pay for Performance with Gainsharing," *Healthcare Financial Management* 60, no. 11 (November 2006), p. 50(6).
78. Markham et al., "The Evolutionary Development of a Scanlon Plan," p. 51.
79. Barry W. Thomas and Madeline Hess Olson, "Gainsharing: The Design Guarantees Success," *Personnel Journal*, May 1998, pp. 73–79.
80. Paraphrased from Woodruff Imbermann, "Boosting Plant Performance with Gainsharing," *Business Horizons*, November–December 1992, p. 77. See also Max Reynolds and Joane Goodroe, "The Return of Gainsharing: Gainsharing Appears to Be Enjoying a Renaissance," *Healthcare Financial Management* 59, no. 11 (November 2005), p. 114(6); and Dong-One Kim, "The Benefits and Costs of Employee Suggestions Under Gainsharing," *Industrial and Labor Relations Review* 58, no. 4 (July 2005), p. 631(22).
81. Paul Rossler and C. Patrick Koelling, "The Effect of Gainsharing on Business Performance at a Paper Mill," *National Productivity Review*, Summer 1993, pp. 365–382.
82. For a discussion of the effects of employee stock ownership on employee attitudes, see John Gamble, "ESOPs: Financial Performance and Federal Tax Incentives," *Journal of Labor Research* 19, no. 3 (Summer 1998), pp. 529–542.
83. Steven Etkind, "ESOPs Create Liquidity for Share Holders and Help Diversify Their Assets," *Estate Planning* 24, no. 4 (May 1998), pp. 158–165. See also S. Coomes, "Employee Stock Plans Can Save Taxes, Attract Talent," *Nation's Restaurant News* 42, no. 36 (September 15, 2008), p. 12.
84. William Smith, Harold Lazarus, and Harold Murray Kalkstein, "Employee Stock Ownership Plans: Motivation and Moral Issues," *Compensation & Benefits Review*, September/October 1990, pp. 37–46. See also "ESOP Trustees Breached Their Fiduciary Duties Under ERISA by Failing to Make Prudent Investigation into Value of Stock Purchased by ESOP," *Tax Management Compensation Planning Journal* 30, no. 10 (October 4, 2002), p. 301(1); and J. D. Mamorsky, "Court Approves ERISA Action Against ENRON Executives, Trustee, and Plan Auditor for Retirement Plan Losses," *Journal of Compensation and Benefits* 20, no. 1 (January–February 2004), p. 46(7).
85. James Sesil et al., "Broad-Based Employee Stock Options in U.S. New Economy Firms," *British Journal of Industrial Relations* 40, no. 2 (June 2002), pp. 273–294.
86. Eric Dash, "Time Warner Stops Granting Stock Options to Most of Staff," *The New York Times*, February 19, 2005, item 128921996.
87. Peter Kurlander, "Building Incentive Compensation Management Systems: What Can Go Wrong?" *Compensation & Benefits Review*, July/August 2001, pp. 52–56. The average

percentage of payroll employers spent on broad-based performance pay plans rose till 2005, and then has fallen for the past few years. "Companies Pull Back from Performance Pay," *Workforce Management,* October 23, 2006, p. 26. For one of many good discussions of why pay for performance tends to be ineffectual, see Fay Hansen, Where's the Merit-Pay Payoff? *Workforce Management,* November 3, 2008, pp. 33–39.

88. Suzanne Peterson and Fred Luthans, "The Impact of Financial and Nonfinancial Incentives on Business Unit Outcomes over Time," *Journal of Applied Psychology* 91, no. 1, 2006, pp. 156–165.
89. Ibid., p. 159.
90. Ibid., p. 159.
91. Ibid., p. 162. See also "Delivering Incentive Compensation Plans That Work," *Financial Executive* 25, no. 7 (September 2009), pp. 52–54.
92. Reed Taussig, "Managing Cash Based Incentives," *Compensation & Benefits Review,* March/April 2002, pp. 65–68. See also Nigel Nicholson, "How to Motivate Your Problem People," *Harvard Business Review,* January 2003, pp. 57–65; and "Incentives, Motivation and Workplace Performance," Incentive Research Foundation, www.incentivescentral.org/employees/whitepapers, accessed May 19, 2007.
93. "Two Frameworks for a More ROI-Minded Rewards Plan," *Pay for Performance Report,* February 2003, p. 1, at http://www.ioma.com/issues/PFP/2003_02/518132-1.html, accessed November 3, 2009; and Alan Robinson and Dean Schroeder, "Rewards That Really Work," *Security Management,* July 2004, pp. 30–34. See also Patricia Zingheim and Jay Schuster, "What Are Key Pay Issues Right Now?" *Compensation & Benefits Review,* May/June 2007, pp. 51–55.
94. See, for example, Jessica Marquez, "Retooling Pay: Premium on Productivity," *Workforce Management* 84, no. 12 (November 7, 2005), pp. 1, 22–23, 25–26, 28, 30; http://www.scribd.com/doc/12824332/NUCOR-CORP-8K-Events-or-Changes-Between-Quarterly-Reports-20090224, accessed November 3, 2009; and http://www.nucor.com/careers, accessed November 3, 2009.
95. Theodore Weinberger, "Evaluating the Effectiveness of an Incentive Plan Design Within Company Constraints," *Compensation & Benefits Review,* November/December 2005, pp. 27–33; Howard Risher, "Adding Merit to Pay for Performance," *Compensation & Benefits Review,* November/December 2008, pp. 22–29.
96. Janet Wiscombe, "Can Pay for Performance Really Work?" *Workforce,* August 2001, p. 30.
97. Susan Marks, "Incentives That Really Reward and Motivate," *Workforce,* June 2001, pp. 108–114.
98. Although not an issue at Nucor, the employer needs to beware of instituting so many incentive plans (cash bonuses, stock options, recognition programs, and so on) tied to so many different behaviors that employees don't have a clear priority of the employer's priorities. See, for example, Stephen Rubenfeld and Jannifer David, "Multiple Employee Incentive Plans: Too Much of a Good Thing?" *Compensation & Benefits Review,* March/April 2006, pp. 35–43.

13 Benefits and Services

When you own about 10,000 stores around the world, you obviously can't be everywhere watching what's going on. Perhaps that's one reason why Starbucks' employee benefits are exceptional. Each partner (employee) gets a "Special Blend" of total pay and benefits that's unique to him or her. Benefits include (just for a start) health care benefits, a retirement savings plan, life and disability coverage, adoption assistance, domestic partner benefits, and (of course) a pound of coffee each week.[1]

Source: Courtesy of Lynne Sladky/AP Wide World Photos.

WHERE ARE WE NOW . . .

We've now covered two of the three pay plan components—salary (or wages) and incentives. The main purpose of Chapter 13 is to discuss employee benefits. We discuss four main types of plans: supplemental pay benefits (such as sick leave and vacation pay); insurance benefits (such as workers' compensation); retirement benefits (such as pensions); and employee services (such as child-care facilities). Because legal considerations loom large in any benefits decision, we cover applicable federal laws and their implications for managers. This chapter completes our discussion of employee compensation. The next chapter, Chapter 14 (Ethics, Justice, and Fair Treatment in HR Management), starts a new part of this book, and focuses on another important human resource task—employee relations.

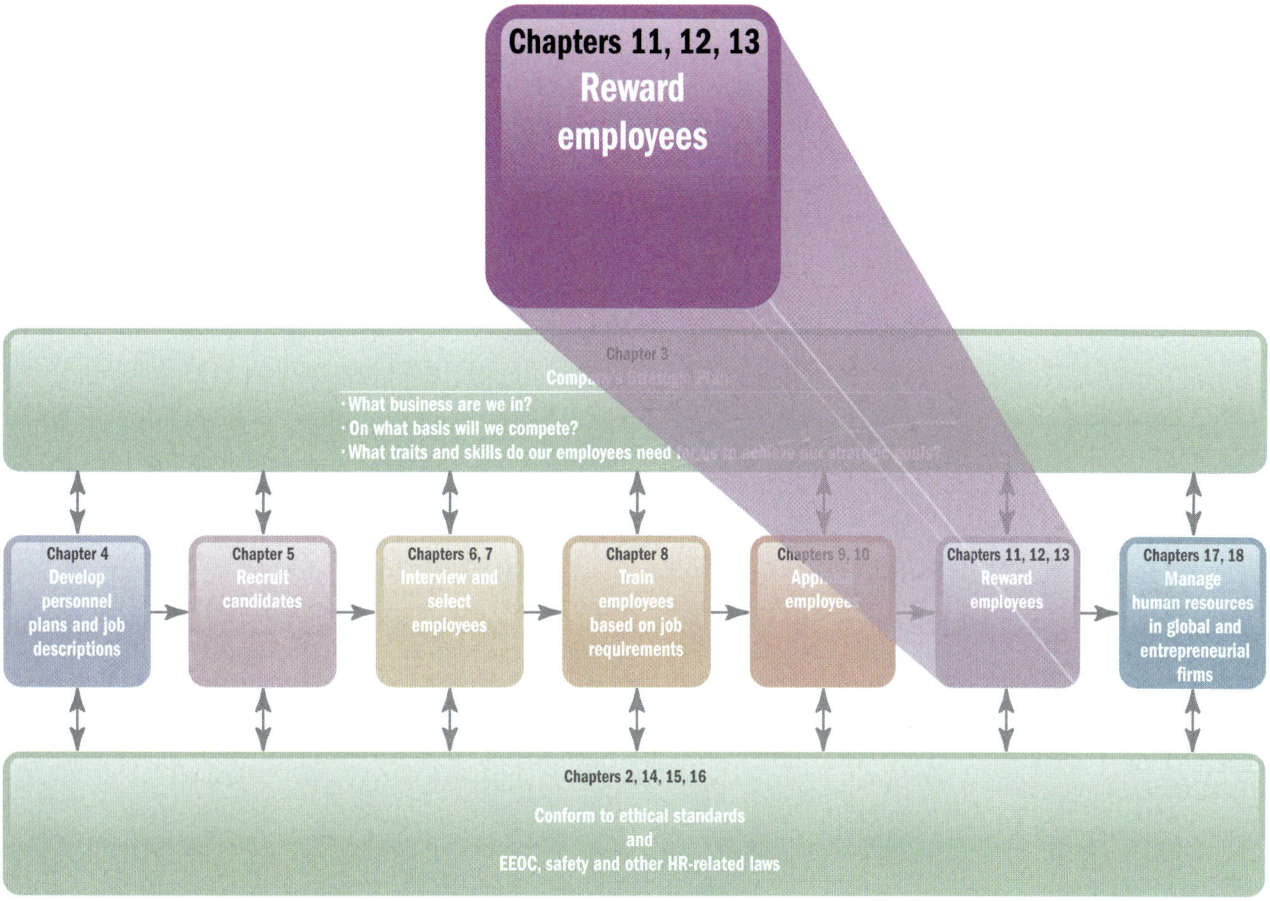

LEARNING OUTCOMES

1. Name and define each of the main pay for time not worked benefits.
2. Describe each of the main insurance benefits.
3. Discuss the main retirement benefits.
4. Outline the main employees' services benefits.
5. Explain the main flexible benefit programs.

THE BENEFITS PICTURE TODAY

"What are your benefits?" is the first thing many applicants ask. **Benefits**—indirect financial and nonfinancial payments employees receive for continuing their employment with the company—are an important part of just about everyone's compensation.[2] They include things like health and life insurance, pensions, time off with pay, and child-care assistance.

Most full-time employees in the United States receive benefits. Virtually all employers offer some health insurance coverage.[3] Employee benefits account for between 33%–40% of wages and salaries (or about 28% of total payrolls); legally required benefits (like unemployment insurance) are the most expensive benefits costs, followed by health insurance.

As Figure 13-1 suggests health care costs are rising. Since 2001, health care premiums have risen about 78%, while inflation rose only 17%.[4] (However, in 2009, employee costs rose only 6.4% compared with an average 15% since 2002, largely because of the employer cost containment efforts we'll discuss shortly.[5]) Consultants Towers Perrin estimate the cost of medical coverage recently was about $888 per month for family coverage.[6] Figure 13-2 summarizes the breakdown of benefits as a percentage of wages and salaries.[7]

Employees understand the value of health benefits. One study concluded that employees whose firms provide such benefits accepted wages about 20% lower than what they would have received working at firms without them.[8] In one survey, 78% of employees cited health care benefits as most crucial to retaining them; 75% cited compensation. But the same survey found that only 34% are satisfied with their health care benefits.[9]

Total Spending on Health Care	$1.9 trillion	$2.9 trillion	$4 trillion
% of GNP	16% 2004	18% 2009	20% 2015

*Note: Figures for 2009 and 2015 estimated. Health care costs rose 7.9% in 2004, about twice the rate of inflation, and are expected to rise at that rate through 2015.

FIGURE 13-1 U.S. Health Care Cost Increases*

Sources: Eric Perlmenter, "Controlling Health Care Costs," *Compensation & Benefits Review*, September/October 2002, p. 44; Victoria Colliver, "Health Care Costs Continue Double Digit Increase," *San Francisco Chronicle*, December 8, 2003; The National Coalition on Health Care, www.nchc.org/facts/cost.shtml, accessed March 21, 2007; http://www.kff.org/insurance/upload/7692_02.pdf, accessed October 29, 2009.

FIGURE 13-2 Private-Sector Employer Benefits Costs by Category, March 2009

Source: www.bls.gov/news.release/pdf/ ecec.pdf, accessed April 29, 2009.

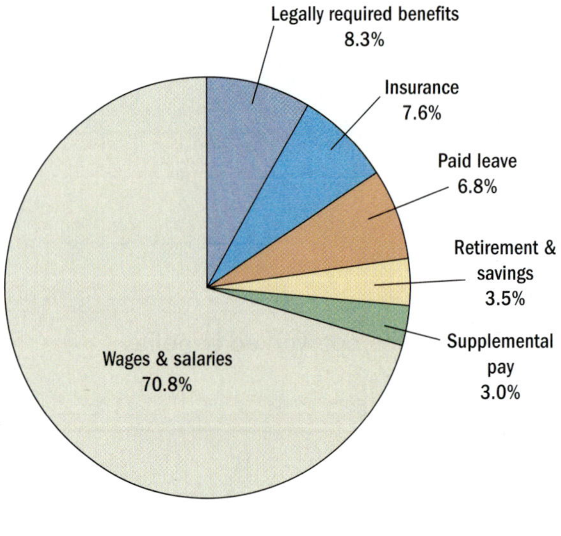

TABLE 13-1 Some Required and Discretionary Benefits

Benefits Required by Federal or Most State Law	Benefits Discretionary on Part of Employer*
Social Security	Disability, Health, and Life Insurance
Unemployment Insurance	Pensions
Workers' Compensation	Paid Time Off for Vacations, Holidays, Sick Leave, Personal Leave, Jury Duty, etc.
Leaves Under Family Medical Leave Act	Employee Assistance and Counseling Programs, "Family Friendly" Benefits for Child Care, Elder Care, Flexible Work Schedules, etc., Executive Perquisites

*Although not required under federal law, all these benefits are regulated in some way by federal law, as explained in this chapter.

Policy Issues Employers therefore need to design benefits packages with care. A short list of policy issues would include what benefits to offer, who receives coverage, whether to include retirees in the plan, whether to deny benefits to employees during initial "probationary" periods, how to finance benefits, the degree of employee choice in determining benefits, cost-containment procedures, and how to communicate benefits options to employees.[10]

Legal issues loom large. Federal laws mandate some benefits (such as Social Security) while other benefits are at the employer's discretion (see Table 13-1). However, federal law kicks in even for discretionary benefits such as vacation leave. And employers must adhere to the laws of the states in which they do business. For example, California requires most state contractors to provide domestic partner benefits for employees.[11]

There are many benefits and various ways to classify them. We will classify them as (1) pay for time not worked, (2) insurance benefits, (3) retirement benefits, and (4) services. We start our discussion with pay for time not worked.

1 Name and define each of the main pay for time not worked benefits.

PAY FOR TIME NOT WORKED

Pay for time not worked—also called **supplemental pay benefits**—is the most costly benefit, because of the large amount of time off that most employees receive. Common time-off-with-pay periods include holidays, vacations, jury duty, funeral leave, military duty, personal days, sick leave, sabbatical leave, maternity leave, and unemployment insurance payments for laid-off or terminated employees.

Unemployment Insurance

All states have **unemployment insurance** or **compensation** laws. These provide benefits if a person is unable to work through no fault of his or her own. The benefits derive from a tax on employers that can range from 0.1% to 5% of taxable payroll in most states. An employer's unemployment tax rate reflects its rate of employee terminations. States have their own unemployment laws, but they all follow federal guidelines.

Firms aren't required to let just everyone they dismiss receive unemployment benefits—only those released through no fault of their own. Thus, strictly speaking, a worker fired for chronic lateness can't legitimately claim benefits. But many managers take a lackadaisical attitude toward protecting their employers. Employers therefore spend thousands of dollars on unemployment taxes that would not be necessary if they protected themselves.

benefits
Indirect financial and nonfinancial payments employees receive for continuing their employment with the company.

supplemental pay benefits
Benefits for time not worked such as unemployment insurance, vacation and holiday pay, and sick pay.

unemployment insurance
Provides benefits if a person is unable to work through some fault other than his or her own.

TABLE 13-2 An Unemployment Insurance Cost-Control Checklist

Do You:

- ☐ Keep documented history of lateness, absence, and warning notices
- ☐ Warn chronically late employees before discharging them
- ☐ Have rule that 3 days' absence without calling in is reason for automatic discharge
- ☐ Request doctor's note on return to work after absence
- ☐ Make written approval for personal leave mandatory
- ☐ Stipulate date for return to work from leave
- ☐ Obtain a signed resignation statement
- ☐ Mail job abandonment letter if employee fails to return on time
- ☐ Document all instances of poor performance
- ☐ Require supervisors to document the steps taken to remedy the situation
- ☐ Document employee's refusal of advice and direction
- ☐ Require all employees to sign a statement acknowledging acceptance of firm's policies and rules
- ☐ File the protest against a former employee's unemployment claim on time (usually within 10 days)
- ☐ Use proper terminology on claim form and attach documented evidence regarding separation
- ☐ Attend hearings and appeal unwarranted claims
- ☐ Check every claim against the individual's personnel file
- ☐ Routinely conduct exit interviews to produce information for protesting unemployment claims

The main rule is to keep a list of written warnings. Beyond that, the checklist in Table 13-2 can help protect employers. Determine whether you could answer, "Yes" to questions such as, "Do you have a rule that 3 days' absence without calling is reason for automatic discharge?" Actions like these should enable you to demonstrate that the dismissal was a result of the person's inadequate performance. (By the way, those you fire during their initial "90-day probation" are eligible for unemployment, so follow that checklist for them, too.)

Vacations and Holidays

Most firms offer vacation leave benefits. Eighty-four percent of human resource professionals said their firms offer paid vacation for employees, and 51% offer paid personal days.[12] On average, American workers get 8.9 days of leave after 1 year's employment. Days off rise to about 11 after 3 years, 14 after 5 years, and 16 after 10 years.[13] Elsewhere, vacation allowances vary from 6 days in Mexico to 10 days in Japan, 25 in Sweden, 25 in France, and 33 in Denmark.

Unemployment insurance/compensation laws provide short-term benefits to people who lose their jobs through no fault of their own.

Source: Courtesy of Reuters NewMedia Inc./CORBIS–NY.

The most common U.S. paid holidays include New Year's Day, Memorial Day, Independence Day, Labor Day, Thanksgiving Day, and Christmas Day. Other common holidays include Martin Luther King, Jr., Day, Good Friday, Presidents' Day, Veterans' Day, the Friday after Thanksgiving, and the days before Christmas Day and New Year's Day.[14]

Firms have to address several holiday- and vacation-related policy issues. They must decide, of course, how many days off employees will get, and which days (if any) will be the paid holidays. Other vacation policy decisions include:

- Will employees get their regular base pay while on vacation, or vacation pay based on average earnings (which may include overtime)?
- Will you pay employees for accrued vacation time if they leave before taking their vacations?
- Will you pay employees for a holiday if they don't come to work the day before and the day after the holiday?
- And, should we pay some premium—such as time and a half—when employees must work on holidays?

More firms are moving to a somewhat more flexible vacation leave approach. For example, all of IBM's 350,000 plus employees get at least 3 weeks' vacation. However, IBM doesn't formally track how much vacation each person takes, or when. Instead, employees simply make informal vacation arrangements with their direct supervisors.[15]

Wage surveys and Web sites like www.hrtools.com provide sample vacation policies for inclusion in the firm's employee manual.

Some Legal Aspects of Vacations and Holidays

Although federal law does not require vacation benefits, the employer must still formulate vacation policy with care. As an example, the employer generally must pay the employee for his or her earned but unused vacation when the employee terminates. Many employers' policies say vacation pay accrues, say, on a biweekly basis. By doing so, they obligate themselves to pay employees when they leave the firm pro rata vacation pay. But if the employer's vacation policy requires that a new employee pass his or her first employment anniversary *before becoming entitled* to a vacation, the employee gets no vacation pay if he or she leaves during that first year.

One question that may arise is whether the employer has the right to cancel an employee's scheduled vacation, for instance, due to a rush of orders. Here it's important that the employer formulate its vacation policy so it's clear that the employer reserves the right to require vacation cancellation and rescheduling if production so demands.

Sick Leave

Sick leave provides pay to employees when they're out of work due to illness. Most sick leave policies grant full pay for a specified number of sick days—usually up to about 12 per year. The sick days usually accumulate at the rate of, say, 1 day per month of service.

Sick leave causes trouble for employers. The problem is that while many employees use their sick days only when they are sick, others use it for personal leave, whether sick or not. In one survey, personal illnesses accounted for only about 45% of unscheduled sick leave absences. Family issues (27%), personal needs (13%), and a mentality of "entitlement" (9%) were other reasons cited.[16] One survey found that the average cost of absenteeism per employee per year was $789, with personal illness accounting for about a third of the absences.[17]

Cost-Reduction Tactics

Employers use several tactics to reduce excessive sick leave absence. Some repurchase unused sick leave at the end of the year by paying

sick leave
Provides pay to an employee when he or she is out of work because of illness.

their employees a sum for each sick leave day not used. The drawback is that this encourages legitimately sick employees to come to work. Others have experimented with holding monthly lotteries in which only employees with perfect monthly attendance are eligible for a cash prize. At Marriott, employees can trade the value of some sick days for other benefits. Others aggressively investigate all absences, for instance, by calling the absent employees at their homes.[18]

Many employers—about 66%—use *pooled paid leave plans.*[19] These plans lump together sick leave, vacation, and personal days into a single leave pool. For example, one hospital previously granted new employees 25 days off per year (10 vacation days, 3 personal days, and 12 sick days). Employees used, on average, 5 of those 12 sick days (as well as all vacations and personal days).[20] The pooled paid leave plan allowed new employees to accrue 18 days to use as they saw fit. ("Catastrophic leaves"—short-term illnesses causing absences for more than 5 consecutive workdays, and special absences like bereavement leave—were handled separately.) The pooled plan reduced absences. The accompanying "Evidence-Based HR" feature expands on this.

EVIDENCE-BASED HR

Tracking Sick Leave

For many employers, sick leave is out of control simply because they don't take the time to measure it. In one survey by Hewitt Associates, only 57% of employers formally tracked sick days for their exempt employees and only 46% tracked personal days.[21] Three-fourths of the employers could not even provide an estimate of what their sick pay was costing as a percentage of payrolls. Therefore, before taking other cost control steps the employer should have a system in place for monitoring sick leaves and for measuring their financial impact. Then, switching to pooled time off plans should make it easier to manage, track, and quantify all employees' time off.

(By the way, the same evidence-based approach applies to controlling health care costs. Some estimate that between 5% and 15% of a medical plan's enrollees may include ineligible dependents such as ex-spouses and grown children. Periodically auditing dependents can therefore translate into significant health care cost savings.[22])

Parental Leave and the Family and Medical Leave Act

Parental leave is an important benefit. About half of workers are women, and about 80% will become pregnant during their work lives. Furthermore, many women and men head single-parent households. Under the Pregnancy Discrimination Act, employers must treat women applying for pregnancy leave as they would any other employee requesting a leave under the employer's policies. Beyond this, Congress passed, as noted, the Family and Medical Leave Act of 1993 (FMLA). Among other things (see Figure 13-3), the FMLA stipulates that:[23]

1. Private employers of 50 or more employees must provide eligible employees (women or men) up to 12 weeks of unpaid leave for their own serious illness, the birth or adoption of a child, or the care of a seriously ill child, spouse, or parent.
2. Employers may require employees to take any unused paid sick leave or annual leave as part of the 12-week leave provided in the law.
3. Employees taking leave are entitled to receive health benefits while they are on unpaid leave, under the same terms and conditions as when they were on the job.
4. Employers must guarantee most employees the right to return to their previous or equivalent position with no loss of benefits at the end of the leave.

Employers have expressed some dissatisfaction with the FMLA. In a survey of 416 human resource professionals, about half said they approved leaves they

FIGURE 13-3 Your Rights Under the Family and Medical Leave Act of 1993

Your Rights
under the
Family and Medical Leave Act of 1993

FMLA requires covered employers to provide up to 12 weeks of unpaid, job-protected leave to "eligible" employees for certain family and medical reasons. Employees are eligible if they have worked for their employer for at least one year, and for 1,250 hours over the previous 12 months, and if there are at least 50 employees within 75 miles. The FMLA permits employees to take leave on an intermittent basis or to work a reduced schedule under certain circumstances.

Reasons for Taking Leave:

Unpaid leave must be granted for *any* of the following reasons:

- to care for the employee's child after birth, or placement for adoption or foster care;
- to care for the employee's spouse, son or daughter, or parent who has a serious health condition; or
- for a serious health condition that makes the employee unable to perform the employee's job.

At the employee's or employer's option, certain kinds of *paid* leave may be substituted for unpaid leave.

Advance Notice and Medical Certification:

The employee may be required to provide advance leave notice and medical certification. Taking of leave may be denied if requirements are not met.

- The employee ordinarily must provide 30 days advance notice when the leave is "foreseeable."
- An employer may require medical certification to support a request for leave because of a serious health condition, and may require second or third opinions (at the employer's expense) and a fitness for duty report to return to work.

Job Benefits and Protection:

- For the duration of FMLA leave, the employer must maintain the employee's health coverage under any "group health plan."
- Upon return from FMLA leave, most employees must be restored to their original or equivalent positions with equivalent pay, benefits, and other employment terms.
- The use of FMLA leave cannot result in the loss of any employment benefit that accrued prior to the start of an employee's leave.

Unlawful Acts by Employers:

FMLA makes it unlawful for any employer to:

- interfere with, restrain, or deny the exercise of any right provided under FMLA.
- discharge or discriminate against any person for opposing any practice made unlawful by FMLA or for involvement in any proceeding under or relating to FMLA.

Enforcement:

- The U.S. Department of Labor is authorized to investigate and resolve complaints of violations.
- An eligible employee may bring a civil action against an employer for violations.

FMLA does not affect any Federal or State law prohibiting discrimination, or supersede any State or local law or collective bargaining agreement which provides greater family or medical leave rights.

For Additional Information:

If you have access to the Internet visit our FMLA website: **http://www.dol.gov.** To locate your nearest Wage-Hour Office, telephone our Wage-Hour toll-free information and help line at 1-866-4USWAGE (1-866-487-9243); a customer service representative is available to assist you with referral information from 8am to 5pm **in your time zone;** or log onto our Home Page at **http://www.wagehour.dol.gov.**

U.S. Department of Labor
Employment Standards Administration
Wage and Hour Division
Washington, D.C. 20210

WH Publication 1420
Revised August 2001

believed were not legitimate, but felt they had to grant because of vague interpretations of the law.[24] Tracking leaves was another problem.[25]

FMLA leaves are usually unpaid, but they're not costless. The costs associated with hiring temporary replacements, training them, and compensating for their lower productivity can be considerable.

FMLA Guidelines Therefore, the manager who wants to avoid granting nonrequired FMLA leaves needs to understand some FMLA details (as the poster in Figure 13-3 summarizes). For example, to be eligible for leave under the FMLA, the employee must have worked for the employer for at least a total of 12 months and have worked (not just been paid, as someone might be if on leave) for 1,250 or more hours in the past 12 consecutive months.[26] If these do not apply, no leave is required.

Employers obviously need clear procedures for all leaves of absence (including those awarded under the Family and Medical Leave Act). These include:

- In general, give no employee a leave until the reason for the leave is clear.
- If the leave is for medical or family reasons, the employer should obtain medical certification from the attending physician or medical practitioner.

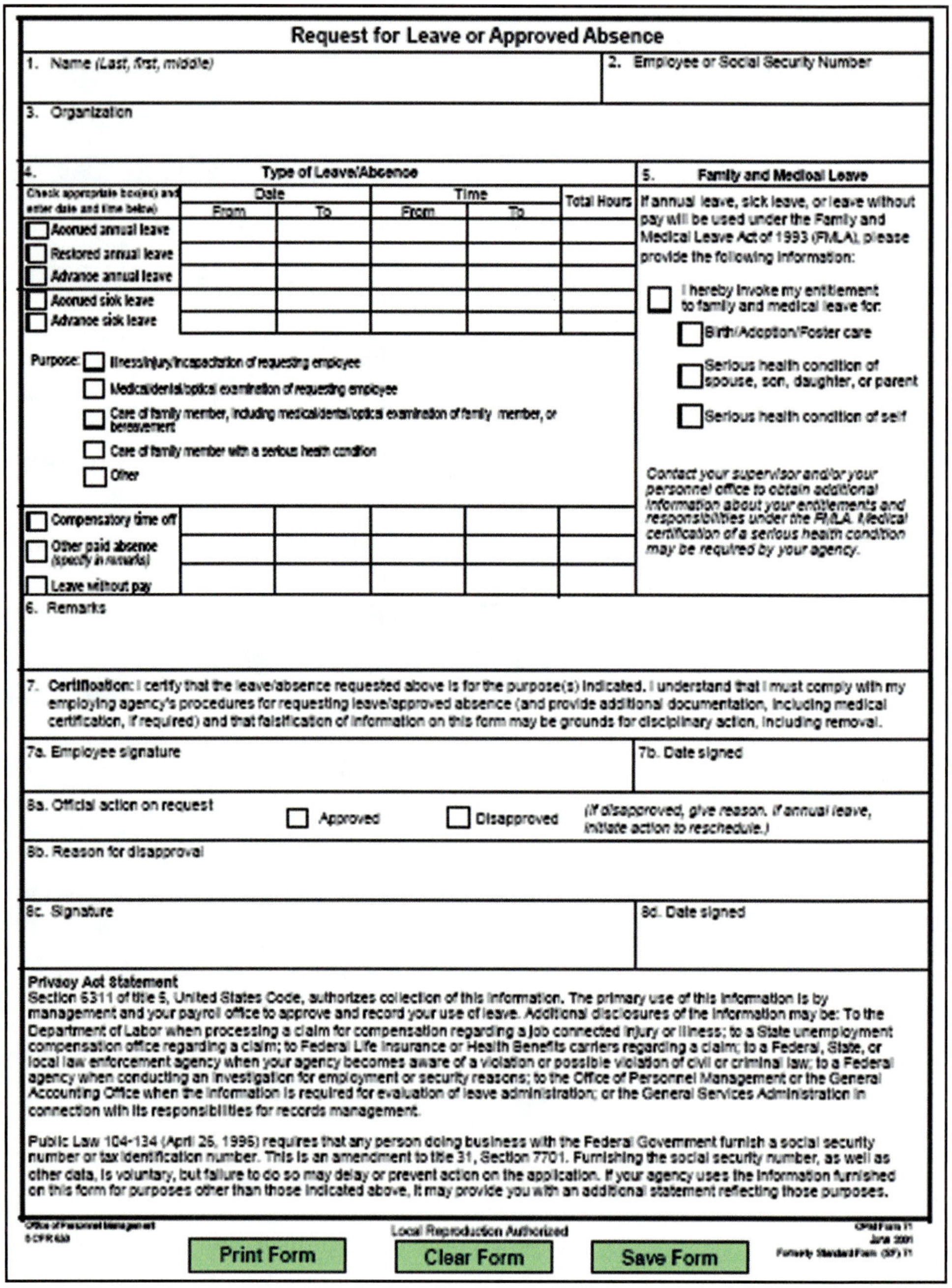

Request for Leave or Approved Absence

1. Name (Last, first, middle)

2. Employee or Social Security Number

3. Organization

4. Type of Leave/Absence

Check appropriate box(es) and enter date and time below)	Date From	Date To	Time From	Time To	Total Hours
☐ Accrued annual leave					
☐ Restored annual leave					
☐ Advance annual leave					
☐ Accrued sick leave					
☐ Advance sick leave					

Purpose: ☐ Illness/injury/incapacitation of requesting employee
☐ Medical/dental/optical examination of requesting employee
☐ Care of family member, including medical/dental/optical examination of family member, or bereavement
☐ Care of family member with a serious health condition
☐ Other

☐ Compensatory time off					
☐ Other paid absence (specify in remarks)					
☐ Leave without pay					

5. Family and Medical Leave

If annual leave, sick leave, or leave without pay will be used under the Family and Medical Leave Act of 1993 (FMLA), please provide the following information:

☐ I hereby invoke my entitlement to family and medical leave for:
☐ Birth/Adoption/Foster care
☐ Serious health condition of spouse, son, daughter, or parent
☐ Serious health condition of self

Contact your supervisor and/or your personnel office to obtain additional information about your entitlements and responsibilities under the FMLA. Medical certification of a serious health condition may be required by your agency.

6. Remarks

7. **Certification:** I certify that the leave/absence requested above is for the purpose(s) indicated. I understand that I must comply with my employing agency's procedures for requesting leave/approved absence (and provide additional documentation, including medical certification, if required) and that falsification of information on this form may be grounds for disciplinary action, including removal.

7a. Employee signature

7b. Date signed

8a. Official action on request ☐ Approved ☐ Disapproved *(If disapproved, give reason. If annual leave, initiate action to reschedule.)*

8b. Reason for disapproval

8c. Signature

8d. Date signed

Privacy Act Statement
Section 6311 of title 5, United States Code, authorizes collection of this information. The primary use of this information is by management and your payroll office to approve and record your use of leave. Additional disclosures of the information may be: To the Department of Labor when processing a claim for compensation regarding a job connected injury or illness; to a State unemployment compensation office regarding a claim; to Federal Life Insurance or Health Benefits carriers regarding a claim; to a Federal, State, or local law enforcement agency when your agency becomes aware of a violation or possible violation of civil or criminal law; to a Federal agency when conducting an investigation for employment or security reasons; to the Office of Personnel Management or the General Accounting Office when the information is required for evaluation of leave administration; or the General Services Administration in connection with its responsibilities for records management.

Public Law 104-134 (April 26, 1996) requires that any person doing business with the Federal Government furnish a social security number or tax identification number. This is an amendment to title 31, Section 7701. Furnishing the social security number, as well as other data, is voluntary, but failure to do so may delay or prevent action on the application. If your agency uses the information furnished on this form for purposes other than those indicated above, it may provide you with an additional statement reflecting those purposes.

Local Reproduction Authorized

Print Form Clear Form Save Form

FIGURE 13-4 Online Request for Leave Form

Source: www.opm.gov/FORMS/PDF_FILL/opm71.pdf, accessed April 28, 2009.

- Use a standard form to place on record both the employee's expected return date and the fact that, without an authorized extension, the firm may terminate his or her employment (see Figure 13-4).
- One employment lawyer says employers should "kind of bend over backward" when deciding if an employee is eligible for leave based on an FMLA situation.[27] However, employers can require independent medical assessments before approving paid FMLA disability leaves.[28]

Some employers are enriching their parental leave plans to make it more attractive for mothers to return from maternity leave. Tactics include communicating benefits and supports proactively, keeping in touch throughout the maternity leave, offering flexible jobs with reduced travel and hours, giving mothers fair access to bonuses and incentives, and facilitating longer leaves.[29]

Other laws apply to sick leaves. Under the Americans with Disabilities Act (ADA), a qualified employee with a disability may be eligible for a leave if such a leave is necessary to accommodate reasonably the employee. Under various state workers' compensation laws, employees may be eligible for leave in connection with work-related injuries. Many states also have their own, more restrictive versions of the FMLA.[30]

Severance Pay

Many employers provide **severance pay**, a one-time separation payment when terminating an employee. Severance pay makes sense. It is a humanitarian gesture, and good public relations. In addition, most managers expect employees to give them 1 or 2 weeks' notice if they plan to quit, so it seems appropriate to provide severance pay when dismissing an employee. Reducing the chances of litigation from disgruntled former employees is another reason. Severance pay plans also help reassure employees who stay on after the employer downsizes its workforce that they'll receive some financial help if they're let go, too.

For whatever reason, severance pay is common. In one survey of 3,000 human resource managers, 82% of responding organizations reported having a severance policy.[31]

The reason for the dismissal affects whether the employee gets severance pay. About 95% of employees dismissed due to downsizings got severance pay, while only about a third of employers offer severance when termination is for poor performance. It is uncommon to pay when employees quit. The average maximum severance is 39 weeks for executives and about 30 weeks for other downsized employees.[32] About half of employers surveyed give white-collar and exempt employees 1 week of severance pay per year of service, and about one-third do the same for blue-collar workers.[33] If the employer obligates itself (for instance, in its employee handbook) to pay severance, then its "voluntary" plan will have to comply with additional rules under ERISA.[34]

Guidelines

In any event, there are several things to keep in mind when designing the severance plan. These include:

- List the situations for which the firm will pay severance, such as layoffs resulting from reorganizations, and that management will take other action as necessary.
- Require signing of a knowing and voluntary waiver/general release prior to remittance of any severance pay, absolving the employer from employment-related liability.
- Reserve the right to terminate or alter the severance policy.
- Make it clear that any severance payments continue until only the stated deadline or until the employee gets a new job, whichever occurs first.
- Remember that as with all personnel actions, the employer must make severance payments, if any, equitably.[35]

Supplemental Unemployment Benefits

In some industries such as auto making, shutdowns to reduce inventories or change machinery are common, and laid-off or furloughed employees must depend on unemployment insurance. As auto firms trooped to Washington for bailouts in 2009, Congress peppered them with questions about their **supplemental unemployment benefits**. As the name implies, these cash payments supplement the employee's unemployment compensation, to help the person maintain his or her standard of living while out of work. They generally cover three contingencies: layoffs, reduced workweeks, and facility relocations.

severance pay
A one-time payment some employers provide when terminating an employee.

supplemental unemployment benefits
Provide for a "guaranteed annual income" in certain industries where employers must shut down to change machinery or due to reduced work. These benefits are paid by the company and supplement unemployment benefits.

2 Describe each of the main insurance benefits.

INSURANCE BENEFITS

Most employers also provide a number of required or voluntary insurance benefits, such as workers' compensation and health insurance.

Workers' Compensation

Workers' compensation laws aim to provide sure, prompt income and medical benefits to work-related accident victims or their dependents, regardless of fault. Every state has its own workers' compensation law and commission, and some run their own insurance programs. However, most require employers to carry workers' compensation insurance with private, state-approved insurance companies. Neither the state nor the federal government contributes any funds for workers' compensation.

How Benefits Are Determined

Workers' compensation can be monetary or medical. In the event of a worker's death or disablement, the person's dependents receive a cash benefit based on prior earnings—usually one-half to two-thirds the worker's average weekly wage, per week of employment. Most states have a time limit—such as 500 weeks—for which benefits can be paid. If the injury causes a specific loss (such as an arm), the employee may receive additional benefits based on a statutory list of losses, even though he or she may return to work. In addition to these cash benefits, employers must furnish medical, surgical, and hospital services as required for the employee.

For workers' compensation to cover an injury or work-related illness, one must only prove that it arose while the worker was on the job. It does not matter that he or she may have been at fault; if the person was on the job when the injury occurred, he or she is entitled to workers' compensation. For example, suppose you instruct all employees to wear safety goggles when at their machines. One worker does not and experiences an eye injury while on the job. The company must still provide workers' compensation benefits.

Keep in mind that ADA provisions generally prohibit employers from inquiring about an applicant's workers' compensation history. Furthermore, failing to let an employee who is on injury-related workers' compensation return to work, or not accommodating him or her, could lead to lawsuits under ADA.

Controlling Workers' Compensation Costs

It is important to control workers' compensation claims (and therefore costs). The employer's insurance company usually pays the claim. However, the costs of the employer's premiums reflect the amount of claims.[36] Workers' comp claims also tend to correlate with injuries, so fewer claims is usually a good sign of fewer accidents.

There are several ways to reduce workers' compensation claims. Screen out accident-prone workers. Reduce accident-causing conditions in your facilities. And reduce the accidents and health problems that trigger these claims—for instance, by instituting effective safety and health programs and complying with government safety standards. Furthermore, although many workers' compensation claims are legitimate, some are not. Supervisors should therefore watch for typical fraudulent claim red flags. These include vague accident details, minor accidents resulting in major injuries, lack of witnesses, injuries occurring late Friday or very early Monday, and late reporting.[37] Other workers' comp cost-control techniques include monitoring health care providers for compliance with their fee schedules and auditing medical bills.[38] *Case management* is a popular cost-control option. It is "the treatment of injured workers on a case-by-case basis by an assigned manager, usually a registered nurse, who coordinates with the physician and health plan to determine which care settings are the most effective for quality care and cost."[39]

It's also important to get injured employees back on the job as fast as possible, since workers' compensation costs accumulate while the person is out. Many firms have rehabilitation programs. These include physical therapy, career counseling to guide injured employees into less strenuous jobs, and nursing assistance to help reintegrate claim recipients into your workforce.[40]

Hospitalization, Health, and Disability Insurance

Health insurance looms large in many people's choice of employer, because it is so expensive. Seventy-five percent of employees in one recent survey called it their most important benefit.[41] Hospitalization, health, and disability insurance helps protect employees against hospitalization costs and the loss of income arising from off-the-job accidents or illness. Many employers purchase insurance from life insurance companies, casualty insurance companies, or Blue Cross (for hospital expenses) and Blue Shield (for physician expenses) organizations. Others contract with health maintenance organizations or preferred provider organizations. The employer and employee usually both contribute to the plan. Table 13-3 illustrates the prevalence of health-related benefits.

Coverage

Most employer health plans provide at least basic hospitalization and surgical and medical insurance for all eligible employees at group rates. Insurance is generally available to all employees—including new nonprobationary ones—regardless of health or physical condition. Most basic plans pay for hospital room and board, surgery charges, and medical expenses (such as doctors' visits to the hospital). Some also provide "major medical" coverage to meet the medical expenses resulting from serious illnesses.

Most employers' health plans also cover health-related expenses like doctors' visits, eye care, and dental services. Other plans pay for general and diagnostic visits to the doctor's office, vision care, hearing aids, and prescription drugs. *Disability insurance* provides income protection for salary loss due to illness or accident. Payments usually start when normal sick leave payments end, and may continue until age 65 or beyond. Disability benefits usually range from 50% to 75% of the employee's base pay if he or she is disabled.

TABLE 13-3 Percentage of Employers Offering Popular Health Benefits—Change Over Time

	Yes (%) 2005	Yes (%) 2009
Prescription drug program coverage	97	96
Dental insurance	95	96
Mail order prescription program	90	91
PPO (preferred provider organization)	87	81
Chiropractic coverage	56	80
Mental health insurance	72	80
Vision insurance	80	76
Employee assistance program	73	75
Medical spending account	80	71
Life insurance for dependants	67	58
HMO (health maintenance organization)	53	35

Source: Adapted from 2009 SHRM Employee Benefits Survey Report, p. 5.

workers' compensation
Provides income and medical benefits to work-related accident victims or their dependents regardless of fault.

HMOs Many employers offer membership in a **health maintenance organization (HMO)** as a hospital/medical insurance option. The HMO is a medical organization consisting of specialists (surgeons, psychiatrists, and so on), often operating out of a health care center. It provides routine medical services to employees who pay a nominal fee. Employees often have general practitioner "gatekeeper" doctors who need to approve appointments with specialist doctors. The HMO receives a fixed annual fee per employee from the employer (or employer and employee), regardless of whether it provides that person service.

PPOs **Preferred provider organizations (PPOs)** are a cross between HMOs and the traditional doctor–patient arrangement: They are "groups of health care providers that contract with employers, insurance companies, or third-party payers to provide medical care services at a reduced fee."[42] Unlike HMOs, PPOs let employees select providers (such as doctors) from a relatively wide list, and see them in their offices, often without gatekeeper doctor approval. The providers agree to provide discounts and submit to certain utilization controls, such as on the number of diagnostic tests they can order.[43]

Mental Health Benefits The World Health Organization estimates that more than 34 million people in the United States between the ages of 18 and 64 suffer from mental illness.[44] Mental illnesses represent about 24% of all reported disabilities, more than disabling injuries, respiratory diseases, cardiovascular diseases, and cancer combined.

Mental health costs are rising. Reasons include widespread drug and alcohol problems, an increase in states that require employers to offer minimum mental health benefits, and the fact that mental health claims tend to trigger other health care claims. The Mental Health Parity Act of 1996 (as amended in 2008) sets minimum mental health care benefits; it also prohibits employer group health plans from adopting mental health benefits limitations without comparable limitations on medical and surgical benefits.[45]

The Legal Side of Health Benefits

With the U.S. introducing new health insurance laws, federal influence over health benefits will increase substantially in the next few years. These laws may even mandate employer health coverage. But even before 2009, federal laws already had a big influence.

COBRA Of these, the ominously titled COBRA—Consolidated Omnibus Budget Reconciliation Act—is the most pressing. COBRA requires most private employers to continue to make health benefits available to separated employees and their families for a time, generally 18 months after separation.[46] The former employee must pay for the coverage.

Employers ignore COBRA's regulations at their peril. Most importantly, you don't want separated employees to leave and be injured, and then claim you never told them they could have continued their insurance coverage. Therefore, when a new employee first becomes eligible for your company's insurance plan, the person *must* receive (and acknowledge receiving) an explanation of his or her COBRA rights. And, all employees separated from the company should sign a form acknowledging that they received and understand those rights. Figure 13-5 provides a COBRA checklist. As the U.S. slid into recession, Congress changed COBRA to support unemployed persons' insurance needs, as the accompanying "Managing HR in Challenging Times" feature explains.

Managing HR in Challenging Times

Providing Extended Health Care Benefits

In normal times, COBRA provides employees who leave the company with a means for maintaining their health and hospitalization coverage, but the (former) employee must pay the premiums. When unemployment began rising, Congress passed, and President Obama signed on February 17, 2009, the American Recovery and Reinvestment Act of 2009.

This new law had the immediate effect of making it easier for qualified employees who were involuntarily dismissed for any reason (other than gross misconduct) anytime after September 1, 2008 (the act was retroactive), to sign up for COBRA. It makes it easier to utilize COBRA because the new law requires that the employer pay 65% of the premium. (The employer then receives a credit for that full amount back from the U.S. government.[47]) The former employee must pay the remaining 35%.

FIGURE 13-5 COBRA Record-Keeping Compliance Checklist

Source: Reprinted from www.HR.BLR.com with permission of the publisher *Business and Legal Resources, Inc.*, 141 Mill Rock Road East, Old Saybrook, CT © 2004. BLR© (Business and Legal Resources, Inc.).

Detailed record keeping is crucial for COBRA compliance. The following checklist is designed to ensure that the proper records are maintained for problem-free COBRA compliance.

	Yes	No
• Do you maintain records so that it is easily determined who is covered by your group health care plan?	☐	☐
• Do you record terminations of covered employees as soon as terminations occur?	☐	☐
• Do you track reduction of hours of employees covered by group health care plans?	☐	☐
• Do you track deaths of employees covered by group health care plans?	☐	☐
• Do you track leaves of absence of employees covered by group health care plans?	☐	☐
• Do you track Medicare eligibility of employees covered by group health care plans?	☐	☐
• Do you track the disability status of employees covered by group health care plans?	☐	☐
• Do you track retirees covered by group health care plans?	☐	☐
• Do you maintain current addresses of employees?	☐	☐
• Do you maintain current addresses of individuals receiving COBRA benefits?	☐	☐
• Do you require employees to provide a written acknowledgment that they have received notice of their COBRA rights?	☐	☐
• Do you have a system to determine who has paid COBRA premiums on time?	☐	☐
• Do you have a system to determine who has obtained other group health coverage so that they are no longer eligible for COBRA under your plan?	☐	☐
• Do you maintain a telephone log of calls received about COBRA?	☐	☐
• Do you maintain a record of changes in your plan?	☐	☐
• Do you maintain a record of how premiums are calculated?	☐	☐
• Do you maintain a log of those employees who are denied COBRA coverage?	☐	☐
• Do you maintain a log of why employees are denied COBRA coverage?	☐	☐

health maintenance organization (HMO)
A prepaid health care system that generally provides routine round-the-clock medical services as well as preventive medicine in a clinic-type arrangement for employees, who pay a nominal fee in addition to the fixed annual fee the employer pays.

preferred provider organizations (PPOs)
Groups of health care providers that contract with employers, insurance companies, or third-party payers to provide medical care services at a reduced fee.

Other Laws Other federal laws are pertinent. For example, among other things, the *Employee Retirement Income Security Act* of 1974 (ERISA) sets minimum standards for most voluntarily established pension and health plans in private industry.[48] *The Newborn Mother's Protection Act of 1996* prohibits employers' health plans from using incentives to encourage employees to leave the hospital after childbirth after less than the legislatively determined minimum stay. Employers who provide health care services must follow the privacy rules of the *Health Insurance Portability and Accountability Act of 1996 (HIPAA)*.[49] Employers must provide the same health care benefits to employees over the age of 65 that they do to younger workers, even though the older workers are eligible for federal Medicare health insurance. Under the *Americans with Disabilities Act,* the plan generally shouldn't make distinctions based on disability. And, as explained earlier, the *Pregnancy Discrimination Act* requires employers to treat women affected by pregnancy, childbirth, or related medical conditions the same as any other employees not able to work, with respect to all benefits.

Trends in Employer Health Care Cost Control

Employers are trying hard to rein in spiraling health care costs. Many retain *cost-containment specialists* who help employers reduce their health care costs. And most now negotiate more aggressively with their health care insurance providers, and require employees to pay higher premiums or deductibles and co-payments.[50] We'll address other important cost-control trends.

Communication and Empowerment Most importantly, *make sure employees know the costs* of their medical benefits.[51] For example, periodically send a statement to each employee listing the employer's costs for each health benefit. As one expert said, "the biggest criticism of managed care . . . is that the health care consumer has little financial stake in treatment decisions."[52] So, for example, employers give employees online access to basic health care coverage and benefits information, promote in-network services, and encourage employees to reevaluate their health care options. Online selection allows employees to choose the best of the employer's health care offerings, based on input from other employees concerning matters like doctor visits and specialists.

Wellness Programs Many illnesses are preventable. In one study "employers who undertook prevention programs aimed at cardiovascular disease . . . reported an average 28% reduction in sick leave, [and] a 26% reduction in direct health-care costs."[53] Many employers therefore offer preventive services.[54] *Clinical prevention* programs include things like mammograms, immunizations, and routine checkups. Walgreens recently purchased two companies that provide *on-site health care services* such as mammograms for employers.[55] *Health promotion and disease prevention* programs include seminars and incentives aimed at improving unhealthy behaviors.[56] Top wellness program trends include obesity management, stress management, senior health improvement, and tobacco cessation programs.[57] But incentives-based wellness programs can backfire. Whirlpool gives nonsmoker discounts on health care premiums worth about $500. It recently suspended 39 workers it caught smoking outside the plant after claiming on their benefits enrollment forms that they were not tobacco users.

Health Savings Accounts The Medicare Modernization Act of 2003 allows employers to establish tax-free health savings accounts (HSA).[58] After the employer, employee, or both deposit pretax (and thus tax sheltered) pay in the employees' HSAs, employees or their families can use their HSA funds to pay for "low dollar" (not catastrophic) medical expenses.[59] The assumption is that this will motivate employees to utilize less expensive health care options, and thus avoid big deductibles.[60]

Claim Audits It makes little sense to initiate prevention plans or HSAs when employers are paying out thousands or millions of dollars in erroneous claims. Unfortunately, with health care plans becoming increasingly complicated, it's much easier for medical claims errors to occur. Human resource consultants Towers Perrin conducted a survey of claims payments. The industry standard for percentage of claims errors is 3%, but in two recent years Towers Perrin found the *actual* percentage of claims with financial errors were 6.3% and 6.6%. The industry standard for percentage of claims dollars actually paid in error was 1%; in two years the *actual* percentage of claims dollars paid in error were 3.5% and 3.3%. So, setting standards for errors and then aggressively auditing all claims may be the most direct way to reduce employer health care expenses.[61]

Other Cost-Control Options

Employers are taking other steps. One is *making online plan enrollment mandatory*.[62] Others use *defined contribution health care plans*. Here each employee gets a specific dollar amount allotment to use for co-payments or discretionary medical costs, rather than a specified health care benefits package with open-ended costs.[63] *Outsourcing* health care plan administration and employee assistance and counseling to outside companies for a fee are other options.[64] One study found that about 13% of surveyed employers had reduced subsidized health benefits for their future *retirees*.[65] Small firms are joining *benefits purchasing alliances*, banding together to purchase health care benefits. Other employers are encouraging *medical tourism*, which means asking employees to have non-urgent medical procedures abroad, where costs are lower.[66] One simple method is just to ensure that any *dependents* enrolled are actually eligible for coverage.[67]

Long-Term Care

Today, baby-boomers are entering their 60s, and long-term care insurance—to support things like nursing assistance to former employees in their old age—is a key employee benefit. The Health Insurance Portability and Accountability Act of 1996 lets employers and employees deduct the cost of long-term care insurance premiums from their annual income taxes, making this benefit more attractive.[68] Employers can provide insurance benefits for several types of long-term care, such as adult day care, assisted living, and custodial care.

Life Insurance

In addition to hospitalization and medical benefits, most employers provide **group life insurance** plans. Employees can usually obtain lower rates in a group plan. And group plans usually accept all employees—including new, nonprobationary ones—regardless of health or physical condition.

Sometimes the employer pays 100% of the base premium, which usually provides life insurance equal to about 2 years' salary. The employee then pays for any additional coverage. Or, the cost of the base premium is split between employer and employee. In general, there are three key personnel policies to address: the benefits-paid schedule (the amount of life insurance benefits is usually tied to the employee's annual earnings), supplemental benefits (continued life insurance coverage after retirement, for instance), and financing (the amount and percent the employee contributes).

Accidental death and dismemberment coverage provides a lump-sum benefit in addition to life insurance benefits when death is accidental. It also provides benefits in case of accidental loss of limbs or sight.

Benefits for Part-Time and Contingent Workers

About 19 million people work part-time (less than 35 hours a week). The recession, more phased retirements, a desire to better balance work and family life, and more women in the workforce help explain this phenomenon. In any case, most firms

group life insurance
Provides lower rates for the employer or employee and includes all employees, including new employees, regardless of health or physical condition.

provide holiday, sick leave, and vacation benefits to part-timers, and more than 70% offer some form of health care benefits to them.[69] Again, employers should take care to not misclassify part-time workers as "independent contractors."[70]

3 Discuss the main retirement benefits.

RETIREMENT BENEFITS

The first contingent of baby-boomers turns 65 in 2011, and many won't wait until then to retire. This presents two challenges for employers. First (as we explained in Chapter 10, Careers), employers are taking steps to entice older workers to keep working in some capacity.[71] Second, retirement funding is a big issue. We'll focus here on retirement benefits, including federal Social Security, and employer pension/retirement plans like the 401(k).

Social Security

Most people assume that **Social Security** provides income only when they are older than 62, but it actually provides three types of benefits. The familiar *retirement benefits* provide an income if you retire at age 62 or thereafter and are insured under the Social Security Act. Second are *survivor's* or *death benefits*. These provide monthly payments to your dependents regardless of your age at death, again assuming you are insured under the Social Security Act. Finally, there are *disability payments*. These provide monthly payments to employees who become disabled totally (and to their dependents) if they meet certain requirements. The Social Security system also administers the Medicare program, which provides health services to people age 65 or older. "Full retirement age" for non-discounted social security benefits traditionally was 65—the usual age for retirement. It is now 67 for those born in 1960 or later.

A tax on the employee's wages, shared equally by employees and employers, funds Social Security (technically, "Federal Old Age and Survivor's Insurance"). As of 2009, the maximum amount of earnings subject to Social Security tax was $106,800.[72] Employer and employee each paid 7.65%.[73]

Pension Plans

Pension plans are financial programs that provide income to individuals in their retirement. About half of full-time workers participate in some type of pension plan at work. However, the actual rate of participation depends on several things. For example, older workers tend to have a higher participation rate, and employees of larger firms have participation rates as much as three times as high as in small firms.

We can classify pension plans in three ways: *contributory versus noncontributory* plans, *qualified versus nonqualified* plans, and *defined contribution versus defined benefit* plans.[74] The employee contributes to the contributory pension plan, while the employer makes all contributions to noncontributory plans. Employers derive tax benefits from contributing to qualified pension plans, such as tax deductions for pension plan contributions (they are "qualified" for improved tax treatment); nonqualified pension plans get less favorable tax treatment.

Defined Benefit Plans With **defined benefit pension plans**, employees know ahead of time the pension benefits they will receive (the benefit is "defined" or specified by amount or formula). The defined pension benefit itself is usually set by a formula that ties the person's retirement pension to an amount equal to a percentage of the person's preretirement pay (for instance, to a fraction of an average of his or her last 5 years of employment), multiplied by the number of years he or she worked for the company. (As with all pay plan components, employers should ensure retirement benefits support their strategic needs by setting guiding principles such as "assist in attracting employees" and "assist in retaining knowledgeable employees.")[75]

Defined Contribution Plans In contrast, **defined contribution pension plans** specify what contribution the employee and/or employer will make to the employee's retirement or savings fund. With a defined *benefit* plan, the employee knows what his or her retirement benefits will be upon retirement. With a defined *contribution* plan, the person's pension will depend on the amounts contributed to the fund and on the retirement fund's investment earnings. Defined contribution plans prevail today. They reduce the employer's balance sheet liabilities (to retirees), have favorable tax treatment, and are easier to administer. While the stock markets were rising, they seemed advantageous to employees too. When markets turn down, those with defined contribution plans sometimes long for the security of defined benefits.

Portability—making it easier for employees who leave the firm prior to retirement to take their accumulated pension funds with them—is enhanced by switching from defined benefit to defined contribution plans. The former are therefore more appropriate for employees who plan to stay with the firm until retirement.

401(k) Plans The most popular defined contribution plans are based on section 401(k) of the Internal Revenue Code, and called **401(k) plans**. The employee authorizes the employer to deduct a sum from his or her paycheck before taxes, and to invest it in the bundle of investments in his or her 401(k). The deduction is pretax, so the employee pays no tax on those dollars until after he or she retires (or removes the money from the 401(k) plan). The person can decide to deduct any amount up to the legal maximum (the IRS sets an annual dollar limit—now about $15,000). The employer arranges, usually with an investment company such as Fidelity Investments, to administer the 401(k) plan and to make investment options available to the plan. The options typically include mutual stock funds and bond funds. As the downturn intensified in 2008, more employees began making "hardship withdrawals" from their 401(k) plans (on which no taxes are due, for a time).[76]

Source: Courtesy of Bill Aron/PhotoEdit Inc.

Firms such as Vanguard, Fidelity, and others can establish online, fully Web-based 401(k) plans even for small firms with 10 to 50 employees.

Employers must choose their 401(k) providers with care. The employer has a fiduciary responsibility to its employees; it must monitor the fund and its administration.[77] Furthermore, changing 401(k) providers can be "grueling."[78] In addition to trustworthiness, the 401(k) plan provider should make it easy to enroll and participate in the plan.[79] Firms such as Vanguard, Fidelity, and others can establish Web-based 401(k) plans with online tools—such as an "asset allocation planner"—even for small firms.

Under the Pension Protection Act of 2006, employers who sponsor plans that facilitate both *automatic enrollment* and allocation to *default investments* (such as age-appropriate "lifestyle funds") reduce their compliance burdens.[80] Post-2008 stories, like that of "David," a 47-year-old engineer, suggest prudence. His adviser said that "if we saved very aggressively, I might be able to retire in my early 70s." Such

Social Security
Federal program that provides three types of benefits: retirement income at the age of 62 and thereafter, survivor's or death benefits payable to the employee's dependents regardless of age at time of death, and disability benefits payable to disabled employees and their dependents. These benefits are payable only if the employee is insured under the Social Security Act.

pension plans
Plans that provide a fixed sum when employees reach a predetermined retirement age or when they can no longer work due to disability.

defined benefit pension plan
A plan that contains a formula for determining retirement benefits.

defined contribution pension plan
A plan in which the employer's contribution to employees' retirement savings funds is specified.

portability
Instituting policies that enable employees to easily take their accumulated pension funds when they leave employer.

401(k) plan
A defined contribution plan based on section 401(k) of the Internal Revenue Code.

experiences underscore the need for employee education, or perhaps directing funds into (relatively) prudent default investments.[81]

Other Defined Contribution Plans The 401(k) plan is one example of a **savings and thrift plan**.[82] In any savings and thrift plan, employees contribute a portion of their earnings to a fund, and the employer usually matches this contribution completely or in part.

As discussed in Chapter 12 (Incentives), employers use a **deferred profit-sharing plan** to contribute a portion of their profits in cash to a pension fund, regardless of the level of employee contribution (income taxes on those contributions are deferred until the employee retires or leaves the employer). An **employee stock ownership plan (ESOP)** is a qualified, tax-deductible defined contribution plan in which employers contribute stock to a trust for eventual use by employees who retire.

Cash Balance Pension Plans Cash balance pension plans are hybrid plans.[83] To get the maximum benefit in a defined benefit plan, the employee generally must "put in" his or her full 30 or so years with the firm. This approach tends to favor older employees (whose income is often higher and who have been with the firm longer). Younger employees (and/or those who want the option of moving on with their vested pension benefits after, say, 7 or 8 years) might prefer defined contribution plans. Here the employee gets the full vested value to that point of his or her pension.

Under **cash balance plans**, the employer contributes a percentage of employees' current pay to the employees' pension plans every year, and employees earn interest on this amount.[84] Cash balance plans provide the portability of defined contribution plans with the more predictable benefits of defined benefit plans.

Pension Planning and the Law

No one wants to wake up and discover that his or her pension has vanished. Therefore, federal laws closely regulate pension planning and administration. As a rule, it is impossible to formulate a plan without expert help.

The **Employee Retirement Income Security Act of 1975 (ERISA)** is the basic law. It requires that employers have written pension plan documents and adhere to certain guidelines, for instance regarding who is eligible for the employer's plan, and at what point the employer's contribution becomes the employee's (more on this later).[85] ERISA protects the employer's pension or health plans' assets by requiring that those who control the plans act responsibly. The Department of Labor says that the primary responsibility of *fiduciaries* is to run the plan solely in the interest of participants and beneficiaries.

Other laws are pertinent. Employers (and employees) want their pension contributions to be "qualified," or tax deductible, so they must adhere to the pertinent *income tax codes*. Under *labor relations laws*, the employer must let its unions participate in pension plan administration. The *Job Creation and Worker Assistance Act* provides guidelines regarding what rates of return employers should use in computing their pension plan values.

PBGC ERISA established the **Pension Benefits Guarantee Corporation (PBGC)** to oversee and insure a pension if a plan terminates without sufficient funds. The PBGC guarantees only defined benefit plans, not defined contribution plans. Furthermore, it will only pay an individual a pension of up to a maximum of about $54,000 per year for someone 65 years of age with a plan terminating in 2009.[86] So, high-income workers may still see most of their expected pensions evaporate if their employers go bankrupt.

Key Pension Policy Issues

In developing pension plans, employers must address several key policy issues. One is the benefits formula. This usually ties the (defined) pension to the employee's final earnings, or an average of his or her last 3 or 4 years' earnings. Plan funding is another issue. Specifically, how will you fund the plan? Will it be contributory or noncontributory? Membership requirements and vesting are two other big issues.

Membership Requirements When does the employee become eligible for a pension? Under the Tax Reform Act of 1986, an employer can require that an employee complete a period of no more than 2 years' service to the company before becoming eligible to participate in the plan. However, if it requires more than 1 year of service before eligibility, the plan must grant employees full and immediate vesting rights at the end of that period.

Vesting *Vested funds* are the money employer and employee have placed in the latter's pension fund that cannot be forfeited for any reason. The employees' contributions are always theirs, of course. However, until the passage of ERISA, the *employers'* contribution in many pension plans didn't vest until the employee retired. So, you could have worked for a company for 30 years and been left with no pension if the company went bust 1 year before you were to retire. That generally can't happen today, given the PBGC's guarantees.

Employers can choose one of two minimum vesting schedules (employers can allow funds to vest faster if they wish). With *cliff vesting*, the period for acquiring a nonforfeitable right to employer matching contributions (if any) is 3 years. So, the employee must have nonforfeitable rights to these funds by the end of 3 years. With the second (*graded vesting*) option, pension plan participants must receive nonforfeitable rights to the matching contributions as follows: 20% after 2 years, and then 20% for each succeeding year, with a 100% nonforfeitable right by the end of 6 years.

Pensions and Early Retirement

To trim their workforces or for other reasons, some employers are encouraging employees to retire early. Many of these plans take the form of **early retirement window** arrangements for specific employees (often age 50-plus). The "window" means that for a limited time, the employees can retire early. The financial incentive is generally a combination of improved or liberalized pension benefits plus a cash payment.

Early retirement programs can backfire for two reasons. Some are too successful. When Verizon Communications offered enhanced pension benefits to encourage what it hoped would be 12,000 employees to retire, more than 21,000 took the plan. Verizon had to replace 16,000 managers.[87]

Discrimination is the other potential problem. Unless structured properly, older employees can challenge early retirement programs as de facto ways for forcing them to retire against their will. Although it is generally legal to use incentives to encourage individuals to choose early retirement, the employee's decision must be voluntary. In one case, the employer told employees on October 12 that they were eligible to retire under a "totally voluntary" early retirement program, and must inform the company of their decision by October 18. However, employees didn't get the details

savings and thrift plan
Plan in which employees contribute a portion of their earnings to a fund; the employer usually matches this contribution in whole or in part.

deferred profit-sharing plan
A plan in which a certain amount of profits is credited to each employee's account, payable at retirement, termination, or death.

employee stock ownership plan (ESOP)
A qualified, tax-deductible stock bonus plan in which employers contribute stock to a trust for eventual use by employees.

cash balance plans
Plans under which the employer contributes a percentage of employees' current pay to employees' pension plans every year, and employees earn interest on this amount.

Employee Retirement Income Security Act (ERISA)
Signed into law by President Ford in 1974 to require that pension rights be vested and protected by a government agency, the PBGC.

Pension Benefits Guarantee Corporation (PBGC)
Established under ERISA to ensure that pensions meet vesting obligations; also insures pensions should a plan terminate without sufficient funds to meet its vested obligations.

early retirement window
A type of offering by which employees are encouraged to retire early, the incentive being liberal pension benefits plus perhaps a cash payment.

of the program until October 15. The court ruled that was unreasonable.[88] The Older Workers' Benefit Protection Act (OWBPA) now imposes limitations. The employee's waiver must be knowing and voluntary, and give the employee ample time to think over the agreement and to seek legal advice, among other things.

Improving Productivity Through HRIS: Online Benefits Management Systems

Benefits administration can be enormously labor-intensive and time-consuming.[89] Left un-automated, it can require the employer to devote hundreds or thousands of human resource professionals' hours to answering employees' questions about comparative benefits and updating employees' benefits information. Typical employee questions include, "In which option of the medical plan am I enrolled?" and "If I retire in 2 years, what will be my monthly retirement income?" Tasks like that cry out for online self-service benefits management applications.

BeneLogic For example, when the organization that assists Pennsylvania school districts with their insurance needs decided to help the school boards automate their benefits administration, they chose a company called BeneLogic.[90] The solution, called the "Employee Benefit Electronic Service Tool," lets users manage all aspects of benefits administration, including enrollment, plan descriptions, eligibility, and premium reconciliation, via their browsers.[91]

BeneLogic hosts and maintains the Web support application on its own servers, and creates customized, Web-based applications for each school district. The system facilitates Web-based employee benefit enrollment, and provides centralized call center support for benefit-related questions. It even handles benefits-related payroll, HRIS, and similar functions by collaborating with companies like ADP (for payroll) and Oracle PeopleSoft (which services many of the school boards' human resource information systems). Each school board employee accesses the BeneLogic site via a link on his or her own board's Web site.

Benefits Web Sites Employers everywhere are adding new services to their own benefits Web sites. In addition to offering things like self-enrollment, the insurance company USAA's Web site (www.usaa.com) helps employees achieve better work life–balance. For example, click on the "today, I'm feeling . . ." menu. Here employees can respond to a list of words (such as "stressed"). From there, they see suggestions for dealing with (in this case) stress. Go to "my child is behaving badly," and the employee gets access to resources like "guide to addressing child behavior problems."[92] Boeing's Pay & Benefits Profile site gives employees real-time information about their salary and bonuses, benefits, pension, and even special services such as child care referrals.[93]

4 Outline the main employees' services benefits.

PERSONAL SERVICES AND FAMILY-FRIENDLY BENEFITS

Although time off, insurance, and retirement benefits account for the lion's share of benefits costs, most employers also provide various services benefits. These include personal services (such as legal and personal counseling), "family-friendly" services (such as child-care facilities), educational subsidies, and executive perquisites (such as company cars for its executives).

Personal Services

Many employers provide the sorts of personal services that employees need at one time or another. These include credit unions, legal services, counseling, and social and recreational opportunities. (Some employers use the term *voluntary benefits* to cover personal services benefits that range from things like pet insurance to automobile insurance.[94]) We'll look at a few of these.

Credit Unions Credit unions are usually separate businesses run by independent companies to help employees with borrowing and saving needs, but some employers establish their own. Employees usually become members by purchasing a share of the credit union's stock for a small fee—perhaps $5 or $10. Members can then deposit savings that accrue interest at a rate determined by the credit union's directors. Loan eligibility and the loan's rate of interest are usually more favorable than are those of banks and finance companies.

Employee Assistance Programs **Employee assistance programs (EAPs)** provide counseling and advisory services, such as personal legal and financial services, child and elder care referrals, adoption assistance, mental health counseling, and life event planning.[95] EAPs are increasingly popular, with more than 60% of larger firms offering such programs. One study found that personal mental health was the most common problem addressed by employee assistance programs, followed by family problems.[96]

For employers, EAPs produce advantages, not just costs. For example, sick family members and problems like depression account for many of the sick days employees take. Employee assistance programs can reduce such absences by providing expert advice on issues like elder care referrals.[97] Few but the largest employers establish their own EAPs. Most contract for the necessary services with vendors such as Magellan Health Services and CIGNA Behavioral Health.[98]

In either case, employers and managers need to keep several issues in mind. Everyone involved with the EAP, including supervisors, secretaries, and support staff, must understand the importance of *confidentiality*. Also, ensure files are locked, access is limited and monitored, and identifying information is minimized. *Be aware of legal issues.* For example, in most states counselors must disclose suspicions of child abuse to state agencies. *Define* the program's purpose, employee eligibility, the roles and responsibilities of EAP and employer personnel, and procedures for using the plan. And ensure the vendors you use fulfill *professional and state licensing requirements.*

Family-Friendly (Work–Life) Benefits

Several trends are changing the benefits landscape. There are more households where both adults work, more one-parent households, more women in the workforce, and more workers older than age 55. Then, there's the "time bind"—people working more, without the time to do all they'd like to do. The issues involve working men, as well as women.[99]

These pressures have led many employers to bolster their **family-friendly (or work–life) benefits**. (The number of Americans who have never married is rising, and the newer "work–life benefits" terminology recognizes the need to improve all employees' work–life situations, not just those with families.)[100] These benefits include child care, elder care, fitness facilities, and flexible work schedules—benefits that help employees balance their family and work lives.[101] For example, a survey by the Society for Human Resource Management (SHRM) found that about 29% of employers provided at least some type of child-care assistance, and 55% offer flexible-schedule work arrangements.[102] We'll look at some examples.

Subsidized Child Care Fulfilling work responsibilities while raising a family is a challenge, particularly for single parents. Most working people make private provisions to take care of their children. For example, relatives accounted for 48% of all child-care providers in one study.[103] Organized day care centers accounted for another 30% of child-care arrangements, and nonrelatives accounted for most of the remaining arrangements.

employee assistance program (EAP)
A formal employer program for providing employees with counseling and/or treatment programs for problems such as alcoholism, gambling, or stress.

family-friendly (or work–life) benefits
Benefits such as child care and fitness facilities that make it easier for employees to balance their work and family responsibilities.

Source: Courtesy of Ann States Photography.

Software giant SAS Institute, Inc., offers generous employee benefits. The North Carolina firm keeps turnover at 4% in an industry where 20% is typical, in large part by offering family-friendly benefits like paid maternity leave, day care on site, lunchtime piano concerts, massages, and yoga classes like this one.

Employers who want to reduce the distractions associated with finding reliable child care can help in various ways. Some employers simply investigate the day care facilities in their communities and recommend certain ones to interested employees. But more employers are setting up company-sponsored and subsidized day care facilities, both to attract employees and to reduce absenteeism. For example, Abbott Laboratories built a $10 million child care center at its headquarters north of Chicago, daytime home to about 400 children of Abbott employees.[104]

By establishing subsidized day care, employers assumedly can benefit in several ways. These include improved recruiting results, lower absenteeism, improved morale, favorable publicity, and lower turnover. But, good planning is required. This often starts with a questionnaire to employees to answer questions like, "What would you be willing to pay for care for one child in a child-care center near work?"

Sick Child Benefits What do you do when your child is sick and you need to get to work? One study found that unexpected absences climbed to about 2.4% of payroll hours recently, with a cost per absence to employers of about $700 per episode (for temp employees and reduced productivity, for instance). More employers are thus offering emergency child-care benefits, for instance for when a young child's regular babysitter is a no-show. Texas Instruments built a Web database its employees use to find last-minute child-care providers. Others, like Canadian financial services company CIBC, are expanding their on-site child-care centers to handle last-minute emergencies.[105]

Elder Care Elder care benefits are important for much the same reason. The responsibility for caring for an aging relative can affect the employee's performance.[106] One study found that, to care for an older relative, 64% of employees took sick days or vacation time, 33% decreased work hours, 22% took leaves of absence, 20% changed their job status from full- to part-time, 16% quit their jobs, and 13% retired early. The problem will grow more acute as the over 65 population rises. One survey found that about 120 million Americans are now caring for—or in the past cared for—an adult relative or friend.[107]

So, more employers are providing elder care services. For example, the United Auto Workers and Ford Motor Company provide elder care referral services for Ford's salaried employees. The service provides a detailed assessment of the elderly relative's needs and recommendations on the care that would be best.[108] The National Council on Aging has a Web site to help elders and caregivers find benefit programs: www.benefitscheckup.org.

Time Off One survey (admittedly conducted prior to the 2008 downturn) found that about half the 2,586 workers surveyed felt they were working too much and putting too little time into "other things in life that really matter." In response, employers such as Hartford Financial Services Group and Nationwide Mutual Insurance are changing their time-off policies. For example, they are handing out time off as a performance reward, tracking employee time off to avert burnout, giving new hires more vacation, and offering employees more long weekends on holidays.[109]

Family-Friendly Benefits and the Bottom Line

But particularly in challenging times, employers need to balance the cost of benefits like these with their advantages. It's not easy to evaluate the "profitability" of such programs. The costs are pretty clear. For example, a few years ago Aetna found it saved $400,000 just by making employees at its Blue Bell, Pennsylvania, office buy their own coffee and tea.[110]

Measuring the program's positive consequences isn't so simple. "Family-friendly" firms such as SAS routinely turn up on "best companies to work for" lists. This almost undoubtedly makes it easier to recruit and retain good employees. Employees may even willingly forego somewhat higher pay for services like built-in day care. And some of the advantages to the employer are indirect. For example, employees who experience work–family conflict may experience anger that affects performance, a situation family-type benefits may improve.[111]

The bottom line is that in challenging times particularly, employers are carefully reviewing which of these benefits to cut back. Even Google, long known for offering benefits that blow almost every other employer's away (free buses from the city, on-campus day care, and restaurants) has been cutting back of late.

Other Job-Related Benefits

Employers provide various other job-related benefits. Some provide subsidized *employee transportation*, such as increased mileage allowances or mass transit discounts.[112] Google's Web site lists benefits such as adoption assistance, the Google Child Care Center, free shuttle service from San Francisco, on-site dry cleaning, backup child-care assistance, and on-site physician and dental care. *Food services* are provided in some form by many employers; they let employees purchase meals, snacks, or coffee, usually at relatively low prices.

Educational Subsidies

Educational subsidies such as tuition refunds are popular benefits. Payments range from all tuition and expenses down to a flat limit of several hundred dollars per year. One survey found that about 72% of the 579 employers surveyed paid for college courses related to an employee's present job. Many employers also reimburse non–job-related courses (such as a Web designer taking an accounting class) that pertain to the company business. Some employers pay for self-improvement classes, such as foreign language study, even though they are unrelated to company business or the employee's job (although there seems to be a trend toward reducing such benefits).[114] Many employers provide college programs, taught on the employer's premises. We've seen that other educational programs include remedial work in basic literacy.

The problem is that you may be paying your best employees to leave. Two researchers studied how employer-sponsored part-time college education reimbursements influenced job mobility. They focused on the U.S. Navy's tuition assistance program. Taking tuition assistance significantly decreased the probability the person stayed in the Navy.[115] So, the employer needs to review the terms of its tuition refund program carefully, and to review the results it has had with the program over the years.

How to extend benefits like these to domestic partners is an important issue for employers. The accompanying "Managing the New Workforce" feature addresses this.

HR APPs 4 U

iPods at Work

Some employers have policies against using devices such as iPods at work. One online columnist wrote supporting such a ban. Of course, many employees wrote in support of having an iPod-at-work benefit. Among their comments:[113]

> "Sitting in a silent office on my own all day with no music or talk radio??!!! May as well send the little men in white coats, because I am off to the funny farm."
>
> "Even in higher level positions, there is a lot of rote work that doesn't require enough thought to light a candle—hence radio has saved my sanity."
>
> "Often the routine part of my job is maddening to me. If I have talk radio on, I am encouraged to stay in my seat and finish up what has to be done in less time."
>
> "It drowns out the constant whining and complaining from co-workers and increases my concentration. I've seen my productivity go up by as much as 20%."

MANAGING THE NEW WORKFORCE

Domestic Partner Benefits

A survey by the Society for Human Resource Management found that of 578 companies responding, about 23% offer same-sex domestic partner benefits, 31% offer opposite-sex partner benefits, and about 2% plan to do one or both.[116] For example, Northrop Grumman Corp. extends domestic partner benefits to the 9,500 salaried workers at its Newport News shipyard.[117]

When employers provide *domestic partner benefits* to employees, it generally means that employees' same-sex or opposite-sex domestic partners are eligible to receive the same benefits (health care, life insurance, and so forth) as do the husband, wife, or legal dependent of one of the firm's employees.[118] Under the Defense of Marriage Act passed in 1996, no state or political subdivision in the United States *need* treat same-sex domestic partners the same as employees' spouses, and the federal government *may not* do so, for purposes of federal law. There is thus some debate as to whether the benefits extended to domestic partners will be federal tax free, as they generally are for the relatives enumerated here.

Executive Perquisites

When you reach the pinnacle of the organizational pyramid—or at least close to the top—you will find, waiting for you, the Executive Perk. As we mentioned in Chapter 11 (Pay Plans), perquisites (perks, for short) usually only go to top executives. Perks can range from substantial (company planes) to relatively insignificant (private bathrooms).

Many popular perks fall between these extremes. These include *management loans* (which typically enable senior officers to exercise their stock options); *salary guarantees* (also known as "golden parachutes") to protect executives if their firms become targets of acquisitions or mergers; *financial counseling* (to handle investments); and *relocation benefits*, often including subsidized mortgages, purchase of the executive's current house, and payment for the actual move.[119] A selection of other executive perks includes time off with pay (including sabbaticals and severance pay), outplacement assistance, company cars, chauffeured limousines, executive dining rooms, physical fitness programs, legal services, tax assistance, liberal expense accounts, club memberships, season tickets, and children's educational subsidies. As you can see, employers have had many ways of making their hardworking executives' lives as pleasant as possible!

The downturn that began in 2008 of course caused many boards of directors and firms to cut back on perks. When the U.S. auto industry's CEOs arrived in Washington aboard private planes to ask Congress for bailouts, many people took offense. Next time, they all drove from Detroit. Many employers are similarly reducing the more lavish perks in particular, such as executive dining rooms. As we noted in Chapter 11, publicly traded companies must now itemize all executives perks if they all total more than $100,000.

5 Explain the main flexible benefit programs.

FLEXIBLE BENEFITS PROGRAMS

Employees prefer choice in their benefits plans. In one survey of working couples, 83% took advantage of flexible hours (when available); 69% took advantage of the flexible-style benefits we'll discuss next; and 75% said that prefer flexible benefits plans.[120] The online job listing service Jobtrak.com asked college students and recent graduates, "Which benefit do you desire most?" Thirty-five percent sought flexible hours; 19%, stock options; 13%, more vacation time; and 12%, a better health plan. Most of the preferred benefits had to do with lifestyle issues rather than financial ones.[121]

Given this, it is prudent to survey employees' benefits preferences, perhaps using a form like that in Figure 13-6. In any case, employers should provide for choice when designing benefits plans.

FIGURE 13-6 Online Survey of Employees' Benefits Preferences

Source: https://data.grapevinesurveys.com/survey.asp?sid=20062143964099, accessed April 29, 2009.

Your Logo Here. 125 px

300 px

Human Resources - Employee Benefits Survey

Please take a moment to tell us your thoughts on the Company benefits plan. Your input is valued and will help us make this better.

Health care

1 **Please rate the following.**
1-Very Satisfied, 5-Very Dissatisfied

	1	2	3	4	5
Medical plan	1	2	3	4	5
Dental plan	1	2	3	4	5
Vision plan	1	2	3	4	5

Retirement and Savings Plan

2 **Please rate the following**
1-Very Satisfied, 5-Very Dissatisfied

	1	2	3	4	5
401K and profit sharing	1	2	3	4	5
Employee Stock Purchase	1	2	3	4	5
Disability (short & long term)	1	2	3	4	5

Other benefits

3 **Please rate the following**
1-Very Satisfied, 5-Very Dissatisfied

	1	2	3	4	5
Accidental death and dismemberment insurance	1	2	3	4	5
Vacation	1	2	3	4	5
Education assistance plan	1	2	3	4	5
Life Insurance plan	1	2	3	4	5

(continued)

FIGURE 13-6 *(continued)*

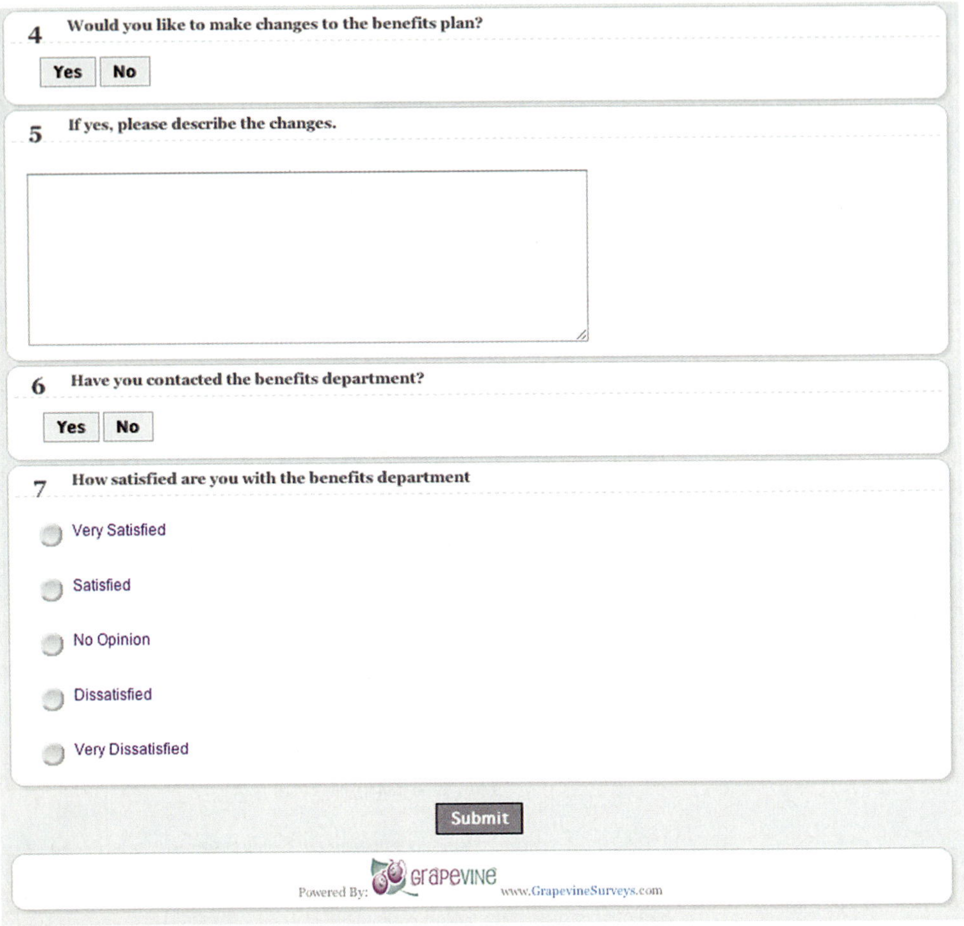

4 **Would you like to make changes to the benefits plan?**

Yes | No

5 **If yes, please describe the changes.**

6 **Have you contacted the benefits department?**

Yes | No

7 **How satisfied are you with the benefits department**

- Very Satisfied
- Satisfied
- No Opinion
- Dissatisfied
- Very Dissatisfied

Submit

Powered By: grapevine www.GrapevineSurveys.com

The Cafeteria Approach

One way to provide a choice is with an aptly named *cafeteria benefits plan.* (Pay specialists use **flexible benefits plan** and **cafeteria benefits plan** synonymously.) A *cafeteria plan* is one in which the employer gives each employee a benefits fund budget, and lets the person spend it on the benefits he or she prefers, subject to two constraints. First, the employer must of course limit the total cost for each employee's benefits package. Second, each employee's benefits plan must include certain required items—for example, Social Security, workers' compensation, and unemployment insurance. Employees can often make midyear changes to their plans if, for instance, their dependent care costs rise and they want to divert contributions.[122] IRS regulations require formal written plans describing the employer's cafeteria plan, including benefits and procedures for choosing them.[123]

Types of Plans Cafeteria plans come in several varieties. To give employees more flexibility in what benefits they use, about 70% of employers offer *flexible spending accounts* for medical and other expenses. This option lets employees pay for certain benefits expenses with pretax dollars (so the IRS, in effect, subsidizes some of the employee's expense). To encourage employees to use this option without laying out cash, some firms are offering *debit cards* that employees can use at their medical provider or pharmacy.[124] *Core plus option plans* establish a core set of benefits (such as medical insurance), which are usually mandatory for all employees. Beyond the core, employees can then choose from various benefits options.[125]

Benefits and Employee Leasing

Many businesses—particularly smaller ones—don't have the resources or employee base to support the cost of many of the benefits we've discussed in this chapter. That's one big reason they turn to "employee leasing."

Employee leasing firms (also called *professional employer organizations* or *staff leasing firms*) assume all or most of the employer's human resources chores. In doing so, they also become the employer of record for the employer's employees, by transferring them all to the employee leasing firm's payroll. The leasing firm thus becomes the employees' legal employer, and usually handles employee-related activities such as recruiting, hiring (with client firms' supervisors' approvals), and paying taxes (Social Security payments, unemployment insurance, and so on).

Insurance and benefits are usually the big attraction. Getting health and other insurance is a problem for smaller firms. Even group rates for life or health insurance can be quite high when only 20 or 30 employees are involved. That's where the leasing firm comes in. Remember that the leasing firm is the legal employer of your employees. The employees therefore are absorbed into a much larger insurable group, along with other employers' former employees. As a result, a small business owner may be able to get insurance for its people that it couldn't otherwise afford. Another advantage is off-loading all or most of the HR-related paperwork. Many small business owners therefore figure what they save on not managing their own human resource activities pays for the employee leasing firm's fees.

First Weigh Example The 40 employees at First Weigh Manufacturing in Sanford, Florida, don't work for a giant company, but they get employee benefits as if they do. That's because Tom Strasse, First Weigh's owner, signed up with ADP Total Source, a professional employee organization that now handles all First Weigh's HR processes. "I didn't have the time or the personnel to deal with the human resources, safety and OSHA regulations," Strasse says. And, "We were always looking for new insurance."[126] Now when Strasse has a question about employee legal issues or safety concerns, he just calls his representative at the employee leasing firm. And more important for Strasse, ADP Total was able to offer his employees better health benefits than he could have gotten through First Weigh.

Employee leasing may sound too good to be true, and it often is. Many employers aren't comfortable letting a third party become the legal employer of their employees. Particularly for employers who build their competitive advantage around employees such as engineers, delegating human resource management duties like screening, training, and career planning to outsiders may be dubious. And, several years ago, the employee leasing industry tarnished itself, when one or two firms manipulated the pension benefits offered to higher-paid employees.[127] Employee leasing can also raise liability concerns. For example, in the typical employee leasing arrangement, the leasing firm and the client employer agree to share certain employee-related responsibilities, a concept known as co-employment. So, for instance, in states where courts have not universally upheld workers' compensation as the sole remedy for injuries at work (there are some such states), one must specify whether the client company or the leasing firm is insuring the workers' compensation exposure.[128] And if the leasing firm suddenly goes out of business, the employer must scramble to obtain new health insurance.

Flexible Work Schedules

Flexible work schedules are increasingly popular.[129] Single parents often find them crucial for balancing work and family responsibilities. And for many millennial employees, flexible work schedules provide a way for them to pursue their careers without surrendering the quality of work life they desire. We'll look at some flexible work schedule options.

flexible benefits plan/cafeteria benefits plan
Individualized plans allowed by employers to accommodate employee preferences for benefits.

Flextime **Flextime** is a plan whereby employees' workdays are built around a core of midday hours, such as 11:00 a.m. to 2:00 p.m. Workers determine their own starting and stopping hours. For example, they may opt to work from 7:00 a.m. to 3:00 p.m. or from 11:00 a.m. to 7:00 p.m. The number of employees in formal flextime programs—from 4% of operators to 17% of executive employees—doesn't tell the whole story. Many more employees, probably almost half, actually take advantage of informal flexible work schedules.[130] In practice, most employers hold fairly close to the traditional 9:00 a.m. to 5:00 p.m. workday. Therefore, the effect of flextime for most employees is to give them about 1 hour of leeway before 9:00 a.m. or after 5:00 p.m.

Compressed Workweeks Many employees, like airline pilots, do not work conventional 5-day, 40-hour workweeks. Similarly, hospitals may want doctors and nurses to provide continuing care to a patient, or manufacturers may want to reduce the productivity lost whenever workers change shifts. Firefighters usually work for several days straight. Workers like these typically have **compressed workweek** schedules, which mean they work fewer days each week, but each day they work longer hours. Nonconventional workweeks come in many flavors. Some firms have 4-day workweeks, with four 10-hour days. Some workers—in hospitals, for instance—work three 12-hour shifts, and then are off for the next 4 days.[131]

Effectiveness of Flexible Work Schedule Arrangements Studies show that flexible work schedules have positive effects on employee productivity, job satisfaction, and employee absenteeism; the positive effect on absenteeism was much greater than on productivity. Compressed workweeks positively affected job satisfaction; absenteeism did not increase, and productivity was not positively affected. Highly flexible programs were actually less effective than less flexible ones.[132]

Some experts argue that longer, 12-hour shifts may increase fatigue and accidents. However, one report suggests 12-hour shifts can actually be safer, in some respects. For example, 12-hour shifts reduce the "general workplace confusion" that often occurs during shift changes, since there are fewer shift changes per day. To reduce potential side effects, some employers install treadmills and exercise bikes, and special "light boxes" that mimic daylight.

Workplace Flexibility As anyone who has flown next to someone tapping away on a laptop knows, employees are increasingly conducting business from nontraditional settings, using technology like iPods and BlackBerry-type devices.[133] **Workplace flexibility** means arming employees with the information technology tools they need to get their jobs done wherever they are. For example, Capital One Financial Corp. has its Future of Work program. Certain Capital One employees received mobile technology tools such as wireless access laptops and BlackBerry-type cell phone devices. The program seems to have led to about a 41% increase in overall workplace satisfaction, a 31% reduction in time needed to get input from peers, and a 53% increase in those who say their workplace enhances group productivity.[134]

Other Flexible Work Arrangements Employers are taking other steps to accommodate employees' scheduling needs. **Job sharing** allows two or more people to share a single full-time job. For example, two people may share a 40-hour-per-week job, with one working mornings and the other working afternoons. About 22% of the firms questioned in one survey indicated that they allow job sharing.[135] Job sharing can be particularly useful for retirement-aged employees, in that it allows them to reduce their hours while enabling the company to retain their expertise.[136] **Work sharing** refers to a temporary reduction in work hours by a group of employees during economic downturns as a way to prevent layoffs. Thus, 400 employees may all agree to work (and be paid for) only 35 hours per week, to avoid a layoff of 30 workers.

REVIEW

CHAPTER SECTION SUMMARIES

1. Because benefits are so important to employees, it's important that all managers understand **the benefits picture today**. In addition to the fact that benefits are very important to employees, the other big issue, of course, is that benefits in general and health care costs in particular are rising very fast. About 78% of employees cite health care benefits as most crucial to retaining them.
2. Employers provide numerous pay **for time not worked benefits**.
   - Unemployment insurance provides benefits if a person is unable to work due to some fault other than his or her own. To avoid unnecessary unemployment taxes, the main rule is to keep a list of written warnings.
   - American workers tend to get about 8 or 9 days of leave after 1 year of employment.
   - Sick pay provides pay to an employee when he or she is out of work because of illness. Minimizing sick leave pay is important, and here cost reduction tactics include repurchasing unused sick leave or simply using paid leave plans that lump sick leave, vacation, and holidays into one leave pool.
   - In formulating parental leave policies, the employer needs to keep in mind the Family and Medical Leave Act, which requires larger employers to provide up to 12 weeks of unpaid leave for family-related issues, and the Americans with Disabilities Act.
   - Severance pay is a one-time payment some employers provide when terminating an employee.
3. Most employers also provide a number of required or voluntary **insurance benefits**. Workers' compensation laws aim to provide sure, prompt medical benefits to work-related accident victims or their dependents, regardless of fault. Hospitalization, health, and disability insurance costs are rising fast, and most employer health plans provide at least basic hospitalization and surgical and medical insurance for eligible employees. Many employers provide these plans via preferred provider organizations or health management organizations. When an employee is terminated or terminates his or her employment, it is essential that the employer make the person aware of his or her COBRA rights. The basic overall trend in health care cost control is to take steps (for instance, in terms of communication and empowerment, health savings accounts, and claims audits) to try to keep the rising cost of health care insurance under control.
4. Particularly with stock markets volatile, **retirement benefits** are important to employees today. Social Security is a federal program that provides retirement income at the age of 62 and thereafter, as well as other benefits. Many employers make available pension plans; these provide an income when employees reach retirement age or when they can no longer work due to disability. Defined benefit plans contain a formula for determining retirement benefits, while defined contribution plans are plans in which the contribution to employees' retirement savings plans is specified. 401(k) plans are perhaps the most well-known of the latter, and are based on section 401(k) of the Internal Revenue Code. The Employee Retirement Income Security Act of 1975 requires that employers have written pension plan documents, and established the Pension Benefits Guarantee Corporation to oversee employers' pension plans. Key pension policy issues include membership requirements and testing.
5. Most employers also provide various **personal services and family-friendly benefits**. These include credit unions, employee assistance programs, and subsidized child care and elder care.
6. Employees prefer choice in their benefits plans, so **flexible benefits programs** are important. Flexible benefits or cafeteria benefits plans are individual plans that accommodate employee preferences for benefits. Some employers turn to employee leasing companies to capitalize on the advantage of the leasing firm's large employee base to get better employee benefits for their employees. Employers also are implementing various types of flexible work schedules, including flextime, compressed workweeks, and other flexible work arrangements such as job sharing.

flextime
A work schedule in which employees' workdays are built around a care of midday hours, and employees determine, within limits, what other hours they will work.

compressed workweek
Schedule in which employee works fewer but longer days each week.

workplace flexibility
Arming employees with the information technology tools they need to get their jobs done wherever they are.

job sharing
Allows two or more people to share a single full-time job.

work sharing
Refers to a temporary reduction in work hours by a group of employees during economic downturns as a way to prevent layoffs.

DISCUSSION QUESTIONS

1. You are applying for a job as a manager and are at the point of negotiating salary and benefits. What questions would you ask your prospective employer concerning benefits? Describe the benefits package you would try to negotiate for yourself.
2. What is unemployment insurance? Is an organization required to pay unemployment benefits to all dismissed employees? Explain how you would go about minimizing your organization's unemployment insurance tax.
3. Explain how ERISA protects employees' pension rights.
4. What is "portability"? Why do you think it is (or isn't) important to a recent college graduate?
5. What are the main provisions of the FMLA?

INDIVIDUAL AND GROUP ACTIVITIES

1. Working individually or in groups, research the unemployment insurance rate and laws of your state. Write a summary detailing your state's unemployment laws. Assuming Company X has a 30% rate of annual personnel terminations, calculate Company X's unemployment tax rate in your state.
2. Assume you run a small business. Working individually or in groups, visit the Web site www.dol.gov/elaws. See the Small Business Retirement Savings Advisor. Write a 2-page summary explaining: (1) the various retirement savings programs available to small business employers, and (2) which retirement savings program you would choose for your small business and why.
3. You are the HR consultant to a small business with about 40 employees. Now the firm offers only 5 days of vacation, 5 paid holidays, and legally mandated benefits such as unemployment insurance payments. Develop a list of other benefits you believe it should offer, along with your reasons for suggesting them.
4. The "HRCI Test Specifications Appendix" (pages 699–706) lists the knowledge someone studying for the HRCI certification exam needs to have in each area of human resource management (such as in Strategic Management, Workforce Planning, and Human Resource Development). In groups of four to five students, do four things: (1) Review that appendix now. (2) Identify the material in this chapter that relates to the required knowledge the appendix lists. (3) Write four-multiple choice exam questions on this material that you believe would be suitable for inclusion in the HRCI exam. And (4) if time permits, have someone from your team post your team's questions in front of the class, so the students in other teams can take each others' exam questions.

EXPERIENTIAL EXERCISE

Revising the Benefits Package

Purpose: The purpose of this exercise is to provide practice in developing a benefits package for a small business.

Required Understanding: Be very familiar with the material presented in this chapter. In addition, review Chapter 11 to reacquaint yourself with sources of compensation survey information, and come to class prepared to share with your group the benefits package for the small business in which you work or in which someone with whom you're familiar works.

How to Set Up the Exercise/Instructions: Divide the class into groups of four or five students. Your assignment is as follows: Maria Cortes runs a small personnel recruiting office in Miami and has decided to start offering an expanded benefits package to her 25 employees. At the current time, the only benefits are seven paid holidays per year and 5 sick days per year. In her company, there are 2 other managers, as well as 17 full-time recruiters and 5 secretarial staff members. In the time allotted, your group should create a benefits package in keeping with the size and requirements of this firm.

APPLICATION CASE

Striking for Benefits

By February 2004, the strike by Southern California grocery workers against the state's major supermarket chains was almost 5 months old. Because so many workers were striking (70,000), and because of the issues involved, unions and employers across the country were closely following the negotiations. Indeed, grocery union contracts were set to expire in several cities later in 2004, and many believed the California settlement—assuming one was reached—would set a pattern.

The main issue was employee benefits, and specifically how much (if any) of the employees' health care costs the employees should pay themselves. Based on their existing contract, Southern California grocery workers had unusually good health benefits. For example, they paid nothing toward their health insurance premiums, and paid only $10 co-payments for doctor visits. However, supporting these excellent health benefits cost the big

Southern California grocery chains over $4.00 per hour per worker.

The big grocery chains were not proposing cutting health care insurance benefits for their existing employees. Instead, they proposed putting any new employees hired after the new contract went into effect into a separate insurance pool, and contributing $1.35 per hour for their health insurance coverage. That meant new employees' health insurance would cost each new employee perhaps $10 per week. And, if that $10 per week weren't enough to cover the cost of health care, then the employees would have to pay more, or do without some of their benefits.

It was a difficult situation for all the parties involved. For the grocery chain employers, skyrocketing health care costs were undermining their competitiveness; the current employees feared any step down the slippery slope that might eventually mean cutting their own health benefits. The unions didn't welcome a situation in which they'd end up representing two classes of employees, one (the existing employees) who had excellent health insurance benefits, and another (newly hired employees) whose benefits were relatively meager, and who might therefore be unhappy from the moment they took their jobs and joined the union.

Questions

1. Assume you are mediating this dispute. Discuss five creative solutions you would suggest for how the grocers could reduce the health insurance benefits and the cost of their total benefits package without making any employees pay more.
2. From the grocery chains' point of view, what is the downside of having two classes of employees, one of which has superior health insurance benefits? How would you suggest they handle the problem?
3. Similarly, from the point of view of the union, what are the downsides of having to represent two classes of employees, and how would you suggest handling the situation?

Source: Based on "Settlement Nears for Southern California Grocery Strike," *Knight-Ridder/Tribune Business News,* February 26, 2004, item 04057052.

CONTINUING CASE

Carter Cleaning Company

The New Benefit Plan

Carter Cleaning Centers has traditionally provided only legislatively required benefits for its employees. These include participation in the state's unemployment compensation program, Social Security, and workers' compensation (which is provided through the same insurance carrier that insures the stores for such hazards as theft and fire). The principals of the firm—Jack, Jennifer, and their families—have individual, family-supplied health and life insurance.

Now, Jennifer can see several potential problems with the company's policies regarding benefits and services. One is turnover. She wants to do a study to determine whether similar companies' experiences with providing health and life insurance benefits suggest they enable these firms to reduce employee turnover and perhaps pay lower wages. Jennifer is also concerned with the fact that her company has no formal policy regarding vacations or paid days off or sick leave. Informally, at least, it is understood that employees get 1 week's vacation after 1 year's work, but in the past the policy regarding paid vacations for days such as New Year's Day and Thanksgiving Day has been very inconsistent. Sometimes employees who had been on the job only 2 or 3 weeks were paid fully for one of these holidays, while at other times employees who had been with the firm for 6 months or more had been paid for only half a day. Jennifer knows that this policy must be made more consistent.

She also wonders whether it would be advisable to establish some type of day care center for the employees' children. She knows that many of the employees' children have either no place to go during the day (they are preschoolers) or have no place to go after school, and she wonders whether a benefit such as day care would be in the best interests of the company.

Questions

1. Draw up a policy statement regarding vacations, sick leave, and paid days off for Carter Cleaning Centers.
2. What would you tell Jennifer are the advantages and disadvantages to Carter Cleaning Centers of providing its employees with health, hospitalization, and life insurance programs?
3. Would you advise establishing some type of day care center for the Carter Cleaning employees? Why or why not?

TRANSLATING STRATEGY INTO HR POLICIES & PRACTICES CASE

The Hotel Paris Case

The New Benefits Plan

The Hotel Paris's competitive strategy is "To use superior guest service to differentiate the Hotel Paris properties, and to thereby increase the length of stay and return rate of guests, and thus boost revenues and profitability." HR manager Lisa Cruz must now formulate functional policies and activities that support this competitive strategy, by eliciting the required employee behaviors and competencies.

Although the Hotel Paris's benefits (in terms of things like holidays and health care) were comparable to those of other hotels, Lisa Cruz knew they weren't good enough to support the high-quality service behaviors her company sought. Indeed, the fact that they were roughly comparable to those of similar firms didn't seem to impress the Hotel Paris's employees, at least 60% of whom consistently said they were deeply dissatisfied with the benefits they were getting. Lisa's concern (with which the CFO concurred) was that dissatisfaction with benefits contributed to morale and commitment being below what they should be, and thus to inhibiting the Hotel Paris from achieving its strategic aims. Lisa therefore turned to the task of assessing and redesigning the company's benefits plans.

As they reviewed the numbers relating to their benefits plan, Lisa Cruz and the CFO became increasingly concerned. They computed several benefits-related metrics for their firm, including *benefits costs as a percentage of payroll, sick days per full-time equivalent employee per year, benefits cost/competitor's benefits cost ratio,* and *workers' compensation experience ratings.* The results, as the CFO put it, offered a "good news–bad news" situation. On the good side, the ratios were generally similar to those of most competing hotels. The bad news was that the measures were strikingly below what they were when compared with the results for high-performing service-oriented businesses. The CFO authorized Lisa to design and propose a new benefits plan.

Lisa knew there were several things she wanted to accomplish with this plan. She wanted a plan that contributed to improved employee morale and commitment. And, she wanted the plan to include elements that made it easier for her employees to do their jobs—so that, as she put it, "they could come to work and give their full attention to giving our guests great service, without worrying about child care and other major family-oriented distractions."

One of the metrics Lisa and her team specifically wanted to address was the relatively high absence rate at the Hotel Paris. Because so many of these jobs are front-line jobs—valets, limousine drivers, and front-desk clerks, for instance—it's impossible to do without someone in the position if there is absence. As a result, poor attendance had a particularly serious effect on metrics like overtime pay and temporary help costs. Here, at the urging of her compensation consultant, Lisa decided to look into a system similar to Marriott's "BENETRADE." With this benefit program, employees can trade the value of some sick days for other benefits. As Lisa put it, "I'd rather see our employees using their sick day pay for things like additional health care benefits, if it means they'll think twice before taking a sick day to run a personal errand."

Questions

1. Because employers typically make benefits available to all employees, they may not have the motivational effects of incentive plans. Given this, list five employee behaviors you believe Hotel Paris could try to improve through an enhanced benefits plan, and explain why you chose them.
2. Given your answer to question 1, explain specifically what benefits you would recommend the Hotel Paris implement to achieve these behavioral improvements.

KEY TERMS

benefits, *p. 467*
supplemental pay benefits, *p. 467*
unemployment insurance, *p. 467*
sick leave, *p. 469*
severance pay, *p. 473*
supplemental unemployment benefits, *p. 473*
workers' compensation, *p. 475*
health maintenance organization (HMO), *p. 477*
preferred provider organizations (PPOs), *p. 477*
group life insurance, *p. 479*
Social Security, *p. 481*
pension plans, *p. 481*
defined benefit pension plan, *p. 481*
defined contribution pension plan, *p. 481*
portability, *p. 481*
401(k) plan, *p. 481*
savings and thrift plan, *p. 483*
deferred profit-sharing plan, *p. 483*
employee stock ownership plan (ESOP), *p. 483*
cash balance plans, *p. 483*
Employee Retirement Income Security Act (ERISA), *p. 483*
Pension Benefits Guarantee Corporation (PBGC), *p. 483*
early retirement window, *p. 483*
employee assistance program (EAP), *p. 485*
family-friendly (or work–life) benefits, *p. 485*
flexible benefits plan/cafeteria benefits plan, *p. 491*
flextime, *p. 493*
compressed workweek, *p. 493*
workplace flexibility, *p. 493*
job sharing, *p. 493*
work sharing, *p. 493*

Part IV Video Cases Appendix

Video 6: Compensating Employees

VIDEO TITLE: COMPENSATION

In this video, two HR staff members, Cheryl and Gina, must determine if an employee, Angelo, is worthy of a pay raise. The company, Focus Pointe, provides market research services. One of these services involves recruiting consumer, medical, and other respondents for the market research industry. It's important to get good, qualified respondents. To distinguish itself from its competitors, Focus Pointe uses a special "triple screening" process to ensure that the respondents it recruits meet its clients' specifications. In this case, Angelo seems to be recruiting inadequate respondents. The two HR staff members are trying to determine if giving Angelo a raise would solve the problem.

As Angelo says in the video, he'd like to be better compensated. Cheryl and Gina point out to him that his pay is falling because his recruits often don't qualify. They ask him what he would like—an increase in salary or an increase in the amount per recruit that he is paid. He responds that he'd like both. They tell them they will go along with his request but that they must see higher levels of recruit qualifications within 3 months. As the panel's human resource managers (including Paul, from BMG) point out in assessing this video, they don't necessarily agree with giving someone who is underperforming a raise. As Paul says, "They should have just told him to improve first."

Discussion Questions

1. Do you think Angelo is underperforming as a result of motivation or something else, such as the need for improved training? How would you find out?
2. Is it a good idea to give someone who is underperforming a raise? Does it send the wrong signal, insofar as it seems to suggest that poor performance leads to rewards?
3. Do you think the idea of paying recruiters like Angelo per recruit might actually backfire, and if so how?

ENDNOTES

1. www.starbucks.com/aboutus/jobcenter_thesbux experience.asp, accessed March 24, 2009.
2. Based on Frederick Hills, Thomas Bergmann, and Vida Scarpello, *Compensation Decision Making* (Fort Worth, TX: The Dryden Press, 1994), p. 424. See also Fay Hansen, "The Cutting Edge of Benefit Cost Control," *Workforce*, March 2003, pp. 36–42; Crain's Benefits Outlook 2009, www.crainsbenefits.com/news/survey-finds-nearly-20-percent-of-employers-plan-to-drop-health-benefits.php, accessed July 28, 2009.
3. "Survey Finds 99 Percent of Employers Providing Health-Care Benefits," *Compensation & Benefits Review*, September/October 2002, p. 11. See also "National Compensation Survey: Employee Benefits in Private Industry in the United States, March 2006," U.S. Department of Labor, U.S. Bureau of Labor Statistics, August 2006.
4. "Health Coverage Premiums: Upward Bound," *HR Trendbook*, 2008, p. 8.
5. "Hewitt Says Employer Measures to Control Increases in Health Care Costs Are Working," *BNA Bulletin to Management*, October 7, 2008, p. 323.
6. "Employers Face Fifth Successive Year of Major Heath Cost Increases, Survey Finds," *BNA Human Resources Report*, October 6, 2003, p. 1050; and "National Compensation Survey: Employee Benefits in Private Industry in the United States, March 2006," U.S. Department of Labor, U.S. Bureau of Labor Statistics, August 2006.
7. It's not clear why, but between 1992/1993 and 2003, the percentage of private-sector workers participating in employer-provided medical care plans declined, as did those participating in retirement plans. "These declines may be the result of shifts in the composition of the labor force, changes in employer decisions to offer coverage, or employee decisions to choose coverage or some combination of these and other factors." William Wiatrowski, "Medical and Retirement Plan Coverage: Exploring the Decline in Recent Years," *Monthly Labor Review* 127, no. 8 (August 2004), pp. 29–36.
8. Craig Olson, "Will Workers Accept Lower Wages in Exchange for Health Benefits?" *Journal of Labor Economics* 20, no. 2 (April 2002), pp. S91–S114.
9. "Trouble Ahead? Dissatisfaction with Benefits, Compensation," *HR Trendbook*, 2008, p. 16.
10. Joseph Martocchio, *Strategic Compensation* (Upper Saddle River, NJ: Prentice Hall, 2001), p. 262.
11. "California Domestic Partner Benefits Mandate Carries Likely Impact Beyond State's Borders," *BNA Bulletin to Management*, November 6, 2003, p. 353.
12. "2007 Benefits," A Survey Report by the Society for Human Research Management, 2007.
13. "National Compensation Survey: Employee Benefits in Private Industry in the United States, March 2006," U.S. Department of Labor, U.S. Bureau of Labor Statistics, August 2006, p. 26.
14. Ibid.
15. Ken Belson, "At IBM, a Vacation Anytime, or Maybe No Vacation at All," *The New York Times*, August 31, 2007, pp. A1–A18.
16. Ibid., p. 116. See also "Spurious Sick-Notes Spiral Upwards," *The Safety and Health Practitioner* 22, no. 6 (June 2004), p. 3.
17. "Unscheduled Employee Absences Cost Companies More Than Ever," *Compensation & Benefits Review*, March/April 2003, p. 19.
18. "Making Up for Lost Time: How Employers Can Curb Excessive Unscheduled Absences," *BNA Human Resources Report*, October 20, 2003, p. 1097. See also W. H. J. Hassink et. al., "Do Financial Bonuses Reduce Employee Absenteeism? Evidence from a Lottery," *Industrial and Labor Relations Review* 62, no. 3 (April 2009), pp. 327–342.
19. "SHRM Benefits Survey Finds Growth in Employer Use of Paid Leave Pools," *BNA Bulletin to Management*, March 21, 2002, p. 89.
20. This is based on M. Michael Markowich and Steve Eckberg, "Get Control of the Absentee-Minded," *Personnel Journal*, March 1996, pp. 115–120. See also "Exploring the Pluses, Minuses, and Myths of Switching to Paid Time Off Banks," *BNA Bulletin to Management* 55, no. 25 (June 17, 2004), pp. 193–194.
21. "Creating Holistic Time Off Programs Can Significantly Reduce Expenses," *Compensation & Benefits Review*, July/August 2007, pp. 18–19.
22. See, for example, Rita Zeidner, "Strategies for Saving in a Down Economy," *HR Magazine*, February 2009, p. 28.
23. The Department of Labor updated its revised regulations for administering the Family and Medical Leave Act in November 2008. See "DOL Issues Long-Awaited Rules; Address a Serious Health Condition, Many Other Issues," *BNA Bulletin to Management*, November 18, 2008, p. 369.
24. "Ten Years After It Was Signed into Law, FMLA Needs Makeover, Advocates Contend," *BNA Bulletin to Management*, February 20, 2003, p. 58.
25. "HR Professionals Face Sundry Challenges Administering FMLA Leave, Survey Asserts," *BNA Bulletin to Management*, July 20, 2007, p. 233.
26. Based on Dennis Grant, "Managing Employee Leaves: A Legal Primer," *Compensation & Benefits Review* 35, No. 4 (2003), p. 41. There are several unresolved issues in what "12 months' employment" means. For example, several courts recently held that an employee *can* count previous periods of employment with the employer to satisfy the 12-month requirement. See Daniel Ritter et al., "Recent Developments Under the Family and Medical Leave Act," *Compensation & Benefits Review*, September/October 2007, p. 33.
27. Gillian Flynn, "Employers Need an FMLA Brush-Up," *Workforce*, April 1997, pp. 101–104. See also "Worker Who Was Employee for Less Than One Year Can Pursue FMLA Claim, Federal Court Determines," *BNA Fair Employment Practices*, April 26, 2001, p. 51.
28. "Workers Who Come and Go Under FMLA Complicate Attendance Policies, Lawyer Says," *BNA Bulletin to Management*, March 16, 2000, p. 81.
29. Sue Shellenbarger, "The Mommy Drain: Employers Beef Up Perks to Lure New Mothers Back to Work," *The Wall Street Journal*, September 28, 2006, p. D1.
30. Jill Fisher, "Reconciling the Family Medical Leave Act with Overlapping or Conflicting State Leave Laws," *Compensation & Benefits Review*, September/October 2007, pp. 39–44.
31. "Severance Practices," *BNA Bulletin to Management*, January 11, 1996, pp. 12–13; and Neil Grossman, "Shrinking the Workforce in an Economic Slowdown," *Compensation & Benefits Review*, Spring 2002, pp. 12–23.

32. "Severance Pay," July 2007, Culpepper Compensation & Benefits Surveys.
33. Terry Baglieri, "Severance Pay," www.SHRM.org, downloaded December 23, 2006.
34. Ibid.
35. Ibid.
36. "Workers' Compensation Costs Are Rising Faster Than Wages," *BNA Bulletin to Management*, July 31, 2003, p. 244.
37. "Workers' Comp Claims Rise with Layoffs, But Employers Can Identify, Prevent Fraud," *BNA Bulletin to Management*, October 4, 2001, p. 313.
38. "Firms Cite Own Efforts as Key to Controlling Costs," *BNA Bulletin to Management*, March 21, 1996, p. 89. See also "Workers' Compensation Outlook: Cost Control Persists," *BNA Bulletin to Management*, January 30, 1997, pp. 33–44; and Annmarie Lipold, "The Soaring Costs of Workers' Comp," *Workforce*, February 2003, p. 42ff.
39. "Using Case Management in Workers' Compensation," *BNA Bulletin to Management*, June 6, 1996, p. 181.
40. See, for example, Betty Bialk, "Cutting Workers' Compensation Costs," *Personnel Journal*, July 1987, pp. 95–97.
41. "Healthcare Tops List of Value Benefits," *BNA Bulletin to Management*, April 24, 2007, p. 132.
42. Hills, Bergmann, and Scarpello, *Compensation Decision Making*, p. 137.
43. George Milkovich and Jerry Newman, *Compensation* (Burr Ridge, IL: McGraw-Hill, 1993), p. 445.
44. Society for Human Resource Management, "Mental Health Trends," *Workplace Visions*, no. 2, http://moss07.shrm.org/Research/FutureWorkplaceTrends/Pages/0303.aspx, accessed July 28, 2009
45. "Mental-Health Parity Measure Enacted as Part of Financial Rescue Signed by Bush," *BNA Bulletin to Management*, October 7, 2008, p. 321.
46. See, for example, Karli Dunkelberger, "Avoiding COBRA's Bite: Three Keys to Compliance," *Compensation & Benefits Review*, March/April 2005, pp. 44–48. As an example of the direction new federal health insurance may take post-2009, see A. Mathews, "Making Sense of the Debate on Health Care," *Wall Street Journal* (Eastern Edition) (September 30, 2009), pp. D1, D5.
47. www.recovery.gov, accessed March 21, 2009.
48. www.DOL.gov, downloaded December 23, 2006.
49. Larri Short and Eileen Kahanar, "Unlocking the Secrets of the New Privacy Rules," *Occupational Hazards*, September 2002, pp. 51–54.
50. "Hewitt Says Employer Measures to Control Increases in Health Care Costs Are Working," *BNA Bulletin to Management*, October 7, 2008, p. 323.
51. Alan Cohen, "Decision-Support in the Benefits Consumer Age," *Compensation & Benefits Review*, March/April 2006, pp. 46–51.
52. Ibid., p. 40. See also "Employers Explore Range of Tactics to Rein In Rising Health Costs for 2005 Plan Year," *BNA Bulletin to Management* 55, no. 27 (July 1, 2004), p. 219.
53. Ron Finch, "Preventive Services: Improving the Bottom Line for Employers and Employees," *Compensation & Benefits Review*, March/April 2005, p. 18. Note that prevention/wellness programs can run afoul of the Americans with Disabilities Act. So, for instance, employers should not make participation in such plans mandatory or use information obtained in such programs in such a way that violates ADA confidentiality requirements or discriminates against employees who are not physically fit. Here, see "Despite Good Intentions, Wellness Plans Can Run Afoul of ADA, Attorney Cautions," *BNA Bulletin to Management* 56, no. 51 (December 20, 2005), p. 41.
54. "Employer Partners to Launch a Three-Year Wellness Initiative," *BNA Bulletin to Management*, August 7, 2007, p. 255.
55. "On-Site Clinics Aimed at Cutting Costs, Promoting Wellness," *BNA Bulletin to Management*, March 25, 2008, p. 103.
56. Ibid. See also Josh Cable, "The Road to Wellness" *Occupational Hazards*, April 2007, pp. 23–27.
57. George DeVries, "The Top 10 Wellness Trends for 2008 and Beyond," *Compensation & Benefits Review*, July/August 2008, pp. 60–63.
58. Christine Keller and Christopher Condeluci, "Tax Relief and Health Care Act Should Prompt Re-Examination of HSAs," *SHRM Legal Report*, July–August 2007, p. 1.
59. In contrast, with health reimbursement arrangements (HRA) only the employer makes contributions. See "Types of Tax Favored Health Accounts," *HR Magazine*, August 2008, p. 76.
60. Michael Bond et al., "Using Health Savings Accounts to Provide Low-Cost Health-Care," *Compensation & Benefits Review*, March/April 2005, pp. 29–32.
61. Vanessa Fuhrmanns, "Oops! As Health Plans Become More Complicated, They're Also Subject to a Lot More Costly Mistakes," *The Wall Street Journal*, January 24, 2005, p. R4.
62. "As Workers Feel the Effect of Cost Hikes, Employers Turn to Health Remedies," *BNA Bulletin to Management*, April 18, 2002, p. 121.
63. "High Deductible Plans Might Catch On," *BNA Human Resources Report*, September 15, 2003, p. 967.
64. "HR Outsourcing: Managing Costs and Maximizing Provider Relations," *BNA, Inc.* 21, no. 11 (Washington, DC: November 2003), p. 10.
65. "One in Five Big Firms May Drop Coverage for Future Retirees, Health Survey Finds," *BNA Bulletin to Management*, December 12, 2002, p. 393. Reducing retiree benefits requires a preliminary legal review. See James McElligott Jr., "Retiree Medical Benefit Developments in the Courts, Congress, and EEOC," *Compensation & Benefits Review*, March/April 2005, pp. 23–28; and Natalie Norfus, "Retiree Benefits: Does an Employer's Obligation to Pay Ever End?" *Compensation & Benefits Review*, January/February 2008, pp. 42–45.
66. Robert Christadore, "Benefits Purchasing Alliances: Creating Stability in an Unstable World," *Compensation & Benefits Review*, September/October 2001, pp. 49–53. Betty Liddick, "Going the Distance for Health Savings," *HR Magazine*, March 2007, pp. 51–55. J. Wojcik "Employers Consider Short-Haul Medical Tourism," *Business Insurance* 43, no. 29 (August 24, 2009), pp. 1, 20.
67. "Dependent Eligibility Audits Can Help Rein In Health Care Costs, Analysts Say," *BNA Bulletin to Management*, September 9, 2008, p. 289.
68. Carolyn Hirschman, "Will Employers Take the Lead in Long-Term Care?" *HR Magazine*, March 1997, pp. 59–66. For recent perspective, see A. D. Postal, "Industry Ramps Up Opposition To LTC Program In Senate Health Bill," *National Underwriter* (Life & Health/Financial Services Edition) 113, no. 14 (July 20, 2009), pp. 10, 32.
69. Bill Leonard, "Recipes for Part-Time Benefits," *HR Magazine*, April 2000, pp. 56–62.
70. As we explained earlier in this book, do not confuse independent contractors with part-time workers. As three attorneys put

it, "Short-term, just-in-time workers provided by staffing agencies are not an issue. However, the employer's policy for workers who are still on the job after 1,000 to 1,500 hours should require that they be provided with benefits, either through the staffing agency or by outsourcing their administration to an administrative employer who can provide benefits." Bob Lanza et al., "Legal Status of Contingent Workers," *Compensation & Benefits Review*, July/August 2003, pp. 47–60.

71. Brenda Paik Sunoo, "Millions May Retire," *Workforce*, December 1997, p. 48. See also "Many Older Workers Choose to 'Un-Retire' or Not Retire at All," *Knight Ridder/Tribune Business News*, September 28, 2003, item 03271012; Patrick Purcell, "Older Workers: Recent Trends in Employment and Retirement," *Journal of Deferred Compensation* 8, no. 3 (Spring 2003), pp. 30–54; and "For Many Seniors, a Job Beats Retirement," *Knight Ridder/Tribune Business News*, February 9, 2003, item 3040001.
72. www.ssa.gov/pressoffice/colafacts.htm, accessed March 6, 2009.
73. The 7.65% tax rate is the combined rate for Social Security and Medicare.
74. Martocchio, *Strategic Compensation*, pp. 245–248; Lin Grensing-Pophal, "A Pension Formula That Pays Off," *HR Magazine*, February 2003, pp. 58–62; Jim Morris, "The Changing Pension Landscape," *Compensation & Benefits Review*, September/October 2005, pp. 30–34.
75. For one recent example of how to do this, see Gail Nichols, "Reviewing and Redesigning Retirement Plans," *Compensation & Benefits Review*, May/June 2008, pp. 40–47.
76. Jessica Marquez, "More Workers Yanking Money Out of 401(k)s," *Workforce Management*, August 11, 2008, p. 4.
77. Nancy Pridgen, "The Duty to Monitor Appointed Fiduciaries Under ERISA," *Compensation & Benefits Review*, September/October 2007, pp. 46—51; "Individual 401(k) Plan Participant Can Sue Plan Fiduciary for Losses, Justices Rule," *BNA Bulletin to Management*, February 20, 2008, p. 65.
78. Lindsay Wyatt, "401(k) Conversion: It's as Easy as Riding a Bike," *Workforce*, April 1997, p. 66. See also Carolyn Hirschman, "Growing Pains. Employers and Employees Alike Have Lots to Learn About 401(k) Plans," *HR Magazine*, June 2002, pp. 30–38.
79. "Benefit Trends: Automatic Enrollment Takes Off," *Compensation & Benefits Review*, September/October 2008, p. 14.
80. Jack VanDerhei, "The Pension Protection Act and 401(k)s," *The Wall Street Journal*, April 20, 2008, p. 12.
81. Jessica Marquez, "Retirement Out of Reach," *Workforce Management*, November 3, 2008, pp. 1, 24.
82. Wyatt, "401(k) Conversion," p. 20.
83. "New Pension Law Plus a Recent Court Ruling Doom Age-Related Suits, Practitioners Say," *BNA Bulletin to Management* 57, no. 36 (September 5, 2006), pp. 281–282.
84. Harold Burlingame and Michael Gulotta, "Cash Balance Pension Plan Facilitates Restructuring the Workforce at AT&T," *Compensation & Benefits Review*, November/December 1998, pp. 25–31; Eric Lekus, "When Are Cash Balance Pension Plans the Right Choice?" *BNA Bulletin to Management*, January 28, 1999, p. 7.
85. This is based on Eric Parmenter, "Employee Benefit Compliance Checklist," *Compensation & Benefits Review*, May/June 2002, pp. 29–38.
86. www.pbgc.gov/workers-retirees/benefits-information/content/page789.html, accessed March 6, 2009.
87. Patrick Kiger, "Early-Retirement Plans Backfire, Driving Up Costs Instead of Cutting Them," *Workforce Management*, January 2004, pp. 66–68.
88. *Paolillo v. Dresser Industries*, 821F.2d81 (2d cir., 1987).
89. "Benefits Cost Control Solutions to Consider Now," *HR Focus* 80, no. 11 (November 2003), p. 1.
90. Johanna Rodgers, "Web Based Apps Simplify Employee Benefits," *Insurance and Technology* 28, no. 11 (November 2003), p. 21.
91. Ibid.
92. Scott Harper, "Online Resources System Boosts Worker Awareness," *BNA Bulletin to Management*, April 10, 2007, p. 119.
93. Drew Robb, "A Total View of Employee Records," *HR Magazine*, August 2007, pp. 93–96.
94. Carolyn Hirschman, "Employees' Choice," *HR Magazine*, February 2006, pp. 95–99.
95. Joseph O'Connell, "Using Employee Assistance Programs to Avoid Crises," *Long Island Business News*, April 19, 2002, p. 10.
96. See Scott MacDonald et al., "Absenteeism and Other Workplace Indicators of Employee Assistance Program Clients and Matched Controls," *Employee Assistance Quarterly* 15, no. 3 (2000), pp. 51–58. See also Paul Courtis et al., "Performance Measures in the Employee Assistance Program," *Employee Assistance Quarterly* 19, no. 3 (2005), pp. 45–58.
97. See, for example, Donna Owens, "EAPs for a Diverse World," *HR Magazine*, October 2006, pp. 91–96.
98. "EAP Providers," *Workforce Management*, July 14, 2008, p. 16.
99. "Fathers Fighting to Keep Work–Life Balance Are Finding Employers Firmly in their Corner," *BNA Bulletin to Management* 56, no. 24 (June 14, 2005), p. 185.
100. Susan Wells, "Are You Too Family-Friendly?" *HR Magazine*, October 2007, pp. 35–39.
101. Maureen Hannay and Melissa Northam, "Low-Cost Strategies for Employee Retention," *Compensation & Benefits Review*, July/August 2000, pp. 65–72. See also Roseanne Geisel, "Responding to Changing Ideas of Family," *HR Magazine*, August 2004, pp. 89–98.
102. Mary Burke, Euren Esen, and Jessica Cullison, "2003 Benefits Survey," SHRM/SHRM Foundation, 1800 Duke Street, Alexandria, VA, 2003, pp. 8–9.
103. "Child Care Options," *BNA Bulletin to Management*, July 4, 1996, p. 212. See also "Child Care Report Boasts of Its Benefit to California Economy," *Knight Ridder/Tribune Business News*, January 9, 2003, item 03009011.
104. Patrick Kiger, "A Case for Childcare," *Workforce Management*, April 2004, pp. 34–40.
105. www.SHRM.org/rewards/library, downloaded December 23, 2006. See also Kathy Gurchiek, "Give Us Your Sick," *HR Magazine*, January 2007, pp. 91–93.
106. Kelli Earhart, R. Dennis Middlemist, and Willie Hopkins, "Elder Care: An Emerging Assistance Issue," *Employee Assistance Quarterly* 8, no. 3 (1993), pp. 1–10. See also, "Finding a Balance Between Conflicting Responsibilities: Work and Caring for Aging Parents," *Monday Business Briefing*, July 7, 2004; and "Employers Feel Impact of Eldercare: Some Expanded Benefits for Workers," *Knight Ridder/Tribune Business News*, June 13, 2004, item 04165011.
107. "Employers Gain from Elder Care Programs by Boosting Workers' Morale, Productivity," *BNA Bulletin to Management* 57, no. 10 (March 7, 2006), pp. 73–74.

108. Rudy Yandrick, "Elder Care Grows Up," *HR Magazine*, November 2001, pp. 72–77.
109. Sue Shellenbarger, "Companies Retool Time Off Policies to Prevent Burnout, Reward Performance," *The Wall Street Journal*, January 5, 2006, p. D1.
110. Matthew Boyle, "How to Cut Perks Without Killing Morale," *Fortune*, February 19, 2001, pp. 241–244.
111. Susan Lambert, "Added Benefits: The Link Between Work Life Benefits and Organizational Citizenship Behavior," *Academy of Management Journal* 43, no. 5 (2000), pp. 801–815. Timothy Judge et al., "Work Family Conflict and Emotions: Effects at Work and Home," *Personnel Psychology* 59 (2006), pp. 779–814.
112. "Rising Gas Prices Prompting Employers to Consider Varied Computer Benefit Options," *BNA Bulletin to Management*, June 20, 2008, p. 201.
113. Quoted from http://hrdailyadvisor.blr.com/tipArchive.aspx, accessed March 23, 2009.
114. SHRM, "2003 Benefits Survey," op. cit., p. 30. See also Michael Laff, "U.S. Employers Tighten Reins on Tuition Reimbursement," *Training & Development*, July 2006, p. 18.
115. Richard Buddin and Kanika Kapur, "The Effect of Employer-Sponsored Education on Job Mobility: Evidence from the U.S. Navy," *Industrial Relations* 44, no. 2 (April 2005), pp. 341–363.
116. SHRM, "2003 Benefits Survey," op. cit., p. 2.
117. Carolyn Shapiro, "More Companies Cover Benefits for Employee's Domestic Partners," *Knight-Ridder/Tribune Business News*, July 20, 2003.
118. "What You Need to Know to Provide Domestic Partner Benefits," *HR Focus* 80, no. 3 (August 2003), p. 3.
119. Martocchio, *Strategic Compensation*, pp. 308–309.
120. "Couples Want Flexible Leave, Benefits," *BNA Bulletin to Management*, February 19, 1998, p. 53; SHRM, "2003 Benefits Survey," op. cit., p. 14. See also Paul Harris, "Flexible Work Policies Mean Business," *Training & Development*, April 2007, pp. 32–36.
121. "Money Isn't Everything," *Journal of Business Strategy* 21, no. 2 (March 2000), p. 4; see also "CEOs in the Dark on Employees' Benefits Preferences," *Employee Benefits News*, September 1, 2006, item 06244007.
122. Carolyn Hirshman, "Kinder, Simpler Cafeteria Rules," *HR Magazine*, January 2001, pp. 74–79.
123. "Employers Should Update Cafeteria Plans Now Based on Proposed Regs, Experts Say," *BNA Bulletin to Management*, September 4, 2007, pp. 281–282.
124. "Debit Cards for Health-Care Expenses Receive Increased Employer Attention," *BNA Bulletin to Management*, September 25, 2003, p. 305.
125. Martocchio, *Strategic Compensation*, p. 263.
126. Jane Applegate, "Employee Leasing Can Be a Savior for Small Firms," *Business Courier Serving Cincinnati–Northern Kentucky*, January 28, 2000, p. 23.
127. Ibid.
128. Diana Reitz, "Employee Leasing Breeds Liability Questions," *National Underwriter Property and Casualty Risk and Benefits Management* 104, no. 18 (May 2000), p. 12.
129. Elka Maria Torpey, "Flexible Work: Adjusting the When and Where of Your Job," *Occupational Outlook Quarterly*, Summer 2007, pp. 14–27.
130. "Slightly More Workers Are Skirting 9–5 Tradition," *BNA Bulletin to Management*, June 20, 2002, p. 197.
131. See, for example, "Compressed Workweeks Gain Popularity, but Concerns Remain About Effectiveness," *BNA Bulletin to Management*, September 16, 2008, p. 297.
132. Boris Baltes et al., "Flexible and Compressed Workweek Schedules: A Meta-Analysis of Their Effects on Work-Related Criteria," *Journal of Applied Psychology* 84, no. 4 (1999), pp. 496–513. See also Charlotte Hoff, "With Flextime, Less Can Be More," *Workforce Management*, May 2005, pp. 65–66.
133. Farrokh Mamaghani, "Impact of Information Technology on the Workforce of the Future: An Analysis," *International Journal of Management* 23, no. 4 (2006), pp. 845–850; Jessica Marquez, "Connecting a Virtual Workforce," *Workforce Management*, September 20, 2008, pp. 1–3.
134. Ann Pomeroy, "The Future Is Now," *HR Magazine*, September 2007, pp. 46–52.
135. SHRM, "2003 Benefits Survey," op. cit., p. 2.
136. "With Job Sharing Arrangements, Companies Can Get Two Employees for the Price of One," *BNA Bulletin to Management* 56, no. 47 (November 22, 2005), pp. 369–370.

14 Ethics, Justice, and Fair Treatment in HR Management

Shortly after the U.S. government spent $170 billion bailing out AIG awhile ago, news spread that AIG was paying $165 million in bonuses to employees in the same department that had allegedly helped to contribute to AIG's huge losses. As noted in Chapter 11 (Incentives), the disclosure enraged Congress, which threatened a new tax to get the bonuses back. The issue triggered ethics-laden debates. One thing not in doubt was that the payments were legal; AIG was paying them to comply with the employees' employment contracts. But was it ethical for employees in that department to get bonuses? Could paying them be legal but not ethical? Was it legal for Congress to tax just these AIG employees? The ethics blogs had a field day.

Source: Courtesy of Roger L. Wollenberg/UPI Photo Landov Media.

WHERE ARE WE NOW . . .

For many managers, recruitment and placement, training and development, and compensation are the heart of human resource management. But people expect something more. They expect their employers to treat them fairly, and to have a safe work environment. Now, in Part 5, we turn to employee justice, safety, and union relations. The main purpose of Chapter 14 is to explain ethics, justice, and fair treatment in human resource management, matters essential for positive employee relations. Topics include ethics and fair treatment at work, factors that shape ethical behavior at work, and managers' roles in fostering improved workplace ethics, employee discipline, and dismissals.

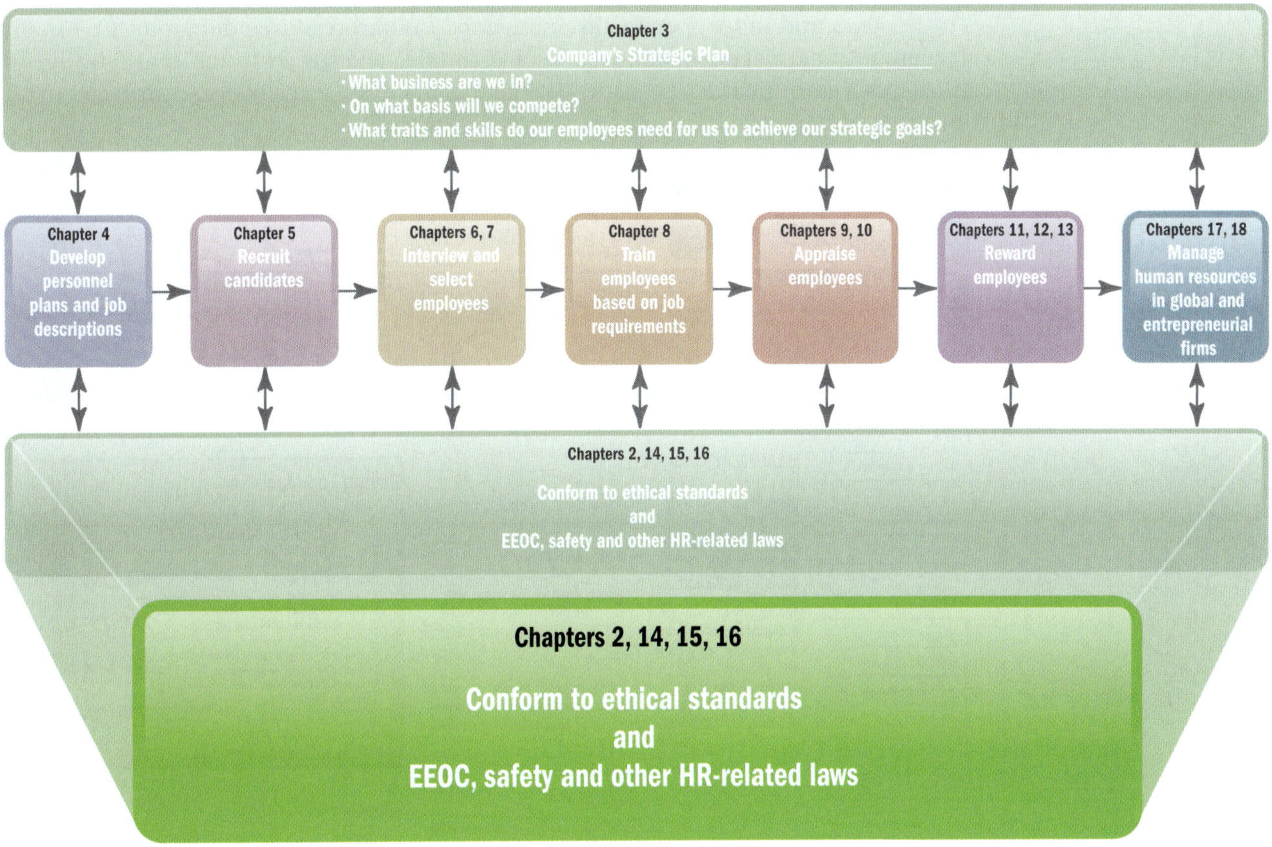

LEARNING OUTCOMES

1. Explain what is meant by ethical behavior at work.
2. Discuss important factors that shape ethical behavior at work.
3. Describe at least four specific ways in which HR management can influence ethical behavior at work.
4. Employ fair disciplinary practices.
5. List at least four important factors in managing dismissals effectively.

1 Explain what is meant by ethical behavior at work.

ETHICS AND FAIR TREATMENT AT WORK

People face ethical choices every day. Is it wrong to use a company credit card for personal purchases? Is a $50 gift to a client unacceptable? Compare your answers by answering the online quiz in Figure 14-1.

Almost everyone reading this book rightfully views himself or herself as an ethical person, so we should start by asking, "Why include ethics in a human resource management book?" For two reasons: First, ethics is not theoretical. Instead, it greases the wheels that make businesses work. Managers who promise raises but don't deliver, salespeople who say "The order's coming" when it's not, production managers who take kickbacks from suppliers—they all corrode the trust that day-to-day business transactions depend on, and eventually run the businesses (or at least the managers) into the ground. According to one recent lawsuit, marketers for Pfizer Inc. influenced Pfizer to suppress unfavorable studies about one of its drugs.[1] Plaintiffs are suing for billions.

Second, and more specifically, managers' human resource decisions are usually replete with ethical consequences.[2] For example, one survey found that 6 of the 10 most serious ethical work issues—workplace safety, employee records security,

FIGURE 14-1 Online Ethics Quiz

Source: http://encarta.msn.com/encnet/departments/elearning/?page=BizEthicsQuiz&Quizid=188&GT1=7004, accessed April 28, 2009.

(continued)

FIGURE 14-1 *(continued)*

employee theft, affirmative action, comparable work, and employee privacy rights—were HR-related.[3] Another survey of human resource professionals found that 54% had observed misconduct ranging from violations of Title VII to violations of the Occupational Safety and Health Act.[4] Table 14-1 lists the percentage of employees observing various unethical behaviors.

Therefore, all managers should understand the basics of ethics and the ethical dimensions of their people-related decisions. We'll start with what *ethics* means.

TABLE 14-1 Specific Observed Unethical Behaviors

Abusive or intimidating behavior toward employees	21%
Lying to employees, customers, vendors, or to the public	19%
A situation that places employee interests over organizational interests	18%
Violations of safety regulations	16%
Misreporting of actual time worked	16%
E-mail and Internet abuse	13%
Discrimination on the basis of race, color, gender, age, or similar categories	12%
Stealing or theft	11%
Sexual harassment	9%
Provision of goods or services that fail to meet specifications	8%
Misuse of confidential information	7%
Alteration of documents	6%
Falsification or misrepresentation of financial records or reports	5%
Improper use of competitors' inside information	4%
Price fixing	3%
Giving or accepting bribes, kickbacks, or inappropriate gifts	3%

Source: From *2005 National Business Ethics Survey: How Employees Perceive Ethics at Work*, 2005, p. 25. Copyright © 2006, Ethics Resource Center (ERC). Used with permission of the ERC, 1747 Pennsylvania Ave., N.W., Suite 400, Washington, DC 2006, www.ethics.org. Reprinted in O. C. Ferrell, John Fraedrich, and Linog Ferrell, *Business Ethics* (Boston: Houghton Mifflin, 2008), p. 61.

The Meaning of *Ethics*

Ethics refers to "the principles of conduct governing an individual or a group; specifically, the standards you use to decide what your conduct should be."[5]

Making ethical decisions always involve two things. First, it always involves *normative judgments.*[6] A normative judgment means that something is good or bad, right or wrong, better or worse. "You are wearing a skirt and blouse" is a nonnormative statement; "That's a great outfit!" is a normative one.

Second, ethical decisions always involve questions of morality. *Morality* is society's highest accepted standards of behavior. Moral standards guide behaviors of the most serious consequence to society's well-being, such as murder, lying, and slander. Authoritative bodies like legislatures can't change what morality means. Moral judgments also trigger strong emotions. Violating moral standards may therefore make someone feel ashamed or remorseful.[7]

It would simplify things if it were always clear when one's decisions were ethical. Unfortunately, it is not. If the decision makes the person feel ashamed or remorseful, or involves doing something with serious consequence such as murder, then, chances are, it's unethical.

Ethics and the Law

Furthermore, asking, "Is what I'm doing legal?" won't necessarily reveal if it is ethical. Firing a 39-year-old employee with 20 years' tenure without cause may be legal, but some would view it as unethical. One executive put it this way: "Ethics means making decisions that represent what you stand for, not just what the laws are."[8] But, some behavior is both illegal and unethical. For example, one huge meat processor had to respond to a federal indictment charging it with smuggling illegal immigrants from Mexico to cut factory costs.[9]

Ethics, Justice, and Fair Treatment

Similarly, fairness is an issue in most human resource decisions. You hire one candidate and reject another, and promote one and demote another. How employees react to these decisions depends, to some extent, on whether they think the decisions and the processes that led up to them were fair.

Fairness is inseparable from what most people think of as "justice." A company that is *just* is, among other things, equitable, fair, impartial, and unbiased in how it does things. With respect to employee relations, experts generally define *organizational justice* in terms of at least two components—distributive justice and procedural justice.

- **Distributive justice** refers to the fairness and justice of the decision's *result* (for instance, did I get an equitable pay raise?).
- **Procedural justice** refers to the fairness of the *process* (for instance, is the process my company uses to allocate merit raises fair?).[10]

In practice, fair treatment reflects concrete actions (see Figure 14-2).[11] These include "employees are treated with respect."[12] In theory, ethics, justice, and fair treatment may be separate but related concepts. But in practice most employees probably can't and won't unscramble what is ethical, fair, or just when it comes to how they're treated at work.[13]

Employee Rights

Of course, few societies rely solely on managers' ethics or sense of fairness to ensure that they do what's right by their employees. They also put in place various laws. Laws like Title VII give employees (or prospective employees, and sometimes past employees) numerous *rights*. For example, the Occupational Safety and Health Act gives employees the right to refuse to work under unsafe conditions.[14] Figure 14-3 lists some other legislated areas under which workers have rights.[15]

FIGURE 14-2 Perceptions of Fair Interpersonal Treatment Scale

Source: Michelle A. Donovan et al., "The Perceptions of Their Interpersonal Treatment Scale: Development and Validation of a Measure of Interpersonal Treatment in the Workplace," *Journal of Applied Psychology* 83, no. 5 (1998), p. 692.

What is your organization like most of the time? Circle Yes if the item describes your organization, No if it does not describe your organization, and ? if you cannot decide.

IN THIS ORGANIZATION:

1. Employees are praised for good work	Yes	?	No
2. Supervisors yell at employees (R)	Yes	?	No
3. Supervisors play favorites (R)	Yes	?	No
4. Employees are trusted	Yes	?	No
5. Employees' complaints are dealt with effectively	Yes	?	No
6. Employees are treated like children (R)	Yes	?	No
7. Employees are treated with respect	Yes	?	No
8. Employees' questions and problems are responded to quickly	Yes	?	No
9. Employees are lied to (R)	Yes	?	No
10. Employees' suggestions are ignored (R)	Yes	?	No
11. Supervisors swear at employees (R)	Yes	?	No
12. Employees' hard work is appreciated	Yes	?	No
13. Supervisors threaten to fire or lay off employees (R)	Yes	?	No
14. Employees are treated fairly	Yes	?	No
15. Coworkers help each other out	Yes	?	No
16. Coworkers argue with each other (R)	Yes	?	No
17. Coworkers put each other down (R)	Yes	?	No
18. Coworkers treat each other with respect	Yes	?	No

Note: R = the item is reverse scored.

ethics
The principles of conduct governing an individual or a group; specifically, the standards you use to decide what your conduct should be.

distributive justice
The fairness and justice of a decision's result.

procedural justice
The fairness of the process.

FIGURE 14-3 Some Areas Under Which Workers Have Legal Rights

- Leave of absence and vacation rights
- Injuries and illnesses rights
- Noncompete agreement rights
- Employees' rights on employer policies
- Discipline rights
- Rights on personnel files
- Employee pension rights
- Employee benefits rights
- References rights
- Rights on criminal records
- Employee distress rights
- Defamation rights
- Employees' rights on fraud
- Rights on assault and battery
- Employee negligence rights
- Right on political activity
- Union/group activity rights
- Whistleblower rights
- Workers' compensation rights

Aside from legislation, employees also have certain rights under common law.[16] For example, under common law, an employee may have the right to sue the employer whose supervisor published embarrassing private and personal information about the employee.[17]

2 Discuss important factors that shape ethical behavior at work.

WHAT DETERMINES ETHICAL BEHAVIOR AT WORK?

Whether a person acts ethically at work is usually not a consequence of any one thing. For example, could it be that everyone running some of the banks that triggered the sub-prime mess was simply unethical? Possibly, but not likely. There must have been more to it.

Research Findings: What Do We Know About Ethical Behavior At Work?

Luckily, we have some hard evidence (not just about banks). Several experts reviewed the research concerning things that influence ethical behavior in organizations. Here's what they found:[18]

- Ethical behavior starts with *moral awareness*. In other words, does the person even recognize that a moral issue exists in the situation?
- *Managers* can do a lot to influence employee ethics by carefully cultivating the right norms, leadership, reward systems, and culture.
- Ethics slide when people undergo *moral disengagement*. Doing so frees them from the guilt that would normally go with violating one's ethical standards. For example, you're more likely to harm others when you view the victims as "outsiders."
- The most powerful morality comes from *within*. In effect, when the moral person asks, "Why be moral?" the answer is, "because that is who I am." Then, failure to act morally creates emotional discomfort and becomes, in effect, a betrayal of oneself.[19]
- Beware the seductive power of an *unmet goal*. Unmet goals pursued blindly can contribute to unethical behavior.[20]
- Offering *rewards* for ethical behavior can backfire. Doing so may actually undermine the intrinsic value of ethical behavior.
- Don't inadvertently reward someone for *bad behavior*. For example, don't promote someone who got a big sale through devious means.[21]
- Employers should *punish unethical behavior*. Employees who observe unethical behavior expect you to discipline the perpetrators.

- The degree to which employees *openly talk about ethics* is a good predictor of ethical conduct. Conversely, organizations characterized by "moral muteness" suffer more ethically problematic behavior.
- People tend to alter their *moral compasses* when they join organizations. They uncritically equate "what's best for this organization (or team, or department)" with "what's the right thing to do?"

Based on this evidence, we'll focus in on several of the things that determine ethical behavior at work.

The Person

The most powerful morality comes from within. Because people bring to their jobs their own ideas of what is morally right and wrong, the individual must shoulder much of the credit (or blame) for ethical choices. For example, one survey of CEOs explored their intention to engage (or not engage) in soliciting a competitor's technological secrets and bribing foreign officials. The researchers concluded that personal inclinations more strongly affected decisions than did environmental pressures or organizational characteristics.[22] How would you rate your own ethics? Figure 14-4 presents a short self-assessment survey to help you answer that question. But beware: Self-deception has a bigger influence than most people realize.[23]

The Boss

Managers do a lot to influence ethics. It's hard to resist even subtle pressure, let alone coercion, from your boss. According to one report, for instance, "the level of misconduct at work dropped dramatically when employees said their supervisors exhibited ethical behavior." Only 25% of employees who agreed that their supervisors "set a good example of ethical business behavior" said they had observed misconduct in the last year, compared with 72% of those who did not feel that their supervisors set good examples.[24] Here are examples of how supervisors knowingly (or unknowingly) can lead subordinates astray:

- Tell staffers to do whatever is necessary to achieve results.
- Overload top performers to ensure that the work gets done.
- Look the other way when wrongdoing occurs.
- Take credit for others' work or shift blame.[25]

Organizational Culture

These examples illustrate an important feature of the boss's influence: The influence is often subliminal. He or she sends signals about the appropriate way to behave. Those signals then create the culture to which employees respond. We can define **organizational culture** as the "characteristic values, traditions, and behaviors a company's employees share." A *value* is a basic belief about what is right or wrong, or about what you should or shouldn't do. ("Honesty is the best policy" would be a value.) Values are important because they guide and channel behavior. Managing people and shaping their behavior therefore depends on shaping the values they use as behavioral guides. The firm's culture should therefore send clean signals about what is and isn't acceptable behavior. For example, if management really believes "honesty is the best policy," the written rules they follow and the things they do should reflect this value.

organizational culture
The characteristic values, traditions, and behaviors a company's employees share.

FIGURE 14-4 How Do My Ethics Rate?

Source: Adapted from A. Reichel and Y. Neumann, *Journal of Instructional Psychology*, March 1988, pp. 25–53.

Instrument

Indicate your level of agreement with these 15 statements using the following scale:

1 = Strongly disagree
2 = Disagree
3 = Neither agree nor disagree
4 = Agree
5 = Strongly agree

1. The only moral of business is making money.	1	2	3	4	5
2. A person who is doing well in business does not have to worry about moral problems.	1	2	3	4	5
3. Act according to the law, and you can't go wrong morally.	1	2	3	4	5
4. Ethics in business is basically an adjustment between expectations and the ways people behave.	1	2	3	4	5
5. Business decisions involve a realistic economic attitude and not a moral philosophy.	1	2	3	4	5
6. "Business ethics" is a concept for public relations only.	1	2	3	4	5
7. Competitiveness and profitability are important values.	1	2	3	4	5
8. Conditions of a free economy will best serve the needs of society. Limiting competition can only hurt society and actually violates basic natural laws.	1	2	3	4	5
9. As a consumer, when making an auto insurance claim, I try to get as much as possible regardless of the extent of the damage.	1	2	3	4	5
10. While shopping at the supermarket, it is appropriate to switch price tags on packages.	1	2	3	4	5
11. As an employee, I can take home office supplies; it doesn't hurt anyone.	1	2	3	4	5
12. I view sick days as vacation days that I deserve.	1	2	3	4	5
13. Employees' wages should be determined according to the laws of supply and demand.	1	2	3	4	5
14. The business world has its own rules.	1	2	3	4	5
15. A good businessperson is a successful businessperson.	1	2	3	4	5

ANALYSIS AND INTERPRETATION

Rather than specify "right" answers, this instrument works best when you compare your answer to those of others. With that in mind, here are mean responses from a group of 243 management students. How did your responses compare?

1. 3.09	6. 2.88	11. 1.58
2. 1.88	7. 3.62	12. 2.31
3. 2.54	8. 3.79	13. 3.36
4. 3.41	9. 3.44	14. 3.79
5. 3.88	10. 1.33	15. 3.38

Managers therefore have to send the right signals to their employees. Guidelines include the following:

- **Clarify expectations.** First, make clear your expectations with respect to the values you think are critical. For example, Johnson & Johnson's ethics code says, "We believe our first responsibility is to the doctors, nurses and patients, to mothers and fathers and all others who use our products and services." That value is one to which the company expects all its employees to adhere.
- **Walk the talk.** Employees take their signals from the boss' actions. Managers need to "walk the talk." They can't say, "Don't fudge the financials," and then do so themselves.
- **Provide physical support.** The physical manifestations of the manager's values—the incentives, appraisal criteria, and disciplinary procedures he or she uses, for instance—send strong signals regarding what employees should and should not do. Do you reward ethical behavior or penalize it?

The Company

People tend to alter their ethical compasses when they join organizations. Is there such a thing as an ethically toxic company? Some think so. An *ethically toxic company* is one in which all the usual procedures that normally diminish bad behavior are simply missing. For example, managers pressure or even reward employees for bad behavior; no one publicizes ethical standards such as "don't bribe officials"; and no one takes the time to follow up on or audit bad behavior. Having ethical meltdowns at companies like these is perhaps understandable. What's strange is that things can go wrong, even in companies that seem to be ethically normal.

However, it may not be so strange. Some years ago, the U.S. government accused the CFO of a large company of instructing subordinates to fraudulently book accounting entries, and of filing false statements with the Securities and Exchange Commission (SEC). Why would the CFO do this? "I took these actions, knowing they were wrong, in a misguided attempt to preserve the company to allow it to withstand what I believed were temporary financial difficulties."[26] So the scary thing about unethical behavior at work is that it's usually not just personal interests driving it. Table 14-2 summarizes the results of one survey. It shows the principal causes of ethical lapses, as reported by six levels of employees and managers. As you can see, being under the gun to meet scheduling pressures was the number-one reported factor. For most of these employees, "meeting overly aggressive financial or business objectives" and "helping the company survive" were the two other top causes. "Advancing my own career or financial interests" ranked toward the bottom. Thus, (at least in this case) most ethical lapses seemed to occur because employees shifted their ethical compasses to "I must help my company." Guarding against such pressures is one way to head off ethical lapses.

What Employers Can Do

Companies do this in several ways. *Manager and employee training* is one; we'll see in a moment that employers invest considerable time and effort on showing all employees the ethically right way to do things. *Whistleblower* policies can help reduce employer unethical behaviors. Whistleblowers are individuals, frequently employees, who use procedural or legal channels to report incidents of unethical behavior to company ethics officers or to legal authorities. While many employers fear whistleblowers, others encourage them, for

TABLE 14-2 Principal Causes of Ethical Compromises

	Senior Mgmt.	Middle Mgmt.	Front-Line Supv.	Prof. Non-Mgmt.	Admin. Salaried	Hourly
Meeting schedule pressure	1	1	1	1	1	1
Meeting overly aggressive financial or business objectives	3	2	2	2	2	2
Helping the company survive	2	3	4	4	3	4
Advancing the career interests of my boss	5	4	3	3	4	5
Feeling peer pressure	7	7	5	6	5	3
Resisting competitive threats	4	5	6	5	6	7
Saving jobs	9	6	7	7	7	6
Advancing my own career or financial interests	8	9	9	8	9	8
Other	6	8	8	9	8	9

Note: 1 is high, 9 is low.
Sources: O. C. Ferrell and John Fraedrich, *Business Ethics*, 3rd ed. (New York: Houghton Mifflin, 1997), p. 28; adapted from Rebecca Goodell, *Ethics in American Business: Policies, Programs, and Perceptions* (1994), p. 54. Permission provided courtesy of the Ethics Resource Center, 1120 6th Street NW, Washington, DC, 2005.

instance, by instituting ethics hotlines.[27] Similarly, an **ethics code** memorializes the standards to which the employer expects its employees to adhere, for instance with respect to bribery. All publicly traded companies in the United States should have one. The Sarbanes-Oxley Act (passed after a series of top corporate management ethical lapses) requires companies to declare whether they have a code of conduct. Federal sentencing guidelines reduce penalties for companies convicted of ethics violations if they have codes of conduct.

Some companies urge employees to apply a quick *ethics test* to evaluate whether what they're about to do fits the company's code of conduct. For example, the Raytheon Company asks employees who face ethical dilemmas to ask themselves:

- Is the action legal?
- Is it right?
- Whom will the decision affect?
- Does it fit Raytheon's values?
- How will it "feel" afterwards?
- How will it look in the newspaper?
- Will it reflect poorly on the company?[28]

3 Describe at least four specific ways in which HR management can influence ethical behavior at work.

HOW MANAGERS USE PERSONNEL METHODS TO PROMOTE ETHICS AND FAIR TREATMENT

Many, of the actions managers can take to promote ethics fall within the realm of human resource management practices. We'll consider some specific examples.

Selection

One writer says, "The simplest way to tune up an organization, ethically speaking, is to hire more ethical people."[29] Employers can start before the applicant even applies by creating recruitment materials that emphasize ethics. (The Microsoft site in Figure 14-5 is an example.) Use tools such as honesty tests and background checks (discussed in Chapter 6) to screen out undesirables.[30] Ask behavioral questions such as, "Have you ever observed someone stretching the rules at work? What did you do about it?[31]

Fairness Managers interviewing applicants also need to make sure the screening process is fair. "If prospective employees perceive that the hiring process does not treat people fairly, they may [also] assume that ethical behavior is not important."[32] Keep several things in mind here:

- Applicants tend to view the *formal procedure* (such as the interview) as fair to the extent that it tests job-related criteria and provides an opportunity to demonstrate competence.
- Applicants expect respect. *Interpersonal treatment* reflects such things as the propriety of the questions, the politeness of the person doing the assessing, and the degree of two-way communication.
- Applicants see a selection system as fair to the extent that the employer provides *useful feedback* about the employee's or candidate's own performance.[33]

Ethics Training

For all practical purposes, ethics training is mandatory. Federal sentencing guidelines reduced penalties for employers accused of misconduct who implemented codes of conduct and ethics training. An amendment to those guidelines now outlines stricter ethics training requirements.[34] Ethics training usually includes showing employees how to recognize ethical dilemmas, how to use ethical frameworks (such

FIGURE 14-5 Using the Company Web site to Emphasize Ethics

Source: www.microsoft.com/industry/government/GovGiftingCompliance.mspx, accessed April 28, 2009.

as codes of conduct) to resolve problems, and how to use human resource activities (such as interviews and disciplinary practices) in ethical ways.

Training like this needn't be complicated. Lockheed Martin provides its employees with short, "what-if" ethical scenarios that highlight how to identify and deal with conflict of interest situations. The training should also emphasize the moral underpinnings of the ethical choice, and the company's deep commitment to integrity and ethics. Top managers' participation underscores that commitment.[35]

Ethics training is often Internet-based. For example, Lockheed Martin's 160,000 employees also take ethics and legal compliance training via the firm's intranet. Lockheed's online ethics program software also keeps track of how well the company and its employees are doing in terms of maintaining high ethical standards. The program helped management see that in one year, 4.8% of the company's ethics allegations

ethics code
A document that memorializes the standards the employer expects its employees to adhere to.

involved conflicts of interest, and that it took about 30 days to complete an internal investigation.[36] Online ethics training tools include *Business Ethics for Managers* from SkillSoft (skillsoftcom).[37]

Figure 14-6 summarizes the tools and techniques employers use as part of their ethics training programs. As you can see, new-hire orientation, annual refresher training, and distributing the companies' policies and handbooks are all quite important.

Performance Appraisal

How you conduct appraisals is important. Studies (and practical experience) confirm that, in practice, some managers ignore accuracy in performance appraisals and instead use the process for political purposes (such as encouraging employees with whom they don't get along to leave the firm).[38] Few things can send a more damaging signal about how fair and ethical the company is. To send the signal that fairness is paramount, standards should be clear, employees should understand the basis upon which you're going to appraise them, and the appraisal itself should be objective.

Reward and Disciplinary Systems

To the extent that behavior is a function of its consequences, the manager needs to reward ethical behavior and penalize unethical behavior. Research suggests "Employees expect the organization to dole out relatively harsh punishment for

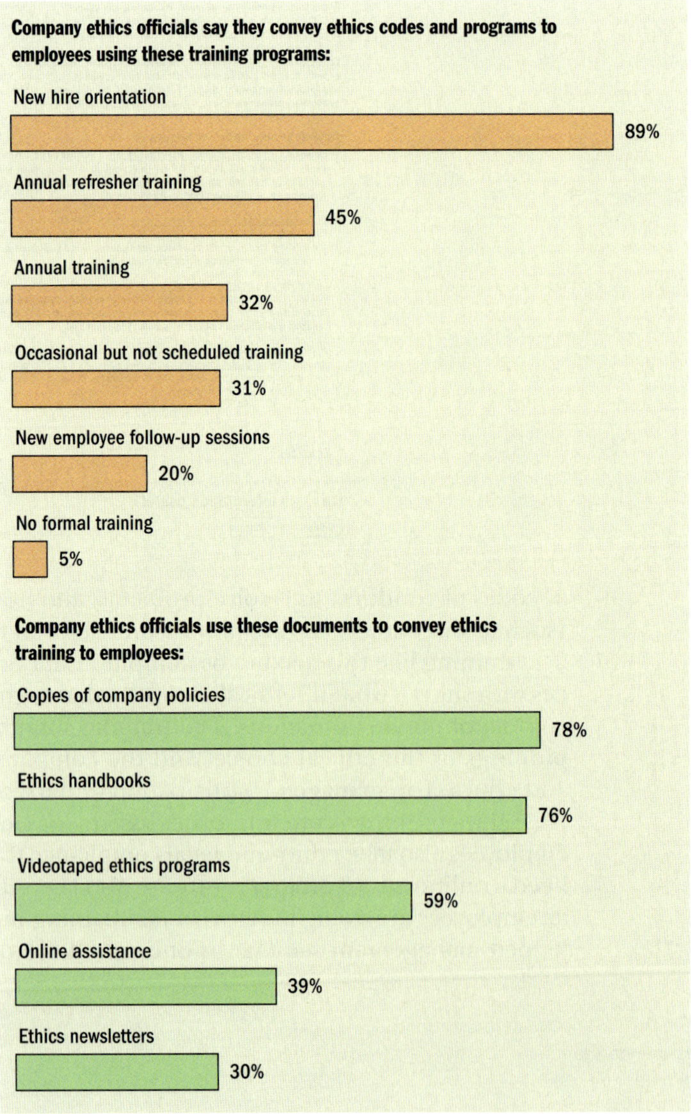

FIGURE 14-6 The Role of Training in Ethics

Source: Susan Wells, "Turn Employees into Saints," *HR Magazine*, December 1999, p. 52. Reproduced with permission via Copyright Clearance Center.

unethical conduct."[39] If the company does not deal swiftly with unethical behavior, often the ethical employees feel punished.

Managing Ethics Compliance

Passage of the Sarbanes-Oxley Act of 2002 made ethics compliance obligatory. As one lawyer put it, "Sarbanes-Oxley has added a wide range of new issues to the traditional compliance function."[40] Among other things, the act requires that the CEO and the CFO of publicly traded companies personally attest to the accuracy of their companies' financial statements, and to the fact that internal controls are adequate.[41] One study of *Fortune* 500 companies concluded than an HR officer was responsible for the program in 28% of responding firms. Another 28% gave the firm's legal officers responsibility, and 16% established separate ethics or compliance departments. The rest of the firms spread the responsibility among auditing departments, or positions such as public affairs and corporate communications.[42]

Personnel-Related Methods for Ensuring Fair Treatment

For most people the answer to "Why treat employees fairly?" is obvious, since most learn, early on, some version of the golden rule. But there are also concrete reasons managers should treat employees fairly. *Arbitrators and the courts* will consider the fairness of the employer's disciplinary procedures when reviewing disciplinary decisions. Fairness also relates to a wide range of *positive employee outcomes.* These include enhanced employee commitment and enhanced satisfaction with the organization, job, and leader and more "organizational citizenship behaviors" (the steps employees take to support their employers' interests).[43] *Job applicants* who felt treated unfairly expressed more desire to appeal the outcome. Those who view the firm's testing programs as fair react more favorably to the selection procedure, and view the company and the job as more attractive.[44] There are thus many practical reasons (beyond the golden rule) for treating employees fairly.

Research Insight A study illustrates this. College instructors completed surveys regarding the extent to which they saw their colleges as treating them with procedural and distributive justice. Procedural justice survey items included "In general, the department/college's procedures allow for requests for clarification for additional information about a decision." Distributive justice items included, "I am fairly rewarded considering the responsibilities I have." The instructors also completed attitude surveys. These included items such as, "I am proud to tell others that I am part of this department/college." Their students also completed surveys. These contained items such as "The instructor put a lot of effort into planning the content of this course," "The instructor was sympathetic to my needs," and "The instructor treated me fairly."

The results were impressive. Instructors who perceived high distributive and procedural justice reported being more committed to the college and to their jobs. Their students reported higher levels of instructor effort, pro-social behaviors, and fairness.[45]

Behaving Unfairly Workplace unfairness is often subtle, but can be blatant. Some supervisors are workplace bullies, yelling at or even threatening subordinates. The employer should, of course, always prohibit such behavior. Many firms have anti-harassment policies. (For example, at one state agency, "It is the policy of the department that all employees, customers, contractors, and visitors to the work site are entitled to a positive, respectful, and productive work environment . . .")[46] Not surprisingly, employees of abusive supervisors are more likely to quit their jobs, and to report lower job and life satisfaction and higher stress.[47] Mistreatment makes it more likely the employee will also show higher levels of "work withdrawal" (show up for work, but not do his or her best).[48] They also exhibit more workplace deviance, for instance, in terms of theft and sabotage.[49]

What Causes Unfair Behavior Some of the things that motivate managers to be fair may (or may not) be surprising. For one thing, the saying, "the squeaky wheel gets the grease" seems to be true. One study investigated the extent to which assertiveness on the subordinate's part influenced the fairness with which the person's supervisor treated him or her.[50] Supervisors treated pushier employees more fairly: "Individuals who communicated assertively were more likely to be treated fairly by the decision maker." Furthermore, supervisors exposed to injustice exhibit abusive behavior against subordinates who they see as vulnerable or provocative.[51] Studies also suggest that large organizations have to work particularly hard to make the workplace seem fair to employees.[52]

Supervisors' Fairness Guidelines What seems "fair" to one person may seem unfair to another. People tend to rate their own performance more highly than do outsiders, and are sensitive to issues of equity and fairness. As a result, even supervisors who try to be fair can expect to have subordinates occasionally say, "You treated me unfairly." One study concluded that three supervisory actions influenced perceived fairness:[53]

- *Involving employees* in the decisions that affect them by asking for their input and allowing them to refute the others' ideas and assumptions;
- Ensuring that everyone involved and affected *understands why* final decisions are made and the thinking that underlies the decisions; and
- Making sure everyone knows up front by what *standards* you will judge him or her.

Practical Communications Opportunities for two-way communication are therefore important in fostering perceptions of fairness. Guidelines here include:

- Ask questions and listen carefully. For example, say, "Can you tell me exactly what you see as unfair about my decision?"[54]
- Set aside your defensive reactions. Instead, perhaps say something like, "I can see why you might feel that way."
- Tactfully deflect distracting statements. For instance, don't get into debates comparing the person's salary raise to someone else's. Instead say, "In fairness to that other person, let's just discuss your situation—you wouldn't want me discussing your salary with him or her."
- Ask, "What would you like me to do?" It could turn out the employee just wants to be heard.
- Deal with specifics. If the employee does want you to change the decision, ask him or her to outline specific reasons.

Many employers establish channels through which employees can air their concerns. For example, Lexington, Kentucky–based Toyota Motor Manufacturing's hotline gives employees an anonymous method of bringing questions or problems to management's attention. Employees can pick up any phone, dial the hotline extension, and record their message. The human resource manager reviews and answers all messages. The FedEx Survey Feedback Action (SFA) program includes an anonymous survey that lets employees express their feelings about the company and their managers. Sample items include:

- I can tell my manager what I think.
- My manager tells me what is expected.
- My manager listens to my concerns.
- My manager keeps me informed.

Each manager then has an opportunity to discuss the department results with subordinates, and create an action plan for improving work group commitment.

4 Employ fair disciplinary practices.

MANAGING EMPLOYEE DISCIPLINE AND PRIVACY

The purpose of *discipline* is to encourage employees to behave sensibly at work (where *sensible* means adhering to rules and regulations). Discipline is necessary when an employee violates a rule.[55]

Proper disciplinary procedures are important for several reasons (beyond the fact that it's the right thing to do). One study surveyed 45 published arbitration awards in which tardiness had triggered discipline and/or discharge. When arbitrators overturned employers' decisions, it was usually because the employer had failed to clarify what it meant by "tardy." A lack of clarity regarding how often an employee may be late and an inappropriately severe penalty were other problems. Unfair disciplinary procedures can backfire in other ways. For example, an unfair disciplinary procedure can trigger retaliatory employee mischief, and thus actually encourage misbehavior.[56]

Establishing a fair disciplinary process isn't as easy at it might appear. The accompanying "Managing the New Workforce" feature addresses one aspect of this.

MANAGING THE NEW WORKFORCE

Comparing Males and Females in a Discipline Situation

Watching a movie like *King Arthur* may lead you to conclude that chivalry in general and a protective attitude toward women in particular is a well-established value in many societies, but that may not be the case. Not only is chivalry not necessarily a prevailing value, but there is even a competing hypothesis in the research literature.[57] What several researchers controversially call the "Evil Woman Thesis" certainly doesn't argue that women are evil. Instead, it "argues that women who commit [certain] offenses violate stereotypic assumptions about the proper behavior of women. These women will [then] be penalized for their inappropriate sex role behavior in addition to their other offenses." In other words, it argues that when a woman doesn't act the way other men and women think she should act, the men and women tend to overreact and treat her more harshly than they might if a man committed it.

While such a thesis might seem ridiculous on its face, the results of at least one careful study seem to support it. In this study, 360 graduate and undergraduate business school students reviewed a labor arbitration case. The case involved two employees, one male and one female, with similar work records and tenure with their employers. Both were discharged for violation of company rules related to alcohol and drugs. The case portrays one worker's behavior as a more serious breach of company rules: The more culpable worker (a male in half the study and a female in the other half) had brought the intoxicant to work. The students had to express their agreement with two alternative approaches to settling the dispute that arose after the discharge.

In their study, the researchers found bias against the woman employee by both the male and female students. The female workers in the case received recommendations for harsher treatment from both the men and women students. As the researchers conclude, ". . . women, as decision makers, appear to be as willing as men to impose harsher discipline on women than upon men."

Basics of a Fair and Just Disciplinary Process

The employer wants its discipline process to be both effective (in terms of discouraging unwanted behavior) and fair. Employers base such a process on three pillars: clear rules and regulations, a system of progressive penalties, and an appeals process.

Rules and Regulations First, rules and regulations address issues such as theft, destruction of company property, drinking on the job, and insubordination. Examples include:

- **Poor performance is not acceptable.** Each employee is expected to perform his or her work properly and efficiently.
- **Alcohol and drugs do not mix with work.** The use of either during working hours and reporting for work under the influence of either are both prohibited.

Rules inform employees ahead of time what is and is not acceptable behavior. Upon hiring, tell employees, preferably in writing, what is not permitted. The employee handbook usually contains the rules and regulations.

Progressive Penalties A system of progressive penalties is a second pillar of effective discipline. Penalties typically range from oral warnings to written warnings to suspension from the job to discharge.

The severity of the penalty is usually a function of the type of offense and the number of times it has occurred. For example, most companies issue warnings for the first unexcused lateness (see form in Figure 14-7). For a fourth offense, discharge is the usual disciplinary action.

Formal Disciplinary Appeals Processes In addition to rules and progressive penalties, the disciplinary process requires an appeals procedure (see Figure 14-8).

FIGURE 14-7 Disciplinary Action Form

Source: Reprinted from www.HR.BLR.com with permission of the publisher *Business and Legal Resources, Inc.*, 141 Mill Rock Road East, Old Saybrook CT, © 2004. BLR© (Business and Legal Resources, Inc.).

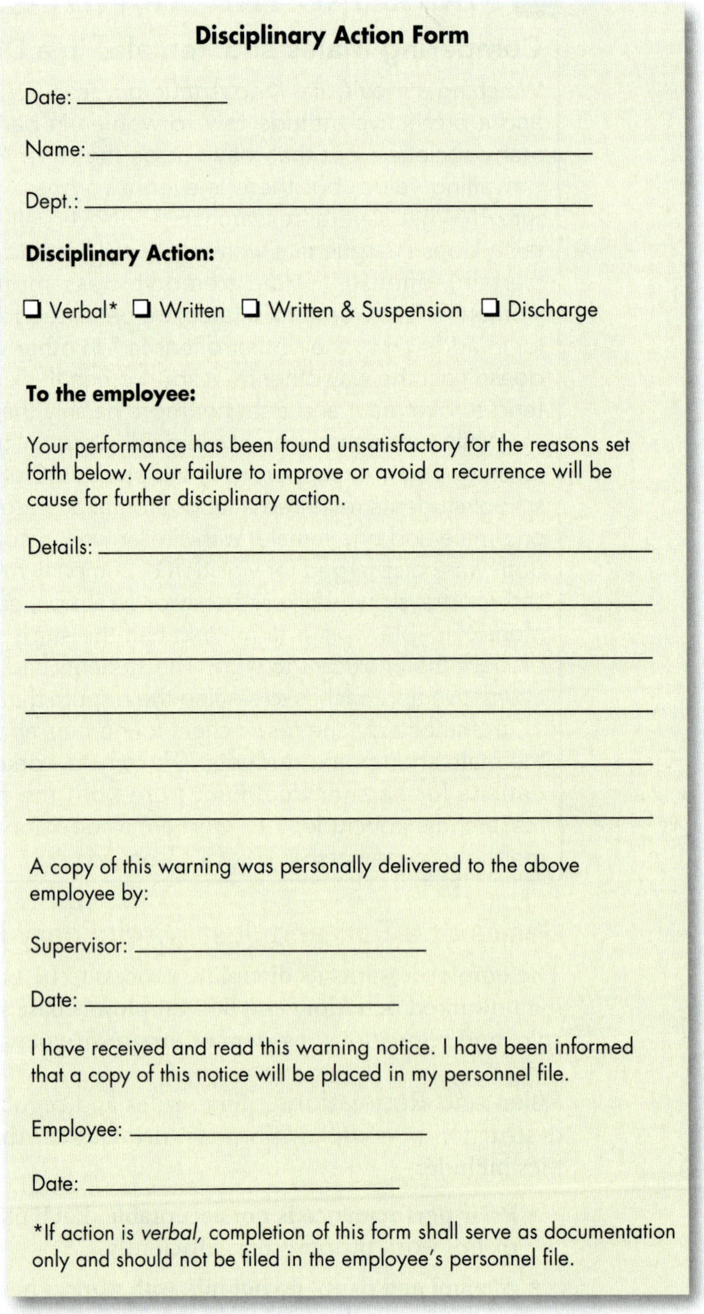

Disciplinary Action Form

Date: ____________

Name: ____________________________________

Dept.: ____________________________________

Disciplinary Action:

❑ Verbal* ❑ Written ❑ Written & Suspension ❑ Discharge

To the employee:

Your performance has been found unsatisfactory for the reasons set forth below. Your failure to improve or avoid a recurrence will be cause for further disciplinary action.

Details: ____________________________________

A copy of this warning was personally delivered to the above employee by:

Supervisor: ____________________

Date: ____________________

I have received and read this warning notice. I have been informed that a copy of this notice will be placed in my personnel file.

Employee: ____________________

Date: ____________________

*If action is *verbal,* completion of this form shall serve as documentation only and should not be filed in the employee's personnel file.

FIGURE 14-8 Grievance Form as Part of Appeal Process

Source: www.wfu.edu/hr/forms/staff-grievance.pdf, accessed May 24, 2007. Used with permission.

WAKE FOREST
UNIVERSITY
HUMAN RESOURCES DEPARTMENT

STAFF GRIEVANCE FORM

This form is to be used by staff employees of Wake Forest University to initiate a **formal** grievance (Step II) that seeks resolution of a work-related problem or condition of employment that an employee believes to be unfair, inequitable, or a hindrance to his/her effective job performance. An employee who wishes to pursue a formal grievance must first have attempted to resolve the grievance informally through a discussion with his/her immediate supervisor (Step I) as outlined in *Staff Employee Grievance and Appeal Process*. Upon completion, this form is to be submitted to the Human Resources Department (Employee Relations), 116 Reynolda Hall.

Grievant: ______________________ Telephone #: ____________

Job Title: ______________________

Employing Department/Office: ______________________

Name of Immediate Supervisor: ______________________

Date Grievance was informally discussed with immediate supervisor (Step I): ____________

EMPLOYEE STATEMENT OF GRIEVANCE: (Provide a concise statement of facts, including dates, to identify the work-related problem or condition of employment you believe to be unfair, inequitable, or a hindrance to your effective job performance – attach a continuation page, if necessary)

REMEDY OR REDRESS SOUGHT BY THE GRIEVANT: (Be specific as to what resolution you are seeking)

______________________ ____________
Grievant's Signature Date

Date the grievance was received by Human Resources: ____________ Initials: ____________

WFU-HR-0013
Issued: 5-17-00
Revised: 5-16-01

Virtually all union agreements contain disciplinary appeal procedures, but such procedures are not limited to unionized firms. For example, FedEx calls its 3-step appeals procedure *guaranteed fair treatment:*

- In *step 1, management review,* the complainant submits a written complaint to a member of management (manager, senior manager, or managing director) within 7 calendar days.
- If not satisfied with that decision, then in *step 2, officer complaint,* the complainant submits a written appeal to the vice president or senior vice president of the division.
- Finally, in *step 3, executive appeals review,* the complainant may submit a written complaint within 7 calendar days of the step 2 decision to the employee relations department. This department then investigates and prepares a case file for the executive review appeals board. The appeals board—the CEO, the COO, the chief personnel officer, and three senior vice presidents—then reviews all relevant information and makes a decision to uphold, overturn, or initiate a board of review, or to take other appropriate action.

Some companies establish independent ombudsman, neutral counselors outside the normal chain of command to whom employees can turn for confidential advice.[58]

Discipline Without Punishment

Traditional discipline has two potential drawbacks. First, no one likes to be punished. Second, punishment tends to gain short-term compliance, but not the sort of long-term cooperation employers often prefer.

Discipline without punishment (or **nonpunitive discipline**) aims to avoid these drawbacks. It does this by gaining employees' acceptance of the rules while reducing the punitive nature of the discipline itself. Here is how it works:[59]

1. **Issue an oral reminder.** The goal is to get the employee to agree to avoid future infractions.
2. **Should another incident arise within 6 weeks, issue a formal written reminder, a copy of which is placed in the employee's personnel file.** In addition, hold a second private discussion with the employee, again without any threats.
3. **Give a paid, 1-day "decision-making leave."** If another incident occurs in the next 6 weeks or so, tell the employee to take a 1-day leave with pay, and to stay home and consider whether the job is right for him or her and whether he or she wants to abide by the company's rules. When the employee returns to work, he or she meets with you and gives you a decision regarding whether or not he or she will follow the rules.
4. **If no further incidents occur in the next year or so, purge the 1-day paid suspension from the person's file.** If the behavior reoccurs, typically the next step is dismissal.

The process would not apply in exceptional circumstances. Criminal behavior or in-plant fighting might be grounds for immediate dismissal, for instance. And if several incidents occurred at very close intervals, you might skip step 2—the written warning.

In Summary: The Hot Stove Rule

Supervisors traditionally apply the four points of what they call the "hot stove rule" when applying discipline. When touching a hot stove that says, "Don't touch," the person has *warning*, and the pain is *consistent*, *impersonal*, and *immediate*. Figure 14-9 summarizes useful fair discipline guidelines.

Employee Privacy

For most people, invasions of privacy are neither ethical nor fair.[60] The four main types of employee privacy violations upheld by courts are intrusion (locker room and bathroom surveillance), publication of private matters, disclosure of medical records, and appropriation of an employee's name or likeness for commercial purposes.[61] (Breaching security of personnel files is a related problem, as we discussed in Chapter 5 (Recruiting). One survey of security professionals ranked human resources last among departments securing such confidential data.[62]) In practice, background checks, monitoring off-duty conduct and lifestyle, drug testing,

FIGURE 14-9 Summary of Fair Discipline Guidelines

- Make sure the evidence supports the charge.
- Make sure the employee's due process rights are protected.
- Warn the employee of the disciplinary consequences.
- The rule that was allegedly violated should be "reasonably related" to the efficient and safe operation of the work environment.
- Fairly and adequately investigate the matter before administering discipline.
- The investigation should produce substantial evidence of misconduct.
- Apply all rules, orders, or penalties evenhandedly.
- The penalty should be reasonably related to the misconduct and to the employee's past work.
- Maintain the employee's right to counsel.
- Don't rob a subordinate of his or her dignity.
- Remember that the burden of proof is on you.
- Get the facts. Don't base a decision on hearsay or on your general impression.
- Don't act while angry.
- In general, do not attempt to deal with an employee's "bad attitude." Focus on improving the specific behaviors creating the workplace problem.

workplace searches, and monitoring of workplace activities trigger most privacy violations.[63] We'll look more closely at monitoring.

Employee Monitoring

As you can see from the screen grab below, monitoring today goes beyond listening in on phone lines. Biometrics—using physical traits such as fingerprints or iris scans for identification—is one example. With fingerprint technology, the user passes his or her fingertip over an optical reader, or presses it onto a computer chip. Bronx Lebanon Hospital in New York uses biometric scanners to ensure that the employee who clocks-in in the morning is really who he or she says he is.[64] Iris scanning tends to be the most accurate authorization device. The Federal Aviation Authority uses it to control employees' access to its information systems.[65] More than half of employers say they monitor their employees' incoming and outgoing e-mail; 27% monitor internal e-mail as well.[66] One survey found that 41% of large employers have someone reading employee e-mails.[67] Ninety-six percent block access to adult Web sites; 61% block access to game sites.[68]

Source: www.imonitorsoft.com, accessed April 28, 2009.

(continued)

nonpunitive discipline
Discipline without punishment, usually involving a system of oral warnings and paid "decision-making leaves" in lieu of more traditional punishment.

IMonitor EAM Professiona Edition (Employee Activity Monitor)
EMPLOYEE
PC ACTIVITY
MONITOR
IMonitor EAM professional edition include all features in EAM standard edition, it also has the following features
EAM Professional edition include a Time Tracker module, it can help your company to analyse what application your employees used and how much time they spend on the application, it has the following fetures.
It can stores 6 months detailed records of used applications of all users in your company.
It can help you to find which user spend more time on web, IM, game or other unwanted application.
It provides Pie Chart and Line Graph report.
It allows you to specify an application and analyse how much time your employee spend on it in one day, one week or one month.
From 25 PCs $1199.95 to buy
More...
Print Job Monitor - Monitor all network printers from one centralized location.
Print Job MONITOR
Print Job Monitor is a well designed software that allows you to audit and log all print jobs, analyse and monitor all network printers from one centralized location. This software can be used by anyone at home, school and office for their own requirements and purposes. Do you lack control of your employee's printing activities? do you want to know how many papers was wasted by your employees who print personal documents? do you want to get a software to protect confidential documents of your business? Print Job Monitor is the best print job monitor software you ever dreamed.
Print Job Monitor allows you to see real time printer's printing status and log all job informations such as printer name, document name, computer name, user name, pages printed, paper size, etc. It also can save the print job informations into centralized database to allow you to analyse and track printer's usage later.
Free Trial
More...
Buy Now!
Power Spy For Office
It can secretly log all document and file used, all clipboard data, and it can secretly log all removable disk added, removed, files/folders copied, modified, renamed, deleted activity.
Power Spy For Office is a well designed and all-in-one spy software for home and office use. Monitor how your computer has been used while you are away. Power Spy Works in stealth mode, silently and smoothly. It can secretly record user's all computer activities and internet activities, such as email, instant message (MSN, ICQ, AOL and Yahoo Messenger), keystrokes, screenshots, websites visited, searching keywords, file or program downloaded, applications used, etc. It also can block unwanted or harmful websites, filter searching keywords, block chat conversations from unwanted people. Additionally it can Send logging reports in text format to a pre-set email box.
Free Trial
More...
Buy Now!
Power Keylogger For Home
Power Spy For Home is a well designed and all-in-one spy keylogger software for home use. Monitor how your computer has been used while you are away. Power Keylogger Works in stealth mode, silently and smoothly. It can secretly record user's all computer activities and internet activities, such as email, instant message (MSN, ICQ, AOL and Yahoo Messenger), keystrokes, screenshots, websites visited, searching keywords, file or program downloaded, applications used, etc. It also can block unwanted or harmful websites, filter searching keywords, block chat conversations from unwanted people. Additionally it can Send logging reports in text format to a pre-set email box.
Free Trial
More...
Buy Now!
IMonitor Time Sheriff (Computer time control software)
IMonitor Time Sheriff is a computer time control software and parental control software for parents and small business.
It allows you to set individual time limits for each application, e.g. allow your kids 2 hours/day of gaming. It also can force kids to take short breaks in computer work to relax the eyes.
Do you know that computers can be a real pain for your kids ? Sitting for a long time in positions that aren't natural for their body can strain their hands, wrists, back, and eyes. If you are concerned your child may be spending too much time online or playing games IMonitor TimeSheriff will offer a solution for you.
Free Trial
More...
Buy Now!
MSN Spy Monitor
MSN
MSN Spy Monitor is a well designed MSN spy software for home & office use. Log all chat conversations and block messages from unwanted people.
MSN Spy Monitor spy software can secretly record all MSN Messenger, ICQ, AOL, Windows Live Messenger and Windows Messenger's incoming and outgoing chat text messages. It runs in a complete invisible mode. It also can block unwanted peoples, and filter message content with pre-set keywords. Additionally it can Send logging reports in text format to a pre-set email box.
Free Trial
More...
Buy Now!
Yahoo Messenger Spy Monitor
Yahoo
Yahoo Messenger Spy Monitor is a well designed spy software for Yahoo Messenger, ICQ, AOL. Log all chat conversations and block messages from unwanted people.
Yahoo Messenger Spy Monitor spy software can secretly record all version of Yahoo Messenger, ICQ and AOl's incoming and outgoing chat text messages. It runs in a complete invisible mode. It also can block unwanted peoples, and filter message content with pre-set keywords. Additionally it can Send logging reports in text format to a pre-set email box.
Free Trial
More...
Buy Now!
Mail Spy Monitor
Mail Spy MONITOR
Mail Spy Monitor is a well designed spy software for home & office use. Log all SMTP and POP3 mails. Mail Spy Monitor can log all emails read in Microsoft Outlook 2000/XP/2003/2007, Microsoft Outlook Express 5/6, Windows Vista WinMail and Incredi Mail. it also can Send logging reports in text format to a pre-set email box.
Free Trial
More...
Buy Now!
Website Blocker
Website BLOCKER
Website Blocker is a well designed spy software for home & office use. Log website usage and block unwanted or harmful websites. Website Blocker can log all webpages opened in Microsoft Internet Explorer, Mozilla Firefox, Netscape Communicator, Netscape Browser, AOL Explorer Browser, Avant Browser, Maxthon, NetCaptor, SlimBrowser and any other web browsers. It also can block unwanted or harmful websites, log file downloaded from HTTP server, log searching keyword user used in google and yahoo and filter searching keyword with pre-set keyword list. Additionally it can Send logging reports in text format to a pre-set email box.
Free Trial
More...
Buy Now!

More employers are using iris scanning to verify employee identity.

Source: Courtesy of Tim Chapman/Newsmakers/Getty Images, Inc.-Liaison.

Location monitoring is becoming pervasive. As its name implies, this involves checking the location and movement of employees.[69] Employers ranging from United Parcel Service to the City of Oakland, California, use GPS units to monitor their truckers' and street sweepers' whereabouts. Cell phone–based GPS technologies will contribute to wider use of location monitoring.[70]

Monitoring Widespread Employee monitoring is widespread. As noted, more than half of employers monitor e-mail activity, three-quarters monitor employee Internet use, and about 40% monitor phone calls.[71] Employers say they do so mostly to improve productivity and protect themselves from computer viruses, leaks of confidential information, and harassment suits.[72] Furthermore, employees who use company computers to do things like swap and download music can ensnare employers in illegal activities.[73] In one case, an employer in New Jersey was found liable when one of its employees used his company computer at work to distribute child pornography. (Someone had previously alerted the employer to the suspicious activity and the employer had not taken action.)[74]

Employers routinely use special software to monitor what their employees are doing online. When one employer noticed that employees were piling up overtime claims, it installed new software and discovered many employees were spending hours each day shopping online instead of working.

Restrictions There are two main restrictions on workplace monitoring: the **Electronic Communications Privacy Act (ECPA)** and *common-law protections* against invasion of privacy. The ECPA is a federal law intended to help restrict interception and monitoring of oral and wire communications. It contains two exceptions. The "business purpose exception" permits employers to monitor communications if they can show a legitimate business reason for doing so. The second, "consent exception," lets employers monitor communications if they have their employees' consent to do so.[75]

Electronic eavesdropping is thus legal—up to a point. Federal law and most state laws allow employers to monitor employees' phone calls in the ordinary course of business, but they must stop listening once it becomes clear that a

Electronic Communications Privacy Act (ECPA)
Intended in part to restrict interception and monitoring of oral and wire communications, but with two exceptions: employers who can show a legitimate business reason for doing so, and employers who have employees' consent to do so.

FIGURE 14-10 Sample E-Mail Monitoring Acknowledgment Statement

I understand that XYZ Company periodically monitors any e-mail communications created, sent, or retrieved using this company's e-mail system. Therefore I understand that my e-mail communications may be read by individuals other than the intended recipient. I also understand that XYZ Company periodically monitors telephone communications, for example to improve customer service quality.

____
Signature | Date

____
Print Name | Department

conversation is personal rather than business related. Employers can also generally monitor their e-mail systems, which are, after all, their property. However, to be safe, employers should warn employees to use those systems for business purposes only. One recent U.S. Court of Appeals case suggests employers may have fewer rights to monitor than previously assumed.[76] Employers should have employees sign e-mail and telephone monitoring acknowledgment statements like that in Figure 14-10.

Videotaped workplace monitoring deserves more caution. In one case, the U.S. Court of Appeals for the First Circuit ruled that an employer's continuous video surveillance of employees in an office setting did not constitute an unconstitutional invasion of privacy.[78] But a Boston employer had to pay more than $200,000 to five workers it secretly videotaped in an employee locker room, after they sued.[79]

HR APPs 4 U

iPods and Ethics at Work

With more employees using their iPod and other MP3 players at work, employers are becoming uneasy. It's not just about wasting time. One employer gave employees iPods as a reward, and then found the employees were clogging the firm's servers with illegal music downloads.[77] Security is a problem, too. One "4-gigabyte MP3 player, such as the first generation of iPod Mini . . . can take home a lot of corporate data," said one employer (a process some graphically describe as "podslurping."[80] Allowing iPod use at work thus seems to require some special planning and policies.

5 List at least four important factors in managing dismissals effectively.

MANAGING DISMISSALS

Dismissal is the most drastic disciplinary step the employer can take. Because of this, it requires special care. There should be sufficient cause for the dismissal, and (as a rule) you should only dismiss someone after taking reasonable steps to rehabilitate or salvage the employee. However, there will undoubtedly be times when dismissal is required, perhaps at once.

The best way to "handle" a dismissal is to avoid it in the first place. Many dismissals start with bad hiring decisions. Using effective selection practices including assessment tests, reference and background checks, drug testing, and clearly defined job descriptions can reduce the need for many dismissals.

Termination at Will and Wrongful Discharge

For more than 100 years, *termination at will* was the prevailing dismissal-related rule in the United States. **Termination at will** means that without a contract, either the employer or the employee could *terminate at will* the employment relationship. The employee can resign for any reason, at will, and the employer can dismiss an employee for any reason, at will.[81]

Today, however, dismissed employees are increasingly taking their cases to court, and many employers are discovering they no longer have a blanket right to fire. Instead, EEO and other laws and court rulings limit management's right to dismiss.

For example, firing a whistleblower might trigger "public policy" exceptions to firing at will. Or, a statement in an employee handbook may imply a contractual agreement to keep an employee. *BusinessWeek* magazine recently described how some employers—even when faced with employee theft—were reluctant to terminate disruptive employees for fear of lawsuits. In practice, though, plaintiffs only win a tiny fraction of such suits. However, the cost of defending the suits is still huge.[82]

Wrongful Discharge

Wrongful discharge refers to a dismissal that violates the law or that fails to comply with contractual arrangements stated or implied by the employer, for instance, in employee manuals.

Three main protections against wrongful discharge have eroded the termination-at-will doctrine—statutory exceptions, common law exceptions, and public policy exceptions.

First, in terms of *statutory exceptions*, federal and state equal employment and workplace laws prohibit specific types of dismissals. As just one example, occupational safety laws prohibit firing employees for reporting dangerous workplace conditions.[83]

Second, numerous *common law exceptions* exist. For example, some state courts recognize the concept of *implied contracts* in employment. Thus, a court may decide that an employee handbook promising termination only "for just cause" may create an exception to the at-will rule.

Finally, under the *public policy exception*, courts have held a discharge to be wrongful when it was against an explicit, well-established public policy (for instance, the employer fired the employee for refusing to break the law).

Grounds for Dismissal

There are four bases for dismissal: unsatisfactory performance, misconduct, lack of qualifications for the job, and changed requirements of (or elimination of) the job. We'll discuss each.

Unsatisfactory performance means persistent failure to perform assigned duties or to meet prescribed job standards.[84] Specific grounds include excessive absenteeism, tardiness, a persistent failure to meet normal job requirements, or an adverse attitude toward the company, supervisor, or fellow employees.

Misconduct is deliberate and willful violation of the employer's rules and may include stealing, rowdy behavior, and insubordination. Sometimes the misconduct is more serious, as when it causes someone else harm. For example, a coworker recently videoed (and posted on YouTube) a cook at a national pizza chain apparently putting all manner of vile foreign matter into the pizzas. Figure 14-11 shows how to identify such *gross misconduct.*

Lack of qualifications for the job is an employee's inability to do the assigned work although he or she is diligent. If the employee may be trying to do the job, it is reasonable to do what's possible to salvage him or her—perhaps by assigning the person to another job.

"Changed requirements of the job" refers to an employee's inability to do the job after the employer changed the nature of the job. Again, the employee may be industrious, so it is reasonable to retrain or transfer this person, if possible.

Insubordination

Insubordination is a form of misconduct, and basically refers to disobedience and/or rebelliousness. While things like stealing, chronic tardiness, and poor-quality work are easily understood grounds for dismissal, insubordination

dismissal
Involuntary termination of an employee's employment with the firm.

termination at will
In the absence of a contract, either the employer or the employee can terminate at will the employment relationship.

wrongful discharge
An employee dismissal that does not comply with the law or does not comply with the contractual arrangement stated or implied by the firm via its employment application forms, employee manuals, or other promises.

insubordination
Willful disregard or disobedience of the boss's authority or legitimate orders; criticizing the boss in public.

FIGURE 14-11 Was It Gross Misconduct?

- Was anyone physically harmed? How badly?
- Did the employee realize the seriousness of his or her actions?
- Were other employees significantly affected?
- Was the employer's reputation severely damaged?
- Will the employer lose significant business or otherwise suffer economic harm because of the misconduct?
- Could the *employer* lose its business license because of the employee's misconduct?
- Will the *employee* lose any license needed to work for the employer (e.g., driver's license)?
- Was criminal activity involved?
- Was fraud involved?
- Was any safety statute violated?
- Was any civil statute violated?
- Was the conduct purposeful?
- Was the conduct on duty?
- Is the violated policy well-known to employees?
- Does the conduct justify immediate termination?
- Has the employer immediately fired other employees who did something similar?

is sometimes harder to translate into words. However, some acts are usually clearly insubordinate. These include, for instance:

1. Direct disregard of the boss's authority
2. Direct disobedience of, or refusal to obey, the boss's orders, particularly in front of others
3. Deliberate defiance of clearly stated company policies, rules, regulations, and procedures
4. Public criticism of the boss
5. Blatant disregard of reasonable instructions
6. Contemptuous display of disrespect
7. Disregard for the chain of command, shown by frequently going around the immediate supervisor with complaints, suggestions, or political maneuvers
8. Participation in (or leadership of) an effort to undermine or remove the boss[85]

Fairness in Dismissals Dismissals are never pleasant. However, there are three things you can do to make sure they are fair.[86] First, "individuals who said that they were given *full explanations* of why and how termination decisions were made were more likely to perceive their layoff as fair . . . and indicate that they did not wish to take the past employer to court."

Second, institute a formal *multistep procedure* (including warning) and a neutral appeal process.

Third, *who actually does the dismissing* is important. Employees in one study whose managers informed them of an impending layoff viewed the dismissal procedure as much fairer than did those told by, say, a human resource manager. (One employer took a less diplomatic approach. The firm had an in-person meeting to announce the downsizing, but telecommuter employees got the news by e-mail. About 10% of respondents in one survey said they've used e-mail to fire employees.[87])

Security Measures Security measures are important whenever dismissals occur. Common sense requires using a checklist to ensure that dismissed employees return all keys and company property, and (often) accompanying them out of their offices and out of the building. The employer should disable Internet-related passwords and accounts of former employees, plug holes that could allow an ex-employee to gain illegal online access, and have rules for return of company laptops and handhelds. "Measures range from simply disabling access and changing passwords to reconfiguring the network and changing IP addresses, remote access procedures, and telephone numbers," says one chief technology officer.[88]

Avoiding Wrongful Discharge Suits

As noted earlier, wrongful discharge occurs when an employee's dismissal does not comply with the law or with the contractual arrangement stated or implied by the employer. (In a *constructive discharge* claim, the plaintiff argues that he or she quit, but had no choice because the employer made the situation so intolerable at work.[89])

Avoiding wrongful discharge suits requires a three-pronged approach.[90] *First*, create employment policies including grievance procedures (like those in this chapter) that help make employees feel you treated them fairly. Similarly, employers can use severance pay to blunt a dismissal's sting.[91] (Figure 14-12 summarizes typical severance policies in manufacturing and service industries.) There is no way to make termination pleasant, but the first line of defense is to handle it justly.[92]

Second, review and refine all employment-related policies, procedures, and documents to limit challenges. Have applicants sign the employment application. Make sure it contains a statement that employment is for no fixed term, and that the employer can terminate at any time. Pay particular attention to the employee handbook. It should include an acknowledgment form as in Figure 14-13. Consider deleting statements such as "employees can be terminated only for just cause." Keep careful confidential records of all actions such as employee appraisals, warnings or notices, and memos outlining how improvement should be accomplished.

Third (but not least), make sure you clearly communicate job expectations to the employee; failing to do so triggers many wrongful termination claims.[93]

Personal Supervisory Liability

Courts sometimes hold managers personally liable for supervisory actions (including discipline and dismissal), particularly with respect to actions covered by the Fair Labor Standards Act and the Family and Medical Leave Act.[94] The former defines *employer* to include "any person acting directly or indirectly in the interest of an employer in relation to any employee . . ." This can mean the individual supervisor.

There are several ways to avoid personal liability. Managers should be fully familiar with applicable federal, state, and local *statutes* (such as Title VII). *Follow company policies and procedures* (since an employee may allege you did not follow company policies and procedures). The essence of many charges is that the

FIGURE 14-12 Median Weeks of Severance Pay by Job Level

Source: Severance Pay: Current Trends and Practices, July 2007, Table 4, www.culpepper.com/info/CS/default.asp.Culpepper eBulletin, accessed July 2007. Complimentary subscriptions at www.culpepper.com/eBulletin.

Severance Calculation Method	Median Weeks of Severance		
	Executives	Managers	Professionals
Fixed	26	6	4
Variable Amount by Employment Tenure			
1 year	4	2	2
3 years	7	5	5
5 years	10	7	7
10 years	20	12	10
15 years	26	16	15
Maximum	39	26	24

FIGURE 14-13 Handbook Acknowledgment Form
Source: www.twc.state.tx.us, accessed April 28, 2009.

Table of Contents | Index | Disclaimer

ACKNOWLEDGMENT OF RECEIPT OF EMPLOYEE HANDBOOK

The Employee Handbook contains important information about the Company, and I understand that I should consult the Administrator/Office Manager/General Manager/Branch Manager/Human Resources Manager [designate one] regarding any questions not answered in the handbook. I have entered into my employment relationship with the Company voluntarily, and understand that there is no specified length of employment. Accordingly, either the Company or I can terminate the relationship at will, at any time, with or without cause, and with or without advance notice.

I understand and agree that no person other than the Executive Director/President/Chief Executive Officer [designate one] may enter into an employment agreement for any specified period of time, or make any agreement contrary to the Company's stated employment-at-will policy.

Since the information, policies, and benefits described herein are subject to change at any time, I acknowledge that revisions to the handbook may occur, except to the Company's policy of employment-at-will. All such changes will generally be communicated through official notices, and I understand that revised information may supersede, modify, or eliminate existing policies. Only the President of the Company has the ability to adopt any revisions to the policies in this handbook.

Furthermore, I understand that this handbook is neither a contract of employment nor a legally-binding agreement. I have had an opportunity to read the handbook, and I understand that I may ask my supervisor or any employee of the Human Resources Department any questions I might have concerning the handbook. I accept the terms of the handbook. I also understand that it is my responsibility to comply with the policies contained in this handbook, and any revisions made to it. I further agree that if I remain with the Company following any modifications to the handbook, I thereby accept and agree to such changes.

I have received a copy of the Company's Employee Handbook on the date listed below. I understand that I am expected to read the entire handbook. Additionally, I will sign the two copies of this Acknowledgment of Receipt, retain one copy for myself, and return one copy to the Company's representative listed below on the date specified. I understand that this form will be retained in my personnel file.

____________________________ ________________
Signature of Employee Date

____
Employee's Name - Printed

____________________________ ________________
Company Representative Date

Return to Businesses & Employers
Return to TWC Home

plaintiff was treated differently than others, so *consistent application* of the rule is important. Administer the discipline in a manner that does not add to the *emotional hardship* on the employee (as dismissing them publicly would). Most employees will try to present *their side* of the story, and allowing them to do so can provide the employee some measure of satisfaction. *Do not act in anger*, since doing so undermines any appearance of objectivity. Finally, *utilize the human resources department* for advice on how to handle difficult disciplinary matters.

The Termination Interview

Dismissing an employee is one of the most difficult tasks a manager faces at work. During one 5-year period, physicians interviewed 791 working people who had just undergone heart attacks to find out what might have triggered them. The researchers concluded that the stress associated with firing doubled the usual risk of a heart attack for the person doing the firing, during the week following the dismissal.[95] Furthermore, the dismissed employee, even if forewarned many times, may still react with disbelief or even violence.[96] Guidelines for the **termination interview** itself are as follows:

1. **Plan the interview carefully.** According to experts at Hay Associates, this includes the following:
   - Make sure the employee keeps the appointment time.
   - Allow 10 minutes as sufficient time for the interview.

- Use a neutral site, not your own office.
- Have employee agreements and release announcements prepared in advance.
- Have phone numbers ready for medical or security emergencies.

2. **Get to the point.** Avoid small talk. *As soon as the employee enters,* give the person a moment to get comfortable and then inform him or her of your decision.
3. **Describe the situation.** Briefly explain why the person is being let go. For instance, "Production in your area is down 6%. We have talked about these problems several times in the past 3 months. We have to make a change." Stress the situation, rather than the employee and his or her shortcomings. Emphasize that the decision is final and irrevocable.
4. **Listen.** To the extent practical, continue the interview for several minutes until the person seems to be talking freely and reasonably calmly about the termination and the support package including severance pay.
5. **Review all elements of the severance package.** Briefly describe severance payments, benefits, access to office support people, and how references will be handled. (Human resources may address this with the employee.) However, make no promises beyond those already in the support package.
6. **Identify the next step.** The terminated employee may be disoriented and unsure what to do next. Explain where the employee should go upon leaving the interview. It's often best to have someone escort him or her until the person is out the door.

Outplacement Counseling

Outplacement counseling is a formal process by which a specialist trains and counsels a terminated person in the techniques of self-appraisal and securing a new position. Outplacement does not imply that the employer takes responsibility for placing the person in a new job. Instead, it is a counseling service whose purpose is to provide the person with advice, instructions, and a sounding board to help formulate career goals and successfully execute a job search him or herself. Outplacement counseling is part of the terminated employee's support or severance package and is done by specialized outside firms.

Outplacement firms don't just counsel displaced employees; they also help the employer devise its dismissal plan. For example, prior to announcing a downsizing, it might be sensible to work with an outplacement firm to decide things like how to break the news and deal with dismissed employees' emotional reactions.

Exit Interview

Many employers conduct **exit interviews** with employees who are leaving the firm for any reason. These are interviews, usually conducted by a human resource professional just prior to the employee leaving; they elicit information about the job or employer with the aim of giving employers insights into what is right—or wrong—about their companies. Exit interview questions include, "Why did you join the company?" "Was the job presented correctly and honestly?" "Were there any special problem areas?"[97] Women and minorities are more likely to quit early in their employment, so this might be one specific issue for which to watch.[98] Figure 14-14 presents an exit interview form.

The assumption of course is that because the employee is leaving, he or she will be candid. However, the information you get may be questionable.[99]

termination interview
The interview in which an employee is informed of the fact that he or she has been dismissed.

outplacement counseling
A formal process by which a terminated person is trained and counseled in the techniques of self-appraisal and securing a new position.

exit interviews
Interviews with employees who are leaving the firm, conducted for obtaining information about the job or related matters, to give the employer insight about the company.

FIGURE 14-14 Employee Exit Interview Questionnaire

Source: http://www.fin.ucar.edu/forms/HR/exit_form/exit.pdf, accessed May 24, 2007. Used with permission.

University Corporation for Atmospheric Research

EXIT INTERVIEW

Employee Name ______________________ Supervisor ______________________

Division ______________________ Job Title ______________________

Hire Date ______________________ Termination Date ______________________

1. Why are you leaving UCAR?

____

____

____

2. What circumstances would have prevented your departure?

____

____

3. What did you like most about your job?

____

____

4. What did you like least about your job?

____

____

5. What did you think of your supervisor on the following points:

	Almost Always	Usually	Sometimes	Never
Was consistently fair	( )	( )	( )	( )
Provided recognition	( )	( )	( )	( )
Resolved complaints	( )	( )	( )	( )
Was sensitive to employees' needs	( )	( )	( )	( )
Provided feedback on performance	( )	( )	( )	( )
Was receptive to open communication	( )	( )	( )	( )
Followed UCAR's policies	( )	( )	( )	( )

Researchers found that at the time of separation, 38% of those leaving blamed salary and benefits, and only 4% blamed supervision. Followed up 18 months later, however, 24% blamed supervision and only 12% blamed salary and benefits. Getting to the real problem during the exit interview may thus require heavy digging. Yet these interviews can be useful. When Blue Cross of Northeastern Pennsylvania dismissed employees, many said, in exit interviews, "This is not a stable place to work." The firm took steps to correct that misperception for those who stayed with Blue Cross.

Layoffs, Downsizing, and the Plant Closing Law

Nondisciplinary separations are a fact of corporate life. For the employer, reduced sales or profits may require *layoffs* or *downsizing*. *Layoff* generally refers to having selected employees take time off, with the expectation that they will come back to work. *Downsizing* refers to permanently dismissing a relatively large proportion of employees in an attempt to improve productivity and competitiveness. Other employees may *resign* to *retire* or to look for better jobs.

The Plant Closing Law Until 1989, there were no federal laws requiring notification of employees when an employer decided to close a facility. However, in that year Congress passed the Worker Adjustment and Retraining Notification Act (popularly known as the *plant closing law*). It requires employers of 100 or more employees to give 60 days' notice before closing a facility or starting a layoff of 50 people or more. The law does not prevent the employer from closing down, nor does it require saving jobs. It simply gives employees time to seek other work or retraining by giving them advance notice. Although there are exceptions, the penalty for failing to give notice is 1 day's pay and benefits to each employee for each day's notice he or she should have received, up to 60 days.

The law is not entirely clear about how to notify employees. However, a paragraph that might suit the purpose would be as follows:

> Please consider this letter to be your official notice, as required by the federal plant closing law, that your current position with the company will end 60 days from today because of a [layoff or closing] that is now projected to take place on [date]. After that day, your employment with the company will be terminated and you will no longer be carried on our payroll records. Any questions concerning the plant closing law or this notice will be answered in the HR office.[100]

The Layoff Process A study illustrates one firm's downsizing process. In this company, senior management first met to make strategic decisions about the size and timing of the layoffs. These managers also debated the relative importance of the skill sets they thought the firm needed going forward. Front-line supervisors assessed their subordinates, rating their nonunion employees either A, B, or C (union employees were covered by a union agreement making layoffs dependant on seniority). The front-line supervisors then informed each of their subordinates about his or her A, B, or C rating, and told each that those employees with C grades were designated "surplus" and most likely to be laid off.[101]

Sensible layoff steps to take therefore include these:[102]

- **Identify objectives and constraints.** For example, decide how many positions to eliminate at which locations, and what criteria to use.
- **Form a downsizing team.** This team should prepare a communication strategy for explaining the downsizing, establish hiring and promotion levels, produce a downsizing schedule, and supervise the displaced employees' benefit programs.
- **Address legal issues.** Review factors such as age, race, and gender before finalizing and communicating any dismissals.
- **Plan post-implementation actions.** For those who remain, activities such as surveys and explanatory meetings can help maintain morale.
- **Address security concerns.** With large layoffs, it may be wise to have security personnel in place.
- **Try to remain informative.** When employees sue after mass layoffs, it's often because they're unhappy with how the employer handled the layoff. Providing advanced notice regarding the layoff and *interpersonal sensitivity* (in terms of the manager's demeanor during layoffs) can both help mitigate negative results.[103] The people who announce the downsizing and deal with the employee questions should explain what is happening truthfully.[104]

Knowing how to prepare for layoffs is an integral part of "Managing HR in Challenging Times," as the accompanying feature explains.

Managing HR in Challenging Times

Preparing for Layoffs

As the U.S. slipped into recession, large layoffs climbed ominously, up by about 9.4% in mid-2009. How do managers prepare for the layoffs that almost invariably result from such challenging times?

Interestingly, the initial focus isn't on the layoffs, but on the employer's appraisal systems. One expert says that in preparing for large scale layoffs, management needs to:[105]

- Make sure appraisals are up-to-date.
- Identify top performers and get them working on the company's future.
- Have leaders committed to the company's turnaround.

Another HR consultant says companies that "don't closely manage their performance appraisal systems suddenly learn during a reduction in force that everyone has been ranked a 'four' out of 'five,'"; "That information is meaningless."[106]

So the essential point about layoffs is to prepare in advance by making sure you have an effective performance appraisal system in place. If you don't, then when the time comes to lay off significant numbers of employers, you may find yourself with no rational basis on which to decide who stays or leaves.

Dismissal's Effects It's not surprising that layoffs often result in harmful psychological and physical health outcomes for employees who lose their jobs, as well as for the survivors who face uncertainty.[107]

Furthermore, not just the "victims" and "survivors" suffer. Researchers collected data from 410 managers who either had or had not been in the position of having to inform subordinates about expected mass layoffs. The researchers ". . . found that the more managers were personally responsible for handing out warning notices to employees, regardless of their age, gender, and marital status, the more likely they were to report physical health problems, to seek treatment for these problems, and to complain of disturbed sleep. . . ."[108]

Bumping/Layoff Procedures As noted, *layoff* generally refers to having some employees take time off, with the expectation that they will come back to work. With layoffs, three conditions are usually present: (1) There is no work available for these employees, (2) management expects the no-work situation to be temporary and probably short term, and (3) management intends to recall the employees when work is again available. A layoff is therefore not a termination, which is a permanent severing of the employment relationship. Many employers, however, do use the term *layoff* as a euphemism for discharge or termination. (Others have taken to calling them "productivity transformation programs.")[109]

Employers who encounter frequent business slowdowns may have bumping/layoff procedures that let employees use their seniority to remain on the job. Most such **bumping/layoff procedures** have these features in common:

1. Seniority is usually the ultimate determinant of who will work.
2. Seniority can give way to merit or ability, but usually only when no senior employee is qualified for a particular job.
3. Seniority is usually based on the date the employee joined the organization, not the date he or she took a particular job.
4. Because seniority is usually company-wide, an employee in one job can usually bump or displace an employee in another job, provided the more senior person can do the job.

Layoff and Downsizing Alternatives Layoffs and downsizings are usually painful for all involved, and have the added disadvantage of stripping away trained personnel. Employers therefore often try to find alternatives.

There are various alternatives. Suggestions include finding *volunteers* who are interested in reducing hours or part-time work, using *attrition*, and even networking with local employers concerning temporary or permanent *redeployments*. With the *voluntary reduction in pay plan*, all employees agree to reductions in pay to keep everyone working. Other employers arrange for all or most employees to *concentrate their vacations* during slow periods. They don't have to hire temporary help for vacationing employees during peak periods, and staffing automatically declines when business declines. For example, Sun (as well as many Silicon Valley employers) had all employees stay home for a week when the economy began slowing. Other employees agree to take *voluntary time off*, which again has the effect of reducing the employer's payroll and avoiding layoffs.

Many employers hire employees with the understanding their work is temporary. When layoffs are required, they are the first to leave. Some seek volunteers as an alternative to dismissing large numbers of employees. For example, many employers offer *early retirement* buyout packages to many of their employees.

Adjusting to Downsizings and Mergers

Firms usually **downsize** to improve their financial positions. Yet many firms discover profits don't improve after major personnel cuts. Low morale among those remaining is often part of the problem.

It therefore makes sense to think through how the firm is going to reduce the surviving employees' uncertainty and boost their morale.[110] When Duracell, Inc. (now part of Dow), downsized, its program included post-downsizing announcement activities. These included a full staff meeting at the facility; an immediate follow-up in which remaining employees split into groups with senior managers to have their questions answered; and long-term support, for instance, by encouraging supervisors to encourage an open-door atmosphere.

Merger Guidelines In terms of dismissal, *mergers and acquisitions* are usually one-sided. In such situations, the acquired firm's surviving employees may be hypersensitive to mistreatment of their soon-to-be former colleagues. It thus behooves the manager to treat those whom you let go fairly. As a rule, therefore:

- Avoid the appearance of power and domination.
- Avoid win–lose behavior.
- Remain businesslike and professional in all dealings.
- Maintain as positive a feeling about the acquired company as possible.
- Remember that the degree to which your organization treats the acquired group with care and dignity will affect the confidence, productivity, and commitment of those who remain.[111]

bumping/layoff procedures
Detailed procedures that determine who will be laid off if no work is available; generally allow employees to use their seniority to remain on the job.

downsizing
The process of reducing, usually dramatically, the number of people employed by a firm.

REVIEW

CHAPTER SECTION SUMMARIES

1. **Ethics and fair treatment** play important roles in managing employees at work. Ethics refers to the principles of conduct governing an individual or a group. The concepts of ethics, justice, and fair treatment are intertwined. For example, fairness is inseparable from what most people think of as "justice" from the individual employee's point of view. Few societies rely solely on managers' ethics or sense of fairness, and therefore legislate employee rights, such as regarding employee pension rights, references rights, defamation rights, and union activity rights.
2. Many things influence **ethical behavior at work**. From research, we know that moral awareness, the managers themselves, moral engagement, morality, unmet goals, and rewards all influence ethical behavior. The person is important, in that people bring to their jobs their own ideas of what is morally right or wrong. The boss and how he or she molds the organizational culture have a prevailing effect on ethical behavior, because it's difficult to resist even subtle pressure from your boss. Employers themselves can take steps to support ethical behavior, for instance via training, whistleblower programs, and ethics codes.
3. Managers can use **personnel methods to promote ethics and fair treatment**. For example, in selection, the manager can hire ethical people and emphasize the fairness of selection procedures. Similarly, ethics training, conducting fair and just performance appraisals, rewarding ethical behavior, and generally treating employees fairly all promote ethics and the perception of fair treatment. Communication plays an important role in fair treatment. For example, ask questions and listen carefully, set aside your defensive actions, and ask, "What would you like me to do?"
4. Managing **employee discipline and privacy** are important management skills. The basics of a fair and just disciplinary process include clear rules and regulations, a system of progressive penalties, and an appeals process. Some employers use nonpunitive discipline, which usually involves a system of oral warnings and paid "decision-making leaves." The "hot stove rule" means administering discipline in such a way that the person has warning, and the pain is consistent, impersonal, and immediate. With more employers using Internet monitoring and technologies such as biometrics, monitoring is widespread. The Electronic Communications Privacy Act and common law protections against invasion of privacy limit, somewhat, workplace monitoring. Employers should have employees sign e-mail and telephone monitoring acknowledgment statements.
5. Dismissals are usually traumatic for both the manager and the dismissed employee, and so managers need to take special care in **managing dismissals**.

   - Termination at will means that without a contract, either the employer or the employee could terminate, at will, the employment relationship.
   - Wrongful discharge refers to a dismissal that violates the law or that fails to comply with contractual arrangements stated or implied by the employer.
   - Grounds for dismissal include unsatisfactory performance, misconduct (including insubordination), lack of qualifications for the job, and changed requirements of the job.
   - Fairness in dismissals is enhanced when employees get explanations of why and how termination decisions were made; there is a formal multistep procedure, including warnings; and the supervisor rather than a third person does the dismissing.
   - Supervisors can be held personally liable for unjust dismissals, and so it is advisable that the supervisor not act in anger, follow company policies and procedures, and avoid adding to the emotional hardship on the employee.
   - The termination interview should be planned carefully, and the supervisor should then get to the point, describe the situation, listen, review all elements of the severance package, and then identify the next step. Some employers use outplacement counselors to facilitate the process.
   - The Worker Adjustment and Retraining Notification Act (plant closing law) requires larger employers to give 60 days' notice before closing a facility or starting to lay off 50 people or more.
   - To avoid wholesale dismissals during what may turn out to be short-term downturns, some employers are using attrition or voluntary reductions in pay plans to temporarily reduce headcount and compensation bills.

DISCUSSION QUESTIONS

1. Explain how you would ensure fairness in disciplining, discussing particularly the prerequisites to disciplining, disciplining guidelines, and the discipline without punishment approach.
2. Why is it important in our highly litigious society to manage dismissals properly?
3. What techniques would you use as alternatives to traditional discipline? What do such alternatives have to do with organizational justice? Why do you think alternatives like these are important, given industry's need today for highly committed employees?
4. Provide three examples of behaviors that would probably be unethical but legal, and three that would probably be illegal but ethical.
5. List 10 things your college or university does to encourage ethical behavior by students and/or faculty.

6. You need to select a nanny for your or a relative's child, and want someone ethical. Based on what you read in this chapter, what would you do to help ensure you ended up hiring someone ethical?
7. You believe your employee is being insubordinate. How would you verify this and what would you do about it if true?
8. Several years ago Walmart instituted a new employee scheduling system that makes it more difficult for its employees to know for sure what hours they would be working. Basically, the store supervisor calls them at the last minute if there's an opening that day. Based on what you read in this chapter, is the new system ethical? Why or why not? Is it fair? What would you do if you were a Walmart employee?

INDIVIDUAL AND GROUP ACTIVITIES

1. Working individually or in groups, interview managers or administrators at your employer or college in order to determine the extent to which the employer or college endeavors to build two-way communication, and the specific types of programs used. Do the managers think they are effective? What do the employees (or faculty members) think of the programs in use at the employer or college?
2. Working individually or in groups, obtain copies of the student handbook for your college and determine to what extent there is a formal process through which students can air grievances. Based on your contacts with other students, has it been an effective grievance process? Why or why not?
3. Working individually or in groups, determine the nature of the academic discipline process in your college. Do you think it is effective? Based on what you read in this chapter, would you recommend any modifications?
4. The "HRCI Test Specifications Appendix" (pages 699–706) lists the knowledge someone studying for the HRCI certification exam needs to have in each area of human resource management (such as in Strategic Management, Workforce Planning, and Human Resource Development). In groups of four to five students, do four things: (1) Review that appendix now. (2) Identify the material in this chapter that relates to the required knowledge the appendix lists. (3) Write four multiple-choice exam questions on this material that you believe would be suitable for inclusion in the HRCI exam. And (4) if time permits, have someone from your team post your team's questions in front of the class, so the students in other teams can take each others' exam questions.
5. In a recent research study at Ohio State University, a professor found that even honest people, left to their own devices, would steal from their employers.[112] In this study, the researchers gave financial services workers the opportunity to steal a small amount of money after participating in an after-work project for which the pay was inadequate. Would the employees steal to make up for the underpayment? In most cases, yes. Employees who scored low on an honesty test stole whether or not their office had an ethics program that said stealing from the company was illegal. Employees who scored high on the honesty test also stole, but only if their office did not have such an employee ethics program—the "honest" people didn't steal if there was an ethics policy.

   In groups of four or five students, answer these questions: Do you think findings like these are generalizable? In other words, would they apply across the board to employees in other types of companies and situations? If your answer is yes, what do you think this implies about the need for and wisdom of having an ethics program?

EXPERIENTIAL EXERCISE

Discipline or Not?

Purpose: The purpose of this exercise is to provide you with some experience in analyzing and handling an actual disciplinary action.

Required Understanding: Students should be thoroughly familiar with the following case, titled "Botched Batch." **Do not read the "award" or "discussion" sections until after the groups have completed their deliberations.**

How to Set Up the Exercise/Instructions: Divide the class into groups of four or five students. Each group should take the arbitrator's point of view and assume that they are to analyze the case and make the arbitrator's decision. Review the case again at this point, but please do not read the award and discussion.

Each group should answer the following questions:

1. Based on what you read in this chapter, including all relevant guidelines, what would your decision be if you were the arbitrator? Why?
2. Do you think that after their experience in this arbitration the parties will be more or less inclined to settle grievances by themselves without resorting to arbitration?

Botched Batch

Facts: A computer department employee made an entry error that botched an entire run of computer reports. Efforts to rectify the situation produced a second set of improperly run reports. Because of the series of errors, the employer incurred extra costs of $2,400, plus a weekend of overtime work by other computer department staffers. Management suspended the employee for 3 days for negligence, and revoked a promotion for which the employee had previously been approved.

Protesting the discipline, the employee stressed that she had attempted to correct her error in the early stages of the run by notifying the manager of computer operations of her mistake. Maintaining that the resulting string of errors could have been avoided if the manager had followed up on her report and stopped the initial run, the employee argued that she had been treated unfairly because the manager had not been disciplined even though he compounded the problem, whereas she was severely punished. Moreover, citing her "impeccable" work record and management's acknowledgment that she had always been a "model employee," the employee insisted that the denial of her previously approved promotion was "unconscionable."

(*Please do* ***not*** *read beyond this point until after you have answered the two questions.*)

Award: The arbitrator upholds the 3-day suspension, but decides that the promotion should be restored.

Discussion: "There is no question," the arbitrator notes, that the employee's negligent act "set in motion the train of events that resulted in running two complete sets of reports reflecting improper information." Stressing that the employer incurred substantial cost because of the error, the arbitrator cites "unchallenged" testimony that management had commonly issued 3-day suspensions for similar infractions in the past. Thus, the arbitrator decides, the employer acted with just cause in meting out an "evenhanded" punishment for the negligence.

Turning to the denial of the already approved promotion, the arbitrator says that this action should be viewed "in the same light as a demotion for disciplinary reasons." In such cases, the arbitrator notes, management's decision normally is based on a pattern of unsatisfactory behavior, an employee's inability to perform, or similar grounds. Observing that management had never before reversed a promotion as part of a disciplinary action, the arbitrator says that by tacking on the denial of the promotion in this case, the employer substantially varied its disciplinary policy from its past practice. Because this action on management's part was not "evenhanded," the arbitrator rules, the promotion should be restored.[113]

APPLICATION CASE

Enron, Ethics, and Organizational Culture

For many people, a company called Enron Corp. still ranks as one of history's classic examples of ethics run amok. During the 1990s and early 2000s, Enron was in the business of wholesaling natural gas and electricity. Rather than actually owning the gas or electric, Enron made its money as the intermediary (wholesaler) between suppliers and customers. Without getting into all the details, the nature of Enron's business, and the fact that Enron didn't actually own the assets, meant that its accounting procedures were unusual. For example, the profit statements and balance sheets listing the firm's assets and liabilities were unusually difficult to understand.

It turned out that the lack of accounting transparency enabled the company's managers to make Enron's financial performance look much better than it actually was. Outside experts began questioning Enron's financial statements in 2001. In fairly short order, Enron collapsed, and courts convicted several of its top executives of things like manipulating Enron's reported assets and profitability. Many investors (including former Enron employees) lost all or most of their investments in Enron.

It's probably always easier to understand ethical breakdowns like this in retrospect, rather than to predict they are going to happen. However, in Enron's case the breakdown is perhaps more perplexing than usual. As one writer recently said,

> "Enron had all the elements usually found in comprehensive ethics and compliance programs: a code of ethics, a reporting system, as well as a training video on vision and values led by [the company's top executives].[114]

Experts subsequently put forth many explanations for how a company that was apparently so ethical on its face could actually have been making so many bad ethical decisions without other managers (and the board of directors) noticing. The explanations ranged from a "deliberate concealment of information by officers" to more psychological explanations (such as employees not wanting to contradict their bosses), and the "surprising role of irrationality in decision-making."[115]

But perhaps the most persuasive explanation of how an apparently ethical company could go so wrong concerns organizational culture. The reasoning here is that it's not the rules but what employees feel they should do that determines ethical behavior. For example (speaking in general, not specifically about Enron), the executive director of the Ethics Officer Association put it this way:

> "[W]e're a legalistic society, and we've created a lot of laws. We assume that if you just knew what those laws meant that you would behave properly. Well, guess what? You can't write enough laws to tell us what to do at all times every day of the week in every part of the world. We've got to develop the critical thinking and critical reasoning skills of our people because most of the ethical issues that we deal with are in the ethical gray areas. Virtually every regulatory body in the last year has come out with language that has said in addition to law compliance, businesses are also going to be accountable to

ethics standards and a corporate culture that embraces them."[116]

How can one tell or measure when a company has an "ethical culture"? Key attributes of a healthy ethical culture include:

- Employees feel a sense of responsibility and accountability for their actions and for the actions of others.[117]
- Employees freely raise issues and concerns without fear of retaliation.
- Managers model the behaviors they demand of others.
- Managers communicate the importance of integrity when making difficult decisions.

Questions

1. Based on what you read in this chapter, summarize in one page or less how you would explain Enron's ethical meltdown.
2. It is said that when one securities analyst tried to confront Enron's CEO about the firm's unusual accounting statements, the CEO publicly used vulgar language to describe the analyst, and that Enron employees subsequently thought doing so was humorous. If true, what does that say about Enron's ethical culture?
3. This case and chapter both had something to say about how organizational culture influences ethical behavior. What role do you think culture played at Enron? Give five specific examples of things Enron's CEO could have done to create a healthy ethical culture.

CONTINUING CASE

Carter Cleaning Company

Guaranteeing Fair Treatment

Being in the laundry and cleaning business, the Carters have always felt strongly about not allowing employees to smoke, eat, or drink in their stores. Jennifer was therefore surprised to walk into a store and find two employees eating lunch at the front counter. There was a large pizza in its box, and the two of them were sipping colas and eating slices of pizza and submarine sandwiches off paper plates. Not only did it look messy, but also there were grease and soda spills on the counter and the store smelled from onions and pepperoni, even with the 4-foot-wide exhaust fan pulling air out through the roof. In addition to being a turnoff to customers, the mess on the counter increased the possibility that a customer's order might actually become soiled in the store.

Although this was a serious matter, neither Jennifer nor her father felt that what the counter people were doing was grounds for immediate dismissal, partly because the store manager had apparently condoned their actions. The problem was, they didn't know what to do. It seemed to them that the matter called for more than just a warning but less than dismissal.

Questions

1. What would you do if you were Jennifer, and why?
2. Should a disciplinary system be established at Carter Cleaning Centers?
3. If so, what should it cover? How would you suggest it deal with a situation such as the one with the errant counter people?
4. How would you deal with the store manager?

TRANSLATING STRATEGY INTO HR POLICIES & PRACTICES CASE

The Hotel Paris Case

The Hotel Paris's New Ethics, Justice, and Fair Treatment Process

The Hotel Paris's competitive strategy is "To use superior guest service to differentiate the Hotel Paris properties, and to thereby increase the length of stay and return rate of guests, and thus boost revenues and profitability." HR manager Lisa Cruz must now formulate functional policies and activities that support this competitive strategy, by eliciting the required employee behaviors and competencies.

As the head of HR for the Hotel Paris, Lisa Cruz was especially concerned about her company maintaining the highest ethical standards. Her concerns were twofold. First, from a practical point of view, there are, in a hotel chain, literally thousands of opportunities on any given day for guests to have bad ethical experiences. For example, in any single hotel each day there are at least a dozen people (including housekeepers, front-desk clerks, security guards, and so on) with easy access to guests' rooms, and to their personal belongings. Guests—many younger, and many unwary—are continually walking the halls unprotected. So, in a service company like this, there is simply no margin for ethical errors.

But she was concerned about ethics for a second reason. She'd been around long enough to know that employees do not like being treated unfairly, and that unfairness in any form could manifest itself in low morale, commitment, and performance. Indeed, perhaps her employees' low morale and commitment—as measured by her firm's attitude surveys—stemmed, in part, from what they perceived as unjust treatment by the hotel's managers. Lisa therefore turned to the task of assessing and redesigning the Hotel Paris's ethics, justice, and fair treatment practices.

To do this, Lisa and her team wanted to proceed methodically through the company's entire HR process, starting with recruitment and selection. For example, working with the company's general counsel, they produced and presented to the CEO a new Hotel Paris code of ethics, as well as a more complete set of ethical guidelines. These now appear on the Hotel Paris's careers Web site link, and are part of each new employee's orientation packet. They contracted with a vendor to provide a customized, Web-based ethics training program, and made it clear that the first employees to participate in it were the company's top executives. However, she knew this was just the start.

Questions

1. List three specific steps Hotel Paris should take with respect to each individual human research function (selection, training, and so on) to improve the level of ethics in the company.
2. Based on what you read in this chapter, create in outline form a strategy map showing how the Hotel's HR functions can foster employee ethics.
3. Based on what you learned in this chapter, write a short (less than one page) explanation Lisa can use to sell to top management the need to improve the hotel chain's fairness and justice processes.

KEY TERMS

ethics, *p. 507*
distributive justice, *p. 507*
procedural justice, *p. 507*
organizational culture, *p. 509*
ethics code, *p. 513*
nonpunitive discipline, *p. 521*
Electronic Communications Privacy Act (ECPA), *p. 523*
dismissal, *p. 525*
termination at will, *p. 525*
wrongful discharge, *p. 525*
insubordination, *p. 525*
termination interview, *p. 529*
outplacement counseling, *p. 529*
exit interviews, *p. 529*
bumping/layoff procedures, *p. 533*
downsizing, *p. 533*

ENDNOTES

1. Keith Winstein, "Suit Alleges Pfizer Spun Unfavorable Drug Studies," *The Wall Street Journal*, October 8, 2008, p. B1.
2. "What Role Should HR Play in Corporate Ethics?" *HR Focus* 81, no. 1 (January 2004), p. 3. See also Dennis Moberg, "Ethics Blind Spots in Organizations: How Systematic Errors in Person Perception Undermine Moral Agency," *Organization Studies* 27, no. 3 (2006), pp. 413–428.
3. Kevin Wooten, "Ethical Dilemmas in Human Resource Management: An Application of a Multidimensional Framework, A Unifying Taxonomy, and Applicable Codes," *Human Resource Management Review* 11 (2001), p. 161. See also Sean Valentine et al., "Employee Job Response as a Function of Ethical Context and Perceived Organization Support," *Journal of Business Research* 59, no. 5 (2006), pp. 582–588.
4. Paul Schumann, "A Moral Principles Framework for Human Resource Management Ethics," *Human Resource Management Review* 11 (2004), p. 94.
5. Manuel Velasquez, *Business Ethics: Concepts and Cases* (Upper Saddle River, NJ: Prentice Hall, 1992), p. 9. See also O. C. Ferrell, John Fraedrich, and Linda Ferrell, *Business Ethics* (Boston: Houghton Mifflin, 2008).
6. The following discussion, except as noted, is based on Manuel Velasquez, *Business Ethics*, pp. 9–12.
7. For further discussion of ethics and morality, see Tom Beauchamp and Norman Bowie, *Ethical Theory and Business* (Upper Saddle River, NJ: Prentice Hall, 2001), pp. 1–19.
8. Richard Osborne, "A Matter of Ethics," *Industry Week*, September 4, 2000, pp. 41–42.
9. Carroll Lachnit, "Recruiting Trouble for Tyson," *Workforce, HR Trends and Tools for Business Results* 81, no. 2 (February 2002), p. 22.
10. Daniel Skarlicki and Robert Folger, "Fairness and Human Resources Management," *Human Resource Management Review* 13, no. 1 (2003), p. 1.
11. Gary Weaver and Linda Trevino, "The Role of Human Resources in Ethics/Compliance Management: A Fairness Perspective," *Human Resource Management Review* 11 (2001), pp. 113–134.
12. Michelle Donovan et al., "The Perceptions of Fair Interpersonal Treatment Scale: Development and Validation of a Measure of Interpersonal Treatment in the Workplace," *Journal of Applied Psychology* 83, no. 5 (1998), pp. 683–692.
13. Gary Weaver and Linda Trevino, "The Role of Human Resources in Ethics/Compliance Management: A Fairness Perspective," *Human Resource Management Review* 11 (2001), p. 115.
14. Kenneth Sovereign, *Personnel Law* (Upper Saddle River, NJ: Prentice Hall, 1999), p. 150.
15. This list is from www.legaltarget.com/employee_rights, accessed January 3, 2008.
16. Basically, *common law* refers to legal precedents. Judges' rulings set precedents, which then generally guide future judicial decisions.
17. Sovereign, op. cit, p. 192.
18. This list is based on Linda K. Trevino, Gary R. Weaver, and Scott J. Reynolds, "Behavioral Ethics in Organizations: A Review," *Journal of Management* 32, no. 6 (2006), pp. 951–990.
19. R. Bergman, "Identity as Motivation: Toward a Theory of the Moral Self." In D. K. Lapsley and D. Narvaez (eds.), *Moral Development, Self and Identity* (Mahwah, NJ: Lawrence Erlbaum, 2004), pp. 21–46.
20. M. E. Schweitzer, L. Ordonez, and B. Douma, "Goal Setting as a Motivator of Unethical Behavior," *Academy of Management Journal* 47, no. 3 (2004), pp. 422–432.

21. N. M. Ashkanasy, C. A. Windsor, and L. K. Treviño, "Bad Apples in Bad Barrels Revisited: Cognitive Moral Development, Just World Beliefs, Rewards, and Ethical Decision Making," *Business Ethics Quarterly* 16 (2006), pp. 449–474.
22. Sara Morris et al., "A Test of Environmental, Situational, and Personal Influences on the Ethical Intentions of CEOs," *Business and Society*, August 1995, pp. 119–247.
23. Vikas Anand et al., "Business as Usual: The Acceptance and Perpetuation of Corruption in Organizations," *Academy of Management Executive* 18 no. 2 (2004), pp. 40–41.
24. "Ethics Policies are Big with Employers, but Workers See Small Impact on the Workplace," *BNA Bulletin to Management*, June 29, 2000, p. 201.
25. From Guy Brumback, "Managing Above the Bottom Line of Ethics," *Supervisory Management*, December 1993, p. 12. See also E. E. Umphress et al., "The Influence of Distributive Justice on Lying for and Stealing from a Supervisor," *Journal of Business Ethics* 86, no. 4 (June 2009), pp. 507–518.
26. "Former CEO Joins WorldCom's Indicted," *Miami Herald*, March 3, 2004, p. 4C.
27. See, for example, Roberta Johnson, *Whistleblowing: When it Works—and Why* (USA: Lynne Rienner Publishers Inc, 2002).
28. Dayton Fandray, "The Ethical Company," *Workforce*, December 2000, pp. 74–77.
29. J. Krohe Jr, "The Big Business of Business Ethics," *Across the Board* 34 (May 1997), pp. 23–29; Deborah Wells and Marshall Schminke, "Ethical Development and Human Resources Training: An Integrative Framework," *Human Resource Management Review* 11 (2001), pp. 135–158.
30. "Ethical Issues in the Management of Human Resources," *Human Resource Management Review* 11 (2001), p. 6; see also Joel Lefkowitz, "The Constancy of Ethics Amidst the Changing World of Work," *Human Resource Management Review* 16 (2006), pp. 245–268.
31. William Byham, "Can You Interview for Integrity?" *Across-the-Board* 41, no. 2 (March/April 2004): 34–38. For a description of how the United States Military Academy uses its student admission and socialization processes to promote character development, see Evan Offstein and Ronald Dufresne, "Building Strong Ethics and Promoting Positive Character Development: The Influence of HRM at the United States Military Academy at West Point," *Human Resource Management* 46, no. 1 (Spring 2007), pp. 95–114.
32. Weaver and Trevino, "The Role of Human Resources," p. 123. See also Linda Andrews, "The Nexus of Ethics," *HR Magazine*, August 2005, pp. 53–58.
33. Russell Cropanzano and Thomas Wright, "Procedural Justice and Organizational Staffing: A Tale of Two Paradigms," *Human Resource Management Review* 13, no. 1 (2003), pp. 7–40.
34. Kathryn Tyler, "Do the Right Thing, Ethics Training Programs Help Employees Deal with Ethical Dilemmas," *HR Magazine*, February 2005, pp. 99–102.
35. Weaver and Trevino, "The Role of Human Resources," p. 123.
36. M. Ronald Buckley et al., "Ethical Issues in Human Resources Systems," *Human Resource Management Review* 11, no. 1, 2 (2001), pp. 11, 29. See also Ann Pomeroy, "The Ethics Squeeze," *HR Magazine*, March 2006, pp. 48–55.
37. Tom Asacker, "Ethics in the Workplace," *Training & Development*, August 2004, p. 44; http://skillsoft.com/catalog/search.asp?title=Business+Ethics&type=Courses&submit.x=45&submit.y=15, accessed August 11, 2009.
38. Weaver and Trevino, "The Role of Human Resources," pp. 113–134.
39. Weaver and Trevino, "The Role of Human Resources," p. 114.
40. Ibid.
41. Michael Burr, "Corporate Governance: Embracing Sarbanes-Oxley," *Public Utilities Fortnightly*, October 15, 2003, pp. 20–22.
42. "Corporations' Drive to Embrace Ethics Gives HR Leaders Chance to Take Reins," *BNA Bulletin to Management*, November 7, 2002, p. 353.
43. Weaver and Trevino, "The Role of Human Resources," p. 117.
44. Russell Cropanzano and Thomas Wright, "Procedural Justice and Organizational Staffing: A Tale of Two Paradigms," *Human Resource Management Review* 13, no. 1 (2003), pp. 7–40.
45. Suzanne Masterson, "A Trickle-Down Model of Organizational Justice: Relating Employees' and Customers' Perceptions of and Reactions to Fairness," *Journal of Applied Psychology* 86, no. 4 (2001), pp. 594–601.
46. Rudy Yandrick, "Lurking in the Shadows," *HR Magazine*, October 1999, pp. 61–68. See also Helge Hoel and David Beale, "Workplace Bullying, Psychological Perspectives and Industrial Relations: Towards a Contextualized and Interdisciplinary Approach," *British Journal of Industrial Relations* 44, no. 2 (June 2006), pp. 239–262.
47. Bennett Tepper, "Consequences of Abusive Supervision," *Academy of Management Journal* 43, no. 2 (2000), pp. 178–190. See also Samuel Aryee et al., "Antecedents and Outcomes of Abusive Supervision: Test of a Trickle-Down Model," *Journal of Applied Psychology*, no. 1 (2007), pp. 191–201.
48. Wendy Boswell and Julie Olson-Buchanan, "Experiencing Mistreatment at Work: The Role of Grievance Filing, Nature of Mistreatment, and Employee Withdrawal," *Academy of Management Journal* 47, no. 1 (2004), pp. 129–139. See also Samuel Aryee et al., 2007, op. cit.
49. Bennett Tepper et al., "Abusive Supervision and Subordinates' Organization Deviance," *Journal of Applied Psychology* 93, no. (2008), pp. 721–732.
50. M. Audrey Korsgaard, Loriann Roberson, and R. Douglas Rymph, "What Motivates Fairness? The Role of Subordinate Assertive Behavior on Manager's Interactional Fairness," *Journal of Applied Psychology* 83, no. 5 (1998), pp. 731–744.
51. Bennett Tepper et al., "Procedural Injustice, Victim Precipitation, and Abusive Supervision," *Personnel Psychology* 59 (2006), pp. 11–23.
52. Marshall Schminke et al., "The Effect of Organizational Structure on Perceptions of Procedural Fairness," *Journal of Applied Psychology* 85, no. 2 (2000), pp. 294–304.
53. W. Chan Kim and Renee Mauborgne, "Fair Process: Managing in the Knowledge Economy," *Harvard Business Review*, July/August 1997, pp. 65–75.
54. Kelly Mollica, "Perceptions of Fairness," *HR Magazine*, June 2004, pp. 169–171.
55. Lester Bittel, *What Every Supervisor Should Know* (New York: McGraw-Hill, 1974), p. 308; and Thomas Salvo, "Practical Tips for Successful Progressive Discipline," SHRM White Paper July 2004, ww.shrm.org/hrresources/whitepapers_published/CMS_009030.asp, accessed January 5, 2008.
56. David Campbell et al., "Discipline Without Punishment—At Last," *Harvard Business Review*, July/August 1995, pp. 162–178.
57. Robert Grossman, "Executive Discipline," *HR Magazine* 50, no. 8 (August 2005), pp. 46–51; "The 'Evil Women' Theses," discussed in Sandra Hartman et al., "Males and Females in a

Discipline Situation: Exploratory Research on Competing Hypotheses," *Journal of Managerial Issues* 6, no. 1 (Spring 1994), pp. 57, 64–68; "A Woman's Place," *The Economist* 356, no. 8184 (August 19, 2000), p. 56.

58. "Employers Turn to Corporate Ombuds to Defuse Internal Ticking Time Bombs," *BNA Bulletin to Management*, August 9, 2005, p. 249.
59. Dick Grote, "Discipline Without Punishment," *Across the Board* 38, no. 5 (September 2001), pp. 52–57.
60. Milton Zall, "Employee Privacy," *Journal of Property Management* 66, no. 3 (May 2001), p. 16.
61. Morris Attaway, "Privacy in the Workplace on the Web," *Internal Auditor* 58, no. 1 (February 2001), p. 30.
62. Rita Zeidner, "Out of the Breach," *HR Magazine*, August 2008, p. 38.
63. Declan Leonard and Angela France, "Workplace Monitoring: Balancing Business Interests with Employee Privacy Rights," *Society for Human Resource Management Legal Report*, May–June 2003, pp. 3–6; "Blogs, Networking Sites Drive Workplace Privacy Disputes," *BNA Bulletin to Management*, August 5, 2008, p. 255.
64. "Time Clocks Go High Touch, High Tech to Keep Workers from Gaming the System," *BNA Bulletin to Management*, March 25, 2004, p. 97.
65. Andrea Poe, "Make Foresight 20/20," *HR Magazine*, February 2000, pp. 74–80.
66. Rita Zeidner, "Keeping E-Mail in Check," *HR Magazine*, June 2007, pp. 70–74.
67. Frederic Leffler and Lauren Palais, "Filter Out Perilous Company E-Mails," *Society for Human Resource Management Legal Report*, August 2008, p. 3.
68. Bill Roberts, "Stay Ahead of the Technology Use Curve," *HR Magazine*, October 2008, pp. 57–61.
69. Gundars Kaupin et al., "Recommended Employee Location Monitoring Policies," www. SHRM.org, downloaded January 2, 2007.
70. "Do You Know Where Your Workers Are? GPS Units Aid Efficiency, Raise Privacy Issues," *BNA Bulletin to Management*, July 22, 2004, p. 233. See also www.WORKRIGHTS.ORG/issue_electronic/NWI_GPS_report.pdf, downloaded January 2, 2007.
71. Eileen Zimmerman, "HR Must Know When Employee Surveillance Crosses the Line," *Workforce*, February 2002, pp. 38–44. See also Rita Zeidner, "Keeping E-Mail in Check," *HR Magazine*, June 2007, pp. 70–74.
72. "Workers Sharing Music, Movies at Work Violates Copyrights, Employer Finds," *BNA Bulletin to Management*, June 19, 2003, p. 193.
73. Cynthia Kemper, "Big Brother," *Communication World* 18, no. 1 (December 2000/January 2001), pp. 8–12.
74. "After Employer Found Liable for Worker's Child Porn, Policies May Need to be Revisited," *BNA Bulletin to Management*, March 21, 2006, p. 89.
75. *Vega-Rodriguez v. Puerto Rico Telephone Company*, CA1, #962061, 4/8/97, discussed in "Video Surveillance Withstands Privacy Challenge," *BNA Bulletin to Management*, April 17, 1997, p. 121.
76. *Quon v. Arch Wireless Operating Co.*, 529f.3d 892 (Ninth Circuit, 2008), "Employers Should Re-Examine Policies in Light of Ruling," *BNA Bulletin to Management*, August 12, 2008, p. 263.
77. Kathy Gurchiek, "iPods Can Hit Sour Note in the Office," *HR Magazine*, April 2006.
78. "Secret Videotaping Leads to $200,000 Settlement," *BNA Bulletin to Management*, January 22, 1998, p. 17.
79. Bill Roberts, "Are You Ready for Biometrics?" *HR Magazine*, March 2003, pp. 95–96.
80. Ibid.
81. Charles Muhl, "The Employment at Will Doctrine: Three Major Exceptions," *Monthly Labor Review* 124, no. 1 (January 2001), pp. 3–11.
82. Michael Orey, "Fear of Firing," *BusinessWeek*, April 23, 2007, pp. 52–54.
83. Robert Lanza and Martin Warren, "United States: Employment at Will Prevails Despite Exceptions to the Rule," *Society for Human Resource Management Legal Report*, October–November 2005, pp. 1–8.
84. Joseph Famularo, *Handbook of Modern Personnel Administration* (New York: McGraw-Hill, 1982), pp. 65.3–65.5. See also Carolyn Hirschman, "Off Duty, Out of Work," *HR Magazine*, www.shrm.org/hrmagazine/articles/0203/0203hirschman.asp, accessed January 10, 2008.
85. Kenneth Sovereign, *Personnel Law* (Upper Saddle River, NJ: Prentice Hall, 1999); Connie Wanberg et al., "Perceived Fairness of Layoffs Among Individuals Who Have Been Laid Off: A Longitudinal Study," *Personnel Psychology* 2 (1999), pp. 59–84.
86. Connie Wanberg et al., "Perceived Fairness of Layoffs Among Individuals Who Have Been Laid Off: A Longitudinal Study," *Personnel Psychology* 2 (1999), pp. 59–84; Brian Klass and Gregory Dell'omo, "Managerial Use of Dismissal: Organizational Level Determinants," *Personnel Psychology* 50 (1997), pp. 927–953; Nancy Hatch Woodward, "Smoother Separations," *HR Magazine*, June 2007, pp. 94–97.
87. "E-Mail Used for Layoffs, Humiliation," *BNA Bulletin to Management*, October 2, 2007, p. 315.
88. Jaikumar Vijayan, "Downsizings Leave Firms Vulnerable to Digital Attacks," *Computerworld* 25 (2001), pp. 6–7.
89. Paul Falcon, "Give Employees the (Gentle) Hook," *HR Magazine*, April 2001, pp. 121–128.
90. James Coil III and Charles Rice, "Three Steps to Creating Effective Employee Releases," *Employment Relations Today*, Spring 1994, pp. 91–94; Richard Bayer, "Termination with Dignity," *Business Horizons* 43, no. 5 (September 2000), pp. 4–10; Betty Sosnin, "Orderly Departures," *HR Magazine* 50, no. 11 (November 2005), pp. 74–78; "Severance Pay: Not Always the Norm," *HR Magazine*, May 2008, p. 28.
91. See, for example, Richard Hannah, "The Attraction of Severance," *Compensation & Benefits Review*, November/December 2008, pp. 37–44.
92. Jonathan Segal, "Severance Strategies," *HR Magazine*, July 2008, pp. 95–96.
93. "Lawyers Say Reasonable Employer Is Best Defense Against Wrongful Termination Claims," *BNA Bulletin to Management*, November 20, 2007, p. 379.
94. Based on Coil and Rice, "Three Steps to Creating Effective Employee Releases," pp. 91–94.
95. "One More Heart Risk: Firing Employees," *Miami Herald*, March 20, 1998, pp. C1, C7.
96. Kemba Dunham, "The Kinder Gentler Way to Lay Off Employees—More Human Approach Helps," *The Wall Street Journal*, March 13, 2001, p. B1.
97. Paul Barada, "Before You Go . . . ," *HR Magazine*, December 1998, pp. 89–102; Marlene Piturro, "Alternatives to Downsizing," *Management Review*, October 1999, pp. 37–42; "How Safe Is Your Job?" *Money*, December 1, 2001, p. 130.

98. Peter Hom et al., "Challenging Conventional Wisdom About Who Quits: Revelations from Corporate America," *Journal of Applied Psychology* 93, no. 1 (2008), pp. 1–34.
99. Joseph Zarandona and Michael Camuso, "A Study of Exit Interviews: Does the Last Word Count?" *Personnel* 62, no. 3 (March 1981), pp. 47–48. For another point of view, see "Firms Can Profit from Data Obtained from Exit Interviews," *Knight Ridder/Tribune Business News*, February 13, 2001, Item 0104 4446.
100. See Nancy Ryan, "Complying with the Worker Adjustment and Retraining Notification Act (WARN act)," *Employee Relations Law Journal* 18, no. 1 (Summer 1993), pp. 169–176; and Emily Nelson, "The Job Cut Buyouts Favored by P&G Pose Problems," *The Wall Street Journal*, June 12, 2001, p. B1. See also Rodney Sorensen and Stephen Robinson, "What Employers Can Do to Stay Out of Legal Trouble When Forced to Implement Layoffs," *Compensation & Benefits Review*, January/February 2009, pp. 25–32.
101. Leon Grunberg, Sarah Moore, and Edward Greenberg, "Managers' Reactions to Implementing Layoffs: Relationship to Health Problems and Withdrawal Behaviors," *Human Resource Management* 45, no. 2 (Summer 2006), pp. 159–178.
102. These are suggested by attorney Ethan Lipsig and discussed in "The Lowdown on Downsizing," *BNA Bulletin to Management*, January 9, 1997, p. 16. See also Stephen Gilliland and Donald Schepers, "Why We Do the Things We Do: A Discussion and Analysis of Determinants of Just Treatment in Layoff Implementation Decisions," *Human Resource Management Review* 13, no. 1 (2003), pp. 59–84.
103. "Communication Can Reduce Problems, Litigation After Layoffs, Attorneys Say," *BNA Bulletin to Management*, April 24, 2003, p. 129.
104. John Kammeyer-Mueller and Hui Liao, "Workforce Reduction and Jobseeker Attraction: Examining Jobseekers' Reactions to Firm Workforce-Reduction Strategies," *Human Resource Management* 45, no. 4 (Winter 2006), pp. 585–603.
105. Adrienne Fox, "Prune Employees Carefully," *HR Magazine*, April 1, 2008.
106. Ibid.
107. Leon Grunberg, Sarah Moore, and Edward Greenberg, "Managers' Reactions to Implementing Layoffs: Relationship to Health Problems and Withdrawal Behaviors," *Human Resource Management* 45, no. 2 (Summer 2006), pp. 159–178.
108. In one recent year, U.S. employers implemented about 1,300 mass layoffs, involving a total of almost 133,000 workers. "Layoffs: 133,914 Workers Idled by Mass Layoffs in April, BLS Says," *BNA Bulletin to Management*, June 3, 2008, p. 181.
109. "Calling a Layoff a Layoff," *Workforce Management*, April 21, 2008, p. 41.
110. See, for example, "Cushioning the Blow of Layoffs," *BNA Bulletin to Management*, July 3, 1997, p. 216.
111. Steve Weinstein, "The People Side of Mergers," *Progressive Grocer* 80, no. 1 (January 2001), pp. 29–31.
112. Based on "Theft Is Unethical," *HR Solutions* 34 (October 2002), p. 66.
113. Bureau of National Affairs, *Bulletin to Management*, September 13, 1985, p. 3.
114. David Gebler, "Is Your Culture a Risk Factor?" *Business and Society Review* 111, no. 3 (Fall 2006), pp. 337–362.
115. John Cohan, "'I Didn't Know' and 'I Was Only Doing My Job': Has Corporate Governance Careened Out of Control? A Case Study of Enron's Information Myopia," *Journal of Business Ethics* 40, no. 3 (October 2002), pp. 275–299.
116. Gebler, op. cit.
117. Ibid.

15 Labor Relations and Collective Bargaining

The U.S. Department of Labor's National Labor Relations Board (NLRB) accused Starbucks of breaking the law by trying to prevent workers in some of its New York shops from unionizing. Among other things, the NLRB accused managers in those stores of retaliating against workers who wanted to unionize by interrogating them about their union inclinations. A Starbucks spokesperson said the company believes the allegations are baseless, and that the firm will vigorously defend itself.[1]

WHERE ARE WE NOW . . .

Chapter 14 focused on employee ethics and justice—important issues in determining employees' tendencies to join unions. The main purpose of this chapter is to help you deal effectively with unions and grievances. After briefly discussing the history of the American labor movement, we describe the basic labor law, including unfair labor practices. We explain labor negotiations, including the union actions you can expect during the union campaign and election. And we explain what you can expect during the actual bargaining sessions, and how to handle grievances.

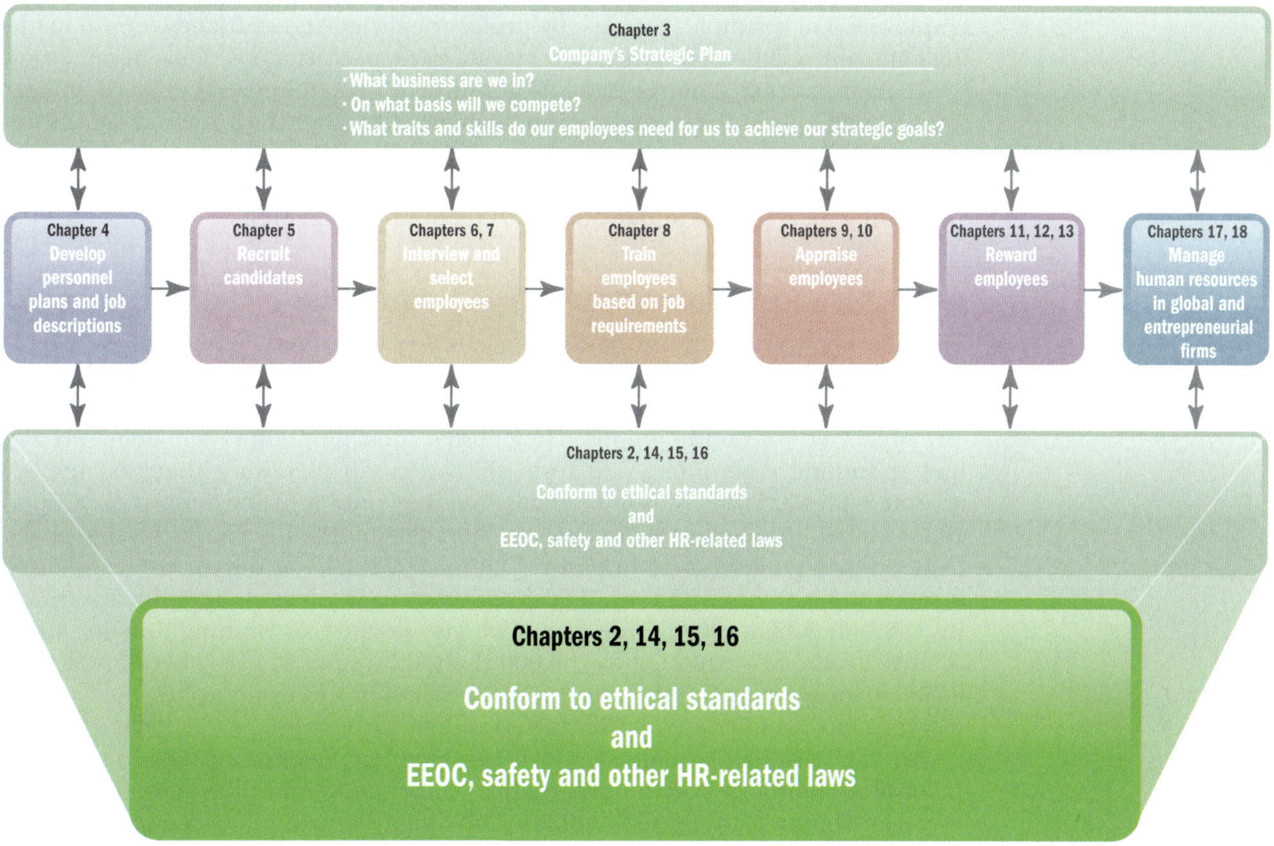

LEARNING OUTCOMES

1. Give a brief history of the American labor movement.
2. Discuss the main features of at least three major pieces of labor legislation.
3. Present examples of what to expect during the union drive and election.
4. Describe five ways to lose an NLRB election.
5. Illustrate with examples bargaining that is not in good faith.
6. Develop a grievance procedure.

THE LABOR MOVEMENT

The labor union movement is important. Just over 17.7 million U.S. workers belong to unions—around 12.4% of the total number of men and women working in this country.[2] Many are still blue-collar workers. But workers including doctors, psychologists, graduate teaching assistants, government office workers, and even fashion models are forming or joining unions.[3] About 40% of America's 20 million federal, state, and municipal public employees belong to unions.[4] And in some industries—including transportation and public utilities, where more than 26% of employees are union members—it's still hard to get a job without joining a union.[5] Union membership in other countries is declining, but still very high (more than 35% of employed workers in Canada, Mexico, Brazil, and Italy, for instance).

Furthermore, it's a mistake to assume that unions only negatively affect employers. For example, perhaps by professionalizing the staff and/or systematizing company practices, unionization may improve performance. Thus in one study, heart attack mortality among patients in hospitals with unionized registered nurses was 5% to 9% lower than in nonunion hospitals.[6] Another study found a significant negative relationship between union membership and employees' intent to leave their jobs.[7]

We'll look at unions and dealing with them in this chapter.

1 Give a brief history of the American labor movement.

A Brief History of the American Union Movement

To understand what unions want, it is useful to understand "where they've been." The history of the U.S. union movement has been one of alternate expansion and contraction.[8] As early as 1790, skilled craftsmen (shoemakers, tailors, printers, and so on) organized into trade unions. They posted their minimum wage demands and had "tramping committees" go from shop to shop to ensure that no member accepted a lesser wage. Union membership grew until a major depression around 1837 resulted in a membership decline. Membership then began increasing as the United States entered its industrial revolution. In 1869, a group of tailors met and formed the Knights of Labor. The Knights were interested in political reform. By 1885, they had 100,000 members, which (because of winning a major strike against a railroad) exploded to 700,000 the following year. Partly because of their focus on social reform, and partly due to a series of unsuccessful strikes, the Knights' membership dwindled rapidly thereafter, and the group dissolved in 1893.

In 1886, Samuel Gompers formed the American Federation of Labor (AFL). It consisted mostly of skilled workers and, unlike the Knights, focused on practical, bread-and-butter gains for its members. The Knights of Labor had engaged in a class

Making fenders at an early Ford factory in Ypsilanti, Michigan. In addition to heavy physical labor, workers faced health hazards—poor lighting, dust, and dangerous machinery.

Source: Courtesy of Culver Pictures, Inc.

struggle to alter the form of society, and thereby get a bigger chunk of benefits for its members. Gompers aimed to reach the same goal by raising day-to-day wages and improving working conditions. The AFL grew rapidly until after World War I, at which point its membership exceeded 5.5 million people.

The 1920s was a period of stagnation and decline for the U.S. union movement. This was a result of several events, including a postwar depression, manufacturers' renewed resistance to unions, Samuel Gompers's death, and the apparent prosperity of the 1920s. By late 1929, due to the Great Depression, millions of workers (including many union members) had lost their jobs. By 1933, union membership was down to less than 3 million workers.

Membership began to rise again in the mid-1930s. As part of his New Deal programs, President Franklin Delano Roosevelt passed the National Industrial Recovery Act, which made it easier for labor to organize. Other federal laws as well as prosperity and World War II also contributed to the rapid increase in members, which topped out at about 21 million workers in the 1970s. Union membership has fallen since then. Reasons include the shift from manufacturing to service jobs and new legislation (such as occupational safety laws) that provides the sorts of protections that workers could once only obtain from their unions.[9]

Why Do Workers Organize?

Experts have spent much time and money trying to discover why workers unionize, and they've proposed many theories. Yet there is no simple answer to the question, partly because each worker probably joins for his or her own reasons.

However, workers don't unionize just to get more pay or better working conditions, though these are important. For example, recent median weekly wages for union workers was $781, while that for nonunion workers was $612.[10] Union workers also generally receive significantly more holidays, sick leave, unpaid leave, insurance plan benefits, long-term disability benefits, and various other benefits than nonunion workers do. Unions also seem to have been able to somewhat reduce the impact of (but obviously not eliminate) downsizings and wage cuts in most industries.[11]

Besides money, two other factors—employer unfairness and the union's power—are also important. In one Australia-based firm, researchers found that "individuals who believe that the company rules or policies were administered unfairly or to their detriment were more likely to turn to unions. . . ."[12] But, to vote pro-union, the employees also had to believe the union could improve their wages, benefits, and treatment.

The Bottom Line

The bottom line is that the urge to unionize often boils down to the belief on the part of workers that it is only through unity that they can protect themselves from unilateral management whims. When Kaiser Permanente's San Francisco Medical Center cut back on vacation and sick leave for its pharmacists and other workers, the pharmacists' union, the Guild for Professional Pharmacists, won back the lost vacation days. As one staff pharmacist said, "Kaiser is a pretty benevolent employer, but there's always the pressure to squeeze a little."[13] One labor relations lawyer puts it this way, "The one major thing unions offer is making you a 'for cause' instead of an 'at will' employee, which guarantees a hearing and arbitration if you're fired."[14] So, in practice, low morale, fear of job loss, and arbitrary management actions help foster unionization. Employers ignore that at their peril.

In some respects, things have not changed in years. Here is how one writer describes the motivation behind the early (1900s) unionization of automobile workers:

> In the years to come, economic issues would make the headlines when union and management met in negotiations. But in the early years, the rate of pay was not the major complaint of the autoworkers. . . . Specifically, the principal grievances of the autoworkers were the speed-up of production and the lack of any kind of job security. As production tapered off, the order in which workers

were laid off was determined largely by the whim of foremen and other supervisors. . . . Generally, what the workers revolted against was the lack of human dignity and individuality, and a working relationship that was massively impersonal, cold, and nonhuman. They wanted to be treated like human beings—not like faceless clock card numbers.[15]

What Do Unions Want?

We can generalize by saying that unions have two sets of aims, one for *union security* and one for *improved wages, hours, working conditions,* and *benefits* for their members.

Union Security

First and probably foremost, unions seek security for themselves. They fight hard for the right to represent a firm's workers, and to be the exclusive bargaining agent for all employees in the unit. (As such, they negotiate contracts for all employees, including those not members of the union.) Five types of union security are possible:

1. **Closed shop.**[16] The company can hire only current union members. Congress outlawed closed shops in interstate commerce in 1947, but they still exist in some states for particular industries (such as printing). They account for fewer than 5% of union contracts.
2. **Union shop.** The company can hire nonunion people, but they must join the union after a prescribed period and pay dues. (If not, they can be fired.) These account for about 73% of union contracts. Unions and employers also tend to negotiate variations of the union shop (for instance, letting older workers quit the union when the contract ends).
3. **Agency shop.** Employees who do not belong to the union still must pay the union an amount equal to union dues (on the assumption that the union's efforts benefit *all* the workers).
4. **Preferential shop.** Union members get preference in hiring, but the employer can still hire union members.
5. **Maintenance of membership arrangement.** Employees do not have to belong to the union. However, union members employed by the firm must maintain membership in the union for the contract period. These account for about 4% of union agreements.

Not all states give unions the right to require union membership as a condition of employment. **Right to work** is a term used to describe "state statutory or constitutional provisions banning the requirement of union membership as a condition of employment."[17] *Right-to-work laws* don't outlaw unions. They do outlaw (within those states) any form of union security. This understandably inhibits union formation in those states. As of 2008, there were 23 right-to-work states.[18] Several years ago, Oklahoma became the 22nd state to pass right-to-work legislation. Some believe that this—combined with a loss of manufacturing jobs—explains why Oklahoma's union membership dropped dramatically in the next 3 years.[19]

Improved Wages, Hours, and Benefits

Once the union ensures its security at the company, it fights to improve its members' wages, hours, and working conditions. The typical labor agreement also gives the union a role in other human resource activities, including recruiting, selecting, compensating, promoting, training, and discharging employees.

The AFL-CIO

The American Federation of Labor and Congress of Industrial Organizations (AFL-CIO) is a voluntary federation of about 56 national and international labor unions in the United States. The separate AFL and CIO merged in 1955. For many people in the United States, the AFL-CIO is synonymous with the word *union*.

There are three layers in the structure of the AFL-CIO (and most other U.S. unions). First, there is the local union. This is the union the worker joins, and to which he or she pays dues. The local union also usually signs the collective bargaining agreement determining the wages and working conditions. The local is in turn a single chapter in the national union. For example, if you were a teacher in Detroit, you would belong to the local union there, which is one of hundreds of local chapters of the American Federation of Teachers, their national union (most unions actually call themselves international unions). The third layer in the structure is the national federation, in this case, the AFL-CIO.

Some people think of the AFL-CIO as the most important part of the labor movement, but it is not. The AFL-CIO itself really has little power, except what its constituent unions let it exercise. Thus, the president of the teachers' union wields more power in that capacity than in his capacity as a vice president of the AFL-CIO. Yet as a practical matter, the AFL-CIO does act as a spokesperson for labor, and its new president, Richard Trumka, has political influence in excess of a figurehead president.

Union federation membership is in flux. Several years ago, six big unions—the Service Employees' International Union (SEIU), the International Brotherhood of Teamsters, the United Food and Commercial Workers, the United Farm Workers, the Laborers International Union, and UNITE HERE (which represents garment and service workers) left the AFL-CIO and established their own federation, called the Change to Win Coalition. Together, the departing unions represented over one-quarter of the AFL-CIO's membership and budget. Change to Win plans to be more aggressive about organizing workers than they say the AFL-CIO was.[20] Then in 2009, UNITE HERE rejoined the AFL-CIO, possibly slowing Change to Win's momentum.

UNIONS AND THE LAW

Until about 1930, there were no special labor laws. Employers were not required to engage in collective bargaining with employees and were virtually unrestrained in their behavior toward unions; the use of spies and firing of union agitators were widespread. "Yellow dog" contracts, whereby management could require nonunion membership as a condition for employment, were widely enforced. Most union weapons—even strikes—were illegal.

This one-sided situation lasted until the Great Depression (around 1930). Since then, in response to changing public attitudes, values, and economic conditions, labor law has gone through three clear periods: from "strong encouragement" of unions, to "modified encouragement coupled with regulation," and finally to "detailed regulation of internal union affairs."[21]

closed shop
A form of union security in which the company can hire only union members. This was outlawed in 1947 but still exists in some industries (such as printing).

union shop
A form of union security in which the company can hire nonunion people, but they must join the union after a prescribed period of time and pay dues. (If they do not, they can be fired.)

agency shop
A form of union security in which employees who do not belong to the union must still pay union dues on the assumption that union efforts benefit all workers.

preferential shop
Union members get preference in hiring, but the employer can still hire union members.

right to work
A term used to describe state statutory or constitutional provisions banning the requirement of union membership as a condition of employment.

2 Discuss the main features of at least three major pieces of labor legislation.

Period of Strong Encouragement: The Norris-LaGuardia (1932) and National Labor Relations or Wagner Acts (1935)

The **Norris-LaGuardia Act of 1932** set the stage for a new era in which union activity was encouraged. It guaranteed to each employee the right to bargain collectively "free from interference, restraint, or coercion." It declared yellow dog contracts unenforceable. And it limited the courts' abilities to issue injunctions (stop orders) for activities such as peaceful picketing and payment of strike benefits.

Yet this act did little to restrain employers from fighting labor organizations by whatever means they could find. So in 1935, Congress passed the **National Labor Relations (or Wagner) Act** to add teeth to Norris-LaGuardia. It did this by (1) banning certain unfair labor practices, (2) providing for secret-ballot elections and majority rule for determining whether a firm's employees would unionize, and (3) creating the **National Labor Relations Board (NLRB)** to enforce these two provisions.

Unfair Employer Labor Practices

The Wagner Act deemed "statutory wrongs" (but not crimes) five unfair labor practices used by employers:

1. It is unfair for employers to "interface with, restrain, or coerce employees" in exercising their legally sanctioned right of self-organization.
2. It is unfair for company representatives to dominate or interfere with either the formation or the administration of labor unions. Among other specific management actions found to be unfair under these first two practices are bribing employees, using company spy systems, moving a business to avoid unionization, and black-listing union sympathizers.
3. Employers are prohibited from discriminating in any way against employees for their legal union activities.
4. Employers are forbidden to discharge or discriminate against employees simply because the latter file unfair practice charges against the company.
5. Finally, it is an unfair labor practice for employers to refuse to bargain collectively with their employees' duly chosen representatives.

Unions file an unfair labor practice charge (see Figure 15-1) with the National Labor Relations Board. The board then investigates the charge and decides if it should take action. Possible actions include dismissal of the complaint, request for an injunction against the employer, or an order that the employer cease and desist.

Such complaints are commonplace. When the former Knight Ridder Company consolidated its separate online operations into what was at the time the new KnightRidder.com, it triggered a labor dispute. Citing possible unfair labor practices, the unions asked the NLRB to investigate whether KnightRidder.com violated labor law by not negotiating the transfer of workers with the union.[22] (The McClatchy Company subsequently bought Knight Ridder's newspapers.)

From 1935 to 1947

Union membership increased quickly after passage of the Wagner Act in 1935. Other factors such as an improving economy and aggressive union leadership contributed to this rise. But by the mid-1940s, after the end of World War II, the tide had begun to turn. Largely because of a series of massive postwar strikes, public policy began to shift against what many viewed as union excesses. The stage was set for passage of the Taft-Hartley Act.

Period of Modified Encouragement Coupled with Regulation: The Taft-Hartley Act (1947)

The **Taft-Hartley (or Labor Management Relations) Act of 1947** reflected the public's less enthusiastic attitude toward unions. It amended the National Labor Relations (Wagner) Act by limiting unions in four ways: (1) prohibiting unfair union labor

FIGURE 15-1 NLRB Form 501: Filing an Unfair Labor Practice

FORM NLRB 501
(2 81)

FORM EXEMPT UNDER
44 U.S.C. 3512

UNITED STATES OF AMERICA
NATIONAL LABOR RELATIONS BOARD
CHARGE AGAINST EMPLOYER

INSTRUCTIONS: File an original and 4 copies of this charge with NLRB Regional Director for the region in which the alleged unfair labor practice occurred or is occurring.	DO NOT WRITE IN THIS SPACE CASE NO.	DATE FILE

1. EMPLOYER AGAINST WHOM CHARGE IS BROUGHT

a. NAME OF EMPLOYER		b. NUMBER OF WORKERS EMPLOYED
c. ADDRESS OF ESTABLISHMENT (*street and number, city, State, and ZIP code*)	d. EMPLOYER REPRESENTATIVE TO CONTACT	e. PHONE NO.
f. TYPE OF ESTABLISHMENT (*factory, mine, wholesaler, etc.*)	g. IDENTIFY PRINCIPAL PRODUCT OR SERVICE	

h. THE ABOVE-NAMED EMPLOYER HAS ENGAGED IN AND IS ENGAGING IN UNFAIR LABOR PRACTICES WITHIN THE MEANING OF SECTION 8(a), SUBSECTIONS (1) AND ______ (*list subsections*) OF THE NATIONAL LABOR RELATIONS ACT, AND THESE UNFAIR LABOR PRACTICES ARE UNFAIR LABOR PRACTICES AFFECTING COMMERCE WITHIN THE MEANING OF THE ACT.

2. BASIS OF THE CHARGE (*be specific as to facts, names, addresses, plants involved, dates, places, etc.*)

BY THE ABOVE AND OTHER ACTS, THE ABOVE-NAMED EMPLOYER HAS INTERFERED WITH, RESTRAINED, AND COERCED EMPLOYEES IN THE EXERCISE OF THE RIGHTS GUARANTEED IN SECTION 7 OF THE ACT.

3. FULL NAME OF PARTY FILING CHARGE (*if labor organization, give full name, including local name and number*)

4a. ADDRESS (*street and number, city, State, and ZIP code*)	4b. TELEPHONE NO.

5. FULL NAME OF NATIONAL OR INTERNATIONAL LABOR ORGANIZATION OF WHICH IT IS AN AFFILIATE OR CONSTITUENT UNIT (*to be filled in when charge is filed by a labor organization*)

6. DECLARATION

I declare that I have read the above charge and that the statements therein are true to the best of my knowledge and belief.

By ______
(signature of representative or person filing charge) (title, if any)

Address ______
(telephone number) (date)

WILLFULLY FALSE STATEMENTS ON THIS CHARGE CAN BE PUNISHED BY FINE AND IMPRISONMENT
(*U.S. CODE, TITLE 18, SECTION 1001*)

Norris-LaGuardia Act (1932)
This law marked the beginning of the era of strong encouragement of unions and guaranteed to each employee the right to bargain collectively "free from interference, restraint, or coercion."

National Labor Relations (or Wagner) Act
This law banned certain types of unfair practices and provided for secret-ballot elections and majority rule for determining whether a firm's employees want to unionize.

National Labor Relations Board (NLRB)
The agency created by the Wagner Act to investigate unfair labor practice charges and to provide for secret-ballot elections and majority rule in determining whether or not a firm's employees want a union.

Taft-Hartley Act (1947)
Also known as the *Labor Management Relations Act*, this law prohibited unfair union labor practices and enumerated the rights of employees as union members. It also enumerated the rights of employers.

practices, (2) enumerating the rights of employees as union members, (3) enumerating the rights of employers, and (4) allowing the President of the United States to bar temporarily national emergency strikes.

Unfair Union Labor Practices

The Taft-Hartley Act enumerated several labor practices that unions were prohibited from engaging in:

1. First, it banned unions from *restraining or coercing employees* from exercising their guaranteed bargaining rights. (Some union actions courts have held illegal include stating to an anti-union employee that he or she will lose his or her job once the union gains recognition, and issuing patently false statements during union organizing campaigns.)
2. It is also an unfair labor practice for a union to *cause an employer to discriminate* in any way against an employee in order to encourage or discourage his or her membership in a union. For example, the union cannot try to force an employer to fire a worker because he or she doesn't attend union meetings or refuses to join a union. There is one exception: Where a closed or union shop prevails (and union membership is therefore a prerequisite to employment), the union may demand the discharge of someone who fails to pay his or her initiation fees and dues.
3. It is an unfair labor practice for a union to *refuse to bargain in good faith* with the employer about wages, hours, and other employment conditions. Certain strikes and boycotts are also unfair practices.
4. It is an unfair labor practice for a union to engage in *featherbedding* (requiring an employer to pay an employee for services not performed).

Rights of Employees The Taft-Hartley Act protected the rights of employees against their unions in other ways. For example, many people felt that compulsory unionism violated the basic right of freedom of association. Legitimized by Taft-Hartley, new right-to-work laws quickly sprung up in 19 (now 23) states (mainly in the South and Southwest). In New York, for example, in many printing firms you can't work as a press operator unless you belong to a printers' union. In Florida, such union shops—except those covered by the Railway Labor Act—are illegal, and printing shops typically employ both union and nonunion operators. Even today, union membership varies widely by state, from a high of 26.8% in New York to a low of 3.7% in South Carolina.[23] This *employee rights provision* also required the employee's authorization before the union could have dues subtracted from his or her paycheck.

In general, the Labor Relations (Taft-Hartley) Act does not restrain unions from unfair labor practices to the extent that the law does employers. It says unions may not restrain or coerce employees. However, "violent or otherwise threatening behavior or clearly coercive or intimidating union activities are necessary before the NLRB will find an unfair labor practice."[24] Examples here would include physical assaults or threats of violence, economic reprisals, and mass picketing that restrains the lawful entry or leaving of a work site.

Rights of Employers The Taft-Hartley Act also explicitly gave *employers* certain rights. First, it gave them full freedom to express their views concerning union organization. For example, you as a manager can tell your employees that in your opinion unions are worthless, dangerous to the economy, and immoral. You can even (generally) hint that unionization and subsequent high-wage demands might result in the permanent closing of the plant (but not its relocation). Employers can set forth the union's record concerning violence and corruption, if appropriate. In fact, the only major restraint is that employers must avoid threats, promises, coercion, and direct interference with workers who are trying to reach a decision. There can be no threat of reprisal or force or promise of benefit.[25]

Furthermore, the employer (1) cannot meet with employees on company time within 24 hours of an election or (2) suggest to employees that they vote against the union while they are at home or in the employer's office (although he or she can do so while in their work area or where they normally gather).

National Emergency Strikes The Taft-Hartley Act also allows the U.S. President to intervene in **national emergency strikes**. These are strikes (for example, by railroad workers) that might "imperil the national health and safety." The President may appoint a board of inquiry and, based on its report, apply for an injunction restraining the strike for 60 days. If the parties don't reach a settlement during that time, the President can have the injunction extended for another 20 days. During this last period, employees take a secret ballot to ascertain their willingness to accept the employer's last offer.

Period of Detailed Regulation of Internal Union Affairs: The Landrum-Griffin Act (1959) In the 1950s, Senate investigations revealed unsavory practices on the part of some unions, and the result was the **Landrum-Griffin Act** (officially, the **Labor Management Reporting and Disclosure Act**) **of 1959**. An overriding aim of this act was to protect union members from possible wrongdoing on the part of their unions. Like Taft-Hartley, it also amended the National Labor Relations (Wagner) Act.

First, the law contains a bill of rights for union members. Among other things, it provides for certain rights in the nomination of candidates for union office. It also affirms a member's right to sue his or her union and ensures that the union cannot fine or suspend a member without due process.

This act also laid out rules regarding union elections. For example, national and international unions must elect officers at least once every 5 years, using some type of secret-ballot mechanism. And it regulates the kind of person who can serve as a union officer. For example, it bars persons convicted of felonies (bribery, murder, and so on) from holding union officer positions for a period of 5 years after conviction.

Senate investigators also discovered flagrant examples of employer wrongdoing. Employers and their "labor relations consultants" had bribed union agents and officers, for example. That had been a federal crime starting with the passage of the Taft-Hartley Act. But Landrum-Griffin greatly expanded the list of unlawful employer actions. For example, companies can no longer pay their own employees to entice them not to join the union, and must report use of labor consultants.

3 Present examples of what to expect during the union drive and election.

THE UNION DRIVE AND ELECTION

It is through the union drive and election that a union tries to be recognized to represent employees. Supervisors need to understand this process, which has five basic steps.

Step 1. Initial Contact

During the initial contact stage, the union determines the employees' interest in organizing, and establishes an organizing committee.

The initiative for the first contact between the employees and the union may come from the employees, from a union already representing other employees of the firm, or from a union representing workers elsewhere. In any case, there is an initial contact.

Once an employer becomes a target, a union official usually assigns a representative to assess employee interest. The representative visits the firm to determine whether enough employees are interested to make a campaign worthwhile. He or she also identifies employees who would make good leaders in the organizing campaign and calls them together to create an organizing committee. The objective

national emergency strikes
Strikes that might "imperil the national health and safety."

Landrum-Griffin Act (1959)
Also known as the *Labor Management Reporting and Disclosure Act*, this law aimed at protecting union members from possible wrongdoing on the part of their unions.

here is to educate the committee about the benefits of forming a union and the law and procedures involved in forming a local union.

The union must follow certain rules when it starts contacting employees. The law allows organizers to solicit employees for membership as long as the effort doesn't endanger the performance or safety of the employees. Therefore, much of the contact takes place off the job, perhaps at home or at eating places near work. Organizers can also safely contact employees on company grounds during off hours (such as lunch or break time). Yet, in practice, there will be much informal organizing going on at the workplace as employees debate organizing. This initial contact stage may be deceptively quiet. Sometimes the first inkling management has of the campaign is the distribution or posting of handbills soliciting union membership.

Much soliciting today will be via e-mail, but prohibiting employees from sending pro-union e-mail messages on company e-mail is easier said than done. You can't discriminate against union activities, so prohibiting only union e-mail may violate NLRB decisions. And barring workers from using e-mail for all non–work-related topics may be futile if the company actually does little to stop it.

Labor Relations Consultants Both management and unions typically use "labor relations consultants," and these are increasingly influencing the unionization process. The consultants may be law firms, researchers, psychologists, labor relations specialists, or public relations firms. Some are former union organizers who now represent the employers.[26]

In any case, their role is to provide advice and related services not just when a vote is expected (although this is when most of them are used), but at other times, too. For the employer, the consultant's services may range from ensuring that the firm properly fills out routine labor relations forms to managing the union campaign. Unions may use public relations firms to improve their image, or specialists to manage corporate campaigns. (These aim to pressure shareholders and creditors to get management to agree to the union's demands.)

The widespread use of such consultants—only some of whom are actually lawyers—raises the question of whether some have advised their clients to engage in questionable activities. One tactic, for instance, is to delay the union vote with lengthy hearings at the NLRB. The longer the delay in the vote, they argue, the more time the employer has to drill anti-union propaganda into the employees.

Union Salting Unions are not without creative ways to win elections. The National Labor Relations Board defines **union salting** as "placing of union members on nonunion job sites for the purpose of organizing." Critics claim that "salts" also often interfere with business operations and harass employees.[27] The U.S. Supreme Court ruled that union salts are "employees" under the National Labor Relations Act; the NLRB will require that employers pay salts if they fire them for trying to organize.[28] For managers, the solution is to make sure you know whom you're hiring. However, not hiring someone simply because, as a member of the local union, he or she might be pro-union or a union salt would be discriminatory.[29]

Step 2. Obtaining Authorization Cards

For the union to petition the NLRB for the right to hold an election, it must show that a sizable number of employees may be interested in organizing. The next step is thus for union organizers to try to get the employees to sign **authorization cards**. Among other things, these usually authorize the union to seek a representation election and state that the employee has applied to join the union. Thirty percent of the eligible employees in an appropriate bargaining unit must sign before the union can petition the NLRB for an election.

This is a dangerous time for supervisors. During this stage, both union and management use propaganda. The union claims it can improve working conditions, raise wages, increase benefits, and generally get the workers better deals. Management can attack the union on ethical and moral grounds and cite the cost of union membership. Management can also explain its accomplishments, express facts and opinions, and explain the law applicable to organizing campaigns. However, neither side can threaten, bribe, or coerce employees. And an employer (or supervisor) may not make promises of benefits to employees or make unilateral changes in terms and conditions of employment that were not planned to be implemented prior to the onset of union organizing activity.

Steps to Take Management can take several steps with respect to the authorization cards themselves. For example, the NLRB ruled an employer might lawfully inform employees of their right to revoke their authorization cards, even when employees have not asked for such information. The employer can also distribute pamphlets that explain just how employees can revoke their cards. However, the law prohibits any material assistance to employees such as postage or stationery.

Similarly, it is an unfair labor practice to tell employees they can't sign a card. What you *can* do is prepare supervisors so they can explain what the card actually authorizes the union to do—including seeking a representation election, designating the union as bargaining representative, and subjecting the employee to union rules. The latter is especially important. The union, for instance, may force the employee to picket and fine any member who does not comply with union instructions. Explaining the serious legal and practical implications of signing the card can thus be an effective weapon. Unions today use the Internet to distribute and collect authorization cards.

One thing managers should *not* do is look through signed authorization cards if confronted with them by union representatives. The NLRB could construe that as an unfair labor practice, as spying on those who signed. Doing so could also later form the basis of a charge alleging discrimination due to union activity, if the firm subsequently disciplines someone who signed a card.

During this stage, unions can picket the company, subject to three constraints: (1) The union must file a petition for an election within 30 days after the start of picketing; (2) the firm cannot already be lawfully recognizing another union; and (3) there cannot have been a valid NLRB election during the past 12 months.

Step 3. Hold a Hearing

Once the union collects the authorization cards, one of three things can occur. If the employer chooses not to contest *union recognition* at all, then the parties need no hearing, and a special "consent election" is held. If the employer chooses not to contest the union's *right to an election,* and/or the scope of the bargaining unit, and/or which employees are eligible to vote in the election, no hearing is needed and the parties can stipulate an election. If an employer *does* wish to contest the union's right, it can insist on a hearing to determine those issues. An employer's decision about whether to insist on a hearing is a strategic one. Management bases it on the facts of each case, and on whether it feels it needs more time to try to persuade employees not to elect a union.

Most companies do contest the union's right to represent their employees, claiming that a significant number of them don't really want the union. It is at this point that the National Labor Relations Board gets involved. The union usually contacts the NLRB, which requests a hearing. The regional director of the NLRB then sends a hearing officer to investigate. The examiner sends both management and union a notice of representation hearing (NLRB Form 852; see Figure 15-2) that states the time and place of the hearing.

union salting
A union organizing tactic by which workers who are in fact employed full-time by a union as undercover organizers are hired by unwitting employers.

authorization cards
In order to petition for a union election, the union must show that at least 30% of employees may be interested in being unionized. Employees indicate this interest by signing authorization cards.

FIGURE 15-2 NLRB Form 852: Notice of Representation Hearing

FORM NLRB-852
(6-61)

UNITED STATES OF AMERICA
BEFORE THE NATIONAL LABOR RELATIONS BOARD

Case No.

NOTICE OF REPRESENTATION HEARING

The Petitioner, above named, having heretofore filed a Petition pursuant to Section 9 (c) of the National Labor Relations Act, as amended, 29 U.S.C. Sec 151 et seq., copy of which Petition is hereto attached, and it appearing that a question affecting commerce has arisen concerning the representation of employees described by such Petition.

YOU ARE HEREBY NOTIFIED that, pursuant to Section 3(b) and 9(c) of the Act, on the
day of , 20 , at

a hearing will be conducted before a hearing officer of the National Labor Relations Board upon the question of representation affecting commerce which has arisen, at which time and place the parties will have the right to appear in person or otherwise, and give testimony.

Signed at on the day of , 20

Regional Director, Region
National Labor Relations Board

The hearing addresses several issues. First, does the record indicate there is enough evidence to hold an election? (For example, did 30% or more of the employees in an appropriate bargaining unit sign the authorization cards?) Second, the examiner must decide what the bargaining unit will be. The **bargaining unit** is the group of employees that the union will be authorized to represent and bargain for collectively. If the entire organization is the bargaining unit, the union will represent all nonsupervisory, nonmanagerial, and nonconfidential employees, even though the union may be oriented mostly toward blue-collar workers. (Professional and nonprofessional employees can be included in the same bargaining unit only if the professionals agree.) If your firm disagrees with the examiner's bargaining unit decision, it can challenge the decision. This will require a separate NLRB ruling.

The NLRB hearing addresses other issues. These include, "Does the employer qualify for coverage by the NLRB?" and "Is the union a labor organization within the meaning of the National Labor Relations Act?"

If the results of the hearing are favorable for the union, the NLRB will order holding an election. It will issue a Notice of Election (NLRB Form 707) to that effect, for the employer to post.

Step 4. The Campaign

During the campaign that precedes the election, union and employer appeal to employees for their votes. The union will emphasize that it will prevent unfairness, set up grievance and seniority systems, and improve wages. Union strength, they'll say, will give employees a voice in determining wages and working conditions. Management will stress that improvements like those don't require unions and that wages are equal to or better than they would be with a union. Management will also emphasize the financial cost of union dues; the fact that the union is an "outsider"; and that if the union wins, a strike may follow. It can even attack the union on ethical and moral grounds, while insisting that employees will not be as well off and may lose freedom. But neither side can threaten, bribe, or coerce employees.

Step 5. The Election

The election occurs within 30 to 60 days after the NLRB issues its Decision and Direction of Election. The election is by secret ballot; the NLRB provides the ballots (see Figure 15-3), voting booth, and ballot box, and counts the votes and certifies the results.

The union becomes the employees' representative if it wins the election, and winning means getting a majority of the votes *cast*, not a majority of the total workers in the bargaining unit. (Also keep in mind that if an employer commits an unfair labor practice, the NLRB may reverse a "no union" election. As representatives of their employer, supervisors must therefore be careful not to commit unfair practices.)

Several things influence whether the union wins the certification election. Unions have a higher probability of success in geographic areas with a higher percentage of union workers. High unemployment seems to lead to poorer results for the union, perhaps because employees fear that unionization efforts might result in reduced job security or employer retaliation. Unions usually carefully pick the size

FIGURE 15-3 Sample NLRB Ballot

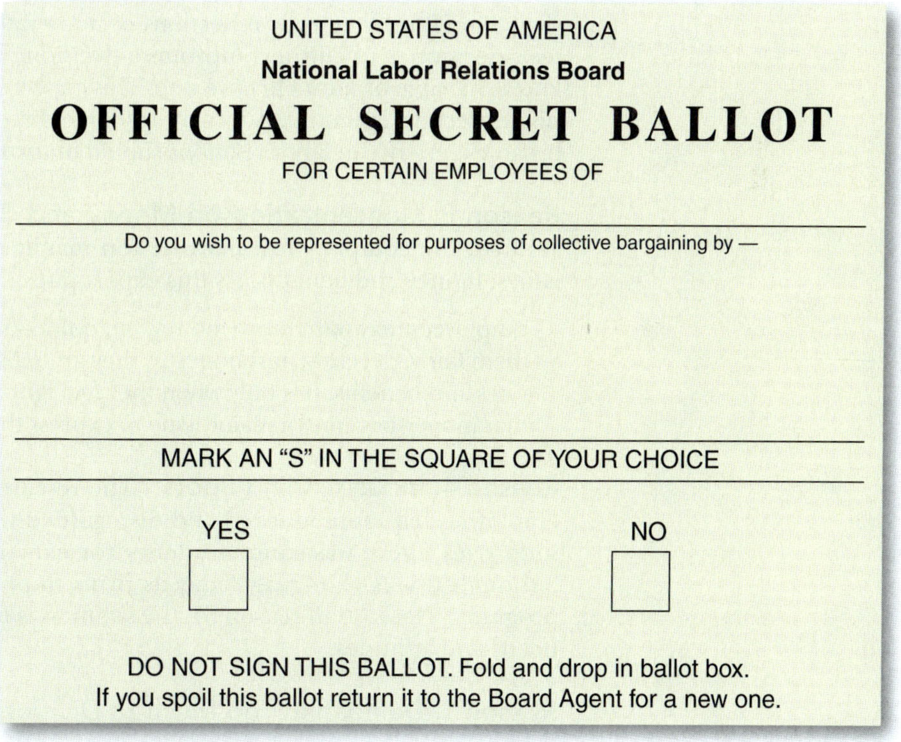
UNITED STATES OF AMERICA

National Labor Relations Board

OFFICIAL SECRET BALLOT

FOR CERTAIN EMPLOYEES OF

Do you wish to be represented for purposes of collective bargaining by —

MARK AN "S" IN THE SQUARE OF YOUR CHOICE

YES ☐ NO ☐

DO NOT SIGN THIS BALLOT. Fold and drop in ballot box.
If you spoil this ballot return it to the Board Agent for a new one.

bargaining unit
The group of employees the union will be authorized to represent.

of their bargaining unit (all clerical employees in the company, only those at one facility, and so on) because the larger the bargaining unit, the smaller the probability of union victory. The more workers vote, the less likely a union victory, probably because more workers who are not strong supporters vote. The union is important, too: The Teamsters union is less likely to win a representation election than other unions, for instance.[30]

4 Describe five ways to lose an NLRB election.

How to Lose an NLRB Election

Over the years, unions typically won about 55% of elections held each year.[31] According to expert Matthew Goodfellow, there is no sure way employers can win elections. However, there are five sure ways to lose one.[32]

Reason 1. Asleep at the Switch In one study, in 68% of the companies that lost to the union, executives were caught unaware. In these companies, turnover and absenteeism had increased, productivity was erratic, and safety was poor. Grievance procedures were rare. When the first reports of authorization cards began trickling back to top managers, they usually responded with a barrage of letters describing how the company was "one big family" and calling for a "team effort." As Goodfellow observes,

> Yet the best strategy is to not be caught asleep in the first place: Overall, prudence dictates that management spend time and effort even when the atmosphere is calm testing the temperature of employee sentiments and finding ways to remove irritants. Doing that cuts down on the possibility that an election will ever take place.[33]

Reason 2. Appointing a Committee Of the losing companies, 36% formed a committee to manage the campaign. According to the expert, there are three problems in doing so: (1) Promptness is essential in an election situation, and committees are notorious for moving slowly. (2) Most committee members are NLRB neophytes. Their views therefore are mostly reflections of hope rather than experience. (3) A committee's decision is usually a compromise decision. The result isn't necessarily the most knowledgeable or most effective one. This expert suggests giving full responsibility to a single, decisive executive. A human resource director and a consultant or adviser with broad experience in labor relations should in turn assist this person.

Reason 3. Concentrating on Money and Benefits In 54% of the elections studied, the company lost because top management concentrated on the wrong issues: money and benefits. As this expert puts it:

> Employees may want more money, but quite often, if they feel the company treats them fairly, decently, and honestly, they are satisfied with reasonable, competitive rates and benefits. It is only when they feel ignored, uncared for, and disregarded that money becomes a major issue to express their dissatisfaction.[34]

Reason 4. Industry Blind Spots The researcher found that in some industries, employees felt more ignored and disregarded than in others. In highly automated industries, there was some tendency for executives to ignore hourly employees, although this is changing today as firms implement more quality improvement programs. Here (as in reason 3), the solution is to pay more attention to employees' needs and attitudes.

Reason 5. Delegating Too Much to Divisions For companies with plants scattered around the country, unionizing one or more plants tends to lead to unionizing others. The solution is, don't abdicate all personnel and industrial relations decisions to plant managers.[35] Dealing effectively with unions—monitoring employees' attitudes, reacting properly when the union appears, and so on—generally requires centralized guidance from the main office and its human resources staff.

The other side of the coin is this: What can unions do to boost their chances they'll win the election? The accompanying "Evidence-Based HR" feature presents evidence concerning union tactics for which managers should be vigilant.

EVIDENCE-BASED HR

What Can I Expect the Union to Do to Win the Election?

A researcher analyzed data from 261 NLRB elections. Her aim was to identify the variables that appear to explain whether the union wins or loses the election.

She found two things. First, the union's tactics explained "more of the variance in election outcomes than any other group of variables, including employer tactics, bargaining unit demographics, organizer background, election background, employer characteristics, and election environment." So, what the union does is pivotal.

Second, she found that the best way for unions to win is to pursue what she calls a "rank and file strategy." You can expect such a campaign to include six specific union tactics.[36]

1. "Reliance on a slow, underground, person-to-person campaign using house calls, small group meetings, and pre-union associations to develop leadership and union commitment, and prepare workers for employer anti-union strategies before the employer becomes aware of the campaign."
2. The union will focus on active rank-and-file participation, including a large rank-and-file organizing committee reflecting the different interest groups in the bargaining unit.
3. The union will pressure for a first contract early in the organizing process.
4. The union will use "inside and outside pressure tactics to build worker commitment and compel the employer to run a fair campaign."
5. There will be an emphasis during the organizing campaign on issues such as respect, dignity, and fairness, not just traditional bread-and-butter issues like wages, benefits, and job security.
6. The union will go all out to win. This includes the involvement of the international union in local union organizing campaigns, and the use of rank-and-file volunteers from already organized bargaining units.

The Supervisor's Role

Supervisors are an employer's first line of defense when it comes to the unionizing effort. They are often in the best position to sense evolving employee attitude problems, for instance, and to discover the first signs of union activity. Unfortunately, there's another side to that coin: They can also inadvertently take actions that hurt their employer's union-related efforts.

Supervisors therefore need special training. Specifically, they must be knowledgeable about what they can and can't do legally to hamper organizing activities. Unfair labor practices could (1) cause the NLRB to hold a new election after your company has won a previous election, or (2) cause your company to forfeit the second election and go directly to contract negotiation.

In one case, a plant superintendent reacted to a union's initial organizing attempt by prohibiting distribution of union literature in the plant's lunchroom. Since solicitation of off-duty workers in nonwork areas is generally legal, the company subsequently allowed the union to post literature on the company's bulletin board and to distribute literature in nonworking areas inside the plant. However, the NLRB still ruled that the initial act of prohibiting distribution of the literature was an unfair labor practice, one not "made right" by the company's subsequent efforts. The NLRB used the superintendent's action as one reason for invalidating an election that the company had won.[37]

Some TIPS Supervisors can use the acronym TIPS to remember what *not* to do during the organizing or preelection campaigns.[38] *Do not* Threaten, Interrogate, make Promises to, or Spy on employees. Use FORE for what you may do. *You may* give employees Facts (like what signing the authorization card means), express your Opinion about unions, explain factually correct Rules (such as that the law permits permanently replacing striking employees), and share your Experiences about unions. Figure 15-4 summarizes some other things supervisors should keep in mind.

Rules Regarding Literature and Solicitation

The employer can legally take steps to restrict union organizing activity.[39]

1. Employers can always bar nonemployees from soliciting employees during their work time—that is, when the employee is on duty and not on a break.
2. Employers can usually stop employees from soliciting other employees for any purpose if one or both employees are on paid-duty time and not on a break.
3. Most employers (generally not including retail stores, shopping centers, and certain other employers) can bar nonemployees from the building's interiors and work areas as a right of private property owners. They can also sometimes bar nonemployees from exterior private areas—such as parking lots—if the reason is not just to interfere with union organizers.[40]
4. Employers can deny on- or off-duty employees access to interior or exterior areas only if they can show the rule is required for reasons of production, safety, or discipline.

Again, such restrictions are valid only if the employer doesn't discriminate against the union. For example, if the employer lets employees collect money for baby gifts, to sell Avon products or Tupperware, or to engage in other solicitation during their working time, it may not be able lawfully to prohibit them from union soliciting during work time. Here are two examples of specific rules aimed at limiting union organizing or other activity:

> Solicitation of employees on company property during working time interferes with the efficient operation of our business. Nonemployees are not permitted to solicit employees on company property for any purpose. Except in break areas where both employees are on break or off the clock, no employee may solicit another employee during working time for any purpose.

FIGURE 15-4 Union Avoidance: What Not to Do

Source: From the BLR Newsletter "Best Practices in HR," *Business & Legal Resources, Inc.*, 141 Mill Rock Road East, Old Saybrook, CT © 2004. Reprinted with permission of the publisher. BLR© (Business and Legal Resources, Inc.).

Human resources professionals must be very careful to do the following during union activities at their companies:

- Watch what you say. Angry feelings of the moment may get you in trouble.
- Never threaten workers with what you will do or what will happen if a union comes in. Do not say, for example, that the business will close or move, that wages will go down or overtime will be eliminated, that there will be layoffs, etc.
- Don't tell union sympathizers that they will suffer in any way for their support. Don't terminate or discipline workers for engaging in union activities.
- Don't interrogate workers about union sympathizers or organizers.
- Don't ask workers to remove union screensavers or campaign buttons if you allow these things for other organizations.
- Don't treat pro-union or anti-union workers any differently.
- Don't transfer workers on the basis of union affiliation or sympathies.
- Don't ask workers how they are going to vote or how others may vote.
- Don't ask employees about union meetings or any matters related to unions. You can listen, but don't ask for any details.
- Don't promise workers benefits, promotions, or anything else if they vote against the union.
- Avoid becoming involved—in any way—in the details of the union's election or campaign, and don't participate in any petition movement against the union.
- Don't give financial aid or any support to any unions.

Any one of these practices may result in a finding of "unfair labor practices," which may in turn result in recognition of a union without an election, as well as fines for your company.

> Distribution of literature on company property not only creates a litter problem but also distracts us from our work. Nonemployees are not allowed to distribute literature on company property. Except in the performance of his or her job, an employee may not distribute literature unless both the distributor and the recipient are off the clock or on authorized break in a break area or off company premises. Special exceptions to these rules may be made by the company for especially worthwhile causes such as United Way, but written permission must first be obtained and the solicitation will be permitted only during break periods.[41]

Decertification Elections: Ousting the Union

Winning an election and signing an agreement do not necessarily mean that the union is in the company to stay. The same law that grants employees the right to unionize also gives them a way to terminate legally their union's right to represent them. The process is **decertification**. There are around 450 to 500 decertification elections each year, of which unions usually win around 30%.[42] That's actually a more favorable win rate for management than the rate for the original, representation elections.

Decertification campaigns don't differ much from certification campaigns.[43] The union organizes membership meetings and house-to-house visits, mails literature into the homes, and uses phone calls, e-mails, NLRB appeals, and (sometimes) threats and harassment to win the election.[44] For its part, management uses meetings—including one-on-one meetings, small-group meetings, and meetings with entire units—as well as legal or expert assistance, letters, improved working conditions, and subtle or not-so-subtle threats to try to influence the votes.

THE COLLECTIVE BARGAINING PROCESS

What Is Collective Bargaining?

When and if the union becomes your employees' representative, a day is set for management and labor to meet and negotiate a labor agreement. This agreement will contain specific provisions covering wages, hours, and working conditions.

What exactly is **collective bargaining**? According to the National Labor Relations Act:

> For the purpose of [this act,] to bargain collectively is the performance of the mutual obligation of the employer and the representative of the employees to meet at reasonable times and confer in good faith with respect to wages, hours, and terms and conditions of employment, or the negotiation of an agreement, or any question arising thereunder, and the execution of a written contract incorporating any agreement reached if requested by either party, but such obligation does not compel either party to agree to a proposal or require the making of a concession.

In plain language, this means that both management and labor are required by law to negotiate wage, hours, and terms and conditions of employment "in good faith."

5 Illustrate with examples bargaining that is not in good faith.

What Is Good Faith?

Good faith bargaining is the cornerstone of effective labor–management relations. It means that both parties communicate and negotiate, that they match proposals with counterproposals, and that both make every reasonable effort to arrive at an agreement. It does not mean that one party compels another to agree to a proposal.

decertification
Legal process for employees to terminate a union's right to represent them.

collective bargaining
The process through which representatives of management and the union meet to negotiate a labor agreement.

good faith bargaining
Both parties are making every reasonable effort to arrive at agreement; proposals are being matched with counterproposals.

Nor does it require that either party make any specific concessions (although as a practical matter, some may be necessary).[45]

How can you tell if bargaining is *not* in good faith? Here are 10 examples.

1. **Surface bargaining.** Going through the motions of bargaining without any real intention of completing an agreement.
2. **Inadequate concessions.** Unwillingness to compromise, even though no one is required to make a concession.
3. **Inadequate proposals and demands.** The NLRB considers the advancement of proposals to be a positive factor in determining overall good faith.
4. **Dilatory tactics.** The law requires that the parties meet and "confer at reasonable times and intervals." Obviously, refusal to meet with the union does not satisfy the positive duty imposed on the employer.
5. **Imposing conditions.** Attempts to impose conditions that are so onerous or unreasonable as to indicate bad faith.
6. **Making unilateral changes in conditions.** This is a strong indication that the employer is not bargaining with the required intent of reaching an agreement.
7. **Bypassing the representative.** The duty of management to bargain in good faith involves, at a minimum, recognition that the union representative is the one with whom the employer must deal in conducting negotiations.
8. **Committing unfair labor practices during negotiations.** Such practices may reflect poorly upon the good faith of the guilty party.
9. **Withholding information.** An employer must supply the union with information, upon request, to enable it to understand and intelligently discuss the issues raised in bargaining.
10. **Ignoring bargaining items.** Refusal to bargain on a mandatory item (one must bargain over these) or insistence on a permissive item (one may bargain over these).[46]

Of course, requiring good faith bargaining doesn't mean that negotiations can't grind to a halt. For example, Northwest Airlines wouldn't let its negotiators meet with mechanics' union representatives because, it said, the union didn't respond to company proposals the last three times they met.[47]

The Negotiating Team

Both union and management send a negotiating team to the bargaining table, and both teams usually go into the bargaining sessions having "done their homework." Union representatives will have sounded out union members on their desires and conferred with representatives of related unions.

Management uses several techniques to prepare for bargaining. First, it prepares the data on which to build its bargaining position.[48] It compiles data on pay and benefits that include comparisons with local pay rates and to rates paid for similar jobs within the industry. Data on the distribution of the workforce (in terms of age, sex, and seniority, for instance) are also important, because these factors determine what the company will actually pay out in benefits. Internal economic data regarding cost of benefits, overall earnings levels, and the amount and cost of overtime are important as well.

Management will also "cost" the current labor contract and determine the increased cost—total, per employee, and per hour—of the union's demands. It will use information from grievances and feedback from supervisors to determine what the union's demands might be, and prepare counteroffers and arguments.[49] Other popular tactics are attitude surveys to test employee reactions to various sections of the contract that management may feel require change, and informal conferences with local union leaders to discuss the operational effectiveness of the contract and to send up trial balloons on management ideas for change.

Collective bargaining experts emphasize the need to cost the union's demands carefully. One says,

> "The mistake I see most often is [HR professionals who] enter the negotiations without understanding the financial impact of things they put on the table. For example, the union wants three extra vacation days. That doesn't sound like a lot, except that in some states, if an employee leaves, you have to pay them for unused vacation time. [So] now your employer has to carry that liability on their books at all times."[50]

Bargaining Items

In practice, saying one must bargain over "wages, hours, and working conditions" is too broad. Labor law sets out categories of specific items that are subject to bargaining: These are mandatory, voluntary, and illegal items.

Voluntary (or permissible) bargaining items are neither mandatory nor illegal; they become a part of negotiations only through the joint agreement of both management and union. Neither party can compel the other to negotiate over voluntary items. You cannot hold up signing a contract because the other party refuses to bargain on a voluntary item. Benefits for retirees might be an example.

Illegal bargaining items are forbidden by law. A clause agreeing to hire union members exclusively would be illegal in a right-to-work state, for example.

Table 15-1 presents some of the 70 or so **mandatory bargaining items**, over which bargaining is mandatory under the law. They include wages, hours, rest periods, layoffs, transfers, benefits, and severance pay. Others, such as drug testing, are added as the law evolves.

TABLE 15-1 Bargaining Items

Mandatory	Permissible	Illegal
Rates of pay	Indemnity bonds	Closed shop
Wages	Management rights as to union affairs	Separation of employees based on race
Hours of employment	Pension benefits of retired employees	Discriminatory treatment
Overtime pay	Scope of the bargaining unit	
Shift differentials	Including supervisors in the contract	
Holidays	Additional parties to the contract such as the international union	
Vacations	Use of union label	
Severance pay	Settlement of unfair labor charges	
Pensions	Prices in cafeteria	
Insurance benefits	Continuance of past contract	
Profit-sharing plans	Membership of bargaining team	
Christmas bonuses	Employment of strikebreaker	
Company housing, meals, and discounts		
Employee security		
Job performance		
Union security		
Management–union relationship		
Drug testing of employees		

Source: Michael R. Carrell and Christina Heavrin, *Labor Relations and Collective Bargaining: Cases, Practices, and Law* (Upper Saddle River, NJ: Prentice Hall, 2001), p. 177.

voluntary (or permissible) bargaining items
Items in collective bargaining over which bargaining is neither illegal nor mandatory—neither party can be compelled against its wishes to negotiate over those items.

illegal bargaining items
Items in collective bargaining that are forbidden by law; for example, a clause agreeing to hire "union members exclusively" would be illegal in a right-to-work state.

mandatory bargaining items
Items in collective bargaining that a party must bargain over if they are introduced by the other party—for example, pay.

Bargaining Stages

The actual bargaining typically goes through several stages.[51] First, each side presents its demands. At this stage, both parties are usually quite far apart on some issues. Second, there is a reduction of demands. Here, each side trades off some of its demands to gain others. Third come the subcommittee studies; the parties form joint subcommittees to try to work out reasonable alternatives. Fourth, the parties reach an informal settlement, and each group goes back to its sponsor. Union representatives check informally with their superiors and the union members; management representatives check with top management. Finally, once everything is in order, the parties fine-tune and sign a formal agreement.

Bargaining Hints

Expert Reed Richardson has the following advice for bargainers:

1. Be sure to set clear objectives for every bargaining item, and be sure you understand the reason for each.
2. Do not hurry.
3. When in doubt, caucus with your associates.
4. Be well prepared with firm data supporting your position.
5. Strive to keep some flexibility in your position.
6. Don't concern yourself just with what the other party says and does; find out why.
7. Respect the importance of face saving for the other party.
8. Be alert to the real intentions of the other party—not only for goals, but also for priorities.
9. Be a good listener.
10. Build a reputation for being fair but firm.
11. Learn to control your emotions and use them as a tool.
12. As you make each bargaining move, be sure you know its relationship to all other moves.
13. Measure each move against your objectives.
14. Remember that collective bargaining is a compromise process. There is no such thing as having all the pie.
15. Try to understand the people and their personalities.[52]

Impasses, Mediation, and Strikes

In collective bargaining, an **impasse** occurs when the parties are not able to move further toward settlement. An impasse usually occurs because one party is demanding more than the other will offer. Sometimes an impasse can be resolved through a third party—a disinterested person such as a mediator or arbitrator. If the impasse is not resolved in this way, the union may call a work stoppage, or strike, to put pressure on management.[53]

Third-Party Involvement

Negotiators use three types of third-party interventions to overcome an impasse: mediation, fact finding, and arbitration. With **mediation**, a neutral third party tries to assist the principals in reaching agreement. The mediator usually holds meetings with each party to determine where each stands regarding its position, and then uses this information to find common ground for further bargaining. The mediator is always a go-between, without authority to dictate terms or make concessions. He or she communicates assessments of the likelihood of a strike, the possible settlement packages available, and the like.

In certain situations, as in a national emergency dispute, a fact finder may be appointed. A **fact finder** is a neutral party who studies the issues in a dispute and makes a public recommendation for a reasonable settlement.[54] Presidential emergency fact-finding boards have successfully resolved impasses in certain critical transportation disputes.

Arbitration is the most definitive type of third-party intervention, because the arbitrator often has the power to determine and dictate the settlement terms. Unlike mediation and fact finding, arbitration can guarantee a solution to an impasse. With *binding arbitration,* both parties are committed to accepting the arbitrator's award. With *nonbinding arbitration,* they are not. Arbitration may also be voluntary or compulsory (in other words, imposed by a government agency). In the United States, voluntary binding arbitration is the most prevalent.

There are two main topics of arbitration. *Interest arbitration* centers on working out a labor agreement; the parties use it when such agreements do not yet exist or when one or both parties are seeking to change the agreement. *Rights arbitration* really means "contract interpretation arbitration." It usually involves interpreting existing contract terms, for instance, when an employee questions the employer's right to have taken some disciplinary action.[55]

Sources of Third-Party Assistance

Various public and professional agencies make arbitrators and mediators available. For example, the American Arbitration Association (AAA) represents and provides the services of thousands of arbitrators and mediators to employers and unions. The U.S. government's Federal Mediation and Conciliation Service provides both arbitrators and mediators (see Figure 15-5).[56] For example, its Office of Arbitration Services maintains a roster of arbitrators qualified to hear and decide disputes over the interpretation or application of collective-bargaining agreements. In addition, most states provide arbitrator and mediation services.

Strikes

A **strike** is a withdrawal of labor, and there are four main types of strikes. An **economic strike** results from a failure to agree on the terms of a contract. Unions call **unfair labor practice strikes** to protest illegal conduct by the employer. A **wildcat strike** is an unauthorized strike occurring during the term of a contract. A **sympathy strike** occurs when one union strikes in support of the strike of another union.[57] For example, in sympathy with employees of the *Detroit News,* the United Auto Workers enforced a nearly 6-year boycott that prevented the papers from being sold at Detroit-area auto plants, cutting sales by about 25,000 copies a day.[58]

The number of major work stoppages (strikes involving 1,000 workers or more) peaked at about 400 per year between 1965 and 1975, and today average around 20.

Picketing, or having employees carry signs announcing their concerns near the employer's place of business, is one of the first activities to occur during a strike. Its purpose is to inform the public about the existence of the labor dispute and often to encourage others to refrain from doing business with the struck employer.

Employers can make several responses when they become the object of a strike. One is to shut down the affected area and halt operations until the strike is over. A second is to

impasse
Collective bargaining situation that occurs when the parties are not able to move further toward settlement, usually because one party is demanding more than the other will offer.

mediation
Intervention in which a neutral third party tries to assist the principals in reaching agreement.

fact finder
A neutral party who studies the issues in a dispute and makes a public recommendation for a reasonable settlement.

arbitration
The most definitive type of third-party intervention, in which the arbitrator usually has the power to determine and dictate the settlement terms.

strike
A withdrawal of labor.

economic strike
A strike that results from a failure to agree on the terms of a contract that involve wages, benefits, and other conditions of employment.

unfair labor practice strike
A strike aimed at protesting illegal conduct by the employer.

wildcat strike
An unauthorized strike occurring during the term of a contract.

sympathy strike
A strike that takes place when one union strikes in support of the strike of another.

picketing
Having employees carry signs announcing their concerns near the employer's place of business.

FIGURE 15-5 Online Request Form for Federal Mediation

FMCS Form F-53
Revised 5-92

Form Approved
OMB No. 3076-0005

FEDERAL SECTOR LABOR RELATIONS
NOTICE TO FEDERAL MEDIATION AND CONCILIATION SERVICE

Mail To:
Notice Processing Unit
FEDERAL MEDIATION AND CONCILIATION SERVICE
2100 K Street, N.W.
Washington, D.C. 20427

THIS NOTICE IS IN REGARD TO: (MARK"X")

① ☐ AN INITIAL CONTRACT (INCLUDED FLRA CERTIFICATION NUMBER) # ______
☐ A CONTRACT REOPENER REOPENER DATE ______
☐ THE EXPIRATION OF AN EXISTING AGREEMENT EXPIRATION DATE: ______

② ☐ ***OTHER REQUESTS FOR THE ASSISTANCE OF FMCS IN BARGAINING (MARK "X")***
SPECIFY TYPE OF ISSUE(S)

③ ☐ ***REQUEST FOR GRIEVANCE MEDIATION (SEE ITEM #10) (MARK "X")***
ISSUE(S)

④ NAME OF FEDERAL AGENCY — NAME OF SUBDIVISION OR COMPONENT, IF ANY
STREET ADDRESS OF AGENCY — CITY — STATE — ZIP
AGENCY OFFICIAL TO BE CONTACTED — AREA CODE & PHONE NUMBER

⑤ NAME OF NATIONAL UNION OR PARENT BODY — NAME AND/OR LOCAL NUMBER
STREET ADDRESS — CITY — STATE — ZIP
UNION OFFICIAL TO BE CONTACTED — AREA CODE & PHONE NUMBER

LOCATION OF NEGOTIATIONS OR WHERE MEDIATION WILL BE HELD
⑥ STREET ADDRESS — CITY — STATE — ZIP

⑦ APPROX. # OF EMPLOYEES IN BARGAINING UNIT(S) >> — IN ESTABLISHMENT>>

⑧ THIS NOTICE OR REQUEST IS FILED ON BEHALF OF ***(MARK "X")*** ☐UNION ☐AGENCY

⑨ NAME AND TITLE OF OFFICIAL(S) SUBMITTING THIS NOTICE OR REQUEST — AREA CODE AND PHONE NUMBER
STREET ADDRESS — CITY — STATE — ZIP

FOR GRIEVANCE MEDIATION, THE SIGNATURES OF BOTH PARTIES ARE REQUIRED:*

⑩ SIGNATURE (AGENCY) — DATE — SIGNATURE (UNION) — DATE

*Receipt of this form does not commit FMCS to offer its services. Receipt of this form will not be acknowledged in writing by FMCS. While use of this form is voluntary, its use will facilitate FMCS service to respondents. Public reporting burden for this collection of information is estimated to average 10 minutes per response, including time for reviewing the collection of information. Send comments regarding this burden estimate or any other aspect of this collection of information, including suggestions for reducing this burden, to FMCS Division of Administrative Services, Washington, D.C. 20427, and to the Office of Management and Budget, Paperwork Reduction Project. Washington, D.C. 20603

For Instructions, See Back

contract out work in order to blunt the effects of the strike. A third response is to continue operations, perhaps using supervisors and other nonstriking workers to fill in for the striking workers. A fourth alternative is hiring replacements for the strikers.

Diminished union influence plus competitive pressures now prompt more employers to replace (or at least consider replacing) strikers with permanent replacement workers. One study of human resource managers found that of those responding, 18% "would not consider striker replacements" in the event of a strike, while 31% called it "not very likely," 23% "somewhat likely" and 21% "very likely."[59] After Northwest Airlines began giving permanent jobs to 1,500 substitute workers it hired to replace striking mechanics, the strike, by the Aircraft Mechanics Fraternal Association, collapsed.[60]

Employers generally can replace strikers. In one very important labor relations case known as *Mackay*, the U.S. Supreme Court ruled that although the National Labor Relations Act does prohibit employers from interfering with employees' right to strike, employers still have the right to continue their operations and, therefore, to replace strikers. Subsequent decisions by the National Labor Relations Board put some limitations on *Mackay*. For example, employers cannot permanently replace

Source: Courtesy of Dennis MacDonald/PhotoEdit Inc.

Picketing is one of the first activities to occur during a strike. The purpose is to inform the public about the labor dispute.

strikers who are protesting unfair labor practices, and must rehire strikers who apply for reinstatement unconditionally.

When a strike is imminent, the employer should make plans to deal with it. For example, as negotiations between the Hibbing Taconite Steel Plant in Minnesota and the United Steelworkers of America headed toward a deadline, the firm brought in security workers and trailers to house them.

Two experts say that, with a strike imminent, following these guidelines can minimize confusion:

- Pay all striking employees what you owe them on the first day of the strike.
- Secure the facility. Management should control access to the property. Consider hiring guards to protect replacements coming to and from workers, if necessary.
- Notify all customers, and prepare a standard official response to all queries.
- Contact all suppliers and other persons who will have to cross the picket line. Establish alternative methods of obtaining supplies.
- Arrange for overnight stays in the facility, and for delivered meals, if necessary.
- Notify the local unemployment office of your need for replacement workers.
- Photograph the facility before, during, and after picketing. If necessary, install videotape equipment to monitor picket line misconduct.
- Record all facts concerning strikers' demeanor and activities and such incidents as violence, threats, mass pickets, property damage, or problems.
- Gather the following evidence: number of pickets and their names; time, date, and location of picketing; wording on every sign carried by pickets; and descriptions of picket cars and license numbers.[61]

Other Alternatives

Management and labor each have other weapons to break an impasse and achieve their aims. The union, for example, may resort to a corporate campaign. A **corporate campaign** is an organized effort by the union that exerts pressure on the employer by pressuring the company's other unions, shareholders, corporate directors, customers, creditors, and government agencies. Thus, the union might surprise individual members of the board of directors by picketing their homes, and organizing a **boycott** of the company's banks.[62]

corporate campaign
An organized effort by the union that exerts pressure on the corporation by pressuring the company's other unions, shareholders, directors, customers, creditors, and government agencies, often directly.

boycott
The combined refusal by employees and other interested parties to buy or use the employer's products.

The Web is a potent union tool. For example, when the Hotel Employees and Restaurant Employees Union, Local 2, wanted to turn up the heat on the San Francisco Marriott, it launched a new Web site. The site explained the union's 8-month boycott and provided a helpful list of union-backed hotels where prospective guests could stay. It also listed organizations that decided to stay elsewhere in response to the boycott.[63]

Inside games are another union tactic. **Inside games** are union efforts to convince employees to impede or to disrupt production—for example, by slowing the work pace, refusing to work overtime, filing mass charges with government agencies, refusing to do work without receiving detailed instructions from supervisors, and engaging in other disruptive activities such as sick-outs.[64] Inside games are basically strikes—albeit "strikes" in which the company continues to pay the employees. In one inside game at Caterpillar's Aurora, Illinois, plant, United Auto Workers' grievances rose from 22 to 336. The effect was to tie up workers and management in unproductive endeavors on company time.[65]

For their part, employers can try to break an impasse with lockouts. A **lockout** is a refusal by the employer to provide opportunities to work. It (sometimes literally) locks out employees and prohibits them from doing their jobs (and being paid). The NLRB views lockouts as an unfair labor practice only when the employer acts for a prohibited purpose. It is not a prohibited purpose to try to bring about a settlement on terms favorable to the employer. Lockouts are not widely used today; employers are usually reluctant to cease operations when employees are willing to continue working (even though there may be an impasse at the bargaining table).

Both employers and unions can seek an injunction from the courts if they believe the other side is taking actions that could cause irreparable harm to the other party. An **injunction** is a court order compelling a party or parties either to resume or to desist from a certain action.[66]

The Contract Agreement

The actual contract agreement may be a 20- or 30-page document; it may be even longer. It may contain just general declarations of policy, or detailed rules and procedures. The tendency today is toward the longer, more detailed contract. This is largely a result of the increased number of items the agreements have been covering.

The main sections of a typical contract cover subjects such as these: (1) management rights, (2) union security and automatic payroll dues deduction, (3) grievance procedures, (4) arbitration of grievances, (5) disciplinary procedures, (6) compensation rates, (7) hours of work and overtime, (8) benefits: vacations, holidays, insurance, pensions, (9) health and safety provisions, (10) employee security seniority provisions, and (11) contract expiration date.

6 Develop a grievance procedure.

GRIEVANCES

Hammering out a labor agreement is not the last step in collective bargaining. No labor contract can cover all contingencies and answer all questions. For example, suppose the contract says you can only discharge an employee for "just cause." You subsequently discharge someone for speaking back to you in harsh terms. Was speaking back to you harshly "just cause"?

The labor contract's grievance procedure usually handles problems like these. The **grievance procedure** provides an orderly system whereby both employer and union determine whether some action violated the contract.[67] It is the vehicle for administering the contract on a day-to-day basis. The grievance process allows both parties to interpret and give meaning to various clauses, and transforms the contract into a "living organism." Remember, though, that this involves interpretation only: It usually doesn't involve negotiating new terms or altering existing ones.

Sources of Grievances

From a practical point of view, it is probably easier to list those items that *don't* precipitate grievances than to list the ones that do. Employees may use just about any factor involving wages, hours, or conditions of employment as the basis of a grievance.

However, certain grievances are more serious, since they're usually more difficult to settle. Discipline cases and seniority problems including promotions, transfers, and layoffs would top this list. Others would include grievances growing out of job evaluations and work assignments, overtime, vacations, incentive plans, and holidays.[68] Here are three examples of grievances:

- **Absenteeism.** An employer fired an employee for excessive absences. The employee filed a grievance stating that there had been no previous warnings related to excessive absences.
- **Insubordination.** An employee on two occasions refused to obey a supervisor's order to meet with him, unless a union representative was present at the meeting. As a result, the employee was discharged and subsequently filed a grievance protesting the discharge.
- **Plant rules.** The plant had a posted rule barring employees from eating or drinking during unscheduled breaks. The employees filed a grievance claiming the rule was arbitrary.[69]

A grievance is often a symptom of an underlying problem. Sometimes, bad relationships between supervisors and subordinates are to blame: This is often the cause of grievances over "fair treatment," for instance. Organizational factors such as ambiguous job descriptions that frustrate employees also cause grievances. Union activism is another cause; the union may solicit grievances from workers to underscore ineffective supervision. Problem employees are yet another underlying cause of grievances. These are individuals, who, by their nature, are negative, dissatisfied, and prone to complaints. Discipline and dismissal, explained in Chapter 14, are also both major sources of grievances.

The Grievance Procedure

Most collective bargaining contracts contain a specific grievance procedure. It lists the steps in the procedure, time limits associated with each step, and specific rules such as "all charges of contract violation must be reduced to writing." Virtually every labor agreement signed today contains a grievance procedure clause. (Nonunionized employers need such procedures, too, as explained in Chapter 14, Ethics.)

Union grievance procedures differ from firm to firm. Some contain simple, two-step procedures. Here, the grievant, union representative, and company representative meet to discuss the grievance. If they don't find a satisfactory solution, the grievance goes before an independent, third-party arbitrator who hears the case, writes it up, and makes a decision. Figure 15-6 shows a grievance record form.

At the other extreme, the grievance procedure may contain six or more steps. The first step might be for the grievant and shop steward to meet informally with the supervisor of the grievant to try to find a solution. If they don't find one, the employee files a formal grievance, and there's a meeting with the employee, shop steward, and the supervisor's boss. The next steps involve the grievant and union

inside games
Union efforts to convince employees to impede or to disrupt production—for example, by slowing the work pace.

lockout
A refusal by the employer to provide opportunities to work.

injunction
A court order compelling a party or parties either to resume or to desist from a certain action.

grievance procedure
Formal process for addressing any factor involving wages, hours, or conditions of employment that is used as a complaint against the employer.

FIGURE 15-6 Sample Online Grievance Form

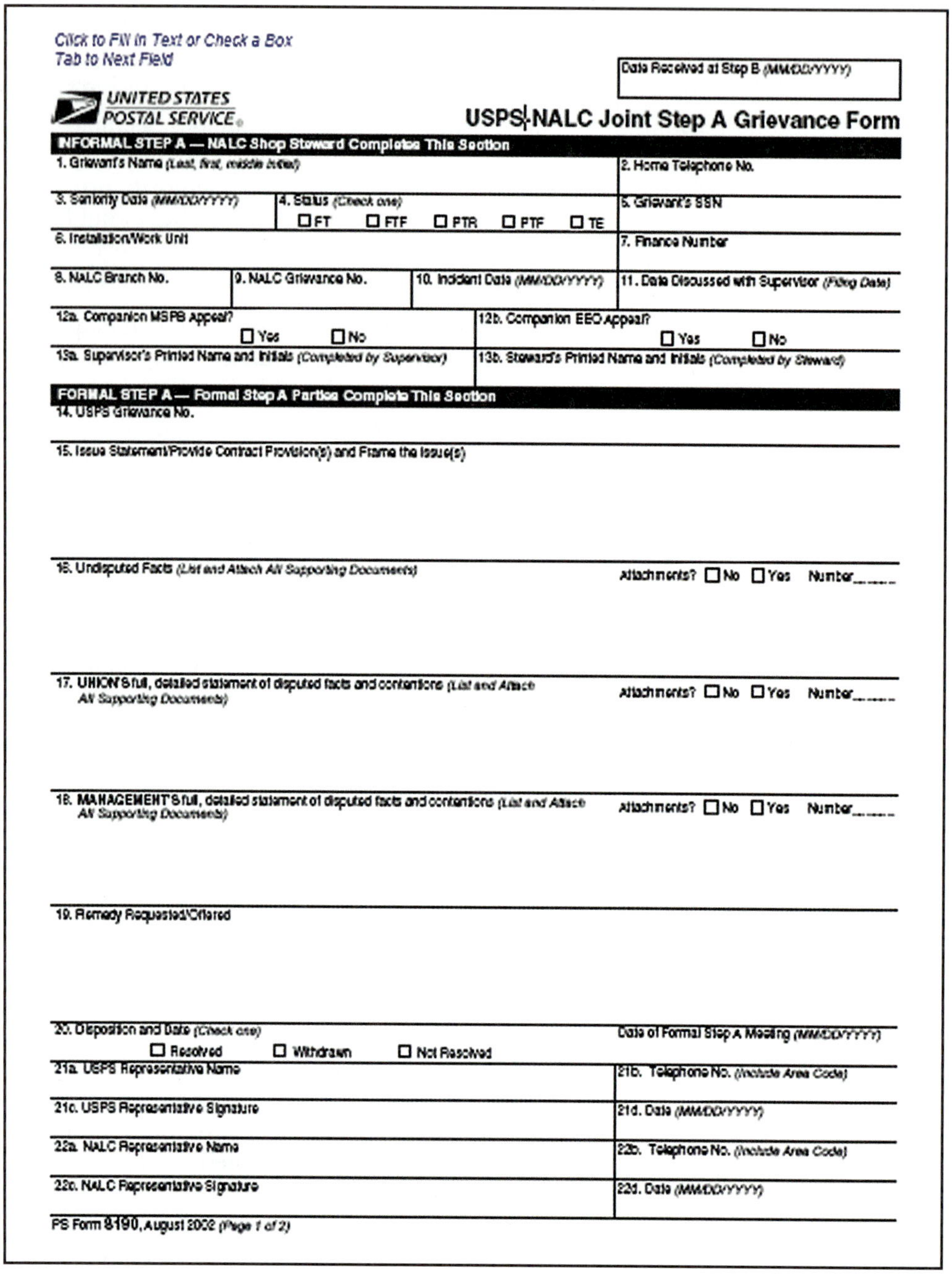
Click to Fill in Text or Check a Box
Tab to Next Field

Date Received at Step B (MM/DD/YYYY)

UNITED STATES POSTAL SERVICE

USPS-NALC Joint Step A Grievance Form

INFORMAL STEP A — NALC Shop Steward Completes This Section

1. Grievant's Name (Last, first, middle initial) | 2. Home Telephone No.
3. Seniority Date (MM/DD/YYYY) | 4. Status (Check one) ☐ FT ☐ FTF ☐ PTR ☐ PTF ☐ TE | 5. Grievant's SSN
6. Installation/Work Unit | 7. Finance Number
8. NALC Branch No. | 9. NALC Grievance No. | 10. Incident Date (MM/DD/YYYY) | 11. Date Discussed with Supervisor (Filing Date)
12a. Companion MSPB Appeal? ☐ Yes ☐ No | 12b. Companion EEO Appeal? ☐ Yes ☐ No
13a. Supervisor's Printed Name and Initials (Completed by Supervisor) | 13b. Steward's Printed Name and Initials (Completed by Steward)

FORMAL STEP A — Formal Step A Parties Complete This Section

14. USPS Grievance No.
15. Issue Statement/Provide Contract Provision(s) and Frame the Issue(s)
16. Undisputed Facts (List and Attach All Supporting Documents) Attachments? ☐ No ☐ Yes Number____
17. UNION'S full, detailed statement of disputed facts and contentions (List and Attach All Supporting Documents) Attachments? ☐ No ☐ Yes Number____
18. MANAGEMENT'S full, detailed statement of disputed facts and contentions (List and Attach All Supporting Documents) Attachments? ☐ No ☐ Yes Number____
19. Remedy Requested/Offered
20. Disposition and Date (Check one) ☐ Resolved ☐ Withdrawn ☐ Not Resolved | Date of Formal Step A Meeting (MM/DD/YYYY)
21a. USPS Representative Name | 21b. Telephone No. (Include Area Code)
21c. USPS Representative Signature | 21d. Date (MM/DD/YYYY)
22a. NALC Representative Name | 22b. Telephone No. (Include Area Code)
22c. NALC Representative Signature | 22d. Date (MM/DD/YYYY)

PS Form 8190, August 2002 (Page 1 of 2)

representatives meeting with higher-level managers. Finally, if top management and the union can't reach agreement, the grievance may go to arbitration.

Sometimes the grievance process gets out of hand. For example, several years ago, members of American Postal Workers Union, Local 482, filed 1,800 grievances at the Postal Service's Roanoke mail processing facility (the usual rate is about 800 grievances per year). The employees apparently were responding to job changes, including efforts to automate its processes.[70]

Guidelines for Handling Grievances

The best way to handle a grievance is to develop a work environment in which grievances don't occur in the first place. Hone your ability to recognize, diagnose, and correct the causes of potential employee dissatisfaction (such as unfair appraisals, inequitable wages, or poor communications) before they become grievances.

The manager is on the firing line and must steer a course between treating employees fairly and maintaining management's rights and prerogatives. One expert has developed a list of do's and don'ts as useful guides in handling grievances.[71] Some critical ones include:

Do:

1. Investigate and handle each case as though it may eventually result in arbitration.
2. Talk with the employee about his or her grievance; give the person a full hearing.
3. Require the union to identify specific contractual provisions allegedly violated.
4. Comply with the contractual time limits for handling the grievance.
5. Visit the work area of the grievance.
6. Determine whether there were any witnesses.
7. Examine the grievant's personnel record.
8. Fully examine prior grievance records.
9. Treat the union representative as your equal.
10. Hold your grievance discussions privately.
11. Fully inform your own supervisor of grievance matters.

Don't:

1. Discuss the case with the union steward alone—the grievant should be there.
2. Make arrangements with individual employees that are inconsistent with the labor agreement.
3. Hold back the remedy if the company is wrong.
4. Admit to the binding effect of a past practice.
5. Relinquish to the union your rights as a manager.
6. Settle grievances based on what is "fair." Instead, stick to the labor agreement.
7. Bargain over items not covered by the contract.
8. Treat as subject to arbitration claims demanding the discipline or discharge of managers.
9. Give long, written grievance answers.
10. Trade a grievance settlement for a grievance withdrawal.
11. Deny grievances because your hands have been "tied by management."
12. Agree to informal amendments in the contract.

THE UNION MOVEMENT TODAY AND TOMORROW

About 35% of the non-farm U.S. workforce belonged to unions in the 1960s. Recently, that figure dropped to about 12.4%. Why has this occurred and what is the future for the union movement?

Why Union Membership Is Down

As we said earlier, several things contributed to union membership decline. *Laws* like OSHA and Title VII reduced the need for union protection. Increased global *competition* and *new technologies* like the Internet and just-in-time production systems forced employers to reduce inefficiencies and cut costs—often by reducing payrolls by automating or by sending jobs abroad. New *foreign-owned* auto plants from Toyota and Daimler largely stayed union free. Only about 15% of U.S. workers now work in *manufacturing and construction*, so unions' traditional membership sources shrank.

All of this squeezes unions. For example, for years, the head of Ford's United Auto Workers union fought for increased benefits for his members. But recently, he's been urging his colleagues to accept productivity-enhancing plans, such as outsourcing Ford's factory jobs to lower paid workers. "Ford is in a desperate situation," he says. "If this company goes down, I want to be able to look in the mirror and say I did everything I could."[72] Other unions, too, are dropping some aggressive tactics.

An Upswing for Unions?

However, the news is not all bleak.[73] For one thing, the 12.4% is up a bit from the preceding few years;[74] for another, it masks unions' real impact. Union membership varies widely by state, so unions are still quite influential in some states (such as Michigan and New York). And, fully 35% of the nation's blue-collar workers—in particular those in manufacturing and construction jobs—belong to unions. Furthermore, a slight majority of all union members (about 51%) are now white-collar workers, which suggests unions are tapping this growing portion of the workforce. For example, an optical physicist at the National Aeronautics and Space Administration is also the president of his local union.[75] White-collar union members include about 40% of all college faculty members, 45,000 physicians, and 50,000 engineers. And almost 100,000 nurses belong to unions (as do most major league baseball, football, basketball, and hockey players). About 40% of all federal, state, and local government employees belong to unions. Union membership declines seem to have leveled off.[76] And, as we'll see, unions themselves are becoming much more aggressive.

Public Employees and Unions

As we said, one bright spot for the union movement is their success in organizing federal, state, and municipal workers. Three public unions—the National Education Association; the American Federation of State, County and Municipal Employees; and the American Federation of Teachers—are among the largest U.S. unions.

The unions' success here reflects, in part, years of changes in public-sector collective-bargaining and labor relations legislation. For example, in 1962, President John F. Kennedy signed Executive Order 10988. This recognized federal employees' rights to join or refrain from joining labor organizations and granted recognition to those organizations. In 1978, Congress passed the Civil Service Reform Act of 1978. Title VII of this act (known as the Federal Labor Relations Act) is similar to the National Labor Relations Act. It gave the new Federal Labor Relations Authority the authority to oversee federal public-sector labor relations. Among other things, this Title VII prohibits the government from restraining or coercing employees in the exercise of their organizational rights, or from encouraging or discouraging union membership.[77]

Organizing Professionals and White-Collar Employees

As noted, unions are also making inroads with professionals and white-collar workers. Recent reports of IBM sending systems analysts' jobs abroad, of Wall Street firms having more security analysis done abroad by foreign nationals, and of hospitals having digitized X-rays read and interpreted by doctors abroad illustrate the concerns many professionals have. Several years ago, Boeing began focusing more on cost-cutting and financial results and (from its engineers' point of view) less on engineering excellence. Engineers' morale reportedly dropped, and Boeing was caught by surprise when its engineers joined the Seattle Professional Engineering Employees Association.[78]

Card Check and Other New Union Tactics

Unions are also becoming much more aggressive. Unions are pushing Congress to pass the Employee Free Choice Act. This would make it more difficult for employers to inhibit workers from organizing. Instead of secret-ballot elections, the act would institute a "card check" system. Here, the union would win recognition when a majority of workers signed authorization cards saying they want the union. (Several large companies, including Cingular Wireless, have already agreed to the card check process.)[79] The act would also require binding arbitration to set a first contract's terms

Unions are making inroads into traditionally hard-to-organize worker segments like professionals and white-collar workers.

Source: Courtesy of Philip James Corwin/CORBIS–NY

if the company and union can't negotiate an agreement within 120 days.[80] Unions are also using class action lawsuits to support employees in nonunionized companies, to pressure employers. For example, unions recently used class action lawsuits to support workers' claims under the Fair Labor Standards Act and the Equal Pay Act.[81]

The steps UNITE took against Cintas Corp. illustrate some of unions' new tactics. In their effort against Cintas, UNITE (which later merged with another union to form UNITE HERE) didn't petition for an NLRB election. Instead, UNITE proposed using the card check process. They also filed a $100 million class action suit against the company. Then, Cintas workers in California filed a lawsuit claiming that the company was violating a nearby municipality's "living wage" law. UNITE then joined forces with the Teamsters union, which in turn began targeting Cintas' delivery people.[82]

Change to Win The priorities of the Change to Win Coalition (whose members broke off from the AFL-CIO) help illustrate what may be the new union strategies. They,

> Make it our first priority to help millions more workers form unions so we can build a strong movement for rewarding work in America; unite the strength of everyone who works in the same industry so we can negotiate with today's huge global corporations for everyone's benefit; reflect the diversity and commitment to change of today's workforce; build a growing, independent voice for working people in politics based on economic issues, and party; modernize the strategies, structure and priorities of the AFL-CIO to make these changes possible.[83]

In practice, this means Change to Win will be very aggressive about organizing workers, both here and abroad.[84]

Unions Go Global Walmart, a company that traditionally works hard to prevent its stores from going union, recently had to agree to let the workers in its stores in China join unions.

Walmart's China experience stems in part from efforts of global union campaigns by the Service Employees' International Union (SEIU). These campaigns reflect the belief that, as SEIU puts it, "huge global service sector companies routinely cross national borders and industry lines as they search for places where they can shift operations to exploit workers with the lowest possible pay and benefits." SEIU is therefore strengthening its alliances with unions in other nations, with the goal of uniting workers in specific multinational companies and industries around the globe.[85] For example, SEIU recently worked with China's All China Federation of Trade Unions (ACFTU) to help the latter organize China's Walmart stores.[86] And recently, the United Steelworkers merged with the largest labor union in Britain to create "Workers Uniting" to better help the new union deal with multinational employers.[87] So, any company that thinks it can avoid unionization by sending jobs abroad may be in for a surprise.

Improving Productivity Through HRIS: Unions Go High-Tech

As one expert asked, "If faster and more powerful ways of communicating enable companies to compete in a quickly changing and challenging environment, shouldn't they also make unions stronger and more efficient?"[88]

In fact, they can. E-mail and the Internet means unions can send mass e-mail announcements to collective-bargaining unit members and use e-mail to reach supporters and government officials for their corporate campaigns.

For example, the group trying to organize Starbucks workers (the *Starbucks Workers' Union*) set up their own Web site (www.starbucksunion.org). It includes notes like "Starbucks managers monitored Internet chat rooms and eavesdropped on party conversations in a covert campaign to identify employees agitating for union representation at the coffee chain, internal emails reveal."[89]

HR APPs 4 U

Union iPod Organizing

Unions are also using mobile devices to support their organizing efforts. The screen grab below shows one slide from a PowerPoint presentation from the National Education Association union.[90]

Web Resources and Techniques for Organizing and Membership Development

Tools	Techniques	Function/Activity
Web Site	○ Forms ○ Polls and Surveys ○ Informational Pages	○ how to join ○ collect contact information ○ Solicit input ○ Provide contact information, news, and union updates.
E-mail/e-newsletters	○ automatic e-mail responses ○ predictable e-news	○ welcome note ○ union news (i.e. grievance updates, meeting notices) ○ Keep membership informed. ○ invites audience back to the web site

High-Performance Work Systems, Employee Participation, and Unions

For some unions, employee participation is too much of a good thing. Many employers encourage employees to work together in quality circles and similar worker participation teams. The aim is to help solve work-related problems and create high-performance work systems. In one such program, at UPS, hourly employees in self-directed teams establish priorities on how to do their jobs. Many unions believe that the result, if not the motive, of such programs is to usurp unions' traditional duties.

That presents a problem for employers. To understand why, it's useful to know that one goal of the National Labor Relations (or Wagner) Act was to outlaw "sham unions." Two years before passage of the NLRA, the National Recovery Act (1933) tried to give employees the right to organize and to bargain collectively. This triggered an increase in unions that were actually company-supported organizations aimed at keeping legitimate unions out. This helped lead to passage of the National Labor Relations Act. The problem is that courts might view some participative programs like UPS's as sham unions. If the committees focus just on issues such as quality and productivity improvement, courts are more likely to view them as outside the scope of the National Labor Relations Act. Being involved in union-type matters such as wages and working conditions may be more questionable.

Employers can take these steps to avoid having their employee participation programs viewed as sham unions:[91]

- Involve employees in the formation of these programs.
- Continually emphasize to employees that the committees exist only to address issues such as quality and productivity, not to deal with management on mandatory bargaining items such as pay.
- Don't try to establish such committees when union organizing activities are beginning in your facility.
- Fill the committees with volunteers rather than elected employee representatives, and rotate membership.
- Minimize your participation in the committees' day-to-day activities to avoid the perception of domination.

A recent review of union research and literature provides an additional insight. The author concludes that unions "that have a cooperative relationship with management can play an important role in overcoming barriers to the effective adoption of practices that have been linked to organizational competitiveness."[92] However, she also concludes that employers who want to capitalize on that potential need to change their way of thinking, avoiding adversarial industrial relations and emphasizing a cooperative partnership with their unions.

REVIEW

CHAPTER SECTION SUMMARIES

1. The **labor movement** is important. Almost 18 million U.S. workers belong to unions, about 12.4% of the total. Workers unionize not just to get more pay or better working conditions; employer unfairness and the union's power are also important. Unions aim for union security, and then for improved wages, hours, and working conditions and benefits for their members. Union security options include the closed shop, union shop, agency shop, preferential shop, and maintenance of membership arrangement. The AFL-CIO plays an important role in the union movement as a voluntary federation of about 56 national and international labor unions in the United States.
2. To understand unions and their impact, it's necessary to understand the interplay between **unions and the law**. In brief, labor law has gone through periods of strong encouragement of unions, to modified encouragement coupled with regulation, and finally to detailed regulation of internal union affairs. Today, the legal environment seems to be moving toward increased encouragement of unions. Historically, the laws encouraging the union movement included the Norris-LaGuardia and National Labor Relations (Wagner) Acts of the 1930s. These outlawed certain unfair employer labor practices and made it easier for unions to organize. The Taft-Hartley or Labor Management Relations Act of 1947 addressed keeping unions from restraining or coercing employees, and listed certain unfair union labor practices. In the 1950s, the Landrum-Griffin Act (technically, the Labor Management Reporting and Disclosure Act) further protected union members from possible wrongdoing on the part of their unions.

3. When unions begin organizing, all managers and supervisors usually get involved, so it's essential to understand the mechanics of **the union drive and election**. The main steps include initial contact, obtaining authorization cards, holding a hearing, the campaign itself, and the election. Supervisors need to understand their role at each step in this process. Follow the acronym TIPS—do not threaten, interrogate, make promises or spy. And follow FORE—provide facts, express your opinions, explain factually correct rules, and share your experiences. Managers need to understand rules regarding literature and solicitation. For example, employers can always bar nonemployees from soliciting employees during their work time, and can usually stop employees from soliciting other employees when both are on duty time and not on a break.
4. The employer and union hammer out an agreement via the **collective bargaining process**. The heart of collective bargaining is good faith bargaining, which means both parties must make reasonable efforts to arrive at agreement, and proposals are matched with counterproposals. Both negotiating teams will work hard to understand their respective clients' needs and to quantify their demands. In the actual bargaining sessions, there are mandatory bargaining items such as pay, illegal bargaining items, and voluntary bargaining items such as benefits for retirees. If things don't go smoothly during collective bargaining, the parties may utilize third-party intermediaries, including mediators, fact finders, and arbitrators. Strikes represent a withdrawal of labor. There are economic strikes resulting from a failure to agree on the terms of the contract, as well as unfair labor practice strikes, wildcat strikes, and sympathy strikes. During strikes, picketing may occur. Other tactics include a corporate campaign by the union, boycotting, inside games, or (for employers) lockouts.
5. Most managers become involved with **grievances** during their careers. Most collective bargaining agreements contain a specific grievance procedure listing the steps in the procedure. In general, the best way to handle a grievance is to create an environment in which grievances don't occur. However if a grievance does occur, things to do include investigate, handle each case as though it may eventually result in arbitration, talk with the employee about the grievance, and comply with the contractual time limits for handling the grievance. On the other hand, don't make arrangements with individual employees that are inconsistent with the labor agreement or hold back the remedy if the company is wrong.
6. In many ways, unions are becoming more influential today, so it's important to understand the **union movement today and tomorrow.** For example, unions are becoming more aggressive in terms of pushing Congress to pass the Employee Free Choice Act, which, among other things, would unable employees to vote for the union by signing authorization cards, rather than going through a formal union election. New union federations, such as Change to Win, are being more aggressive about organizing workers, and unions are going global, for instance, by helping employees in China organize local Walmart stores.

DISCUSSION QUESTIONS

1. Why do employees join unions? What are the advantages and disadvantages of being a union member?
2. Discuss five sure ways to lose an NLRB election.
3. Describe important tactics you would expect the union to use during the union drive and election.
4. Briefly illustrate how labor law has gone through a cycle of repression and encouragement.
5. Explain in detail each step in a union drive and election.
6. What is meant by good faith bargaining? Using examples, explain when bargaining is not in good faith.
7. Define impasse, mediation, and strike, and explain the techniques that are used to overcome an impasse.

INDIVIDUAL AND GROUP ACTIVITIES

1. You are the manager of a small manufacturing plant. The union contract covering most of your employees is about to expire. Working individually or in groups, discuss how to prepare for union contract negotiations.
2. Working individually or in groups, use Internet resources to find situations where company management and the union reached an impasse at some point during their negotiation process, but eventually resolved the impasse. Describe the issues on both sides that led to the impasse. How did they move past the impasse? What were the final outcomes?
3. The "HRCI Test Specifications Appendix" (pages 699–706) lists the knowledge someone studying for the HRCI certification exam needs to have in each area of human resource management (such as in Strategic Management, Workforce Planning, and Human Resource Development). In groups of four to five students, do four things: (1) Review that appendix now. (2) Identify the material in this chapter that relates to the required knowledge the appendix lists. (3) Write four multiple-choice exam questions on this material that you believe would be suitable for inclusion in the HRCI exam. And (4) if time permits, have someone from your team post your team's questions in front of the class, so the students in other teams can take each others' exam questions.
4. Several years ago, 8,000 Amtrak workers agreed not to disrupt service by walking out, at least not until a court hearing was held. Amtrak had asked the courts for a

temporary restraining order, and the Transport Workers Union of America was actually pleased to postpone its walkout. The workers were apparently not upset at Amtrak, but at Congress, for failing to provide enough funding for Amtrak. What, if anything, can an employer do when employees threaten to go on strike, not because of what the employer did, but what a third party—in this case, Congress—has done or not done? What laws would prevent the union from going on strike in this case?

EXPERIENTIAL EXERCISE

The Union-Organizing Campaign at Pierce U.

Purpose: The purpose of this exercise is to give you practice in dealing with some of the elements of a union-organizing campaign.[93]

Required Understanding: You should be familiar with the material covered in this chapter, as well as the following incident, "An Organizing Question on Campus."

INCIDENT: An Organizing Question on Campus: Art Tipton is human resource director of Pierce University, a private university located in a large urban city. Ruth Zimmer, a supervisor in the maintenance and housekeeping services division of the university, has just come into Art's office to discuss her situation. Zimmer's division is responsible for maintaining and cleaning physical facilities of the university. Zimmer is one of the department supervisors who supervise employees who maintain and clean on-campus dormitories.

In the next several minutes, Zimmer proceeds to express her concerns about a union-organizing campaign that has begun among her employees. According to Zimmer, a representative of the Service Workers Union has met with several of her employees, urging them to sign union authorization cards. She has observed several of her employees "cornering" other employees to talk to them about joining the union and to urge them to sign union authorization (or representation) cards. Zimmer even observed this during working hours as employees were going about their normal duties in the dormitories. Zimmer reports that a number of her employees have come to her asking for her opinions about the union. They told her that several other supervisors in the department had told their employees not to sign any union authorization cards and not to talk about the union at any time while they were on campus. Zimmer also reports that one of her fellow supervisors told his employees that anyone who was caught talking about the union or signing a union authorization card would be disciplined and perhaps dismissed.

Zimmer says that her employees are very dissatisfied with their wages and with the conditions that they have endured from students, supervisors, and other staff people. She says that several employees told her that they had signed union cards because they believed that the only way university administration would pay attention to their concerns was if the employees had a union to represent them. Zimmer says that she made a list of employees who she felt had joined or were interested in the union, and she could share these with Tipton if he wanted to deal with them personally. Zimmer closed her presentation with the comment that she and other department supervisors need to know what they should do in order to stomp out the threat of unionization in their department.

How to Set Up the Exercise/Instructions: Divide the class into groups of four or five students. Assume that you are labor relations consultants the university retained to identify the problems and issues involved and to advise Art Tipton on the university's rights and what to do next. Each group will spend the time allotted discussing the issues. Then, outline those issues, as well as an action plan for Tipton. What should he do next?

If time permits, a spokesperson from each group should list on the board the issues involved and the group's recommendations. What should Art do?

APPLICATION CASE

Negotiating with the Writers Guild of America

The talks between the Writers Guild of America (WGA) and the Alliance of Motion Picture & Television Producers (producers) began tense in 2007, and then got tenser. In their first meeting, the two sides got nothing done. As *Law & Order* producer Dick Wolf said, "Everyone in the room is concerned about this."[94]

The two sides were far apart on just about all the issues. However, the biggest issue was how to split revenue from new media, such as when television shows move to DVDs or the Internet. The producers said they wanted a profit-splitting system rather than the current residual system. Under the residual system, writers continue to receive "residuals" or income from shows they write every time they're shown (such as when *Seinfeld* appears in reruns, years after the last original show was shot). Writers Guild executives did their homework. They argued, for instance, that the projections showed producers' revenues from advertising and subscription fees jumped by about 40% between 2002 and 2006.[95]

The situation grew tenser. After the first few meetings, one producers' representative said, "We can see after the dogfight whose position will win out. The open question there, of course, is whether each of us takes several lumps at the table, reaches an agreement, then licks their wounds later—none the worse for wear—or whether we inflict more lasting damage through work stoppages that benefit no one before we come to an agreement."[96] Even after meeting six times, it seemed that, "the parties' only apparent area of agreement is that no real bargaining has yet to occur."[97]

In October 2007, the Writers Guild asked its members for strike authorization, and the producers were claiming that the guild was just trying to delay negotiations until the current contract expired (at the end of October). As the president of the producers' group said, "We have had six across-the-table sessions and there was only silence and stonewalling from the WGA leadership. . . . We have attempted to engage on major issues, but no dialogue has been forthcoming from the WGA leadership. . . . The WGA leadership apparently has no intention to bargain in good faith."[98] As evidence, the producers claimed that the WGA negotiating committee left one meeting after less than an hour at the bargaining table.

Both sides knew timing in these negotiations was very important. During the fall and spring, television series production is in full swing. So, a strike now by the writers would have a bigger impact than waiting until, say, the summer to strike. Perhaps not surprisingly, by January 2008 some movement was discernible. In a separate set of negotiations, the Directors Guild of America reached an agreement with the producers that addressed many of the issues that the writers were focusing on, such as how to divide the new media income.[99] In February 2008, the WGA and producers finally reached agreement. The new contract was "the direct result of renewed negotiations between the two sides, which culminated Friday with a marathon session including top WGA officials and the heads of the Walt Disney Co. and News Corp."[100]

Questions

1. The producers said the WGA was not bargaining in good faith. What did they mean by that, and do you think the evidence is sufficient to support the claim?
2. The WGA did eventually strike. What tactics could the producers have used to fight back once the strike began? What tactics do you think the WGA used?
3. This was a conflict between professional and creative people (the WGA) and TV and movie producers. Do you think the conflict was therefore different in any way than are the conflicts between, say, the Autoworkers or Teamsters unions against auto and trucking companies? Why?
4. What role (with examples) did negotiating skills seem to play in the WGA producers' negotiations?

CONTINUING CASE

Carter Cleaning Company

The Grievance

On visiting one of Carter Cleaning Company's stores, Jennifer was surprised to be taken aside by a long-term Carter employee, who met her as she was parking her car. "Murray (the store manager) told me I was suspended for 2 days without pay because I came in late last Thursday," said George. "I'm really upset, but around here the store manager's word seems to be law, and it sometimes seems like the only way anyone can file a grievance is by meeting you or your father like this in the parking lot." Jennifer was very disturbed by this revelation and promised the employee she would look into it and discuss the situation with her father. In the car heading back to headquarters, she began mulling over what Carter Cleaning Company's alternatives might be.

Questions

1. Do you think it is important for Carter Cleaning Company to have a formal grievance process? Why or why not?
2. Based on what you know about the Carter Cleaning Company, outline the steps in what you think would be the ideal grievance process for this company.
3. In addition to the grievance process, can you think of anything else that Carter Cleaning Company might do to make sure grievances and gripes like this one are expressed and are heard by top management?

TRANSLATING STRATEGY INTO HR POLICIES & PRACTICES CASE

The Hotel Paris Case

The Hotel Paris's New Labor Relations Practices

The Hotel Paris's competitive strategy is "To use superior guest service to differentiate the Hotel Paris properties, and to thereby increase the length of stay and return rate of guests, and thus boost revenues and profitability." HR manager Lisa Cruz must now formulate functional policies and activities that support this competitive strategy, by eliciting the required employee behaviors and competencies.

Lisa Cruz's parents were both union members, and she had no strong philosophical objections to unions. However, as the head of human resources for the Hotel Paris, she did feel very strongly that her employer should do everything legally possible to remain union-free. She knew that this is what the hotel chain's owners and top executives wanted. Furthermore, the evidence seemed to support their position. At least one study that she'd seen concluded that firms with 30% or more of their eligible workers in unions were in the bottom 10% in terms of performance, while those with 8% to 9% of eligible workers in unions scored in the top 10%.[101] The problem was that the Hotel Paris really had no specific policies and procedures in place to help its managers and supervisors deal with union activities. With all the laws regarding what employers and their managers could and could not do to respond to a union's efforts, Lisa knew her company was "a problem waiting to happen." She turned her attention to deciding what steps she and her team should take with regard to labor relations and collective bargaining in the U.S.

Lisa and the CFO knew that unionization was a reality for the Hotel Paris. About 5% of the hotel chain's U.S. employees were already unionized, and unions in this area were quite active. For example, as they were surfing the Internet to better gauge the situation, Lisa and the CFO came across an interesting Web site from the Boston Hotel Employees and Restaurant Employees Union, Local 26 (www. http://hotelworkersrising.org/Campaign/). It describes their success in negotiating contracts and their accomplishments at several hotels, including ones managed by the Westin and Sheraton chains. The CFO and Lisa agreed that it was important that she and her team develop and institute a new set of policies and practices that would enable the Hotel Paris to reduce the likelihood of further unionization and deal more effectively with their current unions. They set about that task with the aid of a labor–management attorney.

Questions

1. How should the details of the Hotel Paris's strategy influence the new union-related HR practices (perhaps such as grievance procedures) it establishes?
2. List and briefly describe what you believe are the three most important steps Hotel Paris management can take to reduce the likelihood unions will organize more of its employees.
3. Write a detailed 2-page outline for a "What You Need to Know When the Union Calls" manual. Lisa will distribute this manual to her company's supervisors and managers, telling them what they need to know about looking out for possible unionizing activity, and how to handle actual organizing process–related supervisory tasks.

KEY TERMS

closed shop, *p. 547*
union shop, *p. 547*
agency shop, *p. 547*
preferential shop, *p. 547*
right to work, *p. 547*
Norris-LaGuardia Act (1932), *p. 549*
National Labor Relations (or Wagner) Act, *p. 549*
National Labor Relations Board (NLRB), *p. 549*
Taft-Hartley Act (1947), *p. 549*
national emergency strikes, *p. 551*
Landrum-Griffin Act (1959), *p. 551*
union salting, *p. 553*
authorization cards, *p. 553*
bargaining unit, *p. 555*
decertification, *p. 559*
collective bargaining, *p. 559*
good faith bargaining, *p. 559*
voluntary (or permissible) bargaining items, *p. 561*
illegal bargaining items, *p. 561*
mandatory bargaining items, *p. 561*
impasse, *p. 563*
mediation, *p. 563*
fact finder, *p. 563*
arbitration, *p. 563*
strike, *p. 563*
economic strike, *p. 563*
unfair labor practice strike, *p. 563*
wildcat strike, *p. 563*
sympathy strike, *p. 563*
picketing, *p. 563*
corporate campaign, *p. 565*
boycott, *p. 565*
inside games, *p. 567*
lockout, *p. 567*
injunction, *p. 567*
grievance procedure, *p. 567*

ENDNOTES

1. Steven Greenhouse, "Board Accuses Starbucks of Trying to Block Union," *The New York Times*, April 3, 2007, p. B2; www.starbucksunion.org, accessed March 25, 2009.
2. www.bls.gov/news.release/union2.nr0.htm, accessed April 2, 2009.
3. Ibid.; "Union Membership Rises," *Compensation & Benefits Review*, May/June 2008, p. 9.
4. Joseph Adler, "The Past as Prologue? A Brief History of the Labor Movement in the United States," *Public Personnel Management*, December 22, 2006, pp. 311–329.
5. Ibid.
6. Michael Ash and Jean Seago, "The Effect of Registered Nurses' Unions on Heart Attack Mortality," *Industrial and Labor Relations Review* 57, no. 3 (April 2004), pp. 422–442.
7. Steven Abraham et al., "The Impact of Union Membership on Intent to Leave: Additional Evidence on the Voice Face of Unions," *Employee Responsibilities and Rights* 17, no. 4 (2005), pp. 21–23.
8. For a good description, see Arthur Sloane and Fred Witney, *Labor Relations* (Upper Saddle River, NJ: Prentice Hall, 2004), pp. 45–78.
9. James Bennett and Jason Taylor, "Labor Unions: Victims of Their Political Success?" *Journal of Labor Research* 22, no. 2 (Spring 2001), pp. 261–273.
10. Paul Monies, "Unions Hit Hard by Job Losses, Right to Work," *The Daily Oklahoman* (via *Knight Ridder/Tribune Business News*), February 1, 2005, accessed May 25, 2005. Now accessible at www.accessmylibrary.com/article-1G1-127994772/unions-hit-hard-job.html, accessed August 11, 2009.
11. Dale Belman and Paula Voos, "Changes in Union Wage Effects by Industry: A Fresh Look at the Evidence," *Industrial Relations* 43, no. 3 (July 2004), pp. 491–519.
12. Donna Buttigieg et al., "An Event History Analysis of Union Joining and Leaving," *Journal of Applied Psychology* 92, no. 3 (2007), pp. 829–839.
13. Kris Maher, "The New Union Worker," *The Wall Street Journal*, September 27, 2005, pp. B1, B11.

14. Robert Grossman, "Unions Follow Suit," *HR Magazine*, May 2005, p. 49.
15. Warner Pflug, *The UAW in Pictures* (Detroit: Wayne State University Press, 1971), pp. 11–12.
16. Arthur Sloane and Fred Witney, *Labor Relations* (Upper Saddle River, NJ: Prentice Hall, 2007), pp. 335–336.
17. Benjamin Taylor and Fred Witney, *Labor Relations Law* (Upper Saddle River, NJ: Prentice Hall, 1992), pp. 170–171.
18. www.dol.gov/esa/programs/whd/state/righttowork.htm, accessed January 13, 2008.
19. Paul Monies, "Unions Hit Hard by Job Losses, Right to Work," *The Daily Oklahoman* (via *Knight Ridder/Tribune Business News*), February 1, 2005, op cit.
20. Steven Greenhouse, "4th Union Quits AFL-CIO in a Dispute over Organizing," *The New York Times*, September 15, 2005, p. A14.
21. The following material is based on Arthur Sloane and Fred Witney, *Labor Relations* (Upper Saddle River, NJ: Prentice Hall, 2001), pp. 46–124.
22. Elizabeth Bennett, "Online Staffers in Dispute with Papers," *Philadelphia Business Journal*, January 12, 2001, p. 6.
23. "Union Membership by State and Industry," *BNA Bulletin to Management*, May 29, 1997, pp. 172–173; "Regional Trends: Union Membership by State and Multiple Jobholding by State," *Monthly Labor Review* 123, no. 9 (September 2000), pp. 40–41.
24. Michael Carrell and Christina Heavrin, *Labor Relations and Collective Bargaining* (Upper Saddle River, NJ: Prentice Hall, 2004), p. 180.
25. Sloane and Witney, *Labor Relations*, p. 121.
26. Kris Maher, "Unions' New Foe: Consultants," *The Wall Street Journal*, August 15, 2005, p. B1.
27. "Some Say Salting Leaves Bitter Taste for Employers," *BNA Bulletin to Management*, March 4, 2004, p. 79; and www.nlrb.gov/global/search/index.aspx?mode=s&qt=salting&col=nlrb&gb=y, accessed January 14, 2008. For a management lawyer's perspective, see www.fklaborlaw.com/union_salt-objectives.html, accessed May 25, 2007.
28. "Spurned Union Salts Entitled to Back Pay, D.C. Court Says, Affirming Labor Board," *BNA Bulletin to Management*, June 21, 2001, p. 193.
29. D. Diane Hatch and James Hall, "Salting Cases Clarified by NLRB," *Workforce*, August 2000, p. 92. See also www.fklaborlaw.com/union_salt-objectives.html, accessed May 25, 2007.
30. Edwin Arnold et al., "Determinants of Certification Election Outcomes in the Service Sector," *Labor Studies Journal* 25, no. 3 (Fall 2000), p. 51.
31. "Number of Elections, Union Wins Increased in 2002," *BNA Bulletin to Management*, June 19, 2003, p. 197.
32. This section is based on Matthew Goodfellow, "How to Lose an NLRB Election," *Personnel Administrator* 23 (September 1976), pp. 40–44. See also Matthew Goodfellow, "Avoid Unionizing: Chemical Company Union Election Results for 1993," *Chemical Marketing Reporter* 246 (July 18, 1994) p. SR14; Gillian Flynn, "When the Unions Come Calling," *Workforce*, November 2000, pp. 82–87.
33. Ibid.
34. Ibid.
35. Harry Katz, "The Decentralization of Collective Bargaining: A Literature Review and Comparative Analysis," *Industrial and Labor Relations Review* 47, no. 1 (October 1993), p. 11.
36. The following are adapted and/or quoted from Kate Bronfenbrenner, "The Role of Union Strategies in NLRB Certification Elections," *Industrial and Labor Relations Review* 50 (January 1997) pp. 195–212.
37. Frederick Sullivan, "Limiting Union Organizing Activity Through Supervisors," *Personnel* 55 (July/August 1978), pp. 55–65. See also Edward Young and William Levy, "Responding to a Union-Organizing Campaign: Do You and Your Supervisors Know the Legal Boundaries in a Union Campaign?" *Franchising World* 39, no. 3 (March 2007), pp. 45–49.
38. Ibid., pp. 167–168.
39. Jonathan Segal, "Unshackle Your Supervisors to Stay Union Free," *HR Magazine*, June 1998, pp. 62–65. See also www.nlrb.gov/workplace_rights/nlra_violations.aspx, accessed January 14, 2008.
40. Whether employers must give union representatives permission to organize on employer-owned property at shopping malls is a matter of legal debate. The U.S. Supreme Court ruled in *Lechmere, Inc. v. National Labor Relations Board* that employers may bar nonemployees from their property if the nonemployees have reasonable alternative means of communicating their message to the intended audience. However, if the employer lets other organizations like the Salvation Army set up at their workplaces, the NLRB may view discriminating against the union organizers as an unfair labor practice. See, for example, "Union Access to Employer's Customers Restricted," *BNA Bulletin to Management*, February 15, 1996, p. 49; "Workplace Access for Unions Hinges on Legal Issues," *BNA Bulletin to Management*, April 11, 1996, p. 113.
41. "Union Access to Employer's Customers Restricted," *BNA Bulletin to Management*, February 15, 1996, pp. 4–65. The appropriateness of these sample rules may be affected by factors unique to an employer's operation, and they should therefore be reviewed by the employer's attorney before implementation.
42. Clyde Scott and Edwin Arnold, "Deauthorization and Decertification Elections: An Analysis and Comparison of Results," *WorkingUSA* 7, no. 3 (Winter 2003), pp. 6–20; www.nlrb.gov/nlrb/shared_files/brochures/rpt_september2002.pdf, accessed January 14, 2008.
43. Carrell and Heavrin, *Labor Relations and Collective Bargaining*, pp. 120–121.
44. See, for example, David Meyer and Trevor Bain, "Union Decertification Election Outcomes: Bargaining Unit Characteristics and Union Resources," *Journal of Labor Research* 15, no. 2 (Spring 1994), pp. 117–136.
45. www.nlrb.gov/nlrb/shared_files/brochures/basicguide.pdf, accessed January 14, 2008.
46. Carrell and Heavrin, *Labor Relations and Collective Bargaining*, pp. 176–177.
47. "No Talks Until Mechanics Union Softens Demand, Northwest Airlines Says," *Knight Ridder/Tribune Business News*, March 28, 2001, Item 01087165.
48. John Fossum, *Labor Relations* (Dallas: BPI, 1982), pp. 246–250.
49. *Boulwareism* is the name given to a strategy, now generally held in disfavor, by which the company, based on an exhaustive study of what it believed its employees wanted, made but one offer at the bargaining table and then refused to bargain any further unless convinced by the union on the basis of new facts that its original position was wrong. The NLRB subsequently found that the practice of offering the same settlement to all units, insisting that certain parts of the package could not differ among agreements, and communicating to the employees about how negotiations were going amounted to an illegal pattern. Fossum, *Labor Relations*, p. 267. See also William Cooke,

Aneil Mishra, Gretchen Spreitzer, and Mary Tschirhart, "The Determinants of NLRB Decision-Making Revisited," *Industrial and Labor Relations Review* 48, no. 2 (January 1995), pp. 237–257.
50. Kathryn Tyler, "Good-Faith Bargaining," *HR Magazine*, January 2005, p. 52.
51. See, for example, Arthur Sloane and Fred Witney, *Labor Relations* (Upper Saddle River, NJ, Prentice Hall, 2004), pp. 177–218.
52. Reed Richardson, *Collective Bargaining by Objectives* (Upper Saddle River, NJ: Prentice Hall, 1977), p. 150.
53. With or without reaching a solution, impasses and union–management conflict can leave union members demoralized. See, for example, Jessica Marquez, "Taking Flight," *Workforce*, June 9, 2008, pp. 1, 18.
54. Fossum, *Labor Relations*, p. 312. See also Thomas Watkins, "Assessing Arbitrator Competence," *Arbitration Journal* 47, no. 2 (June 1992), pp. 43–48.
55. Carrell and Heavrin, *Labor Relations and Collective Bargaining*, p. 501.
56. http://fmcs.gov/assets/files/annual%20reports/FY2006_Annual_Report.pdf, accessed January 14, 2008.
57. Fossum, *Labor Relations*, p. 317.
58. Mark Fitzgerald, "UAW Lifts Boycott," *Editor & Publisher*, February 26, 2001, p. 9.
59. "Striker Replacements," *BNA Bulletin to Management*, February 6, 2003, p. S7.
60. Micheline Maynard and Jeremy Peters, "Northwest Airlines Threatens to Replace Strikers Permanently," *The New York Times*, August 26, 2005, p. C3.
61. Stephen Cabot and Gerald Cuerton, "Labor Disputes and Strikes: Be Prepared," *Personnel Journal* 60 (February 1981), pp. 121–126. See also Brenda Sunoo, "Managing Strikes, Minimizing Loss," *Personnel Journal* 74, no. 1 (January 1995), pp. 50ff.
62. For a discussion, see Herbert Northrup, "Union Corporate Campaigns and Inside Games as a Strike Form," *Employee Relations Law Journal* 19, no. 4 (Spring 1994), pp. 507–549.
63. Jessica Materna, "Union Launches Web Site to Air Grievances Against San Francisco Marriott," *San Francisco Business Times*, May 4, 2001, p. 15.
64. Northrup, "Union Corporate Campaigns and Inside Games," p. 513.
65. Ibid., p. 518.
66. Clifford Koen Jr., Sondra Hartman, and Dinah Payne, "The NLRB Wields a Rejuvenated Weapon," *Personnel Journal*, December 1996, pp. 85–87.
67. Sloane and Witney, *Labor Relations*, 10th ed., pp. 221–227.
68. Carrell and Heavrin, *Labor Relations and Collective Bargaining*, pp. 417–418.
69. Richardson, *Collective Bargaining.*
70. Duncan Adams, "Worker Grievances Consume Roanoke, VA Mail Distribution Center," *Knight Ridder/Tribune Business News*, March 27, 2001, Item 01086009.
71. See M. Gene Newport, *Supervisory Management*, (West Group, 1976), p. 273, for an excellent checklist. See also Mark Lurie, "The Eight Essential Steps in Grievance Processing," *Dispute Resolution Journal* 54, no. 4 (November 1999), pp. 61–65.
72. Jeffrey McCracken, "Desperate to Cut Costs, Ford Gets Union's Help," *The Wall Street Journal*, March 2, 2007, pp. A1, A9.
73. See, for example, Jo Blanden et al., "Have Unions Turned the Corner? New Evidence on Recent Trends in Union Recognition in UK Firms," *British Journal of Industrial Relations* 44, no. 2 (June 2006), pp. 169–190.
74. www.bls.gov/news.release/union2.nr0.htm, accessed April 2, 2009.
75. Kris Maher, "The New Union Worker," *The Wall Street Journal*, September 27, 2005, pp. B1, B11.
76. Andy Meisler, "Who Will Fold First?" *Workforce Management*, January 2004, p. 30.
77. Carrell and Heavrin, *Labor Relations and Collective Bargaining*, pp. 34–36.
78. Woodruff Imberman, "Why Engineers Strike: The Boeing Story," *Business Horizons* 44, no. 6 (November 2001), pp. 35–39.
79. "The Limits of Solidarity," *The Economist*, September 23, 2006, p. 34.
80. Kris Maher, "Specter Won't Support Union-Backed Bill," *The Wall Street Journal*, March 20, 2009, p. A3.
81. "Unions Using Class Actions to Pressure Nonunion Companies," *BNA Bulletin to Management*, August 22, 2006, p. 271. Some believe that today, "long-term observers see more bark than bite in organized labor's efforts to revitalize." For example, Robert Grossman, "We Organized Labor and Code," *HR Magazine*, January 2008, pp. 37–40.
82. Andy Meisler, "Who Will Fold First?" pp. 28–38.
83. Jennifer Schramm, "The Future of Unions," *Workplace Visions* (Society for Human Resource Management, 2005), no. 4, pp. 1–8.
84. Ibid.
85. Ibid, p. 6.
86. Mei Fong and Kris Maher, "US Labor Chief Moves into China," *The Wall Street Journal* (Asia), June 22–24, 2007, p. 1.
87. Steven Greenhouse, "Steelworkers Merge with British Union," *The New York Times*, July 3, 2008, p. C4.
88. Gary Chaison, "Information Technology: The Threat to Unions," *Journal of Labor Research* 23, no. 2 (Spring 2002), pp. 249–260.
89. www.starbucksunion.org, accessed January 14, 2008.
90. Cathie Sheffield-Thompson, "Web Resources and Techniques for Organizing and Membership Development," 2006 Higher Ed State Staff Training, December 7–9, 2006, NEA Research, csheffield@nea.org, accessed March 23, 2009.
91. "Employer's System of Worker Empowerment Does Not Fall Prey to Labor Act, NLRB Rules," *BNA Bulletin to Management*, August 2, 2001, p. 241.
92. Carol Gill, "Union Impact on the Effective Adoption of High Performance Work Practices," *Human Resource Management Review* 19 (2009), pp. 39–50.
93. Raymond Hilgert and Cyril Ling, *Cases and Experiential Exercises in Management* (Upper Saddle River, NJ: Prentice Hall, 1996), pp. 201–203.
94. Chris Pursell, "Rhetoric Flying in WGA Talks," *TelevisionWeek*, July 23, 2007, pp. 3, 35; Peter Sanders, "In Hollywood, a Tale of Two Union Leaderships," *The Wall Street Journal*, January 7, 2008, p. B2.
95. Pursell, "Rhetoric Flying in WGA Talks."
96. Ibid.
97. James Hibberd, "Guild Talks Break with No Progress," *TVWeek* 26, no. 38 (October 8, 2007), pp. 1, 30.
98. Ibid.
99. "DGA Deal Sets the Stage for Writers," *TelevisionWeek*, January 21, 2008, pp. 3, 33.
100. "WGA, Studios Reach Tentative Agreement," UPI NewsTrack, February 3, 2008.
101. Brian Becker et al., *The HR Scorecard* (Boston: Harvard Business School Press, 2001), p. 16.

16 Employee Safety and Health

It must have been a frightening way to die. The worker, 30 years old, "suffocated when the tumbling dirt and debris rose to his chest, creating pressure so great that he could not breathe, even though his head remained uncovered." Other workers had warned the owner of the Brooklyn construction site that the trench was an accident waiting to happen. He allegedly did nothing about it. The prosecutor subsequently charged the owner with manslaughter.[1]

Source: Courtesy of Jim Toomey/Photolibrary.com.

WHERE ARE WE NOW . . .

Ethics and labor relations are both important factors in the quality of employees' work lives. Now, the main purpose of this chapter is to provide you with the basic knowledge you'll need to deal with workplace safety and health issues. Every manager needs a working knowledge of the Occupational Safety and Health Act, and so we discuss its purpose, standards, and inspection procedures, as well as employees' and employers' rights and responsibilities. We'll explain three causes of accidents: chance occurrences, unsafe conditions, and unsafe acts—and several techniques for preventing accidents. And we discuss important employee health problems, such as substance abuse and workplace violence.

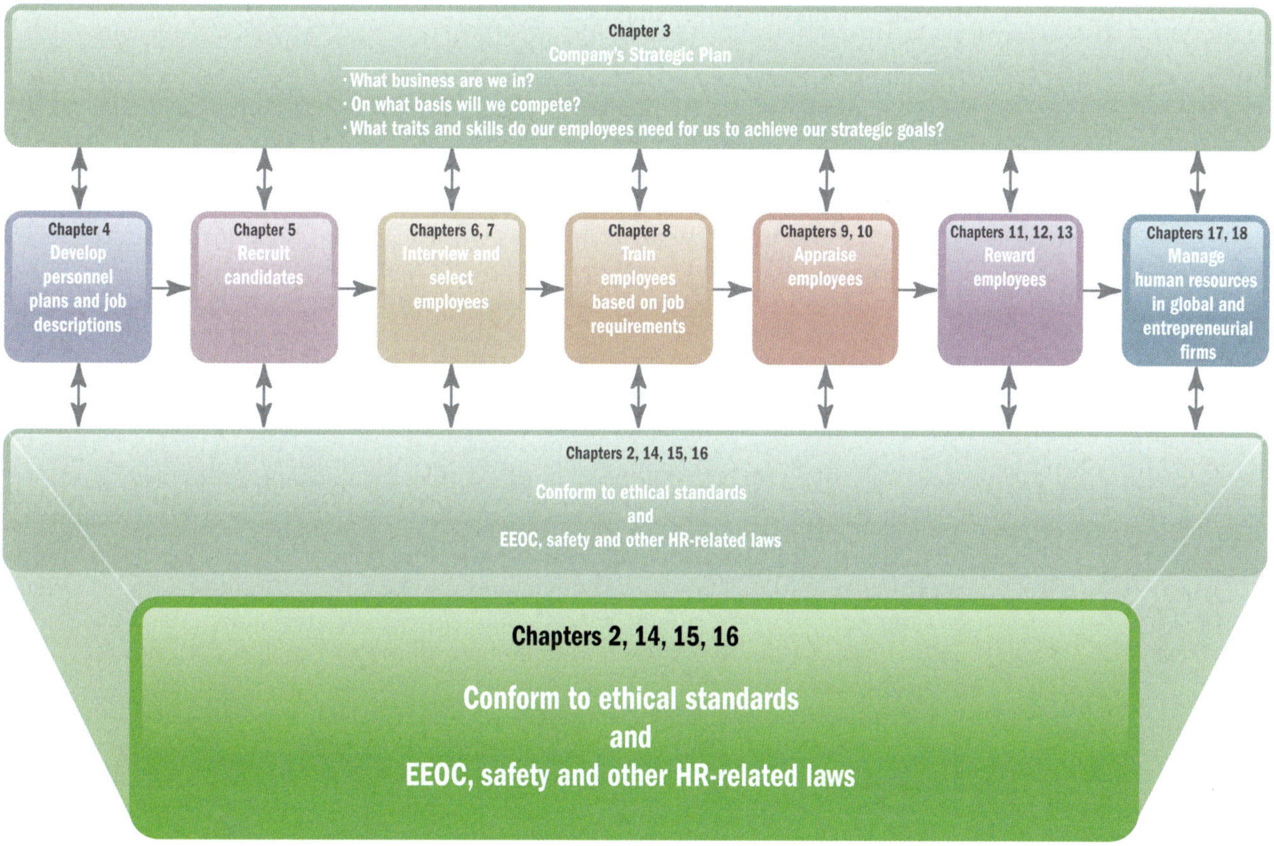

LEARNING OUTCOMES

1. Explain the supervisor's role in safety.
2. Explain the basic facts about safety law and OSHA.
3. Answer the question, "What causes accidents?"
4. List and explain five ways to prevent accidents.
5. Minimize unsafe acts by employees.
6. List five workplace health hazards and how to deal with them.
7. Discuss the prerequisites for a security plan and how to set up a basic security program.

Why Safety Is Important

Safety and accident prevention concern managers for several reasons, one of which is the staggering number of workplace accidents. In one recent year, 5,559 U.S. workers died in workplace incidents.[2] The U.S. Department of Labor says workplace accidents in the United States cause over 3.8 million occupational injuries and illnesses per year—roughly 4.4 cases per 100 full-time workers.[3] Such figures may actually underestimate the real number of injuries and illnesses by two or three times.[4]

And, injuries aren't just problems in dangerous industries like construction. For example, every year more than 15,000 reportable injuries or illnesses occur at manufacturers of computers and computer peripherals. Commercial kitchens have hazards like knives and slippery floors.[5] New computers contribute to "sick building syndrome" symptoms like headaches and sniffles, which some experts blame on poor ventilation.[6] (New computers emit chemical fumes, which diminish after the computer runs constantly for a week.[7]) And office work is susceptible to other health problems, including "repetitive trauma injuries related to computer use, respiratory illnesses stemming from indoor air quality, and high levels of stress."[8]

The Hidden Story But even facts like these don't tell the whole story. They don't show the human suffering incurred by the injured workers and their families or the real economic costs incurred by employers.[9] For example, the direct injury costs of a forklift accident might be $4,500. However, the indirect costs for things like lost production time, maintenance time, and emergency supplies could raise that to $18,000 or more.[10] Nor do they reflect the legal implications. When a boiler explosion at Ford's Rouge Power Plant killed six workers and injured 14, Ford paid a $1.5 million fine, and almost $6 million instituting various safety measures.[11]

Yet, there still are employers who seem to take safety less seriously than they should. For example, the *New York Times* described, in a story titled "A Family's Profits, Wrung from Blood and Sweat," a cast-iron business. It "has been cited for more than 400 safety violations since 1995, four times more than its six major competitors combined."[12]

Management's Role in Safety

All of which brings up a crucial point. On the next few pages, we'll see that reducing accidents often boils down to reducing accident-causing conditions and accident-causing acts. However, safety experts would agree that safety always starts at the top. Telling supervisors to "watch for spills" and employees to "work safely" is futile if everyone thinks management's not serious about safety.

Historically, for instance, DuPont's accident rate has been much lower than that of the chemical industry as a whole. This good safety record is partly due to an organizational commitment to safety, which is evident in the following description:

> One of the best examples I know of in setting the highest possible priority for safety takes place at a DuPont Plant in Germany. Each morning at the DuPont Polyester and Nylon Plant, the director and his assistants meet at 8:45 to review the past 24 hours. The first matter they discuss is not production, but safety. Only after they have examined reports of accidents and near misses and satisfied themselves that corrective action has been taken do they move on to look at output, quality, and cost matters.[13]

What Top Management Can Do

Policies like these start at the top. Ideally, "safety is an integral part of the system, woven into each management competency and a part of everyone's day-to-day responsibilities."[14] The employer should institutionalize top management's commitment with a safety policy, and publicize it. It should give safety matters high priority in meetings: Louisiana-Pacific Corp., which makes building products, starts all meetings, including board of directors' meetings, with a brief safety message.[15] Also analyze the number of accidents and safety incidents and then set specific achievable safety goals.

(Georgia-Pacific reduced its workers' compensation costs by requiring managers to halve accidents or forfeit 30% of their bonuses.) Give the company safety officer high rank and status, and include safety training in new workers' training.

Safety is not just a case of legal compliance or humanitarianism. One study of two organizations concluded that their safety activities paid for themselves by a ratio of 10 to 1, just in direct savings of workers' compensation expenses over 4 years.[16]

1 Explain the supervisor's role in safety.

The Supervisor's Role in Safety

After inspecting a work site where workers were installing pipes in a 4-foot trench, an OSHA inspector cited an employer for violating the rule requiring employers to have a "stairway, ladder, ramp, or other safe means of egress" in deep trench excavations.[17] In the event the trench caved in, workers needed a quick way out. As in most such cases, the employer had the primary responsibility for safety, and the local supervisor was responsible for the day-to-day inspections. Here, the supervisor did not properly do his daily inspection. The trench collapsed, and several employees were severely injured.

The moral is that safety inspections should always be part of the supervisor's daily routine. For example, "a daily walk-through of your workplace—whether you are working in outdoor construction, indoor manufacturing, or any place that poses safety challenges—is an essential part of your work."[18]

What to look for depends on the situation. For example, construction sites and dry cleaners have unique hazards. However, in general you can use a checklist of unsafe conditions such as the one in Figure 16-6 (page 592) to spot problems.

2 Explain the basic facts about safety law and OSHA.

OCCUPATIONAL SAFETY LAW

Congress passed the **Occupational Safety and Health Act of 1970** "to assure so far as possible every working man and woman in the nation safe and healthful working conditions and to preserve our human resources."[19] The only employers it doesn't cover are self-employed persons, farms in which only immediate members of the employer's family work, and some workplaces already protected by other federal agencies or under other statutes. The act covers federal agencies, but usually not state and local governments.

The act created the **Occupational Safety and Health Administration (OSHA)** within the Department of Labor. OSHA's basic purpose is to administer the act and to set and enforce the safety and health standards that apply to almost all workers in the United States. The Department of Labor enforces the standards, and OSHA has inspectors working out of branch offices to ensure compliance.

OSHA Standards and Record Keeping

OSHA operates under the "general" standard clause that each employer:

> . . . shall furnish to each of his [or her] employees employment and a place of employment which are free from recognized hazards that are causing or are likely to cause death or serious physical harm to his [or her] employees.

To carry out this basic mission, OSHA is responsible for promulgating legally enforceable standards. These are contained in five volumes covering general industry standards, maritime standards, construction standards, other regulations and procedures, and a field operations manual.

Occupational Safety and Health Act of 1970
The law passed by Congress in 1970 "to assure so far as possible every working man and woman in the nation safe and healthful working conditions and to preserve our human resources."

Occupational Safety and Health Administration (OSHA)
The agency created within the Department of Labor to set safety and health standards for almost all workers in the United States.

FIGURE 16-1 OSHA Standards Example

Source: www.osha.gov/pls/oshaweb/owadisp.show_document?p_id=9720&p_table=STANDARDS, accessed May 25, 2007.

> Guardrails not less than 2″ ×4″ or the equivalent and not less than 36″ or more than 42″ high, with a midrail, when required, of a 1″ × 4″ lumber or equivalent, and toeboards, shall be installed at all open sides on all scaffolds more than 10 feet above the ground or floor. Toeboards shall be a minimum of 4″ in height. Wire mesh shall be installed in accordance with paragraph [a] (17) of this section.

The standards are very complete and seem to cover in detail just about every conceivable hazard. (Figure 16-1 presents a small part of the standard governing guardrails for scaffolds.) And the regulations don't just list chemical or structural-type standards to which employers should adhere. They also lay out "how." For example, OSHA's respiratory protection standard also covers program administration and employee training.[20]

Under OSHA, employers with 11 or more employees must maintain records of and report certain occupational injuries and occupational illnesses. An **occupational illness** is any abnormal condition or disorder caused by exposure to environmental factors associated with employment. This includes acute and chronic illnesses caused by inhalation, absorption, ingestion, or direct contact with toxic substances or harmful agents.

What the Employer Must Report

As summarized in Figure 16-2, employers must report all occupational illnesses.[21] They must also report most occupational injuries, specifically those that result in medical treatment (other than first aid), loss of consciousness, restriction of work (one or more lost workdays), restriction of motion, or transfer to another job.[22] If an on-the-job accident results in the death of an employee or in the hospitalization of five or more employees, all employers, regardless of size, must report the accident to the nearest OSHA office.

OSHA's current record-keeping rules streamline the job of reporting occupational injuries or illnesses.[23] The rules continue to presume that an injury or illness that resulted from an event in or exposure to the work environment is "work related" (and

FIGURE 16-2 What Accidents Must Be Reported Under the Occupational Safety and Health Act?

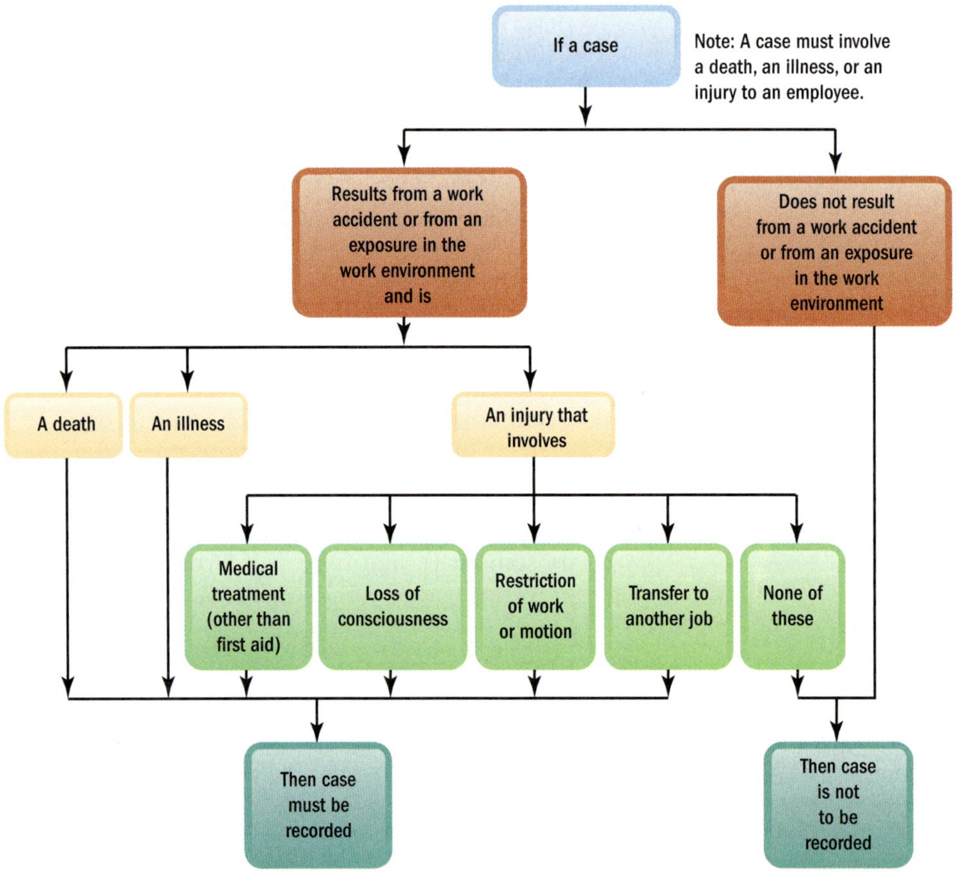

so reportable). However, it allows the employer to conclude that the event needn't be reported if the facts so warrant—such as if a worker breaks an ankle after catching his foot on his car's seat belt when parked on the company lot.

However, OSHA's record-keeping requirements are still broader than you might expect.[24] Examples of recordable conditions include food poisoning suffered by an employee after eating in the employer's cafeteria and ankle sprains that occur during voluntary participation in a company softball game at a picnic the employee was required to attend.

OSHA pursues record-keeping violations during its inspections, so it behooves employers to carefully record injuries or illnesses. Figure 16-3 shows the OSHA form for reporting occupational injuries or illness.

Inspections and Citations

OSHA enforces its standards through inspections and (if necessary) citations. The inspection is usually unannounced. OSHA may not conduct warrantless inspections without an employer's consent. However, it may inspect after acquiring an authorized search warrant or its equivalent.[25] With a limited number of inspectors, OSHA recently has focused on "fair and effective enforcement," combined with outreach, education and compliance assistance, and various OSHA–employer cooperative programs (such as its "Voluntary Protection Programs").[26]

Inspection Priorities However, OSHA still makes extensive use of inspections. OSHA takes a "worst-first" approach in setting inspection priorities. Priorities include, from highest to lowest, imminent dangers, catastrophes and fatal accidents, employee complaints, high-hazard industries inspections, and follow-up inspections.[27] In one recent year, OSHA conducted just over 39,000 inspections. Of these, complaints or accidents prompted 9,176, about 21,500 were high-hazard targeted, and follow-ups and referrals prompted 8,415.[28]

Under its priority system, OSHA conducts an inspection within 24 hours when a complaint indicates an immediate danger, and within 3 working days when a serious hazard exists. For a "nonserious" complaint filed in writing by a worker or a union, OSHA will respond within 20 working days. OSHA handles other nonserious complaints by writing to the employer and requesting corrective action.

The Inspection The inspection itself begins when the OSHA officer arrives at the workplace.[29] He or she displays credentials and asks to meet an employer representative. (Always insist on seeing the credentials, which include photograph and serial number.) The officer explains the visit's purpose, the scope of the inspection, and the standards that apply. An authorized employee representative accompanies the officer during the inspection. The inspector can also stop and question workers (in private, if necessary) about safety and health conditions. The act protects each employee from discrimination for exercising his or her disclosure rights. OSHA rules require employee involvement in OSHA's on-site consultations, and that employees be informed of the inspections' results.[30]

OSHA inspectors look for all types of violations, but some potential problem areas—such as scaffolding and fall protection—grab more of their attention. The five most frequent OSHA inspection violation areas are scaffolding, fall protection, hazard communication, lockout/tagout (electrical disengagement), and respiratory problems.

Finally, after checking the premises and employer's records, the inspector holds a closing conference with the employer's representative. Here the inspector discusses

occupational illness
Any abnormal condition or disorder caused by exposure to environmental factors associated with employment.

OSHA's FORM 301

Injury and Illness Incident Report

Attention: This form contains information relating to employee health and must be used in a manner that protects the confidentiality of employees to the extent possible while the information is being used for occupational safety and health purposes.

U.S. Department of Labor
Occupational Safety and Health Administration

Form approved OMB no. 1218-0176

This *Injury and Illness Incident Report* is one of the first forms you must fill out when a recordable work-related injury or illness has occurred. Together with the *Log of Work-Related Injuries and Illnesses* and the accompanying *Summary*, these forms help the employer and OSHA develop a picture of the extent and severity of work-related incidents.

Within 7 calendar days after you receive information that a recordable work-related injury or illness has occurred, you must fill out this form or an equivalent. Some state workers' compensation, insurance, or other reports may be acceptable substitutes. To be considered an equivalent form, any substitute must contain all the information asked for on this form.

According to Public Law 91-596 and 29 CFR 1904, OSHA's recordkeeping rule, you must keep this form on file for 5 years following the year to which it pertains.

If you need additional copies of this form, you may photocopy and use as many as you need.

Completed by ______________________

Title ______________________

Phone (____)____-______ **Date** ___/___/___

Information about the employee

1) Full name ______________________

2) Street ______________________

City ______________ State ________ ZIP ______

3) Date of birth ___/___/___

4) Date hired ___/___/___

5) ☐ Male
☐ Female

Information about the physician or other health care professional

6) Name of physician or other health care professional ______________________

7) If treatment was given away from the worksite, where was it given?

Facility ______________________

Street ______________________

City ______________ State ________ ZIP ______

8) Was employee treated in an emergency room?

☐ Yes
☐ No

9) Was employee hospitalized overnight as an in-patient?

☐ Yes
☐ No

Information about the case

10) Case number from the *Log* ______________ *(Transfer the case number from the Log after you record the case.)*

11) Date of injury or illness ___/___/___

12) Time employee began work ____________ AM/PM

13) Time of event ____________ AM/PM
☐ Check if time cannot be determined

14) ***What was the employee doing just before the incident occurred?*** Describe the activity, as well as the tools, equipment, or material the employee was using. Be specific. *Examples:* "climbing a ladder while carrying roofing materials"; "spraying chlorine from hand sprayer"; "daily computer key-entry."

15) ***What happened?*** Tell us how the injury occurred. *Examples:* "When ladder slipped on wet floor, worker fell 20 feet"; "Worker was sprayed with chlorine when gasket broke during replacement"; "Worker developed soreness in wrist over time."

16) ***What was the injury or illness?*** Tell us the part of the body that was affected and how it was affected; be more specific than "hurt," "pain," or sore." *Examples:* "strained back"; "chemical burn, hand"; "carpal tunnel syndrome."

17) ***What object or substance directly harmed the employee?*** *Examples:* "concrete floor"; "chlorine"; "radial arm saw," *If this question does not apply to the incident, leave it blank.*

18) ***If the employee died, when did death occur?*** Date of death ___/___/___

Public reporting burden for this collection of information is estimated to average 22 minutes per response, including time for reviewing instructions, searching existing data sources, gathering and maintaining the data needed, and completing and reviewing the collection of information. Persons are not required to respond to the collection of information unless it displays a current valid OMB control number. If you have any comments about this estimate or any other aspects of this data collection, including suggestions for reducing this burden, contact: US Department of Labor, OSHA Office of Statistical Analysis, Room N-3644, 200 Constitution Avenue, NW, Washington, DC 20210. Do not send the completed forms to this office.

FIGURE 16-3 Form Used to Record Occupational Injuries and Illnesses
Source: U.S. Department of Labor.

FIGURE 16-4 Most Frequently Cited Hazards

UNITED STATES DEPARTMENT OF LABOR

OCCUPATIONAL SAFETY & HEALTH ADMINISTRATION

www.OSHA.gov A-Z Index: A B C D E F G H I J K L M N O P Q R S T U V W X Y Z Search OSHA GO

Standards Cited for SIC ALL; All sizes; Federal

ALL *SIC Codes*

Listed below are the standards which were cited by **Federal OSHA** for the specified SIC during the period October 2007 through September 2008. Penalties shown reflect current rather than initial amounts. For more information, see definitions.

Standard	#Cited	#Insp	$Penalty	Description
Total	115044	29042	105224214	
19260451	10223	3962	9497057	General requirements.
19260501	7081	6422	9664000	Duty to have fall protection.
19101200	7061	3712	1808357	Hazard Communication.
19100147	4271	2262	4201860	The control of hazardous energy (lockout/tagout).
19100134	4187	1811	1662891	Respiratory Protection.
19100305	3484	2144	2050473	Wiring methods, components, and equipment for general use.
19100178	3427	2286	2826717	Powered industrial trucks.
19261053	3061	2270	1863798	Ladders.
19100212	2937	2414	3558430	General requirements for all machines.

apparent violations for which OSHA may issue or recommend a **citation** and penalty. At this point, the employer can produce records to show compliance efforts. Figure 16-4 lists the hazards that accounted for the greatest number of citations in one recent year. Inadequate scaffolding/fall protection was one of the most frequently cited hazards.

Penalties OSHA can impose penalties. These generally range from $5,000 up to $150,000 for willful or repeat serious violations, although the penalties can be far higher—$1.5 million at the Ford Rouge plant, for instance.[31] The parties settle many OSHA cases before litigation, in "precitation settlements." Here, OSHA issues the citation and agreed-on penalties simultaneously, after negotiations with the employer.[32] There is also a maximum of $7,000 a day in penalties for failure to correct a violation. Other-than-serious violations often carry no penalties.

In general, OSHA calculates penalties based on the gravity of the violation and usually takes into consideration factors like the size of the business, the firm's compliance history, and the employer's good faith.[33] In practice, OSHA must have a final order from the independent Occupational Safety and Health Review Commission (OSHRC) to enforce a penalty.[34] An employer who files a notice of contest can drag out an appeal for years. Many employers do appeal, at least to the OSHA district office.[35]

To the chagrin of some employers, OSHA is publicizing its inspection results online. For example, OSHA's Web site (www.osha.gov) gives you easy access to your company's (or your competitors') OSHA enforcement history.

Managers' Inspection Guidelines What should you do when OSHA inspectors unexpectedly show up? Guidelines include the following:

Initial Contact

- Restrict admittance until the manager in charge/OSHA coordinator is on site.[36]
- Check the inspector's credentials.
- Ask the inspector why he or she is inspecting your workplace. Is it complaints? A scheduled visit?
- If the inspection stems from a complaint, you are entitled to know whether the person is a current employee, though not the person's name.
- Notify your counsel, who should review all documents and information.

citation
Summons informing employers and employees of the regulations and standards that have been violated in the workplace.

Opening Conference

- Establish the focus and scope of the planned inspection.
- Discuss the procedures for protecting trade secret areas.
- Show the inspector you have safety programs in place. He or she may not even go to the work floor if your paperwork is complete and up to date.

Walk-Around Inspection

- Accompany the inspector and take detailed notes.
- If the inspector takes a photo or video, you should, too.
- Ask for duplicates of all physical samples and copies of all test results.
- Be helpful and cooperative, but don't volunteer information.
- To the extent possible, immediately correct any violation the inspector identifies.[37]

The magazine *Occupational Hazards* conducted a survey of 12 safety experts and asked them to identify the "10 best ways" to get into trouble with OSHA.[38] Several "best ways" were inspection-related. They include the following:

1. Antagonize or lie to OSHA during an inspection.
2. Keep inaccurate OSHA logs and have disorganized safety files.
3. Fail to control the flow of information during and after an inspection. (The employer should not give the OSHA inspector any information he or she does not ask for, and should also keep tabs on everything the employer has given to the inspector.)

OSHA's Free On-Site Inspections OSHA provides free on-site safety and health services for small businesses.[39] This service uses safety experts from state governments and provides consultations, usually at the employer's workplace. Employers can contact their nearest OSHA area office to speak to the compliance assistance specialist. According to OSHA, it issues no citations or penalties based on these inspections.

The employer triggers the process by requesting a voluntary consultation. There is then an opening conference with a safety expert, a walk-through, and a closing conference at which the employer and safety expert discuss the latter's observations. The consultant then sends a detailed report explaining the findings. The employer's only obligation is to commit to correcting serious job safety and health hazards in a timely manner. Said one small business owner, "Our workers' compensation costs have decreased significantly, we have had no accidents, and there is an awareness that we take safety seriously."[40]

Source: Courtesy of ENSR.

Employees have rights and responsibilities under OSHA standards, such as to wear their hardhats, but OSHA can't cite them if they violate their responsibilities.

Responsibilities and Rights of Employers and Employees

Both employers and employees have responsibilities and rights under the Occupational Safety Health Act. *Employers* are responsible for providing "a workplace free from recognized hazards," for being familiar with mandatory OSHA standards, and for examining workplace conditions to make sure they conform to OSHA standards. Employers have the right to seek advice and off-site consultation from OSHA, request and receive proper identification of the OSHA compliance officer before inspection, and to be advised by the compliance officer of the reason for an inspection.

Employees also have rights and responsibilities, but OSHA can't cite them for violations of their responsibilities. Employees are responsible, for example, for complying with all applicable OSHA standards, for following all employer safety and health rules and regulations, and for reporting hazardous conditions to the supervisor. Employees have a right to demand safety and health on the job without fear of punishment. The act prohibits employers from punishing or discriminating against workers who complain to OSHA about job safety and health hazards. (See the accompanying OSHA safety poster, in Figure 16-5.)

FIGURE 16-5 OSHA Safety Poster

Dealing with Employee Resistance

Although employees have a responsibility to comply with OSHA standards, they often resist; the employer usually remains liable for any penalties. The refusal of some workers to wear hard hats typifies this problem.

Employers have attempted to defend themselves against penalties for such noncompliance by citing worker intransigence and their own fear of walkouts. In most cases, courts still hold employers liable for workplace safety violations.

Yet employers can reduce their liability, since "courts have recognized that it is impossible to totally eliminate all hazardous conduct by employees."[41] In the event of a problem, the courts may take into consideration facts such as whether the employer's safety procedures were adequate; whether the training really gave employees the understanding, knowledge, and skills required to perform their duties safely; and whether the employer really required employees to follow the procedures.

There are several other ways to reduce liability.[42] The employer can bargain with its union for the right to discipline any employee who disobeys an OSHA standard. A formal employer–employee arbitration process could provide a relatively quick method for resolving an OSHA-related dispute. Other employers turn to positive reinforcement and training for gaining employee compliance; more on this shortly. The independent three-member Occupational Safety and Health Review Commission that reviews OSHA decisions says employers must make "a diligent effort to discourage, by discipline if necessary, violations of safety rules by employees."[43] However, the only surefire way to eliminate liability is to ensure that no safety violations occur.

WHAT CAUSES ACCIDENTS?

There are three basic causes of workplace accidents: chance occurrences, unsafe conditions, and employees' unsafe acts. Chance occurrences (such as walking past a window just as someone hits a ball through it) are more or less beyond management's control. We will therefore focus on unsafe conditions and unsafe acts.

Unsafe Conditions and Other Work-Related Factors

Unsafe conditions are a main cause of accidents. They include things like:

- Improperly guarded equipment
- Defective equipment
- Hazardous procedures in, on, or around machines or equipment
- Unsafe storage—congestion, overloading
- Improper illumination—glare, insufficient light
- Improper ventilation—insufficient air change, impure air source[44]

The solution here is to identify and eliminate the unsafe conditions. The main aim of the OSHA standards is to address these mechanical and physical accident-causing conditions. The employer's safety department (if any), and its human resource managers and top managers should take responsibility for identifying unsafe conditions.

3 Answer the question, "What causes accidents?"

Danger Zones

While accidents can happen anywhere, there are some high-danger zones. About one-third of industrial accidents occur around forklift trucks, wheelbarrows, and other handling and lifting areas. The most serious accidents usually occur by metal and woodworking machines and saws, or around transmission machinery like gears, pulleys, and flywheels. Falls on stairs, ladders, walkways, and scaffolds are the third most common cause of industrial accidents. Hand tools (like chisels and screwdrivers) and electrical equipment (extension cords, electric droplights, and so on) are other major causes of accidents.[45]

Certain jobs are inherently more dangerous. For example, the job of crane operator results in about three times more hospital visits than does the job of supervisor.[46]

Work schedules and fatigue also affect accident rates. Accident rates usually don't increase too noticeably during the first 5 or 6 hours of the workday. But after that, the accident rate increases faster. This is due partly to fatigue and partly to the fact that accidents occur more often during night shifts.

Unfortunately, some of the most important working-condition–related causes of accidents are not as obvious, because they involve workplace "climate" or psychology. One researcher reviewed the official hearings regarding the fatal accidents offshore oil workers suffered in the British North Sea.[47] A strong pressure to complete the work as quickly as possible, employees who are under stress, and a poor safety climate—for instance, supervisors who never mention safety—were a few of the psychological conditions leading to accidents. Similarly, accidents occur more frequently in plants with high seasonal layoff rates, hostility among employees, many garnished wages, and blighted living conditions.

What Causes Unsafe Acts? (A Second Basic Cause of Accidents)

Unsafe acts can undo even the best attempts to reduce unsafe conditions. The problem is that there are no easy answers to the question of what causes people to act recklessly.

It may seem intuitively obvious that some people are simply accident prone, but the research isn't that clear.[48] On closer inspection it turns out some "accident repeaters" were just unlucky, or may have been more meticulous about reporting their accidents.[49] However, there is growing evidence that people with specific traits may indeed be accident prone. For example, people who are impulsive, sensation seeking, extremely extroverted, and less conscientious (in terms of being less fastidious and dependable) are more likely to have accidents.[50]

Furthermore, the person who is accident prone on one job may not be so on another. Driving is one example. Personality traits that correlate with filing vehicular insurance claims include *entitlement* ("think there's no reason they should not speed"), *impatience* ("were 'always in a hurry'"), *aggressiveness* ("the first to move when the light turns green"), and *distractibility* ("frequently distracted by cell phones, eating, and so on"). A study in Thailand similarly found risky drivers were naturally competitive and prone to anger.[51]

We'll turn to how employers can reduce unsafe acts and conditions next.

4 List and explain five ways to prevent accidents.

HOW TO PREVENT ACCIDENTS

In practice, accident prevention boils down to two basic activities: (1) reducing unsafe conditions and (2) reducing unsafe acts. In large facilities, the chief safety officer (often called the "Environmental Health and Safety Officer") is responsible for this.[52] In smaller firms, managers, including those from human resources, plant management, and first-line managers, share these responsibilities.

Reducing Unsafe Conditions

Reducing unsafe conditions is always an employer's first line of defense in accident - prevention. Safety engineers should design jobs to remove or reduce physical hazards. In addition, we saw that supervisors and managers play a role. Checklists

unsafe conditions
The mechanical and physical conditions that cause accidents.

like the ones in Figures 16-6 and 16-7 or the self-inspection checklist in Figure 16-11 (page 619) can help identify and remove potential hazards.

Employers increasingly use computerized tools to design safer equipment. For example, Designsafe (from Designsafe Engineering, Ann Arbor, Michigan) helps automate the tasks of hazard analysis, risk assessment, and identifying safety options. Designsafe helps the safety designer choose the most appropriate safety control device for keeping the worker safe, such as adjustable enclosures, presence-sensing devices, and personal protective equipment.[53]

I. GENERAL HOUSEKEEPING

Adequate and wide aisles—no materials protruding into aisles
Parts and tools stored safely after use—not left in hazardous positions that could cause them to fall
Even and solid flooring—no defective floors or ramps that could cause falling or tripping accidents
Waste cans and sand pails—safely located and properly used
Material piled in safe manner—not too high or too close to sprinkler heads
Floors—clean and dry
Firefighting equipment—unobstructed
Work benches orderly
Stockcarts and skids safely located, not left in aisles or passageways
Aisles kept clear and properly marked; no air lines or electric cords across aisles

II. MATERIAL HANDLING EQUIPMENT AND CONVEYANCES

On all conveyances, electric or hand, check to see that the following items are all in sound working conditions:
Brakes—properly adjusted
Not too much play in steering wheel
Warning device—in place and working
Wheels—securely in place; properly inflated
Fuel and oil—enough and right kind
No loose parts
Cables, hooks, or chains—not worn or otherwise defective
Suspended chains or hooks conspicuous
Safely loaded
Properly stored

III. LADDERS, SCAFFOLD, BENCHES, STAIRWAYS, ETC.

The following items of major interest to be checked:
Safety feet on straight ladders
Guardrails or handrails
Treads, not slippery
No cracked, or rickety
Properly stored
Extension ladder ropes in good condition
Toeboards

IV. POWER TOOLS (STATIONARY)

Point of operation guarded
Guards in proper adjustment
Gears, belts, shafting, counterweights guarded
Foot pedals guarded
Brushes provided for cleaning machines
Adequate lighting
Properly grounded
Tool or material rests properly adjusted
Adequate work space around machines
Control switch easily accessible
Safety glasses worn
Gloves worn by persons handling rough or sharp materials
No gloves or loose clothing worn by persons operating machines

V. HAND TOOLS AND MISCELLANEOUS

In good condition—not cracked, worn, or otherwise defective
Properly stored
Correct for job
Goggles, respirators, and other personal protective equipment worn where necessary

VI. WELDING

Arc shielded
Fire hazards controlled
Operator using suitable protective equipment
Adequate ventilation
Cylinder secured
Valves closed when not in use

VII. SPRAY PAINTING

Explosion-proof electrical equipment
Proper storage of paints and thinners in approved metal cabinets
Fire extinguishers adequate and suitable; readily accessible
Minimum storage in work area

VIII. FIRE EXTINGUISHERS

Properly serviced and tagged
Readily accessible
Adequate and suitable for operations involved

FIGURE 16-6 Checklist of Mechanical or Physical Accident-Causing Conditions

Source: Courtesy of the American Insurance Association. From "A Safety Committee Man's Guide," pp. 1–64.

FIGURE 16-7 Online Safety Inspection Checklist

FORM **CD-574**
(9/02)

U.S. Department of Commerce
Office Safety Inspection Checklist for
Supervisors and Program Managers

Name:	**Division:**
Location:	**Date:**
Signature:	

This checklist is intended as a guide to assist supervisors and program managers in conducting safety and health inspections of their work areas. It includes questions relating to general office safety, ergonomics, fire prevention, and electrical safety. Questions which receive a "**NO**" answer require corrective action. If you have questions or need assistance with resolving any problems, please contact your safety office. More information on office safety is available through the Department of Commerce Safety Office website at http://ohrm.doc.gov/safetyprogram/safety.htm.

Work Environment

Yes	No	N/A	
○	○	◉	Are all work areas clean, sanitary, and orderly?
○	○	◉	Is there adequate lighting?
○	○	◉	Do noise levels appear high?
○	○	◉	Is ventilation adequate?

Walking / Working Surfaces

Yes	No	N/A	
○	○	◉	Are aisles and passages free of stored material that may present trip hazards?
○	○	◉	Are tile floors in places like kitchens and bathrooms free of water and slippery substances?
○	○	◉	Are carpet and throw rugs free of tears or trip hazards?
○	○	◉	Are hand rails provided on all fixed stairways?
○	○	◉	Are treads provided with anti-slip surfaces?
○	○	◉	Are step ladders provided for reaching overhead storage areas and are materials stored safely?
○	○	◉	Are file drawers kept closed when not in use?
○	○	◉	Are passenger and freight elevators inspected annually and are the inspection certificates available for review on-site?
○	○	◉	Are pits and floor openings covered or otherwise guarded?
○	○	◉	Are standard guardrails provided wherever aisle or walkway surfaces are elevated more than 48 inches above any adjacent floor or the ground?
○	○	◉	Is any furniture unsafe or defective?
○	○	◉	Are objects covering heating and air conditioning vents?

Ergonomics

Yes	No	N/A	
○	○	◉	Are employees advised of proper lifting techniques?
○	○	◉	Are workstations configured to prevent common ergonomic problems? (Chair height allows employees' feet to rest flat on the ground with thighs parallel to the floor, top of computer screen is at or slightly below eye level, keyboard is at elbow height. Additional information on proper configuration of workstations is available through the Commerce Safety website at http://ohrm.doc.gov/safetyprogram/safety.htm)
○	○	◉	Are mechanical aids and equipment, such as; lifting devices, carts, dollies provided where needed?
○	○	◉	Are employees surveyed annually on their ergonomic concerns?

(continued)

FIGURE 16-7 *(continued)*

FORM **CD-574**
(9/02)

Emergency Information (Postings)

Yes	No	N/A	
○	○	⊙	Are established emergency phone numbers posted where they can be readily found in case of an emergency?
○	○	⊙	Are employees trained on emergency procedures?
○	○	⊙	Are fire evacuation procedures/diagrams posted?
○	○	⊙	Is emergency information posted in every area where you store hazardous waste?
○	○	⊙	Is established facility emergency information posted near a telephone?
○	○	⊙	Are the OSHA poster, and other required posters displayed conspicuously?
○	○	⊙	Are adequate first aid supplies available and properly maintained?
○	○	⊙	Are an adequate number of first aid trained personnel available to respond to injuries and illnesses until medical assistance arrives?
○	○	⊙	Is a copy of the facility fire prevention and emergency action plan available on site?
○	○	⊙	Are safety hazard warning signs/caution signs provided to warn employees of pertinent hazards?

Fire Prevention

Yes	No	N/A	
○	○	⊙	Are flammable liquids, such as gasoline, kept in approved safety cans and stored in flammable cabinets?
○	○	⊙	Are portable fire extinguishers distributed properly (less than 75 feet travel distance for combustibles and 50 feet for flammables)?
○	○	⊙	Are employees trained on the use of portable fire extinguishers?
○	○	⊙	Are portable fire extinguishers visually inspected monthly and serviced annually?
○	○	⊙	Is the area around portable fire extinguishers free of obstructions and properly labeled ?
○	○	⊙	Is heat-producing equipment used in a well ventilated area?
○	○	⊙	Are fire alarm pull stations clearly marked and unobstructed?
○	○	⊙	Is proper clearance maintained below sprinkler heads (i.e., 18" clear)?

Emergency Exits

Yes	No	N/A	
○	○	⊙	Are doors, passageways or stairways that are neither exits nor access to exits and which could be mistaken for exits, appropriately marked "NOT AN EXIT," "TO BASEMENT," "STOREROOM," etc.?
○	○	⊙	Are a sufficient number of exits provided?
○	○	⊙	Are exits kept free of obstructions or locking devices which could impede immediate escape?
○	○	⊙	Are exits properly marked and illuminated?
○	○	⊙	Are the directions to exits, when not immediately apparent, marked with visible signs?
○	○	⊙	Can emergency exit doors be opened from the direction of exit travel without the use of a key or any special knowledge or effort when the building is occupied?
○	○	⊙	Are exits arranged such that it is not possible to travel toward a fire hazard when exiting the facility?

FIGURE 16-7 *(continued)*

FORM **CD-574**
(9/02)

Electrical Systems
(Please have your facility maintenance person or electrician accompany you during this part of the inspection)

Yes	No	N/A	
○	○	⊙	Are all cord and cable connections intact and secure?
○	○	⊙	Are electrical outlets free of overloads?
○	○	⊙	Is fixed wiring used instead of flexible/extension cords?
○	○	⊙	Is the area around electrical panels and breakers free of obstructions?
○	○	⊙	Are high-voltage electrical service rooms kept locked?
○	○	⊙	Are electrical cords routed such that they are free of sharp objects and clearly visible?
○	○	⊙	Are all electrical cords grounded?
○	○	⊙	Are electrical cords in good condition (free of splices, frays, etc.)?
○	○	⊙	Are electrical appliances approved (Underwriters Laboratory, Inc. (UL), etc)?
○	○	⊙	Are electric fans provided with guards of not over one-half inch, preventing finger exposures?
○	○	⊙	Are space heaters UL listed and equipped with shutoffs that activate if the heater tips over?
○	○	⊙	Are space heaters located away from combustibles and properly ventilated?
○	○	⊙	In your electrical rooms are all electrical raceways and enclosures securely fastened in place?
○	○	⊙	Are clamps or other securing means provided on flexible cords or cables at plugs, receptacles, tools, equipment, etc., and is the cord jacket securely held in place?
○	○	⊙	Is sufficient access and working space provided and maintained about all electrical equipment to permit ready and safe operations and maintenance? (This space is 3 feet for less than 600 volts, 4 feet for more than 600 volts)

FORM **CD-574**
(9/02)

Material Storage

Yes	No	N/A	
○	○	⊙	Are storage racks and shelves capable of supporting the intended load and materials stored safely?
○	○	⊙	Are storage racks secured from falling?
○	○	⊙	Are office equipment stored in a stable manner, not capable of falling?

Sometimes the solution for eliminating an unsafe condition is obvious, and sometimes it's more subtle. For example, slips and falls are often the result of debris or slippery floors.[54] Obvious remedies include floor mats and better lighting. Perhaps less obviously, personal safety gear, like slip-resistant footwear with grooved soles, can also reduce slips and falls. Cut-resistant gloves reduce the hazards of working with sharp objects.[55] (Hand injuries account for about 1 million emergency department visits annually by U.S. workers.[56]) Figure 16-8 illustrates what's available.

Personal Protective Equipment Getting employees to wear personal protective equipment (PPE) is a famously difficult chore. Wearability is important. In addition to providing reliable protection, protective gear should fit properly; be easy to care for, maintain, and repair; be flexible and lightweight; provide comfort and reduce heat stress; have rugged construction; be relatively easy to put on and take off; and be easy to clean, dispose of, and recycle.[57] Many employers, such as Kimberly-Clark and MCR Safety, are tapping into the new fibers and fabrics used by runners, skiers, and NASCAR drivers to design easier wearing high-tech solutions.[58] Including employees in planning the safety program and addressing comfort issues contribute to employees' willingness to use the protective gear.[59] The accompanying "Managing the New Workforce" feature expands on this.

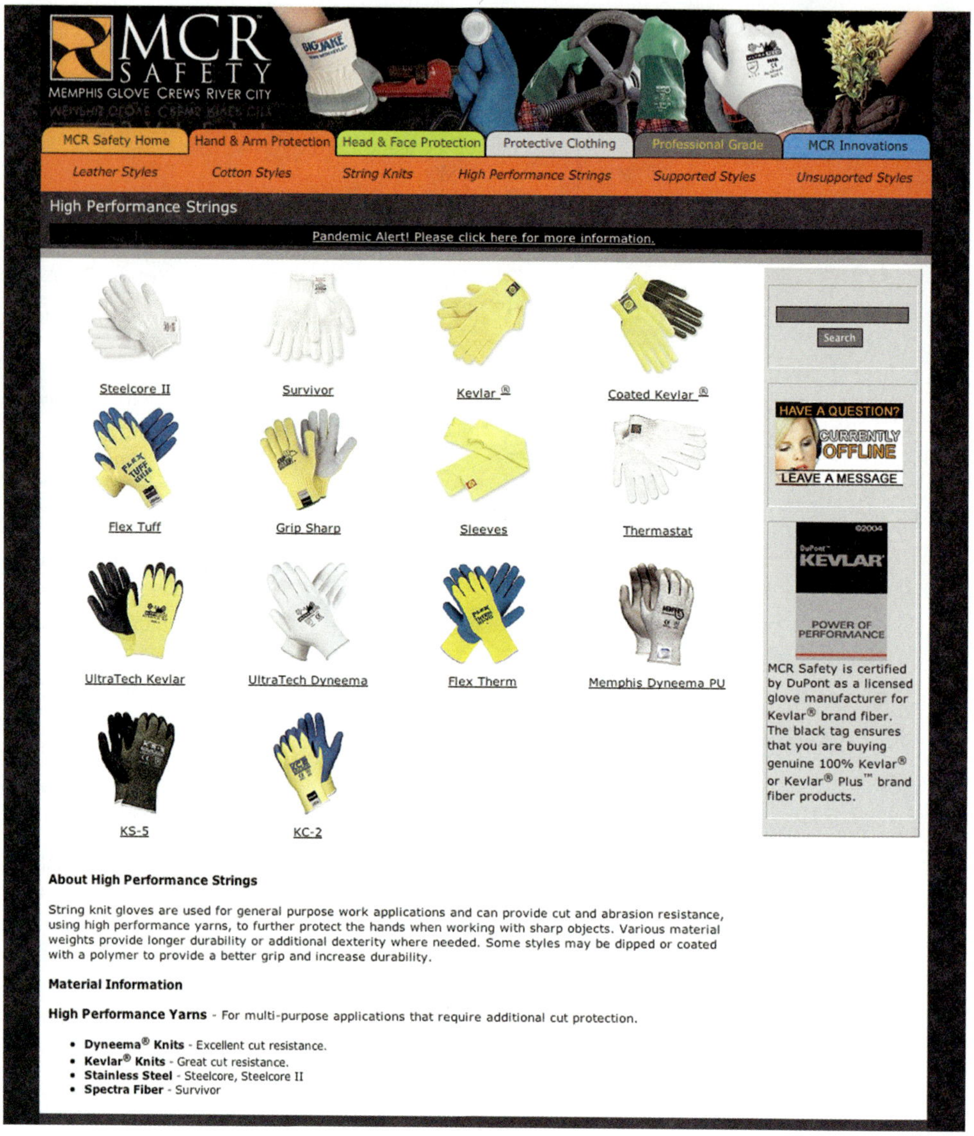

FIGURE 16-8 Cut-Resistant Gloves Web Ad
Hand protection from MCR provides both the wear-ability and safety that employers want in safety equipment for their employees

Source: Courtesy of Occupational Hazards, Penton Media, Inc.

Managing the New Workforce

Protecting Vulnerable Workers

In designing safe and healthy environments, employers need to pay special attention to vulnerable workers, those who are "unprepared to deal with hazards in the workplace," either due to lack of education, ill-fitting personal protective equipment, physical limitations, or cultural reasons. Among others, these may include young workers, immigrant workers, aging workers, and women workers.[60] (The Fair Labor Standards Act strictly limits young people's exposure to dangerous jobs, but about 64 workers under age 18 died from work-related injuries in one recent year.[61])

For example, although about half of all workers today are women, most machinery and personal protective equipment (like gloves) are designed for men. Women may thus have to use makeshift platforms or stools to reach machinery controls, or safety goggles that don't fit. The solution is to make sure the equipment and machines women use are appropriate for their size.[62]

Similarly, with more workers postponing retirement, older workers are doing more manufacturing jobs. For example, at one ATI Allegheny Ludlum facility (which makes stainless steel), about two-thirds of the workers are within 10 years of retirement.[63] They can do these jobs very effectively. However, there are numerous potential physical changes associated with aging, including loss of strength, loss of muscular flexibility, and reduced reaction time.[64] This means that employers should make special provisions such as designing jobs to reduce heavy lifting, and boosting lighting levels.[65] The fatality rate for older workers is about three times that of younger workers.[66]

But again, reducing unsafe conditions (such as enclosing noisy equipment) is always the first line of defense. Then use administrative controls (such as job rotation to reduce long-term exposure to the hazard). Only then, turn to PPE.[67]

Reducing unsafe acts—by emphasizing safety and through screening, training, or incentive programs, for example—is the second basic way to reduce accidents. Let's look at how to do this.

5 Minimize unsafe acts by employees.

Reducing Unsafe Acts

Although reducing unsafe conditions is the first line of defense, human misbehavior can short-circuit even the best safety efforts. Sometimes the misbehavior is intentional, but often it's not. For example, distractions—not noticing moving or stationary objects or that a floor is wet—often cause accidents.[68] And, ironically, ". . . making a job safer with machine guards or PPE lowers people's risk perceptions and thus can lead to an increase in at-risk behavior."[69]

As mentioned earlier, the manager plays a central role in reducing unsafe acts. For example, supervisors should:

- Praise employees when they choose safe behaviors;
- Listen when employees offer safety suggestions, concerns, or complaints; and
- Be a good example, for instance, by following every safety rule and procedure.[70]

Unfortunately, praising employees is usually not enough to banish unsafe acts. Instead, it requires a process. First, identify and try to eliminate potential risks, such as unguarded equipment. Next, reduce potential distractions, such as noise, heat, and stress. Then, carefully screen and train employees, as we explain next.

Reducing Unsafe Acts Through Selection and Placement

Proper employee screening and placement reduces unsafe acts. Here, the employer's aim is to identify the traits that might predict accidents on the job in question, and then screen candidates for this trait. For example, the Employee Reliability Index (ERI) (see www.ramsaycorp.com/products/eriphone.asp) measures reliability dimensions such as emotional maturity, conscientiousness, and safe job performance.[71] Though not definitive, using the ERI in selection did seem to be associated with reductions in work-related accidents in one study. Others use *job simulation tests* (which attempt to measure the applicant by simulating physically demanding work activities) and *physical capabilities tests* (which measure muscle strength and motion) to predict who will have more accidents.[72]

Similarly, behavioral interview questions can be revealing. For example, ask, "What would you do if you saw another employee working in an unsafe way?" and "What would you do if your supervisor gave you a task, but didn't provide any training on how to perform it safely?"[73]

Asking about a candidate's workers' compensation history might at first glance seem sensible. However, under the Americans with Disabilities Act (ADA) it is unlawful to inquire (prior to hiring) about an applicant's workers' compensation injuries and claims. You also cannot ask applicants whether they have a disability, or require them to take tests that tend to screen out those with disabilities. However, you can usually ask whether an applicant has the ability to perform a job. You can even ask, "Do you know of any reason why you would not be able to perform the various functions of the job you are seeking?"[74]

Reducing Unsafe Acts Through Training

Safety training reduces unsafe acts, especially for new employees. You should instruct them in safe practices and procedures, warn them of potential hazards, and work on developing a safety-conscious attitude. OSHA has two useful booklets, "Training Requirements under OSHA" and "Teaching Safety and Health in the Workplace." OSHA, the National Institute for Occupational Safety and Health (NIOSH), and numerous private vendors provide online safety training solutions.[75] OSHA also supplies training at its Institute in Chicago, or at one of 20 education centers located at U.S. colleges and universities.

OSHA's standards require more than training. Employers must demonstrate that employees actually learned what to do. For example, OSHA's respiratory standard requires that each employee be able to demonstrate how to inspect, put on, and remove respirator seals.[76] The accompanying "Managing the New Workforce" feature provides an additional perspective.

Managing the New Workforce

Safety Training for Hispanic Workers

With increasing numbers of Spanish-speaking workers in the United States, experts express concern about their safety. For example, the number of Hispanic fatalities in construction rose by almost 50% in the early 2000s, because so many more Hispanics are now working in construction jobs.[77]

Faced with statistics like these, many construction companies are offering specialized training programs for Hispanic workers. One example is a 40-hour training course provided for construction workers at the Dallas–Fort Worth airport expansion project. The construction firms here credit part of the airport site's safety improvements to the new training program.

Based on this program's apparent success, there are several useful conclusions one can draw about what a program like this should look like.

- First, the program should *speak the workers' language.*
- Second, teaching the program in Spanish (or another appropriate language) is only part of "speaking the workers' language." The employer should also recruit instructors who are from the ethnic groups they are training.
- Third, provide for some *multilingual cross-training* for specific phrases. For example, the course teaches non-Hispanic trainees to say "peligro" (danger) or "cuidado" (be careful).[78]
- Fourth, *don't skimp on training.* Because of the added cultural and multilingual aspects, experts contend that a 24-hour course is the absolute minimum. The 40-hour course at the Dallas–Fort Worth airport cost about $500 tuition per student (not counting the workers' wages).

Employers also turn to the Web to support their safety training programs.[79] For example, PureSafety (www.puresafety.com) enables firms to create their own training Web sites, complete with a "message from the safety director." Once an employer installs the PureSafety Web site, it can populate the site with courses from companies that supply health and safety courses via that site. The courses themselves are available in various formats, including digital versions of videotape training, and PowerPoint presentations.[80]

Reducing Unsafe Acts Through Motivation: Posters, Incentives, and Positive Reinforcement

Employers also use various tools to *motivate* workers to work safely. *Safety posters* are one. Safety posters can apparently increase safe behavior, but they are no substitute for a comprehensive safety program. Employers should combine them with other techniques (like screening and training) to reduce unsafe conditions and acts, and also change the posters often.

Incentive programs are also useful.[81] Management at the Golden Eagle refinery in California instituted one such plan. Employees earn "WINGS" points for engaging in one or more of 28 safety activities, such as conducting safety meetings, and taking emergency response training. Employees can each earn up to $20 per month by accumulating points.[82] Other employers award gift cards.

Some contend that safety incentive programs are misguided. OSHA has argued, for instance, that they don't cut down on actual injuries or illnesses, but only on injury and illness *reporting*. One expert argues that by encouraging habitual behavior they can lull employees into letting their guard down.[83] One option is to emphasize nontraditional incentives, like recognition. For instance, recognize employees for identifying hazards.[84] In any case, the incentive program needs to be part of a comprehensive safety program.[85]

Research Insight: Positive Reinforcement Many employers successfully use *positive reinforcement programs* to improve safety. Such programs provide workers with continuing positive feedback, usually in the form of graphical performance reports and supervisory support, to shape the workers' safety-related behavior.

Source: Courtesy of Richard Pasley.Stock Boston.

One way to motivate and encourage safety in a factory is to tell employees how much management values it: This safety poster on an exterior factory wall tells employees how well they are doing.

Researchers introduced one program in a wholesale bakery.[86] An analysis of the safety-related conditions in the plant before the study suggested areas that needed improvement. For example, new hires received no formal safety training, and managers rarely mentioned safety.

The new safety program included training and positive reinforcement. The researchers set and communicated a reasonable safety goal (in terms of observed incidents performed safely). Next, employees participated in a 30-minute training session by viewing pairs of slides depicting scenes that the researchers staged in the plant. One slide, for example, showed the supervisor climbing over a conveyor; the parallel slide showed the supervisor walking around the conveyor. After viewing an unsafe act, employees had to describe, "What's unsafe here?" Then, the researchers demonstrated the same incident again but performed in a safe manner, and explicitly stated the safe-conduct rule ("go around, not over or under, conveyors").

At the conclusion of the training phase, supervisors showed employees a graph with their pretraining safety record (in terms of observed incidents performed safely) plotted. Supervisors then encouraged workers to consider increasing their performance to the new safety goal for their own protection, to decrease costs, and to help the plant get out of its last place safety ranking. Then the researchers posted the graph and a list of safety rules.

Whenever observers walked through the plant collecting safety data, they posted on the graph the percentage of incidents they had seen performed safely by the group as a whole, thus providing the workers with positive feedback. Workers could compare their current safety performance with both their previous performance and their assigned goal. In addition, supervisors praised workers when they performed selected incidents safely. Safety in the plant subsequently improved markedly.

Use Behavior-Based Safety

Behavior-based safety means identifying the worker behaviors that contribute to accidents and then training workers to avoid these behaviors. For example, Tenneco Corporation (which manufactures Monroe brand suspensions) implemented a behavior-based safety program at its 70 manufacturing sites in 20 countries. The firm selected internal consultants from among its quality managers, training managers, engineers, and production workers. After training, the internal consultants identified five critical behaviors for Tenneco's first safety program, such as, *Eyes on task: Does the employee watch his or her hands while performing a task?* The consultants made observations, collected data regarding the behaviors, and then instituted training programs to get employees to perform these five behaviors properly.[87]

Use Employee Participation

There are two good reasons to involve employees in designing the safety program. First, employees are often your best source of ideas about what the problems are and how to solve them. Second, employee involvement tends to encourage employees to accept the safety program.

For example, when the International Truck and Engine Corp. began designing its new robot-based plant in Springfield, Ohio, management chose to involve employees in designing the new facility.[88]

Management appointed joint labor–management safety teams for each department. These worked with project engineers to start designing safeguards for the robot equipment. The company even sent one safety team to Japan to watch the robot machines in action, and to develop a checklist of items that the safety teams needed to address. Back in Ohio, this team worked with employees to identify possible hazards and to develop new devices (such as color-coded locks) to protect the employees.[89]

FIGURE 16-9 Employee Safety Responsibilities Checklist

Source: Reprinted from www.HR.BLR.com with permission of the publisher Business and Legal Resources, Inc., 141 Mill Rock Road East, Old Saybrook, CT © 2004. BLR© (Business and Legal Resources, Inc.).

Employee Safety Responsibilities Checklist

- ❑ Know what constitutes a safety hazard.
- ❑ Be constantly on the lookout for safety hazards.
- ❑ Correct or report safety hazards immediately.
- ❑ Know and use safe work procedures.
- ❑ Avoid unsafe acts.
- ❑ Keep the work area clean and uncluttered.
- ❑ Report accidents, injuries, illnesses, exposures to hazardous substances, and near misses immediately.
- ❑ Report acts and conditions that don't seem right even if you aren't sure if they're hazards.
- ❑ Cooperate with internal inspections and job hazard analyses.
- ❑ Follow company safety rules.
- ❑ Look for ways to make the job safer.
- ❑ Participate actively in safety training.
- ❑ Treat safety as one of your most important job responsibilities.

Once they are committed to the idea of safety, a checklist as in Figure 16-9 can provide employees with a useful reminder.

Conduct Safety and Health Audits and Inspections

Again, however, reducing unsafe acts is no substitute for eliminating hazards. Managers should therefore routinely inspect for possible problems, using safety audit/checklists as aids. Investigate all accidents and "near misses." Enable employees to notify managers about hazards.[90] Employee safety committees should evaluate safety adequacy, conduct and monitor safety audit findings, and suggest strategies for improving health and safety performance.[91]

Research Insight: High-Performance Systems and Safety

Finally, it is important not to miss the forest for the trees. Individual practices like safety training and incentives often reflect good overall management practices.

A study of high performance management systems illustrates this. We've seen that high-performance work systems, usually include practices like employment security, selective hiring, extensive training, self-managed teams, empowered decision making, and measurement of management practices.[94]

This study found that one consequence of high-performance work practices is that such systems incur fewer injuries. The researchers concluded, ". . . We can no longer assume that occupational safety is the primary prerogative of individual workers, ergonomic design, and government regulations of collective agreements. Rather, our data demonstrates that a high-performance work system is significantly associated with occupational safety."[95] In sum, great companies tend to be safer ones, too.

Table 16-1 summarizes suggestions for reducing unsafe conditions and acts.[96]

HR APPs 4 U

PDA Safety Audits

Managers expedite safety audits by using personal digital assistants (PDAs).[92] For example, Process and Performance Measurement (PPM) is a Windows application for designing and completing safety audit questionnaires. To use this application, the manager gives the safety audit a name, enters the audit questions, and lists possible answers. Typical questions for a fire extinguisher audit might include, "Are fire extinguishers clearly identified and accessible?" and "Are only approved fire extinguishers used in the workplace?"[93] The supervisor or employee then uses his or her PDA to record the audit and transmit it to the firm's safety office.

behavior-based safety
Identifying the worker behaviors that contribute to accidents and then training workers to avoid these behaviors.

TABLE 16-1 Reducing Unsafe Conditions and Acts: A Summary

Reduce Unsafe Conditions
Identify and eliminate unsafe conditions.
Use administrative means, such as job rotation.
Use personal protective equipment.

Reduce Unsafe Acts
Emphasize top management commitment.
Emphasize safety.
Establish a safety policy.
Reduce unsafe acts through selection.
Provide safety training.
Use posters and other propaganda.
Use positive reinforcement.
Use behavior-based safety programs.
Encourage worker participation.
Conduct safety and health inspections regularly.

Controlling Workers' Compensation Costs

In the event an accident does occur, the employee may turn to the employer's workers' compensation insurance to cover his or her expenses and losses. In turn, the employer's workers' compensation premiums reflect the number and size of its claims. Workers' compensation claims tend to spike on Mondays, possibly because some workers represent weekend injuries as work-related ones.[97] We addressed workers' compensation in Chapter 13 (Benefits), but address several relevant points here.

Before the Accident

The time to start "controlling" workers' compensation claims is before the accident happens. This involves taking all the safety steps described earlier.[98] The approach doesn't have to be complicated. For example, LKL Associates, Inc., of Orem, Utah, cut its workers' compensation premiums in half by communicating written safety and substance abuse policies to workers and then strictly enforcing those policies.[99]

After the Accident

The injury can be traumatic for the employee, and how the employer handles it is important. The employee will have questions, such as where to go for medical help and whether he or she is paid for time off. It's also usually at this point that the employee decides whether to retain a workers' compensation attorney to plead his or her case.

Here it is important to be supportive and proactive. Provide first aid, and make sure the worker gets quick medical attention; make it clear that you are interested in the injured worker; document the accident; file required accident reports; and encourage a speedy return to work.[100]

It doesn't help that half the employees who return after workers' comp face indifference, criticism, or dismissal.[101] Perhaps the most important thing an employer can do is develop an aggressive return-to-work program, including making light-duty work available. The best solution, for both employer and employee, is for the worker to become a productive member of the company again instead of a victim living on benefits.[102]

Analyzing Claims

Claims-tracking software is crucial for helping employers understand what's causing their workers' compensation claims. For example, a health services agency in Bangor, Maine, purchased CompWatch, a workers' compensation claims management and tracking program, from Benefit Software, Inc. CompWatch enables an employer to track and analyze each of its workers' compensation claims. The agency entered all its previous claims, and used CompWatch to analyze trends. The agency discovered some of its auto accidents were apparently due to its drivers' need for training, so the agency introduced a driver safety program. In one department, this apparently led to a 42% reduction in auto accidents from one year to the next.[103]

Controlling safety and health costs of all types becomes a more pressing issue in challenging times, as the accompanying "Managing HR in Challenging Times" feature explains.

Managing HR in Challenging Times

Cutting Safety Costs Without Cutting Costs

When economic times turn challenging, it's hard to think of a more dubious way to cut costs than by cutting what the employer spends on employee safety and health. Reducing expenditures on activities like safety training or safety incentives may reduce expenses short term. But they may well drive up accident-related costs, including workers' compensation, almost as quickly.

The solution isn't to cut safety costs across the board, but to cut costs selectively and intelligently. For example, employers are migrating from more expensive classroom training to less expensive online training. And within online safety training, many in these challenging times are migrating from paid programs to free online programs, like those offered by NIOSH, or at Web sites such as www.free-training.com. They are also applying practices we explained in this chapter such as more diligently reviewing workers' compensation claims and reducing accidents before they occur, for instance, with more diligent safety checks and audits and more careful employee background checks.

This is also a good time to review how you actually administer your safety programs, with an eye toward reducing costs there. For example, there are online safety management Web sites (which charge a monthly fee) as well as PC-based packages for this that reside on your company's server. ZeraWare (www.zeraware.com) is one example.[104]

The ZeraWare safety package consists of four modules:

Together, these modules help employers control the costs of their safety and health programs by helping them to:

- Track accidents, investigations, and inspections.
- Customize safety and OSHA inspection checklists.
- Track corrective actions from inspections and investigations.
- Analyze and compile accident data; produce reports.
- Identify accident patterns and problems quickly and easily.
- Establish safety responsibilities and accountability.
- Unify safety functions at multiple locations.
- Fill in OSHA forms #300, 301, and 300A

6 List five workplace health hazards and how to deal with them.

WORKPLACE HEALTH HAZARDS: PROBLEMS AND REMEDIES

Most workplace hazards aren't obvious like unguarded equipment or slippery floors. Many are unseen hazards (like mold) that the company inadvertently produces as part of its production processes. Other problems, like drug abuse, the employees may create for themselves. In either case, these hazards are often as much or more dangerous to workers' health and safety than are obvious hazards like slippery floors. Typical workplace exposure hazards include chemicals and other hazardous materials, temperature extremes, biohazards (including those that are normally occurring, such as mold, and man-made, such as anthrax), and ergonomic hazards (such as poorly designed, uncomfortable equipment).[105]

Source: Courtesy of Philip A. Savoie.

Exposure to asbestos is a major potential source of occupational respiratory disease. This worker wears protective clothing and a respirator to remove asbestos from ceiling panels in a classroom.

The Basic Industrial Hygiene Program

OSHA standards list exposure limits for about 600 chemicals. Table 16-2 lists some OSHA substance-specific health standards. Hazardous substances like these require air sampling and other preventive and precautionary measures. They are also more widespread than most managers realize. For example, cadmium pigments provide color to many paints and coatings, and manufacturers use ethyl alcohol as a solvent in industrial processes.

Managing exposure hazards like these comes under the area of *industrial hygiene* and involves recognition, evaluation, and control. First, the facility's health and safety officers (possibly working with teams of supervisors and employees) must *recognize* possible exposure hazards. This typically involves conducting plant/facility walk-around surveys, employee interviews, records reviews, and reviews of government (OSHA) and nongovernmental standards.

Having identified a possible hazard, the *evaluation* phase involves determining how severe the hazard is. This requires measuring the exposure, comparing the measured exposure to some benchmark (as in Table 16-2), and determining whether the risk is within tolerances.[106]

Finally, the hazard *control* phase involves eliminating or reducing the hazard. Note that personal protective gear (such as face masks) is generally the *last* option for dealing with such problems. Before relying on these, the employer must install engineering controls (such as process enclosures or ventilation) and administrative controls (including training and improved housekeeping); this is mandatory under OSHA.

TABLE 16-2 OSHA Substance-Specific Health Standards

Substance	Permissible Exposure Limits
Asbestos	.1001
Vinyl chloride	.1017
Inorganic arsenic	.1018
Lead	.1025
Cadmium	.1027
Benzene	.1028
Coke oven emissions	.1029
Cotton dust	.1043
1,2-Dibromo-3-chloropropane	.1044
Acrylonitrile	.1045
Ethylene oxide	.1047
Formaldehyde	.1048
4,4'-Methylene-dianaline	.1050
Methylene chloride	.1051

Source: John F. Rekus, "If You Thought Air Sampling Was Too Difficult to Handle, This Guide Can Help You Tackle Routine Sampling with Confidence, Part I," *Occupational Hazards,* May 2003, p. 43.

Asbestos Exposure at Work

There are four major sources of occupational respiratory diseases: asbestos, silica, lead, and carbon dioxide. Of these, asbestos is a major concern, in part because of publicity surrounding asbestos in buildings constructed before the mid-1970s. Major efforts are still underway to rid these buildings of the substance.

OSHA standards require several actions with respect to asbestos. Employers must monitor the air whenever they expect the level of asbestos to rise to one-half the allowable limit (which is 0.1 fibers per cubic centimeter). Engineering controls—walls, special filters, and so forth—are required to maintain an asbestos level that complies with OSHA standards. Only then can employers use respirators if additional efforts are required to achieve compliance.

Improving Productivity Through HRIS: Internet-Based Safety Improvement Solutions

In today's business environment, companies need to obtain efficiencies wherever they can, and Internet-based systems can help them manage their safety programs much more efficiently. For example, employees handling hazardous chemicals must be familiar with those chemicals' *material safety data sheets (MSDS).* In a dry-cleaning store, for instance, the cleaner–spotter should be knowledgeable about the MSDS for chemicals like hydrofluoric acid (used for stain removal) and perchloroethylene (used for cleaning).

For large firms, managing the MSDS can cost millions of dollars annually. The employer needs to distribute the appropriate MSDS to each employee, ensure that the employees study and learn their contents, and continually update the data sheets based on new OSHA information. Web-based systems now provide a platform upon which the employer can mount all its relevant MSDS, make these available to the employees who need them, monitor and test employees on the sheets' use, and update the MSDS as required.[107]

Infectious Diseases

With many employees traveling to and from international destinations, monitoring and controlling infectious diseases has become an important safety issue.[108]

Employers can take steps to prevent the entry or spread of infectious diseases into their workplaces. These steps include:

1. Closely monitor Centers for Disease Control and Prevention (CDC) travel alerts. These inform travelers about health concerns and provide precautions. Access this information at www.cdc.gov.
2. Provide daily medical screenings for employees returning from infected areas.
3. Deny access to your facility for 10 days to employees or visitors returning from affected areas, particularly those who have had contact with suspected infected individuals.
4. Tell employees to stay home if they have a fever or respiratory system symptoms.
5. Clean work areas and surfaces regularly.
6. Stagger breaks. Offer several lunch periods to reduce overcrowding.
7. Emphasize the importance of frequent hand washing and make sanitizers containing alcohol easily available.

Alcoholism and Substance Abuse

Alcoholism and substance abuse are widespread problems at work. About two-thirds of people with an alcohol disorder work full-time.[109] About 15% of the U.S. workforce (just over 19 million workers) "has either been hung over at work, been drinking shortly before showing up for work, or been drinking or impaired while on the job at least once during the previous year."[110] Some experts estimate that as many as 50% of all "problem employees" are actually alcoholics.[111] Drug-using employees are more than three and a half times more likely to be involved in workplace accidents.[112]

Effects of Alcohol Abuse

The effects of alcoholism on the worker and work are severe.[113] Both the quality and quantity of the work decline in the face of a sort of on-the-job absenteeism. The alcoholic's on-the-job accidents usually don't increase significantly, apparently, because he or she becomes much more cautious. However, the off-the-job accident rate is higher. Morale of other workers drops, as they have to shoulder the alcoholic's burdens.

Recognizing the alcoholic on the job is a problem. Early symptoms such as tardiness are similar to those of other problems and thus hard to classify. The supervisor is not a psychiatrist, and without specialized training, identifying—and dealing with—the alcoholic is difficult.

Table 16-3 presents a chart showing observable behavior patterns that indicate alcohol-related problems. As you can see, alcohol-related problems range from tardiness in the earliest stages of alcohol abuse to prolonged, unpredictable absences in its later stages.

Dealing with Substance Abuse

For many employers, dealing with alcohol and substance abuse begins with substance abuse testing. It's increasingly unusual to find employers who don't at least test job candidates for substance abuse before formally hiring them. And many states are instituting mandatory random drug testing for high-hazard workers. For example, as of 2008, New Jersey requires random drug testing of electrical workers.[114]

There's some debate about whether drug tests reduce workplace accidents. One answer seems to be that preemployment tests pick up only about half the workplace drug users, so ongoing random testing is advisable. One study, conducted in three hotels, concluded that preemployment drug testing had little effect on workplace accidents. However, a combination of preemployment and random ongoing testing was associated with a significant reduction in workplace accidents.[115]

TABLE 16-3 Observable Behavior Patterns Indicating Possible Alcohol-Related Problems

Alcoholism Stage	Some Possible Signs of Alcoholism Problems	Some Possible Alcoholism Performance Issues
Early	Arrives at work late Untrue statements Leaves work early	Reduced job efficiency Misses deadlines
Middle	Frequent absences, especially Mondays Colleagues mentioning erratic behavior Mood swings Anxiety Late returning from lunch Frequent multi-day absences	Accidents Warnings from boss Noticeably reduced performance
Advanced	Personal neglect Unsteady gait Violent outbursts Blackouts and frequent forgetfulness Possible drinking on job	Frequent falls, accidents Strong disciplinary actions Basically incompetent performance

Sources: Gopal Patel and John Adkins Jr., "The Employer's Role in Alcoholism Assistance," *Personnel Journal* 62, no. 7 (July 1983), p. 570; Mary-Anne Enoch and David Goldman, "Problem Drinking and Alcoholism: Diagnosis and Treatment," *American Family Physician*, February 1, 2002, www.aafp.org/afp/20020201/441.html, accessed July 20, 2008; and Ken Pidd et al., "Alcohol and Work: Patterns of Use, Workplace Culture, and Safety," www.nisu.flinders.edu.au/pubs/reports/2006/injcat82.pdf, accessed July 20, 2008.

Preemployment drug testing also discourages those on drugs from applying for work or going to work for employers who test. One study found that more than 30% of regular drug users employed full-time said they were less likely to work for a company that conducted preemployment screening.[116] Some applicants or employees may try to evade the test, for instance, by purchasing "clean" specimens to use. Several states have laws making drug-test fraud a crime.[117] However, a newer oral fluid drug test eliminates the "clean specimen" problem and is less expensive to administer.[118]

The big question is what to do when a *current* employee tests positive. Disciplining, discharge, in-house counseling, and referral to an outside agency are the four traditional prescriptions. Most professionals seem to counsel treatment rather than outright dismissal, at least initially. They also emphasize that whether it's the supervisor or just a friend who notices the employee's problem, the worst thing to do is ignore it.

In practice, each employer tends to develop its own approach to dealing with substance abuse. One human resource manager says,

> Some employers have zero tolerance and terminate immediately. Some employers don't have a choice (pharmaceutical labs, for example). Others are lenient. Our policy is a three-strikes-and-you're-out process. The first step is a warning notification and permission given to us to test the employee at any time we want—for a period of five years. The second step is a mandatory substance abuse rehabilitation program at the employee's own expense . . . the third step is immediate termination for cause.[119]

Substance Abuse Policies Employers should establish and communicate a substance abuse policy. This policy should state management's position on alcohol and drug abuse and on the use and possession of illegal drugs on company premises. It should also list the methods (such as urinalysis) used to determine the causes of poor performance; state the company's views on rehabilitation, including workplace counseling; and specify penalties for policy violations. Additional steps employers take include conducting workplace inspections (searching employees for illegal substances) and using undercover agents.

Supervisor Training Training supervisors to identify alcoholics or drug abusers and the problems they create is advisable. However, supervisors are in a tricky position: They should be the company's first line of defense in combating workplace drug abuse, but should avoid becoming detectives or medical diagnosticians. Guidelines supervisors should follow include these:

- If an employee appears to be under the influence of drugs or alcohol, ask how the employee feels and look for signs of impairment such as slurred speech. (See Table 16-3.) Send an employee judged unfit for duty home.
- Make a written record of your observations and follow up each incident. In addition, inform workers of the number of warnings the company will tolerate before requiring termination.
- Refer troubled employees to the company's employee assistance program.

Legal Aspects of Workplace Substance Abuse The federal Drug-Free Workplace Act requires employers with federal government contracts or grants to ensure a drug-free workplace by taking a number of steps. For example, employers must agree to:

- Publish a policy prohibiting the unlawful manufacture, distribution, dispensing, possession, or use of controlled substances in the workplace.
- Establish a drug-free awareness program that informs employees about the dangers of workplace drug abuse.
- Inform employees that they are required, as a condition of employment, not only to abide by the employer's policy but also to report any criminal convictions for drug-related activities in the workplace.[120]

The U.S. Department of Transportation has rules regarding drug testing in the transportation industry.[121] These rules require random breath alcohol tests as well as preemployment, postaccident, reasonable suspicion, and return-to-duty testing for workers in safety-sensitive jobs in transportation industries.

In general, employers can hold alcohol dependent employees to the same performance standards as they hold nonalcoholics. Whether the alcohol abuse reflects a "disability" under the ADA depends on several things, including whether the person is alcohol dependant.[122] However, there are other legal risks. Employees have sued for invasion of privacy, wrongful discharge, defamation, and illegal searches. Therefore, before implementing any drug control program:

- Use employee handbooks, bulletin board postings, pay inserts, and the like to publicize your substance abuse plans.
- Explain the conditions under which testing may occur and the procedures for handling employees who refuse to be tested.
- Explain what accommodations you make for employees who voluntarily seek treatment. Substance abuse may be a physical handicap under federal and some state laws.

Stress, Burnout, and Depression

Problems such as alcoholism and drug abuse sometimes reflect underlying psychological causes such as stress and depression. In turn, a variety of workplace factors can lead to stress. These include work schedule, pace of work, job security, route to and from work, workplace noise, poor supervision, and the number and nature of customers or clients.[123]

Personal factors also influence stress. For example, Type A personalities—people who are workaholics and who feel driven to be on time and meet deadlines—normally place themselves under greater stress than do others. Add to job stress the stress caused by nonjob problems like divorce and, as you might imagine, many workers are problems waiting to happen.

Job stress has serious consequences for both employer and employee. The human consequences include anxiety, depression, anger, cardiovascular disease, headaches, accidents, and even early onset Alzheimer's disease.[124] For the employer, consequences include diminished quantity and quality of performance, and increased absenteeism and turnover. A study of 46,000 employees concluded that high-stress workers' health care costs were 46% higher than those of their less-stressed coworkers.[125] Yet only 5% of surveyed U.S. employers say they're addressing workplace stress.[126]

Reducing Job Stress There are a number of ways to alleviate dysfunctional stress. These range from commonsense remedies (such as getting more sleep and eating better) to remedies like biofeedback and meditation. Finding a more suitable job, getting counseling, and planning and organizing each day's activities are other sensible responses.[127] In his book *Stress and the Manager*, Dr. Karl Albrecht suggests the following ways for a person to reduce job stress:[128]

- Build rewarding, pleasant, cooperative relationships with colleagues and employees.
- Don't bite off more than you can chew.
- Build an especially effective and supportive relationship with your boss.
- Negotiate with your boss for realistic deadlines on important projects.
- Learn as much as you can about upcoming events and get as much lead time as you can to prepare for them.
- Find time every day for detachment and relaxation.
- Take a walk around the office to keep your body refreshed and alert.
- Find ways to reduce unnecessary noise.
- Reduce the amount of trivia in your job; delegate routine work whenever possible.
- Limit interruptions.
- Don't put off dealing with distasteful problems.
- Make a constructive "worry list" that includes solutions for each problem.
- Get more and better quality sleep.[129]

Meditation is another option. Choose a quiet place with soft light and sit comfortably. Then meditate by focusing your thoughts, for instance by counting breaths or by visualizing a calming location such as a beach. When your mind wanders, bring it back to focusing your thoughts on your breathing, or the beach.[130]

The employer and its human resource team and supervisors also play a role in reducing stress. Supportive supervisors and fair treatment are two obvious steps. Other steps include reducing personal conflicts on the job and encouraging open communication between management and employees. Huntington Hospital in Pasadena, California, introduced an on-site concierge service to help its employees reduce work-related stress. It takes care of tasks like mailing bills and making vacation plans for them.[131]

One British firm follows a three-tiered employee stress-reduction approach.[132] First, is *primary prevention*, and focuses on ensuring that things like job designs and workflows are correct. Second involves *intervention*, including individual employee assessment, attitude surveys to find sources of stress at work and personal conflicts on the job, and supervisory intervention. Third is *rehabilitation*, through employee assistance programs and counseling.

Burnout **Burnout** is a phenomenon closely associated with job stress. Experts define burnout as the total depletion of physical and mental resources caused by excessive striving to reach an unrealistic work-related goal. Burnout builds gradually, manifesting itself in symptoms such as irritability, discouragement, exhaustion, cynicism, entrapment, and resentment.[133]

burnout
The total depletion of physical and mental resources caused by excessive striving to reach an unrealistic work-related goal.

Employers can head off burnout, for instance, by monitoring employees in potentially high-pressure jobs.[134] What can a burnout candidate do? In his book *How to Beat the High Cost of Success*, Dr. Herbert Freudenberger suggests:

- **Break your patterns.** First, are you doing a variety of things or the same one repeatedly? The more well rounded your life is, the better protected you are against burnout.
- **Get away from it all periodically.** Schedule occasional periods of introspection during which you can get away from your usual routine.
- **Reassess your goals in terms of their intrinsic worth.** Are the goals you've set for yourself attainable? Are they really worth the sacrifices?
- **Think about your work.** Could you do as good a job without being so intense?

RESEARCH INSIGHT If you're thinking of taking a vacation to reduce your burnout, you might as well save your money, according to one study.[135] In this study, 76 clerks in the headquarters of an electronics firm in Israel completed questionnaires measuring job stress and burnout twice before a vacation, once during the vacation, and twice after the vacation.

The clerks' burnout did decline during the vacation. The problem was the burnout quickly returned. Burnout moved partway back toward its pre-vacation level by 3 days after the vacation, and all the way by 3 weeks after they returned to work.[136] One implication, as these researchers point out, is that minivacations during the workday—"such as time off for physical exercise, meditation, power naps, and reflective thinking"—might help reduce stress and burnout. A later, separate study concluded that the quality of a vacation—for instance, in terms of relaxation and nonwork hassles—affected the vacation's fade-out effects.[137]

Employee Depression *Employee depression* is a serious problem at work. Experts estimate that depression results in more than 200 million lost workdays in the United States annually, and may cost U.S. businesses $24 billion or more per year just in absenteeism and lost productivity.[138] Depressed people also tend to have worse safety records.[139]

Employers need to work harder to ensure that depressed employees utilize available support services. One survey found that while about two-thirds of large firms offered employee assistance programs covering depression, only about 14% of employees with depression said they ever used one.[140]

Employers therefore need to train supervisors to identify depression's warning signs and to counsel those who may need such services to use the firm's employee assistance program.[141] Depression is a disease. It does no more good to tell a depressed person to "snap out of it" than it would to tell someone with a heart condition to stop acting tired. Typical warning signs of depression (if they last for more than 2 weeks) include persistent sad, anxious, or "empty" moods; sleeping too little; reduced appetite; loss of interest in activities once enjoyed; restlessness or irritability; and difficulty concentrating.[142]

Solving Computer-Related Ergonomic Problems

Even with advances in computer screen technology, there's still a risk of monitor-related health problems at work. Problems include short-term eye burning, itching, and tearing, as well as eyestrain and eye soreness. Backaches and neck aches are also widespread. These often occur because employees try to compensate for monitor problems (such as glare) by maneuvering into awkward body positions. There may also be a tendency for computer users to suffer from cumulative motion disorders, such as carpal tunnel syndrome, caused by repetitive use of the hands and arms at uncomfortable angles.[143] OSHA has no specific standards that apply to computer workstations. It does have general standards that might apply, regarding, for instance, radiation, noise, and electrical hazards.[144]

NIOSH provided general recommendations regarding computer screens. Most relate to *ergonomics* or design of the worker–equipment interface. These include:

1. Employees should take a 3–5 minute break from working at the computer every 20–40 minutes, and use the time for other tasks, like making copies.
2. Design maximum flexibility into the workstation so it can be adapted to the individual operator. For example, use adjustable chairs with midback supports. Don't stay in one position for long periods.
3. Reduce glare with devices such as shades over windows and recessed or indirect lighting.
4. Give workers a complete preplacement vision exam to ensure properly corrected vision for reduced visual strain.[145]
5. Allow the user to position his or her wrists at the same level as the elbow.
6. Put the screen at or just below eye level, at a distance of 18 to 30 inches from the eyes.
7. Let the wrists rest lightly on a pad for support.
8. Put the feet flat on the floor or on a footrest.[146]

Workplace Smoking

Smoking is a serious health and cost problem for both employees and employers. For employers, these costs derive from higher health and fire insurance, as well as increased absenteeism and reduced productivity (which occurs, for instance, when a smoker takes a 10-minute break behind the store).

Furthermore, nonsmoking employees who are concerned with secondhand smoke are suing their employers. The California Environmental Protection Agency estimates that each year in the United States, secondhand smoke causes 3,000 deaths due to lung cancer and 35,000 to 62,000 illnesses due to heart problems (not all work related).[147]

What You Can and Cannot Do

Can the employer institute a smoking ban? The answer depends on several things, including the state in which you are located and whether or not your firm is unionized. For example, instituting a smoking ban in a unionized facility that formerly allowed employees to smoke may be subject to collective bargaining.[148] Many states and municipalities now ban indoor smoking in public areas (see www.smokefreeworld.com/usa.shtml for a list).

In general, you can deny a job to a smoker as long as you don't use smoking as a surrogate for some other kind of discrimination. A "no-smokers-hired" policy does not, according to one expert, violate the Americans with Disabilities Act (since smoking is not considered a disability), and in general "employers' adoption of a no-smokers-hired policy is not illegal under federal law." About 72% of the 270 human resources professionals responding to a SHRM online survey said their companies have designated smoking areas outside of the office; 32% offer smoking cessation programs; 27% have policies limiting the number of breaks employees can take; and 19% ban workplace smoking, both inside and outside the facility.[149]

Some firms take a hard-line approach. WEYCO Inc., a benefits services company in Michigan, first gave employees 15 months' warning and offered smoking secession assistance. Then they began firing or forcing out all its workers who smoke, including those who do so in the privacy of their homes.[150]

Violence at Work

A disgruntled employee walked into Chrysler's Ohio Jeep assembly plant and fatally shot one worker, after reportedly being involved in an argument with a supervisor.[151]

Violence against employees is an enormous problem at work. Homicide is the second biggest cause of fatal workplace injuries. Surveys by NIOSH found that nonfatal workplace assaults resulted in more than 1 million lost workdays in one recent year. While robbery was the main motive for homicide at work, a coworker or personal associate committed roughly one of seven workplace homicides.[152] In one survey, over half of human resource or security executives reported that disgruntled employees had threatened senior managers in the past 12 months.[153]

Who Is at Risk? Violence is more associated with some jobs. In one study, researchers constructed a "risk for violence scale." This listed 22 job characteristics that the researchers found correlated with violence on the job. Jobs with a high likelihood for violence include those jobs that involve physical care of others or decisions that influence other people's lives, handling guns, security functions, physical control over others, interacting with frustrated individuals, and handling weapons other than guns.[154]

Although men have more fatal occupational injuries than do women, the proportion of women who are victims of assault is much higher. The Gender-Motivated Violence Act, part of the Violence against Women Act Congress passed in 1994, imposes significant liabilities on employers whose women employees become victims.[155] Most women (many working in retail establishments) murdered at work were victims of random criminal violence by an assailant unknown to the victim, as during a robbery. Coworkers, family members, or previous friends or acquaintances carried out the remaining homicides.

You can predict and avoid many workplace incidents. *Risk Management* magazine estimates that about 86% of past workplace violence incidents were apparent earlier to coworkers, who had brought them to management's attention prior to the incidents. Yet, in most cases, management did little or nothing.[156] Employers can take several steps to reduce workplace violence. Let's look at them.

Heightened Security Measures Heightened security measures are an employer's first line of defense. NIOSH suggests the following: Improve external lighting, use drop safes to minimize cash on hand and post signs noting that only a limited amount of cash is on hand, install silent alarms and surveillance cameras, increase the number of staff on duty, provide staff training in conflict resolution and nonviolent response, and close establishments during high-risk hours late at night.[157] Employers can also issue a weapons policy, for instance barring firearms and other dangerous weapons.

Because about half of workplace homicides occur in the retail industry, OSHA issued voluntary recommendations aimed at reducing homicides and injuries in such establishments. Particularly for late-night or early-morning retail workers, the suggestions include the following: Install mirrors and improved lighting, provide silent and personal alarms, reduce store hours during high-risk periods, install drop safes and signs that indicate little cash is kept on hand, erect bullet-resistance enclosures, and increase staffing during high-risk hours.[158]

Improved Employee Screening That testing can screen out those prone to workplace aggression is clear. In one study researchers measured the relationship among personal characteristics such as "trait anger" (for instance, how someone reacts when they do not receive recognition for doing good work) and "attitude toward revenge" (which, of course, measures a person's attitude toward revenge). The researchers concluded that measurable individual differences like trait anger "account for more than 60% of the variance in our measure of the incidence of workplace aggression."[159]

At a minimum, carefully check references. Obtain a detailed employment application. Solicit and verify the applicant's employment history, educational background, and references. A personal interview, personnel testing, and a review and verification of all information provided should also be included. Sample interview questions to ask might include, "What frustrates you?" and "Who was your worst supervisor and why?"[160]

Certain background facts suggest the need for a more in-depth background investigation. Red flags include:[161]

- An unexplained gap in employment
- Incomplete or false information on the résumé or application
- A negative, unfavorable, or false reference
- Prior insubordinate or violent behavior on the job
- A criminal history involving harassing or violent behavior
- A prior termination for cause with a suspicious (or no) explanation

- A history of significant psychiatric problems
- A history of drug or alcohol abuse
- Strong indications of instability in the individual's work or personal life, for example, frequent job changes or geographic moves
- Lapsed or lost licenses or accreditations[162]

Workplace Violence Training Vendors offer video violence training programs. These explain what workplace violence is, identify its causes and signs, and offer tips to supervisors on how to prevent it and what to do when it occurs.

Employers should also train supervisors to identify the clues that typically precede violent incidents. These include:[163]

- **Typical profiles.** The typical perpetrator is male, between the ages of 25 and 40, and exhibits an inability to handle stress, manipulative behavior, and steady complaining. Of course, many nonviolent people exhibit such traits, too. However, perpetrators also tend to exhibit other behaviors, such as the following.
- **Verbal threats.** They harbor grudges and often talk about what they may do, such as, "That propane tank in the back could blow up easily."
- **Physical actions.** Troubled employees may try to intimidate others, gain access to places where they do not belong, or flash a concealed weapon.
- **Frustration.** Most cases involve an employee who has a frustrated sense of entitlement to a promotion, for example.
- **Obsession.** An employee may hold a grudge against a coworker or supervisor, and some cases stem from romantic interest.[164]

Organizational Justice At work, as three researchers said, ". . . [Violence] typically occurs in response to a perceived injustice."[165] These researchers asked respondents to reply to this: "Think back over your time as an employee in your current organization when you've been offended by another person." The researchers also asked the respondents how they reacted to the offense. An employee who blamed another for some personal affront was more likely to try to seek revenge (especially against less powerful offenders) and less likely to seek reconciliation.[166] Bear in mind one executive suspected of sabotaging his former employer's computer system, thus causing about $20 million in damage. He'd been earning $186,000 a year; what made him do it? A note he wrote anonymously to the president provides some insight:

> "I have been loyal to the Company in good and bad times for over thirty years. . . . What is most upsetting is the manner in which you chose to end our employment. I was expecting a member of top management to come down from his ivory tower to face us directly with a layoff announcement, rather than sending the kitchen supervisor with guards to escort us off the premises like criminals. . . . We will not wait for God to punish you—we will take measures into our own hands."[167]

The moral is, to reduce violence, strive for fairness.

Enhanced Attention to Employee Retention/Dismissal Employers also need effective procedures for identifying and dealing with potentially lethal employees. Start with adopting a workplace violence policy that outlines unacceptable employee behavior and a zero-tolerance policy toward workplace violence.[168] Behaviors to watch out for include:

- An act of violence on or off the job
- Erratic behavior evidencing a loss of awareness of actions
- Overly defensive, obsessive, or paranoid tendencies
- Overly confrontational or antisocial behavior

- Sexually aggressive behavior
- Isolationist or loner tendencies
- Insubordinate behavior with a suggestion of violence
- Tendency to overreact to criticism
- Exaggerated interest in war, guns, violence, catastrophes
- The commission of a serious breach of security
- Possession of weapons, guns, knives at the workplace[169]
- Violation of privacy rights of others, such as searching desks or stalking
- Chronic complaining and frequent, unreasonable grievances
- A retribution-oriented or get-even attitude[170]

Dismissing Violent Employees You should use caution when firing or disciplining potentially violent employees.

In dismissing potentially violent employees:

- Analyze and anticipate, based on the person's history, what kind of aggressive behavior to expect.
- Have a security guard nearby when the dismissal takes place.
- Clear away furniture and things the person might throw.
- Don't wear loose clothing that the person might grab.
- Don't make it sound as if you're accusing the employee; instead, say that according to company policy, you're required to take action.
- Maintain the person's dignity and try to emphasize something good about the employee.
- Provide job counseling for terminated employees, to help get the employee over the traumatic post-dismissal adjustment.[171]
- Consider obtaining restraining orders against those who have exhibited a tendency to act violently in the workplace. Human resource managers should understand restraining orders and the process for obtaining them.[172]

Dealing with Angry Employees What do you do when confronted by an angry, potentially explosive employee? Here are some suggestions:[173]

- Make eye contact.
- Stop what you are doing and give your full attention.
- Speak in a calm voice and create a relaxed environment.
- Be open and honest.
- Let the person have his or her say.
- Ask for specific examples of what the person is upset about.
- Be careful to define the problem.
- Ask open-ended questions and explore all sides of the issue.
- Listen: As one expert says, "Often, angry people simply want to be listened to. They need a supportive, empathic ear from someone they can trust."[174]

Legal Issues in Reducing Workplace Violence It is sensible to try to screen out potentially violent employees, but doing so incurs legal risks. Most states have policies that encourage the employment and rehabilitation of ex-offenders, and some states therefore limit the use of criminal records in hiring decisions.[175] For example, except in certain limited instances, Article 23-A of the New York Corrections Law makes it unlawful to discriminate against job applicants based on their prior criminal convictions. Similarly, courts have interpreted Title VII of the Civil Rights Act of 1964 as restricting employers from making employment decisions based on arrest records, since doing so may unfairly discriminate against some minority groups.

Aside from federal law, most states prohibit discrimination under any circumstances based on arrest records and on prior convictions unless a direct relationship exists between the prior conviction and the job, or the employment presents an unreasonable risk.[176] And developing a "violent employee" profile could end up merely describing a mental impairment and violate the Americans with Disabilities Act.[177]

7 Discuss the prerequisites for a security plan and how to set up a basic security program.

OCCUPATIONAL SECURITY AND SAFETY

A majority of employers have security arrangements.[178] Figure 16-10 illustrates this. For example, about 46% of the surveyed employers issued security-related gloves, masks, or other personnel protective equipment to at least specific employees (such as mail room workers). Forty-three percent instituted new, more stringent, building entry procedures. Those instituting identification requirements or hiring security personnel rose after November 2001. A SHRM survey found that about 85% of responding organizations now have some type of formal disaster plan.[179] Many firms have also instituted special handling procedures for suspicious mail packages and hold regular emergency evacuation drills.

Many of these actions stemmed from employers' heightened focus on risk management in the past few years. Identifying security and other corporate risks falls within the domain of *enterprise risk management,* which means identifying risks, and planning to mitigate and actually mitigating these risks. Thus, as part of its risk management, WalMart asks questions such as, "What are the risks? And what are we going to do about these risks?"[180] Eliminating crime and enhancing facility security are two important issues here.

Basic Prerequisites for a Crime Prevention Plan

As one corporate security summary put it, "workplace security involves more than keeping track of who comes in a window, installing an alarm system, or employing guards for an after-hours watch. Organizations that are truly security conscious plan and implement policies and programs that involve employees in protecting against identified risks and threats."[181]

Ideally, a comprehensive corporate anticrime program should start with the following:

1. Company philosophy and policy on crime—In particular, make sure employees understand that no crime is acceptable and that the employer has a zero-tolerance policy with respect to workers who commit crimes.

FIGURE 16-10 Safety, Security, and Emergency Planning Initiatives Following Terrorist Incidents

Source: Adapted from "After Sept. 11th, Safety and Security Moved to the Fore," *BNA Bulletin to Management*, January 17, 2002, p. 52.

Initiatives	Percent of Employers
	(146)
Safety and Security	
Personal protective equipment	46%
New/more stringent building entry procedures	43
Restricted access to some areas	19
Closed entrances/areas	17
New/additional security personnel	12
Extended work hours for security personnel	10
New security devices (e.g., metal detectors)	10
New/more stringent applicant screening	7
Physical barriers to building entry	5
Emergency Planning and Disaster Recovery	
Review emergency/disaster recovery plan(s)	46
Revise emergency/disaster recovery plan(s)	32
New/revised evacuation drills	23
Form committee or task force to address emergency planning/disaster recovery	15
Develop emergency/disaster recovery plan(s)	14
Develop/revise procedures for data backup	14
Develop/revise procedures for tracking employee whereabouts	10

2. Investigations of job applicants—Conduct full background checks as part of your selection process for every position.
3. Crime awareness training—Make it clear, during training and orientation, that the employer takes a tough approach to workplace crime.
4. Crisis management—Establish and communicate the procedures employees should follow in the event of a bomb threat, fire, or other emergency.

Setting Up a Basic Security Program

In simplest terms, actually instituting a basic facility security program requires four steps: analyzing the current *level* of risk, and then installing *mechanical, natural,* and *organizational* security systems.[182]

Security programs ideally start with an analysis of the facility's *current level of risk.* The employer, preferably using security experts, should assess the company's exposure. Here, it is logical to start with the obvious. For example, what is the neighborhood like? Does your facility (such as the office building you're in) house other businesses or individuals (such as law enforcement agencies) that might bring unsafe activities to your doorstep? As part of this initial threat assessment, also review at least these six matters

1. **Access to the reception area,** including number of access points, and need for a "panic button" for contacting emergency personnel;
2. **Interior security,** including possible need for key cards, secure restrooms, and better identification of exits;
3. **Authorities' involvement,** in particular emergency procedures developed with local law enforcement authorities;
4. **Mail handling,** including how employees screen and open mail and where it enters the building;
5. **Evacuation,** including a full review of evacuation procedures and training; and
6. **Backup systems,** for instance that let the company store data off site if disaster strikes.

Having assessed the potential current level of risk, the employer then turns its attention to assessing and improving natural, mechanical, and organizational security.[183]

Source: Courtesy of Getty Images–Stockbyte, Royalty Free.

Many employers install video security cameras to monitor areas in and around their premises.

Natural Security

Natural security means taking advantage of the facility's natural or architectural features in order to minimize security problems. For example, are there unlit spots in your parking lot? Does having too many entrances mean it is difficult to control facility access?

Mechanical Security

Mechanical security is the utilization of security systems such as locks, intrusion alarms, access control systems, and surveillance systems to reduce the need for continuous human surveillance.[184] Technological advances are making this easier. Many mail rooms now use scanners to check the safety of incoming mail. And for access security, biometric scanners that read thumb or palm prints or retina or vocal patterns make it easier to enforce plant security. (Critics say these also may undermine employee privacy, for instance, by identifying where the employee is at any point in time.[185])

Organizational Security

Finally, *organizational security* means using good management to improve security. For example, it means properly training and motivating security staff and lobby attendants. Also ensure that the security staff has written orders that define their duties, especially in situations such as fire, elevator entrapment, hazardous materials spills, medical emergencies, hostile intrusions, suspicious packages, civil disturbances, and workplace violence.[186] Other questions to ask include the following: Are you properly investigating the backgrounds of new hires? Are you requiring the same types of background checks for the contractors who supply security and other personnel to your facility? And, do you provide new employees with security orientations?

Evacuation Plans

The possibility of emergencies prompted by fires, explosions, and similar issues means that employers need facility notification and evacuation plans.[187] Such plans should contain several elements. These include *early detection of a problem, methods for communicating the emergency externally*, and *communications plans for initiating an evacuation and for providing information to those the employer wants to evacuate.* A simple alarm often does not suffice. Ideally, an initial alarm should come first. The employer should then follow the initial alarm with an announcement providing specific information about the emergency and letting employees know what action they should take next. Some use text messaging.[188]

Company Security and Employee Privacy

Security programs like these have been accompanied by a significant rise in the monitoring of employee communications and workplace activities; this has prompted many to ask, are employee privacy rights being violated?

As noted earlier in this book, employers must consider employee privacy when using monitoring to control or investigate possible employee security breaches. Ideally, employers should get employees' consent for monitoring, for instance, when employees sign for receipt of company handbooks during orientation. But he employer may also use monitoring if it is clear from its policies and notices that employees should have known that monitoring might take place.

The employer can take several steps to make it easier to investigate employees for potential security breaches. These include:[189]

1. Distribute a policy that (a) says the company reserves the right to inspect and search employees as well as their personal property, electronic media, and files; and (b) emphasizes that company-provided conveniences such as lockers and desks remain the property of the company and are subject to its control and search.
2. Train investigators to focus on the facts and avoid making accusations.
3. Make sure your investigators know that employees can request that an employee representative be present during the interview.
4. Make sure all investigations and searches are evenhanded and nondiscriminatory.

REVIEW

CHAPTER SECTION SUMMARIES

1. Safety and accident prevention concerns managers for several reasons, one of which is the staggering number of workplace accidents. Because of this, all managers need to be familiar with **occupational safety law**. The Occupational Safety and Health Act was passed by Congress in 1972 to ensure so far as possible every working man and woman in the nation safe and healthful working conditions and to preserve human resources. The act created the Occupational Safety and Health Administration (OSHA). OSHA, in turn, promulgates thousands of specific policies and standards with which employers must comply. It enforces these standards via a system of inspections and citations and, where necessary, penalties. Inspectors cannot make warrantless inspections, and managers need to make sure a designated OSHA coordinator is present if an inspector demands admittance.
2. There are three basic **causes of workplace accidents**: chance occurrences, unsafe conditions, and employees' unsafe acts. Unsafe conditions include things like improperly guarded equipment and hazardous procedures. Unsafe acts sometimes reflect personality traits such as impatience and distractibility.

3. In practice, **how to prevent accidents** boils down to reducing unsafe conditions and reducing unsafe acts. Reducing unsafe conditions is always the first line of defense and includes using checklists and following OSHA standards. Once all necessary steps are taken here, employers need to encourage employees to use personal protective equipment. There are then several basic approaches to reducing unsafe acts, for instance, through proper selection and placement, training, motivation and positive reinforcement, behavior-based safety, employee participation, and conducting safety and health audits.
4. Most **workplace health hazards** aren't obvious, like unguarded equipment.
   - Typical exposure hazards include, for instance, chemicals, biohazards, and improperly designed equipment.
   - Managing exposure hazards like these comes under the area of industrial hygiene, and involves recognition, evaluation, and control. Obvious areas of concern include asbestos exposure and infectious diseases.
   - Managers need to be familiar with alcoholism, substance abuse, and their manifestations at work and particularly be familiar with signs of these problems and how to deal with them.
   - Stress, burnout, and depression are more serious at work than many people realize and both the employee and employer can take steps to deal with them. Employers especially need to train supervisors to identify depression's warning signs and to counsel those who may need special services.
   - Violence against employees is an enormous problem. Women in particular are at risk. Heightened security measures are an employer's first line of defense and include, for instance, improving external lighting and using drop safes to minimize cash on hand.
   - Improved employee screening can reduce the risk of hiring potentially violent employees. However employers also need to provide workplace violence training (for instance, including what to watch for such as verbal threats) and enhanced attention to employee retention and dismissal processes.
5. Most employers today have **occupational security and safety programs**. Instituting a basic facility security program involves analyzing the current level of risk, and then installing mechanical, natural, and organizational security systems.

DISCUSSION QUESTIONS

1. Explain how to reduce the occurrence of unsafe acts on the part of your employees.
2. Discuss the basic facts about OSHA—its purpose, standards, inspections, and rights and responsibilities.
3. Explain the supervisor's role in safety.
4. Explain what causes unsafe acts.
5. Describe at least five techniques for reducing accidents.
6. Explain how you would reduce stress at work.
7. Describe the steps employers can take to reduce workplace violence.

INDIVIDUAL AND GROUP ACTIVITIES

1. Working individually or in groups, answer the question, "Is there such a thing as an accident-prone person?" Develop your answer using examples of actual people you know who seemed to be accident prone on some endeavor.
2. Working individually or in groups, compile a list of the factors at work or in school that create dysfunctional stress for you. What methods do you use for dealing with the stress?
3. The "HRCI Test Specifications Appendix" (pages 699–706) lists the knowledge someone studying for the HRCI certification exam needs to have in each area of human resource management (such as in Strategic Management, Workforce Planning, and Human Resource Development). In groups of four to five students, do four things: (1) Review that appendix now. (2) Identify the material in this chapter that relates to the required knowledge the appendix lists. (3) Write four multiple-choice exam questions on this material that you believe would be suitable for inclusion in the HRCI exam. And (4) if time permits, have someone from your team post your team's questions in front of the class, so the students in other teams can take each others' exam questions.
4. The journal *Occupational Hazards* presented some information about what happens when OSHA refers criminal complaints about willful violations of OSHA standards to the U.S. Department of Justice (DOJ). Between 1982 and 2002, OSHA referred 119 fatal cases allegedly involving willful violations of OSHA to the DOJ for criminal prosecution. The DOJ declined to pursue 57% of them, and some were dropped for other reasons. Of the remaining 51 cases, the DOJ settled 63% with pretrial settlements involving no prison time. So, counting acquittals, of the 119 cases OSHA referred to the DOJ, only 9 resulted in prison time for at least one of the defendants. "The Department of Justice is a disgrace," charged the founder of an organization for family members of workers killed on the job. One possible explanation for this low conviction rate is that the crime in cases like these is generally a misdemeanor, not a felony, and the DOJ generally tries to focus its attention on felony cases. Given this information, what implications do you think this has for how employers and their managers should manage their safety programs, and why do you take that position?
5. Recently, a 315-foot-tall, 2-million-pound crane collapsed on a construction site in East Toledo, Ohio, killing four ironworkers. Do you think catastrophic failures like this are avoidable? If so, what steps would you suggest the general contractor take to avoid a disaster like this?

EXPERIENTIAL EXERCISE

How Safe Is My University?

Purpose: The purpose of this exercise is to give you practice in identifying unsafe conditions.

Required Understanding: You should be familiar with material covered in this chapter, particularly that on unsafe conditions and that in Figures 16-6, 16-7, and 16-11.

How to Set Up the Exercise/Instructions: Divide the class into groups of four.

Assume that each group is a safety committee retained by your college's or university's safety engineer to identify and report on any possible unsafe conditions in and around the school building. Each group will spend about 45 minutes in and around the building you are now in for the purpose of identifying and listing possible unsafe conditions. (Make use of the checklists in Figures 16-6, 16-7, and 16-11.)

Return to the class in about 45 minutes. A spokesperson for each group should list on the board the unsafe conditions you think you have identified. How many were there? Do you think these also violate OSHA standards? How would you go about checking?

Develop your own checklist.

These are only sample questions.

GENERAL	OK	ACTION NEEDED
1. Is the required OSHA workplace poster displayed in your place of business as required where all employees are likely to see it?	☐	☐
2. Are you aware of the requirement to report all workplace fatalities and any serious accidents (where five or more are hospitalized) to a federal or state OSHA office within 48 hours?	☐	☐
3. Are workplace injury and illness records being kept as required by OSHA?	☐	☐
4. Are you aware that the OSHA annual summary of workplace injuries and illnesses must be posted by February 1 and must remain posted until March 1?	☐	☐
5. Are you aware that employers with 10 or fewer employees are exempt from the OSHA recordkeeping requirements, unless they are part of an official BLS or state survey and have received specific instructions to keep records?	☐	☐
6. Have you demonstrated an active interest in safety and health matters by defining a policy for your business and communicating it to all employees?	☐	☐
7. Do you have a safety committee or group that allows participation of employees in safety and health activities?	☐	☐
8. Does the safety committee or group meet regularly and report, in writing, its activities?	☐	☐
9. Do you provide safety and health training for all employees requiring such training, and is it documented?	☐	☐
10. Is one person clearly in charge of safety and health activities?	☐	☐
11. Do all employees know what to do in emergencies?	☐	☐
12. Are emergency telephone numbers posted?	☐	☐
13. Do you have a procedure for handling employee complaints regarding safety and health?	☐	☐

WORKPLACE ELECTRICAL WIRING, FIXTURES, AND CONTROLS	OK	ACTION NEEDED
1. Are your workplace electricians familiar with the requirements of the National Electrical Code (NEC)?	☐	☐
2. Do you specify compliance with the NEC for all contract electrical work?	☐	☐
3. If you have electrical installations in hazardous dust or vapor areas, do they meet the NEC for hazardous locations?	☐	☐
4. Are all electrical cords strung so they do not hang on pipes, nails, hooks, etc.?	☐	☐
5. Is all conduit, BX cable, etc., properly attached to all supports and tightly connected to junction and outlet boxes?	☐	☐
6. Is there no evidence of fraying on any electrical cords?	☐	☐
7. Are rubber cords kept free of grease, oil, and chemicals?	☐	☐
8. Are metallic cable and conduit systems properly grounded?	☐	☐
9. Are portable electric tools and appliances grounded or double insulated?	☐	☐
10. Are all ground connections clean and tight?	☐	☐
11. Are fuses and circuit breakers the right type and size for the load on each circuit?	☐	☐
12. Are all fuses free of "jumping" with pennies or metal strips?	☐	☐
13. Do switches show evidence of overheating?	☐	☐
14. Are switches mounted in clean, tightly closed metal boxes?	☐	☐
15. Are all electrical switches marked to show their purpose?	☐	☐
16. Are motors clean and kept free of excessive grease and oil?	☐	☐
17. Are motors properly maintained and provided with adequate overcurrent protection?	☐	☐
18. Are bearings in good condition?	☐	☐
19. Are portable lights equipped with proper guards?	☐	☐
20. Are all lamps kept free of combustible material?	☐	☐
21. Is your electrical system checked periodically by someone competent in the NEC?	☐	☐

(continued)

FIGURE 16-11 Self-Inspection Safety and Health Checklist

Develop your own checklist. These are only sample questions.

EXITS AND ACCESS	OK	ACTION NEEDED
1. Are all exits visible and unobstructed?	☐	☐
2. Are all exits marked with a readily visible sign that is properly illuminated?	☐	☐
3. Are there sufficient exits to ensure prompt escape in case of emergency?	☐	☐
4. Are areas with restricted occupancy posted and is access/egress controlled by persons specifically authorized to be in those areas?	☐	☐
5. Do you take special precautions to protect employees during construction and repair operations?	☐	☐

FIRE PROTECTION	OK	ACTION NEEDED
1. Are portable fire extinguishers provided in adequate number and type?	☐	☐
2. Are fire extinguishers inspected monthly for general condition and operability and noted on the inspection tag?	☐	☐
3. Are fire extinguishers recharged regularly and properly noted on the inspection tag?	☐	☐
4. Are fire extinguishers mounted in readily accessible locations?	☐	☐
5. If you have interior standpipes and valves, are these inspected regularly?	☐	☐
6. If you have a fire alarm system, is it tested at least annually?	☐	☐
7. Are employees periodically instructed in the use of extinguishers and fire protection procedures?	☐	☐
8. If you have outside private fire hydrants, were they flushed within the last year and placed on a regular maintenance schedule?	☐	☐
9. Are fire doors and shutters in good operating condition?	☐	☐
Are they unobstructed and protected against obstruction?	☐	☐
10. Are fusible links in place?	☐	☐
11. Is your local fire department well acquainted with your plant, location, and specific hazards?	☐	☐
12. Automatic sprinklers:		
Are water control valves, air, and water pressures checked weekly?	☐	☐
Are control valves locked open?	☐	☐
Is maintenance of the system assigned to responsible persons or a sprinkler contractor?	☐	☐
Are sprinkler heads protected by metal guards where exposed to mechanical damage?	☐	☐
Is proper minimum clearance maintained around sprinkler heads?	☐	☐

HOUSEKEEPING AND GENERAL WORK ENVIRONMENT	OK	ACTION NEEDED
1. Is smoking permitted in designated "safe areas" only?	☐	☐
2. Are NO SMOKING signs prominently posted in areas containing combustibles and flammables?	☐	☐
3. Are covered metal waste cans used for oily and paint-soaked waste?	☐	☐
Are they emptied at least daily?	☐	☐
4. Are paint spray booths, dip tanks, etc., and their exhaust ducts cleaned regularly?	☐	☐
5. Are stand mats, platforms, or similar protection provided to protect employees from wet floors in wet processes?	☐	☐
6. Are waste receptacles provided and are they emptied regularly?	☐	☐
7. Do your toilet facilities meet the requirements of applicable sanitary codes?	☐	☐
8. Are washing facilities provided?	☐	☐
9. Are all areas of your business adequately illuminated?	☐	☐
10. Are floor load capacities posted in second floors, lofts, storage areas, etc.?	☐	☐
11. Are floor openings provided with toe boards and railings or a floor hole cover?	☐	☐
12. Are stairways in good condition with standard railings provided for every flight having four or more risers?	☐	☐
13. Are portable wood ladders and metal ladders adequate for their purpose, in good condition, and provided with secure footing?	☐	☐
14. If you have fixed ladders, are they adequate, and are they in good condition and equipped with side rails or cages or special safety climbing devices, if required?	☐	☐
15. For loading docks:		
Are dockplates kept in serviceable condition and secured to prevent slipping?	☐	☐
Do you have means to prevent car or truck movement when dockplates are in place?	☐	☐

FIGURE 16-11 *(continued)*

MACHINES AND EQUIPMENT

	OK	ACTION NEEDED
1. Are all machines or operations that expose operators or other employees to rotating parts, pinch points, flying chips, particles, or sparks adequately guarded?	☐	☐
2. Are mechanical power transmission belts and pinch points guarded?	☐	☐
3. Is exposed power shafting less than 7 feet from the floor guarded?	☐	☐
4. Are hand tools and other equipment regularly inspected for safe condition?	☐	☐
5. Is compressed air used for cleaning reduced to less than 30 psi?	☐	☐
6. Are power saws and similar equipment provided with safety guards?	☐	☐
7. Are grinding wheel tool rests set to within $1/8$ inch or less of the wheel?	☐	☐
8. Is there any system for inspecting small hand tools for burred ends, cracked handles, etc.?	☐	☐
9. Are compressed gas cylinders examined regularly for obvious signs of defects, deep rusting, or leakage?	☐	☐
10. Is care used in handling and storing cylinders and valves to prevent damage?	☐	☐
11. Are all air receivers periodically examined, including the safety valves?	☐	☐
12. Are safety valves tested regularly and frequently?	☐	☐
13. Is there sufficient clearance from stoves, furnaces, etc., for stock, woodwork, or other combustible materials?	☐	☐
14. Is there clearance of at least 4 feet in front of heating equipment involving open flames, such as gas radiant heaters, and fronts of firing doors of stoves, furnaces, etc.?	☐	☐
15. Are all oil and gas fired devices equipped with flame failure controls that will prevent flow of fuel if pilots or main burners are not working?	☐	☐
16. Is there at least a 2-inch clearance between chimney brickwork and all woodwork or other combustible materials?	☐	☐
17. For welding or flame cutting operations:		
Are only authorized, trained personnel permitted to use such equipment?	☐	☐
Have operators been given a copy of operating instructions and asked to follow them?	☐	☐
Are welding gas cylinders stored so they are not subjected to damage?	☐	☐
Are valve protection caps in place on all cylinders not connected for use?	☐	☐
Are all combustible materials near the operator covered with protective shields or otherwise protected?	☐	☐
Is a fire extinguisher provided at the welding site?	☐	☐
Do operators have the proper protective clothing and equipment?	☐	☐

Develop your own checklist.

These are only sample questions.

MATERIALS

	OK	ACTION NEEDED
1. Are approved safety cans or other acceptable containers used for handling and dispensing flammable liquids?	☐	☐
2. Are all flammable liquids that are kept inside buildings stored in proper storage containers or cabinets?	☐	☐
3. Do you meet OSHA standards for all spray painting or dip tank operations using combustible liquids?	☐	☐
4. Are oxidizing chemicals stored in areas separate from all organic material except shipping bags?	☐	☐
5. Do you have an enforced NO SMOKING rule in areas for storage and use of hazardous materials?	☐	☐
6. Are NO SMOKING signs posted where needed?	☐	☐
7. Is ventilation equipment provided for removal of air contaminants from operations such as production grinding, buffing, spray painting and/or vapor degreasing, and is it operating properly?	☐	☐
8. Are protective measures in effect for operations involved with x-rays or other radiation?	☐	☐
9. For lift truck operations:		
Are only trained personnel allowed to operate forklift trucks?	☐	☐
Is overhead protection provided on high lift rider trucks?	☐	☐
10. For toxic materials:		
Are all materials used in your plant checked for toxic qualities?	☐	☐
Have appropriate control procedures such as ventilation systems, enclosed operations, safe handling practices, proper personal protective equipment (such as respirators, glasses or goggles, gloves, etc.) been instituted for toxic materials?	☐	☐

(continued)

FIGURE 16-11 *(continued)*

Develop your own checklist.

These are only sample questions.

EMPLOYEE PROTECTION	OK	ACTION NEEDED
1. Is there a hospital, clinic, or infirmary for medical care near your business?	☐	☐
2. If medical and first-aid facilities are not nearby, do you have one or more employees trained in first aid?	☐	☐
3. Are your first-aid supplies adequate for the type of potential injuries in your work-place?	☐	☐
4. Are there quick water flush facilities available where employees are exposed to corrosive materials?	☐	☐
5. Are hard hats provided and worn where any danger of falling objects exists?	☐	☐
6. Are protective goggles or glasses provided and worn where there is any danger of flying particles or splashing of corrosive materials?	☐	☐
7. Are protective gloves, aprons, shields, or other means provided for protection from sharp, hot, or corrosive materials?	☐	☐
8. Are approved respirators provided for regular or emergency use where needed?	☐	☐
9. Is all protective equipment maintained in a sanitary condition and readily available for use?	☐	☐
10. Where special equipment is needed for electrical workers, is it available?	☐	☐
11. When lunches are eaten on the premises, are they eaten in areas where there is no exposure to toxic materials, and not in toilet facility areas?	☐	☐
12. Is protection against the effect of occupational noise exposure provided when the sound levels exceed those shown in the OSHA noise standard?	☐	☐

FIGURE 16-11 *(continued)*

APPLICATION CASE

The New Safety and Health Program

At first glance, a dot-com company is one of the last places you'd expect to find potential safety and health hazards—or so the owners of LearnInMotion.com thought. There's no danger of moving machinery, no high-pressure lines, no cutting or heavy lifting, and certainly no forklift trucks. However, there are safety and health problems.

In terms of accident-causing conditions, for instance, the one thing dot-com companies have cables and wires. There are cables connecting the computers to screens and to the servers, and in many cases separate cables running from some computers to separate printers. There are 10 telephones in this particular office, all on 15-foot phone lines that always seem to be snaking around chairs and tables. There is, in fact, an astonishing amount of cable considering this is an office with fewer so-called wireless connections and with fewer than 10 employees. When the installation specialists wired the office (for electricity, high-speed cable, phone lines, burglar alarms, and computers), they estimated they used well over 5 miles of cables of one sort or another. Most of these are hidden in the walls or ceilings, but many of them snake their way from desk to desk, and under and over doorways. Several employees have tried to reduce the nuisance of having to trip over wires whenever they get up by putting their plastic chair pads over the wires closest to them. However, that still leaves many wires unprotected. In other cases, they brought in their own packing tape and tried to tape down the wires in those spaces where they're particularly troublesome, such as across doorways.

The cables and wires are only one of the more obvious potential accident-causing conditions. The firm's programmer, before he left the firm, had tried to repair the main server while the unit was still electrically alive. To this day, they're not sure exactly where he stuck the screwdriver, but the result was that he was "blown across the room," as one manager put it. He was all right, but it was still a scare. And while they haven't received any claims yet, every employee spends hours at his or her computer, so carpal tunnel syndrome is a risk, as are a variety of other problems such as eyestrain and strained backs.

One recent accident particularly scared the owners. The firm uses independent contractors to deliver the firm's book- and DVD-based courses in New York and two other cities. A delivery person was riding his bike east at the intersection of Second Avenue and East 64th Street in New York when he was struck by a car going south on Second Avenue. Luckily, he was not hurt, but the bike's front wheel was wrecked, and the narrow escape got the firm's two owners, Mel and Jennifer, thinking about their lack of a safety program.

It's not just the physical conditions that concern the two owners. They also have some concerns about potential health problems such as job stress and burnout. Although the business may be (relatively) safe with respect to physical conditions, it is also relatively stressful in terms of the demands it makes in hours and deadlines. It is not at all unusual for employees to get to work by 7:30 or 8 o'clock in the morning and to work through until 11 or 12 o'clock at night, at least 5 and sometimes 6 or 7 days per week.

The bottom line is that both Jennifer and Mel feel quite strongly that they need to do something about implementing a health and safety plan. Now, they want you, their management consultants, to help them do it. Here's what they want you to do for them.

Questions

1. Based upon your knowledge of health and safety matters and your actual observations of operations that are similar to theirs, make a list of the potential hazardous conditions employees and others face at LearnInMotion.com. What should they do to reduce the potential severity of the top five hazards?
2. Would it be advisable for them to set up a procedure for screening out stress-prone or accident-prone individuals? Why or why not? If so, how should they screen them?
3. Write a short position paper on the subject, "What should we do to get all our employees to behave more safely at work?"
4. Based on what you know and on what other dot-coms are doing, write a short position paper on the subject, "What can we do to reduce the potential problems of stress and burnout in our company?"

CONTINUING CASE

Carter Cleaning Company

The New Safety Program

Employees' safety and health are very important matters in the laundry and cleaning business. Each facility is a small production plant in which machines, powered by high-pressure steam and compressed air, work at high temperatures washing, cleaning, and pressing garments, often under very hot, slippery conditions. Chemical vapors are produced continually, and caustic chemicals are used in the cleaning process. High-temperature stills are almost continually "cooking down" cleaning solvents in order to remove impurities so that the solvents can be reused. If a mistake is made in this process—like injecting too much steam into the still—a boilover occurs, in which boiling chemical solvent erupts out of the still and over the floor, and on anyone who happens to be standing in its way.

As a result of these hazards and the fact that chemically hazardous waste is continually produced in these stores, several government agencies (including OSHA and the Environmental Protection Agency) have instituted strict guidelines regarding the management of these plants. For example, posters have to be placed in each store notifying employees of their right to be told what hazardous chemicals they are dealing with and what the proper method for handling each chemical is. Special waste-management firms must be used to pick up and properly dispose of the hazardous waste.

A chronic problem the Carters (and most other laundry owners) have is the unwillingness on the part of the cleaning–spotting workers to wear safety goggles. Not all the chemicals they use require safety goggles, but some—like the hydrofluoric acid used to remove rust stains from garments—are very dangerous. The latter is kept in special plastic containers, since it dissolves glass. The problem is that wearing safety goggles can be troublesome. They are somewhat uncomfortable, and they become smudged easily and thus cut down on visibility. As a result, Jack has always found it almost impossible to get these employees to wear their goggles.

Questions

1. How should the firm go about identifying hazardous conditions that should be rectified? Use checklists such as Figures 16-6 and 16-11 to list at least 10 possible dry-cleaning store hazardous conditions.
2. Would it be advisable for the firm to set up a procedure for screening out accident-prone individuals? How should they do so?
3. How would you suggest the Carters get all employees to behave more safely at work? Also, how would you advise them to get those who should be wearing goggles to do so?

TRANSLATING STRATEGY INTO HR POLICIES & PRACTICES CASE

The Hotel Paris Case

The New Safety and Health Program

The Hotel Paris's competitive strategy is "To use superior guest service to differentiate the Hotel Paris properties, and to thereby increase the length of stay and return rate of guests, and thus boost revenues and profitability." HR manager Lisa Cruz must now formulate functional policies and activities that support this competitive strategy, by eliciting the required employee behaviors and competencies.

Although "hazardous conditions" might not be the first thing that comes to mind when you think of hotels, Lisa Cruz knew that hazards and safety were in fact serious issues for the Hotel Paris. Indeed, everywhere you look—from the valets leaving car doors open on the driveways to slippery areas around the pools, to tens of thousands of pounds of ammonia, chlorine, and other caustic chemicals that the hotels use each year for cleaning and laundry—hotels provide a fertile environment for accidents. Obviously, hazardous conditions are bad for the Hotel Paris. They are inhumane for the workers. High accident rates probably reduce employee morale and thus service. And accidents raise the company's costs and reduce its profitability, for instance in terms of workers' compensation claims and absences. Lisa knew that she had to clean up her firm's occupational safety and health systems.

Lisa and the CFO reviewed their company's safety records, and what they found disturbed them deeply. In terms of every safety-related metric they could find, including accident costs per year, lost time due to accidents, workers' compensation per employee, and number of safety training programs per year, the Hotel Paris compared unfavorably with most other hotel chains and service firms. "Why, just in terms of extra workers' compensation costs, the Hotel Paris must be spending $500,000 a year more than we should be," said the CFO. And that didn't include lost time due to accidents, or the likely negative effect accidents had on employee morale, or the cost of litigation (as when, for instance, one guest accidentally burned himself with chlorine that a pool attendant had left unprotected). The CFO authorized Lisa to develop a new safety and health program.

Questions

1. Based on what you read in this chapter, what's the first step the Hotel Paris should take as part of its new safety and health program, and why?
2. List 10 specific high-risk areas in a typical hotel you believe Lisa and her team should look at first, including examples of the safety or health hazards that they should look for there.
3. Give three specific examples of how Hotel Paris can use HR practices to improve its safety efforts.
4. Write a 1-page summary addressing the topic, "How improving safety and health at the Hotel Paris will contribute to us achieving our strategic goals."

KEY TERMS

Occupational Safety and Health Act of 1970, *p. 583*
Occupational Safety and Health Administration (OSHA), *p. 583*
occupational illness, *p. 585*
citation, *p. 587*
unsafe conditions, *p. 591*
behavior-based safety, *p. 601*
burnout, *p. 609*

ENDNOTES

1. Michael Wilson, "Manslaughter Charge in Trench Collapse," *The New York Times*, June 12, 2008, p. B1.
2. For a discussion of specific strategies for reducing fatalities at work, see, for example, Laura Walter, "Facing the Unthinkable: Fatality Prevention in the Workplace," *Occupational Hazards*, January 2008, pp. 32–39.
3. All data refer to 2006. See www.bls.gov/iif/oshwc/osh/os/ostb1757.txt, accessed January 19, 2008.
4. "BLS Likely Underestimating Injury and Illness Estimates," *Occupational Hazards*, May 2006, p. 16; Tahira Probst et al., "Organizational Injury Rate Underreporting: The Moderating Effect of Organizational Safety Climate," *Journal of Applied Psychology* 93, no. 5 (2008), pp. 1147–1154.
5. Greg Hom, "Protecting Eyes from High-Tech Hazards," *Occupational Hazards*, March 1999, pp. 53–55; "Workplace Injuries by Industry, 2002," *Safety Compliance Letter*, no. 2438 (February 2004), p. 12. See also Katherine Torres, "Stepping into the Kitchen: Protection for Food Workers," *Occupational Hazards*, January 2007, pp. 29–30.
6. "Blame New Computers for Sick Buildings," *USA Today* 129, no. 2672 (May 2001), p. 8.
7. Michael Pinto, "Why Are Indoor Air Quality Problems So Prevalent Today?" *Occupational Hazards*, January 2001, pp. 37–39.
8. Sandy Moretz, "Safe Havens?" *Occupational Hazards*, November 2000, pp. 45–46.
9. See, for example, "Workplace Fatalities: The Impact on Coworkers," *Occupational Hazards*, March 2008, p. 18.
10. David Ayers, "Mapping Support for an E. H. S. Management System," *Occupational Hazards*, June 2006, pp. 53–54.
11. Todd Nighswonger, "Rouge Settlement Sparks Safety Initiative at Ford," *Occupational Hazards*, October 1999, pp. 101–102; Karen Gaspers, "It's Painful for the Bottom Line, Too," *Safety and Health* 168, no. 14 (October 2003), p. 323.

12. David Barstow and Lowell Bergman, "Family's Profits, Wrung from Blood and Sweat," *The New York Times*, January 9, 2003, p. 81.
13. Willie Hammer, *Occupational Safety Management and Engineering* (Upper Saddle River, NJ: Prentice Hall, 1985), pp. 62–63. See also "DuPont's 'STOP' Helps Prevent Workplace Injuries and Incidents," *Asia Africa Intelligence Wire*, May 17, 2004.
14. F. David Pierce, "Safety in the Emerging Leadership Paradigm," *Occupational Hazards*, June 2000, pp. 63–66. See also, for example, Josh Williams, "Optimizing the Safety Culture," *Occupational Hazards*, May 2008, pp. 45–49.
15. Sandy Smith, "Louisiana-Pacific Corp. Builds Safety into Everything It Does," *Occupational Hazards*, November 2007, pp. 41–42.
16. Donald Hantula et al., "The Value of Workplace Safety: A Time Based Utility Analysis Model," *Journal of Organizational Behavior Management* 21, no. 2 (2001), pp. 79–98.
17. Ibid. In a similar case, in 2008 the owner of a Brooklyn, New York, construction site was arrested for manslaughter when a worker died in a collapsed trench. Michael Wilson, "Manslaughter Charge in Trench Collapse," *The New York Times*, June 12, 2008, p. B1.
18. "A Safety Committee Man's Guide," Aetna Life and Casualty Insurance Company, Catalog 87684, pp. 17–21.
19. Based on "All About OSHA" (Washington, DC: U.S. Department of Labor, 1980), www.OSHA.gov, accessed January 19, 2008.
20. "Safety Rule on Respiratory Protection Issues," *BNA Bulletin to Management*, January 8, 1998, p. 1.
21. "OSHA Hazard Communication Standard Enforcement," *BNA Bulletin to Management*, February 23, 1989, p. 13. See also William Kincaid, "OSHA vs. Excellence in Safety Management," *Occupational Hazards*, December 2002, pp. 34–36.
22. "What Every Employer Needs to Know About OSHA Record Keeping," U.S. Department of Labor, Bureau of Labor Statistics (Washington, DC), Report 412-3, p. 3.
23. Arthur Sapper and Robert Gombar, "Nagging Problems Under OSHA's New Record-Keeping Rule," *Occupational Hazards*, March 2002, p. 58.
24. Brian Jackson and Jeffrey Myers, "Just When You Thought You Were Safe: OSHA Record-Keeping Violations," *Management Review*, May 1994, pp. 62–63.
25. "Supreme Court Says OSHA Inspectors Need Warrants," *Engineering News Record*, June 1, 1978, pp. 9–10; W. Scott Railton, "OSHA Gets Tough on Business," *Management Review* 80, no. 12 (December 1991), pp. 28–29; Steve Hollingsworth, "How to Survive an OSHA Inspection," *Occupational Hazards*, March 2004, pp. 31–33.
26. http://osha.gov/as/opa/oshafacts.html, accessed January 19, 2008; Edwin Foulke Jr., "OSHA's Evolving Role in Promoting Occupational Safety and Health," *EHS Today*, November 2008, pp. 44–49. Some believe that under the new Democratic administration of President Obama, OSHA may move from voluntary programs back to increased attention on inspections. See, for example, Laura Walter, "Safety Roundtable: The View from the End of an Era," *EHS Today*, December 2008, pp. 30–31.
27. www.osha.gov/Publications/osha2098.pdf+OSHA+inspection+priorities&hl=en&ct=clnk&cd=1&gl=us, accessed January 19, 2008.
28. www.OSHA.gov, downloaded May 28, 2005, and http://osha.gov/pls/oshaweb/owadisp.show_document?p_table=NEWS_RELEASES&p_id=14883, accessed January 19, 2008.
29. This section is based on "All About OSHA," pp. 23–25. See also "OSHA Final Rule Expands Employees' Role in Consultations, Protects Employer Records," *BNA Bulletin to Management*, November 2, 2000, p. 345.
30. D. Diane Hatch and James Hall, "A Flurry of New Federal Regulations," *Workforce*, February 2001, p. 98.
31. For example, OSHA recently settled with Murphy Oil USA, with Murphy paying just over $179,000 in OSHA fines for a variety of violations and OSHA recently proposed a penalty of $195,200 against a masonry contractor with a total of 21 violations. See "Enforcement Briefs," *Occupational Hazards*, March 2008, p. 13.
32. www.osha.gov/Publications/osha2098.pdf+OSHA+inspection+priorities&hl=en&ct=clnk&cd=1&gl=us, accessed January 19, 2008.
33. "Enforcement Activity Increased in 1997," *BNA Bulletin to Management*, January 29, 1998, p. 28. See also www.osha.gov/as/opa/osha-faq.html, accessed May 26, 2007.
34. Ibid., p. 28.
35. For a discussion of how to deal with citations and proposed penalties, see, for example, Michael Taylor, "OSHA Citations and Proposed Penalties: How to Beat the Rap," *EHS Today*, December 2008, pp. 34–36.
36. Patricia Poole, "When OSHA Knocks," *Occupational Hazards*, February 2008, pp. 59–61.
37. Robert Grossman, "Handling Inspections: Tips from Insiders," *HR Magazine*, October 1999, pp. 41–50; and "OSHA Inspections," OSHA, www.osha.gov/Publications/osha2098.pdf, accessed May 26, 2007.
38. These are based on James Nash, "The Top Ten Ways to Get into Trouble with OSHA," *Occupational Hazards*, December 2003, pp. 27–30.
39. Sean Smith, "OSHA Resources Can Help Small Businesses with Hazards," *Westchester County Business Journal*, August 4, 2003, p. 4. See also www.osha.gov/as/opa/osha-faq.html, accessed May 26, 2007.
40. Lisa Finnegan, "Industry Partners with OSHA," *Occupational Hazards*, February 1999, pp. 43–45.
41. Charles Chadd, "Managing OSHA Compliance: The Human Resources Issues," *Employee Relations Law Journal* 20, no. 1 (Summer 1994), p. 106.
42. These are based on Roger Jacobs, "Employee Resistance to OSHA Standards: Toward a More Reasonable Approach," *Labor Law Journal*, April 1979, pp. 227–230. See also "Half of All Working Americans Feel Immune to Workplace Injuries," https://www.mem-ins.com/newsroom/pr072803.htm, accessed August 11, 2009.
43. Arthur Sapper, "The Oft-Missed Step: Documentation of Safety Discipline," *Occupational Hazards*, January 2006, p. 59.
44. "A Safety Committee Man's Guide," Aetna Life and Casualty Insurance Company, Catalog 87684. See also Dan Petersen, "The Barriers to Safety Excellence," *Occupational Hazards*, December 2000, pp. 37–39.
45. "Did This Supervisor Do Enough to Protect Trench Workers?" *Safety Compliance Letter*, October 2003, p. 9.
46. Julian Barling et al., "High-Quality Work, Job Satisfaction, and Occupational Injuries," *Journal of Applied Psychology* 88, no. 2 (2003), pp. 276–283.
47. For a discussion of this, see David Hofmann and Adam Stetzer, "A Cross-Level Investigation of Factors Influencing Unsafe Behaviors and Accidents," *Personnel Psychology* 49 (1996), pp. 307–308. See also David Hofman and Barbara Mark, "An

Investigation of the Relationship Between Safety Climate and Medication Errors as Well as Other Nurse and Patient Outcomes," *Personnel Psychology* 50, no. 9 (2006), pp. 847–869.

48. Duane Schultz and Sydney Schultz, *Psychology and Work Today* (Upper Saddle River, NJ: Prentice Hall, 1998), p. 351.
49. Robert Pater and Robert Russell, "Drop That 'Accident Prone' Tag: Look for Causes Beyond Personal Issues," *Industrial Safety and Hygiene News* 38, no. 1, (January 2004): 50, http://findarticles.com/p/articles/mi_hb5992/is_200401/ai_n24195869/ accessed August 11, 2009.
50. Discussed in Douglas Haaland, "Who's the Safest Bet for the Job? Find Out Why the Fun Guy in the Next Cubicle May Be the Next Accident Waiting to Happen," *Security Management* 49, no. 2 (February 2005), pp. 51–57.
51. "Thai Research Points to Role of Personality in Road Accidents," http://www.driveandstayalive.com/info%20section/news/individual%20news%20articles/x_050204_personality-in-crash-causation_thailand.htm, February 2, 2005, accessed August 11, 2009; Donald Bashline et al., "Bad Behavior: Personality Tests Can Help Underwriters Identify High-Risk Drivers," *Best's Review* 105, no. 12 (April 2005), pp. 63–64.
52. Todd Nighswonger, "Threat of Terror Impacts Workplace Safety," *Occupational Hazards*, July 2002, pp. 24–26.
53. Michael Blotzer, "Safety by Design," *Occupational Hazards*, May 1999, pp. 39–40; and www.designsafe.com/dsesoftware.php, accessed May 26, 2007.
54. Susannah Figura, "Don't Slip Up on Safety," *Occupational Hazards*, November 1996, pp. 29–31. See also Russ Wood, "Defining the Boundaries of Safety," *Occupational Hazards*, January 2001, pp. 41–43.
55. See, for example, Laura Walter, "What's in a Glove?" *Occupational Hazards*, May 2008, pp. 35–36.
56. Donald Groce, "Keep the Gloves On!" *Occupational Hazards*, June 2008, pp. 45–47.
57. James Zeigler, "Protective Clothing: Exploring the Wearability Issue," *Occupational Hazards*, September 2000, pp. 81–82.
58. Sandy Smith, "Protective Clothing and the Quest for Improved Performance," *Occupational Hazards*, February 2008, pp. 63–66.
59. Tim Andrews, "Getting Employees Comfortable with PPE," *Occupational Hazards*, January 2000, pp. 35–38. Note that personal protective equipment can backfire. As one expert says, ". . . making a job safer with machine guards or PPE lowers people's risk perceptions and thus can lead to an increase in at-risk behavior." Therefore, also train employees not to let their guards down. E. Scott Geller, "The Thinking and Seeing Components of People-Based Safety," *Occupational Hazards*, December 2006, pp. 38–40.
60. Sandy Smith, "Protecting Vulnerable Workers," *Occupational Hazards*, April 2004, pp. 25–28.
61. Katherine Torres, "Challenges in Protecting a Young Workforce," *Occupational Hazards*, May 2006, pp. 24–27.
62. Linda Tapp, "We Can Do It: Protecting Women Workers." *Occupational Hazards*, October 2003, pp. 26–28.
63. Katherine Torres, "Don't Lose Sight of the Older Workforce," *Occupational Hazards*, June 2008, pp. 55–59.
64. Robert Pater, "Boosting Safety with an Aging Workforce," *Occupational Hazards*, March 2006, p. 24.
65. Michael Silverstein, M.D., "Designing the Age Friendly Workplace," *Occupational Hazards*, December 2007, pp. 29–31.
66. Elizabeth Rogers and William Wiatrowski, "Injuries, Illnesses, and Fatalities Among Older Workers," *Monthly Labor Review* 128, no. 10 (October 2005), pp. 24–30.
67. "The Complete Guide to Personal Protective Equipment," *Occupational Hazards*, January 1999, pp. 49–60. See also Edwin Zalewski, "Noise Control: It's More Than Just Earplugs: OSHA Requires Employers to Evaluate Engineering and Administrative Controls Before Using Personal Protective Equipment," *Occupational Hazards* 68, no. 9 (September 2006), p. 48(3). You can find videos about new spersonal protective products at "SafetyLive TV" at www.occupationalhazards.com, accessed March 14, 2009.
68. Robert Pater and Ron Bowles, "Directing Attention to Boost Safety Performance," *Occupational Hazards*, March 2007, pp. 46–48.
69. E. Scott Geller, "The Thinking and Seeing Components of People-Based Safety," *Occupational Hazards*, December 2006, pp. 38–40.
70. William Kincaid, "10 Habits of Effective Safety Managers," *Occupational Hazards*, November 1996, pp. 41–43. See also Sandy Smith, "Breakthrough Safety Management," *Occupational Hazards*, June 2004, p. 43.
71. Gerald Borofsky, Michelle Bielema, and James Hoffman, "Accidents, Turnover, and the Use of a Preemployment Screening Inventory: Further Contributions to the Validation of the Employee Reliability Inventory," *Psychological Reports*, 1993, pp. 1067–1076.
72. Ibid., p. 1072. See also Keith Rosenblum, "The Companion Solution to Ergonomics: Pretesting for the Job" *Risk Management* 50, no 11 (November 2003), p. 26(6).
73. Dan Hartshorn, "The Safety Interview," *Occupational Hazards*, October 1999, pp. 107–111.
74. Gaye Reese and Joy Waltemath, *Workers' Compensation Manual for Managers and Supervisors: A Guide to Effective Workers' Compensation Management* (Chicago, IL: CCH Incorporated, 1996), pp. 22–23.
75. Laura Walter, "Surfing for Safety," *Occupational Hazards*, July 2008, pp. 23–29.
76. John Rekus, "Is Your Safety Training Program Effective?" *Occupational Hazards*, August 1999, pp. 37–39.
77. James Nash, "Rewarding the Safety Process," *Occupational Hazards*, March 2000, pp. 29–34.
78. Quoted in Josh Cable, "Seven Suggestions for a Successful Safety Incentives Program," *Occupational Hazards* 67, no. 3 (March 2005), pp. 39–43. See also Jill Bishop, "Create a Safer Work Environment by Bridging the Language and Culture Gap," *EHS Today*, March 2009, pp. 42–44.
79. See, for example, Ron Bruce, "Online from Kazakhstan to California," *Occupational Hazards*, June 2008, pp. 61–65.
80. Michael Blotzer, "PDA Software Offers Auditing Advances," *Occupational Hazards*, December 2001, p. 11. See also Erik Andersen "Automating Health & Safety Processes Creates Value," *Occupational Hazards*, April 2008, pp. 53–63.
81. See, for example, Josh Cable, "Seven Suggestions for a Successful Safety Incentive Program," *Occupational Hazards* 67, no. 3 (March 2005), pp. 39–43. See also J. M. Saidler, "Gift Cards Make Safety Motivation Simple," *Occupational Health & Safety* 78, no. 1 (January 2009), pp. 39–40.
82. Don Williamson and Jon Kauffman, "From Tragedy to Triumph: Safety Grows Wings at Golden Eagle," *Occupational Hazards*, February 2006, pp. 17–25.
83. See, for example, Josh Cable, "Safety Incentives Strategies," *Occupational Hazards* 67, no. 4 (April 2005), p. 37; E. Scott Geller, op. cit.
84. James Nash, "Construction Safety: Best Practices in Training Hispanic Workers," *Occupational Hazards*, February 2004, pp. 35–38.

85. Ibid., p. 37.
86. Judi Komaki, Kenneth Barwick, and Lawrence Scott, "A Behavioral Approach to Occupational Safety: Pinpointing and Reinforcing Safe Performance in a Food Manufacturing Plant," *Journal of Applied Psychology* 63 (August 1978), pp. 434–445. See also Anat Arkin, "Incentives to Work Safely," *Personnel Management* 26, no. 9 (September 1994), pp. 48–52; Peter Makin and Valerie Sutherland, "Reducing Accidents Using a Behavioral Approach," *Leadership and Organizational Development Journal* 15, no. 5 (1994), pp. 5–10; Sandy Smith, "Why Cash Isn't King," *Occupational Hazards*, March 2004, pp. 37–38.
87. Stan Hodson and Tim Gordon, "Tenneco's Drive to Become Injury Free," *Occupational Hazards*, May 2000, pp. 85–87. For another example, see Terry Mathis, "Lean Behavior-Based Safety," *Occupational Hazards*, May 2005, pp. 33–34.
88. Tim McDaniel, "Employee Participation: A Vehicle for Safety by Design," *Occupational Hazards*, May 2002, pp. 71–76.
89. For another good example, see Christopher Chapman, "Using Kaizen to Improve Safety and Ergonomics," *Occupational Hazards*, February 2006, pp. 27–29.
90. Linda Johnson, "Preventing Injuries: The Big Payoff," *Personnel Journal*, April 1994, pp. 61–64; David Webb, "The Bathtub Effect: Why Safety Programs Fail," *Management Review*, February 1994, pp. 51–54. See also www.osha.gov/Publications/osha2098.pdf, accessed May 26, 2007.
91. Lisa Cullen, "Safety Committees: A Smart Business Decision," *Occupational Hazards*, May 1999, pp. 99–104. See also www.osha.gov/Publications/osha2098.pdf, accessed May 26, 2007; and D. Kolman, "Effective Safety Committees," *Beverage Industry* 100, no. 3 (March 2009), pp. 63–65.
92. www.aihaaps.ca/palm/occhazards.html, accessed April 26, 2009.
93. Michael Blotzer, "PDA Software Offers Auditing Advances," *Occupational Hazards*, December 2001, p. 11.
94. Anthea Zacharatos et al., "High-Performance Work Systems and Occupational Safety," *Journal of Applied Psychology* 90, no. 1 (2005), pp. 77–93.
95. Ibid., p. 89.
96. Note that the vast majority of workers' injury-related deaths occur not at work, but when the employees are off the job, often at home. More employers, including Johnson & Johnson, are therefore implementing safety campaigns encouraging employees to apply safe practices at home, as well as at work. Katherine Torres, "Safety Hits Home," *Occupational Hazards*, July 2006, pp. 19–23.
97. Michele Campolieti and Douglas Hyatt, "Further Evidence on the 'Monday Effect' in Workers' Compensation," *Industrial and Labor Relations Review* 59, no. 3 (April 2006), pp. 438–450.
98. See, for example, Rob Wilson, "Five Ways to Reduce Workers' Compensation Claims," *Occupational Hazards*, December 2005, pp. 43–46.
99. "Strict Policies Mean Big Cuts in Premiums," *Occupational Hazards*, May 2000, p. 51.
100. See, for example, *Workers' Compensation Manual for Managers and Supervisors*, pp. 36–39.
101. "Study: No Warm Welcome After Comp Leave," *Occupational Hazards*, February 2001, p. 57.
102. Ibid., p. 51.
103. Donna Clendenning, "Taking a Bite Out of Workers' Comp Costs," *Occupational Hazards*, September 2000, pp. 85–86.
104. www.zeraware.com, accessed March 22, 2009.
105. This is based on Paul Puncochar, "The Science and Art to Identifying Workplace Hazards," *Occupational Hazards*, September 2003, pp. 50–54.
106. Ibid., p. 52.
107. Mark Wysong, "A Prescription for Managing Chemicals: Use These Strategies for Successful Electronic MSDS," *Industrial Safety and Hygiene News* 37, no. 1 (January 2003), p. 42.
108. Sandy Smith, "SARS: What Employers Need to Know," *Occupational Hazards*, July 2003, pp. 33–35.
109. Based on the report "Workplace Screening and Brief Intervention: What Employers Can and Should Do About Excessive Alcohol Use," http://www.ensuringsolutions.org/resources/resources_show.htm?doc_id=673239, accessed August 11, 2009.
110. "15% of Workers Drinking, Drunk, or Hungover While at Work, According to New University Study," *BNA Bulletin to Management*, January 24, 2006, p. 27.
111. "Facing Facts About Workplace Substance Abuse," *Rough Notes* 144, no. 5 (May 2001), pp. 114–118.
112. Todd Nighswonger, "Just Say Yes to Preventing Substance Abuse," *Occupational Hazards*, April 2000, pp. 39–41. See also L. Claussen, "Can You Spot the Meth Addict?," *Safety & Health* 179, no. 4 (April 2009), pp. 48–52.
113. See, for example, Kathryn Tyler, "Happiness from a Bottle?" *HR Magazine*, May 2002, pp. 30–37.
114. "New Jersey Union Takes on Mandatory Random Drug Tests," *Record* (Hackensack, NJ), January 2, 2008.
115. Frank Lockwood et al., "Drug Testing Programs and Their Impact on Workplace Accidents: A Time Series Analysis," *Journal of Individual Employment Rights* 8, no. 4 (2000), pp. 295–306; and Sally Roberts, "Random Drug Testing Can Help Reduce Accidents for Construction Companies; Drug Abuse Blamed for Heightened Risk in the Workplace," *Business Insurance* 40 (October 23, 2006), p. 6.
116. William Current, "Pre-Employment Drug Testing," *Occupational Hazards*, July 2002, p. 56. See also William Current, "Improving Your Drug Testing ROI," *Occupational Health & Safety* 73, no. 4 (April 2004), pp. 40, 42, 44.
117. Diane Cadrain, "Are Your Employees' Drug Tests Accurate?" *HR Magazine*, January 2003, pp. 41–45.
118. Sally Roberts, "Random Drug Testing Can Help Reduce Accidents for Construction Companies; Drug Abuse Blamed for Heightened Risk in the Workplace," *Business Insurance* 40 (October 23, 2006), p. 6.
119. Ibid., p. 94. See also Carrie Printz, "No Practice Is Immune," *American Medical News* 49, no. 2 (January 16, 2006), p. 21(2).
120. "Alcohol Misuse Prevention Programs: Department of Transportation Final Rules," *BNA Bulletin to Management*, March 24, 1994, pp. 1–8. See also www.dol.gov/elaws/drugfree.htm and www.dot.gov/ost/dapc, both accessed May 26, 2007.
121. "Stress, Depression Cost Employers," *Occupational Hazards*, December 1998, p. 24. See also Charlene Solomon, "Stressed to the Limit," *Workforce*, September 1999, pp. 48–54; and "To Slash Health-Care Costs, Look to the Company Culture," *Managing Benefits Plans*, December 2004, p. 1(5).
122. Beth Andrus, "Accommodating the Alcoholic Executive," *Society for Human Resource Management Legal Report*, January 2008, pp. 1, 4.
123. Eric Sundstrom et al., "Office Noise, Satisfaction, and Performance," *Environment and Behavior*, no. 2 (March 1994), pp. 195–222; and "Stress: How to Cope with Life's Challenges," *American Family Physician* 74, no. 8 (October 15, 2006).

124. "Failing to Tackle Stress Could Cost You Dearly," *Personnel Today*, September 12, 2006; http://www.sciencedaily.com/releases/2007/06/070604170722.htm, accessed November 3, 2009.
125. This is quoted from "Drug-Free Workplace: New Federal Requirements," *BNA Bulletin to Management*, February 9, 1989, pp. 1–4. Note that the Drug-Free Workplace Act does not mandate or mention testing employees for illegal drug use. See also www.dol.gov/elaws/drugfree.htm and www.dot.gov/ost/dapc (this site contains detailed guidelines on urine sampling, who's covered, etc.), both accessed May 26, 2007.
126. "Few Employers Addressing Workplace Stress, Watson Wyatt Surveys Find," *Compensation & Benefits Review*, May/June 2008, p. 12.
127. See, for example, Elizabeth Bernstein, "When a Coworker Is Stressed Out," *The Wall Street Journal*, August 26, 2008, pp. B1, B2.
128. Karl Albrecht, *Stress and the Manager* (Englewood Cliffs, NJ: Spectrum, 1979). For a discussion of the related symptoms of depression, see James Krohe Jr., "An Epidemic of Depression?" *Across-the-Board*, September 1994, pp. 23–27; and Todd Nighswonger, "Stress Management," *Occupational Hazards*, September 1999, p. 100.
129. Sabine Sonnentag et al., "'Did You Have a Nice Evening?' A Day-Level Study on Recovery Experiences, Sleep, and Affect," *Journal of Applied Psychology* 93, no. 3 (2008), pp. 674–684.
130. "Meditation Gives Your Mind Permanent Working Holiday; Relaxation Can Improve Your Business Decisions and Your Overall Health," discussed in *Investors Business Daily*, March 24, 2004, p. 89. See also "Meditation Helps Employees Focus, Relieve Stress," *BNA Bulletin to Management*, February 20, 2007, p. 63.
131. Kathryn Tyler, "Stress Management," *HR Magazine*, September 2006, pp. 79–82.
132. "Going Head to Head with Stress," *Personnel Today*, April 26, 2005, p. 1.
133. See, for example, Christina Maslach and Michael Leiter, "Early Predictors of Job Burnout and Engagement," *Journal of Applied Psychology* 93, no. 3 (2008), pp. 498–512.
134. Christina Maslach and Michael Leiter, "Early Predictors of Job Burnout and Engagement," *Journal of Applied Psychology* 93, no. 3 (2008), pp. 498–512.
135. Mina Westman and Dov Eden, "Effects of a Respite from Work on Burnout: Vacation Relief and Fade-Out," *Journal of Applied Psychology* 82, no. 4 (1997), pp. 516–527.
136. Ibid., p. 516.
137. Ibid., p. 526. See also Charlotte Fritz and Sabine Sonnentag, "Recovery, Well-Being, and Performance-Related Outcomes: The Role of Workload and Vacation Experiences," *Journal of Applied Psychology* 91, no. 4 (July 2006), p. 936(10).
138. Todd Nighswonger, "Depression: The Unseen Safety Risk," *Occupational Hazards*, April 2002, pp. 38–42.
139. Ibid., p. 40.
140. "Employers Must Move from Awareness to Action in Dealing with Worker Depression," *BNA Bulletin to Management*, April 29, 2004, p. 137.
141. See, for example, Felix Chima, "Depression and the Workplace: Occupational Social Work Development and Intervention," *Employee Assistance Quarterly* 19, no. 4 (2004), pp. 1–20.
142. Ibid.
143. "Risk of Carpal Tunnel Syndrome Not Linked to Heavy Computer Work, Study Says," *BNA Bulletin to Management*, June 28, 2001, p. 203.
144. www.OSHA.gov, downloaded May 28, 2005.
145. Anne Chambers, "Computer Vision Syndrome: Relief Is In Sight," *Occupational Hazards*, October 1999, pp. 179–184; and www.OSHA.gov/ETOOLS/computerworkstations/index.html, downloaded May 28, 2005.
146. Sandra Lotz Fisher, "Are Your Employees Working Ergosmart?" *Personnel Journal*, December 1996, pp. 91–92. See also www.cdc.gov/od/ohs/Ergonomics/compergo.htm, accessed May 26, 2007.
147. Ronald Davis, "Exposure to Environmental Tobacco Smoke: Identifying and Protecting Those at Risk," *Journal of the American Medical Association*, December 9, 1998, pp. 147–148; see also Al Karr, "Lighting Up," *Safety and Health* 162, no. 3 (September 2000), pp. 62–66.
148. Kenneth Sovereign, *Personnel Law* (Upper Saddle River, NJ: Prentice Hall, 1999), pp. 76–79.
149. Daniel Warner, "We Do Not Hire Smokers: May Employers Discriminate Against Smokers?," *Employee Responsibilities and Rights Journal*, 7, No. 2 (1994), p. 138. See also "Workplace Smoking: How Far Should You Go?" *Managing Benefits Plans* 5, no. 6 (June 2005), p. 2(2).
150. Steve Bates, "Where There Is Smoke, There Are Terminations: Smokers Fired to Save Health Costs," *HR Magazine* 50, no. 3 (March 2005), pp. 28–29.
151. "Worker Opens Fire at Ohio Jeep Plant," *Occupational Hazards*, March 2005, p. 16.
152. Guy Toscano and Janice Windau, "The Changing Character of Fatal Work Injuries," *Monthly Labor Review*, October 1994, p. 17. See also Robert Grossman, "Bulletproof Practices," *HR Magazine*, November 2002, pp. 34–42; and Chuck Manilla, "How to Avoid Becoming a Workplace Violence Statistic," *Training & Development*, July 2008, pp. 60–64.
153. Kelly Gurchiek, "Workplace Violence on the Upswing," *HR Magazine*, July 2005, p. 27.
154. Manon Mireille LeBlanc and E. Kevin Kelloway, "Predictors and Outcomes of Workplace Violence and Aggression," *Journal of Applied Psychology* 87, no. 3 (2002), pp. 444–453.
155. Kenneth Diamond, "The Gender-Motivated Violence Act: What Employers Should Know," *Employee Relations Law Journal* 25, no. 4 (Spring 2000), pp. 29–41.
156. Paul Viollis and Doug Kane, "At Risk Terminations: Protecting Employees, Preventing Disaster," *Risk Management Magazine* 52, no. 5 (May 2005), pp. 28–33.
157. "Workplace Violence: Sources and Solutions," *BNA Bulletin to Management*, November 4, 1993, p. 345. See also "Creating a Safer Workplace: Simple Steps Bring Results," *Safety Now*, September 2002, pp. 1–2; and L. Claussen, "Disgruntled and Dangerous," *Safety & Health* 180, no. 1 (July 2009), pp. 44–47.
158. "OSHA Addresses Top Homicide Risk," *BNA Bulletin to Management*, May 14, 1998, p. 148. See also www.osha.gov/Publications/osha3148.pdf, accessed May 26, 2007.
159. Scott Douglas and Mark Martinko, "Exploring the Role of Individual Differences in the Prediction of Workplace Aggression," *Journal of Applied Psychology* 86, no. 4 (2001), p. 554.
160. Dawn Anfuso, "Deflecting Workplace Violence," *Personnel Journal*, October 1994, pp. 66–77.
161. Alfred Feliu, "Workplace Violence and the Duty of Care: The Scope of an Employer's Obligation to Protect Against the Violent Employee," *Employee Relations Law Journal*, 20, no. 3 (Winter 1994–5), p. 395.
162. Ibid., p. 395.
163. "Preventing Workplace Violence," *BNA Bulletin to Management*, June 10, 1993, p. 177. See also Paul Viollis and Doug

Kane, "At-Risk Terminations: Protecting Employees, Preventing Disaster," *Risk Management* 52, no. 5 (May 2005), p. 28(5).

164. Quoted or paraphrased from Beverly Younger, "Violence Against Women in the Workplace," *Employee Assistance Quarterly* 9, no. 3/4 (1994), p. 177, and based on recommendations from Chris Hatcher. See also Paul Viollis and Doug Kane, "At-Risk Terminations: Protecting Employees, Preventing Disaster," op. cit.
165. Karl Aquino et al., "How Employees Respond to Personal Offense: Effect of Blame Attribution, Victim Status, and Offender Status on Revenge and Reconciliation in the Workplace," *Journal of Applied Psychology* 86, no. 1 (2001), pp. 52–59. See also M. Sandy Hershcovis et al., "Predicting Workplace Aggression: A Meta-Analysis," *Journal of Applied Psychology* 92, no. 1 (2007), pp. 228–238.
166. Ibid. p. 57.
167. Eve Tahmincioglu, "Employers Maintaining Vigilance in the Face of Layoff Rage," *The New York Times*, August 1, 2001, pp. C1, C6.
168. Jean Thilmany, "In Case of Emergency," *HR Magazine*, November 2007, pp. 79–82; Chuck Mannila, "How to Avoid Becoming a Workplace Violence Statistic," *Training & Development*, July 2008, pp. 60–64.
169. Florida recently passed a law giving employees the right to carry guns in cars parked at work. See "Right to Carry Guns in Cars Parked at Work Becomes Loaded Issue in Florida, Elsewhere," *BNA Bulletin to Management*, May 13, 2008, p. 153.
170. Feliu, "Workplace Violence," pp. 401–402.
171. Shari Caudron, "Target HR," *Workforce*, August 1998, pp. 44–52.
172. Diane Cadrain, "And Stay Out! Using Restraining Orders Can Be an Effective and Proactive Way of Preventing Workplace Violence," *HR Magazine*, August 2002, pp. 83–86.
173. Donna Rosato, "New Industry Helps Managers Fight Violence," *USA Today*, August 8, 1995, p. 1.
174. Helen Frank Bensimon, "What to Do About Anger in the Workplace," *Training & Development* 51, no. 9 (September 1997), pp. 28–32. See also Paul Viollis and Doug Kane, "At-Risk Terminations: Protecting Employees, Preventing Disaster," *Risk Management* 52, no. 5 (May 2005), p. 28(5).
175. Louis P. DiLorenzo and Darren J. Carroll, "The Growing Menace: Violence in the Workplace," *New York State Bar Journal*, January 1995, p. 25.
176. Quoted from Feliu, "Workplace Violence," p. 393.
177. DiLorenzo and Carroll, "The Growing Menace," p. 27.
178. This is based on "New Challenges for Health and Safety in the Workplace," *Workplace Visions* (Society for Human Resource Management, 2003), no. 3, pp. 2–4. See also J. L. Nash, "Protecting Chemical Plants from Terrorists: Opposing Views," *Occupational Hazards*, February 2004, pp. 18–20.
179. "Survey Finds Reaction to September 11 Attacks Spurred Companies to Prepare for Disasters," *BNA Bulletin to Management*, November 29, 2005, p. 377.
180. Sources of *external* risk include legal/regulatory, political, and business environment (economy, e-business, etc.). *Internal* risks nclude financial, strategic, operational (including safety and security), and integrity (embezzlement, theft, fraud, etc.). William Atkinson, "Enterprise Risk Management at Wal-Mart," www.rmmag.com/MGTemplate.cfm?Section=RMMagazine&NavMenuID=128&template=/Magazine/DisplayMagazines.cfm&MGPreview=1&Volume=50&IssueID=205&AID=2209&ShowArticle=1, accessed April 1, 2009.
181. "Focus on Corporate Security," *BNA HR Executive Series*, Fall 2001, p. 4.
182. Unless otherwise noted, the following is based on Richard Maurer, "Keeping Your Security Program Active," *Occupational Hazards*, March 2003, pp. 49–52.
183. Ibid., p. 50.
184. Ibid., p. 50.
185. Bill Roberts, "Are You Ready for Biometrics?" *HR Magazine*, March 2003, pp. 95–99.
186. Maurer, "Keeping Your Security Program Active," p. 52.
187. Craig Schroll, "Evacuation Planning: A Matter of Life and Death," *Occupational Hazards*, June 2002, pp. 49–51.
188. Ibid., p. 52; and Li Yuan et al., "Texting When There's Trouble," *The Wall Street Journal*, April 18, 2007, p. B1.
189. Louis Obdyke, "Investigating Security Breaches, Workplace Theft, and Employee Fraud," *Society for Human Resource Management Legal Report*, January–February 2003, pp. 1–2.

17 Managing Global Human Resources

Wal-Mart, a company famously resistant to unions in America, recently had a surprise. Opening stores in China at a fast clip, it attempted to dissuade local unions there from organizing Walmart's employees. However, the All China Federation of Trade Unions (ACFTU), with strong government backing, quickly established itself in several Walmart stores. At first, it seemed likely that the union would succeed in unionizing many Walmart China workers. But Walmart was vigorously resisting.[1]

Source: Courtesy of Elizabeth Dalziel, File/AP Wide World Photos.

WHERE ARE WE NOW . . .

More managers and employers today find themselves managing people internationally. The purpose of this chapter is to improve your effectiveness at applying your human resource knowledge and skills when global issues are involved. The topics we'll discuss include the internationalization of business, inter-country differences affecting HR, improving international assignments through selection, and training and maintaining international employees.

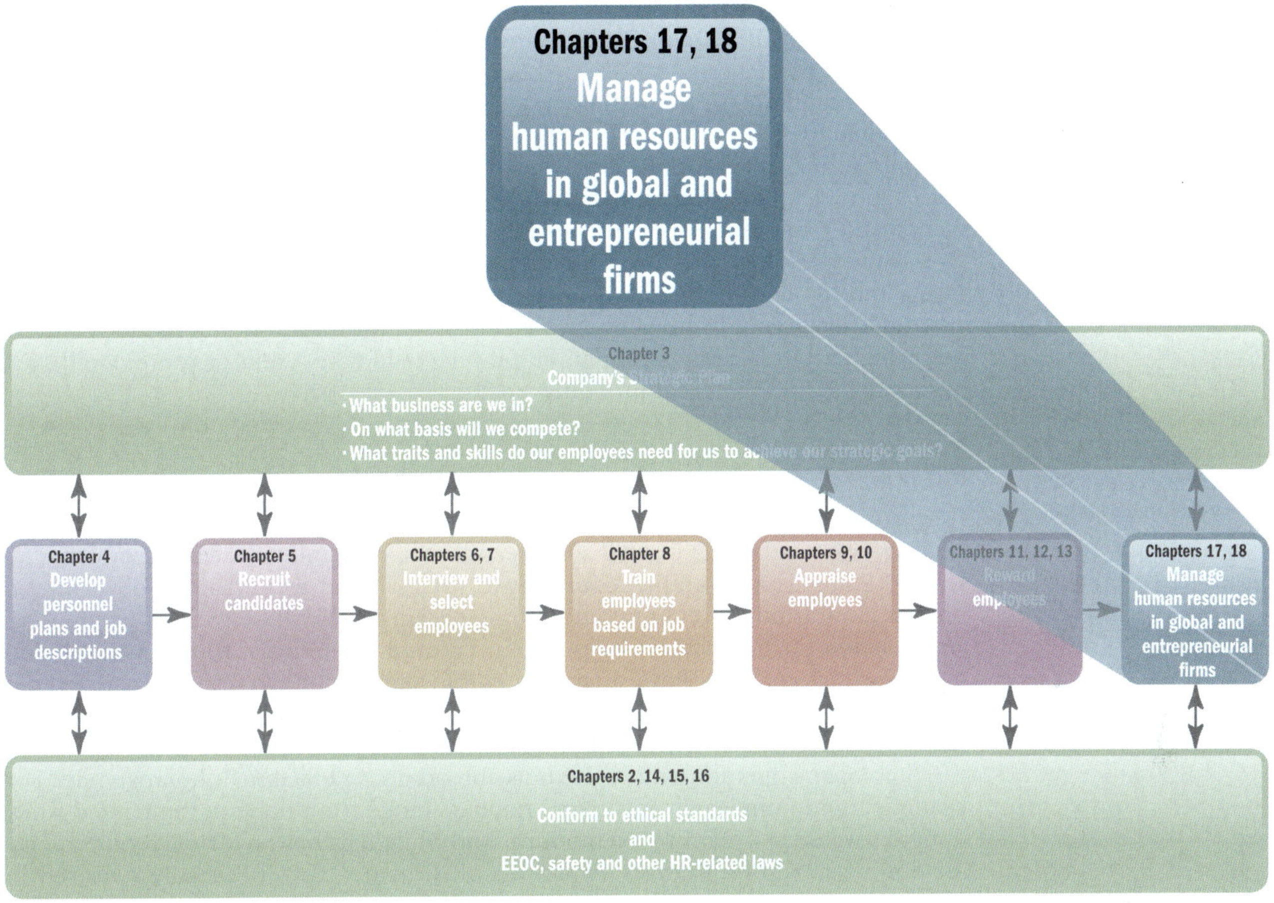

LEARNING OUTCOMES

1. List the HR challenges of international business.
2. Illustrate with examples how intercountry differences affect HRM.
3. List and briefly describe the main methods for staffing global organizations
4. Discuss some important issues to keep in mind in training, appraising, and compensating international employees.
5. Explain with examples how to implement a global human resource management program.

1 List the HR challenges of international business.

HR AND THE INTERNATIONALIZATION OF BUSINESS

Huge firms like IBM have long had extensive overseas operations, of course.[2] But with the globalization of the world economy, even small firms are discovering that success depends on marketing and managing overseas.[3]

The Manager's Global Challenge

Taking the company global triggers various management challenges. The employer has to install all those management systems it needs to manage its overseas activities. These management systems include organization structures, managerial controls, worldwide banking relationships, and, of course, human resource management systems for recruiting, selecting, training, and appraising and compensating its workers abroad.

Managing human resources internationally creates unique challenges. For example, "Should we staff the local offices abroad with local or U.S. managers?" "How should we appraise and pay our local employees?" "How should we deal with the unions in our offices abroad?" "How do we identify and get the right talent and skills to where we need them?" and "How do we spread state-of-the-art knowledge to our operations abroad?"[4]

Challenges like these don't just come from the vast distances involved (though this is important). The bigger issue is coping with the cultural, political, legal, and economic differences among countries. In China, for instance, unions are relatively powerful, and in Europe, firing an employee could take a year or more. We'll start by looking at these intercountry differences.

2 Illustrate with examples how intercountry differences affect HRM.

How Intercountry Differences Affect HRM

Companies operating only within the United States generally have the luxury of dealing with a relatively limited set of economic, cultural, and legal variables. The United States is a capitalist, competitive society. And while the U.S. workforce reflects a multitude of cultural and ethnic backgrounds, shared values (such as an appreciation for democracy) help to blur cultural differences. Different states and municipalities certainly have their own employment laws. However, a basic federal framework helps produce a predictable set of legal guidelines regarding matters such as employment discrimination, labor relations, and safety and health.

A company operating multiple units abroad doesn't face such homogeneity. For example, minimum legally mandated holidays range from none in the United Kingdom to 5 weeks per year in Luxembourg. And while Italy has no formal requirements for employee representatives on boards of directors, they're usually required in Denmark. The point is that managers have to be cognizant of and generally adapt their human resource policies and practices to the countries in which they're operating. We'll consider some examples.

Cultural Factors

Countries differ widely in their *cultures*—in other words, in the basic values their citizens adhere to, and in how these values manifest themselves in the nation's arts, social programs, and ways of doing things. For example, in a study of about 330 managers from Hong Kong, Mainland China, and the United States, the U.S. managers tended to be most concerned with getting the job done. Chinese managers were most concerned with maintaining a harmonious environment. Hong Kong managers fell between these extremes.[5]

A classic study by Professor Geert Hofstede identified other international cultural differences. For example, Hofstede says societies differ in *power distance*—in other words, the extent to which the less powerful members of institutions accept and expect an unequal distribution of power.[6] He concluded that acceptance of such inequality was higher in some countries (such as Mexico) than in others (such as Sweden).

Source: Courtesy of Michael Rosenfeld/Stone/Getty Images.

Employers need to adapt their HR practices to the cultures of the countries where they do business.

Similarly, compared to U.S. employees, "Mexican workers expect managers to keep their distance rather than to be close, and to be formal rather than informal."[7] In Germany, you should never arrive even a few minutes late and should address senior people formally, with their titles.[8] Such cultural differences are a two-way street.[9] For example, in the Intel Corp. booklet "Things You Need to Know About Working in the U.S.A.," topics for incoming workers from abroad include sexual harassment and recognition of gay and lesbian rights.[10] (At the same time, globalization is blurring national differences in cultures, as people come to share common cultural experiences like McDonalds.[11])

Such cultural differences influence human resource policies and practices. For example, Americans' heavier emphasis on individuality may help to explain why European managers have more constraints, such as in dismissing workers.[12] As another example, in countries with a history of autocratic rule, employees often had to divulge information about their coworkers. Here, whistleblower rules, popular in America, are frowned upon.[13]

Economic Systems

Differences in *economic systems* also translate into differences in human resource management policies. For one thing, some countries are less wedded to the ideals of laissez-faire (hands off) capitalism. For instance, some countries in the Euro zone tend to put more restrictions on the number of hours an employee can legally work each week. Portuguese workers average about 1,980 hours of work annually, while German workers average 1,648 hours.

Differences in labor costs are also substantial. Hourly compensation costs for production workers range from \$2.75 in Mexico to \$6.43 in Taiwan, \$23.82 in the United States, \$27.10 in the United Kingdom, and \$34.21 in Germany, for instance.[14]

Several European countries, including the United Kingdom and Germany, require substantial severance pay to departing employees, usually equal to at least 1 years' service in Germany. Workers in France can expect two and a half days of paid holiday per full month of service per year, and Germans get about 18 vacation days per year.

Legal, Political, and Labor Relations Factors

Legal differences blindside even sophisticated companies. After spending billions expanding into Germany, Walmart discovered that Germany's commercial laws discourage ads based on price comparisons. They soon left Germany.

As other examples, the U.S. practice of employment at will does not exist in Europe, where firing or laying off workers is usually expensive. And in many European countries, *work councils* replace the worker–management mediations typical in U.S. firms. *Work councils* are formal, employee-elected groups of worker representatives that meet monthly with managers to discuss topics ranging from no-smoking policies to layoffs.[15]

Codetermination is the rule in Germany and several other countries. **Codetermination** means employees have the legal right to a voice in setting company policies. Workers elect their own representatives to the supervisory board of the employer.[16] In the United States, by comparison, HR policies on most matters (such as wages and benefits) are set by the employer, or in negotiations with its labor unions.

codetermination
Employees have the legal right to a voice in setting company policies.

Managing globally also requires monitoring political risks. *Political risks* "are any governmental actions or politically motivated events that could adversely affect the long run profitability or value of the firm."[17] For example, the president of Venezuela moved to nationalize his country's oil industries.

Ethics and Codes of Conduct

With operations in several countries, employers also need to make sure their employees abroad are adhering to their firm's ethics codes.

Doing so is not easy. Exporting a firm's ethics rules requires more than having employees abroad use versions of its U.S. employee handbook. Relying on such handbooks can cause problems. For example, few countries adhere to "employment at will," so even handbooks with at-will disclaimers "can become binding contracts."[18]

Instead of exporting the employee handbook, one expert recommends creating and distributing a global code of conduct. The employer's main concern here may be establishing global standards for adhering to U.S. laws that have cross-border impacts. These employers should set policies on things like discrimination, harassment, bribery, and Sarbanes-Oxley. For other firms, like Mattel, the main concern may be with enforcing codes of conduct for avoiding, for instance, sweatshop conditions.

We'll zero on in two examples of cultural, economic, and legal/political differences: Europe and China.

HR Abroad: The European Union

Over the past two decades, the separate countries of the former European Community (EC) unified into a common market for goods, services, capital, and even labor called the *European Union (EU)*. Tariffs for goods moving across borders from one EU country to another generally disappeared, and employees (with some exceptions) now move freely between jobs in EU countries. The introduction of a single currency—the euro—further blurred differences.

Companies doing business in Europe must adjust their human resource policies and practices to European Union (EU) directives, as well as to country-specific employment laws. The directives are basically EU-wide laws. The directives' objectives are binding on all member countries (although each country can implement the directives as they wish). For example, the EU directive on confirmation of employment requires employers to provide employees with written terms and conditions of their employment. However, these terms vary from country to country.[19] In England, a detailed written statement is required, including things like rate of pay, date employment began, and hours of work. Germany doesn't require a written contract, but it's still customary to have one specifying most particulars about the job.

This interplay of directives and country laws means that an employer's human resource practices must vary from country to country. For example:[20]

- **Minimum EU wages.** Most EU countries have minimum wage systems. Some set national limits. Others allow employers and unions to work out their own minimum wages.
- **Working hours.** The EU sets the workweek at 48 hours, but most EU countries set it at 40 hours a week.
- **Employee (union) representation.** Europe has many levels of employee representation. In France, for instance, employers with 50 or more employers must consult with their employees' representatives on matters including working conditions, training, and profit-sharing plans and layoffs. In Italy, all employers with 15 or more employees must consult with their work councils on internal work rules. As of 2008, most companies—including all those with 50 or more employees in the EU—had to "inform and consult" employees about employee-related actions, even if the firms don't operate outside their own countries' borders.[21]
- **Termination of employment.** Required notice periods when dismissing employees in Europe range from none in Spain to 2 months in Italy.

HR Abroad: China

All employers in China deal with issues including relatively scarce employment services and an increasingly active union movement. However, how they deal with these issues depends on the ownership of the firm. State-owned enterprises use fewer modern human resource management tools than do giant Chinese multinationals like Lenova, for instance. There are therefore wide variations in human resource management practices among companies in China, and between Chinese and Western firms.[22] For example:

Recruiting Because of governmental constraints on migration and other legal constraints, it is relatively difficult to recruit, hire, and retain good employees. At least until the downturn starting in 2008, sporadic labor shortages were widespread and will likely return. China's new Employment Contract Law (enacted in 2007) requires, among many other things, that employers report the names, sexes, identification numbers, and contract terms for all employees they hire within 30 days of hiring to local labor bureaus.[23]

In China, recruiting effectiveness depends largely on nonrecruitment human resource management issues. Employees are highly career oriented and gravitate toward employers that provide the best career advancement training and opportunities.[24] Firms like Siemens China, with impressive training and development programs, have the least difficulty attracting good candidates. Poaching employees is a serious matter in China. The employer must verify that the applicant is free to sign a new employment agreement.

Selection The dominant employee selection method involves analyzing the applicant's résumé and then interviewing him or her. The ideal way to do this, as we saw in Chapter 6, is to institute a structured interview process, as many of the foreign firms in China have done.

Appraising Employee appraisal is particularly sensitive to the cultural realities in China. The appraisal therefore needs to follow the formalities of saving face and avoiding confrontational, tension-producing situations. In general, it's best to talk in terms of objective work data (as opposed to personal comments like "you're too slow").

Compensation Although many managers endorse performance-based pay in China, many employers, to preserve group harmony, make incentive pay a small part of the pay package. And, as in other parts of Asia, team incentives are advisable.[25]

3 List and briefly describe the main methods for staffing global organizations.

STAFFING THE GLOBAL ORGANIZATION

Filling your company's jobs abroad has traditionally been the heart of international human resource management. The process involves identifying and selecting the people who will fill the positions, and then placing them in those positions.

International Staffing: Home or Local?

Companies doing business internationally employ several types of international employees. *Locals* are citizens of the countries where they are working. **Expatriates ("expats")** are noncitizens of the countries in which they are working (an American working in France is an expat).[26] **Home-country nationals** are citizens of the

expatriates (expats)
Noncitizens of the countries in which they are working.

home-country nationals
Citizens of the country in which the multinational company has its headquarters.

country in which the multinational company has its headquarters (so an American working for GM's subsidiary in China is a home-country national, as well as an expat). **Third-country nationals** are citizens of a country other than the parent or the host country—for example, a British executive working in the Tokyo branch of a U.S. multinational bank.[27] Expatriates still represent a minority of multinationals' managers. Locals fill most positions.[28]

Using Locals There are many reasons employers rely more on locals. Many people don't want to work in a foreign country, and the cost of using expatriates is usually far greater than the cost of using local workers.[29] In one survey, employers reported a 21% attrition rate for expatriate employees, compared with an average of 10% for their general employee populations.[30] Local people may view the multinational as a "better citizen" if it uses local management talent; some governments even press for staffing with local management.[31] There may also be a fear that expatriates, knowing they're at the foreign subsidiary for only a few years, may overemphasize short-term results.[32] Some companies are surprised at what it costs to post someone abroad. Agilent Technologies routinely estimated that it cost about three times the expatriate's annual salary to keep the person abroad for 1 year. When Agilent outsourced is expatriate program, it discovered that the costs were much higher. The firm then dramatically reduced the number it sent abroad, from about 1,000 to 300 per year.[33]

It's also become more difficult to bring workers into the United States from abroad. Under rules in effect since 2005, U.S. employers must now try to recruit U.S. workers before filing foreign labor certification requests with the Department of Labor. In particular, employers must now first post open positions in the Department of Labor's job bank and (at least) run two Sunday newspaper advertisements before filing such requests.[34]

Using Expats Yet there are also reasons for using expatriates—either home-country or third-country nationals—for staffing subsidiaries. The main reason is usually that employers can't find local candidates with the required technical qualifications. Multinationals have also viewed a successful stint abroad as a required step in developing top managers. (For instance, after a term abroad, the head of General Electric's Asia–Pacific region returned as vice chairman at GE.) Control is another important reason for using expatriates. The assumption here is that home-country managers are already steeped in the firm's policies and culture, and thus more likely to apply headquarters' ways of doing things.

However, for the past 10 years or so the trend has definitely been toward using locals or toward other solutions. Posting expatriates abroad is very expensive, security problems increasingly give potential expatriates' pause, returning expatriates often leave for other employers within a year or two of returning, educational facilities are turning out top-quality candidates abroad, and the recent global recession made the cost of posting employees abroad even more unattractive. As a result, new expatriate postings are not only down, but many employers are actually bringing them home early.[35]

Other Solutions Today, the choice is not just between expatriate versus local employees; there are other solutions. Some dub these "short-term," "commuter," or "frequent-flier" assignments. They involve much travel but no formal relocation.[36] Other firms use Internet-based video technologies and group decision-making software to enable global virtual teams to do business without either travel or relocation.[37]

One survey found that about 78% of surveyed employers had some form of "localization" policy. This is a policy of transferring a home-country national employee to a foreign subsidiary as a "permanent transferee." The employer here does not treat the employee (who assumedly wants to move abroad) as an expatriate, but instead as, say, a French local hire.[38] For example, U.S. IBM employees originally from India eventually filled many of the 5,000 jobs that IBM recently shifted from the United States to India. These employees elected to move back to India, albeit at local, India pay rates.

Offshoring

As explained in Chapter 4 (Recruiting), offshoring is an important international staffing issue. *Offshoring* means having local employees abroad do jobs that the firm's domestic employees previously did in-house. Offshoring is increasingly popular. As noted, IBM recently announced that it was shifting about 5,000 U.S. software and sales jobs to India.[39] Forrester Research projects that about 1.5 million jobs will move offshore by 2010, 2.5 million jobs will go by 2013, and more than 3 million jobs will go by 2015.[40]

Offshoring and HR

Offshoring tends to be a uniquely human resource management–dependent activity. The traditional reason firms went abroad was to develop new markets or to open up new manufacturing facilities to serve local markets. Here marketing, sales, and production executives played the pivotal roles. Offshoring, on the other hand, mostly involves human resource management. Employers seeking to gain cost advantages by offshoring, say, a call center, look to their HR managers to help identify high-quality, low-cost talent abroad, and to provide the necessary information on things like literacy, foreign wage rates, and working conditions. (For example, the percentage of younger workers with postsecondary educations ranges from 5% or 10% in Indonesia up to 60% or more in South Korea and Singapore. See Figure 17-1.)

Finding a country abroad that provides sufficiently low-paid, technically competent workers is only part of the task of making offshoring succeed. Among other things, the human resource manager also needs to make sure that all the employees receive the screening and training that they require. It may be advisable to retain local legal counsel, both to navigate local laws and for advice on cultural hiring practices.[41] And of course, human resource managers will want to ensure that the compensation policies and working conditions are satisfactory.

Management Values and International Staffing Policy

We've seen that various factors like technical competence determine whether firms use, say, locals or expatriates abroad. But it's not just facts that influence such decisions. In addition, the top executives' values also play a role. Some executives are

FIGURE 17-1 Workers With Postsecondary Education

Source: Reprinted in Damien DeLuca and Han Hu, "Evaluate Workforces in Emerging Economies," *HR Magazine*, September 2008, p. 67.

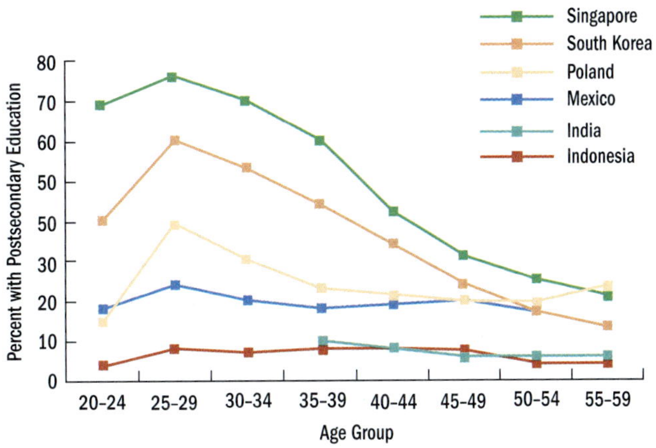

third-country nationals
Citizens of a country other than the parent or the host country.

just more "expat-oriented." For example, some experts classify top executives' values as *ethnocentric, polycentric,* or *geocentric.* We'll look at each.

Ethnocentric Practices

In an ethnocentrically oriented corporation, "the prevailing attitude is that home-country attitudes, management style, knowledge, evaluation criteria, and managers are superior to anything the host country might have to offer."[42]

Such values translate into particular employment practices. With an **ethnocentric** staffing policy, the firm fills key management jobs with parent-country nationals.[43] At Royal Dutch Shell, for instance, financial officers around the world are often Dutch nationals. Reasons given for ethnocentric staffing policies include lack of qualified host-country senior management talent, a desire to maintain a unified corporate culture and tighter control, and the desire to transfer the parent firm's core competencies (for instance, a specialized manufacturing skill) to a foreign subsidiary more expeditiously.[44]

Polycentric Practices

In the **polycentric** corporation, "there is a conscious belief that only host-country managers can ever really understand the culture and behavior of the host-country market; therefore, the foreign subsidiary should be managed by local people."[45]

A polycentric-oriented firm would staff its foreign subsidiaries with host-country nationals, and its home office with parent-country nationals. This may reduce the local cultural misunderstandings that might occur if it used expatriate managers. It will also almost undoubtedly be less expensive.[46]

Geocentric Practices

Geocentric executives believe they must scour the firm's management staff on a global basis, on the assumption that the best manager for a specific position anywhere may be in any of the countries in which the firm operates. Thus, Sony appointed as CEO someone from Wales who'd run the firm's U.S. operations.

A **geocentric** staffing policy "seeks the best people for key jobs throughout the organization, regardless of nationality."[47] This can let the global firm use its human resources more efficiently by transferring the best person to the open job, wherever he or she may be. Such cross-breeding can also help build a stronger and more consistent culture and set of values among the entire global management team.

Selecting Expatriate Managers

The processes that firms use to select managers for their domestic and foreign positions obviously have many similarities. For either assignment, candidates need the technical knowledge and skills to do the job, and the intelligence and people skills to be successful managers.[48] Testing, interviewing, and background checks are as applicable for selecting expatriates as for domestic assignments.

However, foreign assignments are different. For example, there is the stress that being alone in a foreign land can put on the single manager. And if spouse and children will share the assignment, there are the pressures that the family will have to confront abroad. Furthermore, it's not just how different culturally the host country is from the person's home country. Rather, the person's adaptability is important. Some people adapt anywhere; others fail to adapt anywhere.[49]

Selecting managers for assignments abroad therefore means testing them for traits that predict success in working abroad. One study asked 338 international assignees from various countries to specify which traits were important for the success in a foreign assignment. The researchers identified five factors. These were job knowledge and motivation, relational skills, flexibility/adaptability, extra-cultural openness, and family situation (spouse's positive opinion, willingness of spouse to live abroad, and so on). Figure 17-2 shows some of the specific items that make up each of the five

FIGURE 17-2 Five Factors Important in International Assignee Success and Their Components

Source: Adapted from Arthur Winfred Jr. and Winston Bennett Jr., "The International Assignee: The Relative Importance of Factors Perceived to Contribute to Success," *Personnel Psychology* 18 (1995), pp. 106–107.

I. Job Knowledge and Motivation
- Managerial ability
- Organizational ability
- Imagination
- Creativity
- Administrative skills
- Alertness
- Responsibility
- Industriousness
- Initiative and energy
- High motivation
- Frankness
- Belief in mission and job
- Perseverance

II. Relational Skills
- Respect
- Courtesy
- Display of respect
- Kindness
- Empathy
- Nonjudgmental
- Integrity
- Confidence

III. Flexibility/Adaptability
- Resourcefulness
- Ability to deal with stress
- Flexibility
- Emotional stability
- Willingness to change
- Tolerance for ambiguity
- Adaptability
- Independence
- Dependability
- Political sensitivity
- Positive self-image

IV. Extracultural Openness
- Variety of outside interests
- Interest in foreign cultures
- Openness
- Knowledge of local language(s)
- Outgoingness and extroversion
- Overseas experience

V. Family Situation
- Adaptability of spouse and family
- Spouse's positive opinion
- Willingness of spouse to live abroad
- Stable marriage

factors. "Family situation was generally found to be the most important factor, a finding consistent with other research on international assignments and transfers." A recent review of the research reported "strong support" for the importance of factors like interpersonal skills and family adjustment for expatriate adjustment.[50]

Adaptability Screening

With adaptability appearing high in studies like these, adaptability screening should be part of the expatriate screening process. Often conducted by a psychologist or psychiatrist, **adaptability screening** aims to assess the assignees' (and spouses') probable success in handling the foreign transfer, and to alert them to issues (such as the impact on children) the move may involve.[51] Here, experience is often the best predictor of future success. Companies like Colgate-Palmolive therefore look for overseas candidates whose work and nonwork experience, education, and language skills already demonstrate a commitment to and facility for living and working with different cultures.[52] Even several summers traveling overseas or participating in foreign student programs might provide some basis to believe that the potential transferee can adjust when he or she arrives overseas.

ethnocentric
The notion that home-country attitudes, management style, knowledge, evaluation criteria, and managers are superior to anything the host country has to offer.

polycentric
A conscious belief that only the host-country managers can ever really understand the culture and behavior of the host-country market.

geocentric
The belief that the firm's whole management staff must be scoured on a global basis, on the assumption that the best manager of a specific position anywhere may be in any of the countries in which the firm operates.

adaptability screening
A process that aims to assess the assignees' (and spouses') probable success in handling a foreign transfer.

Many firms also use tests such as the Overseas Assignment Inventory (OAI). This identifies the characteristics and attitudes international assignment candidates should have. Its publisher establishes local norms and conducts ongoing validation studies.[53] Figure 17-3 illustrates the OAI.

Realistic previews are also important. These should cover the problems to expect in the new job (such as extensive travel) as well as the cultural benefits, problems, and idiosyncrasies of the target country. The rule, say experts, should always be to "spell it all out" ahead of time, as many multinationals do for their international transferees.[54]

Unfortunately, theory doesn't always translate into practice. The importance of adaptability screening notwithstanding, 70% of respondents in one survey listed "skills or competencies" as the most important selection criteria when choosing candidates for international assignments. They ranked "job performance" second. The ability to adapt to new cultural conditions—as measured by items like "prior international living experience or assignment" and "familiarity with assignment country"—rarely ranked as first or second.[55] One study found that selection for positions abroad is so informal that the researchers called it "the coffee machine system." Two colleagues meet at the office coffee machine, strike up a conversation about the possibility of a position abroad, and based on that and little more a selection decision is made.[56] Perhaps this helps explain the high failure rate of foreign assignees.

The accompanying "Managing the New Workforce" feature provides a perspective on how such informality can affect women managers.

Managing the New Workforce

Sending Women Managers Abroad

Recently, 56% of the overseas workforce was under age 40, single (43%), and female (21%). So although women represent about 50% of the middle management talent in U.S. companies, they represent only 21% of managers sent abroad. That's up from about 3% in the 1980s and 15% in 2005, but still low.[57] What accounts for this?

Actually, many of the misperceptions that impeded women's progress over the years still exist.[58] Line managers make these assignments, and many assume that women don't want to work abroad, are reluctant to move their families abroad, or can't get their spouses to move.[59] In fact, this survey found that women do want international assignments, they are not less inclined to move their families, and that male spouses are not necessarily reluctant to move.

Safety is another issue. Employers tend to assume that women abroad are more likely to become crime victims. However, most surveyed women expats said that safety was no more an issue with women than it was with men. As one said, "It doesn't matter if you're a man or woman. If it's a dangerous city, it's dangerous for whomever."[60]

Fear of cultural prejudices against women is another common issue. In some cultures, women do have to follow different rules than do men, for instance, in terms of attire. But as one expat said, "Even in the more harsh cultures, once they recognize that the women can do the job, once your competence has been demonstrated, it becomes less of a problem."[61]

Employers take several steps to short-circuit misperceptions like these, and to identify more women to assign abroad. For example, *formalize a process* for identifying employees who are willing to take assignments abroad. (At Gillette, for instance, supervisors use the performance review to identify the subordinate's career interests, including for assignments abroad.) *Train managers* to understand how employees really feel about going abroad, and what the real safety and cultural issues are. Let successful female expats *help recruit* prospective female expats, and discuss with them the pros and cons of assignments abroad. Provide the expat's spouse with employment assistance.[62]

Sample excerpt from the OVERSEAS ASSIGNMENT INVENTORY

Welcome!

Enter the login information you were provided in the box on the left. This will direct you to a registration page before proceeding to your survey.

This site contains:

Overseas Assignment Inventory–A tool designed to assess cultural adaptability for employees and spouses going on international expatriate assignments.

Global Assessment Inventory–A development tool designed to assess factors related to success in multicultural interactions.

Demographics

Please complete the demographic information requested. Note, your answers will not impact the survey results. Upon completion, you will be directed to the survey.

Background Information

Employee or Spouse/Partner:	☐ Employee	☐ Spouse/Partner
Gender:	☐ Male	☐ Female
Nationality:	____________	
Age:	____________	
Number of Children:	____________	
Have Traveled Outside of Country of Citizenship:	☐ Yes	☐ No
Have Lived Outside of Country of Citizenship:	☐ Yes	☐ No

Employment

Destination Country:	____________
Current Country Location:	____________

Submit

Survey Questions *(page 1 of 6)*

Read each survey question carefully and select the bubble that corresponds to your choice. When answering the questions, keep in mind that there are no "right" or "wrong" answers. Choose the response that is reflective of what you think and do most of the time. Some of the questions appear similar; actually no two are exactly alike. Please answer each one without regard to the others.

Strongly Agree	Agree	Uncertain	Disagree	Strongly Disagree
1	2	3	4	5

1. I do not want to compromise my present standard of living.	☐1 ☐2 ☐3 ☐4 ☐5
2. The environment I am comfortable with is similar to that in my destination country.	☐1 ☐2 ☐3 ☐4 ☐5
3. Generally, my spouse/partner and I understand each other.	☐1 ☐2 ☐3 ☐4 ☐5
4. I am generally one of the first to speak and take charge in a group.	☐1 ☐2 ☐3 ☐4 ☐5
5. It is very clear to me how my work on this assignment will be evaluated.	☐1 ☐2 ☐3 ☐4 ☐5
6. I am fluent in the language spoken in my destination country.	☐1 ☐2 ☐3 ☐4 ☐5

FIGURE 17-3 Overseas Assignment Inventory

Source: Copyright © 2008. Prudential Relocation. Reprinted with permission of Prudential Relocation. All rights reserved. May not be further copied, reproduced or republished in any medium without the express written permission of Prudential Relocation.

In selecting (or training, and so on) employees for assignments abroad, don't ignore the legal issues. As we explained in Chapter 2 (EEOC), American equal employment opportunity laws, including Title VII, the ADEA, and the ADA, affect qualified employees of U.S. employers doing business abroad, and foreign firms doing business in the United States or its territories.[63] If equal employment opportunity laws conflict with the laws of the country in which the U.S. employer is operating, the laws of the local country generally take precedence.[64]

Making Expatriate Assignments Successful

Many employers post expatriates abroad, but it's disconcerting to see how often such assignments fail.[65] Knowing how to make a successful assignment is an important management skill. Start by systematizing your expatriate process. Make sure there's an expatriate policy covering matters such as compensation and transfer costs. Have procedures, for instance, requiring that the managers responsible for the expat's budget understand the projected costs, and for obtaining all chain of command approvals.[66] Then, before selecting someone to send abroad, understand where the main potential problems lie.

Traits of Successful Expatriates

We've seen that having the right personality is one issue. For example, in a study of 143 expatriate employees, extroverted, agreeable, and emotionally stable individuals were less likely to leave early.[67] (So, not surprisingly, sociable outgoing people are more likely to do better abroad.[68]) Furthermore, the person's *intentions* are important; people who want expatriate careers try harder to adjust to them.[69] Similarly, expatriates who are more satisfied with their jobs are more likely to adapt to the foreign assignment.[70] And some people are so culturally at ease that they do fine transferred anywhere; others will fail anywhere.[71]

Family Pressures

Nonwork factors like *family pressures* loom large in expatriate failures. In one study, U.S. managers listed, in descending order of importance for leaving early: inability of spouse to adjust, managers' inability to adjust, other family problems, managers' personal or emotional immaturity, and inability to cope with larger overseas responsibility.[72] Other studies similarly emphasize dissatisfied spouses' effects on the international assignment.[73]

These findings underscore a truism about selecting international assignees: The difficulty is usually not incompetence, but family and personal problems. Yet, as noted, employers still tend to select expatriates almost entirely based on technical competence.[74]

Given the role of family problems in expatriate failures, the employer should understand just how unhappy and cut off the expatriate manager's spouse can feel in a foreign environment. Here is how the spouse of one expat put it:[75]

> It's difficult to make close friends. So many expats have their guard up, not wanting to become too close. Too many have been hurt, too many times already, becoming emotionally dependent on a friend only to have the inevitable happen—one or the other gets transferred. It's also difficult to watch your children get hurt when their best friend gets transferred. Although I have many acquaintances, I have nowhere near the close friends I had in the States. My spouse therefore has become my rock.[76]

One study identified three things that helped make it easier for the spouse to adjust. First is *language fluency*, since spouses will feel even more cut off if they can't make themselves understood. Second, having *preschool-age children* (rather than school-age children or no children) seemed to make it easier for the spouse to adjust. "This suggests that younger children, perhaps because of their increased dependency, help spouses retain that part of their social identities: as parents, their responsibilities for these children remain the same."[77] Third, it helps that there be a *strong bond of closeness* between spouse and expat partner. This provides the continuing emotional and social support many spouses find lacking abroad.

What Employers Can Do So, employers can do several things to boost the odds that assignments abroad will go smoothly. Providing realistic previews of what to expect, carefully screening expat and souse, improved orientation, and improved benefits packages are obvious solutions. Another is simply to shorten the length of the assignment. Person–job match is also important, insofar as expatriates who are more satisfied with their jobs are more likely to adapt to the foreign assignment.[78] Helping spouses get jobs abroad and providing more support to the expat and his or her family are also important.[79] Some employers set up "global buddy" programs. Here local managers mentor new expatriates.[80]

4 Discuss some important issues to keep in mind in training, appraising, and compensating international employees.

TRAINING AND MAINTAINING EXPATRIATE EMPLOYEES

After deciding who you'll send abroad, attention turns to providing the person with the training, pay, and other support he or she needs to be successful.

Orienting and Training Employees on International Assignment

When it comes to the orientation and training required for success overseas, the practices of most U.S. employers reflect more talk than substance. Executives tend to agree that international assignees do best when they receive the special training (in things like language and culture) that they require. However, few companies actually provide such training.

Predeparture Training What sort of special training do overseas candidates need? One firm specializing isn such programs prescribes a 4-step approach.[81]

- Level 1 training focuses on the impact of cultural differences, and on raising trainees' awareness of such differences and their impact on business outcomes.
- Level 2 aims at getting participants to understand how attitudes (both negative and positive) form and how they influence behavior. (For example, unfavorable stereotypes may subconsciously influence how a new manager responds to his or her new foreign subordinates.)
- Level 3 training provides factual knowledge about the target country.
- Level 4 provides skills in areas like language and adjustment and adaptation skills.

More employers use software and the Internet for such cross-cultural training. For example, *Bridging Cultures* is a self-training multimedia package for people who will be traveling and/or living overseas. It uses short video clips to introduce case-type intercultural problems. It then guides users to selecting the best response for the situation. Cross-cultural training firms' Web sites include www.livingabroad.com and www.globaldynamics.com.[82]

Some employers use returning managers as resources to cultivate the "global mind-sets" of those departing. For example, Bosch holds regular seminars. Here newly arrived returnees pass on their knowledge and experience to relocating managers and their families.

Ongoing Training Beyond such predeparture training, more firms are providing continuing, in-country cross-cultural training during the early stages of an overseas assignment.

For example, after settling in, managers abroad continue to need traditional skills-oriented development. At many firms, including IBM, such development includes rotating assignments to help overseas managers grow professionally. IBM and other firms also have management development centers around the world where executives can hone their skills. And classroom programs (such as those at the London Business School or at INSEAD in France) provide overseas executives the educational opportunities (to acquire MBAs, for instance) that similar stateside programs do for their U.S.-based colleagues.

In addition to honing these managers' skills, international development activities hopefully have other, less tangible benefits. For example, rotating assignments can help managers form bonds with colleagues around the world. These can help the managers make cross-border decisions more expeditiously. Bringing together managers from their global subsidiaries for seminars can also help employers cultivate a unifying set of values, standards, and corporate culture.

Compensating Expatriates

The whole area of international compensation presents some tricky problems. On the one hand, there is logic in maintaining company-wide pay scales and policies so that, for instance, you pay divisional marketing directors throughout the world within the same range. This reduces the risk of perceived inequities, and dramatically simplifies the job of keeping track of disparate, country-by-country wage rates.

Yet not adapting pay scales to local markets will produce more problems than it solves. The fact is it can be enormously more expensive to live in some countries (like Japan) than others (like India); if these cost-of-living differences aren't considered, it will be almost impossible to get managers to take "high-cost" assignments. However, the answer is usually not just to pay, say, marketing directors more in one country than in another. One way to handle the problem is to pay a similar base salary company-wide, and then add on various allowances according to individual market conditions.[83]

However, determining equitable wage rates in many countries is not simple. There is a wealth of "packaged" compensation survey data available in the United States, but such data are not so easy to come by overseas. As a result, one of the greatest difficulties in managing multinational compensation is obtaining consistent compensation measures between countries.

Many global employers bring their international managers together periodically for training seminars.

Source: Courtesy of INSEAD

Some multinational companies conduct their own local annual compensation surveys. For example, Kraft conducts an annual study of total compensation in Belgium, Germany, Italy, Spain, and the United Kingdom. It focuses on all forms of compensation paid to each of 10 senior management positions held by local nationals in these firms.

The Balance Sheet Approach The most common approach to formulating expatriate pay is to equalize purchasing power across countries, a technique known as the *balance sheet approach*.[84] More than 85% of North American companies reportedly use this approach.

The basic idea is that each expatriate should enjoy the same standard of living he or she would have had at home. The balance sheet approach focuses on four groups of expenses—income taxes, housing, goods and services, and discretionary expenses (child support, car payments, and the like). The employer estimates what each of these four expenses is in the expatriate's home country, and what each will be in the host country. The employer then pays any differences—such as additional income taxes or housing expenses.

For example, the base salary will normally be in the same range as the manager's home-country salary. In addition, however, there might be an overseas or foreign service premium. The executive receives this as a percentage of his or her base salary, in part to compensate for the cultural and physical adjustments he or she will have to make.[85] There may also be several allowances, including a housing allowance and an education allowance for the expatriate's children. To help the expatriate manage his or her home and foreign financial obligations, most employers use a *split pay* approach; they pay, say, half a person's actual pay in home-country currency and half in the local currency.[86]

Table 17-1 illustrates the balance sheet approach for someone transferring from the U.S. to Belgium. In this case, the manager's annual earnings are $80,000, and she faces a U.S. income tax rate of 28% and a Belgium income tax rate of 70%. Other costs are based on the index of living costs abroad published in the "U.S. Department of State Indexes of Living Costs Abroad, Quarters Allowances, and Hardship Differentials," available at www.state.gov.

Incentives Employers use two types of incentives in international compensation. First, as mentioned, employers pay various incentives to encourage the employee to take the job abroad. For example, **foreign service premiums** are financial payments

TABLE 17-1 The Balance Sheet Approach (Assumes U.S. Base Salary of $80,000)

Annual Expense	Chicago, U.S.	Brussels, Belgium (US$ Equivalent)	Allowance
Housing & utilities	$35,000	$67,600	$32,600
Goods & services	6,000	9,500	3,500
Taxes	22,400	56,000	33,600
Discretionary income	10,000	10,000	0
Total	$73,400	$143,100	$69,700

Source: Joseph Martocchio, *Strategic Compensation: A Human Resource Management Approach*, 2nd ed. (Upper Saddle River, NJ: Prentice Hall, 2001), Table 12-15, p. 294.

foreign service premiums
Financial payments over and above regular base pay, typically ranging between 10% and 30% of base pay.

over and above regular base pay. These typically range from 10% to 30% of base pay, and appear as weekly or monthly salary supplements. **Hardship allowances** compensate expatriates for hard living and working conditions at certain foreign locations. (U.S. diplomats posted to Iraq receive about a 70% boost in base salary, among other incentives.[87]) **Mobility premiums** are typically lump-sum payments to reward employees for moving from one assignment to another.

Employers also pay their expatriates and local managers abroad performance incentives. In general, executive compensation systems around the world are becoming more similar.[88] And, as in the United States, more multinational employers are granting more stock options to a broader group of their employees overseas. U.S. firms that offer overseas managers long-term incentives often use overall corporate performance criteria (like worldwide profits) when awarding incentive pay.

Although the situation is changing, employers still use performance-based incentives less in Europe. Here firms traditionally emphasized a guaranteed annual salary and company-wide bonus.[89] European firms are moving toward incentive pay. However, they still have to overcome several problems—including (given recent revelations about global bankers' bonuses) the public relations aspects of such a move. In Japan, a worker might expect to receive as much as half his or her total annual compensation near year end, as a sort of profit-sharing bonus. In Asia, including the People's Republic of China, incentives, even for production workers, are popular. To maintain group harmony, team incentives are advisable.[90]

However, the bottom line is that in buying power, American managers rank nowhere near the top in terms of managerial pay. "Companies are operating in an increasingly open and competitive global economy, and emerging markets are offering managers higher disposable incomes than established countries." Average disposable income for managers ranges from about $72,000 in Indonesia to $98,000 in France; $105,000 in the United States; $124,000 in Brazil; $149,000 in the Ukraine; and $229,000 in Saudi Arabia.[91]

Steps in Establishing a Global Pay System Balancing global consistency in compensation with local considerations starts with establishing a rewards program that makes sense in terms of the employer's strategic needs.[92] In practice, doing so involves five steps (probably over several years).[93]

Step 1: Global philosophy framework. First, step back and ask how you want each pay component to help achieve the company's strategic goals.

Step 2: Identify any gaps. Next, review your existing rewards programs around the world. The question here is, "To what extents do our pay plans around the world support our strategic aims?"

Step 3: Systematize pay systems. Next, systematize job descriptions and performance expectations around the world. For example, create more consistent performance assessment practices, and establish consistent job requirements and performance expectations for similar jobs worldwide.

Step 4: Adapt pay policies. Fourth, review your global pay policies (for setting salary levels, incentives, and so forth). Next, conduct surveys and analyses to assess local pay practices. Then, fine-tune the firm's global pay policies so they make sense for each location.

Step 5: Ongoing program assessment. Finally, periodically reevaluate the global pay policies, given your firm's strategic needs and competitors' pay practices.

The accompanying "Managing HR in Challenging Times" feature explains why applying practices like these are especially important today.

Managing HR in Challenging Times

Getting a Handle on Global Compensation

A recent report on global pay from Hewitt Associates highlights the challenge facing many managers with operations abroad. As the report says, "[W]ith exponential growth in the past years, many U.S. multinational organizations have not given prudent consideration to their compensation cost structures outside the U.S."

Therefore, economic challenges now are forcing many employers to refocus on the effectiveness of their global compensation pay practices. For one thing, they're looking more carefully at who exactly is making the global compensation pay decisions, and how they're making them. Are managers abroad involved? Is it the home-office human resources team? Is it clear who is responsible for what and that the people making these decisions are doing so within the framework of the company's overall pay practices? The aim here is to "ensure that overall compensation spending is managed effectively. . . ."

Employers are also focusing more diligently on the details of their overseas pay decisions. For example, is how we're paying our employees abroad competitive? And are we basing our overseas pay decisions by referencing (as the Hewitt report says) "credible and defendable market data"?[94] Good pay practices are always important, but particularly so in economically changing times.

Appraising Expatriate Managers

Several things complicate the task of appraising an expatriate's performance. For one thing, the question of who actually appraises the expatriate is crucial.[95] Obviously, local management must have some input, but cultural differences here may distort the appraisals. Thus, host-country bosses might evaluate a U.S. expatriate manager in India somewhat negatively if they find his or her use of participative decision making culturally inappropriate. On the other hand, home-office managers may be so out of touch that they can't provide valid appraisals. Similarly, the procedure may be to measure the expatriate by objective criteria such as profits and market share. However, local events (such as political instability) may affect the manager's performance while remaining "invisible" to home-office staff. Some suggestions for improving expatriate appraisals follow.

1. Stipulate the assignment's difficulty level, and adapt the performance criteria to the situation.
2. Weigh the evaluation more toward the on-site manager's appraisal than toward the home-site manager's appraisal.
3. If the home-office manager does the actual written appraisal, have him or her use a former expatriate from the same overseas location for advice.

International Labor Relations

Firms opening subsidiaries abroad will find substantial differences in labor relations practices among countries and regions. This is important, because, while union membership is dropping in the United States, it is still relatively high abroad, and unions abroad therefore tend to be more influential. Walmart, for instance, has successfully neutralized attempts to organize its U.S. employees, but may have to accept unions in many of its stores in China.

Consider, for example, Europe.

hardship allowances
Compensate expatriates for exceptionally hard living and working conditions at certain locations.

mobility premiums
Typically, lump-sum payments to reward employees for moving from one assignment to another.

Unions in Europe are influential and labor–management bargaining and relations reflect this fact. In general, four issues characterize European labor relations:

- **Centralization.** Collective bargaining in Western Europe tends to be industry-wide, whereas in the United States it generally occurs at the enterprise or plant level.
- **Employer organization.** Due to the prevalence of industry-wide bargaining in Europe, employers tend to bargain via employer associations, rather than as individual employers.
- **Union recognition.** Union recognition is less formal than in the United States. For example, even if a union represents 80% of an employer's workers, another union can try to organize the other 20%.
- **Content and scope of bargaining.** U.S. labor–management agreements specify wages, hours, and working conditions. European agreements tend to be brief and to leave individual employers free to institute more generous terms.

Terrorism, Safety, and Global HR

From drug wars on the U.S.–Mexico border to pirates capturing ships off Somalia, the increased threat of terrorism is affecting human resource activities in many ways. For one thing, more prospective expatriates are reluctant to take their families abroad, and those who do are demanding more compensation. The other side of the coin is that getting working papers for foreign workers to come to the United States now takes weeks or months instead of days. This is because, in most cases, the prospective employee must first have an interview at his or her local U.S. Embassy. And for employees and facilities abroad, employers have had to institute more comprehensive safety plans, as well as other measures.

Taking Protective Measures

Employers are doing so in a variety of ways. Many employers retain crisis management teams' services. They then call on these teams, for instance, when they receive notice that criminal elements have kidnapped one of their managers. As one insurance executive puts it, "When you have a specialist, there's a better chance to get the person back."[96] Many employers purchase intelligence services for monitoring potential terrorist threats abroad. The head of one intelligence firm estimates such services at costing $6,000–$10,000 per year.[97]

Kidnapping and Ransom (K&R) Insurance

Hiring crisis teams and paying ransoms can be prohibitively expensive for all but the largest firms, so many employers buy kidnapping and ransom (K&R) insurance. Any one or more of several events may trigger payments under such policies. The obvious ones are kidnapping (for instance, the employee is a hostage until the employer pays a ransom), extortion (threatening bodily harm), and detention (holding an employee without any ransom demand).

The insurance typically covers several costs associated with kidnappings, abductions, or extortion attempts. These costs might include, for instance, hiring a crisis team, the actual cost of the ransom payment to the kidnappers or extortionists, insuring the ransom money in transit, legal expenses, and employee death or dismemberment.[98]

Keeping business travelers out of crime's way is a specialty all its own, but suggestions here include the following.[99]

- Provide expatriates with general training about traveling, living abroad, and the place they're going to, so they're more oriented when they arrive.
- Tell them not to draw attention to the fact that they're Americans—by wearing flag emblems or by using American cars, for instance.
- Have travelers arrive at airports as close to departure time as possible and wait in areas away from the main flow of traffic where they're not as noticeable.
- Equip the expatriate's car and home with adequate security systems.
- Tell employees to vary their departure and arrival times and take different routes to and from work.

- Keep employees current on crime and other problems by regularly checking, for example, the State Department's travel advisory service and consular information sheets (click on Country Specific Information at http://travel.state.gov/).
- Advise the employees to remain confident at all times: Body language can attract perpetrators, and those who look like victims often become victimized.[100]

HR APPs 4 U

Traveling Safely with Google Maps

As almost everyone knows, Maps is one of Google's most popular applications. It's also one that can keep you a bit safer when traveling abroad. Few things put international travelers at risk quite like being lost (and looking lost!). In case you haven't done so already, downloading Google Maps to your smart phone (from www.google.com/mobile) provides several mapping services, almost anywhere you may be. As just a few examples, *My Location* shows your current location on the map. Google Maps offers turn-by-turn driving directions. You can search Google Maps for local businesses and points of interest. And, IT managers can install Google Maps on corporate BlackBerrys using Google's BlackBerry Enterprise Server options.[101]

Repatriation: Problems and Solutions

One of the most worrisome facts about sending employees abroad is that 40% to 60% of them will probably quit within 3 years of returning home.[102] Given the investment the employer makes in training and sending these high-potential people abroad, it obviously makes sense to do everything possible to make sure they stay with the firm. For this, formal repatriation programs can be quite useful.[103] One study found that about 5% of returning employees resigned if their firms had formal repatriation programs, while about 22% of those left if their firms had no such programs.[104]

The heart and guiding principle for any repatriation program is this: Make sure that the expatriate and his or her family don't feel that the company has left them adrift. For example, AT&T has an effective 3-part repatriation program, one that actually starts before the employee leaves for the assignment abroad.[105] First, AT&T *matches the expat and his or her family with a psychologist* trained in repatriation issues. The psychologist meets with the family before they go abroad. The psychologist discusses the challenges they will face abroad, assesses with them how well he or she thinks they will adapt to their new culture, and stays in touch with them throughout their assignment. (Other firms, like Dow, also provide written repatriation agreements. These guarantee in writing that the company won't keep the expat abroad for more than some period, such as 3 years, and that on return he or she will receive a mutually acceptable job.)

Second, AT&T makes sure that *the employee always feels that he or she is still "in the loop"* with what's happening back at the home office. For example, AT&T assigns the expatriate a mentor. It also periodically brings the expat back to the home office to meet with and to socialize with colleagues.

Third, once it's time for the expatriate employee and his or her family to return home, AT&T *provides formal repatriation services.* About 6 months before the overseas assignment ends, the psychologist and an HR representative meet with the expat and the family, to start preparing them for the return. For example, they help plan the employee's next career move, help the person update his or her résumé, and begin putting the person in contact with supervisors back home. They work with the person's family on the logistics of the move back. Then, about a month after returning home, the expat and family attend a "welcome home" seminar, where they discuss matters like the stress of repatriation.[106]

Improving Productivity Through HRIS: Taking the HRIS Global

As a company grows, relying on manual HR systems to manage activities like worldwide safety, benefits administration, payroll, and succession planning becomes unwieldy. As we've seen, more firms are therefore automating and integrating their HR systems into human resource information systems (HRIS).

For global firms, it makes particular sense to expand the firm's human resource information systems to the firm's operations abroad. For example, electrical components manufacturer Thomas & Betts once needed 83 faxes to get a head count of its 26,000 employees in 24 countries; it can now do so with the push of a button, thanks to its global HRIS system.[107] Similarly, without a database of a firm's worldwide management talent, selecting employees for assignments abroad and keeping track of each unit's compensation plans and personnel practices can be overwhelming.

When Buildnet, Inc., decided to automate and integrate its separate systems for things like applicant tracking, training, and compensation, it chose a Web-based software package called MyHRIS, from NuView, Inc. (www.nuviewinc.com). This is an Internet-based system that includes human resource and benefits administration, applicant tracking and résumé scanning, training administration, and succession planning and development.[108] With MyHRIS, managers at any of the firm's locations around the world can access and update more than 200 built-in reports such as "termination summary" or "open positions."[109] The firm's home-office managers can access data on and monitor global human resource activities on a real-time basis.

Employers are also increasingly taking their employee self-service HR portals international. For example, consider Time Warner's "Employee Connection" portal. It lets Time Warner's 80,000 worldwide employees self-manage much of their benefits, compensation planning, merit review, and personal information updating online.[110]

5 Explain with examples how to implement a global human resource management program.

HOW TO IMPLEMENT A GLOBAL HR SYSTEM

With employers increasingly relying on local rather than expatriate employees, transferring one's selection, training, appraisal, pay, and other human resource management practices abroad is a top priority. In other words, there's less emphasis today on expatriate issues, and more on how to manage your local employees abroad. Of course, the attractive way to do this is by exporting your current HR practices abroad.

Given the cross-cultural differences in human resource management practices, one could reasonably ask, "Is it realistic for a company to try to institute a standardized human resource management system in its facilities around the world?" A study suggests that the answer is "yes." In brief, the study's results show that employers may have to defer to local managers on some specific human resource management policy issues. However, in general, the findings also suggest that big intercountry HR practice differences are often not necessary or even advisable. The important thing is how you implement the global human resource management system.

In this study, the researchers interviewed human resource personnel from six global companies—Agilent, Dow, IBM, Motorola, Procter & Gamble, and Shell Oil Co.—as well as international human resources consultants.[111] The study's overall conclusion was that employers who successfully implement global HR systems do so by applying several best practices. This enables them to install uniform global human resource policies and practices around the world. The basic idea is to *develop* systems that are *acceptable* to employees in units around the world, and ones that the employers can *implement* more effectively. We'll look at each of these three requirements' best practices.

Developing a More Effective Global HR System

First, these employers engage in two best practices in developing their worldwide human resource policies and practices.

Form Global HR Networks To head off resistance, human resource managers around the world should feel that they're part of a greater whole, namely, the firm's global human resource management network. The researchers found that in developing global HR systems, the most critical factor is "creating an infrastructure of partners around the world that you use for support, for buy-in, for organization of local activities, and to help you better understand their own systems and their own challenges."[112] Treat the local human resource managers as equal partners, not just implementers. These six firms accomplished this solidarity in various ways. For instance, they formed global teams to help develop the new human resources systems.

Remember That It's More Important to Standardize Ends and Competencies Than Specific Methods For example, IBM uses a more or less standardized recruitment and selection process worldwide. However, "details such as who conducts the interview (hiring manager versus recruiter) or whether the prescreen is by phone or in person, differ by country."[113]

Making the Global HR System More Acceptable

Next, employers engage in three best practices so that the global human resource systems they develop will be *acceptable* to local managers around the world. These best practices include the following:

Remember That Truly Global Organizations Find it Easier to Install Global Systems

Employers like these don't just install globally uniform human resource management systems; everything they do is global. For example, truly global companies require their managers to work on global teams, and identify and recruit and place the employees they hire globally. As one Shell manager put it, "If you're truly global, then you are hiring here [the United States] people who are going to immediately go and work in The Hague, and vice versa."[114] This global mind-set makes it easier for managers everywhere to accept the wisdom of having a standardized human resource management system.

Investigate Pressures to Differentiate and Determine Their Legitimacy

Standardizing selection, training, or other HR practices worldwide will still meet resistance from local managers. They will insist, "You can't do that here, because we are different culturally." These researchers found that these "differences" are usually not persuasive. For example, when Dow wanted to implement an online recruitment and selection tool abroad, the hiring managers there said that there was no way their managers would use it. After investigating the supposed cultural roadblocks, Dow implemented the new system. "What we found is that the number of applicants went through the roof when we went online, and the quality of the applicants also increased."[115]

The operative word here is "investigate." Carefully assess whether the local culture or other differences might in fact undermine the new system. Be knowledgeable about local legal issues, and be willing to differentiate where necessary. Then, market-test the new method.

Try to Work Within the Context of a Strong Corporate Culture

Companies that create a strong corporate culture find it easier to obtain agreement among far-flung employees. For example, because of how Procter & Gamble recruits, selects, trains, and rewards them, its managers have a strong sense of shared values. For instance, P&G encourages a relatively high degree of conformity among managers. New recruits quickly learn to think in terms of "we" instead of "I." They learn to value thoroughness, consistency, self-discipline, and a methodical approach. Because all P&G managers worldwide tend to share these values, they are in a sense more similar to each other than they are geographically different. Having such global unanimity in values makes it easier to develop and implement standardized human resource practices worldwide.

Implementing the Global HR System

Finally, two best practices helped ensure success in actually *implementing* the globally consistent human resource policies and practices.

"You Can't Communicate Enough"

For one thing, "There's a need for constant contact with the decision makers in each country, as well as the people who will be implementing and using the system."[116]

Dedicate Adequate Resources

For example, don't require the local human resource management offices to implement new job analysis procedures unless the head office provides adequate resources for these additional activities. Table 17-2 below summarizes these best practices for instituting global HR systems.

TABLE 17-2 Summary of Best Global HR Practices

Do . . .	Don't . . .
• Work within existing local systems—integrate global tools into local systems	• Try to do everything the same way everywhere
• Create a strong corporate culture	• Yield to every claim that "we're different"—make them prove it
• Create a global network for system development—global input is critical	• Force a global system on local people
• Treat local people as equal partners in system development	• Use local people just for implementation
• Assess common elements across geographies	• Use the same tools globally, unless you can show that they really work and are culturally appropriate
• Focus on what to measure and allow flexibility in how to measure	• Ignore cultural differences
• Allow for local additions beyond core elements	• Let technology drive your system design—you can't assume every location has the same level of technology investment and access
• Differentiate when necessary	• Assume that "if we build it they will come"—you need to market your tools or system and put change management strategies in place
• Train local people to make good decisions about which tools to use and how to do so	
• Communicate, communicate, communicate!	
• Dedicate resources for global HR efforts	
• Know, or have access to someone who knows, the legal requirements in each country	

Source: Ann Marie Ryan et al., "Designing and Implementing Global Staffing Systems: Part 2—Best Practices," *Human Resource Management* 42, no. 1 (Spring 2003), p. 93. Reproduced with permission of Society for Human Resource Management in the format Textbook via Copyright Clearance Center.

REVIEW

CHAPTER SECTION SUMMARIES

1. The **internationalization of business influences employers' HR processes.** The big issue is coping with the cultural, political, legal, and economic differences among countries. For example, citizens of different countries adhere to different values, and countries have differing economic systems as well as different legal, political, and labor relations systems.
2. **Staffing the global organization** is a major challenge. Companies may use expatriates, home-country nationals, or third-country nationals. Offshoring means having local employees abroad do jobs that domestic employees previously did in-house. Employers seeking to gain cost advantages by offshoring rely on their HR managers to help identify high-quality, low-cost talent abroad. Top management values will influence how they staff their operations abroad. Ethnocentric companies tend to emphasize home-country attitudes, polycentric companies focus more on host-country employees, and geocentric employers try to pick the best candidates from wherever they might be. Selecting employees to successfully work abroad depends on several things, most importantly on adaptability screening and on making sure that each employee's spouse and family get the realistic previews, counseling, and support necessary to make the transition abroad. Successful expatriates tend to be extroverted, agreeable, and emotionally stable individuals.
3. After selecting the employees to send abroad, attention turns to **training and maintaining your expatriate employees.**
   - In terms of predeparture preparation, training efforts ideally first cover the impact of cultural differences; then, the focus moves to getting participants to understand how attitudes influence behavior, providing factual knowledge about the target country, and developing skills in areas like language and adjustment.

- In compensating expatriates, most employers use the balance sheet approach; this focuses on four groups of expenses: income taxes, housing, goods and services, and discretionary expenses. The balance sheet approach aims to provide supplements in such a way that the employee's standard of living abroad is about what it would have been at home. It's usual to apply incentives such as foreign service premiums and hardship allowances to get employees to move abroad.
- Distance complicates the issue of appraising expatriate managers, so it's prudent to let both the home-office supervisor and the manager's local superior contribute to the appraisal.
- Labor relations tend to be different abroad from what they are in the United States. For instance, there's a much greater emphasis on centralized bargaining in Europe.
- With terrorism a threat, most employers today take protective measures, including buying kidnapping and ransom insurance.
- To reduce the chronic problem of turnover among newly returned employees, it's important to have well-thought-out repatriation programs. These emphasize keeping employees in the loop as far as what's happening in their home offices, bringing them back to the office periodically, and providing formal repatriation services for the expatriate and his or her family to start preparing them for the return.

4. With employers increasingly relying on local rather than expatriate employees, it's important for managers to understand **how to implement a global HR system**. Studies suggest that it is realistic for a company to try to institute standardized human resource management practices at their facilities around the world, although it may be necessary to "fine-tune" them to the needs of the specific facility. The basic approach involves three steps. (1) Develop a more effective global HR system (by forming global HR networks and remembering that it's more important to standardize ends rather than specific methods). (2) Make the global HR system more acceptable (for instance, by taking a global approach to everything the company does, by investigating pressures to differentiate and determining their legitimacy, and by creating a strong company culture). (3) Implement the global system (by emphasizing continuing communications and by ensuring that adequate resources are available).

DISCUSSION QUESTIONS

1. You are the president of a small business. What are some of the ways you expect "going international" will affect HR activities in your business?
2. What are some of the specific, uniquely international activities an international HR manager typically engages in?
3. What intercountry differences affect HRM? Give several examples of how each may specifically affect HRM.
4. You are the HR manager of a firm that is about to send its first employees overseas to staff a new subsidiary. Your boss, the president, asks you why such assignments often fail, and what you plan to do to avoid such failures. How do you respond?
5. What special training do overseas candidates need? In what ways is such training similar to and different from traditional diversity training?
6. How does appraising an expatriate's performance differ from appraising that of a home-office manager? How would you avoid some of the unique problems of appraising the expatriate's performance?
7. As an HR manager, what program would you establish to reduce repatriation problems of returning expatriates and their families?

INDIVIDUAL AND GROUP ACTIVITIES

1. Working individually or in groups, outline an expatriation and repatriation plan for your professor, whom your school is sending to Bulgaria to teach HR for the next 3 years.
2. Give three specific examples of multinational corporations in your area. Check on the Internet or with each firm to determine in what countries these firms have operations. Explain the nature of some of their operations, and summarize whatever you can find out about their international employee selection and training HR policies.
3. Choose three traits useful for selecting international assignees, and create a straightforward test to screen candidates for these traits.
4. Use a library or Internet source to determine the relative cost of living in five countries as of this year, and explain the implications of such differences for drafting a pay plan for managers being sent to each country.
5. The "HRCI Test Specifications Appendix" (pages 699–706) lists the knowledge someone studying for the HRCI certification exam needs to have in each area of human resource management (such as in Strategic Management, Workforce Planning, and Human Resource Development). In groups of four to five students, do four things: (1) Review that appendix now. (2) Identify the material in this chapter that relates to the required knowledge the appendix lists.

(3) Write four multiple-choice exam questions on this material that you believe would be suitable for inclusion in the HRCI exam. And (4) if time permits, have someone from your team post your team's questions in front of the class, so the students in other teams can take each others' exam questions.

6. An issue of *HR Magazine* contained an article titled "Aftershocks of War," which said that soldiers returning to their jobs from Iraq would likely require HR's assistance in coping with "delayed emotional trauma." The term *delayed emotional trauma* refers to the personality changes such as anger, anxiety, or irritability and associated problems such as tardiness or absenteeism that exposure to the traumatic events of war sometimes triggers in returning veterans. Assume you are the HR manager for the employer of John Smith, who is returning to work next week after 1 year in Iraq. Based on what you read in this chapter, what steps would you take to help ensure that John's reintegration into your workforce goes as smoothly as possible?

EXPERIENTIAL EXERCISE

A Taxing Problem for Expatriate Employees

Purpose: The purpose of this exercise is to give you practice identifying and analyzing some of the factors that influence expatriates' pay.

Required Understanding: You should be thoroughly familiar with this chapter and with the Web site www.irs.gov.

How to Set Up the Exercise/Instructions: Divide the class into teams of four or five students. Each team member should read the following: One of the trickiest aspects of calculating expatriates' pay relates to the question of the expatriate's U.S. federal income tax liabilities. Go to the Internal Revenue Service's Web site, www.irs.gov. Scroll down to Individuals, and go to Overseas Taxpayers. Your team is the expatriate-employee compensation task force for your company, and your firm is about to send several managers and engineers to Japan, England, and Hong Kong. What information did you find on the site that will help your team formulate expat tax and compensation policies? Based on that, what are the three most important things your firm should keep in mind in formulating a compensation policy for the employees you're about to send to Japan, England, and Hong Kong?

APPLICATION CASE

"Boss, I Think We Have a Problem"

Central Steel Door Corporation has been in business for about 20 years, successfully selling a line of steel industrial-grade doors, as well as the hardware and fittings required for them. Focusing mostly in the United States and Canada, the company had gradually increased its presence from the New York City area, first into New England and then down the Atlantic Coast, then through the Midwest and West, and finally into Canada. The company's basic expansion strategy was always the same: Choose an area, open a distribution center, hire a regional sales manager, and then let that regional sales manager help staff the distribution center and hire local sales reps.

Unfortunately, the company's traditional success in finding sales help has not extended to its overseas operations. With the introduction of the new "Euro" European currency in 2002, Mel Fisher, president of Central Steel Door, decided to expand his company abroad, into Europe. However, the expansion has not gone smoothly at all. He tried for 3 weeks to find a sales manager by advertising in the *International Herald Tribune*, which is read by businesspeople in Europe and by American expatriates living and working in Europe. Although the ads placed in the *Tribune* also run for about a month on the *Tribune*'s Web site, Mr. Fisher so far has received only five applications. One came from a possibly viable candidate, whereas four came from candidates who Mr. Fisher refers to as "lost souls"—people who seem to have spent most of their time traveling aimlessly from country to country, sipping espresso in sidewalk cafés. When asked what he had done for the last 3 years, one told Mr. Fisher he'd been on a "walkabout."

Other aspects of his international HR activities have been equally problematic. Fisher alienated two of his U.S. sales managers by sending them to Europe to run temporarily the European operations, but neglecting to work out a compensation package that would cover their relatively high living expenses in Germany and Belgium. One ended up staying the better part of the year, and Mr. Fisher was rudely surprised to be informed by the Belgian government that his sales manager owed thousands of dollars in local taxes. The two managers had hired about 10 local people to staff each of the two distribution centers. However, without full-time local European sales managers, the level of sales was disappointing, so Fisher decided to fire about half the distribution center employees. That's when he got an emergency phone call from his temporary sales manager in Germany: "I've just been told that all these employees should have had written employment agreements and that in any case we can't fire anyone without at least 1 year's notice, and the local authorities here are really up in arms. Boss, I think we have a problem."

Questions

1. Based on this chapter and the case incident, compile a list of 10 international HR mistakes Mr. Fisher has made so far.
2. How would you have gone about hiring a European sales manager? Why?
3. What would you do now if you were Mr. Fisher?

CONTINUING CASE

Carter Cleaning Company Going Abroad

With Jennifer gradually taking the reins of Carter Cleaning Company, Jack decided to take his first long vacation in years and go to Mexico for a month in January 2008. What he found surprised him: While he spent much of the time basking in the sun in Acapulco, he also spent considerable time in Mexico City and was surprised at the dearth of cleaning stores, particularly considering the amount of air pollution in the area. Traveling north, he passed through Juarez, Mexico, and was similarly surprised at the relatively few cleaning stores he found there. As he drove back into Texas, and back toward home, he began to think about whether it would be advisable to consider expanding his chain of stores into Mexico.

Quite aside from the possible economic benefits, he had liked what he saw in the lifestyle in Mexico and was also attracted by the idea of possibly facing the sort of exciting challenge he had faced 20 years ago when he started Carter Cleaning in the United States: "I guess entrepreneurship is in my blood," is the way he put it.

As he drove home to have dinner with Jennifer, he began to formulate the questions he would have to ask before deciding whether to expand abroad.

Questions

1. Assuming they began by opening just one or two stores in Mexico, what do you see as the main HR-related challenges he and Jennifer would have to address?
2. How would you go about choosing a manager for a new Mexican store if you were Jack or Jennifer? For instance, would you hire someone locally or send someone from one of your existing stores? Why?
3. The cost of living in Mexico is substantially below that of where Carter is now located: How would you go about developing a pay plan for your new manager if you decided to send an expatriate to Mexico?
4. Present a detailed explanation of the factors you would look for in your candidate for expatriate manager to run the stores in Mexico.

TRANSLATING STRATEGY INTO HR POLICIES & PRACTICES CASE

The Hotel Paris Case

Managing Global Human Resources

The Hotel Paris's competitive strategy is, "To use superior guest service to differentiate the Hotel Paris properties, and to thereby increase the length of stay and return rate of guests, and thus boost revenues and profitability." HR manager Lisa Cruz must now formulate functional policies and activities that support this competitive strategy, by eliciting the required employee behaviors and competencies.

With hotels in 11 cities in Europe and the United States, Lisa knew that the company had to do a better job of managing its global human resources. For example, there was no formal means of identifying or training management employees for duties abroad (either for those going to the United States or to Europe). As another example, recently, after spending upwards of $600,000 sending a U.S. manager and her family abroad, they had to return her abruptly when the family complained bitterly of missing their friends back home. Lisa knew this was no way to run a multinational business. She turned her attention to developing the HR practices her company required to do business more effectively internationally.

On reviewing the data, it was apparent to Lisa and the CFO that the company's global human resource practices were probably inhibiting the Hotel Paris from being the world-class guest services company that it sought to be. For example, high-performing service and hotel firms had formal departure training programs for at least 90% of the employees they sent abroad; the Hotel Paris had no such programs. Similarly, with each city's hotel operating its own local hotel HR information system, there was no easy way for Lisa, the CFO, or the company's CEO to obtain reports on metrics like turnover, absences, or workers' compensation costs across all the different hotels. As the CFO summed it up, "If we can't measure how each hotel is doing in terms of human resource metrics like these, there's really no way to manage these activities, so there's no telling how much lost profits and wasted efforts are dragging down each hotel's performance." Lisa received approval to institute new global human resources programs and practices.

Questions

1. Provide a 1-page summary of what individual hotel managers should know in order to make it more likely incoming employees from abroad, like those in the Hotel Paris's management development program, will adapt to their new surroundings.
2. In previous chapters you recommended various human resource practices Hotel Paris should use. Choose one of these, and explain why you believe they could take this program abroad, and how you suggest they do so.
3. Choose one Hotel Paris human resources practice that you believe is essential to the company achieving its high-quality-service goal, and explain how you would implement that practice in the firm's various hotels worldwide.

KEY TERMS

codetermination, *p. 633*
expatriates (expats), *p. 635*
home-country nationals, *p. 635*
third-country nationals, *p. 637*
ethnocentric, *p. 639*
polycentric, *p. 639*
geocentric, *p. 639*
adaptability screening, *p. 639*
foreign service premiums, *p. 645*
hardship allowances, *p. 647*
mobility premiums, *p. 647*

ENDNOTES

1. http://talkingunion.wordpress.com/2008/09/27/is-union-reform-possible-in-china, accessed March 25, 2009.
2. There is considerable debate regarding the pros and cons of globalization. Many economists, and, most recently, the international monetary fund, have concluded that globalization in the form of technology transfer and foreign investment may actually be fueling income inequality. See, for example, Bob Davis, "IMF Fuels Critics of Globalization," *The Wall Street Journal*, October 10, 2007, p. 89.
3. See, for example, Kimberly Manion, "Venturing Abroad," *HR Magazine*, June 2008, pp. 86–90.
4. See, for example, Chris Rowley and Malcolm Warner, "Introduction: Globalizing International Human Resource Management," *International Journal of Human Resource Management* 18, no. 5 (May 2007), p. 703(14).
5. David Ralston, David Gustafson, Priscilla Elsass, Fannie Cheung, and Robert Terpstra, "Eastern Values: A Comparison of Managers in the United States, Hong Kong, and the People's Republic of China," *Journal of Applied Psychology* 71, no. 5 (1992), pp. 664–671. See also P. Christopher Earley and Elaine Mosakowski, "Cultural Intelligence," *Harvard Business Review*, October 2004, pp. 139–146.
6. Geert Hofstede, "Cultural Dimensions in People Management," in Vladimir Pucik, Noel Tichy, and Carole Barnett (eds.), *Globalizing Management* (New York: John Wiley & Sons, 1992), p. 143.
7. Randall Schuler, Susan Jackson, Ellen Jackofsky, and John Slocum Jr., "Managing Human Resources in Mexico: A Cultural Understanding," *Business Horizons*, May–June 1996, pp. 55–61.
8. Valerie Frazee, "Establishing Relations in Germany," *Global Workforce*, April 1997, p. 17.
9. Charlene Solomon, "Destination U.S.A.," *Global Workforce*, April 1997, pp. 19–23.
10. Ibid., p. 21.
11. Tyler Cowen, "Creative Destruction: How Globalization Is Changing the World's Cultures," Princeton University Press, Princeton, New Jersey, 2002.
12. Chris Brewster, "European Perspectives on Human Resource Management," *Human Resource Management Review* 14 (2004), pp. 365–382.
13. "SOX Compliance, Corporate Codes of Conduct Can Create Challenges for U.S. Multinationals," *BNA Bulletin to Management*, March 28, 2006, p. 97.
14. Annual 2006 figures, www.bls.gov/news.release/ichcc.nro.htm, accessed January 27, 2008.
15. See, for example, http://www.fedee.com/ewc1.html, accessed November 4, 2009.
16. This is discussed in E. Gaugler, "HR Management: An International Comparison," *Personnel*, 1988, p. 28. E. Poutsma et. al., "The Diffusion of Calculative and Collaborative HRM Practices in European Firms," *Industrial Relations* 45, no. 4 (October 2006), p9. 513–546.
17. Helen Deresky, *International Management* (Upper Saddle River, NJ: Prentice Hall, 2008), p. 17.
18. Donald Dowling Jr., "Export Codes of Conduct, Not Employee Handbooks," *Society for Human Resource Management Legal Report*, January/February 2007, pp. 1–4.
19. Phillips Taft and Cliff Powell, "The European Pensions and Benefits Environment: A Complex Ecology," *Compensation & Benefits Review*, January/February 2005, pp. 37–50.
20. Ibid.
21. "Inform, Consult, Impose: Workers' Rights in the EU," *The Economist*, June 16, 2001, p. 3. See also J. Banyuls et. al., "European Works Council at General Motors Europe: Bargaining Efficiency in Regime Competition?," *Industrial Relations Journal* 39, no. 6 (November 2008), pp. 532–547.
22. See, for example, Syed Akhtar et al., "Strategic HRM Practices and Their Impact on Company Performance in Chinese Enterprises," *Human Resource Management* 47, no. 1 (Spring 2008), pp. 15–32.
23. Andreas Lauffs, "Chinese Law Spurs Reforms," *HR Magazine*, June 2008, pp. 92–98.
24. See, for example, Kathryn King-Metters and Richard Metters, "Misunderstanding the Chinese Worker," *The Wall Street Journal*, July 7, 2008, p. R11.
25. Gary Dessler, "Expanding into China? What Foreign Employers Entering China Should Know About Human Resource Management Today," *SAM Advanced Management Journal*, August 2006. See also Joseph Gamble, "Introducing Western-Style HRM Practices to China: Shop Floor Perceptions in a British Multinational," *Journal of World Business* 41, no. 4 (December 2006), pp. 328–340; and Adrienne Fox, "China: Land of Opportunity and Challenge," *HR Magazine*, September 2007, pp. 38–44.
26. John Daniels and Lee Radebaugh, *International Business*, (Upper Saddle River, N.J., Prentice Hall, 2001), p. 767.
27. Arvind Phatak, *International Dimensions of Management* (Boston: PWS Kent, 1989), p. 106. See also Charles Hill, *International Business: Competing in the Global Marketplace* (Burr Ridge, IL: Irwin McGraw-Hill, 2001), pp. 564–566.
28. Daniels and Radebaugh, *International Business*, p. 767.
29. Ibid., p. 769; Phatak, *International Dimensions of Management*, p. 106.
30. "Survey Says Expatriates Twice as Likely to Leave Employer as Home-Based Workers," *BNA Bulletin to Management*, May 9, 2006, p. 147.
31. Phatak, *International Dimensions of Management*, p. 108.
32. Daniels and Radebaugh, *International Business*, p. 769.

33. Leslie Klass, "Fed Up with High Costs, Companies Winnow the Ranks of Career Expats," *Workforce Management*, October 2004, pp. 84–88.
34. "DOL Releases Final Rule Amending Filing, Processing of Foreign Labor Certifications," *BNA Bulletin to Management*, January 11, 2005, p. 11.
35. Michelle Rafter, "Return Trip for Expats," *Workforce*, March 16, 2009, pp. 1, 3.
36. Helene Mayerhofer et al., "Flexpatriate Assignments: A Neglected Issue in Global Staffing," *International Journal of Human Resource Management* 15, no. 8 (December 2004), pp. 1371–1389; and Martha Frase, "International Commuters," *HR Magazine*, March 2007, pp. 91–96.
37. Michael Harvey et al., "Global Virtual Teams: A Human Resource Capital Architecture," *International Journal of Human Resource Management* 16, no. 9 (September 2005), pp. 1583–1599.
38. Timothy Dwyer, "Localization's Hidden Costs," *HR Magazine*, June 2004, pp. 135–144.
39. William Bulkeley, "IBM to Cut US Jobs, Expand in India," *The Wall Street Journal*, March 26, 2009, p. B1.
40. Based on Pamela Babcock, "America's Newest Export: White Collar Jobs," *HR Magazine*, April 2004, pp. 50–57.
41. Mary Medland, "Setting Up Overseas," *HR Magazine*, January 2004, p. 71.
42. Phatak, *International Dimensions of Management*, p. 129.
43. Charles Hill, *International Business: Competing in the Global Marketplace* (Burr Ridge, IL: Irwin, 1994), p. 507.
44. Ibid., pp. 507–510.
45. Ibid.
46. Ibid., p. 509.
47. Ibid. See also M. Harvey et al., "An Innovative Global Management Staffing System: A Competency-Based Perspective," *Human Resource Management* 39, no. 4 (Winter 2000), pp. 381–394.
48. Mason Carpenter et al., "International Assignment Experience at the Top Can Make a Bottom-Line Difference," *Human Resource Management* 30, no. 223 (Summer–Fall 2000), pp. 277–285. See also Gunter Stahl and Paula Caligiuri, "The Effectiveness of Expatriate Coping Strategies: The Moderating Role of Cultural Distance, Position Level, and Time on the International Assignment," *Journal of Applied Psychology* 90, no. 4 (2005), pp. 603–615.
49. Sunkyu Jun and James Gentry, "An Exploratory Investigation of the Relative Importance of Cultural Similarity and Personal Fit in the Selection and Performance of Expatriates," *Journal of World Business* 40, no. 1 (February 2005), pp. 1–8. See also Jan Selmer, "Cultural Novelty and Adjustment: Western Business Expatriates in China," *International Journal of Human Resource Management* 17, no. 7 (2006), pp. 1211–1222.
50. Winfred Arthur Jr. and Winston Bennett Jr., "The International Assignee: The Relative Importance of Factors Perceived to Contribute to Success," *Personnel Psychology* 48 (1995), p. 110; Gretchen Spreitzer, Morgan McCall Jr., and Joan Mahoney, "Early Identification of International Executive Potential," *Journal of Applied Psychology* 82, no. 1 (1997), pp. 62–69. For recent, similar conclusions, see, for example, Handan Kepir Sinangil and Deniz Ones, "Expatriate Management," in Neil Anderson, Deniz Ones, Handan Kepir Sinangil, and Chockalingam Viswesvaran (eds.), *Handbook of Industrial, Work and Organizational Psychology, Vol. 1: Personnel Psychology* (Thousand Oaks, CA: Sage Publications, 2002), pp. 424–443; Regina Hechanova, Terry Beehr, and Neil Christiansen, "Antecedents and Consequences of Employees' Adjustment to Overseas Assignment: A Meta-Analytic Review," *Applied Psychology: An International Review* 52, No. 2, (April 2003), pp. 213–236; and Raymond Edward Branton, "A Multifaceted Assessment Protocol for Successful International Assignees," *Dissertation Abstracts International: Section B: The Sciences and Engineering* 64, no. 8B, (2004), p. 4024.
51. Phatak, *International Dimensions of Management*, p. 119. See also Arno Haslberger, "The Complexities of Expatriate Adaptation," *Human Resource Management Review* 15, no. 2 (June 2005), pp. 160–180.
52. See, for example, Paul Blocklyn, "Developing the International Executive," *Personnel*, March, 1989, p. 45.
53. www.performanceprograms.com/Surveys/Overseas.shtm, accessed January 31, 2008.
54. Blocklyn, "Developing the International Executive," p. 45. See also Eric Krell, "Evaluating the Returns on Expatriates," *HR Magazine* 50, no. 3 (March 2005), pp. 61–65.
55. "International Assignment Policies and Practices," *BNA Bulletin to Management*, May 1, 1997, pp. 140–141, based on a survey by Organization Resources Counselors, Inc., New York City. See also Michael Stevens et al., "HR Factors Affecting Repatriate Job Satisfaction and Job Attachment for Japanese Managers," *International Journal of Human Resource Management* 17, no. 5 (2006), pp. 831–841.
56. Hilary Harris and Chris Brewster, "The Coffee Machine System: How International Selection Really Works," *International Journal of Human Resource Management* 10, no. 3 (June 1999), pp. 488–500.
57. "More Women, Young Workers on the Move," *Workforce Management*, August 20, 2007, p. 9.
58. For a good discussion of this, see Yochanan Altman and Susan Shortland, "Women and International Assignments: Taking Stock—A 25-Year Review," *Human Resource Management* 47, no. 2 (Summer 2008), pp. 199–216.
59. Kathryn Tyler, "Don't Fence Her In," *HR Magazine* 46, no. 3 (March 2001), pp. 69–77.
60. Ibid.
61. Ibid.
62. See Nancy Napier and Sully Taylor, "Experiences of Women Professionals Abroad," *International Journal of Human Resource Management* 13, no. 5 (August 2002), pp. 837–851; I. C. Fischlmayr, "Female Self-Perception as a Barrier to International Careers?" *International Journal of Human Resource Management* 13, no. 5 (August 2002), pp. 773–783; and Yochanan Altman and Susan Shortland, op cit.
63. The following is quoted from or adapted from "The Equal Employment Opportunity Responsibilities of Multinational Employers," The U.S. Equal Employment Opportunity Commission, www.EEOC.gov/facts/multi-employers.html, downloaded February 9, 2004.
64. See Donald Dowling Jr., "Choice of Law Contract Clauses May Not Fly Abroad," *Society for Human Resource Management Legal Report*, October–November 2008, pp. 1–2.
65. Margaret Shaffer and David Harrison, "Expatriates' Psychological Withdrawal from International Assignments: Work, Nonwork, and Family Influences," *Personnel Psychology* 51 (1998), p. 88. See also Jan Selmer, "Psychological Barriers to Adjustment of Western Business Expatriates in China: Newcomers

vs. Long Stayers," *International Journal of Human Resource Management* 15, no. 4–5 (June–August 2004), p. 794(21).

66. Chuck Csizmar, "Does Your Expatriate Program Follow the Rules of the Road?" *Compensation & Benefits Review*, January/February 2008, pp. 61–69.
67. P. Caligiuri, "The Big Five Personality Characteristics as Predictors of Expatriates' Desire to Terminate the Assignment and Supervisor-Rated Performance," *Personnel Psychology* 53, no. 1 (Spring 2000), pp. 67–88. See also Margaret A. Shaffer, David A. Harrison, Hal Gregersen, J. Stewart Black, and Lori A. Ferzandi, "You Can Take It with You: Individual Differences and Expatriate Effectiveness," *Journal of Applied Psychology* 91, no. 1 (January 2006), p. 109(17).
68. Quoted in Meredith Downes, Iris I. Varner, and Luke Musinski, "Personality Traits as Predictors of Expatriate Effectiveness: A Synthesis and Reconceptualization," *Review of Business* 27, no. 3 (Spring–Summer 2007), p. 16(8).
69. Jan Selmer, "Expatriation: Corporate Policy, Personal Intentions and International Adjustment," *International Journal of Human Resource Management* 9, no. 6 (December 1998), pp. 997–1007.
70. Hung-Wen Lee and Ching-Hsing, "Determinants of the Adjustment of Expatriate Managers to Foreign Countries: An Empirical Study," *International Journal of Management* 23, no. 2 (2006), pp. 302–311.
71. Sunkyu Jun and James Gentry, "An Exploratory Investigation of the Relative Importance of Cultural Similarity and Personal Fit in the Selection and Perfozrmance of Expatriates," *Journal of World Business* 40, no. 1 (February 2005), pp. 1–8. See also Jan Selmer, "Cultural Novelty and Adjustment: Western Business Expatriates in China," *International Journal of Human Resource Management* 17, no. 7 (2006), pp. 1211–1222.
72. Discussed in Charles Hill, *International Business*, pp. 511–515.
73. Charlene Solomon, "One Assignment, Two Lives," *Personnel Journal*, May 1996, pp. 36–47; Michael Harvey, "Dual-Career Couples During International Relocation: The Trailing Spouse," *International Journal of Human Resource Management* 9, no. 2 (April 1998), pp. 309–330.
74. Barbara Anderson, "Expatriate Selection: Good Management or Good Luck?" *International Journal of Human Resource Management* 16, no. 4 (April 2005), pp. 567–583.
75. Margaret Shaffer and David Harrison, "Forgotten Partners of International Assignments: Development and Test of a Model of Spouse Adjustment," *Journal of Applied Psychology* 86, no. 2 (2001), pp. 238–254.
76. Ibid., p. 251.
77. Ibid., p. 250.
78. Hung-Wen Lee and Ching-Hsing, "Determinants of the Adjustment of Expatriate Managers to Foreign Countries: An Empirical Study," *International Journal of Management* 23, no. 2 (2006), pp. 302–311.
79. Gary Insch and John Daniels, "Causes and Consequences of Declining Early Departures from Foreign Assignments," *Business Horizons* 46, no. 6 (November–December 2002), pp. 39–48.
80. Eric Krell, "Budding Relationships," *HR Magazine* 50, no. 6 (June 2005), pp. 114–118.
81. This is based on Krell, "Budding Relationships," p. 30. See also Jill Elswick, "Worldly Wisdom: Companies Refine Their Approach to Overseas Assignments, Emphasizing Cost-Cutting and Work-Life Support for Expatriates," *Employee Benefit News*, June 15, 2004, Item 0416600B.
82. Mark Mendenhall and Gunter Stahl, "Expatriate Training and Development: Where Do We Go from Here?" *Human Resource Management* 39, no. 223 (Summer–Fall 2000), pp. 251–265.
83. See, for example, Victor Infante, "Three Ways to Design International Pay: Headquarters, Home Country, Host," *Workforce*, January 2001, pp. 22–24; and Gary Parker and Erwin Janush, "Developing Expatriate Remuneration Packages," *Employee Benefits Journal* 26, no. 2 (June 2001), pp. 3–51.
84. Stephenie Overman, "Focus on International HR," *HR Magazine*, March 2000, pp. 87–92; Sheila Burns, "Flexible International Assignee Compensation Plans," *Compensation & Benefits Review*, May/June 2003, pp. 35–44; Thomas Shelton, "Global Compensation Strategies: Managing and Administering Split Pay for an Expatriate Workforce," *Compensation & Benefits Review*, January/February 2008, pp. 56–59.
85. Phatak, *International Dimensions of Management*, p. 134. See also "China to Levy Income Tax on Expatriates," *Asia Africa Intelligence Wire*, August 3, 2004, Item A120140119.
86. Thomas Shelton, "Global Compensation Strategies: Managing and Administering Split Pay for an Expatriate Workforce," *Compensation & Benefits Review*, January/February 2008, pp. 56–59.
87. Mark Schoeff Jr., "Danger and Duty," *Workforce*, November 19, 2007, pp. 1, 3.
88. See, for example, "More Multinational Organizations Are Taking a Global Approach to Compensation," *Compensation & Benefits Review*, May/June 2008, p. 5.
89. Except as noted, this section is based on Joseph Martocchio, *Strategic Compensation* (Upper Saddle River, NJ: Prentice Hall, 2001), pp. 280–283. See also Gary Parker, "Establishing Remuneration Practices Across Culturally Diverse Environments," *Compensation & Benefits Review* 17, no. 2 (Spring 2001), p. 23.
90. Gary Dessler, "Expanding into China? What Foreign Employers Entering China Should Know About Human Resource Management Today," *SAM Advanced Management Journal*, in press. See also Joseph Gamble, "Introducing Western-style HRM Practices to China: Shop Floor Perceptions in a British Multinational," *Journal of World Business* 41, no. 4 (December 2006), pp. 328–340; and Adrienne Fox, "China: Land of Opportunity and Challenge," *HR Magazine*, September 2007, pp. 38–44.
91. "Managers Are Paid More in Emerging Economies," *Compensation & Benefits Review*, September/October 2007, p. 19.
92. Robin White, "A Strategic Approach to Building a Consistent Global Rewards Program," *Compensation & Benefits Review*, July/August 2005, p. 25.
93. Ibid., pp. 23–40.
94. "Recommendations for Managing Global Compensation Clause in a Changing Economy," Hewitt Associates, www.hewittassociates.com/_MetaBasicCMAssetCache_/Assets/Articles/2009/hewitt_pov_globalcomp_0109.pdf, accessed March 22, 2009.
95. See, for example, Jie Shen, "Effective International Performance Appraisals: Easily Said, Hard to Do," *Compensation & Benefits Review*, July/August 2005, pp. 70–78.
96. Ibid.

97. Fay Hansen, "Skirting Danger," *Workforce*, January 19, 2009, pp. 1, 3.
98. Ibid.
99. These are based on or quoted from Samuel Greengard, "Mission Possible: Protecting Employees Abroad," *Workforce*, August 1997, pp. 30–32. See also Z. Phillips, "Global Firms Consider Additional Cover for Overseas Execs," *Business Insurance* 43, no. 23 (June 15–22, 2009), pp. 4, 22.
100. Ibid., p. 32.
101. www.google.com/mobile/default/maps.html, accessed March 24, 2009.
102. Carla Joinson, "Save Thousands Per Expatriate," *HR Magazine*, July 2002, p. 77.
103. Kathryn Tyler, "Retaining Repatriates," *HR Magazine*, March 2006, pp. 97–102.
104. Quoted in Leslie Klaff, "The Right Way to Bring Expats Home," *Workforce*, July 2002, p. 43.
105. Ibid., p. 43.
106. Ibid.
107. Bill Roberts, "Going Global," *HR Magazine*, August 2000, pp. 123–128.
108. Diane Turner, "NuView Brings Web-Based HRIS to Buildnet," *Workforce*, December 2000, p. 90.
109. Jim Meade, "Web-Based HRIS Meets Multiple Needs," *HR Magazine*, August 2000, pp. 129–133. See also "Dynamic HR: Global Applications from IBM," *Human Resource Management* 48, no. 4 (July/August 2009), pp. 641–648.
110. Drew Robb, "Unifying Your Enterprise with a Global HR Portal," *HR Magazine*, March 2006, pp. 119–120.
111. Ann Marie Ryan et al., "Designing and Implementing Global Staffing Systems: Part 2—Best Practices," *Human Resource Management* 42, no. 1 (Spring 2003), pp. 85–94.
112. Ibid., p. 89.
113. Ibid., p. 90.
114. Ryan et al., op cit., p. 86. See also M. Schoeff, "Adopting an HR Worldview," *Workforce Management* 87, no. 19 (November 17, 2008), p. 8.
115. Ryan et al., op cit., p. 87.
116. Ryan et al., op cit.., p. 92.

18 Managing Human Resources in Entrepreneurial Firms

It's not easy running a restaurant. Customers are notoriously fickle, food hygiene is always a concern, and, perhaps most unnerving to many restaurant owners, it's become exceedingly difficult to hire and keep good employees. Half of all restaurant employees are less than 30 years old, and turnover of more than 100% per year is the norm.[1] So, when Joe Scripture, whose company runs 11 IHOP restaurants around Atlanta, looked at the industry's turnover statistics, he knew he and his partner needed to do something, but what?[2]

Source: Courtesy of Emile Wamsteker/Bloomberg News/Landov Media.

WHERE ARE WE NOW . . .

Particularly in challenging times, many people graduating in the next few years either will work for small businesses or will create new small businesses of their own. Entrepreneurs have some special human resource management needs. The main purpose of this chapter is to help you apply what you know about human resource management to running a small business. The main topics we'll address include the small business challenge; using Internet and government tools to support the HR effort; leveraging small size with familiarity, flexibility, fairness, and informality; using professional employer organizations; and managing HR systems, procedures, and paperwork.

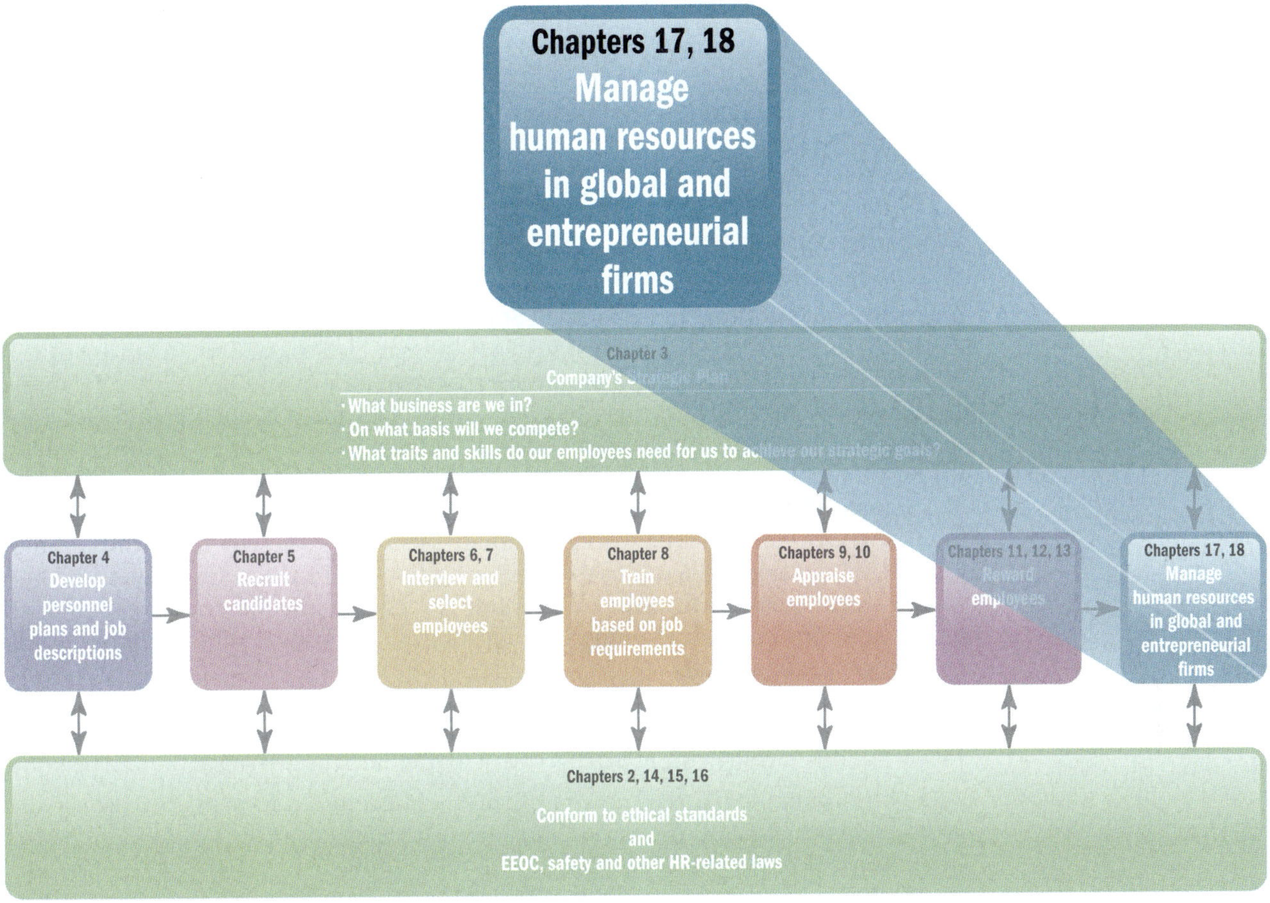

LEARNING OUTCOMES

1. Explain why human resource management in small companies is different from that in larger companies.
2. Give at least five specific examples of how you would use the Internet and government tools to support the HR effort in a small business.
3. Answer the question, "Why are *familiarity, flexibility,* and *informality* important tools that entrepreneurs can use to improve human resource management practices in their small businesses?"
4. Explain what professional employers' organizations are and how entrepreneurs can use them.
5. Describe how HR systems traditionally evolve in a small business and give examples of how small businesses can use human resource management information systems.

Source: Curtesy of Richard Levine/Alamy Images.

THE SMALL BUSINESS CHALLENGE

Why Entrepreneurship Is Important

In terms of the U.S. economy, the phrase *small business* is a misnomer. More than half the people working in the United States—about 68 million out of 118 million—work for small firms.[3] Small businesses as a group also account for most of the 600,000 or so new businesses created every year, as well as for most of business growth (small firms grow faster than big ones). And small firms account for about three-quarters of the employment growth in the U.S. economy—in other words, they create most of the new jobs in the United States.[4]

Statistically speaking, therefore, most people graduating from college in the next few years either will work for small businesses or will create new small businesses of their own—those with fewer than 200 or so employees. Anyone interested in small businesses (or human resource management) thus needs to understand how managing human resources in small firms is different from doing so in huge multinationals.

1 Explain why human resource management in small companies is different from that in larger companies.

How Small Business Human Resource Management Is Different

Managing human resources in small firms is different for four main reasons: *size, priorities, informality*, and the nature of the *entrepreneur.*

Size For one thing, it would be very unusual to find a really small business—say, fewer than 90 or so employees—with a dedicated human resource management professional.[5] The rule of thumb is that it's not until a company reaches the 100-employee milestone that it can afford an human resources specialist. That's not to say that small businesses don't have human resource tasks to which they must attend. Even 5- to 6-person retail shops must recruit, select, train, and compensate employees, for instance. It's just that in such situations, it's usually the owner and (sometimes) his or her assistant that does all the human resource management paperwork and tasks involved. SHRM's *Human Capital Benchmarking Study* found, for instance, that even firms with fewer than 100 employees often spend the equivalent of two-or-so peoples' time each year addressing human resource management issues.[6] But, that time is usually just coming out of the owner's very long workday.

Priorities It's not just size but the realities of the entrepreneur's situation that drive them to focus their time on non-HR issues. For example, one researcher studied small e-commerce firms in the United Kingdom. He concluded that, as important as human resource management is, it simply wasn't a high priority for these firms. He said,

> ". . . given their shortage of resources in terms of time, money, people and expertise, a typical SME [small and midsize enterprise] manager's organizational imperatives are perceived elsewhere, in finance, production and marketing, with HR of diminished relative importance."[7]

Informality One effect of this is that human resource management activities tend to be more informal in smaller firms. For example, one study analyzed training practices in about 900 family and nonfamily small companies.[8] Training tended to be informal, with an emphasis, for instance, on methods like coworker and supervisory on-the-job training.

Such informality isn't just due to a lack of expertise and resources (although that's part of it); it's also partly a "matter of survival." Entrepreneurs must be able to react quickly to changes in competitive conditions. Given that, there's some logic in keeping things like compensation policies flexible. As one researcher says, the need for small businesses to adapt quickly to environmental realities like competitive challenges often means handling matters like raises, appraisals, and time off "on an informal, reactive basis with a short time horizon."[9]

The Entrepreneur *Entrepreneurs* are "people who create businesses under risky conditions," and starting new businesses from scratch is always risky. Entrepreneurs therefore need to be highly dedicated and visionary. Researchers therefore believe that small firms' relative informality partly stems from entrepreneurs' unique personalities. Entrepreneurs tend (among other things) to be somewhat controlling: "Owners tend to want to impose their stamp and personal management style on internal matters, including the primary goal and orientation of the firm, it's working conditions and policies, and the style of internal and external communication and how this is communicated to the staff."[10] Is entrepreneurship for you? The accompanying "Evidence-Based HR" feature may help you answer that.

EVIDENCE-BASED HR

Is Entrepreneurship for You?

Do you have what it takes to be a successful entrepreneur? Psychologists have studied entrepreneurs' personality traits, and produced some useful insights. Based on several studies, researchers say that the entrepreneur's personality characteristics include self-confidence, a high level of motivation, a high energy level, persistence, initiative, resourcefulness, the desire and ability to be self-directed, and a relatively high need for autonomy.[11] Other studies of entrepreneurs focus on the "proactive personality." Proactive behavior reflects the extent to which people ". . . take action to influence their environments."[12] One study found that proactive small business owners did at least seem to have the most innovative companies.[13] Still others study what they call the "dark side" of the entrepreneur. They say that entrepreneurs are driven by less positive traits, such as the need for control, a sense of distrust, the need for applause, and a tendency to defend one's operations.[14]

Still not sure? Additional advice comes from the accumulated wisdom of the U.S. Small Business Administration, which has seen many good, and not so good, entrepreneurs. They suggest answering the following questions if you want to know whether entrepreneurship is for you:

- Are you a self-starter?
- How well do you get along with different personalities?
- How good are you at making decisions?
- Do you have the physical and emotional stamina to run a business (often 16 hours a day, 6 or 7 days per week)?

- How well do you plan and organize?
- Is your drive strong enough to maintain your motivation in the face of relentless opposition, reversals, and burnout?
- How will the business affect your family (which, after all, will have to absorb much of the strain)?

The Entrepreneur's Risky Human Resource Management Situation

All this (relative) lack of attention and expertise means you're facing at least five HR-type risks if you're managing a small business.

- First, small business owners run the risk that their relatively rudimentary human resource practices will put them at a *competitive disadvantage*. We saw that big firms use practices such as Web-based recruiting, computerized testing, and intranet-based employee benefits enrollments to reduce the resources they must spend on them. A small business owner not using tools like these is probably deriving inferior results than (larger) competitors.
- Second, there is a *lack of specialized HR expertise*.[15] In most larger small businesses, there are at most one or two dedicated human resource management people responsible for the full range of HR functions, from recruitment to compensation and safety. This makes it more likely that they'll miss problems in specific areas, such as equal employment law. This may produce legal or other problems.
- Third, the smaller firm is probably not adequately addressing potential *workplace litigation*. Most small business owners are well aware of the threat of employment-related litigation. However, their size and lack of HR expertise makes it unlikely that they'll address the problem. For example, most don't provide adequate (or any) employment discrimination or sexual harassment training.
- Fourth, the small business owner may not be fully complying with *compensation regulations and laws*. We saw that compensation and benefits laws impose many restrictions on employers. These include (as examples) how to pay compensatory time for overtime hours worked, and distinguishing between employees and independent contractors. Violations have serious consequences.
- Fifth, duplication and paperwork leads to inefficiencies and *data entry errors*. For small businesses, many of which don't use human resource information systems, employee data (name, address, marital status, and so on) often appears on multiple human resource management forms. These forms include, for instance, medical enrollment forms, dental enrollment forms, W-4 forms, and so on. Any change requires manually changing all forms. This is not only time-consuming and inefficient, but can precipitate errors.

Why HRM Is Important to Small Businesses

Smart entrepreneurs take these risks to heart. Small firms need all the advantages they can get, and for them effective human resource management is a competitive necessity. Small firms that have effective HR practices do better than those with less effective practices.[16] For example, researchers studied 168 family-owned fast-growth small and medium-size enterprises (SMEs). They concluded that successful high-growth SMEs placed greater importance on training and development, performance appraisals, recruitment packages, maintaining morale, and setting competitive compensation levels than did low-performing firms: "These findings suggest that these human resource activities do in fact have a positive impact on performance [in smaller businesses]."[17]

For many small firms, effective human resource management is also a condition for getting and keeping big customers. Most suppliers (and therefore *their* suppliers) today must comply with international quality standards. This means even smaller businesses must attend to their human resource processes. Thus, to comply with ISO-9000 requirements, large customers "either directly checked for the presence of certain HR policies, or [satisfying the customer] necessitated changes in, for example, [the small vendor's] training and job design."[18]

We'll turn in this chapter to methods entrepreneurs in particular can use to improve their human resource management practices, starting with Internet and government tools.

2 Give at least five specific examples of how you would use the Internet and government tools to support the HR effort in a small business.

USING INTERNET AND GOVERNMENT TOOLS TO SUPPORT THE HR EFFORT

Texas-based City Garage's original hiring process consisted of a paper-and-pencil application and one interview, followed by a hire/don't hire decision.[19] The process ate up valuable management time, and was not particularly effective. City Garage's solution was to purchase the Personality Profile Analysis (PPA) online test from Thomas International USA. Now, after a quick application and background check, likely candidates take the 10-minute, 24-question PPA. City Garage staff then enter the answers into the PPA Software system, and receive test results in less than 2 minutes.

Like City Garage, no small business owner needs to cede the advantage to big competitors when it comes to human resource management. One way to even the terrain is to use Internet-based HR resources, as City Garage has done. Another is to tap into the free resources of the U.S. government. We'll see how in this section.

Complying with Employment Laws

Small business owners spend much of their time tackling employment law–type issues. "What can I ask a job candidate?" "Must I pay this person overtime?" and "Must I report this injury?" are typical questions that may arise.[20] They can quickly find the answers to many such questions online at federal agencies' Web sites like the following.

The DOL The U.S. Department of Labor's "*FirstStep* Employment Law Advisor" (see www.DOL.gov/elaws/firststep) helps small employers determine which laws apply to their business. First, the elaws wizard takes the owner through a series of questions, such as "What is the maximum number of employees your business or organization employs or will employ during the calendar year? (See Figure 18-1.)

Proceeding through the wizard, you'll arrive at a "results" page. This says, "Based on the information you provided in response to the questions in the Advisor, the following employment laws administered by the Department of Labor (DOL) may apply to your business or organization."[21] For a typical small firm, these laws might include the Consumer Credit Protection Act, Employee Polygraph Protection Act, Fair Labor Standards Act, Immigration and Nationality Act, Occupational

City Garage's managers knew they would never implement their firm's growth strategy without changing how they tested and hired employees.

Source: Courtesy of Paul Rapson/ Alamy Images.

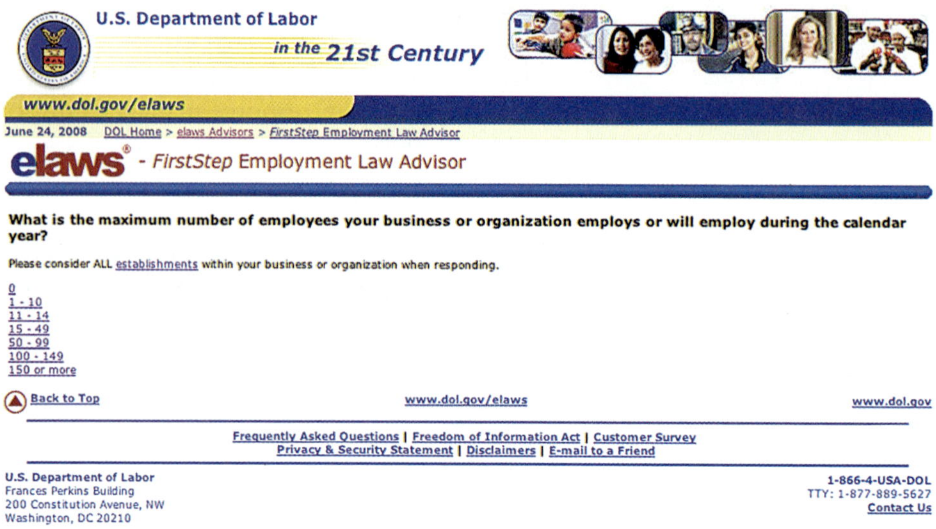

FIGURE 18-1 *FirstStep* Employment Law Advisor

Source: www.dol.gov/elaws/firststep, accessed June 2008.

Safety and Health Act, Uniformed Services Employment and Reemployment Rights Act, and Whistleblower Acts.

A linked DOL site (www.dol.gov/esa/whd/flsa) provides information on the Fair Labor Standards Act (FLSA). It contains several specific "*elaws advisors.*" Each one provides practical guidance on questions such as when to pay overtime. Figure 18-2 presents, from this Web site, a list of elaws advisors.

The EEOC The U.S. Equal Employment Opportunity Commission (EEOC) administers Title VII of the Civil Rights Act of 1964 (Title VII), the Age Discrimination in Employment Act of 1967 (ADEA), Title I of the Americans with Disabilities Act of 1990 (ADA), and the Equal Pay Act of 1963 (EPA). Its Web site (www.EEOC.gov/employers) contains important information regarding EEOC matters, in particular:

- How do I determine whether EEOC laws apply to my size business?
- Who may file a charge of discrimination with the EEOC?
- When can a charge of discrimination be filed?
- Can a small business resolve a charge without undergoing an investigation or facing a lawsuit?

Linked Web pages (see www.EEOC.gov/employers/smallbusinesses.html) provide practical advice. For example, "What should I do when someone files a charge against my company?"

OSHA The DOL's Occupational Safety and Health Administration site (www.OSHA.gov) similarly supplies guidance for small business owners. (See

FIGURE 18-2 Sample DOL elaws Advisors

Source: www.dol.gov/esa/whd/flsa, accessed April 28, 2008.

- The Coverage and Employment Status Advisor helps identify which workers are employees covered by the FLSA.
- The Hours Worked Advisor provides information to help determine which hours spent in work-related activities are considered FLSA "hours worked" and, therefore, must be paid.
- The Overtime Security Advisor helps determine which employees are exempt from the FLSA minimum wage and overtime pay requirements under the Part 541 overtime regulations.
- The Overtime Calculator Advisor computes the amount of overtime pay due in a sample pay period based on information from the user.
- The Child Labor Rules Advisor answers questions about the FLSA's youth employment provisions, including at what age young people can work and the jobs they can perform.
- The Section 14(c) Advisor helps users understand the special minimum wage requirements for workers with disabilities.

FIGURE 18-3 OSHA Web Site

Source: www.osha.gov/dcsp/smallbusiness/index.html.

Figure 18-3). OSHA's site provides, among other things, easy access to the *OSHA Small Business Handbook*. This contains practical information for small business owners, including industry-specific safety and accident checklists.

Employment Planning and Recruiting

Internet resources can make small business owners almost as effective as their large competitors at writing job descriptions and building applicant pools.

As we saw in Chapter 4 (Recruiting), the Department of Labor's O*NET (http://online.onetcenter.org) illustrates this well. Its online wizard enables business owners to quickly create accurate and professional job descriptions and job specifications.

Web-Based Recruiting

Small business owners can use the online recruiting tools we discussed in Chapter 4. You'll find a full description there, but, for example, most employers (including small ones) post positions on Internet job boards such as Careerbuilder.com and Monster.com, on the sites of professional associations (such as the American Institute of Chemical Engineers), or on the sites of local newspapers.

For businesses with their own company Web sites, the dot-jobs domain can be effective. As explained in Chapter 4, this gives job seekers a simple, one-click way for finding jobs at the employers who registered at dot-jobs. (Employers register at www.goto.jobs.) For example, applicants seeking a job at Shula's Steak Houses can go to www.shula.jobs.

Employment Selection

For the small business, one or two hiring mistakes could wreak havoc. A formal testing program, like the one at City Garage, is thus advisable.

Some tests are so easy to use they are particularly good for smaller firms. One is the *Wonderlic Personnel Test*, which measures general mental ability. With questions somewhat similar to the SAT, it takes less than 15 minutes to administer the 4-page booklet. The tester reads the instructions, and then keeps time as the candidate works through the 50 problems. The tester scores the test by totaling the number of correct answers. Comparing the person's score with the minimum scores recommended for various occupations shows whether the person achieved the minimally acceptable score for the type of job in question.

The *Predictive Index* is another example. It measures work-related personality traits, drives, and behaviors—in particular dominance, extroversion, patience, and blame avoidance—on a 2-sided sheet. A template makes scoring simple. The Predictive Index program includes 15 standard benchmark personality patterns. For example, there is the "social interest" pattern, for a person who is generally unselfish, congenial, persuasive, patient, and unassuming. This person would be good with people and a good personnel interviewer, for instance.

Wonderlic Example Several vendors, including both Wonderlic and Praendex (which publishes the Predictive Index) offer online applicant compilation and screening services. Wonderlic's service (which costs about $8,500 per year for a firm with, say, 35 employees) provides job analyses for the employer's jobs. Wonderlic then provides a Web site that the small business applicants log into to take one or several selection tests (including the Wonderlic Personnel Test). Figure 18-4 shows the report for an applicant sample.

Online arrangements like these have many benefits, beyond just saving the time the owners' employees might have to spend testing employees. For example, because it's available 24/7, prospective candidates can log in and apply anytime, wherever they are. That means a larger potential pool of applicants, and hopefully more likelihood of getting an outstanding employee.

Employment Training

Although small companies can't compete with the training resources of giants like General Electric, Internet training can provide, at a relatively low cost, the sorts of professional employee training that was formerly beyond most small employers' reach.

FIGURE 18-4 Wonderlic Personnel Test: Part of a Sample Report

Source: Wonderlic (www.wonderlic.com).

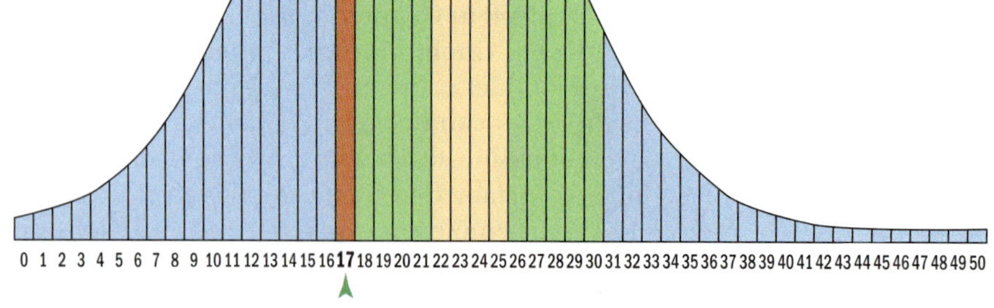

Score Interpretation

Job Fit: Test takers who score in this range do not meet the cognitive ability requirements identified for this job. The complexity present within this position may make it difficult for these individuals to meet minimum standards for job performance.

Training Potential: This test taker is likely to receive maximum benefit from training that follows a programmed or mastery approach to learning. Given enough time, this individual may have the ability to learn a limited number of lengthy, routine procedures. Allow for sufficient time with hands-on-training before requiring this individual to work independently.

Private Vendors The small business owner can tap hundreds of suppliers of prepackaged training solutions. These range from self-study programs from the American Management Association (www.amanet.org) and SHRM (www.shrm.org) to specialized programs (for example, trade journals like EHS Today (for environment, health, and safety managers), (www.ehs.com) that contain information on specialized prepackaged training program suppliers (in this case, for occupational safety and health). For example, the employer might arrange with one of these suppliers, www.puresafety.com, to have its employees take occupational safety courses.

SkillSoft is another example (http://skillsoft.com/catalog/default.asp). Its offerings include software development, business strategy and operations, professional effectiveness, and desktop computer skills. As an example, the course "Interviewing Effectively" is aimed at managers, team leaders, and human resource professionals. About 2 1/2 hours long, it shows trainees how to use behavioral questioning to interview candidates.[22]

The buyer's guide from the American Society of Training and Development (click on Find a Supplier at http://www.astd.org/) is a good place to start to find a vendor.

The SBA The federal government's Small Business Administration (www.SBA.gov/training) provides a virtual campus that offers online courses, workshops, publications, and learning tools aimed toward supporting entrepreneurs.[23] For example, the small business owner can link to "Writing Effective Job Descriptions," "Employees versus Contractors: What's the Difference?" and "The Interview Process: How to Select the Right Person." The SBA also has a growing list of online training courses (www.SBA.gov/services/training/onlinecourses/index.html). It includes online courses in areas such as developing a business plan (see Figure 18-5).

NAM The National Association of Manufacturers (NAM) is the largest industrial trade organization in the United States. It represents about 14,000 member manufacturers, including 10,000 small and midsized companies.

NAM's Virtual University (www.namvu.com) helps employees maintain and upgrade their work skills and continue their professional development. It offers almost 650 courses.[24] There are no long-term contracts to sign. Employers simply pay about $10–$30 per course taken by each employee. The catalog includes OSHA, quality, and technical training as well as courses in areas like business and finance, personal development, and customer service.

Employment Appraisal and Compensation

We've seen that even small employers now have easy access to computerized and online appraisal and compensation services.

For example, small employers can contract with vendors that enable them to do performance appraisals online. Thus, Employee Appraiser, an employee appraisal software package from Successfactors, Inc., (www.employeeappraiser.com/index.php) presents a menu of more than a dozen evaluation dimensions, including dependability, initiative, communication, decision making, leadership, judgment, and planning and productivity.[25] Within each dimension are various performance factors, again in menu form. The eAppraisal system from Halogen Software is another example.[26]

Similarly, lack of easy access to salary surveys once made it difficult and time-consuming for smaller businesses to fine-tune their pay scales. Today, sites like www.salary.com make it easy to determine local pay rates.

Employment Safety and Health

Safety is an important issue among small employers. One European study found that the majority of workplace accidents and serious workplace accidents occur in firms with fewer than 50 employees.[27] In addition to the handbooks at osha.gov, OSHA also provides several free services for small employers.

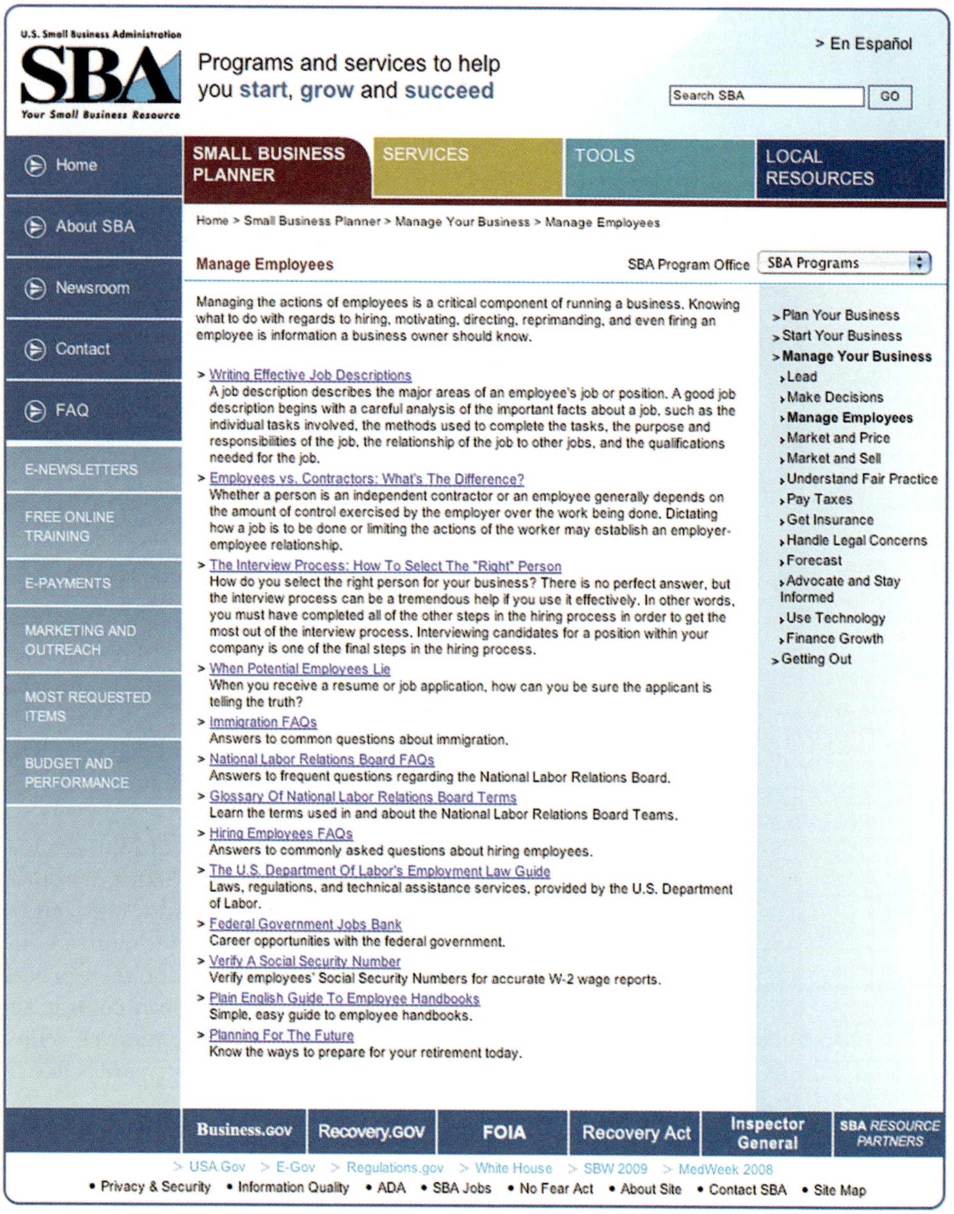

FIGURE 18-5 Part of Small Business Administration's Virtual Campus for Small Business Training

OSHA Consultation Without human resource managers or safety departments, small businesses often don't know where to turn for advice on promoting employee safety. Many even have the (inaccurate) notion that the Occupational Safety and Health Act doesn't cover small firms.[28]

OSHA provides free on-site safety and health services for small businesses. This service uses safety experts from state governments who provide consultations, usually at the employer's workplace.

For example, when Jan Anderson, president of her own steel installation company in Colorado, realized her workers' compensation costs were higher than her payroll, she knew she had to do something. OSHA helped draft new safety systems, created educational materials, and provided inspections that were more cooperative than adversarial. As a result, says Anderson, "Our workers' compensation costs have decreased significantly, we have had no accidents, and there is an awareness that we take safety seriously."[29]

OSHA Sharp The OSHA Sharp program is a certification process through which OSHA certifies that small employers have achieved commendable levels of safety awareness. Employers request a consultation and visit, and undergo a complete hazard identification survey. The employer agrees to correct all hazards identified, and to implement and maintain a safety and health management system that, at a minimum, addresses OSHA's safety and health program management guidelines. In addition to producing a certifiably safe workplace, OSHA's on-site project manager may recommend that OSHA exempt the Sharp employer for 2 years from scheduled inspections.

3 Answer the question, "Why are *familiarity, flexibility,* and *informality* important tools that entrepreneurs can use to improve human resource management practices in their small businesses?"

LEVERAGING SMALL SIZE: FAMILIARITY, FLEXIBILITY, INFORMALITY, AND HRM

Small businesses need to capitalize on their strengths, so in dealing with employees they should capitalize on their smallness. Smallness should translate into personal *familiarity* with each employee's strengths, needs, and family situation. And it should translate into the luxury of being able to be relatively *flexible* and *informal* in the human resource management policies and practices the company follows. As we said earlier, smaller businesses often need to adapt quickly to environmental realities like competitive challenges. This often means that entrepreneurs tend to conduct matters such as raises, appraisals, and time off "on an informal, reactive basis with a short time horizon."[30] Flexibility is often key.

Flexibility in Benefits and Rewards

For example, the Family and Work Institute surveyed the benefits practices of about 1,000 small and large companies. They examined benefits such as flexible work, child-care assistance, and health care.[31] Not surprisingly, they found that large firms offer more *extensive* benefits packages than do smaller ones. However, many small firms seemed to overcome their bigger competitors by offering more flexibility.

A Culture of Flexibility Basically the study found that small companies, because of the familiarity that comes from owners personally interacting with the employees each day, did a better job of fostering a "culture of flexibility." Most importantly, "supervisors are more supportive and understanding when work/life issues emerge."[32] Ward's Furniture in Long Beach, California, exemplifies this. Many of Ward's 17 employees have been with the firm for 10 to 20 years. Brad Ward, an owner, attributes this in part to his firm's willingness to adapt to its workers' needs. For example, workers can share job responsibilities, and work part-time from home.

At Ward Furniture, workers can share job responsibilities and work part-time from home.

Source: Courtesy of PhotoEdit Inc.

Work–Life Benefits The point is that even without the deep pockets of larger firms, small firms can offer employees work–life benefits that large employers usually can't match. Here are some examples:[33]

- **Extra time off.** For example, some small business owners offer Friday afternoons off in the summer.
- **Compressed workweeks.** For example, in the summer, offer compressed workweeks that allow employees to take longer weekends.
- **Bonuses at critical times.** Small business owners are more likely to know what's happening in the lives of their employees. They often use this knowledge to provide special bonuses, for instance, if an employee has a new baby.
- **Flexibility.** Small businesses should excel at helping employees deal with the demands of personal issues like child care and eldercare. For example "if an employee is having a personal problem, help him or her create a work schedule that allows the person to solve problems without feeling like they're going to be in trouble."[34]
- **Sensitivity to employees' strengths and weaknesses.** The relative intimacy of the small business should enable the owner to be better attuned to his or her employees' strengths, weaknesses, and aspirations. Therefore, be attentive about what each of your employees does. Ask them which jobs they feel most comfortable doing, and give them an opportunity to train for and move into the jobs they desire.
- **Help them better themselves.** For example, pay employees to take a class to help them develop their job skills.
- **Feed them.** Particularly after a difficult workweek or when some milestone (like a big sale) occurs, provide free meals, perhaps by taking your employees to lunch.
- **Make them feel like owners.** "Job enrichment" is relatively easy to achieve in small firms. For example, give your employees input into major decisions, let them work directly with clients, get them client feedback, share company performance data with them, and let them share in the company's financial success.
- **Make sure they have what they need to do their jobs.** Having highly motivated employees is only half the challenge. Also ensure that they have the tools they need to do their jobs—for instance, the necessary training, procedures, and computers.[35]

Recognition Studies show that recognition can often be as powerful as financial rewards. The relatively personal nature of small business interactions makes it both easier and more important to recognize employees. We saw in Chapter 12 (Incentives) that you can use numerous *recognition rewards* daily. A short list would include:[36]

- Challenging work assignments
- More of preferred task
- Job rotation
- Encouragement of learning and continuous improvement
- Expression of appreciation in front of others
- Note of thanks
- Special commendation
- Bigger office or cubicle

Simple Retirement Benefits Access to retirement benefits is more prevalent in large firms than small ones. Roughly 75% of large firms offer such benefits, while about 35% of small ones do.[37]

There are several straightforward ways that small firms can provide retirement plans for their employees. The *Pension Protection Act of 2006* contains a provision for a new type of retirement benefit that combines traditional defined benefit and 401(k) plans.[38] Only available to employers with fewer than 500 employees, this provision exempts employers from the complex pension rules large employers must adhere to. With this new benefit, the employees get a retirement plan that blends a defined pension set by the plan, plus returns on the part of the investment that employee-participants contributed.[39]

Probably the easiest way for small businesses to provide retirement benefits is through a *SIMPLE IRA plan*. With the SIMPLE (for *Savings Incentive Match Plan for Employees*) IRA, employers must (and employees may) make contributions to traditional employee IRAs. These plans are for employers or small businesses with 100 or fewer employees and no other type of retirement plan.

SIMPLE IRAs have many advantages—starting with simplicity. The owner need only contact an eligible financial institution and fill out several IRS forms. The IRS needs to have previously approved the financial institution. However, banks, mutual funds, and insurance companies that issue annuity contracts are generally eligible.[40] The plan has very low administrative costs. Employer contributions are tax deductible. With a SIMPLE IRA, each employee is always 100% vested.[41]

Under these plans, the employer *must* contribute and employees *may* contribute. A typical employer contribution might match employee contributions dollar for dollar up to 3% of pay. The financial institution usually handles the IRS paperwork and reporting.

Simple, Informal Employee Selection Procedures

We saw earlier that small business managers could easily use Internet-based recruitment and selection tools to help level the recruitment/selection terrain. (For example, Wonderlic's service includes a Web site that a small firm's applicants can use to take prescreening tests.) But, in general, small firms tend to rely on more informal employee selection and recruitment practices (like employee referrals and unstructured interviews) than do large firms.[42] Large firms simply have more time, resources, and specialized support to invest in formal recruiting and testing programs.

However, there are low-tech and costless things a small business can do to improve its selection process. We discussed several in Chapters 6 (Selection) and 7 (Interviewing). One was "How to Conduct an Effective Interview" in Chapter 7. Another is the work sampling test.

Work Sampling Tests

What should you do if you are, say, trying to hire a marketing manager, and want a simple but more formal way to screen your job applicants?

Devising a *work sampling test* is one simple solution. A work sampling test means having the candidates perform actual samples of the job in question. Such tests have obvious face validity (they should clearly measure actual job duties) and are easy to devise.

The process is simple. Break down the job's main duties into component tasks. Then have the candidate complete a sample task. For example, for the marketing manager position, ask the candidate to spend an hour designing an ad, or to spend a half-hour writing out a marketing research program for a hypothetical product.

Flexibility in Training

Small companies also typically take a more informal approach to training and development. For example, one study of 191 small and 201 large firms in Europe found that smaller firms were much more informal in their approaches to training and development.[43] Many of the small firms didn't systematically monitor their managers' skill needs, and fewer than 50% (as opposed to 70% of large firms) had management career development programs. The smaller firms also tended to focus any management development training on learning specific firm-related competencies (such as how to sell the firm's products). They generally downplayed developing longer-term management skills.[44] They did so due to a reluctance to invest too much in managers who may then leave.

Limited resources or not, small businesses must have training procedures. Having high-potential employees doesn't guarantee they'll succeed. Instead, they must know what you want them to do and how you want them to do it. If they don't, they will improvise or do nothing productive at all. We discussed one less complex but still effective *4-step training process* in Chapter 8 (Training).

Informal Training Methods

Training expert Stephen Covey says small businesses can do many things to provide job-related personal improvement without actually establishing expensive formal training programs. His suggestions include:[45]

- Offer to cover the tuition for special classes.
- Identify online training opportunities.
- Provide a library of tapes and DVDs for systematic, disciplined learning during commute times.
- Encourage the sharing of best practices among associates.
- When possible, send people to special seminars and association meetings for learning and networking.
- Create a learning ethic by having everyone teach each other what they are learning.

Fairness and the Family Business

Most small businesses are family businesses, in that the owner and one or more managers (and possibly employees) are family members.

Being a nonfamily employee here isn't always easy. They sometimes feel like outsiders. Furthermore, treating inequitably family and nonfamily employees can undermine perceptions of fairness, as well as morale. If so, as one writer puts it, "It's a sure bet that their lower morale and simmering resentments are having a negative effect on your operations and sapping your profits."[46] Reducing such "fairness" problems involves several steps. These include the following:[47]

- **Set the ground rules.** One family business consultant says,

  > "During the hiring process the [management] applicant should be informed as to whether they will be essentially placeholders, or whether there will be some potential for promotion. The important thing is to make the expectations clear, including in matters such as the level of authority and decision-making they can expect to attain in the company."[48]

- **Treat people fairly.** Most employees in a family business understand that they're not going to be treated exactly the same as family members. However, they do expect you to treat them fairly. In part, this means working hard to avoid "any appearance that family members are benefiting unfairly from the sacrifice of others."[49] That's why family members in many family businesses avoid ostentatious purchases like expensive cars. (Several years ago, a book titled *The Millionaire Next Door* explained, among other things, that some small business owners were so frugal that their neighbors didn't realize they were millionaires.)
- **Confront family issues.** Discord and tension among family members at work distracts and demoralizes other employees. Family members must therefore confront and work out their differences.
- **Erase privilege.** Family members "should avoid any behavior that would lead people to the conclusion that they are demanding special treatment in terms of assignments or responsibilities."[50] Family employees should come in earlier, work harder, and stay later than other employees do. Make it clear that family members earned their promotions.

Building Communications

Effective communications are important for any manager, but especially for those managing small businesses. With a thousand or more employees, one or two disgruntled employees who feel you're not treating them fairly may get lost in the crowd. But in a small restaurant or retail shop, one or two disgruntled employees can destroy the businesses' quality service. Yet small business owners generally don't have the means to implement expensive communications programs. That's why simple programs, like the following ones, are important.

Online Reporting Seeking to shield their 11 IHOP restaurants from the industry's sky-high turnover rates, the owners hit on a solution. They dramatically reduced turnover with a new online system. It lets new employees anonymously report their opinions about the hiring process.[51] Feedback from that simple communication tool enabled them to recalibrate their firm's training and orientation methods, and reduce turnover by about a third.

Newsletter In Bonita Springs, Florida, Mel's Gourmet Diner keeps employees informed with a quarterly newsletter. It distributes copies at the chain's 10 locations, but also posts it on the company Web site, and plans to translate it into Spanish. "It sounds like a cliché, but our people are the keys to our success," says the owner. "We want to make sure we give them all the information and tools they need."[52]

Online Each time employees of Tampa, Florida–based Let's Eat go to one of the firm's computers to input a guest's order, they can quickly review the chain's menu changes, special promotions, and mandatory employee meetings.[53]

The Huddle Sea Island Shrimp House in San Antonio, Texas, keeps employees in its seven restaurants communicating with what it calls "cascading huddles." As in football parlance, the huddles are very quick meetings. At 9 A.M. top management meets in the first of the day's "huddles." The next huddle is a conference call with store managers. Then, store managers meet with hourly employees at each location before the restaurants open, to make sure the news of the day gets communicated. "It's all about alignment and good, timely communications," says the company. "Any issues on that day that needed to be communicated would happen in that huddles sequence."[54]

4 Explain what professional employers' organizations are and how entrepreneurs can use them.

USING PROFESSIONAL EMPLOYER ORGANIZATIONS

As we first explained in Chapter 13 (Benefits), the 40 employees at First Weigh Manufacturing in Sanford, Florida, don't work for a giant company, but they get employee benefits and services as if they do. That's because Tom Strasse, First Weigh's owner, signed with ADP Total Source, a *professional employer organization* that now handles all First Weigh's HR processes.[55]

At the end of the day, many small business owners, like Tom Strasse, understandably look at all the issues involved with managing personnel, and decide to outsource all or most of their human resource functions to outside vendors (generally called *professional employer organizations* (PEOs), *human resource outsourcers* (HROs), or sometimes *employee* or *staff leasing firms*). As we discussed briefly in Chapter 13 (Benefits), many employers turn to these mostly to get improved employee benefits. But there are other reasons.

How Do PEOs Work?

These vendors range from payroll companies to those that handle all an employer's human resource management requirements.[56] At a minimum these firms take over the employer's payroll tasks.[57] Usually, however, PEOs assume most of the employer's human resources chores.

PEOs have several characteristics. By transferring the client firm's employees to the PEO's payroll, PEOs become co-employers of record for the employer's employees. That enables the PEO to fold the client's employees into the PEOs' insurance and benefits program, usually at a lower cost. The PEO usually handles employee-related activities such as recruiting, hiring (with client firms' supervisors' approvals), and payroll and taxes (Social Security payments, unemployment insurance, and so on). Most PEOs focus on employers with less than 100 employees, and charge fees of 2% to 4% of a company's payroll. In contrast, HROs usually handle these functions on an "administrative services only"—they're your "HR office," but your employees still work for you.[58]

Why Use a PEO?

Employers turn to PEOs for several reasons:

Lack of Specialized HR Support Up to 100 or so employees, small firms typically have no dedicated HR managers, and even larger ones may have few specialists. That means the owner has all or most of the human resource management burden on his or her shoulders.

Paperwork The Small Business Administration estimates that small business owners spend up to 25% of their time on personnel-related paperwork. This includes background checks, benefits sign-ups, and so on.[59] The association that represents employee leasing firms estimates that the average cost of regulations, paperwork, and tax compliance for smaller firms is about $5,000 per employee per year.[60] The PEO assumes responsibility for all or most of this. Many small business owners therefore figure that what they save on not managing their own human resource activities pays for the employee leasing firm's fees. For instance, when First Weigh's Strasse has a question about employee legal issues, he just calls his ADP representative.

Liability Staying in compliance with pension plan rules, Title VII, OSHA, COBRA, the Fair Labor Standards Act, and other personnel-related laws can be distracting. Legally, PEOs generally "contractually share liability with clients and have a vested interest in preventing workplace injuries and employee lawsuits."[61] The PEO should thus help ensure the small business fulfills all its personnel-related legal responsibilities. The issues that Peter McCann and his embroidery company Ideal Images faced help illustrate the liability issue. His 27-employee firm was studiously nondiscriminatory. However, a former employee still filed a charge of racial discrimination. The investigation absorbed several tense weeks of McCann's time. Between that, and the fact that he was starting to find his chores "nearly all-consuming," he turned to Alliance Group, a PEO.[62]

Benefits We saw that insurance and benefits are often the big PEO attraction. Getting health and other insurance is a problem for smaller firms. First Weigh Manufacturing's health insurance carrier dropped the firm after its first 2 years, and Strasse had to scramble to find a new carrier—which he did, with premiums that were 30% higher.

That's where First Weigh's leasing firm comes in. Remember that the leasing firm is the legal employer of your employees. The employees therefore are absorbed into a much larger insurable group, along with other employers' former employees. As a result, a small business owner may be able to get insurance (as well as benefits like 401(k)) for its people that it couldn't otherwise.[63]

Performance Last, but not least, the professionalism that the PEO brings to recruiting, screening, training, compensating, and maintaining employee safety and welfare will hopefully translate into improved employee and business results.

Caveats

Remember that using vendors like these may sound too good to be true, and often is. "If your PEO is poorly managed, or goes bankrupt, you could find out with an office full of uninsured workers."[64] Many employers view their human resource management processes as a strategic advantage, and aren't inclined to turn over strategy-sensitive tasks like screening and training to third-party firms. Many employers aren't comfortable letting a third party become the legal employer of their employees.[65]

"Problem PEOs" often unknowingly send several signals. One is *lax due diligence.* They share liability with the employer, and so *should* question you extensively about your firm's workplace safety and human resource policies and practices.[66] Another is a *recent name change.* Search the Internet and Better Business Bureaus to see if there's been a recent name change, a possible signal of past problems. Finally, it's unlikely that the employer will gain more than a modest savings (if any) by collaborating with a PEO (relative to overseeing its own HR). Therefore, be suspect of anyone *promising you substantial savings.*

Guidelines for Finding and Working with PEOs

Small business managers need to choose and manage the PEO relationship carefully. Suggestions for doing so follow.

Conduct a needs analysis. Know ahead of time exactly what human resource and risk management concerns your company wants to address.

Review the services of all PEO firms you're considering. Determine which can meet all your requirements.

Determine if the PEO is accredited. There is no rating system for PEOs. However, the Employer Services Assurance Corporation of Little Rock, Arkansas (www.Esacorp.org), imposes higher financial, auditing, and operating standards on its members.[67] Also check the Web site of the National Association of Professional Employer Organizations (www.NAPEO.org).[68]

Check the provider's bank, credit, and professional *references.* Make sure to demand specifics on things like insurance providers and creditors.

Understand how the *employee benefits are funded.* Is it fully insured or partially self-funded? Who is the third-party administrator or carrier? Confirm the participating employers will receive first-day coverage.

See if the provider contract assumes the employment law *compliance liabilities in the applicable states.*

Review the service agreement carefully. Are the respective parties' responsibilities and liabilities clearly delineated?[69]

Investigate *how long the PEO has been in business.* The vendor should show a history of staying power to show that it's well-managed.

Check out the prospective PEO's staff. Do they seem to have the depth and expertise to deliver on its promises?

Ask *how will the firm deliver its services.* In person? By phone? Via the Web?

Ask about *upfront fees* and how these are determined.

Periodically get proof that payroll taxes and insurance premiums are being paid properly and that any legal issues are handled correctly.[70]

5 Describe how HR systems traditionally evolve in a small business and give examples of how small businesses can use human resource management information systems.

MANAGING HR SYSTEMS, PROCEDURES, AND PAPERWORK

Introduction

Consider the paperwork required to run a 5-person retail shop. Just to start with, recruiting and hiring an employee might require a help wanted advertising listing, an employment application, interviewing checklist, various verifications—of education, and immigration status, for instance—and a telephone reference checklist. You then might need an employment agreement, confidentiality and noncompete agreements, and an employer indemnity agreement. To process that new employee, you might need an employee background verification, new-employee checklist, and forms for withholding taxes and new employee data. And to keep track of the employee once on board, you'd need—just to start—a personnel data sheet, daily and weekly time records, an hourly employee's weekly time sheet, and an expense report. Then there are the performance appraisal forms, a disciplinary notice, a job description, an employee checkout record, separation notice, and employment reference response.

In this last section, we'll see that the preceding list barely scratches the surface of the policies, procedures, and paperwork you'll need to run the human resource management part of your business. Perhaps with just one or two employees you could keep track of everything in your head, or just write a separate memo for each HR action, and place it in a manila folder for each worker. But with more than a few employees, you'll need to create a human resource system comprised of standardized forms. Then, as your company grows, you'll probably want to computerize various parts of the HR system—payroll, or appraising, for instance—to remain competitive. We'll cover manual and computerized HR systems in this final section.

Basic Components of Manual HR Systems

Very small employers (say, with 10 employees or less) will probably start with a manual human resource management system. From a practical point of view, this generally means obtaining and organizing a set of standardized personnel forms covering each important aspect of the HR—recruitment, selection, training, appraisal, compensation, safety process—as well as some means for organizing all this information for each of your employees.

Basic Forms

The number of forms you could conceivably need even for a small firm is quite large. This is illustrated by the menu of forms shown in Table 18-1, which is adapted from the table of contents of a compilation of HR agreements and forms.[71] A reasonable way to obtain the basic component forms of a manual HR system is to start with a *compilation of forms book* like that one. The forms you want can then be adapted for your particular situation. Office supply stores (such as Office Depot and Staples) also sell packages of personnel forms. For example, Office Depot sells packages of individual personnel forms as well as a "Human Resource Kit" containing 10 copies of each of the following: Application, Employment Interview, Reference Check, Employee Record, Performance Evaluation, Warning Notice, Exit Interview, and Vacation Request, plus a Lawsuit-Prevention Guide.[72] Also available (and highly recommended) is a package of Employee Record Folders. Use the folders to maintain a file on each individual employee; on the outside of the pocket is printed a form for recording information such as name, start date, company benefits, and so on.

Sources of Forms

Several direct-mail catalog companies similarly offer a variety of HR materials. For example, HRdirect (100 Enterprise Place, Dover, DE, 19901, phone: 1-800-346-1231, www.hrdirect.com) offers packages of personnel forms. These include, for instance, Short- and Long-Form Employee Applications, Applicant Interviews, Employee Performance Reviews, Job Descriptions, Exit Interviews, and Absentee Calendars and Reports. There are also various legal-compliance forms, including standardized Harassment Policy and FMLA Notice forms, as well as posters (for instance, covering legally required postings for matters such as the Americans with Disabilities Act and Occupational Safety and Health Act) available.

G. Neil Company of Sunrise, Florida (phone: 1-800-999-9111, www.gneil.com), is another direct-mail personnel materials source. In addition to a complete line of personnel forms, documents, and posters, it also carries manual systems for matters like attendance history, job analyses, and for tracking vacation requests and safety records. They have a complete HR "start-up" kit containing 25 copies of each of the basic components of a manual HR system. These include Long Form Application

TABLE 18-1 Some Important Employment Forms

New Employee Forms	Current Employee Forms	Employee Separation Forms
Application	Employee Status Change Request	Retirement Checklist
New Employee Checklist	Employee Record	Termination Checklist
Employment Interview	Performance Evaluation	COBRA Acknowldgment
Reference Check	Warning Notice	Unemployment Claim
Telephone Reference Report	Vacation Request	Employee Exit Interview
Employee Manual Acknowledgment	Probation Notice	
Employment Agreement	Job Description	
Employee Application Disclaimer	Direct Deposit Acknowledgment	
Probationary Evaluation	Absence Report	
	Disciplinary Notice	
	Employee Secrecy Agreement	
	Grievance Form	
	Expense Report	
	401(k)Choices Acknowledgment	
	Injury Report	

for Employment, Attendance History, Performance Appraisal, Payroll/Status Change Notice, Absence Report, and Vacation Request & Approval, all organized in a file box.

Automating Individual HR Tasks

As the small business grows, it becomes increasingly unwieldy and uncompetitive to rely on manual HR systems. For a company with 40 or 50 employees or more, the amount of management time devoted to things like attendance history and performance appraisals can multiply into weeks. It is therefore at about this point that most small- to medium-sized firms begin computerizing individual human resource management tasks.

Packaged Systems Here again there are a variety of resources available. For example, at the Web site for the International Association for Human Resource Information Management (www.ihrim.org), you'll find, within the Buyers Guide tab, a categorical list of HR software vendors.[73] These firms provide software solutions for virtually all personnel tasks, ranging from benefits management to compensation, compliance, employee relations, payroll, and time and attendance systems.

The G. Neil Company sells software packages for controlling attendance, employee record keeping, writing job descriptions, writing employee handbooks, and conducting computerized employee appraisals. HRdirect offers software for writing employee policy manuals, writing performance reviews, creating job descriptions, tracking attendance and hours worked for each employee, employee scheduling, writing organizational charts, managing payroll, conducting employee surveys, scheduling and tracking employee training activities, and managing OSHA compliance. *People Manager* maintains employee records (including name, address, marital status, number of dependents, emergency contact and phone numbers, hire date, and job history). It also enables management to produce quickly 30 standard reports on matters such as attendance, benefits, and ethnic information.

As the company grows, the owner will probably decide to transition to an integrated human resource management system; we turn to this next.

Human Resource Management Information Systems (HRIS)

Companies need information systems to get their work done. For example, the sales team needs some way to tell accounting to bill a customer, and to tell production to fill the order. The term *information system* refers to the interrelated people, data, technology, and organizational procedures a company uses to collect, process, store, and disseminate information. Information systems may or may not be computerized. However they often are. All the HR paperwork systems we described—for collecting information on new employees, and for keeping track of their appraisals, benefits, and training, for instance—are information systems, although they're not computerized. Of course, as the company grows, it makes sense to computerize its information systems.

Levels of Information Systems

Companies tend to install information systems from the bottom up, level by organizational level. *Transaction-processing systems* often come first; they provide the company's managers and accountants with detailed information about short-term, daily activities, such as accounts payables, tax liabilities, and order status.

Management information systems (MIS) are a level up; they help managers make better decisions by producing standardized, summarized reports on a regular basis. For example, an MIS may take raw data (say, on sales by location), and show the sales manager the trend of sales for the past 2 weeks; or show the production manager a graph of weekly inventory levels; or show the CEO a report summarizing the company's revenues, expenses, and profits for the quarter.

One more level up, *executive support systems* provide top managers with information for making decisions on matters such as 5-year plans. For example, the CEO of Ford might use his executive support system to put the sales of each of Ford's various cars last month into context, by comparing them with sales of competing brands.

As companies grow, they also often turn to integrated human resource information systems (HRIS). We can define an *HRIS* as interrelated components working together to collect, process, store, and disseminate information to support decision making, coordination, control, analysis, and visualization of an organization's human resource management activities.[74] There are several reasons for installing an HRIS. The first is improved transaction processing.

Improved Transaction Processing

The day-to-day minutiae of maintaining and updating employee records takes an enormous amount of time. One study found that 71% of HR employees' time was devoted to transactional tasks like checking leave balances, maintaining address records, and monitoring employee benefits distributions.[75] HRIS packages substitute powerful computerized processing for a wide range of the firm's HR transactions. For example, they automatically update an employee's name on all forms when the employee gets married.

Online Self-Processing

HR information systems make it possible (or easier) to make the company's employees part of the HRIS. For example, at Provident Bank, an HR compensation system called Benelogic lets the bank's employees self-enroll in all their desired benefits programs over the Internet at a secure site. It also "support[s] employees' quest for 'what if' information relating to, for example, the impact on their take-home pay of various benefits options, W-4 changes, insurance coverage, retirement planning and more."[76] That's all work that HR employees would previously have had to do for Provident's employees.

Improved Reporting Capability Because the HRIS integrates numerous individual HR tasks (training records, appraisals, employee personal data, and so on), installing an HRIS boosts HR's reporting capabilities. In practice, the variety of reports possible is limited only by the manager's imagination. For a start, for instance, reports might be available (company-wide and by department) for health care cost per employee, pay and benefits as a percent of operating expense, cost per hire, costs of training, volunteer turnover rates, turnover costs, time to fill jobs, and return on human capital invested (in terms of training and education fees, for instance).

HR System Integration Because the HRIS' software components (record keeping, payroll, appraisal, and so forth) are integrated (linked together), the employer can dramatically reengineer its HR function. The system PeopleSoft (now part of Oracle Corporation) installed in its own offices provides an illustration. For example, its HRIS routes promotions, salary increases, transfers, and other forms through the organization to the proper managers for approval. As one person signs off, it's routed to the next. If anyone forgets to process a document, a smart agent issues a reminder until the task is completed. That eliminates the need for all the clerks who previously did those jobs.

HRIS Vendors Many firms today offer HRIS packages. The Web site for the International Association for Human Resource Information Management (www.ihrim.org), for instance, lists Automatic Data Processing, Inc., Business Information Technology, Inc., Human Resource Microsystems, Lawson Software, Oracle Corporation, SAP America, Inc., and about 25 other firms as HRIS vendors.

HR and Intranets We've seen that employers are creating intranet-based HR information systems. For example, LG&E Energy Corporation uses its intranet for benefits communication. Employees can access the benefits home page and (among other things) review the company's 401(k) plan investment options, get answers to frequently asked questions about the company's medical and dental plans, and report changes in family status. Other uses for human resource intranets include, for instance, job postings, applicant tracking, training registration, providing electronic pay stubs, electronic employee handbooks, and to let employees update their personal profiles and access their 401(k) accounts.

REVIEW

CHAPTER SECTION SUMMARIES

1. Many people reading this book will work for or own their own small businesses, so it's important to understand **the small business challenge**. In terms of managing human resources, small businesses are different in terms of size (not enough employees for a dedicated HR manager), priorities (sales come first), informality, and the nature of the entrepreneur. Without effective human resource management, small business owners run the risk that they'll be at a competitive disadvantage or that without the necessary HR expertise they may commit mistakes that lead to litigation.
2. Being small, small businesses can particularly capitalize on freely available **Internet and government tools to support their HR efforts**. For example, you can use Department of Labor elaws advisers to answer overtime questions, the EEOC's Web sites for answers on questions like "How can we resolve the charge?" and the Department of Labor's OSHA Web site to review, for instance, their small business handbook. To better compete, small business owners can also use online recruiting tools like those we discussed in Chapter 5 and training programs available online from companies such as puresafety.com, and from the SBA and National Association of Manufacturers.
3. Small businesses need to capitalize on their strengths, and in this case, it means capitalizing on **familiarity, flexibility, and informality**. For example, in many respects it's easier for small businesses to be flexible about extra time off, compressed workweeks, and job enrichment. They can also use relatively informal but still effective employee selection procedures such as the work sampling test we discussed.

Informal training methods include online training opportunities, encouraging the sharing of best practices among associates, and sending employees to seminars. Because small businesses are often family businesses, it's important to make sure that nonfamily members are treated fairly, something that requires setting ground rules (for instance, regarding promotions), treating employees fairly, dealing with family discord and issues, and erasing privilege. Small businesses can also use simple methods for improving communications, for instance, online newsletters.

4. After reviewing all the challenges of managing human resources, many small business owners turn to **using professional employer organizations.** Also called *human resource outsourcers*, or *employee or staff leasing firms*, these firms generally transfer the client firm's employees to the PEO's own payroll and thus become the employer of record for the employer's employees. Reasons to turn to the PEOs include a lack of specialized HR support, a desire to reduce the paperwork burden, avoiding HR-related liability, obtaining better benefits for employees, and providing improved employee and business results.
5. Small business managers need to understand how their **HR systems, procedures, and paperwork** will evolve. At first, there may be a simple manual human resource management system, for instance, with employee records compiled on forms from office supply companies and maintained in manual files. The employer then may purchase one or more packaged systems for automating individual HR tasks, for instance, such as applicant tracking and performance appraisal. As companies grow, they will look to integrate the separate systems with a human resource information system, i.e., interrelated components working together to collect, process, store, and disseminate information to support decision making, coordination, control, analysis, and visualization of the company's human resource management activities.

DISCUSSION QUESTIONS

1. How and why is HR in small businesses different than that in large firms?
2. Explain why HRM is important to small businesses.
3. Explain and give at least four examples of how entrepreneurs can use Internet and government tools to support the HR effort.
4. Explain and give at least five examples of ways entrepreneurs can use small size—familiarity, flexibility, and informality—to improve their HR processes.
5. Discuss what you would do to find, retain, and deal with a professional employee organization on an on-going basis.
6. Describe with examples how you would create a start-up, paper-based human resource system for a new small business.

INDIVIDUAL AND GROUP PROJECTS

1. Form teams of five or six persons, each with at least one person who owns or has worked for a small business. Based on their experiences, make a list of the "inadequate-HR risks" the business endured, in terms of competitive disadvantage, lack of specialized HR expertise, workplace litigation, compensation laws compliance, and paperwork/data-entry errors.
2. You own a small business, and you are confused about which of your employees is eligible for overtime pay. The employees in question include your secretary, two accounting clerks, one engineer, and two inside salespeople. Individually or in groups of four or five students, use the DOL's Overtime Security Advisor and DOL's Calculator to determine who gets overtime pay.
3. You have about 32 employees working in your factory. Working individually of in teams of four or five students, find and create a list of five online sources you could use to provide training to them, at no cost to you or to them.
4. The "HRCI Test Specifications Appendix" (pages 699–706) lists the knowledge someone studying for the HRCI certification exam needs to have in each area of human resource management (such as in Strategic Management, Workforce Planning, and Human Resource Development). In groups of four to five students, do four things: (1) Review that appendix now. (2) Identify the material in this chapter that relates to the required knowledge the appendix lists. (3) Write four multiple-choice exam questions on this material that you believe would be suitable for inclusion in the HRCI exam. And (4) if time permits, have someone from your team post your team's questions in front of the class, so the students in other teams can take each others' exam questions.

EXPERIENTIAL EXERCISE

Building an HRIS

Purpose: The purpose of this exercise is to give you practice in creating a human resource management system (HRIS).

Required Understanding: You should be fully acquainted with the material in this chapter.

How to Set Up the Exercise/Instructions: Divide the class into teams of five or six students. Each team will need access to the Internet.

Assume that the owners of a small business come to you with the following problem. They have a company with less than 40 employees and have been taking care of all types of HR paperwork informally, mostly on little slips of paper and with memos. They want you to build them a human resource management information system—how computerized it is will be up to you, but they can only afford a budget of $5,000 upfront (not counting your consulting), and then about $500 per year for maintenance. You know from your HR training that there are various sources of paper-based and online systems. Write a 2-page proposal telling them exactly what your team would suggest, based on its accumulated existing knowledge, and from online research.

APPLICATION CASE

The Liquidity Crisis and the New Hedge Fund[77]

After 12 years working for various hedge funds, Emily Thomas was laid off as a managing director with one of the midsize funds in January 2009. As the sub-prime and liquidity crises worsened, the fund she managed, in the media industry, was actually doing fairly well. Unfortunately, several of her colleagues in the hedge fund's other industry sectors had taken huge gambles, which did not pan out. As a result, the hedge fund's investors were clamoring to redeem their investments, and Emily was let go as part of a consolidation. Sitting in a small restaurant just off Water Street in lower Manhattan with two friends, Guy and Bill, the three decided that if they were ever going to start their own hedge fund, now was the time. "The time to start something like this is at the bottom, not at the top," as Guy put it, so the three of them began making plans. They pooled their savings and incorporated as EGB Funds.

Because of regulatory and tax issues, there is much more to starting a hedge fund than just hanging a sign on the door.[78] The fund must have local accounting and valuations expertise. For example, U.S. investors expect accounting reports to follow America's "generally accepted accounting procedures," or GAAP. Many hedge funds establish a "master-feeder structure" to attract investors' capital in a tax-efficient way. This involves establishing on- and offshore feeder funds, which in turn invest directly into the master fund, where all trading activity takes place. In the past, most funds performed everything from trading to back office support in-house. The rationale was that with such specialized work to do, the hedge fund operators want total control of all the operations. Increasingly, however, fund managers have been outsourcing some activities to cut costs. But like all funds, EGB will have to appoint an internal fund manager. That person will in turn essentially be the operational head of the firm. He or she will work with lawyers to establish the fund's corporate legal structure. Here she will have to make sure that all of the necessary policies and procedures are clearly documented and in place; for a financial institution such as this, these necessarily include not just the usual office administrative types of matters but also, for instance anti-money laundering procedures for investors. In addition, the fund manager (in this case, working with Emily, Guy, and Bill) will find and rent office space and determine staffing requirements.

Given all of the legal, compliance, and accounting issues they face, the minutiae of staffing the company and instituting human resource policies and procedures frankly seemed secondary. On the other hand, they weren't foolish, and they understood that at its heart, their hedge fund was going to be no better than the people that they hired. They planned to hire about seven people, including a fund manager, chief financial officer, four analysts, and a secretary/receptionist. Knowing that you are a human resource management expert, they've come to you for advice. Here's what they want to know.

Questions

1. In terms of staffing or human resource management, where should we start? Do we put in the HR system first? Or hire the people first?
2. Should we hire the fund manager first, and let him or her do all the necessary staffing/human resource management? Or should we have some HR processes in place first, so that we do a better job of hiring the fund manager?
3. If we are going to institute an HR system first, what's the best way to go about doing that? What would you suggest in terms of the sorts of HR policies, procedures, and practices we will need, and where should we get them?
4. We know there are professional employment organizations that will essentially handle most of the personnel-related matters for our fund. In our brief case synopsis, we've told you something about starting a hedge fund and the sorts of employees we need. Based on that, would you suggest we use a PEO? Why?

CONTINUING CASE

Carter Cleaning Company

Cleaning in Challenging Times

As the economic turndown worsened, revenues at the Carter stores fell off steeply. Many of their customers were simply out of work and didn't need (or couldn't afford) dry cleaning. Working customers were cutting back wherever they could. The Carters actually found themselves giving away some free cleaning services. They started a new program wherein existing customers could get one suit or dress cleaned free each month if they needed it for a job interview.

In the midst of this downturn, the Carters knew they had to do something to get their employment costs under control. The problem was that, realistically, there wasn't much room for cutting staffing in a store. Of course, if a store got very slow, they could double up by having a cleaner spotter spend some of his or her time pressing, or having the manager displace the counter person. But if sales only fall 15% to 20% per store, there really wasn't much room for reducing employee head count because each store never really employed that many people in the first place.

The question therefore naturally arose as to whether the Carters could cut their employment expenses without dismissing too many people. Jennifer Carter has several questions for you.

Questions

1. Assume that we don't want to terminate any of our employees. What work-scheduling–related changes could we make that would reduce our payrolls by, say, 20% per week but still keep all our employees on board?
2. We are currently handling most of our personnel-related activities, such as sign-ons, benefits administration, and appraisals manually. What specific suggestions would you have for us in terms of using software systems to automate our HR processes?
3. Suggest at least five free Internet-based sources we could turn to for helping us to lower our total employment costs.

TRANSLATING STRATEGY INTO HR POLICIES & PRACTICES CASE

The Hotel Paris Case

The Hotel Paris's competitive strategy is "To use superior guest service to differentiate the Hotel Paris properties, and to thereby increase the length of stay and return rate of guests, and thus boost revenues and profitability." HR manager Lisa Cruz must now formulate functional policies and activities that support this competitive strategy, by eliciting the required employee behaviors and competencies.

Challenging economic times brought the drawbacks of the Hotel Paris relatively small size into sharp relief. Large chains like Marriott had vast online reservations capabilities with huge centralized systems that easily and economically handled reservations requests from throughout the world. By comparison, the Hotel Paris still handled reservations much as hotels did 20 years ago, either with separate Web sites for each of their hotel locations, or by phone. Their human resource management information systems were similarly primitive. Lisa had managed to install several separate information systems, for instance for performance appraisals. However, as she discussed one day over lunch with the CFO, these systems were not integrated. Therefore, if an employee changed his or her name, for instance, through marriage, people in Lisa's office had to execute all those name changes manually on all the various employee rosters and benefits plans.

This lack of integration was bad enough in boom times, but was increasingly unacceptable as the economy soured. In one of the most difficult discussions she ever had with the CFO, he pointed out to her that the amount of money they were spending on human resource management administration was about 30% higher than it was at larger chains such as Marriott. He understood that large size brings economies of scale. But on the other hand, he believed there had to be something they could do to bring down the cost of administering human resource management.

Questions

1. Using any benchmark data that you can find, including information from this textbook, what are some benchmark metrics that Lisa could be using to assess the efficiency of her human resource management operations? To what extent does the Hotel Paris's quality service orientation enter into how Lisa's metrics should compare?
2. Throughout this textbook, we've discussed various specific examples of how human resource management departments have been reducing the cost of delivering their services. Keeping in mind the Hotel Paris's service quality orientation, please list and explain with examples how Lisa Cruz could use it at least five of these.
3. Focusing only on human resource information systems for a moment, what sorts of systems would you suggest Lisa consider recommending for the Hotel Paris?
4. Explain with detailed examples how Lisa can use free online and governmental sources to accomplish at least part of what you propose in your previous answers.
5. Give three examples of fee-based online tools you suggest Lisa use.
6. Do you suggest Lisa use a PEO? Why?

Appendix for Chapter 18

HRCI Test Specifications Appendix

This appendix contains the complete test specifications for the Human Resource Certification Institute's certification exams. Note the specific areas of *knowledge* ("knowledge of") listed for each HR functional area. (Note that, while we haven't done so here, HRCI numbers all *knowledge* questions sequentially, with, for instance, the last Strategic Management question numbered 6, and the first Workforce Planning knowledge question numbered 7.)

HRCI TEST SPECIFICATIONS APPENDIX

The percentages that follow each functional area heading are the PHR and SPHR percentages, respectively.

1. Strategic Management (12%, 26%) The processes and activities used to formulate HR objectives, practices, and policies to meet the short- and long-range organizational needs and opportunities, to guide and lead the change process, and to evaluate HR's contributions to organizational effectiveness.

Responsibilities

1. Interpret information related to the organization's operations from internal sources, including financial/accounting, marketing, operations, information technology, and individual employees, in order to participate in strategic planning and policy making.
2. Interpret information related to the general business environment, industry practices and developments, and technological developments from external sources (for example, publications, government documents, media and trade organizations) in order to participate in strategic planning and policy making.
3. Participate as a partner in the organization's strategic planning process.
4. Establish strategic relationships with individuals in the organization, to influence organizational decision making.
5. Establish relationships/alliances with key individuals in the community and in professional capacities to assist in meeting the organization's strategic needs.
6. Evaluate HR's contribution to organizational effectiveness, including assessment, design, implementation and evaluation of activities with respect to strategic and organizational measurement in HR objectives.
7. Provide direction and guidance during changes in organizational processes, operations, planning, intervention, leadership training, and culture that balances the expectations and needs of the organization, its employees, and other stakeholders (including customers).
8. Develop and shape organizational policy related to the organization's management of its human resources.
9. Cultivate leadership and ethical values in self and others through modeling and teaching.
10. Provide information for the organizational budgeting process, including budget development and review.
11. Monitor legislative environment for proposed changes in law and take appropriate action to support, modify, or stop the proposed action (for example, write to a member of Congress, provide expert testimony at a public hearing, lobby legislators).

Knowledge of

1. Lawmaking and administrative regulatory processes.
2. Internal and external environmental scanning techniques.
3. Strategic planning process and implementation.
4. Organizational social responsibility (for example, welfare to work, philanthropy, alliances with community-based organizations).
5. Management functions, including planning, organizing, directing, and controlling.
6. Techniques to sustain creativity and innovation.

2. Workforce Planning and Employment (26%, 16%) The processes of planning, developing, implementing, administering, and performing ongoing evaluation of recruiting, hiring, orientation, and organizational exit to ensure that the workforce will meet the organization's goals and objectives.

Responsibilities

1. Identify staffing requirements to meet the goals and objectives of the organization.
2. Conduct job analyses to write job descriptions and develop job competencies.
3. Identify and document the essential job functions for positions.
4. Establish hiring criteria based on the competencies needed.
5. Assess internal workforce, labor market, and recruitment agencies to determine the availability of qualified applicants.
6. Identify internal and external recruitment methods and implement them within the context of the organization's goals and objectives.
7. Develop strategies to market the organization to potential applicants.
8. Establish selection procedures, including interviewing, testing, and reference and background checking.
9. Implement selection procedures, including interviewing, testing, and reference and background checking.
10. Develop and/or extend employment offers.
11. Perform or administer post-offer employment activities (for example, employment agreements, completion of I-9 verification form, relocation agreements, and medical exams).
12. Facilitate and/or administer the process by which non-U.S. citizens can legally work in the United States.
13. Design, facilitate, and/or conduct the orientation process, including review of performance standards for new hires and transfers.
14. Evaluate selection and employment processes for effectiveness and implement changes if indicated (for example, employee retention).
15. Develop a succession planning process.
16. Develop and implement the organizational exit process, including unemployment insurance claim responses.
17. Develop, implement, manage, and evaluate affirmative action program(s), as may be required.

Knowledge of

7. Federal/state/local employment-related laws (for example, Title VII, ADA, ADEA, Vietnam Veterans, WARN) and regulations (for example, EEOC Uniform Guidelines on Employee Selection Procedures).

8. Immigration law (for example, visas, I-9).
9. Quantitative analyses required to assess past and future staffing (for example, cost-benefit analysis, costs per hire, selection ratios, adverse impact).
10. Recruitment methods and sources.
11. Staffing alternatives (for example, telecommuting, outsourcing).
12. Planning techniques (for example, succession planning, forecasting).
13. Reliability and validity of selection tests/tools/methods.
14. Use an interpretation of selection tests (for example, psychological/personality, cognitive and motor/physical assessments).
15. Interviewing techniques.
16. Relocation practices.
17. Impact of compensation and benefits plans on recruitment and retention.
18. International HR and implications of international workforce for workforce planning and employment.
19. Downsizing and outplacement.
20. Internal workforce planning and employment policies, practices, and procedures.

3. Human Resource Development (15%, 13%) The processes of ensuring that the skills, knowledge, abilities, and performance of the workforce meet the current and future organizational and individual needs through developing, implementing, and evaluating activities and programs addressing employee training and development, change and performance management, and the unique needs of particular employee groups.

Responsibilities

1. Conduct needs analyses to identify and establish priorities regarding human resource development activities.
2. Develop training programs.
3. Implement training programs.
4. Evaluate training programs.
5. Develop programs to assess employees' potential for growth and development in the organization.
6. Implement programs to assess employees' potential for growth and development in the organization.
7. Evaluate programs to assess employees' potential for growth and development in the organization.
8. Develop change management programs and activities.
9. Implement change management programs and activities.
10. Evaluate change management programs and activities.
11. Develop performance management programs and procedures.
12. Implement performance management programs and procedures.
13. Evaluate performance management programs and procedures.
14. Develop programs to meet the unique needs of particular employees (for example, work/family programs, diversity programs, outplacement programs, repatriation programs, and fast-track programs).
15. Implement programs to meet the unique needs of particular employees (for example, work/family programs, diversity programs, outplacement programs, repatriation programs, and fast-track programs).
16. Evaluate programs to meet the unique needs of particular employees (for example, work/family programs, diversity programs, outplacement programs, repatriation programs, and fast-track programs).

Knowledge of

21. Applicable international, federal, state, and local laws and regulations regarding copyrights and patents.
22. Human resource development theories and applications (including career development and leadership development).
23. Organizational development theories and applications.
24. Training methods, programs, and techniques (design, objectives, methods, etc.).
25. Employee involvement strategies.
26. Task/process analysis.
27. Performance appraisal and performance management methods.
28. Applicable international issues (for example, culture, local management approaches/ practices, societal norms).
29. Instructional methods and program delivery (content, building modules of program, selection of presentation/delivery mechanism).
30. Techniques to assess HRD program effectiveness (for example, satisfaction, learning, and job performance of program participants, and organizational outcomes such as turnover and productivity).

4. Compensation and Benefits (20%, 16%) The processes of analyzing, developing, implementing, administering, and performing ongoing evaluation of a total compensation and benefits system for all employee groups consistent with human resource management goals.

Responsibilities

1. Ensure the compliance of compensation and benefits with applicable federal, state, and local laws.
2. Analyze, develop, implement, and maintain compensation policies and a pay structure consistent with the organization's strategic objectives.
3. Analyze and evaluate pay rates based on internal worth and external market conditions.
4. Develop/select and implement a payroll system.
5. Administer payroll functions.
6. Evaluate compensation policies to ensure that they are positioning the organization internally and externally according to the organization's strategic objectives.
7. Conduct a benefit plan needs assessment and determine/select the plans to be offered, considering the organization's strategic objectives.
8. Implement and administer benefit plans.
9. Evaluate benefits program to ensure that it is positioning the organization internally and externally according to the organization's strategic objectives.
10. Analyze, select, implement, maintain, and administer executive compensation, stock purchase, stock options and incentive, and bonus programs.
11. Analyze, develop, select, maintain, and implement expatriate and foreign national compensation and benefit programs.
12. Communicate the compensation and benefits plan and policies to the workforce.

Knowledge of

31. Federal, state, and local compensation and benefit laws (for example, FLSA, ERISA, COBRA).
32. Accounting practices related to compensation and benefits (for example, excess group term life, compensatory time).

33. Job evaluation methods.
34. Job pricing and pay structures.
35. Incentive and variable pay methods.
36. Executive compensation.
37. Noncash compensation methods (for example, stock option plans).
38. Benefit needs analysis.
39. Benefit plans (for example, health insurance, life insurance, pension, education, health club).
40. International compensation laws and practices (for example, expatriate compensation, socialized medicine, mandated retirement).

5. Employee and Labor Relations (21%, 24%) The processes of analyzing, developing, implementing, administering, and performing ongoing evaluation of the workplace relationship between employer and employee (including the collective bargaining process and union relations), in order to maintain effective relationships and working conditions that balance the employer's needs with the employees' rights in support of the organization's strategic objectives.

Responsibilities

1. Ensure compliance with all applicable federal, state, and local laws and regulations.
2. Develop and implement employee relations programs that will create a positive organizational culture.
3. Promote, monitor, and measure the effectiveness of employee relations activities.
4. Assist in establishing work rules and monitor their application and enforcement to ensure fairness and consistency (for union and nonunion environments).
5. Communicate and ensure understanding by employees of laws, regulations, and organizational policies.
6. Resolve employee complaints filed with federal, state, and local agencies involving employment practices.
7. Develop grievance and disciplinary policies and procedures to ensure fairness and consistency.
8. Implement and monitor grievance and disciplinary policies and procedures to ensure fairness and consistency.
9. Respond to union organizing activity.
10. Participate in collective bargaining activities, including contract negotiation and administration.

Knowledge of

41. Applicable federal, state, and local laws affecting employment in union and nonunion environments, such as antidiscrimination laws, sexual harassment, labor relations, and privacy.
42. Techniques for facilitating positive employee relations (for example, small group facilitation, dispute resolution, and labor/management cooperative strategies and programs).
43. Employee involvement strategies (for example, alternate work schedules, work teams).
44. Individual employment rights issues and practices (for example, employment at will, negligent hiring, defamation, employees' rights to bargain collectively).
45. Workplace behavior issues/practices (for example, absenteeism and discipline).
46. Methods for assessment of employee attitudes, opinions, and satisfaction (for example, opinion surveys, attitude surveys, focus panels).
47. Unfair labor practices.

48. The collective bargaining process, strategies, and concepts.
49. Public-sector labor relations issues and practices.
50. Expatriation and repatriation issues and practices.
51. Employee and labor relations for local nationals (i.e., labor relations in other countries).

6. Occupational Health, Safety, and Security (6%, 5%) The processes of analyzing, developing, implementing, administering, and performing ongoing evaluation of programs, practices, and services to promote the physical and mental well-being of individuals in the workplace, and to protect individuals and the workplace from unsafe acts, unsafe working conditions, and violence.

Responsibilities

1. Ensure compliance with all applicable federal, state, and local workplace health and safety laws and regulations.
2. Determine safety programs needed for the organization.
3. Develop and/or select injury/occupational illness prevention programs.
4. Implement injury/occupational illness prevention programs.
5. Develop and/or select safety training and incentive programs.
6. Implement safety training and incentive programs.
7. Evaluate the effectiveness of safety prevention, training, and incentive programs.
8. Implement workplace injury/occupational illness procedures (for example, workers' compensation, OSHA).
9. Determine health and wellness programs needed for the organization.
10. Develop/select, implement, and evaluate (or make available) health and wellness programs.
11. Develop/select, implement, and evaluate security plans to protect the company from liability.
12. Develop/select, implement, and evaluate security plans to protect employees (for example, injuries resulting from workplace violence).
13. Develop/select, implement, and evaluate incident and emergency response plans (for example, natural disasters, workplace safety threats, evacuation).

Knowledge of

52. Federal, state, and local workplace health and safety laws and regulations (for example, OSHA, Drug-Free Workplace Act, ADA).
53. Workplace injury and occupational illness compensation laws and programs (for example, workers' compensation).
54. Investigation procedures of workplace safety, health, and security enforcement agencies (for example, OSHA).
55. Workplace safety risks.
56. Workplace security risks (for example, theft, corporate espionage, information systems/technology, and vandalism).
57. Potential violent behavior and workplace violence conditions.
58. General health and safety practices (for example, fire evacuation, HAZCOM, ergonomic evaluations).
59. Incident and emergency response plans.
60. Internal investigation and surveillance techniques.
61. Employee assistance programs.
62. Employee wellness programs.
63. Issues related to chemical use and dependency (for example, identification of symptoms, drug testing, discipline).

CORE Knowledge Required by HR Professionals

64. Needs assessment and analysis.
65. Third-party contract management, including development of requests for proposals (RFPs).
66. Communication strategies.
67. Documentation requirements.
68. Adult learning processes.
69. Motivation concepts and applications.
70. Training methods.
71. Leadership concepts and applications.
72. Project management concepts and applications.
73. Diversity concepts and applications.
74. Human relations concepts and applications (for example, interpersonal and organizational behavior).
75. HR ethics and professional standards.
76. Technology and human resource information systems (HRIS) to support HR activities.
77. Qualitative and quantitative methods and tools for analysis, interpretation, and decision-making purposes.
78. Change management.
79. Liability and risk management.
80. Job analysis and job description methods.
81. Employee records management (for example, retention, disposal).
82. The interrelationships among HR activities and programs across functional areas.

CERTIFICATION HANDBOOK RECERTIFICATION GUIDE APPENDIX

Introduction

What Is Certification? Certification is a voluntary action by a professional group to establish a system to grant recognition to professionals who have met a stated level of training and work experience. Certified individuals are usually issued a certificate attesting that they have met the standards of the credentialing organization and are entitled to make the public aware of their credentialed status, usually through the use of acronyms (i.e., PHR, SPHR, or GPHR) after their names.

Certifications differ from certificate programs because certifications, by definition, include a work experience component. Certificate programs, on the other hand, award certificates once a course of study has been completed and do not require previous work experience.

Why Is Certification Desirable? Certification sets those with the credential apart—or above—those without it. There are a number of advantages to seeking certification. Certification becomes a public recognition of professional achievement—both within and outside of the profession. For many, achieving certification becomes a personal professional goal—a way to test knowledge and to measure it against one's peers. Others see certification as an aid to career advancement.

Purpose and Use of Certification PHR and SPHR certifications show that the holder has demonstrated mastery of the HR body of knowledge and, through recertification, has accepted the challenge to stay informed of new developments in the HR field.

The PHR and SPHR exams are completely voluntary. Organizations or individuals incorporating PHR or SPHR certification as a condition of employment or advancement do so of their own volition. Individuals should determine for themselves whether the use of this process, including its eligibility and recertification requirements, when coupled with any other requirements imposed by individuals or organizations, meets their needs and complies with any applicable laws.

The PHR and SPHR designations are a visible reminder to peers and coworkers of the holder's significant professional achievement. PHR and SPHR certified professionals should proudly display their certificates and use the credentials on business correspondence.

Certification Denial and Revocation Certification may be denied or revoked for any of the following reasons:

- Falsification of work experience or other information on the exam application.
- Misrepresentation of work experience or other information on the exam application.
- Violation of testing procedures.
- Failure to pass the certification exam.
- Failure to meet recertification requirements.

Candidates whose certifications are denied or revoked should contact HRCI for more information about how to appeal the denial or revocation. There is no appeal based on failure to pass the exam or to recertify.

Exam Overview

- 225 multiple choice questions.
- Four hours to complete.
- Administered by computer.
- Administered only in English.

Are You Ready?

- Take the HRCI Online Assessment Exam (www.hrci.org).

There are two levels of certification, the Professional in Human Resources (PHR®) and the Senior Professional in Human Resources (SPHR®).[79] Both exams are generalist (i.e., they assess all the functional areas of the HR field) but differ in terms of focus and the cognitive level of questions. PHR questions tend to be at an operational/technical level. SPHR questions tend to be more at the strategic and/or policy level. HRCI exams are offered only in English.

Test questions on both exams reflect the most recently published test specifications (see the previous "HRCI Test Specifications Appendix"). The exams are multiple choice and consist of 200 scored questions plus 25 pretest questions randomly distributed throughout the exam (a total of 225 questions). Each question lists four possible answers, only one of which is the correct or "best possible answer." The answer to each question can be derived independently of the answer to any other question. Four hours are allotted to complete the exam. All exams are administered by computer at more than 250 Prometric testing centers. There are no paper-and-pencil exam administrations.

Pretest questions are not counted in scoring. They are, however, essential in building the PHR and SPHR item (or test question) banks and are on the exam to statistically assess their difficulty level and effectiveness at discriminating between candidates who meet the passing standard and those who do not. The information gathered in the pretest process determines whether or not the question will be included on a future exam.

On test day, answer questions that are easy first and mark the more difficult ones to return to later. There is no penalty for guessing, so try to answer all the questions. Unanswered questions are counted as incorrect.

There are survey questions at the end of the exam that candidates are encouraged to answer if time allows. These questions are optional. Responses are confidential. The information collected is used for statistical purposes only.

Exam questions represent the following functional areas in HR. The percentages indicate the extent to which each functional area is emphasized at either exam level.

Exams reflect the percentages listed below and are reviewed by a panel of certified professionals with subject matter expertise to ensure that the questions are up to date and reflect the published test specifications.

PHR and SPHR Exam Functional Areas

	PHR	SPHR
Strategic Management	12%	26%
Workforce Planning and Employment	26%	16%
Human Resource Development	15%	13%
Compensation and Benefits	20%	16%
Employee and Labor Relations	21%	24%
Occupational Health, Safety, and Security	6%	5%

Passing Score The passing score for both exams (based on a scaled score) is 500. The minimum possible score is 100. The maximum possible score is 700.

For more information about scaled scoring, please see "Understanding the Score Report" and "How the Passing Score Was Set" in the separate HRCI handbook.

HRCI Online Assessment Exam HRCI offers an online assessment exam comprised of actual exam questions that have appeared on previous exams but were removed from the item bank to develop the assessment exam. Before registering for the exam, consider taking this online assessment exam. The assessment exam exposes candidates to the types of questions that are on the actual exam. For more information about the assessment exam (including fees), visit the HRCI Web site at www.hrci.org.

About Computer-Based Testing (CBT) Starting in 2004, HRCI has delivered all PHR and SPHR exams by computer at Prometric test centers. Here's what you need to know about this exciting development:

Advantages to Computer-Based Exam Delivery

- Exams will be administered exclusively by computer. Exams will no longer be available in paper-and-pencil format.
- The exams will be administered at more than 250 test centers across the United States, U.S. territories, and Canada. Exams will also be offered internationally wherever a Prometric test center is located. See HRCI's separate Appendix D for more information about taking the exam outside the United States, U.S. territories, or Canada.
- There are two annual testing windows—May 1–June 30, 2009 and December 1, 2009–January 31, 2010 for 2009–2010.
- Exams will no longer be offered at SHRM conferences.
- Candidates can schedule their exams Monday through Friday and take their exams Monday through Saturday, during the testing windows.
- Candidates will have access to a built-in clock and calculator.
- Individual testing stations will allow for more privacy and test security.

- Immediate (preliminary) pass/fail score results will be provided to candidates before they leave the testing center. Official score reports will be mailed within two to three weeks of testing.
- There are more testing dates.
- There are more test center locations.
- There will be consistent exam administration and test-taking environments.
- Candidates are able to mark more difficult questions to return to later.
- Computer-based testing provides ease of use (no computer experience necessary).
- A self-paced tutorial shows you how to take the test (including how to mark questions to return to later) to ensure that you are comfortable with the exam administration process.
- Prometric, the leading provider of computer-based testing, will deliver the exams.

What Will Stay the Same

- Exam content, number of questions (225), and duration (4 hours).
- Eligibility requirements.
- Strict deadline dates.
- Official score reports will be mailed to candidates.
- PES will review exam applications, process payments, score the exams, and mail score reports.

For more information about CBT, visit the HRCI homepage at www.hrci.org.

Part V Video Cases Appendix

Video 7: Ethics and Fair Treatment in Human Resource Management

VIDEO TITLE: GLOBAL BUSINESS AND ETHICS

This video suggests, among other things, that there is no absolute statement on what constitutes ethical behavior. Instead, ethics tends to be determined by social, cultural, and other value-laden factors, such as religion. Similarly, as the video points out, the degree of enforcement (for instance, regarding ethical lapses like bribery of customers) tends to vary with social, cultural, and other factors, so what is considered ethical or unethical in one society might not be in another.

This video also discusses the interplay between ethics and management practices. For example, the video points out that "most people look first at how a company treats its employees when viewing its ethics." Focus primarily on the introductory material in the video, the part on ethics and management practices.

Discussion Questions

1. What is the meaning of ethics, and how does the social and cultural context of the business affect what it means to be "ethical" as we move from country to country and society to society?
2. What does the video say about how the company's social and cultural context (in particular, the country in which it does business) affects how you might define what is, or is not, ethical treatment of employees?
3. Based on what you saw in this video, assume for a moment that child labor (as defined by the U.S. Fair Labor Standards Act) is acceptable behavior in some country. How, based on this video, should American companies deal with child labor issues in their own plants in these countries? Why?

Video 8: Managing Labor Relations and Collective Bargaining

VIDEO TITLE: LABOR RELATIONS

In this video, Sarah has just accepted a position in HotJobs' computer programming department as a full-time programmer. She has come to the HR department a bit nervously, to ask whether she has the option of joining the union there. As Sarah says, "I had a lot of benefits with my previous job and there was a union there." HotJobs does not offer union membership. The human resource representative goes on to explain that HotJobs is committed to its employees, and grievances are dealt with on a case-by-case basis. Therefore there is no need for a third party to intercede between the union and the employee, she says. This video also explains the importance of union membership in specific industries and the benefits that union membership provides to employees.

Discussion Questions

1. If you were the company's human resource representative, would you be at all concerned that Sarah might become a leader in a unionization movement at HotJobs, and if so what if anything would you suggest the human resource representative do about it? Why?
2. Do you think human resources provided as comprehensive an answer to Sarah about why she does not need a union as HR could have? If not, what else would you have told Sarah?
3. Do you believe, based on what you read in this part of the book and saw in the video, that union membership may be more important in some industries than others, and if so why?
4. If you were Sarah, would you have even brought a question like this to HR? Why or why not?

Video 9: Protecting Safety and Health

VIDEO TITLE: STRESS

As Chapter 16 explains, stress is an ever-present and potentially debilitating factor at work. In this video, the sources of stress include the employees' own dedication and sense of responsibility, changes in job scope and workload that resulted from the company's rapid growth, and the pressure to make the company a success. At Student Advantage, the stressors appear to be counterbalanced somewhat by most employees' feeling that it's fun to work at the company, and that the atmosphere is collegial and the challenges are worthwhile.

The fun and psychic rewards notwithstanding, it's apparent from the video that stress at this company is a fact of life. For example, Vinny mentions that one source of stress is when someone comes to him and says something needs to be done "an hour ago." Another source of stress here is that employees have to do a sort of balancing act, balancing the needs of their workplace and job with outside interests and family. Sympathy from coworkers helps, but employers still need to be able to refresh themselves and keep stress at tolerable levels.

Discussion Questions

1. What other sources of stress are articulated by the people in this video, and do you think any of the employees seem to be candidates for burnout? Why?
2. What prescriptions for reducing or dealing with stress did the employees in this video mention?
3. What additional methods of dealing with stress would you suggest based upon what you read in Chapter 16?
4. How many potential safety hazards can you identify at this company by watching the video? What are they?

ENDNOTES

1. Dina Berta, "Job Trekker's Odyssey Offers HR Insights," *Nation's Restaurant News* 42, no. 6 (February 11, 2008), pp. 1, 12.
2. Dina Berta, "IHOP Franchise Employs Post-Hiring Surveys to Get Off Turnover 'Treadmill,'" *Nation's Restaurant News* 41, no 39 (October 1, 2007), p. 6.
3. "Statistics of U.S. Businesses and Non-Employer Status," www.sba.gov/advo/research/data.html, accessed November 5, 2009.
4. "Small Business Economic Indicators 2000," Office of Advocacy, U.S. Small Business Administration (Washington, D.C., 2001), p. 5. See also "Small Business Laid Foundation for Job Gains," www.sba.gov/advo, accessed March 9, 2006.
5. Studies show that the size of the business impacts human resource activities such as executive compensation, training, staffing, and HR outsourcing. Peter Hausdorf and Dale Duncan, "Firm Size and Internet Recruiting in Canada: A Preliminary Investigation," *Journal of Small-Business Management* 42, no. 3 (July 2004), pp. 325–334.
6. Society for Human Resource Management, *SHRM Human Capital Benchmarking Study 2007*, p. 12.
7. Graham Dietz et al., "HRM Inside UK E-Commerce Firms," *International Small Business Journal* 24, no. 5 (October 2006), pp. 443–470.
8. Bernice Kotey and Cathleen Folker, "Employee Training in SMEs: Effect of Size and Firm Type—Family and Nonfamily," *Journal of Small-Business Management* 45, no. 2 (April 2007), pp. 14–39.
9. Graham Dietz et al., op cit.
10. Ibid.
11. Mary Coulter, *Entrepreneurship in Action* (Upper Saddle River, NJ: Prentice Hall, 2001), p. 18.
12. Ibid. See also N. Wasserman, "Planning a Start-Up? Seize the Day . . . Then Expect to Work All Night," *Harvard Business Review* 87, no. 1 (January 2009), p. 27.
13. Jill Kickul and Lisa Gundry, "Prospecting for Strategic Advantage: The Proactive Entrepreneurial Personality and Small Firm Innovation," *Journal of Small-Business Management* 40, no. 2 (April 2002), pp. 85–98.
14. S. McKenna, "The Darker Side of the Entrepreneur," *Leadership & Organization Development Journal* 17, no. 6 (November 1996), pp. 41–46. See also L. Farrell, "Welcome to The Dark Side," *Conference Board Review* 44, no. 6 (November/December 2007), pp. 63-64.
15. The following four points based on Kathy Williams, "Top HR Compliance Issues for Small Businesses," *Strategic Finance*, February 2005, pp. 21–23.
16. However, one study concluded that the increased labor costs associated with high-performance work practices offset the pay productivity increases associated with high-performance work practices. Luc Sels et al., "Unraveling the HRM–Performance Link: Value Creating and Cost Increasing Effects of Small-Business HRM," *Journal of Management Studies* 43, no. 2 (March 2006), pp. 319–342. For supporting evidence of HR's positive effects on small companies, see also Andrea Rauch, et al., "Effects of Human Capital and Long-Term Human Resources Development and Utilization on Employment Growth of Small-Scale Businesses: A Causal Analysis," *Entrepreneurship Theory and Practice* 29, no. 6 (November 2005), pp. 681–698; Andries de Grip and Inge Sieben, "The Effects of Human Resource Management on Small Firms' Productivity and Employees' Wages," *Applied Economics* 37, no. 9 (May 20, 2005), pp. 1047–1054.
17. Dawn Carlson et al., "The Impact of Human Resource Practices and Compensation Design on Performance: An Analysis of Family-Owned SMEs," *Journal of Small-Business Management* 44, no. 4 (October 2006), pp. 531–543.
18. Graham Dietz et al., op cit.
19. Gilbert Nicholson, "Automated Assessments for Better Hires," *Workforce*, December 2000, pp. 102–107.
20. www.EEOC.gov/employers/overview.html, accessed February 10, 2008.
21. www.DOL.gov/elaws, accessed February 10, 2008.
22. Paul Harris, "Small Businesses Bask in Training's Spotlight," *Training & Development* 59, no. 2 (Fall 2005), pp. 46–52.
23. Ibid.
24. Ibid.
25. www.employeeappraiser.com/index.php, accessed January 10, 2008.
26. www.halogensoftware.com/products/halogen-eappraisal/, accessed January 10, 2008.
27. Jan de Kok, "Precautionary Actions Within Small and Medium-Sized Enterprises," *Journal of Small-Business Management* 43, no. 4 (October 2005), pp. 498–516.
28. Sean Smith, "OSHA Resources Can Help Small Businesses Spot Hazards," *Westchester County Business Journal*, August 4, 2003, p. 4. See also www.osha.gov/as/opa/osha-faq.html, accessed May 26, 2007.
29. Lisa Finnegan, "Industry Partners with OSHA," *Occupational Hazards*, February 1999, pp. 43–45.
30. Graham Dietz et al., op cit.
31. Gina Ruiz, "Smaller Firms in Vanguard of Flex Practices," *Workforce Management* 84, no. 13 (November 21, 2005), p. 10.
32. Ibid.
33. These are from Ty Freyvogel, "Operation Employee Loyalty," *Training Media Review*, September–October 2007.
34. Ibid.
35. Ibid.
36. Based on Bob Nelson, *1001 Ways to Reward Employees* (New York: Workman Publishing, 1994), p. 19. See also Sunny C. L. Fong and Margaret A. Shaffer, "The Dimensionality and Determinants of Pay Satisfaction: A Cross-Cultural Investigation of a Group Incentive Plan," *International Journal of Human Resource Management* 14, no. 4 (June 2003), p. 559(22).
37. Jeffrey Marshall and Ellen Heffes, "Benefits: Smaller Firm Workers Often Getting Less," *Financial Executive* 21, no. 9 (November 1, 2005), p. 10.
38. www.dol.gov/ebsa/pdf/ppa2006.pdf, accessed February 18, 2008.
39. Bill Leonard, "New Retirement Plans for Small Employers," *HR Magazine* 51, no. 12 (December 2006), p. 30.
40. Kristen Falk, "The Easy Retirement Plan for Small Business Clients," *National Underwriter* 111, no. 45 (December 3, 2007), pp. 12–13.
41. Ibid.
42. Adrienne Fox, "McMurray Scouts Top Talent to Produce Winning Results," *HR Magazine* 51, no. 7 (July 2006), p. 57.
43. Colin Gray and Christopher Mabey, "Management Development: Key Differences Between Small and Large Businesses in Europe," *International Small Business Journal* 23, no. 5 (October 2005), pp. 467–485.

44. Ibid. See also Essi Saru, "Organizational Learning and HRD: How Appropriate Are They for Small Firms?" *Journal of European Industrial Training* 31, no. 1 (January 2007), pp. 36–52.
45. From Stephen Covey, "Small Business, Big Opportunity," *Training* 43, no. 11 (November 2006), p. 40.
46. Phillip Perry, "Welcome to the Family," *Restaurant Hospitality* 90, no. 5 (May 2006), pp. 73, 74, 76, 78.
47. Ibid.
48. Ibid.
49. Ibid.
50. Ibid.
51. Dina Berta, "IHOP Franchisee Employs Post-Hiring Surveys to Get Off Turnover 'Treadmill,'" *Nation's Restaurant News* 41, no 39 (October 1, 2007), p. 6.
52. Kate Leahy, "The 10 Minute Manager's Guide to . . . Communicating with Employees," *Restaurants & Institutions* 116, no. 11 (June 1, 2006), pp. 22–23.
53. Ibid.
54. Ibid.
55. Jane Applegate, "Employee Leasing Can Be a Savior For Small Firms," *Business Courier Serving Cincinnati–Northern Kentucky,* January 28, 2000, p. 23.
56. Robert Beck and J. Starkman, "How to Find a PEO That Will Get the Job Done," *National Underwriter* 110, no. 39 (October 16, 2006), pp. 39, 45.
57. Layne Davlin, "Human Resource Solutions for the Franchisee," *Franchising World* 39, no. 10 (October 2007), pp. 27–28.
58. Robert Beck and Jay Starkman, "How to Find a PEO That Will Get the Job Done," *National Underwriter* 110, no. 39 (October 16, 2006), pp. 39, 45.
59. Lyle DeWitt, "Advantages of Human Resources Outsourcing," *The CPA Journal* 75, no. 6 (June 2005), p. 13.
60. Harriet Tramer, "Employee Leasing Agreement Can Ease Personnel Concerns," *Crain's Cleveland Business,* July 24, 2000, p. 24.
61. Max Chafkin, "Fed Up with HR?" *Inc.* 28, no. 5 (May 2006), pp. 50–52.
62. Ibid.
63. Ibid.
64. Ibid.
65. Jane Applegate, op cit.
66. Max Chafkin, op cit.
67. Robert Beck and J. Starkman, op cit.
68. Lyle DeWitt, op cit and www.peo.com/dnn, accessed April 28, 2008.
69. The following items are from Layne Davlin, "Human Resource Solutions for the Franchisee," *Franchising World* 39, no. 10 (October 2007), p. 27.
70. Ibid.
71. Sondra Servais, *Personnel Director* (Deerfield Beach, FL: Made E-Z Products, 1994).
72. Office Depot, Winter 2003 Catalog (Delray Beach, FL: Office Depot, 2008).
73. www.ihrim.org, accessed April 28, 2008.
74. Adapted from Kenneth Laudon and Jane Laudon, *Management Information Systems: New Approaches to Organization and Technology* (Upper Saddle River, NJ: Prentice Hall, 1998), p. G7. See also Michael Barrett and Randolph Kahn, "The Governance of Records Management," *Directors and Boards* 26, no. 3 (Spring 2002), pp. 45–48; Anthony Hendrickson, "Human Resource Information Systems: Backbone Technology of Contemporary Human Resources," *Journal of Labor Research* 24, no. 3 (Summer 2003), pp. 381–395.
75. "HR Execs Trade Notes on Human Resource Information Systems," *BNA Bulletin to Management,* December 3, 1998, p. 1. See also Brian Walter, "But They Said Their Payroll Program Complied with the FLSA," *Public Personnel Management* 31, no. 1 (Spring 2002), pp. 79–94.
76. "HR Execs Trade Notes on Human Resource Information Systems," *BNA Bulletin to Management,* December 3, 1998, p. 2. See also Ali Velshi, "Human Resources Information," *The Americas Intelligence Wire,* February 11, 2004.
77. 2009 Copyright © Gary Dessler PhD.
78. Portions based on Gustavo Rodriguez, "Starting a Hedge Fund," *LatinFinance* 47, no. 201 (2008), http://vnweb.hwwilsonweb.com.ezproxy.fiu.edu/hww/results/results_single_fulltext.jhtml;hwwilsonid=VIMPEAQW53NMFQA3DIKSFGOADUNGIIV0, accessed March 26, 2009.
79. Not addressed here is the more specialized GPHR global human resources certification.

Appendix A
Applying HR Content, Personal Competencies, and Business Knowledge

SUPPLEMENTARY STUDY AND DISCUSSION ASSIGNMENTS*

I INTRODUCTION: SHRM'S HUMAN RESOURCE CURRICULUM GUIDEBOOK

SHRM, the Society for Human Resource Management, distributed its *SHRM Human Resource Curriculum Guidebook and Templates for Undergraduate and Graduate Programs* several years ago. It contains SHRM's recommended curriculum templates or guides "to assist university faculty, deans, program directors, and other stakeholders in the dissemination of HR knowledge that will better prepare students and the organizations they support. . . ."

In a nutshell, the *Guidebook* advocates building human resource management programs and courses around 24 major and minor "HR Learning Modules." Each module contains three interrelated components—*HR Content* (such as "employment law"), *Personal Competencies* (such as "ethical decision making"), and *Business or Policy Knowledge Applications* (such as "business law, public policy, and corporate social responsibility"). SHRM's stated aims are to systematize and standardize the knowledge and skills HR students leave the classroom with, and to make sure that they learn, not just human resource management skills, but also how to apply personal skills (like communicating) as well as business knowledge to the human resource problems at hand. SHRM wants schools to use the modules to build multi-course programs in human resource management.

II THE PURPOSES OF THIS APPENDIX

The exercises in the following sections III, IV, and V serve two purposes. *First,* they provide an opportunity to learn more about SHRM-recommended HR Content Areas, Personal Competencies, and Business/Policy Areas. For example, section III lets you practice applying some of what you learned in the book about most of SHRM's main HR Content Areas. *Second* (since not all adopters will cover the new SHRM guidelines in detail), we also prepared this appendix so that all adopters and readers can use these exercises to supplement the behavioral objectives and case questions now in each chapter and case, simply as supplementary exercises.

III ASSESSING WHAT YOU KNOW ABOUT MAJOR SHRM *HR CONTENT AREAS*

List of SHRM-Recommended *HR Content Areas*	Supplementary Discussion Questions for Assessing Your *Knowledge and Skills* with Respect to SHRM HR Content Areas
History of HR and Its Role (*we covered in Ch. 1*)	**1.** Briefly discuss the evolution of the personnel/HR field in the United States over the last 100 years to its current role in modern globally competitive societies. **2.** Describe HR's role in developing human capital. **3.** Describe HR's impact on firm success. **4.** Discuss the partnership of line managers and HR managers and departments.
Employment Law (*Ch. 2*)	**1.** List and discuss the major equal employment laws, and give examples of how they influence the various HR functions such as recruiting and training employees. **2.** Describe the basic equal employment law enforcement procedure, from complaint to conclusion.
Managing a Diverse Workforce (*Ch. 2*)	**1.** List and discuss several important strategies for successfully increasing workforce diversity. **2.** Explain with examples how diversity management can improve business results. **3.** Give some examples of how creating a diverse workforce can enhance employee perceptions of fairness and equity throughout the organization.
HR and Organizational Strategy (*Ch. 3*)	**1.** List and explain with examples the basic types of corporate, competitive, and functional strategies. **2.** Define "strategic human resource management" and explain with examples how managers devise HR practices to support their companies' strategies. **3.** Answer the question, "How do firms gain sustainable competitive advantage through effective human resource management strategies and practices?"
HR and Mergers and Acquisitions (*Ch. 3*)	**1.** Give several examples of how HR practices can contribute to the success of corporate mergers and acquisitions.
Measuring HR Outcomes and the Bottom Line (*Ch. 3*)	**1.** Explain and provide examples of at least five HR metrics. **2.** Discuss how you as a manager could use HR and broader business metrics to link HR practices to achieving bottom-line business results.
Job Analysis (*Ch. 4*)	**1.** List and describe the methods and procedure you would use to conduct a job analysis. **2.** Briefly discuss the main factors that must be taken into account in designing a job. **3.** List and briefly describe the main sections in a job description.
Workforce Planning and Talent Management (*Ch. 5*)	**1.** Describe the basic process and methods of human resource planning, and explain, in doing so, how they relate to corporate strategy. **2.** Show how you would create a simple staffing plan.
Outsourcing (*Chs. 5, 13*)	**1.** Explain the difference between employee leasing and outsourcing. **2.** Discuss the pros and cons of outsourcing.

(continued)

List of SHRM-Recommended *HR Content Areas*	Supplementary Discussion Questions for Assessing Your *Knowledge and Skills* with Respect to SHRM HR Content Areas
Recruiting and Selection (Ch. 5)	**1.** Describe the various methods of locating qualified job candidates and the advantages and disadvantages of each. **2.** Briefly discuss what you believe would illustrate a successful strategy for developing a diverse talent pool of qualified candidates.
Recruiting and Selection (Chs. 6, 7)	**1.** List and compare and contrast the main assessment methods an employer can use for identifying a candidate's suitability for employment. **2.** Discuss the main legal implications associated with employment selection techniques, including interviewing.
Organizational Entry and Socialization (Ch. 8)	**1.** Answer the question, "Why is it important to familiarize new employees with the organization, and with their new jobs and work units?"
Training and Development (Ch. 8)	**1.** Explain how you would link training objectives to organizational goals. **2.** List and discuss the principles of learning, and describe how they facilitate training. **3.** Explain how you would create a training program. **4.** List and briefly describe five important training methods. **5.** Why is it important to assess training effectiveness, and how would you go about doing so?
Performance Appraisal and Feedback (Ch. 9)	**1.** Explain what you would consider to be the main *purposes, characteristics, methods,* and *communication techniques* of an effective performance appraisal program. **2.** Answer the question, "How would you use performance management techniques to develop a clear 'line of sight' connecting the employees' performance and the company's goals?"
Career Planning (Ch. 10)	**1.** Answer the question, "How would you use HR management functions to better match individual and organizational needs?" **2.** List and describe the basic stages of one's career development. **3.** Describe five methods employers can use to support their employees' career development needs.
Compensation Benefits and Total Rewards (Ch. 11)	**1.** Discuss the major federal laws affecting compensation. **2.** What role does "equity" play in devising a compensation plan? **3.** Define "strategic compensation" and explain how you would go about linking pay, employee performance, and organizational objectives.
Compensation Benefits and Total Rewards (Ch. 12)	**1.** What is meant by "variable pay"? **2.** List and explain the nature and pros and cons of at least one individual, group, and companywide incentive plan.
Employee Benefits (Ch. 13)	**1.** List the employee benefits required by law. **2.** What are the trends with respect to employee benefits costs and what strategies are employers using to control these costs? **3.** What are the major trends in retirement policies and pension plans? **4.** What strategic considerations should guide the design of benefits programs?

(*continued*)

List of SHRM-Recommended *HR Content Areas*	Supplementary Discussion Questions for Assessing Your *Knowledge and Skills* with Respect to SHRM HR Content Areas
Employee and Labor Relations (Chs. 14, 2)	**1.** Explain the concepts of employment at will, wrongful discharge, implied contract, and constructive discharge. **2.** What is "discipline" and what are the characteristics of a defensible discipline system? **3.** Answer the question, "How can effective employee relations policies and practices create a positive organizational culture and improved employee commitment and performance?" **4.** With respect to fair and equitable treatment, what are employees' rights and responsibilities?
HR and Downsizing (Ch. 14)	**1.** Identify the legal issues associated with organizational downsizings and layoffs. **2.** What are some other, business and people, issues to consider when making downsizing and/or layoff decisions?
Employee and Labor Relations (Ch. 15)	**1.** List and discuss each of the principal federal laws that provide a framework for labor relations. **2.** Briefly define collective bargaining, union representation, union organizing, and bargaining and negotiation. **3.** Discuss the main types of alternative dispute resolution procedures.
Occupational Health, Safety, and Security (Ch. 16)	**1.** Explain the general provisions of the Occupational Safety and Health Act of 1970. **2.** Answer the question, "How would you go about creating a safe work environment?"
HR and Globalization (Ch. 17)	**1.** For the manager, HR manager, and employer, what are the main challenges that influence designing HR policies and practices when managing across borders?
Managing Human Resources in Entrepreneurial Firms (Ch. 18)	**1.** List and briefly discuss what to look for when retaining an HR vendor.
HR Information Systems (Chs. 1–18)	**1.** In general, how can employers use technology to improve the efficiency and effectiveness of their human resource management operations? **2.** Explain how HR information systems can lessen time spent on transactional HR activities and thereby allow HR professionals to focus more on strategic activities. **3.** Give specific examples of how employers use HR information systems to improve HR practices in each of the main HR functions such as recruiting and training. **4.** Answer the question, "How can technology help HR and other managers to make better short- and long-term decisions?"

IV APPLYING YOUR KNOWLEDGE OF SHRM *PERSONAL COMPETENCIES* TO SOLVE HR ISSUES

List of SHRM-Recommended *Personal Competencies* Needed for Effectively Carrying Out the Manager's Various HR Activities	Supplementary Discussion Questions for Assessing Your Ability to Apply SHRM *Personal Competencies* in Solving HR Issues
Change Management: Demonstrate an ability to develop a planned approach to help employees adjust to changes within the organization.	**1.** Bandag Automotive case (Appendix B, pp. 707–709): Assuming Jim Bandag's father decides to step back in and implement the required changes, what issues might he encounter, and how exactly would you suggest he plan and execute the changes (using guidelines like those in Chapter 8)? **2.** BP Texas City case (Appendix B, pp. 718–722): In 2007, Lord Browne stepped down as BP's CEO, and the firm's president took charge. Based on the case, what organizational changes should BP make now and how would you suggest the new CEO go about executing them? **3.** Jack Nelson case (Ch. 1, p. 26): Assuming the bank decides to set up a central HR office, what employee resistance issues would you expect them to face and how (in outline form) do you suggest they implement the change?
Communication Skills: Demonstrate an ability to effectively convey information both verbally and in writing.	**1.** Video 3: Recruitment and Placement (Ch. 7, p. 257): In this video, Paul and BMG's vice president have a heated and not particularly productive exchange regarding the firm's hiring practices. What did each of these two people do right and wrong with respect to communicating, and what do you think they each should have done to make the discussion more useful? **2.** "Helping 'The Donald,'" experiential exercise (Ch. 1, p. 25): Would you consider Mr. Trump's communication style in the evaluation sessions entirely effective or not, and if not how would you suggest he improve his style?
Conflict Management: Demonstrate an ability to develop strategies to help productively resolve disagreements between individuals or groups within the organization.	**1.** **Carter Cleaning Case: The Grievance** (Ch. 15, p. 576): Was Murray the manager's summary suspension of George fair? Possibly, but Jennifer also knows that such decisions occasionally flow from personal conflicts, or from a lack of clear rules. If you were Jennifer in this case, what would you have done at this point to reduce the potential for ongoing conflict between Murray and George? If you are the firm's HR manager (assuming they had one), what if anything would you do to reduce the potential that the conflict will escalate? **2.** Video 4: Training and Development (Ch. 10, p. 381): In this video the training director handles a fairly confrontational meeting with the firm's marketing director. What was the source of the conflict, how well do you think the parties managed the conflict, and what would you have done differently?

(continued)

List of SHRM-Recommended *Personal Competencies* Needed for Effectively Carrying Out the Manager's Various HR Activities	Supplementary Discussion Questions for Assessing Your Ability to Apply SHRM *Personal Competencies* in Solving HR Issues
Cross-Cultural Effectiveness: Demonstrate an ability to successfully recognize and deal with cultural differences that may affect behavior in the workplace.	**1.** Google case (Appendix B, pp. 712–715): What sorts of factors will Google have to take into consideration as it tries transferring its culture and reward systems and way of doing business to its operations abroad? **2.** Carter Cleaning Company Going Abroad case (Ch. 17, p. 655): What do you see as the two or three main cultural challenges Carter would face in opening a store in Mexico? How (in terms of specific HR policies and practices) would you suggest the Carters deal with these challenges?
Ethical Decision Making: Demonstrate an ability to make decisions that reflect a high standard of professional behavior.	**1.** BP Texas City case (Appendix B, pp. 718–722): The textbook defines ethics as "the principles of conduct governing an individual or a group," and specifically as the standards one uses to decide what their conduct should be. To what extent do you believe that what happened at BP is as much a breakdown in the company's ethical systems as it is in its safety systems, and how would you defend your conclusion? What would you have done differently, ethically? What should the new CEO do now?
Leadership: Demonstrate the ability to direct, lead, and inspire others toward a shared vision.	**1.** Carter Cleaning Company Guaranteeing Fair Treatment case (Ch. 14, p. 537): "To change her employees' behavior in this matter, Jennifer will have to exhibit effective leadership." Explain why you do (or do not) agree with that statement, and (if you do agree) explain exactly what you would do now if you were Jennifer with respect to exercising effective leadership to improve the situation. **2.** Reinventing the Wheel at Apex Door Company case (Ch. 8, pp. 294–295): In what ways is Apex's current problem a failure of leadership, what leadership mistakes has president Jim Delaney made, and what leadership steps would you take now if you were in his shoes?
Managing Organizational Culture: Demonstrate an ability to recognize and influence organizational norms and values.	**1.** BP Texas City case (Appendix B, pp. 718–722): Based on the case, how would you characterize the organizational culture at BP companywide and at its refineries, and what exactly would you do to change that culture (assuming it needs changing)? **2.** Honesty Testing at Carter Cleaning Company case (Ch. 6, pp. 222–223): Often, the best way to reduce problems like the one now facing the Carters is to create an organizational culture that strongly supports ethical behavior. How exactly could the Carters have fostered such a culture, and what exactly should they do now to do so?
Negotiation Skills: Demonstrate an ability to communicate, discuss, and agree on something among people with differing objectives.	**1.** Video 6: Compensation (Ch. 13, p. 497): In this case Angelo is negotiating a pay raise with Cheryl and Gina. How would you rate each person's negotiating skills? Why? What would you advise Cheryl and Gina to do with respect to their negotiating technique? **2.** Salary Inequities at Acme Manufacturing case (Ch. 11, pp. 417–418): Joe Black may well now find himself negotiating with the female supervisors in order to reach an equitable salary arrangement with them. What negotiating strategy (for instance, "take it or leave it" vs. "collaboration") would you suggest he use in this situation, and why?

(continued)

List of SHRM-Recommended *Personal Competencies* Needed for Effectively Carrying Out the Manager's Various HR Activities	Supplementary Discussion Questions for Assessing Your Ability to Apply SHRM *Personal Competencies* in Solving HR Issues
Quantitative Analysis: Demonstrate an ability to ascertain quantitatively, for example, the attributes, behavior, or opinions of the entity you are measuring.	**1.** Muffler Magic case (Appendix B, pp. 715–718): Create a spreadsheet showing the titles of the main measurable factors owner Ron Brown should take into consideration in analyzing whether to take the professor's pay plan advice. **2.** Carter Cleaning Company Incentive Plan case (Ch. 12, pp. 458–459): What measurable factors should the Carters take into consideration in costing out and deciding on the new incentive plan?
Team Building: Demonstrate an ability to engage in a planned effort to improve the working relationships within a group of people in an organizational setting.	**1.** Angelo's Pizza case (Appendix B, pp. 709–712): If Angelo wants to open more stores, he will have to take steps to make sure that teamwork prevails in each store—that employees in each store work together collaboratively, supportively, and in support of each store's goals. What concrete steps can Angelo take to make sure that teamwork prevails in each store?

V SHRM'S *BUSINESS/POLICY AREAS:* WHY MANAGERS APPLYING HR PRACTICES NEED A BROAD-BASED BUSINESS BACKGROUND

SHRM's Recommended List of *Business or Policy Area* Knowledge and Skills Managers Require for Executing HR Activities	***Assignment:*** *Give specific examples of how dealing with the following HR activities depends on your knowledge and skills in the business or policy areas listed in the left column. We've provided general examples.*
Accounting	Ch. 3, Strategic HR—computing costs and benefits of various HR activities
Business Law	Chs. 2, 11, 15, 16, HR's legal framework—understanding the context of equal employment, safety, compensation, labor relations law
Corporate Social Responsibility	Ch. 13, Fair treatment—exercising fairness in downsizings
Economics	Ch. 5, Personnel planning—labor supply and demand forecasting
Entrepreneurship	Chs. 1–18, When you're on your own—How does understanding the entrepreneur's unique challenges make it possible to formulate HR policies and practices that are appropriate for the small business's needs?
Finance	Chs. 11–13, Compensation—formulating possible pay plans
General Management	Ch. 3, Strategic HR—How does understanding how interplay of various business functions influences company strategy, and how HR can support various departments' (sales, production, etc.) strategic aims?

(continued)

SHRM's Recommended List of *Business or Policy Area* Knowledge and Skills Managers Require for Executing HR Activities	***Assignment:* *Give specific examples of how dealing with the following HR activities depends on your knowledge and skills in the* business or policy areas *listed in the left column. We've provided general examples.***
Information Technology	Ch. 5, Recruitment—using technology-based services such as applications service providers to support the recruitment function
International Business	Ch. 17, Managing global human resources—creating international HR services (such as testing and compensation) that make sense in terms of the company's global sales, production, and finance operations
Managing Information Systems	Chs. 1–18, HRIS—instituting companywide human resource information systems
Organizational Behavior	Chs. 9, 12, 14, Applying your knowledge of human behavior in counseling, motivating, and disciplining employees
Statistics	Ch. 6, Testing and selection—assessing the effectiveness of various selection tools
Strategic Management	Ch. 3, Strategic HR—being able to formulate an HR strategy that supports the company's broader strategic aims
Supply Chain Management	Chs. 11–13, Compensation—creating a compensation plan that motivates employees to work cooperatively with supply chain partners such as vendors, distributors, and customers.

Appendix B Comprehensive Cases

BANDAG AUTOMOTIVE*

Jim Bandag took over his family's auto supply business in 2005, after helping his father, who founded the business, run it for about 10 years. Based in Illinois, Bandag employs about 300 people, and distributes auto supplies (replacement mufflers, bulbs, engine parts, and so on) through two divisions, one that supplies service stations and repair shops, and a second that sells retail auto supplies through five "Bandag Automotive" auto supply stores.

Jim's father, and now Jim, have always endeavored to keep Bandag's organization chart as simple as possible. The company has a full-time controller, managers for each of the five stores, a manager that oversees the distribution division, and Jim Bandag's executive assistant. Jim (and his father, working part-time) handles marketing and sales.

Jim's executive assistant administers the firm's day-to-day human resource management tasks, but they outsource most HR activities to others, including an employment agency that does their recruiting and screening, a benefits firm that administers their 401(k) plan, and a payroll service that handles their paychecks. Bandag's human resource management systems consist almost entirely of standardized HR forms they purchase from an HR supplies company. It supplies HR tools including forms such as application forms, performance appraisal forms, and an "honesty" test Bandag uses to screen the staff that works in the five stores. The company performs informal salary surveys to see what other companies in the area are paying for similar positions, and use these results for awarding annual merit increases (which in fact are more accurately cost-of-living adjustments).

Jim's father took a fairly paternal approach to the business. He often walked around speaking with his employees, finding out what their problems were, and even helping them out with an occasional loan—for instance, when he discovered that one of their children was sick, or for part of a new home down payment. Jim, on the other hand, tends to be more abrupt, and does not enjoy the same warm relationship with the employees as did his father. Jim is not unfair or dictatorial. He's just very focused on improving Bandag's financial performance, and so all his decisions, including his HR-related decisions, generally come down to cutting costs. For example, his knee-jerk reaction is usually to offer fewer days off rather than more, fewer benefits rather than more, and to be less flexible when an employee needs, for instance, a few extra days off because a child is sick.

It's therefore perhaps not surprising that over the past few years Bandag's sales and profits have increased markedly, but that the firm has found itself increasingly enmeshed in HR/equal employment–type issues. Indeed, Jim now finds himself spending a day or two a week addressing HR problems. For example, Henry Jaques, an employee of one of their stores, came to Jim's executive assistant and told her he was "irate" about his recent firing and was probably going to sue. On Henry's last performance appraisal, his store manager had said Henry did the technical aspects of his job well, but that he had "serious problems interacting with his coworkers."

He was continually arguing with them, and complaining to the store manager about working conditions. The store manager had told Jim that he had to fire Henry because he was making "the whole place poisonous," and that (although he felt sorry because he'd heard rumors that Henry suffered from some mental illness) he felt he had to go. Jim approved the dismissal.

Gavin was another problem. Gavin had worked for Bandag for 10 years, the last two as manager of one of the company's five stores. Right after Jim Bandag took over, Gavin told him he had to take a Family and Medical Leave Act medical leave to have hip surgery, and Jim approved the leave. So far so good, but when Gavin returned from leave, Jim told him that his position had been eliminated. They had decided to close his store and open a new, larger store across from a shopping center about a mile away, and appointed a new manager in Gavin's absence. However, the company did give Gavin a (nonmanagerial) position in the new store as a counter salesperson, at the same salary and with the same benefits as he had before. Even so, "This job is not similar to my old one," Gavin insisted. "It doesn't have nearly as much prestige." His contention is that FMLA requires that the company bring him back in the same or equivalent position, and that this means a supervisory position, similar to what he had before he went on leave. Jim said no, and they seem to be heading toward litigation.

In another sign of the times at Bandag, the company's controller, Miriam, who had been with the company for about 6 years, went on pregnancy leave for 12 weeks in 2005 (also under the FMLA), and then received an additional 3 weeks' leave under Bandag's extended illness days program. Four weeks after she came back, she asked Jim Bandag if she could arrange to work fewer hours per week, and spend about a day per week working out of her home. He refused, and about 2 months later fired her. Jim Bandag said, "I'm sorry, it's not anything to do with your pregnancy-related requests, but we've got ample reasons to discharge you—your monthly budgets have been several days late, and we've got proof you may have forged documents." She replied, "I don't care what you say your reasons are, you're really firing me because of my pregnancy, and that's illegal."

Jim felt he was on safe ground as far as defending the company for these actions, although he didn't look forward to spending the time and money that he knew it would take to fight each. However, what he learned over lunch from a colleague undermined his confidence about another case that Jim had been sure would be a "slam dunk" for his company. Jim was explaining to his friend that one of Bandag's truck maintenance service people had applied for a job driving one of Bandag's distribution department trucks, and that Jim had turned him down because the worker was deaf. Jim (whose wife has occasionally said of him, "No one has ever accused Jim of being politically correct") was mentioning to his friend the apparent absurdity of a deaf person asking to be a truck delivery person. His friend, who happens to work for UPS, pointed out that the U.S. Court of Appeals for the Ninth Circuit had recently decided that UPS had violated the Americans with Disabilities Act by refusing to consider deaf workers for jobs driving the company's smaller vehicles.

Although Jim's father is semi-retired, the sudden uptick in the frequency of such EEO-type issues troubled him, particularly after so many years of labor peace. However, he's not sure what to do about it. Having handed over the reins of the company to his son Jim, he was loath to inject himself back into the company's operational decision making. On the other hand, he was afraid that in the short run, these issues were going to drain a great deal of Jim's time and resources, and that in the long run they might be a sign of things to come, with problems like these eventually overwhelming Bandag Auto. He comes to you, who he knows consults in human resource management, and asks you the following questions.

Questions

1. Given Bandag Auto's size, and anything else you know about it, should we reorganize the human resource management function, and if so why and how?
2. What, if anything, would you do to change and/or improve upon the current HR systems, forms, and practices that we now use?

3. Do you think that the employee that Jim fired for creating what the manager called a poisonous relationship has a legitimate claim against us, and if so why and what should we do about it?
4. Is it true that we really had to put Gavin back into an equivalent position, or was it adequate to just bring him back into a job at the same salary, bonuses, and benefits as he had before his leave?
5. Miriam, the controller, is basically claiming that the company is retaliating against her for being pregnant, and that the fact that we raised performance issues was just a smokescreen. Do you think the EEOC and/or courts would agree with her, and, in any case, what should we do now?
6. An employee who is deaf has asked us to be one of our delivery people and we turned him down. He's now threatening to sue. What should we do, and why?
7. In the previous 10 years, we've had only one equal employment complaint, and now in the last few years we've had four or five. What should I do about it? Why?

Based generally on actual facts, but Bandag is a fictitious company. Bandag source notes: "The Problem Employee: Discipline or Accommodation?" *Monday Business Briefing*, March 8, 2005; "Employee Says Change in Duties After Leave Violates FMLA," *BNA Bulletin to Management*, January 16, 2007, p. 24; "Manager Fired Days After Announcing Pregnancy," *BNA Bulletin to Management*, January 2, 2007, p. 8; "Ninth Circuit Rules UPS Violated ADA by Barring Deaf Workers from Driving Jobs," *BNA Bulletin to Management*, October 17, 2006, p. 329.

ANGELO'S PIZZA*

Angelo Camero was brought up in the Bronx, New York, and basically always wanted to be in the pizza store business. As a youngster, he would sometimes spend hours at the local pizza store, watching the owner knead the pizza dough, flatten it into a large circular crust, fling it up, and then spread on tomato sauce in larger and larger loops. After graduating from college as a marketing major, he made a beeline back to the Bronx, where he opened his first Angelo's Pizza store, emphasizing its clean, bright interior, its crisp green, red, and white sign, and his all-natural, fresh ingredients. Within 5 years, Angelo's store was a success, and he had opened three other stores and was considering franchising his concept.

Eager as he was to expand, his 4 years in business school had taught him the difference between being an entrepreneur and being a manager. As an entrepreneur/small-business owner, he knew he had the distinct advantage of being able to personally run the whole operation himself. With just one store and a handful of employees, he could make every decision and watch the cash register, check in the new supplies, oversee the takeout, and personally supervise the service.

When he expanded to three stores, things started getting challenging. He hired managers for the two new stores (both of whom had worked for him at his first store for several years) and gave them only minimal "how to run a store"–type training, on the assumption that, having worked with him for several years, they already knew pretty much everything they needed to know about running a store. However, he was already experiencing human resource management problems, and he knew there was no way he could expand the number of stores he owned, or (certainly) contemplate franchising his idea, unless he had a system in place that he could clone in each new store, to provide the manager (or the franchisee) with the necessary management knowledge and expertise to run their stores. Angelo had no training program in place for teaching his store managers how to run their stores. He simply (erroneously, as it turned out) assumed that by working with him they would learn how to do things on the job. Since Angelo really had no system in place, the new managers were, in a way, starting off below zero when it came to how to manage a store.

There were several issues that particularly concern Angelo. Finding and hiring good employees was number one. He'd read the new National Small Business Poll from the National Federation of Independent Business Education Foundation. It found that 71% of small-business owners believed that finding qualified employees was "hard." Furthermore, "the search for qualified employees will grow more difficult as demographic and education factors" continue to make it more difficult to find employees. Similarly, reading *The Kiplinger Letter* one day, he noticed that just about every type of business couldn't find enough good employees to hire. Small firms were particularly in jeopardy; the *Letter* said: Giant firms can outsource many (particularly entry-level) jobs abroad, and larger companies can also afford to pay better benefits and to train their employees. Small firms rarely have the resources or the economies of scale to allow outsourcing or to install the big training programs that would enable them to take untrained new employees and turned them into skilled ones.

Although finding enough employees was his biggest problem, finding enough honest ones scared him even more. Angelo recalled from one of his business school courses that companies in the United States are losing a total of well over $400 billion a year in employee theft. As a rough approximation, that works out to about $9 per employee per day and about $12,000 lost annually for a typical company. Furthermore, it was small companies like Angelo's that were particularly in the crosshairs, because companies with fewer than 100 employees are particularly prone to employee theft. Why are small firms particularly vulnerable? Perhaps they lack experience dealing with the problem. More importantly: Small firms are more likely to have a single person doing several jobs, such as ordering supplies and paying the delivery person. This undercuts the checks and balances managers often strive for to control theft. Furthermore, the risk of stealing goes up dramatically when the business is largely based on cash. In a pizza store, many people come in and just buy one or two slices and a cola for lunch, and almost all pay with cash, not credit cards.

And, Angelo was not just worried about someone stealing cash. They can steal your whole business idea, something he learned from painful experience. He had been planning to open a store in what he thought would be a particularly good location, and was thinking of having one of his current employees manage the store. Instead, it turned out that this employee was, in a manner of speaking, stealing Angelo's brain—what Angelo knew about customers, suppliers, where to buy pizza dough, where to buy tomato sauce, how much everything should cost, how to furnish the store, where to buy ovens, store layout—everything. This employee soon quit and opened up his own pizza store, not far from where Angelo had planned to open his new store.

That he was having trouble hiring good employees, there was no doubt. The restaurant business is particularly brutal when it comes to turnover. Many restaurants turn over their employees at a rate of 200% to 300% per year—so every year, each position might have a series of two to three employees filling it. As Angelo said, "I was losing two to three employees a month." As he said, "We're a high-volume store, and while we should have [to fill all the hours in a week] about six employees per store, we were down to only three or four, so my managers and I were really under the gun."

The problem was bad at the hourly employee level: "We were churning a lot at the hourly level," said Angelo. "Applicants would come in, my managers or I would hire them and not spend much time training them, and the good ones would leave in frustration after a few weeks, while often it was the bad ones who'd stay behind." But in the last 2 years, Angelo's three company-owned stores also went through a total of three store managers—"They were just blowing through the door," as Angelo put it, in part because, without good employees, their workday was brutal. As a rule, when a small-business owner or manager can't find enough employees (or an employee doesn't show up for work), about 80% of the time the owner or manager does the job himself or herself. So, these managers often ended up working 7 days a week, 10 to 12 hours a day, and many just burned out in the end. One night, working three jobs himself with customers leaving in anger, Angelo decided he'd never just hire someone because he was desperate again, but would start doing his hiring more rationally.

Angelo knew he should have a more formal screening process. As he said, "If there's been a lesson learned, it's much better to spend time up-front screening out candidates that don't fit than to hire them and have to put up with their ineffectiveness." He also knew that he could identify many of the traits that his employees needed. For example, he knew that not everyone has the temperament to be a waiter or waitress (he has a small pizza/Italian restaurant in the back of his main store). As Angelo said, "I've seen personalities that were off the charts in assertiveness or overly introverted, traits that obviously don't make a good fit for a waiter a waitress."

As a local business, Angelo recruits by placing help wanted ads in two local newspapers, and he's been "shocked" at some of the responses and experiences he's had in response to his help wanted ads. Many of the applicants left voice mail messages (Angelo or the other workers in the store were too busy to answer), and some applicants Angelo "just axed" on the assumption that people without good telephone manners wouldn't have very good manners in the store either. He also quickly learned that he had to throw out a very wide net, even if only hiring one or two people. Many people, as noted, he just deleted because of the messages they left, and about half the people he scheduled to come in for interviews didn't show up. He'd taken courses in human resource management, so (as he said) "I should know better," but he hired people based almost exclusively on a single interview (he occasionally made a feeble attempt to check references). In total, his HR approach was obviously not working. It wasn't producing enough good recruits, and the people he did hire were often problematical.

What was he looking for? Service-oriented courteous people, for one. For example, he'd hired one employee who used profanity several times, including once in front of a customer. On that employee's third day, Angelo had to tell her, "I think Angelo's isn't the right place for you," and he fired her. As Angelo said, "I felt bad, but also knew that everything I have is on the line for this business, so I wasn't going to let anyone run this business down." Angelo wants reliable people (who'll show up on time), honest people, and people who are flexible about switching jobs and hours as required.

Angelo's Pizza business has only the most rudimentary human resource management system. Angelo bought several application forms at a local Office Depot, and rarely uses other forms of any sort. He uses his personal accountant for reviewing the company's books, and Angelo himself computes each employee's paycheck at the end of the week and writes the checks. Training is entirely on-the-job. Angelo personally trained each of his employees. For those employees who go on to be store managers, he assumes that they are training their own employees the way that Angelo trained them (for better or worse, as it turns out). Angelo pays "a bit above" prevailing wage rates (judging by other help wanted ads) but probably not enough to make a significant difference in the quality of employees that he attracts. If you asked Angelo what his reputation is as an employer, Angelo, being a candid and forthright person, would probably tell you that he is a supportive but hard-nosed employer who treats people fairly, but whose business reputation may suffer from disorganization stemming from inadequate organization and training. He approaches you to ask you several questions.

Questions

1. My strategy is to (hopefully) expand the number of stores and eventually franchise, while focusing on serving only high-quality fresh ingredients. What are three specific human resource management implications of my strategy (including specific policies and practices)?
2. Identify and briefly discuss five specific human resource management errors that I'm currently making.

3. Develop a structured interview form that we can use for hiring (1) store managers, (2) waiters and waitresses, and (3) counter people/pizza makers.
4. Based on what you know about Angelo's, and what you know from having visited pizza restaurants, write a one-page outline showing specifically how you think Angelo's should go about selecting employees.

Based generally on actual facts, but Angelo's Pizza is a fictitious company. Angelo's Pizza source notes: Dino Berta, "People Problems: Keep Hiring from Becoming a Crying Game," *Nation's Business News* 36, no. 20 (May 20, 2002), pp. 72–74; Ellen Lyon, "Hiring, Personnel Problems Can Challenge Entrepreneurs," *Patriot-News*, October 12, 2004; Rose Robin Pedone, "Businesses' $400 Billion Theft Problem," *Long Island Business News*, no. 27 (July 6, 1998), pp. 1B–2B; "Survey Shows Small-Business Problems with Hiring, Internet," *Providence Business News* 16 (September 10, 2001), pp. 1B; "Finding Good Workers Is Posing a Big Problem as Hiring Picks Up," *The Kiplinger Letter* 81 (February 13, 2004).

GOOGLE*

Fortune magazine named Google the best of the 100 best companies to work for, and there is little doubt why. Among the benefits they offer are free shuttles equipped with Wi-Fi to pick up and drop off employees from San Francisco Bay area locations, unlimited sick days, annual all-expense-paid ski trips, free gourmet meals, five on-site free doctors, $2,000 bonuses for referring a new hire, free flu shots, a giant lap pool, on-site oil changes, on-site car washes, volleyball courts, TGIF parties, free on-site washers and dryers (with free detergent), Ping-Pong and foosball tables, and free famous people lectures. For many people, it's the gourmet meals and snacks that make Google stand out. For example, human resources director Stacey Sullivan loves the Irish oatmeal with fresh berries at the company's Plymouth Rock Cafe, near Google's "people operations" group. "I sometimes dream about it," she says. Engineer Jan Fitzpatrick loves the raw bar at Google's Tapis restaurant, down the road on the Google campus. Then, of course, there are the stock options—each new employee gets about 1,200 options to buy Google shares (recently worth about $480 per share). In fact, dozens of early Google employees ("Googlers") are already multimillionaires thanks to Google stock. The recession that began around 2008 did prompt Google and other firms to cut back on some of these benefits (cafeteria hours are shorter today, for instance), but Google still pretty much leads the benefits pack.

For their part, Googlers share certain traits. They tend to be brilliant, team oriented (teamwork is the norm, especially for big projects), and driven. *Fortune* describes them as people who "almost universally" see themselves as the most interesting people on the planet, and who are happy-go-lucky on the outside, but type A—highly intense and goal directed—on the inside. They're also super-hardworking (which makes sense, since it's not unusual for engineers to be in the hallways at 3 A.M. debating some new mathematical solution to a Google search problem). They're so team oriented that when working on projects, it's not unusual for a Google team to give up its larger, more spacious offices and to crowd into a small conference room, where they can "get things done." Historically, Googlers generally graduate with great grades from the best universities, including Stanford, Harvard, and MIT. For many years, Google wouldn't even consider hiring someone with less than a 3.7 average—while also probing deeply into the why behind any B grades. Google also doesn't hire lone wolves, but wants people who work together and people who also have diverse interests (narrow interests or skills are a turnoff at Google). Google also wants people with growth potential. The company is expanding so fast that they need to hire people who are capable of being promoted five or six times—it's only, they say, by hiring such overqualified people that they can be sure that the employees will be able to keep up as Google and their own departments expand.

The starting salaries are highly competitive. Experienced engineers start at about $130,000 a year (plus about 1,200 shares of stock options, as noted), and new MBAs can expect between $80,000 and $120,000 per year (with smaller option grants). Most recently, Google had about 10,000 staff members, up from its start a few years ago with just three employees in a rented garage.

Of course, in a company that's grown from three employees to 10,000 and from zero value to hundreds of billions of dollars in about 5 years, it may be quibbling to talk about "problems," but there's no doubt that such rapid growth does confront Google's management, and particularly its "people operations" group, with some big challenges. Let's look at these.

For one, Google, as noted earlier, is a 24-hour operation, and with engineers and others frequently pulling all-nighters to complete their projects, the company needs to provide a package of services and financial benefits that supports that kind of lifestyle, and that helps its employees maintain an acceptable work–life balance.

As another challenge, Google's enormous financial success is a two-edged sword. While Google usually wins the recruitment race when it comes to competing for new employees against competitors like Microsoft or Yahoo!, Google does need some way to stem a rising tide of retirements. Most Googlers are still in their late twenties and early thirties, but many have become so wealthy from their Google stock options that they can afford to retire. One 27-year-old engineer received a million-dollar founder's award for her work on the program for searching desktop computers, and wouldn't think of leaving "except to start her own company." Similarly a former engineering vice president retired (with his Google stock profits) to pursue his love of astronomy. The engineer who dreamed up Gmail recently retired (at the age of 30).

Another challenge is that the work not only involves long hours but can also be very tense. Google is a very numbers-oriented environment. For example, consider a typical weekly Google user interface design meeting. Marisa Meyer, the company's vice president of search products and user experience, runs the meeting, where her employees work out the look and feel of Google's products. Seated around a conference table are about a dozen Googlers, tapping on laptops. During the 2-hour meeting, Meyer needs to evaluate various design proposals, ranging from minor tweaks to a new product's entire layout. She's previously given each presentation an allotted amount of time, and a large digital clock on the wall ticks off the seconds. The presenters must quickly present their ideas, but also handle questions such as "what do users do if the tab is moved from the side of the page to the top?" Furthermore, it's all about the numbers—no one at Google would ever say, for instance, "the tab looks better in red"—you need to prove your point. Presenters must come armed with usability experiment results, showing, for instance, that a certain percent preferred red or some other color, for instance. While the presenters are answering these questions as quickly as possible, the digital clock is ticking, and when it hits the allotted time, the presentation must end, and the next team steps up to present. It is a tough and tense environment, and Googlers must have done their homework.

Growth can also undermine the "outlaw band that's changing the world" culture that fostered the services that made Google famous. Even cofounder Sergi Brin agrees that Google risks becoming less "zany" as it grows. To paraphrase one of its top managers, the hard part of any business is keeping that original innovative, small-business feel even as the company grows.

Creating the right culture is especially challenging now that Google is truly global. For example, Google works hard to provide the same financial and service benefits every place it does business around the world, but it can't exactly match its benefits in every country because of international laws and international taxation issues. Offering the same benefits everywhere is more important than it might initially appear. All those benefits make life easier for Google staff, and help them achieve a work–life balance. Achieving the right work–life balance is the center-piece of Google's culture, but also becomes more challenging as the company grows. On the one hand, Google does expect all of its employees to work super hard; on the other hand, it realizes that it needs to help them maintain some sort of balance. As one manager says, Google acknowledges "that we work hard but that work is not everything."

Recruitment is another challenge. While Google certainly doesn't lack applicants, attracting the right applicants is crucial if Google is to continue to grow successfully. Working at Google requires a special set of traits, and screening employees is easier if they recruit the right people to begin with. For instance, they need to attract people who are super-bright, love to work, have fun, can handle the stress, and who also have outside interests and flexibility.

As the company grows internationally, it also faces the considerable challenge of recruiting and building staff overseas. For example, Google now is introducing a new vertical market–based structure across Europe, to attract more business advertisers to its search engine. (By vertical market–based structure, Google means focusing on key vertical industry sectors such as travel, retail, automotive, and technology.) To build these industry groupings abroad from scratch, Google promoted its former head of its U.S. financial services group to be the vertical markets director for Europe; he moved there recently. Google is thus looking for heads for each of its vertical industry groups for all of its key European territories. Each of these vertical market heads will have to educate their market sectors (retailing, travel, and so on) so Google can attract new advertisers. Most recently, Google already had about 12 offices across Europe, and its London office had tripled in size to 100 staff in just 2 years.

However, probably the biggest challenge Google faces is gearing up its employee selection system, now that the company must hire thousands of people per year. When Google started in business, job candidates typically suffered through a dozen or more in-person interviews, and the standards were so high that even applicants with years of great work experience often got turned down if they had just average college grades. But recently, even Google's cofounders have acknowledged to security analysts that setting such an extraordinarily high bar for hiring was holding back Google's expansion. For Google's first few years, one of the company's cofounder's interviewed nearly every job candidate before he or she was hired, and even today one of them still reviews the qualifications of everyone before he or she gets a final offer.

The experience of one candidate illustrates what Google is up against. They interviewed a 24-year-old for a corporate communications job at Google. Google first made contact with the candidate in May, and then, after two phone interviews, invited him to headquarters. There he had separate interviews with about six people and was treated to lunch in a Google cafeteria. They also had him turn in several "homework" assignments, including a personal statement and a marketing plan. In August, Google invited the candidate back for a second round, which they said would involve another four or five interviews. In the meantime, he decided he'd rather work at a start-up, and accepted another job at a new Web-based instant messaging provider.

Google's new head of human resources, a former GE executive, says that Google is trying to strike the right balance between letting Google and the candidate get to know each other while also moving quickly. To that end, Google recently administered a survey to all Google's current employees, in an effort to identify the traits that correlate with success at Google. In the survey, employees had to respond to questions relating to about 300 variables, including their performance on standardized tests, how old they were when they first used a computer, and how many foreign languages they speak. The Google survey team that went back and compared the answers against the 30 or 40 job performance factors they keep for each employee. They thereby identified clusters of traits that Google might better focus on during the hiring process. Google is also trying to move from the free-form interviews they've had in the past to a more structured process.

Questions

1. What do you think of the idea of Google correlating personal traits from the employee's answers on the survey to their performance, and then using that as the basis for screening job candidates? In other words, is it or is it not a good idea and please explain your answer.
2. The benefits that Google pays obviously represent an enormous expense. Based on what you know about Google and on what you read in this book, how would you defend all these benefits if you're making a presentation to the security analysts who were analyzing Google's performance?
3. If you wanted to hire the brightest people around, how would you go about recruiting and selecting them?
4. To support its growth and expansion strategy, Google wants (among other traits) people who are super-bright and who work hard, often round-the-clock, and who are flexible and maintain a decent work–life balance. List five specific HR policies or practices that you think Google has implemented or should implement to support its strategy, and explain your answer.
5. What sorts of factors do you think Google will have to take into consideration as it tries transferring its culture and reward systems and way of doing business to its operations abroad?
6. Given the sorts of values and culture Google cherishes, briefly describe four specific activities you suggest they pursue during new-employee orientation.

Source notes for Google: "Google Brings Vertical Structure to Europe," *New Media Age*, August 4, 2005, p. 2; Debbie Lovewell, "Employer Profile—Google: Searching for Talent," *Employee Benefits*, October 10, 2005, p. 66; "Google Looking for Gourmet Chefs," *Internet Week*, August 4, 2005; Douglas Merrill, "Google's 'Googley' Culture Kept Alive by Tech," *eWeek*, April 11, 2006; Robert Hof, "Google Gives Employees Another Option," *BusinessWeek Online*, December 13, 2005; Kevin Delaney, "Google Adjusts Hiring Process as Needs Grow," *The Wall Street Journal*, October 23, 2006, pp. B1, B8; Adam Lishinsky, "Search and Enjoy," *Fortune*, January 22, 2007, pp. 70–82; www.nypost.com/seven/10302008/business/frugal_google_cuts_perks_136011.htm, accessed July 12, 2009.

MUFFLER MAGIC*

Muffler Magic is a fast-growing chain of 25 automobile service centers in Nevada. Originally started 20 years ago as a muffler repair shop by Ronald Brown, the chain expanded rapidly to new locations, and as it did so Muffler Magic also expanded the services it provided, from muffler replacement to oil changes, brake jobs, and engine repair. Today, one can bring an automobile to a Muffler Magic shop for basically any type of service, from tires to mufflers to engine repair.

Auto service is a tough business. The shop owner is basically dependent upon the quality of the service people he or she hires and retains, and the most qualified mechanics find it easy to pick up and leave for a job paying a bit more at a competitor down the road. It's also a business in which productivity is very important. The single largest expense is usually the cost of labor. Auto service dealers generally don't just make up the prices that they charge customers for various repairs; instead, they charge based on standardized industry rates for jobs like changing spark plugs or repairing a leaky radiator. Therefore, if, for instance, someone brings a car in for a new alternator, and the standard number of hours for changing the alternator is an hour, but it takes the mechanic 2 hours, the service center's owner may end up making less profit on the transaction.

Quality is a persistent problem as well. For example, "rework" has recently been a problem at Muffler Magic. A customer recently brought her car to a Muffler Magic to have the car's brake pads replaced, which the store did for her. Unfortunately, when she drove off, she only got about two blocks before she discovered that she had no brake power at all. It was simply fortuitous that she was going so slowly she was able to stop her car by slowly rolling up against a parking bumper. It subsequently turned out that the mechanic who replaced the brake pads had failed to properly tighten a fitting on the hydraulic brake tubes and the brake fluid had run out, leaving the car with no braking power. In a similar problem the month before that, a (different) mechanic replaced a fan belt, but forgot to refill the radiator with fluid; that customer's car overheated before he got four blocks away, and Muffler Magic had to replace the whole engine. Of course problems like these not only diminish the profitability of the company's profits, but, repeated many times over, have the potential for ruining Muffler Magic's word-of-mouth reputation.

Organizationally, Muffler Magic employs about 300 people total, and Ron runs his company with eight managers, including Mr. Brown as president, a controller, a purchasing director, a marketing director, and the human resource manager. He also has three regional managers to whom the eight or nine service center managers in each area of Nevada report. Over the past 2 years, as the company has opened new service centers, company-wide profits have actually diminished, rather than gone up. In part, these diminishing profits probably reflect the fact that Ron Brown has found it increasingly difficult to manage his growing operation ("Your reach is exceeding your grasp" is how Ron's wife puts it).

The company has only the most basic HR systems in place. They use an application form that the human resource manager modified from one that she downloaded from the Web, and they use standard employee status change request forms, sign-on forms, I-9 forms, and so on that they purchased from a human resource management supply house. Training is entirely on-the-job. They expect the experienced technicians that they hire to come to the job fully trained; as noted, to that end, the service center managers generally ask candidates for these jobs basic behavioral questions that hopefully provide a window into these applicants' skills. However, most of the other technicians they hire to do jobs like rotating tires, fixing brake pads, and replacing mufflers are untrained and inexperienced. They are to be trained by either the service center manager or by more experienced technicians, on-the-job.

Ron Brown faces several HR-type problems. One, as he says, is that he faces the "tyranny of the immediate" when it comes to hiring employees. Although it's fine to say that he should be carefully screening each employee and checking their references and work ethic, from a practical point of view, with 25 centers to run, the centers' managers usually just hire anyone who seems to be breathing, as long as they can answer some basic interview questions about auto repair, such as, "What do you think the problem is if a 2001 Camry is overheating, and what would you do about it?"

Employee safety is also a problem. An automobile service center may not be the most dangerous type of workplace, but it is potentially dangerous. Employees are dealing with sharp tools, greasy floors, greasy tools, extremely hot temperatures (for instance, on mufflers and engines), and fast-moving engine parts including fan blades. There are some basic things that a service manager can do to ensure more safety, such as insisting that all oil spills be cleaned up immediately. However, from a practical point of view, there are a few ways to get around many of the problems—such as when the technician must check out an engine while it is running.

With Muffler Magic's profits going down instead of up, Brown's human resource manager has taken the position that the main problem is financial. As he says, "You get what you pay for" when it comes to employees, and if you compensate technicians better then your competitors do, then you get better technicians, ones who do their jobs better and stay longer with the company—and then profits will rise. So, the HR manager scheduled a meeting between himself, Ron Brown, and a professor of business who teaches compensation management at a local university. The HR manager has asked this professor to spend about a week looking at each of the service centers, analyzing the situation, and coming up with a compensation plan that will address Muffler Magic's quality and productivity problems. At this meeting, the professor makes three basic recommendations for changing the company's compensation policies.

Number one, she says that she has found that Muffler Magic suffers from what she calls "presenteeism," in other words employees drag themselves into work even when they're sick, because the company does not pay them at all if they are out—there are no sick days. In just a few days the professor couldn't properly quantify how much Muffler Magic is losing to presenteeism. However, from what she could see at each shop, there are typically one or two technicians working with various maladies like the cold or flu, and it seemed to her that each of these people was probably really only working about half of the time (although they were getting paid for the whole day). So, for 25 service centers per week, Muffler Magic could well be losing 125 or 130 personnel days per week of work. The professor suggests that Muffler Magic start allowing everyone to take 3 paid sick days per year, a reasonable suggestion. However, as Ron Brown points out, "Right now, we're only losing about half a day's pay for each employee who comes in and who works unproductively; with your suggestion, won't we lose the whole day?" The professor says she'll ponder that one.

Second, the professor also recommends putting the technicians on a skill-for-pay plan. Basically, here's what she suggests. Give each technician a letter grade (A through E) based upon that technician's particular skill level and abilities. An "A" technician is a team leader and needs to show that he or she has excellent diagnostic troubleshooting skills, and the ability to supervise and direct other technicians. At the other extreme, an "E" technician would typically be a new apprentice with little technical training. The other technicians fall in between those two levels, based on their individual skills and abilities.

In the professor's system, the "A" technician or team leader would assign and supervise all work done within his or her area but generally not do any mechanical repairs himself or herself. The team leader does the diagnostic troubleshooting, supervises and trains the other technicians, and test drives the car before it goes back to the customer. Under this plan, every technician receives a guaranteed hourly wage within a certain range, for instance:

A tech = \$25–\$30 an hour

B tech = \$20–\$25 an hour

C tech = \$15–\$20 an hour

D tech = \$10–\$15 an hour

E tech = \$8–\$10 an hour

Third, to directly address the productivity issue, the professor recommends that at the end of each day, each service manager calculate each technician-team's productivity for the day and then at the end of each week. She suggests posting the running productivity total conspicuously for daily viewing. Then, the technicians as a group get weekly cash bonuses based upon their productivity. To calculate productivity, the professor recommends dividing the total labor hours billed by the total labor hours paid to technicians, in other words: Total labor hours billed, *divided by* total hours paid to technicians.

Having done some homework, the professor says that the national average for labor productivity is currently about 60%, and that only the best-run service centers achieve 85% or greater. By her rough calculations, Muffler Magic was attaining about industry average (about 60%—in other words, they were billing for (as an example) only about 60 hours for each 100 hours that they actually had to pay technicians to do the jobs). (Of course, this was not entirely the technicians' fault. Technicians get time off for breaks, and for lunch, and if a particular service center simply didn't have enough business on a particular day or during a particular week, then several technicians may well sit around idly waiting for the next car to come in.) The professor recommends setting a labor efficiency goal of 80% and posting each team's daily productivity results in the workplace to provide them with additional feedback. She recommends that if at the end of a week the team is able to boost its productivity ratio from the current 60% to 80%, then that team would get an additional 10% weekly pay bonus. After that, for every 5% boost of increased productivity above 80%, technicians would receive an additional 5% weekly bonus. (So, if a technician's normal weekly pay is $400, that employee got an extra $40 at the end of the week when his team moved from 60% productivity to 80% productivity.)

After the meeting, Ron Brown thanked the professor for her recommendations and told her he would think about it and get back to her. After the meeting, on the drive home, Ron was pondering what to do. He had to decide whether to institute the professor's sick leave policy, and whether to implement the professor's incentive and compensation plan. Before implementing anything, however, he wanted to make sure he understood the context in which he was making his decision. For example, did Muffler Magic really have an incentive pay problem, or were the problems more broad? Furthermore, how, if at all, would the professor's incentive plan impact the quality of the work that the teams were doing? And should they really start paying for sick days? Ron Brown had a lot to think about.

Questions

1. Write out a one-page summary outline listing three or four recommendations you would make with respect to each HR function (recruiting, selection, training, and so on) that you think Ron Brown should be addressing with his HR manager now.
2. Develop a 10-question structured interview form Ron Brown's service center managers can use to interview experienced technicians.
3. If you were Ron Brown, would you implement the professor's recommendation addressing the presenteeism problem—in other words, start paying for sick days? Why or why not?
4. If you were advising Ron Brown, would you recommend that he implement the professor's skill-based pay and incentive pay plans as is? Why? Would you implement it with modifications? If you would modify it, please be specific about what you think those modifications should be, and why.

Based generally on actual facts, but Muffler Magic is a fictitious company. This case is based largely on information in Drew Paras, "The Pay Factor: Technicians' Salaries Can Be the Largest Expense in a Server Shop, as Well as the Biggest Headache. Here's How One Shop Owner Tackled the Problem," *Motor Age*, November 2003, pp. 76–79; see also Jennifer Pellet, "Health Care Crisis," *Chief Executive*, June 2004, pp. 56–61; "Firms Press to Quantify, Control Presenteeism," *Employee Benefits*, December 1, 2002.

BP TEXAS CITY*

In March 2005, an explosion and fire at British Petroleum's (BP) Texas City, Texas, refinery killed 15 people and injured 500 people in the worst U.S. industrial accident in more than 10 years. The disaster triggered three investigations: one internal investigation by BP, one by the U.S. Chemical Safety Board, and another, independent investigation chaired by former U.S. Secretary of State James Baker and an 11-member panel, and organized at BP's request.

To put the results of these three investigations into context, it's useful to understand that under its current management, BP has pursued, for the past 10 or so years, a strategy emphasizing cost-cutting and profitability. The basic conclusion of the investigations was that cost-cutting helped compromise safety at the Texas City refinery. It's useful to consider each investigation's findings.

The Chemical Safety Board's (CSB) investigation, according to Carol Merritt, the board's chairwoman, showed that "BP's global management was aware of problems with maintenance, spending, and infrastructure well before March 2005." Apparently, faced with numerous earlier accidents, BP did make some safety improvements. However, it focused primarily on emphasizing personal employee safety behaviors and procedural compliance, and on thereby reducing safety accident rates. The problem (according to the CSB) was that "catastrophic safety risks remained." For example, according to the CSB, "unsafe and antiquated equipment designs were left in place, and unacceptable deficiencies in preventive maintenance were tolerated." Basically, the CSB found that BP's budget cuts led to a progressive deterioration of safety at the Texas City refinery. Said Ms. Merritt, "In an aging facility like Texas City, it is not responsible to cut budgets related to safety and maintenance without thoroughly examining the impact on the risk of a catastrophic accident."

Looking at specifics, the CSB said that a 2004 internal audit of 35 BP business units, including Texas City (BP's largest refinery), found significant safety gaps they all had in common, including for instance, a lack of leadership competence, and "systemic underlying issues" such as a widespread tolerance of noncompliance with basic safety rules and poor monitoring of safety management systems and processes. Ironically, the CSB found that BP's accident prevention effort at Texas City had achieved a 70% reduction in worker injuries in the year before the explosion. Unfortunately, this simply meant that individual employees were having fewer accidents. The larger, more fundamental problem was that the potentially explosive situation inherent in the depreciating machinery remained.

The CSB found that the Texas City explosion followed a pattern of years of major accidents at the facility. In fact, there had apparently been an average of one employee death every 16 months at the plant for the last 30 years. The CSB found that the equipment directly involved in the most recent explosion was an obsolete design already phased out in most refineries and chemical plants, and that key pieces of its instrumentation were not working. There had also been previous instances where flammable vapors were released from the same unit in the 10 years prior to the explosion. In 2003, an external audit had referred to the Texas City refinery's infrastructure and assets as "poor" and found what it referred to as a "checkbook mentality," one in which budgets were not sufficient to manage all the risks. In particular, the CSB found that BP had implemented a 25% cut on fixed costs between 1998 and 2000 and that this adversely impacted maintenance expenditures and net expenditures, and refinery infrastructure. Going on, the CSB found that in 2004, there were three major accidents at the refinery that killed three workers.

BP's own internal report concluded that the problems at Texas City were not of recent origin, and instead were years in the making. It said BP was taking steps to address them. Its investigation found "no evidence of anyone consciously or intentionally taking actions or making decisions that put others at risk." Said BP's report, "The underlying reasons for the behaviors and actions displayed during the incident are complex, and the team has spent much time trying to understand them—it is evident that they were many years in the making and will require concerted and committed actions to address." BP's report concluded that there were five underlying causes for the massive explosion:

- A working environment that had eroded to one characterized by resistance to change, and a lack of trust
- Safety, performance, and risk reduction priorities had not been set and consistently reinforced by management
- Changes in the "complex organization" led to a lack of clear accountabilities and poor communication
- A poor level of hazard awareness and understanding of safety resulted in workers accepting levels of risk that were considerably higher than at comparable installations
- A lack of adequate early warning systems for problems, and no independent means of understanding the deteriorating standards at the plant.

The report from the BP-initiated but independent 11-person panel chaired by former U.S. Secretary of State James Baker contained specific conclusions and recommendations. The Baker panel looked at BP's corporate safety oversight, the corporate safety culture, and the process safety management systems at BP at the Texas City plant as well at BP's other refineries.

Basically, the Baker panel concluded that BP had not provided effective safety process leadership and had not established safety as a core value at the five refineries it looked at (including Texas City).

Like the CSB, the Baker panel found that BP had emphasized personal safety in recent years and had in fact improved personal safety performance, but had not emphasized the overall safety process, thereby mistakenly interpreting "improving personal injury rates as an indication of acceptable process safety performance at its U.S. refineries." In fact, the Baker panel went on, by focusing on these somewhat misleading improving personal injury rates, BP created a false sense of confidence that it was properly addressing process safety risks. It also found that the safety culture at Texas City did not have the positive, trusting, open environment that a proper safety culture required. The Baker panel's other findings included:

- BP did not always ensure that adequate resources were effectively allocated to support or sustain a high level of process safety performance
- BP's refinery personnel are "overloaded" by corporate initiatives
- Operators and maintenance personnel work high rates of overtime
- BP tended to have a short-term focus and its decentralized management system and entrepreneurial culture delegated substantial discretion to refinery plant managers "without clearly defining process safety expectations, responsibilities, or accountabilities"
- There was no common, unifying process safety culture among the five refineries
- The company's corporate safety management system did not make sure there was timely compliance with internal process safety standards and programs
- BP's executive management either did not receive refinery specific information that showed that process safety deficiencies existed at some of the plants, or did not effectively respond to any information it did receive.[1]

The Baker panel made several safety recommendations for BP, including these:

1. The company's corporate management must provide leadership on process safety.
2. The company should establish a process safety management system that identifies, reduces, and manages the process safety risks of the refineries.
3. The company should make sure its employees have an appropriate level of process safety knowledge and expertise.
4. The company should involve "relevant stakeholders" in developing a positive, trusting, and open process safety culture at each refinery.
5. BP should clearly define expectations and strengthen accountability for process safety performance.
6. BP should better coordinate its process safety support for the refining line organization.
7. BP should develop an integrated set of leading and lagging performance indicators for effectively monitoring process safety performance.

8. BP should establish and implement an effective system to audit process safety performance.
9. The company's board should monitor the implementation of the panel's recommendations and the ongoing process safety performance of the refineries.
10. BP should transform into a recognized industry leader in process safety management.

In making its recommendations, the panel singled out the company's chief executive at the time, Lord Browne, by saying, "In hindsight, the panel believes if Browne had demonstrated comparable leadership on and commitment to process safety [as he did for responding to climate change] that would have resulted in a higher level of safety at refineries."

Overall, the Baker panel found that BP's top management had not provided "effective leadership" on safety. It found that the failings went to the very top of the organization, to the company's chief executive, and to several of his top lieutenants. The Baker panel emphasized the importance of top management commitment, saying, for instance that "it is imperative that BP leadership set the process safety tone at the top of the organization and establish appropriate expectations regarding process safety performance." It also said BP "has not provided effective leadership in making certain its management and U.S. refining workforce understand what is expected of them regarding process safety performance."

Lord Browne, the chief executive, stepped down about a year after the explosion. About the same time, some BP shareholders were calling for the company's executives and board directors to have their bonuses more closely tied to the company's safety and environmental performance in the wake of Texas City. In October 2009, OSHA announced it was filing the largest fine in its history for this accident, for $87 million, against BP.

Questions

1. The textbook defines ethics as "the principles of conduct governing an individual or a group," and specifically as the standards one uses to decide what their conduct should be. To what extent do you believe that what happened at BP is as much a breakdown in the company's ethical systems as it is in its safety systems, and how would you defend your conclusion?
2. Are the Occupational Safety and Health Administration's standards, policies, and rules aimed at addressing problems like the ones that apparently existed at the Texas City plant? If so, how would you explain the fact that problems like these could have continued for so many years?
3. Since there were apparently at least three deaths in the year prior to the major explosion, and an average of about one employee death per 16 months for the previous 10 years, how would you account for the fact that mandatory OSHA inspections missed these glaring sources of potential catastrophic events?
4. The textbook lists numerous suggestions for "how to prevent accidents." Based on what you know about the Texas City explosion, what do you say Texas City tells you about the most important three steps an employer can take to prevent accidents?
5. Based on what you learned in Chapter 16, would you make any additional recommendations to BP over and above those recommendations made by the Baker panel and the CSB? If so, what would those recommendations be?
6. Explain specifically how strategic human resource management at BP seems to have supported the company's broader strategic aims. What does this say about the advisability of always linking human resource strategy to a company's strategic aims?

Source notes for BP Texas City: Sheila McNulty, "BP Knew of Safety Problems, Says Report," *The Financial Times,* October 31, 2006, p. 1; "CBS: Documents Show BP Was Aware of Texas City Safety Problems," *World Refining & Fuels Today,* October 30, 2006; "BP Safety Report Finds Company's Process Safety Culture Ineffective," *Global Refining & Fuels Report,* January 17, 2007; "BP Safety Record Under Attack," *Europe Intelligence Wire,* January 17, 2007; Mark Hofmann, "BP Slammed for Poor Leadership on Safety, Oil Firm Agrees to Act on Review Panel's Recommendations," *Business Intelligence,* January 22, 2007, p. 3; "Call for Bonuses to Include Link with Safety Performance," *The Guardian,* January 18, 2007, p. 24; www.bp.com/genericarticle.do?categoryId=9005029&contentId=7015905, accessed July 12, 2009. Steven Greenhouse, "BP Faces Record Fine For '05 Blast," *The New York Times,* October 30, 2009, pp. 1, 6.

ENDNOTE

1. These findings and the following suggestions based on "BP Safety Report Finds Company's Process Safety Culture Ineffective," *Global Refining & Fuels Report,* January 17, 2007.

Glossary

action learning A training technique by which management trainees are allowed to work full-time analyzing and solving problems in other departments.

adaptability screening A process that aims to assess the assignee's (and spouse's) probable success in handling a foreign transfer.

adverse impact The overall impact of employer practices that result in significantly higher percentages of members of minorities and other protected groups being rejected for employment, placement, or promotion.

affirmative action Making an extra effort to hire and promote those in protected groups, particularly when those groups are underrepresented.

Age Discrimination in Employment Act of 1967 (ADEA) The act prohibiting arbitrary age discrimination and specifically protecting individuals over 40 years old.

agency shop A form of union security in which employees who do not belong to the union must still pay union dues on the assumption that union efforts benefit all workers.

alternation ranking method Ranking employees from best to worst on a particular trait, choosing highest, then lowest, until all are ranked.

alternative dispute resolution or ADR program Grievance procedure that provides for binding arbitration as the last step.

alternative staffing The use of nontraditional recruitment sources.

Americans with Disabilities Act (ADA) The act requiring employers to make reasonable accommodations for disabled employees; it prohibits discrimination against disabled persons.

annual bonus Plans that are designed to motivate short-term performance of managers and are tied to company profitability.

applicant tracking systems Online systems that help employers attract, gather, screen, compile, and manage applicants.

application form The form that provides information on education, prior work record, and skills.

appraisal interview An interview in which the supervisor and subordinate review the appraisal and make plans to remedy deficiencies and reinforce strengths.

apprenticeship training A structured process by which people become skilled workers through a combination of classroom instruction and on-the-job training.

arbitration The most definitive type of third-party intervention, in which the arbitrator usually has the power to determine and dictate the settlement terms.

at-risk variable pay plans Plans that put some portion of the employee's weekly pay at risk, subject to the firm's meeting its financial goals.

authority The right to make decisions, direct others' work, and give orders.

authorization cards In order to petition for a union election, the union must show that at least 30% of employees may be interested in being unionized. Employees indicate this interest by signing authorization cards.

bargaining unit The group of employees the union will be authorized to represent.

behavior modeling A training technique in which trainees are first shown good management techniques in a film, are asked to play roles in a simulated situation, and are then given feedback and praise by their supervisor.

behavior modification Using contingent rewards or punishment to change behavior.

behavioral interviews A series of job-related questions that focus on how the candidate reacted to actual situations in the past.

behaviorally anchored rating scale (BARS) An appraisal method that aims at combining the benefits of narrative critical incidents and quantified ratings by anchoring a quantified scale with specific narrative examples of good and poor performance.

behavior-based safety Identifying the worker behaviors that contribute to accidents and then training workers to avoid these behaviors.

benchmark job A job that is used to anchor the employer's pay scale and around which other jobs are arranged in order of relative worth.

benefits Indirect financial and nonfinancial payments employees receive for continuing their employment with the company.

bias The tendency to allow individual differences such as age, race, and sex to affect the appraisal ratings employees receive.

bona fide occupational qualification (BFOQ) Requirement that an employee be of a certain religion, sex, or national origin where that is reasonably necessary to the organization's normal operation. Specified by the 1964 Civil Rights Act.

boycott The combined refusal by employees and other interested parties to buy or use the employer's products.

broadbanding Consolidating salary grades and ranges into just a few wide levels or "bands," each of which contains a relatively wide range of jobs and salary levels.

bumping/layoff procedures Detailed procedures that determine who will be laid off if no work is available; generally allow employees to use their seniority to remain on the job.

burnout The total depletion of physical and mental resources caused by excessive striving to reach an unrealistic work-related goal.

business plan Provides a comprehensive view of the firm's situation today and of its company-wide and departmental goals and plans for the next 3 to 5 years.

candidate-order (or contrast) error An error of judgment on the part of the interviewer due to interviewing one or more very good or very bad candidates just before the interview in question.

career The occupational positions a person has had over many years.

career anchors Pivots around which a person's career swings; require self-awareness of talents and abilities, motives and needs, and attitudes and values.

career cycle The various stages a person's career goes through.

career development The lifelong series of activities that contribute to a person's career exploration, establishment, success, and fulfillment.

career management The process for enabling employees to better understand and develop their career skills and interests, and to use these skills and interests most effectively.

career planning The deliberate process through which someone becomes aware of personal skills, interests, knowledge, motivations, and other characteristics and establishes action plans to attain specific goals.

case study method A development method in which the manager is presented with a written description of an organizational problem to diagnose and solve.

cash balance plans Defined benefit plans under which the employer contributes a percentage of employees' current pay to employees' pension plans every year, and employees earn interest on this amount.

central tendency A tendency to rate all employees the same way, such as rating them all average.

citation Summons informing employers and employees of the regulations and standards that have been violated in the workplace.

Civil Rights Act of 1991 (CRA 1991) It places burden of proof back on employers and permits compensatory and punitive damages.

classes Grouping jobs based on a set of rules for each group or class, such as amount of independent judgment, skill, physical effort, and so forth, required. Classes usually contain similar jobs.

closed shop A form of union security in which the company can hire only union members. This was outlawed in 1947 but still exists in some industries (such as printing).

coaching Educating, instructing, and training subordinates.

codetermination Employees have the legal right to a voice in setting company policies.

collective bargaining The process through which representatives of management and the union meet to negotiate a labor agreement.

college recruiting Sending an employer's representatives to college campuses to prescreen applicants and create an applicant pool from the graduating class.

comparable worth The concept by which women who are usually paid less than men can claim that men in comparable rather than in strictly equal jobs are paid more.

compensable factor A fundamental, compensable element of a job, such as skills, effort, responsibility, and working conditions.

competencies Demonstrable characteristics of a person, including knowledge, skills, and behaviors, that enable performance.

competency model Consolidates, usually in one diagram, a precise overview of the competencies (the knowledge, skills, and behaviors) someone would need to do a job well.

competency-based job analysis Describing a job in terms of the measurable, observable, and behavioral competencies an employee must exhibit to do a job well.

competency-based pay Where the company pays for the employee's range, depth, and types of skills and knowledge, rather than for the job title he or she holds.

competitive advantage Any factors that allow an organization to differentiate its product or service from those of its competitors to increase market share.

competitive strategy A strategy that identifies how to build and strengthen the business's long-term competitive position in the marketplace.

compressed workweek Schedule in which employee works fewer but longer days each week.

content validity A test that is content valid is one that contains a fair sample of the tasks and skills actually needed for the job in question.

controlled experimentation Formal methods for testing the effectiveness of a training program, preferably with before-and-after tests and a control group.

corporate campaign An organized effort by the union that exerts pressure on the corporation by pressuring the company's other unions, shareholders, directors, customers, creditors, and government agencies, often directly.

corporate-level strategy Type of strategy that identifies the portfolio of businesses that, in total, comprise the company and the ways in which these businesses relate to each other.

criterion validity A type of validity based on showing that scores on the test (predictors) are related to job performance (criterion).

critical incident method Keeping a record of uncommonly good or undesirable examples of an employee's work-related behavior and reviewing it with the employee at predetermined times.

Davis-Bacon Act (1931) A law that sets wage rates for laborers employed by contractors working for the federal government.

decertification Legal process for employees to terminate a union's right to represent them.

decline stage Period where many people face having to accept reduced levels of power and responsibility, and must learn to develop new roles as mentors or confidantes for younger people.

deferred profit-sharing plan A plan in which a certain amount of profits is credited to each employee's account, payable at retirement, termination, or death.

defined benefit pension plan A plan that contains a formula for determining retirement benefits.

defined contribution pension plan A plan in which the employer's contribution to employees' retirement savings funds is specified.

diary/log Daily listings made by workers of every activity in which they engage along with the time each activity takes.

digital dashboard Presents the manager with desktop graphs and charts, and so a computerized picture of where the company stands on all those metrics from the HR Scorecard process.

direct financial payments Pay in the form of wages, salaries, incentives, commissions, and bonuses.

dismissal Involuntary termination of an employee's employment with the firm.

disparate rejection rates A test for adverse impact in which it can be demonstrated that there is a discrepancy between rates of rejection of members of a protected group and of others.

distributive justice The fairness and justice of a decision's result.

diversity The variety or multiplicity of demographic features that characterize a company's workforce, particularly in terms of race, sex, culture, national origin, handicap, age, and religion.

downsizing The process of reducing, usually dramatically, the number of people employed by a firm.

early retirement window A type of offering by which employees are encouraged to retire early, the incentive being liberal pension benefits plus perhaps a cash payment.

economic strike A strike that results from a failure to agree on the terms of a contract that involve wages, benefits, and other conditions of employment.

Electronic Communications Privacy Act (ECPA) Intended in part to restrict interception and monitoring of oral and wire communications, but with two exceptions: employers who can show a legitimate business reason for doing so, and employers who have employees' consent to do so.

electronic performance monitoring (EPM) Having supervisors electronically monitor the amount of computerized data an employee is processing per day, and thereby his or her performance.

electronic performance support systems (EPSS) Sets of computerized tools and displays that automate training, documentation, and phone support; integrate this automation into applications; and provide support that's faster, cheaper, and more effective than traditional methods.

employee assistance program (EAP) A formal employer program for providing employees with counseling and/or treatment programs for problems such as alcoholism, gambling, or stress.

employee compensation All forms of pay or rewards going to employees and arising from their employment.

employee orientation A procedure for providing new employees with basic background information about the firm.

employee recruiting Finding and/or attracting applicants for the employer's open positions.

Employee Retirement Income Security Act (ERISA) Signed into law by President Ford in 1974 to require that pension rights be vested and protected by a government agency, the PBGC.

employee stock ownership plan (ESOP) A qualified, tax-deductible stock bonus plan in which employers contribute stock to a trust for eventual use by employees.

employment (or personnel) planning The process of deciding what positions the firm will have to fill, and how to fill them.

Equal Employment Opportunity Commission (EEOC) The commission, created by Title VII, is empowered to investigate job discrimination complaints and sue on behalf of complainants.

Equal Pay Act of 1963 The act requiring equal pay for equal work, regardless of sex.

establishment stage Spans roughly ages 24 to 44 and is the heart of most people's work lives.

ethics The principles of conduct governing an individual or a group; specifically, the standards you use to decide what your conduct should be.

ethics code Memorializes the standards to which the employer expects its employees to adhere.

ethnocentric The notion that home-country attitudes, management style, knowledge, evaluation criteria, and managers are superior to anything the host country has to offer.

executive coach An outside consultant who questions the executive's boss, peers, subordinates, and (sometimes) family in order to identify the executive's strengths and weaknesses, and to counsel the executive so he or she can capitalize on those strengths and overcome the weaknesses.

exit interviews Interviews with employees who are leaving the firm, conducted for the purpose of obtaining information about the job or related matters, to give the employer insight about the company.

expatriates (expats) Noncitizens of the countries in which they are working.

expectancy A person's expectation that his or her effort will lead to performance.

expectancy chart A graph showing the relationship between test scores and job performance for a group of people.

exploration stage The period (roughly from ages 15 to 24) during which a person seriously explores various occupational alternatives.

fact finder A neutral party who studies the issues in a dispute and makes a public recommendation for a reasonable settlement.

factor comparison method A widely used method of ranking jobs according to a variety of skill and difficulty factors, then adding up these rankings to arrive at an overall numerical rating for each given job.

fair day's work Standards of output which employers should devise for each job based on careful, scientific analysis.

Fair Labor Standards Act (1938) This act provides for minimum wages, maximum hours, overtime pay, and child labor protection. The law has been amended many times and covers most employees.

family-friendly (or work–life) benefits Benefits such as child care and fitness facilities that make it easier for employees to balance their work and family responsibilities.

Federal Violence Against Women Act of 1994 Provides that a person who commits a crime of violence motivated by gender shall be liable to the party injured.

financial incentives Financial rewards paid to workers whose production exceeds some predetermined standard.

flexible benefits plan/cafeteria benefits plan Individualized plans allowed by employers to accommodate employee preferences for benefits.

flextime A plan whereby employees' workdays are built around a core of mid-day hours, such as 11:00 A.M. to 2:00 P.M.

forced distribution method Similar to grading on a curve; predetermined percentages of ratees are placed in various performance categories.

foreign service premiums Financial payments over and above regular base pay, typically ranging between 10% and 30% of base pay.

4/5ths rule Federal agency rule that minority selection rate less than 80% (4/5ths) that of group with highest rate evidences adverse impact.

401(k) plan A defined contribution plan based on section 401(k) of the Internal Revenue Code.

functional authority (or functional control) The authority exerted by an HR manager as coordinator of personnel activities.

functional strategies Strategy that identifies the broad activities that each department will pursue in order to help the business accomplish its competitive goals.

gainsharing plan An incentive plan that engages employees in a common effort to achieve productivity objectives and share the gains.

geocentric The belief that the firm's whole management staff must be scoured on a global basis, on the assumption that the best manager of a specific position anywhere may be in any of the countries in which the firm operates.

globalization The tendency of firms to extend their sales, ownership, and/or manufacturing to new markets abroad.

golden parachutes Payments companies make in connection with a change in ownership or control of a company.

good faith bargaining Both parties are making every reasonable effort to arrive at agreement; proposals are being matched with counterproposals.

good faith effort strategy Employment strategy aimed at changing practices that have contributed in the past to excluding or underutilizing protected groups.

grade definition Written descriptions of the level of, say, responsibility and knowledge required by jobs in each grade. Similar jobs can then be combined into grades or classes.

grades A job classification system like the class system, although grades often contain dissimilar jobs, such as secretaries, mechanics, and firefighters. Grade descriptions are written based on compensable factors listed in classification systems.

graphic rating scale A scale that lists a number of traits and a range of performance for each. The employee is then rated by identifying the score that best describes his or her level of performance for each trait.

grievance procedure Formal process for addressing any factor involving wages, hours, or conditions of employment that is used as a complaint against the employer.

group life insurance Provides lower rates for the employer or employee and includes all employees, including new employees, regardless of health or physical condition.

growth stage The period from birth to age 14 during which a person develops a self-concept by identifying with and interacting with other people.

halo effect In performance appraisal, the problem that occurs when a supervisor's rating of a subordinate on one trait biases the rating of that person on other traits.

hardship allowances Compensate expatriates for exceptionally hard living and working conditions at certain locations.

health maintenance organization (HMO) A prepaid health care system that generally provides routine round-the-clock medical services as well as preventive medicine in a clinic-type arrangement for employees, who pay a nominal fee in addition to the fixed annual fee the employer pays.

high-performance work system An integrated set of human resources policies and practices that together produce superior employee performance.

home-country nationals Citizens of the country in which the multinational company has its headquarters.

HR audit An analysis by which an organization measures where it currently stands and determines what it has to accomplish to improve its HR function.

HR Scorecard Measures the HR function's effectiveness and efficiency in producing employee behaviors needed to achieve the company's strategic goals.

human capital The knowledge, education, training, skills, and expertise of a firm's workers.

human resource management (HRM) The policies and practices involved in carrying out the "people" or human resource aspects of a management position, including recruiting, screening, training, rewarding, and appraising.

human resource metric The fundamental financial and nonfinancial measures you will use to assess the HR unit's status and progress.

illegal bargaining items Items in collective bargaining that are forbidden by law; for example, a clause agreeing to hire "union members exclusively" would be illegal in a right-to-work state.

impasse Collective bargaining situation that occurs when the parties are not able to move further toward settlement, usually because one party is demanding more than the other will offer.

indirect financial payments Pay in the form of financial benefits such as insurance.

in-house development center A company-based method for exposing prospective managers to realistic exercises to develop improved management skills.

injunction A court order compelling a party or parties either to resume or to desist from a certain action.

inside games Union efforts to convince employees to impede or to disrupt production—for example, by slowing the work pace.

instrumentality The perceived relationships between successful performance and obtaining the reward.

insubordination Willful disregard or disobedience of the boss's authority or legitimate orders; criticizing the boss in public.

interest inventory A personal development and selection device that compares the person's current interests with those of others now in various occupations so as to determine the preferred occupation for the individual.

job aid A set of instructions, diagrams, or similar methods available at the job site to guide the worker.

job analysis The procedure for determining the duties and skill requirements of a job and the kind of person who should be hired for it.

job classification (or grading) method A method for categorizing jobs into groups.

job description A list of a job's duties, responsibilities, reporting relationships, working conditions, and supervisory responsibilities—one product of a job analysis.

job enlargement Assigning workers additional same-level activities, thus increasing the number of activities they perform.

job enrichment Redesigning jobs in a way that increases the opportunities for the worker to experience feelings of responsibility, achievement, growth, and recognition.

job evaluation A systematic comparison done in order to determine the worth of one job relative to another.

job instruction training (JIT) Listing each job's basic tasks, along with key points, in order to provide step-by-step training for employees.

job posting Publicizing an open job to employees (often by literally posting it on bulletin boards) and listing its attributes, like qualifications, supervisor, working schedule, and pay rate.

job-related interview A series of job-related questions that focus on relevant past job-related behaviors.

job rotation Systematically moving a worker from one job to another to enhance work team performance and/or to broaden his or her experience and identify strong and weak points to prepare the person for an enhanced role with the company.

job sharing Allows two or more people to share a single full-time job.

job specifications A list of a job's "human requirements," that is, the requisite education, skills, personality, and so on—another product of a job analysis.

Landrum-Griffin Act (1959) The law aimed at protecting union members from possible wrongdoing on the part of their unions.

lifelong learning Providing employees with continuing learning experiences over their tenure with the firm, with the aims of ensuring they have the opportunity to learn the skills they need to do their jobs and to expand their horizons.

line authority The authority exerted by an HR manager by directing the activities of the people in his or her own department and in service areas (like the plant cafeteria).

line manager A manager who is authorized to direct the work of subordinates and is responsible for accomplishing the organization's tasks.

lockout A refusal by the employer to provide opportunities to work.

maintenance stage Period between ages 45 and 65 when many people slide from the stabilization substage into an established position and focus on maintaining that place.

management assessment center A simulation in which management candidates are asked to perform realistic tasks in hypothetical situations and are scored on their performance. It usually also involves testing and the use of management games.

management by objectives (MBO) Involves setting specific measurable goals with each employee and then periodically reviewing the progress made.

management development Any attempt to improve current or future management performance by imparting knowledge, changing attitudes, or increasing skills.

management game A development technique in which teams of managers compete by making computerized decisions regarding realistic but simulated situations.

management process The five basic functions of planning, organizing, staffing, leading, and controlling.

manager The person responsible for accomplishing the organization's goals, and who does so by managing the efforts of the organization's people.

managing diversity Maximizing diversity's potential benefits while minimizing the potential barriers that can undermine the company's performance.

mandatory bargaining items Items in collective bargaining that a party must bargain over if they are introduced by the other party—for example, pay.

mass interview A panel interviews several candidates simultaneously.

mediation Intervention in which a neutral third party tries to assist the principals in reaching agreement.

mentoring Formal or informal programs in which mid- and senior-level managers help less experienced employees—for instance, by giving them career advice and helping them navigate political pitfalls.

merit pay (merit raise) Any salary increase awarded to an employee based on his or her individual performance.

midcareer crisis substage Period during which people often make major reassessments of their progress relative to original ambitions and goals.

miniature job training and evaluation Training candidates to perform several of the job's tasks, and then evaluating the candidates' performance prior to hire.

mission statement Summarizes your answer to the question, "What business are we in?"

mixed motive case A discrimination allegation case in which the employer argues that the employment action taken was motivated, not by discrimination, but by some nondiscriminatory reason such as ineffective performance.

mobility premiums Typically, lump-sum payments to reward employees for moving from one assignment to another.

national emergency strikes Strikes that might "imperil the national health and safety."

National Labor Relations (or Wagner) Act This law banned certain types of unfair practices and provided for secret-ballot elections and majority rule for determining whether or not a firm's employees want to unionize.

National Labor Relations Board (NLRB) The agency created by the Wagner Act to investigate unfair labor practice charges and to provide for secret-ballot elections and majority rule in determining whether or not a firm's employees want a union.

negligent hiring Hiring workers with questionable backgrounds without proper safeguards.

negligent training A situation where an employer fails to train adequately, and the employee subsequently harms a third party.

nonpunitive discipline Discipline without punishment, usually involving a system of oral warnings and paid "decision-making leaves" in lieu of more traditional punishment.

Norris-LaGuardia Act (1932) This law marked the beginning of the era of strong encouragement of unions and guaranteed to each employee the right to bargain collectively "free from interference, restraint, or coercion."

occupational illness Any abnormal condition or disorder caused by exposure to environmental factors associated with employment.

Occupational Safety and Health Act The law passed by Congress in 1970 "to assure so far as possible every working man and woman in the nation safe and healthful working conditions and to preserve our human resources."

Occupational Safety and Health Administration (OSHA) The agency created within the Department of Labor to set safety and health standards for almost all workers in the United States.

Office of Federal Contract Compliance Programs (OFCCP) This office is responsible for implementing the executive orders and ensuring compliance of federal contractors.

offshoring Having local employees abroad do jobs that the firm's domestic employees previously did in-house.

on-demand recruiting services (ODRS) A service that provides short-term specialized recruiting to support specific projects without the expense of retaining traditional search firms.

on-the-job training Training a person to learn a job while working on it.

organization Consists of people with formally assigned roles who work together to achieve the organization's goals.

organization chart A chart that shows the organizationwide distribution of work, with titles of each position and interconnecting lines that show who reports to and communicates to whom.

organizational culture The characteristic values, traditions, and behaviors a company's employees share.

organizational development A special approach to organizational change in which employees themselves formulate and implement the change that's required.

organizationwide incentive plans Plans in which all or most employees can participate, and that generally tie the reward to some measure of company-wide performance.

outplacement counseling A systematic process by which a terminated person is trained and counseled in the techniques of self-appraisal and securing a new position.

paired comparison method Ranking employees by making a chart of all possible pairs of the employees for each trait and indicating which is the better employee of the pair.

panel interview An interview in which a group of interviewers questions the applicant.

pay grade A pay grade is comprised of jobs of approximately equal difficulty.

pay ranges A series of steps or levels within a pay grade, usually based upon years of service.

Pension Benefits Guarantee Corporation (PBGC) Established under ERISA to ensure that pensions meet vesting obligations; also insures pensions should a plan terminate without sufficient funds to meet its vested obligations.

pension plans Plans that provide a fixed sum when employees reach a predetermined retirement age or when they can no longer work due to disability.

performance analysis Verifying that there is a performance deficiency and determining whether that deficiency should be corrected through training or through some other means (such as transferring the employee).

performance appraisal Evaluating an employee's current and/or past performance relative to his or her performance standards.

performance management Taking an integrated, goal-oriented approach to assigning, training, assessing, and rewarding employees' performance.

personnel replacement charts Company records showing present performance and promotability of inside candidates for the most important positions.

picketing Having employees carry signs announcing their concerns near the employer's place of business.

piecework A system of pay based on the number of items processed by each individual worker in a unit of time, such as items per hour or items per day.

point method The job evaluation method in which a number of compensable factors are identified and then the degree to which each of these factors is present on the job is determined.

polycentric A conscious belief that only the host-country managers can ever really understand the culture and behavior of the host-country market.

portability Making it easier for employees who leave the firm prior to retirement to take their accumulated pension funds with them.

position analysis questionnaire (PAQ) A questionnaire used to collect quantifiable data concerning the duties and responsibilities of various jobs.

position replacement card A card prepared for each position in a company to show possible replacement candidates and their qualifications.

preferential shop Union members get preference in hiring, but the employer can still hire union members.

preferred provider organizations (PPOs) Groups of health care providers that contract with employers, insurance companies, or third-party payers to provide medical care services at a reduced fee.

Pregnancy Discrimination Act (PDA) An amendment to Title VII of the Civil Rights Act that prohibits sex discrimination based on "pregnancy, childbirth, or related medical conditions."

procedural justice The fairness of the process.

process chart A work flow chart that shows the flow of inputs to and outputs from a particular job.

profit-sharing plan A plan whereby employees share in the company's profits.

programmed learning A systematic method for teaching job skills involving presenting questions or facts, allowing the person to respond, and giving the learner immediate feedback on the accuracy of his or her answers.

promotions Advancements to positions of increased responsibility.

protected class Persons such as minorities and women protected by equal opportunity laws, including Title VII.

qualifications (or skills) inventories Manual or computerized records listing employees' education, career and development interests, languages, special skills, and so on, to be used in selecting inside candidates for promotion.

qualified individuals Under ADA, those who can carry out the essential functions of the job.

ranking method The simplest method of job evaluation that involves ranking each job relative to all other jobs, usually based on overall difficulty.

ratio analysis A forecasting technique for determining future staff needs by using ratios between, for example, sales volume and number of employees needed.

reality shock Results of a period that may occur at the initial career entry when the new employee's high job expectations confront the reality of a boring, unchallenging job.

recruiting yield pyramid The historical arithmetic relationships between recruitment leads and invitees, invitees and interviews, interviews and offers made, and offers made and offers accepted.

reliability The consistency of scores obtained by the same person when retested with the identical tests or with alternate forms of the same test.

restricted policy Another test for adverse impact, involving demonstration that an employer's hiring practices exclude a protected group, whether intentionally or not.

reverse discrimination Claim that due to affirmative action quota systems, white males are discriminated against.

right to work A term used to describe state statutory or constitutional provisions banning the requirement of union membership as a condition of employment.

role playing A training technique in which trainees act out parts in a realistic management situation.

salary compression A salary inequity problem, generally caused by inflation, resulting in longer-term employees in a position earning less than workers entering the firm today.

salary survey A survey aimed at determining prevailing wage rates. A good salary survey provides specific wage rates for specific jobs. Formal written questionnaire surveys are the most comprehensive, but telephone surveys and newspaper ads are also sources of information.

savings and thrift plan Plan in which employees contribute a portion of their earnings to a fund; the employer usually matches this contribution in whole or in part.

Scanlon plan An incentive plan developed in 1937 by Joseph Scanlon and designed to encourage cooperation, involvement, and sharing of benefits.

scatter plot A graphical method used to help identify the relationship between two variables.

scientific management Management approach based on improving work methods through observation and analysis.

severance pay A one-time payment some employers provide when terminating an employee.

sexual harassment Harassment on the basis of sex that has the purpose or effect of substantially interfering with a person's work performance or creating an intimidating, hostile, or offensive work environment.

sick leave Provides pay to an employee when he or she is out of work because of illness.

situational interview A series of job-related questions that focus on how the candidate would behave in a given situation.

situational test Examinees respond to situations representative of the job.

Social Security Federal program that provides three types of benefits: retirement income at the age of 62 and thereafter; survivor's or death benefits payable to the employee's dependents regardless of age at time of death; and disability benefits payable to disabled employees and their dependents. These benefits are payable only if the employee is insured under the Social Security Act.

stabilization substage Firm occupational goals are set and the person does more explicit career planning.

staff authority Gives the manager the right (authority) to advise other managers or employees.

staff manager A manager who assists and advises line managers.

standard hour plan A plan by which a worker is paid a basic hourly rate but is paid an extra percentage of his or her rate for production exceeding the standard per hour or per day. Similar to piecework payment but based on a percent premium.

Standard Occupational Classification (SOC) Classifies all workers into one of 23 major groups of jobs which are subdivided into minor groups of jobs and detailed occupations.

stock option The right to purchase a stated number of shares of a company stock at today's price at some time in the future.

straight piecework An incentive plan in which a person is paid a sum for each item he or she makes or sells, with a strict proportionality between results and rewards.

strategic human resource management Formulating and executing human resource policies and practices that produce the employee competencies and behaviors the company needs to achieve its strategic aims.

strategic management The process of identifying and executing the organization's mission by matching its capabilities with the demands of its environment.

strategic plan The company's plan for how it will match its internal strengths and weaknesses with external opportunities and threats in order to maintain a competitive advantage.

strategy The company's long-term plan for how it will balance its internal strengths and weaknesses with its external opportunities and threats to maintain a competitive advantage.

strategy map Diagram that summarizes the chain of major activities that contribute to a company's success.

stress interview Interviewer seeks to make the applicant uncomfortable with occasionally rude questions.

strictness/leniency The problem that occurs when a supervisor has a tendency to rate all subordinates either high or low.

strike A withdrawal of labor.

structured (or directive) interview An interview following a set sequence of questions.

structured sequential interview An interview in which the applicant is interviewed sequentially by several persons; each rates the applicant on a standard form.

structured situational interview A series of job-oriented questions with predetermined answers that interviewers ask of all applicants for the job.

succession planning The ongoing process of systematically identifying, assessing, and developing organizational leadership to enhance performance.

supplemental pay benefits Benefits for time not worked such as unemployment insurance, vacation and holiday pay, and sick pay.

supplemental unemployment benefits Provide for a "guaranteed annual income" in certain industries where employers must shut down to change machinery or due to reduced work. These benefits are paid by the company and supplement unemployment benefits.

sympathy strike A strike that takes place when one union strikes in support of the strike of another.

Taft-Hartley Act (1947) Also known as the Labor Management Relations Act, this law prohibited unfair union labor practices and enumerated the rights of employees as union members. It also enumerated the rights of employers.

talent management The automated end-to-end process of planning, recruiting, developing, managing, and compensating employees throughout the organization.

task analysis A detailed study of a job to identify the specific skills required.

team (or group) incentive plan A plan in which a production standard is set for a specific work group, and its members are paid incentives if the group exceeds the production standard.

termination at will Without a contract, either the employer or the employee could *terminate at will* the employment relationship.

termination interview The interview in which an employee is informed of the fact that he or she has been dismissed.

test validity The accuracy with which a test, interview, and so on measures what it purports to measure or fulfills the function it was designed to fill.

third-country nationals Citizens of a country other than the parent or the host country.

Title VII of the 1964 Civil Rights Act The section of the act that says an employer cannot discriminate on the basis of race, color, religion, sex, or national origin with respect to employment.

training The process of teaching new employees the basic skills they need to perform their jobs.

transfers Reassignments to similar positions in other parts of the firm.

trend analysis Study of a firm's past employment needs over a period of years to predict future needs.

trial substage Period that lasts from about ages 25 to 30 during which the person determines whether or not the chosen field is suitable; if not, changes may be attempted.

unclear standards An appraisal that is too open to interpretation.

unemployment insurance Provides benefits if a person is unable to work through some fault other than his or her own.

unfair labor practice strike A strike aimed at protesting illegal conduct by the employer.

uniform guidelines Guidelines issued by federal agencies charged with ensuring compliance with equal employment federal legislation explaining recommended employer procedures in detail.

union salting A union organizing tactic by which workers who are in fact employed full-time by a union as undercover organizers are hired by unwitting employers.

union shop A form of union security in which the company can hire nonunion people, but they must join the union after a prescribed period of time and pay dues. (If they do not, they can be fired.)

unsafe conditions The mechanical and physical conditions that cause accidents.

unstructured (or nondirective) interview An unstructured conversational-style interview in which the interviewer pursues points of interest as they come up in response to questions.

unstructured sequential interview An interview in which each interviewer forms an independent opinion after asking different questions.

valence The perceived value a person attaches to the reward.

value chain Identifies the primary activities that create value for customers and the related support activities.

variable pay Any plan that ties pay to productivity or profitability, usually as one-time lump payments.

video-based simulation A situational test in which examinees respond to video simulations of realistic job situations.

virtual classroom Special collaboration software used to enable multiple remote learners, using their PCs or laptops, to participate in live audio and visual discussions, communicate via written text, and learn via content such as PowerPoint slides.

vision statement A general statement of the firm's intended direction and shows, in broad terms, "what we want to become."

Vocational Rehabilitation Act of 1973 The act requiring certain federal contractors to take affirmative action for disabled persons.

voluntary (or permissible) bargaining items Items in collective bargaining over which bargaining is neither illegal nor mandatory—neither party can be compelled against its wishes to negotiate over those items.

wage curve Shows the relationship between the value of the job and the average wage paid for this job.

Walsh-Healey Public Contract Act (1936) A law that requires minimum wage and working conditions for employees working on any government contract amounting to more than $10,000.

wildcat strike An unauthorized strike occurring during the term of a contract.

work samples Actual job tasks used in testing applicants' performance.

work sampling technique A testing method based on measuring performance on actual basic job tasks.

work sharing Refers to a temporary reduction in work hours by a group of employees during economic downturns as a way to prevent layoffs.

workers' compensation Provides income and medical benefits to work-related accident victims or their dependents regardless of fault.

workplace flexibility Arming employees with the information technology tools they need to get their jobs done wherever they are.

wrongful discharge An employee dismissal that does not comply with the law or does not comply with the contractual arrangement stated or implied by the firm via its employment application forms, employee manuals, or other promises.

Name/Organization Index

C

E

F

G

H

K

L

M

Q

R

S

X

Y

Z

Subject Index

Page numbers with *f* represent figures; those with *t* represent tables.

F

N

O

P

Q

R